THE OXFORD HANDBOOK OF

BUSINESS AND GOVERNMENT

THE OXFORD HANDBOOK OF

BUSINESS AND GOVERNMENT

Edited by

DAVID COEN
WYN GRANT
and
GRAHAM WILSON

OXFORD
UNIVERSITY PRESS

OXFORD
UNIVERSITY PRESS

Great Clarendon Street, Oxford OX2 6DP

Oxford University Press is a department of the University of Oxford.
It furthers the University's objective of excellence in research, scholarship,
and education by publishing worldwide in

Oxford New York

Auckland Cape Town Dar es Salaam Hong Kong Karachi
Kuala Lumpur Madrid Melbourne Mexico City Nairobi
New Delhi Shanghai Taipei Toronto

With offices in

Argentina Austria Brazil Chile Czech Republic France Greece
Guatemala Hungary Italy Japan Poland Portugal Singapore
South Korea Switzerland Thailand Turkey Ukraine Vietnam

Oxford is a registered trade mark of Oxford University Press
in the UK and in certain other countries

Published in the United States
by Oxford University Press Inc., New York

British Library Cataloguing in Publication Data

Data available

Library of Congress Cataloguing in Publication Data

Data available

Typeset by SPI Publisher Services, Pondicherry, India
Printed in Great Britain
on acid-free paper by
CPI Antony Rowe, Chippenham, Wiltshire

ISBN 978–0–19–921427–3

1 3 5 7 9 10 8 6 4 2

PREFACE

....

Business is one of the major power centers in modern society. The state seeks to check and channel that power so as to serve broader public policy objectives. However, if the way in which business is governed is ineffective or over burdensome, it may become more difficult to achieve desired goals such as economic growth or higher levels of employment. In a period of international economic crisis, the study of how business and government relate to each other in different countries is of more central importance than ever.

These relationships have been studied from a number of different disciplinary perspectives—business studies, economics, law, and political science—and all of these are represented in this Handbook. The first part of the book provides an introduction to the ways in which five different disciplines have approached the study of business and government. The second part, on the firm and the state, looks at how these entities interact in different settings, emphasizing such phenomena as the global firm and varieties of capitalism. The third part examines how business interacts with government in different parts of the world, including the United States, the EU, China, Japan, and South America. The fourth part reviews changing patterns of market governance through a unifying theme of the role of regulation. Business–government relations can play out in divergent ways in different policy and the fifth part examines the contrasts between different key arenas such as competition policy, trade policy, training policy, and environmental policy. The volume provides an authoritative overview with chapters by leading authorities on the current state of knowledge of business–government relations, but also points to ways in which this work might be developed in the future, for example, through a political theory of the firm.

In preparing this volume, we owe our greatest debt to the contributors. They have all been superbly professional in delivering drafts and final chapters. We could not have asked for a more cooperative group of scholars and colleagues. We also owe a huge debt to David Musson and Mathew Derbyshire at Oxford University Press for their support and patience in waiting for the final version to arrive. Finally, David would like to thank the Fulbright Foundation and the Center for Business and Government at the Kennedy School Harvard University for their support and providing a home in the final days of editing with Graham in Boston.

The final editing of this volume, like its subject, was a truly global event with meetings in Boston, Brussels, and London and email exchanges from Australian airports. Somehow in all this international exchange we managed to coordinate thirty-seven leading business government scholars as well as, somewhat harder, the three of us. Events in "the real" world as the book was nearing completion served to remind us of both the unpredictability of politics and the importance of the topic. If anyone in 2006 when we started this project had predicted that President George W. Bush would have ordered major US banks to sell stock to the government they would have been thought insane. On the other hand, the real problems that people were experiencing around the world reminded us of the importance of this topic for the futures of our children Adam, Alexandria, Sophia, Rosalind, and Amelia and we dedicate this book to them and our wives Gina, Maggie, and Natasha.

CONTENTS

PART III   COMPARATIVE BUSINESS SYSTEMS

PART IV   CHANGING MARKET GOVERNANCE

PART V   POLICY

LIST OF FIGURES

LIST OF TABLES

LIST OF CONTRIBUTORS

Tim Büthe is Assistant Professor in the Department of Political Science and Associate Director of the Center for European Studies at Duke University.

Pamela Camerra-Rowe is Associate Professor of Political Science in the Department of Politics at Kenyon College.

Martin Chick is Reader in Economic and Social History in the School of History, Classics, and Archeology at Edinburgh University.

David Coen is Professor of Public Policy at the Department of Political Science, School of Public Policy, University College London.

Colin Crouch is Professor of Governance and Public Management at the Warwick Business School, University of Warwick.

Pepper D. Culpepper is an Associate Professor of Public Policy at Harvard Kennedy School, Harvard University.

Michelle Egan is Associate Professor and Director of the European Studies Program at the School of International Service at the American University in Washington.

Francis J. Greene is Associate Professor of Enterprise at Warwick Business School, University of Warwick.

Carsten Greve is Professor at the International Center for Business and Politics in the Copenhagen Business School.

Jean-Pascal Gond is a Lecturer in Corporate Social Responsibility at Nottingham University Business School, Nottingham University.

Wyn Grant is Professor of Politics in the Department of Politics and International Studies at the University of Warwick.

Yukihiko Hamada is a research and media officer at the Japan Embassy in London and a Post Doctoral Fellow at University College London.

Bob Hancké is a Reader in European Political Economy at the London School of Economics.

David M. Hart is Associate Professor of Public Policy, School of Public Policy, George Mason University, Arlington, Va., USA.

Jason Heyes is a Reader in Human Resource Management at Birmingham Business School, Birmingham University.

Torben Iversen is Professor of Political Science in the Department of Government at Harvard University.

Nahee Kang is an ESRC Post-Doctoral Fellow at Nottingham University Business School, Nottingham University.

Thomas Lawton is Professor of Strategic Management at Cranfield School of Management, Cranfield University, UK.

Christopher Magee is Associate Professor at the Department of Economics at Bucknell University.

Stephen P. Magee is the Bayless/Enstar Chair and Professor of Finance and Economics in the Department of Finance, University of Texas, Austin.

Cathie Jo Martin is Professor of Political Science in the Department of Political Science at Boston University.

Walter Mattli is Professor of International Political Economy and Official Fellow of St John's College at the University of Oxford.

Jill J. McCluskey is Professor and Chair of Graduate Studies in the School of Economic Sciences at Washington State University.

Jeremy Moon is Professor of Corporate Social Responsibility and Director of the International Centre for Corporate Social Responsibility at Nottingham University Business School.

Michael Moran is the WJM Mackenzie Professor of Government in the Department of Politics at Manchester University.

Christos N. Pitelis is a Reader in International Business and Competitiveness at Judge Business School and Fellow in Economy Queens' College, University of Cambridge.

Helen Rainbird is Professor of Human Resource Management at Birmingham Business School, Birmingham University.

Philippe Schmitter is Emeritus Professor of Political Science in the Department of Social and Political Science at the European University Institute.

Ben Ross Schneider is Professor of Political Science in the Department of Political Science at Massachusetts Institute of Technology.

Gregory C. Shaffer is Melvin C. Steen Professor of Law, University of Minnesota Law School.

Timothy J. Sinclair is Associate Professor of International Relations in the Department of Politics and International Studies at the University of Warwick.

David Soskice is a Research Professor in the Department of Political Science at Duke University.

David J. Storey is Professor of Enterprise and Director of the Centre for Small and Medium-Sized Enterprise at the Warwick Business School, University of Warwick.

Jonathan Story is Emeritus Professor of International Political Economy at INSEAD, France, and Marusi Chair of Global Business and Political Economy, Lally School of Management & Technology, Rensselaer Polytechnic Institute, Troy, NY.

Johan F. M. Swinnen is Professor at the Department of Economics and Director of LICOS Centre for Institutions and Economic Performance at the Catholic University of Leuven.

Gunnar Trumbull is Associate Professor at the Harvard Business School, Harvard University.

David Vogel is the Solomon P. Lee Distinguished Professor of Business Ethics at the Haas Business School at the University of California Berkeley.

Timothy Werner is Assistant Professor of Political Science at Grinnell College.

Stephen Wilks is Professor of Politics at the University of Exeter. He is a Member of the UK Competition Commission. None of the views expressed in his chapter should be attributed to the Competition Commission.

Graham Wilson is Professor of Political Science in the Department of Political Science at Boston University.

OVERVIEW

DAVID COEN

WYN GRANT

GRAHAM WILSON

THE relationship between business and government is undeniably important: both are major forces in our lives. They are locked inextricably in a relationship with each other, but the nature of that relationship varies over time and between countries, firms, and sectors of the economy. At a fundamental level, the exercise of power by business has implications for democracy. Some would see it as a threat to democracy, while others would regard a successful free market economy as a precondition for the existence of democracy.

That is an important literature, but our concern here is also with the efficacy of the relationship between business and government. If it does not work well, desired economic goals such as growth and employment will not be secured. It also makes it difficult to tackle global public bads such as climate change. If business is constrained too much by poorly designed and executed government interventions, the tax base that funds merit goods such as public health services and education will be undermined.

Markets are not naturally occurring phenomena; they need to be embedded in a structure of laws and rules. Without such a framework, markets cannot function and deliver net welfare gains. Governments are therefore impelled to make interventions in markets, although their extent and nature varies over time in response to prevalent ideological frameworks and the state of the economy. The quality of government interventions in markets conditions their long-term success in developing such benefits. Equally, sometimes the state has to intervene to save markets from themselves and to guarantee their continued existence, as in the crisis of 2008. Particularly in response to such crises, but also at other times, governments, depending in part on their partisan composition and long-term national perspectives on the legitimacy and desirability of intervention, may intervene to try to restructure their national economies. The reproduction of such interventions at an EU level has been advocated and even attempted, but with relatively limited impact.

Business is a key political actor. It dwarfs other interest groups in terms of resources and political displacement. It touches most areas of public policy. Business helps to shape policy agendas, formulation, and implementation. The driver of this involvement is that the costs of doing nothing can be considerable. It may result in legislation or regulation that has substantial intended or unintended consequences for business and competitiveness. For its part government has to become involved with business because left unchecked it can inflict substantial costs on society in terms of various forms of market failure, for example, anti-competitive behavior that prevents the benefits of competition being realized and negative externalities such as pollution. Following Polanyi's argument that labor cannot be treated as a commodity without having a dehumanizing effect, there also needs to be a framework of employment protection for workers and provision for health and safety at work. If training is simply left to employers, the result is likely to be an undersupply of the skills needed to maintain an economy's international competitiveness. A much broader issue than making the market work effectively is the use of government taxation and spending to redistribute income. The existence of a much skewed redistribution, as in Brazil, can affect a nation's ability to function effectively economically, socially, and even politically. There is also a moral case derived from Rawlsian notions of justice, among other arguments, for redistribution.

The study of business–government relations has grown from a low base point. The subject area is still undersupplied with theory. Early Marxist accounts of business power were often crude "reading off" that ignored the subtleties in Marx's own work. Later work became more aware of the existence of "fractions of capital," permitting a more nuanced account from a Marxist perspective, but still failed to capture the range and variability of business political activity. Simplistic business accounts of business as one pressure group among many were challenged by Lindblom's account of the structural power of business. The corporatist debate stimulated considerable empirical research on intermediate structures such as trade associations, but deflected attention from the growing phenomenon of political action on their own behalf by large firms. It is in this area of micropolitical activity, exploring the motivations of firms and the extent and or organization of their political activity, that the greatest theoretical deficit exists and one that this volume seeks to remedy.

A number of disciplines have contributed to the study of business–government relations and they are all represented in this volume. Political science has been interested in how business organizes to operate politically and the opportunity structures it encounters. Historical institutionalism and its emphasis on path dependency has been a substantial influence, notably through the Varieties of Capitalism debate which seeks to identify distinctive national patterns of interaction that are shaped by the historical form that the state had adopted. How much these patterns have been undermined by globalization, the core paradigm of international political economy, remains a highly contested issue.

Another approach has been to look at the historical development of ideal typical state forms in which one form supplants another while retaining elements of the earlier form. Thus the regulatory state has become the increasingly predominant state form in developed countries, but substantial elements of the preceding form, the "Keynesian welfare state," remain in place. Keynes set out a model which enabled capitalist economies to run at a higher level of employment equilibrium than had been possible in the depression of the 1930s, although his model was less useful in coping with the inflation problem that arose when economies were run at a higher level of employment. However, it was only possible to afford an extensive welfare state if unemployment levels were not so high that a great deal of expenditure was spent on benefit to those out of work. The Keynesian model, as developed by his disciples, ran into considerable difficulty in the 1970s and this was one of the factors that led many countries to reduce their involvement in the economy. However, where natural monopolies remained, some sort of regulatory framework was required and this was one of the factors contributing to the emergence of the regulatory state. The concept of the regulatory state has been developed in the work of Moran (see his chapter in this volume). The state has understandably played a central role in political science analysis, particularly after it was "brought back in," but this has arguably produced an imbalance in analysis that has led to an insufficient focus on the firm as a political actor with the political side of the equation often been conceived in terms of the intermediaries privileged by the neo-corporatist tradition. The state sets the rules of the game for business, but the game can be played in different ways both strategically and tactically.

Economics, and in particular the microeconomic tradition of rational choice that is concerned with understanding the behavior of utility maximizing agents, has drawn our attention to rent-seeking behavior by interest groups. By modeling the firm as a profit maximizing entity, economics has provided us with robust and testable models of micro-level behavior. These have not been matched in political science by a political theory of the firm. Economics identifies cases of market failure that may justify state intervention, but also reminds us that attempts to remedy a market failure may simply lead to government failure. From economic history we learn that abstention from intervention, or the wrong interventions, may worsen an economic slump as in the 1930s.

Business studies have led the analysis of the growing phenomenon of corporate social responsibility, its motivations and consequences. It has also drawn our attention to the distinctive characteristics, agendas, and needs of small firms. Through the use of the case study method it has brought out the complexity and dynamic nature of the challenges facing the individual firm. A longer term perspective on these challenges has been provided by the work of business historians which has helped us to understand the importance and consequences of changes in the management structures of firms over time as ownership and control became separated.

Legal studies focus on what it means to be a corporation in terms of rights, responsibilities, and liabilities. What are the political consequences of the legal personalities of corporations? How are corporate executives constrained by law? Thus as Shaffer notes in this volume corporations are not naturally occurring phenomena but are created and structured by laws.

Unfortunately, this work within different disciplines has not been well integrated. Each captures a bit of the reality. Knowing one piece without having any sense of the whole gives incomplete, even misleading results, such as being impressed by the poor lobbying performance of US business in the 1950s without appreciating their more general strength in US society (notably the "military–industrial complex") and the global economy could lead to misleading inferences about their weakness. There have, of course, been cross-disciplinary influences, notably through Olson's work on the logic of collective action which has had a profound impact on the debate in political science about business political activity.

While there are considerable continuities in business–government relations in particular countries which have not been swept away by globalization there is also substantial instability. Some of this is evident in short-term fluctuations. The nature of the exchange between business and government can change over quite a short time period, shorter than might be implied by some of the propositions of the Varieties of Capitalism literature. Fluctuations in the policy cycle and policy outputs will influence the nature of business–government exchanges. In periods of high legislative activity, the emphasis is on speedily available informational outputs. In periods of low legislative output, the focus is more on building downstream relationships and consultation. This could involve deepening relationships with one set of interests or it could lead to a process of broadening out to other interests. However, business–government interactions can also shift in the longer term in response to changes in market structure and the political system.

In the post-war period the dominant economic model was that of the mixed economy, a market economy with substantial government involvement. Government often owned public utilities or at least regulated them very tightly. Many governments engaged in indicative planning, although such efforts often foundered on the autonomy of the firm when it came to key investment decisions. This was succeeded by a period in which the market was seen as the preferred logic of economic activity, reflected in the preferences of the Thatcher government in the UK and the Reagan administration in the US and at an international level by the "Washington consensus." Neo-liberalism began a long march through the institutions. It should be emphasized that neo-liberalism was about redesigning markets and restructuring them, rather than simply relying on the market to deliver desired outcomes. The role of the state did not diminish as much as was sometimes claimed, but it was seen more as the servant of the market and of business than its controller. Thus, while regulatory frameworks generally remained in place, they were often interpreted in a looser way or enforced less strictly, although there was considerable variation by country and in terms of forms of regulation.

Does the financial crisis of 2008 represent the start of a new era in business–government relations? It is difficult to believe that it will be "business as usual." In particular, regulation of the financial system is likely to be tighter given that it represents a distinctive and particularly serious form of market failure. Trust in business, and in particular in banks, has been damaged and will take a long time to recover. However, there is no viable alternative model to free market capitalism on offer, even if it is likely to experience a period of state market capitalism. This has already involved the provision of very substantial sums of government money to bail out banks and industrial firms, but the US and UK governments have seen these as temporary interventions from which they have remained at arm's length. New formulations may arise, not least in France with its "dirigiste" tradition, but President Sarkozy's call for a European industrial policy received an unsympathetic reception from other member states. Governments are eager to disengage from their involvement in banks and troubled automobile companies, but it is often easier to get in than get out.

The relationships analyzed in this volume are therefore of fundamental importance. This book reviews the state of the literature across a number of disciplines, but it also identifies areas for future work. The debate has been going on for over fifty years, and many insights have accumulated, but there is a sense in which it has only just begun.

PART I

DISCIPLINARY PERSPECTIVES

POLITICAL SCIENCE

PERSPECTIVES ON BUSINESS AND GOVERNMENT

DAVID COEN

WYN GRANT

GRAHAM WILSON

WHAT does political science as a discipline contribute to understanding the relationship between business and government? The field has long been a stepchild within the discipline with many fewer practitioners than the study of fields such as voting behavior, political parties, or legislatures. And yet, the relatively small number of political scientists involved in the field has generated at least four distinct debates on business and government.

The first debate ironically concerns claims that the study of politics has relatively little to contribute to understanding business and government. In a highly influential book published four decades ago, the then prominent American political scientist, Charles Lindblom, argued that markets constituted a prison that robbed democratic governments of effective choice (Lindblom 1977). Business controlled investment; any government that displeased business or that failed to create a favorable business environment would be punished automatically by the rational response of business executives; they would invest elsewhere, in cities, states, or countries that treated them more favorably. Lindblom argued memorably that business executives did not need to pressure, coerce, or bribe politicians to do their bidding. The economic well-being of their constituents—and politicians' chances of re-election—were dependent on pleasing business. Lindblom's argument appeared on the eve of the era of globalization and was directed more to dynamics within nations than between them; the obvious application of his argument was to the constraints on state and local governments in the US. Within a few years, however, political scientists were more preoccupied with the international application of Lindblom's argument. The near total abolition of tariffs on manufactured goods and the widespread relaxing of controls on capital movements facilitated the ease of "exit" as a strategy for businesses displeased with a government's policies. Ironically, therefore, policy decisions made by governments on trade and capital movements arguably has the effect of weakening the power of governments. The impact of these decisions was amplified by technological changes such as cheap international air travel, low-cost international phone calls, email, the internet, and the development of containerized shipping—all of which facilitated the movement of money and goods around the world. When Lindblom published *Politics and Markets* it was plausible to argue that city and state governments were prisoners of the market; two decades later it was commonplace to argue that national governments had lost autonomy and were doomed to pursue policies as "competition states" (Cerny 1997). We return to this discussion later in this chapter. We should note, however, that many political scientists have disagreed with both Lindblom's original argument and subsequently with claims that globalization had destroyed the power and autonomy of national governments (Ohmae 1995; Strange 1996). Thus the first debate in political science on the relative power of governments and of market forces continues to be of central importance.

A second debate has focused on whether or not business has enjoyed unfair advantages in politics. Pluralists contended that power was widely distributed among numerous competing and conflicting interests—that, as Madison had intended for the United States, interest was set against interest and the competition benefited public policy. This claim has been consistently and energetically challenged by political scientists. Schattschneider (1960) famously argued when pluralism was at its peak that the trouble with its vision of heaven was that the choir sang with an upper-class accent. In more recent times, critics of pluralism have argued that business has been consistently over-represented and has inbuilt advantages in the political system. As Werner and Wilson (this volume) note, study after study has concluded that the vast majority of lobbyists in Washington are employed by business and the majority of campaign contributions from interest groups come from business (Gray and Lowery 1997; Baumgartner et al. 2009). Even when (as with President Obama) candidates eschew direct contributions from interest groups, they still receive a very large proportion of their funds from individuals associated with particular interests including in his case financial institutions such as Goldman Sachs. No group in the United States—certainly not the groups such as unions or public interest groups—that might be expected to clash with business commands anything like equal resources. And yet without claiming that the distribution of resources is ideal or adequately equal, a number of political scientists have argued that the resource advantage enjoyed by business is not decisive (Baumgartner et al. 2009). Indeed, it is when American business is most united and cohesive that it is most likely to lose politically (Smith 2000). Public interest groups may be short of money but they have been able to outmaneuver and defeat business on key issues such as environmental protection (Vogel 1995; Berry 1999: 4). Thus, while nearly all political scientists agree that business as interest in most democracies enjoys formidable resources advantages, a vigorous debate persists within political science over the degree to which this results in disproportionate influence for business over government and public policy (Culpepper 2009 and this volume).

A third debate within political science has focused on aspects of business–government relations that result in suboptimal public policy. This can be distinguished from the preceding debate because suboptimal policy can result from decisions that are hostile to business as well as from business pressure. Of course venerable tradition in the discipline has focused on the dangers of the capture of government agencies by corporations that it might be supposed they exist to control (Bernstein 1955; Kolko 1965). Thus, over half a century ago political scientists such as Huntington and Bernstein argued that rent-seeking corporations had captured control of regulatory agencies to ensure that they worked to enhance market stability and profitability for business, not the interests of consumers. Some decades later economists rediscovered this argument (generally without acknowledging the earlier work of political scientists) in discussions of how "rent seeking" by corporations resulted in the exploitation of government by business to increase profits and reduce competition (Becker 1985; Austen-Smith 1997; Austen-Smith and Bank 2002). The negative view of regulation—that it is a means of advancing sectional not public interests—contributed to the development of the "Washington consensus" propagated by the World Bank in the late twentieth century. Economic success was best achieved through minimizing government size and intrusion into the economy, lest it facilitate rent-seeking behavior; a belief that many economic historians think conflicts with the patterns of industrialization in the nineteenth century in countries such as Japan, South Korea, and even arguably the United States. Again, we shall return to this argument later. A contrasting position in this debate was to argue that business is the victim of excessive government zeal. A powerful argument has been made that regulatory officials in the United States can be so legalistic and adversarial in their approach that they contribute to a substantial waste of resources in complying with unwise, overly costly, and unnecessary regulations (Bardach and Kagan 2002). Officials may be motivated by ideology or by fear of endangering their jobs if any unlikely danger actually materializes; better to stray on the side of caution. Regulators, therefore, push for the adoption of costly and inconvenient measures by industry to guard against remote risks thereby reducing not only business profits but societal welfare (Greaves 2009). Similar fears have been expressed in the UK and in relation to the regulatory activities of the EU.

The fourth debate has been almost the mirror image of the first. Instead of arguing that market forces totally control government and politics, "statists" suggest that government, or more accurately, the state, is the fundamental determinant. The state determines the structure of markets and even businesses themselves. Business corporations themselves are products of the state in that they are organized and constituted under policies and laws created by the state. Exxon or Siemens are not products of nature; they are social formations made possible by corporate law. "Free markets" are also products of state action. Without legal frameworks for trading and exchange, the means of settling disputes and enforcing payments through the legal system and the specification of the rights or duties of stockholders, managers, consumers, and workers, markets would not exist. Belatedly, economists recognized the centrality of governance—and therefore the state. From the mid-1990s onwards, the World Bank stressed that an effective and reasonable state—good governance— was a precondition for economic development. States are not only providers of frameworks for economic activity but can be purposive actors in steering and promoting economic growth. We explore below what forms state activity can take in terms of variation between countries in relation to these forms of state involvement and whether globalization has reduced state autonomy and capacity.

Underlying these debates are analyses of the interrelated motivation and behavior of firms on the one hand and, on the other hand, the analyses of the context in which they operate on business associations, governmental institutions, and the broader structures of the state itself. We might make an analogy with the study of the firm on the one hand and the study of markets on the other. While everyone knows that the economic behavior of firms is related to the structure of the markets in which they operate, it is also the case that we can analyze the actions of the firm as a purposive actor. In practice, political scientists have been more focused on understanding the institutional structures and political environments in which firms operate than on understanding the actions and strategies of firms themselves. There is, however, a growing literature that approaches the topic from the perspective of the firm and it is here that we see the greatest opportunity for analytical development. In the next section we propose a typology for studying the political behavior of the firm before turning to the more familiar literature on business, intermediary organizations, and the state.

A POLITICAL THEORY OF THE FIRM

It is a striking feature of this debate that in fact little research exists on when, why, and how individual businesses become involved in politics (but see Wilson 1990; Coen 1998; Grant 2000). There are in fact substantial differences among businesses—large as well as small—in terms of how much political activity they undertake and, if they become involved, the choices they make on how to pursue their objectives. We lack a micro-theory of business and politics that explains the motivations of individual corporations and that explains the choices they make on tactics and strategy. We attempt to remedy this failing ourselves later in this chapter, as do other contributors to this volume, especially Hart and Crouch.

The most systematic micropolitical theories of the firm have been developed in the US institutional setting. Here, traditional profit maximizing models of the firm have sought to explain political action in terms of rent-seeking activity of business and power utility maximizing activity of decision-makers (politicians and bureaucrats). Both the financial and informational aspects of lobbying play an important role in this body of literature. In such models decision-makers provide policy in exchange for political resources (be that money, expertise, information) up to the marginal point when funds and information no longer facilitate political re-election; good policy or association with such policy mobilizes countervailing interests against the proposed policy (see Broschied 2006). From the firm perspective such rent-seeking logic has opened up a huge formal and empirical literature debate in the US about the costs and effectiveness of political campaign contributions (see Brier and Munger 1986; Grier, Munger, and Roberts 1994; Hansen and Mitchel 2000; Milyo, Primo, and Groseclose 2000; de Figueiredo 2002; Werner and Wilson this volume); and the risk of political capture and inefficient allocation of political resources (see Stiglitz 1986; Grossman and Helpman 1994; Pitelis this volume). This first body of literature has been US-centric as campaign contributions play such a prominent role in the American electoral system. American public disclosure laws ensure that data about interest group and candidate expenditures are more readily available than in the EU or other Western democracies (see Wilson and Grant, and Werner and Wilson this volume).

A second literature on corporate political behavior has emerged in game theory (Austen-Smith and Wright 1992). The general conclusion of those models is that the interest representatives are indeed able to influence policy by misrepresenting and/or selectively providing information to decision-makers; while decision-makers minimize misinformation by carefully selecting the interest representatives whose information they take into account (see Austen-Smith 1997 for the US models; and Potters and Sloof 1996; Broschied and Coen 2003). These models assumed "that decisions to lobby are narrowly driven by the pursuit of specific and immediate policy benefits" (Brasher and Lowery 2006: 2) when in reality the lobbying nexus is a much more diverse and complex long run game where variables such as reputation and political goodwill play a role. Relationships between lobbyists and policy-makers are generally iterative. If we broaden our micro-behavioral model of the firm to assume learning on the part of business and government, bounded rationality on the part of both players, and a longer term political horizon, the conventional models of the profit maximizing firm begin to predict less of the actual political activity by firms. Moreover, purely profit maximizing activity could incur significant costs, not just financial costs, but also the potential for reputational damage if the firm took an unpopular stance or offended politicians who subsequently became powerful. Reputational damage has become an increasingly important consideration for firms as investment in brands has become a more significant aspect of strategy for many of them, particularly those making consumer goods (Klein 2000; Tucker 2008). On the other hand, the benefits of political activity may be difficult to identify in terms of a contribution to firms' profits. This is a practical as well as a theoretical problem. Government relations or public affairs divisions in firms often find it a challenge to quantify their contribution to the bottom line and find themselves under pressure when there is an economic downturn or "sponsors" on the board are replaced.

The literature on the behavioral theory of the firm suggests that firms often behave in practice rather differently from what theories of profit maximization would suggest (Cyert and March 1992) and this could also be argued for the political logic of the firm (Baumgartner and Leech 1998; Lowery 2007). Large firms are complex organizations and particular components of the firm may pursue objectives that do not necessarily contribute to profit maximization. For example, those engaged in marketing may pursue a market share objective which is actually detrimental to profits. Of course, if profits become too depressed, then the firm will become vulnerable to takeover or even bankruptcy, so the profit maximization objective remains a powerful constraint and shaping force. However, there is enough organizational "slack" in big firms to permit activities whose contribution to profit maximization cannot be readily demonstrated. If that was not the case, corporate social responsibility would have not developed to the extent that it is evident from more than one chapter in this volume (see Moon Kang and Gond and Vogel). Finally, we must also ask how far big business reaches its lobbying rationality threshold when we consider that for a giant oil firm, the total cost of government relations activities in one year may amount to no more than fifteen minutes of turnover.

One of the key themes of the behavioral theory of the firm literature is that firms operate in conditions of bounded rationality, that is they tend to tend to satisfice (accept a "good enough" solution) rather than maximize. Some economists would object that satisficing behavior is still optimizing behavior that takes the costs of acquiring information into account. Most firms would consider that they know enough about their markets to operate successfully in them: indeed, if they do not, they are likely to fail. However, in the political sphere they face conditions of information asymmetry. They are unlikely to have a good understanding of how the political process operates. Sophisticated and experienced business executives often make simple errors when they have to operate politically. Businesses also face an increasingly complex and demanding operating environment as regulation becomes the predominant mode of government intervention.

There are two potential consequences to this asymmetry. The first is to reduce information by pooling information with other firms through a trade or other business association. This reduces the costs of obtaining relevant information, reduces uncertainty, and to some extent shares out risks. The association may not, however, reach a policy position that represents interests of an individual business adequately, forcing the firm to undertake its own political action. Alternatively, firms can learn to deal with uncertainty with decision-makers via a process of iterative exchanges that help the firm identify the relative costs of non-action, outright opposition, or compliance and transparency. Iterative exchanges may change the appropriate strategy for both firms and regulators; deception generally does work as a strategy in iterative exchanges. Iteration may also change the balance of power through equalizing information. In early business–agency exchanges, firms may have an informational advantage over regulators that may result in suboptimal policy outcomes. However, as the process evolves over time policy-makers can identify businesses or groups that have misled or failed to disclose appropriate information and may use their discretion in controlling the policy-making process to exclude them or treat their arguments as inconsequential. Under such conditions we can envisage a situation where reverse capture emerges and firms provide additional information in an attempt to become insiders in the policy process (Willman et al. 2003 for the UK; Coen this volume for the EU; Lowery 2007 for the US).

In the preceding discussion, policy-making took place in a very simplified setting in which there was business on the one hand and a set of policy-makers on the other dealing with a single issue. In practice, business is affected by a wide variety of policies and numerous policy-makers. Not surprisingly, political activity by firms varies considerably from one to another. Indeed, we suggest that all firms can evolve through all the categories set out below; as the situation and preferences change, firms may move from one category to another. We propose five categories.

Denial
Helplessness
Delegation
Insurance
Sophistication

Denial occurs when a firm or entrepreneur denies that government has any relevance to the activities that the business is undertaking. Given the pervasiveness of the regulatory state, not least in the United States, there are very few business activities that are not affected in some way by government. Indeed, one possibility is that businesses seek to evade government altogether and operate in the black economy. However, the discussion here is confined to legitimate businesses and does not consider criminal organizations, even though they are major participants in the economy.

Denial is a high-risk strategy. It is most likely to work in a sector that is not tightly regulated and where enforcement of regulations is spasmodic and slipshod or where, even if there are penalties, they are light. Indeed, for some businesses, the threat of civil litigation by customers who are dissatisfied is probably a greater risk. For some businesses operated as franchises, effective quality control may be exercised by the franchise holder who can ultimately withdraw the license to operate. In general, however, denial is a calculated gamble. It involves a construction of reality by the business person which may make their life simpler in the short run but may land them in trouble in the longer run.

Helplessness is a more typical response, particularly among smaller businesses. In this case, there is a grudging acceptance that government does affect the operation of the business, but this is seen as posing a threat rather than an opportunity. Businesses may claim that they are overtaxed and over-regulated and that the uncertainty of their operating environment is increased by apparently capricious decisions by government (see Greene and Storey this volume). However, they may feel unable to do anything to counter these forces or at least calculate that the costs of doing so exceed the likely benefits. This is not a totally unrealistic position, as it is evident that the growth of the regulatory state is at least in part a response by politicians seeking electoral popularity to demands from the media or non-governmental organizations.

Delegation is probably the most typical response of businesses to the political environment. In this instance businesses accept that they are affected by government decisions. As a single business, they are unlikely to be able to affect such decisions. However, if they band together with other businesses, most usually on the basis of product or industry sector, they may be able at least to modify government policy. If sufficient numbers of them join an association, they will be able to afford to employ professional staff with an understanding of the political process. The costs for each business are not likely to be that large in relation to potential turnover or if the number of firms is relatively small, the slice of the collective good they obtain is likely to be larger ("privileged groups" in Olson's terminology). As Olson put it, "A 'privileged' group is a group such that each of the members, or some of them, has an incentive to see that the collective good is provided, even if he has to bear the full burden of providing it himself" (Olson 1965: 49–50). Hence a characteristic of all developed economies, and many developing ones, is the presence of a large variety of associations representing business. Once Communist economies were freed, associations also developed there. Indeed, in some cases (e.g. Hungary) this happened in anticipation of the transition process (Grant 1993).

Insurance is differentiated from delegation in that it represents an individual rather than a collective response. In this case, a firm gives a donation to a political party (perhaps more than one) or to legislators not in anticipation of corrupt favors (although that does happen) but as an insurance policy that will give access to decision-makers if needed. If a firm is a donor, then the legislator or political party will at least feel obligated to listen to their concerns. An alternative insurance policy could be large-firm funding and participating in collective trade associations. Unlike for small firms, the selective benefits are unlikely to motivate large-firm active membership. When they are able to engage, individual lobbying is always an option. However, large firms may participate in collective action to gain the long-term positive externality of "reputation and good will" in the policy process that can be utilized on a private issues in later policy debates (Coen 1998, 2007). Such a quest for reputation and goodwill may create a dynamic process as firms respond to political activity by rivals. That said, as one firm becomes a prominent and respected actor other firms must develop a similar high profile or lose political advantage (Wilson 1990; Broschied and Coen 2003).

Sophisticated strategies are most typically found in the largest firm, particularly those operating at an international level and dealing with entities such as the EU. One general statement can be made: as a generalization, the larger the firm, the greater the range and sophistication of political activity (Vogel 1989; Wilson 1990; Coen 1997).

There are of course exceptions; IBM used to act as though it were too grand to need to use common strategies such as having a political action committee. Nonetheless, large firms have important opportunities that small firms do not. Managements of small firms have to multi-task and are less likely to have resources available for political activity. Their associative activity is more likely to focus on the selective incentives in the form of support services that an external organization can provide (Olson 1965; Moe 1980; Grant 2000; Hart 2004; Jordan and Halpin 2004). This does not mean that small firms cannot have quite a sophisticated appreciation of their political activities, particularly those run by younger graduate entrepreneurs. For example, they may use a general small business association for representation and support services; use a local chamber of commerce for networking to develop business; and join a trade association to qualify for public procurement contracts. However, the resources they can devote to such activity are limited. The large firm will develop its own specialized government relations division but will also be actively involved in a range of business associations, including in some cases associations of chief executive officers with membership restricted to those who are invited. In some cases it may use political consultants or lobbyists to undertake particular work, e.g. if this is thought to be a more effective way of contacting the legislature or operating at subnational level. In Washington and Brussels, law firms may play a key role. The exact combination of influence tactics used will depend on the issue being addressed, but will be influenced by the overall strategy of the firm. In some cases, it may also be necessary to pursue internal coordination of government relations activities within the firm as different divisions may have divergent and even contradictory commercial and political interests (see Werner and Wilson, and Coen this volume).

What influences the choice of these responses, apart from size of firm? Agency may play a role: a new chief executive may give greater emphasis to governmental work, in part to boost his own personal profile. Some established small-business owners may decide to pursue a career as a "business politician:" there is no lack of offers for entrepreneurs willing to undertake public roles. However, it is argued that there are underlying structural factors which shape the choices a firm makes about political involvement. These are strategies and goals; market setting; the culture of the firm; the political setting and party systems.

Strategies

If firms were engaged only in short-term profit maximization, we would need to spend little time discussing strategy. However, reality is more complex. Some firms may pursue goals such as size or status that are unrelated to short-term profitability and may be only loosely linked to even a long-term profit maximizing strategy. In at least some societies, business leaders may pursue social status as well as profits. If we turn to understanding corporate behavior based on profit maximization, a key question is the degree to which the firm operates in areas which are dependent on government decisions such as extractive industries (for example needing mining or exploration permits), government contracting, or that are otherwise highly regulated. For example, utility firms, even if privately owned, are continuously engaged with government because in practice governments set limits on their behavior in charging and servicing customers. (See Baldwin and Cave 1999; Besley 2006; Chick this volume). There are therefore important differences within specific industries. For example, in the entertainment industry, gambling establishments and sports stadia are highly politicized, theaters and cinemas much less so because of differences in the degree to which they are regulated. Alcohol and tobacco are the targets of significant regulatory interventions and are therefore among the most politically active firms. In general, the more regulated the industry, the more politically active are the firms within it (Hart and Coen this volume). The same can be said of government contracting; the greater the dependence of a firm on government contracting, the more active the firm politically. It is very difficult to function successfully in such industries without continuous engagement with government. While we argue that firms that are highly dependent on government decisions are more likely to adopt a sophisticated strategy, we would not make this an iron law as many firms are multi-sectoral and have a range of subsidiaries (Grier, Munger, and Roberts 1994; Brasher and Lowery 2006).

Strategies and goals involve choices by firms: they can exit some activities and enter others. Of course, the "sunk costs" and the rewards involved in some sectors mean that firms are unlikely to leave them, for instance, oil companies are unlikely to stop extracting oil, even if they invest in renewable energy. A firm that is embedded in a particular sector encounters a set of market conditions that, in terms of their regulatory component, are generally fixed in the short term. For example, the market strategies of airlines are strongly influenced by the rules governing access to "slots" at an airport. New entry airlines can use spare capacity at less popular airports, but this shapes the commercial strategy they follow (Lawton 2002). In general, the more regulated the industry, the more active politically are the firms within it.

Culture

The culture of the firm can be an important intervening variable, sometimes shaped by a chief executive who has founded the firm. A classic example would be the Irish airline, Ryanair, which has consistently adopted a confrontational and adversarial stance towards the European Union and member state governments, possibly to the detriment of the firm's interests. In the oil industry, BP and Shell have tended to seek partnership relationships with governments, admittedly not always successfully, while Exxon has historically taken a more adversarial stance. Some firms have stronger corporate and cultural identities than others and most of them base their political strategies and tactics on a calculation of how their interests can be maximized. Nevertheless, some firms adopt a more "capitalist aggressive" stance than others. The importance of the firm's reputation to its commercial success may be one key factor that influences how far it needs to safeguard that reputation by adopting a cooperative stance.

Political setting

"Political setting" refers to the type of state that a firm encounters. It is these differences which the "Varieties of Capitalism" literature attempts to capture (Hall and Soskice 2001; see Hancké and Culpepper this volume). As we discuss later in this chapter, states vary in the extent to which they intervene in the economy and society (Schmidt 2006). This is not merely a matter of what percentage of GDP is accounted for by government expenditure. For example, the United States and Japan dispose of a relatively low share of GDP in the public sector, in part because the United States does not have universal health care and Japan has relatively ungenerous social security provision. However, as we shall see, government is a larger influence than this figure suggests. Japan has been characterized by what is probably the closest relationship in the developed world between business, the state, and the usual ruling party (Johnson 1982; Tiberghien 2007; Hamada this volume). The United States pioneered the regulatory state as a form of governance and American business is extensively regulated, not just by the federal government, but also by state and local governments (Vogel 1995). Similar arguments can be made in Europe where the EU is often characterized as the regulatory state or a network of regulators (Majone 2005; Coen and Thatcher 2008; Camerra-Rowe and Egan this volume). As we discuss below, states also differ in the degree to which interaction between government and business is based on interaction with individual firms or with business associations.

Firms also have to adjust to the development of multi-level systems of government. This was always a consideration in strong federal systems such as Australia and Canada, while in the United States attention always had to be paid to the "agenda setting" role of California (Vogel 1995). Scotland is moving towards a similar role in the devolved government of the United Kingdom. The development of the EU, and the increasing importance of international bodies such as the World Trade Organization (WTO), mean that firms are impelled to develop strategies that can cope with many different levels of government activity. Political setting is one of the strongest influences on how firms develop their government relations strategies and activities.

Party structure

Party structure remains an important influence on the choice of political strategy. In "party states" such as Italy, Greece, and Japan where business can align itself with factions or groupings within the ruling party, insurance strategies can become particularly important (see Wilson and Grant, and Iversen and Soskice this volume). In states which do not display these particular characteristics, a particular party may be sympathetic to business interests, even if pure "business parties" are relatively rare because too close an alignment with business may be electorally damaging in a democracy. This consideration has made the British Conservative Party's relationship with business more problematic than a superficial analysis might suggest and often business has enjoyed a closer working relationship with the Labour Party, especially New Labour. Schnattschneider, argued (1956) that the biggest advantage that business can enjoy in the United States is to have the Republicans in power (and this would appear to have been the case during the George W. Bush administration).

We have attempted to delineate key determinants of firms' political strategy. Political strategy is, however, dynamic. As Baumgartner and Jones (1993) describe, policy issues can be redefined and redescribed, which in turn results in major change in the political setting and balance of forces involved. As policy questions are refined and moved to different policy arenas, the appropriate strategy may also change. The fluidity of policy definition necessarily results in fluidity in successful political strategies (see Baumgartner et al. 2009 for Washington; and Coen and Richardson 2009 for EU). Increasingly over the last fifty years we have been able to say with confidence that large businesses are political actors. The extent and form of their activity is influenced by a range of variables, but the structure of political institutions is especially important. The study of government–business relations thus becomes a key task for social scientists as it raises important questions about the effectiveness of government, about democracy, and about the distribution of power in modern societies.

A SECOND LEVEL OF ANALYSIS: BUSINESS, STATES, AND GOVERNMENT

Two fundamental changes in social organization in the last 500 years have been the rise of the modern state (Tilly 1974; Spruyt 1994) and the emergence of large business corporations as the dominant force in economic life (Chandler 1962). The relationship between these two developments is obviously central to the study of business and government and has generated a large literature to which political scientists have been active contributors in recent decades. Political scientists have focused on three themes: the structuring role of the state, the directive role of the state, and the autonomy of the state.

States as structuring agents

Although many think of "free markets" as naturally occurring phenomena, it is difficult to imagine them operating without some form of state (Polanyi 1944). The degree of state intervention and the legitimacy of such action have varied over time and are dependent on the dominant economic paradigms. At the very least, states provide some protection for property without which theft might displace trade and exchange. Moreover, states provide not only currencies that are the means of exchange but also the legal framework that makes economic activity possible. Without courts to enforce contracts, capitalism could not exist unless some non-state actor (such as the Mafia) took over the role of enforcing contracts and agreements, as does indeed happen in Sicily (Gambetta 1993). However, most modern activity is not of course conducted between individuals. A particularly important role for the state is in determining the rules under which economic actors can combine. The legal innovation of the joint stock company or corporation made possible modern capitalism. The legal structure that permitted individuals to combine some but not all of their assets to create corporations with defined liability if they failed was a significant departure from prior law. Indeed, extensive legal changes were required to create modern capitalism. As Morton Horwitz (1977) has described, the creation of modern markets in the US required the courts to make major changes from established understandings of common law. Unless courts had issued decisions that took away common-law rights such as not having one's property overshadowed by a neighboring building or water taken upstream from a river that flows through one's property, nineteenth-century entrepreneurs would have faced severe difficulties in building factories. On the other hand, courts in both the UK and USA used common law to impede the development of labor unions.

Labor law today is a rich and complex field establishing how workers can be hired or fired and covering many aspects of working conditions. It illustrates well how the structuring role of the state is not a neutral process but can be used to favor one interest over another; the rules of the economic game are deliberately changed in order to advance or restrain the power of actors. This can be seen in terms of changing labor laws in the United States which boosted union activity in the New Deal and later restrained it through the Taft Hartley Act and laws passed under the Reagan administration. A similar pattern can be observed in the UK.

There are notable differences between states in how this structuring power is used and the differences between states are more complex than can be captured by calling some pro-business and others not. Take, for example, the contrasts between France and the United States. The French state imposes restrictions on the ability of employers to fire workers while labor market flexibility is much higher in the US. On the other hand, American legal procedures have long facilitated the pursuit of class action suits against corporations. This makes corporations more vulnerable to legal challenges from consumers which can lead to punitive damages. Then again, French corporations are more constrained in terms of labor law, but are less vulnerable to trial lawyers. Deciding which state is or more or less pro-business is complicated.

The state does not merely define the relationship between the corporation and potential opponents such as unions and consumers; it shapes the very nature of the corporation itself. One of the most important differences within capitalism that has been linked to the structuring role of the state concerns the degree to which the managers of major corporations are subject to short-term financial forces. Frequent reporting to stockholders, and the dominance of the publicly traded stock company (rather than the privately owned firm) have allegedly made American and British managers attentive to short-term results. Poor results would result quickly in them being fired or the company being subject to hostile takeover bids. In contrast, German businesses are more likely to be privately owned and be responsive to local stakeholders such as *länder* (state) governments, banks, and workers. German corporations can also focus on longer term investments that may take some years to generate profits. (Zysman 1983; Porter 1992; Deeg 1999; Deeg 2001). Whether this results in companies having a better long-term strategy is hotly debated. There would be general agreement, however, that differences in the types of corporate law created by states result in the creation of what have been seen as fundamentally different modes of capitalism—the organized capitalisms of Germany and Japan versus the liberal market economies of the US and UK (Hall and Soskice 2001).

The directive role of the state

Was there ever a time when states were not significantly involved in the promotion of their economies? Germany and the United States were avid practitioners of protectionism in the nineteenth century and perhaps only Great Britain truly opened all its markets to the world. States played a major role in fostering development. States can also influence the structure of interest groups. The comparative weakness of American trade associations, for example, has been linked to the strong anti-trust laws of the USA that restrict collaboration between businesses (Lynn and McKeown 1988). At least indirectly, the structure of the state is reflected in the structure of interest groups, including employers' organizations. The deliberate fragmentation of governmental power in the United States into overlapping branches of government and competing institutions makes it unimaginable that there could ever be an effective policy of compelling businesses to enroll in the monopolistic and hierarchical structures found in neo-corporatist and developmental states. This, of course is to invite a further question which is fortunately beyond the scope of this chapter: what determines variations in the nature of states?

While perhaps all states have played a role in fostering economic development, the means they have used to do so have varied. States can be placed into one of three broad groupings that we may array along a continuum of interventionism.

The first consists of those states that have limited their direct involvement in industry while pursuing macroeconomic policies aimed at maximizing long-term growth and financial stability. In the thirty years following the Second World War, the dominant policy approach was Keynesian demand management. In theory, governments would secure stable long-term growth by boosting demand (through tax cuts or higher spending) when recession threatened and by reducing demand (through higher taxes or reduced spending) when inflation threatened. Keynesianism was pronounced dead in the last decades of the twentieth century. However, when the Great Crash of 2008 occurred, prominent politicians including President George W. Bush responded with calls for fiscal stimuli in the classic Keynesian mode. Even if Keynesianism had been unfashionable for a few decades preceding the Great Crash of 2008, however, demand management had not. Monetarism as actually practiced—as opposed to its theory—in the UK and USA was also focused on the fine tuning of the economy usually relying on variations in interest rates to boost or restrain the economy. The pure monetarist doctrine that central banks should merely focus on increasing the money supply at a fixed and stable rate was honored in the theory but not in practice. Even if states have limited direct and explicit involvement in industry does not mean that they have avoided it totally. Defence spending has fostered the development of immensely successful commercial products ranging from the Boeing 747 jumbo jet to the internet, which was originally intended to maintain government communications after nuclear attack (see Werner and Wilson this volume). However, government involvement in industry is indirect and often the product of political pressure for support or spending rather than outcome of long-range economic planning.

In the second group of states, direct intervention in the economy was also limited but the state fostered and participated in collaborative partnerships between the main economic actors such as unions and employers. These are the so called neo-corporatist states such as the Scandinavian countries, the Netherlands, and Austria (Katzenstein 1985). Governments avoided detailed intervention in industry but coordinated economic management with representatives of capital and labor. Government demand management policies were agreed with unions and employers' organizations. By agreeing to restrain wage increases, unions helped maintain competitiveness in export markets and full employment. Employers committed to maintaining investment and governments made improvements in welfare state policies or the social wage with some of the growth that was achieved. Thus, incomes policies were implemented by the "social partners" not by the state itself. The allocation of resources within and between industries was emphatically left to market forces, however, and the state played little role in the allocation of resources or investment between industries. Neo-corporatist states performed well economically for some four decades following the Second World War (Schmitter 1974; Streeck 1997; Martin 2000; Eichengreen 2007) but thereafter many concluded that the model had outlived its usefulness. It was alleged that a combination of globalization and centrifugal forces in the ranks of labor unions had made the model obsolete (see Schmitter in this volume). Class decomposition had made it harder to achieve a united front among unions as different groups of workers felt that they had less in common with each other than in the past (Streeck and Schmitter 1991). Globalization contributed to this fragmentation. Some industries are unable to compete with overseas producers and workers in those industries lose from globalization. Some industries are able to compete successfully in world markets and their workers are winners. Finally, many people work in government or in services so they are largely unaffected by globalization as workers but benefit as consumers from lower prices for imports. These seemed powerful factors that would make the continuation of neo-corporatism unlikely. In practice, however, it seems that there is no simple trend evident. There is even some evidence that neo-corporatist pacts have become more common and have evolved rather than disappearing (Regini 2002; but see Schmitter in this volume).

The third group of states practiced the most explicit interventionist policies found in capitalist countries; common examples were Japan, South Korea, and France (Johnson 1982; Woo-Cumings 1999). These developmental stages generally started in varying degrees to lag behind the top economies (obviously more the case in Japan and South Korea than for France). Economic development was a national priority mandated and led by government. Government agencies such as the Ministry of International Trade and Industry (MITI) in Japan (Yukihiko Hamada in this volume) or the Commissariat du Plan in France identified which industries should be developed and which industries were likely to decline. The obvious danger of this process being used for political patronage was reduced because it was managed and controlled primarily by a professional, permanent, and prestigious bureaucracy. Government-set priorities were reinforced by a variety of measures in different periods. In Japan in the 1950s and 1960s, the government could enforce its priorities through controls such as import licenses. One of the most important and consistent weapons that gave teeth to government planning was the ability to provide favored industries with lower interest loans from the large state-owned savings banks such as the Post Office Bank in Japan (Zysman 1983).

The viability of a developmental state strategy has been called into question by several changes. The very success of developmental states has made the task of planning for further growth more difficult. When Japan was a comparatively poor country, it could look to other countries for models of which industries to promote. Once Japan was a leader, this approach was necessarily impossible. The development of stronger international institutions such as the WTO or EU to enforce liberal trading regimes has inhibited the use of traditional tactics of the developmental state (Pempel 1998). More recent scholarship has argued that that developmental states adapted successfully to globalization (Wright 2002; Vogel 2006; Tiberghien 2007). Fairly broad brushstrokes are required in characterizing to which groups a country belongs. States were never totally and consistently in one or other category. The UK, for example, which is generally characterized as a liberal market economy, had a lengthy period in which there was extensive government ownership of industry and largely unsuccessful attempts at national planning. Japan is the model of state-directed development. And yet if the Japanese government had had its way, Honda would not be an automobile manufacturer because MITI had intended to limit it to motorcycle production, leaving cars to Nissan and Toyota. Honda's success was achieved through classic entrepreneurship. After the Crash of 2008, a conservative Republican Administration in the United States took partial ownership of the nine largest banks and the insurance giant, AIG.

The balance of power between business and the state

Perhaps *the* classic question about business and the state has been the power relationship between them. Is business dominated and controlled by the state or are states dominated and controlled by businesses? For some the answer is clear: the capitalist class exists to serve the needs of business. Marx's comment in the *Communist Manifesto* that the state is but the committee for the management of the common affairs of the bourgeoisie is well known but he was not consistent on this point. He was certainly aware that the Prussian and French states, for example, were more complicated entities than that slogan suggests. Contemporary Marxists take even more nuanced positions.

For example Bieling's (2007) description of the state seems compatible with the approach that has traditionally emphasized the idea that contending groups struggled to control the state, namely pluralism. Pluralists claim that wide varieties of groups enjoy some form of political power and are able to influence public policy. Contrary to what their critics have claimed, pluralists do not necessarily believe, for example, that all interests have an equal chance of influencing public policy; they are well aware that inequalities in resources among interest groups have important consequences for their ability to influence policy. What does perhaps set pluralists apart from other schools is that they do not believe that there is any fundamental way in which the democratic state is biased towards business interests. If other interests such as consumers, workers, and environmentalists mobilize and win politically, they can harness state power to their purposes. The opposite tendency which we encountered at the beginning of this chapter, which we might term "structuralism," holds that there is a fundamental dependence of the state on business. States need the resources and revenue that business generates. It is therefore essential for states to attract and retain business investment (Lindblom 1977). Yet even without embracing structuralism, it is difficult to regard business as just another interest group.

Although there are important variations on who is consulted, so that it is sometimes leaders of business organizations and sometimes top business executives, governments do pay far more attention to business leaders than, say, leaders of environmental groups. There have been very few governments in advanced democracies that have not worried about the "business climate" or have not held meetings with business representatives to emphasize their commitment to growth. The utter numerical domination of the interest group scene by representatives of business (Werner and Wilson in this volume) suggests that even if business is just one interest among many, it is a very special type of interest group. In some countries, there are also extensive connections between business and the state in terms of the common background or careers of business executives and bureaucracy. For example the "grandes Ecoles" of France nurtured future top civil servants (Schmidt 2006), politicians, and executives of French companies.

A large number of political appointees in US administrations come from business. Major positions in some departments such as Treasury and Commerce are nearly always given to business executives irrespective of whichever party is in power. Administrations that wish to favor business over other interests such as that of George W. Bush have also placed business executives in key positions in agencies charged with environmental and consumer protection. While the quest by scholars such as C. Wright Mills (1956) in the 1950s to find an elite that ran the country behind the scenes now seems charmingly naive, it is the case that in some countries officials and executives have important social linkages.

Yet structuralist explanations of business power also have their difficulties. First, as is well known, "business" is a very encompassing label. There are numerous different types of businesses and their interests diverge. Business interests differ depending on not only the size but nature of a business. Some industries, such as textiles and apparel, by and large want simply a low wage workforce and low taxes. High-tech industries have more complex needs, including highly skilled workers and investment in research. Some industries are relatively mobile and can indeed shift investment to locations that offer lower wages and taxes. The mobility of other industries is limited by the nature of their business or market. Extractive industries must be where their raw material is found. Service industries generally must be near their customers although outsourcing overseas (for example to call centers in India) represents an attempt to escape this constraint. States also differ tremendously in their capacity. In some third world countries, states have very limited administrative capacity and not even much physical control over their territory. In the most extreme cases, they become "failed" states unable even to guarantee the basic infrastructure, a degree of economic stability, and freedom from random violence that business needs to function. Even among advanced democracies, state capacity differs in terms of the degree to which the bureaucracy has detailed knowledge of business, administrative controls over it (e.g. through licensing requirements) or the ability to influence the cost or availability of credit.

It is unlikely, therefore, that there can be a single theory of the relationship between business and the state. Both business and the state differ too much and can be understood as variables, not constants. The balance of power between a highly mobile industry (e.g. apparel) and a state with little administrative capacity is different from the balance between a state with high administrative capacity and an industry that because of its product or market has limited capacity to relocate. The balance between finance—which can increasingly be located around the globe— and the state is not the same as the balance between an extractive industry such as coal mining and the state. Finally, states differ in terms of what they are trying to achieve. Not every state wants to have a detailed or directive role in managing the economy.

Structuralist interpretations of business power received a powerful boost from concern about globalization (Ohmae 1995; Strange 1996). Most of the claims about the consequences of globalization were variants on the structuralist argument discussed above. If, to quote Friedman (2005), "the world is flat," however, structural forces can operate more forcefully thereby reducing state autonomy. The volume of currencies traded daily far outstrips the capacity not only of individual states but of combinations of states to shape the market. Markets, not governments, rule.

Globalization itself generates countervailing forces. For example, the freedom that globalization provides to ship goods around the world may strengthen the desire of industries to cluster in locations that maximize their productivity because of the presence there of markets, skilled workers, or raw materials. An interesting empirical literature has developed that explores whether or not globalization has stripped contemporary states of their ability to tax business or business executives without them relocating to a lower tax environment. If it were necessary to compensate, theorists suggested, taxes would rise on immobile factors or groups such as less mobile workers and on consumers. Empirical evidence has not supported these expectations, however. There has seemed to be a positive not a negative relationship between globalization and taxation (Garrett 1998). Steinmo (2002) argues that "wage rates, quality of workforce, infrastructure, access to markets, and a host of other factors are generally more important factors used when deciding whether to invest new capital (i.e. whether to "exit" or "enter"). Dreher (2007) argues that globalization does indeed lower *marginal* tax rates on capital while Swank (1998) argues that lower tax rates on corporations have been accompanied by the abolition of many incentives and allowances. There are few if any known instances of governments repealing environmental or consumer protection regulations to attract or retain businesses. Indeed, as Vogel (1995) notes there are more instances in which globalization leads to "trading up" as states that are regulatory leaders seek to insure that others adopt similar and similarly expensive standards.

Much of the literature on globalization points out that many of its features are not new (Weiss 1998). Capital movements were freer prior to the First World War than they were until the late 1990s (Eichengreen 1985). International trade and capital movements were less restricted prior to the First World War until several decades after the Second. The US economy was more dependent on foreign trade in 1914 than it was again until the 1970s. Perhaps the odd period out historically was from the 1930s to the 1960s when state was more autarkic, trade was a lower proportion of GDP for many states, and there was the most faith in the ability of governments to steer their economies. States are not mere victims of historical change. States created the gold standard and free trade; states ended the gold standard and moved in a more autarkic, protectionist direction in the 1930s. In the late twentieth century, states moved to liberalize trade by reducing tariffs and creating the WTO. It took conscious state action to liberalize capital movements. In recent years, there have been fears (or hopes) that globalization has been slowed or even reversed. Both the terrorist attacks of 9/11 and the Great Crash of 2008 have resulted in policy changes that impede the free movement of goods and capital. It seems unlikely, however, that there will be a full-scale retreat from globalization even if the regulation of the financial sector is tightened.

How might states be reshaped in responding to the challenges for dealing with business in a globalized world? There has been increased awareness that states cannot rely on traditional forms of governance in meeting the challenge. Obvious possible strategies for states are to merge sovereignty, cooperate loosely, delegate to private sector organizations, or change in character.

Probably the only clear example of states merging sovereignty to a significant degree is the European Union. The EU has emerged as a major regulatory force setting policy in a large number of policy areas of vital concern to business including environmental policy, the rights of workers, and consumer protection. States may hope to achieve some of the benefits provided by collaboration within the

EU without the attendant costs of loss of sovereignty and democracy through looser forms of coordination. Slaughter (2004) has suggested that less binding forms of cooperation between states such as benchmarking and peer review may help states establish meaningful standards to which business can be held. This strategy has even made some ground within the EU as an alternative to complex and legalistic regulation (Zeitlin and Trubeck 2003). Finally states might encourage business to establish meaningful standards itself through self-regulation. Prakash and Potosi suggest that processes such as the ISO 14001 in which business itself develops and polices standards resulting in meaningful improvements in business behavior. The growth of international social movements that can damage the reputation of a company's brand in the first world in response to its behavior in the third world gives businesses a motive to follow this strategy (Büthe and Mattli this volume; but see Vogel 2006). Only time will tell whether the great hopes for self-regulation can withstand the downward pressure on corporate profits. More pessimistic perspectives suggest that the more probable responses by states in governing strategies to globalization is to reorientate themselves domestically. Cerny (1997) noted a development of the "competition state" in which states were more concerned with international economic success than with goals such as social justice. Are states likely to refocus resources on promoting competitiveness? As Pierson (2002a, 2002b) has stressed some of the most generous welfare states have been almost immune from serious criticism or pressure while the weakest (e.g. the American) have been more vigorously assailed. Certainly alternatives to reliance on the private provision of welfare by business look less attractive than in the past. While in general public welfare states have been remarkably resilient, private sector welfare states (e.g. employer-provided pensions and health insurance) have been subject to major cuts (Hacker 2002, 2006). The belief that, encouraged by tax incentives, the private sector will provide adequate levels of protection and security looks less convincing, if economic crises are to persist. As a result, the financial crises will have unpredictable consequences for the structure of corporations and may result in an increase in the regulatory role of the state.

Conclusions

As the above illustrates, political science has deployed a variety of theoretical perspectives and methodologies—both rationalist and constructivist—in the study of business and government relations, and these have generated some useful insights. What is evident is that there is a considerable body of empirical material on the variety of forms of business interaction across countries (see Hall and Soskice 2001; Hancké, and Culpepper in this volume) and at the EU and international level (Schmidt 2006; Büthe and Mattli, and Coen in this volume), but what is still lacking, given the evident importance of the firm as an actor, is a political theory of the firm. While the above varieties of capitalism debates move political science on from Lindblom's dialogue about business interests and business power to the more fruitful debate about the definition of business interest (or preferences), we are still struggling with our notions of political influence (Culpepper 2008). While many have built on Olson's seminal work to understand the logic of collective action (Moe 1980; Jordan and Halpin 2004), today political scientists are still left utilizing the economic profit maximizing rationale for individual political activity (Austen-Smith 1997). It is hoped that this chapter and others in this volume can expand our understanding of the firm's political action beyond the economic and management debates of profitability and competitiveness to provide the foundations for a more political science theory of the firm.

At the state level we hope to show that although many think of them as overwhelming forces, both business and corporations, and the state are in fact historically contingent. States have changed considerably in character as they have adapted to changed circumstances. In recent decades the challenge of globalization followed by the challenge of deep recession has prompted considerable experimentation in governance techniques. We can be reasonably confident that both states and corporations will look significantly different in the future than today even while it is impossible to be certain what their future character or the balance between them will be. The dominant theme of the 1990s was "from governing to governance." States would adapt to new circumstances through measures that included contracting out, relying on indirect policy measures such as tax incentives or rewards schemes and networks.

Similarly, the nature of corporations and business is changing but in ways that are much debated. We have noted the increased competitive pressures experienced in many industries. As capital has become more mobile, pressure on managers to produce higher short-term rates of return has increased. Corporations adopted first the techniques such as contracting and outsourcing later urged on governments. Developments in corporations therefore paralleled those in the state—a movement towards a less formalized, less hierarchical "post-Fordist" structure (such as the European Union that has been characterized as a postmodern polity). Whether or not these trends will continue in either business or government is hard to say. Some have suggested that a "re-bureaucratization" of the state is likely as the failures of contracting out become ever more apparent. The privatization and liberalization of industries such as electricity and energy supply in Europe has been followed by the creation of complex national specific regulatory systems operated by wholly new government agencies (Coen and Heritier 2005).

Financial crises may have unpredictable consequences for the structure of corporations and almost certainly lead to new regulatory governance structures sponsored by the state. However, the balance between state and market is subject to long-run cyclical fluctuations. The state advances and the market retreats, only for the market to advance again, followed in turn by a reinvigoration of state power as awareness of the deficiencies of the market as a form of social organization is renewed.

This pendulum effect was anticipated by Polanyi (1944). Hence, even if one wants as much market as possible, there is no final answer to how much state is necessary. What is clear is that capitalism is subject to recurrent crises and out of these new forms of capitalist organization emerge, setting the framework for business–government relations.

REFERENCES

AUSTEN-SMITH, D. 1997. "Interest groups: money, information and influence," in D. Mueller, ed., *Perspectives on Public Choice: A Handbook*. Cambridge: Cambridge University Press.

—— 1998. "Allocating access for information and contributions," *Journal of Law, Economics, and Organization* 14(2): 277–303.

—— and BANK, J. 2002. "Costly signalling and cheap talk in models of political influence," *European Journal of Political Economy* 18(4): 263–80.

—— and WRIGHT, J. 1992. "Competitive lobbying for legislators' votes," *Social Choice and Welfare* 9: 229–57.

BALDWIN, R., and CAVE, M. 1999. *Understanding Regulation: Theory, Strategy, and Practice*. Oxford: Oxford University Press.

BARDACH, E., and KAGAN, R. A. 2002. *Going by the Book: The Problem of Regulatory Unreasonableness*. New Brunswick, NJ: Transaction.

BAUMGARTNER, F. R., and JONES, B. D. 1993. *Agendas and Instability in American Politics*. Chicago: University of Chicago Press.

—— and LEECH, B. 1998. *Basic Interests: The Importance of Groups in Politics and Political Science*. Princeton: Princeton University Press.

—— BERRY, J. M., HOJNACKI, M., KIMBALL, D. C., and LEECH, B. L. 2009. *Lobbying and Policy Change: Who Wins, Who Loses, and Why*. Chicago: Chicago University Press.

BECKER, G. 1985. "Public politics, pressure groups and deadweight cost," *Journal of Public Economics* 28: 329–47.

BERNSTEIN, M. 1955. *Regulating Business by Independent Commission*. Princeton: Princeton University Press.

BERRY, J. 1999. *The New Liberalism and the Rising Power of Citizen Groups*. Washington, DC: Brookings Institute.

BESLEY, T. 2006. *Principled Agents: The Political Economy of Good Government*. Oxford: Oxford University Press.

BIELING, H.-J. 2007. "The other side of the coin: conceptualizing the relationship between business and the state in the age of globalization," *Business and Politics* 9(3): 1–20.

BRASHER, H., and LOWERY, D. 2006. "The corporate context of lobbying activity," *Business and Politics* 8(1): 1–23.

BRIER, K., and MUNGER, M. 1986. "The impact of legislator attitudes on interest group campaign contributions," *Journal of Labour Research* 7(4): 344–61.

BROSCHIED, A. 2006. "Distributional and informational models of business and government interaction," in D. Coen and W. Grant, eds., *Business and Government: Methods and Practice*. Berlin: Leske and Bundrich.

—— and COEN, D. 2003 "Insider outsider lobbying of the European Commission", *European Union Politics* 4(2): 165–89.

—— —— 2007 "Lobbying activity and forum creation in the EU: Empirically exploring the nature of the Policy God," *Journal of European Public Policy* 14(3): 333–46.

CERNY, P. G. 1997. "Paradoxes of the competition state: the dynamics of globalization," *Government and Opposition* 32: 351–74.

CHANDLER, A. 1962. *Strategy and Structure.* Cambridge: MIT Press.

COEN, D. 1997. "The evolution of the large firm as a political actor in the European Union," *Journal of European Public Policy* 4(1): 91–108.

—— 1998. "The European business interest and the nation state: large-firm lobbying in the European Union and member states," *Journal of Public Policy* 18(1): 75–100.

—— 2007. "Empirical and theoretical studies in EU lobbying," *Journal of European Public Policy* 14: 333–45.

—— and HERITIER, A. 2005. *Refining Regulatory Regimes: Utilities in Europe.* Cheltenham: Edward Elgar.

—— and RICHARDSON, J. 2009. *Lobbying the European Union: Institutions, Actors and Policy.* Oxford: Oxford University Press.

—— and THATCHER, M. 2008. "Network governance and delegation in European networks of regulation agencies," *Journal of Public Policy* 28(1): 49–71.

CULPEPPER, P. D. 2008. "Business power, policy salience and the study of politics," *European Studies Forum* 38(2): 1–7.

—— 2009. *Business Power in Contemporary Capitalism: Corporate Control and Public Policy in Europe and Japan.* Cambridge: Cambridge University Press.

CYERT, R. M., and MARCH, J. G. 1992. *Behavioral Theory of the Firm.* Englewood Cliffs, NJ: Prentice-Hall.

DEEG, R. 1999. *Finance Capital Unveiled: Banks and the German Political Economy.* Ann Arbor: University of Michigan Press.

—— 2001. *Institutional Change and the Uses and Limits of Path Dependency: The Case of German Finance.* Max Plank Institute Discussion Paper 01/6. Cologne: Max Plank Institute.

DREHER, A. 2007. "The influence of globalization on taxes and social policy: an empirical analysis for OECD countries," *European Journal of Political Economy* 22(1): 179–201.

EICHENGREEN, B. 1985. *Who Elected Bankers? Surveillance and Control in the World Economy.* Ithaca, NY: Cornell University Press.

—— 2007. *The European Economy Since 1945: Coordinated Capitalism and Beyond.* Princeton: Princeton University Press.

—— ed. 2008. *The Gold Standard in Theory and History.* New York: Methuen.

FRIEDMAN, T. L. 2005. *The World Is Flat: A Brief History of the Twenty First Century.* New York: Farar Straus and Giroux.

FIGUEIREDO J. DE. 2002. "Lobbying and information politics," *Business and Politics* 4(2): 125–30.

GAMBETTA, D. 1993. *The Sicilian Mafia: The Business of Private Protection.* Cambridge, Mass.: Harvard University Press.

GARRETT, G. 1998. *Partisan Politics in the Global Economy.* New York: Cambridge University Press.

GRANT, W. 1993. "Business associations in Eastern Europe and Russia," *Journal of Communist Studies* 9(2): 21–33.

—— 2000. *Business and Politics.* London: McMillan.

GRAY, V., and LOWERY, D. 1997. "Reconceptualising PAC formation: it's not a collective action problem and may be an arms race," *American Political Quarterly* 25(3): 319–46.

GREAVES, J. 2009. "Bio pesticides, regulation, innovation and the regulatory state," *Public Policy and Administration* 24(3): 245–64.

GRIER, K., MUNGER, M., and ROBERTS, B. 1994. "The determinants of industrial political activity, 1978–1986," *American Political Science Review* 88: 911–26.

GROSSMAN, G., and HELPMAN, E. 1994 "Protection for sale," *American Economic Review* 84(1): 833–50.

HACKER, J. 2002. *The Divided Welfare State: The Battle over Public and Private Social Benefits in the United States.* Cambridge: Cambridge University Press.

—— 2006. *The Great Risk Shift: The Assault on American Jobs, Families, Health Care and Retirement and How You Can Fight Back.* Oxford: Oxford University Press.

HALL, P. A., and SOSKICE, D. W. 2001. *Varieties of Capitalism: The Institutional Foundations of Comparative Advantage.* Oxford: Oxford University Press.

HANSEN, W., and MITCHELL, N. 2000. "Disaggregating and explaining corporate political activity: domestic and foreign corporations in national politics," *American Political Science Review* 94: 891–903.

HART, D. 2003. "Political representation in concentrated industries: revisiting the Olsonian hypothesis," *Business and Politics* 5 (3): 261–86.

—— 2004. "Business is not an interest group: on companies in American National Politics", *Annual Review of Political Science* 7: 47–67.

HORWITZ, M. 1977. *The Transformation of American Administrative Law 1780–1860.* Cambridge, Mass.: Harvard University Press.

JOHNSON, C. A. 1982. *MITI and the Japanese Miracle: The Growth of Industrial Policy 1925–75.* Stanford, Calif.; Stanford University Press.

JORDAN, G., and HALPIN, D. 2004. "Olson triumphant? Recruitment strategies and the growth of a small business organisation," *Political Studies* 52: 431–49.

KATZENSTEIN, P. J. 1985. *Small States in World Markets: Industrial Policy in Europe.* Ithaca, NY: Cornell University Press.

KLEIN, N. 2000. *No Logo: Taking Aim at the Brand Bullies.* London: Random House.

KOLKO, G. 1965. *Railroads and Regulation 1877–1916.* Princeton: Princeton University Press.

LAWTON, T. 2002. *Cleared for Take-Off: Structure and Strategy in the Low Fare Airline Business.* London: Ashgate.

LINDBLOM, C. E. 1977. *Politics and Markets: The World's Political Economic Systems.* New York: Basic.

LOWERY, D. 2007. "Why do organised interests lobby? A multi-goal, multi-level theory of lobbying," *Polity* 39: 29–54.

LYNN, L. N., and McKEOWN, T. J. 1988. *Organizing Business: Trade Associations in America and Japan.* Washington, DC: AEI.

MAJONE, G. 2005. *Dilemmas of European Integration: The Ambiguities and Pitfalls of Integration by Stealth.* Oxford: Oxford University Press.

MARTIN, C. J. 2000. *Stuck in Neutral: Business and the Politics of Human Capital Investment Policy.* Princeton: Princeton University Press.

—— 2004. "Reinventing welfare regimes: employers and the implementation of active social policy," *World Politics* 57: 39–69.

MILLS, C. W. 1956. *The Power Elite.* New York: Oxford University Press.

MILYO, J., PRIMO, D., and GROSECLOSE, T. 2000. "PAC campaign contributions in perspective," *Business and Politics* 2(1): 74–90.

MOE, T. 1980. *The Organization of Interests.* Chicago: University of Chicago Press.

NETTL, J. 1965. "Consensus or elite domination: the case of business," *Political Studies*, 13(1): 22–44.

OHMAE, K. 1995. *The End of the Nation State.* New York: Free Press.

OLSON, M. 1965. *The Logic of Collective Action: Public Good and the Theory of Groups.* New York: Harvard University Press.

PEMPEL, T. J. 1998. *Regime Shift: Comparative Dynamics of the Japanese Political Economy.* Ithaca, NY: Cornell University Press.

PIERSON, P. 2002a. *Dismantling the Welfare State: Reagan, Thatcher and the Politics of Retrenchment.* Cambridge: Cambridge University Press.

—— 2002b. "Coping with permanent austerity: welfare state restructuring in affluent democracies," *Revue Française de Sociologie* 43(2): 369–406.

POLANYI, K. 1944. *The Great Transformation.* New York: Farrar and Reinhart.

PORTER, M. 1992. "Capital disadvantage: America's failing capital investment system," *Harvard Business Review* 70: 65–82.

POTTERS, J., and SLOOF, R. 1996. "Interest groups: a survey of empirical models that try to access their influence," *European Journal of Political Economy* 12(3): 403–42.

REGINI, M. 2002. "Between de-regulation and social pacts: the response of European economies to globalization," *Politics and Society* 28: 5–33.

SCHATTSCHNEIDER, E. E. 1956. "United States: the functional approach to party government," in S. Neumann, ed., *Modern Political Parties: Approaches to Comparative Politic.* Chicago: University of Chicago Press, 194–215.

—— 1960. *The Semisovereign People: A Realist's View of Democracy in America.* New York: Holt, Rinehart & Winston.

SCHMIDT, V. A. 2006. *Democracy in Europe: The EU and National Polities.* Oxford: Oxford University Press.

SCHMITTER, P. C. 1974. "Still the century of corporatism?" *The Review of Politics* 36(1): 85–131.

SLAUGHTER, A.-M. 2004. *A New World Order.* Princeton: Princeton University Press.

SMITH, M. 2000. *American Business and Political Power: Public Opinion, Elections and Democracy.* Chicago: Chicago University Press.

SPRUYT, H. 1994. *The Sovereign State and its Competitors.* Princeton: Princeton University Press.

STEINMO, S. 2002. "Taxation and globalization: challenges to the Swedish welfare state," *Comparative Political Studies* 35(7): 839–62.

STIGLER, G. 1971. "The theory of economic regulation," *Bell Journal of Econometrics and Management Science* 2: 3–21.

STIGLITZ, J. 1986. *Economics of the Public Sector.* New York: Norton Press.

STRANGE, S. 1996. *The Retreat of the State: The Diffusion of Power in the World Economy.* Cambridge: Cambridge University Press.

STREECK, W. 1997. "German capitalism: does it exist? Can it survive?" *New Political Economy* 2 (2): 237–56.

—— and SCHMITTER, P. C. 1991. "From national corporatism to transnational pluralism: organized interests in the single European market," *Politics and Society* 19(2): 133–65.

—— GROTE, J., SCHNIEDER, V., and VISSER, J. 2005. *Governing Interests: Business Associations Facing Internationalization.* London: Routledge.

SWANK, D. 1998. "Funding the welfare state: globalization and the taxation of business in advanced market economies," *Political Studies* 3: 671–92.

TIBERGHIEN, Y. 2007. *Entrepreneurial States: Reforming Corporate Governance in France, Japan and Korea.* Ithaca, NY: Cornell University Press.

TILLY, C. (ed.) 1974. *The Formation of National States in Western Europe.* Princeton: Princeton University Press.

TUCKER, A. 2008. "Trade associations as industry reputation agents: a model of reputational trust," *Business and Politics* 10(1): 1–26.

VOGEL, D. 1989. *Fluctuating Fortunes: The Political Power of Business in America.* New York: Basic Books.

VOGEL, D. 1995. *Trading up: Consumer and Environmental Regulation in a Global Economy.* Cambridge, Mass.: Harvard University Press.

VOGEL, S. K. 2001. "The crisis of German and Japanese capitalism," *Comparative Political Studies* 34(10): 1103–33.

—— 2006. *Japan Remodeled: How Government and Industry are Reforming Japanese Capitalism.* Ithaca, NY: Cornell University Press.

WEISS, L. 1998. *The Myth of the Powerless State.* Ithaca, NY: Cornell University Press.

WILLMAN, P., COEN, D., CURRIE, D., and SINER, M. 2003. "Regulatory institutions and firm behaviour: the evolution of regulatory relationships in the UK," *Industrial and Corporate Change* 12(1): 69–89.

WILSON, G. 1990. "Corporations' political strategies," *British Journal of Political Science* 20: 281–8.

WOO-CUMINGS, M. (ed.) 1999. *The Developmental State.* Ithaca, NY: Cornell University Press.

WRIGHT, M. 2002. "Who governs Japan? Politicians and bureaucrats in the policymaking process," *Political Studies* 47: 939–54.

ZEITLIN, J., and TRUBECK, D. 2003. *Governing Work and Welfare in a New Economy: European and American Experience.* Oxford: Oxford University Press.

ZYSMAN, J. 1983. *Governments, Markets and Growth: Financial Systems and the Politics of Industrial Change.* Ithaca, NY: Cornell University Press.

CHAPTER 2

ECONOMICS

ECONOMIC THEORIES OF THE FIRM, BUSINESS, AND GOVERNMENT

CHRISTOS N. PITELIS

INTRODUCTION

THE aim of this chapter is to provide a short critical account of extant economic theory(ies) of the firm, business (and industry organization), and the state and government. We explore competing perspectives, such as the neoclassical economics, transaction costs, evolutionary, resource, capabilities, and system-based as well as Marxist and identify common ground and differences. We also attempt a limited eclectic synthesis. The task of covering such apparently diverse topics in the context of a single entry is facilitated by the fact that extant alternative economic perspectives have implications on all the aforementioned theories. (However, we do not enter the important issue of public and/or business policy, due to space considerations). We also try to show that the issues at hand are central to an appreciation of international organization and system-wide economic performance.

Structure-wise, the second section discusses alternative theories of the firm, industry, and business organization; the third section discusses economic theories of the state; and the fourth explores their interrelationships, commonalities, and differences, and the scope for an eclectic synthesis. The fifth section concludes.

ALTERNATIVE PERSPECTIVES ON MARKETS, FIRMS, BUSINESS (AND INDUSTRY ORGANIZATION)

The Market(-Failure)-based Theory (MFT)

The major elements of MFT are expounded in Alfred Marshall's 1920 *Principles of Economics*. While Marshall himself had a rather nuanced approach to firms and their internal operations and capabilities, subsequent developments in microeconomics and Industrial Organization (IO) economics focused on the industry as the unit of analysis.[1] The main economic question raised by this perspective is how the price-output decisions (equilibrium) of firms operating in industries (collection of firms producing similar products, such as cars) impact on the efficient allocation of scarce resources and therefore on the optimality of the market system as a whole.

The method used to answer this question involves the assumption of "optimizing behavior" (firms are assumed to maximize profits). Given this objective, all one needs in order to determine the price-output "equilibrium" in an industry is knowledge of the cost structure, the demand conditions, and the type of industry structure. The last mentioned can be perfectly competitive or imperfectly competitive. "Perfect competition" exists when firms are numerous, produce homogeneous products, and there exists free entry and exit in the industry. Under these assumptions firms can only make "normal" (or zero economic) profits, that is they will simply cover their average costs (defined to include compensation for all factors of production, including managers and entrepreneurs).

"Imperfect competition" refers to all types of non-perfectly competitive markets, such as monopoly (a single seller in the industry) or oligopoly (relatively few sellers whose actions impact on each other—there exists interdependence). A limiting case of oligopoly is duopoly (two firms in the industry). In the case of imperfect competition, profit maximizing behavior often leads to prices in excess of the perfectly competitive ones, therefore to super-normal profits or, in the case of monopoly, to "monopoly profits."

Assuming the same cost and demand conditions, the "monopoly profit" represents an equivalent reduction in the "consumer surplus" (the benefit consumers receive by not paying the highest possible price they would be willing to pay for lower quantities as portrayed by their demand curve). This simply represents a redistribution from consumers to producers and it is not seen as necessarily bad per se (this depends on how monopolists use their profits). The real problem with monopoly, however, is that in order to maximize profits, monopolies need to restrict output. This leads to lower levels of output than are possible under perfect competition, leading to underutilization (misallocation) of scarce resources. This is the anathema of neoclassical microeconomics, which explains why in this perspective monopoly is bad. It represents a structural market failure and needs to be addressed, through government intervention (see below).

Monopoly and perfect competition are two extremes; in practice most industries will tend to be oligopolistic. Analyzing oligopolies is more exciting but not as straightforward. Given the many possibilities available for the possible behavior of oligopolies, there exist many oligopoly models. In the original duopoly models of Bertrand and Cournot, different equilibria follow depending on assumptions of oligopolistic behavior. Betrand assumed that oligopolies will compete over price and thus derived competitive pricing behavior, despite oligopolistic market structures. Cournot instead assumed firms compete over output and derived a positive relationship between firm numbers and output—the more firms exist the higher the output will be (see Cabral 2000).

Starting with the classic work of Joe Bain in 1956 on *Barriers to New Competition*, modern IO theory built oligopoly models that derive equilibria which range between perfectly competitive and monopolistic, depending on assumptions of entry and exit. For example, in the limit pricing model of Modigliani (1958), it is shown that oligopolies will charge a price above the competitive one (because, and up to the point where, they are protected from barriers to entry, notably economies of scale), but below the monopolistic one because of fear of entry and in order to deter it. Others, notably Cowling and Waterson (1976) argue that firms do not need to reduce prices; instead they can deter entry through strategy, for example by investing in excess capacity. If their threat of using this capacity post-entry is credible (in that it involves pre-entry commitments that make it more profitable for firms to act on their threats post-entry), entry will not occur and incumbents will be able to charge prices, which can be as high as the monopoly price (depending also on the degree of price collusion). In stark contrast to this, Baumol's (1982) "contestable markets" theory claims that even oligopolistic industries will behave competitively (charge competitive prices), if there exists powerful potential competition (other firms that may be attracted to the industry). Potential competition renders markets contestable, re-establishing the perfectly competitive ideal even in the presence of oligopolistic structures.

All the above can be examined using simple game theory (Dixit 1982). Building on such earlier works, the "new IO" puts emphasis on the conduct of firms (in contrast to the focus on structure of the industry of the Bain tradition, which in effect posited a mostly unidirectional causal link from structure to conduct to performance).[2] The emphasis on conduct allows a more realistic approach to the link between structure and performance that allows for co-determination of structure–conduct performance links and simultaneity. It can also be mathematically more rigorous. On the minus side however, game theoretic models of oligopoly have been plagued by the possibility of "multiple equilibria"—in effect a good mathematician can prove anything he or she may wish depending on the initial specification of the "game" (see Tirole 1988). More recently, Sutton (1998) made a very important contribution towards marrying formal modeling with reality. His "bounds" approach employs stylized facts and theoretical insights to predict where, within expected bounds, price–output equilibrium should lie—and adopts formal modeling to analyze and test for such a reality-bound range of expected outcomes.

In the absence of perfect competition or perfect contestability, there exists scope for the government to step in to restore perfectly competitive conditions. A problem here is that in the absence of perfect competition across all industries in the economy, intervention in one market is not guaranteed to improve efficiency (the problem of "second best") except under rather restrictive assumptions (Gilbert and Newberry 1982). This limits the power of IO to provide useful public prescriptions, which is its purported aim.[3]

The above is just one of the problems of the microeconomic and IO approach. Other related problems include the restrictive assumptions (which include perfect information/knowledge, optimizing behavior, inter-firm cooperation being seen only as price collusion and technology/innovations being exogenous). In this context perfect competition in effect implies the absence of any competition at all. In addition, the whole focus on efficient allocation of scarce resources ignores the fundamental issue of resource creation. While changes in resource allocation can lead to changes in resource creation, it is far from evident that the efficient resource allocation at any given time is the only way to affect resource creation. Indeed resource creation is automatically related to intertemporal issues, which poses another problem for the neoclassical perspective—its focus is on comparative statics, not on intertemporal efficiency. The last mentioned involves knowledge and innovation, which the neoclassical view considers to be exogenously given.

The difficulties of the IO perspective to deal with knowledge and innovation, therefore with intertemporal efficiency (the theme of the founding father of economics Adam Smith and many leading economists since, such as Joseph Schumpeter), led IO scholars such as Baumol (1991; the inventor of contestability theory), to lament the suboptimal properties or "perfect competition" and "perfect contestability," as regards innovation, thus dynamic intertemporal economic performance. A reason, Baumol observed, echoing Schumpeter (1942), is that both these types of market structure remove any incentive to innovate, which is of course the above-competitive rates of return.

The usefulness of the neoclassical IO perspective has been questioned widely, both from within and from without economics. From within, "managerial theories" drew on Berle and Means's (1932) classic statement of separation of ownership from control to claim that controlling professional managers maximize their own utility, not profits. This includes sales, discretionary expenditures, growth, and other (see Marris 1996). Subsequent developments in economics tried to address the resultant problem of "agency" (for example, Alchian and Demsetz 1972; and Jensen and Meckling 1976). The emergent "agency" literature gradually became the foundation of the "shareholder value" approach to corporate governance (see Pitelis 2004 and below).

In contrast to IO, Joseph Schumpeter suggested that competition should be viewed as a process of creative destruction through innovation, not a type of market structure. Hayek (1945) pointed to the efficiency of markets, in terms not of allocative efficiency, attributed to perfectly competitive structures, but instead in terms of their ability to address the problem of coordination in the presence of dispersed knowledge. Cyert and March's (1963) classic book questioned the ability of firms to maximize profits, in the presence of uncertainty, and intra-firm conflict. They suggested "satisficing" as a better objective of firms. Coase (1937) lamented the failure of mainstream theory to enter the "black box" (the firm), while Penrose (1959) pointed to the failure of mainstream theory to deal with the issue of firm growth. Building on Penrose, Richardson (1972) viewed cooperation, not just as a form of price collusion, but as a mode of organizing production, such as markets and firms, explicable in terms of firm capabilities relevant to such activities.

From the aforementioned economic theories-critiques, it is only Penrose and Cyert and March that really entered the "black box" (Coase "merely" tried to explain its existence). The former, by focusing on intra-firm resources and knowledge creation; the latter by considering intra-firm decision-making and conflict. It is therefore hardly surprising that these two economic theories proved to be very influential to non-economists (Pitelis 2007a), with Penrose claiming motherhood of the currently influential resource-based view (RBV) and the dynamic capabilities (DCs) approach (Teece 2007). We explore these theories and their implications on industry structure in the next subsection.

Given the strength and prominence of its critics and the unrealism of its assumptions, a non-economist can be baffled as to what, if any, is the usefulness of the MFT. It is ironic, perhaps, that many microeconomic textbooks provide extensive treatment of the "Theory of the Firm," with little if any reference to what a firm is. In Penrose's apt observation, in traditional theory firms are simply points in a cost curve. This seems clearly unsatisfactory, but it need not be—the main issue is the objective such theories aim to satisfy, whether they achieve it, and whether the objective is a useful one.

The above is a big debate that cannot be addressed satisfactorily in an entry of this length. However, some points are worth making. On the realism of assumptions, Friedman (1967) claimed that it is predictive ability that counts, not the realism or the assumptions per se. On this basis, traditional theory is claimed to fare well. On "objectives," profit maximization has been re-justified in terms of survival of the fittest arguments and the market for corporate control (takeover of ineffective firms). Alchian and Demsetz (1972) claimed that markets and firms do not really differ, firms are simply "internal markets"; the crucial issue for them being incentive alignment through monitoring and self-monitored "residual claimants" of profits. The view that even firms (hierarchies) are markets could serve as a pure neoclassical MFT. However, both Alchian and Demsetz have subsequently conceded that markets and firms could not be seen as being the same (Pitelis 1991).

Little discussed in the literature are the objectives the traditional theory tried to serve. These were mainly two. The first was to explain price–output decisions of firms under different types of industry structures, with an eye to predicting changes by suitably modifying the assumptions. The second aim was grander—to prove the efficiency of the market system vis-à-vis alternatives such as central planning, in terms of allocative efficiency. A major achievement of economic theory was its ability to prove that under perfect competition a market economy can affect Pareto-efficient allocation of scarce resources (a situation where no change can make one person better off, without making someone else worse off). This is suitably celebrated as the First Fundamental Theorem of Welfare Economics.

It is arguable that the apparent irrelevance of MFT in terms of explaining firms and organizations is due to its focus on static allocative efficiency, which renders any relation to real-life firms, organizations, and the organization of industry very distant indeed. Real life is, if anything, dynamic and the objective of any agents, be they firms or nations is to improve their conditions over time (that is intertemporal performance). MFT is ill suited for this purpose. Considering that issues such as knowledge and innovation are critical determinants of long-term performance (Pitelis 2009), given that firms, organizations, and the organization of industry can impact crucially on them; and considering that economic performance over time is certainly an important economic issue (arguably *the* important one), one would be forgiven for believing the MFT are patently useless, even in terms of their own objective. That would be wrong.

The resilience and strength of MFT is quite amazing and needs explaining. First, most currently popular discussions of organization and strategy, notably transaction costs economics, the RBV, and corporate governance rely heavily on ideas originally developed within economics (even as critiques of the mainstream paradigm). Importantly the very mainstream paradigm still serves as the only available analysis of the role of industry structure on firms' price–output decisions, and has led to the first conceptual framework for the industry-based analyses on firm performance in the context of Porter's (1980) five- forces model of competition. Porter's approach was fully reliant on the neoclassical IO model of industry structures, where Porter himself had contributed significantly before turning to business strategy.

Despite its failures to account for firm heterogeneity and the role of the intra-firm environment (resources, decision-making, conflict, etc.), industry is arguably an influential concept and an important determinant on performance. It is not surprising that Penrose (1959) combined her focus on internal resources with the role of the external environment (which includes the industry), in the context of her concept of "productive opportunity" (the dynamic interaction between internal resources and capabilities and the external environment). Evidence shows that with regard to firm performance, firm-level factors are more important than industry-level ones, but the latter are still significant (McGahan and Porter 1997).

Other potential purposes of the mainstream approach are that it serves as a benchmark against which to compare reality. Moreover, in mature industries, characterized by stability, and high knowledge of the environment, the mainstream model can even help approximate reality (Pitelis 2002). In addition, the model may help provide a neat, rigorous diagrammatical and mathematical exposition, which can help facilitate student learning. For others, however, the static, unrealistic models used by mainstream economists do not lead gradually to a more nuanced understanding of reality described above, but are often seen as *the* reality, especially by younger students. This does not help them be critical and think outside the box.

To conclude, MFT has a long history of distinction (and frustration). Its concepts and models have proven resilient, influential, and of import to other disciplines.

Many fundamental ideas have emerged as its criticisms and have helped further the appreciation of organizations, markets, and economies. To date there exists no alternative explanation of price–output decisions by firms operating in industries, of equal generality and rigor. In its Porterian version, MFT has informed management theory and managerial practice. Then again, it is important to look at MFT as it is—an abstraction, potentially dangerous when taken at face value. Last, but not least, it is not clear whether more or less progress could have been made in economics and organization scholarship, were the mainstream approach not so dominant.

The search for an alternative perspective, which focuses on organizations, not markets (as required by reality and proposed by Nobel Laureate Herbert Simon, 1995) yet is rigorous, can explain price–output decisions with a degree of generality, and have applications to other disciplines, has not been achieved yet. The nearest we have is arguably Nelson and Winter's (1982) evolutionary theory (see below). Despite its significance, however, this has been more influential outside mainstream economics. The lack of an alternative approach that commands wide recognition by economists is explicable in part by the input spent on MFT. This has been disproportional (until at least recently), partly due to its ideological underpinnings and prescriptions (its reliance on, and defense of, the free market system and ideology). Whether economics will ever change, remains to be seen. Our guess is not so soon. What now helps the paradigm going on is the huge sunk investment in education, careers, textbooks, and lives. Changing this may require generations. However, there are some positive signs—not least the endogenous growth theory (Romer 1990), North's (1990) institutional approach, and more recently the work by Acemoglu, Johnson, and Robinson (2001) on institutions and intertemporal economic performance. Such works, at the very least, legitimize the idea that intertemporal economic performance and the factors that affect it are within the scope of mainstream economics.

Transaction Costs, Property Rights and Resource, Evolutionary and System-Based Views

A major challenge to the mainstream IO approach has been Coase's (1937) transaction costs perspective. This is still a market-failure-based approach, only now market failure is "natural" (not structural) and attributable to high market transaction costs. In addition, the private firm is seen as a device that can solve market failure, by internalizing market transactions.

In Coase's (1937) article, the nature of the firm was considered to be the "employment contract" between an entrepreneur and laborers. While, conceptually, it is always possible to organize production through the exclusive use of the market mechanism (where hierarchical relationships are absent and relative price changes determine the allocation of resources), Coase observed that the employment contract-firm can have advantages in terms of transaction costs. These can be the result of fewer transactions, but also lower average cost of transaction. The former is the case when an entrepreneur directs resources (notably employees), instead of having to transact with an equal number of independent contractors (who may also liaise between themselves), and when a single general longer term contract replaces spot market contracting (which would involve continuous renegotiations of contractual terms). The latter is the case when hierarchy (or fiat) leads to less protracted intra-firm negotiations, for example because of the fear of redundancy by employees. As intra-firm transactions also involve costs, the internalization of market transactions will take place up to the point where the transaction costs involved in having a transaction organized by the market are equal to the (organizational) costs of undertaking this transaction intra-firm. According to Coase, both horizontal integration and vertical integration can be explained in terms of this logic (Pitelis and Pseiridis 1999). Accordingly the nature and boundaries of the firm can be explained in terms of overall market and organizational costs minimization (Teece 1982; Pitelis 1991).

The development of Coase's work, mainly by Oliver Williamson (1975, 1985), focused on asset specificity (assets whose redeployment involves loss of value) as the driver of integration (in particular vertical) but also through conglomerate diversification and cross-border (Williamson 1991). Buckley and Casson (1976) zeroed in on the public good (non-excludability in use) nature of knowledge, to explain integration (foreign direct investment—FDI) by multinational corporations (MNCs). Teece (1977) and Kogut and Zander (1993), instead, explained FDI in terms of differential costs–benefits of transferring tacit knowledge intra- versus inter-firm. Coase (1991) questioned the importance of asset specificity and even the concept of rationality (Pitelis 2002). Moreover he has later expressed regret for his almost exclusive focus on the "employment relationship," claiming that one should not just focus on the (Coasean) nature of the firm, but also its essence, which is "running a business." In his view, this involves more than the employment contract and includes the use of human and non-human resources and one's own time and capabilities to produce for a profit (Coase 1991; Pitelis 2002).

Despite a very extensive literature on transaction costs, which includes support and criticisms (see David and Han 2004 for an assessment of the evidence, which is found to be mixed), Coase's distinction between the "nature" and the "essence" was little noticed. Subsequent developments zeroed in on "property rights" (Grossman and Hart 1986; Hart 1995) and problems of metering and (self-)monitoring (Alchian and Demsetz 1972), to address the question of the existence and scope of the firm, as well as the question why does capital employ labor rather than the other way around. The answer was in terms of the efficiency benefits of property rights, and the need for (self-)monitoring, in the context of team production respectively; see Kim and Mahoney (2002), Foss and Foss (2005), and Pitelis (2007a) for more detailed critical assessments and syntheses. None of these theories attempted to deal with Coase's "running a business" challenge.

Subsequent contributions by Demsetz (1988, 1994) and Kogut and Zander (1996) as well as the emergence of the resource-based view (RBV) drew on earlier works by Edith Penrose (1959) and Demsetz (1973) (see among others Teece 1982; Wernerfelt 1984; Barney 1991; Peteraf 1993), and went some way toward explicating what firms do, thus addressing in part the problem of the "essence." A critical concern, for example, of the strategy literature is to explain how firms aim to acquire sustainable competitive advantage (SCA) (see for example Lippman and Rumelt 2003; Peteraf and Barney 2003). This involves definitionally issues pertaining to "running a business." For example, in the resource-based view (RBV), the diagnosis, building, reconfiguration, and leveraging of intra-firm resources that are valuable, rare, inimitable, and non-substitutable (VRIN), may help firms acquire SCAs. This is at least part and parcel of Coase's "essence" (Pitelis and Teece 2009).

Early contributions in the RBV did not aim to also explain the nature of the firm (see Barney 2001; Priem and Butler 2001). For Pitelis and Wahl (1998), the Penrosean version of the RBV, however, could be interpreted as a theory of the nature of the firm too. The superiority of firms in terms of knowledge creation, innovation, endogenous growth, and productivity for production for sale in the market for a profit (attributed by Penrose to learning by doing and teamwork in the context of the cohesive shell of the organization) could be seen as an alternative and complementary to Coase's efficiency-based explanation of the employment relationship, thus the nature and boundary of firms. Subsequent literature, summarized in Mahoney (2005) has used the two theories as partly complementary, partly incompatible. Issues of potential incompatibility revolved around the question of "opportunism" (self-interested behavior that also involves guile) and "asset specificity" (Mahoney 2005).

It is arguable that the most relevant recent development on the Coasean "essence" of the firm is the dynamic capabilities perspective (Teece et al. 1997; Eisenhardt and Martin 2000; Zollo and Winter 2002; Helfat et al. 2007; Teece 2007). While Penrose (1959), Richardson (1972), and resource-based scholars used the concept of capabilities to explain the growth, scope, and boundaries of firms, as well as the institutional division of labor between market, firm, and inter-firm cooperation (Richardson 1972), they have not gone far enough in terms of analyzing how firms can leverage these resources and capabilities so as to obtain SCA, in the context of uncertainty and radical change. Additionally there has been limited discussion on the nature and types of capabilities that can help engender SCA. This has been the agenda of the DCs perspective. By focusing on DCs as higher order capabilities that help create, reconfigure, and leverage more basic, such as operational (Helfat et al. 2007), organizational resources and capabilities, and by identifying the sensing and seizing of opportunities, as well as the need to maintain SCA, as key objective and functions of DCs, the DC perspective has arguably been the major advance in terms of explicating Coase's "essence" of the firm. In addition, Pitelis and Teece (2009) claimed that the Coasean distinction between the "nature" and the "essence" is suspect and that DCs in market, value, and price co-creation can help explain both. This claim also questions the widely popular approach to define the nature of the firm independently of the objective of its principals or principals-to-be (Pitelis 1991).

The transaction costs, property rights RBV, and DC-based theories of the firm have efficiency implications on industry structure; they both explain more concentrated industry structures in terms of transaction costs and/or productivity-related efficiencies. In the transaction costs view, integration strategies can lead to more concentrated industry structures, but in so doing they reduce transaction costs. Similarly, firm heterogeneity in the RBV can explain firm-level sustainable competitive advantages (SCA), thus provide a reason why more efficient firms can grow faster, increasing industry concentration. Despite such similarities, however, the RBV and DCs and related evolutionary and system-based views (see below), also differ in many significant respects from both the IO and transaction costs perspectives. In particular, despite differences, these perspectives share between them the view that competition is not a type of market structure, and that what is important is not just the efficient allocation of scarce resources, but also the creation and capture of value and wealth through innovation. Efficient resource allocation through perfectly competitive market structures, moreover, is not seen as the best way to effect value and wealth creation and capture. There is a wide belief that firms are very important contributors to value/wealth creation and capture, and also that each firm is an individual entity, which differs from other firms primarily in terms of its distinct resources, capabilities, and knowledge.

The lineage of this perspective can be claimed to include founding fathers in economics, such as Adam Smith (1776) and Karl Marx (1959). Smith and Marx focused on wealth creation, not just resource allocation. They both saw competition as a process, regulating prices and profit rates, not a type of market structure. Smith described the productivity gains through specialization, the division of labor, the generation of skills, and inventions within the (pin) factory. Marx also suggested there is a dialectical relation between monopoly and competition (whereby competition leads to monopoly and monopoly can only maintain itself through the competitive struggle) and their impact on technological change, the rate of profit and the "laws of motion" of capitalism at large. Marx focused in addition to competition (conflict) within the factory, and at the society at large, between employers and employees.

Building critically on Marx, Joseph Schumpeter (1942) described competition as a process of creative destruction through innovations. He saw monopoly as a necessary and just (yet only temporary) reward for innovations. He attributed firm differential performance to differential innovativeness and saw concentration to be the result of such innovativeness.

Penrose's now classic 1959 book on *The Theory of the Growth of the Firm*, is arguably a glue that can bind such contributions together. In her book, firms are seen as bundles of resources, which interaction generates knowledge, which releases resources. "Excess resources" are an incentive to management for (endogenous) growth and innovation as they can be put to use at almost zero marginal cost (since they have already been employed and their release is hindered by indivisibilities). Differential innovations and growth lead to concentration, which, however, can also be maintained through monopolistic practices. The world is seen as one of big business competition, where competition is god and the devil at the same time. It drives innovativeness, yet it is through its restrictions that monopoly profit can be maintained.

Building on Penrose, Richardson (1972) observed that firms compete but also cooperate extensively. Such cooperation is not just price collusion as the neoclassical theory assumes. It lies between market and hierarchy, and occurs when firm activities are complementary but dissimilar (require different capabilities).

Nelson and Winter (1982) developed ideas currently of import to the resource-based view. Notable are those of firm "routines," which simultaneously encapsulate firms' unique package of knowledge, skills, and competences, allow firms to operate in an evolving environment with a degree of path-dependent institutionalization that does not necessarily rely on continuous redesign, and pass on the evolving "routines" to the also evolving organization.

The focus on the evolutionary and resource-based view on change, knowledge, and innovation, as well as its "systemic" (as opposed to market) perspective, has arguably facilitated the emergence of a major change in the economics of firms, business, and industry organization, one that emphasizes the knowledge and innovation-promoting potential of different institutional configurations. The "national," regional, and sectoral systems of innovation approach, the literature on clusters of firms, and the work of Michael Porter (1990) on national competitiveness, as well as the varieties of capitalism perspective (Hall and Soskice 2001) draw upon, and relate to, the evolutionary/resource system-based view; see Wignaraja (2003), Edquist (2005), Lundvall (2007), Pitelis (2009) for various contributions.

There are various other implications of the evolutionary/resource and systems-based perspective. First, the focus on value and wealth creation suggests a broader welfare criterion than just the consumer surplus. Second, superior capabilities provide another efficiency-based reason for concentrated industry structures. Third, competition as a dynamic process of creative destruction through innovation implies a need to account for the determinants to innovate, when considering the effects of "monopoly," but also more widely, including business organization and strategy. Fourth, competition with cooperation (co-opetition), as in Richardson, implies the need to account for the potential productivity benefits of co-opetition, in devising business strategy and public policies.[4]

Economic Theories of the State

Background: Private and public ownership

The abovementioned theories of the firm, business, and industry organization have implications on the theory of the state and government intervention. We explore these below and draw on them to examine the relationship between firms, markets, business (and industry organization), and states.

The state is widely acknowledged to be one of the most important institutional devices for resource allocation and creation along with the market and the firm. In centrally planned economies, the state has been the primary such device. However, in market economies, too, the role of the state has been mostly increasing steadily since the Second World War. In most OECD countries today, government receipts and outlays as a proportion of GDP are very high, in cases as high as 60 per cent (Mueller 2006). Many theories tried to explain the growth of the public sector in market economies, the so-called Wagner's Law, originating from a number of different perspectives. In brief, neoclassical theories consider such growth as a result of increasing demand for state services by sovereign consumers, while "public choice" theorists regard it as a result of state officials, politicians, and bureaucrats' utility maximizing policies. In the Marxist tradition, the growth of the state is linked to the laws of motion of capitalism—increasing concentration and centralization of capital, and declining profit rates—which generate simultaneous demands by capital and labor on the state to enhance their relative distributional shares, for example, through infrastructure provisions and increased welfare services, respectively. There are variations on these views within each school as well as other views from institutional, feminist, and post-Keynesian perspectives (see Pressman 2006; Hay, Lister, and Marsh 2007).

Besides explaining why states increase their economic involvement over time, many economists in the 1980s focused their attention on why states fail to allocate resources efficiently and, more particularly, on the relative efficiency properties of market versus non-market resource allocation. Particularly well known here are the views of the Chicago School, in particular Friedman (1962) and Stigler (1988). Friedman emphasized the possibility of states becoming captive to special interests of powerful organized groups, notably business and trade unions. In addition, Stigler pointed to often unintentional inefficiencies involved in cases of state intervention. Examples are redistributional programs by the state which dissipate more resources (for example in administrative costs) than they redistribute. These reasons and the tendency generated by utility maximizing bureaucrats and politicians towards excessive growth and rising and redundant costs, tend to lead to government failure. Wolf (1979) has a classification of such failures in terms of derived externalities (the Stigler argument), rising and redundant costs because of officials' "more is better" attitude, and distributional inequities, in favor of powerful pressure groups.

On a more general theoretical level, the case for private ownership and market allocation is based on three well-known theories. First, the property rights school, which suggests that the communal ownership (the lack of property rights) will lead to dissipation—the "tragedy of the commons." Second, Hayek's (1945) view of dispersed knowledge, according to which knowledge is widely dispersed in every society and efficient acquisition and utilization of such knowledge can be achieved only through price signals provided by markets. Third, Alchian and Demsetz's (1972) residual claimant's theory which suggests, much in line with the property rights school, that private ownership of firms is predicated on the need for a residual claimant of income-generating assets, in the absence of which members of a coalition, would tend to free ride, thus leading to inefficient utilization of resources.

There is a large literature on the merits and limitations of these theories (see for example Eggertson 1990 for a coverage). Some weaknesses have been exposed in each defense of private ownership and market allocation. Concerning the "tragedy of the commons," it has been observed that, historically, communal ownership could have efficiency enhancing effects (Chang 1994). Hayek's critique of pure planning loses some of its force when one considers choices of degree in "mixed economies." The residual claimant theory downplays the potential incentive-enhancing attributes of cooperatives and, moreover, becomes weaker when applied to modern joint-stock companies run by a controlling management group, as well as to knowledge workers (Pitelis and Teece 2009).

Other well-known mainstream arguments relating to the problem of government failure are Bacon and Eltis's (1976) claim that services, including state services, tend to be unproductive and Martin Feldstein's (1974) view that pay-as-you-go social security schemes reduce aggregate savings-capital accumulation. The reason is that rational individuals consider their contributions to such schemes as their savings, and reduce their personal savings accordingly to remain at their optimal consumption-savings plans. Given, however, that the schemes are pay-as-you-go (contributions are used by government to finance current benefits), no actual fund is available, so that individuals' reduction of personal savings represents an equivalent reduction of aggregate saving.

Some of the above are in line with Marxist criticism of the role of the state, for example, the views that the state is captive to capitalists' interests (Miliband 1969), and that some state services involve no surplus value-generating labor (Gouph 1979). This is often linked to the falling tendency of the rate of profits, and the tendency for government spending under advanced capitalism to exceed government receipts, for reasons related to demands by both capital and labor on state funds and resistance on both sides to taxation, which are particularly intensified under conditions of monopoly capitalism (O'Connor 1973).

Concerning more specifically the relative efficiency properties of private sector versus public sector enterprises, the focus of attention has been on issues of managerial incentives, competitive forces, and differing objectives. It was claimed that public sector enterprises achieve inferior performance in terms of profits or the efficient use of resources. While private sector managers are subject to various constraints leading them to profit maximizing policies, this is not be the case with public sector managers. Such constraints arise from the market for corporate control (that is, the possibility of takeover of inefficiently managed firms by ones which are run more efficiently), the market for managers (that bad managers will be penalized in their quest for jobs), and the product market, including the idea that consumers will choose products of efficiently run firms for their better price for given quality (Pitelis 1994).

Among other factors which tend to ensure that private sector agents (managers) behave in conformity with the wishes of the principals (shareholders)—by maximizing profits in private firms—are the concentration of shares in the hands of financial institutions; the emergence of the M-form organization which tends to ensure that divisions operate as profit centers; and the possibility of contestable markets, that is, markets where competitive forces operate through potential entry by new competitors, as a result of free entry and costless exit. It is assumed that public sector enterprises are not subject to such forces to the same degree, which implies the possibility that managerial incentives for efficient use of resources and profit maximization may be less pressing in public sector firms (Pitelis 1994).

Many of the above factors are linked to competition and competitive forces. The claim is that public sector enterprises may be more insulated from such forces and are less likely to pursue efficiency and profit maximization. The latter will also be true if public sector enterprises do not aim at such policies, for example, because they are used as redistribution vehicles by the government; and/or for non-economic reasons, such as the need for electoral support; and/or because they aim at correcting structural market failure of private sector monopolies. All these tend to establish the economic-theoretical rationale for the superior efficiency of private firms, and therefore for privatization. Kay, Mayer, and Thompson (1986), Vickers and Yarrow (1987), and Rodrik and Hausmann (2006) offer discussions and critiques.

Various limitations can be identified in the case for the superior efficiency of the private sector. One arises from the possibility that the various constraints on private sector firms' managers are not as strong as they are suggested to be. For example, large size may protect inefficient firms from the threat of takeover, it may be difficult to tell when a manager has performed well, given the often long-term nature of managerial decisions; and bounded rational consumers may often fail to tell differences in the quality of similarly priced products. Concerning competition, a private sector monopoly is as insulated from it as a public sector monopoly, *ceteris paribus* (assuming no difference in the forces of potential competition). Furthermore, the absence of competition is not per se a reason for privatization: it could well be a reason for opening up the public sector to competitive forces, for example, through competitive tendering and franchising (Yarrow 1986). Such considerations led many commentators to the conclusion that the issue is not so much that of the change in ownership structures as the nature of competitive forces and of regulatory policies themselves (Kay and Silberston 1984; Yarrow 1986; Vickers and Yarrow 1987; Clarke and Pitelis 1993).

An important issue often downplayed by proponents of privatization is that the very reason for public sector enterprises has often been market, not government, failure (Rees 1986). The first fundamental of welfare economics shows that markets can allocate resources efficiently without state intervention, provided that market failures do not exist. Such failures, however, are widely observed, famous instances of market failure being the existence of externalities (interdependencies not conveyed through prices); public goods (goods which are jointly consumed and non-excludable); and monopolies, which tend to increase prices above the competitive norm.

The observation, among others, that efficient government itself is a public good, has led to the idea of pervasive market failure (Dasgupta 1986), which is viewed as the very *raison d'être* of state intervention (Stiglitz 2002). The very reason why public sector enterprises are run by the state is that they have been seen as natural monopolies (firms in which the minimum efficient size is equal to the size of the market as a result of economies of scale, leading to declining costs). If private, it is assumed that these firms would induce structural market failure in terms of mon-opoly pricing. The undertaking of the activities of such natural monopolies (often known as public utilities) by the state could solve the problem through, for example, the introduction of marginal cost-pricing policies. Although such policies need not necessarily re-establish a first-best Pareto optimal solution (given imperfections elsewhere in the economy), they could question the value of the critique that public utilities do not maximize profits, given that this was not their objective to start with.

Theory and evidence seem to be less clear-cut on the issue of the relative efficiency properties of different ownership structures than would appear to be the case on the basis of the privatization drive of the 1980s and 1990s. This is not to say that ownership does not matter, but rather that the issue of market versus non-market allocation is far more complex than sometimes acknowledged (Pitelis 2003).

Recent work by Rodrik (2006) and colleagues (e.g. Hausmann et al. 2008) focused on wider market-failure-related issues (such as information, coordination, and missing linkages) to defend the need for regulation. Despite progress, such work remains market-failure based. It is arguable that we need to go beyond this, to explore the differential capabilities of the public (versus the private) sector. Such a differential-capabilities-based perspective is adopted below, and is applied to the private–public interaction at the national but also supra-national levels. This is because of the currently topical concern with global governance, especially in view of the current crisis.

FIRMS–BUSINESS–STATE INTERACTIONS AND SUPRA-NATIONAL ORGANIZATION

The firm, particularly the multinational enterprise (MNE) and the state, most commonly in the form of a nation state, are today arguably the two major institu-tional devices of resource allocation and creation globally, along with the market. The voluminous and fast-growing literature on the market and the hierarchy, particularly their *raisons d'être*, evolution, attributes, and interrelationships, represents a recog-nition of their importance (see, for example, Mahoney 2005). The relationship between MNEs and nation states and international organizations such as the WTO has also received interest in recent years, see Hill (2009).

As noted already, the neoclassical economic perspective considers the state to be a result of market failure. In Adam Smith (1776) the state is required mainly for the provision of justice and public works. More recent accounts point to prisoner's dilemma, coordination, asymmetric information, and missing linkages-related market failures (Hardin 1997; Rodrik 2004). Coase (1960) and Arrow (1970) generalized the neoclassical perspective of instances of market failure leading to the state, in terms of transaction costs. This has been taking up and extended by North (1991) and Pitelis (1991)—see below.

There is limited detailed discussion in the neoclassical literature of the relationship between the firm and the state. Coase (1960) briefly refers to the issue, to the effect that both firm and market transactions have to take place within the general legal framework imposed by the state. The implication is that firms and markets (the private sector) are seen as substitutes to the state. This implies a need for an explanation of the state in terms of private sector (not just market) failure. This approach still leaves unresolved the question of why states do not substitute (fully) markets and firms (the private sector); i.e. why market and not planning. An explanation can be offered in terms of the—nowadays popular—concept of government failure, generalized in terms of transaction costs, but also Coase's claim that in market economies the optimal mix between market and plan emerges endogenously and not from the top down (Coase 1960; Pitelis 1991).

Concerning the relationship between nation states and MNEs, the neoclassical view is that MNEs tend to enhance welfare by increasing global efficiency. The latter is more evident in the transaction-cost perspective, but it is also true of proponents of ownership advantage perspective, such as Charles Kindleberger (e.g. 1984). Here the reasons are not transaction costs but rather technology diffusion, know-how, employment creation, etc. A problem emerges when the power of the one actor (the state) is being undermined by that of the other, the MNE. This, Vernon (1971) observed, is possible as a result of the mobility of MNEs versus the immobility of the state. The original suggestion was that of "sovereignty at bay," qualified, however, ten years later (Vernon 1981) in view of increasing expropriations of MNE assets by third-world countries, and the increasing resistance (and militancy) of at least some states. Nye (1988) added a new interesting insight, by pointing to the possible complementarity between MNE and nation states, each with a comparative advantage: MNEs on production, nation states on legitimization. This supports the argument favouring complementarity between the private sector (firm, in this case) and public sector and it is nearer to the capabilities-based perspective (Pitelis 1991).

The emergence of international state apparatus can, in principle, be explained in parallel to the development of the state in the neoclassical tradition. Kindleberger (1986), pointed to the relationship between international public goods (such as international stability) and international governments, i.e. organizations such as the UN and WTO. Such goods can, in principle, be provided by hegemonic powers. For example, the UK, first, and the USA, more recently, played such a role in recent history. For a multitude of reasons, however, hegemons decline and/or lose their appetite for the provision of such goods. International government can be a solution to this problem.

Kindleberger's framework is one of international market failure, leading to international government, in the absence of a sufficiently strong (or interested) national government-hegemons. The relationship between international government and the MNE is seen as one of complementarity. An interesting new dimension is added in terms of the relationship between national states and inter-nation states, which again is seen as one of complementarity (in the absence of hegemons). Following Nye, it could be claimed that comparative advantage in the provision of international public goods and international production, respectively, explain the need for complementarity between international state apparatus and MNEs. International market failures morever could in principle also be generalized in terms of transaction costs (Pitelis 1991).

In summary, the neoclassical perspective on the firm, including the MNE, the nation state, and international organizations can be described as one of both substitutability and complementarity. This can also be suggested as regards the private sector (firm and price mechanism), because the transaction-costs perspective, which views the market and the firm as substitutes, provides no adequate justification for this view. It is possible therefore to claim that, given also firms' possible failures (e.g. excessive transaction costs within firms, or management costs (see Demsetz 1988), after a certain size, as Coase and Williamson suggest), and the concept of comparative advantage advanced by Nye, this relationship too should be seen as one of complementarity within the mainstream. If this is accepted, all of them—the market, the MNE, and state (and international organizations)—should be seen as complementary institutions of resource allocation, each specializing in what they can do more efficiently (in terms, for example but not exclusively, of economizing in transaction costs). This way the prevailing institutional mix can be attributed to overall efficiency-related factors.

The major alternative to the mainstream tradition is the radical left. Regarding the *raison d'être* of the firm (the factory system), the major contribution here is Marglin's (1974). Developed independently of the Williamson perspective on markets and hierarchies, Marglin's ideas represent the major alternative to the transaction cost-efficiency argument. For Marglin, the main reason for the rise of the factory system from the previously existing putting-out system was the result of capitalist attempts to increase control over labor. In this sense, the factory system was due to control-distribution-related reasons. Any efficiency gains resulting from increased control should be seen as the outcome, but not the driving force.

Coming to the MNE, Stephen Hymer is the leading contributor in the radical left tradition and arguably the father-figure of the modern theory of the MNE as a whole, see Dunning and Pitelis (2008). Similar to Ronald Coase, Hymer regarded the market and the firm as alternative institutional devices for the division of labor. Hymer focused primarily on the evolution of firms (rather than their existence per se), from the small family-controlled firm to the joint-stock company, and then through the multidivisional (M-form) firm to the MNE. He focused on the latter in his now classic 1960 PhD thesis (Hymer 1976) and extended his analysis on the MNE and the multinational corporate capitalist system as a whole in his subsequent writings, some of the best of which are collected in Cohen et al. (1979).

In brief, Hymer explained the ability of US firms to become MNEs (i.e. to compete successfully with domestic firms of host countries, despite the latter's inherent advantages of knowledge of language, customs, etc.) in terms of monopolistic advantages derived during their process of growth. Such were know-how, managerial expertise, technology, organization, etc. He then explained the willingness of US firms to become MNEs in terms of oligopolistic rivalry, in particular as a defensive attack to guard against the threat of the rising European and Japanese firms and a means to reduce international rivalry. He also used transaction-cost-related theorizing to explain FDI vis-à-vis market-based international activities, for example licensing, and referred to locational factors, and divide-and-rule (of both labor and nation states) factors. It is for these reasons that most existing perspectives on the MNE can be seen as developments of Hymer's early insights (Dunning and Pitelis 2008).

Although the Marxist tradition explored the issue of internationalization of production and the MNE, their focus is primarily on the former, rather than on an explanation of the particular institutional form of the MNE. From a large literature, the contributions of Baran and Sweezy (1966) and Palloix (1976) are noteworthy. The latter considered internationalization as a process inherent in the development of capitalism, itself the result of the process of competition. The former focus on effective demand problems (of the under-consumptionist type) in order to explain the need of capital to seek foreign markets.

As already noted, the Marxist theory paid particular attention to the theory of the state. Views here range from the instrumentalist theory, which sees the state as an instrument of capital, through the structural-functional perspective for which capitalist cohesion is achieved through the state, to the capital logic or state form derivation debate, where the state is seen as an outcome of the very logic of capital accumulation, see below.

Variations apart, all Marxist theories view the state's existence and functions as the result of a quest and/or need to nurture the class interests of the capitalist class. Hymer (in Cohen et al. 1979) has an historical justification of this need-quest. Marxists, most notably O'Connor (1973), also acknowledge the possibility of government (capitalist state) failure, but attribute it to a structural gap between receipts and outlays. Some of the Marxist perspective can be translated into mainstream terms, such as government failure. What remains as different is the focus on a distributional, class-based perspective, as opposed to the efficiency focus of the mainstream.

Marxist theory also paid attention to the relationship between MNEs and nation states. However, views here vary greatly. On the general relationship between the relative power of the state and MNEs, Murray (1971) claimed that the power of MNEs tends to undermine that of nation states, while Warren (1971) has made the opposite claim. These and other contributions are collected in Radice (1975). Concerning the relationship between MNEss and developing host-states (the hinterland or periphery), views vary from the Monthly Review school's perspective of imperialism (see for example Sweezy 1978) to Warren's (1973) claim that MNEs are a major factor contributing to the economic development of the periphery. In between lie the concepts of unequal exchange, uneven development, and dependent development (Pitelis 1991).

Stephen Hymer's perspective on MNEs and nation states is insightful (see Cohen et al. 1979). On the general relationship, he claimed that MNEs erode the powers of nation states, but unequally; more so for the weak (typically developing) states and less so for the strong (developed) ones. The latter possess more leverage against MNEs, in part by being themselves home-bases to MNEs. Concerning MNEs and developing host states, he conceded that MNEs can contribute to the economic development of the periphery, but described the relationship as one of inequality and self-perpetuating dependency. In part, this was the result of the incentives for local entrepreneurs to cooperate or sell to rather than compete with MNEs. Observing a more general tendency of the world's wealthy to increase the global surplus, Hymer went on to describe a tendency for global collusion by global firms through interpenetration of investments.

Globalization of production, for Hymer, also creates the need for international capital markets and international government (organizations)—the latter in order to assist the global operations of MNEs. This observation provides a Marxist perspective on MNEs and international organizations, akin to the more general Marxist focus on control-distribution (in particular in regarding the dominant classes as the locomotive of history). Given the influence of this class on the state, too, as already discussed, one would expect nation states not to oppose the development at least of some types of international organization, see Dunning and Pitelis (2008) for a critical assessment.

To summarize, the Marxist perspective considers the firm, the market, and the state, including MNEs, national states, and international organizations, as complementary devices, for the exploitation of (the division of) labor. The emphasis, however, is on sectional (capitalist) interests, not efficiency. The latter could be the outcome, or the means, but not the driving force. Put differently, efficiency could be sacrificed for the sake of sectional-class interests.

From the discussion thus far, it could be suggested that there is an emerging consensus in economic theory to the effect that institutions of capitalism should be seen as both complementary and substitutes. The exclusive focus on either power efficiency or capitalist class interests, on the other hand, is, we think, far-fetched. Efficiency and sectional interests can often go hand in hand, or be different sides of the same coin. Consider, for example, the view that firms maximize their utility (cultivate their own interests). If such utility can be enhanced, for example, by increasing market power and charging monopoly prices, it is not obvious that firms should not do so (Penrose 1959). Similarly, if profits can be increased by reducing labor costs, this will, if possible, be done. On the other hand, if profit increases follow from policies associated with transaction-cost reductions, such policies are likely to be pursued, "despite" their benign effects of efficiency. The point is simply that efficiency and sectional interest can go hand in hand. Interestingly, neoclassical economic historian Douglass North (1981) suggests that efficiency by state functionaries will tend to be pursued, provided that their own utility is first maximized. This may point to some emerging consensus.

The possibility of inefficiencies of state intervention (government failure), owing to opportunistic (or, more mildly, utility-maximizing) behavior by state functionaries (bureaucrats, politicians) is explicitly entertained by the public choice and Chicago perspectives. Here internalities and redundant and rising costs result from state functionaries' desire to increase their utility (status, size of bureaus, etc.). Moreover, even though the state may emerge spontaneously in an attempt by individuals to raise themselves above the anarchy of the market (Hobbesian state of nature) in this scenario, states can be captured by organized interest groups which (thus) hinder the efficient allocation of resources. If so, markets should be left to operate freely, while the state should limit itself to the provision of stable rules of the game, for example clear delineation of property rights. The maximization of state functionaries' utility and the demands by powerful organized groups of producers and trades unions which have captured the state, helps to explain, in this scenario, its growth in OECD countries (see Mueller 2006).

The transaction-cost and new-right perspectives on the state have been brought together in Douglass North's (1981) attempt to provide a neoclassical theory of the state. Here a wealth or utility maximizing ruler trades a group of services (e.g., protection, justice) for revenue, acting as a discriminating monopolist, by devising property rights for each so as to maximize state revenue, subject to the constraint of potential entry by other rulers (other states or parties). The objective is to maximize rents to the ruler and, subject to that, to reduce transaction costs in order to foster maximum output, thus the tax revenues accruing to the ruler. The existing competition from rivals and the transaction costs of state activities typically tend to produce inefficient property rights: the former, as it implies, favoring powerful constituents, while transaction costs in metering, policing, and collecting taxes provide incentives for states to grant monopolies. The existence of the two constraints gives rise to a conflict between a property rights structure which produces economic growth and one which maximizes rents to the ruler, and thus accounts for widespread inefficient property rights. North regards this idea as the neoclassical variant of the Marxian notion of the contradictions in the mode of production, in which the ownership structure is incompatible with potential gains from existing technological opportunities.

The similarities between the public choice and North's view of the state, on the one hand, and that of the Marxian school, on the other, do not end here. Marx and his followers were among the first to contemplate a capture theory, which Marx moreover considered to be part and parcel of capitalism's existing inequalities in production (capitalists–workers). This inherent inequity, for Marx, implied a bias of the state in favor of capitalists. This view has been elaborated by latter-day Marxists, who pointed to instrumental reasons (links of state personnel with capital, see Miliband

1969) and/or structural reasons (control of capital over investments, see Poulantzas 1969) for this capitalist capture of the state. Marxists explained the autonomous form of the capitalist state in terms of the control of labor directly by capital in the production process (thus no need for the state to assume direct control of labor) and the need of the state to support production (provision of infrastructure, etc.) as a result of the anarchy of the market (the existence of many capitals), see Holloway and Picciotto (1978). For the Marxist school, the growth of the state and fiscal crises can be explained in terms of laws of motion of capitalism, such as the concentration and centralization of capital, declining profit rates, and thus class struggle over state expenditures (see, for example, O'Connor 1973).

North's and the Marxist theories underplay the power of consumers as electors and as a source of tax revenues. Electoral defeats and reductions in the rents accruing to the state, resulting from reduced employment levels, are further constraints on the behavior of state functionaries, whether they try to maximize their own utility or that of capital. On the other hand, the possibility of capture is an important point of consensus between the public choice, Marxian and North's theories. It is not alien to the conventional neoclassical tradition either (Chang 1994). Last, but not least, the Marxian focus on the need to reduce production costs (already there in the conventional neoclassical focus on public goods, see Adam Smith 1776) counterbalances the exclusive reliance of transaction-cost theorists on the exchange side.

The above summary of alternative perspectives on the possibility of capture allows a generalization of North's theory. According to this, the state exists because of excessive private sector transaction and production costs, and aims to reduce them, so as to increase output and thus, revenue for state functionaries. Increased output also helps to legitimize any income inequities. A constraint on the state's functionaries' attempt to achieve their objectives arises from the possibility of capture (inherent for Marxists, but arising ex-post for public choice) which tends to generate inefficient property rights, which in turn hinder increases in output. Transaction costs in metering, policing, and enforcing taxes also lead to inefficiency in terms of states granting monopolies. Moreover, costs of governing put a limit on the ability of the state to replace the private sector, leading to a need for a plurality of institutional forms.

It follows that the aim of the state is, or should be, to reduce private sector transaction and production costs, by removing the constraints which hinder the realization of this, notably the problem of capture by powerful constituents. This points towards the need to establish competitive conditions in product and labor markets. Competition would tend to reduce but not eliminate, if they are inherent in production the power of such constituents. It would, moreover, tend to reduce problems with governing costs associated, for example, with powerful opportunist private sector suppliers of required state services. Competitive conditions, however, should not be limited to the private sector only, but should be extended to a lesser extent (so as not to facilitate capture and/or inefficiency due to discontinuities of state personnel) to the market for government control, so that political positions should also be contestable. This would provide useful sources of information on possible differences in the efficiency of governing. The reduction of private and public sector transaction and production costs by the state is aimed at providing the conditions for the efficient production of goods and services by the economy, i.e. to increase supply-side output and facilitate the realization of this output (its purchase by consumers, domestic or overseas). This introduces the concept of national strategy for growth, as the set of state policies intended to reduce production and transaction costs so as to increase realized output in the form of income. The internalization of private sector activities by the state should be pursued up to the point where an additional transaction or production activity would be produced at equal cost in the private sector. This reinforces the concept of pluralism in institutional forms, i.e. the complementarity between the public and private sectors for the efficient production and allocation of resources.

The notion of national strategy takes the revenue side as given, i.e. as the prerogative purely of the private sector. However, besides affecting production and transaction costs, a government can also affect the revenue side, if it consciously directs its production-transaction cost-reducing activities to particular areas, and/or by directly undertaking production activities. This is particularly important in open economies with trade. In such a world, growth can be achieved via domestic and foreign demand, while income-rent will be affected positively through both reductions in transaction-production costs and increases in revenues through, for example, a focus on high-return sectors and/or the creation of agglomeration and clusters (Pitelis 2009). It follows that, especially in open economies, national strategy could be designed to reduce overall production and transaction costs for the economy, but also influence the revenue side, so as to increase the income accruing to the nation and (thus) taxes to the state. In this context, the state functionaries could be argued to act as political entrepreneurs (Yu 1997). This would also tend to endogenize the public–private nexus and require a theory of political entrepreneurship and its interaction with economic entrepreneurship. Despite recent progress, economic theory is still far off such an analysis, which is more akin to political science, management, and entrepreneurship scholarship (Klein et al. 2009).

CONCLUDING REMARKS

Economic theories of the firm, business (and industry organization), and the state draw on alternative economic perspectives. Dominant among these is the market-failure-based one, albeit in more recent years evolutionary, knowledge, dynamic capabilities, and systems-based views are making significant inroads— especially on the theory of the firm and business strategy.

Our relatively short account of the extensive literature pointed to commonalities and remaining differences and provided some scope for syntheses. Moreover, we claimed that a truly endogenous evolutionary theory of the above-mentioned issues would need to go beyond economic approaches to include at the very least an analysis of political agency-entrepreneurship. Attempts to provide an integrative framework would also be welcome, especially as they would help inform specific business and public policy issues. This is beyond the scope of this chapter.

Notes

1. Indicative IO texts are Tirole (1988); Scherer and Ross (1990); and Cabral (2000). To varying degrees of sophistication and detail, they all tend to cover the ground surveyed in this subsection.
2. Thus Structure, Conduct, Performance (SCP) model, see Scherer and Ross (1990) for an account.
3. For an account of alternative approaches to competition and competition policy within and without IO, see Hunt (2000); Pitelis (2007b).
4. Another dimension on competition relates to its strength, and the role of proximity and location. This links to the work of Richardson, but has been developed by Porter (1990); Krugman (1991); Audretsch (1998); Dunning (1998); and others. For example, Porter claims that local competition is more potent than distant (foreign) for example competition. This may have important implications in devising public policies.

References

ACEMOGLU, D., JOHNSON, S., and ROBINSON, J. 2001. "The colonial origins of comparative development: an empirical investigation," *American Economic Review* 91: 1369–401.

ALCHIAN, A., and DEMSETZ, H. 1972. "Production, information costs and economic organization," *American Economic Review* 62(5): 777–95.

ARROW, K. 1970. "The organization of economic activity: issues pertinent to the choice of market versus non-market allocation," in R. H. Haveman and J. Margolis, eds., *Public Expenditure and Policy Analysis*. Chicago: Markham.

AUDRETSCH, D. B., ed. 1998. *Industrial Policy and Competitive Advantage. Volume 1: The Mandate for Industrial Policy*. Cheltenham: Edward Elgar.

BACON, R., and ELTIS, W. 1976. *Britain's Economic Problem: Too Few Producers*. London: Macmillan.

BAIN, J. 1956. *Barriers to New Competition: Their Character and Consequences for Manufacturing Industries*. Boston, Mass.: Harvard University Press.

BARAN, P., and SWEEZY, P. 1966. *Monopoly Capital*. Harmondsworth: Penguin.

BARNEY, J. B. 1991. "Firm resources and sustained competitive advantage," *Journal of Management* 17(1): 99–120.

—— 2001. "Resource-based theories of competitive advantage: a ten-year retrospective on the resource-based view," *Journal of Management* 27(6): 643–50.

BAUMOL, W. J. 1982. "Contestable markets: an uprising in the theory of industry structure," *American Economic Review* 72(1): 1–15.

BAUMOL, W. J. 1991. *Perfect Markets and Easy Virtue: Business Ethics and the Invisible Hand.* Cambridge, Mass.: Blackwell.

BERLE, A., and MEANS, G. 1932. *The Modern Corporation and Private Property.* New York: Commerce Clearing House.

BUCKLEY, P. J., and CASSON, M. C. 1976. *The Future of the Multinational Enterprise.* London: Macmillan.

CABRAL, L. M. B. 2000. *Introduction to Industrial Organization.* Cambridge, Mass.: MIT Press.

CHANDLER, A. D. 1990. *Scale and Scope: The Dynamics of Industrial Capitalism.* Cambridge, Mass.: The Belknap Press of Harvard University Press.

CHANG, H.-J. 1994. *The Political Economy of Industrial Policy.* London: Macmillan.

CLARKE, T., and PITELIS, C. N., eds. 1993. *The Political Economy of Privatization.* London: Routledge.

COASE, R. H. 1937. "The nature of the firm," *Economica* 4: 386–405.

——1960. "The problem of social cost," *Journal of Law and Economics* 3: 1–44.

——1991. "The nature of the firm: influence," in O. E. Williamson and S. G. Winter, eds., *The Nature of the Firm: Origins, Evolution and Development.* Oxford: Oxford University Press.

COHEN, R. B., FELTON, N., VAN LIERE, J., and NIKOSI, M., eds. 1979. *The Multinational Corporation: A Radical Approach, Papers by Stephen Herbert Hymer.* Cambridge: Cambridge University Press.

COWLING, K., and WATERSON, M. 1976. "Price–cost margins and market structure," *Economica* 43(171): 267–74.

CYERT, R. M., and MARCH, J. G. 1963. *A Behavioral Theory of the Firm.* Englewood Cliffs, NJ: Prentice Hall.

DASGUPTA, P. 1986. "Positive freedom, markets and the welfare state," *Oxford Review of Economic Policy* 2(4): 25–36.

DAVID, R. J., and HAN, S. H. 2004. "A systematic assessment of the empirical support for transaction cost economics," *Strategic Management Journal* 25: 39–58.

DEMSETZ, H. 1973. "Industry structure, market rivalry, and public policy," *Journal of Law and Economics* 16: 1–9.

——1988. "The theory of the firm revisited," *Journal of Law, Economics, and Organization* 4 (1): 141–62.

—— and JACQUEMIN, A. 1994. *Anti-trust Economics: New Challenges for Competition Policy.* Bromley: Chartwell-Bratt.

DIXIT, A. 1982. "Recent developments in oligopoly theory," *American Economic Review* 72(2): 12–17.

DUNNING, J. H. 1998. "Location and the multinational enterprise: a neglected factor?" *Journal of International Business Studies* 29(1): 45–66.

—— and PITELIS, C. N. 2008. "Stephen Hymer's contribution to international business scholarship: an assessment and extension," *Journal of International Business Studies* 39: 167–76.

EDQUIST, C. 2005. "Systems of innovation: perspectives and challenges," in J. Fagerberg, D. C. Mowery, and R. R. Nelson, eds., *The Oxford Handbook of Innovation.* Oxford: Oxford University Press, 181–208.

EGGERTSON, T. 1990. *Economic Behaviour and Institutions.* Cambridge: Cambridge University Press.

EISENHARDT, K. M., and MARTIN, J. A. 2000. "Dynamic capabilities: what are they?" *Strategic Management Journal* 21: 1105–21.

FELDSTEIN, M. 1974. "Social security, induced retirement and aggregate capital accumulation in the United States," *Journal of Political Economy* 82: 905–26.

FRIEDMAN, M. 1962. *Capitalism and Freedom*. Chicago: University of Chicago Press.

——1967. *Essays in Positive Economics*. University of Chicago Press: Chicago.

FOSS, K., and FOSS, N. J. 2005. "Resources and transaction costs: how property rights economics furthers the resource-based view," *Strategic Management Journal* 26: 541–53.

GILBERT, R., and NEWBERY, D. 1982. "Preemptive patenting and the persistence of monopoly," *American Economic Review* 72(2): 514–26.

GOUPH, I. 1979. *The Political Economy of the Welfare State*. London: Macmillan Educational.

GROSSMAN, S. J., and HART, O. D. 1986. "The costs and benefits of ownership: a theory of vertical and lateral integration," *Journal of Political Economy* 94(4): 691–718.

HALL, P. A., and SOSKICE, D. 2001. *Varieties of Capitalism: The Institutional Foundations of Comparative Advantage*. New York: Oxford University Press.

HARDIN, R. 1997. "Economic theories of the state," in D. Mueller, ed., *Perspectives on Public Choice: A Handbook*. Cambridge: Cambridge University Press.

HART, O. 1995. *Firms, Contracts, and Financial Structure*. Oxford: Clarendon.

HAUSMANN, R., RODRIK, D., et al. 2008. "Reconfiguring industrial policy: a framework with an application to South Africa," paper presented at the 25th DRUID Celebration Conference 2008. Copenhagen.

HAY, C., LISTER, M., and MARSH, D., eds. 2007. *The State: Theories and Issues*. Basingstoke: Macmillan.

HAYEK, F. A. 1945. "The use of knowledge in society," *The American Economic Review* 35(4): 519–30.

HELFAT, C., FINKELSTEIN, S., et al. 2007. *Dynamic Capabilities: Understanding Strategic Change in Organizations*. Oxford: Blackwell.

HILL, J. S. 2009. *International Business*. Thousand Oaks, Calif.: Sage Publications, Inc.

HOLLOWAY, J., and PICCIOTTO, S. 1978. *State and Capital: A Marxist Debate*. London: Edward Arnold.

HUNT, S. D. 2000. *A General Theory of Competition: Resources, Competences, Productivity, Economic Growth (Marketing for a New Century)*. Thousand Oaks, Calif.: Sage Publications, Inc.

HYMER, S. H. 1960. *The International Operations of National Firms: A Study of Direct Foreign Investment*. Cambridge, Mass.: MIT Press.

——1968. "The large multinational 'corporation,'" in M. Casson, ed., *Multinational Corporations*. London: Edward Elgar, 6–31.

——1976. *The International Operations of National Firms: A Study of Foreign Direct Investment*. Cambridge, Mass.: MIT Press.

JENSEN, M. C., and MECKLING, W. 1976. "Theory of the firm: managerial behaviour, agency costs and ownership structure," *Journal of Financial Economics* 3(4): 304–60.

KAY, J. A., and SILBERSTON, Z. A. 1984. "The new industrial policy: privatization and competition," *Midland Bank Review* (Spring): 8–16.

——MAYER, C., and THOMPSON, D. 1986. *Privatization and Regulation: The UK Experience*. Oxford: Clarendon Press.

KIM, J., and MAHONEY, J. T. 2002. "Resource-based and property rights perspectives on value creation: the case of oil field unitization," *Managerial and Decision Economics* 23(4): 225–45.

KINDLEBERGER, C. P. 1984. "Plus ça change: a look at the new literature," in C. P. Kindleberger, ed., *Multinational Excursions*. Cambridge, Mass.: MIT Press, 180–8.

——1986. "International public goods without international government," *American Economic Review* 76(1): 1–13.

KLEIN, P., MCGAHAN, A., MAHONEY, P., and PITELIS, C. 2009. "The Economic Organization of Public Entrepreneurship," *European Management Review*, Forthcoming.

KOGUT, B., and ZANDER, U. 1993. "Knowledge of the firm and the evolutionary theory of the multinational corporation," *Journal of International Business Studies* 24(4): 625–45.

————1996. "What firms do? Coordination, identity, and learning," *Organization Science* 7(5): 502–18.

KRUGMAN, P. R. 1991. "Increasing returns and economic geography," *Journal of Political Economy* 99: 183–99.

LIPPMAN, S. A., and RUMELT, R. P. 2003. "The payments perspective: micro-foundations of resource analysis," *Strategic Management Journal* 24: 903–27.

LUNDVALL, B. 2007. "National innovation systems: analytical concept and development tool," *Industry and Innovation* 14(1) 95–119.

MCGAHAN, A., and PORTER, M. 1997. "How much does industry matter, really?" *Strategic Management Journal* 18(4): 15–30.

MAHONEY, J. T. 2005. *Economic Foundations of Strategy*. Thousand Oaks, Calif.: SAGE Publications Inc.

MARGLIN, S. 1974. "What do bosses do? The origins and functions of hierarchy in capitalist production," *Review of Radical Political Economics* 6: 60–112.

MARSHALL, A. 1920. *Principles of Economics*. London: Macmillan.

MARRIS, R. 1996. "Managerial theories of the firm," in *International Encyclopaedia of Business and Management*. London: Routledge, 3117–25.

MARX, K. 1959. *Capital*. London: Lawrence & Wishart.

MILIBAND, R. 1969. *The State in Capitalist Society*. London: Quarter Books.

MODIGLIANI, F. 1958. "New developments on the oligopoly front," *Journal of Political Economy* 66(3): 215–32.

MUELLER, D. C. 2006. "Corporate governance and economic performance," *International Review of Applied Economics* 20(5): 623–43.

MURRAY, R. 1971. "The internationalisation of capital and the nation state," in H. Radice, ed., *International Firms and Modern Imperialism*. Harmondsworth: Penguin.

NELSON, R. R., and WINTER, S. G. 1982. *An Evolutionary Theory of Economic Change*. Cambridge, Mass.: Belknap/Harvard University Press.

NORTH, D. C. 1981. *Structure and Change in Economic History*. New York: Norton.

————1990. *Institutions, Institutional Change and Economic Performance*. Cambridge: Cambridge University Press.

————1991. "Institutions," *Journal of Economic Perspectives* 5(1): 97–112.

NYE, J. S. 1988. "The multinational corporation in the 1980s," in C. Kindleberger and P. Audretsch, eds., *The Multinational Corporation in the 1980s*. Cambridge, Mass.: MIT.

O'CONNOR, J. 1973. *The Fiscal Crisis of the State*. New York: St Martin's Press.

PALLOIX, C. 1976. *L'Internationalisation du capital: élements critiques*. Paris: François Maspero.

PENROSE, E. T. 1959/1995. *The Theory of the Growth of the Firm*. Oxford: Oxford University Press.

PETERAF, M. 1993. "The cornerstone of competitive advantage," *Strategic Management Journal* 14: 179–91.

————and BARNEY, J. B. 2003. "Unravelling the resource based tangle," *Managerial and Decision Economics* 24(4): 309–23.

PITELIS, C. N. 1991. *Market and Non-Market Hierarchies: Theory of Institutional Failure*. Oxford: Blackwell Publishing.

————1994. "Industrial strategy: for Britain, in Europe and the world," *Journal of Economic Studies* 21(5): 2–92.

————2002. *The Growth of the Firm: The Legacy of Edith Penrose*. Oxford: Oxford University Press.

—— 2003. "Privatization, regulation and domestic competition policy," in G. Wignaraja, ed., *Competitiveness Strategy and Industrial Performance in Developing Countries: A Manual for Policy Analysis.* Oxford: Routledge.

—— 2004. "Edith Penrose and the resource-based view of (international) business strategy," *International Business Review* 13(4): 523–32.

—— 2007a. "A behavioral resource-based view of the firm: the synergy of Cyert and March (1963) and Penrose (1959)," *Organization Science* 18(3): 337–49.

—— 2007b. "European industrial and competition policy: perspectives, trends and a new approach," *Policy Studies* 28(4): 365–81.

—— 2009. "The sustainable competitive advantage and catching-up of nations: FDI, clusters and liability (asset) of smallness," *Management International Review* 49(1): 95–120.

—— and PSEIRIDIS, A. N. 1999. "Transaction costs versus resource value," *Journal of Economic Studies* 26(3): 221–40.

—— and TEECE, D. J. 2009. "The (new) nature and essence of the firm," *European Management Review* 6(1) (Spring): 5–15.

—— and WAHL, M. 1998. "Edith Penrose: Pioneer of Stakeholder Theory," *Long Range Planning* 31(2): 252–61.

PRIEM, R. L., and BUTLER, J. E. 2001. "Is the resource-based theory a useful perspective for strategic management research?" *Academy of Management Review* 26(1): 22–40.

PORTER, M. E. 1980. *Competitive Strategy: Techniques for Analyzing Industries and Competitors.* New York: The Free Press.

—— 1990. *The Competitive Advantage of Nations.* Basingstoke: Macmillan.

POULANTZAS, N. 1969. *Political Power and Social Class.* London: New Left Books.

PRESSMAN, S. 2006. *Alternative Theories of the State.* Basingstoke: Palgrave Macmillan.

RADICE, H., ed. 1975. *International Firms and Modern Imperialism.* Harmondsworth: Penguin.

REES, R. 1986. *Public Enterprise Economics.* Oxford: Philip Allan.

RICHARDSON, G. 1972. "The organisation of industry," *Economic Journal* 82: 883–96.

RODRIK, D. 2004. "Industrial policy for the twenty-first century," *CEPR Discussion Paper No. 4767.*

—— and HAUSMANN, R. 2006. "Doomed to choose: industrial policy as predicament," paper prepared for the *First Blue Sky Seminar* organized by the Center for International Development, Harvard University.

ROMER, P. M. 1990. "Endogenous technological change," *Journal of Political Economy* 98: 71–101.

SCHERER, F. M., and ROSS, D. 1990. *Industrial Market Structure and Economic Performance.* Boston, Mass.: Houghton & Mifflin Company.

SCHUMPETER, J. 1942. *Capitalism, Socialism and Democracy.* London: Unwin Hyman. 5th edn. 1987.

SIMON, H. 1993. "Strategy and organizational evolution," *Strategic Management Journal* 14: 131–42.

—— 1995. "Organizations and markets," *Journal of Public Administration Res. & Theory (Transaction)* 5(3): 273–95.

SMITH, A. 1776. "An enquiry into the nature and causes of the wealth of nations," *The Glasgow Edition of the Works and Correspondence of Adam Smith.* C. R. H. S. A. S. London: Strahan & Cadell.

STIGLER, G. 1988. "The effect of government on economic efficiency," *Business Economics* 23: 7–13.

STIGLITZ, J. 2002. *Economics of the Public Sector: Third Edition.* London: W. W. Norton & Company.

SUTTON, J. 1998. *Technology and Market Structure: Theory and History.* Cambridge: MIT Press.

SWEEZY, P. M. 1978. "Corporations: the state and imperialism," *Monthly Review* (November): 1–10.

TEECE, D. J. 1981. "The multinational enterprise: market failure and market power considerations," *Sloan Management Review* 22(3): 3–17.

—— 1982. "Towards an economic theory of the multiproduct firm," *Journal of Economic Behavior and Organization* 3(1): 39–63.

—— 1985. "Multinational enterprise, internal governance and industrial organization," *American Economic Review* 75(2): 233–8.

—— 2006. "Reflections on 'profiting from innovation'," *Research Policy* 35(8): 1131–46.

—— 2007. "Explicating dynamic capabilities: the nature and microfoundations of (sustainable) enterprise performance," *Strategic Management Journal* 28(13): 1319–50.

—— PISANO, G., and SHUEN, A. 1997. "Dynamic capabilities and strategic management," *Strategic Management Journal* 18(7): 509–33.

TIROLE, J. 1988. *The Theory of Industrial Organization.* Cambridge, Mass.: MIT Press.

VERNON, R. 1971. *Sovereignty at Bay.* Harlow: Longman.

—— 1981. "Sovereignty at bay ten years after," *International Organization* 35(3): 517–29.

VICKERS, J., and YARROW, G. 1987. *Privatization: An Economic Analysis.* London: The MIT Press.

WARREN, B. 1971. "The internationalisation of capital and the nation state: a comment," *Law Review* 68.

—— 1973. "Imperialism and capitalist development," *New Left Review* 81: 3–44.

WERNERFELT, B. 1984. "The resource-based view of the firm," *Strategic Management Journal* 5: 171–80.

WIGNARAJA, G., ed. 2003. *Competitiveness Strategy and Industrial Performance in Developing Countries: A Manual Policy Analysis.* London: Routledge.

WILLIAMSON, O. E. 1975. *Markets and Hierarchies: Analysis and Antitrust Implications: A Study in the Economics of Internal Organization.* New York: The Free Press.

—— 1979. "A theory of non-market behaviour: framework for implementation analysis," *Journal of Law and Economics* 22(1): 107–40.

—— 1985. *The Economic Institutions of Capitalism.* New York: Free Press.

—— 1991. "Strategizing, economizing, and economic organization," *Strategic Management Journal* 12: 75–94.

WOLF, C. 1979. "A theory of non-market behaviour: framework for implementation analysis," *Journal of Law and Economics* 22(1): 107–40.

YARROW, G. 1986. *Governments, Markets and Growth.* Oxford: Martin Robertson.

YU, T. F. 1997. "Entrepreneurial state: the role of government in the economic development of the Asian newly industrialising economies," *Development Policy Review* 15: 47–64.

ZOLLO, M., and WINTER, S. G. 2002. "Deliberate learning and the evolution of dynamic capabilities," *Organization Science* 13: 339–51.

CHAPTER 3

LAW AND BUSINESS

GREGORY C. SHAFFER[1]

THIS chapter puts business center stage as a means to understand law. Law consists of systems of rules, standards, and procedures that social institutions create and apply. These social institutions may be public or private. The rules, standards, and procedures that they create provide a framework in which business strategizes and operates. Business, in turn, uses law as a resource to advance and defend business aims.[2] This chapter assesses the reciprocal interaction of business and law. Law helps constitute business by recognizing business organizational forms, and business helps constitute law.

Business interests may be united or divided vis-à-vis government and the laws government creates. Regulation provides some businesses with competitive advantages over others, dividing business and creating incentives for different public-private alliances (Vogel 1995). Business is divided on account of economic competition, and public actors are divided on account of political and ideological competition. Different factions within business thus ally with different factions within government. Business interests, however, may also converge to oppose government measures, as when government sides with consumer or environmental groups at the national level, and business believes it will be disadvantaged vis-à-vis foreign competition. With the rise of transnational institutions, businesses can also look to public actors at different levels of social organization to promote their interests.

Much legal scholarship addresses issues of compliance with law. This chapter reverses the telescope, addressing what shapes law, and, more particularly, what are the mechanisms through which business shapes law. To understand the relationship of business and law, we must look at the following three sets of institutional interactions: (i) horizontal public institutional interaction among legislative, administrative, and judicial processes, in each of which business typically plays a critical role; (ii) vertical public institutional interaction involving national and transnational institutional processes, with transnational processes becoming more prominent in our economically globalized age; and (iii) the interaction among these public institutional processes and parallel private rule-making, administrative, and dispute settlement mechanisms that business creates, again at different levels of social organization. It is these dynamic, reciprocal interactions that constitute the legal field in which business operates.

This chapter addresses the advantages that business holds in public and private law-making, and assesses the reciprocal interaction among these public and private legal systems. First, business has advantages before the different public institutions that make and apply law, be they legislatures, administrative bodies, or courts. Second, business creates its own private legal systems, including what is traditionally referred to as *lex mercatoria* (or private merchant law) and private institutions to enforce it (such as arbitral bodies).[3] These two sources of law, publicly and privately made law, interact dynamically. Privately made law is adopted in response to the public legal system, to preempt public law's creation as unnecessary, to internalize public law through creating new organizational policies and procedures, or to exit from the public legal system through the development of alternative dispute resolution bodies. Publicly made law is made in response to developments in the private sphere, sometimes addressing privately made law's purported deficiencies, and sometimes codifying or otherwise taking into account private business law, business custom, and business institutional developments (such as alternative dispute resolution) in national statutes, regulations, and institutional practices. The reciprocal interaction of public and private legal systems at different levels of social organization constitutes the legal field in which economic activity takes place. In short, to assess the relation of business to law, we need to examine how law is created and applied through public institutions, how it is created and applied through private entities, and how these systems interact, including between the national and the transnational levels.

The first section addresses business's role in shaping law through public institutions. The next section addresses business's creation of private legal rules and institutions. The third section examines how public and private legal systems interact, and, in particular, how private business-made law and business practice affect publicly made law over time. Although these three sections focus on the relationship of law and business in the United States, the chapter's aim is to provide a general framework for analysis which builds from existing empirical and theoretical work in discrete areas. The fourth section addresses the interaction of business and law in comparative and global context. It shows how, on the one hand, much of international business law has developed in response to business demands and practices, in the process affecting national law. On the other hand, it explains why national law and legal practice nonetheless retain significant variation in reflection of local interests, institutional structures, and business and legal cultures.

BUSINESS AND PUBLIC LEGAL SYSTEMS

Business and law interact in mutually supportive and mutually constraining ways. On the one hand, law can significantly constrain business choice so that business attempts to constrain law's reach. On the other hand, law not only helps to stabilize expectations and thus create greater business certainty, it provides legitimacy for business and business operations, shielding them from fundamental challenge,[4] and it can provide competitive advantages for some businesses over others. Business thus invests in law, both to shape law to support business interests and to legitimize business conduct, as well as to thwart law's potential constraints.

Business has a complex relationship with law, which, at a minimum, must appear autonomous from business or law lacks legitimacy. Yet as Yves Dezalay and Bryant Garth write, "the autonomy of the law, which is necessary to its legitimacy, is not inconsistent with serving the needs of political and economic power" (Dezalay and Garth 1996: 98). There often exists an "unspoken deference of administrations, legislatures, and the courts to the needs of business" (Lindblom 1977: 179; Galanter 2006: 1399). Moreover, the processes of legitimation go both ways. Business also legitimates law through passive compliance and active support. This phenomenon is particularly salient at the transnational level where public institutions are weak and may seek allies with business, as exemplified by the United Nations' Global Compact and its attempt to align business conduct with "universally accepted principles in the areas of human rights, labour, environment, and anti-corruption."[5]

Business and legislation

Legislators may respond to business demands for many reasons, ranging from self-interest in campaign support, a desire not to harm business in light of business's importance for the economy, and persuasion based on information that business provides. The extent to which they do so depends on "a larger number of factors— among them the nature of the issue, the nature of the demand, the structure of political competition, and the distribution of resources" (Schlozman and Tierney 1986: 317; Farber and Frickey 1991). Organized business enjoys significant advantages in the legislative process over other constituencies because of businesses' monetary and organizational resources, arguably facilitated in the United States by a pro-business ideological orientation (Lindblom 1977; Farnsworth and Holden 2006: 475). They can fund political campaigns, hire well-connected lobbyists, create think tanks to circulate business-friendly ideas, access the media, and promote the exchange of their personnel into government positions. Because of these resources, organized business tends to have preferential access to the political process so that legislators take account of businesses' views (Vogel 1983: 29; Farnsworth and Holden 2006: 475–80).

Business interests have long held a preferential position in law-making for structural reasons. Their importance for investment and employment in capitalist economies provides them with a privileged position in dealings with government, since critical market functions such as jobs, prices, production, growth, standard of living and economic security depend on business activity (Lindblom 1977: 172). Government thus has incentives to facilitate business performance by providing business with benefits, whether tax breaks, subsidies, or business-favorable regulation (Lindblom 1977: 174). The globalization of production arguably "enhances the structural power of corporate capital" because business can threaten to invest elsewhere if national regulation is unfavorable (Rodrik 1997; Held et al. 1999: 270).

Political representatives respond to popular concerns regarding business power, the intensity of which varies over time. In the United States, for example, the regulatory state grew significantly during the New Deal in the 1930s and in response to the public interest movement of the 1970s.[6] Yet when faced with potentially constraining regulation, business lobbying can produce compromises that safeguard business interests, such as the inclusion of exceptions, loopholes, and open-ended language subject to subsequent interpretation. In some cases, "public interest" statutes may serve as a façade, providing a symbol of government concern while masking government inaction (Edelman 1964, 1971).

Business and administration

Statutes often contain language that is sufficiently ambiguous so that their application depends on who mobilizes law before administrative agencies to advance their ends. There is a large literature, including that of public choice in law-and-economics, debating whether or not agencies are "captured" or "co-opted" by special interests, and, in particular, business interests (cf. Bernstein 1955; Noll 1971; Posner 1974). While it is an overstatement to maintain that agencies are simply captured by business (Wilson 1980), most agree that agencies are subject to significant business pressure and influence, and that business often occupies a privileged position. Explanations for business's influence range from sociological ones, with regulators learning to think like the regulated through constant interaction with them, to interest-based ones, where it is in regulators' interest to accommodate business so as to avoid adverse consequences, such as contestation before legislative committees and the courts. Well-organized business groups can sometimes shape the application of regulation that is nominally to protect a public interest (such as clean air) to suit producer interests (such as the producers of "dirty coal") (Ackermann and Hassler 1981). Business groups can also press legislatures to thwart regulation that business does not like, including through threats to limit agency funding for the relevant programs (Quirk 1981: 176; Skrzycki 2003: 106-7). Administrative law ultimately can be viewed as a negotiated legal order in which public officials and private actors must coordinate if public goals are to be achieved (Freeman 2000).

Representatives of organized interests are in constant contact with agency officials and the two sides have opportunities to exercise influence over each other. Regulatory officials deploy "soft" persuasive mechanisms and threaten "hard" enforcement to affect business conduct (Hawkins 1983; Kagan, Gunningham, and Thornton 2003).

Reciprocally, even lower level officials who see their specialized position as technocratic can have their views shaped over time through regular interaction with business representatives, and the information that business provides (Coglianese, Zeckhauser, and Parson 2004).

A "revolving door" political culture also furthers business access to administrative law-making and application. In the United States, business is often able to obtain the appointment of supportive political appointees to lead government agencies.[7] More generally, lawyers and lobbyists in Washington, DC, enhance their résumés by splashing a few years in public life to subsequently—and lucratively—serve private commercial clients. As former United States Trade Representative Robert Strauss observes, lawyers often go to work for the US government because "they know that [government work] enables them to move on out in a few years and become associated with a lobbying or law firm [where] their services are in tremendous demand."[8] Whether or not regulators accommodate business to prop their own career prospects, a "revolving door" political culture forges better understanding among public and private representatives so that each side better appreciates the perspectives and needs of the other.

Business and the courts

Law is also driven from below by litigants who initiate and defend cases resulting in law's application, interpretation, and elaboration over time (Black 1973; Scheingold 1974).[9] Even where a statute or administrative regulation does not favor business, business can attempt to mobilize litigation and dispute settlement resources to build favorable judicial precedent. Just as in political and administrative processes, well-resourced actors have advantages. To start, organized businesses tend to have greater financial resources to attract the best lawyers to gather evidence and put forward legal arguments, and they benefit from economies of scale because of their experience with litigation. Corporate in-house counsel can hire leading external law firms employing scores of legal associates to scour statutes and jurisprudence and develop sophisticated factual and legal arguments.[10] Legal counsel can also deploy procedural mechanisms to draw out litigation and impose costs on less-resourced parties to induce favorable settlements. Moreover, business can attempt to use soft law processes, such as through the American Law Institute which compiles "restatements" of the existing state of law, where business has been less successful in hard law processes, such as before legislatures (Rubin 1993; Schwartz and Scott 1995; Elson 1998). In this way, business can aim to affect subsequent hard law interpretation by courts. These advantages, however, can be countered, in part, where mechanisms exist—such as attorney fee awards and class action lawsuits—which incentivize attorneys to bring lawsuits on behalf of consumers, investors, and other constituencies.[11]

Marc Galanter has theorized the limited prospects of social change through adjudication in his classic work "Why the Haves Come Out Ahead" (Galanter 1974). As Galanter states, certain actors are more likely to be "repeat players" in litigation. These repeat players do not use the adjudicative process solely for the adjudication of single, unrelated cases; they also play for rules. As repeat players, they are well positioned to settle unfavorable cases and litigate and appeal cases that are more likely to result in a favorable legal precedent. By selecting which cases to settle and thus extract them from the adjudicative process, repeat players are better positioned to reduce the likelihood of adverse precedent affecting their future operations (Galanter 1974: 103). Even where subsequent legislation overturns a judicial precedent favorable to a repeat player, such new legislation triggers a new process of legal interpretation where well-resourced repeat players are favored.

Galanter defines a repeat player as a larger unit "which has had and anticipates repeated litigation, which has low stakes in the outcome of any one case, and which has the resources to pursue its long-run interests" (Galanter 1974: 97–8). He defines a "one-shotter," in contrast, as a smaller unit whose stakes in a given case are high relative to the actor's total worth. One-shotters, as a result, are more likely to focus on the particular result from settling a dispute rather than the creation of long-term precedent affecting future operations. Galanter finds that "organizations roughly correspond to [repeat players]," whether the organizations be a business or government actor (Galanter 1974: 97, 113, 1975: 348).

K. T. Albiston has examined how businesses have strategically used litigation to shape the interpretation of aspects of employment law over time. Applying Galanter's framework, she finds that "[e]mployers may settle strong cases likely to produce adverse decisions, ensuring that these cases never become the basis for a published judicial opinion," while they "may dispose of weak cases...through motions to dismiss or motions for summary judgment, which often do become part of the judicial interpretation of the law" (Albiston 1999: 894). She finds that "published judicial determinations of rights...occur primarily when employers win" (902), which affects understandings of law in subsequent employment disputes. Employees' successful settlements come "at the price of silence in the historical record of the common law" (906).

In the United States, businesses have successfully used litigation to be recognized as "persons" benefiting from constitutional rights, such as involving search and seizure, free speech, and campaign finance, as opposed to mere instruments of natural persons. Mayer characterizes Supreme Court decisions recognizing constitutional rights protections for corporations against government action as symbolic of "the transformation of our constitutional system from one of individual freedoms to one of organizational prerogatives" (Mayer 1990: 578). In contrast, although there have been stirrings of some change, corporations have remained relatively "immune from criminal punishment" since criminal laws are typically designed in contemplation of natural persons (Galanter 1999: 1118).

Negotiating in the shadow of law

Reading statutes, administrative regulations, and judicial decisions tells us little about law's operation. As socio-legal scholars have long shown, there is a difference between the law in the books (whether in statutes or published judicial decisions) and the law in practice, what they refer to as the "gap."[12] Only a few disputes are fully litigated. Most are settled through negotiation. As Galanter reminds us, "the career of most cases does not lead to full-blown trial and adjudication but consists of negotiation and maneuver in the strategic pursuit of settlement through mobilization of the court process" (Galanter 2001: 579). Galanter calls this process "litigotiation" (Galanter 1984).

Two primary aspects of the law exercise shadow effects on bargaining: the law's substance, and the law's procedures. The substance of law, as set forth in statutes and administrative regulations and as interpreted in case law, can inform and constrain settlement negotiations conducted in the law's shadow. As Robert Mnookin and Lewis Kornhauser (1979: 950) observe in their famous study of divorce law, "the outcome that the law will impose if no agreement is reached gives each [party] certain bargaining chips—an endowment of sorts."[13] Those more legally astute are more likely to be aware of the bargaining chips that they may deploy in order to use them strategically to their advantage. Repeat players in dispute settlement who can "play for rules" may also affect the very nature of the bargaining chips.

The judicial decision itself may be viewed in terms of its "shadow effect" on the resolution of a dispute. Negotiations may take place in the context of, and be informed by, a judicial decision. As Stewart Macaulay (2003: 89) writes regarding contract law, "[w]hat appears to be a final judgment at the trial level may be only a step toward settlement. The judgment may affect the balance of power between the parties, but often it will not take effect as written." Parties can settle the dispute in the shadow of a potential appeal, or they can settle it in light of their ongoing business relations with each other and third parties.

In addition, the law's "shadow" effects include the costs of deploying the law procedurally. As Herbert Kritzer (1991: 73) states, "the ability to impose costs on the opponent and the capability of absorbing costs" affect how the law operates. Where large businesses can absorb high litigation costs by dragging out a case, while imposing them on weaker complainants, they can seriously constrain a person's incentives to initiate a claim, and correspondingly enhance a person's incentives to settle a dispute unfavorably (Trubek et al. 1983). Law casts a weaker shadow for parties that lack the ability to hire and retain skilled lawyers, unless there are mechanisms, such as attorney fee awards and class actions, which create incentives for the plaintiff's bar. When legal resources cannot be mobilized cost-effectively, then a party's threat to invoke legal procedures against a business that wields greater legal resources has less credibility. A party may not even consider the threat of litigation, knowing the challenges that it faces. It has less of an incentive to even study the details of law, affecting what is called in socio-legal studies its "legal consciousness" (Cortese 1966). These aspects of the legal system most adversely affect individuals with fewer resources.

In sum, businesses have advantages in each of the public institutions discussed above and can look for allies in each of them when their interests are at stake. At times, businesses may find the legislature more favorable to their views, at others the executive, and at others courts. Businesses can thus search for allies in one public institution to counter or constrain another. These institutional processes interact over time, giving rise to the public law system.

THE PRIVATE LEGAL SPHERE: BUSINESS DISPLACEMENT AND INTERNALIZATION OF PUBLICLY MADE LAW

Law-in-action refers to how law is received, interpreted by, and subsequently given meaning through practice—what Ehrlich (1936) called "the living law." Law, whether formed through statute, administrative regulation, or judicial judgment, not only must be put into action through practice; it also competes and interacts with private ordering mechanisms. Business can respond in three ways to publicly made law. First, it can create its own private legal ordering regimes which, if accepted as legitimate, can displace the demand for public law (a private law alternative that is more *centralized*). Second, it can ignore existing law, even that in its favor, because of other concerns such as long-term client relations and reputation (a market-oriented alternative based on business relations and norms that is more *decentralized*). Third, it can implement public law requirements through internal organizational policies and procedures in which it translates and potentially transforms the meaning of public law (an *internal organizational* business alternative which, in turn, may be diffused through customary practice and thus lies between the first two alternatives). Through the first and third mechanisms, in particular, the corporate organization can act, "to varying extents, as a legislator, adjudicator, lawyer, and constable," constituting a private legal system (Macaulay 1986; Edelman and Suchman 1999: 961).[14]

Business has long created its own private legal systems, such as to govern commercial transactions under merchant law (or *lex mercatoria*) (Trakman 1983), or to govern the listing and trading of securities on stock exchanges (such as the New York Stock Exchange), although some self-regulatory organizations have become more regulated. These private business law regimes can be transnational or national in scope. At the national level, for example, business can create model contracts which effectively become the law in areas of industry, as has been the case with standards set by the American Institute of Architects for the design and construction of buildings (Macaulay 1986: 448). Similarly, Lloyd's of London syndicates were effectively responsible for insurance law in the UK, and Lloyd's power extended internationally because London was the financial center for international trade (Braithwaite and Drahos 2000: 113). Business self-regulation plays a central role in international harmonization today, often under the auspices of the International Chamber of

Commerce (ICC) as we explore further in the fourth section. To give just one example, the ICC periodically revises "Incoterms," which set forth the definitions of, and interpretative guidance for, sales terms used for the shipment of goods. Through its creation of new institutions, this alternative is the most centralized of the privately made variants.

Second, a business can simply disregard law in light of long-term client relations and reputational concerns. As Macaulay (1963: 61) found in his famous study of business contracts and the settlement of business disputes, "there is a hesitancy to speak of legal rights or to threaten to sue in these settlement negotiations."[15] Ian Macneil elaborated such insights in terms of "relational contract theory" under which social norms underpin contractual relations so that individual contracts and contract disputes are best viewed as "part of a relational web" (Macneil 2001: 18). In such cases, a business may not even engage with law to determine what legal rights, claims, or defenses it may have. Non-legal sanctions, such as damaged reputation, are available if a business does not act in good faith. This alternative which relies on business relations and social norms is the most decentralized; law (in terms of formal rules, standards, and procedures) plays the most limited role.

Third, business responds to public law by creating business-internal organizational policies and procedures which parallel and overlap with public law. Like the external public legal system, organizations adopt increasingly detailed rules, policies, and programs, and create new departments and positions to oversee regulatory compliance. In some cases, these new programs and institutions can facilitate other parties' awareness and activation of the law. In other areas, they can lead to interpretations and applications of law that neutralize the law's normative ambitions. In short, business internalization processes can help both to expand and weaken the law's reach.

By internalizing public law, business can further law's reach by internally incorporating public law norms and principles. Philip Selznick (Selznick, Nonet, and Vollmer 1969) labeled such internalization "legalization," arguing that legalization transforms business organizations into polities that provide substantial "citizenship" rights for their members. Public law, for example, in spurring the creation of internal corporate rules, can expand the "rights consciousness" of internal stakeholders, such as employees, who have reinforced expectations of social justice (Edelman 1990: 1410). Public law can, in parallel, spur the creation of new corporate compliance personnel within corporations. Company employees in these positions attend conferences on the applicable law, write memoranda on the relevant issues which they distribute within firms, and generally increase firm awareness of the legal issues in question. In formulating and overseeing the implementation of company policies, they affect internal business organizational culture, fostering company compliance with existing legal requirements and norms even where state enforcement is weak (Dobbin and Sutton 1998).

Business lawyers who defend their clients against advocates' claims may aid advocates' ends in creating legal compliance procedures to avoid legal challenge. Even if the risk of restrictions is minute, in-house lawyers can benefit if their clients take the law seriously. In-house counsel has an interest in being heard within the firm's hierarchy. When consulted by the firm's business personnel, in-house counsel, together with employees from the firm's human resources division, may overstate the risks to an enterprise from non-compliance by focusing on a legal reading of the law, its substantive requirements and sanctions, including any draconian risks such as imprisonment of company executives. Outside law firms and other consultants likewise distribute to clients and prospective clients memoranda, manuals, and other private assessments of the law. At symposia, they market contractual and other precautions which can be drafted and implemented to reduce the risk of legal intervention.

In the field of wrongful discharge law, for example, Edelman, Abraham, and Erlanger (1992: 75) note how "employer's in-house counsel may benefit from increased demands for their services within the firm and, like personnel professionals, may attain power by helping to curb the perceived threat of wrongful discharge lawsuits... The threat of wrongful discharge, then, may [also] help practicing lawyers [of outside firms] in the field of employment law expand the market for their services." They conclude that "the personnel profession, with some help from the legal profession, has constructed the law in a way that significantly overstates the threat it poses to employers" (1992: 47). Ironically, in providing legal counsel to their clients on the law's provisions and risks, in-house and external business lawyers and internal human resource employees can become unconscious abettors of the aims of otherwise underfunded and disparate advocates.

Data privacy regulation provides another example of private law regimes that complement and parallel public law regimes (Shaffer 2000). In the United States, private privacy seal programs are funded by business to adopt private privacy codes. This is done in part to ward off public regulation by demonstrating that business self-regulation is sufficient. Yet these private regimes also interact with public law regimes. For example, if a business does not comply with the rules it advertizes, it is subject to challenge by the US Federal Trade Commission for deceptive practices. Moreover, through the threat of data transfer restrictions and foreign litigation under European Union (EU) law (the data privacy directive), the EU helps raise the bar of what US business is willing to sign. Existing public law and the threat of new public law, in this case domestic and foreign, stimulate business demand for privacy policies and independent certification of them.

These professionals serve as carriers and filters of law and the magnitude of law's threat, giving rise to a convergence in business practice. Over time, business policies can become isomorphic in light of these professionals' interactions, and business desires to gain legitimacy through the adoption of what is perceived as "fair" governance procedures (Meyer and Rowan 1977; DiMaggio and Powell 1983). In this way, business-internal policies affect organizational fields through parallel adoption of policies by individual firms (Edelman and Suchman 1999: 979). For example, internal US business policies and procedures parallel civil rights laws (Edelman 1990) and health and safety laws (Bardach and Kagan 1982: 95).

The creation of internal business practices more than simply reflects and furthers law's reach. In creating organizational policies and procedures, business has an incentive to interpret public law requirements to suit business interests. In some cases, business may do so to market itself as a good citizen in protecting the environment or labor rights or otherwise (Prakash 2000; Prakash and Potoski 2006). Businesses may even require their suppliers to conform to these policies, extending their effects. In other cases, business may do so in ways designed to limit regulation's constraints. Law's textual ambiguities facilitate their opportunity to do so. In internalizing public law business translates and transforms it. Corporate internal policies and administrative procedures, for example, mimic central legal principles of due process, but do so by displacing the intervention of public legal authorities. Adopting internal rules allows the organization to "symbolize compliance" and borrow the legitimacy accorded public law, while exercising greater control of its implementation and, in the process, its meaning (Edelman and Suchman 1999: 961).

Business can attempt to preempt public law by removing disputes from external controls, such as by including mandatory arbitration provisions in business contracts (Edelman and Suchman 1999: 963). Businesses have long created dispute settlement institutions to resolve conflict between them. *Lex mercatoria*, for example, was enforced by specialized merchant courts at trade fairs in the middle ages (Milgram, North, and Weingast 1990; Braithwaite and Drahos 2000: 46). In contemporary international transactions, businesses still seek to avoid the biases and complexities of conflicts of law by avoiding adjudication before public courts. National legal systems recognize and enforce these private arbitration rulings (Leservoisier 2002: 256). The US Federal Arbitration Act even curtails US states' ability to limit the use and enforceability of arbitration provisions in contracts with consumers.[16] The rise of the alternative dispute resolution (ADR) movement further facilitates businesses' ability to resolve disputes outside the public domain (Stipanowich 2004).

The rise of in-house counsel also contributes to the internalization of law by business. Since the 1970s, the number and status of in-house counsel has grown dramatically. "Between 1970 and 1980, there was a forty percent increase in the number of lawyers working in-house; and between 1980 and 1991, there was a thirty-three percent increase" (Daly 1997: 1059). The use of in-house counsel involves lawyers at an earlier stage of transactions in strategic planning (Chayes and Chayes 1985: 281). In-house counsel not only helps business manage outside legal counsel, but also to manage the businesses' internalization of legal regimes as part of programmatic prevention policies (Chayes and Chayes 1985). In the process, in-house counsel can help give law more of a business orientation since in-house counsel tends to blend both legal and business advice, blurring the distinction between doing law and doing business (Rosen 1989; Nelson and Nielsen 2000).

By symbolically incorporating public requirements in internal policies, by internalizing administrative control over its routine activities through complaint procedures, and by preempting external intervention through private alternative dispute resolution, business creates its own legal field which helps to legitimize its practices. While Galanter earlier explored the ability of repeat players to exploit the judicial process, internalizing the legislative and judicial processes circumvents the public law system. In a reflection piece twenty-five years after his article speculating "why the haves come out ahead," Galanter finds that corporate internalization policies represent a "recoil against law" in response to reduced leeway afforded to business by the public law system (Galanter 1999: 1116). Internalization policies remove issues from public rule-making and adjudication. By usurping the role of external legal processes and supplanting them with internal rules, large organizations can enhance their ability to limit legal change (Edelman and Suchman 1999: 944). Under these internal systems, the "haves" are arguably even more advantaged (Edelman and Suchman 1999: 944).

LAW IN THE SHADOW OF BUSINESS PRACTICE

Rather than being viewed as distinct, public law and business internal policies are interpenetrated, reciprocally affecting each other (Macaulay 1986: 449). On the private side, private legal systems do not exist in a vacuum. Even in domains where publicly made law does not exist and business creates its own private standards, business does so in the shadow of the public law system's potential intervention. The public legal system can also provide default rules around which businesses contract.[17] On the public side, public legal systems can also be viewed as operating in the shadow of business practice. Legislators and courts have responded to private regimes by codifying and enforcing them. In addition, when business responds to new public regulation through adopting internal policies and practices, business may reciprocally shape the understanding of law within public institutions, including courts. While legal interpretation and enforcement affect economic behavior, organizational behavior, including business internalization practices, in turn, affects public law (Stryker 2003: 342).

To give an example, national courts have long enforced contracts based on customary business practices. As Braithwaite and Drahos (2000: 49) write, "the common law absorbed and adapted the Law Merchant," such as private business regimes pertaining to bills of exchange, promissory notes and letters of credit. "Specialist commercial courts...in England bound themselves to the principle of recognizing the customary practices of merchants, which in turn helped to produce and reinforce the Law Merchant" (Braithwaite and Drahos 2000: 65). In civil law countries, this customary private law was codified in the commercial codes of Western Europe.[18] In the United States, codification took place through the model Uniform Commercial Code which was subsequently adopted in all US states but one (Braithwaite and Drahos 2000: 50). These codes and institutional practices then spread to other parts of the world through colonization and a general "modeling" of Western commercial law (Braithwaite and Drahos 2000: 49–50).

Internal business policies and procedures may also shape how public law is perceived, transforming its meaning. To start, business practices under internal organizational policies and procedures can affect what individuals perceive to be the law through everyday social practice, shaping their "legal consciousness." Corporate compliance officers share their policies and procedures in symposia, workshops, electronic list-serves, trade journals, and other fora, leading to similar institutionalized practices in the field. By "redefining what is seen as normal, reasonable, rational and compliant in terms of internal business grievance procedures created in response to public law," internal business law and practice can colonize public law (Edelman and Suchman 1999: 963). For example, Edelman, Fuller, and Mara-Drita (2001: 1591) find that managerial discretion in applying civil rights laws has appropriated legal ideas, transforming how the public views the scope and application of civil rights laws.[19] They (2001: 1599) find that, "as legal ideas move into managerial and organizational arenas, law tends to become 'managerialized,' or progressively infused with managerial values."

These business practices can affect courts' interpretation and application of public law. In the civil rights field, internal business grievance procedures are not required by the laws themselves. Yet they can shape our understandings of the laws. As Edelman, Uggen, and Erlanger (1999) find in their study of internal business practices applying the civil rights laws, professionals "promote a particular compliance strategy, organizations adopt this strategy to reduce costs and symbolize compliance, and courts adjust judicial constructions of fairness to include these emerging organizational practices" (406). The authors' study finds that "courts have become more likely to defer to organizations' grievance procedures and to consider them relevant to determinations of liability" (409). These socio-legal scholars have found that even where disputants ultimately bring their claims to the public legal system, courts "often defer to the results of internal hearings," and "dismiss claims where plaintiffs' have failed to exhaust their in-house remedies" (Edelman and Suchman 1999: 964). Judges in overstretched and underfunded public law systems have incentives to do so (Komesar 2001). In sum, public law acquires meaning and has effects through the intermediation of business practice.

BUSINESS AND LAW IN COMPARATIVE AND GLOBAL CONTEXT

Legal rules, norms, and institutions have diffused globally through processes of colonization, economic exchange, and the growth of international and transnational institutions. This diffusion interacts with national and local legal cultures so that we find significant variation in outcomes despite these processes of convergence (Nelken 2007). We first address international developments and then turn to national law in comparative context.

The international level

Business plays an important role in international law-making, which has spread, directly or indirectly, to most regulatory areas. As John Braithwaite and Peter Drahos find in their masterful study of thirteen areas of global business regulation, business actors frequently play leading roles, whether through exporting their internal standards globally, through the creation of transnational private orders, or through "enrolling" states to create public law. They find, for example, that "state regulation follows industry self-regulatory practice more than the reverse" (481). In some cases, international standards may simply formalize and legitimize informal practices of large dominant businesses (492).

Private parties have long engaged in private rule-making to facilitate cross-border transactions. When law merchant norms are codified by states, conflict-of-law issues arise between different national variants. Business has responded by trying to harmonize the law at the international level, giving rise to what is called a "new Law Merchant" (Trakman 1983).

Among international business organizations, the International Chamber of Commerce (ICC) stands apart as the premier lobbying body on behalf of business interests (Braithwaite and Drahos 2000: 488). The ICC lobbies the full spectrum of UN organizations, looking "for key loci of decision-making in the globe and build [ing] a poultice of influence around them" (Braithwaite and Drahos 2000: 488). The ICC has, for example, been central to international commercial law (70); tax law (and in particular the creation of model tax treaties to avoid double taxation of business) (120); telecommunications and e-commerce law (344); and the drafting of environmental treaties (273).

In the field of international trade finance, transnational letters of credit are governed by a set of rules known as the Uniform Customs and Practice for Documentary Credit (UCP), written by the ICC. The ICC's goal is to codify "international banking practices, as well as to facilitate and standardize developing practices" (Levit 2008: 1171). Most banks will not issue letters-of-credit unless they are subject to the UCP (Levit 2008: 1177). When exporters and importers identify the UCP as their choice of law, these rules are applied by national courts that enforce them (Levit 2005: 141). Levit finds that "domestic courts, which are frequently called upon to hear actual letter-of-credit disputes, apply the UCP 500 even in the face of a domestic statute designed for related issues" (Levit 2005: 141). The ICC interprets its own rules through issuing hundreds of "advisory opinions" intended to clarify ambiguities (Levit 2008: 1174–5).

International private law-making has particularly evolved in the area of technical standard setting. Within the European Union, the Comité Européen de Normalisation (CEN) and Comité Européen de Normalisation Electrotechnique (CENELEC) play central roles. At the international level, business works through the Geneva-based International Organization for Standardization (ISO). Practically, businesses are pressed by market forces to apply those standards, and national courts can impose tort liability if they fail to do so and someone is harmed (Basedow 2008: 710).

Business also affects international law through enrolling state representatives to advance business goals. Examples of private international law include international treaties like the United Nations Convention on Contracts for the International Sale of Goods (CISG) and the International Convention for the Unification of Certain Rules of Law relating to Bills of Lading, as well as "soft law" norms such as the UNIDROIT Principles of International Commercial Contracts and the UNCITRAL Legislative Guide on Insolvency Law. A common form of regulatory export occurs where national industry associations shape the law in a dominant state, and this law becomes the model for other states, including through international regimes. While such influence varies by industry and country, Braithwaite and Drahos (2000: 482) find that "US corporations exert more power in the world system than corporations of other states because they can enroll the support of the most powerful state in the world."

Private business also enrolls states to advance its interests through inter-state litigation. Corporations frequently lie behind the claims that state representatives bring in international trade litigation. They lobby them, provide them with requisite background factual information, and hire outside lawyers to help write the legal briefs. As a result, most litigation before the renowned dispute settlement system of the World Trade Organization (WTO) involves the formation of partnerships between state representatives, private business interests, and the lawyers that business hires (Shaffer 2003; Shaffer, Sanchez, and Rosenberg 2008).

International law of course can also be used against business. Non-business actors can deploy international law to challenge business conduct, including before national courts; this again exemplifies how international and national institutions interact. Human rights activists, for example, have repeatedly brought suits under inter-national law before US courts to challenge business conduct in third countries, such as mining in Indonesia, oil exploration in Burma and Nigeria, and aiding and abetting the apartheid regime in South Africa (Davis 2008; Stephens and Ratner 2008).

Comparative legal context

The relation of business to law varies in comparative national and local context as a function of the configuration of interests in a regulatory area, institutional structures, the role of elites, traditions of business–government relations, and differences in "legal culture" and "business culture." By legal culture, we refer to attitudes and behavior as to "when, why and where people look for help to law or to other institutions, or decide just to 'lump it' " (Friedman 1994; Nelken 2007: 370). By business culture, we refer to patterns of norms and behavior within which people and institutions in the business world operate.[20] These norms and behaviors vary widely between (and within) countries, and they interact with and are shaped by local institutional structures and political interests. Any assessment thus must be careful not to reify or essentialize culture, especially without an appreciation of how norms are channeled by institutional structures which reflect political choices.[21]

Robert Kagan's work, in this respect, depicts how business–government relations in the United States are often characterized by "adversarial legalism," which he defines as "policymaking, policy implementation, and dispute resolution by means of lawyer-dominated litigation" (Kagan 2001: 3). Kagan finds that both cultural and institutional factors give rise to adversarial legalism. He maintains that US attitudes that governmental power should be constrained and that individuals should invoke the law to protect their rights and achieve their goals further an adversarial legal culture (Kagan 2001: 15). He likewise maintains that, in the United States, "adversarial legalism arises from the relative *absence* of institutions that effectively channel contending parties and groups into less expensive and more efficient ways of resolving disputes, ensuring accountability, regulating business, and compensating victims of injury or economic misfortune" (Kagan 2001: 34).

Adversarial legalism is viewed as less prevalent in Europe, although there is disagreement about the extent to which Europe is changing (cf. Levi-Faur 2005; Kelemen 2006; Kagan 2007). In a famous article from the 1970s, Rueschemeyer maintained that attitudes toward law in Germany are affected by more authoritarian traditions of rule "by an enlightened and supposedly neutral bureaucracy" (Rueschemeyer 1996: 274). He contended that lawyers within the German bar retained a greater "reserve toward the world of business" (Rueschemeyer 1996: 278). In France, Dyson (1996: 395) found that "state–industry relations remain notably intertwined," reflected in "the prevalence of members of the elite *grand corps* in the top management positions of the public and private sectors," giving rise to "a web of patronage spanning the public–private sector divide." Cohen-Tanugi (1996: 270) contended that French society is "sensitive to the power relations underlying a given legal framework" which leads to a "quasi-exclusive attention to power, whether political or economic, rather than to law, which is seen as either mere window-dressing or simply the result of the power relations." He argued that the French thus manifest "a fair amount of tolerance for failure to respect the rule of law" (Cohen-Tanugi 1996: 269). The place of law is changing in Europe, in reflection of global competition, economic restructuring, the rise of the European Union, and citizen demands. Change nonetheless takes place in the context of institutional path dependencies and different legacies of government–business relations.

It is commonly touted that people are more reluctant in Asia to use formal legal processes compared to Western nations, and especially in the United States, and thus there is less adversarial legalism. The explanation for Japan's lower litigation rates, compared to the United States, for example, has sparked debate among those stressing cultural and institutional factors (Feldman 2007). A focus on culture as an explanation, such as the importance of "social harmony" and "social consensus" in Asian countries, sparks charges of Orientalism in scholars' characterization of Asian legal systems, which, in themselves, vary significantly. Many scholars today stress how political choices determine the availability of formal institutions for dispute settlement.[22] Ginsburg and Hoetker (2006), for example, show how litigation rates have risen in Japan in response to structural reforms and institutional changes, including relaxed controls over the licensing of lawyers. Rapid economic development, followed by the bursting of the Japanese economic bubble and the 1997 Asian financial crisis, has significantly affected the role of law for business. China, for example, has moved dynamically toward a market economy, and has developed "new structures and processes for resolving disputes," and, in particular, commercial ones (Potter 2001: 26; Peerenboom and He 2008). In India, where courts are plagued by a large backlog of cases, frequent adjournments, and long delays, companies have increasingly sought to resolve legal disputes through alternative dispute resolution processes, including arbitration, but these processes also have given rise to delay, backlog, and frustration (Krishnan 2007). In sum, the articulation of competing political and economic interests continues to be mediated by different institutional structures and cultural norms, producing variations in the law-in-action in each country.

Scholars have used Marc Galanter's framework to compare patterns of dispute settlement by repeat players in different countries. A number of empirical studies have found that Galanter's general thesis that "repeat player 'haves' tend to fare well and that one-shot litigants lose frequently appear[s] to have considerable cross-national validation, at least among countries in the English common law tradition" (Songer, Sheehan, and Haire 1999: 814). In contrast, some studies of courts in other countries, particularly of higher courts, have come to different conclusions. Once again, however, we need to be careful to generalize the implications of these studies since higher court judgments represent only a small part of law and thus law's implications for business. In a study of business dispute settlement in Russia, Hendley, Murrell, and Ryterman (1999: 836–7) found Russian repeat players lack the impetus to "play for" rules because such efforts are pointless in light of the role of courts in the Russian legal system. However, they also noted the crisis situation in Russia at the time, with Russian enterprises "struggling for their very survival," so that the business focus was short-term (859). In a study of litigation before the Israeli High Court of Justice (HCJ), Dotan (1999: 1062–3) found that the "haves" benefit from only limited advantages over "have nots." He attributed this situation, in part, to the accessibility and marginal expense of litigation before the HCJ and, in part, to the HCJ's view of itself as a "protector" and "representative of the common citizen." Similarly, Haynie (1994) found that, before the Philippine Supreme Court, individuals have higher success rates in court judgments than government or business litigants, the prototypical repeat players. She postulated that in less-developed countries generally, courts may tend to favor the "have nots" out of concern for "their own legitimacy" and domestic social "stability," while nonetheless balancing elite concerns (754). Haynie's study, however, only focused on Supreme Court decisions which may play a constrained role in practice, especially if repeat players have a long-term privileged relation with lower court judges, in some cases being able to buy them off. Moreover, the role of formal courts and law have not held as prominent a position in many less developed countries, in part because they have other political and economic priorities.[23]

The central point here is not to enter a debate as to which countries are governed to a greater extent by the "rule of law," but rather that, in an era of economic and cultural globalization, even when law is harmonized at the international level, the impact varies significantly. Carruthers and Halliday's path-breaking work (2006, 2007) on international harmonization of corporate bankruptcy law provides a leading example. Their work depicts how bankruptcy law prescribed at the international level is differentially received in China, Korea, and Indonesia. They examine the different types of mechanisms used to diffuse international bankruptcy norms, with coercive measures being relatively more effective in Indonesia (such as IMF loan conditionality) than in Korea, which is more likely to require persuasion to effect legal change, or in China, in which change is more likely to occur through Chinese modeling of reforms based on others' practices. They address how different interests and institutional legacies at the national level, and a country's position of relative power in global context, affect the implementation of international harmonization efforts. They show how the indeterminacy of law, internal contradictions within law, diagnostic struggles over problem definition, and the fact that different actors (and, in particular, different business interests) participate in struggles over national implementation result in ongoing national divergences.

CONCLUSION

In sum, to understand the relation of business and law, one must assess business influence on the formation and application of public law before legislatures, administrative bodies, and courts, together with business creation and application of private legal systems, whether to preempt public law, exit from public law, or internalize and, in the process, translate and transform public law. One next needs to assess the dynamic and reciprocal interaction of these public and private legal systems in different national and transnational contexts which constitutes the legal field in which business operates. Although public and private law-making for most regulatory fields has spread to the international level, the domestic implementation of harmonized rules and standards still varies considerably in light of ongoing differences in the relative power of business, government, and law at the domestic level, as well as differences in local institutional structures and business and legal cultures. Thus, the relationship of business and law can be viewed in terms of three sets of institutional interactions: (i) horizontal public institutional interaction among legislative, administrative, and judicial processes, in each of which business can play a critical role; (ii) vertical public institutional interaction involving national and transnational institutional processes, with transnational processes becoming more prominent; and (iii) the interaction among these public institutional processes and parallel private rule-making, administrative, and dispute settlement mechanisms that business creates.

Notes

1. Melvin C. Steen Professor of Law, University of Minnesota Law School. I would like to thank Fabrizio Cafaggi, Howard Erlanger, Claire Hill, Herbert Krtizer, Brett McDonnell, Randall Peerenboom, Joachim Savelsberg, and Veronica Taylor for their comments, and Katie Staba, Carla Kupe, Kyle Shamberg, Ryan Griffin, Mary Rumsey, and Suzanne Thorpe for their extensive research assistance. All errors, of course, remain my own.

2. By business, we refer to all institutional forms, including peak business trade associations, sectoral lobbying groups, large corporations, and small proprietorships. Although we have made clear that the interests of business as regards law are rarely, if ever, monolithic, we will at times focus on business as a whole in this chapter to simplify analysis. Corporate organization and state regulation have both grown dramatically in number and complexity over the last century, with each responding to the other. On the rise and global diffusion of the corporate form, see Braithwaite and Drahos (2000: 144). On the growing pervasiveness of law during the latter half of the twentieth century, as reflected in more regulation, litigation, number of lawyers and other legal actors, and greater diffusion of information and public awareness about law, see Galanter (1992: 1–2); Friedman (2002).

3. By private legal systems and private law, we mean law made by and through private bodies, as opposed to traditional contract, property, and family law. Cf. Michaels and Jansen (2006) (providing conceptual clarifications of private law in light of processes of globalization and privatization).

4. This is true not only of property and contract law which facilitate and legitimize business economic activity (Hurst 1970: 61), but of regulatory law more broadly in a capitalist economy.

5. See http://www.unglobalcompact.org/AboutTheGC/index.html, I thank Fabrizio Cafaggi for our discussion on this point.

6. As Willard Hurst (1970: 59) wrote concerning developments of law affecting business in the United States, "[b]efore the late nineteenth century questions of legitimacy relating to the business corporation concerned in the main the legitimacy of the ends and means of government's power as it affected corporations, rather than the legitimacy of corporations' use of the facilities the law provided for them." While progressive regulation of corporations grew in the twentieth century, corporate law limits withdrew. From the 1890s to 1930s, "[t]he function of corporation law [in the United States became] to enable businessmen to act, not to police their action" (Hurst 1970: 70).

7. See Skrzycki (2003: 84; chart noting industry background of regulators in the George W. Bush administration, taken from the Brookings Institution, Presidential Appointee Initiative Analysis).

8. Abramson (1998: A1; quoting Strauss).

9. Although this is clearly true in common law systems, it is also arguably the case in civil law systems where judges and legal scholars refer to judicial decisions as regards the law's meaning and give weight to them, which helps to preserve legal certainty and consistency. See e.g. Cappelletti (1981: 392; "there is no sharp cleavage between the two major legal traditions, not even to the topic [stare decisis] discussed in this article").

10. These law firms have grown in size, as have litigation expenses, favoring those with greater resources (Galanter and Palay 1991). Heinz and Laummann (1982: 127) found that legal "fields serving big business clients" are at the top in ranking of prestige, and "those serving individual clients ... at the bottom".

11. These attorneys also have their own interests, complicating the assessment of the costs and benefits of these mechanisms.

12. See, e.g., Feeley (1979) demonstrating gap between law "on the books" and its implementation in criminal justice system); Macaulay (1963; documenting differences between written contracts and actual practices followed by parties); Stryker (2003; institutions generally).

13. But compare Macaulay (1963) regarding the role of non-legal norms in the settlement of business disputes.

14. Edelman and Suchman contend that business organizations have internalized elements of the public legal system in at least four major ways which interact: "(1) the legalization of organizational governance [through internal policies and procedures]; (2) the expansion of private dispute resolution; (3) the rise of in-house counsel; and (4) the re-emergence of private policing" (Edelman and Suchman 2007: xxv). On the latter point, businesses use private police forces to patrol their premises and oversee their workforce. It is estimated that private police outnumber public police by 3:1 (Suchman and Edelman 1999: 958).

15. See also Bernstein (1992: 115; "The diamond industry has systematically rejected state-created law. In its place, the sophisticated traders who dominate the industry have developed an elaborate, internal set of rules, complete with distinctive institutions and sanctions, to handle disputes among industry members").

16. State attempts to protect consumers from mandatory arbitration "have been rendered irrelevant by [a] series of Supreme Court decisions" (Brunet et al. 2006: 159).

17. See, for example, the adoption by corporations of Board Audit Committees, which the New York Stock Exchange required for listing, but which non-listed companies adopted out of concern that courts in lawsuits claiming director liability might consider the practice as a standard for responsible conduct (Braithwaite and Drahos 2000: 171).

18. Moreover, in France, the lowest-level court for commercial matters, the Tribunal de Commerce, is composed of lay members from the business community. Many German *Länder* have created special chambers for commercial matters that include lay judges (Basedow 2008: 707).

19. Edelman, Fuller, and Mara-Drita (2001: 1591) suggest that managerial discretion in implementing civil rights laws within organizations reframe diversity issues to include not only gender and race, but also issues of personality and cultural lifestyle traits. Including such issues changes not only the scope of civil rights laws, but transforms the legal ideals underlying civil rights.

20. DiMaggio 1994 (within organizational studies, "culture" refers to the "shared cognitions, values, norms, and expressive symbols" associated with a discrete group).

21. The literature on pluralist, centralized, and corporatist political systems provides institutional-oriented explanations for national approaches (Wilson 2003).

22. For assessments of dispute settlement within Japan cf. Kawashima (1963), Haley (1978), Upham (1987), Ramseyer (1988); within China, Macauley (1998), Peerenboom and He (2008); within Korea, Choi and Kahei (2007), Yoon (2000); and within Asia generally, Taylor and Pryles (2003).

23. Cf. Carruthers and Halliday (2006: 544; noting "historic irrelevance of law and the courts as institutions of market regulation, and hence the ineptness of current courts and their vulnerability to corruption"); Henderson (2006; finding judicial corruption in 18 of 23 countries surveyed); and Peerenboom (2004: 26; identifying problems common to Asian

countries' judicial systems—impaired access to justice, inefficient and expensive courts, corruption, and incompetence).

REFERENCES

ABRAMSON, J. 1998. "The business of persuasion thrives in nation's capital," *New York Times*, September 29, p. A1.

ACKERMAN, B., and HASSLER, W. 1981. *Clean Coal/Dirty Air: Or How the Clean Air Act Became a Multibillion-Dollar Bail-out for High-Sulfur Coal Producers and What Should be Done about it.* New Haven: Yale University Press.

ALBISTON, C. 1999. "The rule of law and the litigation process: the paradox of losing by winning," *Law and Society Review* 33: 869–910.

BARDACH, E., and KAGAN, R. A., eds. 1982. *Social Regulation: Strategies for Reform.* San Francisco: Institute for Contemporary Studies.

BASEDOW, J. 2008. "The state's private law and the economy: commercial law as an amalgam of public and private rule-making," *American Journal of Comparative Law* 56: 703–21.

BERNSTEIN, M. H. 1955. *Regulating Business by Independent Commission.* Princeton: Princeton University Press.

BERNSTEIN, L. 1992. "Opting out of the legal system: extralegal contractual relations in the diamond industry," *Journal of Legal Studies* 21: 115–57.

BLACK, D. 1973. "The mobilization of law," *Journal of Legal Studies* 2: 125–49.

BRAITHWAITE, J., and DRAHOS, P. 2000. *Global Business Regulation.* Cambridge: Cambridge University Press.

BRUNET, E., SPEIDEL, R. E., WARE, S. J., and STERNLIGHTET, J. R. 2006. *Arbitration Law in America: A Critical Assessment.* Cambridge: Cambridge University Press.

CAPPELLETTI, M. 1981. "The doctrine of stare decisis and the civil law: a fundamental difference—or no difference at all?," in K. Zweigert, H. Bernstein, U. Drobnig, and H. Kötz, eds., *Festschrift für Konrad Zweigert zum 70. Geburtstag.* Tübingen: Mohr Siebeck, 388.

CARRUTHERS, B. G., and HALLIDAY, T. C. 2006. "Negotiating globalization: global scripts and intermediation in the construction of Asian insolvency regimes," *Law and Social Inquiry* 31: 521–84.

——— 2007. "The recursivity of law: global norm-making and national law-making in the globalization of corporate insolvency regimes," *American Journal of Sociology* 112: 1135–202.

CHAYES, A., and CHAYES, A. H. 1985. "Corporate counsel and the elite law firm," *Stanford Law Review* 37: 277–300.

CHOI, D.-K. C., and ROKUMOTO, K., eds. 2007. *Judicial System Transformation in the Globalizing World: Korea and Japan.* Seoul: Seoul National University Press.

COGLIANESE, C., ZECKHAUSER, R., and PARSON, E. 2004. "Seeking truth for power: informational strategy and regulatory policymaking," *Minnesota Law Review* 89: 277–341.

COHEN-TANUGI, L. 1996. "The law without the state," in *European Legal Cultures.* Brookfield, Vt.: Dartmouth Publishing Company, 269–73. Originally published in *Le Droit sans l'état.* Paris: Presses Universitaires de France, 1985.

CORTESE, C. 1966. "A study in knowledge and attitudes toward the law: the legal knowledge inventory," *Rocky Mountain Social Science Journal* 3: 192–204.

DALY, M. C. 1997. "The cultural, ethical, and legal challenges in lawyering for a global organization: the role of the general counsel," *Emory Law Journal* 46: 1057–112.

DAVIS, J. 2008. *Justice across Borders: The Struggle for Human Rights in US Courts.* Cambridge: Cambridge University Press.

DEZALAY, Y., and GARTH, B. 1996. *Dealing in Virtue: International Commercial Arbitration and the Construction of a Transnational Legal Order.* Chicago: University of Chicago Press.

DiMAGGIO, P. 1994. "Culture and economy," in N. J. Smelser and R. Swedberg, eds., *The Handbook of Economic Sociology.* Princeton: Princeton University Press, 27–8.

—— and POWELL, W. W. 1983. "The iron cage revisited: institutional isomorphism and collective rationality in organizational fields," *American Sociological Review* 48(2): 147–60.

DOBBIN, F., and SUTTON, J. R. 1998. "The strength of a weak state: the rights revolution and the rise of human resources management divisions," *American Journal of Sociology* 104(2): 441–76.

DOTAN, Y. 1999. "Do the 'haves' still come out ahead? Resource inequalities in ideological courts: the case of the Israeli High Court of Justice," *Law and Society Review* 33: 1059–80.

DYSON, K. 1996. "Cultural issues and the single European Market: barriers to trade and shifting attitudes," in *European Legal Cultures.* Brookfield, Vt.; Dartmouth Publishing Company, 387–97. Originally published in *Political Quarterly* 64(1) (1993): 84–98.

EDELMAN, L. B. 1990. "Legal environments and organization governance: the expansion of Due Process in the American workplace," *American Journal of Sociology* 95: 1401–40.

—— and SUCHMAN, M. C. 1999. "When the 'haves' hold court: speculations on the organization internalization of law," *Law and Society Review* 33: 941–91.

—— —— 2007. *The Legal Lives of Private Organizations.* Aldershot: Ashgate.

—— ABRAHAM, S. E., and ERLANGER, H. S. 1992. "Professional construction of law: the inflated threat of wrongful discharge," *Law and Society Review* 25: 47–84.

—— FULLER, S. R., and MARA-DRITA, I. 2001. "Diversity rhetoric and the managerialization of law," *American Journal of Sociology* 106: 1589–641.

EDELMAN, M. 1964. *The Symbolic Uses of Politics.* Urbana: University of Illinois Press.

—— 1971. *Politics as Symbolic Action: Mass Arousal and Quiescence.* Chicago: Markham Publishing Co.

—— UGGEN, C., and ERLANGER, H. S. 1999. "The endogeneity of legal regulation: grievance procedures as rational myth," *American Journal of Sociology* 105(2): 406–54.

EHRLICH, E. 1936. *Fundamental Principles of the Sociology of Law.* Cambridge, Mass.: Harvard University Press.

ELSON, A. 1998. "The case for an in-depth study of the American Law Institute," *Law and Social Inquiry* 23: 625–40.

FARBER, D. A., and FRICKEY, P. P. 1991. *Law and Public Choice: A Critical Introduction.* Chicago: University of Chicago Press.

FARNSWORTH, K., and HOLDEN, C. 2006. "The business–social policy nexus: corporate power and corporate inputs into social policy," *Journal of Social Policy* 35: 473–94.

FEELEY, M. M. 1979. *The Process is the Punishment: Handling Cases in a Lower Criminal Court.* New York: Russell Sage Foundation.

FELDMAN, E. A. 2007. "Law, culture and conflict: dispute resolution in postwar Japan," in D. H. Foote, eds., *Law in Japan: A Turning Point.* Seattle: University of Washington Press.

FREEMAN, J. 2000. "The private role in public governance," *New York University Law Review* 75 (101): 543 ff.

FRIEDMAN, L. M. 1994. "Is there a modern legal culture?" *Ratio Juris* 7: 117–31.

—— 2002. *American Law in the Twentieth Century.* New Haven: Yale University Press.

GALANTER, M. 1974. "Why the 'haves' come out ahead: speculations on the limits of legal change," *Law and Society Review* 9: 95–160.

—— 1975. "Afterword: explaining litigation," *Law and Society Review* 9: 347–68.

—— 1984. "Worlds of deals: using negotiation to teach about legal process," *Journal of Legal Education* 34: 268–76.

—— 1992. "Law abounding: legislation around the North Atlantic," *Modern Law Review* 55: 1–24.

—— 1999. "Farther along," *Law and Society Review* 33: 1113–23.

—— 2001. "Contract in court; or almost everything you may or may not want to know about contract litigation," *Wisconsin Law Review* 1: 577–628.

—— 2006. "Planet of the APs: Reflections on the scale of law and its users," *Buffalo Law Review* 53: 1369–417.

—— and PALAY, T. 1991. *Tournament of Lawyers: The Transformation of the Big Law Firm.* Chicago. University of Chicago Press.

GINSBURG, T., and HOETKER, G. 2006. "The unreluctant litigant? An empirical analysis of Japan's turn to litigation," *Journal of Legal Studies* 35(1): 31–59.

HALEY, J. O. 1978. "The myth of the reluctant litigant," *Journal of Japanese Studies* 4: 359–90.

HAWKINS, K. 1983. "Bargain and bluff: compliance strategy and deterrence in the enforcement of regulation," *Law and Policy Quarterly* 5: 35–73.

HAYNIE, S. L. 1994. "Resource inequalities and litigation outcomes in the Philippine Supreme Court," *Journal of Politics* 56: 752–72.

HEINZ, J. P., and LAUMMANN, E. O. 1982. *Chicago Lawyers: The Social Structure of the Bar.* New York: Russell Sage Foundation.

HELD, D., McGREW, A., GOLDBLATT, D., and PERRATON, J. 1999. *Global Transformations: Politics, Economics and Culture.* Oxford: Polity Press.

HENDERSON, K. E. 2006. "Global lessons and best practices: corruption and judicial independence—a framework for an annual State of the Judiciary Report," in G. Canivet, M. Andenas, and D. Fairgrieve, eds., *Independence, Accountability and the Judiciary.* London: British Institute of International and Comparative Law, 439–92.

HENDLEY, K., MURRELL, P., and RYTERMAN, R. 1999. "Do repeat players behave differently in Russia? Contractual and litigation behavior of Russian enterprises," *Law and Society Review* 33: 833–67.

HURST, J. W. 1970. *The Legitimacy of the Business Corporation in the Law of the United States 1780-1970.* Charlottesville: University Press of Virginia.

KAGAN, R. A. 2001. *Adversarial Legalism: The American Way of Law.* Cambridge, Mass.: Harvard University Press.

—— 2007. "Globalization and legal change: the 'Americanization' of European law?," *Regulation and Governance* 1: 99–120.

—— GUNNINGHAM, N., and THORNTON, D. 2003. "Explaining corporate environmental performance: how does regulation matter?" *Law and Society Review* 37: 51–90.

KAWASHIMA, T. 1963. "Dispute resolution in contemporary Japan," in A. T. von Mehren, eds., *Law in Japan: The Legal Order in a Changing Society.* Cambridge, Mass.: Harvard University Press, 41–72.

KELEMAN, R. D. 2006. "Suing for Europe: adversarial legalism and European governance," *Comparative Political Studies* 39: 101–27.

KOMESAR, N. 2001. *Law's Limits: The Rule of Law and the Supply and Demand of Rights.* Cambridge: Cambridge University Press.

KRISHNAN, J. K. 2007. "Outsourcing and the globalizing legal profession," *William and Mary Law Review* 48: 2189–246.

KRITZER, H. 1991. *Let's Make a Deal: Understanding the Negotiation Process in Ordinary Litigation.* Madison: University of Wisconsin Press.

LESERVOISIER, L. 2002. "Enforcing arbitration awards and important conventions," in D. Campbell, ed., *The Arbitration Process: Comparative Law Yearbook of International Business*. The Hague: Kluwer Law International, 255–64.

LEVI-FAUR, D. 2005. "The political economy of legal globalization: juridification, adversarial legalism, and responsive regulation," *International Organization* 59: 451–62.

LEVIT, J. K. 2005. "A bottom–up approach to international lawmaking: the tale of three trade finance instruments," *Yale Journal of International Law* 30: 125–210.

—— 2008. "Bottom–up lawmaking through a pluralist lens: the ICC Banking Commission and the transnational regulation of letters of credit," *Emory Law Journal* 57: 1147–225.

LINDBLOM, C. E. 1977. *Politics and Markets: The World's Political Economic Systems*. New York: Basic Books.

MACAULAY, S. 1963. "Non-contractual relations in business: a preliminary study," *American Sociological Review* 28: 1–19.

—— 1986. "Private government," in L. Lipson and S. Wheeler, eds., *Law and Social Science*. Beverly Hills, Calif.: Russell Sage Foundation, 445–518.

—— 2003. "The real and the paper deal: empirical pictures of relationships, complexity and the urge for transparent simple rules," *Modern Law Review* 66: 44–79.

MACAULEY, M. 1998. *Social Power and Legal Culture: Litigation Masters in Late Imperial China*. Stanford, Calif.: Stanford University Press.

MACNEIL, I. 2001. *The Relational Theory of Contract: Selected Works of Ian Macneil*, ed. David Campbell. London: Sweet and Maxwell.

MAYER, C. J. 1990. "Personalizing the impersonal: corporations and the Bill of Rights," *Hastings Law Journal* 41: 577–668.

MEYER, J. W., and ROWAN, B. 1977. "Institutional organizations: formal structure as myth and ceremony," *American Journal of Sociology* 83(2): 340–63.

MICHAELS, R., and JANSEN, N. 2006. "Private law beyond the state? Europeanization, globalization, privatization," *American Journal of Comparative Law* 54: 843–90.

MILGRAM, P., NORTH, D. C., and WEINGAST, B. R. 1990. "The role of institutions in the revival of trade: the medieval law merchant, private judges, and the Champagne fairs," *Economics and Politics* 1: 1–23.

MNOOKIN, R., and KORNHAUSER, L. 1979. "Bargaining in the shadow of the law: the case of divorce," *Yale Law Journal* 88: 950–97.

NELKEN, D. 2007. "Culture, legal," in *Encyclopedia of Law and Society: American and Global Perspectives*. Los Angeles: Sage Publications, i. 370–5.

NELSON, R., and NIELSEN, L. B. 2000. "Cops, counsel, and entrepreneurs: constructing the role of inside counsel in large corporations," *Law and Society Review* 34: 457–94.

NOLL, R. G. 1971. *Reforming Regulation: An Evaluation of the Ash Council Proposals*. Washington, DC: Brookings Institute.

PEERENBOOM, R. 2004. "Varieties of rule of law," in R. Peerenboom, ed., *Asian Discourses of Rule of Law: Theories and Implementation of Law in Twelve Asian Countries, France and the US*. London: RoutledgeCurzon.

—— and XIN HE. 2008. "Dispute resolution in China: patterns, causes and prognosis," in *Dispute Resolution in China*. Oxford: Oxford Foundation for Law, Justice and Society.

POSNER, R. A. 1974. "Theories of economic regulation," *Bell Journal of Economics and Management Science* 5: 335–58.

POTTER, P. B. 2001. *The Chinese Legal System: Globalization and Local Legal Culture*. London: RoutledgeCurzon.

PRAKASH, A. 2000. *Greening the Firm: The Politics of Corporate Environmentalism*. Cambridge: Cambridge University Press.

—— and POTOSKI, M. 2006. *The Voluntary Enviornmentalists: Green Clubs, ISO 14001, and Voluntary Environmental Regulations*. Cambridge: Cambridge University Press.

QUIRK, P. J. 1981. *Industry Influence in Federal Regulatory Agencies*. Princeton: Princeton University Press.

RAMSEYER, M. 1988. "Reluctant litigant revisited: rationality and disputes in Japan," *Journal of Japanese Studies* 14: 111–23.

RODRIK, D. 1997. *Has Globalization Gone Too Far*. Washington, DC: Institute for International Economics.

ROSEN, R. E. 1989. "The inside counsel movement, professional judgment and organizational representation," *Indiana Law Journal* 64: 479–554.

RUBIN. E. L. 1993. Thinking like a lawyer, acting like a lobbyist: some notes on the process of revising UCC Articles 3 and 4," *Loyola of Los Angeles Law Review* 26: 743–88.

RUESCHEMEYER, D. 1996. "Lawyers and their society," in *European Legal Cultures*. Brookfield, Vt.: Dartmouth Publishing Company, 274–8. Originally published in *Lawyers and their Society: A Comparative Study of the Legal Profession in Germany and in the United States*. Cambridge, Mass.: Harvard University Press, 1973.

SCHEINGOLD, S. 1974. *The Politics of Rights: Lawyers, Public Policy, and Political Change*. New Haven: Yale University Press.

SCHLOZMAN, K., and TIERNEY, J. 1986. *Organized Interests and American Democracy*. New York: Harper and Row.

SCHWARTZ, A., and SCOTT, R. E. 1995. "The political economy of private legislatures," *University of Pennsylvania Law Review* 143: 595–654.

SELZNICK, P., NONET, P., and VOLLMER, H. 1969. *Law, Society, and Industrial Justice*. New York: Russell Sage Foundation.

SHAFFER, G. 2000. "Globalization and social protection: the impact of foreign and international rules in the ratcheting up of US privacy standards," *Yale Journal of International Law* 25: 1–88.

—— 2003. *Defending Interest: Public–Private Partnerships in WTO Litigation*. Washington, DC: Brookings Institution Press.

—— SANCHEZ, M. R., and ROSENBERG, B. 2008. "The trials of winning at the WTO: what lies behind Brazil's success," *Cornell International Law Journal* 41(2): 383–501.

SKRZYCKI, C. 2003. *The Regulators: Anonymous Power Brokers in American Politics*. Lanham, Md.: Rowman & Littlefield Publishers.

SONGER, D. R., SHEEHAN, R. S., and HAIRE, S. B. 1999. "Do the 'haves' come out ahead over time? Applying Galanter's framework to decisions of the US Courts of Appeals, 1925–1988," *Law and Society Review* 33: 811–32.

STEPHENS, B., and RATNER, M. 2008. *International Human Rights Litigation in US Courts*. Boston: Martinus Nijhoff Publishers.

STIPANOWICH, T. J. 2004. "ADR and the 'Vanishing Trial': the growth and impact of 'Alternative Dispute Resolution,'" *Journal of Empirical Legal Studies* 1: 843–912.

STRYKER, R. 2003. "Mind the gap: law, institutional analysis, and socioeconomics," *Socio-Economic Review* 1: 335–67.

TAYLOR, V. L., and PRYLES, M. 2003. "The cultures of dispute resolution in Asia," in M. Pryles, ed., *Dispute Resolution in Asia*, 2nd edn. The Hague: Kluwer, 1–23.

TRAKMAN, L. E. 1983. *The Law Merchant: The Evolution of Commercial Law*. Littleton, Colo.: Fred B. Rothman.

TRUBEK, D. M., SARAT, A., FELSTINER, W. L. F., KRITZER, H. M., and GROSSMAN, J. B. 1983. "The costs of ordinary litigation," *UCLA Law Review* 31: 72–127.

UPHAM, F. K. 1987. *Law and Social Change in Postwar Japan*. Cambridge, Mass.: Harvard University Press.

VOGEL, D. 1983. "The power of business in America: a re-appraisal," *British Journal of Political Science* 13: 19–43.

——1995. *Trading up: Consumer and Environmental Regulation in a Global Economy.* Cambridge, Mass.: Harvard University Press.

WILSON, G. K. 2003. *Business and Politics: A Comparative Introduction*, 3rd edn. New York: Chatham House Publishers.

WILSON, J. Q. 1980. *The Politics of Regulation.* New York: Basic Books.

YOON, DAE-KYU, ed. 2000. *Recent Transformations in Korean Law and Society.* Seoul: Seoul National University Press.

CHAPTER 4

BUSINESS STUDIES

THE GLOBAL DYNAMICS OF BUSINESS–STATE RELATIONS

JONATHAN STORY
THOMAS LAWTON

INTRODUCTION

BUSINESS people increasingly ask "how can we make corporate strategy in such a volatile world?" An answer to the question requires us to take a more holistic approach to corporate strategy and company policy than we conventionally do when considering the challenges facing top management teams. Conventional strategy divides conveniently into three parts, like Caesar's description of Gaul: first, the development and deployment of resources, competences, and capabilities of the firm; second, dynamics and shifts in the firm's market positions caused by customers and competition and by the goals, policies, and actions of governments; and third, what both inquiries hold for the firm's future. What is going on inside the corporation, within its value chain and its wider business ecosystem and in its existing and emergent markets, are certainly major drivers of corporate strategy. But corporate strategies have to be elaborated, and opportunities and risks assessed in full recognition of the dynamics at work in a world undergoing complex transformation. In this chapter, we take the position that strategy and policy must be seen as complementary because they provide a different lens to look on the future as the holism through which current resources in the firm are developed and allocated. In a static presentation of our theme—and where time is absent—we may say that business leaders need to develop a deeper understanding of the issues underpinning what we call the politics, markets, and business triangle. We start with time as the key variable to consider, and sketch a stylized survey of how corporate strategy thinking has evolved, with a view to teasing out the key tensions that businesses encounter when operating in a semi-integrated world market and polity. We then look closer at the relation of corporate policies to the diversity of states, discuss the evolution of the global state and market system, and spell out some of the key challenges facing corporate leaders making strategies and policies to both shape and understand the future. This should condition their allocation of current scarce resources. The key parameter of risk for top management is by definition the exigency of dealing with a future about which little is known, but where some things can be learnt.

The Corporate Focus

For most of the Twentieth Century, Big Business and Big Government reigned supreme. Modern industrial organization may be dated from 1913, when Henry Ford is said to have observed how cattle entered a Chicago slaughterhouse at one end and exited as steak cuts at the other. Always looking to lower costs of production, he had moving assembly belts introduced into his plants (Ford and Crowther 1992). Frederick Winslow Turner had already outlined the Principles of Scientific Management, whereby tasks were divided into discrete forms and executed by specialists, in turn supervised by managers whose job was to control and motivate. Motivation was ensured through force and fear in the factory, and control over the tiers of managers required to run the organization was maintained through capital budgeting techniques. As Stalin, a great admirer of Ford and Turner observed, as he prepared to turn Russia into a giant factory for tractors and tanks, "The combination of the Russian revolutionary sweep with American efficiency is the essence of Leninism" (Hughes 2004).

There were four enduring features of these earlier experiments with scientific management. The first, represented in the mind-numbing experience of an industrial worker's life as a cog in a huge machine—immortalized in Charlie Chaplin's *Modern Times*—was to generate the human relations movement which, since the 1920s, has aimed to improve human satisfaction in the workplace (Bruce 2006). The second was the assumption that as scientific management played an ever greater part in shaping the fortunes of corporations, the managerial function came to overshadow that of owners and shareholders (Bearle and Means 1932). The third was the contribution of the Ford Motor Company, and of "scientific management" to allied victory in both world wars, encapsulated in President Roosevelt's description of Detroit (Ford's headquarters) as the "arsenal of democracy." The fourth was the spread of scientific principles of management across activities and worldwide, their development in the 1940s and 1950s into operations research, and their renewed salience as the world economy opened up from the late 1970s onwards, associated with the notoriety of the "Toyota Production System."[1]

New technologies in the 1920s enabled corporations to diversify production into new markets by linking economies of scale to a wider scope of products. The emblematic corporation to emerge in this decade, and to overtake the Ford Company as the world's largest automobile corporation in terms of yearly units sold, was General Motors (GM). This position was held for over seven decades. Alfred P. Sloan became President of GM in 1923, and was associated with the development of tools to manage a multi-product company, compared to Ford's focus, at the time, on the company's unique Model-T car. Two tools are worth mentioning: one was the financial metric of return on investment, yielding a figure comparable across product divisions; the other was a multi-product pricing strategy to keep customers loyal as their incomes rose. His integrative concept for good management was "decentralisation with co-ordinated control" (Sloan 1965), where decentralization encourages initiative, responsibility, and decisions based on facts, and coordination promotes efficiencies and economies of scale. The management process, though, depended heavily on coordination by committee, and also on the availability of consumer finance to bring the customer to buy. As long as banks in the 1920s arranged for loans to customers on hire-purchase, the mass consumer markets experienced unprecedented growth.

But the collapse of the money and credit system in 1929, led subsequently to Roosevelt's New Deal and the closer association of Big Labor with Big Business. Big Government came in the 1940s, when the captains of US industry and finance in effect took over the running of the US war efforts. Federal outlays rose from around 10 per cent in the 1930s, to 42 per cent of GDP by 1945, and have remained around 20 per cent of GDP since. Allied victory paved the way for the spread around the world of the US experience in technology and science policy (Smith 1990) and the export of US business practice and experience to Europe (Bjarnar and Kipping 1998), Japan, and beyond (Maier 1978). US outward investment expanded as world markets slowly opened up again, generating an extensive literature on the effect of control over production by internationally invested corporations (multi- or trans-nationals) on states' divestment of their sovereign powers (Kindleberger 1969; Vernon 1971; Barnet and Muller 1974). But the very different reactions of states in the global system to the oil crises of the 1970s revealed the peculiarities of their domestic structures, and their continuing autonomy to respond to markets and to their status as home or host countries for multinationals (Katzenstein 1978). Rather, states and corporations came to be seen as enmeshed in a web of political and market interdependence. The conditions for this complex interdependence are provided with the existence of multiple channels for exchanges between societies. This is complemented by extensive consultative networks, which are indicative of the overlap between domestic and foreign policy. This overlap is characteristic of relations between developed industrial countries (Keohane and Nye 1977). States, in this view, remain the central pillars of the global system. This was borne out during the global credit crunch of 2008, when governments around the world stepped in to bolster business and prevent the collapse of financial markets.

From a corporate perspective, the managerial issues seemed more pertinent. Running large organizations required senior management to elaborate broad strategies to guide policy over the longer term, and to adapt the organization to changing conditions and new opportunities. The typical US corporation had initially developed along functional lines, but this created major problems of coordination between the purchasing, production, finance, or marketing departments as the number of products sold multiplied. Some decided, like GM, to centralize authority, risking "analysis paralysis" among a senior management far removed from the humbler but vital tasks of production and sales, while others, like 3M, managed to delegate authority and initiative down the organizational hierarchy. To facilitate assessment of the profitability of operations, the trend set in to split the organization into product divisions, with their own functional sub-units. An international division was added to this as markets developed abroad.

John Stopford and Louis Wells (1972) recorded the problems inherent in such an arrangement. The usual international division held a mandate to run business within a geographic area, and competed for home attention with the foreign desks of product divisions. This led to endless bureaucratic efforts to "coordinate" activities, prompting corporations to take one of two options. Those firms who sold few products and were still organized along functional lines tended to opt for worldwide and regional area structures. Regional structures duplicated the functions back home, and to a degree were able to respond to local conditions. Multi-product firms took the other tack, and tended to expand the responsibilities of their product divisions worldwide. Their strengths played to the demand by consumers for quality and price competitiveness. Marrying local responsiveness with price competitiveness could be achieved by having local managers report to two chiefs in a matrix organization, run on joint regional and product lines.

That was in 1972. Then came the oil shock, and the whirlwind of Japanese competition across a swathe of industries, notably automobiles and consumer electronics. President Nixon's visit to China, and then Washington's pressure on US oil multinationals to heed US interests above their commercial instincts, delivered Japan's political and business elites a double shock. The impressive response was to tighten up on consumption, and to make a concerted drive for efficiency in Japan's major export industries. Research has shown that Japan's corporations were the first to reverse the general trend among developed country corporations to an ever slower turnover in stocks (Schonburger 1998), and to take the lead in "lean production." The method—an elaboration of scientific management—was made famous in the best selling book, *The Machine that Changed the World* (Womack, Jones, and Roos 1990), which recorded how Toyota learnt to combine US lessons on mass production with a skilled workforce, who were given responsibility for quality control throughout the manufacturing process. Japanese corporations rode to victory in market after market in the course of the 1970s and 1980s, as Western corporations made desperate efforts to chase down their cost and experience curves. In 2007, it became the world's largest automobile manufacturer.

The corporate strategy fraternity, headquartered at that time in Harvard Business School, took on the challenge by plunging into the study of all things Japanese. Two broad schools of thinking emerged over time, one being championed by Harvard's Michael Porter, and his studies on corporate and national competitiveness (Porter 1980, 1990). Porter identifies the national conditions required to promote competitiveness—a competitive context for firms, demand conditions, related and supporting industries, created factors of production such as skilled labor, and a government which promotes competition and excellence. He then examines how "clusters" of firms in different countries can create enduring competitive advantages on world markets. For the analysis of firms' strategies and performance, he introduced neoclassical microeconomics and industrial organization theory. In essence, he presents firms as competing among each other to make profits by selling products that consumers value at the going price.

He thereby proposes three broad categories of corporate strategy. The first is that of cost leadership, where the corporation supplies products and services to the market that are made at the lowest cost, but also the most attractive quality and price. This is an update of Henry Ford's insight. Lower costs may be achieved by economies of scale, which refers to reducing the cost of each unit through volume production. The more experience firms have in making or delivering a product or service, the cheaper they learn to do it (Hall and Howell 1985). An example is a leading low fare airline like Ryanair or Southwest Airlines. The second category of strategy emphasizes product differentiation through superior design, quality, or functionality. This is Sloan's strategy updated for modern consumption. The implication is that the corporation invests in its employees, their ideas, and the knowledge that they accumulate, and that firms permanently search for ways to cut costs while preserving know-how in the organization. Think of a product like Apple's iPod and you can see how successful this approach can be. The third strategy is focus, understood as a niche strategy, whereby a firm focuses on one or two market segments, and brings scarce resources to bear to meet specific needs. Suitable for smaller firms, the suggestion is that firm's objectives are met by effectiveness, rather than by efficiency. The firm is sensitive to the particular market's requirements. Any good local provider you can think of, from a family-owned restaurant to your favorite hair stylist employs this type of strategy.

The second school of strategic management thinking took a more political view of the corporation. Corporations were analyzed as social constructs, rooted in their home and host country contexts, with their own sources of legitimacy and their own measures of performance. The distinct tone of this approach is evident in the definition of Yves Doz and C. K. Prahalad, when they speak of corporate strategy as "the dominant world view" among senior managers on the nature of competition, the key success factors in sustaining a competitive advantage, the type of risk incurred, and the resource base on which they draw (Pralahad and Doz 1987). This approach in turn spawned what came to be known as the resource-based view of the firm, based on an earlier study by Edith Penrose (1995), and emphasizing the internal learning process of firms as providing the structure within which knowledge is accumulated and deployed. This differed from the emphasis of Porter and others on advantage derived from external responsiveness and positioning.

The two dominant schools of corporate strategy thinking have been able to meet on a significant common terrain. As Prahalad and Doz put it, managers must be able to "recognise the balance of the forces of global integration and local responsiveness to which a business is subject" (Pralahad and Doz 1987: 30). The present from which senior managers start to consider their competitive position is the result of the inheritance from past policies, structures, and performances. Senior managers must understand the history which makes their corporations as they are, in order to anticipate where they may lead them.

The European decentralized federation

European corporations, such as Philips, Unilever, or Nestlé moved abroad in the early decades of the twentieth century, organizing in worldwide area structures. Local subsidiaries became highly independent of the parent company. Scale economies for the corporation as a whole were sacrificed in favor of servicing local tastes, and establishing sound working relationships with local governments. There was some sharing between the parent company and its units in terms of flows of information about research and development, appointments to senior positions, and the transfer of capital and dividends. Coordination mechanisms between parent and unit took the form of bureaucratic and budgetary mechanisms of control. Contacts between the units were limited. Such a structure was eminently suited to Europe's fragmentation in discrete national markets well in to the 1980s, but proved highly vulnerable to cost pressures as markets opened and competition sharpened.

The US coordinated federalist

The post-war years were the era of US dominance, when GM, Ford, IBM, Coca-Cola, Caterpillar, and Proctor & Gamble became household names. US corporations operated abroad through relatively autonomous subsidiaries. Their key asset was the size and opulence of their home market. Overseas subsidiaries exploited products first developed there. They were not customized to local tastes, but competed on quality at competitive prices. Senior management kept research and development facilities in the US, and managed the transfer of skills and technologies through the life cycle of the product. But there were serious deficiencies in this method. Headquarters controlled the main resources, and left operations to the locals. Locals met glass ceilings for promotion to senior positions. Budgetary and bureaucratic controls from the center suffered from upward creep, as did demands from local governments. US corporations also proved highly vulnerable to super-competitors from Japan.

Japanese global strategists

In the 1970s and 1980s, the Japanese competitive onslaught occurred. The strategic intent of corporations, such as Toyota, NEC, or Matsushita, was to achieve global dominance in their respective markets in order to fund the switch from competition on the basis of low labor costs towards high-tech, lean manufacturing systems. Such corporations treated the world as one market. Knowledge was developed and retained centrally. Their plants were scaled to produce mass standardized products, which were sold with aggressive price strategies. Integration between the central product division and each subsidiary was achieved through top–down strategic plans and controls, the fostering of a strong corporate identity, and through socialization of personnel. Subsidiaries were concentrated in a few locations. But such "global strategists" were vulnerable to trade retaliation, consumer reactions to standardized products, and to glass ceilings for promotions of locals that were set very low in the organization.

The transnational corporate citizen

A transnational corporation, Bartlett and Ghoshal (1989) maintain, has to achieve all three virtues of local responsiveness, efficiency, and knowledge management simultaneously. Its key feature is that it functions as an integrated network. Local units provide a source of skills, ideas, and capabilities, and attain global scale by becoming the corporation's local champion for a product or service sold worldwide. It adopts flexible manufacturing techniques and takes optimum choices with regard to pricing, sourcing of inputs, and product design. This implies a very different role for headquarters, as all units must develop mechanisms for integration and coordination among themselves. Transnational corporations speak English as a common language, develop inclusive management networks, acquire a corporate-wide global scanning capability, and promote a common culture through incentives, corporate visions, and leadership selection. In short, they become a learning organization in a permanent process of renewal (Ghoshal and Bartlett 1997). We shall return to this in our last section.

STATES AND CORPORATE RESPONSIVENESS

In this section, we focus on the corporate–state policy nexus. Despite some advances (Baron 1996, 1997, 1999; Shaffer and Hillman 2000; Pearce 2001), the corporate environment remains relatively uncharted territory for both scholars and practitioners of strategic management. In particular, "the state," a subset of the non-market context, is a largely unexplained and indeterminate variable within companies' strategic decision-making processes. Although considerable research exists on state-business relations (Boddewyn 1988, 1993, 1995; Ring, Lenway and Govekar 1990; Lenway and Rehbein 1991; Brewer 1992; Boddewyn and Brewer 1994; Baron 1995; Czinkota and Ronkainen 1997; Rugman and Verbeke 1998) and more specifically, on the influence of firms on public policy formulation (Richardson and Jordan 1979; Streeck and Schmitter 1984; Mazey and Richardson 1993; Green-Cowles 1995; Coen 1997, 1998; Lawton 1997; Baron 1999), less work has been done on how top management teams factor the external political environment into their strategic decisions and actions (Hambrick 1981).

The point of departure for political scientists is states, with their distinct peoples, public policies, very divergent capabilities, and their relations with other members of the society of states.[2] Learning about them constitutes a central component of the ability of corporations to act upon what is happening within these territories, and how they are affected by the forces of global integration—the global efficiency and local diversity which Doz, Prahalad, and others have written about in the management literature. In current usage, "politics" is what happens and is talked about within states about public policy, and what the public realm should or should not encompass. A less state-centric view of politics would stress that it is not just what politicians do, but embraces all undertakings where the wills of two or more people are harnessed to a particular task (Jouvenel 1957). This broader definition allows for politics as ubiquitous across organizations, but also allows us to specify more closely the relations of firms to states.

Corporate strategies have to be implemented in the context of markets which are fragmented between states. Clearly, corporations prefer to operate within the context of market-supporting institutions, which ensure that property rights and the rule of law are respected, people can be trusted to live up to their promises, externalities are held in check, competition is fostered, and information flows smoothly. In policy terms, we look at institutional arrangements within a state that are directly involved in markets: these include the financial system and its regulation; the labor market institutions and their regulation (trade unions, dispute settlement mechanisms, training, education); product markets (standards setting, norms); the corporate sector (ownership types, trade associations; value/supply chain relationships); the business culture of the country (the legal system; attitudes towards business, as expressed, for instance, through the tax system; attitudes towards entrepreneurship and wealth creation). There is a huge literature on this. This literature states that capitalisms are embedded in cultures and states, and that they differ.

As a step towards presenting the complex linkages between global dynamics and country-level factors, we turn here to the notion of a national business system, which we simply define as holding three key, related components (Whitley 1999). First come the *state institutions* dealing with financial markets structures and labor market regulations. Most emerging market countries have bank-based financial systems, while their financial markets have traditionally been used to allocate financial resources authoritatively for use by state corporations (France) or private *chaebols* (Korea). Labor market regulations are the product of national social contracts, the details of which can make all the difference as to whether an investment goes ahead or not. The second component of a business system relates to the coordination of economic activities between stakeholders. This yields a spectrum of types from loose coordination among firms, as in the UK, through highly hierarchical and authoritative structures of business interest representation, such as in Germany and Austria, or state-centered business representation as in France or China. The third component relates to the way firm policy is made—its governance—and the organizational attributes that enable firms to transform resource inputs into product or service outputs using the skills and knowledge of their employees in codified or tacit routines. This touches on the level of workforce skills in the short term, the development of collective competences in the medium term, and, in the long term, the dynamic capability of innovation (Nelson and Winter 1982; Teece, Pisano, and Shuen 1997).

Given the variety of business systems in the world, it follows that there is not one, but many types of capitalism (Crouch and Streeck 1997; Hall and Soskice 2001). Markets are embedded in social and political institutions, and do not exist independently of the rules and institutions that establish them (Zysman 1994). Such institutional structures foster their own incentives for agents in markets and their continuation is dependent on particular forms of policy processes (North 1991). They generate typical strategies, routine approaches to problems, and shared decision rules that create predictable patterns in the way governments and companies go about their business in a particular national political economy. Some scholars maintain that global capitalism's workings weaken labor and endanger social stability as domestic norms and institutions are challenged (Rodrick 1997; Burtless et al. 1998); as globalization deepens, conflicts emerge within and between nations. This may lead to bad policy, endangering the open trading system on which prosperity is based (Ruggie 1995). Definitely, it raises the stakes in international negotiations. Governments tend to project their own demands into these negotiations, which become political markets for trade-offs on regulations, exemptions, transition periods, and on a host of details (Story and Walter 1997). The global "competition system" which results is thus a negotiated construct, which reflects the institutional arrangements—national, regional or global—from which they emerged (Whitley 1997). Governance in this global economy is necessarily multi-tiered, as in the middle ages, where nation states are one class of power in a complex system of power from world to local levels.

It follows that in a context where multiple forces at work in global markets impact upon national economies differentially, states have very different capabilities to adapt to changing conditions (Katzenstein 1978; Weiss 1998). Globalization does not force states to follow a linear path of accommodation to markets. They retain discretion to choose between options, which are shaped by the cognitive patterns of their leadership, the types of state they govern, or the policy processes that they operate in (Mény and Thoenig 1989). This process of public policy may be illustrated in the form of a feedback loop, where the elements in the chain are interactive, and the flow of influences and events are in the form of feedback, so that past policies condition the present situation and future options (Lasswell 1950; Easton 1965; Almond and Powell 1966). Take, for instance, the omnipresence of interventionist governments, operating as a "megaforce" (Austin 1990) in nationally protected markets. The ostensible rationale of the multiple actors in the policy process was to reduce dependency on foreign suppliers, to build up local productive capabilities, or to develop a national technological base. Public officials controlled financial flows, issued licenses, deployed procurement, promoted labor "aristocracies," kept high tariffs or quotas, and regulated foreign exchange. They supervised competition in domestic markets among state enterprises, large private businesses, local firms, and multinationals. Over time, typically, the signs multiplied that all was not well: resource misallocations, unemployment, inflation, external deficits, devaluations. To escape from these conditions, each had to start thinking of reform in their own context. Their discrete policy processes, and the specific features of their political economies, would ensure that the path towards a more market-oriented regime would remain particular with regard to the time required to negotiate the transition, the sequencing of reforms, and their detailed content and impact. Just as Bartlett and Ghoshal depict the development of corporate strategy paths away from their original configurations, so the transformation of state institutions and policies can be stylized as different paths of adaptation in national political and business systems (Rustow 1970; Morlino 1980). *Ex ante*, the future is open, and the possible outcomes are multiple. It is only *ex post* that the path of history can look predetermined. Convergence is not written in stone.

Different capabilities underpin the hierarchy of wealth and power in the world as it is. This is the essence of the realist school of thinking about world affairs—the most widely held view of international politics, as of corporate strategy—which holds that there exists an unremitting clash between states and competition between corporations and business networks for wealth and power in world politics and markets (Morgenthau 1967; Waltz 1979; Porter 1990). In the political domain, states remain the prime units in world affairs, but capabilities between states are highly unevenly distributed. The tenet is predicated on the presumption of the separability of the domestic domain of the territorial state, and the system of states where no authority is endowed with a monopoly of power and authority, despite periods of hegemony. The major political issue is how to preserve some minimal order and to prevent or minimize the risk of conflict between states. Security trumps economic interdependence, as the lack of trust between states sets some limit to their readiness to depend on world markets, and draws an invisible ring of defences around their producers. Global capitalism is the instrument of the powers, their competing interests, and the way they are articulated through markets, corporate alliances, or in legislation and international negotiations. States seek alliances in order to supplement their own limited resources for their own purposes by borrowing the resources of their ally, and on their own terms as far as possible. But as all allies make the same calculation, who gets what out of the alliance depends very much on relative bargaining skills and on the hierarchy of the allies' priorities in any particular situation. Great powers by definition are concerned with a broader canvas of interests than smaller states, and maximize their returns from alliance by minimizing their commitments as far as possible to local rivals. They seek to sell their alliance as dearly to local contestants as the calculations of other great powers permit. Ultimately, the nature of the international system is shaped by relations among the great powers.

The global market structure is equally built on inherited inequalities, and these are reflected in international economic relations. This observation lay at the heart of the major conflict between the capitalist powers and the Soviet Union, over the course of "the short twentieth century" (Hobsbawm 1994). From a realist perspective, world affairs after 1945 were played out within a dangerous but predictable system structured around the competing alliances of the two great powers, their allies, and their clients. US containment strategy aimed to bottle up communism within the boundaries of the Soviet Union, and to contest its expansion abroad. There were two variants of containment (Gaddis 1982): one was to promote "a working economy in the world so as to permit the emergence of political and social conditions in which free institutions can exist." The other was predicated on global military containment. The US as a continental island was pre-eminent throughout Latin America and the Caribbean, with key positions in Germany, Japan, and the Persian Gulf. The US dominated the world seas and air traffic. US bilateral alliances with Germany and Japan formed the cornerstone of their domestic and foreign policies. The flow of provisions in raw materials were ensured through US control of the world sea-lanes, trade and investments flowed within the boundaries of the Western alliance, Japan, and the Asia-Pacific states. The communist party-states predicated their mission to free the world from capitalism on the primacy of class war. Once in power, communist party-states tolerated no alternative to their rule, suspended the market, and allocated resources by a central plan. They thus erected a monopoly on political power, on economic resources, and on "truth." All economic decisions relating to production and distribution were centralized. Consumers had the limited freedom not to buy whatever was on offer, and to keep their opinions to themselves. This was the party-states' Achilles heel: by 1990, America's affluent alliance, representing 16 per cent of the world's population, held 80 per cent of the world's income and output, compared to the Soviet Union's 2 per cent. The Soviet Union's demise delivered a mortal blow to the world communist system, but also to US containment strategy.

As the dust lifted slowly from the wreckage of the Soviet Union's collapse, and the cold war drifted into history, the contours of the global system appeared in sharp outline. The US stood without equal, in a world of unprecedented inequalities of power and wealth. The Soviet collapse also ended the separation of world labor markets between the advanced industrial countries, the communist party-states, and the developing countries sheltering behind high tariff barriers. Its most immediate effect was to precipitate upwards of three billion people on to the world labor market, from the former Soviet Union, central eastern Europe, China, and India. In addition, the resolution of the 1980s debt crisis under a plan advanced by US Treasury Secretary Brady enabled mid-income endebted countries to restructure their debt to commercial banks through officially supported debt reduction programs tied to broad policies of liberalization, stabilization, and privatization. Brady's debt relief plan spurred Mexico to negotiate the North American Free Trade Agreement (NAFTA) accords with the US and Canada, while Brazil and Argentina formed the Mercosur customs union with Uruguay and Paraguay. By comparison, the "world market" of the cold war had expanded its total workforce by about 270 million, as Japan, Spain, Turkey, Korea, and the South East Asian countries moved to industrialize. In other words, whereas 1 unit of capital in the 1980s had at its disposal, say, 10 units of labor, after the end of the cold war, one unit of capital had, say, 100 units of labor. The average cost of labor around the world fell correspondingly. Given the availability of global finance for corporations, and the development of multinational corporations during the period of the cold war, the implication for high wage countries was that their relative wage advance depended on productivity continuing to outstrip that of cheaper wage locations, to which multinationals were now freer to move.

There were two competing visions of where the world was heading in the twenty-first century. Conventional wisdom had the world converging on Western political norms, Western economic policy, and a market-driven process of world integration (Fukuyama 1989; Huntingdon 1991). The view was encapsulated in the word "globalization," depicting a One World driving towards shared prosperity, democracy, and better living conditions for all. A cascade of new technologies was accelerating the pace of innovation, combined with an unprecedented opening of all on to world markets. Western corporations would pour technologies into the poorer regions of the world, where labor was abundant, cheap, and talented. Global financial markets, no longer under political lock and key, provided capital, ending the historic capital shortages of developing countries. All countries which wished to sign up to prosperity were advised to end controls on capital flows. Within a couple of decades, there would arise a huge transnational market for consumers. This drive towards a more efficient allocation of resources worldwide would promote more educated populations, encourage the world's democratization, promote greater security between states with similar values and regimes, and eventually equalize incomes at an unprecedented high level of well-being. The world economy's productivity levels would likely lift historic growth rates, and within a couple of decades, the great planetary debate would have opened. The history of the twenty-first century would be one of a civilization of civilizations, where achievement of a more harmonious world would require the development of a global governance architecture. That was the prime contention of the world's convergence-at-a-high-level-of-wealth story.

The alternative view was that nothing was written in advance, rather the reverse. The historical world in which we live is one of inherited inequalities, different capabilities, and very diverse motivations. It is characterized by diversity and divergence, rather than linearity, integration, and convergence. Globalization in this light was not a dissolvent to old conflicts, so much as a stimulus to old tensions as well as to new. Other ideals besides liberalism had survived the cold war's end, such as the fascist ideals of the supremacy of political will in the ordering of human affairs, economic nationalism, or the millenary vision of religious prophets. Enduring imbalances in the world economy bore testimony to the propensities of states to pursue relative or absolute gains over competitors. Far from states following a linear path of accommodation to markets, states with state-corporate linkages forged in discrete, historic circumstances (Weiss 1998; Whitley 1999), were bound to adapt to global changes in their own way and in their own time. The abilities of states to adapt to changing conditions would continue to diverge, not converge, and because globalization advanced under a Western, primarily US guise, it was as often as not experienced as a diktat for non-Western civilizations to align on Western cultural norms (Huntingdon 1993; Mahbubani 1995). Indeed, globalization was none other than global capitalism unchained, intent on imposing its own world-view of "market democracy" on a diverse world. The project was argued to be as unrealizable as was worldwide communism, and just as likely to end in failure (Goldsmith 1994; Gray 1998; Soros 1998).

In effect, the new world system to emerge in the course of the 1990s came to be characterized by both convergent and divergent trends, which we can see as complementary opposites: a diversity of states in a non-homogeneous world, penetrated and shaped by global markets, operating powerfully to create a more homogeneous world civilization; alongside aspirations to create a system of global governance out of the world's existing institutional framework as the counterpart to a world of relentless competition between states, corporations, or currencies. At the same time, the prospects for an increasingly wealthy and inclusive world as global civil society develops towards a higher civilization are juxtaposed with a world of history where the forces of globalization operate as a stimulant to divergence, to conflicts, and to a ruthless competition between peoples, states, and corporations. It is this double movement between the forces driving towards the prospect of a radiant future and the world's very divergent capabilities to adapt that lie at the heart of the new dialectics in global affairs. Cold war dialectics was structured by the global configuration of the international system; the post-cold-war dialectics is a global process working at the level of cultures, markets, and politics, and where corporations are often the leading revolutionaries.

Global Dynamics and Structural Power

The state-centric view of world affairs, with which we introduced the last section, has long been criticized as an inadequate lens through which corporate leaders should incorporate the external political environment—and associated political uncertainty—into their strategic decisions and actions. We argue that through adapting and applying Strange's realist structuralism approach from international relations, corporate leaders will be better able to understand and respond to what

Gilpin describes as the reciprocal and dynamic interaction in the world economy between the pursuit of wealth and the pursuit of power (Gilpin 1975; Strange 1985, 1987, 1988). These twin forces complicate and often confound the decision-making process of corporate leaders, as they involve variables outside of the control of the organization and beyond the scope of rational economic actor analysis. As Gilpin (1987) argues, both economics and political science, as separate, compartmentalized disciplines are inadequate to explain the state–market nexus: economics does not integrate power analysis into its explanatory models and political science often treats economics as exogenous or even dependent on the political setting—the autonomy of market forces is missing. Strange argues for a structural approach that seeks to integrate the Marxist concern with production and the realist concern with security into a wider analysis of the world political economy around a concept of structural power. The structural power approach is a useful conceptual lens for top management teams seeking to make sense of the external political context of their organizations. Understanding power, its main conduits in the world and the forces that determine it in international business, allows strategic leaders to understand and account for external political forces in corporate strategy.

The dynamics of change in the second half of the twentieth century, and especially from the 1960s on, were not located in states and international organizations—the focus of realist and idealist approaches to the study of international relations—but in markets and corporations. That is Strange's central thesis. Most of the string of "vague and often woolly words" (Strange 1997), such as "globalization," "interdependence," or "multinational corporation," conceived to describe the diffusion of power in the world economy, are state-centric or plain euphemisms for the export of American culture and preferences. Yet Strange acknowledges that the US, with its federal law, huge state sector, large corporations and financial institutions, universities, publicly and privately funded research laboratories, and vast internal market, is the epicenter of a world market, reconstituted under US patronage after 1945. What has happened, Strange maintains, is that "the impersonal forces of world markets, integrated over the post-war period more by private enterprise in finance, industry and trade than by the cooperative decisions of governments, are now more powerful than the states to whom ultimate political authority over society and economy is supposed to belong" (Strange 1997: 4).

From this flow four propositions central to Strange's conception of international political economy. First, war and peace between states is no longer a prime concern, at least for the materialist citizens of the affluent alliance for whom war with other major states is too dangerous an option. Because populations want trade and investment, states are primarily concerned with ensuring that business conditions within their own jurisdiction are sufficiently attractive to foster wealth-creating activities and to attract inward investment by multinational corporations. Second, all states have found their power and authority hollowed out, as they have to share functions with an ever wider range of interested parties. Their powers are shared with other governments, firms, or technologies outside the state's territorial jurisdiction. The third proposition is that there has been a shift in power from states to markets

(Strange 1970), generated by two key agents of change. One is the multinational corporation, and the globalization of production which has been the result of the corporations' need to recuperate the cost of investment in new technologies. The other agent of change is global financial markets, which have expanded on the back of competition between financial centers, governments' thirst for funding, and corporations' search for cheap financing. Corporations, states, and global financial markets have become unequal partners. Corporations are establishing transnational networks of alliances and arrangements with other corporations, and by entering bargains on a bilateral basis with states. The "new diplomacy" (Stopford and Strange 1991) is characterized by bargains between states and corporations, where control over outcomes can be negotiated. By contrast, traditional economic diplomacy is unable to control the outcomes decided by the global financial markets (Strange 1988).

The fourth proposition holds that, after three centuries in which state authority over society was centralized, we have moved towards a "new medievalism" (Strange 1988) of dispersed power, and competing authorities. There is no Pope, as the world is materialist, driven by greed and self-interest, while the emperor—the US—is unwilling or unable to behave responsibly. The best way to describe this world, Strange says, is through the lens of pluralism, halfway to a world economy and a world society. The pluralist perspective reduces the significance of the traditional distinction between domestic and international, and populates the world system with more authorities than states. This definition presents politics as ubiquitous, and populates its arena with a broad fauna of organizations and individuals. Following Easton's famous definition of politics as "the authoritative allocation of values in the system" (Easton 1965), Strange defines politics as those processes and structures through which the mix of values in the system—freedom, equality, security, justice—are distributed among groups and individuals. She also deploys Lasswell's formulation, of politics as who gets what, when, and how (Lasswell 1950), and refers to Dahl and Lindblom's concept of "polyarchy"—the power structures of public officials and societal elites and their ability to define "issue areas" in promotion of particular interests (Dahl and Lindblom 1953; Lindblom 1977). If these are the definitions to work with, then any study of politics must examine the sources of authority, the process and the values by which these "issue areas" are defined. Who defines the "what"—the contested issues—and how the process is decided is the task of the political economist (Strange 1994).

The global financial crisis of 2008 indicates that Strange's assertion of corporate and even market autonomy from—if not pre-eminence over—the state may have run its course. The response of governments in the US, Europe, and elsewhere demonstrates a reassertion and a rebalancing of the global system. But Strange's ideas, especially her structural power framework, remain relevant for an understanding of business–state relations, even in an era of multilateral government intervention in the workings of the market economy. Strange (1988) advances a framework for analyzing the who-gets-what of world society based on four basic structures. In these, power over others and over the mix of values in the system is exercised within and across frontiers by those who are in a position to offer *security*, or to threaten it; by those who are in a position to offer, or to withhold, *credit*; by those who decide what to *produce*, where and by whom and on what terms and conditions; and by those who control access to *knowledge* and information and who are in a position to define the nature of knowledge (Strange 1996). Of the four kinds of structural power outlined by Strange, the state takes the lead role in only one— security—and even there needs the support of other systemic agents. In all the other structures, non-state authorities—primarily firms—play a large part in determining the allocation of resources. Strange therefore argues that structural power is the unevenly distributed systemic ability to define the basic structures of the world economy: security, credit, production, and knowledge (Strange 1988). All other elements of the international political economy (e.g. global issues such as trade or more specific sectoral items such as aerospace or microchips) are secondary struc- tures, being molded by the four fundamental power structures. Strange further argues that structural changes in finance, information and communications systems, defense equipment, and production methods have together played the most import- ant role in redefining the relationship between authority (government) and market (firms). To clarify the determinants of change at a systemic level, it is accepted that the state and the market (through its corporate agents) together comprise the broad vehicles of transformation (Strange 1991). Each of these systemic players shapes the nature of the four pillars of structural power.

LEADERSHIP, STRATEGY, POLICY AND THE FUTURE

A corporate actor that understands this systemic dynamic and gains first mover advantage in bringing about structural change can wield considerable power, both relative to government and to other companies. So let us take the position that the corporation is the central unit of analysis in the world economy, and that the corporation cannot survive and prosper unless top management teams incorporate the lessons they take from these dynamics into their strategic decisions and actions. Our suggestion is for business leaders to start by distinguishing between corporate strategy and corporate policy. Strategy is about setting vision, marshaling resources, selecting markets, and so on. Policy comes both prior to and after strategy. It comes prior to strategy because policy is crafted by cultivating sensitivity to context— national cultures, macroeconomic trends, currency fluctuations, social change, and politics (international/global, regional, national, and local); and it comes after strategy because policy is also about implementation—delivery of results and adding value. Corporate policies have to be crafted relating location decision, recruitment and retention, and marketing and finance—as well as relations between subsidiaries and with headquarters—to varied conditions around the world. Similarly corporate strategies have to be elaborated, and opportunities and risks assessed in full recognition of the external environment in which they take place. It is through this holistic lens that business leaders may integrate markets and politics into strategic management, and it is through policy that corporate strategies are implemented to deliver results. In this last section, we focus on corporate leadership, identify a typology of different strategies available to corporate leaderships, introduce the concept of non-market strategy, and end by sketching out the triangle linking business, to markets and policy, as a way of summarizing the many domains linking corporate politics and strategy to the broader context facing corporations.

Corporate leadership

We start with leadership, and the exercise of power in corporations. Here, the literature from political science and economics may be serviceable. Attempts have been made by economists such as Frey to explain politics and power through the prism of rational choice (Frey 1984). But as Strange (1996) argues, this is too clinical an approach to be serviceable. For instance, an industry leader may choose to forgo profit to enable price reduction in order to drive new entrants out of the market. Such action is not rational if we apply the strict economic logic of firm action as being motivated by profit maximization. Of course the rebuttal to the scenario just mentioned is that forgoing profit in the short term can result in greater profit in the long term. However, this is not assured and there is risk associated with such action, e.g. regulatory authorities may deem such action illegal or the new entrant(s) may successfully resist predatory behavior and subsequently use it to undermine the dominant firm's market position. Witness for instance the clash between British Airways and Virgin Atlantic in the early 1990s, where British Airways attempted to undermine Virgin Atlantic's market entry into the lucrative transatlantic routes by engaging in price competition and negative advertising. Virgin Atlantic weathered the storm, won a court ruling against British Airways practices, and subsequently subverted its arch-rival through appealing to airline customers as the David to British Airway's Goliath. Identifying the players is the first step to studying their motivations and the non-market and market arenas in which they operate.

To explain why organizations act as they do Herbert Simon has advanced the case for his concept of "bounded rationality," whereby governments and corporations have multiple objectives in mind when they take decisions (Simon 1982, 1997). They are not always seeking the optimal outcome but are looking for a result that satisfies multiple objectives. As Michael Crozier, the French sociologist, pointed out (Crozier 1971), Max Weber's stylization of official decision-making in "rational-legal hierarchies" was misleading. Graham Allison argued in a similar fashion in contesting the then dominant view in foreign policy analysis using the rational actor model, that it was equally possible to explain the Cuban missile crisis through an organizational process model and a bureaucratic politics model. Allison's revolutionizing of the study of decision-making in political science fed into teaching in business schools, alongside studies of power relations within organizations (French and Raven 1959; Emerson 1962; Hambrick 1981). Corporate strategies, this literature suggests, may be guided by the concepts, ambitions, and personality of the leader or their team, as contrasted to the longer term interests of the corporation. They may also be the result of bureaucratic battles within the organization fought over ideas and careers, or simply the outcome of organizational processes. In such conditions, the assumption of static objectives, implicit in the concept of bounded rationality, may not hold. As Crozier and Friedberg argued, the rationality of actors may originate from the "game structures" that channel and stabilize power and bargaining relations between a set of strategically interdependent actors (Crozier and Friedberg, 1977). New "game structures" may emerge, the personalities engaged change, markets may rise or fall, and new technologies emerge forth. If static goals are assumed their content may be informed by deeply held and pre-existing beliefs, which suffuse collective identities (Smith, 1991), or they may be created as visions by corporate leaders.[3] We have to be able to identify the hymns that "a community sings to justify and make legitimate what it is doing" (Lodge and Vogel 1987).

Leaders, of course, have policy instruments, the most important of which is their leadership team. Leadership involves choosing the personnel for the top team; permanently keeping in touch with the details of the organization; knowing as many of the personnel as one reasonably can; setting priorities; defining and communicating the vision to all stakeholders; fostering enthusiasm; ensuring fair process; promoting and, if necessary, changing the culture of the business. The most successful business leaders invariably, as a matter of habit, give expression to strategic principles and practices that dramatically increase the possibility of establishing and retaining a strong market position.[4] The pursuit of a carefully crafted yet essentially simple strategy provides the best means for a business leader or entrepreneur to maximize corporate value. The optimal strategy, if properly implemented, bestows industry power on a company, enabling it to change or modify the rules of competition and increase its supply chain authority. A well-defined and clearly communicated strategy facilitates the acquisition of new customers while retaining existing customers. Strategic innovation, practically grounded, confers authority on the business leader, creating a window of opportunity for the introduction of far-reaching, transformational change. In the broadest sense, strategic excellence is the proven key to value creation in modern business, and as such, is of vital importance to the well-being of shareholders, employees, customers, and society at large.

Unfortunately, strategic excellence is not the norm. A wealth of detail on industry and market trends often serves as a substitute for more fundamental thinking as to what makes a product or service appealing, or how that product or service can reliably be delivered to the customer (Finkelstein, Harvey, and Lawton 2007). As a result, managers down the line all too often are confronted with the task of implementing strategies they don't fully understand, based on strategic thinking that doesn't always appear to make sense. It is a painful truth that confused or misapplied strategies continue to blight the business landscape and up-end companies. The flaws inherent in some of the major strategic disasters of modern times—Enron, Parmalat, and Vivendi Universal to name just three—that are so apparent in retrospect, might well have been recognized much earlier had corporate leaders approached strategy with the rigor the subject requires.

In an intensely competitive world, business leaders are challenged to demonstrate the ability to work with strategy to create and take control of the future of their companies. Whatever its defects and disadvantages, capitalism remains a dynamic and self-renewing system, populated by companies large and small that are striving to get on the fast track to business growth and sustained profitability. In this world, it is corporations that are center stage. It is a world in which change is endemic, and companies whose positions appear unchallengeable are unseated by nimbler competitors in what Joseph Schumpeter in his book *Capitalism, Socialism and Democracy* (1942) termed "creative destruction." New companies are created, while others change in form and purpose as they try to survive and prosper. Those that fail to make the grade are taken over by rivals or are driven out of business. Value creation is the reward of success; value destruction is the price of failure.

A corporate strategy typology

All practical business strategies are contingent, dependent in form and substance upon the specific circumstances, internal and external, of the individual company. However, there are three broad perspectives regarding the realities of strategy and strategy making in successful companies. The first perspective is that what is amazing about successful companies is not the sophistication of their approach to strategy, but rather the brilliance with which they execute a *simple strategy*. Consider how the most successful companies lead with a straightforward, easy to understand value proposition—but one backed up with robust and finely tuned business models. Successful retailers like Wal-Mart and Tesco illustrate the point perfectly, as do the best budget airlines like Southwest Airlines and Ryanair. Rather than being constrained by overly sophisticated, yet essentially wrong-headed, strategies, high performance companies have found that the most successful strategies are often the simplest. They adhere to the realistic and comprehensible practices that are at the heart of winning strategies: creating a workable vision by understanding needs and aspirations; facing customers with a value proposition that covers all the important bases; aligning what you do with what the customer really wants; balancing the people and process sides of business to deliver on your promises; and liberating the energies of any strategy's toughest critic—those who work within the business (Finkelstein, Harvey, and Lawton 2007).

The second broad perspective we offer is that companies that successfully break out, from whatever starting point, have in place well-thought-out and participative strategy processes. As might be expected, such processes vary considerably in form and substance between organizations: there is no evidence of widespread employment of commonplace methodologies, templates, tools, or techniques. Yet, while high-growth companies favor the application of organizationally distinctive strategy routines, these routines are to some extent similar to those found elsewhere. They involve, for example, strategy reviews, business planning, formalized setting of strategic objectives and performance targets, and the establishment and monitoring of strategic projects and programs. What makes these processes stand out in high-performance, breakout companies is the careful alignment with strategy, and world-class execution. Integral to strategy-making in many high-growth companies are processes for acquisition and assimilation, innovation and new product development, business growth, and knowledge management. In the case of a Mexican success story, CEMEX (a producer of cement, ready-mix concrete and aggregates), for example, its expansion into emerging markets on a global scale has been made possible through the application of comprehensive acquisition and assimilation procedures. The rapid incorporation of acquired businesses into a global framework, supported by advanced information systems, has enabled tight cost management, correspondingly high returns on investment, and the generation of high levels of free cash flow to fund further acquisitions in emerging markets.

The third broad perspective we put forward is that close familiarity with organizational context and industry dynamics are prerequisites for effective strategy-making. When companies like Marconi are brought to their knees it is most often because of a monumental failure on the part of the leadership team to recognize and understand the difficulties of the strategic course embarked upon—in this case making a significant play in a market already populated by knowledge rich and dominant enterprises. In contrast to the experience of Marconi, it is conspicuous that many of the most brilliant corporate success stories of modern times are associated with CEOs steeped in the realities of their companies, industries, and markets. Strategic leaders like Terry Leahy of Tesco, Lorenzo Zambrano of CEMEX, Pierre Bellon of Sodexho, Lindsay Owen Jones of L'Oréal, and Jim Koch of Boston Beer Company each served their companies for more than two decades and took a deep personal interest in all aspect of their business, particularly in the experiences and changing demands of customers. These are CEOs lauded as strategists, as value creators on a grand scale, yet whenever they are interviewed what impresses most is their supreme command of operational detail and industry knowledge. It is their sureness of touch and grasp of market realities that enables them to be confident that big strategic moves will maintain profitable growth and strengthen their companies further.

Strategy-making is different from business planning. It is a bigger idea. Sound planning is necessary for the effective delivery of a strategy, but it should be conceived as part of a process rather than a discrete activity. Likewise, a business plan is not a strategy: it is just one of a series of outputs that may emerge from the strategy process. Planning is valuable when dealing with changes that are relatively discrete and predictable, defined parts of the jigsaw, whereas strategy deals with the bigger picture, with fundamentals such as the market space the company is seeking to occupy and how customers or clients will be won and retained. In this sense, strategy may usefully be conceived as the mechanism for binding the many parts of an organization together, expressing unity of purpose, establishing direction, and building the momentum needed for growth and beneficial change.

A further defining feature of strategy, as a practical endeavor, is the ongoing tension that exists between the omnipresent organizational impulses towards continuity and change. For a strategy to serve its purpose as a mechanism for beneficial change, it cannot be subject to significant alteration on a frequent basis. Continuity of purpose is essential to the successful implementation of a strategy, and a strategy without implementation is not a strategy at all: it is window dressing. At the same time, however, no organization can completely control its external environment and, for most companies, markets and competitors regularly deliver shocks to the system, demanding a series of appropriate responses. Learning and flexibility are therefore just as essential to strategy as underlying continuity of purpose, and the incorporation of refinements and changes on a regular and systematic basis is a feature of any sound strategy process. Small changes at regular intervals, of course, may have a significant compound effect on business performance.

Non-market strategy

Where state policies and corporate strategies interact to shape international business outcomes, there is a significant body of literature (Vernon 1971; Boarman and Schollhamer 1975; Doz and Prahalad 1980; Fagre and Wells 1982; Boddewyn 1988; Kim 1988; Behrman and Grosse 1990; Ring, Lenway, and Govekar 1990; Stopford and Strange 1991; Brewer 1992; Murtha and Lenway 1994; Rugman and Verbeke 1998; Hillman, Zardkoohi, and Bierman 1999; Ramamurti 2001; Schuler, Rehbein, and Cramer 2002). International diplomacy regularly associates state institutions with corporations and non-governmental organizations. Corporations negotiate the terms of their investments and the distribution of its rents around the world with other firms, through direct discussions with governments, and more indirectly through government channels. These channels may be bilateral, for instance China pressuring France to desist from arms sales to Taiwan by depriving French corporations of mainland Chinese contracts. They may be multilateral, such as EU negotiations for enlargement to incorporate the candidate countries of central-eastern Europe. Or they may focus on global trade negotiations in the World Trade Organization (WTO) on patent policies and non-tariff barriers. Corporations thus establish transnational networks of alliances, and enter bilateral bargains with states, where control over outcomes are negotiated. This is the "new diplomacy" between states and corporations, which overlays and differs from the bi- or multilateral diplomacy of states (Stopford and Strange 1991). It has considerable significance for corporations, which have become— whether they like it or not—political players in what many people around the world consider a nascent world polity. The three strategic implications of the entrance of multinational corporations into international diplomacy are:

(1) Managers, like politicians before them, should assess their relative bargaining power in negotiations with governments, multi-lateral bodies and non-governmental organizations (Vernon 1977; Kobrin 1979; Fagre and Wells 1982).

(2) Managers must negotiate with foresight. The outcome of a negotiation depends not only on the terms of the final agreement but also on negotiating skills, as well as on the credibility that such terms will in fact be realized. However, much of the literature stops short of examining how firms with knowledge of governments factor this into their decision-making process and in turn, leverage it into industry authority and market power.

(3) Corporations are not just responsible to shareholders, but should expect to be held accountable for their actions to a wider world community. In other words, when determining corporate strategy, it is wise to factor the external, non-business environment into the decision-making process. Baron (1995: 73) describes this as consisting of: "the social, political and legal arrangements that structure interactions among companies and their public."

For example, the law of contract is an important part of this external environment that enables companies and their public to contract for the exchange of goods, services, labor, and capital. Variations in contract law between different countries and industries impact the strategic choices of firms. These various social, political, and legal arrangements are collectively referred to as "*regulation.*" In advanced industrialized nations, regulation pervades the competitive environment within which firms select and execute their strategies (Shaffer 1995). Trade policy, competition policy, employment policy, environmental policy, fiscal policy, monetary policy—government policies in general and the particular regulations to which they give birth—have the ability to alter the size of markets through government purchases and regulations affecting substitute and complimentary products; to affect the structure of markets through entry and exit barriers and antitrust legislation; to alter the cost structure of firms though various types of legislation pertaining to multiple factors, such as employment factors and pollution standards (Gale and Buchholz 1987); to affect the demand for product and services by charging excise taxes and imposing regulations that affect consumer patterns (Wilson 1990); to affect access to scarce resources (Boddewyn 1998); and to have an impact on firms' profitability by increasing costs and restricting markets (Schuler 1996). Consequently, there is substantial interdependence between regulation and the competitive environment within which firms operate (Porter 1990; Baron 1995; Bonardi, Hillman, and Keim 2005).

These issues have taken on increasing importance as the regulatory reach of the state has evolved. Between the end of the Second World War and the end of the 1970s oil crises, Western governments (particularly in Europe) managed industrial policy by taking direct ownership of certain of the means of production, i.e. full or partial nationalization of key firms and industries. But from the early 1980s those governments eschewed direct ownership, privatized those formerly nationalized industries, and relied instead on regulation to manage their industrial policies. In particular, regulation was used to manage the (inappropriately named) process of deregulation: of creating a framework that encouraged competition amongst firms and addressed instances of market failure such as price collusion and monopoly. Ironically, deregulation significantly increased the influence of regulation on firm strategy, hence the unexpected phenomenon of "freer markets, more rules" (Vogel 1996). Indeed, the penetration of business strategy by regulation has become so substantial that Weidenbaum (1980) argues it has fundamentally altered the relationship between business and government and that these changes are tantamount to a second managerial revolution. Weidenbaum contends that the shift of decision-making away from the firm to government regulators (through increased regulation and selected deregulation) is as significant for management as the separation of ownership and control was earlier this century (Bearle and Means 1932).

Firms therefore take an interest in regulation: an interest in minimizing the cost of existing and proposed regulation upon strategy and business models; an interest in lobbying for regulations which are consistent with and supportive of preferred strategy and business models; and an interest in regulation as a source of competitive advantage. The interest that firms take in regulation is described in management literature as their "nonmarket strategy." A nonmarket strategy is defined by Baron (1995) as that component of a firm's business strategy that helps it navigate the nonmarket environment. This is distinct from a firm's market strategy, which is understood as that component of a firm's business strategy that helps it navigate the competitive environment, which consists of the market choices of competitors, customers, distributors, and suppliers. The market environment sits within the nonmarket environment: choices in the former are prescribed (to a greater or lesser degree) by the latter.

In many industries the success of firms' nonmarket strategy is no less important than their broader market strategy. For example, MCI's initial strategy was political. It created a market opportunity by influencing regulators to deregulate the US long-distance telephone market (Yoffie and Bergenstein 1985). Firms also use nonmarket strategies to ensure competitive advantage or possibly even survival. In the late 1990s, Pepsi Co. Inc., losing a fierce competitive battle for soft drink market share to rival Coca-Cola, turned to the governments of Venezuela, France, India, and the US for help in regaining market share (Light 1998). In a study of the US steel industry, Schuler (1996) found that domestic steel producers used the government's control over access to the US market as a political tool to enjoy stabilized process and profits in a declining market and to gain temporary relief from downsizing by lobbying for trade protection. Subsequent to Schuler's study, in 2002 US steel producers again persuaded the American government to provide trade protection, but failed to simultaneously pursue that nonmarket strategy through the WTO, with the effect that the trade protection was ruled illegal and the political strategy ultimately failed (Lawton and McGuire 2002). Similarly as the tobacco industry faces serious threats in the US market, tobacco firms are using nonmarket strategies to ward off similar threats in the European and Asian markets. Finally, Boeing and Airbus pursue overt and elaborate political strategies, as each seeks access to the others market (McGuire 1997).

Since regulation increasingly permeates the competitive environment, nonmarket strategy must be a business priority (Yoffie 1988). The purported objective of firms' nonmarket strategies is to produce regulatory outcomes that are favorable to their continued economic survival and success (Baysinger 1984; Keim and Baysinger 1988). Firms can use their influence over regulation for a number of strategic ends: to bolster their economic positions; to hinder both their domestic and foreign competitors' progress and ability to compete; and to exercise their right to a voice in government affairs (Keim and Zeithaml 1986; Wood 1986). Through nonmarket strategy, firms can potentially increase overall market size; gain an advantage related to industrial competition, thereby reducing the threats of substitutes and entry; and increase their bargaining power relative to suppliers and customers. However, a problem persists: how can a top management team gain, leverage, and retain nonmarket power?

Conclusions: Scanning the Global Context

We suggest the key to this question lies in the concept of the transnational corporation, wherein Bartlett and Ghoshal argue that their three types of context or structured corporate strategies—the European, North American, and Japanese—have to acquire the best characteristics of each in terms of local responsiveness, efficiency, and knowledge management. The world trend to global markets requires large, diversified corporations to take the path to becoming transnationals. This means that the transformation strategies of the first three types involve different trajectories:

- The loose European federation has to have its units specialize while retaining their local responsiveness, transform relations between headquarters and local management, develop global scanning skills, or recruit skills worldwide.
- The Japanese-type global strategist must develop local responsiveness, decentralize and export the domestic skills for network relationships to their worldwide organization, and—the biggest challenge of all—become a multicultural corporation.
- The US-type centralized federation has to decentralize research and development, learn to be locally responsive and acquire the skills to manage a networked organization.

Alongside the other characteristics that the two authors list and that are required to operate in the global political economy, the feature we wish to identify here as crucial for a transnational corporation is to acquire a corporate-wide global scanning capability. Transnational corporations, they argue, have to become learning organizations in a permanent process of renewal (Ghoshal and Bartlett 1997). The model predicts the growth of highly flexible and competitive transnationals who treat the world as their oyster. As Bartlett and Ghoshal warn, this is no easy task, and above all depends on an in-built corporate capacity to tolerate a high degree of ambiguity in the organization while retaining vital control over far-flung operations. This entails senior management moving away from detailed strategies to clearly defining corporate purposes, to think in terms of managing a process rather than a structure, and to place people rather than systems center stage. People management lies at the heart of corporations' ability to survive and prosper in a highly dynamic world political economy. It follows that business leaders have to be able to scan the context, ask probing questions about it, elaborate a strategy, and implement it through policy.

The global context to survey may be presented abstractly as a triangle, linking business, markets, and politics to the future, as the key prism through which we suggest corporate leaders link their decisions to allocate resources now in preparation for a future, in which they can act through strategy, but which is co-shaped by powerful forces at work in the world, and outside their control. But these forces are nonetheless amenable to be incorporated into policy. From the perspective of our business firm, the interactions of businesses, markets, and politics together shape the future. The first angle is the business perspective—leadership (including organizational culture, management style, and vision); resources and capabilities (both hard and soft); and innovation (across business units and functional activities). The second is the market perspective—diverse systems of capitalism; market structure (defined perhaps by Porter's five forces of rivalry, supplier power, barriers to entry, threat of substitutes, and buyer power); and international economics (trade policy and performance, foreign direct investment, capital flows, foreign exchange markets, global bond and equity markets, and media markets). Third is the politics perspective—states, international organizations, and a multitude of policy regimes on trade, finance, or on new security issues; the long list of players—such as multinational corporations, media, the global communications infrastructure, non-governmental organizations, religions, criminal gangs, terrorists, sports organizations, and so on—which condition the world in which states, markets, and business evolve, and the interdependence between them. This is the "medieval" world of multiple authorities over diverse markets, which we have discussed.

In the center of the triangle is a point which represents sometime in the future. We argue that the salient feature of business is that business people have to deal with a future they know little about because that is where risk and reward lie. Paradoxically, the only things we know about the future reside in the past. The past is recorded in accounts, enduring structures and institutions, or cultures and belief systems. How we read this past is the clue to how we analyze the future, and act upon it. So let us drop a line from the business end of the triangle to the point in the triangle center, representing the future. We may observe that this depicts the domain of activity and concern which it is within the power of management to influence and to shape through strategy. Here the future is being created by the activity of the leadership team, but especially by the business as a collective unit. Let us now drop an imaginary line from the market angle of the triangle to the future point in the triangle's center. The interactions of different, territorially defined market institutions, of global markets, and of interdependent market structures of different industries also shape the future. The business unit and its leadership have little to no influence over the operations of "markets." To the extent they do not shape the operations of markets (as, for instance, IBM did in its heydays of the 1960s, or Microsoft has done since the mid-1980s), they can only hope to anticipate how they work, or to react in good time to the signals which markets send out. Interpreting these signals is very controversial, and depends to a large part on the intellectual prism through which they are analyzed. Finally, drop a line from the politics angle of the triangle to the future point in the center. Here again the future is being created by the complex of political factors at play in the world. The business has little to do, other than to accept its broad political context as a given, and to work on it for its own benefit.

The interim conclusion is that the future can be segmented into two parts: the future which business leadership can shape by its own actions; and the future to which business leadership can be sensitive. For us, strategy is the means by which leaders create and take control of the future (Finkelstein, Harvey, and Lawton 2007), whereas policy relates more to organizational structures, processes, and routines that cumulatively orchestrate and deliver on strategic objectives. Put another way, strategy is about vision, analysis, and configuration, whereas policy is concerned with implementation and the delivery of results. Effective corporate policy is heavily dependent on context—national cultures, macroeconomic trends, currency fluctuations, social change, and politics (international/global, regional, national, and local). Inherently, environmental uncertainty is not easily described or encapsulated as a risk parameter in a simple accounting formula but rather interacts with corporate strategy in global, national, and industrial contexts. The best measure of a country's risk level is of little use if managers do not appreciate its strategic implications and limitations. Peter Wack of Royal Dutch Shell Petroleum explained it best when he implored managers to recognize that forecasts are typically wrong when you need them most (Wack 1985). Wack argues that uncertainty should not be merely measured, but accepted and planned for. In other words, that corporate resources should be allocated now in the light of the senior management's view of the future. Assessing and preparing for the future therefore lies at the heart of corporate strategy, just as sensitivity to context lies at the heart of corporate policies.

This implies that business leaderships have to "go beyond" conventional business strategies and policies. They have to use the forces over which they have little control to complement and enrich their corporate quest into the future as a going concern. They have to incorporate the "global players" into their policies; they have to know about different political systems of states, and of relations between states in order to make sensible corporate policies going forward. They have to be able to use the interdependencies created by global players and markets as facilitators to their corporate policy. Further they are advised to carefully study the evolution of market institutions, as these have a significant impact on competitiveness and business conditions. This does not mean that business leaders have to know and learn everything. What they need to know is that these dimensions do bear upon the business's future. The conclusion is that business leaders are advised to formulate their own questions in light of their existing knowledge about the business and its context. And as they investigate the future towards which they are moving the business, they reformulate their original question in light of the evidence and insights they have won from their consultations with experts. Corporate strategy and policy is scientific management in action.

Ultimately, transnational corporations flourish if they build trust, the vital complement to inbuilt ambiguities in relations between interdependent units strung out across the world. Transnationals become pillars of an open world order in which they have a crucial stake, and on which they depend, but over which they cannot reign.

NOTES

1. There is an abundant literature on the "Toyota system." See Womack, Jones, and Roos (1990) and Womack and Jones (2003).
2. The concept of the society of states as contrasted to the state system is developed by Bull (1980).
3. For instance, the vision of Konosuke Matsushita, who announced on May 5, 1932, the fourteenth anniversary of the company's founding, his business philosophy and a 250-year plan for the company, broken down into ten 25-year segments (Bartlett and Ghoshal 1989).
4. Our perspective on strategy is largely based on Finkelstein, Harvey, and Lawton (2007).

REFERENCES

ALMOND, G., and POWELL, G. 1966. *Comparative Politics: A Developmental Approach.* Boston: Little Brown.

AUSTIN, J. 1990. *Managing in Developing Countries: Strategic Analysis and Operating Techniques.* New York: Free Press.

BARNET, R., and MULLER, R. 1974. *Global Reach: The Power of the Multinational Corporations.* New York: Simon & Schuster.

BARON, D. 1995. "Integrated strategy: market and nonmarket components," *California Management Review* 37(2): 47–65.

——1996. *Business and its Environment.* 2nd edn. Upper Saddle River, NJ: Prentice-Hall.

——1997. "Integrated strategy in international trade disputes: the Kodak-Fujifilm case," *Journal of Economics and Management Strategy* 6 (Summer): 291–346.

——1999. "Integrated market and nonmarket strategies in client and interest group politics," *Business and Politics* 1(1): 7–34.

BARTLETT, C., and GHOSHAL, S. 1989. *Managing across Borders: The Transnational Solution.* Boston: Harvard Business School Press.

BAYSINGER, B. 1984. "Domain maintenance as an objective of business political activity: an expanded typology," *Academy of Management Review* 9: 248–58.

BEARLE, A., and MEANS, G. 1932. *The Modern Corporation and Private Property.* London: Transaction Publishers.

BEHRMAN, J., and GROSSE, R., 1990. *International Business and Governments: Issues and Institutions.* Columbia: University of South Carolina Press.

BJARNAR, O., and KIPPING, M. 1998. *The Americanisation of European Business, the Marshall Plan and the Transfer of US Management Models.* London: Routledge.

BOARMAN, P., and SCHOLLHAMER, H., eds. 1975. *Multinational Corporations and Governments.* New York: Praeger.

BODDEWYN, J. 1988. *Advertising Self-Regulation and Outside Participation: A Multinational Comparison.* London: Quorum Books.

—— 1993. "Political resources and markets in international business: beyond Porter's generic strategies," in J. Post, ed., *Research in Global Strategic Management,* vol. iv. Greenwich: JAI Press, 162–84.

—— 1995. "The legitimacy of international-business political behavior," *The International Trade Journal* 9(1) 143–61.

—— 1998. "The domain of international management: mission statement impossible?" Paper presented at the preconvention workshop on exploring the domain of international management at the Academy of Management annual meeting in San Diego, August.

—— and BREWER, T. 1994. "International-business political behavior: new theoretical directions," *Academy of Management Review,* 19(1): 119–43.

BONARDI, J-P., HILLMAN, A., and KEIM, G. 2005. "The attractiveness of political markets: implications for firm strategy," *Academy of Management Review* 30(2): 397–413.

BREWER, T. 1992. "MNC–Government relations: strategic networks and foreign direct investment in the United States in the automotive industry," *The International Executive* 34: 113–29.

BRUCE, K. 2006. "Henry S. Dennison, Elton Mayo, and human relations historiography," *Management and Organizational History* 1: 177–99.

BULL, H. 1980. *The Anarchical Society: A Study of Order in World Politics.* London: Macmillan.

BURTLESS, G., LAWRENCE, R., LITAN, R., and SHAPIRO, R. 1998. *Globaphobia: Confronting Fears about Open Trade.* Washington, DC: Brookings Institution.

COEN, D. 1997. "The evolution of the large firm as a political actor in the European Union," *Journal of European Public Policy* 4: 91–108.

—— 1998. "The European business interest and the nation state: large-firm lobbying in the European Union and member state," *Journal of Public Policy* 18: 75–100.

CROUCH, C., and STREECK, W. 1997. *Political Economy of Modern Capitalism: Mapping Convergence and Diversity.* London: Sage.

CROZIER, M. 1971. *Le Phénomène bureaucratique.* Paris: Le Seuil.

—— and FRIEDBERG, E. 1977. *L'Acteur et le système.* Paris: Le Seuil.

CZINKOTA, M., and RONKAINEN, I. 1997. "International business and trade in the next decade: report from a delphi study," *Journal of International Business Studies* 28(4): 827–44.

DAHL, R., and LINDBLOM, C. 1953. *Politics, Economics and Welfare.* New York: Harper.

DOZ, Y., and PRAHALAD, C. 1980. "How MNCs cope with host government intervention," *Harvard Business Review* 58 (March–April): 147–57.

EASTON, D. 1965. *A Systems Analysis of Political Structure.* New York: Wiley.

EMERSON, R. 1962. "Power dependency relationships," *American Sociological Review* 27: 31–41.

FAGRE, N., and WELLS, L. 1982. "Bargaining power of multinationals and host governments," *Journal of International Business Studies* 13(2): 9–23.

FINKELSTEIN, S., HARVEY, C., and LAWTON, T. 2007. *Breakout Strategy: Meeting the Challenges of Double-Digit Growth.* New York: McGraw-Hill.

FORD, H., and CROWTHER, S. 1992. *My Life and Work.* New York: Garden City Publishing Company.

FRENCH, J., and RAVEN, B. 1959. "The basis of social power," in D. Cartwright, *Studies in Social Power.* Ann Arbor: University of Michigan Press.

FREY, B. 1984. "The public choice view of international political economy," *International Organization* 38(1): 199–207.

FUKUYAMA, F. 1989. "The end of history?" *The National Interest* 16: 3–18.

GADDIS, J. 1982. *Strategies of Containment: A Critical Appraisal of Post-war American National Security Policy.* New York: Oxford University Press.

GALE, J., and BUCHHOLZ, R. 1987. "The political pursuit of competitive advantage," in A. Marcus, A. Kaufman, and D. Beam., ed., *Business Strategy and Public Policy.* New York: Quorum, 43–60.

GHOSHAL, S., and BARTLETT, C. 1997. *The Individualized Corporation: A Fundamentally New Approach to Management.* New York: Harper Collins.

GILPIN, R. 1975. *US Power and the Multinational Corporation: The Political Economy of Foreign Direct Investment.* New York: Basic Books.

—— 1987. *The Political Economy of International Relations.* Princeton: Princeton University Press.

GOLDSMITH, J. 1994. *The Trap.* London: MacMillan.

GRAY, J. 1998. *False Dawn: The Delusions of Global Capitalism.* London: Granta.

GREEN-COWLES, M. 1995. "Setting the agenda for a new Europe: The ERT and EC 1992," *Journal of Common Market Studies* 33(4): 501–26.

HALL, G., and HOWELL, S. 1985. "The experience curve from an economist's perspective," *Strategic Management Journal* 6: 197–212.

HALL, P., and SOSKICE, D. 2001. *Varieties of Capitalism: The Institutional Foundations of Comparative Advantage.* Oxford: Oxford University Press.

HAMBRICK, D. 1981. "Environment, strategy, and power within top management teams," *Administrative Science Quarterly* 26(2): 253–75.

HILLMAN, A., ZARDKOOHI, A., and BIERMAN, L. 1999. "Corporate political strategies and firm performance: indications of firm-specific benefits from personal service in the US government," *Strategic Management Journal* 20(1): 67–81.

HOBSBAWM, E. 1994. *Age of Extremes: The Short Twentieth Century.* London: Little Brown.

HUGHES, T. 2004. *American Genesis: A Century of Invention and Technological Enthusiasm, 1870-1970,* 2nd edn. Chicago: University of Chicago Press, 115.

HUNTINGDON, S. 1991. *The Third Wave: Democratization in the Late Twentieth Century.* Norman: University of Oklahoma Press.

—— 1993. *The Clash of Civilizations.* New York: Foreign Affairs.

JOUVENEL, B. 1957. *Sovereignty: An Inquiry into the Political Good.* Chicago: University of Chicago Press.

KATZENSTEIN, P. 1978. *Between Power and Plenty: The Foreign Economic Policies of Advanced Industrial Countries.* Madison: University of Wisconsin Press.

KEIM, G., and BAYSINGER, B. 1988. "The efficacy of business political activity: competitive considerations in a principal-agent context," *Journal of Management* 14: 163–80.

—— and ZEITHAML, C. 1986. "Corporate political strategy and legislative decision making: a review and contingency approach," *Academy of Management Review* 11: 828–43.

KEOHANE, R., and NYE, J. 1977. *Power and Interdependence: World Politics in Transition.* Boston: Little Brown.

KIM, W. C. 1988. "The effects of competition and corporate political responsiveness on multinational bargaining power," *Strategic Management Journal* 9(3): 289–95.

KINDLEBERGER, C. 1969. *American Business Abroad: Six Lectures on Direct Investment.* Boston: Little Brown.

KOBRIN, S. 1979. "Political risk: a review and reconsideration," *Journal of International Business Studies* 10(1): 67–80.

LASSWELL, H. 1950. *Politics: Who Gets What, When and How?* New York: P. Smith.

LAWTON, T. 1997. *Technology and the New Diplomacy: The Creation and Control of EC Industrial Policy for Semiconductors.* Aldershot: Avebury.

LAWTON, T., and McGUIRE, S. 2002. "Constraining choice: exploring the influence of WTO regulation and domestic politics on US trade policy for steel." Academy of International Business, San Juan, Puerto Rico, June 28–July 2.

LENWAY, S., and REHBEIN, K. 1991. "Leaders, followers, and free riders: an empirical test of variation in corporate political involvement," *Academy of Management Journal* 34: 893–905.

LIGHT, L. 1998. "Litigation: the choice of a new generation," *Business Week* May 25: 42.

LINDBLOM, C. 1977. *Politics and Markets: The World's Political-Economic Systems.* New York: Basic Books.

LODGE, G., and VOGEL, E. 1987. *Ideology and Competitiveness: An Analysis of Nine Countries.* Cambridge, Mass.: Harvard Business School.

McGUIRE, S. 1997. *Airbus Industrie: Conflict and Cooperation in US–EC Trade Relations,* New York: St Martin's Press.

MAHBUBANI, K. 1995. "The pacific impulse," *Survival* 37(1): 105–20.

MAIER, C., 1978. "The politics of productivity: the foundations of American economic policy after World War II," in P. Katzenstein, ed., *Between Power and Plenty: The Foreign Economic Policies of Advanced Industrial Countries.* Madison: University of Wisconsin Press, 607–33.

MAZEY, S., and RICHARDSON, J. 1993. *Lobbying in the European Community.* Oxford: Oxford University Press.

MÉNY, Y., and THOENIG, J. 1989. *Politiques publiques.* Paris: Presses Universitaires de France, 129–58.

MORGENTHAU, H. 1967. *Politics among Nations,* 4th edn. New York: Knopf.

MORLINO, L. 1980. *Como cambiano i regimi politici: strumenti di analisi.* Milan: Franco Angeli.

MURTHA, T., and LENWAY, S. 1994. "Country capabilities and the strategic state: how national political institutions affect multinational corporations' strategies," *Strategic Management Journal* 15 (special issue): 113–29.

NELSON, R., and WINTER, S. 1982. *An Evolutionary Theory of Economic Change.* Cambridge, Mass.: Belknap Press.

NORTH, D. 1991. *Institutions, Institutional Change and Economic Performance: Political Economy of Institutions and Decisions.* Cambridge: Cambridge University Press.

PEARCE, J. L. 2001. "How we can learn how governments matter to management and organization," *Journal of Management Inquiry* 10(2): 103–12.

PENROSE, E. 1995. *The Theory of the Growth of the Firm.* Oxford: Oxford University Press.

PORTER, M. 1980. *Competitive Strategy: Techniques for Analyzing Industries and Competitors.* London: Free Press.

—— 1990. *The Competitive Advantage of Nations.* New York: Free Press.

PRAHALAD, C., and DOZ, Y. 1987. *The Multi-National Mission: Balancing Local Demands and Global Vision.* New York: Free Press.

RAMAMURTI, R. 2001. "The obsolescing 'bargaining model': MNC-host developing country relations revisited," *Journal of International Business Studies* 32: 23–39.

RICHARDSON, J., and JORDAN, A. 1979. *Governing under Pressure: The Policy Process in a Post-Parliamentary Democracy.* Oxford: Martin Robertson.

RING, P. S., LENWAY, S. A., and GOVEKAR, M. 1990. "Management of the political imperative in international business," *Strategic Management Journal* 11(2): 141–51.

RODRICK, D. 1997. *Has Globalization Gone Too Far?* Washington, DC: Institute for International Economics.

RUGGIE, J. 1995. "At home abroad, abroad at home: international liberalization and domestic stability in the new world economy," *Millennium: Journal of International Studies* 24(3): 507–26.

RUGMAN, A., and VERBEKE, A. 1998. "Multinational enterprises and public policy," *Journal of International Business Studies* 29(1): 115–36.

RUSTOW, D. 1970. "Transitions to democracy: towards a dynamic model," *Comparative Politics* 2(3): 337–63.

SCHONBURGER, R. 1998. *World Class Manufacturing: The Next Decade.* New York: Free Press.

SCHULER, D. 1996. "Corporate political strategy and foreign competition: the case of the steel industry," *Academy of Management Journal* 39: 720–37.

—— REHBEIN, K., and CRAMER, R. 2002. "Pursuing strategic advantage through political means: a multivariate approach," *Academy of Management Journal* 45: 659–72.

SCHUMPETER, J. 1942. *Capitalism, Socialism and Democracy.* New York: Harper.

SHAFFER, B., and HILLMAN, A. 2000. "The development of business–government strategies by diversified firms," *Strategic Management Journal* 21(2): 175–90.

SHAFFER, C. 1995. "Firm-level responses to government regulation: theoretical and research approaches," *Journal of Management* 21: 495–514.

SIMON, H. A. 1982–1997. *Models of Bounded Rationality,* vols. i–iii. Cambridge, Mass.: MIT Press.

SLOAN, A. 1965. *My Years with General Motors.* New York: MacFadden Books.

SMITH, B. 1990. *American Science Policy Since World War II.* Washington, DC: Brookings Institution.

SMITH, A. 1991. *National Identity.* Harmondsworth: Penguin.

SOROS, G. 1998. *The Crisis of Global Capitalism.* New York: Public Affairs Press.

STOPFORD, J., and STRANGE, S. 1991. *Rival States, Rival Firms: Competition for World Market Share.* Cambridge: University of Cambridge Press, 1–31.

—— and WELLS, L. 1972. *Managing the Multinational Enterprise.* New York: Basic Books.

STORY, J., and WALTER, I. 1997. *Political Economy of Financial Integration in Europe.* Manchester: Manchester University Press.

STRANGE, S. 1970. "International economics and international relations: a case of mutual neglect," *International Affairs* 46(2): 305–15.

—— 1985. "Protectionism and world politics," *International Organisation* 39(2): 233–59.

—— 1987. "The persistent myth of lost hegemony," *International Organisation* 41(4): 551–74.

—— 1991. "Big business and the state," *Millennium: Journal of International Studies* 20(2): 245–50.

—— 1988. *States and Markets: An Introduction to International Political Economy.* London: Pinter.

—— 1994. "Who governs? Networks of power in world society," *Hitotsubashi Journal of Law and Politics* Special Issue (June): 5–17.

—— 1996. *The Retreat of the State: The Diffusion of Power in the World Economy.* Cambridge: Cambridge University Press.

—— 1997. *The Retreat of the State: The Diffusion of Power in the World Economy,* 2nd edn. Cambridge: Cambridge University Press.

STREECK, W., and SCHMITTER, P., eds. 1984. *Private Interest Government: Beyond Market and State.* London: Sage.

TEECE, D., PISANO, G., and SHUEN, A. 1997. "Dynamic capabilities and strategic management," *Strategic Management Journal* 18: 509–33.

VERNON, R. 1971. *Sovereignty at Bay.* New York: Basic Books.

—— 1977. *Storm over the Multinationals: The Real Issues.* Cambridge, Mass.: Harvard University Press.

VOGEL, D. 1996. "The study of business and politics," *California Management Review* 38(3): 146–65.

WACK, P. 1985. "Scenarios: uncharted waters ahead," *Harvard Business Review,* 1 (September–October): 73–89.

WALTZ, K. 1979. *Theory of International Politics.* New York: McGraw-Hill.

WEIDENBAUM, M. 1980. "Public policy: no longer a spectator sport for business," *Journal of Business Strategy* 3(4): 46–53.

WEISS, L. 1998. *The Myth of the Powerless State: Governing the Economy in a Global Era.* London: Polity Press.

WHITLEY, R. 1997. "Internationalization and varieties of capitalism: the limited effects of cross-national coordination of economic activities on the nature of business systems," *Review of International Political Economy* 5(3): 445–81.

——1999. *Divergent Capitalisms: The Social Structuring and Change of Business Systems.* Oxford: Oxford University Press.

WILSON, G. 1990. *Business and Politics.* London: Chatham House.

WOMACK, J., and JONES, D. 2003. *Lean Thinking: Banish Waste and Create Wealth in your Corporation.* New York: Free Press.

——— and ROOS, D. 1990. *The Machine that Changed the World.* New York: MacMillan.

WOOD, D. 1986. *Strategic Uses of Public Policy,* Marshfield, Mass.: Pitman Publishing.

YOFFIE, D. 1988. "How an industry builds political advantage," *Harvard Business Review* 3 (May–June): 82–9.

——and BERGENSTEIN, S. 1985. "Creating political advantage: the rise of the corporate political entrepreneur," *California Management Review* 28(1): 124–39.

ZYSMAN, J. 1994. "How institutions create historically rooted trajectories of growth," *Industrial and Corporate Change* 3(1): 243–83.

PART II

FIRM AND STATE

CHAPTER 5

VARIETIES OF CAPITALISM AND BUSINESS

BOB HANCKÉ

THE 1990s taught students of comparative business two important things: one was that capitalism was indeed a more effective way of allocating resources in an economy, the other—slightly paradoxically—that there was no such thing as a singular mode of capitalist organization. By the late 1990s, several parallel efforts were under way to map diversity in the advanced capitalist world, which slowly converged on an understanding of capitalism and especially of firms and business in capitalism that was very different from the standard neoclassical one that has dominated training and research in business.

The comparative study of capitalism has a long pedigree in the social sciences. In some form or other, it was part of the foundation of modern economics (then still called "political economy"): classical thinkers such as Smith, Ricardo, Mill, and Marshall were keenly aware that modern capitalism was as much a generic economic system as a particular one that was embedded in its moral, political, institutional, and social environment. Similarly, Weber, and (the young) Marx drew our attention to the non-economic elements of capitalism. By the 1920s, "institutional economics," an intellectual current that counted among its practitioners, such names as John Commons and Thorsten Veblen, had become a respectable field in the then modern social sciences including economics. But this idea of a capitalist economy embedded in a broader social, political, and institutional system that influences how economic activities are organized very early on coexisted uneasily with a different set of arguments that claimed to have discovered the essential principles of economic behavior and, in the Marxist version, the immutable laws of motion of capitalism. This second but increasingly dominant strand ultimately overshadowed the more relativist positions. Instead of an embedded economic agent, it posited the *homo economicus*; instead of contextualized economic systems, it posited convergence toward a single capitalist system, usually the one that existed in the UK and the USA (Bronk 2009). The basic drivers of convergence in these arguments sound remarkably familiar to today's ears: technology, trade, finance, and competition. Technology offers a plateau for efficient production, which spreads as competitors start to copy the techniques of the market leader. Free trade produces one growing market, in which competition weeds out old production methods. And smart money, in turn, invests in companies with the highest return. In some form or other these arguments have found an expression in practically every generation of thinkers and scholars since the initial statements by the classical political economists.

Since the mid-1960s, the comparative position has again gained in importance: capitalism embodies within it different politically and institutionally determined subspecies. Andrew Shonfield's (1965) magisterial account of the different capitalist systems emerging in Europe, and subsequently the debates in the 1970s and 1980s about the economic performance of neo-corporatism (Schmitter 1981; Cameron 1984), reflected the prevailing unease with the view that capitalist systems would converge on a single system driven by efficiency, trade and competition.

Today's generation of comparative capitalism studies, which found its earliest expressions in Zysman's (1983) work on the effects of different financial systems, and Piore and Sabel's (1984) analysis of the different productive models within "Fordist" capitalism, builds on these analytical traditions. Three more or less fully specified approaches to capitalist diversity exist: "national business systems," typologies of "social systems of innovation and production," and "Varieties of Capitalism." National business systems (NBS) approaches (Hollingsworth and Boyer 1997; Whitley 1999; Crouch 2005; Streeck 2009) organize diversity within capitalist systems along two dimensions: the provision of capital (via direct ownership, banks, or stock markets, etc.) and the relations between management and workers (cooperation, dependence, conflict, etc.). Relying on a wide variety of different constellations of capital provision and employment relations, Whitley (1999: 42) identifies a handful of business systems, with different capitalist countries being close to different types of business system: South Korea, for example, is a state-organized business system, Germany (at least until recently) a collaborative model, and the Third Italy a coordinated district business system. Amable (2003: 14) examines, in a parallel way, five spheres in an economy: product market competition, wage setting systems and labor markets, finance and corporate governance, social protection and the welfare state, and the educational system. His approach establishes close mutual links through correlation analysis and then uses principal component analysis to bring out underlying commonalities that tie the different dimensions into coherent models. He thus identifies five capitalist models where different spheres are articulated in a complementary way: the market-based, the social-democratic, the continental European, the Mediterranean, and the Asian models.

We have learnt a lot from the NBS and SSIP approaches. However, they both alert us to a problem which consists in trading off analytical sophistication against empirical coverage. These approaches draw on impressive collections of variables that allow us to identify types of capitalism in more or less systematic ways. What they lack, however, is a limited set of organizing principles, theoretically embedded in a wider literature. Whitley's characterizations, for example, encompass many more or—usually—less interrelated and diverse spheres in a political economy, but without laying down the rules along which they have been selected. Amable's analysis suffers from a parallel problem. His analysis adds dimensions of an economy until they are mathematically coherent, but without saying much about the organizing principles that focused our attention on these dimensions in the first place.

"Varieties of Capitalism" approaches the question from a different angle (Hall and Soskice 2001a), which allows for such a combination of empirical range and analytical sharpness. Diversity within capitalism follows from the institutional solutions to the perennial information and coordination problems that firms face. Since such institutional solutions come in a limited number of discrete blocks, only a handful of them can be coherent enough to survive. In the balance of this chapter, I will first present the basic outline and the main criticisms of VoC, and, based on that review and debate, explore three key dimensions of modern capitalist economies that influence business–state relations: the nature of business networks, cross-class coalitions between labor and capital, and the role of the state. That discussion will lead to a revised typology of VoC which pays more attention to relations between the state and different coalitions of producer groups. The final section concludes.

"Varieties of Capitalism": The Basics

The VoC approach starts axiomatically with the firm in the center of the analysis. In contrast to standard economic analyses, however, it treats the firm as a relational network: the firm, operating in its markets and other aspects of the relevant environment, is institutionally embedded. These institutional frameworks, in turn, are mutually attuned in systemic ways, leading to institutional complementarities, in which the presence of one institution reinforces the positive effects that another one might have, and confer comparative and competitive advantages to countries, which are reinforced through specialization in rapidly integrating international markets. What emerges, in ideal typical form, is two (or more, but at least two) institutional equilibria, one where coordination takes the form of contractual relations (in LMEs) and another which relies on strategic forms of coordination (in CMEs).

By placing the firm at the core of the analysis, VoC explores capitalism from the vantage point of what it considers as its central actor—business. Where other perspectives have focused on descriptive macro-level attributes, and to a large extent have regarded the shape of markets and the nature of market participants as a function of these macro-structures, VoC instead starts with the analytics underlying the coordination problems that firms face in their strategic environment. That world, according to VoC, is riddled with information and hold-up problems: for example, how do owners know that managers maximize their profits, managers that workers perform to the level of their abilities, and who or what guarantees workers that owners will not fire them after they have put in their effort? The solution to these potentially debilitating information asymmetries is offered by the historically given institutional frameworks within which management finds itself. Firms are permanently exposed to markets—product markets which structure relations between firms and their customers; labor markets where workers and management meet; and capital markets which provide firms with capital—and the organization of these markets takes very different shapes in different capitalist economies. Labor markets in Germany, Sweden, and other countries in north-western Europe, for example, are highly structured arrangements, where strong employers' associations meet strong trade unions and collectively negotiate wages. Capital provision has, up until very recently, been organized through banks in those countries, and even if international investors have made a dramatic and massive appearance on these capital markets over the last decade, the relations between firms and banks remain tightly coordinated. Compare this with the dispersed shareholder systems associated with the City of London and Wall Street, or with the loose hire and fire labor market regulations in most Anglo-Saxon (but very few continental European) economies, and the differences are clear. Firms in these two types of systems do not operate in the same labor and capital markets.

This is not a coincidence: it makes little sense to link long-term capital provision along the lines of what banks usually provide to short-term, deregulated labor markets or vice versa. Long-term investors are usually very willing to invest in the provision of specific skills for workers and accept that regulated labor markets are a useful way of doing so. Nervous institutional investors such as mutual funds, on the other hand, are loathe to sink capital in a long-term training project with uncertain (and often long-term) pay-offs, which ties their capital to the effort and skills of workers. The crucial issue is that once labor and product markets are linked in such systemic ways, the options for a company in terms of product markets are considerably narrower as well. Building machine tools in a competitive way, for example, requires that both employer and employee invest in skills that further a deep knowledge of the technology deployed and of the type of customers that would want to buy such complex capital goods. Specific skills and long-term capital are combined, in other words, in ways that produce important competitive advantages in narrow market niches, where long-term, relationship-specific links between producers and consumers emerge.

VoC systematizes this insight into a key argument: the presence of several "correctly calibrated" institutions that govern different markets determines the efficiency of the overall institutional framework. This argument of "institutional complementarities" implies that for a framework to have the desired strong effect, the constituent institutions in the different markets—between labor relations and corporate governance, labor relations and the national training system, and corporate governance and inter-firm relations—reinforce each other. The tightness of the links between these institutional complementarities between institutional sub-systems determines the degree to which a political economy is "coordinated." Coordinated market economies (CMEs) are characterized by the prevalence of non-market relations, collaboration, and credible commitments among firms. The essence of its "liberal market economy" (LME) counterpart is one of arm's-length, competitive relations, formal contracting, and supply-and-demand price signalling (Hall and Soskice 2001b; Hall and Gingerich 2004). VoC argues that these institutional complementarities lead to different kinds of firm behavior and investment patterns. In LMEs, fluid labor markets fit well with easy access to stock market capital, producing "radical-innovator" firms in sectors ranging from bio-technology, semi-conductors, software, and advertising to corporate finance. In CMEs, long-term employment strategies, rule-bound behavior, and the durable ties between firms and banks that underpin patient capital provision predispose firms to "incre-mental innovation" in capital goods industries, machine tools, and equipment of all kinds. While the logic of LME dynamics is centered on mobile "switchable assets" whose value can be realized when diverted to multiple purposes, CME logic derives from "specific or co-specific assets" whose value depends on the active cooperation of others (Hall and Soskice 2001b; Hall and Gingerich 2004).

The persistence of capitalist diversity is largely attributed to "positive feedbacks": the different logics of LMEs and CMEs, each with their own return-on-investment schedules, create different incentives for economic actors, which, in turn, generate different politics of economic adjustment. In LMEs, holders of mobile assets (work-ers with general skills, investors in fluid capital markets) will seek to make markets still more fluid and accept further deregulatory policies. In CMEs, holders of specific assets (workers with industry-specific skills and investors in co-specific assets) will more often oppose greater market competition and form status quo supporting cross-class coalitions (Hall and Gingerich 2004: 28–9). Globalization reinforces this logic of divergent adjustment (Hall and Soskice 2001b; Gourevitch and Hawes 2002): since FDI will flow to locations rich in either specific or co-specific assets, depending on the sector or firm-specific requirements that investors are searching for, global-ization will often reinforce comparative institutional advantage. CMEs and LMEs are therefore likely to be located at different points in international production chains: high value-added, high skill-dependent, high-productivity activities will tend to remain in the core CMEs, while lower value-added, lower-skill, price-oriented production will relocate to lower-cost jurisdictions.

The final step in the argument thus links the development of these coherent institutional frameworks to the processes of economic integration associated with globalization and European economic integration. It builds on two key insights in classical political economy. Ricardo's theory of comparative advantage suggests that if two trading nations specialize in what they do relatively better, the overall outcome will be beneficial. VoC suggests that in today's world the intricate institutional frameworks in different capitalist economies confer such comparative advantages.

Adam Smith's idea that the division of labor is determined by the extent of the market—the larger the market, the more market participants specialize—is the second. Globalization increases the size of the market, and therefore nations in a global economy will specialize according to their comparative advantages.

VARIETIES OF CAPITALISM: THE DEBATE

This political-economic approach to capitalism, which emphasizes the role of business in advanced capitalism, has come under fire from many different corners. The main theoretical criticism has been that it is functionalist, focusing on permanency and path-dependence, and therefore ignores important dynamic elements of economic change (Streeck and Thelen 2005). VoC thus misunderstands endogenous sources of change in national business systems and diversity within the systems (Boyer 2005b; Coates 2005; Crouch 2005; Panitch and Gindin 2005). Others have criticized VoC's "institutional determinism" and equilibrium thinking, and its relative neglect of power, including class, in processes of change, and more generally the role of politics and the state in the political economy (Schmidt 2002, 2003; Howell 2003; Regini 2003; Thelen and Van Wijnbergen 2003; Watson 2003; Crouch and Farrell 2004; Coates 2005; Kinderman 2005; Pontusson 2005; Jackson and Deeg 2006). The second large set of critiques deals with the methodological approach underlying VoC. Firms and business are, according to these critiques, institution-takers rather than autonomous, creative, or disruptive actors (Allen 2004; Crouch and Farrell 2004; Crouch 2005; Martin 2005), usually found in the relatively small manufacturing sector (Blyth 2003). National institutional frameworks are treated as insulated from globalization and whatever forces of cross-national convergence might reside there (Crouch and Farrell 2004; Martin 2005; Panitch and Gindin 2005; Pontusson 2005). The final set of critiques is that VoC artificially divides the world into LMEs and CMEs and either tries to shoehorn countries in that typology or define away less clear-cut cases, neglecting many CME elements which are, have been, or might be present in LMEs and vice versa. Finally, it ignores most countries outside north-west Europe, the UK, and the US, where business and labor are not necessarily organized along carefully constructed industry lines, and the state plays a considerably larger direct and indirect role in the supply side of the economy (Schmidt 2002, 2003; Watson 2003; Boyer 2005b; Hay 2005; Pontusson 2005).

Four areas from among these critiques which have a direct bearing on relations between business and government will be explored in this chapter: the role of conflicts and coalitions; the link between institutional complementarities and institutional change; the nature of political economies that fall outside the crisp CME/LME distinction; and the relation between state and economy in contemporary advanced capitalism.

Conflict, shocks, and change

Two important recent developments raise questions for VoC. The first is the attempts by employers in CMEs to break with long-established commitments to coordination. The VoC argument suggests that businesses in a CME would be very hesitant to liberalize their main factor markets, since their product market and profit strategies are intimately tied to the institutional framework of CMEs. While this appeared to be the case in the 1980s (Wood 2001), today businesses seem to be pushing a more competitive, "deregulatory" agenda in both labor and financial markets. In Germany these changes are making coordination on both the employer and union sides more difficult and may ultimately threaten the long-term viability of the system (Thelen and Van Wijnbergen 2003; Kinderman 2005). The second big recent development is economic and financial internationalization. VoC predicts that competition and the spread of global production networks will further institutional differences and drive divergence by exploiting comparative institutional advantages. In this world, multi-nationals scan different national systems in search of optimal locations for discrete activities in their value chain, by acquiring dynamic radically innovative companies in LMEs while keeping development and commercialization in the core CMEs. However, a subversion of institutional structures and relations in *home* locations is another possible result of such processes of economic integration (Berger et al. 1999, 2001; Berger 2000; Lane 2003; Herrigel and Wittke 2005). Both of these recent developments upset the careful class balance in CMEs, and often pave the way for new distributional conflicts, which are difficult to handle for VoC (Regini 2003; Watson 2003). Howell (2003: 122) claims that VoC renders "invisible the exercise of class power that underlies co-ordination and equilibrium in the political economy," while Allen (2004) and Crouch (2005) attribute these weaknesses to the axiomatic conception of the strategic preferences of firms as endogenous to their environments. When existing coalitions and alliances are reconfigured, new lines of conflict may open. Often this process will involve new alliances with external actors such as multinationals and pension funds, as economies open up to foreign capital (Rhodes and van Apeldoorn 1998). One of the predictions of VoC (Hall and Soskice 2001b: 64) is that the response in LMEs will consist of calls for more deregulation, while actors in CMEs defend strategic interaction and coordination. Yet new coalitions may, especially in CMEs, disrupt rather than strengthen existing alliances. Contemporary Germany offers many such instances. In recent years an alliance between domestic and international investors has formed in favor of a reform of the German financial system (Deeg 2005b). Conflicts over the shareholder value orientation in German companies have been crucial in reconfiguring long-standing coalitions between shareholders, management, and employees (Höpner 2001). Small and medium-sized firms in Germany are working towards a break with the conventional industrial relations bargains that mainly reflect the interests of large firms (Berndt 2000). And even within the large German business associations opposition to the wage bargain-ing system is growing (Kinderman 2005). This suggests the need for specifying more clearly when firms will "exit" or exercise "voice" and exploring how exit or voice in turn imperil or are shaped by existing systems of coordination and complementar-ities. In part this comes down to identifying the conditions under which firms will behave *creatively* and possibly challenge the prevailing institutional environment by transforming it (Hancké and Goyer 2005: 5).

Institutional complementarities and change

A strong criticism of VoC has been that by focusing on systemic coherence and institutional complementarities, it is unable to accommodate contradiction, disjunc-tion, and politics as a source of both stability and change. The basic idea in VoC is that "nations with a particular type of co-ordination in one sphere of the economy should tend to develop complementary practices in other spheres as well" (Hall and Soskice 2001b: 18). Others, however, reject such a focus on "coherent logics of ordering," since it ignores "incongruencies, incoherence and within-system diver-sities" (Crouch and Farrell 2004: 8–9). Streeck and Thelen (2005), in turn, contrast VoC's overemphasis on system stability with other approaches (including their own) that are more open to the dynamics of institutional innovation and punctuated equilibria.

Deeg (2005c) suggests three ways of thinking about the relation between institu-tional complementarities and change. A useful scenario to start is the one where change occurs, but where the nature of core complementarities remains stable, because of the existence of institutional and functional equivalents, and strong incentives for key actors to preserve the existing system of coordination. Compare changes in French and German corporate governance (Goyer 2002, 2007). When firms in both countries were confronted with similar external stimuli or shocks following a shift in financial regimes, they responded using the tools within their institutional context, and thus ended up adjusting in very different ways. Similarly, while formal institutions governing sectors in MMEs such as France or CMEs such as Germany may at some level begin to emulate their LME counterparts, informal networks, opportunity structures, and strategies (including those of governments) may remain very distinct (Thatcher 2007) and thus lead to very different de facto governance mechanisms and outcomes. Or wage setting in Germany seems to have been able to adapt quite easily by changing slightly in the way it operates. Whilst its form, built on strong central employers' organizations and trade unions, has sur-vived the (mainly decentralizing) shifts in the wage setting system, it is now more flexible and responsive to newly emerging forms of cost competition (Hassel and Rehder 2001; Hassel 2007).

In another scenario, change may be limited to one sub-sector of the economy, which may find itself significantly transformed, but where the rest of the system remains intact. In the last decade, for example, and in part as a result of the shifts in wage setting alluded to above, an increasing degree of dualism in the German labor market indicates a loosening of coordination in these spheres of the economy; strategic coordination, however, remains as important as it was in other areas of the economy, including the labor market (Hall 2007; Hassel 2007)—for example in training or standard setting. Höpner's (2006) insight that some elements in a political economy may be redundant while appearing complementary helps us understand these dynamics. Because of their redundant character, their demise may well have few consequences for the evolution of the overall production regime as such.

But complementarities, especially of the tightly linked type that we can find in some of the CMEs, can magnify pressures for change in one sphere of the economy, thus forcing change in other spheres as well. Shareholder value-driven shifts in corporate governance change the background parameters of labor relations, which themselves then come under pressure to comply with these constraints imposed by shifts in ownership and management. In a similar vein, complementarities between different fields of corporate governance are also unwinding the ties that bind the country's large companies together, threatening strategic coordination (Höpner 2001; Höpner and Krempel 2003). The key question here is how far strategic coordination will erode. Will it ultimately collapse, or will firms change the system while retaining those elements that served them well in the past? Most evidence points to the latter scenario. Peter Hall (2007), for example, argues that countries in Europe have indeed adapted their institutions to new domestic challenges and changing international conditions—yet those changes seem to have followed tracks laid down by the linkages and performance of previous institutional frameworks.

Mixed and emerging market economies

A further set of questions concerning the nature of complementarities is raised by developments in "mid-spectrum," mixed-market political economies, or MMEs (Hall and Gingerich 2004). "Mid-spectrum" MMEs (and what we refer to as EMEs—emerging market economies—in Central and Eastern Europe) mix market regulation with some elements of coordinated regulation as well as state-compensating coordination, sustaining sub-systems that are, in the ideal typical concepts that VoC applies, far from "correctly calibrated" (Molina and Rhodes 2007). These economies, thus the standard VoC argument, will eventually be forced to transform themselves into one of the two pure types (Hall and Gingerich 2004). The lack of systemic efficiency that follows from the incomplete nature of institutional complementarities will ultimately lead to diminishing returns, and the MMEs and EMEs will adapt and adopt the institutional features of CMEs or LMEs. Since the capacity for coordination appears asymmetrically distributed, in the sense that it is far easier to deregulate and destroy the basis for coordination than it is to build coordinating capacity which may often have evolved over many decades (Culpepper 2003), change in these economies will tend to favor liberal market solutions over coordinated ones. Hybrid capitalist systems, in other words, will either always underperform compared to their pure cousins, or transform themselves, often into LME-type economies.

One relevant criticism leveled at this view questions the national homogeneity assumption. Höpner, for example (2005: 383), suggests that, even if the broad national institutional contexts lack coherence because of conflicting governance modes, it is always possible that institutions or clusters of institutions within them may still be complementary in a functional, mutually reinforcing sense. An example might be the large firms and the localized industrial districts found in northern Italy. Such sub-national variation, however, may not be randomly distributed, and possibly such sectoral or regional "islands" of quasi-coordination are themselves determined by characteristics of the national system operating in the background. Another critique of this view questions the functionalist assumptions underlying the idea that high performance is associated with pure capitalist types. While the tightly coupled frameworks associated with these pure types may have demonstrated strong performance during the stable period of mass production of the 1960s and 1970s, that may no longer be the case today. The basic idea is borrowed from biology: as environments become more unstable, species that combine different strengths have a competitive advantage over "pure" species, since they can thrive in very different ecological niches (Boyer 2005a, 2005b; Crouch 2005). Eichengreen (2006) develops this argument most forcefully in his analysis of the comparative strengths and weaknesses of European and American capitalism. In his analysis the "extensive growth" model underlying CMEs, which relied on cooperation between different actors in the economy to mobilize resources, may be running out of steam now that gains are obtained from "intensive growth," which favors production factor intensity.

The state in capitalist variety

The preoccupation in VoC with economic regimes has led many critics to stress the role of the state in coordinating and shaping the political economies of many advanced capitalist countries and to develop alternative typologies in which the state is a major determining variable. Whitley (2005), for example, argues that the state plays two crucial roles. The first is to provide regulatory and institutional frameworks that influence the basic characteristics of the business system; the second more specifically to induce (or not) employers to cooperate and coordinate. Moreover, direct intervention by the state in the economy through industrial policies, ownership, or credit may lead to increased diversity with regard to labor relations or capital provision between targeted firms and sectors and the others in an economy. Other authors identify separate models of capitalism in which the state is, if not the dominant economic actor, then at least one on a par with business. Schmidt (2002), for example, distinguishes "state capitalism" (France) from "managed" and "market capitalisms" (Germany and Britain). In Amable's (2003) typology the state plays a determining role in the European-integration/public social system of innovation and production alongside three other such systems in Europe (the market-based, meso-corporatist, and social-democratic) (cf. also Boyer 2005b).

What remains unclear is the extent to which the role of the state is a defining characteristic of different capitalist economies. If we start from the idea that inter-firm coordination defines capitalist varieties, then the emphasis on the state can be accommodated by seeing it everywhere as providing a broad framework for coordination, and sometimes as one of its key elements in the absence of strong capacity for business coordination. The state is therefore an element of coordination that can be found everywhere—in different forms, with different functions, and to varying degrees. Adding a separate variety of capitalism built on the state seems to add little analytical value precisely because the state is important everywhere. Schmidt's (2002) attempt to build a state-led model based on the experience of France until the 1980s disregards the different, mostly *compensating*, role that the state has played in other Mediterranean economies up until today (Molina and Rhodes 2007). Similarly, adding dimensions to political economies that build on the state, as Amable (2003) does, increases the number of varieties of capitalism, but also dilutes the analytical strength of such typologies.

Interests, Coalitions, and Institutional Frameworks

Building on the discussion so far allows for these different elements to be brought together in one analytical framework that is both attuned to the criticisms directed at VoC and offers a more dynamic way of understanding contemporary capitalism without losing its analytical power. In what follows (which is largely based on Hancké et al. 2007) I will concentrate on institutional frameworks as outcomes rather than causes, and on the ways in which networks and class coalitions evolve (and potentially also devolve) around "friction points" in relations between institutional subsystems.

Business interests and networks

In their introduction to VoC, Hall and Soskice (2001b) repeatedly refer to different modes of coordination in terms of business networks, but give less attention to the ways in which such networks might emerge and operate, essentially reducing that question to the shared interests between economic actors. A confluence of interests is, however, an insufficient condition for collective action to ensue—however, locating the capacity for collective action in the distribution of sanctions and rewards, as Olson (1965) does, is unsatisfactory because of its implicit functionalism. A historical perspective on the emergence and reproduction of such networks offers a more appropriate entry point.

The character of the social–institutional matrices for coordination is strongly influenced by pre-existing legal arrangements. As a result, in LMEs strong business networks find it hard to emerge because the competition regimes in these economies preclude trusts and "collusion." In the UK, moreover, business networks have in any case been fractured by historical divisions between financial and industrial capital. The origins of post-war German "organized" capitalism, however, can be traced back to the networks that tied many large firms and banks together in powerful industrial-financial groups before the Second World War (Hilferding 1910; Gerschenkron 1962; Herrigel 1996). Even after the break-up of large cartels by the Allies, these groups reconstituted themselves quickly to become the key organizational structure of the German political economy (Berghahn 1996). In France, modernizing elites constructed such business networks after the Second World War (Kuisel 1981). The founding of new, and the revamping of old, elite schools (*Grandes Écoles*), against the background of the Treasury's central role in allocating industrial credit, produced a state-centered system (Zysman 1983). Italy's pyramidal ownership structures and conglomerates with strong horizontal ties, spanning firms and banks, allowed pre- and post-war elites to create collaborative, defensive, and closed business networks. And in Central and Eastern Europe, as King (2007) argues, the roots of contemporary CEE economies lie in their pre-1989 class structure, in which party bureaucrats wielded power and technocrats managed production. Depending on which of these sectors gained the upper hand prior to the 1990s transition, the emerging form of economic governance reflected these relative positions of power—liberal capitalist in the case of the technocrats; oligarchic in the case of the party bureaucrats.

These business elite networks achieved their centrality because they managed to control key parts of the economy and state at politically strategic moments: the post-war governments led by De Gaulle; the reconstruction of the post-war German economy along "ordo-liberal" lines; the large public sector under the investment holding IRI in Italy which merged and modernized a scattered small- and medium-sized industrial sector; and the political and economic chaos of the post-communist transition. The role and function of the state is important in all these instances, and contributes to both the structural coherence of economic governance and the potential for functional complementarities. In the German case it has provided a strong legal framework for intensive interaction between the core elements of the corporate governance system—finance, firms, and labor; in France (and other Mediterranean economies) state intervention has both impeded autonomous interest intermediation and articulation and compensated for the consequent weakness of business coordination; in the communist countries, the suppression of freely coordinating actors has given way to different forms of market governance, depending on the pre-capitalist balance of power between bureaucrats and technocrats.

The mechanisms that reproduce network structures determine the capacity of business to coordinate activities. For networks to become and remain building blocks for coordination, they require both *external* reproduction (the recruitment of new members into the network) and *internal* reproduction (the development of sanctioning mechanisms that secure compliance). The *Grandes Écoles* in France, family-based, holding-type ownership patterns in Italy, the importance of industry associations built on technical knowledge in Germany, and party membership in the former Soviet bloc countries have all performed such functions. Internal reproduction mechanisms run from simple reputation games in France (see Hancké and Soskice 1996; Hancké 2001), via binding sanctions for club members in Germany (Soskice 1999; Wood 2001), to family-dominated, firm–finance linkages in Italy, to political promotion in the former communist countries.

What does this network-focused analysis of business coordinating capacity imply for the construction of broader institutional frameworks? The standard VoC answer to this question is that institutions reflect the needs of business. This conception has come under criticism: capital may indeed be crucial in capitalist economies, but, paraphrasing Marx, it does not choose the conditions under which it operates. We therefore introduce the two other central actors in capitalist economies that influence these conditions: labor (and especially its relationship with capital) and the state.

Business, labor, and cross-class coalitions

Labor constrains business in two ways: directly, because business needs workers and their skills to produce goods and services; and indirectly via the constraints of collective organization. National "settlements" between capital and labor in the post-war era reflected their relative positions of power, which can be conceptualized as equilibrium strategies (see also Iversen 2005; and Iversen and Soskice 2006).

If skills are predominantly industry- or firm-specific, labor will prefer CME-type institutions and policies. As Iversen (2005, 2007) argues, employees in CME countries who have a high proportion of specific skills will also prefer a higher level of social insurance (and hence redistributive spending) than employees in LME nations where the proportion of general skills is higher. But when the predominant skill profile in an economy is more of a general nature, the choices are more complex. Employees in the primary segments of the labor market (lawyers, consultants, investment bankers, etc.) are likely to prefer liberal market institutions and individual rather than collective action. The rest of the labor market may then be forced to fall in line and develop strategies to increase their survival in highly competitive labor markets. As for capital, two equilibrium strategies are available since the nature of skills is tightly linked to other labor market institutions. Specific skills, plant- and firm-level workers' participation, and coordinated wage bargaining all help safeguard the high value-added product market strategies of large CME firms, while general skills, unilateral management, and decentralized wage setting allow for quite different company strategies in LMEs. Cross-class coalitions in CMEs can be understood as the point where the strategies of labor and capital meet: both have strong preferences for thick, inclusive, and well-institutionalized frameworks. Because both benefit, they will therefore fight for their survival. In LMEs, the interests of both employers and highly skilled employees tend to converge on a less well-regulated institutional framework.

Institutional frameworks are thus not simply reflections of the strategic needs of firms, but express underlying cross-class coalitions, which in turn reflect the relative power of important sections of capital and labor. In addition, such a class analysis suggests that coordination is not a function of strategies by the business class *as a whole*, but by its dominant sections, primarily those that are found in the large firms in CMEs and in the labor markets surrounding the leading sectors in LMEs—and often only after protracted struggles for control of the class agenda. CME-type institutions are, as Hassel (2007) shows, in the interest of large firms in CMEs, which may derive significant complementarity-like benefits from the institutional relationships that underpin the cross-class coalition. It is considerably less evident, however, that they also reflect the interests of small firms, for whom collectively bargained labor costs, and other concessions related to the cross-class settlement, may simply be prohibitively high.

Such cross-class coalitions and their institutional settlements therefore face a perennial problem: they are permanently subject to defections. Large and small firms in an economy, for example, do not necessarily have the same interests, nor do firms that produce primarily for export as compared with those based in domestic markets. The interests of large firms in the exposed manufacturing sector will diverge substantially from those of small firms in the sheltered sector, and as employment in the latter expands, the potential for disruption of the cross-class settlement will increase (Gourevitch 1986; Rogowski 1989; Frieden 1991; Franzese 2002). Similarly, workers in small companies do not necessarily share the priorities of workers in large firms. Intra-class politics, and the codification of institutional arrangements in favor of the winners who lay down the rules for others, is an important part of the answer why defections are not more common. Swenson's (1989) analysis of labor politics in Sweden and Germany showed how in inter-war Sweden the export sector and the metalworkers' union forged a coalition against the interests of firms and their workers in the sheltered sector to impose a centralized wage bargaining system. More generally, the post-war settlements in most of Europe primarily reflected the interests of the fast-growing modern sector—business and workers in large, mass-producing firms (Piore and Sabel 1984). And even today, collective bargaining systems frequently use large firms, with standardized job classifications and wage scales, as their main point of reference.

Yet these struggles were not settled by power alone: side-payments made the settlement acceptable to those whose interests were inadequately reflected. On the workers' side, institutionalized subservience has come with an important benefit: in most (non-LME) European economies, wages for workers outside the core sectors of the economy are negotiated in the shadow of the modern large firm-led sector, and their wages are usually set following the prevailing rules in large industrial firms. Wages for these workers thus acquired a level of protection, predictability, and standardization that they would not have had otherwise. Small firms gain from the arrangement as well, since they are allowed to exploit the benefits of coordination, including well-developed skill provision and technology transfer systems, standard-ized wage grids, and social peace, without incurring the costs associated with these public goods. In most countries, small firms have choices with regard to the menu offered by the institutional framework: workers' representation thresholds exclude the vast majority of small firms, negotiated wages set a maximum for them (while frequently providing a de facto minimum for large firms), employment protection may differ between large and small firms, and escape clauses for small firms have either been in existence for a while or were recently introduced in the more "rigid" systems such as Germany.

Organized interests and the state in contemporary capitalism

This brings us to the third neglected issue regarding the nature and origins of coordination in VoC: the state. The dual equilibrium strategies and stable class coalitions examined above are obviously ideal types, closely resembling LMEs and CMEs. But most empirical instances will differ from these ideal types. For example, business coordination may be underdeveloped, and/or labor representation may be far from unitary and based on ideological divisions. Under those conditions, strategic interaction may only occur sporadically and rarely produce stable institutional settlements (Molina and Rhodes 2007). Since economies with these characteristics lack the institutional complementarities that allow for the provision of public goods and thus increase the overall efficiency of the system as a whole, they will, according to VoC, be permanently outperformed by the pure LMEs and CMEs who can rely on strategic links between different sub-systems of the economy. However, instead of facing permanent economic adjustment problems, these economies—France, Italy, or Spain, for example—appear to be stable as well, and their performance on the whole does not lag that of CMEs and LMEs. In these mid-spectrum economies, the state provides that element of stability by compensating for weaknesses elsewhere in the political economy.

The state is too often regarded as a reflection of the existing mode of coordination without an autonomous role. Somewhat schematically, in the VoC framework, the state reflects the key interests of business: if reforms are articulated with the underlying interests of business, they work; where they are not, they fail (see Wood 2001 on Germany). In many advanced capitalist economies, however, the state is considerably more autonomous and activist (Evans, Rueschmeyer, and Skocpol 1985). In countries as diverse as France, Japan, Italy, and Korea, the state played a crucial role in defining, supporting, or organizing the post-war growth model. In later arrivals on the capitalist scene, the state's role has been both more (e.g. in Latin America and southern Europe) and less (as in Central Europe) than the simple LME/CME dichotomy suggests. The transition to capitalism involved a dramatic *expansion* of the state's activities in the economy in the former, and a forced *reduction* in the latter, sometimes against the immediate interests of a nascent business class at the time (Innes 2005). The diversity in state–economy relations that persists until today suggests there is a benefit in establishing the state and the mode of business coordination as analytically independent categories of any given model of capitalism.

A revised typology of capitalist varieties

Combining the insights from these discussions on the nature of business, cross-class coalitions, and the state allows us to rethink the basic typology underlying VoC. The starting point is provided by the two basic forms that relations between the state and the (supply side of the) economy can take in advanced capitalism: either the state has close direct influence over the economy, e.g. as the owner of industries and/or main provider of industrial credit, or the state is a primarily a regulator operating at arm's length. Post-war France and to some extent post-war Italy, as well as some Central European economies, fall into the first category, while the UK, Sweden, and Germany fall into the second. Following the discussion on cross-class alliances earlier, class-based interest organization, in turn, can run from being highly structured to being highly fragmented (in most countries, the levels of business and labor organization tend to mirror one another in this respect). In the first (highly structured) category, individual companies and industry associations or industrial groups balance their respective strategies and are able to strike bargains with organized labor. In the second (fragmented) category, collective interest definition above the company level is more or less absent, either among firms or between their representatives and (similarly fractured) trade union organizations. Dichotomizing these two continuums into a matrix (cf. Figure 5.1) leads to the following four ideal types of coordination.

The first "type" or mode of coordination, *étatisme*, has traditionally been associated with post-war France, where the state controlled the strategic levers of the economy through outright ownership of many companies and control of industrial credit (Hall 1986: 204). Partly as a result of the state's dominance and partly due to

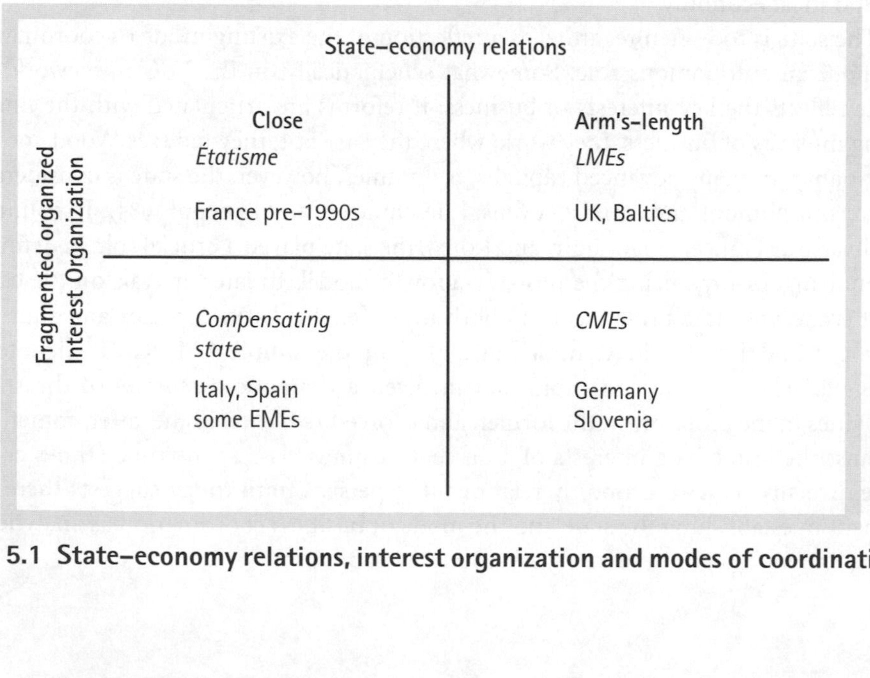

	State–economy relations	
	Close	**Arm's-length**
Fragmented organized Interest Organization	*Étatisme* France pre-1990s	*LMEs* UK, Baltics
	Compensating state Italy, Spain some EMEs	*CMEs* Germany Slovenia

Fig. 5.1 State–economy relations, interest organization and modes of coordination

the deep interpenetration of the state and the economic elites, business organization in France has been weak. In privately owned companies, management and owners have typically relied on themselves for providing the resources they needed, refusing to allow external agents, including associations, to play a role in that process. Similarly, unions have been weakened by ideological fragmentation and their weak roots in the workplace (outside the public sector), while they lack effective vertical links between confederal, sectoral, and firm levels. Since both business and unions were weakly organized, and the state predominant in economic governance, the capitalist model was built upon the state (Levy 2000). Strategic complementarities, to the extent that they have existed at all, could be found in state–business linkages in the large-firm sector, based in the credit-allocation system, and predominantly in traditional manufacturing and public utilities (see Börsch 2007; Thatcher 2007). State-protected markets and business in high-technology sectors have, by contrast, been highly dysfunctional, delivering poor results and high-profile policy failures (Rhodes 1988). In industrial relations, atomized business finds a parallel in the weak and ideologically divided labor movement. The result is less a class compromise or coalition than a permanently contested truce that frequently breaks down into conflict.

A different constellation can be found where the state is important as an actor in industrial policy, but where business is also relatively well organized, usually a result of the nature of ownership structures. Italy exemplifies this type (Molina and Rhodes 2007). The Italian state organized a large state-controlled business sector that has provided key basic industrial inputs and compensated for the absence of autonomous arrangements for capital and labor, primarily through state-funded wage-compensation schemes during industrial restructuring and a social transfer-oriented welfare state. Business and labor tend to be better organized, and wage bargaining more coordinated than in France. But the scope for synergistic, VoC-type complementarities is limited. Interest organizations are strong enough to make demands on the state but insufficiently cohesive to provide it with dependable bargaining partners. Attempts to build more effective coordination also run up against collective action problems, including anti-collective behavior on the part of firms (and employees); an acquiescence in "inefficient inertia," due to the sunk costs confronting agents for change; and the capacity, especially of large firms, to offset the lack of complementarities by seeking competitive advantage by other means. In Italy, the latter included frequent competitive devaluations, government subsidies, cheap immobile factors of production, and evasion of taxation and labor laws.

The third type of state–business relations is the one we usually associate with LMEs. The state sets detailed legal frameworks, leaving business to operate within them, and guards the integrity of market operations by closely monitoring ownership arrangements and market concentration. In part resulting from its history and ownership structures business is weakly organized, and the regulatory frameworks set by the state reinforce this by precluding most forms of deep cooperation. The labor movement, in turn, is decentralized and poorly coordinated, contributing to a conflict-ridden form of industrial relations and strong, endemic weaknesses in employer–employee relations—until submitted, that is, to the market discipline of a Thatcher–Reagan type re-regulation of employment law and labor markets. In LMEs, the political strategies of business are primarily oriented towards influencing the regulatory framework, and considerably less towards finding a compromise with labor (Wood 2001). Some CEE emerging market economies (e.g., the Baltics) have also rapidly moved towards this model.

The fourth and final type of coordination is conventionally associated with the north-west European economies (or CMEs in VoC), of which Germany is the prime example. The state plays a small direct role in the economy (but organizes a large and robust welfare state), and offers broad frameworks for companies to operate within. Business is highly organized and relies on strong industry and employer associations for the provision of collective goods. The high level of economic regulation is less the result of state intervention, but follows from voluntary agreements by associations (including labor unions) to set limits on the behavior of individual companies. In this model, state policies only appear to have an effect if they are carried out or sanctioned by these associations.

The state thus plays an important role everywhere, but in different ways. In some forms of capitalism the state is a central actor in the sense that it provides both a framework for business activities and a means for pursuing them. In other forms of capitalism, the state is less a promoter of economic activity than a compensator for coordination deficits and provider of political consensus and legitimacy. In still others, the state allows markets to operate within a broad set of regulatory frameworks and refrains from direct interference.

CONCLUSION

Over the last decade, VoC has dramatically altered our understanding of capitalism—both in terms of how to approach it and in terms of how it works. This chapter has concentrated on one particular area—business–government relations and their antecedents. Understanding business–government relations from this particular institutionalist political-economic perspective has two advantages over competing frameworks. The first is that VoC concentrates on business as economic actors—i.e. firms—and thus understands capitalism "from within." Its focus on coordination problems and on the types of institutional solutions that are on offer forces us to think of capitalism with capital in mind. But at the same time, such a comparative historical-institutionalist framework also alerts us to the crucial role of the state and (organized) labor. Depending on the degree of organization of labor, often as much a function of the nature of skills deployed in particular product market strategies as it is of the institutional power base of trade unions, and the particular nature of cross-class coalitions between dominant factions of business and labor, relations between business and the state take different shapes. In one large set of OECD economies, found in north-western Europe, this relation is best understood as framework-providing, enabling rather than steering, and on the whole organized in an arm's-length way. In economies where business is weakly organized, such as France, Italy, and other Mediterranean economies, the state plugs the holes by substituting in whole or in part for the lack of endogenous capacity of business to coordinate. Finally, in Anglo-Saxon economies the state fiercely guards the free operation of markets, and limits its intervention on the whole to what is necessary for a well-functioning supply side. The state and governments therefore have an important part everywhere in contemporary advanced capitalism, but the roles they play vary along the different capitalist models. Making sense of that diversity, which appears to be with us for the long haul, despite the pervasive influence of neo-liberal ideas and cross-border institutional and policy borrowing, may well be the most important contribution that VoC has made to the study of business–government relations.

ACKNOWLEDGEMENTS

This chapter is based on joint work with Martin Rhodes and Mark Thatcher (Hancké et al. 2007). Discussions with Martin and Mark, David Soskice, Peter Hall, and especially my students over the years, have helped me tremendously in formulating important elements of this assessment. A declaration of interest: I contributed to the original statement in *Varieties of Capitalism*.

REFERENCES

ALLEN, M. 2004. "The varieties of capitalism paradigm: not enough variety?" *Socio-Economic Review* 2(1): 87–108.

AMABLE, B. 2003. *The Diversity of Modern Capitalism*. Oxford: Oxford University Press.

AOKI, M. 1994. "The contingent governance of teams: analysis of institutional complementarity," *International Economic Review* 35(3): 657–76.

BEBCHUCK, L. A., and ROE, M. J. 2004. "A theory of path dependence in corporate ownership and governance," in J. N. Gordon and M. J. Roe, eds., *Convergence and Persistence in Corporate Governance*. Cambridge: Cambridge University Press, 69–113.

BERGER, S. 2000. "Globalization and politics," *Annual Review of Political Science* 3: 43–62.

——STURGEON, T., KURZ, C., VOSKAMP, U., and WITTKE, V. 1999. "Globalization, value networks and national models," MIT IPC Globalization Working Paper 99–000.

BERGER, S., KURZ, C., STURGEON, T., VOSKAMP U., and WITTKE, V. (2001), "Globalization, production networks and national models of capitalism: on the possibilities of new productive systems and institutional diversity in an enlarging Europe," *SOFI-Mitteilungen* 29: 59–72.

BERGHAHN, V. R., ed. 1996. *German Big Business and Europe, 1918–1992*. New York: Berg Publishers.

BERNDT, C. 2000. "Regulation, power and scale: 'reworking' capital–labour relations in German SMEs," ESRC Centre for Business Research, University of Cambridge, Working Paper No. 157.

BLYTH, M. 2003. "Same as it never was: temporality and typology in the varieties of capitalism," *Comparative European Politics* 1(2): 215–25.

BOHLE, D., and GRESKOVITS B. 2004. "Capital, labor and the prospects of the European social model in the East," Central and Eastern Europe Working Paper Series, No. 58. Cambridge, Mass.: Harvard University, Center for European Studies.

BÖRSCH, A. 2007. "Institutional variation and coordination patterns in CMEs: Swiss and German corporate governance in comparison," in B. Hancké, M. Rhodes, and M. Thatcher, eds., *Beyond Varieties of Capitalism: Conflict, Contradictions and Complementarities in the European Economy*. Oxford: Oxford University Press.

BOYER, R. 2005a. "Complementarity in regulation theory," *Socio-Economic Review* 3(2): 366–71.

—— 2005b. "How and why capitalisms differ," *Economy and Society* 34(4): 509–57.

BRONK, R. 2009. *The Romantic Economist*. Cambridge: Cambridge University Press.

CALLAGHAN, H. 2004. "The domestic politics of EU legislation: British, French and German attitudes towards takeover regulation, 1985–2003," paper presented to the Conference of Europeanists, Chicago.

CAMERON, D. 1984. "Social democracy, corporatism, labor quiescence and the representation of economic interests in advanced capitalist society," in J. Goldethorpe, ed., *Order and Conflict in Contemporary Capitalism*. Oxford: Clarendon, 143–78.

CARLIN, W., and SOSKICE D. 2006. *Macroeconomics: Imperfections, Institutions and Policies*. Oxford: Oxford University Press.

COATES, D. 2005. "Paradigms of explanation," in D. Coates, ed., *Varieties of Capitalism, Varieties of Approaches*. Houndmills: Palgrave-Macmillan, 1–25.

COEN, D., and HÉRITIER, A., eds. 2005. *Redefining Regulatory Regimes: Utilities in Europe*. Cheltenham: Edward Elgar.

CROUCH, C. 2005. *Capitalist Diversity and Change: Recombinant Governance and Institutional Entrepreneurs*. Oxford: Oxford University Press.

—— and FARRELL H. 2004. "Breaking the path of institutional development? Alternatives to the new determinism," *Rationality and Society* 16(1): 5–43.

CULPEPPER, P. D. 2003. *Creating Cooperation: How States Develop Human Capital in Europe*. Ithaca, NY: Cornell University Press.

DEEG, R. 2005a. "Path dependency, institutional complementarity, and change in national business systems," in G. Morgan, R. Whitley, and E. Moen, eds., *Changing Capitalisms? Internationalization, Institutional Change and Systems of Economic Organization* Oxford: Oxford University Press, 21–52.

—— 2005b. "Change from within: German and Italian finance in the 1990s," in W. Streeck and K. Thelen, eds., *Beyond Continuity: Institutional Change in Advanced Political Economies*. Oxford: Oxford University Press, 169–202.

—— 2005c. "Complementarity and institutional change: how useful a concept," discussion Paper SP 11 2005-21, Wissenschaftszentrum Berlin.

EICHENGREEN, B. 2007. *The European Economy Since 1945: Coordinated Capitalism and Beyond.* Princeton, NJ: Princeton University Press.

ESTÉVEZ-ABE, M. 2005. "Gender bias in skills and social policies: the varieties of capitalism perspective on sex segregation," in L. McCall and A. Orloff, eds., "Gender, class and capitalism," *Social Politics Special Issue* 12(2): 180–215.

European Commission. 2003. *2003 European Innovation Scoreboard: Technical Paper No. 2, Analysis of National Performances.* Brussels: European Commission–Enterprise Directorate-General.

EVANS, P., RUESCHMEYER, D., and SKOCPOL, T. 1985. *Bringing the State Back In.* Cambridge: Cambridge University Press.

FRANZESE, R. J., JR. 2002. *Macroeconomic Policies of Developed Democracies.* Cambridge: Cambridge University Press.

FRIEDEN, J. 1991. "Invested interests: the politics of national economic policies in a world of global finance," *International Organization* 45(4): 425–41.

GERSCHENKRON, A. 1962. *Economic Backwardness in Historical Perspective.* Cambridge, Mass.: Harvard University Press.

GOUREVITCH, P. A. 1986. *Politics in Hard Times: Comparative Responses to International Economic Crises.* Ithaca, NY: Cornell University Press.

——and HAWES, M. B. 2002. "The politics of choice among national production systems," in R. Boyer, ed., *L'Année de la régulation, No. 6.* Paris: Presses de Sciences Po, 241–70.

——and SHINN, J. 2005. *Political Power and Corporate Control: The New Global Politics of Corporate Governance.* Princeton: Princeton University Press.

GOYER, M. 2002. "The transformation of corporate governance in France and Germany: the role of workplace institutions," Max-Planck-Institut für Gesellschaftsforschung Working Paper 02/10, July.

——2007. "Capital mobility, varieties of institutional investors and the transforming stability of corporate governance in France and Germany," in B. Hancké, M. Rhodes, and M. Thatcher, eds., *Beyond Varieties of Capitalism: Conflict, Contradictions and Complementarities in the European Economy.* Oxford: Oxford University Press.

HACKETHAL, A., SCHMIDT, R. H., and TYRELL, M. 2005. "Banks and corporate governance: on the way to a capital market-based system?" *Corporate Governance* 11(3): 397–407.

HALL, P. 1986. *Governing the Economy.* Oxford: Oxford University Press.

——2005. "Institutional complementarity: causes and effects," *Socio-Economic Review* 3(2): 373–8.

——2007. "The evolution of varieties of capitalism in Europe," in B. Hancké, M. Rhodes, and M. Thatcher, eds., *Beyond Varieties of Capitalism: Conflict, Contradictions and Complementarities in the European Economy.* Oxford: Oxford University Press.

——and GINGERICH, D. W. 2004. "Varieties of capitalism and institutional complementarities in the macroeconomy: an empirical analysis," Max-Planck-Institut für Gesellschaftsforschung, Cologne, Discussion Paper 04/5.

——and SOSKICE, D., eds. 2001a. *Varieties of Capitalism: The Institutional Foundations of Comparative Advantage.* Oxford: Oxford University Press.

————2001b. "An introduction to varieties of capitalism," in P. A. Hall and D. Soskice, eds., *Varieties of Capitalism: The Institutional Foundations of Comparative Advantage.* Oxford: Oxford University Press, 1–68.

————2003. "Varieties of capitalism and institutional change: a response to three critics," *Comparative European Politics* 1(2): 241–50.

——and THELEN, K. 2005. "Institutional change in varieties of capitalism," paper prepared for presentation to the Annual Meeting of the American Political Science Association, Washington, DC, September 1, 2005.

HANCKÉ, B. 2001. "Revisiting the French model: coordination and restructruing in French industry," in P. A. Hall and D. Soskice, eds., *Varieties of Capitalism: The Institutional Foundations of Comparative Advantage*. Oxford: Oxford University Press, 307–36.

—— 2009. "Varieties of capitalism: introducing the debate," in B. Hancké, *Debating Varieties of Capitalism: A Reader*. Oxford: Oxford University Press.

—— and GOYER, M. 2005. "Degrees of freedom: rethinking the institutional analysis of economic change" in G. Morgan, R. Whitley, and E. Moen, eds., *Changing Capitalisms? Internationalization, Institutional Change and Systems of Economic Organization*. Oxford: Oxford University Press, 53–77.

—— RHODES, M., and THATCHER, M., eds. 2007. *Beyond Varieties of Capitalism: Conflict, Contradictions and Complementarities in the European Economy*. Oxford: Oxford University Press.

—— and SOSKICE, D. 1996. "Coordination and restructuring in large French firms: the evolution of French industry in the 1980s," discussion Paper 96-303, Wissenschaftszentrum Berlin.

HASSEL, A. 2007. "What does business want? Labour market reforms in CMEs and its problems," in B. Hancké, M. Rhodes, and M. Thatcher, eds., *Beyond Varieties of Capitalism: Conflict, Contradictions and Complementarities in the European Economy*. Oxford: Oxford University Press.

—— and REHDER, B. 2001. "Institutional change in the German wage bargaining system: the role of big companies," Max-Planck-Institut für Gesellschaftsforschung, Working Paper 01/9, December.

HAY, C. 2005. "Two can play at that game—or can they? Varieties of capitalism, varieties of institutionalism," in D. Coates, ed., *Varieties of Capitalism, Varieties of Approaches*. Houndmills: Palgrave-Macmillan, 106–21.

HERRIGEL, G. 1996. *Industrial Constructions: The Sources of German Industrial Power*. Cambridge: Cambridge University Press.

—— and WITTKE, V. 2005. "Varieties of vertical disintegration: the global trend towards heterogeneous supply relations and the reproduction of difference in US and German manufacturing," in G. Morgan, R. Whitley, and E. Moen, eds., *Changing Capitalisms? Internationalization, Institutional Change and Systems of Economic Organization*. Oxford: Oxford University Press.

HILFERDING, R. 1910 [1981]. *Finance Capital*. London: Routledge and Kegan Paul.

HOLLINGSWORTH, R., and BOYER, R., eds. 1997. *Contemporary Capitalism: The Embeddedness of Institutions*. Cambridge: Cambridge University Press.

HÖPNER, M. 2001. "Corporate governance in transition: ten empirical findings on shareholder value and industrial relations in Germany," Max-Planck-Institut für Gesellschafts-forschung, Discussion Paper, 01/5, October.

—— 2005. "What have we learnt? Complementarity, coherence and institutional change," *Socio-Economic Review* 3(2): 383–7.

—— 2006. "What is organized capitalism? The two dimensions of non-liberal capitalism," paper presented to the International Centre for Business and Politics conference on "Institutional Emergence, Stability and Change," Copenhagen Business School, June 1–2.

—— and KREMPEL, L. 2003. "The politics of the German company network," Max-Planck-Institut für Gesellschaftsforschung, Working Paper 03/9, September.

HOWELL, C. 2003. "Varieties of capitalism: and then there was one?" *Comparative Politics* 36 (1): 103–24.

INNES, A. 2005. "*State* retreat and democracy," paper presented at the workshop on "Post-communist State and Society: Transnational and National Politics," Maxwell School, Syracuse University. September 30 – October 1, 2005.

IVERSEN, T. 2005. *Capitalism, Democracy and Welfare*. Cambridge: Cambridge University Press.

——2007. "Economic shocks and varieties of government responses," in B. Hancké, M. Rhodes, and M. Thatcher, eds., *Beyond Varieties of Capitalism: Conflict, Contradictions and Complementarities in the European Economy*. Oxford: Oxford University Press.

——ROSENBLUTH, F., and SOSKICE, D. 2005. "Divorce and the gender division of labor in comparative perspective," in L. McCall, and A. Orloff, eds., "Gender, class and capitalism," *Social Politics* Special Issue 12(2): 216–42.

——and SOSKICE, D. 2006. "Electoral institutions, parties and the politics of class: why some democracies distribute more than others," *American Political Science Review* 100(2): 165–81.

JACKSON, G., and DEEG, R. 2006. "How many varieties of capitalism? Comparing the comparative institutional analysis of capitalist diversity," Max-Planck-Institut für Gesellschaftsforschung, Discussion Paper 06/2, Cologne.

——HÖPNER, M., and KURDELBUSCH, A. 2005. "Corporate governance and employees in Germany: changing linkages, complementarities and tensions," in H. Gospel and A. Pendleton, eds., *Corporate Governance and Labour Management: An International Comparison*. Oxford: Oxford University Press, 84–121.

JONES, E., and RHODES, M. 2006. "Europe and the global challenge," in P. Heywood, E. Jones, M. Rhodes, and U. Sedelmeier, eds., *Developments in European Politics*. New York: Palgrave-Macmillan, 13–34.

KERR, C., DUNLOP, J. T., HARBISON, F. H., and MYERS, C. A. 1964. *Industrialism and Industrial Man*. Cambridge, Mass.: Harvard University Press.

KINDERMAN, D. 2005. "Pressure from without, subversion from within: the two-pronged German employer offensive," *Comparative European Politics* 3(4): 432–63.

KING, L. 2007. "Central European capitalism in comparative perspective," in B. Hancké, M. Rhodes, and M. Thatcher, eds., *Beyond Varieties of Capitalism: Conflict, Contradictions and Complementarities in the European Economy*. Oxford: Oxford University Press.

KOGUT, B., and WALKER, G. 2001. "The small world of Germany and the durability of national networks," *American Sociological Review* 66(3): 317–35.

KUISEL, R. F. 1981. *Capitalism and the State in Modern France: Renovation and Economic Management in the Twentieth Century*. Cambridge: Cambridge University Press.

LANE, C. 2003. "Changes in corporate governance of German corporations: convergence to the Anglo-American model?" ESRC Centre for Business Research, University Cambridge, Working Paper No. 259.

——2005. "Institutional transformation and system change: changes in the corporate governance of German corporations" in G. Morgan, R. Whitley, and E. Moen, eds., *Changing Capitalisms? Internationalization, Institutional Change and Systems of Economic Organization*. Oxford: Oxford University Press, 78–109.

LEVY, J. 2000. *Tocqueville's Revenge: Dilemmas of Institutional Reform in Post-Dirigiste France*. Cambridge, Mass.: Harvard University Press.

——2005. "Redeploying the state: liberalization and social policy in France," in *Beyond Continuity: Institutional Change in Advanced Political Economies*. Oxford: Oxford University Press, 103–26.

LINDBECK, A., and SNOWER, D. J. 1989. *The Insider–Outsider Theory of Employment and Unemployment*. Cambridge, Mass.: MIT Press.

McCALL, L., and ORLOFF, A., eds. 2005a. "Introduction to Special Issue of *Social Politics*: 'Gender, class, and capitalism.' " *Social Politics* 12(2): 159–69.

————2005b. "Gender, class and capitalism," *Social Politics* Special Issue 12(2).

MARTIN, C. J. 2005. "Beyond bone structure: historical institutionalism and the style of economic growth," in D. Coates, ed., *Varieties of Capitalism, Varieties of Approaches*. Houndmills: Palgrave-Macmillan, 63–82.

MOLINO, Ó., and RHODES, M. 2007. "The political economy of adjustment in mixed market economies: a study of Spain and Italy," in B. Hancké, M. Rhodes, and M. Thatcher, eds., *Beyond Varieties of Capitalism: Conflict, Contradictions and Complementarities in the European Economy*. Oxford: Oxford University Press.

NORTH, D. C. 1990. *Institutions, Institutional Change and Economic Performance*. Cambridge: Cambridge University Press.

OLSON, M. 1965. *The Logic of Collective Action: Public Goods and the Theory of Groups*. Cambridge, Mass.: Harvard University Press.

PANITCH, L., and GINDIN, S. 2005. "Euro-Capitalism and American empire," in D. Coates, ed., *Varieties of Capitalism, Varieties of Approaches*. Houndmills: Palgrave-Macmillan, 139–59.

PIORE, M., and SABEL, C. 1984. *The Second Industrial Divide*. New York: Basic.

PONTUSSON, J. 2005. "Varieties and commonalities of capitalism," in D. Coates, ed., *Varieties of Capitalism, Varieties of Approaches*. Houndmills: Palgrave-Macmillan, 163–88.

RADOSEVIC, S. 2005. "Are systems of innovation in Central and Eastern Europe inefficient?" paper presented at the conference on "Dynamics of Industry and Innovation: Organizations, Networks and Systems," Copenhagen, June 27–9.

REGINI, M. 2003. "Dal neo-corporativismo alle varietà dei capitalismi", *Stato e mercato* 3: 384–93.

RHODES, M. 1988. "The state and the modernisation of French industry," in J. Gaffney, ed., *France and Modernization*. Aldershot: Avebury, 66–95.

——— 2000. "Restructuring the British welfare state: between domestic constraints and global imperatives," in F. W. Scharpf and V. Schmidt, eds., *Welfare and Work in the Open Economy: Diverse Responses to Economic Challenges*. Oxford: Oxford University Press, 19–68.

——— 2005. "Varieties of capitalism and welfare states," *New Political Economy* 10(3): 363–70.

——— and VAN APELDOORN, B. 1997. "Capitalism versus capitalism in Western Europe," in M. Rhodes, P. Heywood, and V. Wright, eds., *Developments in West European Politics*. London: Macmillan Press Ltd, 171–89.

——— ——— 1998. "Capital unbound? The transformation of European corporate governance," *Journal of European Public Policy* 5(3): 406–27.

ROGOWSKI, R. 1989. *Commerce and Coalitions: How Trade Affects Domestic Political Alignments*. Princeton: Princeton University Press.

RUEDA, D. 2005. "Insider–outsider politics in industrialized democracies: the challenge to social democratic parties," *American Political Science Review* 99(1): 61–74.

SCHMIDT, V. 1996. *From State to Market? The Transformation of French Business and Government*. Cambridge: Cambridge University Press.

——— 2002. *The Futures of European Capitalism*. Oxford: Oxford University Press.

——— 2003. "French capitalism transformed, yet still a third variety of capitalism," *Economy and Society* 32(4): 526–54.

SCHMITTER, P. 1981. "Interest intermediation and regime governability in contemporary Western Europe and North America," in S. Berger, ed., *Organizing Interests in Western Europe*. New York: Cambridge University Press, 285–337.

SHONFIELD, A. 1965. *Modern Capitalism: The Changing Balance of Public and Private Power*. London: Oxford University Press.

SIEBERT, H. 2004. "Germany's social market economy: how sustainable is the welfare state?" American Institute for Contemporary German Studies/German–American Dialogue Working Paper Series, http://www.ifw-kiel.de/pub/siebert/pdf/Washington2003.pdf

SOSKICE, D. 1999. "Divergent production regimes: coordinated and uncoordinated market economies in the 1980s and 1990s," in H. Kitschelt, P. Lange, G. Marks, and J. D. Stephens, eds., *Continuity and Change in Contemporary Capitalism*. Cambridge: Cambridge University Press, 101–34.

—— 2005. "Varieties of capitalism and cross-national gender differences," in L. McCall and A. Orloff, eds., "Gender, class and capitalism," *Social Politics* Special Issue 12(2): 170–9.

STREECK, W. 2005a. "Rejoinder: on terminology, functionalism, (historical) institutionalism and liberalization," *Socio-Economic Review* 3(3): 577–87.

—— 2005b. "Requirements for a useful concept of complementarity," *Socio-Economic Review* 3(2): 363–6.

—— 2009. *Re-forming Capitalism: Institutional Change in the German Political Economy*. Oxford: Oxford University Press.

—— and THELEN, K. 2005. "Introduction: institutional change in advanced political economies" in W. Streeck and K. Thelen, eds., *Beyond Continuity: Institutional Change in Advanced Political Economies*. Oxford: Oxford University Press, 1–39.

SWENSON, P. 1989. *Fair Shares: Unions, Pay and Politics in Sweden and West Germany*. Ithaca, NY: Cornell University Press.

THATCHER, M. 2004. "Varieties of capitalism in an internationalized world: domestic institutional change in European telecommunications," *Comparative Political Studies* 37(7): 1–30.

—— 2005. "The third force? Independent regulatory agencies and elected politicians in Europe," *Governance: An International Journal of Policy, Administration and Institutions* 18 (3): 347–74.

—— 2007. "Reforming national regulatory institutions: the EU and cross-national variety in European network industries," in B. Hancké, M. Rhodes, and M. Thatcher, eds., *Beyond Varieties of Capitalism: Conflict, Contradictions and Complementarities in the European Economy*. Oxford: Oxford University Press.

THELEN, K., and KUME, I. 2006. "Co-ordination as a political problem in co-ordinated market economies," *Governance: An International Journal of Policy, Administration and Institutions* 19(1): 11–42.

—— and VAN WIJNBERGEN C. 2003. "The paradox of globalization: labor relations in Germany and beyond," *Comparative Political Studies* 36(8): 859–80.

VITOLS, S. 2004. "Changes in Germany's bank-based financial system: a varieties of capitalism perspective," Wissenschaftszentrum Berlin, Discussion Paper SP II 2004–03.

WATSON, M. 2003. "Ricardian political economy and the 'varieties of capitalism' approach: specialization, trade and comparative institutional advantage," *Comparative European Politics* 1(2): 227–40.

WHITLEY, R. 2005. "How national are business systems? The role of states and complementary institutions in standardizing systems of economic coordination and control at the national level", in G. Morgan, R. Whitley, and E. Moen, eds., *Changing Capitalisms? Internationalization, Institutional Change, and Systems of Economic Organization*. Oxford: Oxford University Press, 190–231.

—— 1999. *Divergent Capitalisms: The Social Structuring and Change of Business Systems*. Oxford: Oxford University Press.

WOOD, S. 2001. "Business, government, and patterns of labour market policy in Britain and the Federal Republic of Germany," in P. A. Hall and D. Soskice, eds., *Varieties of Capitalism: The Institutional Foundations of Comparative Advantage*. Oxford: Oxford University Press, 247–74.

ZYSMAN, J. 1983. *Governments, Markets and Growth: Financial Systems and the Politics of Industrial Change*. Ithaca, NY: Cornell University Press.

CHAPTER 6

THE GLOBAL FIRM

THE PROBLEM OF THE GIANT FIRM IN DEMOCRATIC CAPITALISM

COLIN CROUCH

POLITICAL theory has never satisfactorily resolved the ambiguities presented by the political role of the firm in a capitalist economy and democratic polity. On the one hand, the rules of the free market require a mutual separation of economy and polity; on the other, the individuals who constitute the leadership of firms enjoy the democratic rights of citizens to work for their political interests. They must therefore be expected to try to mobilize the resources of their firms in order to advance those interests, whether law tries to limit such practices in various ways or not. There is also a possibility of conflict among different important interests within firms, which means that the firm cannot be treated as a simple actor. It is indeed a political actor in a double sense: first, it may be active within the general polity; second, there is an internal politics of the firm, which may or may not be relevant to the issue of the firm's role in the wider polity. The general issues raised here are discussed elsewhere in this Handbook (see Hart, this volume). Here our particular concern is with the "giant" firm.

This in itself vague adjective can be made more scientific by giving it two specific attributes. A "giant" firm is one that is sufficiently dominant within its markets to be able to influence the terms of those markets by its own actions, using its organizational capacity to develop market-dominating strategies. Second, a giant firm will be active across more than one national jurisdiction. These two attributes intensify the general question of the importance to political theory of the role of the firm, as capacity for market-dominating strategy can include having a political strategy, and transnational corporations (TNCs) can sometimes play off national governments against each other. The full implications of both points will become clear during the following discussion.

First, some clarification is needed of these definitional criteria. In economic theory, firms respond to price signals from the market; they can develop strategy in the sense of moving to advantageous positions as indicated by those prices, but they are always price takers—of prices of stocks and shares, of labor, of supplies, of products. No one firm can by its sole actions affect a price: prices move in response to actions by large aggregates of firms and individuals. If this characteristic of the pure market is lacking, if some firms and individuals acting alone can produce a change in a price, there is a problem for both economic theory itself and for its political implications. There is a failure for theory, because the mathematical models on which economics is based assume large numbers of uncoordinated actors who can produce effects on prices only in aggregate. The political problem will be considered in more detail below. In brief, if firms are always dependent on the market, they do not present a problem of power. Indeed, economics has no use for a concept of power because it is assumed away in the conditions of the pure market. However, in practice firms who are able to affect prices by their sole actions do exist. They occupy monopolistic or oligopolistic positions in markets and therefore do not conform to the criterion of needing to be part of an uncoordinated aggregate of firms in order to affect prices. This can happen at very local levels, as in the case of a single shop in an isolated village, and by itself is not enough to define a giant firm. For this reason we add the second definitional criterion, that the firm operates over more than one national jurisdiction, that is, it is trans- or multinational. Such corporations develop large organizational structures, which they use in order to develop market-changing strategies.

Both definitional criteria are needed to constitute a "giant" firm: market dominance and multi-national character. There are today many examples of firms that have branches in a number of countries but which are relatively small within their markets and subject to the full weight of the laws of supply and demand.

So far emphasis has been placed on the capacity of the giant firm to act alone. Different issues are raised by the possibility that they may act together. Some of these issues are particularly important for politics, as is the decision that firms might make whether to act together or separately. These questions will also be considered below.

Three potential resolutions exist in the political theory literature to the problem of how to subject the giant firm to political science analysis. Under pluralist theory, the existence of high levels of competition in both economy and polity prevent concentrations of either economic or political power, and thereby limit or even cancel out any undue influence exercised by particular firms. Under neo-corporatist theory, firms exercise their political influence through formally constituted associations. This both maintains a level playing field among firms, at least within the sectors represented by an association, and makes transparent the way in which influence is exercised. In the theory of international political economy (IPE), the firm is treated more seriously, but is seen as a simple economic actor maximizing its profits, exercising political influence only in order to achieve that goal. This last comes closest to confronting issues of political analysis raised by the giant firm, but does so by "importing" economic theory into political analysis.

All three approaches have their limitations. It will be argued below that no solution exists for the analysis of these firms within the political theory of nation state-based democracy, and that the only way forward requires acceptance that there is a non-democratic component of politics in advanced capitalism. This acceptance has important normative implications, but the task of the present article is limited to considering the analytical issues.

We shall initially consider why the political role of the giant firm presents a problem for theory. Subsequent sections then consider the solutions presented respectively by pluralist, neo-corporatist, and IPE theory. A final section explores a possible analytical solution.

THE POLITICAL ANALYSIS OF THE FIRM

In the perfectly competitive economy understood by neoclassical theory the individual firm does not need to be treated as either an economic or a political actor. Economically the firm is nothing other than a nexus of markets, a point where resources in a number of markets come together and are traded off against each other. The firm's behavior can be read off from the signals that the market gives to its decision-makers about the most rational path that it should follow given its taken for granted goal of profit maximization. Firms that do not maximize rationally in this way will be out-performed by those that do and will disappear from the market. In fact, the concept of "actor" is not used in economic theory, since human actors are little other than calculating machines for working out the appropriate logic of maximization in any given situation. Pure economic theory and indeed practical commercial law in the Anglo-American tradition treat firms as particular kinds of individuals, because these schools of thought do not have a concept of an organization that pays attention to the internal complexities of organization as such.

As noted above, it is a condition of the perfect market that all individuals (including firms) are price takers and not price makers: no one individual can by its actions affect the price of any commodity. Prices result as mathematical properties from the transactions of masses of individuals. If there is evidence that, say, the actions of an individual investor have begun to influence the price of a firm's shares, then that is evidence that the market is not pure.

While economic theory does not have much to say about politics, some implications for political behavior can be read off from this neoclassical model. First, in a pure market economy there is a strong separation between politics and economics. All but extreme libertarian forms of neoclassical economics recognize a role for the state in safeguarding the rules necessary for the market to operate: enforcement of contracts; maintenance of currency; maintenance of rules of corporate accountability and transparency. But this role itself requires that the worlds of economy and polity do not interfere with each other. Governments should not interfere with markets, or the mathematical rationality of price setting will be disturbed; individuals active in the market should not use their economic resources to interfere in politics to get privileged outcomes for themselves, or this too will distort the market. There is a vulnerable spot in this account, in that, individuals being free to use their resources as they wish in the democratic polity,[1] and economic resources being capable of being used politically, there are no means to prevent individuals from using their wealth in a way that produces mutual interference by economic and political forces.

This is the fundamental problem of the political role of the firm: the market requires the separation of polity and economy, but political and economic resources can be translated into each other. Wealth can be used to buy political influence, and political influence can be used to purchase favorable conditions for a firm. This process is self-reinforcing, which threatens to exempt it from the diminishing returns to scale that are assumed by economic theory to prevent the long-term reinforcement of trends.

Neoclassical economics has its own answer to this, which is then paralleled by analogy in pluralist political theory: in the pure market economy, economic inequalities are limited, and therefore the influence exercised by any one individual will be quickly canceled out by others. Since in political debate free markets are often considered to be associated with inequalities, this may seem a surprising statement. It is therefore important to understand the basic egalitarianism of the pure market. An essential feature of such a market is that entry barriers to any one activity are low: if barriers are high, competition is reduced and becomes imperfect and the market is no longer pure. In a pure market, if larger profits or incomes arise in a particular sector than are available elsewhere, individuals in other sectors will quickly switch their resources to the more profitable one until, as a result of competition and the operation of the law of supply and demand, profit and income levels reach the mean of other sectors, at which point there is no longer an incentive to shift to it. In the long run, therefore, a pure market economy is one without sharp inequalities. As a consequence, no one will be able to use extreme wealth to accumulate political privileges.[2]

In practice, actually existing capitalist economies do not conform to the pure neoclassical model. Barriers to entry can be high and irremediable, as where vast investment is required for research and development or where extensive distribution networks have to be developed before a firm can establish itself. Also, information, a resource fundamental to the operation of market rationality, is itself unequally distributed. To operate efficiently in capital markets, for example, it is necessary to have kinds of information that can be provided only by highly skilled teams of experts; and it takes a high level of existing resources to be able to construct such teams in the first place. Therefore, those firms and individuals with the resources to acquire professional advice are able to make better use of information concerning capital markets than those who lack them, leading to a spiraling exacerbation of inequalities rather than the tendency for them to diminish predicted by neoclassical theory on the strength of assumptions of low entry barriers. High entry barriers both create and are created by "giant" firms, according to the first attribute that we have given such firms of being organizations capable of strategy and acting beyond the strict constraints of the market (Yoffie and Bergenstein 1985).

The fact that the firm, particularly the large one, is an organization and not just a nexus of markets was first recognized in economic theory in the 1930s, in the theory of the firm developed by Robert Coase (1937). The central idea is most easily understood through the labor market. When a firm wants to make use of labor, it can do this by making a contract with some individuals that they will perform certain tasks in exchange for a set fee; if, when that task is completed, another one is needed, a new contract is made. This is common practice for tasks that a firm needs only sporadically, such as formulation of a new advertising strategy. When firms operate in this way, they can be understood fully by pure market analysis. However, when they want continuous and repeated performance of a set of tasks for an indefinite future, they are likely to find it inefficient to keep making new contracts and introducing new workers to the firm. They therefore usually make general contracts, known as employment contracts, under which the supplier of labor services is guaranteed payment for a prolonged period in exchange for placing him- or herself under the general authority of the employer, carrying out such tasks as the employer may require. These are the terms under which the majority of people in modern economies work. The firm here becomes more than a nexus of markets and is an organization with a hierarchy through which orders are transmitted rather than contracts made.

The main use that orthodox economics makes of the theory of the firm is in considering a trade-off that confronts companies. Use of the market enables frequent testing of prices and quality being offered in the external market, at the expense of possibly costly market searches and training to induct new employees and suppliers in the ways of the firm. Operation through hierarchy ensures continuity and reduced transaction costs at the expense of some inefficiency through neglect of market testing. Most large firms will reappraise the trade-offs in their use of markets and hierarchy from time to time in the operation of their businesses. Economics can also analyze imperfect competition and information asymmetries; it is certainly not limited to the study of perfectly functioning markets. However, it has been left to unconventional ("institutional") economists and organization theorists to consider some of the wider implications of the idea of the firm as an organization, in particular the political implications.[3]

Within the scope of neoclassical analysis, Oliver Williamson has developed the original Coasian concepts, and in particular the idea of transaction costs, to explore a wide range of organizational issues affecting firms (Williamson 1975, 1985; Williamson and Masten 1995). These prominently include the fact that information, seen in simple neoclassical theory as something which rational actors necessarily possess, is in reality difficult to acquire. One reason for firms developing and deploying organizational resources is to be able to acquire information. An interesting and important example of this concerns the way in which, for example, staff members of commissioning firms and their contractors, engaged together on complex tasks, often create informal shared organizational structures bridging their respective employing organizations. According to neoclassical theory one side is the principal, the other the agent; they must keep themselves separate and relate only through the terms of the contract, which will have anticipated everything necessary for governance of the relationship. In reality, information about the task was always incomplete, so the contract was also incomplete. The gaps can be filled only by close, informal collaboration. As we shall see below, this idea is capable of extension to the study of relations between governments and contractors, with political implications not particularly anticipated by transaction-cost economics, but fully compatible with it.

Large firms that have developed the ability to act as organizations, choosing when to go straight to market and when to use organizational resources, have acquired a capacity for strategy. They have not liberated themselves fully from the market; they remain subject to it in order to buy and sell successfully. But they also have some ability to act proactively, to shape markets, and to determine how they will respond to them. For example, instead of responding passively to market signals that there is a demand for a certain product, they will mount aggressive marketing and advertising campaigns to *create* demand. This is what entrepreneurship is all about.

Competition law, especially in the USA, has accommodated itself to the inevitability of the domination of large firms and limited competition. Classical US antitrust law, developed in the first part of the twentieth century, aimed at breaking up major accumulations of corporate power, so that there was a limit to how far any one firm or group of firms could go in dominating a particular set of markets. One of the strongest examples of this was US banking law, which for many decades prevented US banks from having branches outside an individual state. It is no coincidence that US pluralist political theory (see below) developed from exactly this intellectual environment. It was as essential for democracy as it was for economic efficiency that there should not be concentrations of power so strong that they faced no effective competition. To the extent that economic power could be a major source of political power too, antitrust policy served the purpose of protecting democratic pluralism as much as it did market competition.

It proved impossible to maintain all markets with low entry barriers and full competition, and by the late twentieth century American law and political practice had changed. Economic theorists, principally at the University of Chicago, and corporate lawyers defending antitrust suits for large corporations developed a new set of principles that abandoned earlier perspectives that had insisted on the need for actual competition and numbers of competitors if the liberal capitalist model was to work. The doctrine of "consumer welfare" was developed, which argued that, if it could be shown that economies of scale resulting from the existence of a small number of firms meant lower prices than if there was a large number of competing firms, then consumers' welfare could be considered to be better protected by the domination of markets by a small number of giant enterprises than by a purer neoclassical market with many producers (see Bork 1978 and Posner 2001 for leading expositions of this view). Such arguments were used successfully in cases before the courts to roll back the antitrust bias of US corporate law (Schmidt and Rittaler 1989). It can be argued that the strong capacity for judge-made law given by the common law system in the USA, together with the ability of wealth to secure the services of the best lawyers, constitutes one of the ways in which giant corporations in that country exercise a power over law-making (van Waarden 2002).

European Union competition policy, paradoxically trying harder to hold on to the earlier US model than the US itself, has developed a kind of second-best policy under which market-dominant firms are required to maintain the possibility of survival for competitors in some aspects of their operations. This can be seen in such measures as the EU's insistence that Microsoft maintain access to its platforms so that competitors can produce software that is compatible with them.

In several countries, particularly the UK, a new regulatory approach to monopoly has also developed in those industries that had previously been maintained in state ownership because of the difficulty of maintaining effective competition within them. Instead of requiring the break-up of monopolies, regulatory agencies develop mathematical models to work out the prices and practices that would emerge if a particular industry were competitive, even if in practice it is monopolistic—as for example with privatized railways and water services.[4] The agencies would then have the power to require the monopolist to follow these "as if" competitive approaches. Unlike EU competition law, which requires the survival of actual competitors, this approach leaves the monopolist unchallenged as an organization but required to act as though there were competitors.

It is not our task here to examine the economic efficacy of these different approaches to grappling with monopoly and imperfect competition, but to assess their political implications. As noted above, economic and political power can be translated into each other; this is why it is so difficult in practice to maintain the separateness alongside interdependence required by liberal capitalism. Because they do not exist in perfect markets, giant firms generate very high concentrations of wealth. Not only can they convert this wealth into political influence, but they can use the capacity for strategy given to them by their organizational hierarchies to pursue political purposes and to become political actors. Seeing the firm as an organization and not just as a nexus of markets enables us to perceive the implications of this for political theory. Doctrines of consumer welfare and the role of regulatory agencies may check the economic implications of corporate gigantism, but they cannot address these political implications. To consider this further we need to examine the responses that political theory had made to the existing problem of the firm in general within the democratic polity.

THE RESPONSE OF PLURALIST THEORY

The theory of political pluralism comes from the same intellectual stable as neoclassical economics, though it lacks the elegance of the economic argument, being based on a large number of empirical possibilities rather than the single theoretical one of the existence of pure markets. According to this theory, to prevent major inequalities of political power arising, it is important that power resources are scattered around a society in autonomous centers, and not aggregated into large blocks. In such a situation, all decision-making requires the assembly of numbers of these centers. Different classes, religious faiths, ethnic groups might all constitute the building blocks of such a system; and different elements of these blocks might separate off and join with others if they consider that the dominant forces of a currently governing block are accumulating too much power. As with economic theory, protection against the abuses that might flow from powerful concentrations of resources is found in large numbers of separate participants in the system. Also as with economic theory, a more or less egalitarian economy is one of the conditions for political pluralism, as a polity in which economic resources were very unequally shared would be likely to be one in which political power was also concentrated, economic resources being so easily capable of conversion into political ones.

The rise of giant firms clearly challenges the balance implied here, in ways that current purely economic regulatory approaches, which leave the "giants" in place, do not address. Political scientists have not ignored this problem. Thirty years ago two of the most prominent exponents of both the analytical and normative concepts of American political pluralism— Charles Lindblom (1977) and Ronald Dahl (1982)— both warned that the large corporation was becoming a threat to the balance of democratic pluralism. Lindblom based his analysis, not so much on the implications of the size of individual firms, as on the absolute dependence of governments for their popularity and legitimacy on economic success, and their perception that they depended for that success on the business community. Governments were therefore likely to listen intently and uncritically to whatever that community said it wanted from public policy.

Dahl and Lindblom were writing when the current trend towards economic globalization following the international deregulation of financial markets was just beginning. This, the second attribute of giant firms established above, has further enhanced their capacity to translate their economic strength into political power in two ways. First, they have some capacity to "regime shop," that is to direct their investments to countries where they find the most favorable rules. Second, the global economy itself constitutes a space where governmental actors are (compared with the national level within stable nation states) relatively weak, and corporations therefore have more autonomy. There are many studies of the political implications of these developments. Some authors have seen it as a benign development, with corporations being likely to act more rationally and creatively than states (Ohmae 1985). Others have been highly critical, as had Dahl and Lindblom at national level, seeing a shift away from democracy to the power of business. There are also many examples of more analytical studies, concerned to study rather than evaluate the phenomenon. Baumgartner and Jones (1993) and Baumgartner and Leech (1998) looked generally at the US economy. Mörth (2006) and Jacobsson and Sahlin-Andersson (2006) studied the role of "soft" regulation, regulatory forms which depend on voluntary cooperation by the firms being regulated. Botzem and Quack (2006) and Morgan (2006) examined respectively the power of major Anglo-American accountancy firms and law firms in determining regulation and standards in the global economy; when we think of "giant" firms today it is essential to include enterprises of this kind and not just manufacturers and banks. Engwall (2006) looked generally at the role of giant firms in global governance.

The first of the arguments here seems straightforward: if firms have a choice between two countries for maintaining their investments, they should be predicted to choose that which presents better opportunities for profit maximization, which will mean lower costs, and therefore lower levels of corporate taxation, lower labor protection and social standards, lower levels of environmental and other regulation. In the short run we should therefore expect a shift of investments from the more costly to the cheaper country. In the longer run the more costly country should be expected to adjust its own standards downwards in order to be able to compete for investments with the cheaper country. The result would be a general lowering of standards to meet the preferences of multinational enterprises—a process often known as "the race to the bottom."

In practice matters are not as simple as this. Existing investments in plant, distribution, and supplier networks, as well as social links, are not so easily moved. Firms have what are called "sunk costs" in their existing locations, and in order to move existing investments from one jurisdiction to another they need confidence that profits in the new location will be sufficient to outweigh these costs (Sutton 1991).[5] The more likely threat is not so much a transfer of existing investments as a preference in favor of the cheaper country for future new investments being planned by the firm. Even here, there is not necessarily a consistent preference among firms for the cheapest locations. Firms, especially those that are capable of strategy, choose in which market niches to locate themselves, and this does not always mean a preference for the lowest costs. Chobanova (2007), in a study of investment by western European giant food industry firms in Central and Eastern European countries, found surprising results of this kind. High quality of the good or service being produced is often a criterion, and this may require highly paid staff with good working conditions, or a strong social infrastructure, requiring high taxation. It is therefore not the case that high-wage, high-tax economies have lost out in competition for direct inward investment, as the strong performance of the Nordic countries shows.

Nevertheless, this argument still places the initiative with the firms: it is their market strategy that determines (or at least strongly affects) whether particular government policies will be "rewarded" with investment or not. Globalization does not necessarily means a race to the bottom, but it does increase the power of firms in setting public policy.

The second argument maintains that, there being no government at global level, MNCs are left fairly free to make what rules they like, including deals they make between each other for setting standards or rules of trade. There appears to be no higher level than deals among firms for making regulations at the global level; and since this is the level at which there is currently most economic dynamism, this global level of firm-determined regulation feeds back into national levels, undermining government authority.

This argument too may be exaggerated, as there clearly are elements, albeit weak, of a civil society emerging at global level (Djelic and Sahlin-Andersson 2006; Scholte 2007; Levy and Kaplan 2008). Alongside the growth of the global economy has come a growth of regulatory activity by international agencies whose members comprise national governments and which therefore constitute delegated governmental authority. Since the post-war period some (but not much) of the work of the United Nations, and the activities of the World Bank and International Monetary Fund (IMF) have had some authority of this kind. The Organization for Economic Cooperation and Development (OECD), for long mainly a source of data and statistics on national economies, has gradually acquired more of an international policy-coordinating role—for example, in the field of corruption in governments' business deals with MNCs. Most recently, the World Trade Organization has begun to regulate terms of international trade, though its authority extends more over governments than over corporations. Finally, at a level between the nation state and the global level itself there has been a growth of intergovernmental organizations regulating economic affairs in a more detailed way across world regions: the European Union (EU); the Association of South-East Asian Nations (ASEAN); the North American Free Trade Area (NAFTA); the organization of South American states called Mercosur. However, of these only the EU has developed extensive policies across a wide range of fields.

Global economic space is therefore not entirely without regulation, but individual giant firms do occupy a more directly regulatory role at this level than at national level in a number of areas. An important example is standardization (Mattli 2001; Schepel 2005; Botzem and Quack 2006). The standardization of products and components is essential for the conduct of a market economy, as it is a major means for lowering entry barriers. For example, if individual firms were able to patent the design of electrical plugs and sockets, dominant firms could ensure that wall sockets in domestic and commercial premises would accept only the plugs of their patented design, preventing competition by creating an entry barrier of having the owners of premises install more than one type of socket if competitors' plugs were to be used.

In the case of the example given, standardization has been at the national (or to some extent EU) level, giving the users of electrical equipment some inconvenience when they move between countries. In other cases (such as mobile telephones) standardization exists at world-regional level, with some inter-authority cooperation at global level. The key players here are both giant firms (who produce the equipment concerned), national standards authorities acting in collaboration, and the International Standards Organization (ISO), which comprises representatives of governments and trade associations.

However, there are important areas of the economy where individual giant firms set their own standards with little reference to international or national authorities, and doing so in a manner deliberately intended to raise entry barriers against competitors. This is particularly likely to happen in high-technology areas where product innovation is so rapid that there is no time to secure agreement on a standard among a wide range of different governments. For this reason this form of standard setting has become accepted, though from a strict neoclassical point of view it threatens market competition. The frequent disputes between the European Commission and Microsoft are examples of this issue: Microsoft establishes de facto standards for computer software because of its global monopoly position; the Commission regards these corporate standards as erecting excessive market entry barriers to competitors, and therefore requires Microsoft to facilitate access to its platforms by other firms.

In other cases, where single firms are not sufficiently powerful to impose global standards, groups of them may form and together produce standards and regulation. An outstanding example of this, already referred to above, concerns the recent more or less global imposition of a system of corporate accounting devised by an association of accounting firms (Botzem and Quack 2006). This might look like an instance of corporatism (see below) at a transnational level. In practice, however, the association concerned comprises just the "big four" UK and US accountancy firms.

It is clear that classical pluralist theory cannot cope with these developments.

Neo-Corporatist Theory

When Dahl considered the inability of pluralist theory to deal adequately with the political role of firms in the modern US economy, he looked for potential solutions in the organized capitalism of the Nordic economies. Here, firms exercised political influence mainly through business associations, partly at the sectoral level, but partly through peak associations representing the whole private sector. Because this representation was formal and open, it could be used to impose some kind of collective social responsibility on member firms in exchange for any success of their lobbying activities. In addition, lobbying through associations maintained a level playing field among firms, at least within a sector, and could not be used to secure anti-competitive privileges for individual companies.

Dahl was here moving from US pluralist theory to the more European approach of neo-corporatist analysis. While most often used for the analysis of relations between organized workers and organized employers (e.g. Crouch 1993; Traxler, Blaschke, and Kittel 2004), the concept of interest representation through organizations that simultaneously lobbied and imposed codes of behavior on members could also be used more generally to describe the politics of business in certain contexts. In addition to the Nordic countries, it has been mainly applied to Germany, Austria, the Netherlands, and Japan. While neo-corporatism might avoid some of the polit-ical problems presented by single-firm political action, it presents a new one that whole sectors might become privileged at the expense of others, or functional economic interests privileged over other kinds of interest (for example, the environ-ment). As Mancur Olson (1982) argued, in a market economy organizations of particular interests operate by means of rent-seeking behavior: extracting gains for their members from the general public. They would abstain from this only if their membership was so extensive within the society concerned ("encompassing" in Olson's term) that they must internalize any negative consequences of their action: there is not enough of the society outside the group's membership on to which negative consequences can be dumped. This tended to be the case where neo-corporatist structures operated most successfully (Crouch 2006a).

Olson's concept of encompassingness assumes a manageable and definable uni-verse across which organizations can be said to be encompassing. His theory, and all others that concern the logic of neo-corporatist stability, hold only to the extent that there is a relatively bounded universe linking fiscal and monetary policy, and the scope of firms. Throughout most of the history of industrial societies the nation state has provided such a universe. Neo-corporatism is therefore severely challenged by the rise of the global economy and in particular the global firm.

Neo-corporatist organizations can respond positively to this kind of situation by shifting their point of activity to a higher level, such as the EU, joining forces with their opposite numbers in other nation states to recapture encompassingness. But incentives to do this have been rather weak. Governments, trade unions, and smaller firms remain organized primarily at national levels, and governments and unions have to respond to national constituencies. MNCs operate at the global level, but have little incentive to participate, as they can operate alone. It is difficult for any system of organized interests that is not itself global to achieve encompassingness.

A further problem with neo-corporatism is that, being based on associations representing existing industries and sectors, it loses effectiveness at times of rapid economic and technical change. During such times the old, organized sectors of the economy become less important—or, worse, their organizations try to slow down a decline that will be inevitable. Meanwhile, new sectors are not yet organized, and may not even see themselves as sectors. For example, what we now see as a biotechnical industry existed for several years before its existence as such was noted. Now, it and other new industries, such as information technology, have acquired self-awareness and have developed organizations. But it remains the case that, at any moment during a period of high change and innovation, old, declining sectors will be better represented than new, dynamic ones.

A further cause of a decline in associations to the benefit of individual giant firms has been an unanticipated consequence of neo-liberalism and globalization: a trend away from self-regulation by business interests to statutory regulation. This happens because pure markets, particularly transnational ones, require transparent, easily comparable behavioral rules. National associational regulation cannot provide this, but statutes formulated to common standards can (Moran 2006). This can be seen particularly clearly in the financial sector (Lütz 2003). In some cases, particularly perhaps the UK, a decline in the importance of labor issues, the core of associational activity in earlier decades, reduced firms' reliance on collective action (Moran 2006).

In such a situation, individual giant firms, rather than associations, become the main representatives of business interests—as demonstrated above with the case of standardization, and as analyzed by a range of perceptive authors (Grant 1981, 1984, 2000; Coen 1997, 1998; Coen and Grant 2006b; Schneider 2006). This fundamentally important development for both economy and polity reduces the level playing field among firms, considerably restricting the chances of influence for small ones, who have often relied on large corporations to bear the main costs of sustaining business associations. Individual giant firms, in contrast, are given a strong incentive and possibility to act politically.[6] This issue has been particularly important in certain Western European economies (Austria, Germany, the Netherlands, the Nordic countries), where associations have historically been important in business politics, and where major change is now taking place (Coen 1997; Streeck 1997; Schneider 2006). In the UK, where associations have always been weak, there is now evidence of them becoming even weaker, again to the advantage of individual giant corporations (Moran 2006).

The dominance of firm-level over associational types of organization also takes a further form: regulatory activity itself, normally thought of as a public function, can be marketized, and firms might offer regulatory services to an industry, firms essentially buying their own regulation. This is again especially important at the transnational level, where individual national regulators do not have adequate reach. This development is seen particularly strongly in the rise of ratings agencies, which assess the performance of firms and even governments according to various financial or other indicators (Kerwer 2001; Coen and Thatcher 2005). These agencies are necessarily themselves giant firms. It might be objected that impartial regulation is not likely to emerge where the regulated is the customer of the regulator; and indeed, the ratings agencies came under criticism for not noticing the high risks that banks were taking in the activities that led to the 2007–8 credit crisis.

There can therefore be no formal guarantees that extremely skewed influence will be excluded from a democratic political system through either pluralism or neo-corporatism. Problems of entry barriers blocking access to resources and capacity to be heard apply to both.

INTERNATIONAL POLITICAL ECONOMY

"Political economy" has been a label adopted by a number of different groups of scholars trying to bridge the gap that exists between neoclassical economics and political theory—a gap that is particularly damaging to attempts to tackle the problem being identified in this chapter. They are agreed in taking seriously the political implications of corporate behavior, and more generally of economic action, but beyond that there are important divisions. Some come from a background in mainstream political analysis (e.g. Grant 1981, 1984; Strange 1986, 1996; Strange and Stopford 1991; Mitchell, Hansen, and Jepsen 1997; Pauly and Reich 1997; Coen 1999; Parkinson, Kelly, and Gamble 2000), or sociology (Trigilia 1999; Fligstein 2001). They tend to be critical of the unwillingness of neoclassical economics to embrace variables adequately complex to tackle these questions, but as a result their work often lacks a theoretical focus. A further group, which usually adopts the name of international political economy (IPE), takes the opposite approach, and seeks to solve this problem through the use of rational choice theory, adopting the theoretical apparatus of economics, applying it to political issues (in general, Tullock 1980; Becker 1985; applied specifically to the question of the political role of firms, Mitchell and Munger 1991; Austin-Smith 1994; Grossmann 2001; Broscheid 2006). There is a cost to this achievement, in that an economics approach requires a simplification of motivation and of the identity of actors. Firms are therefore conceived as acting politically with their normal profit-maximization motive, which means that more complex, or more purely political, actions are usually, though not necessarily, ignored. Also, just as orthodox economics has some difficulty with the idea of a firm as an internally complex organization, so IPE authors do not normally treat firms as the sites of intra-organizational political conflict.

BEYOND THE "LOBBYING" MODEL: TOWARDS A NEW APPROACH

From the perspective of pluralist political theory, firms constitute "lobbies", and the kind of role that giant firms are able to play in the global economy makes them disturbingly powerful lobbies, threatening the balance of both democracy and pluralism. This was the burden of the critique of Dahl and Lindblom, and of a large number of subsequent critics. The main alternative view is that: (i) provided the economy remains a market one, these firms are still constrained to accept consumer sovereignty in their economic activities; (ii) provided the political system is transparent, firms' lobbying activities will be subject to criticism and public debate; and

(iii) the activities of firms bring jobs and new consumer products, and so public welfare is enhanced by even their political lobbying activities.

There are some studies of the politics of individual giant firms seen as lobbies. Examples are Grant (2007) on the chemicals industry and the challenge of environmental politics; and Singer (2008) on the role of privately owned military firms. Not surprisingly, these and similar studies are concentrated among industries that are politically salient, either (as in the examples cited) because of their connection with major political issues or national security, or because the industry (or even the individual companies) are so large within a country that their health is relevant to the national economy, and therefore to the polity. There is considerable literature on this latter issue from earlier periods, when governments were concerned to establish "national champion" firms through strategies of "industrial patriotism" in key sectors (such as ICI Ltd. in the UK in the 1920s (Kennedy 1993: ch. 3), or French national and European policy until very recently (Hayward 1986, 1995)). The response of governments in both Europe and the USA to the credit crisis of 2007–8 is likely to lead to a revival of such studies, as considerable state assistance was given to selected firms, primarily in the banking and automotive industries.

But this kind of activity cannot really be subsumed under the concepts of either lobbying or corporatism. The firms are too much insiders to the governmental process to be called lobbies; and they operate alone and not in associations, as is necessary for corporatism. To embrace this we need to reconceptualize the large firm as a political entity, which in turn requires rethinking the scope of the political and its characteristic institutions.

The standard model of a polity in political science, rational choice theory, constitutional law, and the assumptions of everyday political discussion alike, takes the following form. At the peak is the sovereign entity, the state. These states recognize no authority above them: that is what defines them as the units of the global system and as the peaks of their own sub-systems. It is taken for granted that these states are "nation states," that is that they constitute a large area of usually coterminous territory, both open country and urban centers, with a population that recognizes that it is joined by certain ties to form a "nation," even if these are sometimes little more than being part of the same territorial state. These states do make treaties with each other, and sometimes these treaties can be very demanding in the terms they impose and strict in enforcing sanctions in the case of disobedience of the terms. The treaties may even construct organizations charged with the task of enforcing their terms and charting the common tasks that should be confronted by the treaty's members. These treaties therefore constitute important de facto compromises with the concept of "sovereignty," but because they are treaties (contracts among equals) rather than constitutions (implying subordination within an organizational hierarchy) they are held not to make *de jure* compromises. Within each nation state there will be regional and local levels of political authority; these are subordinate within the organizational hierarchy of the state and are bound together through its structures, not through treaties.

The nation states, the structures produced by treaties among them, and the states' internal sub-structure of delegated authority constitute the only "political" entities within society. This does not mean that they can do what they like. Where the state is defined as being one within the rule of law, the things it may do and the powers it may take in relation to its citizens or others are carefully prescribed and limited. Within a liberal polity citizens have opportunities to lobby for, request, demand, beseech various actions (or abstention from action) by the state; and, as we have seen, some organizations (in particular, giant firms) can attain such power that governments have little practical choice than to give in to their demands. But they remain "lobbies," as the political power to implement the demands remains in the hands of government. In the terminology of an earlier age, these lobbies constitute "over mighty subjects," but it is still possible to see an important formal difference between the "subject" making a demand and the constituted authority responding to it.

This framework has become inadequate for analyzing the early twenty-first-century giant firm for the following reasons:

1. The framework assumes that those engaged in lobbying are members of the polity of the nation state concerned, or physically within it and therefore subject to its authority for the time being. This is not the case with MNCs bargaining over the terms of their investments. International law requires firms to have a place somewhere on the planet where they have their formal location, but from that base they can deal with governments all over the world, never putting themselves into a position of subordination to their authority, unless and until they set up facilities. During the crucial period of negotiations, where they are deciding among a number of potential locations for an investment, they remain external and therefore do not "lobby" for terms, an action implying at least formal subordination. Their relations are more like those of ambassadors of other states, but they cannot be assimilated to this concept as it belongs only to the world of political entities.

2. It is difficult to apply the concept of a lobby to the relationship of large global firms to a global polity seen as constituted by nation states and organizations formed by treaties among them. This can perhaps be seen most clearly in that autonomous role in standard-setting of individual corporations, which is a kind of legislative activity. They exist out there *alongside* the international and transnational agencies, not generally subordinate to them.

3. When large corporations from the advanced countries invest in very poor countries, there is usually a major imbalance between the institutions of the corporations and those of the local state (Dixon, Drakakis-Smith, and Watts 1986; Rondinelli 2002; Ite 2004). The former will be well equipped and staffed, with a high level of resources, and with clear hierarchies and internal procedures. The local state is likely to have very low levels of resources and poor means of internal communications and enforcement. In such circumstances it is very difficult for the local state to live up to the legal fiction that it constitutes an "authority" and the investing firm a private entity subject to its authority.

The firm is likely to be able to pick and choose which local laws it obeys and which ignores, as enforcement and inspection are likely to be poor. The firm becomes its own law enforcement agency. This imbalance can also work the other way (Visser 2008). Within the society governed by the local state there may well be only meager political debate, while the home base of the investing firm may have lively debate, even over affairs in the country where the firm is investing. For example, a European firm employing child labor in an African country is likely to experience more difficulties about the issue at home than it is in the country where the abuse is occurring. In response to domestic pressure the firm might become a more vigorous guardian of children's rights than the African government. Again, the firm becomes its own law enforcement agency.

4. The last example raises the general issue of corporate social responsibility. This concept refers to the acceptance by firms that their responsibilities as organizations extend beyond that of immediate profit maximization and that they should recognize those for the externalities produced by their actions (i.e., those effects of their activities that are not represented in the market forces operating on them, such as pollution caused by production processes) (Crouch 2006b). There is much debate in the literature on whether firms do or should accept social responsibilities for moral reasons, in order to preempt tougher government action if they do not act, or because for various reasons social responsibility will be associated with higher long-run profitability (see Carroll 1999 for a view broadly favorable to the concept; Henderson 2001 for a hostile one; Crane et al. 2008 and Scherer and Palazzo 2008 for overviews of the entire field). It is not our present task to try to resolve this debate. We need only note that firms are here taking on themselves responsibility for defining public priorities, and deciding and then implementing the actions that seem to be required by those priorities.

For example, some Western firms operating in African countries have decided that, because their activities lead to the concentration together of large numbers of young people as employees, they have some responsibility for education and medical treatment relating to HIV/AIDS among their workforces, and beyond in their workers' local communities (Campbell and Williams 1998, 1999; Distlerath and Macdonald 2004). This is public policy action going beyond the immediate remit of the firm as a profit-maximizing concern. The decisions whether or not to do anything about the issue, and if so what to do, are public policy actions. The firm may or may not liaise with local government about the matter; that also is its decision. The example given is from a third-world country, but CSR issue are also presented within the advanced economies, at the present time particularly in relation to environmental concerns and climate changes.

CSR has to be distinguished from charitable activities, or the establishment of charitable trusts and foundations by firms. These activities are usually governed by separate bodies of law, recognizing and regulating the existence of a particular form of publicly oriented activity that is part of neither the state nor profit-making activity. CSR is undertaken by firms within the ambit of normal company law, the firms' directors and senior management using the capacity for strategy of their corporate hierarchies to pursue their public policy preferences. In seeking concepts by which this process might be understood, some authors have developed the idea of "corporate citizenship." This can have a banal meaning, signifying little more than that firms ought to behave like good citizens. But in the hands of Crane, Matten, and Moon (2008) it has been brought to a higher pitch of analysis. Strictly speaking, firms cannot "be" citizens as in democracies this quality belongs solely to the individual human beings who possess the right to vote. But these authors see firms as administering the general rights of citizens, in so far as firms enter the field of making corporate-level public policy, which is what CSR amounts to. The idea remains deeply problematic, as citizens have no formal capacity to access the corporation (which remains governed by corporate law, recognizing only the rights of shareholders) in the way that they can in theory put political pressure on governments. On the other hand, firms can be responsive to citizens qua customers. An interesting example of this was seen in the late 1990s when British supermarkets were quicker than the government to respond to consumers' uneasiness over the use of genetically modified organisms (GMO) in food, and removed such products from their shelves while government was still supporting the food-producing industry's insistence that they should be sold.

5. Finally, we need to consider a series of developments that flow from the general adoption of neo-liberal economic and social policies that has been developing in many countries since the late 1970s. An important element of this has been the view that, because they are not subject to competitive pressures in the same way as firms, the activities of government are likely to be less efficient than those of firms, and that there would be efficiency gains if governments increasingly modeled themselves on firms or, better still, delegated the execution of many of their administrative and service-delivery tasks to firms. The general movement towards policies of this kind is known as New Public Management and has been adopted officially by many governments, the EU and by the OECD. It has had a number of implications for the political role of the corporation:

i. The delivery of many public services, from schools to prisons, has been contracted out to private firms. Strictly speaking, government continues to make policy and the contractor only provides what has been decided. However, knowledge of relations between principals and agents in contracting within the private sector suggests that this is naive. In a contract of any complexity there is usually lengthy and even post-contractual negotiation during which the agent proposes amendments to the contract to suit its own preferences, and these may result in considerable amendment of the contract's terms. We are reminded here of Williamson's work (1975, 1985), cited above, on the way in which employers from both commissioning and contracting firms often come together to form single work teams when working on complex contracts, overriding any precise concepts of differences between principal and agent. This may also happen between government departments and contractors, obliterating the formal distinction between policy-making and implementation, and giving the contractor a role in the latter. Singer (2008: 236) argues that this can extend to the role of private military contractors influencing the conduct of wars and invasions.

ii. As Freedland (2001) has shown, privatization of service delivery alters the relationship between citizen and public authority in a manner analogous to that identified in relation to CSR by Crane, Matten, and Moon (2008). The firm's customer is the public authority that placed the contract; the consumer has no relationship to the firm. The consumer has a citizenship relationship to the public authority, but the authority has delegated delivery of the service to the firm, so the citizenship route cannot be used to express any concerns over service delivery. Any responsiveness of firms to consumers therefore stands outside both the public (citizenship) and market (customer) spheres.

iii. Firms being seen as almost inevitably more efficient than governments, the latter have been encouraged to model their own internal practices on firms as far as possible, and to bring firms right into government as consultants, even to the extent of permitting them to recommend the sale of their own services. This challenges the important criterion of the neoclassical economy discussed above, that state and market need to be kept separate from each other. This had, under late nineteenth- and twentieth-century concepts of that separation, led to public service codes of conduct that kept ministers and civil servants at arm's length from representatives of private firms. Under new public management that arm's-length relationship came to be seen as a factor preventing government from learning about efficient private sector practices. That has however left in confusion ideas about the correct separation that is needed between government and business for the proper functioning of markets. Firms that become government insiders must be presumed to benefit from the existence of entry barriers inevitably faced by competitors for public contracts who are not insiders, with self-perpetuating consequences. In addition to doubts raised about the long-term efficiency of competition with high entry barriers, there is a political concern that some private firms are becoming public policy monopolists.

iv. As governments withdraw in favor of firms from areas of social policy that they had dominated for much of the twentieth century, firms become the main policy makers. This happens, for example, in the trend towards company-level pensions policy and the definition of the rights and responsibilities of different kinds of employee.

v. Several of the processes described above have contributed to the construction of a global economy with high entry barriers in many sectors, a consequence of which is growing inequality and the emergence of some individuals and corporations with very high concentrations of wealth. Various "causes" (welfare, educational, cultural, etc.) which are unable to flourish within the market and which therefore depend upon "public" support of various kinds have turned to these individuals and corporations for financial help. There has often been a generous response to these appeals, but of course the wealthy express their personal preferences when deciding to what causes they shall give. This enables them to use their private wealth to make public decisions. Governments have sought to encourage this private giving, as it reduces the pressure on themselves to help support the causes. They do this by allowing tax remission on money used to make charitable donations, reinforcing the amount of the gift by the amount of taxation remitted. This therefore increases the wealthy individual's effect on public policy, as he or she is able to affect the destination of public funds in the form of the taxation foregone. Governments then want to encourage charitable causes to be more active in seeking donations, in order further to reduce their own burden; they therefore inform charities that government funding will go disproportion- ately to those who have successfully raised money from the private sector— extending further the ability of the wealthy individual to determine the allocation of public funds. Finally, in a further attempt to bring private sector efficiencies to the public sector, governments tend to appoint individuals who have acquired corporate wealth to preside over public bodies, enabling these individuals to extend their public policy reach even further.

The concept of "powerful lobby" is inadequate to analyze this multifaceted role of today's large private firms: they are part of the polity, insiders, not a part of an external civil society that powerfully lobbies the polity (Schneider 2006). The ideal that the economic and the political can be mutually separated is nearly always compromised in practice: their mutual dependence and their capacity to be translated into each other are too great. As a result political formulae that depend on their separation will be false and misleading. The consequence of this is that democracy operates in relation to only part of the actual polity. If an issue arises in relation to a private firm acting in a public capacity (whether as a sub-contractor, in CSR policy, or its global governance activ- ities), it can become a political question only if it can be tracked back to government. This is guaranteed by the character of electoral politics in mass democracies, whereby a question can acquire political salience only if it can be shown to offer opportunities for mutual blaming between government and opposition. Even if firms are somehow implicated in the affair, they are secondary to the democratic politics of the issue.

This raises important normative issues, but our present concerns are analytical. Despite the risk of compromising the reductionism of modern political theory, we need to conceptualize firms, at least large ones operating multinationally, as locations of political power and authority, to be analyzed alongside governments, parties, and other obviously political actors. They might operate by lobbying, but that is not always the right way to describe their relations with government; but they also operate in their own right on the political stage, and not through government.

These firms may also be internally divided; as anticipated above, giant firms, as organizations often coping with uncertain or inadequate information, are vulnerable to internal dispute and should not be taken for granted as unitary players, even if they are usually better able to keep this secret than democratic governments operating under the glare of publicity. There are several studies of internal conflicts in firms, though these are usually concerned with managerial and corporate issues as such, rather than any relationship between these conflicts and wider politics. Making these connections is another field where there is considerable scope for research (for important contributions to such study, see Thompson 1982; Amoore 2000; Fligstein 2001; Martin 2006).

Giant corporations constitute a non-democratic part of the modern polity, in that they are not formally answerable to a public. On the other hand, they are vulnerable to campaigning by social movement organizations, particularly when these can negatively affect a firm's reputation among its customers. At the international economic level and in poor countries with undeveloped institutional infrastructure, they may constitute the most important objects for political study.

Notes

1. Strictly speaking, it is necessary only to specify a "liberal," not necessarily a "democratic," polity for the problem to occur. By "liberal" is meant a polity in which individuals are able to use their private property to engage in public and political affairs; by "democratic" is defined one in which all persons who meet certain criteria of age, nationality, and (possibly) gender enjoy that right, irrespective of their property status. The political rights of capitalists are adequately ensured if a polity is liberal, and historically the establishment of the rules of the capitalist economy took place more easily where liberal rather than democratic rights were in place. At certain points this distinction becomes very important to understanding the politics of capitalism. However, for present purposes I shall talk mainly in terms of democracy, as this is the more usually understood concept.

2. There are many important empirical demonstrations of this. In developing societies the introduction of free markets into economies previously dominated by non-capitalist elites is often associated with a reduction in equalities, as new firms enter markets that had been the preserve of privileged monopolies.

3. The author who has done most to demonstrate the importance of institutions, including political ones, in studying the market economy is Douglas North (1990). For a general discussion of institutional economics, including its political implications, see Hodgson (1993).

4. In several previously publicly owned industries technical or physical characteristics of the sector made effective competition virtually impossible. This is the case with railways and water supply. In some others, just as electricity, gas, and most forms of telecommunications, technological development has made possible the introduction of some true competition.

5. Orthodox economists tend to be skeptical of the importance of sunk costs, arguing that the rational firm will have discounted the costs of one day liquidizing an investment when originally deciding to make it. This cannot however help with cases where cheap new investment locations arise that could not have been expected to exist at the time

the firm first chose its locations. This has been particularly the case in recent years, as new, previously unpredicted opportunities have appeared in East Asia and the former Soviet bloc.

6. Paradoxically, while neoclassical economists normally see neo-corporatism as more hostile to the free market than a pluralist arrangement, in practice neo-corporatist associational representation is better able to restrain market distortions stemming from unequal size among firms than is a pluralist system.

REFERENCES

AMOORE, L. 2000. "International political economy and the 'contested firm,' " *New Political Economy* 5(2): 183–204.

AUSTIN-SMITH, D. 1994. "Counteractive lobbying," *American Journal of Political Science* 38: 25–44.

BAUMGARTNER, F., and JONES, B. 1993. *Agendas and Instability in American Politics.* Chicago: Chicago University Press.

——— and LEECH, B. 1998. *Basic Interests: The Importance of Groups in Politics and Political Science.* Princeton: Princeton University Press.

BECKER, G. S. 1985. "Public policies, pressure groups, and dead-weight costs," *Journal of Public Economics* 28: 329–47.

BORK, R. H. 1978. *The Antitrust Paradox: A Policy at War with Itself.* New York: Free Press.

BOTZEM, S., and QUACK, S. 2006. "Contested rules and shifting boundaries: international standard setting in accounting," in M.-L. Djelic and K. Sahlin-Andersson, eds., *Transnational Governance: Institutional Dynamics of Regulation.* Oxford: Oxford University Press, 266–86.

BROSCHEID, A. 2006. "Public choice models of business lobbying," in D. Coen and W. Grant, eds., *Business and Government: Methods and Practice.* Opladen: Budrich, 79–108.

CAMPBELL, C., and WILLIAMS, B. 1998. "Managing disease on the gold mines: 'work-related' and 'non-work-related' diseases," *South African Medical Journal* 88: 789–95.

——— ——— 1999. "Beyond the biomedical and behavioural: towards an integrated approach to HIV prevention in the Southern African mining industry," *Social Sciences and Medicine* 48: 1625–39.

CARROLL, A. B. 1999. "Corporate social responsibility: evolution of a definitional construct," *Business in Society* 38(3): 268–95.

CHOBANOVA, Y. 2007. "MNEs in the CEECs: shaping the microeconomic architecture of states in the context of European integration. The cases of Unilever, Nestlé and InBev," unpublished Ph.D. thesis. Florence: European University Institute.

COASE, R. 1937. "The nature of the firm," *Economica* 4: 386–405.

COEN, D. 1997. "The evolution of the large firm as a political actor in the European Union," *Journal of European Public Policy* 4(1): 91–108.

——— 1998. "The European business interest and the nation state: large-firm lobbying in the European Union and member states," *Journal of Public Policy* 18(1): 75–100.

——— 1999. "The impact of US lobbying practice on the European business–government relationship," *California Management Review* 41(4): 27–44.

——— and GRANT, W., eds. 2006a. *Business and Government: Methods and Practice.* Opladen: Budrich.

——— ——— 2006b. "Managing business and government relations," in D. Coen and W. Grant, eds., *Business and Government: Methods and Practice.* Opladen: Budrich, 13–32.

COEN, D., and THATCHER, M. 2005. "The new governance of markets and non-majoritarian regulators," *Governance* 18(3): 329–46.

CRANE, A., MATTEN, D., and MOON, J. 2008. *Corporations and Citizenship.* Cambridge: Cambridge University Press.

——McWILLIAMS, A., MATTEN, D., MOON, J., and SIEGEL, D. S., eds. 2008. *The Oxford Handbook of Corporate Social Responsibility.* Oxford: Oxford University Press.

CROUCH, C. 1993. *Industrial Relations and European State Traditions.* Oxford: Oxford University Press.

——2006a. "Neo-corporatism and democracy," in C. Crouch and W. Streeck, eds., *The Diversity of Democracy.* Cheltenham: Elgar, 46–70.

——2006b. "Modelling the firm in its market and organizational environment: methodologies for studying corporate social responsibility," *Organization Studies* 27(10): 1533–51.

DAHL, R. A. 1982. *Dilemmas of Pluralist Democracy: Autonomy Versus Control.* New Haven: Yale University Press.

DISTLERATH, L., and MACDONALD, G. 2004. "HIV/AIDS partnerships: a new role for MNCs in global health policy," *Yale Journal of Health Policy, Law, and Ethics* (Winter): 147–55.

DIXON, C., DRAKAKIS-SMITH, D., and WATTS, H. D., eds. 1986. *Multinational Corporations and the Third World.* London: Croom Helm.

DJELIC, M.-L., and SAHLIN-ANDERSSON, K., eds. 2006. *Transnational Governance: Institutional Dynamics of Regulation.* Oxford: Oxford University Press.

ENGWALL, L. 2006. "Global enterprises in fields of governance," in M.-L. Djelic and K. Sahlin-Andersson, eds., *Transnational Governance: Institutional Dynamics of Regulation.* Oxford: Oxford University Press, 161–79.

FLIGSTEIN, N. 2001. *The Architecture of Markets: An Economic Sociology of 21st Century Capitalist Societies.* Princeton: Princeton University Press.

FREEDLAND, M. 2001. "The marketization of public services," in C. Crouch, K. Eder, and D. Tambini, eds., *Citizenship, Markets, and the State.* Oxford: Clarendon Press.

GRANT, W. 1981. "The development of the government relations function in UK Firms: a pilot study of UK-based companies," Labor Market Policy Discussion Paper 81/20. International Institute of Management, Berlin.

——1984. "Large firms and public policy in Britain," *Journal of Public Policy* 4(1): 1–17.

——2000. *Pressure Groups and British Politics.* London: Palgrave.

——2007. "Government environmental policy and the chemical industry," in L. Galambos, T. Hikino, and V. Zamagni, eds., *The Global Chemical Industry in the Age of Petroleum.* Cambridge: Cambridge University Press, 114–37.

GROSSMANN, G. M. 2001. *Special Interest Politics.* Cambridge, Mass.: MIT Press.

HAYWARD, J. 1986. *The State and the Market Economy: Industrial Patriotism and Economic Intervention in France.* Brighton: Wheatsheaf.

——ed. 1995. *Industrial Enterprise and European Integration: From National to International Champions in Western Europe.* Oxford: Oxford University Press.

HENDERSON, D. 2001. *Misguided Virtue: False Notions of Corporate Social Responsibility.* Wellington: New Zealand Business Roundtable.

HODGSON, G. M. 1993. *Economics and Evolution: Bringing Life back into Economics.* Cambridge: Polity Press.

ITE, U. 2004. "Multinationals and corporate social responsibility in developing countries: a case study of Nigeria," *Corporate Social Responsibility and Environmental Management* 11: 1–11.

JACOBSSON, B., and SAHLIN-ANDERSSON, K. 2006. "Dynamics of soft regulations," in M.-L. Djelic and K. Sahlin-Andersson, eds., *Transnational Governance: Institutional Dynamics of Regulation.* Oxford: Oxford University Press, 247–65.

KENNEDY, C. 1993. *The Company that Changed our Lives*, 2nd edn. London: Chapman.

KERWER, D. 2001. "Standardizing as governance: the case of credit rating agencies," Working Paper 2001: 3. Max-Planck-Projektgruppe Recht der Gemeinschaftsgüter, Bonn.

LEVY, D. L., and KAPLAN, R. 2008. "Corporate social responsibility and theories of global governance: strategic contestation in global issue areas," in A. Crane, D. Matten, and Moon, J., eds., *Corporations and Citizenship*. Cambridge: Cambridge University Press, 432–51.

LINDBLOM, C. 1977. *Politics and Markets: The World's Politico-Economic Systems*. New York: Basic Books.

LÜTZ, S. 2003. "Convergence within national diversity: a comparative perspective on the regulatory state in finance," MPIfG Discussion Paper 03/7. Cologne: Max-Planck-Institut für Gesellschaftsforschung.

MARTIN, C. J. 2006. "Consider the source! Determinants of corporate preferences for public policy", in D. Coen and W. Grant, eds., *Business and Government: Methods and Practice*. Opladen: Budrich, 51–78.

MATTLI, W. 2001. "The politics and economics of international institutional standards setting," *Journal of European Public Policy* 8(3): 328–44.

MITCHELL, N., HANSEN, W., and JEPSEN, E. 1997. "The determinants of domestic and foreign corporate political activity," *Journal of Politics* 59(4): 1096–113.

MITCHELL, W. C., and MUNGER, M. C. 1991. "Economic models of interest groups: an introductory survey," *American Journal of Political Science* 35(2): 512–46.

MORAN, M. 2006. "The company of strangers," *New Political Economy* 11(4): 453–77.

MORGAN, G. 2006. "Transnational actors, transnational institutions, transnational spaces: the role of law firms in the internationalization of competition regulation," in M.-L. Djelic and K. Sahlin-Anderson, eds., *Transnational Governance: Institutional Dynamics of Regulation*. Oxford: Oxford University Press, 139–60.

MÖRTH, U. 2006. "Soft regulation and global democracy," in M.-L. Djelic and K. Sahlin-Anderson, eds., *Transnational Governance: Institutional Dynamics of Regulation*. Oxford: Oxford University Press, 119–35.

NORTH, D. C. 1990. *Institutions, Institutional Change, and Economic Performance*. Cambridge: Cambridge University Press.

OHMAE, K. 1985. *Triad Power: The Coming Shape of Global Competition*. New York: Collier Macmillan.

OLSON, M. 1982. *The Rise and Decline of Nations: Economic Growth, Stagflation and Social Rigidities*. New Haven: Yale University Press.

PARKINSON, J., KELLY, J., and GAMBLE, A. 2000. *The Political Economy of the Company*. Oxford: Hart.

PAULY, L., and REICH, S. 1997. "National structures and multinational corporate behaviour: enduring differences in the age of globalization," *International Organization* 51: 1–30.

POSNER, R. A. 2001. *Antitrust Law*, 2nd edn. Chicago: University of Chicago Press.

RONDINELLI, D. 2002. "Transnational corporations: international citizens of new sovereigns?" *Business and Society Review* 107(4): 391–413.

SCHEPEL, H. 2005. *The Constitution of Private Governance: Standards in the Regulation of Integrating Markets*. Oxford: Hart.

SCHERER, A. G., and PALAZZO, G., eds. 2008. *Handbook of Research on Global Corporate Citizenship*. Cheltenham: Edward Elgar.

SCHMIDT, I. L. O., and RITTALER, J. B. 1989. *A Critical Evaluation of the Chicago School of Antitrust Analysis*. London: Kluwer.

SCHNEIDER, V. 2006. "Business in policy networks: estimating the relative importance of corporate direct lobbying and representation by trade associations," in D. Coen and W. Grant, eds., *Business and Government: Methods and Practice*. Opladen: Budrich, 109–27.

SCHOLTE, J. A. 2007. "Civil society and the legitimation of global governance," CSGR Working Paper. University of Warwick Centre for the Study of Globalization and Regionalization, Coventry.

SINGER, P. W. 2008. *Corporate Warriors. The Rise of the Privatized Military Industry*. Ithaca, NY: Cornell University Press.

STRANGE, S. 1986. *Casino Capitalism*. Oxford: Basil Blackwell.

——1996. *The Retreat of the State: The Diffusion of Power in the World Economy*. Cambridge: Cambridge University Press.

——STOPFORD, J. M., with HENLEY, J. S. 1991. *Rival States, Rival Firms: Competition for World Market Shares*. Cambridge: Cambridge University Press.

STREECK, W. 1997. "German capitalism: does it exist? Can it survive?," in C. Crouch and W. Streeck (eds.), *Political Economy of Modern Capitalism*. London: Sage.

SUTTON, J. 1991. *Sunk Costs and Market Structure*. Cambridge, Mass.: MIT Press.

THOMPSON, G. 1982. "The firm as a 'dispersed' social agency," *Economy and Society* 11: 233.

TRAXLER, F., BLASCHKE, S., and KITTEL, B. 2004. *National Labor Relations in Internationalized Markets*. Oxford: Oxford University Press.

TRIGILIA, C. 1999. *Economic Sociology*. Oxford: Blackwell.

TULLOCK, G. 1980. "Efficient rent seeking," in G. Tullock, J. M. Buchanan, and R. D. Tollison, eds., *Toward a Theory of the Rent-Seeking Society*. College Station: Texas A and M University.

VAN WAARDEN, F. 2002. "Market institutions as communicating vessels: changes between economic coordination principles as a consequence of deregulation policies," in J. R. Hollingsworth, K. H. Müller, and E. J. Hollingsworth, eds., *Advancing Socio-Economics: An Institutionalist Perspective*. Lanham, Md.: Rowman and Littlefield.

VISSER, W. 2008. "Corporate social responsibility in developing countries," in A. Crane, D. Matten, and J. Moon, eds., *Corporations and Citizenship*. Cambridge: Cambridge University Press, 473–99.

WILLIAMSON, O. E. 1975. *Markets and Hierarchies: Analysis and Antitrust Implications: A Study in the Economics of Internal Organization*. New York: Free Press.

——1985. *The Economic Institutions of* Capitalism. New York: Free Press.

——and MASTEN, S. E. 1995. *Transaction Cost Economics*. Aldershot: Edward Elgar.

YOFFIE, D., and BERGENSTEIN, S. 1985. "Creating political advantage: the rise of the political entrepreneur," *California Management Review* 28: 124–39.

CHAPTER 7

THE POLITICAL THEORY OF THE FIRM[1]

DAVID M. HART

INTRODUCTION: BEYOND THE "ARTIFICIAL PERSON"

IN the late nineteenth century, American courts accepted the counter-intuitive proposition that corporations were, for certain legal purposes, persons (Lamoreaux 2004). They were therefore endowed with some inalienable rights, although not exactly the same rights as those to which "natural persons" (as we corporeal beings thus became known) were entitled by the US Constitution. "Artificial persons" cannot vote in the US, but, among other things, they can and do "petition the government for a redress of grievances" and exercise freedom of speech, individual rights that are protected by the First Amendment. A tangled web of law tries to distinguish between the rights held by the two kinds of legal persons, but litigation over the exact boundaries is ongoing.

Scholars of business–government relations, too, typically treat firms as if they were persons. Like consumers in microeconomic theory, firms' actions are assumed to manifest individual tastes and preferences. Like states in much of international relations theory, firms are taken to be unitary, rational decision-makers. As in law, the concept of corporate personhood can help social science to make sense of a complex reality. Yet, as the law also recognizes, this simplification, useful as it is, must sometimes be rejected, lest we misinterpret what we seek to explain and jeopardize values that we hold dear.

This chapter argues for balancing corporate personhood—or, more precisely, the unitary rational actor political theory of the firm, which predominates in the social science literature—with two other theories of the firm that have not yet been as fully developed. These alternatives treat the firm as a complex nexus of contracts among individual rational actors or as a set of organizational routines enacted by individuals playing roles. Although the three theories sometimes yield conflicting hypotheses, they more often direct analytical attention to different phenomena. From this perspective, as I argue at the end of the chapter, they are, at the broadest level, complementary, like the blind men who feel different parts of the elephant in the Indian folk tale.

Greater scholarly attention to the political theory of the firm is justifiable on both empirical and normative grounds. The empirical case rests on the ubiquity of firms in contemporary politics in the advanced industrial nations and, increasingly, in developing countries as well. US data compiled by Baumgartner and Leech (2001), for instance, show that individual firms spend more money on Washington lobbying than all other types of organizations combined, including business associations. Interest representation in Brussels, too, is dominated by business lobbyists, with individual firms playing an increasingly important role (John and Schwarzer 2006; Coen 2007).

If the empirical case is powerful, the normative case is profound. For contemporary capitalism to function, "artificial persons" must exercise substantial power over "natural persons" in their roles as workers and consumers. In their roles as citizens, however, the people ought to be able to exert a counterweight (Lindblom 1977). If they are subject to unnecessary risks when they do their jobs or purchase the necessities of life, for instance, citizens should be able to "broaden the scope of conflict" beyond the private sphere (Schattschneider 1960) and invoke the power of the state to hold firms liable, regulate them, or otherwise mitigate the danger. If firms hold the reins of public power as well as private power, this recourse is lost and injustice prevails.

The political theory of the firm provides the conceptual framework for understanding what firms are doing and what it means for the polities in which they operate. This chapter proceeds by explicating each of the three theories—unitary rational actor, nexus of contracts, and behavioral. Within each of these sections I offer a brief assessment of the empirical findings and opportunities associated with the theory at hand and of its limits. I conclude with the synthesis alluded to above.

UNITARY RATIONAL ACTOR THEORY

The concept of corporate personhood is a legal one, but its manifestation in political science derives primarily from microeconomics. This approach treats the firm "as if" it is an individual and "as if" it is rational (Becker 1976). This individual knows what it wants from the political system, can calculate the cost of getting what it wants, and acts on the basis of these calculations. These "as if" assumptions may be demonstrably false, as advocates of the alternative theories like to point out, yet they nonetheless provide a starting point for empirical research that has yielded significant findings.

Each of the assumptions is worth spelling out in a bit more detail. "Natural persons" want to maximize utility in microeconomic theory, a concept that encompasses not just material pleasures but ethereal ones as well. What "artificial persons" want is less complicated and easier to measure: profits. Profits (and expectations of them) determine whether a firm grows or shrinks and, ultimately, survives or fails. Unlike the theory of the rational voter, in which the material payoffs from taking action are infinitesimal, there is no need in the unitary rational actor theory of the firm to invoke "psychic benefits" or "duty" (Ferejohn and Fiorina 1974) to explain behavior.

Another assumption of this theory is that a firm can assess the impact of political expenditures on its bottom line (Baron 1995). These calculations are comprised of two interlinked elements. First, a firm must determine the degree to which alternative policies will benefit it. Second, it must predict how much each political activity that it might undertake will enhance the probability of the preferred policy being enacted. The information required to make these calculations is taken to be readily available in the political environment in combination with the firm's proprietary knowledge base.

Finally, the unitary rational actor theory of the firm assumes that there is no "slip twixt cup and lip," as the saying goes. If the expected benefit of a political expenditure is greater than the expected benefits of alternative investments that the firm might make, the cost is incurred. The firm thus operates on what might be called a "political possibility frontier" (analogous to the production possibility frontier in economics) in which its political resources are efficiently invested across policy areas, jurisdictions, and tactics. Innovation in political "technologies" (defined broadly) may shift the frontier out, allowing the firm to do more with the same resources, just as technological innovation in production technology shifts out the production possibility frontier.

Mancur Olson's *The Logic of Collective Action* (1965) is the *locus classicus* for the unitary rational actor theory. Olson's foray into political science was one of the first by an economist, and his analytical framework proved to be so attractive that the American Political Science Association now awards a dissertation prize in his honor in the field of political economy. Although Olson's *Logic* has been applied to phenomena as diverse as military alliances (Olson and Zeckhauser 1966), state formation (Levi 1988), and environmental policy (Ostrom 1990) (to name but a few), he initially intended that it explain the behavior of economic interests, including businesses.

Olson deduced that most firms, especially small firms, would choose not to undertake political activities, especially activities aimed at providing collective benefits for business as a whole. Such firms would instead free ride on the efforts of others or simply accept the consequences of inactivity, because the costs of political activity at the level of the individual firm outweighed the expected benefits at that level. This prediction has been confirmed by many studies, such as those showing that many US firms do not make campaign contributions or lobby (Hansen, Mitchell, and Drope 2004; Drope and Hansen 2006). Olson's work overturned the conventional wisdom in political science, exemplified in David Truman's (1951) *magnum opus, The Governmental Process,* that action would follow without complication whenever a political interest emerged.

Olson's *Logic* also challenged the view, widely held among left-leaning scholars, that a unified business class dominates politics in capitalist societies (Mills 1956; Miliband 1969). Rational calculation by firms, according to Olson, should generally preclude the formation of a "power elite" or "executive committee of the bourgeoisie." Defections from such entities by individual benefit-seekers should be common when they do form. Research on pluralism and corporatism generally confirms this expectation; business unity is more likely to be sustained in smaller countries in which a few firms are able to make credible commitments to one another and in which the state has the authority to punish defectors (Goldthorpe 1984; Hall and Soskice 2001). In the US, on the other hand, a big country with a weak state in this respect, business unity is rare (Vogel 1989).

The unitary rational actor theory of the firm ought to direct attention away from peak business associations (Smith 2000) that seek collective benefits for all firms and toward "private goods" that benefit individual firms (Brasher and Lowery 2006). Godwin and Seldon (2002: 216) provide evidence that private goods dominate the agendas of large firms. "Airline lobbyists," they write, "reported spending 75–95 percent of their time on issues affecting only their firm or their firm and one other." The theory also supplies a lens for reinterpreting the activities of industry associations, coalitions, and the like. Individual firms may use nominally collective entities that they actually control to provide "cover" to pursue private goods without appearing to do so publicly. They may also use these entities to block similar efforts by rival firms.

Private goods that have a measurable effect on the corporate bottom line and those that can be divided easily among contending interests are the most likely targets of business political activity under the unitary rational actor theory of the firm. Government contracts are an obvious case in point. Substantial empirical research shows a strong association between dependence of a firm on government contracts and its political activity, such as lobbying and campaign contributions (Lichtenberg 1989; Hansen and Mitchell 2000). Firm-specific regulatory issues similarly motivate political activity (de Figueiredo and Tiller 2001). Brady and his colleagues (2007), for instance, find that regulated broadcasters and energy firms are substantially over-represented in US lobbying reports.

Taxes and trade protection are easily measurable and divisible, too, and they have been the subjects of substantial research that rests on the unitary rational actor theory. A recent study, for instance, finds that the more a firm spends on lobbying in the US, the lower the effective tax rate it pays (Richter, Samphantharak, and

Timmons 2008). Similar associations have been found in research on anti-dumping petitions lodged with US trade authorities (Drope and Hansen 2004).[2]

Corporate government affairs managers vouch in interviews for the importance of expending effort on political activities that can be directly linked to the bottom line. Sometimes, the senior executives to whom these managers report (such as an executive vice-president with broad oversight responsibilities) only recognize the value of an activity if it is placed in the familiar terms of monetary return on investment (ROI). Indeed, firms in which the government affairs function is controlled by executives with this mindset may explicitly impose an ROI framework on the function when they allocate budgets and headcount each year.

Yet, the same interviews also suggest that such myopia is far from universal. Most firms with well-developed government affairs functions take the idea of "investment" seriously. They expect returns over a period of years and recognize that their political activities comprise a portfolio that will yield payoffs in aggregate, not individually. This approach is perfectly compatible with the unitary rational actor theory of the firm (Snyder 1992); in fact, one would expect a sophisticated "person" with a potentially infinite lifespan to adopt a long time horizon and a probabilistic risk assessment. Too often, researchers working within this tradition have operationalized the unitary, rational actor theory of the firm in its most simplistic form.

However, as one's model of rationality becomes more complex, the information requirements that the model places on the decision-making process become more demanding. Over a long time horizon, for instance, major national and world events, such as wars, economic panics, and electoral upsets, may overturn the political order. The probability of such events cannot be estimated in any rigorous way and must therefore be omitted from the model. Similarly, in a complex political environment—London, Paris, Tokyo, Washington, etc.—the range of tactical choices available to actors with substantial political resources is quite wide, and the choices of any individual firm interact with those of all the other players. The marginal effect of any particular choice is very hard to estimate. The behavioral theory of the firm (see below) finds analytic purchase in this critique of information and how it is processed in the unitary rational actor theory.

The nexus of contracts theory, by contrast, largely accepts that rational choices are possible and instead targets the dominant theory's assumption that the firm is unitary. Celebrity CEOs who use corporate resources to indulge a "taste" for politics (Ansolabehere, de Figueiredo, and Snyder 2003) in order to satisfy their personal utility functions, for instance, are commonly sighted at the World Economic Forum in Davos, Switzerland. Similarly, government affairs managers who catch "Potomac fever" and choose to pursue their personal political ambitions, rather than those of the firm for which they work, are hardly unheard of, as the existence of such slang suggests.

George Stigler, one of the great contributors to the development of the unitary rational actor theory, once offered the perplexing statement that it has become "essentially inconceivable (but not impossible) that the theory of utility-maximizing is wrong... Indeed there is no alternative hypothesis" (1975: 140). Stigler and his colleagues of the University of Chicago often emphasized that monopolies left unchallenged quickly become inefficient and reap undeserved rents. The unitary rational actor theory has achieved something of a monopoly on the political theory of the firm. The critiques offered in the preceding paragraphs, and the political theories of the firm to which they lead, are worth pursuing if for no other reason than to provide plausible alternative hypotheses against which to pit the unitary rational actor theory. As I argue below, however, I believe the alternatives have more to offer than this minimal contribution.

NEXUS OF CONTRACTS THEORY

In reality, if not always in law or social science, firms are not people, but are rather composed of people. These people may be well coordinated, responding to a common set of incentives and inspired by a shared framework of values—but, then again, they may not. If a firm's employees are "looking out for number one," as the best-selling business book of a few years back put it, they may use corporate resources to advance their own agendas, instead of their employer's. The "new institutional economics" (Williamson 2000) which entered the disciplinary mainstream of economics in recent years and has begun to make its way into the study of business–government relations as well, takes this possibility very seriously.

The godfather of this approach is Ronald Coase, who argued in 1937 that firms exist because hierarchy is sometimes a more efficient way of organizing transactions than the market (Coase 1937). Workers agree to employment contracts, according to this line of thought, in part because it would be very costly to have to constantly re-establish the value of complex labor services through frequent bargaining, as a spot labor market would require.[3] Contracts reduce the cost of bargaining by making it infrequent, while also specifying mutually agreed-upon contingencies that might otherwise cause the deal to break down. Coase's insights were generalized and formalized by Jensen and Meckling (1976), among others, who conceived of the firm as a "nexus of contracting relationships."

Scholars in the Coasian tradition are alert to the possibility that the goals of the contracting parties may be different. To be sure, one function of any contract is to align these goals, for instance, by imposing penalties for failure to perform as the contract stipulates. But the theory also assumes that the parties will take full advantage of any opportunities that may arise within the framework of the contract and its enforcement mechanisms to advance their interests. If we imagine the government affairs function of the firm as a nexus of contracts engaging politically savvy individuals, the goals of those involved may include fame (as in the case of "Davos man"), election to public office ("Potomac fever"), enactment of policies of personal interest, and personal wealth, in addition to improving the collective fortunes embodied by the firm.

Opportunities to maximize individual self-interest, at the expense of the shared interests to which the contract is supposed to be directed, are more likely to arise in complex and uncertain environments. In such environments, according to the nexus of contracts theory, the information available to the contracting parties is often asymmetrical, and the party with better information may be able to use the asymmetry to her advantage. The political environment fits the bill; it is often complex and uncertain, and opportunism is therefore rife. Like elected officials who exploit their informational advantage over voters through unwarranted "credit claiming" and "blame avoidance" (Pierson 1996), the political agents of the firm are well-situated to favorably interpret (or even to misrepresent) their actions to the principals who are supposed to oversee them.

The nexus of contracts theory also points toward several "governance mechanisms" that could reduce opportunistic behavior of this sort. The most obvious is more elaborate contracting; more sophisticated criteria for the principal to assess the performance of the agent, for instance, could be incorporated into the contract terms. Another possibility is to provide for more active monitoring; site visits might reduce information asymmetry. A third option is more careful advance screening; knowledge of the agents' reputation on the part of the principal *ex ante* may limit opportunistic behavior. Finally, the organization could invest in team-building; shared norms may align goals more tightly. All of these mechanisms might be employed by a firm that seeks to keep a tighter leash on its interface with the government.

The nexus of contracts theory points to an agenda for empirical research that is both deeper and broader than the agenda inspired by the unitary rational actor theory. One might well see the unitary rational actor theory as a special case of the nexus of contracts theory, in which goals and incentives of all the political agents acting on the firm's behalf happen to be tightly aligned. More commonly, the nexus of contracts theory suggests, the internal processes of the firm will be worth scrutinizing, along with the environment in which the firm operates.

Recent empirical research has challenged one bit of conventional wisdom that is consistent with the unitary rational actor theory, but not necessarily with the nexus of contract theory: that corporate lobbyists are faithful agents of their employers (Heinz et al. 1993). As Dexter (1969: 143) noted nearly forty years ago, "lack of trust [between the lobbyist and her client] is partly justified." Kersh (2002) explored this issue by employing ethnographic methods to follow eleven lobbyists, including several corporate government affairs managers, around Washington. He concludes that his subjects had substantial autonomy to act on their own policy preferences, which were sometimes irrelevant to or even in tension with the stated preferences of their employers.

Like corporate lobbyists, CEOs may also be quite autonomous in their political activities, seeking to maximize immediate personal gains in the tax code, for instance, rather than looking out for the long-term interests of their firms (Englander and

Kaufman 2004). In the corporate hierarchy, CEOs control so many resources that their subordinates are unlikely to object to such behavior. Corporate boards of directors, their nominal principals, may benefit personally from the CEO's activities or may not recognize any divergence between the interests of the CEO and those of the firm.[4]

Indeed, the nexus of contracts theory leads us to anticipate such failures. As Kersh writes of his lobbyists' superiors, "most clients know little of Washington activity and decisions, in part because of the ambiguous and complex nature of the policy process" (Kersh 2002: 236). Similar findings might be expected in other large national capitals and within large firms, which may themselves be complex political environments. (As one executive in a large multinational company who had also served in senior positions in the US government told me, politics at corporate headquarters is just as byzantine as that in Washington and "there's no *Washington Post* to tell you what's going on.") On the other hand, in smaller polities and within smaller firms, the theory suggests that the political environment will be less permissive of opportunism, because there are fewer players (Lowery and Gray 1995).

We know relatively little about how and with what effect firms try to control their political agents through human resources practices (hiring, firing, and compensation), budgeting for the government affairs function, and other governance mechanisms. Among government affairs professionals, there has been a lively discourse about the performance metrics that ought to be applied to the function (Wartick and Rude 1986; Heath 1995). Goldstein (1999) notes that some firms now include participation in government affairs activities in their evaluation of key managers.

Ex ante screening of key hires is perhaps more important as a means of solving the principal/agent problem than *ex post* performance assessment in corporate government affairs. Large firms such as IBM (Hart 2007) used to transfer personnel from other corporate functions to their Washington offices, in part to assure their loyalty to the firm's goals. However, as the Washington environment became more complex in the 1980s and 1990s, they shifted to hiring former Congressional staff and other Washington insiders who come to their jobs with more inside-the-beltway savvy. This new breed of corporate government affairs manager may be less loyal to the firm than the "true blue" IBMer of old, but she may be more sensitive to her reputation for professional competence and responsiveness as perceived by potential employers the next time she wants to change jobs.

The effectiveness of such governance mechanisms is difficult to assess. My interview-based research (e.g. Hart 2002) exploring possible tensions within firms was often blocked by a wall of "spin," as all parties to the nexus of contracts sought to maintain the appearance of unity. Kersh's ethnographic method was more successful, but requires great skill to implement effectively; he evidently sustained the trust of subjects who have little to gain and might have much to lose from his study. We will need more creative and determined efforts along these lines if we are to be able to judge how often principals and agents diverge in this sensitive domain.

The contracting out of the firm's political activities, not surprisingly, constitutes another important area for developing and testing the nexus of contracts theory.

Oliver Williamson (1971), one of Coase's most distinguished followers, focused attention on the "make or buy" decision of firms in general, and some of Williamson's students have extended his analysis to the political domain. De Figueiredo and Kim (2004), for instance, explore whether telecommunications firms represent themselves in the regulatory process or rely on outside entities, such as trade associations, to do their bidding. The decision hinges, in this analysis, on the potential for opportunism and information leakage to competitors with respect to particular issues under regulatory consideration.

The study of contracting out is also fraught with data collection challenges. Clients and consultants have even stronger incentives to "spin" a positive portrayal of their relationships with their business counterparts than do their in-house counterparts. Yet, the enormous growth of the "politics industry," encompassing public relations, advertising, "grassroots" management, and many other specialized services, commends this subject to our research agenda nonetheless. Loomis and Struemph (2004) estimate that this "industry" at the federal level in the US alone has $8 billion annual turnover and employs about 100,000 people. Whether this represents a triumph of efficiency, as traditional Coasian logic might suggest, or a cancerous process that feeds on "fud" (fear, uncertainty, and doubt), as an alternative interpretation of the nexus of contracts theory might suppose, seems worth trying to discover.

By opening up the "black box" of the firm and directing attention to its "make or buy" decision, the nexus of contracts theory leads scholars to explore important issues that emerge when the unitary rational actor theory's assumption that the firm is a unitary decision-maker is relaxed. The nexus of contracts theory also diverges from the unitary rational actor theory by assuming that rationality operates at the individual, rather than the firm, level. Yet, in the complex environment so ably identified by the nexus of contracts theory, individuals may well have difficulty managing all of the information available and calculating all of the factors that are relevant to their interests, as that theory requires. Rather than operating on the basis of rational calculation, these individuals may turn to short-cuts that permit them to reach decisions without overtaxing their cognitive abilities. The decisions that result from such short-cuts may not be optimal, either for the individual or for the firm. Instead, they may simply be good enough for the firm and the people who comprise it to carry on.

BEHAVIORAL THEORY

This premise—that informational short-cuts are required by environmental complexity and the limits of human cognition—points toward the third political theory of the firm reviewed here, in which the firm is viewed as a bundle of routines (Nelson and Winter 1982). These routines are enacted by individuals who fill roles within the organization (Meyer and Rowan 1977). Organizational routines tend to continue until environmental stimuli, such as threats to revenue, profits, or freedom to operate, signal the need for change. When such stimuli are perceived, the firm experiments with new routines, usually in an incremental fashion, until the threat is reduced to a tolerable level. This behavioral theory of the firm, as Cyert and March entitled their path-breaking 1963 book, has led a nascent but fruitful research agenda in business-government relations that emphasizes institutional and historical analysis of firms and issues.

Cyert and March built upon earlier work by their Carnegie-Mellon University colleague Herbert Simon. Simon (1957), who helped to establish the discipline of computer science as well as make foundational contributions to the social sciences, argued that rationality is "bounded." Humans are simply unable to perceive everything going on in their environments that is relevant to their interests. Moreover, their ability to process the information that they do perceive is restricted by neurobiology and by mental habit. These limitations are compounded when such boundedly rational individuals must work together to achieve collective objectives in organizations. Organizational routines and the roles that enact them simplify the challenges of perception and processing by focusing attention and trimming decision trees.

The internal structure of the firm may be the most important determinant of the routines and roles that, in turn, influence which signals the firm receives from the political environment and how it reacts to them (Fligstein 1990; Schuler 1999). Firms that maintain specialized units devoted to sensing political threats and that employ experts who have sophisticated mental models of policy-making, for instance, are likely to behave differently than those that do not. The behavioral theory acknowledges that the organizational chart is not the only source of roles and routines; informal norms that constitute the firm's culture are also pertinent. Thus, the political behavior of a strongly hierarchical firm will tend to reflect the CEO's personal experiences and political ideology more than that of a firm in which decision-making is more collective and deliberative.

Inertia is a defining motif of the behavioral theory of the firm. Unlike the opportunists who populate the political world described by nexus of contracts theorists, the role-enactors of the behavioral theory are not looking for any edge they can find but rather to get through each day. If the routines that they carry out are not perceived by anyone in the firm to cause damage, these routines will usually be maintained (Harris 1997). Failure to "satisfice"—that is, to meet a minimum standard of adequacy—rather than failure to maximize personal utility or firm profits, as in the unitary rational actor and nexus of contract theories, is the threshold for change in the behavioral theory (Miles 1982).

Such failures occur relatively rarely. The political environment may be complex, but it is generally forgiving, in the view of the behavioral theory. A firm's inability to attain its electoral, legislative, or regulatory objectives only rarely threatens its existence or even makes a noticeable dent in its bottom line. In addition, lack of knowledge within the firm and the sheer opacity of policy-making make it difficult to link specific routines to specific outcomes. As a result, "the inefficiencies of history" (Cyert and March 1992) tend to cumulate, rather than being continually squeezed out by the struggle to survive (as would be the case in a harsher environment) or by optimizing behavior (as postulated by the other two theories).

When an environmental stimulus prompts a change in a firm's organizational routines, that change is typically incremental. The "search space" (McKelvey 1997) that defines the options is dominated by modest variations on existing routines. The firm may also seek to imitate the routines that are common within the "organizational field" (DiMaggio and Powell 1983) to which it regularly pays attention. The organizational field might be comprised of firms within its industry, firms of a similar size, or organizations of comparable power, any of which key decision-makers may look to as a model.

The empirical agenda flowing from the behavioral theory thus emphasizes history more than choice and continuity more than change. "Processes of information and communication" (Bauer, Pool, and Dexter 1972), both within firms and across their boundaries, are an important focus, particularly when they involve selective attention and interpretive flexibility. The research also inquires into the kinds of environmental turbulence that evoke a search for new routines and the ways that such searches get resolved.

Martin (2000), for instance, develops the concept of "corporate policy capacity," a set of specialized roles and routines devoted to managing the firm's interface with government and civil society. She argues that firms that have substantial policy capacity will take different policy positions and adopt different political strategies than those without such capacity. In the domain of US health policy that she studied, such capacity derives in part from the experiences of human resource managers who must comply with the intricate regulations of government insurance programs and in part from health policy "issue managers" within the government affairs function. Martin argues that coalitions within the firm (March 1962) of these two types of policy experts can exert a powerful influence on its internal "conversation" about how to position itself politically. Corporate policy capacity is correlated with firm size, but "the way size matters" (Martin 2000: 126) here is not the same as the monopoly rents that are stressed in the Olsonian tradition.

Small firms, family-owned firms, and firms run by their founders, by contrast, are more likely to have idiosyncratic political routines in which the views of the CEO drive the political roles of subordinates. Epstein's (1969) classic work on US business politics supplies a number of examples of this type, including Henry Ford and his eponymous automobile company, which supported extremely conservative causes, far beyond the more pragmatic anti-statism (Vogel 1978) of most of his big business peers. William McGowan of MCI exemplifies a different type of CEO, the "corporate political entrepreneur" (Yoffie and Bergenstein 1985). McGowan was utterly pragmatic, adopting any available political tactic that would allow him to break the hold of AT&T over US telecommunications policy, which MCI ultimately did, with spectacular consequences (Noam 2003).

Empirical phenomena that excite intense interest among scholars drawing on the unitary rational actor and nexus of contracts theories, such as organizations for collective action and campaign contributions, are imbued with different meanings in the behavioral tradition. Trade association membership is more a matter of habit than of calculation; its primary value lies in access to information about other members of the association and about the firm's broader political environment (Bauer, Pool, and Dexter 1972), rather than the attainment of specific instrumental objectives. Campaign contributions may be interpreted as a means to create social and informational networks as well, rather than as a price for political favors; they are "gifts" in the anthropological sense, "not bribes" (Clawson, Neustadtl, and Weller 1998: 61; Milyo, Primo, and Groseclose 2000). Ansolabehere, de Figueiredo, and Snyder (2003: 127), who would prefer to find a rational choice explanation for their data, conclude to the contrary: there may be "so little money in US politics" simply because "executives and managers may value being part of the Washington establishment."

Thomas Watson, Sr., the founder of IBM, and his son, namesake, and successor as IBM CEO illustrate some of these points. Both deeply enjoyed their associations with the global political elite, including a series of US Presidents. To be sure, they pursued numerous policy objectives of great importance to the firm through these relationships, but they did so obliquely, at times imposing constraints on the firm's political activities to avoid the appearance of influence-seeking. Watson, Jr., for instance, forbade IBM from giving corporate campaign contributions in the 1970s; in 2000, IBM was one of only nine firms in the *Fortune* 100 that had neither formed a PAC nor contributed soft money. Watson Jr.'s successors maintained this policy because IBM's organizational routines, public reputation, and corporate culture made changing the policy hard for them to imagine and even harder to effect (Hart 2007).

Inertia does not account for all firm political behavior. Suarez's (2000) longitudinal case study of the pharmaceutical industry explores what happens when environmental stimuli prompt incremental change. Large firms in this industry made significant manufacturing investments in Puerto Rico over several decades in response to federal tax breaks that favored that location. This policy came under attack in Congress from time to time, and the industry mobilized to defend it. When these efforts failed, as they did on a couple of occasions, the firms adjusted their routines for cooperating with one another, in order to gain an edge in the next battle. The new routines were innovative only in the narrowest sense. Firms formed temporary coalitions or committed greater resources to industry associations than they had in the past.

The political history of Microsoft provides an instance of more dramatic change in organizational routines in response to an existential threat to the firm. The threat was a 1998 government antitrust lawsuit; Department of Justice lawyers eventually proposed breaking up the firm. Prior antitrust enforcement efforts had not been taken seriously by Microsoft, which was perceived in Washington as a "wimp." Microsoft CEO Bill Gates's appearance before a Congressional antitrust committee in 1998 apparently broke through the firm's organizational and cultural barriers to perceiving the threat. Soon, it was acting as a virtual full employment agency for the city's lobbying industry. Ironically, this over-reaction failed to stem the threat and may even have exacerbated it. Only the election of a new Republican president, for which Microsoft could hardly claim credit, led to a resolution of the suit on favorable terms (Hart 2003).

These cases bring out the limits of the behavioral theory of the firm as well as its strengths. Its stress on routines and inertia seems to preclude consideration of systematic learning across firms and within the community of policy practitioners and executives. Its emphasis on response to threat means that neither firms nor individuals within them are seen to seek out opportunities, much less create them. Agency, in short, is rarely observed in this depiction of the political realm, a realm that in most other accounts is replete with human creativity and foibles.

Scholars deploying the behavioral theory of the firm in empirical domains other than politics have sought with some success to address this weakness. More room can be made for agency relative to structure, and will relative to inertia, without undermining the theory's core concepts. Yet, those concepts do impose constraints; they must, in order to give definition to the research agenda. So, they must be questioned and challenged. A robust and constructive discourse among the political theories of the firm ought to complement efforts to perfect each of them individually.

CONCLUSION: OF BLIND MEN AND ELEPHANTS

A single political theory of the firm cannot do justice to the complexity of the organizations involved, their interactions, and the environments in which they operate. Scholars of business–government relations have elaborated the three theories discussed above for good reasons. All serious theories entail simplifying assumptions; reality, for better or worse, often violates them. The varied circumstances of corporate political behavior demand a diversity of perspectives on it.

The unitary rational actor theory of the firm assumes the firm to be a profit-maximizing machine, in its relations with government as in its relations with competitors, workers, suppliers, and customers. Evidence that corroborates this assumption is widespread, across government procurement policy, economic regulation, taxation, and international trade, to name just a few of the most prominent areas. Yet, there is also plenty of evidence that firms are often confused, ignorant, or simply wrong about how to maximize profits through their political activities.

The nexus of contracts theory of the firm views the firm as the sum of many individual parts, each of which seeks to maximize his or her own utility function, however that function may be constructed. Although less effort has been expended compiling evidence consistent with this view (in part due to the difficulty of doing so), political agents of firms clearly exploit the informational advantages that they enjoy and the murkiness of the environment in which they operate from time to time. Whether they can do so consistently—or whether they would even want to try—is a matter for further inquiry.

The behavioral theory of the firm postulates satisficing as the governing rule of behavioral change, and limited attention as the human condition. Anyone who has participated in politics and policy-making, especially in the specialized domains that occupy the time of most corporate issue managers, will acknowledge that routine, inertia, accident, and drift explain much of what happens. But not all: entrepreneurial behavior and even radical change must be incorporated for many narratives of the policy process to be fully told.

I return then, to the folk tale of the blind men and elephant. We must first describe this large beast and then explain it. These three theories direct researchers' attention to different parts of the animal as well as prompt distinctive interpretations of their observations. As a field, we should encourage all three (and there may be room for more[5]) without expecting any one of them to provide complete understanding.

Moreover, the beast is growing and changing and will keep doing so. The "globally integrated enterprise" (Palmisano 2007) faces different issues and mobilizes different capabilities than the multinational corporation that preceded it. Preference formation and decision-making within networks of specialty firms (Lamoreaux, Raff, and Temin 2003) differ from those of their vertically integrated forebears. In this dynamic context, limiting our vision to a single paradigm would be costly. And, as an ever-larger fraction of the world's population is drawn into the global market economy and thus within the impact zone of business-government relations, the costs of misunderstanding corporate political behavior are rising, too.

NOTES

1. This chapter builds upon and draws from Hart (2004). Thanks to Lee Drutman for his advice.
2. I should note, however, that many studies of taxes and trade protection take the industry, rather than the firm, as the unit of analysis, and, ironically, essentially assume away the collective action problem. Grossman and Helpman (1994) simply state "we do not at this point have a theory of lobby formation."
3. Of course, for relatively simple tasks such as crop harvesting and construction clean-up, labor may be hired on a daily basis, rather than through longer term contracts. Markets may be preferred to hierarchies in such instances, according to the new institutional economics, because bargaining costs are low for homogeneous labor services.
4. The nexus of contracts theory of the firm helped to justify stock option-heavy compensation packages for many US CEOs during the 1980s and 1990s, ostensibly to align managerial and investor interests. Ironically, these packages created incentives for CEOs to manipulate stock prices for their personal benefit during the boom of the late 1990s

(with the complicity of board members who were supposed to represent investors), setting the stage for the ensuing stock market crash and recession, in which investors were pummeled.

5. An emerging "entrepreneurial theory of the firm," which focuses on risk and uncertainty, for instance, might be adapted to the political arena (Alvarez and Barney 2007).

REFERENCES

ALVAREZ, S. A., and BARNEY, J. B. 2007. "The entrepreneurial theory of the firm," *Journal of Management Studies* 44: 1057–63.

ANSOLABEHERE, S., DE FIGUEIREDO, J. M., and SNYDER, JR., J. M. 2003. "Why is there so little money in US politics?," *The Journal of Economic Perspectives* (Winter): 105–30.

BARON, D. P. 1995. "Integrated strategy: market and nonmarket components," *California Management Review* (Winter): 47–65.

BAUER, R., POOL, I. S., and DEXTER, L. A. 1972. *American Business, Public Policy, and the Politics of Foreign Trade*, 2nd edn. Chicago: Aldine-Atherton.

BAUMGARTNER, F. R., and LEECH, B. L. 2001. "Interest niches and policy bandwagons: patterns of interest group involvement in national politics," *The Journal of Politics* 63: 1191–213.

BECKER, G. S. 1976. *The Economic Approach to Human Behavior*. Chicago: University of Chicago Press.

BRADY, H. E., DRUTMAN, L., SCHLOZMAN, K. L., and VERBA, S. 2007. "Corporate lobbying activity in American politics," *the annual meeting of the American Political Science Association.*

BRASHER, H., and LOWERY, D. 2006. "The corporate context of lobbying activity," *Business and Politics* 8(1), Art. 1.

CLAWSON, D., NEUSTADTL, A., and WELLER, M. 1998. *Dollars and Votes: How Business Campaign Contributions Subvert Democracy*. Philadelphia: Temple University Press.

COASE, R. 1937. "The nature of the firm," *Economica* 4: 386–405.

COEN, D. 2007. "Empirical and theoretical studies in EU lobbying," *Journal of European Public Policy* 14: 333–45.

CYERT, R. M., and MARCH, J. G. 1992. *A Behavioral Theory of the Firm*, 2nd edn. Cambridge: Blackwell Business.

DE FIGUEIREDO, J. M., and KIM, J. J. 2004. "When do firms hire lobbyists? The organization of lobbying at the Federal Communications Commission," *Industrial abd Corporate Change* 13: 883–900.

—— and TILLER, E. H. 2001. "The structure and conduct of corporate lobbying: how firms lobby the Federal Communications Commission," *Journal of Economics and Management Strategy* 10: 91–122.

DEXTER, L. A. 1969. *How Organizations Are Represented in Washington.* Indianapolis: Bobbs-Merrill.

DIMAGGIO, P. J., and POWELL, W. W. 1983. "The iron cage revisited: institutional isomorphism and collective rationality in organizational fields," *American Sociological Review* 48: 147–60.

DROPE, J. M., and HANSEN, W. L. 2004. "Purchasing protection? The effect of political spending on US trade policy," *Political Research Quarterly* 57: 27–37.

—— —— 2006. "Does firm size matter? Analyzing business lobbying in the United States," *Business and Politics* 8(2), Art. 4.

ENGLANDER, E., and KAUFMAN, A. 2004. "The end of managerial ideology: from corporate social responsibility to corporate social indifference," *Enterprise and Society* 5: 404–50.

EPSTEIN, E. M. 1969. *The Corporation in American Politics*. Englewood Cliffs, NJ: Prentice-Hall.

FLIGSTEIN, N. 1990. *The Transformation of Corporate Control.* Cambridge, Mass.: Harvard University Press.

FEREJOHN, J. A., and FIORINA, M. P. 1974. "The paradox of not voting: a decision theoretic analysis," *American Political Science Review* 68: 525–36.

GODWIN, R. K., and SELDON, B. J. 2002. "What corporations really want from government: the public provision of private goods," in A. J. Cigler and B.A. Loomis, eds., *Interest Group Politics*, 6th edn. Washington, DC: CQ Press, 205–24.

GOLDSTEIN, K. M. 1999. *Interest Groups, Lobbying, and Participation in America.* New York: Cambridge University Press.

GOLDTHORPE, J. 1984. *Order and Conflict in Contemporary Capitalism.* New York: Oxford University Press.

GROSSMAN, G. M., and HELPMAN, E. 1994. "Protection for sale," *The American Economic Review* 84: 833–50.

HALL, P.A., and SOSKICE, D. 2001. *Varieties of Capitalism: Institutional Foundations of Comparative Advantage* New York: Oxford University Press.

HANSEN, W. L., and MITCHELL, N. J. 2000. "Disaggregating and explaining corporate political activity: domestic and foreign corporations in national politics," *American Political Science Review* 94: 891–903.

——— and DROPE, J. M. 2004. "Collective action, pluralism, and the legitimacy tariff," *Political Research Quarterly* 57: 421–9.

HARRIS, R. A. 1997. "Boundary spanners, legitimacy, and corporate communications," in J. Garnett and A. Kouzmin, eds., *Handbook of Administrative Communication.* Oxford: Marcel Dekker, 309–27.

HART, D. M. 2002. "High-tech learns to play the Washington game, or the political education of Bill Gates and other nerds," in A. J. Cigler and B. A. Loomis, eds., *Interest Group Politics*, 6th edn. Washington: CQ Press, 293–312.

——— 2003. "Political representation among dominant firms: revisiting the Olsonian hypothesis," *Business and Politics* 5: 261–86.

——— 2004. "Business is not an interest group: on companies in American national politics," *Annual Review of Political Science* 7: 47–67.

——— 2007. "Red, white, and 'big blue': IBM and the business-government interface in the U.S., 1956-2000," *Enterprise and Society* 8: 1–34.

HEATH, R. L. 1995. *Strategic Issues Management: Organizations and Public Policy Challenges.* Thousand Oaks, Calif.: Sage.

HEINZ, J. P., et al. 1993. *The Hollow Core: Private Interests in National Policy-Making* Cambridge, Mass.: Harvard University Press.

JENSEN, M. C., and MECKLING, W. H. 1976. "Theory of the firm: managerial behavior, agency costs, and ownership structure," *Journal of Financial Economics* 3: 305–60.

JOHN, S., and SCHWARZER, D. 2006. *Industrial Lobbying within the European Union.* Washington, DC: American Institute for Contemporary German Studies.

KERSH, R. T. 2002. "Corporate lobbyists as political actors: a view from the field," in A. J. Cigler and B. A. Loomis, eds., *Interest Group Politics*, 6th edn. Washington: CQ Press, 225–48.

LAMOREAUX, N. R. 2004. "Partnerships, corporations, and the limits on contractual freedom in US history: an essay in economics, law, and culture," in K. Lipartito and D. B. Sicilia, eds., *Constructing Corporate America: History, Politics, Culture.* New York: Oxford University Press, 29–65.

——— RAFF, D., and TEMIN, P. 2003. "Beyond markets and hierarchies: toward a new synthesis of American business history," *American Historical Review* 108: 404–33.

LEVI, M. 1988. *Of Rule and Revenue.* Berkeley: University of California Press.

LICHTENBERG, F. R. 1989. "Contributions to federal elections campaigns by government contractors," *Journal of Industrial Economics* 38: 31–48.

LINDBLOM, C. 1977. *Politics and Markets.* New York: Basic.

LOOMIS, B., and STRUEMPH, M. 2004. "Growing larger, going abroad, getting acquired," the annual meeting of the American Political Science Association.

LOWERY, D., GRAY, V. 1995. "The population ecology of Gucci Gulch, or the natural regulation of interest group numbers in the American states," *American Journal of Political Science* 39: 1–29.

McKELVEY, M. 1997. "Using evolutionary theory to define systems of innovation," in C. Edquist, ed., *Systems of Innovation: Technologies, Institutions, and Organizations.* London: Pinter.

MARCH, J. G. 1962. "The business firm as a political coalition," *Journal of Politics* 24: 662–78.

MARTIN, C. J. 2000. *Stuck in Neutral: Business and the Politics of Human Capital Investment Policy.* Princeton: Princeton University Press.

MEYER, J. W., and ROWAN, B. 1977. "Institutionalized organizations: formal structure as myth and ceremony," *American Journal of Sociology* 83: 340–63.

MILES, R. H. 1982. *Coffin Nails and Corporate Strategies.* Englewood Cliffs, NJ: Prentice-Hall.

MILIBAND, R. 1969. *The State in Capitalist Society.* New York: Basic.

MILLS, C. W. 1956. *The Power Elite.* New York: Oxford University Press.

MILYO, J., PRIMO, D., and GROSECLOSE, T. 2000. "Corporate PAC contributions in perspective," *Business and Politics* 2: 75–88.

NELSON, R. R., and WINTER, S. G. 1982. *Evolutionary Theory of Economic Change.* Cambridge, Mass.: Harvard University Press.

NOAM, E. 2003. "Entrepreneurship and government in telecommunications," in D. M. Hart, ed., *The Emergence of Entrepreneurship Policy: Governance, Start-Ups, and Growth in the Knowledge Economy.* New York: Cambridge University Press.

OLSON, M. 1965. *The Logic of Collective Action.* Cambridge, Mass.: Harvard University Press.

—— and ZECKHAUSER, R. 1966. "An economic theory of alliances," *Review of Economics and Statistics* 48: 266–79.

OSTROM, E. 1990. *Governing the Commons: Evolution of Institutions for Collective Action.* New York: Cambridge University Press.

PALMISANO, S. J. 2006. "The globally integrated enterprise," *Foreign Affairs* (May/June): 127–36.

PIERSON, P. 1996. "The new politics of the welfare state," *World Politics* 48: 143–79.

RICHTER, B. K., SAMPHANTHARAK, K., and TIMMONS, J. F. 2008. "Lobbying and taxes," unpublished MS, http://ssrn.com/abstract=1082146

SCHATTSCHNEIDER, E. E. 1960. *The Semi-Sovereign People.* New York: Holt, Rinehart & Winston.

SCHULER, D. A. 1999. "Corporate political action: rethinking the economic and organizational influences," *Business and Politics* 1: 83–97.

SIMON, H. A. 1957. *Administrative Behavior,* 2nd edn. New York: MacMillan.

SMITH, M. A. 2000. *American Business and Political Power: Public Opinion, Elections, and Democracy.* Chicago: University of Chicago Press.

SNYDER JR., J. M. 1992. "Long-term investing in politicians; or give early, give often," *Journal of Law and Economics* 35: 15–43.

STIGLER, G. J. 1975. *The Citizen and the State: Essays on Regulation.* Chicago: University of Chicago Press.

SUAREZ, S. L. 2000. *Does Business Learn? Tax Breaks, Uncertainty, and Political Strategies.* Ann Arbor: University of Michigan Press.

TRUMAN, D. B. 1951. *The Governmental Process: Political Interests and Public Opinion.* New York: Knopf.

VOGEL, D. J. 1978. "Why American businessmen distrust their state: the political consciousness of American corporate executives," *British Journal of Political Science* 8: 45–78.

VOGEL, D. J. 1989. *Fluctuating Fortunes: The Political Power of Business in America.* New York: Basic.

WARTICK, S. L., and RUDE, R. E. 1986. "Issues management: corporate fad or corporate function," *California Management Review* 29: 124–40.

WILLIAMSON, O. E. 1971. "The vertical integration of production: market failure considerations," *The American Economic Review* 61: 112–23.

——2000. "The new institutional economics: taking stock, looking ahead," *Journal of Economic Literature* 38: 595–613.

YOFFIE, D. B., and BERGENSTEIN, S. 1985. "Creating political advantage: the rise of the corporate political entrepreneur," *California Management Review* 28 (1): 124–39.

CHAPTER 8

BUSINESS AND POLITICAL PARTIES

GRAHAM WILSON
WYN GRANT

INTRODUCTION

As numerous contributions to this volume make clear, businesses and business organizations seek to influence policy through standard techniques of interest group politics such as lobbying. A powerful tradition in political science urges us to pay attention not only to lobbying, however, but to the role of business in party systems. Perhaps the exemplar of this approach is a giant of twentieth-century American political science, E. E. Schattschneider, who argued that the primary "political instrument of business" was the Republican Party (Schattschneider 1956: 197). McMenamin and Schoenman (2007: 153) have drawn attention to the fact that "the political party remains a relatively understudied actor in government–business relations. Indeed, there is very little systematic literature on the relationship between two key organisations of capitalism and representative democracy."

Although it is conventional in political science to distinguish between political parties and interest groups in practice the distinction is less clear. The conventional definitions suggest that political parties seek to capture power; interest groups aspire to influencing public policy. Even the names of political parties make it obvious, however, that in practice this distinction is not absolute. The linkage in the UK between Labour parties and unions is usually clear. In the United States, the Minnesota branch of the Democratic Party is still called the Democratic Farm Labor Party. Farmers' parties used to be fairly common although as in the Swedish case they have generally adopted labels that are more encompassing such as, to continue the Swedish example, the Center Party.

Parties do not call themselves "The Business Party" but are often described as such. What does this mean? On what basis is it reasonable to identify a party as the business party? There are a number of different indicators that can be used. First a party may be the business party in the sense that it is openly and explicitly endorsed by the leading business organization or organizations. Second, we might label a party the business party because a large majority of business people identify with and vote for the party so that they constitute the party's major Course of support. Third, a party might receive most of its financial support from businesses or business people. Finally, the party might be seen to be consistently favoring business in its policies and manifestos. It is not obvious, however, what favoring business means. There are also very important differences across sectors and across countries in terms of what business wants. While some are willing to label the German Free Democrats a pro-business party on the basis of their support for liberal economic policies, it is abundantly clear that many German employers there have not been enthusiastic advocates of liberal reforms of the labor market and have often felt more comfortable with the more collectivist views of the CDU/CSU (Deeg 1999). Similarly in Japan, the Keidanren in Japan has worked with sympathetic legislators in the Liberal Democratic Party (LDP) to slow or in some cases prevent the adoption of liberal economic reforms (Tiberghien 2007). While some academics have conflated support for liberal economic reforms with support for business interests and wishes, there are many examples that prove that this is a mistake.

While the programmatic or ideological consequences may vary, in most if not all democracies, one of the major parties is generally thought of as being the natural party for business to support. The Conservative Party in the UK and the Republican Party in the USA are familiar examples. Similarly the Liberal Democratic Party has been associated with the interests of Japanese corporations. Business relates to political parties in several ways—financial, ideological, and organizational. Yet political parties are coalitions varying in size and complexity but invariably bringing together varied interests and even viewpoints. To our knowledge there is no political party in any stable democracy that can be described as *simply* a business party dedicated to advancing the interests of business as a whole or of particular types of business with no other major interest or ideology within its ranks. This is not to say that business is not an extremely important influence—even a dominating influence—in some political parties. As we shall see, even when the case for business dominance of a party seems strongest, there are nearly always competing ideological and material interests with which business has to be balanced. Finally, almost all political parties in democracies including those to which business is allied seek to maximize their vote. This has implications for the degree to which a party can be explicitly aligned with business. Even in the most pro-business environments, it is rarely a successful strategy for a politician to run for office on the claim that he or she is the most uncritical friend of business.

Iversen and Soskice (this volume) explore the link between electoral systems and modes of business representation. In this chapter we explore the variations among parties linked to business in stable democracies and offer some theoretical conclusions. We begin with the familiar and often linked cases of the UK and USA.

THE ANGLO-AMERICAN CASES

As we have noted already, many people identify the Conservative Party in the UK and the Republican Party in the United States as pro-business parties. In both cases, the links between business and the parties can be traced back to the late nineteenth century.

The Republican Party had emerged immediately before the Civil War as the party of free labor (as opposed to slavery) and of the family farmer (as opposed to the plantation.) Shortly after the Civil War it linked manufacturing interests and labor through a commitment to a highly protectionist trade policy based on high tariffs. It also retained a commitment to the family farm and benefited in important regions such as the upper Midwest from the legacy of being the party of the Union; Republicans waved "the bloody shirt" of Civil War memories as vigorously in the North as did Democrats in the South. The alliance between the party and business was highlighted in the 1890s when the Democrats attempted to co-opt the populists of the Midwest and South by nominating William Jennings Bryant whose monetary policies were seen as advantaging farmers at the cost of bankers. Mark Hannah, the Republican campaign consultant guru of the age, attracted vast contributions from business in order to defeat Bryant. Yet business was by no means monolithically in support of the Republicans either then, or even after Franklin Roosevelt's New Deal. Regional loyalties, especially in the South where the Democrats retained a virtual monopoly on power until the 1970s, overwhelmed appeals to business or class interest (Bensell 1984; Martin 2006; Martin and Swank 2008). Thus, to take a celebrated example, Lyndon Johnson, although elected as a strong New Dealer, soon developed a mutually beneficial relationship with the oil industry supply firm Haliburton (Caro 1982, 2002). Although the more usual error is to assume that all Southern politicians were conservative on economic and social policy issues, it is also often forgotten that many of them combined great influence within the Democratic Party with loyalty to business interests. Even in the modern era, some business people are very loyal to the Democratic Party: Wall Street contributed generously to President Obama's campaign; Goldman Sachs executives were a particularly important source of money for Obama in the crucial and difficult early stages of the presidential campaign ("In Race for Wall Street Funds Obama has Early Lead," Dealbook *New York Times*, April 17, 2007).

The history of the relationship between the Conservative Party and business also developed in the nineteenth century. Originating as the party of the landed interests, the Conservatives gradually detached business from what had seemed a more natural relationship between businessmen and what became the Liberal Party. While the exact process of this change is the subject of much debate a few key moments can be identified. The Whigs/Liberals generally took the lead in extending the right to vote to commercial classes. However, the repeal of agricultural protection (the Corn Laws) by a Conservative Prime Minister (Peel) in the face of opposition from the landed gentry showed the willingness of at least some Conservatives to place business interests ahead of their traditional base. As business became an established interest as the Industrial Revolution receded into the past, the Liberals' willingness to play with radical change—first in relation to Ireland, later (1906–16) in introducing the beginnings of the welfare state financed by taxes on the wealthy and furthering democracy—concerned the property-owning classes. A lasting relationship developed between the Conservatives and certain industries (notably brewing) that had an uneasy relationship with parts of the Liberal Party's base. Ironically, the greater willingness of the Conservatives to abandon free trade in the late nineteenth century as the competitiveness of British manufacturing industry declined made them attractive to industrialists who now feared foreign competition. Finally, the displacement of the Liberal Party by a competitor (the Labour Party) ostensibly committed to socialism and financed by the unions completed the linking of business and the Conservative Party (Ramsden 1998).

The limited linkage between Republicans and business in the United States is demonstrated both by the varying levels of support the party receives in the form of campaign contributions from business and in the prominence of other interests in its campaign strategies. As Werner and Wilson discuss (this volume), the Democrats have always received a significant minority of campaign contributions from business. In general, the business contributions they have received have been in proportion to their power or prospects for power. It seems that business's heart has generally been with the Republicans but its head has sometimes dictated alliances with powerful Democrats in Congress. The Republicans tended to see this as a betrayal, and during the period in which they controlled Congress from 1994 to 2006 they launched the "K Street Project" aimed at forcing corporations to be closer to the party in terms of both making a higher proportion of campaign contributions and hiring only its supporters as lobbyists. However, the Republicans' success in controlling Congress and the White House was based on appealing to groups very different from the base among long-established businesses with which it had been associated. The Republicans assiduously cultivated a base among far from privileged voters by showing sympathy for evangelical Christians, Catholic values on issues such as abortion rights, gun ownership, and antipathy to increased rights for homosexuals, a combination often known as the Three Gs—God, Guns, and Gays. Even the Republicans' avid pursuit of tax cuts irrespective of the condition of the government's budget was cast in populist terms—allowing ordinary people to keep money that would otherwise be pilfered by Big Government or transferred to the undeserving. The impact of these issues on voting behavior has been much debated, and Bartells (2008) in particular has criticized that the idea that these issues won the Republicans a significant working-class base. There can be little debate that the Republicans followed this strategy whether or not it worked. A recent and complete expression came in the selection of Governor Sarah Palin to be the Republican vice presidential candidate in 2008.

British political parties are somewhat less *openly* coalitional than American but are certainly not monoliths. The Conservatives, like the Republicans, have generally tried to project an image of being the more patriotic party at least since their opposition to devolution for Ireland in the nineteenth century. They would not have enjoyed the success that they did after the extension of the franchise to all following the 1918 Representation of the People Act if they had not had significant working-class support. The swift acceptance of the welfare state by the Conservatives after their defeat in the 1945 election was generally seen as an attempt to keep a working-class base. The nature of this support in the decades immediately following the Second World War was much debated, with some arguing that it reflected deferential attitudes in the British working class and others that this support was based on rational calculations of economic advantage. The "Thatcher Project" of the 1980s, as it was often called, involved a determined effort to win support from skilled workers through measures such as income tax cuts, the sale of government-owned housing to its occupants, and of stock in government-owned business to consumers on favorable terms. Meanwhile, Thatcher herself was far from sympathetic to the main business interest group, the CBI. Relations between her and the Director General in her early years as Prime Minister were particularly rocky. The Department of Trade and Industry deliberately weakened links with trade associations, and a rival group to the CBI, the Institute of Directors, was promoted.

Thus the Conservative Party has not had a simple, friendly relationship with business and business interest groups. This has left it free to pursue attempts to build a wide coalition. Apart from appeals to working-class voters, the Conservatives also continued to be identified in most but not all of Britain as the party of the farmer and the countryside. Moreover, until Thatcherism came to dominate the party in the 1980s, there had been a strong tradition in the party of limiting market forces in order to promote social cohesion and to protect the national culture. Conservatives were fond of mentioning the fact that some of the first legislation to protect workers in the nineteenth century had been promoted by Conservatives. Conservative governments created and sustained the BBC as a monopoly in its early days lest commercialism lower standards. In the 1930s Conservatives such as Harold Macmillan pressed for measures to alleviate the consequences of the Great Depression; in late old age he made clear in the House of Lords his discomfort with Margaret Thatcher's embrace of market forces. The Party was heavily dependent on business financially for much of the modern era but had the political sense to realize that a wider electoral base was needed. The attempts by David Cameron to lead the party out of the political wilderness after the 2005 election included significant efforts to dissociate it from total loyalty to market forces and identification with business.

Several factors have limited the closeness of both the Republican and Conservative Parties and business. Three deserve particular emphasis. First, both parties have generally followed strategies of widening their electoral base far beyond business. Both have emphasized issues and traditions that are unrelated to business interests and in some cases (such as the Republican alliance with conservative evangelicals) may even be a source of discomfort to business supporters. Third, and most importantly, business interests have been eager to avoid being overly identified as partisans of these parties. Business interests have been well aware in both countries that Democrats and the Labour Party often win elections and hold power. Not only groups such as the CBI but individual corporations have been well aware of the need to be able to lobby successfully whichever party is in power. Whenever major businesses or the CBI have felt that there was some conflict between identification with Conservatives on the one hand and on keeping open the links between them and government departments during periods of Labour government, they have overwhelmingly favored the latter. Labour governments in the twentieth century were more consistently interested in organized links between business and government than were the Conservatives. The creation of the CBI itself was encouraged by the 1964–70 Labour government. The CBI and major businesses have generally cultivated an image of non-partisan expertise and when given the chance during the high tide of neo-corporatism in the UK in the 1960s and 1970s were eager to be full participants in tripartism.

Does this mean that the Conservative and Republican parties have not been business parties? If we use most of the criteria at the opening of this chapter, the answer is clearly negative. Both parties have consistently received the majority of votes from business executives and their families even though this majority has declined in the UK in recent times. Similarly, the parties have received the bulk of financial contributions from business and business executives. Finally, both parties have advanced policies that are generally seen as being more in line with the interests and wishes of business. If we tried the thought experiment of imaging what British or American politics would be like without the Conservative and Republican parties, the balances struck in public policy would be much less sympathetic to business and more sympathetic to contending interests (unions, environmentalists, consumers, etc.). Even when these parties are out of power, Downsian party competition helps to pull their opponents in a more pro-business direction. It was of course central to both Clinton and Blair's political strategies to make their parties seem more sympathetic to business. Business does have its favorite party in both countries. However, the relationship between business and the parties is complicated by the consequences of history, ideology, and electoral politics.

Labour governments in Britain have necessarily had to have an effective working relationship with business because of the extent to which their policies have been concerned with economic management. The relationship with the Labour Party has necessarily been more distant, in part because of the institutional relationship with the trade unions, in part because relatively few business persons have openly identified them as Labour supporters and those that have done so have been viewed as curiosities in business circles.

Nevertheless, the Labour Party has employed a variety of mechanisms to mobilize the advice and support of such business persons as it has among its supporters. In 1932, the semi-secret XYZ club was formed to bring together Labour sympathizers in the City, economist, and a few politicians, with the future Labour leader Hugh Gaitskell as secretary. Hugh Dalton, a future finance minister, linked its activities to party policy-making and "much of the financial policy in Labour's 1934 document, *For Labour and Peace,* was a product of XYZ deliberations" (Pimlott 1985: 223). At the end of the Second World War, it contributed to work on post-war employment policy, but it eventually became little more than a dining club for Gaitskellites.

Harold Wilson relied on ad hoc links with industrialists he trusted, but a more formal mechanism was revived with the creation of the Labour Party Finance and Industry Group in 1972, recruited from long-term Labour supporters. It was not an affiliated organization, but was eventually registered with the party. In opposition, the committee offered practical help on the development of policy. However, the Labour Party's links with business suffered a blow with the formation of the breakaway Social Democratic Party. About 30 to 40 per cent of the membership of the 1972 committee defected to the new party. Another organization that emerged in the late 1980s was Enterprise for Labour, an organization of young business persons that met in a Soho wine bar and were known as "Yuppies for Kinnock."

However, the real transformation in the Labour Party's relationship with business took place with the development of New Labour under the leadership of Tony Blair. Blair and Gordon Brown embarked on a "prawn cocktail offensive" to win support in the City of London. Blair made it clear that he wanted Labour to be "the natural party of business." One consequence was a substantial increase in the value of business donations to Labour. However, these fell away as the party's relationship with business became more strained, even though Gordon Brown was determined to maintain a good relationship with business.

Although not normally identified as the natural choice for business, the Democratic Party has had a somewhat easier time of maintaining links with business. Unlike the Labour Party before the repeal of Clause IV of its Constitution, the Democrats never had an explicitly anti-capitalist stance. (Of course, Clause IV never had that much of an impact on the actual behaviour of Labour governments after 1951, but Clause IV still had symbolic significance.) The Democratic Party in the United States has also been able take advantage of its much looser structure to maintain links with business *and* its opponents (unions, environmentalists, consumer groups) simultaneously. The fragmented nature of American institutions helps; one Democratic Representative can be more pro-business and another assertively environmentalist. However, even individual Democratic politicians often find ways of combining support from business and its critics.

THE LIBERAL DEMOCRATIC PARTY

Experts on Japanese politics agree that the Liberal Democratic Party was an essential component of the regime that brought about the emergence of Japan as the world's second largest economy. The conventional view expressed by Chalmers Johnson (1982) portrayed the party as essentially the political insulation that allowed the bureaucracy to make policy. Ramseyer and Rosenbluth (1993) in contrast suggested that the party was the principal controlling the bureaucracy, its agent. For Johnson in his original writing, the LDP was almost irrelevant to the governance of Japan; for Ramseyer and Rosenbluth the LDP was the controlling force behind economic policy—and for that matter even judicial policy. The Policy Advisory Research Committees (PARCS) of the Diet determined policy which the bureaucracy merely implemented.

The LDP was formed in 1955 by the merger of two conservative parties. Most LDP deputies are career politicians, different in background and style from the bureaucratic elite. A substantial minority of LDP deputies, however, have been members of the elite civil service. Interestingly creating a mildly redistributionist influence, the former bureaucrats tend to represent the more rural and poorer parts of Japan. We should be careful to note that conservativism in this context does not necessarily mean support for laissez-faire economics. Indeed as Stephen Vogel notes, there has never been consistent support—let alone pressure—from the party for economic liberalization (Vogel 2006). Any public discontent with policies of liberalization was unlikely to find strong resistance from the Party. Between 1955 and 1994, the LDP had a system of highly developed factions, something that was generally ascribed to the consequences of the Single Non Transferable Vote (SNTV) system combined with multiple member constituencies. In other words, LDP candidates competed against each other as well as against opposition parties. Thus although the LDP has been the majority party for all but a brief period in the 1990s, its candidates have operated in a competitive environment. This competition has fueled the quest for pork barrel spending, the many bridges (and roads) to nowhere noted by Pempel (1998). LDP candidates have been eager for the support of many local interests including farmers and, to take another celebrated example, the operators of post offices. Indeed, Estevez-Abe (2008) argues that the entire character of the Japanese welfare state was shaped by the logic of electoral competition created by the multi-member constituencies and SNTV.

One of the reasons for the sharp difference of opinion that developed between Chalmers Johnson on the one hand and Ramseyer and Rosenbluth on the other is that they were writing about different eras in a changing situation. As Maurice

Wright (1999) has argued, the model of Japanese governance developed by Johnson in his seminal book was one that was gradually disappearing by the time it was published. Most authorities, perhaps even Johnson himself, admit that the idea that Japan was ruled by the bureaucracy in close but dominating partnership with big business was outdated by the 1980s. Political leaders were becoming more assertive on policy issues. This change was supposed to be reinforced by the change in the electoral law, when the SNTV system was abolished in 1994 and was replaced with a single member system modified by the presence of deputies elected through proportional representation. It was hoped that these changes would produce more policy-centered politics. Whether the changes have had the desired effect has been debated (Schaede and Grimes 2003) and the factions have been more resilient than expected. However, the reforms have increased public confidence in the Party. Estevez-Abe (2008) argues that the reforms did indeed move Japan towards a more Westminster style of government with concentrated, centralized power in the hands of the prime minister. Tiberghien (2007) believes that it was the effective leadership of a prime minister with effective control over the LDP, Koizumi, that made possible what structural reforms of both government and business were achieved by Japan's leaders in the late 1990s. In preceding decades the LDP had proved incapable of providing leadership as power within the party was divided among the half-dozen party leaders and leaders of the four to six factions. However, Tiberghien believes that the period of effective leadership and reform was brief. There is general agreement that LDP politicians pushed hard for greater influence in policy-making in the 1990s. They contributed to the widespread attacks on the honesty and competence of the higher bureaucracy that Pempel (1998) saw as bringing about the "regime change" ending bureaucratic dominance of policy-making. While the exact balance of power between the bureaucracy and the LDP remains unclear, it is generally agreed to have shifted considerably towards the party in the last decade of the twentieth century. However, change was not total. Vogel concludes that "The Japanese model is changing but the change is continuous, not discontinuous" (Vogel 2006: 224). The LDP often acting on behalf of business interests including the Keidanren has often been a brake on change towards a liberal market economy (Tiberghien 2007). The Party as such has not been the motor of change which has been provided by the prime ministers with enhanced standing and autonomy.

The LDP was never the primary means through which Japanese business sought to exert influence. Contacts with government departments such as MITI (now METI) were more important. The LDP was clearly preferred by business to the alternatives, particularly the Socialist Party. It has received financial and other support from corporations. However, its behavior and roles have been shaped by a wider variety of factors including electoral dynamics and shifts in relationships between the elements of the political system. During the heydays of economic growth, most scholars saw the primary role of the LDP was being the provider of the political insulation or casing within which the bureaucracy in partnership with business could make policy. So low was the standing of LDP ministers that it was their top civil servants who answered Parliamentary Questions, a task that was thought to be beyond ministers' capacities (Estevez- Abe 2008). In contrast, when Japan was seen to need fundamental reform in the 1990s, it was hoped that LDP politicians could provide the necessary impetus for change. The LDP has provided Japan with leaders such as Prime Minister Koizumi who have sought to make important changes in Japan's political economy. However, aided by a surprisingly high institutional capacity to block government legislation because of the procedural rules of the Japanese parliament, the LDP has also been a major barrier to more extensive reform (Tiberghien 2007).

BALANCING OUT INTERESTS: THE GERMAN CASE

Germany is the prototypical associative state. Associations are seen as having a crucial and legitimate role in mediating between business and government. This does not mean that there is not a role for business interaction with political parties. The Christian Democratic Union (the CDU) and its Bavarian sister party (the Christian Social Union, CSU) are factionalized parties that seek to balance out competing interests. Indeed, this balancing out is more generally characteristic of Germany. The political system in Germany makes reform difficult, a phenomenon referred to as *Reformstau*, "reform logjam" (Vogel 2001: 1104). Those who favor liberal reforms "cannot forge a strong political coalition because the major industry associations and conservative political parties incorporate both the potential winners and the potential losers from reform. Thus the associations and the parties must work out internal compromises between constituent groups before proposing reforms" (Vogel 2001: 1005). One view of the consequences would be that this creates a classic case of "Eurosclerosis," inhibiting the development of a flexible labor market and incurring high regulatory costs. An alternative view would be that the slow pace of reform has protected Germany from the worst excesses of neo-liberalism and the rundown of the manufacturing sector.

One of the distinctive characteristics of the CDU is the strength of the labor wing within the party. A whole series of proposed reforms have been moderated by the actions of the labor wing. Arguably an important political cleavage in Germany is "the one between the labour wing of the CDU on the one hand and the business wing of the same party and the FDP on the other" (Zohlnhöfer 1999: 152). There are limits, however, in the extent to which the FDP can act as a spokesperson for business. It has placed an increasing emphasis on liberal ideas in recent years, but without reaping any electoral dividend. Moreover, "The FDP garners considerable support from small business owners and professionals who themselves benefit from government regulation, so it has refrained from endorsing unbridled deregulation" (Vogel 2001: 1116).

The various factions of the CDU map onto policy domains, institutionalizing them within the state apparatus. Thus, " 'classical' economic policy...is in the hands of the middle classes' organisation (MIT), and labour and social policy...is controlled by the CDA" representing worker interests. Similarly, "The business wing dominates the ministry of finance and represents the party in the (Parliamentary) committees of finance and economic affairs, while the ministry of social affairs and the corresponding committee is in the hands of the labour wing" (Zohlnhöfer 1999: 154). Although there have been significant changes in Germany, the political system still has a strong productionist emphasis which encourages the development of networks between business the CDU/CSU and the FDP. Nevertheless, these links are not as important as those between business associations and the state.

ITALY AND THE PARTY STATE

In Grant (1989, 1993) an attempt was made to develop a typology of government–business relations in terms of the predominant form of interaction between government and business. In the party state, interaction takes place through a political party or, in particular, through the factions of a dominant political party. This is in contrast to the associative state where intermediation is through business associations or the company state where direct contacts between large firms and government are encouraged.

It is argued that over time party states tend to be displaced by associative states or company states. The associative state sits easily with a social-democratic scenario (which may be pursued by parties that are not formally social democratic) which "requires some capacity for collective action and, as a second step, an agreement over the pursuit of agreed societal objectives through interactive adjustments between political compromise and interest intermediation" (Lanza and Lavdas 2000: 203). Similarly, the company state is compatible with the paradigm of neo-liberalism and globalization.

However, apart from this compatibility with familiar political scenarios enjoyed by the other forms of interaction, the party state has a more fundamental flaw: it is incompatible with economic and political modernity. It is typified by patron–client relationships, the grant of personal favors, privileges awarded on the basis of network ties, and, in extreme cases, corruption. Decisions about the economy are influenced by considerations of political favoritism, invariably leading to suboptimal outcomes that undermine economic efficiency and international competitiveness. Political skills become more important than technical skills in managers.

Under the formerly prevalent party state arrangement in Italy, "the style of managers was political, not entrepreneurial, the criterion for evaluating performance was party allegiance rather than professional achievements, and corporate strategies were important to political competition than to market competition" (Grant and Martinelli 1991: 87). Within Italy's large complex of state holding companies, "Public managers started to support political groups, especially within the DC (Christian Democrats), and these groups started to offer protection to public managers. The main result was to create a vicious circle for the mutual promotion of politicians and public managers" (Bianchi 1987: 277). Public funds were wasted and corporate strategies paralyzed at a time when competitors were restructuring more rapidly.

The Italian case helps us to understand how a party state was created in the first place and how it eventually came to be displaced: in the case of another party state, Greece, the process of displacement has been slower and less complete. Post-war Italy was characterized by a weak state and a strong civil society. However, the later industrialization of Italy meant that employer organizations were weakly developed and often territorial in character. The Christian Democrats pursued a conscious strategy of controlling the main power centers of civil society through party-connected managers. The Christian Democrats sought "to control sectors of civil society, and colonize state institutions" (Martinelli and Grant 1991: 278). Their legitimacy in doing so was reinforced by their links with the Vatican in what was then a deeply religious society, with Catholic conceptions of an organic and unified social order having a strong influence. Within this context interest groups were subordinated to parties:

[It] must be said that *colonization* of groups by the parties was more widespread than *penetration* of parties by the groups. Parties were founding members of many interest groups and maintained throughout the years a considerable power of appointment within the groups themselves.   (Lanza and Lavdas 2000: 211)

These arrangements probably were more functional in the 1950s when industry was relatively homogeneous. The business class was still tainted by its association with Fascism, while the Christian Democrats were the embodiment of the new era, standing firm in a Cold War context against their main domestic rivals, the Communist Party. Thus, "Throughout the period of the so-called first republic, the relation between Confindustria and political parties was marked by an early imbalance in favour of the parties" (Lanza and Lavdas 2000: 207). Business interests had nowhere to turn but the Christian Democrats. Indeed, "the three main political parties, the Christian Democrats, the Communist Party and the Socialist Party were in different ways the bearers of an anti-capitalist culture, whose referent social groups were the petty and middle bourgeoisie and employed workers, rather than the industrial bourgeoisie" (Lanza and Lavdas 2000: 207). What this produced was a business class that was lacking in collective political self-confidence and was over-reliant on its ties with the Christian Democrats.

The very success of industrialization in Italy produced new lines of division. "The once close link between a unified party and a rather homogeneous business class became instead a fragmented network of influences in which different party factions were allied to different centres of economic power" (Martinelli and Treu 1984: 16). This tended to increase the transaction costs and the dysfunctional character of the relationships. The consequences can be clearly seen in the case of the chemical industry. This became "the site of complex political exchanges, combining oligopoly competition with political conflict among parties and party fractions." The combination of oligopoly and political conflict delayed needed restructuring and permitted the survival of "an obsolete managerial culture which was too production-oriented and insufficiently market-oriented, too dependent on government financial support, too centralised and insufficiently internationalised" (Grant, Martinelli, and Paterson 1989: 79). The tentacles of the party state extended into the firms themselves, distorting their decision-making and ossifying their cultures.

A grouping centered around capital intensive firms favored the breakdown of the relationship with the dominant party, also backed by the so-called "Young Entrepreneurs" and smaller businesses from the north-east who subsequently showed some sympathy with the Northern League (a movement that has drawn on smaller businesses as a significant support base). The "Italian business class acquired a new legitimacy and business values became more central to Italian society" (Grant, Martinelli, and Paterson 1989: 82). A more autonomous business class reduced its dependency on the Christian Democrats. "After the late 1980s Confindustria sight to abandon its time-old privileged relationship with the DC" (Lanza and Lavdas 2000: 213). The Christian Democrats were held responsible for a number of ills in the Italian economy and society. At the time of the 1992 election "Confindustria replaced its privileged relationship with the DC with the *multiparty appeal* to whomever agreed to support industrial proposals" (Lanza and Lavdas 2000: 213). Thus, Confindustria sought to act like an intermediary organization in any modern democratic regime which is not to say that the alliance with the DC had not served many industrialists well, perhaps too well. The collapse of the Christian Democrats created a vacuum that needed to be filled.

THE BUSINESS FIRM MODEL OF PARTY ORGANIZATION

The vacuum on the centre-right of Italian politics was filled by Silvio Berlusconi and his *Forza Italia* (FI). There is an interesting parallel between Berlusconi and the former Thai Prime Minister Thaksin Shinawatra and his Thai Rak Tai party. Both are businessmen who had specific interests to defend, media in the case of Berlusconi, telecommunications in the case of Thaksin. Both have been subject to allegations that their conduct in business and political life has not always met the highest standards of probity. Both set up populist political movements based around their own charisma which they control on a highly personal basis. Both set themselves up against the established political class of their countries, Thaksin by appealing to disenfranchised rural voters.

However, FI is "probably the most extreme example to date of a new political party organising as a business firm...the organisation of the party is largely conditioned by the prior existence of a business firm" (Hopkin and Paolucci 1999: 307). FI was designed to be different from what were seen as failed traditional political parties in Italy. "The model adopted stemmed from a belief in the organisational superiority of the private business firm, which in turn reflected FI's emphasis on modern entrepreneurialism as an effective substitute for a discredited political class composed of professional politicians, academics and lawyers" (Hopkin and Paolucci 1999: 329).

The business firm model does not represent a re-creation of the party state. Rather it is a distinctive form of the company state in which a company forms the basis for a political party. The claim is that business success is a form of legitimacy which can be translated to the democratic sphere. The business person is free from association with traditional political formations and can engage in the pragmatic pursuit of the national interest. Berlusconi used what was effectively a football chant for the name of his party, while Thaksin managed to insert the word "Thai" twice in his party title which translates as "Thais love Thais." At its worst, such an approach to politics can lead to the appropriation of the state apparatus to serve the interests of particular businesses. For example, in December 2009 Berlusconi proposed to double the value added tax charged on pay-TV, a market dominated in Italy by the main rival of his family company, Sky. The move led to half a million emailed complaints by Sky subscribers to the Prime Minister's office (http://www.guardian.co.uk/media/2008/dec/08/berlusconi-vat-pay-tv accessed 16 January 2009). The business form model of party organization hardly represents a step forward for democratic government with its tendency to political incoherence and the service of particularistic interests.

Conclusions

Political parties are complex political institutions that balance ideologies and interests while seeking to win elections. If the above examples have any single linking theme, it is that parties cannot reduced to labels that portray them as representatives of a single interest such as capital or labor. Parties are rarely policy-framing institutions. Center-right parties that are generally regarded as being pro-business contain important elements with which business interests have to share power; the Christian Democratic parties of continental Europe are perhaps the clearest examples containing as they do labor as well as business interests. There is as far we know nowhere an example of a party that can be described simply and exclusively as the party of business. As is true of parties in general, the parties generally aligned with business interests rarely make and articulate specific defined policies. They more typically set the general direction of policy and articulate the clues that will be expressed in trade-offs such as equity versus growth, employment versus inflation. Yet even these trade-offs are very general and mask important internal disagreements over specific policies as evidenced by the fights between Koizumi and the anti-reformers in the LDP or, in earlier era, between Thatcher and the "wets" in the Conservative Party in the UK. Perhaps ironically the most important contribution of pro-business parties to business—government relations has been somewhat contradictory. On the one hand, these parties have provided the means through which leaders such as Thatcher or Koizumi have been selected who have gone on to implement transformative policy changes. On the other hand, these parties have also been institutions that have slowed or limited the changes unwelcome to specific business interests that these leaders have been able to make.

Pro-business political parties have been influenced by two trends. The first has been the tendency for the influence and power of party organizations to decline. In most advanced democracies, parties—as opposed to their leaders—are playing a less meaningful role in politics and policy-making. Perhaps the primary role of parties recently has been to provide a vehicle through which political entrepreneurs (Blair, Obama, Sarkozy) achieve power (Panebianco 1988). Such leaders have been determined to prevent their parties from adopting policies that compromise the image they wish to project to voters. Party politics never could replace the needs of individual corporations, trade associations, and business peak organizations to articulate priorities and concerns on detailed policy issues such as a specific regulation or tax change. A perhaps temporary exception to this occurs in post-communist countries, where so far business associations have been weak and informal ties more important. Business interests have therefore placed greater reliance on often short-lived alliances with shallowly rooted and somewhat transient political parties (McMenamin and Schoenman 2007). The reduction in the importance of parties more generally makes this even truer. Pro-business parties in advanced democracies have also been influenced and generally weakened by the near disappearance after 1989 of democratic parties that are theoretically or in practice committed to ending capitalism. As parties that were once anti-capitalist (socialists, communists) have declined, disappeared, or changed, the central task of pro-business parties, namely keeping the left out of office, has become less significant. With varying speed and enthusiasm, center-left parties have embraced capitalism and their leaders have been eager to demonstrate their understanding of business's needs. Schattschneider's notion that the Republican Party was the supreme expression of business politically seems more an echo of a previous era when political scientists such as Seymour Martin Lipset were tempted to portray elections as "the democratic form of the class struggle." Unless the Great Crash of 2008 and consequent recession revive socialism, the articulation of business interests and the workings of the party system are likely to be increasingly separated.

References

BARTELLS, L. 2008. *Unequal Democracy: The Political Economy of the New Gilded Age.* Princeton: Princeton University Press.

BENSELL, R. 1984. *Sectionalism and American Political Development.* Madison: University of Wisconsin Press.

BIANCHI, P. 1987. "The IRI in Italy: strategic role and political constraint," *West European Politics* 10(2): 269–90.

CARO, R. 1982. *The Path to Power: The Years of Lyndon Johnson.* New York: Alfred Knopf.

—— 2002. *Master of the Senate: The Years of Lyndon Johnson.* New York: Knopf.

DEEG, R. 1999. *Finance Capital Unveiled: Banks and the German Political Economy.* Ann Arbor: University of Michigan Press.

—— 2006. "Path dependency, institutional complementarity and change in national business systems," in G. Morgan, R. Whitley, and E. Moen, eds., *Changing Capitalisms: Internationalization, Institutional Change and Systems of Economic Organization.* Oxford: Oxford University Press.

ESTEVEZ-ABE, M. 2008. *Welfare and Capitalism in Postwar Japan.* Cambridge: Cambridge University Press.

GRANT, W. 1989. "Government–industry relations in Britain, Germany and Italy: the company state, associative state and party state," Universität Konstanz, Sozialwissenschaftliche Fakultät, Sonderforschungsbereich 221.

—— 1993. *Business and Politics in Britain,* 2nd edn. Basingstoke: Macmillan.

—— and MARTINELLI, A. 1991. "Political turbulence, enterprise crisis and industrial recovery: ICI and Montedison," in A. Martinelli (ed.), *International Markets and Global Firms: A Comparative Study of Organized Business in the Chemical Industry.* London: Sage, 61–90.

—— —— and PATERSON, W. 1989. "Large firms as political actors: a comparative analysis of the chemical industry in Britain, Italy and West Germany," *West European Politics* 12(1): 72–90.

HOPKIN, J., and PAOLUCCI, C. 1999. "The business firm model of party organization: cases from Spain and Italy," *European Journal of Political Research* 35: 307–39.

JOHNSON, C. 1982. *MITI and the Japanese Economic Miracle: The Growth of Industrial Policy.* Ithaca, NY: Cornell University Press.

LANZA, O., and LAVDAS, K. 2000. "The distentanglement of interest politics: business associability, the parties and policy in Italy and Greece," *European Journal of Political Research* 37: 203–35.

MARTIN, C. J. 2006. "Sectional parties, divided business," *Studies in American Political Development* 20: 160–84.

—— and SWANK, D. 2008. "The political origins of coordinated capitalism: business organizations party systems and state structure in the age of innocence," *American Political Science Review* 102: 181–98.

MARTINELLI, A., and GRANT, W. 1991. "Conclusion," in A. Martinelli (ed.), *International Markets and Global Firms: A Comparative Study of Organized Business in the Chemical Industry.* London: Sage, 272–88.

—— and TREU, T. 1985. "Employers associations in Italy," in I. P. Windmuller and A. Gladstone (eds.), *Employers Associations and Industrial Relations.* Oxford: Clarendon Press, 264–92.

McMENAMIN, I., and SCHOENMAN, R. 2007. "Together forever? Explaining exclusiivity in party–firm relations," *Political Studies* 55: 155–73.

PANEBIANCO, A. 1988. *Political Parties: Organization and Power.* Cambridge: Cambridge University Press.

PEMPEL, T. J. 1998. *Regime Shift: Comparative Dynamics of the Japanese Political Economy.* Ithaca, NY: Cornell University Press.

PIMLOTT, B. 1985. *Hugh Dalton.* London: Jonathan Cape.

PRZEWORSKI, A., and WALLERSTEIN, M. 1988. "Structural dependence of the state on capital," *American Political Science Review* 82: 11–30.

RAMSEYER, M. J., and ROSENBLUTH, F. M. 1993. *Japan's Political Marketplace.* Cambridge, Mass.: Harvard University Press.

RAMSDEN, J. 1998. *An Appetite for Power.* London: Harper Collins.

SCHAEDE, U., and GRIMES, W., eds. 2003. *Japan's Managed Globalization: Adapting to the Twenty First Century.* Armonk, NY: M. E. Sharpe.

SCHATTSCHNEIDER, E. E. 1956. "United States: the functional approach to party government," in S. Neumann, ed., *Political Parties' Approaches to Comparative Politics.* Chicago: University of Chicago Press, 194–215.

—— 1960. *The Semi Sovereign People: A Realist's View of American Democracy.* New York: Holt, Reinhart and Winston.

TIBERGHIEN, Y. 2007. *Entrepreneurial States: Reforming Corporate Governance in France, Japan and Korea.* Ithaca, NY: Cornell University Press.

VOGEL, S. K. 2001. "The crisis of German and Japanese capitalism," *Comparative Political Studies* 34(10): 1103–33.

—— 2006. *Japan Remodeled: How Government and Industry are Reforming Japanese Capitalism.* Ithaca, NY: Cornell University Press.

WRIGHT. M. 1999. "Who governs Japan? Politicians and bureaucrats in the policy-making processes," *Political Studies* 47: 939–54.

—— 2002. "Who governs Japan? Politicians and bureaucrats in the policymaking process," *Political Studies* 47: 939–54.

ZOHLNHÖFER, R. 1999. "Institutions, the CDU and policy change: explaining German economic policy in the 1980s," *German Politics* 8(3): 141–60.

CHAPTER 9

ECONOMIC INTERESTS AND POLITICAL REPRESENTATION

COORDINATION AND DISTRIBUTIVE CONFLICT IN HISTORICAL PERSPECTIVE

TORBEN IVERSEN

DAVID SOSKICE

INTRODUCTION

A long line of research has inquired into the relationship between democratic institutions and public policy, especially economic policies to reduce inequality. Much of this research is motivated by a striking empirical puzzle. Contrary to intuition and one of the most celebrated models in economics by Allen Meltzer and Scott Richard, democracy does not appear to compensate for market inequality through redistribution.[1] At least for advanced democracies, data consistently show that equality in market income is associated with high redistribution.[2] This "Robin Hood paradox" is illustrated in Fig. 9.1 for a sample of countries where we have good data on redistribution from the Luxembourg Income Study. Redistribution is measured here by the percentage reduction in the poverty rate (left axis) and in the Gini coefficient (right axis) from before taxes and transfers to after taxes and transfers (based on income for working age households). Individual market inequality is measured by d5/d1 and d9/d5 earnings ratios for full-time workers. As is clear, the overall relationship is the reverse of the predicted regardless of the particular measure we use for either market inequality or government redistribution (we comment briefly on the "outliers," especially France and Switzerland, below). In this chapter we argue that the explanation for this puzzle takes us back to differences in the organization of capitalist production at the beginning of the twentieth century. These differences in production regimes shaped the structure of employer and worker

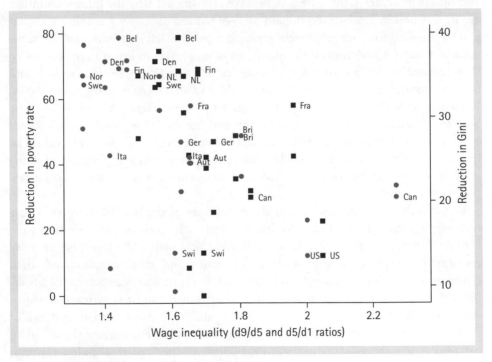

Fig. 9.1 Inequality and redistribution, c.1970–95

Notes: For each country there are four markers. Squares are for the d9/d5 earnings ratio; circles for the d5/d1 earnings ratios. Each marker identified by a country label refers to the reduction in the poverty rate (left axis), which is the percentage reduction of the poverty rate (the percentage of families with income below 50 per cent of the median) from before to after taxes and transfers. Right below each labeled marker is a marker for the corresponding reduction in the Gini coefficient (right axis) from before taxes and transfers to after. The redistribution measures for Italy is from after taxes to after taxes and transfers. The data are limited to the countries included in Bradley et al. (2003).

Sources: OECD Electronic Data Base on Wages (n.d.); Bradley et al. (2003), based on the Luxembourg Income Study.

interests and affected how they became represented through democratic institutions. The structure of political and economic institutions in turn determined distributive outcomes.

Our argument stands in contrast to power resource theory (PRT), which explains the clustering of countries on distribution and redistribution as a function of the organizational strength of the working class. A large literature in this tradition documents how the size and structure of the welfare state is related to the historical strength of the political left, mediated by alliances with the middle classes (Stephens 1979; Korpi 1983, 1989, 2006; Esping-Andersen 1990; Huber and Stephens 2001). Yet, we see some important limitations in this approach—especially in its lack of attention to employer interests, the absence of any systematic account of the origins of left government strength, and the lack of a credible explanation for capitalist investment in political economies dominated by the political left.

The alternative explanation that we outline in this chapter not only solves the Robin Hood puzzle, but explains why some countries are dominated by center-left, and others by center-right, governments. We also suggest why the former countries are in fact dominated by exceptionally well-organized and strong employer associations. In addition our approach explains why the left partisan bias in some countries has not undermined the incentives of employers to invest in the economy. Our account builds on work in the varieties of capitalism tradition by Hall and Soskice (2001), Estevez-Abe, Iversen, and Soskice (2001), Iversen (2005), and Cusack, Iversen, and Soskice (2007), as well as on employer-centered historical work by Swenson (2002), Mares (2003), and Martin and Swank (2008), and unlike PRT we emphasize the complementarities that exist between economic, political, and social institutions. Our aim is to provide a comprehensive causal explanation for the contemporary patterns of distribution and redistribution going back to the late nineteenth century.

Very briefly, our argument is that the economies of the last half century with a relatively egalitarian distribution of income and high levels of redistribution were organized economically before industrialization and before the franchise in more coordinated ways (especially in terms of guilds and rural cooperatives) than economies with high inequality and little redistribution. And even before the breakthrough of democracy these non-liberal countries had (limited) systems of representation whose consequences were not too different from current systems of proportional representation (PR). During the early twentieth century the coupling between economic coordination and PR became institutionalized under universal suffrage, and this, we argue, produced the correlation between distribution and redistribution illustrated in Fig. 9.1. Unions and left parties certainly played a role in this process, as argued in PRT, but we can only understand this role if we take into account the organization of the economy and why employers in some cases had an interest in cross-class collaboration. The strength of the left is in some measure a function of the institutional choices made by employers and the right in the 1920s and earlier. More critically from our point of view, institutions that promoted equality in the distribution of wages co-evolved with institutions that promoted redistribution, thus producing the pattern we observe today.

In developing our argument we begin by explaining the positive relationship between distributional equality and redistribution. We propose in the second section that the correlation is indirect: two factors, the electoral system and the degree of economic coordination, each impact on both distribution and redistribution. Proportional representation (PR) promotes both distributive equality and especially redistribution; so does coordinated capitalism with an even greater impact on distribution. PR promotes center-left coalitions; and coordinated capitalism, by encouraging investment in co-specific skills, reinforces both median voter and business support for wage compression and strong welfare state insurance.

The positive correlation between distributional equality and redistribution is in turn explained by a positive correlation between PR and coordinated capitalism. Using a composite measure of PR[3] and two measures of non-market coordination,[4] Fig. 9.2 illustrates how countries cluster into a PR-coordinated group and a majoritarian-uncoordinated group (even if there are some questions about where Ireland and France, according to one of the measures, belong). Because coordinated capitalism and PR determine distribution and redistribution, a full account of the correlation between the two pulls us back into the nineteenth century where these

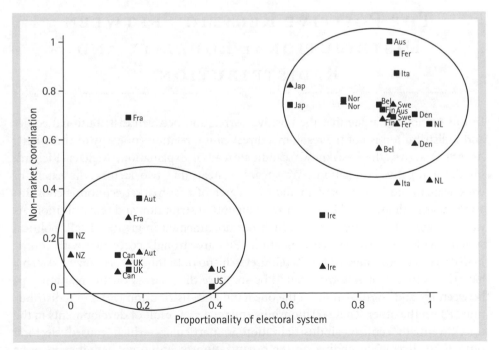

Fig. 9.2 PR and non-market coordination

Sources: Proportionality of electoral system: Lijphart (1984); non-market coordination index (squares): Hall and Gingerich (2004); cooperation index (triangles): Hicks and Kenworthy (1998).

institutions became linked up in the process of industrialization and democratization. We argue that these historical origins, and the process of institutional co-evolution they set in motion, cannot be understood as a simple function of power resources.

In this chapter we outline a historical explanation of the positive correlation between PR and coordinated capitalist systems based on Cusack, Iversen, and Soskice (2007). We then revisit power resource theory and point out that our explanation is fundamentally different from power resource theory because it is not the power resources on the left that have *caused* the institutional differences that we observe. Employers and the right did not choose PR because they feared the power of the left, but because of the opportunities this representative system created for collaborative arrangements with labor. Once in place PR and center-left dominance increased redistribution beyond the ideal point of employers, but it was a price they were willing to pay to realize the economic potential of their enterprises. We also discuss the implications of our argument for understanding changes in inequality and redistribution over time. In particular, we argue that the rise in inequality starting in the 1980s is due to changes in technology that affect the bargaining power of low-skilled workers—not to an overall decline in the power of the left.

THE POSITIVE RELATION BETWEEN DISTRIBUTIONAL EQUALITY AND REDISTRIBUTION

In this section we argue that the positive correlation between distributional equity and redistribution is not the result of a direct causal relation (one way or the other). As noted above, the best-known candidate causal explanation, Meltzer–Richard, implies a *negative* correlation.[5] We suggest instead that two factors, the extent of consensus in the political system and the degree of non-market economic coordination, have both impacted in similar ways on both distribution and redistribution. As we illustrated above, and as Gourevitch has documented in greater detail, political systems with proportional representation (PR) are strongly correlated with coordinated market economies or CMEs (Gourevitch 2003). In the next section we sketch a historical account of why that should be so. Here the focus is on the relationships between PR and coordination on the one hand and distribution (D) and redistribution (R) on the other. These relationships emerged as a result of developments in the early twentieth century—industrialization in particular—which caused electoral systems to diverge depending on the organization of economic activities in place around the turn of the previous century. The argument follows the rough causal sketch in Fig. 9.3.

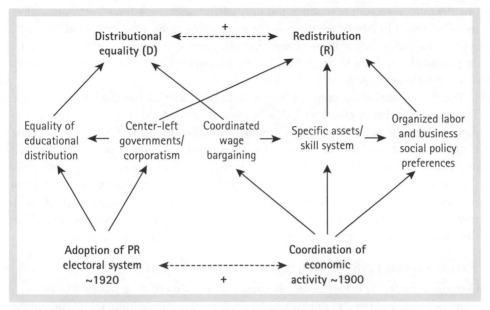

Fig. 9.3 A sketch of the causal argument

Coordinated economies

The more the organization of firms and economic institutions facilitates the coordination of economic activity, especially wage setting and skill formation, the more likely the political economy is to promote both distributive equality and redistribution (for detailed evidence see Hicks 2000: chs. 5–6; Swank 2003: ch. 3). We look at two mechanisms through which this occurs and which have been the subject of considerable research.

Social policy preferences and redistribution

There is a substantial amount of literature which argues that one of the comparative advantages of CMEs is that they provide incentives for employees and companies to invest in industry, occupation, and/or company-specific assets. A key condition for employee preparedness to make such investments is that there are adequate protections in the event of company or industry failure. As argued in Estevez-Abe, Iversen, and Soskice (2001), some combination of three types of protection is directly involved: First, wage protection is needed to guarantee that relative earnings in the industry or occupation do not fall; this protection normally takes the institutional form of coordinated wage bargaining.[6] Second, employment protection reduces the likelihood that companies dismiss employees. Third, unemployment protection in the form of high replacement rates and conditions on acceptable reemployment is important, and the more so to the extent that company-level employment protection is reduced. Of these three protections the third, protection of income in the event of unemployment, impacts most directly on redistribution and can be conceived more broadly as a protection of income, not only when workers are forced into unemployment but also into jobs where their skills are not fully employable. Any social insurance system that helps maintain a certain level of expected income regardless of adverse employment conditions—including health insurance and public pensions—serves as a protection of specific skills (Iversen 2005).

There is an important contrast here with LMEs, especially in the last thirty years. The institutional framework in LMEs has not permitted major programs of investment in specific skills. Vocational training, whether in professional schools (law, engineering) or community colleges, provides relatively general skills which enable movement across company and industry boundaries as well as retraining. And while skill-specificity and consequent long tenure in CMEs can limit mid-career labor markets, labor markets in LMEs are becoming more flexible over time. Portable skills mean that employment insecurity is less of a concern, and that more people can use their market power to gain adequate insurance against illness and old age.

Business social policy preferences and redistribution

Governments decide on replacement rates, and in doing so they respond to pressure from organized interests. Organized labor will naturally support unemployment protection. But against widely held views, the pioneering work of Peter Swenson, Cathie Jo Martin, and Isabela Mares has provided a wealth of historical evidence that employers are not necessarily advocating a minimal welfare state (Martin 2000; Swenson 2002; Mares 2003). In CMEs the combination of strong employer organizations and their acceptance of the case for non-minimal replacement rates has meant that there is a floor to replacement rates as well as duration of benefits. There may be more than one reason why employers should want non-minimal replacement rates. An important argument is that they are necessary for persuading employees to invest in deep specific skills. Of course, actual replacement rates are also influenced by government partisanship; CMEs tend to have more than average left of center governments, so business associations in CMEs may well call for reductions in replacement rates (we will return to this point below). The critical point is that organized business in CMEs has not engaged, nor had the motivation to engage, in promoting the wholesale dismantling of the welfare state.

Organized business in LMEs has played a different role.[7] Concerned to promote unilateral management control within companies, its interest has been in flexible labor markets and weak unions. For both reasons, having a minimal welfare state has been important to it. However, organized business has been weaker in LMEs than in CMEs. This reflects the lack of business coordinating capacity in LMEs. It also reflects, as we will see, political systems based on majoritarian elections and single party governments, which undermine the incentives of parties to cater to business interests (Martin 2006). Thus, although business has been anti-welfare state in LMEs, its impact has been blunted by its lack of political power. The exception is the US, where weak party discipline and power-sharing between executive and legislature enable business in effect to promote a minimal welfare state agenda through individual members of Congress.

Voters' social policy preferences and redistribution

Employees with specific skills have an interest in wage and unemployment protection, and insofar as skills are firm-specific also in employment protection. In Iversen and Soskice (2001) we show the relatively weak conditions (especially on risk aversion) that have to be satisfied in order for specific skills workers to vote for more redistributive spending at given levels of income. Using ISSP comparative surveys we show that this is indeed the case. Insofar as CMEs encourage investment in specific skills, therefore, we expect voters in CMEs to prefer higher replacement rates than voters with the same income level in LMEs. This translates into higher actual spending and redistribution assuming that political parties are able to commit to long-term platforms that insure currently employed against future loss of income. As we argue below, such commitment capacity tends to be greater in PR electoral systems where, unlike majoritarian systems, winning the next election is not everything, and where parties can ally themselves openly with groups (such as unions) that promote long-term social spending (see also Iversen 2005: ch. 4). The empirical correlation between vocational training activity (as a measure of specific skill) and redistribution through taxes and transfers is illustrated in Fig. 9.4.

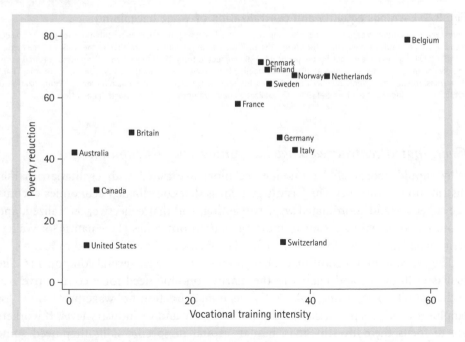

Fig. 9.4 Vocational training and redistribution

Notes: Poverty reduction is defined the same way as in Fig. 9.1. Vocational training intensity is the share of an age cohort in either secondary or post-secondary (ISCED5) vocational training. The data are limited to the countries included in Bradley et al. (2003).

Sources: UNESCO (1999). The poverty reduction data are from Bradley et al. (2003) based on Luxembourg Income Study.

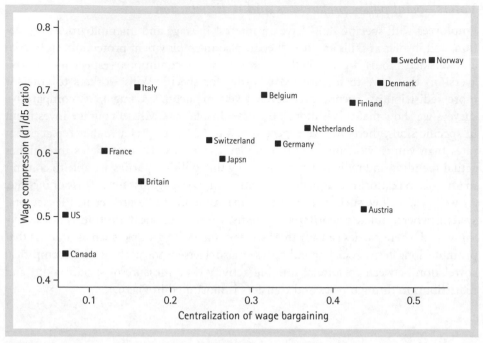

Fig. 9.5 Earnings equality and centralization of wage bargaining

Notes: Wage equality is measured as the ratio of gross earnings (including all employer contributions for pensions, social security, etc.) of a full-time worker at the bottom decile of the earnings distribution relative to the worker at the median (d1/d5 ratios). Figures are averages for the period 1977–93 computed from OECD (n.d.). Centralization is measured as the one divided by the number of unions at different bargaining levels weighted by relative union size ("concentration") and then transformed into a single number depending on the importance of different bargaining levels ("centralization of authority"). The index is from Iversen (1999). Centralization data are not available for Australia and New Zealand.

Coordinated/centralized wage bargaining and distribution

Why should coordinated economies be more associated with egalitarian market distribution of income? The basic argument is that coordinated economies encourage collective and coordinated wage bargaining, and that collective, centralized, and coordinated bargaining leads to more egalitarian outcomes (Freeman 1980; Wallerstein 1999; Rueda and Pontusson 2000). The relationship is illustrated in Fig. 9.5.

The explanation for coordinated bargaining in CMEs has several components. The first is well-known and related to the macroeconomic need for a competitive real exchange rate. The second links to the insurance function of "wage protection" for employees with deep specific skills at the company and/or industry level. If workers are to focus their investment in human capital in specific skills they need some guarantee that their earnings will not drop dramatically relatively to those of other occupations. Hence the support of skilled unions for wage coordination across different bargaining units (or for centralized wage bargaining).

The next question is then why coordinated bargaining should lead to a more compact distribution of earnings. A key reason has to do with the nature of inter-union bargaining. Loosely speaking, effective bargaining requires that union threats of action are credible; this in turn requires that there is wide support within the bargaining unit for the union's position; and that in turn implies that the bottom half of the workforce is not unrewarded. Another way of phrasing this is that unions representing different income groups have to consent to the bargaining proposal of the union central before it can be credibly proposed to employers. This gives low wage unions the capacity to demand their fair share of any agreement, as long as low-skilled labor is a complement to skilled labor in production (Iversen 1999). The more centralized the wage bargaining system and the more encompassing the bargaining unit, the more compact the resulting distributional outcomes (we discuss recent decentralization trends in collective bargaining in the fourth section).

Summary

CMEs have positive effects relative to LMEs on both the extent of redistribution and the degree of distributional equality. Both voters and business in CMEs have interests in higher replacement rates on average. And business has a more substantial influence on government in CMEs via corporatist arrangements. As Moene and Wallerstein (2003) have emphasized, we need to more pay attention to the insurance function of the welfare state rather than simply the redistributive function. That is the argument in "Social policy preferences and redistribution," above. Because CMEs have a comparative advantage in the creation of specific skills, there is an insurance need for high replacement rates,[8] and these in turn reinforce the comparative advantage of companies in international competition.

CMEs equally have more centralized and coordinated wage bargaining than LMEs. An important reason for this is the insurance function which wage protection offers those with specific skills who get locked into companies or occupations. Moreover CMEs need effective employee representation at the plant and company level (Hall and Soskice 2001); but this raises the danger of competitive wage bargaining in the absence of centralized and/or coordinated unions. And for reasons explained in "Coordinated/centralized wage bargaining and distribution", above, the more centralized is collective bargaining the greater the distributional equity.

PR political systems

As Gourevitch has pointed out, and as Fig. 9.1 above illustrated, electoral systems with proportional representation are closely linked statistically to coordinated market economies (Gourevitch 2003). It is also related to corporatist forms of interest representation (Katzenstein 1985). In the third section we seek to explain why that is the case. In this sub-section we discuss the consequences of PR systems for distribution and redistribution.

Three linkages from PR to R and D seem of particular importance. In the first place, PR electoral systems in advanced economies have a bias towards left of center

Table 9.1 Electoral system and the number of years with governments farther to the left or to the right than the median legislator, 1945–98

Electoral system	Government partisanship		Proportion of right governments
	Left	Right	
Proportional	291 (9)	171 (0)	0.37
Majoritarian	116 (1)	226 (7)	0.66

Note: Excludes governments coded as centrist on the Castles–Mair scale.
Source: Cusack and Engelhardt (2002).

governments over the period since the Second World War; this is almost the inverse of majoritarian systems (see Table 9.1). We sketch in "Electoral systems and redistribution: the PR bias towards center-left," below, an analytic argument as to why this may be the case and why it will lead to an increase in redistribution. The second linkage is via the educational system. Standard microeconomic theory says that the relative wages of two individuals will be equal to the ratio of their marginal productivities, absent any influences which might result from market imperfections, including collective bargaining. Since the ratio of marginal productivities is closely related to the human capital ratio, the distribution of educational attainments will play a large part in determining the underlying distribution of earnings from employment. We show in "Electoral systems and educational outcomes," below, that the electoral system is correlated with the educational attainments of low income groups and argue that there is a good reason why this should be the case.

Electoral systems and redistribution: the PR bias towards center-left governments

Table 9.1 shows the data on government partisanship in advanced economies between 1945 and 1998, derived from Cusack and his associates (Cusack and Engelhardt 2002). The scale is a composite index of three expert surveys of the left–right position of political parties in each country. The partisanship of the government is a weighted average of the ideological position of each party times its proportional share of government seats.[9] Note we compare this measure to the position of the median legislator (which is defined as the left–right position of the party with the median legislator). This should take account of any factor that may shift the whole political spectrum in one direction or another—such as the possibility identified in "Social policy preferences and redistribution," above, that the demand for "left" policies is greater in specific skills countries.

What accounts for this surprising relationship? We sketch out here an argument developed in detail elsewhere (Iversen and Soskice 2006). There are three income groups in an economy, L, M, and H. Under PR there are three parties, L, M, and H, each representing one of the groups and sharing the respective group's goals ("representative" parties). M is formateur and has to choose a coalition partner. The key intuition is that a party is less capable of looking after its interest if it is excluded from the coalition. Since M benefits more from taxing an unprotected H than from taxing an unprotected L, M will choose L as coalition partner. This can be modeled in a number of different ways; the only bargaining structure which is excluded is a take-it-or leave-it offer from M.[10] The basic point is that it pays L and M to form a coalition and take resources from the excluded H party, rather than H and M forming a coalition to take resources from an excluded L. PR systems therefore tend to privilege center-left coalitions and such coalitions will redistribute more than center-right coalitions.

Majoritarian systems operate quite differently. The three parties are replaced by two, a center-left (LM) and a center-right (MH) party, both competing for M. If both parties could commit to an M platform, then each would win 50 per cent of the time. But they cannot: M-voters believe that there is some possibility that an LM government will be tempted to move left and an MH government to move right. The fundamental bias in majoritarian systems arises because, under reasonable assumptions, M has less to fear from an MH government moving right than from an LM government moving left. The former leads to lower benefits going to M but also to lower taxes on M, while the latter implies higher taxes on M with the proceeds redistributed to L. Parties will try to deal with this problem by electing strong leaders who are willing and capable of ignoring the pressures from the party base ("leadership parties"). But as long as platform commitment is incomplete, there will be a center-right bias.[11]

Note that the insights of this model are completely lost in one-dimensional models such as Meltzer–Richard's, or indeed power resource theory. The reason is that these models artificially impose a symmetry on the distributive game where the interests of M are always equally well aligned with the interests of L and M. With three parties in a PR system this means that M is equally likely to ally with H as it is to ally with L. Likewise, in a majoritatian system, any deviation from an M platform is equally threatening to M whether it comes from the center-left or the center-right party (e.g., the center-left party is forced to share with M even if L sets policies).

There is one important qualification to our argument. The center-left bias of PR systems is less pronounced in countries with large Christian democratic parties. Among the latter, the proportion of center-left governments, measured as in Table 9.1, reduces to 57 per cent, whereas it is 63 per cent for the sample as a whole. This also implies that for PR countries without strong CD parties, notably Scandinavia, the center-left advantage is more pronounced: 71 per cent. The reason for this difference, we believe, has to do with the cross-class nature of CD parties (Manow and Kersbergen 2007). Because these parties include constituencies from L, M, as well as H, differences in distributive preferences between these groups have to be bargained out within the party. This produces a more center-oriented platform than we would usually associate with a center-right party, and this in turn makes CD parties more attractive coalition partners for "pure" center, or middleclass, parties. The logic that leads center parties to ally with the left is therefore broken, and in countries (such as Germany and Italy) where CD and center parties have at times held a majority of seats, the influence of the left has been reduced. Where such CD–center majority coalitions have not been feasible, as has often been the case in Belgium and the Netherlands, we observe frequent coalitions between CD and left parties, producing a unique blend of policies where transfers are high and somewhat redistributive, but some of these nevertheless are directed to those with high incomes (H).

Electoral systems and educational outcomes

The center-left bias in PR systems increases redistribution of income towards lower income groups, by comparison with majoritarian systems. Using analogous reasoning electoral systems will also affect the distribution of educational spending, and educational outcomes in turn affect the distribution of income.

Center-left governments have an incentive to spend more on L's education than do center-right or middle of the road governments in majoritarian countries. And they have a lesser incentive to spend on H's education. The model in Iversen and Soskice (2006) assumes that policies are limited to redistributive transfers. But a similar argument can be run with the three groups competing for expenditure on education for their own group (see Iversen and Stephens 2008). Indeed, if H opts for private education, and if there are positive externalities for M from educational expenditure on L (for example, economies of scale in school buildings), then M has an increased incentive to opt for an LM coalition.[12]

Ansell (2008) and Busemeyer (2007) have recently documented that left governments spend relatively more on primary and secondary education than right governments, which benefits low-income groups more than high-income groups. Boix (1998) has likewise shown that the left governments spend more on public education than right governments. Ansell demonstrates that similar effects can be attributed to PR electoral systems, though Iversen and Stephens (2008) show that this is less true in PR countries where Christian democratic parties are strong.

The limitation of these results is that they do not speak directly to the skills acquired by students, which could vary with the effectiveness of educational institutions across countries. However, the OECD and Statistics Canada have run an international adult literacy survey in the years 1995–8 (OECD 2000), which does consider more directly the level and distribution of skill acquisition. We confine our attention to the advanced economies included in the survey.[13] The survey conducted three tests, testing writing, comprehension, and quantitative skills. Figure 9.6 summarizes the results. The top bars (using top scale) show the percentage of adults who have not completed an upper secondary education but have high scores on document literacy. The bottom bars (using bottom scale) show

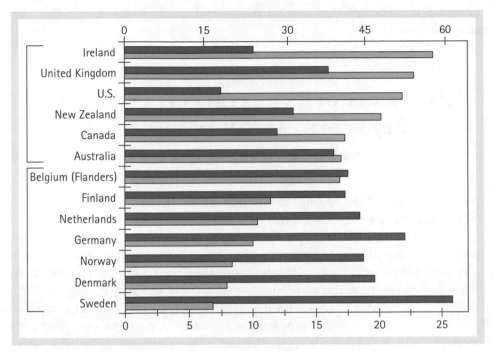

Fig. 9.6 The percentage of adults with poor literacy scores (bottom scale), and the percentage of adults with low education and high scores (top scale), thirteen OECD countries, 1994–8

Notes: The top bars (using top scale) show the percentage of adults who have not completed an upper secondary education but have high scores on document literacy. The bottom bars (using bottom scale) show the percentage of adults taking the test who get the lowest score, averaged across three test categories.

Source: OECD/Statistics Canada Literacy study (OECD 2000).

the percentage of adults taking the test who get the lowest score, averaged across the three test categories.[14]

Compared to majoritarian systems at the top of the figure, it can be seen that the PR countries have far fewer adults who get the lowest scores, and they also tend to produce higher scores among those with little formal education. There is therefore a prima facie case that the electoral system is an important determinant of the compactness of the skill distribution. Since PR and coordination are co-linear, it is of course also possible that the pattern is related to the prevalence of vocational training in CMEs. Indeed we argue below that this is likely to be a reinforcing factor and related to the fact that PR and corporatist representation are linked: in addition to affecting distributive coalition formation PR also permits consensus bargaining over regulatory policies—typically through legislative committees closely linked to bureaucratic agencies with union and employer representation. A key regulatory area is the structure and curriculum of the school system, which intersects the vocational training systems directly and indirectly. PR and corporatist bargaining thus provide organized interests influence over the educational system and indirectly therefore also distribution.

PATTERNS OF INDUSTRIALIZATION AND REPRESENTATION IN THE LATE NINETEENTH CENTURY

PR systems and CMEs explain at least partially both distributive equality and redistribution (with the qualification we noted concerning Christian democracy). In turn, PR systems are strongly positively correlated with CMEs. It is this correlation that is key to explaining the clustering of countries into relatively egalitarian ones with high redistribution and relatively inegalitarian ones with low redistribution. The historical origins of this correlation are the focus of this section.

Specifically, we need to answer the following set of questions. First, what explains why some countries adopted proportional representation in the early twentieth century? (As is well known, almost all advanced countries which have PR today adopted PR early in the twentieth century; before that electoral systems were largely majoritarian, some with run-offs.) Second, why had the same countries developed at least proto-coordinated institutions at the national level by the same period? And third, what explains the different coalitional patterns across these same PR countries—dividing roughly the Scandinavian from the Continental (or Christian democratic) welfare states?

In answering these questions we claim that it is economic interests that are the ultimate drivers. In doing so we go against the accepted wisdom of comparative political science of the last thirty plus years: Since Rokkan's analysis of 1970 (Lipset and Rokkan 1967; Rokkan 1970), Cusack, Iversen, and Soskice (2007) is to our knowledge the only serious challenge to the view that social cleavages (religious, territorial, and ethnic) explain PR. And since Esping-Andersen's analysis in 1990 (Esping-Andersen 1990) it has also been generally accepted that these same cleavages, in particular the religious, help explain patterns of welfare states—at least between Scandinavian and continental European countries. We believe that this reflects a failure of both political scientists and historians to work on the bridge between party politics and the economic interests that are embedded in production systems; and also the failure of economists seriously to consider the possibility that systems of representation are complements to systems of production.

Two of the books on which we most rely to make our argument are Herrigel (1995)—on decentralized production regions—and Thelen (2004)—on the development of training systems. Yet key though they are neither of them mentions religion, nor party politics except in passing. Another book which has proved of great value to us, Manow and van Kersbergen (2007) on religion and the welfare state, focuses on the role of political parties and religion, but largely neglects detailed discussion of production systems. Based on Cusack, Iversen and Soskice (2007), in this section we attempt to link the development of party politics and electoral systems with the representation of economic interests. We emphasize its inevitably tentative nature at this stage, but believe it points to a major historical research agenda.

Economic interests and systems of representation

We first want to stress the need to analyze PR systems more broadly than has been customary. There are two quite different analyses of PR in the existing literature: on the one hand, PR has been analyzed by Huber and Stephens (2001), Iversen and Soskice (2006), Manow and van Kersbergen (2007), and implicitly by Baron and Ferejohn (1989), in terms of minimum winning coalitions—an approach going back to the theoretical work of Riker (1962). By contrast to this *exclusionary* view of PR, a quite different *inclusionary* approach, that of "consensus" bargaining, has been promoted by Lijphart (1984); Crepaz (1998); Powell (2000); and Colomer (2006); among others. The focus here is on the effectiveness of PR in enabling Pareto improvements in welfare (Rogowski 1989). Here we follow Cusack, Iversen, and Soskice (2007) in arguing that PR systems typically embody both approaches. But they relate to different policy areas: The minimum winning coalition logic determines distributive outcomes, so that after PR adoption what matters for the redistributive aspects of the welfare state is the governing coalition. We argued in the last section that PR will be biased to the center-left, though we also noted how a centrist coalition involving a Christian democratic party might exclude the social democrats and thus generate a welfare state with less redistribution. The precise nature of coalitions is discussed further in the third part of this section.

The consensus aspect of PR is reflected *inter alia* in the strength of opposition parties in legislative committees (Powell 2000). This relates to regulatory politics if there is general agreement that a wider range of interests, represented by government and opposition parties, should have a role in decision-making. Our basic contention is that this arises in corporatist-type societies in which associational activities are widespread and in which investments in co-specific assets are important (Iversen 2005). This is the case, as for example, in major schemes of vocational training, when many different agents (workers, companies, unions, business associations) make serious investments which depend upon commonly agreed regulatory frameworks. Under such circumstances political systems which can systematically exclude particular interests (as is the case under majoritarian systems) are inimical to the development of co-specific assets and institutions to regulate these. The last part of the nineteenth and the first part of the twentieth century was a period of intense economic institution building at the national level, and these issues were of great importance for the construction of the political system.

The core argument of this section takes industrialization as the key independent variable. Throughout the period we consider local economic networks were developing into national networks, just as labor was moving into industry from agriculture and from artisan or unskilled pre-industrial work in the towns.[15] At the same time entrepreneurs and financers grew up both from the bourgeoisie and perhaps state officialdom and from small-scale artisan owners and farmers and independent peasants.

The argument rests on the quite different impact industrialization had on economies depending on two related dimensions of those economies: one that refers to the organization of production and the organization of the state. Specifically, we observe the following patterns across these two dimensions:

(i) Pre-industrial rural and urban local economic system—all the states which subsequently emerged as PR/coordinated states had locally coordinated rural and urban economies with some mixture of rural cooperatives and regulated artisan systems; peasants owned or had tenure over their land. We will argue that both Scandinavian and Continental states apart from France fit into this description; and that their differences arise from the nature of rural and urban production systems in the two areas. By contrast, those states which emerged as majoritarian/liberal had large independent farms and landless agricultural labor, and/or rural communities with low entry and exit costs, and weakly or unregulated artisan systems.

(ii) The pre-existing structure of the state—all the states which subsequently emerge as PR/coordinated states were originally Ständestaaten, with functional representation of economic interests, while none of the majoritarian/liberal states were.

We use these two dimensions to explain the origins of liberal, Continental, and Scandinavian systems of representation, the task of the following three sections. We stress that the three systems are ideal types in the Weberian sense that they highlight key differences while ignoring numerous similarities and finer distinctions. In particular, since all three types blend in elements from others, we implicitly downplay sectoral differences. Even though the artisan sector in nineteenth-century America was smaller and less well organized than in most of continental Europe this does not imply that no company, especially in the Midwest and North-east, was able to draw on the sector to develop skill-intensive product market strategies. It does imply, however, that these firms were in a comparative disadvantage in doing so and that this undermined their capacity to impose their institutional preferences on the rest of industry. Likewise, there were large continental European companies in the coal and steel industry (in the Ruhrgebiet especially) which relied heavily on unskilled workers as in Britain. These firms consequently did not share the concerns of other employers in developing a cooperative training and industrial relations system, but they did not have the organizational power to prevent such developments. Our argument implies sectoral differences in interests, but our account in this brief chapter focuses on those that were advantaged by the structural and institutional conditions we highlight and that came to dominate institutional developments.

Liberal economies and majoritarian political systems

In the liberal case local economies were relatively uncoordinated historically: guild traditions were weak and their power limited or non-existent; the acquisition of craft skills was haphazard, formal certification did not exist and the supply of craft skills was relatively low; equally in agriculture, farming was dominated by large farmers, so the agricultural labor force was largely a dependent one of landless workers; alternatively, in areas such as the American West, small farmers had low entry and exit costs, making embedded long-run cooperation rare.

The consequence of these local arrangements was twofold. The absence of local coordination implied an absence of major areas of co-specific assets. Hence as local economic networks became regional or national, there was no corresponding push to develop coordinating mechanisms at the national level to manage investment in co-specific assets by different economic groups.

The second consequence was that the industrial labor force as it developed could not call on a major pool of craft workers, nor was there an available mechanism for training. The industrial workforce in these liberal economies was relatively unskilled. This impacted on the form which unions took: since it was very difficult in this pre-Fordist world to build effective unions from unskilled workers, unions were largely craft-based.

Union strategies also depended on the organization of employers. The liberal state was anti-corporatist and businesses consequently found it difficult to develop strong self-disciplining associations. This in turn meant that businesses were nervous of investing heavily in training workers in transferable skills. Because employers' associations could not sanction individual employers who stepped out of line, it was not possible to force unions into becoming highly disciplined bodies themselves, with whom they might negotiate on a long-term basis. Instead the interest of craft unions was to reduce the supply of skills to maximize their bargaining power and to control job content within companies to prevent dilution of skill needs by substitutions of unskilled labor. Because union discipline was not easy to maintain, craft unions were at risk of fragmentation, especially where labor market conditions were heterogeneous. This reinforced the political interest of employers in deregulated labor markets and minimizing welfare and unemployment benefits in order to weaken the power of unions. To circumvent job control employers, especially in America, introduced technologies which reduced the need for skilled labor.

There is an important political distinction to be made at this point between the US and other liberal economies. In the latter with centralized political systems skilled workers (Disraeli's "respectable working men") were median voters and the state underwrote legal protection for unions. But the decentralized nature of the American polity, with economic competition between states and labor law at state level, and lack of Federal or even state control over the means of violence—autonomous local police forces as well as private companies such as Pinkertons—allowed employers a free hand to crush unions. But in both environments the consequence of these mutually reinforcing centrifugal incentive structures between unions and employers during this

critical formative period for labor market arrangements was to put the liberal economies firmly onto the zero-sum game, or minimal winning coalition, trajectory.

From the discussion of this subsection, two conclusions emerge. First, the industrialized economy which developed in the nineteenth and early twentieth centuries
was liberal and uncoordinated, without encompassing unions and strong business
associations. Second, there was no pressure for a political system which represented
group interests and which allowed longer term consensus agreements to be made,
hence no pressure for PR. Business had no need for a consensus political system from
which an institutional framework labor market regulation and skill formation might
develop; on the contrary they saw unions as a threat to their autonomy. The split of
interests between skilled workers and unskilled workers meant that the working-class
representation which developed during this period paid no attention to the socialist
notion of a unified working class, still less to expanding skills (by contrast to the
social democratic parties of the continent).

Our central contention, contra Rokkan, is that PR and consensus-based political
systems were chosen when economic interests were organized and when major
societal framework understandings needed to be legally embedded. When that was
not the case, as in the liberal economies, majoritarian systems protected the right and
the middle classes against the left.

Rokkan instead saw the choice of PR as the reflection of deep social cleavages. It is
appropriate to finish this subsection by noting that such deep cleavages were equally
present in the Anglo-Saxon world at this time. There were religious cleavages in
England (between the dissenting churches and the Anglican established church—
with almost equally sized congregations), in the US between Catholics, Anglicans,
and Lutherans, in Australia between Catholics and Anglicans, let alone in Ireland.
Moreover in both New South Wales and Ireland Catholic education had been sharply
attacked. There were major ethnic divisions in the US, Ireland, and Australia. And,
within the right, England was divided socially, religiously, and territorially, between
the dissenting, urban, industrial class and the Anglican, rural, landowners, and
tenant farmers. None of these divisions played a role in hindering the continuation
of majoritarianism.

Continental states: proportional representation and coordination

We now turn to explain the adoption of PR and economic proto-coordination in the
continental states during the period of the late nineteenth and early twentieth
centuries. We also want to explain the post-PR adoption pattern of coalitions: in
these states Christian democratic parties played a major role in most coalitions,
generating a particular welfare state that we discussed earlier—so-called conservative, Christian democratic, or continental welfare states.[16]

The first major difference in the starting points from those in the liberal economies
relates to agriculture and urban economic life. Both peasantry and artisans operated
within locally coordinated frameworks. Peasants owned or had strong tenure on their
land, and the artisan urban sector was formally or informally regulated.[17] Moreover

there was substantial skilled artisan and small-scale industrial work in the peasant countryside. This is also true of the Scandinavian states to be discussed in the next subsection. Indeed the important common consequence for all these non-liberal states—Continental and Scandinavian—was that more or less effective and more or less formalized artisan training systems existed. These implied that a larger proportion of the workforce had craft skills than was the case in the liberal economies. Thus industrialization in all these economies could draw on a potentially large supply of skilled workers.

This had in turn, as Thelen (2004) insightfully noted, major implications for the development of union strategies. For, while unions initially developed along craft lines, they could not build strategies based on the control of the supply of skills since these were monopolized by the artisan sector. Nor (given that unions could not control how craft skills were defined) could they build strategies based on the control of job content. In both Continental and Scandinavian economies, therefore, union strategies developed differently from those of craft unions in liberal economies. Over time and not without considerable conflict unions saw a common interest with industrial employers in extending the training system and deepening the skills of workers—effectively breaking the monopoly on training of the artisan sector. But for companies to use skilled workers effectively required that workers behaved cooperatively and without costly monitoring; for then skilled workers could be given responsibility, and there would be no danger to the company of hold-up. Consequently, while most companies were initially deeply hostile to unions, union strategy gradually evolved into one of offering cooperation in exchange for collective bargaining rights. This in turn required that unions were in a position to discipline their members effectively.

Here a second exogenous factor enters the argument. Governance in the Continental and Scandinavian states derived from a Ständestaat or corporative state tradition in which government operated partially through groups (estates). Although the original interests represented through the Ständer were pre-capitalist (landowners, small-holders, guilds, the church, and so on), the Ständestaat can be thought of as at the institutional origin of neo-corporatist regimes (Crouch 1993). Thus little constraint was put on associational activity in developing industries—putting them in line with the way in which handwork and agriculture was organized. This is in turn reflected in the different ways in which liberalism was interpreted outside the Anglo-Saxon world and France in the nineteenth century.

As Swenson has argued, organized industry in these economies put strong pressure on unions to structure themselves so as to be able to discipline their membership (Swenson 1991). This was the price which the unions had to pay for representation and collective bargaining. Thus unions centralized, even if internally they remained organized across crafts until the 1920s or later (Kocka 1986). Moreover, as skill formation in industry became part of the industrialization agenda, unions and industry became the representative partners in massive investment in co-specific assets. And with such investments came the need and demand for related developments in the welfare state and employee representation within the company. While many of these positive-sum issues were primarily negotiated out between industry and unions, they were also put into legal frameworks. For this reason business and the unions were deeply concerned to be represented politically in a consensus-based regulatory process.

If business could have bargained everything out with the unions through some form of what Schmitter (1979) has called state corporatism this may have been its preferred option. But it could not prevent democracy, at least for a while, and then the right representing business had a strong reason to favor proportional representation, even if it could see that a majoritarian system would guarantee a focus on the redistributive needs of the middle classes, thus pushing out the redistributive claims of low-income groups. Business wanted a sweep of labor market and training reforms that would help modernize the economy, and it had no guarantee that the median voter would support these reforms or that the unions would be cooperative in such a setting.

These developments also had profound implications for the political left which led social democracy to have different strategic interests to left parties in liberal states. For social democratic parties in both Continental and Scandinavian countries represented the whole working class in ways which for example the British Labour Party did not. This was because they had an interest, as did their social democratic union counterparts, in extending skills throughout the working class. Yet this strategy would hardly have been compatible in the long run with a majoritarian electoral system: for a social democratic party would be unable to pursue an egalitarian strategy with any hope of capturing middle-class voters. Thus the political left in non-liberal countries had a double interest in proportional representation: it could be a part of minimum winning coalitions without having to focus on middle-class voters, and it allowed the indirect presence of unions—representing co-specific skilled workers—in a consensus-based regulatory framework.

We want to stress that the adoption of PR did not in our view present a sharp break with previous forms of representation. When economic interests were locally rooted, not only was most regulation local, but the single-member district systems that preceded PR had ensured essentially proportional representation of local interests at the national level by politicians who had a strong incentive to cater to their own local constituencies. It was because industrialization threatened the continuation of a consensus-based negotiation over regulatory issues—threatening, in effect, to turn locally based SMD systems into majoritarian national-level systems—that PR was adopted in some countries. This did not require exceptional rational forecasting: once the move to the national level of industry and politics made it apparent that the pre-existing majoritarian institutions of representation were producing stark disproportionalities, PR was a natural choice to restore representivity. Contrary to the impression from the literature, this did not involve intense conflict or position-taking by organized interests. Political parties representing these interests (both on the right and the left) for the most part agreed on the move to PR. PR was everywhere adopted with the support of center-right parties and with near unanimity (Blais, Dobrzynska, and Indridason 2005). It is possible that the distributive consequences of PR were not fully understood on the right, but with the exception of France there were no reversals of the electoral system even though the center-right everywhere enjoyed subsequent periods of majorities.

Scandinavian and Continental countries had much in common in their Ständestaat and guild backgrounds, but continental countries differed from the Scandinavian in one key respect.[18] In the Continental countries the peasant-dominated countryside was *more closely integrated* into the urban economies than in the Scandinavian (Hechter and Brustein 1980; Katzenstein 1985; Herrigel 1995). If the formerly strongly feudalized areas (mentioned in n. 17) are excluded, something like these patterns seem to be traceable a long way back in history (Katzenstein 1985). Hechter and Brustein use the term "petty commodity production" areas to describe the Continental pattern and "sedentary pastoral" the Scandinavian, and they begin their account in the twelfth century (Hechter and Brustein 1980). While a great deal more work is needed to pin down the connections, the petty commodity production areas seem clearly related to the decentralized production regions identified by Herrigel (1995) in south and west Germany. Herrigel pointed to the most notable of these districts in Germany, but we can imagine that on smaller scales they were widespread in the areas of Western Europe where autonomous urban centers had dominated non-feudal surrounding countrysides.

Guilds were sometimes but not always integrated in these networks, and there was substantial putting-out of work to small farms; there was also significant development of rural artisans; most generally the production process of goods could be spread over many different locations. Hechter and Brustein (1980) also emphasize the integration of farms and towns, and they emphasize the dispersion of ownership and the lack of a rigid class structure. As Herrigel makes clear, these urban–rural networks are in fact complex co-specific asset groups:

The [producers] are absolutely dependent upon one another...they essentially engage in highly asset-specific exchanges every time they engage in an exchange...Producers in the decentralized industrial order are part of a thick network of specialized producers that is much more than the sum of its parts. The institutions they create to govern their activities...constitute important fora to engage in negotiation and to establish understanding regarding... their individual and collective interests.   (Herrigel 1995: 29)

We want to argue that the urban–rural networks of the Continental coordinated economies created in the Catholic Christian democratic parties political coalitions which tied together lower income groups (largely peasant) with higher income artisan and small-producer groups. The regions Herrigel identifies are largely in the south and west of Germany, as are the major areas of Catholicism—though they were by no means universally Catholic (neither Saxony (pre-1871 Kingdom), nor North Wurttemberg was Catholic). In Switzerland there were some predominantly strong rural cooperative cantons, but all were Protestant (Rokkan 1970). Austria and Belgium were largely Catholic countries. In the Netherlands the Catholic community was separated economically and socially from the Protestant, and urban–rural networks characterized both. What is important for our argument is the assumption that in broad terms many of these networks were confined to Catholic areas.

This matters for how we understand the support of Christian democratic parties for PR, as well as their distinct approach to the welfare state.

In the standard Rokkan story, which is used by Esping-Andersen and others to separate out a distinct welfare state type, Christian democratic parties are a reflection of the *Kulturkampf* against the Catholic church, especially over education, which led to a deep division between Catholics and other social forces on the right in continental European states. So deep was the distrust by Catholics for non-Catholics on the right, that though both groups were anti-socialist they were unable to combine in a single right-wing political movement. Therefore right-wing parties chose proportional representation, and whenever Christian democrats participated in governments they were under the influence of the church to choose a welfare state that would prevent the rise of socialism and promote Catholic values of the family.

Yet, while Christian democratic parties did indeed emerge from the *Kulturkampf*, it was clearly not a sufficient condition for their creation: Christian democratic parties did not appear in either France or the then independent self-governing crown colony of New South Wales in both of which Catholic education was fiercely attacked by their respective governments. A necessary condition for founding a highly organized Christian democratic party, we surmise, was that the Catholic adherents were already members of organized economic groups, which was the case in neither France nor New South Wales. The *Kulturkampf* may also have been a necessary condition for the emergence of Christian democratic parties but not for their persistence since they remained strong long after the attack on the church had subsided. Indeed, if all that held Catholics to Christian democratic parties was their priest we might have expected Christian democratic parties to have remained responsive to their hierarchies. But in fact Christian democratic parties were fighting largely successfully for their independence from the church by the 1890s (Kalyvas 1996). The idea that they would have accepted social policies from the church against the interests of their voters is not persuasive. Nor is it necessary: compellingly, Kalyvas further shows that the different Christian democratic parties were organizing themselves by the turn of the twentieth century as representative parties with committees for different economic interests—as indeed they are still organized. And the Catholic welfare state, with its emphasis on insurance, fits well as a negotiated outcome between these interest.

The reason that Catholics with different economic interests remain with a party which is Catholic largely only in name is explained, we submit, by the interdependencies of these economic interests. The rural–urban, peasant–artisan–small employer–merchant co-specific asset network acted, if our hypothesis is correct, to create a peasant–Mittelstand constituency which had an incentive to remain within the Catholic party. Another way of putting this, very consistent with Manow and van Kersbergen (2007), is to see the Christian democratic party as a negotiating community with a range of different economic interests in terms of income levels and hence redistribution, but a common interest in sharing and managing co-specific assets. Moreover, as local and regional networks developed in part into national networks, and as regulations over a wide range of issues germane to these urban–rural networks were increasingly set at the national political level as well as regional and local ones, so the importance of supporting a party capable of representing these co-specific asset groups grew in significance.

The intra-party Christian democratic compromise played down redistribution because of its cross-class nature, and focused instead on insurance and agricultural protection. Yet, as compared to traditional liberal and conservative parties, Christian democratic parties were clearly much more favorably disposed towards the welfare state, precisely as we would expect given the structure of economic interests they represented. As we noted in the second section, this moderate position made Christian democratic parties attractive coalition partners with more traditional middle-class, or center, parties. So long as Christian democratic parties could govern with these parties, redistribution remained moderate. Only when centrist parties were too weak to ensure a majority, as has been the case during periods in the Netherlands and Belgium after the Second World War or indeed Weimar, they formed coalitions with Social Democrats, and then we see more redistribution as a consequence (though relatively insurance-based compared to the Scandinavian). This logic is entirely consistent with our coalitional model of redistribution, whereas for PRT Christian democracy is a residual category with no obvious linkage to power resources or economic interests.

Scandinavian states: Proportional representation, coordinated institutions, and agrarian social democratic coalitions

We have already set out much of the argument for the adoption by Scandinavian economies of PR, since the incentive structures for unions and business developed in a similar way to those in the Continental economies. This too explains why economic coordination was important in both groups of economies. Moreover, as in the Continental economies, the nature of the broad framework agreement as it evolved through this period reinforced social democratic parties as representing the whole working class. They believed that skill formation should be universal rather than seeing themselves as representing de facto skilled workers as was the case for the major left parties in the liberal economies and in France. Thus social democracy in Scandinavia as in the Continental countries stood for redistribution by comparison to counterparts in the liberal economies. Skilled workers remained important in social democratic parties, nonetheless; and their basic stance was one which favored income-related benefits rather than universalism.

Our claim is that the major difference with the Continental economies lay in the nature of the agricultural sector. While Scandinavian peasants owned their own land and coordinated activities as in the Continental countries, Scandinavian agriculture did not have the same tight links and dependency upon urban economies. Instead, the agricultural communities were tightly knit and heavily invested in co-specific asset relationships within autonomous rural cooperative frameworks. There was thus not the same logic in Scandinavia to support a peasant–Mittelstand party. Instead the logic of co-specificity led to agrarian parties from which the occasional large landowner was excluded. In these agrarian parties, by contrast to Christian democratic parties, homogeneous economic interests reinforced co-specific assets. The economic interests of peasants as discussed above favored redistribution. And because of the nature of agricultural uncertainty, agrarian parties were *more* predisposed to egalitarianism and universality than the social democratic parties.

Thus the coalitions which emerged after PR linked social democracy with agrarian parties and hence to both redistribution and universalism.

Recasting the relationship between PR, business, and the left

Our account of the origins of electoral institutions is very different from the dominant ones, which, in one form or another, build on work by Stein Rokkan. Consistent with power resource theory, these accounts suggest that PR emerged as a result of a strong left. But if one examines the historical data there is in fact no relationship between the electoral support of the left and the adoption of PR (Cusack, Iversen, and Soskice 2007). This is also true if one examines the interaction of left strength and divisions on the right, as in Boix (1999), and it can be easily illustrated (see Table 9.2). Countries with a dominant right party were no more likely to retain majoritarian institutions than countries that did not (compare the columns). The table also shows that the countries in bold where support for left parties was strong before the adoption of PR (or universal male suffrage in cases that

Table 9.2 Type of economy, party dominance on the right, and electoral system

Organization of production and labor	Single right party dominance?	
	Yes	*No*
No guilds/cooperatives, weak employer coordination, and craft unions	*United Kingdom, United States*	*Australia, Canada, New Zealand*
Guilds/cooperatives, employer coordination, and industrial unions	**Belgium, Denmark,** Greece, **Switzerland,** Italy	**Germany, Norway,** Sweden, the Netherlands
Ambiguous cases		*France, Japan*

Notes: *Italicized* countries retained majoritarian institutions. Bolded countries had left parties with above median electoral strength in the last election before the adoption of PR, or, in the cases where countries remained majoritarian, the first election under universal male suffrage. Referring to the same elections, single party dominance is measured by the percentage lead of the largest party over the next largest party. The "right party dominance" cut-off point is the value that would produce a number of countries with a dominant right party that is equivalent to the number of countries (7) that actually remained majoritarian.

remained majoritarian) were as likely to remain majoritarian as were countries without a strong left.

The critical variable, we maintain, was the organization of production and labor at the eve of the national industrial revolution (indicated on the left in Table 9.2). Where guilds and agricultural cooperatives were strong, employers well-organized and highly coordinated, and unions organized along industry lines, both right and left parties ended up supporting PR as a political mechanism to protect their mutual investments in co-specific assets. Where guilds and agricultural cooperatives were weak, employers poorly organized and coordinated, and unions divided by crafts, the right opposed PR in order to protect their class interests.

Long-Run Dynamics

We have argued in this chapter that economic and political institutions co-evolved over long stretches of time, creating a remarkable persistence in the comparative patterns of inequality and redistribution. The high-equality, high-redistribution economies today appear to be the same during most of the twentieth century and even earlier. Yet while the cross-national rankings may not have changed very much there are large changes in inequality and redistribution over time. The government today plays a much greater role in redistributing income than at the beginning of the previous century. Likewise wage dispersion has waxed and waned, falling from the 1930s and then showing a sharp upturn since the late 1970s. How do we explain these changes?

Our answer focuses on the interaction between the structure of skill investments, political institutions, and technological change. In this section we provide a brief sketch of these interactions for the purpose of illustrating the kind of explanations that our approach invites.

Redistribution over a century

Figure 9.7 shows the trends in social spending as a share of GDP for sixteen advanced democracies beginning in 1880 (we only include countries that were democracies during the entire period). Note that before the 1920s the government did not play much of a role in the provision of social insurance or redistribution. What arrangements existed were largely "private" ones and operated through the guilds, the church, the burgeoning unions, and the emerging industrial relations system. But with massive industrialization, urbanization, and expansion of the franchise came demand for insurance against risks that could no longer be addressed through decentralized, private arrangements. It is our contention that the role of universal suffrage and left parties cannot be separated from either the design of democratic institutions (PR vs. majoritarian institutions) or the structure of production (CME vs LME).

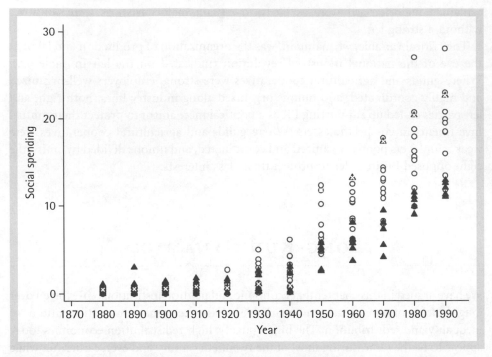

Fig. 9.7 Social spending in sixteen industrialized democracies, 1880–1990

Notes: Filled circles indicate PR electoral institutions, triangles indicate majoritarian institutions. The figures for 1940 are estimates using the growth in total general government non-military spending from 1930 to 1940 (the correlation between general government spending and social spending is 0.92). The observations marked with an x are for France. The other countries for which data are available are Austria, Australia, Belgium, Britain, Canada, Denmark, Finland, Germany, Italy, Japan. Netherlands, Norway, Sweden, Switzerland, and United States.

Sources: Data assembled by Thomas Cusack and presented in Cusack and Englehardt (2002) based on Lindert (2004) and various volumes of the OECD's *Economic Outlook* and *Yearbook of National Accounts*.

Seen in this light it is remarkable that starting with the adoption of PR in Western European countries in the 1920s, the trajectory of social spending began to diverge. By the end of the Second World War (or at least by the 1950s) there was an almost complete separation of PR and majoritarian countries with the former spending notably more than the latter. It is easy to confirm this econometrically using a fixed effect model with a lagged dependent variable and time dummies. Controlling for the size of the electorate, the elderly population, and GDP per capita, PR has a strong and statistically significant effect on spending.[19]

Yet the entire gap between PR and majoritarian countries today cannot be attributed to the accumulated effects of the introduction of PR in the 1920s. Instead, the string of social reforms introduced since the 1920s can sensibly be seen as conditioned by electoral institutions, with differences being reinforced through international specialization. On the first point, since risks tend to be concentrated at the middle and lower end of the income distribution (Cusack, Iversen, and Soskice 2007), and because PR favors the center-left, we would expect the response to shocks to be more pronounced in PR countries. These "shocks" include major upheavals such as the industrial revolution, the Great Depression, the Second World War, and so on. Indeed, if we interact PR with a set of decade dummies representing the (unobserved) exogenous shocks, the results indicate that PR countries respond much more aggressively to pressures for protection against social risks.[20] This pattern is probably magnified by cross-national differences in the structure of skills since, as we have argued, PR countries are associated with specific skills production systems and high demand for insurance. Here the role of specialization also enters the story because trade allows countries to specialize in production where they have a comparative advantage, which implies that differences in skills and their associated institutions of social protection will grow. In this sense we agree with the literature that assigns an important role to the international economy in explaining social welfare regimes.

There is one exception to the general pattern, which is highlighted in Fig. 9.7: France. France adopted PR after the Second World War but changed back in 1958 under the Fifth Republic. The shift to PR was associated with a jump in spending, but there was no subsequent reversal. To understand this it must be recalled that France developed along a distinct path where large companies dominated the skill formation process and where workers became closely tied to their workplace as a result of highly firm-specific skills. Even though unions were weak and management enjoyed unilateral control over hiring and firing, and even though most governments in France have been center-right, the middle class appears to expect and demand high levels of social insurance from the state. Certainly it is hard to explain the large welfare state in France by the strength of the left.

Wage compression and (post-)Fordism, 1930s to today

There appears to be a long-run U-shaped evolution in wage, or pre-fisc income, inequality in a majority of OECD countries: First a decline from 1920s until the middle of the century followed by a sharp increase starting in the 1970s (Atkinson 2003). It also appears that periods of compression have been characterized by smaller differences in inequality across countries, while periods of greater dispersion have been marked by greater differences.

Significant changes in dispersion notwithstanding, the cross-national ranking of countries appears to have been quite stable, at least in the post-war period. The correlation between pre-tax d5/d1 ratios for the 1970s and 1990s is .97 for nine countries where data are available (OECD n.d.), and using evidence for pre-tax income inequality, the correlation between the 1950s and 1990s is .92 for ten countries. This persistence is notable because the 1980s and 1990s were decades of dramatic increases in wage inequality in some countries. In other words, while inequality changes quite dramatically over time the ranking of countries does not.

This conclusion is much harder to corroborate for the pre-war period where comparable data are scarce. Tax return data have recently become available for top incomes in a number of countries (see Piketty 2005; Piketty and Saez 2006) and there has been considerable volatility in these over time (Scheve and Stasavage 2007). But top incomes include a large component of capital income and inequality at the lower end of the income scale appears to be much more stable (Atkinson 2003). As Roine and Waldenström (2008) conclude based on the Swedish tax data:

The income share going to the lower half of the top decile (P90–P95), which consists mainly of wages, has been remarkably stable over the entire period [between] 1903 and 2004.   (367)

Based on this type of evidence we may conjecture that country rankings were also relatively stable in the pre-war period. Still, we need to account for the U-shaped change in the wage distribution over time—a change that appears to have occurred everywhere to some degree. PRT would point to changes in unionization rates and the level of centralization of bargaining institutions. Certainly these variables are correlated with wage compression (see Wallerstein 1999; Rueda and Pontusson 2000). But why did unions become stronger and more centralized in this period?

Our perspective roots union power in co-specific assets. Changes over time, including institutional change, are in large measure a reflection of changes in technology. The notable move towards centralized bargaining and compression of inter-occupational wages that occurred across OECD countries from the 1950s until the end of the 1970s must be understood in the context of the spread of Fordist mass production, which generated strong complementarities between skilled and semi-skilled workers and gave the latter a level of bargaining power they heretofore had lacked.

Correspondingly, our explanation for the sharp rise in wage inequality in the 1980s and 1990s is that the complementarities between skilled and unskilled workers were undone by the widespread application of the microprocessor as well as the segmentation of the occupational structure caused by deindustrialization. Unlike the old assembly line, low-skilled workers in the new types of production are not strong complements to skilled workers and therefore cannot easily extract rents from skilled workers. In relatively fragmented bargaining systems such as the British this has meant a loss in power of semi-skilled unions with union membership declining as a consequence. In some northern European countries with highly centralized systems the changes have caused skilled workers and their employers (especially in the engineering sector) to break out of the centralized systems (see Iversen 1996; and Pontusson; and Swenson 1996 for related accounts).

Yet in all the countries where skilled workers and employers had made major investments in co-specific assets, wage coordination was re-established at the industry or sectoral levels, with a more marginal position for semi-skilled workers. The central role that unions continue to play in these counties is explained by the fact that skilled workers are still co-owners of major production assets that are irreplaceable for employers. This is less true in countries like Britain and the US and has resulted in a more widespread collapse of union membership. While this collapse was furthered by partisan attacks on the organizational foundation of unions, as PRT would point out, such attacks were made possible by the liberal underpinnings of the economy.

Finally, it is important to consider the dimensions of distribution and redistribution together. It is precisely in liberal countries where the decline of unions was most severe that a majoritarian political system militated against political coalitions that could compensate for rising inequality though redistribution. By contrast, in coordinated economies with PR systems, especially of the social democratic variety, the rise in labor market inequality was less dramatic and the political system facilitated the formation of redistributive coalitions that could compensate losers through the welfare state and active labor market policies.

Co-evolving Systems: Welfare States, Varieties of Capitalism, and Political Institutions

In this concluding section, we draw out the central aspects of our approach to distribution and redistribution and more generally to welfare states and the analysis of power and institutions. There are points of contact with Power Resource Theory, but our work is different in its micro analysis, in its understanding of modern welfare states, and in its historical account of their origins. At a quite fundamental level we suggest how the power balance between employers and workers, as well as among workers, cannot be taken as exogenous but instead reflects differences in the level and type of investments economic agents have made in the economy. Because PRT takes power as the starting point, it cannot explain why it varies across time and space. This is true both in the analysis of economic institutions, such as unions and coordinated wage bargaining, and in the analysis of political institutions, such as strong left parties and PR. We have to treat these institutions as endogenous to the structure of production and investments in economic assets. And these differences in turn depend on economic, welfare, and political institutions, which themselves depend on earlier patterns of investment, and so on: varieties of capitalism, welfare states, and political institutions thus co-evolve.

More specifically, the main elements of our approach can be summarized as follows:

1. *Welfare states as skill insurance systems in varieties of capitalism.* Most fundamentally, in our perspective welfare states are the insurance systems which accompany the different nature of skill formation in different varieties of capitalism. The institutions of *coordinated* economies encourage widespread investment in *deep co-specific skills*, where the co-specificity covers companies, sectors, and/or occupations. Hence, such systems require unemployment insurance and pensions offering high replacement rates as in Scandinavian or Continental welfare states.

The institutions of *liberal* economies encourage by contrast widespread investment in *general* or mobile skills. Since reinsertion into employment is relatively easy after separations or to supplement pensions the need for state-provided insurance is low, and liberal safety-net welfare states are the consequence. This is an argument about high *horizontal* mobility between firms and industries; it does not imply that vertical mobility between income groups is high. In fact, investment in high general education, such as college degrees, is an insurance against permanent income loss and hence poverty. In such a system, there will be little sense of commonality of interests between the middle class and the poor. This conclusion is reinforced when we look beyond insurance and consider the welfare state as a system of redistribution, discussed below in (4).

2. *Wage coordination as regulation of co-specific assets.* Union centralization and/or coordinated wage bargaining plays a major role in our argument—as it does in Power Resources Theory—in determining the equality of the earnings distribution (D). But for us this derives from the different nature of skills in different varieties of capitalism. Groups of workers are strong when they can credibly threaten to hold up employers. This is a consequence not of employment or skills per se—employers can in principle replace workers with general skills at low cost—but of skills which are costly to replace and whose withdrawal is costly to the employer in lost production. Thus *co-specific* skills cause particular problems for employers; and for employers to invest in them, they need the assurance that wages will be set *outside* the company, whether across the industry or more widely, hence disciplined unions and industry or economy-wide bargaining. Clearly, this requires solutions to collective action problems, and in our account such solutions were only possible in countries which had initially been organized into strong guilds and Ständestaaten (see (6) below).

Workers with co-specific assets also have an insurance need for strong unions and coordinated wage bargaining. For they need to know that the return on their investment in co-specific assets is not going to be eroded by employer hold-up or more generally by changing demand patterns. Hence we see coordinated wage bargaining and egalitarian distributions as stemming in part from an insurance need of co-specific asset investment by both employers and workers in coordinated economies (Estevez-Abe, Iversen, and Soskice 2001; Iversen 2005).[21]

In part wage compression also reflects the relative power of workers with different skills. When skilled and semi-skilled labor are strong complements in production, even small groups of workers have the capacity to cause serious interruptions in production. Semi-skilled workers in that situation in effect become co-owners of a specific asset (specialized machinery), and they gain bargaining power as a consequence. The most prominent example of this logic is the rise of Fordist mass production, where interruptions anywhere in the assembly line could shut down the entire production process. Not surprisingly, this is a period with falling wage dispersion across countries. Conversely, the end of Fordism in the 1980s was associated with a rise in wage inequality as the complementarities between semi-skilled and skilled workers unraveled.

3. *Implications for consensus and majoritarian political systems.* We also argue that the type of political system is central to our analysis. Empirically, coordinated market economies cluster with strong welfare states and consensus political systems; and liberal market economies cluster with weak welfare states and majoritarian political systems. This clustering follows directly from our logic of the set of rules and understandings governing the production and maintenance of skills and their insurance. Whatever that set of rules and understandings, its framework is underwritten by the political system. Where skills are co-specific assets, multiple actors—business, labor, and handwork organizations covering many different sectors of the economy—will only be prepared to invest in them if they are represented directly, as well as indirectly via political parties, in their political regulation. Hence a consensus system of political regulation is necessary for co-specific skill formation to be widely viable. In practical terms this means proportional representation of different parties in legislative institutions, especially parliamentary committees, which are themselves closely integrated with a bureaucracy where major interest groups enjoy direct representation ("corporatism").

4. *The partisan and redistributional consequences of political systems.* Proportional representation has two aspects which the literature has traditionally kept apart: the consensus (or inclusive) regulatory politics explained in (3) above, and a minimum winning coalition (or exclusive) politics of redistribution. As explained in the second section, the politics of redistribution in PR systems favors the center-left, at least in a simple three party—Left, Center, Right—legislature. If the Center cannot govern by itself it will prefer a Center-Left coalition to impose high taxes on an excluded Right.

But this makes the precise pattern of coalition partners centrally important for understanding redistribution in PR systems. And it points to the critical importance of understanding parties in terms of the economic interests of the groups they represent, rather than social cleavages. PR permitted a center-left alliance between social democrats and independent peasants in Scandinavia, allowing substantial redistribution as well as insurance. By contrast—we suggest tentatively—the linkage of the economic interests of independent small-holding peasants, parts of the handwork sector, and small business was behind the success of Christian democracy in a range of countries, and this enabled center–Christian-democratic alliances with insurance but less redistribution.

Our analysis also explains why the relation between redistribution and center-left governments needs to be mediated by electoral systems. With a majoritarian system, where a center-left party has to credibly commit to a median voter platform, center-left governments—such as Blair's—will imply low redistribution. This is of course in addition to the fact that majoritarian systems are less likely to produce center-left governments.

5. *Choosing political systems.* The type of capitalism determines national political systems. In our argument embryonic patterns of capitalist industrialization—the presence or absence of coordinated co-specific investments at different territorial levels, and whether or not co-specificity linked town and country—pre-date and explain the

choice of *national* political systems. Proportional representation (consensus) as opposed to the retention of majoritarian systems in the early twentieth century was adopted by countries with coordinated co-specific investment systems as industrialization pushed the centre of gravity of economic networks to the national level from the local and regional; it reflected the need for national representation as standard setting increasingly took place at the national level instead of the local and regional.[22]

In most cases PR was chosen by the center and right (the left not having a full franchise). Given the redistributional consequences of PR in (4), its choice implied that the center and right put the positive representational benefits above the redistributive costs. It mattered for this calculation that redistribution simultaneously serves insurance purposes, which is a precondition for investment in skills that employers in coordinated systems rely on (see (1) above). In particular, redistributive policies that reduce the loss of income in the event of adverse shocks to firms or industries are at the same time forms of income insurance.

6. *Origins.* The third section explains the origins of the quite different broad arrangements which start to emerge at the end of the nineteenth century and build up over the next decades for the structuring of labor markets and skill formation— on the one hand, the essentially deregulated systems of the liberal economies, and on the other the more regulated systems permitting workforce cooperation and systematic skill formation in the coordinated economies. In the deregulated liberal case, there is a zero-sum game between fragmented craft unions and hostile employers, with neither side strongly organized. In the regulated coordinated case, broad framework agreements gradually emerge between increasingly centralized business and union organizations.

The observer in the mid-nineteenth century would not necessarily have predicted these divergences: embryonic unions were everywhere craft unions, and companies were almost everywhere hostile to them. Why then this ultimately fundamental divergence? In our view, which draws heavily on Crouch (1993) and Thelen (2004), both on the union side and on the employer side there were key differences between the liberal and the coordinated world: in the liberal world the possibility of sustained collective action did not exist on either side; that reflected the dominance of a liberal state tradition and the absence of a serious guild tradition. In addition, consequence of the absence of guilds and of the demise or nonexistence of a widespread independent but collectively organized peasantry, the labor force available to meet the demands of industrialization was primarily unskilled. Thus industrializing companies in the liberal economies built their operations with a bias towards unskilled and semi-skilled labor. The skilled workers that employers needed were likely to be craft union members. But neither individual businesses nor unions could solve the collective action problems needed for more regulated labor markets and skill formation systems, and neither side had a strong incentive to do so: hence business strategies towards skills focused either on developing technologies which minimized the use of skills or on excluding unions or on minimizing their power within plants.

By contrast in the economies which became nationally coordinated, collective action was encouraged by the background traditions of guilds and Ständestaaten (Crouch 1993), as well as the coordination in decentralized industrial districts. While late industrialization may be a part of the story (Gerschenkron 1966), Herrigel's (1996) work makes it plain that it is only one part. Given that collective action is possible, both employers and unions have incentives to develop a coordinated solution to specific skill formation and workplace cooperation. In addition in our argument pre-industrial localized traditions of skill formation are important. This is because an effective guild system implied that industrializing companies could call on a ready supply of skilled labor, thus having an incentive to focus on skill-biased production—at least if they could solve the problems of hold up associated with skilled workers. An effective guild system also removed the incentive for embryonic unions to attempt to control the supply of skills or to control their job content (Thelen 2004). Thus both employers and unions had a joint incentive to exchange skilled workforce cooperation for collective bargaining, and ultimately for joint engagement in creating a skill formation system fashioned for the needs of industry.

In relation to the perspective sketched in this chapter, a view which focuses on left power as the fundamental exogenous determinant of high redistribution and of egalitarian distribution of income seems inadequate. We have important points in common with Power Resources Theory, and see PRT as the catalytic intellectual development behind welfare state analysis. But in our view business and its political representation is as important as labor in understanding strong welfare states. Note, though, that this implies that an approach which is largely "employer-centered," highly influential though it has been on our thinking, is *also* incomplete (Swenson, Mares, Martin). Although Crouch was looking at the origins of different systems of industrial relations, his broad conclusion in relation to corporatist systems is echoed by ours: the advanced countries with strong welfare states today are those in which economies were locally coordinated a century and a half ago; and whose state tradition was one of functional representation and limited autonomy of government to different interests.

Acknowledgements

A previous version of this chapter was presented at the annual meeting of the American Political Science Association, Philadelphia, August 31 – September 3, 2006. We would like to thank Sven Beckert, Suzanne Berger, Tom Cusack, Charles Maier, Peter Gourevitch, Robert Hancke, Jurgen Kocka, Cathie Jo Martin, Kathleen Thelen, Daniel Ziblatt, and three anonymous reviewers for many helpful comments. We are particularly grateful to Peter Hall who gave us detailed comments on all parts of an early version of this chapter.

Notes

1. Meltzer and Richard (1981).
2. See Bénabou (1996); Perotti (1996); Lindert (1996); Alesina and Glaeser (2004); Moene and Wallerstein (2001). Milanovic (2000) finds a positive relationship between inequality and redistribution to the poor in a sample of countries that includes transition economies. Milanovic uses inequality in household income, not inequality in earnings, which is the focus of this chapter. Household income inequality is strongly affected by households without income and therefore says very little about individual labor market inequality. Besides, Milanovic is explicit that the results do not confirm the Meltzer and Richard's median voter model because the median voter turns out not to benefit more from redistribution in countries with high household inequality.
3. The proportionality of the electoral system measure in the last column is a composite index of two widely used indices of electoral system. One is Lijphart's measure of the effective threshold of representation based on national election laws. It indicates the actual threshold of electoral support that a party must get in order to secure representation. The other is Gallagher's measure of the disproportionality between votes and seats, which is an indication of the extent to which smaller parties are being represented at their full strength. The data are from Lijphart (1984).
4. One (marked by triangles) is Hall and Gingerich's (2004) measure of non-market coordination, based on the existence of coordinating institutions in industrial relations and the corporate governance system. The other (marked by squares) is Hicks and Kenworthy's (1998) index of cooperation, which measures the extent to which interactions between firms, unions, and the state are cooperative as opposed to adversarial.
5. Moene and Wallerstein (2001) derive a positive relation based on an insurance argument. But though elegant the implication that there is a positive relationship between income and preferences for spending in the relevant interval around the median voter is in our view implausible as a general proposition, and it is inconsistent with evidence presented in Iversen and Soskice (2001).
6. We shall see that this is not the only use of coordinated wage bargaining.
7. At least in recent decades, though see Swenson for the US in the inter-war period.
8. The insurance function operates of course in LMEs as well, but with a greater weight of general skills less insurance is needed.
9. We excluded governments that were coded as centrist by the one expert survey (Castles and Mair 1984) which explicitly identified parties as such.
10. If M can make a take-it-or-leave it offer, it can enforce M's ideal point on either L or H. But this is not the reality of most coalition formation where counter-offers are invariably both made and considered.
11. Note that since the LM party is at an electoral disadvantage it has a greater need and incentive to elect centrist leaders than the MH party. If this holds, the distribution of wins and losses will be more even, but the political spectrum will be shifted to the right. The contrast between the centrist Clinton and the rightist G. W. Bush is a case in point.
12. Though note too that this weakens the center-right bias in majoritarian systems, since a left deviation is less frightening for M.
13. Flanders has been included for the sake of completeness, but linguistic ability testing in Flemish and internal migration may account for lower than expected performance.
14. A more detailed analysis of the literacy data is provided in Iversen and Stephens (2008).

15. Some of the literature on corporatism (especially Katzenstein 1985) and PR (especially Rogowski 1987) also emphasize the importance of economic openness. Yet openness per se is not particularly strong correlated with the distinctions we make in this chapter. Austrialia, New Zealand, and Ireland are small countries which developed liberal economic institutions and majoritarian political institutions (with some qualifications in the case of Ireland). Germany and (northern) Italy, on the other hand, are large countries that developed coordinated capitalism with PR. However, Katzenstein's argument may be read to mean that *specialization* is important for the development of corporatism, and our argument is entirely consistent with that view. We also believe that the international economy reinforces the institutional differences we discuss through the mechanism Hall and Soskice (2001) call "comparative institutional advantage"—namely the process by which institutions that are complements to particular types of production are reinforced as countries can specialize through international trade. We return to this issue below, in "Co-evolving systems: welfare states, varieties of capitalism and political institutions."

16. The French welfare state has much in common with this, but its genesis is quite different. So it is excluded from this group of states.

17. There are exceptions on land ownership, including East Prussia and the Mezzogiorno, as well as the Ruhr region in West Prussia.

18. No work that we know of has taken this route, so we should both caution, and perhaps encourage, the reader that more historical research is needed to fill out the argument we are tentatively putting forward.

19. The estimated parameter for the PR dummy is 1.213 (s.e. = 0.539) and for the lagged dependent variable 0.855 (s.e. = 0.062). The result stands in contrast to a recent paper, Aidt, Dutta, and Loukoianova (2006), which finds no effect of PR on spending in twelve European countries 1830–1938. But they only have data for central government spending and without separating out social spending.

20. The model is

$$y_{i,t} = \lambda \cdot y_{i,t-1} + (\Sigma \delta_t \cdot D_t) \cdot (1 + \beta_1 \cdot PR_i) + \beta_2 \cdot PR_i + \Sigma \gamma^k \cdot X_{i,t}^k + \alpha_i + \varepsilon_{i,t},$$

where y refers to social spending, D to the time dummies, and i indexes countries, t time, and k a set of control variables ($X_{i,t}$). The model is estimated using non-linear least squares. The model described in the previous paragraph sets $\beta_1 = 0$.

21. Reinforcing this is the fact that in coordinated economies, employers and unions have the capacity to resolve, and share an interest in resolving, the negative externalities of uncoordinated bargaining on inflation or competitiveness, because otherwise higher unemployment is needed to stabilize inflation or the real exchange rate.

22. Herrigel points in Germany to a similar phenomenon structuring federalist institutions (1996).

REFERENCES

AIDT, T. S., DUTTA, J., and LOUKOIANOVA, E. 2006. "Democracy comes to Europe: franchise extension and fiscal outcomes," *European Economic Review* 50: 249–83.

ALESINA, A., and GLAESER, E. 2004. *Fighting Poverty in the US and Europe.* Oxford: Oxford University Press.

ANSELL, B. 2008. "University challenges: explaining institutional change in higher education," *World Politics* 60(2): 189–230.

ATKINSON, A. B. 2003. "Income inequality in OECD countries: data and explanations," *CESifo Economic Studies* 49(4): 479–513.

BARON, D. P., and FEREJOHN, J. A. 1989. "Bargaining in legislatures," *American Political Science Review* 83(4): 1181–206.

BARTELS, L. 2004. "Homer gets a tax cut: inequality and public policy in the American mind," typescript, Department of Politics, Princeton.

BÉNABOU, R. 1996. "Inequality and Growth," in B. S. Bernanke and J. J. Rotemberg, eds., *National Bureau of Economic Research Macro Annual* 11: 11–74.

BLAIS, A., DOBRZYNSKA, A., and INDRIDASON, I. H. 2005. "To adopt or not to adopt proportional representation: the politics of institutional choice," *British Journal of Political Science* 35 (January): 182–90.

BOIX, C. 1998. *Political Parties, Growth and Equality.* New York: Cambridge University Press.

—— 1999. "Setting the rules of the game: the choice of electoral systems in advanced democracies," *American Political Science Review* 93: 609–24.

BRADLEY, D., HUBER, E., MOLLER, S., NIELSEN, F., and STEPHENS, J. 2003. "Distribution and redistribution in postindustrial democracies," *World Politics* 55(2): 193–238.

BUSEMEYER, M. 2007. "Determinants of public education spending in 21 OECD democracies, 1980-2001," *Journal of European Public Policy* 14(4): 582–610.

CASTLES, F., and MAIR, P. 1984. "Left–right political scales: some 'expert' judgments," *European Journal of Political Research* 12: 73–88.

COLOMER, J. H. 2006. *Political Institutions: Democracy and Social Choice.* Oxford: Oxford University Press.

CREPAZ, M. 1998. "Inclusion versus exclusion: political institutions and welfare expenditures," *Comparative Politics* 31(1): 61–80.

CROUCH, C. 1993. *Industrial Relations and European State Traditions.* Oxford: Oxford University Press.

CUSACK, T. 1997. "Partisan politics and public finance: changes in public spending in the industrialized democracies, 1955–1989," *Public Choice* 91: 375–95.

—— and ENGELHARDT, L. 2002. "The PGL file collection: file structures and procedures," Wissenschaftszentrum Berlin für Sozialforschung.

—— IVERSEN, T., and SOSKICE, D. 2007. "Economic Interests and the origins of electoral institutions," *American Political Science Review* 101(3).

ESPING-ANDERSEN, G. 1990. *The Three Worlds of Welfare Capitalism.* Princeton: Princeton University Press.

ESTEVEZ-ABE, M., IVERSEN, T., and SOSKICE, D. 2001. "Social protection and the formation of skills: a reinterpretation of the welfare state," in P. Hall and D. Soskice, eds., *Varieties of Capitalism.* Oxford: Oxford University Press, 145–83.

FREEMAN, R. B. 1980. "Unionization and the dispersion of wages," *Industrial and Labor Relations Review* 34: 3–24.

GERSCHENKRON, A. 1966. *Economic Backwardness in Historical Perspective: A Book of Essays.* Cambridge, Mass.: Harvard University Press.

GOUREVITCH, P. 2003. "The politics of corporate governance regulation," *Yale Law Journal* 112 (7): 1829–80.

HALL, P. A., and GINGERICH, D. W. 2004. "Varieties of capitalism and institutional complementarities in the macroeconomy: an empirical analysis," MPIfG Discussion Paper 04/5.

—— and SOSKICE, D., eds. 2001. *Varieties of Capitalism: The Institutional Foundations of Comparative Advantage.* Oxford, Oxford University Press.

HECHTER, M., and BRUSTEIN, W. 1980. "Regional modes of production and patterns of state formation in Western Europe," *American Journal of Sociology* 85(5): 1061–94.

HERRIGEL, G. 1996. *Industrial Constructions: The Sources of German Industrial Power.* Cambridge: Cambridge University Press.

HICKS, A. 2000. *Social Democracy & Welfare Capitalism: A Century of Income Security Politics.* Ithaca, NY: Cornell University Press.

—— and KENWORTHY, L. 1998. "Cooperation and political economic performance in affluent democratic capitalism," *American Journal of Sociology* 103(6): 1631–72.

—— and SWANK, D. 1992. "Politics, institutions, and welfare spending in industrialized democracies, 1960–82," *American Political Science Review* 86(3): 649–74.

HUBER, E., and STEPHENS, J. D. 2001. *Development and Crisis of the Welfare State : Parties and Policies in Global Markets.* Chicago: University of Chicago Press.

IVERSEN, T. 1996. "Power, flexibility, and the breakdown of centralized wage bargaining: Denmark and Sweden in comparative perspective," *Comparative Politics* 28(4): 399–436.

—— 1999. *Contested Economic Institutions: The Politics of Macroeconomics and Wage Bargaining in Advanced Democracies.* Cambridge: Cambridge University Press.

—— 2005. *Capitalism, Democracy and Welfare.* Cambridge: Cambridge University Press.

—— and SOSKICE, D. 2001. "An asset theory of social policy preferences," *American Political Science Review* 95(4): 875–93.

—— —— 2006. "Electoral institutions and the politics of coalitions: why some democracies redistribute more than others," *American Political Science Review* 100(2): 165–81.

—— and STEPHENS, J. 2008. "Partisan politics, the welfare state, and three worlds of human capital formation," *Comparative Political Studies*, forthcoming.

KALYVAS, S. 1996. *The Rise of Christian Democracy in Europe.* Ithaca, NY: Cornell University Press.

KATZENSTEIN, P. 1985. *Small States in World Markets.* Ithaca, NY: Cornell University Press.

KOCKA, J. 1986. "Problems of working-class formation in Germany: the early years, 1800–1875," in I. Katznelson and A. R. Zolberg, eds., *Working Class Formation: Nineteenth-Century Patterns in Western Europe and the United States.* Princeton: Princeton University Press, 279–351.

KORPI, W. 1983. *The Democratic Class Struggle.* London: Routledge & Kegan Paul.

—— 1989. "Power, politics, and state autonomy in the development of social citizenship: social rights during sickness in 18 OECD countries since 1930," *American Sociological Review* 54(3): 309–28.

—— 2006. "Power resources and employer-centered approaches in explanations of welfare states and varieties of capitalism. protagonists, consenters, and antagonists," *World Politics* 58 (January): 167–206.

KWON HYEOK YONG and PONTUSSON, J. 2005. "The rise and fall of government partisanship: dynamics of social spending in OECD countries, 1962–2000." Princeton: Department of Politics, Princeton University.

LAVER, M., and SCHOFIELD, N. 1990. *Multiparty Government: The Politics of Coalition in Western Europe.* Oxford: Oxford University Press.

LIJPHART, A. 1984. *Democracies: Patterns of Majoritarian and Consensus Government in Twenty-One Countries.* New Haven: Yale University Press.

—— 1997. "Unequal participation: democracy's unresolved dilemma," *American Political Science Review* 91: 1–14.

LINDBLOM, CHARLES E. 1980. *Politics and Markets: The World's Political Economic Systems.* New York: Harper Collins.

LINDERT, PETER H. 1996. "What limits social spending?" *Explorations in Economic History* 33 (1): 1–34.

—— 2004. *Growing Public*, vol. i: *The Story.* Cambridge: Cambridge University Press.

LIPSET, S. M., and ROKKAN, S. 1967. "Cleavage structures, party systems and voter alignments: an introduction, in S. M. Lipset and S. Rokkan, eds., *Party Systems and Voter Alignments: Cross-National Perspectives*. New York: Free Press, 1–64.

MANOW, P., and VAN KERSBERGEN, K., eds. 2007. "Religion, class coalitions and welfare state regimes," manuscript.

MARES, I. 2003. *The Politics of Social Risk: Business and Welfare State Development*. Cambridge: Cambridge University Press.

MARTIN, C. J. 2000. *Stuck in Neutral: Business and the Politics of Human Capital Investment Policy*. Princeton: Princeton University Press.

—— 2006. "Sectional parties, divided business," *Studies in American Development 20 (Fall)*. 160–84.

—— and SWANK, D. 2008. "The political origins of coordinated capitalism: business organizations, party systems, and state structure in the age of innocence," *American Political Science Review* 102(2): 181–98.

MELTZER, A., and RICHARD, S. 1981. "A rational theory of the size of government," *Journal of Political Economy* 89: 914–27.

MILANOVIC, B. 2000. "The median-voter hypothesis, income inequality, and income redistribution: an empirical test with the required data," *European Journal of Political Economy* 16(2): 367–410.

MOENE, K. O., and WALLERSTEIN, M. 2001. "Inequality, social insurance and redistribution," *American Political Science Review* 95(4): 859–74.

—— —— 2003. "Earnings inequality and welfare spending," *World Politics* 55: 485–516.

OECD. 2000. *Literacy in the Information Age: Final Report of the Adult Literacy Survey*. Paris: OECD.

—— n.d. *OECD Electronic Data Base on Wages*. Paris: OECD.

PEROTTI, R. 1996. "Growth, income distribution and democracy: what the data say," *Journal of Economic Growth* 1(2): 149–87.

PIKETTY, T. 2005. "Top income shares in the long run: an overview," *Journal of the European Economic Association* 3(2–3): 382–92.

—— and SAEZ, E. 2006. "The evolution of top incomes: a historical and international perspective," NBER Working Paper No. 11955.

PONTUSSON, J. 2005. *Inequality and Prosperity: Social Europe vs. Liberal America*. Ithaca, NY: Cornell University Press.

—— and SWENSON, P. 1996. Labor markets, production strategies, and wage bargaining institutions: the Swedish employer offensive in comparative perspective. *Comparative Political Studies*, 29 (April): 223–50.

POWELL, G. B. 2000. *Elections as Instruments of Democracy: Majoritarian and Proportional Visions*. New Haven: Yale University Press.

PRZEWORKI, A. 1986. *Capitalism and Social Democracy*. Cambridge: Cambridge University Press.

—— and SPRAGUE, J. 1988. *Paper Stones: A History of Electoral Socialism*. Chicago: University of Chicago Press.

RIKER, W. 1962. *The Theory of Political Coalitions*. New Haven: Yale University Press.

ROGOWSKI, R. 1987. "Trade and the variety of democratic institutions," *International Organization* 41(2): 203–23.

—— 1989. *Commerce and Coalitions: How Trade Affects Domestic Political Arrangements*. Princeton: Princeton University Press.

ROINE, J., and WALDENSTRÖM, D. 2008. "The evolution of top incomes in an egalitarian society: Sweden, 1903–2004," *Journal of Public Economics* 92(1–2): 366–87.

ROKKAN, S. 1970. *Citizens, Elections, Parties: Approaches to the Comparative Study of the Processes of Development*. Oslo: Universitetsforlaget.

RUEDA, D., and PONTUSSON, J. 2000. "Wage inequality and varieties of capitalism," *World Politics* 52(3): 350–83.

SCHEVE, K., and STASAVAGE, D. 2007. "Political institutions, partisanship, and inequality in the long run," typescript, Yale University.

SCHMITTER, P. 1979. "Still the century of corporatism?," in P. Schmitter and G. Lehmbruch, eds., *Trends Towards Corporatist Intermediation.* Beverly Hills: Sage, 7–48.

STEPHENS, J. D. 1979. *The Transition From Capitalism to Socialism.* London: Macmillan.

SWANK, D. 2003. *Global Capital, Political Institutions, and Policy Change in Developed Welfare States.* Cambridge: Cambridge University Press.

SWENSON, P. 1991. "Bringing capital back in, or social democracy reconsidered: employer power, cross-class alliances, and centralization of industrial relations in Denmark and Sweden," *World Politics* 43(4): 513–45.

—— 2002. *Capitalists against Markets.* Oxford: Oxford University Press.

THELEN, K. 2004. *How Institutions Evolve: The Political Economy of Skills in Germany, Britain, the United States and Japan.* Cambridge: Cambridge University Press.

UNESCO. 1999. *UNESCO Statistical Yearbook.* New York: UNESCO.

WALLERSTEIN, M. 1999. "Wage setting institutions and pay inequality in advanced industrial societies," *American Journal of Political Science* 43(3): 649–88.

WILENSKY, H. 2006. "Trade-offs in public finance: comparing the well-being of big spenders and lean spenders," *International Political Science Review* 27(4): 333–85.

CHAPTER 10

BUSINESS AND NEO-CORPORATISM

PHILIPPE C. SCHMITTER

THE advent of neo-corporatism has been a rare occurrence among advanced capitalist liberal democracies—and virtually unheard of elsewhere. Of the twenty or so original members of that club of rich countries, the OECD, only about one-third have managed to practice it for any length of time, despite the demonstrable benefits that this mode of interest intermediation has had for many aspects of macroeconomic performance from the end of the Second World War until the end of the 1970s. The most pervasive reason for this has been the opposition of organized business interests. Only under exceptional conditions of a "balance of class forces" between capital and labor has it emerged and persisted at the national level. Periods of war and its aftermath, socialist or social democratic party hegemony, or incipient revolutionary threat have contributed to creating such a balance, but under more normal conditions, the representatives of business have refused to enter into such arrangements or repudiated them when they could do so.

Whether defined as a way of organizing interests or of making policy, modern neo-corporatism may share its conceptual root with earlier, more compulsory, arrangements for managing conflicts between class, sectoral, and professional interests, but its contemporary emergence and persistence are contingent upon the voluntary consent of those organizations that participate in it. Under authoritarian auspices, its existence depended primarily upon the coercive power of state authority and neither business nor labor had much choice in the matter. Granted that in retrospect, the interests of the former in Italy under Mussolini, Spain under Franco, Portugal under Salazar, and Brazil under Vargas prevailed over those of the latter, this "functionally benign" outcome was no proof of causal intent or collective consent by business.

When the isomorphism between the state and societal versions of corporatism was discovered in the mid-1970s, analysts (such as myself) made three mistakes: (1) they focused attention exclusively on the national or macro-level of interest conflict resolution; (2) they privileged the interaction between capital, labor, and the state (so-called "Tripartism"); and (3) they assumed that such arrangements were stable since they seemed to be firmly anchored in both the pattern of interest associability and public policy-making. Now, almost thirty years later, we know that all three of these assumptions are dubious. Neo-corporatism can be practiced at multiple levels of aggregation from the micro- to the meso- to the supra-national; it can involve a much wider set of organized interests in its negotiations; and it can evolve and shift relatively quickly, especially in response to changes in political context and policy content. In short, what we thought was a constant turned out to be a variable—and we seemed to have first caught that variable at the very moment when it went into decline (Schmitter 1989: Schmitter and Grote 1997).

Right from the start, the concept of corporatism was "essentially contested." Apart from the obvious problem of the historical confusion occasioned by using the same term to refer to state and societal, authoritarian and democratic versions of it, there was also the initial distinction between its application to a system of organized interest intermediation and the contrast between it and pluralist systems (Schmitter 1974, 1981), and its application to a mode of making public policy by incorporating interest associations within the process and the contrast between this and "pressure group" arrangements in which they were excluded and acted upon the process from outside (Lehmbruch 1982, 1984). Once these conceptual confusions were clarified, attention was focused upon the voluntary relationship between organizational structure and policy-making (Williamson 1985; Cawson 1986). The prevailing hypothesis was that the two were closely interrelated, even reciprocally causal. In order to practice concertation in the making and (often) implementing of policies, the organizations involved had to be officially recognized, monopolistically organized, and hierarchically structured so that they could cover broad, class-based, constituencies of interest. It was also presumed that this had to occur at the national level and that once it had been established between interlocutors representing capital, labor, and the state, it would persist into the foreseeable future.

As we have already noted above, these assumptions have proven incorrect. The ensuing thirty years have witnessed significant transformations both in the participating organizations and in the purposes to which neo-corporatism has been applied. Needless to say, these have affected the extent to which business interests have supported or opposed such an arrangement. Right from the start, it demonstrated some disturbing trends when seen from this perspective: (1) the longer it persisted, the greater was the tendency for it to expand its purview by incorporating new substantive issues in order to satisfy working-class demands; (2) the more binding and extensive its policy scope, the greater was the tendency toward an equalization of income across skill levels, economic sectors, and territorial units; (3) the wider the scope of issues subject to interorganizational concertation, the more rigid became the conditions determining the labor contract, especially during downturns in the business cycle; (4) the longer neo-corporatist bargaining continued, the greater increased the influence that business associations could potentially exert over their member firms; and (5) the more important and encompassing the role of peak associations of business, the greater the likelihood became that large firms would have to defer to the interests of small and medium size ones. None of these trends were particularly welcomed by business—especially by its most prominent units, but as long as this mode of intermediation produced greater social peace, more stable exchange rates, predictable wage agreements below productivity increases and, therefore, enhanced competitive advantage, they could be ignored or tolerated as the unavoidable side effects of a "second best" solution.

The acceleration of globalization after the 1980s changed that situation (Gobeyn 1993; Walsh 1995). Countries that liberalized trade and, especially, financial flows, imposed strict monetary discipline, privatized public enterprises, and deregulated product and service markets seemed to perform better—and the flood of cheap consumer goods from China and elsewhere made the contention of wage costs in order to lower inflation rates a much less salient macroeconomic objective. The result of neo-corporatist negotiations (where they persisted) seemed to impose excessively rigid constraints on labor practices that interfered with the exciting prospects offered by new "globalized" markets for products and services. Pluralist bargaining with its shifting variety of less well-organized actors (and, often, operating at the level of firms or even individuals) looked much more appealing. Greater "flexibility" increasingly became the declared objective of business interests and neo-liberal economic theorists (backed by newly elected conservative politicians such as Margaret Thatcher) identified "corporatism" as the arch-enemy to attaining it. The business-oriented press made it single-handedly responsible for what was perceived as the inexorable decline of Europe vis-à-vis the United States (Wolf 2007).

Despite this much less favorable context, neo-corporatism did not completely disappear from the practice of European interest politics after the 1970s (Kenworthy 2003; Visser 2009). In a few countries, e.g. Austria, Finland, and Norway, it survived at the macro-level but only by shifting a good deal of bargaining to the meso-level of economic sectors and even by permitting micro-level arrangements at the level of individual firms (Traxler 1995; Crouch 2005). It also required increasingly direct intervention by state authorities, either to reach agreements or to ensure their implementation (Traxler, Blaschke, and Kittel 2001). The most frequent and persistent form of neo-corporatism in Europe came to rest on so-called "pattern bargaining" whereby organizations representing one industrial sector (usually metalworking) reached an agreement on wages and other issues and this was then generalized from sector to sector to cover almost the entire economy—without any need for a formal national accord. Germany, Greece, and Switzerland have long had such a system; Denmark and Sweden moved in that direction during the 1980s and 1990s. Spain and Portugal practiced it more erratically, reflecting no doubt broader political calculations stemming from their recent democratization (Royo 2002). In one case, Ireland, macro-corporatism made its first appearance during this period (Hardiman 2002) and in the Netherlands it re-emerged after an absence of over twenty years, but soon shifted downward to the meso-level (Visser and Hemerijck 1997). Many advanced capitalist economies have proven immune to the corporatist temptation, much to the delight of neo-liberal economists who persisted in asserting their belief in the superior performance of pluralist systems or, even better, in systems where no collective bargaining at all took place. Australia, Canada, New Zealand, the United Kingdom, and the United States are prominent examples, although the first experienced brief bouts of national social pacting in the 1980s. France's system of bargaining was consistently pluralist during this period, but only due to a heavy dose of direct state intervention in the process. Italy stands out as the most extreme example of a national economy that tried almost every conceivable variety of interest intermediation—from coordinated national pact-making to completely uncoordinated sectoral agreements—without institutionalizing any one of them.

In a previous article, Jürgen Grote and I argued that the practice of neo-corporatism had been following a cyclical pattern since the last third of the nineteenth century with roughly twenty to twenty-five years between its peaks and troughs—although we were not able to come up with a convincing hypothesis to explain this periodicity (Schmitter and Grote 1997). In most cases, the inversion of trend was triggered by the resistance or outright defection of capitalists, but why this should be the case remains a mystery (at least, to me). One might consider invoking the impact of so-called Kondratiev Waves with their fifty-year cycles, but their very existence is controversial and their causality with regard to the behavior of capitalists is even more mysterious.

Now, in retrospect, one is entitled to question whether one can legitimately use neo-corporatism to cover such a lengthy period and such a diversity of practices. In other words, how far and in how many directions can one stretch a concept before it snaps? Granted that neo-corporatism always was a "radial" concept that sheltered many sub-types and covered a wide range of activities, but are there not limits to its utility?

Consider the following major changes that have transformed many, if not most contemporary neo-corporatist arrangements:

1. Change in Identity of Actors. The initial specifications assumed that the key participants were representatives of capital and labor with some occasional and usually unobtrusive intervention by the state. With the introduction of organizations representing other interests such as the environment, women, consumers, youth, patients *e cosí via*, can it be the same?
2. Change in the Organization of Actors. The participants were supposed to be monopolistic, hierarchically structured, broadly comprehensive and officially recognized organizations; whereas, many of the more recent ones are pluralistic, autonomous, fragmented, and informally tolerated ones.

3. Change in Substantive Policy Content. Incomes policy or wage contention under inflationary pressure generated by full employment used to provide the core concern; whereas these are no longer so significant and the agenda has shifted to other issues, some of which have only a marginal relationship to class conflict.

4. Change in Level of Decision-Making. Setting rules and standards for the entire national economy was supposed to be the normal practice. This has been largely replaced by the increased resort to more specialized forums operating at the meso-level of economic sectors or sub-national regions.

5. Change in the Capacity of Actors. It was assumed that the organizations entering into neo-corporatist negotiations were capable of subsequently governing the behavior and, therefore, delivering the compliance of their respective members. How can that be the case with interest organizations and social movements that manifestly lack such a capacity and that, at best, can only try to convince their members to conform to the policies that they have agreed upon?

6. Change in Decision-Making Rules. Previously, most decisions in these arrangements were supposedly to be produced by the consensus of all participants and their implementation dependent upon the organizations' delivering the compliance of their members. What difference does it make when some participants refuse to sign the agreement (but do nothing to defeat it) and/or when state agencies are called upon to ensure eventual compliance by coercive means?

If "it" is no longer exclusively negotiated between organizations representing business and workers, if "it" is no longer about incomes policy and containing inflation, if "it" no longer involves encompassing and self-enforcing agreements at the national level, is "it" still "it"? Or, are we in the presence of something new that deserves a substantively different label? There has been no shortage of scholars who have proposed to replace it with such things as "social pacts or accords," "governance arrangements," "associational orders," or (my favorite) "systems of political exchange integrated within policy networks" (Molina and Rhodes 2002). I have chosen to put "neo-corporatism" in the title of this chapter and will continue to use it to the very end, but the reader is forewarned that this may be an anachronism.

Certainly the most challenging of these recent transformations involve Items 1 and 2, i.e. changes in the identity and the organizational structures of the actors involved. Since the 1980s, neo-corporatist bargaining has been taking place without the presumed covariance between *organizational structures* that were hierarchical, monopolistic and broadly encompassing and *policy-making structures* that involved officially sanctioned but nonetheless private actors in producing a variety of "social pacts" (Fajertag and Pochet 1997; Rhodes 1998; Hassel 2003). This unanticipated disjuncture had two effects: (1) It opened up the possibility for neo-corporatism in countries whose structures of organized interest previously seemed inappropriate (viz. Italy, Spain, Portugal, and Ireland); and (2) it opened up the possibility for concerted policy-making in issue arenas that are dominated by pluralist interest associations—even very weak and dispersed ones (viz. consumer protection, environmental standards, health insurance, and public safety). Ergo, the sites and instances of policy concertation over the past thirty years—including those involving capital and labor—have probably not declined in number (but they may have become much less binding in nature and more specialized in content). And they have even increased to cover new policy issues (where actors may be quite differently organized, if barely organized at all).

The following hypotheses might help to explain this puzzling disjuncture between organizational structure and decision-making process that was so central to initial speculation about neo-corporatism:

1. Associations representing the interests of business and workers have become increasingly "divorced" or, at least, "dissociated" from their respective "friendly" political parties, along with considerable convergence in the appeals and programs of these parties which has resulted in an abandonment of the commitment to full employment by Leftist or Social-Democratic parties.

2. Globalization has had a disruptive impact upon the "balance of class forces" between Capital and Labor and this has inhibited both the need for and the willingness of the former to engage in mutually concerted policy-making.

3. The ideological hegemony of "neo-liberalism" and the (alleged) greater success of "Liberal Market Economies" have provoked a process of convergence among "Coordinated Market Economies" where neo-corporatist practices were most firmly entrenched and this—along with the prescriptions of international financial and trade organizations (IMF, IBRD, WTO, etc.)—has discredited these practices, as well as the Keynesian paradigm that had previously justified the need for them.

4. European integration and its imposition of an additional layer of policy-making upon its member states has contributed to "embedding" liberal economic policies at the supra-national level and this was extended even further by European Monetary Unification and the autonomous powers arrogated to the European Central Bank.

5. The decline in working-class collective identity and in the distinctively "solidaristic" demands that this implies is due to individuation in the nature of workplace—combined with the growth of service sector employment where class relations are more fragmented and ambiguous.

6. The rise in the relative importance of public employment has given its representatives a privileged status within a generally shrinking trade union movement at the expense of manual working-class organizations that were more inclined to favor concertation arrangements.

7. Contemporary liberal democracies have witnessed the emergence of new lines of political cleavage around issues that cut across and, hence, divide the

previously overriding cleavage between Capital and Labor, e.g. environmental, gender equality, gay rights, *e così via*.

8. Political militants, especially youths, have shifted in their effort and attention from "orthodox" channels of partisan and associational representation to social movements—many of which have no stable organizational connection with either parties or interest associations.

9. Countries have to engage in greater competition with each other in order to attract foreign direct investment and this has undermined the rights of workers to collective representation and their potential for disrupting production which in turn has led to a decline in the power of trade unions and the attractiveness for capitalists of compromising with them.

10. Trade liberalization on a global scale—especially when extended to China and other low wage countries—has diminished inflationary pressures, even under conditions of full employment, and this makes containing wage pressures a much less salient issue than in the past for neo-corporatism.

11. An ageing population has meant that more and more trade union members are retired and, hence, less concerned with pressing current demands for wages and working conditions than with protecting future welfare benefits, and that lies more in the domain of state policy-making than that of social concertation.

12. The trend toward increasing the political independence of national central banks and, especially, the European Central Bank has deprived policy concertation of one of its most flexible mechanisms, i.e. the ability to make side-payments in social and/or fiscal policy in exchange for wage and working condition concessions.

13. The shift in substantive content from moderating wage demands and lowering inflation to improving international competitiveness by lowering non-wage costs and containing welfare spending has also detracted from the appeal of "orthodox" concertation arrangements.

Whatever the validity of each of these hypotheses, there is not a single one of them that is not welcome from the perspective of business interests and the associations that defend them. Together, they make a massive presumptive case against the perpetuation of neo-corporatism—unless, of course, it changes its practices beyond recognition with the original version.

And yet, *e pur si mouve*! Neo-corporatism has not completely disappeared from the policy process, even as practiced between consenting adults representing capital and labor at the macro-level of aggregation in Europe. According to a recent systematic survey by Lucio Baccaro (2007), it has actually been on the increase since 1975. Seen from the perspective of advocacy, ten of the fifteen EU + Norway governments called for it in 1975 and fourteen were doing so by 2000 (although the number fell back to eleven by 2003). Seen from the perspective of actual practice, eight were using some version of it for purposes of negotiating either salaries or welfare issues in 1975 and eleven were doing so by 2000 (again, with a subsequent decline to nine by 2003). Presumably, every time it was practiced, organized capital was a voluntary participant, since no one has invented a way to apply it without its consent. Australia tried to do so in the early 1980s, but this collapsed rather quickly. Inversely, Japan has been quietly, protractedly, and more-or-less effectively been accomplishing this without the participation of labor.

Why this should be the case when there are so many good reasons why organized business interests should have definitively rejected neo-corporatism in any form and at any level is puzzling. "Path dependence" is currently the most fashionable explanation for the persistence of such apparently irrational or improbable outcomes. Actors persist in their practices simply out of habit or because the short-term costs of changing them outweigh the longer term benefits. It seems unlikely, however, that unsentimental marginalist calculators like business executives would remain in such constraining arrangements unless they generated demonstrable and immediate comparative advantage over their more pluralist competitors. As noted above, neo-corporatism at the national level after the Second World War until the late 1970s was associated with key aspects of economic performance in the advanced capitalist democracies of the OECD: greater ruliness of the citizenry, lower strike rates, more balanced budgets, high fiscal effectiveness, lower rates of inflation, less unemployment, less income inequality, less instability at the level of political elites, and less of a tendency to exploit the "political business cycle"—all of which suggested that countries scoring high on this property were more governable and, hence, attractive in terms of long-term investment in material goods and human capital (Schmitter 1981). Econometricians such as Calmfors and Driffill (1988) even concluded that countries with "corporatist bargaining structures" were as capable of economic success as those following more orthodox neo-liberal and pluralist practices.

Largely on the strength of that endorsement, a substantial literature on "varieties of capitalism" emerged in which well-entrenched neo-corporatist bargaining was considered an integral part of a set of institutions labeled as composing "coordinated market economies" by Hall and Soskice (2001) that performed comparatively as well as their polar opposite, "liberal market economies." The defining characteristics of each variety of capitalism have tended to vary from author to author, but have included such other institutions as corporate governance, equity markets, regulatory mechanisms, and even vocational training systems. This approach tends to deny any particular salience or significance to the system of interest intermediation. Moreover, it comes accompanied with the hypothesis that whether it is pluralist or corporatist, its contribution to performance depends on its "complementarity" with the other institutions. "Hybrid" varieties that combined neo-corporatist bargaining with the wrong type of corporate governance arrangements are presumed to be less successful.

Subsequent econometric studies with more recent data have called into question some of the "benevolent" findings regarding the impact of neo-corporatism alone (Crepaz 1993; Traxler 2000), even in the its heartland of small European social democracies (Woldendorp 1997). No one has ever been able to show that neo-corporatist systems have been correlated with persistently higher rates of economic growth. In the turbulent times at the end of the 1990s and the beginning of this century, as we have noted above, policy concertation between social classes, sectors, and professions shifted away from the contention of wage costs and reduction in inflationary pressures toward such matters as improving productivity, encouraging worker flexibility, and reforming welfare systems. At least one major study has concluded that its impact has been disappointing in these policy arenas—unless backed up with the coercive intervention of state authority (Brandl and Traxler 2005). The previous assumption that such agreements between business and labor could be voluntarily enforced by the private contracting "social partners" was shown to be much more dubious under the new conditions of enhanced global competition.

With the dramatic crash of late 2008, the conditions that have previously promoted or impeded neo-corporatism, tripartism, policy concertation, social pacting, systems of political exchange, or whatever it should be called, have radically altered. After years of decline in the balance of forces between capital and labor in favor of the former, the terms of encounter are no longer the same. The ideological hegemony of business interests has been seriously undermined by the collapsed credibility of neo-liberalism, as well as by the revelations of fraud and misconduct by financial interests. Materially speaking, many enterprises have been devastated in their balance sheets and recovery to profitability—especially in those that depend heavily on the export of high-quality products—will require the willful cooperation of a skilled (and still unionized) labor force. If recovery of demand comes relatively soon and order books for investment goods fill quickly, then, regular negotiations between employers' associations and trade unions are likely to follow in many European countries, although admittedly, given previous trends, this could be satisfied at the meso-level of industrial sectors or even, in those cases where unions have been especially weakened, at the micro-level of individual enterprises. "Classical" macro-corporatist agreements covering the entire economy would not have much to offer—and it is difficult to imagine a scenario under which rejuvenated labor confederations coupled with triumphant Social Democratic political parties would be in a position to impose them. It is even dubious that they would have a joint interest in doing so.

The initial reaction by state authorities to the present crisis—even in governments dominated by conservative parties—demonstrates that they are not just disposed but anxious to intervene (previous ideological protestations to the contrary, notwithstanding). So far, their emergency measures have involved distributing massive welfare to capitalists and no concertation with labor at any visible level. On the one hand, there has simply not been sufficient time for tripartite negotiations, but on the other it is by no means clear what solutions such negotiations would presently be capable of reaching and delivering. The organizations for collective action by both capital and labor have been weakened by internal divisions and virtually all consultation has been directly (and clandestinely) between public monetary and budgetary authorities and large private firms. However, this unprecedented level of subsidization of the very enterprises whose decisions produced the present crisis has already begun to generate a popular backlash. It is not difficult to imagine a scenario in which governments—of whatever partisan composition—would eventually seek to divert this criticism by creating various forums for "social partnership" rather than to have it spill over into the much less predictable arenas of partisan competition and legislative process. This combination of factors could well lead to yet another revival of neo-corporatism, probably at the sectoral level and especially in small, relatively homogeneous and internationally vulnerable European countries. For those countries with larger, more heterogeneous and externally sheltered economies that have had no (or only unsuccessful) experience with such arrangements—and whose structures of organized interests tend to be much less centralized, monopolistic, and comprehensive—this prospect is much less likely.

Finally, the worst case scenario should not be excluded. Momentary recession could turn into protracted depression with mass unemployment reaching levels attained in the 1930s and aggregate output taking more than a decade to recover. This was precisely the context in which the initial experiments with macro-corporatist bargaining emerged voluntarily in Denmark, Norway, Switzerland, and Sweden, but one should not forget that it was also the context in which state corporatist structures were imposed on the entire system of interest intermediation by authoritarian regimes in Italy, Portugal, Spain, and most of Central Europe—not to mention in National Socialist Germany and its conquered states of Belgium, France, and the Netherlands.

REFERENCES

BACCARO, L. 2007. "*Political Economy* della concertazione sociale," *Stato e Mercato* 79 (April): 47–78.

BRANDL, B., and TRAXLER, F. 2005. "Industrial relations, social pacts and welfare expenditures: a cross-national comparison," *British Journal of Industrial Relations* 43(4): 635–58.

CALMFORS, L., and DRIFFILL, J. 1988. "Bargaining structure, corporatism and macro-economic performance," *Economic Policy* 6: 13–61.

CAWSON, A. 1986. *Corporatism and Political Theory*. Oxford: Basil Blackwell.

CREPAZ, M. 1993. "Corporatism in decline? An empirical analysis of the impact of corporatism on macroeconomic performance and industrial disputes in 18 industrialized economies," *Comparative Political Studies* 25(2): 139–68.

CROUCH, C. 1993. *Industrial Relations and European State Traditions*. Oxford: Oxford University Press.

—— 2005. *Capitalist Diversity and Change*. Oxford: Oxford University Press.

FAJERTAG, G., and POCHET, P., eds. 1997. *Social Pacts in Europe*. Brussels: European Trade Union Institute.

GOBEYN, M. J. 1993. "Explaining the decline of macro-corporatist political bargaining structures in advanced capitalist societies," *Governance* 6(1): 3–22.

HALL, P., and GINGERICH, D. 2004. "Varieties of capitalism and institutional complementarities in the macroeconomy: an empirical analysis," Max Planck Institute for the Study of Societies, Discussion Paper 04/5.

—— and SOSKICE, D., eds. 2001. *Varieties of Capitalism*. Oxford: Oxford University Press.

HARDIMAN, N. 2002. "From Conflict to coordination: economic governance and political innovation in Ireland," *Western European Politics* 25(4): 1–24.

HASSELL, A. 2003. "The politics of social pacts," *British Journal of Industrial Relations* 41(1): 707–26.

KENWORTHY, L. 2003. "Quantitative indicators of corporatism," *International Journal of Sociology* 33(3): 10–44.

LASH, S., and URRY, J. 1987. *The End of Organized Capitalism*. Oxford: Polity Press.

LEHMBRUCH, G. 1982. "Introduction: neo-corporatism in comparative perspective," in G. Lehmbruch and P. C. Schmitter, *Patterns of Corporatist Decision-Making*. London: Sage.

—— 1984. "Concertation and the structure of corporatist networks," in J. Goldthorpe, ed., *Order and Conflict in Contemporary Capitalism*. Oxford: Clarendon Press, 60–80.

MOLINA, O., and RHODES, M. 2002. "Corporatism: the past, present and future of a concept," *Annual Review of Political Science* 5.

RHODES, M. 1998. "Globalisation, labour markets and welfare states: a future of "competitive corporatism?," in M. Rhodes and Y. Meny, eds., *The Future of European Welfare: A New Social Contract*, London: Macmillan, 178–203.

ROYO, S. 2002. "A new century of corporatism? corporatism in Spain and Portugal," *Western European Politics* 25(3): 77–104.

SCHMITTER, P. 1974. "Still the century of corporatism?" *Review of Politics* 36: 85–131.

—— 1981. "Interest intermediation and regime governability in contemporary Western Europe and North America," in S. Berger, ed., *Organizing Interests in Western Europe: Pluralism, Corporatism and the Transformation of Politics*. Cambridge: Cambridge University Press, 287–327.

—— 1989. "Corporatism is dead! Long live corporatism," *Government and Opposition* 24(1): 54–73.

—— and GROTE, J. 1997. "The corporatist sisyphus: past, present and future," EUI Working Papers, No. 97/4.

—— and LEHMBRUCH, G., eds. 1979. *Trends Towards Corporatist Intermediation*. Beverly Hills, Calif.: Sage Publications.

TRAXLER, F. 1995. "Farewell to labour market associations? Organized versus disorganized decentralization as a map for industrial relations," in C. Crouch and F. Traxler, eds., *Organized Industrial Relations in Europe: What Future?* Aldershot: Avebury, 3–19.

—— 2000. "The bargaining system and performance," *Comparative Political Studies* 33: 1154–90.

—— BLASCHKE, S., and KITTEL, B. 2001. *National Labour Relations in Internationalized Markets: A Comparative Study of Institutions, Change, and Performance*. Oxford: Oxford University Press.

VISSER, J. 2009. *The ICTWSS Data Base: Database on Institutional Characteristics of Trade Unions, Wage Setting, State Intervention and Social Pacts in 34 Countries between 1960 and 2007*. Amsterdam Institute for Advanced Labor Studies, University of Amsterdam, Version 2.

—— and HEMERIJCK, A. 1997. *A Dutch Miracle: Job Growth, Welfare Reform and Corporatism in the Netherlands*. Amsterdam: Amsterdam University Press.

WALSH, J. 1995. "Convergence or divergence? Corporatism and the dynamics of European wage bargaining," *International Review of Applied Economics*, 9(2): 196–91.

WILLIAMSON, P. J. 1985. *Varieties of Corporatism: A Conceptual Discussion*. New York: Macmillan.

WOLDENDORP, J. 1997. "Neo-corporatism and macroeconomic performance in eight small West European countries," *Acta Politica* 32: 49–79.

WOLF, M. 2007. "European corporatism needs to embrace market-led change," *Financial Times* January 27.

PART III

COMPARATIVE BUSINESS SYSTEMS

CHAPTER 11

BUSINESS REPRESENTATION IN WASHINGTON, DC

TIMOTHY WERNER

GRAHAM WILSON

THE GENERAL PICTURE

WRITING in 1964, Peter Drucker famously described big business as a leading, if not the leading, institution of American society. Drucker was writing at the end of a golden age for US business, when arguably its position in US society was so strong that it did not need to mobilize vigorously to protect its political interests. Opinion polls reported great public confidence in major corporations and their leaders. Public interest groups were more or less absent from the Washington scene and the book that many credit for reviving environmentalism, Rachel Carson's *Silent Spring*, had only just been published. Political scientists reported that business representation in Washington was unimpressive, perhaps because not much political effort had been needed (Bauer, Pool, and Dexter 1963). In the years that followed, American business experienced greater criticism and a sharp fall in public confidence. Business was less able to take its position in American society for granted (Wilson 1981; Vogel 1989). Its political representation increased in quantity and quality in the 1980s and 1990s though, to the point that there was little doubt forty years later that Drucker's comment still applied to politics. However, in the wake of the financial and related crises of 2008, it appears that businesses' efforts in Washington now will be geared not toward retaining their prominence but, in many ways, toward ensuring their very survival.

At least numerically, business has towered over the American interest group scene in recent decades. Businesses employ a high proportion of all the lobbyists in Washington, DC, and provide a high proportion of the campaign contributions made by organized interests. Based on a survey they conducted in the early 1980s, Schlozman and Tierney (1986) concluded that business accounted for nearly three-quarters (72 per cent) of all organizations represented in Washington. As Baumgartner and Leech (1998) summarize, later studies have confirmed this numerical dominance of the Washington interest group scene by businesses. In a later work Baumgartner and Leech (2001) found that businesses accounted for 56 per cent of all of the spending on lobbying, and the Center for Responsive Politics (2003) reported that by 2000, businesses were spending $1.3 billion to lobby Congress, fifteen times the total spending of single-interest groups and forty-eight times the spending of labor groups. Indeed, the number of business representatives in Washington has been increasing at a fairly rapid rate. Heinz et al. (1993) found that individual businesses have become more directly involved in DC since the 1970s, supplementing their traditional representation through peak and industry associations by hiring their own representatives and opening their own offices. The number of corporations represented increased from 2,500 in 1981 to about 4,000 in 2001, and the number of trade associations represented in DC also increased, from 900 to 1,200 over the same period.

Businesses thus comprise a large proportion of the total interest group system. This is not *necessarily* to argue that businesses dominate the interest group system, let alone the political system as a whole; there are certainly sources of power and influence other than lobbying and campaign contributions. It is to say nevertheless, that business is by far the largest component of the interest group system and the DC policy community.

Several broad generalizations about the nature of business representation in Washington would command general agreement. First, business representation is organizationally fragmented and competitive (Berry 1997). In contrast to the situation in countries such as Japan, Sweden, Germany, or even the UK, there is no one body or small set of bodies that can plausibly claim to be the authoritative voice of business. The organization that comes the closest, the Chamber of Commerce, is generally identified with small business while the National Association of Manufacturers (NAM), as its title suggests, represents only part of business. The Business Roundtable represents very large firms, and the National Federation of Independent Business (NFIB) competes with the Chamber to be the voice of small business.

Second, there is no hierarchical relationship between business organizations. Peak associations such as the NAM or the Chamber of Commerce do not have authority over trade associations representing specific industries. With very few exceptions—most notably the American Chemistry Council (Prakash 2000)—trade associations have no authority to oversee, regulate, or commit individual corporations. The sovereign unit in American business is the firm. Peak and trade associations are organizations that exist in a competitive environment and seek to recruit corporations as members by offering them services, a pattern of behavior akin to that of most interest groups (see, e.g., Olson 1965). The contrast with neo-corporatist business organizations described elsewhere in this volume is stark.

Third, peak and trade organizations are not the only source of business representation in Washington. Large corporations increasingly have their own "in-house" lobbyists in a governmental affairs unit; although, this trend varies by industry and firm size, there was a marked increase between 1991 and 2001 across industries in the emphasis firms placed upon hiring in-house lobbyists (Brady et al. 2007). Corporations may supplement or replace these lobbyists with outside representatives they hire. Traditionally outside representation came from expensive, prestigious, and politically well-connected law firms such as Arnold and Porter. In recent decades a vigorous profession of contract lobbying has developed, leading to the creation of firms such as the Livingstone Group or Capitol Associates. These firms are often created and led by former legislators or congressional staffers and aim to have both Democratic and Republican partners (Salisbury 1986; Solomon 1987). A similar pattern of bipartisanship can be seen within the Congress: current legislators often work to advance or defend business interests even when it might seem inconsistent with their ideology to do so. For example, liberal Democrats often work to secure defense contracts for corporations located in their district or state.

Fourth, business groups are often part of short-lived coalitions that can link businesses with other types of organizations or pit one group of businesses against another (Hula 1999). Tax legislation, in particular, has a high potential to set one group of businesses against another (Martin 1991). For example, capital-intensive firms are likely to want different tax allowances to those that are labor intensive. Research dependent businesses (such as pharmaceuticals) are also likely to have distinct interests and goals.

What We Do—and Don't—Know about What Business Does in Washington

The trade-off in producing a summary of businesses' activities in DC that commands general acceptance is that it provides us few details about what businesses actually do in practice. Investigating deeper still allows us to make more specific claims about what businesses do, but it also exposes the methodological difficulties and the limits of this research.

First, as we have seen, businesses lobby. Although most lobbying studies are focused on lobbyists in general and not on business lobbyists in particular, the fact that business lobbyists are such a high proportion of the total number of lobbyists makes it likely that findings of these studies will indeed apply to business. Contrary to the shock journalism view of lobbying (see, e.g., Birnbaum and Murray 1987), most political scientists tend to see it as an aid to better policy-making. Business lobbyists, in particular, may be able to provide information and technical guidance that other interests (Bauer, Pool, and Dexter 1963; Heinz et al. 1993) or the political parties (Hansen 1991) may not be able to share. This information may, in short, be a "subsidy" that interest groups provide to legislators (Hall and Deardorff 2006).

The traditional picture of lobbyists suggested that they talk only to their allies and argued that they go through a range of contacts, starting by meeting with legislators to gauge their attitude towards the interest group and proceeding later on to delivering their message to those that are receptive to it (Milbrath 1963). When Milbrath wrote, there would have been general agreement that the old adage that "Congress at work is Congress in committees" was correct, enabling lobbyists to focus on a limited number of legislators in any policy area. Although the statement would not be accepted today at face value, the committee and subcommittee stages remain the best time for lobbyists to influence legislation before it comes up for a vote on the floor. Hojnacki and Kimball (1998) explored how lobbyists strategize about handling committee members. They found that the initial focus is on allies, particularly those in leadership positions on committees, but that if time and resources permit (highly likely for corporations), they extend their lobbying to legislators whose attitude toward the interest is more ambiguous. This suggests some change from the findings of political scientists that in the pre-reform Congress of the early 1960s successful lobbying was based on a close long-term relationship of trust with legislators (Bauer, Pool, and Dexter 1963; Milbrath 1963). This is not to say that lobbyists do not still focus their greatest efforts on legislators already predisposed to support them (Wright 1996). After all, this strategy is not irrational: even good allies may need to be mobilized and may be unaware of the implications of a bill for the business or other interest that they support, and once mobilized, allies might still need evidence and arguments to use that business lobbyists can supply.

Tighter lobby registration rules and requirements for reports have allowed political scientists in recent years to study the activities of lobbyists more systematically through the creation and use of large data sets. Recent studies do not dispute the importance of the relationship between lobbyists and legislators, even if their findings with regard to the effects of lobbying remain ambiguous (see, e.g., Ansolabehere, de Figueiredo, and Snyder 2003). However, others suggest that traditional tactics should be supplemented with an integrated political strategy that involves trying to influence public opinion, the media, and a legislator's constituents, particularly those who may be active in his or her campaigns (Kollman 1998; Goldstein 1999). Lobbying "inside the Beltway" (that is, within Washington, DC) is now often supplemented by campaigns outside the Beltway. This trend in lobbying strategy is of course fully consistent with broader trends in the American political system such as the shift towards "the permanent campaign" as a mode of governing (Ornstein and Mann 2000) and the importance of the strategy of "going public" to presidents

(Kernell 1986). Smith (2000) emphasizes the importance of public opinion to business success in Washington; even a strong effort by business as a whole in Washington, DC, will fail if business does not also succeed in winning over public opinion.

It is generally assumed that most lobbying is focused on Congress, and nearly all large-scale studies of DC lobbying focus more or less exclusively on interest group lobbying of Congress. However, interest groups also target the executive branch. Aberbach and Rockman (2000) report that high proportions of both political appointees and the most senior civil servants who report to them have weekly or more contact with interest groups; indeed for the civil servants this frequency of contact was higher than with any part of the government itself, including the White House and their own department head (116). This relatively open access for lobbyists to the executive does not carry over to the Executive Office of the President (EOP) itself though; for as Peterson (1992) reports, less than 10 per cent of DC lobbyists claim frequent and cooperative contact with any part of the EOP.

Second, businesses give money. Due to the comparatively high cost of American political campaigns, money would appear to be one of the greatest advantages that business has in politics, and its opponents have consistently tried to limit the amount that each interest group and individual can contribute. Equally often, money, like water moving downhill, has found alternative routes into politics as regulations or barriers have been erected. Following revelations about illegal corporate gifts to campaigns in the Watergate hearings, the 1974 Federal Elections Campaign Finance Act specified that corporations could make donations to campaigns only from Political Action Committees (PACs) that were separated from the corporation's basic structure and received their money as contributions from stockholders, executives, or, on a restricted basis, appeals to employees in general. It was easy to imagine how money could be routed to the PAC through contributions from ambitious and cooperative executives whose salaries could be increased to facilitate their ability to contribute.

Indeed, business appeared to have a strong hand in this environment. Wright's (1996) analysis of Federal Election Commission (FEC) data from 1992 shows that approximately 41 per cent of PACs were corporate sponsored and that these PACs were responsible for over 31 per cent of all donations from PACs, and Franz's (2005) longer-term study (1983–2002) of the same data shows that corporate PACs (not including trade associations) made up 31 per cent of all PACs and 41 per cent of active PACs (those actually making donations).

But one limit on business's influence is the limit on the amount PACs could contribute to a campaign—$5,000. This is a small proportion of the cost of a serious campaign for a House or Senate seat. During the 1990s, however, limits on PAC contributions were rendered almost inconsequential by a rapid increase in the practice of making large payments ("soft money") from the general funds of corporations to political parties, allegedly for "party building" activities. This was an exemption specifically allowed by FEC interpretations of the 1974 law in order to bolster what were then seen as declining party organizations, but it was easily abused.

Party building funds could easily be redirected into campaigns to support specific candidates. This practice was ended by the McCain–Feingold Act, which also raised the amount that individuals can contribute to campaigns from $1,000 to $2,500. Lobbyists now increasingly collect checks for this amount from individuals within corporations and "bundle" them into a significant contribution. After all, $2,500 from each of twenty executives creates a gift ($50,000) that dwarfs the amount a PAC can contribute. Money can also be contributed to so-called 527s, advocacy organizations that, except within a month of an election, can campaign freely for a candidate as long as they operate independently of the candidate's own campaign. In *McConnell v FEC* (2002, 540 US 93), the Supreme Court upheld the constitutionality of limiting advertisements by such groups close to an election that explicitly supported (or opposed) a candidate. However, the Supreme Court in *FEC v Wisconsin Right to Life* (2007, 551 US 449) struck down McCain–Feingold's attempts to limit issue advertisements by 527s within sixty days of the election, even though the issue advertisements might have well an impact on its outcome.

In spite of the limited role that PACs have played in campaign finance, great controversy has raged about the impact of PACs in general and business PACs in particular. Do PACs buy votes in Washington? If not, why do they give money? On the principle that people—and certainly corporations—do not spend money for no reason, it would seem obvious that PAC contributions are given for a purpose. However, studies have generally failed to find evidence that PACs buy votes (Wright 1996). In the words of Richard Smith, "the real story, as pieced together from dozens of scholarly studies, seems to be that interest group contributions have far less influence than is commonly thought" (1995: 91). Smith analyzes carefully eight quantitative studies of the impact of campaign contributions and finds that they generate very conflicting and modest conclusions. Baumgartner and Leech (1998) have a very similar impression of the results of quantitative studies, and Sorauf (1992) is dismissive of the easy assumption so often made by journalists and activists that campaign contributions purchase Congressional votes.

Legislators' ideological predispositions, party pressures, electoral considerations, and ambition may all be more important (Kingdon 1989). Legislators may have more important reasons to vote for or against a bill than a contribution of $5,000. However, it should be noted that there is no definitive proof of the negative—that campaign contributions have no impact. As both Baumgartner and Leech (1998) and Smith (1995) note, it may well be that campaign contributions are more likely to have an impact under some conditions than under others. The most favorable circumstances for influence include situations common to issues affecting business: technical complexity, lack of awareness by the general public about the issue involved, lack of strong views on the part of the legislator, and the absence of an opposing interest group.

Supposing, however, that the general conclusion that campaign contributions do not buy votes in Congress is correct, why do corporations—and other interest groups— bother to give them? Ansolabehere, Snyder, and Tripathi (2002) and Hansen and Mitchell (2000) note the close relationship between making campaign contributions and engaging in lobbying; as Ansolabehere et al. (2002) note, 86 per cent of PAC expenditures are made by interest groups that lobby in Washington. This seems consistent with the often-made argument that PAC contributions are made to improve the opportunities for access (Hall and Wayman 1990). Indeed, interest group officials often complain privately that politicians are assiduous in demanding PAC contributions and, when they were allowed, "soft money" donations, in effect, "shaking down" and imposing an "access tax" on lobbyists (Sitkoff 2003).

This helps to explain one of the more distinctive features of business PACs. Unlike the PACs of both "cause" groups and labor unions, as Herrnson (2007) notes, business PACs give money to both Republicans and Democrats. Much to the dismay of Republicans, corporations have always given a significant amount to liberal and moderate Democrats, not just to conservatives (Wilson 1981). Why? The most plausible explanation is that corporations behave pragmatically even if they have a conservative soul (Romer and Snyder 1994). If Democrats are in powerful positions, then corporations will buy access to them. Once the Republicans had gained control of Congress after the 1994 midterm elections, corporations were free to concentrate their giving more on Republicans, probably as they would always have preferred. For their part, Republican leaders such as Tom DeLay tried to impose partisan discipline on corporations. In the "K Street Project," (named after the Washington, DC, street on which many corporations and lobbyists have their offices) DeLay told corporations that if they wished to have influence in the new Republican Congresses, they must give only to Republicans, hire Republicans as their lobbyists, and support Republican policy goals. Those who live by the sword die by it also; the logic of the K Street Project suggests that after the Democrats gained control of Congress in 2006, the appropriate strategy for corporations would be to shift all their support to them and away from Republicans. There are indications that this may be happening. The *New York Times* reported on October 29, 2007, that contributions to Democrats by the health industries—including pharmaceutical corporations—were heavily outrunning contributions to Republicans. The explanation apparently was that because the Democratic candidates for president (Clinton, Obama, etc.) were proposing major healthcare reforms, healthcare businesses felt the need to make contributions that would provide access to them and therefore the opportunity to influence their thinking.

Third, business is not reluctant to go to court to get its way. Interest group use of the courts is well-known, and there is good evidence that the more *amicus curiae* briefs that groups file, the higher the probability the Supreme Court will accept a particular case (Caldeira and Wright 1988). Most of the discussion on interest group use of the courts is linked to dramatic issues of individual rights—abortion, gay rights, affirmative action—but businesses are heavier users of the courts. Federal administrative law (the Administrative Procedures Act and statutes governing individual regulatory agencies) provides that regulations issued by federal agencies can be challenged in federal appeals courts not only on the grounds that they misapply the statute under which they were made but also on the grounds that the evidence used to justify their adoption was inadequate. Such cases generally go straight to the federal appeals courts, particularly to the DC Circuit Court of Appeals, which Congress has mandated should hear cases from many agencies. Some 40 per cent of the workload of DC Circuit Court consists of such cases (Banks 1999). As the Supreme Court rarely finds room on its docket to review such cases, the reality is that the appeals court is likely to have both the first and last word on whether a regulation stands or falls (Humphries and Songer 1999). In theory, courts show deference to expert regulators; in reality, after the upsurge of judicial activism in general in the 1960s, judges proved very willing to override expert regulators, even when the statutes seemed to give regulators discretion by providing that they should be overruled only when the supporting evidence was so slight as to make their actions seem "arbitrary and capricious." A second and higher standard, "substantive evidence on the record," provided that judges should be convinced themselves that the evidence was compelling—in practice, however, the two standards of justification became blurred rather quickly (Stewart 1975).

In recent years, a "counter-reformation" has taken place in which a more conservative, pro-business Supreme Court has rolled back some of the procedural rules that had allowed public interest groups to press regulators to act (Shapiro 2005). For example, in *Chevron USA v National Resources Defense Council* (1984, 467 US 837), the Court ordered lower courts to give deference to agencies' interpretations of their statutory powers. Fortunately for business, perhaps, the regulatory agencies subsequently were controlled either by Republican administrations or, in the case of the Clinton administration, one committed to finding less adversarial approaches to regulation. In a similar development, the once expansive definition of standing that allowed public interest groups through the courthouse door was narrowed in *Lujon v Defenders of Wildlife* (1992, 504 US 555).

It is not clear—from business's point of view—that these reversals for public interest groups necessarily reduce the ability of business to use the courts to challenge regulators; after all, no one doubts their standing to sue in such cases. Moreover, judges on the crucial DC Circuit Court seem likely to continue to use the supposedly different standards of review interchangeably and are much more likely to overturn a regulatory agency when it makes a new rule than when it enforces one. In other words, the deference to regulatory agencies in statutory interpretation mandated in *Chevron* does not seem to be accompanied by "evidentiary" deference to regulatory agencies in determining whether the facts support a proposed regulation (Caruson and Bitzer 2004).

The importance of the courts to business both in general and in particular as means of controlling the regulatory agencies necessarily makes the politics of judicial appointments important to business. In particular, as Cross and Tiller (1998) demonstrate, there is a substantial relationship between the partisanship of judges on the federal appeals courts and their reactions to decisions by regulatory agencies. Regulatory politics might become more challenging for business if there were a Democrat in the White House for a sustained period, particularly if he or she appointed both more liberal judges to the appeals courts and more aggressive regulators to the agencies.

Fourth, business attempts to influence public opinion. Smith (2000) indeed believes that this is the most important tactic for business. If the public is hostile, not even a united stand by business will prevail in policy-making (Mitchell 1997). As Smith (2000) and West, Heith, and Goodwin (1996) describe, business has fought its corner vigorously in the battle of ideas using a wide variety of tactics: for example, oil companies have placed advertisements arguing their point of view on the op-ed pages of prestigious newspapers such as the *New York Times*, and corporate partici-pants in mid-1990s national healthcare debate targeted the districts of persuadable members of Congress with television advertisements that questioned the proposed reforms. Corporations also attempt to cultivate a good image that can be used as political tool by encouraging employees to undertake voluntary work in the com-munity and by making contributions to charities (Neiheisel 1994; Sims 2003).

Both business organizations and individual corporations have increased substantially their capacity to engage in grassroots campaigning (Kollman 1998; Goldstein 1999). Indeed, the enormously successful but controversial retailer, Wal-Mart, despite for years lacking a strong capacity to respond to public relations threats, now has created a "war room" modeled on those in presidential campaigns and staffed it with politically experienced operators ready to take on any issue that emerged concerning the company. This corporate activity is no longer motivated simply by political considerations. Perhaps because of enhanced awareness of the commercial value of brand image, corporations have been eager to forestall or defeat criticisms of them from public interest groups, as well as from agents internal to the firm (Baron and Diermeier 2005; Werner 2008). For corporations that make products that are sold to consumers at far more than the cost of manufacturing them—such as sports apparel—or products that are easily replaced by competitors'—such as petrol/gasoline—maintaining the attractiveness of the brand is crucial. If the marketing strategy is to sell shoes that allow you to "Bend it Like Beckham" or to "Be Like Mike" (Michael Jordan), protesters outside the store alleging that the shoes were made in sweat shops can puncture the image. Thus, the political need to promote a positive public image and a real commercial need to protect the brand can often coincide.

The fifth and most far-sighted activity of all that business has undertaken has been to fund ideologically committed think tanks such as the Heritage Foundation and the American Enterprise Institute (Weaver 1989; Smith 1991). In contrast to the Brookings Institution, which carefully nurtures a non-partisan image with a balance between moderates leaning to liberalism and moderates leaning to conservatism, Heritage and AEI are unabashedly conservative, pro-business organizations. They have contributed substantially to shifting the balance of debate towards lower taxation, less regulation, and away from the welfare state towards welfare reform, education vouchers, and charter schools. It is an open legal question as to how protected (if at all) these attempts by corporations to shape public opinion—either directly through public relations or indirectly through think tanks—are; however, it is probably the case that the current Supreme Court would protect the rights of firms in a manner similar to how it protects the rights of individuals. This question is important though, as corporations are making their voices heard more vigorously and effectively than ever before.

WHAT WE DON'T KNOW—OR AT LEAST DON'T KNOW ENOUGH ABOUT

The major defect in our knowledge of how business operates in Washington comes in understanding how these pieces fit together. When do corporations rely on trade associations or peak associations? When do they use Washington law firms or contract lobbyists instead of their in-house staff? We have enough evidence to make some plausible suggestions.

Most obviously, corporations are more likely to expect trade associations to take the lead when the issue involved affects everyone in an industry. Legislation to restrict the use of a chemical used by more or less all businesses in an industry would be a typical case. Trade associations can also be useful when the issue involved is unpopular or may be construed in a way that would harm the corporation's image (Prakash 2000). Opposition to health and safety or environmental policies would be typical examples. However, corporations may find that, outside of oligopolistic industries, the trade association lacks the resources and ability to represent them adequately. Moreover, corporations often have diverging or conflicting interests when faced with regulations that would appear to affect all of them equally. Attempts to mandate better mileage per gallon for automobiles standards through CAFE (Corporate Average Fuel Economy) regulations are an interesting case in point. What at first sight seems a neutral rule (for example, that every manufacturer's cars should average thirty-five miles per gallon) affects manufacturers very differently. The American manufacturers (Ford, GM, Chrysler) make what limited profits they achieve on large, inefficient vehicles and vehemently oppose higher CAFE standards. Honda, in contrast, has made a substantial investment in improving fuel efficiency, and its product range achieves higher fuel economy standards. Honda therefore supports higher CAFE requirements. Although—as in this instance—differences among firms in an industry can be explained in terms of their market position and strategy, there are also important contrasts in individual firms' internal culture and the values of their leaders that can result in contrasting political approaches across issues (Werner 2008).

The use of Washington law firms or contract lobbyists rather than in house lobbyists may be the result of superior access or the need to form temporary collations (Wolpe and Levine 1996). Both law firms and contract lobbyists employ people who have worked in the executive branch recently and may therefore know the political appointees or officials who are drafting regulations and making policy. Heinz et al. (1993) found that lawyers working as lobbyists tended to have relatively narrow focus, perhaps suggesting that trading on relatively few contacts and networks was the service they provided. Contract lobbyists can also be the fulcrum of temporary coalitions—now a common feature of Washington—that come together to support or oppose a particular bill, such as changes in tax allowances. The contract lobbyist takes on the work of bringing together disparate interests and groups.

We also know far too little about the contacts between lobbyists and executive branch agencies. In spite of the evidence from Aberbach and Rockman (2000) discussed above that top officials and political appointees spend much of their time dealing with interest groups, political scientists remain drawn to studying lobbying solely in terms of Congress. Specifically, there was a long tradition of seeing relations between interest groups and executive agencies in terms of an "iron triangle" that bound agency, congressional committees, and interest group in a relationship of mutual support (McConnell 1966) that shut out the political appointees of the executive. In this conceptualization, legislators tended to come from districts or states where the agency had a major impact, and many of their constituents were members of interest groups that focused on the agency. Thus, to please the legislators on the congressional committees on which it depends for its budget and legislation, the agency had to please the interest groups in its field.

The iron triangle has been much less accepted in recent decades since Heclo's (1978) pivotal chapter. In brief, critics of the concept argue that it is not so much wrong as outdated. In particular, the explosion in the number and range of interests represented in Washington makes it much less likely that there can be a cozy triangle linking an agency, congressional committees, and a single interest group (Berry 1997). To take an obvious example, the Bureau of Land Management that has authority over federal lands used to worry only about pleasing the American beef Cattlemen's Association and Western legislators. In recent decades it also has to concern itself with criticisms from environmental groups worried about the degradation of the landscape caused by intensive grazing.

Although some argue that there are still numerous issues in which there is only one interest or interest group represented (Schlozman 2004), it is also the case that changes in Congress and the executive branch make iron triangles less likely. The increased intensity of party divisions and the greater importance of the party leaderships have made committees less autonomous and capable of sustaining sub-governments (Cox and McCubbins 2005). At least in the House during the Republican majority years (1995–2007), committee or subcommittee chairs that strayed from the party line were likely to be removed. Cross-party alliances also became rarer. Similarly, the Reagan and Bush 41 and 43 administrations have asserted vigorously their power to control the executive branch regulatory agencies, using the Office of Management and Budget (OMB) to impose more and stringent controls on when and how new regulations could be developed (Cooper and West 1988). The "theory of the unitary executive" promoted assiduously by Vice President Cheney argued that agencies such as EPA and OSHA were as subject as any other government department to the direction of a president who, in this case, was avowedly pro-business.

The iron triangle concept has not been replaced with an equally graphic and satisfactory image. The prevailing view is one of complexity; there are important differences both from issue area to issue area and also over time. The character of issue networks in one area (such as labor policy) is very different from that in another (such as agriculture) (Heinz et al. 1993). The character of a policy area can also change significantly over time particularly if there is a re-definition of the policy question or field (Bosso 1987; Baumgartner and Jones 1993).

The consequences of election results for business also appear to be much greater in recent decades. For example, most observers would accept that the Bush 43 administration tilted heavily towards business in policies and appointments. In one notorious example, the advisory committee on energy policy, whose proceedings and membership were kept secret, is known to have been heavily dominated by representatives from energy corporations; further, reports to the committee from scientific agencies that stated conclusions unwelcome to business (for example, on global warming) were edited to weaken their arguments. Other startling examples of business's influence in the current administration were the nominations of a former NAM official, Michael Baroody, to lead the Consumer Product Safety Commission (it was unsuccessful); of a long-standing critic of government regulation, Susan Dudley, to head the Office of Information and Regulatory Affairs; and of a former representative of mining companies, David Bernhardt, to the senior legal position in the Department of the Interior. None of these appointments by an avowedly pro-business administration were illegitimate. They do illustrate, however, the increased representation within the Executive Branch—not merely access to it—that the current Bush administration has provided business.

Finally, we know too little about the type of argument that lobbyists make, beyond their general emphasis on maintaining their personal credibility when providing information to elected officials (Ainsworth 1993). It seems reasonable to suppose that corporations take advantage of the fact that they can generate technical information more readily than most public interest groups. Perhaps supporting this, Heinz et al. (1993) found that lobbyists for corporations were relatively narrowly focused in terms of the number of issues they covered in comparison with lobbyists for labor unions and other organizations. However, politicians may still be more interested in relatively straightforward information about the effects of a policy on their district or state. It is almost certainly the case that different politicians respond to different arguments, but it would be valuable to have a clearer sense of what the different types of arguments being made are.

WHAT DOES BUSINESS WANT?

The stereotype of American business in politics is that it simply wants less—less regulation, lower taxes, and less government "interference." As with many stereotypes, although there are notable exceptions—the bailouts of the financial and automotive industries being two prominent examples—there is also an element of truth in this picture. The Chamber of Commerce and NFIB in particular give the stereotype some foundation in reality. They fight to keep taxes down, unions weak, and mandates on employers (such as healthcare or parental leave) light.

However, the political needs of business are complex and sometimes highly specific to a single business. Government controls some very individualized private benefits (or "rents" in economic parlance; see, e.g., Godwin and Sheldon 1998), such as contracts, wavelengths for terrestrial broadcasting, and cell phones or airline routes to foreign countries (e.g., China), where treaties limit the number of flights and operators. Government can also play an indispensable role in pressing other countries to adopt policies a corporation wants such as market access, ending subsidies to competitors, or not adopting regulations that a corporation would find damaging such as the EU's ban on genetically engineered seeds. We may think of these goals in terms of a spectrum from firm specific goals (getting a contract) to interests shared by a group of companies (such as tax allowances for research and investment or barriers to entry in a particular market or industry via regulation) to concerns for an industry as whole (such as avoiding regulatory restrictions on inputs all use) to finally, concerns shared by most corporations (such as limiting liability lawsuits, changes in labor law that would help unions and general levels of taxation—as opposed to tax allowances).

We should not assume that it is obvious how business interests should be defined in practice or that there is unanimity within an industry or even within a single corporation on what these are. Martin (2000) has emphasized that the interests of business are capable of being understood in quite different ways. National health insurance, long opposed by business organizations, would in fact be quite helpful to the remaining US auto manufacturers as they are increasingly admitting. Indeed, recently, new plants have been located across the Canadian border from Detroit because the cost savings of not having to pay for private health insurance for employees in Canada are so great. However, during the last serious attempt at achieving national health insurance (1992–3), corporations and business organizations (notably the Chamber of Commerce) that had flirted with the idea of supporting reform were dissuaded from doing so partly through pressure from Republican leaders in Congress. Large corporations that would clearly have gained from reform fell silent as a result of pressure from small business, which they value as a political ally because of its presence in every congressional district (Skocpol 1996). The definition of business interests can be a highly political process about which we know little. Competition between business groups also has an impact, as the story of health reform also illustrates. The Chamber of Commerce backed off from supporting national health insurance because it was losing members to NFIB, which alleged that the Chamber had "gone soft."

COMPARISONS AND TRENDS

Until the 1990s, it was easy to regard the US as a laggard in terms of business–government relations. The general features of the American system of business representation that we outlined at start of this chapter—notably the absence of strong trade associations or a single authoritative employers' organization—seemed to demonstrate a lack of development. From time to time the US seemed about to "catch up" with countries that had more authoritative, monopolistic, and hierarchically organized forms of business representation but somehow never quite made it. The characteristic untidiness of the process of consultation between business and government in the US was easily explained by the sharing of powers among the different branches of government, the decentralized nature of those institutions internally, and the absence of a coherent structure among business organizations. Again, however, it seemed to many academic observers in the 1970s and 1980s to contrast poorly during the 1970s with the more formalized processes of partnership between business and government found in some of the other advanced democracies (Lindberg 1976; Hollingsworth, Schmitter, and Streek 1994). Schmitter demonstrated at least to his own satisfaction that the neocorporatist countries such as the Netherlands and Sweden through formalized partnerships between business, labor, and government achieved better results on a number of key policy dimensions than the countries with less organized relationships. (Later scholarship would formalize this contrast as being between organized capitalism and liberal market economies, see Hall and Soskice 2001.) Indeed, this perception was apparently shared by policymakers as well as academics: between the early 1960s and late 1970s, some of the least neo-corporatist countries such as the UK made attempts to change their ways and become more so. Even the US was influenced by these trends too—certainly in terms of the intellectual and academic climate and briefly in terms of public policy—when Nixon attempted to operate a system of wage and price controls in 1970. His policy shift immediately, if briefly, generated a need for more formalized linkages with the AFL-CIO and employers. In the aftermath of the breakdown of the Bretton Woods system and the oil shocks of the 1970s, structured partnerships between governments and authoritative representatives of business and labor seemed to offer a way through the crises of economic management and governance that afflicted advanced democracies.

In more recent years, the idea that the US is a laggard in terms of its mode of business representation is harder to sustain. This is partly because of the strengthening of business representation in Washington, DC, that we have described above and partly because of the decline of competing modes in other countries. Neo-corporatism, for example, lost favor in academic circles in the 1980s and 1990; the question became more whether it could survive rather than whether it could spread to other countries. In an era of globalization with some industries benefiting from market expansion and others losing out to imports, even Sweden struggled to maintain the industry-wide collective bargaining that had underpinned its neo-corporatist system. Not only in the UK but in Europe more generally and in Japan, individual corporations became more politically active in their own right while trade associations and employers' organizations lost stature. As neo-corporatism struggled in its heartlands, countries that had been tempted to move in that direction (again the UK being a good example) veered away sharply. Nixon's flirtation with a more organized mode of capitalism was indeed brief. Its long-term impact may have been more to mobilize pro-market thinkers than to influence the US system of business representation. The flexible labor market in the US also seemed to generate superior results to countries operating more organized forms of capitalism particularly in terms of economic growth and employment. In brief, more organized modes of capitalism seemed both hard to sustain globally and more likely to deliver inferior results to the American model.

The decline in the popularity of more organized modes of capitalism in policy-making circles has significant consequences for business representation. In the US as we have noted, the sovereign and dominant component of the system of business representation is and has always been the individual corporation. Trade associations and the competing employers' organizations are service providers, not organizations with autonomous power or authority. In recent years this feature of the American system has seemed to be more the wave of the future worldwide rather than a sign of arrested development. Not only in UK but even in Sweden, the major employers' organization has struggled to maintain its authority. Divisions between individual sectors and corporations intensified as globalization created winners and losers from market integration. In brief, the trend seemed to be towards a more "American" model of individual corporations acting autonomously and employers' organizations having limited stature.

The tendency to argue that the rest of the world will inexorably become more like the US is at least as old as Tocqueville's masterpiece, *Democracy in America*. It would no doubt be as foolish to argue that the rest of the world will become the same as the US as it had been in the 1970s to suppose that the US interest group system would become like Sweden's. There are, however, at least some characteristics of the US that have become more common elsewhere and that have consequences for trends in business representation. First, market integration achieved in the US through decisions of the Supreme Court in the nineteenth century and technology thereafter has been achieved in other places through integration (the EU) or through international trade agreements such as the Uruguay Round and decisions of the World Trade Organization (WTO). Larger markets reshape the character of business representation. As noted above, globalization has created different winners and losers than existed in more national markets, thereby breaking established political coalitions and organizations and disrupting business organization. Second, democracies have tended to move towards a situation long common in the US of having overlapping and competing institutions making public policy. The old story of the French Education Minister who told a visitor that he knew (because he and his predecessors had decided) what every schoolchild in France was studying at that hour no longer applies in France or in similarly centralized states. Some of the most centralized countries such as the UK, Italy, and Spain have deliberately decentralized. Federalism has reached new heights in Canada. European nation states also share power with the institutions of the EU. International organizations such as the WTO have significant power. In the US, institutional complexity has long been associated with a high degree of decentralization in the organization of business: multiple overlapping institutions create multiple opportunities for influencing public policy. Shifts in this direction in other advanced democracies may, if American experience is relevant, also shift them away from monopolistic and hierarchical forms of business representation. Just as Epstein (1986) argued about American political parties, the American form of business representation may be less a fossil than a glimpse of the future.

THE BROADER SCENE

Everyone agrees that there have been substantial changes in business representation in Washington in the last forty years. Scarcely was the ink dry on the work of Bauer, Pool, and Dexter's (1972) second edition when their conclusions were invalidated. Bauer et al. had argued that business was poorly represented by a disproportionately small number of incompetent lobbyists. A slew of studies in their wake (Schlozman and Tierney 1986; Wilson 1990a; Heinz et al. 1993) reported that there had been an explosion in the number of business lobbyists, trade association representatives, and corporations with their own governmental affairs offices in DC. The questions that remain to be answered definitively are why this explosion occurred and its significance.

A plausible explanation offered early in this transformation was that business was responding to the growth in the political power of its critics—the consumer and environmental groups (Berry 1977; Vogel 1978; Wilson 1981). American business had earlier basked in the luxury of not needing to do much politically to win (Vogel 1989). The public had a highly favorable impression of business and business executives; public interest groups were almost non-existent in Washington, DC. The explosion in regulation that brought many businesses face to face with federal authority for the first time in the form of new agencies such as the EPA and OSHA convinced business that it need to beef up its political strength quickly (Herman 1981; Wilson 1985).

Reform in America has a long history of surge and decline (Huntington 1981). The Progressives, for example, did much to transform America in the early years of the twentieth century and yet faded away thereafter. The consumer and environmental groups that sprouted in the late 1960s and early 1970s have been remarkably success-ful in sustaining themselves, however (Berry 1999; Bosso 2005). Clear shifts to the right in national politics have if anything strengthened them organizationally as potential members rushed to join to try to stop Republicans such as James Watt (Reagan's Interior Secretary) or similar appointments made by George W. Bush from undermining their favorite programs or agencies. Although American politics in general has become more conservative, public interest groups have survived or even flourished, remaining a potential threat to corporations. What remains to be answered, however, is whether or not the rise of such groups can effectively replace labor as a counterweight to business's strength.

More cynical explanations might point to the growth in government spending in recent decades. Although there have been well-publicized tax cuts, government expenditure has increased in both absolute terms and as a percentage of gross domestic product. While corporations tend not volunteer this as a reason for their political presence in Washington, there is a statistically positive correlation between federal contracting and the scale of a corporation's political efforts (Wilson 1990b; Grier, Munger, and Roberts 1994; Brady et al. 2007). Wilson argued that in an era when by no means all large businesses were represented in Washington, contracting had sensitized the politically active corporations to the importance of politics and thus possibly explained who was and who was not politically active, not that contracting necessarily explained political activism directly. However, it is reasonable to assume that, given the greater resources contractors dedicate to relations with the government, resulting contracts soften the blow of the bill for the DC office.

The case for businesses maintaining robust representation in Washington remains strong on general policy grounds too. Even after an era of deregulation, government retains the capacity to make decisions that have enormous commercial consequences for corporations in certain industries, such as pharmaceuticals and energy. Further, the financial crisis of 2008 and the resulting Troubled Assets Relief Program or financial bailout has strengthened those who were critical of the repeal of New Deal legislation, such as the Glass–Steagall Act, and of the lack of substantial regulations in other Clinton-era legislation, especially the Commodity Futures Modernization Act. The leverage—and in some cases, the ownership stakes—gained by the government as a result of the financial and automotive industry bailout plans, in combination with the strong electoral victories scored by the Democrats in 2008, may lead to a new wave of legislation that is much less friendly to firms and free-marketers.

Moreover, just as the public interest groups have survived, so too have the regulatory agencies. Notwithstanding the best efforts of conservative appointees to leadership positions within them, these agencies retain a continuing capacity and in terms of their staffs, a tendency to produce new regulations. Even during a Republican era, politicians may respond to popular concerns or scandals with legislation that poses problems for business. Thus the financial regulatory system know as Sarbanes–Oxley, one of the most intrusive pieces of legislation affecting American business for many years, was passed after several major corporate governance and accounting scandals by margins of 423–3 in the House and 99–0 in the Senate. President Bush signed it into law saying it was the most significant reform of its type since the days of President Franklin Roosevelt. The requirements of Sarbanes–Oxley have been difficult and costly to implement and may have resulted in significant shift of business form Wall Street to the City of London. The episode serves as a warning against assuming that generally favorable political circumstances warrant business lowering its guard and reducing its presence in DC.

At the same time, there is little doubt that many factors have improved the political situation of business since the 1970s. First, avowedly conservative and pro-business administrations have held power for most of the period since 1970 (all but twelve of the thirty-seven years). Further, Republicans controlled both chambers of Congress from 1995 to 2007 and the Senate from 1981 to 1987. This naturally produced an atmosphere conducive to business's political success: a vice president for government affairs at a major firm told one of the authors that he thought "he had died and gone to heaven" during the Reagan administration. This conservative trend reflected political changes and tensions—conflict over culture and questions of personal morality, race, crime, and foreign policy—that cannot be linked to business. Yet business was undoubtedly a beneficiary of this conservative shift. For example, even when the Democrats held the presidency under Clinton (1993–2001), they were at pains to emphasize that they were "new" Democrats sympathetic to the needs of business (Baer 2000).

Second, a whole host of technological and economic developments often lumped together as "globalization" have, in some ways, advantaged business (see, e.g., Kahler and Lake 2003). These changes, discussed extensively throughout this volume, are of course not unique to the US but here, as elsewhere, have had important consequences. There has been a sharp decline in the proportion of the workforce employed in manufacturing; total manufacturing employment dropped by 21 per cent between 1990 and 2005, a time of particularly strong growth for the economy as a whole (US Department of Commerce 2005). Partly because of this there has been a severe reduction in the number of people employed in industries that used to be the bedrock of the union movement. For example, total employment in the American automobile industry declined from 271,400 in 1990 to 249,700 in 2005 (Commerce 2005). Employment in the apparel industry also has collapsed, as more and more clothes—even those sold under prestigious labels—are made in China. These are of course important developments in their own right. However, they also have important political implications. Unions such as UAW or ILGWU used to be the bedrock of the Democratic Party. They continue to provide money for and volunteers for campaigns and lobbyists in Washington that work on a variety of issues, including liberal reforms of little direct relevance to unions. The decline in these unions, due in large measure to globalization, has important political consequences. Although unions are still a vital component in the liberal, Democratic coalition, their ability to contribute has been diminished (Asher 2001). The major countervailing interest to business on many issues has withered.

More generally, the unease over the economic future that globalization engenders has contributed to an environment in which elected officals are reluctant to challenge business. It is now thirty years since Lindblom (1977) argued that business's power was primarily structural. In the years that have elapsed since the publication of his book, the ease with which business can exercise its ultimate power—to pick up and leave for a country that will treat it better—has increased. Cheaper international phone calls and air transport, lower freight rates due to containerization and bulk transport and electronic communication have all facilitated moving production and, increasingly, services to low cost, low regulation countries.

As a country with lower taxes and less regulated labor markets than most in the first world, globalization had fewer consequences for the US than for countries such as France. Republican administrations have reduced the incidence of taxation on corporations and executives. They have also interpreted or enforced labor laws in ways more favorable to employers and, as discussed earlier, reined in the regulatory agencies. While these trends are probably not due primarily to globalization, the lack of coordinated opposition to them might be. In the US as elsewhere, the left has suffered from a feeling that such policies are inevitable. Attempts to redefine strategy for the left in the US (the New Democrats) as in the UK (New Labour) nearly always start from accepting the necessity in an era of globalization of collaborating with, not confronting business. Although there have been few demands for the formal repeal of policies or laws unpopular with business (with the exception of certain taxes), it is striking how few new proposals that might be seen as unwelcome to enterprise commanded a wide hearing prior to 2008.

The implications of the Great Crash of 2008 on business and government relations in the United States will be profound and long lasting. This close to events, it is hard to comprehend in full what those consequences will be. Some forecasts are easy to make. First, the faith that markets are always efficient whereas government is subject to rent seeking and inefficiency is utterly discredited. The incapacity of the most prestigious investment banks and other leading financial institutions to assess the true value of complex financial derivatives based on mortgages and other forms of collateralized debt shocked even Alan Greenspan into wondering his lifelong faith in markets had been misguided. Second, the crisis had brought about a close and direct involvement of government in business that was inconceivable only months before the crisis. Astonishingly, government became a major stock or stake holder in the major banks, the largest insurance company (AIG), and two of the three remaining US auto manufacturers. Once created, this situation may be difficult to unravel. Only if and when the enterprises that have been partially socialized return to full profitability will it be possible for the government to privatize its holdings and retrieve its loans. Yet these almost cataclysmic events may also be interpreted as proof of the importance of an effective political and lobbying operation for corporations. In the closing months of the Bush Administration it was the government, not the markets, that decided which companies should live (the auto companies, AIG) and which should die (Lehman Brothers). The auto companies had a near death experience in part because of the ineptness of their chief executives in the manner in which they approached Washington for help. In a situation in which government was so intimately involved with business and its decisions so consequential, it should not be difficult for government affairs offices to make a case they play an essential role in the modern American corporation.

The commercial and financial difficulties of US business may make the case for extensive political involvement all the stronger. This political involvement will have to be managed skillfully. The public's intense anger over the combination of the professional ineptness of US business executives and the extraordinarily high rewards they granted themselves could make clumsy or overt tactics counter-productive.

For at least the next few years, lobbying, for example, will most definitely have to be based on technically informed argument rather than anything that could be denounced as "influence pedaling."

It is likely that in responding to the Obama administration's approach to solving the current economic crisis, businesses will have to give serious thought as to how they can reorganize themselves in Washington, DC. The last major development, the formation of the Business Roundtable, came during a period when, in the words of Proctor and Gamble's Bryce Harlow, executives feared that business was about to be rolled up and put in the trash can. It is surely likely that the crisis following the Crash of 2008 will result in some significant innovations.

David Vogel has argued that there is an inverse relationship between the economic and political success of American business. When business—and therefore the economy—flourishes, political challenges to business are greatest. When the economy falters, business is more successful politically perhaps as people fear taking actions that might weaken it further. The circumstances at the end of the Bush Administration might be an interesting test of Vogel's thesis. Adverse economic and political circumstances for business coincide. The severity of the economic situation has already resulted in remarkable policy reversals such as the extensive socialization of industry by a right wing Republican Administration. The question now will be whether this will be followed by regulatory and other measures such as changes in the tax code to reduce the advantages for very highly paid executives that many have demanded.

The last few decades have represented a modern golden era for American businesses' influence in Washington: big business seems to have had less to fear during the Clinton Democratic presidency than during the Nixon Republican. Fissures in this strong foundation began to form with the passage of Sarbanes–Oxley in the wake of the Enron and WorldCom scandals and have continued to develop throughout the 2000s. Although, Harlow's claim that business's strength was about to disappear would have appeared quite foreign just years ago, in today's Washington, dominated by Democrats and full of anger toward executives on Wall Street and at the Big Three automakers due to both their professional failures and their seeming aloofness, it is Drucker's claim about the prominence and advantages accorded to business in American society and politics that is now exceptional.

REFERENCES

ABERBACH, J. D., and ROCKMAN, B. A. 2000. *In the Web of Politics: Three Decades of the US Federal Executive.* Washington, DC: Brookings Institution Press.

AINSWORTH, S. 1993. "Regulating lobbyists and interest group influence," *Journal of Politics* 55 (1): 41–56.

ANSOLABEHERE, S., SNYDER, J. S., and TRIPATHI, M. 2002. "Are PAC contributions and lobbying linked? New evidence from the 1995 Lobby Disclosure Act," *Business and Politics* 4(2): 131–55.

—— FIGUEIREDO, J. M. de, and SNYDER, J. M. 2003. "Why is there so little money in US politics?" *Journal of Economic Perspectives* 17(1): 105–30.

ASHER, H. B. 2001. *American Labor Unions in the Electoral Arena*. Lanham, Md.: Rowman & Littlefield.

BAER, K. S. 2000. *Reinventing Democrats: The Politics of Liberalism from Reagan to Clinton*. Lawrence: University Press of Kansas.

BANKS, C. P. 1999. *Judicial Politics in the DC Circuit Court*. Baltimore: Johns Hopkins Press.

BARON, D. P., and DIERMEIER, D. 2005. "Strategic activism and nonmarket strategy," Research Paper No. 1909, Graduate School of Business, Stanford University.

BAUER, R. A., POOL, I. de SOLA, and DEXTER, L. A. 1963. *American Business and Public Policy: The Politics of Foreign Trade*. New York: Atherton Press.

BAUMGARTNER, F. R., and JONES, B. D. 1993. *Agendas and Instability in American Politics*. Chicago: University of Chicago Press.

—— and LEECH, B. L. 1998. *Basic Interests: The Importance of Groups in Politics and in Political Science*. Princeton: Princeton University Press.

—— —— 2001. "Interest niches and policy bandwagons: patterns of interest group involvement in national politics," *Journal of Politics* 63(4): 1191–213.

BERRY, J. M. 1977. *Lobbying for the People: The Political Behavior of Public Interest Groups*. Princeton: Princeton University Press.

—— 1997. *The Interest Group Society*, 3rd edn. New York: Longman.

—— 1999. *The New Liberalism: The Rising Power of Citizen Groups*. Washington, DC: Brookings Institution.

BIRNBAUM, J. H., and MURRAY, A. S. 1987. *Showdown at Gucci Gulch*. New York: Random House.

BOSSO, C. J. 1987. *Pesticides and Politics: The Life Cycle of a Public Issue*. Pittsburgh: University of Pittsburgh Press.

—— 2005. *Environment, Inc.: From Grassroots to Beltway*. Lawrence: University Press of Kansas.

BRADY, H., DRUTMAN, L., SCHLOZMAN, K., and VERBA, S. 2007. "Corporate lobbying activity in American politics," paper presented at the annual meeting of the American Political Science Association, Chicago, August 30 – September 2.

CALDEIRA, C., and WRIGHT, J. R. 1988. "Organized interests and agenda setting in the US Supreme Court," *American Political Science Review* 82(4): 1109–27.

CARUSON, K., and BITZER, M. J. 2004. "At the crossroads of policymaking: executive politics, administrative action, and judicial deference by the DC Circuit Court of Appeals (1985–1996)," *Law and Policy* 26(3–4): 347–69.

Center for Responsive Politics. 2003. "Lobbyist spending by sector in 2000," http://www.opensecrets.org/lobbyists/index.asp

COOPER, J., and WEST, W. F. 1988. "Presidential power and Republican government: the theory and practice of OMB Review of Agency Rules," *Journal of Politics* 50(4): 864–89.

COX, G. W., and McCUBBINS, M. D. 2005. *Setting the Agenda: Responsible Party Government in the US House of Representatives*. New York: Cambridge University Press.

CROSS, F. B., and TILLER, E. H. 1998. "Judicial partisanship and obedience to legal doctrine: whistleblowing on the Federal Courts of Appeals," *Yale Law Journal* 107(7): 2155–76.

DRUCKER, P. F. 1964. *The Concept of a Corporation*. New York: Mentor.

EPSTEIN, L. D. 1986. *Political Parties in the American Mold*. Madison: University of Wisconsin Press.

FRANZ, M. M. 2005. "Choices and changes: interest groups and the electoral process," Ph.D. thesis. University of Wisconsin, Madison.

GODWIN, R. K., and SHELDON, B. J. 1998. "What corporations really want from government: the public provision of private goods," in A. J. Cigler and B. A. Loomis, eds., *Interest Group Politics*. Washington, DC: Congressional Quarterly Press.

GOLDSTEIN, K. M. 1999. *Interest Groups, Lobbying, and Participation in America*. New York: Cambridge University Press.

GRIER, K., MUNGER, M., and ROBERTS, B. 1994. "The determinants of industry political activity, 1978–1986," *American Political Science Review* 88(4): 911–26.

HALL, P. A., and SOSKICE, D. 2001. *Varieties of Capitalism: The Institutional Foundations of Comparative Advantage*. New York: Oxford University Press.

HALL, R. L., and DEARDORFF, A. V. 2006. "Lobbying as legislative subsidy," *American Political Science Review* 100(1): 69–84.

—— and WAYMAN, F. 1990. "Buying time: moneyed interests and the mobilization of bias in congressional committees," *American Political Science Review* 84(3): 797–820.

HANSEN, J. M. 1991. *Gaining Access: Congress and the Farm Lobby, 1919–1981*. Chicago: University of Chicago Press.

HANSEN, W. L., and MITCHELL, N. J. 2000. "Disaggregating and explaining corporate political activity: domestic and foreign corporations in national politics," *American Political Science Review* 94(4): 891–903.

HECLO, H. 1978. "Issue networks and the executive establishment," in A. King, ed., *The New American Political System*, 1st edn. Washington, DC: American Enterprise Institute Press.

HEINZ, J. P., LAUMANN, E. O., NELSON, R. L., and SALISBURY, R. H. 1993. *The Hollow Core: Private Interests in National Policy Making*. Cambridge, Mass.: Harvard University Press.

HERMAN, E. S. 1981. *Corporate Control, Corporate Power*. New York: Cambridge University Press.

HERRNSON, P. 2007. *Congressional Elections: Campaigning at Home and in Washington*, 5th edn. Washington, DC: Congressional Quarterly Press.

HOJNACKI, M., and KIMBALL, D. C. 1998. "Organized interests and the decision whom to lobby," *American Political Science Review* 92(4): 775–90.

HOLLINGSWORTH, J. R., SCHMITTER, P., and STREECK, W., eds. 1994. *Governing Capitalist Economies: Performance and Control of Economic Sectors*. New York: Oxford University Press.

HULA, K. W. 1999. *Lobbying Together: Interest Group Coalitions in Legislative Politics*. Washington, DC: Georgetown University Press.

HUMPHRIES, M., and SONGER, D. R. 1999. "Law and politics in judicial oversight of administrative agencies," *Journal of Politics* 61(1): 207–20.

HUNTINGTON, S. P. 1981. *American Politics: The Promise of Disharmony*. Cambridge, Mass.: Harvard University Press.

KAHLER, M., and LAKE, D. A. 2003. "Globalization and changing patterns of political authority," in M. Kahler and D. A. Lake, eds., *Governance in a Global Economy*. Princeton: Princeton University Press.

KERNELL, S. P. 1986. *Going Public: New Strategies of Presidential Leadership*. Washington, DC: Congressional Quarterly Press.

KINGDON, J. W. 1989. *Congressmen's Voting Decisions*, 2nd ed. Ann Arbor: University of Michigan Press.

KOLLMAN, K. 1998. *Outside Lobbying: Public Opinion and Interest Group Strategies*. Princeton: Princeton University Press.

LINDBERG, L. N. ed. 1976. *Politics and the Future of Industrial Society*. New York: D. McKay Co.

LINDBLOM, C. E. 1977. *Politics and Markets: The World's Political-Economic Systems*. New York: Basic Books.

McCONNELL, G. 1966. *Private Power and American Democracy*. New York: Knopf.

MARTIN, C. J. 1991. *Shifting the Burden: The Struggle over Growth and Corporate Taxation*. Chicago: University of Chicago Press.

—— 2000. *Stuck in Neutral: Business and the Politics of Human Capital Investment Policy.* Princeton: Princeton University Press.

MILBRATH, L. W. 1963. *The Washington Lobbyists.* Chicago: Rand McNally.

MITCHELL, N. J. 1997. *The Conspicuous Corporation: Business, Public Policy, and Representative Democracy.* Ann Arbor: University of Michigan Press.

NEIHEISEL, S. R. 1994. *Corporate Strategy and the Politics of Goodwill: A Political Analysis of Corporate Philanthropy in America.* New York: Peter Lang Publishing.

OLSON, M. 1965. *The Logic of Collective Action: Public Goods and the Theory of Groups.* Cambridge, Mass.: Harvard University Press.

ORNSTEIN, N. J., and MANN, T. E., ed. 2000. *The Permanent Campaign and its Future.* Washington, DC: American Enterprise Institute Press.

PETERSON, M. 1992. "The presidency and organized interests: White House patterns of interest group liaison," *American Political Science Review* 86(3): 612–25.

PRAKASH, A. 2000. "Responsible care: an assessment," *Business and Society* 39(2): 183–209.

ROMER, T., and SNYDER, J. 1994. "An empirical investigation of the dynamics of PAC contributions," *American Journal of Political Science* 38(3): 745–69.

SALISBURY, R. 1986. "Washington lobbyists: a collective portrait," in A. J. Cigler and B. A. Loomis, *Interest Group Politics*, 2nd edn. Washington, DC: Congressional Quarterly Press.

SCHLOZMAN, K. 2004. "Still an upper-class accent? Organized interest politics and equality of political voice," paper presented at the Annual Meeting of the American Political Science Association, Chicago, September 2–5.

—— and TIERNEY, J. T. 1986. *Organized Interests and American Democracy.* New York: Harper and Row.

SHAPIRO, S. A. 2005. "Pragmatic administrative law," Legal Studies Paper No. 05-02, Wake Forest University School of Law.

SIMS, G. C. 2003. "Rethinking the political power of American business: the role of corporate social responsibility," Ph.D. diss. Stanford University.

SITKOFF, R. H. 2003. "Politics and the business corporation," *Regulation* 26(4): 30–6.

SKOCPOL, T. 1996. *Boomerang: Clinton's Health Security Effort and the Turn against Government in US Politics.* New York: W.W. Norton.

SMITH, J. A. 1991. *Idea Brokers: Think Tanks and the Rise of the New Policy Elite.* New York: Free Press.

SMITH, M. A. 2000. *American Business and Political Power: Public Opinion, Elections, and Democracy.* Chicago: University of Chicago Press.

SMITH, R. 1995. "Interest group influence in the US Congress," *Legislative Studies Quarterly* 20(1): 89–139.

SOLOMON, B. 1987. "Clout merchants," *National Journal* March 21: 662–6.

SORAUF, F. J. 1992. *Inside Campaign Finance: Myths and Realities.* New Haven: Yale University Press.

STEWART, R. B. 1975. "The reformation of American administrative law," *Harvard Law Review* 88(8): 1669–813.

US Department of Commerce. 2005. "US automobile industry employment trends," http://www.ita.doc.gov/td/auto/domestic/staffreports/Jobloss.pdf

VOGEL, D. J. 1978. *Lobbying the Corporation: Citizen Challenges to Business Authority.* New York: Basic Books.

—— 1989. *Fluctuating Fortunes: The Political Power of Business in America.* New York: Basic Books.

WEAVER, K. R. 1989. "The changing world of think tanks," *PS: Political Science and Politics* 22 (3): 563–78.

WEST, D. M., HEITH, D. J., and GOODWIN, C. 1996. "Harry and Louise go to Washington: political advertising and health care reform," *Journal of Health Policy, Politics, and Law* 21 (1): 35–68.

WERNER, T. 2008. "Business vulnerability and self-regulation: gay politics inside the *Fortune 1000*," paper presented at the annual meeting of the Southern Political Science Association, New Orleans, January 10–12.

WILSON, G. K. 1981. *Interest Groups in the United States*. Oxford: Clarendon Press.

—— 1985. *The Politics of Safety and Health: Occupational Safety and Health in the United States and Britain*. New York: Oxford University Press.

—— 1990a. *Interest Groups*. Cambridge, Mass.: Blackwell.

—— 1990b. "Corporate Political Strategies," *British Journal of Political Science* 20(2): 281–8.

WOLPE, B. C., J. LEVINE, B. J. 1996. *Lobbying Congress: How the System Works*. Washington, DC: Congressional Quarterly Press.

WRIGHT, J. 1996. *Interest Groups and Congress: Lobbying, Contributions, and Influence*. Boston: Allyn & Bacon.

CHAPTER 12

EUROPEAN BUSINESS– GOVERNMENT RELATIONS

DAVID COEN

INTRODUCTION[1]

THE role of the firm in European public policy and integration process has been a long-standing contentious issue for academics, practitioners, and policy-makers. Business has had a presence in Brussels since the foundation of the European Economic Community; but it is only in recent years as business has become a key player in the EU that appropriate EU models of business have emerged. In addition to moving beyond the early academic and empirical writing, which tended to focus the emergence of Euro-corporatism and the growth of EU collective action models (Streeck and Schmitter 1991), in recent years new studies have attempted to develop an understanding of individual business lobbying capacities that take account of the distinct nature of EU public policy process (Coen 1997, 2007; Woll 2008). These new studies have recognized that large firms played a significant role in the integration process and the creation of the European Single Market (Sandholtz and Zysman 1989; Cowles 1995, 1996) and became significant and regulatory interlocutors with the EU bureaucracy (Coen 1998; Bouwen 2009; Lehmann 2009).

What are less well-defined are the new EU behavioral logics of business, their allocation of political resources across the European policy process and between EU institutions, and the effectiveness of specific strategies. Moreover, in explaining the individual business logic of political action in the EU it is important that we develop lobbying models that take account of the distinct European institutional environment and move beyond the US-centric concentration on Political Action Committees (PACs) and rent-seeking literature (see Werner and Wilson, this volume), especially when there is limited empirical evidence that these forms of campaign finance have any effect on policy outcomes even in the USA (see Baumgartner and Leech 2001; de Figueiredo 2002). Rather, much more attention must be attached to the role of informational exchanges and the emergence of trust and reputation in Brussels (Broscheid and Coen 2003). Especially, as European public policy is highly discretionary and technocratic, in its dealings with interest groups, and conciliatory in its inter-institutional relationships. Consequently, this chapter attempts to look at EU business–government relations by discussing not just at how business has learned to lobby and the resources that it can mobilize in terms of expertise and resources, but also what the European Commission, European Parliament, and European Council have learned to demand from business interests.

Empirically, like their cousins in Washington, business interests make up the largest percentage of political actors in Brussels—representing approximately 66 per cent of the 1,800 recognized interest groups in the EU (Greenwood 2007). Moreover, in addition to the hundreds of sector trade associations, it is estimated that some 300 large firms have a government affairs office in Brussels and many more have a dedicated European affairs capacity located at headquarters (Coen 2007; Berkhout and Lowery 2008). In fact, lobbying is big business in the EU with an estimated 30–60 billion Euros spent on funding approximately 20,000 lobbyists in Brussels each year. Much of this business lobbying activity takes the form of commissioning reports and statistical studies, funding Brussels offices, and arranging forums and meetings with technical experts and senior executives (see Coen and Richardson 2009).

With their numerical presence and their significant economic and informational resources, business interests are one of the few interest groups to exert an influence along the whole policy process from agenda setting to implementation in the nation states. However, this is not to say that business has captured the European policy process, rather business has increasingly had to learn to work in complex advocacy coalitions with societal and environmental groups (Mahoney 2007; Long and Lorinzi 2009) in order to gain access to the EU institutions and establish political reputation. Accordingly, this chapter argues that a distinct "reputational" based model of business lobbying has emerged that is unique to the EU political setting and has huge implications for the forthcoming EU disclosure and Transparency debates (European Commission 2006, 2008; European Parliament 2008; Obradovic 2009).

In making the claim for a unique European business–government relationship this chapter sets out in the first part why firms located to Brussels and how they and EU institutions learned to play a specific lobbying game. In so doing the chapter describes how the creation of the single market and the concurrent increases in regulatory competencies of the Commission and the increasing fiscal and monetary convergence of member states (Schmidt 2007) reduced the ties to home capital lobbying and incentives for individual lobbying of the EU. Having identified what motivated lobbying of the EU and the creation of government affairs offices in Brussels, the first section attempts to explain how best practice and lobbying norms emerged over time—especially as interest group overloading created a more competitive political environment and pressure on EU institutions to manage interest group representation via the creation of an elite pluralist process of fora and consultations (Coen 2007). The second part assesses how large firms have organized their political affairs functions and developed increasingly sophisticated government and EU affairs offices in Brussels. In recognizing the emergence of an individual and professional lobbying capacity the chapter explores the potential impact on the logic of collective action in the EU (Coen 1998, 2007) and the development of new ad hoc and short life alliances (Mahoney 2007). Finally, the chapter briefly explores the consequences for policy-making.

BUSINESS LOBBYING AND EVOLVING INSTITUTIONAL RELATIONS

While there has been an extensive historical literature on the politics of business and government relations in the US (Vogel 1989; Wilson 1990), there have been fewer studies of the role of business in the EU policy system (see Coen 1997, 1998, 2009; Eising 2007). This chapter represents an attempt to chart the rise of the firm as a political actor in Brussels and explains the changing behavioral logic of individual business lobbying over a twenty-year period from 1985 to 2005. This was a significant period for economic and political European integration after a long period of economic stagnation. More specifically, with the creation of the single market and single currency, the delegation of significant regulatory functions to the EU institutions and regulatory agencies, and the increasing agenda setting roles of the Commission and co-decision activity of the European Parliament, business was pulled into the political orbit of the EU institutions (Coen 1997; Richardson 2006).

In the context of these economic and institutional changes this chapter attempts to illustrate how the business lobby mobilized, so that we can assess how to regulate and monitor business–government relations in the future. The analysis is derived from two surveys completed in 1994/5 (n94) and 2004/5 (n50) of 200 firms with European government affairs functions in Brussels (see Coen 1997, 2009). Using this empirical evidence, the chapter pursues the idea that large firms have developed sophisticated EU political affairs functions that are capable of complex political alliances and EU identity building in response to EU institutional informational demands and access requirements.

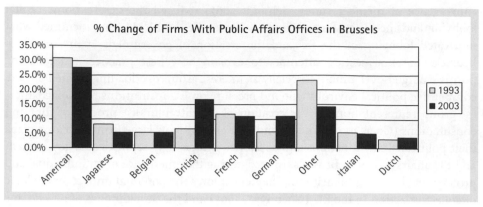

Fig. 12.1 Firms with public affairs offices, 1993–2003
Source: Landmarks Publications (1993, 2003).

In charting the rise of business activity it is clear that the number and activity of firms with government affairs has risen. Between 1983 and 2003 the number of firms with European government affairs rose dramatically from an estimate of 50 in 1980, to 200 in 1993, and some 300 in 2003. As Fig. 12.1 illustrates, in addition to the total numbers rising, the distribution of nationalities present has altered. Significantly, large US companies, such as Ford, GM, and IBM, British and Dutch multinationals such as BP, Philips, and Shell, and EU conglomerates such as Fiat and Daimler Benz have had a presence in Brussels since the early 1980s. In fact all played important roles in the creation of the European industrial round table, restructuring of UNICE (Business Europe) and the American chamber of commerce (AMCHAM), and in the push for the creation of the Single Market program and subsequent regulatory integration process (Sandholtz and Zysman 1989; Cowles 1995, 1996; Majone 2005). Today, as Fig. 12.1 illustrates, a variety of companies from most of the EU 27 have some presence in Brussels working in direct competition with US, Japanese, Swiss, and South Korean firms. However, what is notable is that even those firms of non-EU origin and those that have recently located to Brussels must all learn the rules of EU business–government relations (see Coen 1999; Hamada 2007).

With the creation of the single market, the introduction of qualified majority voting at the Council of Ministers, and the creeping regulatory competencies of the EU institutions, we saw the locus of business–government relations shift from national institutions towards European institutional channels over the last twenty years. Moreover, as regulatory issues delegated to the European Commission began to impact directly on the day-to-day running of companies, we began to see the rise of direct individual lobbying by firms. Such activity was rational as firms could no longer ignore the regulatory activity of the European Commission nor allow their positions to be only collectively presented via Trade associations. They needed to get reliable information directly about proposed legislation and impact the development of future market and social regulations—see Fig. 12.2. However, for all these changes

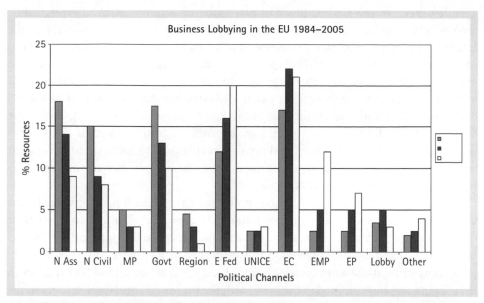

Fig. 12.2 Changing nature of business political activity in the EU

Note: Fig. 12.2 shows the lobbying pattern for large firms seeking to influence the European policy process and represents the mean average who responded to the question: How would you allocate 100 units of political resources (time, money, expertise) between the channels listed to influence the European Union today? The percentage data therefore represent firms' revealed preference for various political channels, as opposed to their actual expenditure.

Source: Coen (1997 and 2009).

in business–government activity there was also a realization that all the political channels were mutually reinforcing and that an integrated approach to lobbying involving all national and regional government and EU institutions along the policy process was needed to exert influence (Coen 1997, 2007; Constantelos 2007). This early multi-level lobbying mirrored in many ways the classic US literature on pluralism (see Truman 1951; Vogel 1989).

Business lobbies using a variety of political channels ranging from individual meetings with the European Commission (EC) and European Parliament (EP), National government (MP and Govt), and civil services (N Civil) through collective arrangements at the National association (N Ass) and European Federations (E Fed). Moreover, the voice of the lobby can take the form of constructive consultation and meetings through to media public relation offensives and direct action on the streets of Brussels.

In the early period of the European Community business lobbying was primarily focused on the nation state and therefore indirectly on reactive and destructive lobbying via the veto of the Council of Ministers. However, between 1984 and 1994 a significant shift in political activity occurred in favor of the European institutions and most specifically towards individual lobbying of the European Commission. With the gradual transfer of political, administrative, and fiscal authority to the EU, business recognized that the Commission was becoming the new economic policy agenda setter. However, while much of new lobbying activity could be explained by the single market legislative boom acting as a pull factor, it should be noted that the introduction of qualified majority voting at Maastricht also acted as a push factor out of the national lobbying model. Responding to the changing European institutional architecture large firms recognized the need to shift from reactive and destructive EU lobbying strategies towards a more proactive EU strategy that was focused on the EU decision-makers and formulators. Logically, the Commission as the EU legislative agenda setter and initial policy formulator became the primary port of call. Consequently, in the early 1990s, firms and regulators alike had to learn to establish clear business–government terms of engagement, and as such we moved incrementally towards a new form of EU public policy.

The emergence of a distinct EU public policy system was further encouraged by the willingness of the European Commission and European Parliament to open their doors to more lobbyists. In reality, this new openness was recognition by the EU institutions that they no longer had the resources to deal with the expansion of legislation without the active participation of technical experts. However this boom in lobbying was not confined to business, with the increased regulatory activity of the Commission, also encouraging civil society groups to gravitate to Brussels. Thus by 1992 it was estimated that more than 3,000 public and economic lobbies were active in Brussels (OJ93/C63/02). Moreover, the Commission (recognizing the democratic deficit and policy legitimacy issues) facilitated many civil and society groups to overcome their collective action problems and partially fund the creation of European secretariats—to the tune of one billion euros.

However, with EU lobbying continuing to grow over the 1990s and business recognized that it was faced with an increasingly crowded political market, with multiple access points, and a growing number of interrelated policy areas. In such a politically noisy environment, businesses realized that it was important to establish individual reputation with the functionaries—who determined who were consulted. Moreover, in a political market where numerous interest groups and businesses were trying to influence an open political system, greatest weight was given to those actors who were prepared to establish their European credentials and/or solidarity links with societal interests (Coen 1998; Mahoney 2007).

Yet, for all the growth in direct representation in the EU policy process, EU collective action remains an important lobbying option for big business (Streeck and Visser 2006; Greenwood 2007). Like individual lobbyist, collective action exploded in the 1990s due to the increased regulatory activity of the EU, and it is estimated today that there are around 1,000 business associations active in the EU public policy process (Greenwood 2000b, 2002a, 2007). However, significantly, as the numbers increased, so too have the variety of collective arrangements ranging from high-level business clubs to sector-specific European federations constituted of national trade associations (Greenwood 2007; Berkhout and Lowery 2008). As a result big business altered its collective action logics and attempted to rebuild the existing European federations by encouraging more large-firm direct participation (see Greenwood 2007), used them in a selective and focused form for issues where a common collective voice could be found, and on occasion used them to mask an individual lobbying position. The result of this reorganization and allocation of new functions was the rebirth of European trade association from 1984 and 2004 (see Fig. 12.2) after a period of stagnation and a perception that they only represented lowest common denominator positions in the 1980s.

In the mid-1990s, as these new alliances matured and the lobbying environment continued to overload, it became apparent that large firms that wished to continue to exert a direct influence on the European public policy process would have to marshal a greater number of skills than merely monitoring the progress of European directives and responding to consultation calls from the European Commission. Successful lobbying of the European Commission meant establishing an organizational capability (office) to coordinate potential ad hoc political alliances and to develop and reinforce existing political channels at the national and European level. To achieve good access for individual lobbying of the European Commission—the primary focus—large firms were encouraged to develop a broad political profile across a number of issues and to participate in the creation of collective strategies. Accordingly, the cost of identity building would be discounted against better access to "company specific" issues at a later date. However, as a result of this professionalization and increased contact some firms were establishing themselves as political "insiders" through a process of regular and broad-based political activity. It was these new insiders which stood to benefit most from the gradual "closing down" of access to the European Commission in face of the "interest overload" in the late 1990s. In many ways this mirrored what Vogel had observed for US firms: as big business favored access and was challenged by the rise of the politics of consumerism, firms had to develop new identities, and the notion of corporate social responsibility emerged (Vogel 1989).

In the twenty years of business–government relations the importance of economic business cycles and the influence of cost considerations have increased. It is fair to assume that the importance of cost grows with the uncertainty attributed to the political channel. With many of the functions and roles of the EU institutions changing with successive treaties it is not surprising that business has been slow to alter its political activity. Moreover, this responsiveness is slowest during periods of recession—when corporate affairs budgets are the first to be cut back. This conservative political nature is best illustrated by the slow lobbying take-up of the European Parliament even after the Maastricht and Nice treaties in the 1990s had conferred co-decision and increased consultation powers.

While many interviewees in the 1984–94 period recognized the increasing policy-making powers of the European Parliament and the emergence of new lobbying opportunities, the reality was that until a time came when they had additional resources or they had suffered a clear cost of non-participation, the focus of lobbying remained the European Commission. Moreover, for much of the early 1990s the ambiguous political outcomes of EP policy committees and the subsequent risk of log-rolling at the Strasbourg plenary votes more than outweighed the perceived benefits of lobbying to influencing the co-decision process (Lehmann 2009).

This perception changed in the late 1990s with some high-profile lobbying campaigns on bio-technology patenting and tobacco by civic and health lobbies alerting business to the cost of non-action at the Parliament (Earnshaw and Judge 2006). At the same time the European Parliament stepped up its activism vis-à-vis the Council and Commission—so providing more lobbying opportunities via co-decision and consultation (Hix 2005). Hence, by 2005 we observed almost a doubling in the utilization of the European Parliament and its near parity with the European Commission as a focal point in lobbying the EU—see Fig. 12.2.

The result of bringing politics into an EU bureaucratic and technocratic policy process is that business has had to learn greater awareness of public interests, public relations, and the media. While still seeking to influence the European Parliament officials on the grounds of quality information, business has become aware that the MEPs wish to consult with a wider range of societal interest groups than the European Commission. That is to say that the lobbying game at the EP is about influencing and providing political legitimacy as opposed to policy legitimacy.

This reputation and legitimacy argument is important in the utilization of the professional lobbying consultancy in Brussels. In the early 1990s the low take-up of hired lobbyists was explained by the realization by business that they were capable of lobbying the EU institutions directly. The private lobbyist's position worsened with the green papers on open access and transparency in the European Union (OJ 93/C166/04), especially as the report made a clear distinction between representatives from business and society and those making representations for profit. However, more damaging to take-up was the fact that in the increasingly competitive and reputation-based public arena they did not establish "goodwill" or political reputations for the client (that could facilitate private business access at a later date). That said, professional lobbyists and, increasingly, law firms continued to grow in the 1990s and maintained a specialist niche as many firms used them in the busy 1990s legislative period to identify new political issues and trends (Lahusen 2002).

In the 2000s, the profession continued to grow as big business start to use them for profile building as well as monitoring (see Fig. 12.2). Moreover, as lobbyists themselves recognized the importance of reputation building and public interest lobbying at the European Parliament, we have seen traditional lobbying firms augmented by the arrival and expansion of a number of large public relations companies and think tanks. These new lobbyists have attempted to help manage the international media, coordinate the ad hoc alliances, and build policy identities for business clients.

However, the increasing numbers of lobbyists in Brussels at the turn of the century has become a concern for EU institutions and interest groups alike. Unable to process information from some 20,000 lobbying voices, EU institutions have attempted to informally manage access to committees and fora, and are currently debating transparency and codes of conduct procedures (Commission European Transparency Initiative 2006, EC2008).

As already noted with only 20,000 officials responsible for hundreds of directives European institutions looked to interest representation and business for information and initiatives. As a consequence there was reluctance in the early 1990s to regulate lobbying and no system of accreditation emerged—regardless of the debates on transparency and openness. However, as the lobbying boom escalated the need and incentive to regulate and restrict access began to emerge. The initial response to create a self-regulatory code of conduct that only applied to consultants (and therefore only covered about 5 per cent of all lobbying activity) was deemed by many too little too late. Thus, in the late 2000s both EU institutions looked into systems of accreditation and transparency as a response to criticisms over account-ability and democratic deficits in the policy process (Obradovic 2009). At present the European Parliament has established a registry and code of conduct for lobbyists (EP 2005) and the European Commission has introduced a register of interest groups and code of conduct (EC 2008). The Commission's regulation proposes financial disclos-ure of lobbying budgets but is still unclear on what constitutes lobbying: i.e. is it funding a study, office, flying a CEO into Brussels, or running a PR campaign just before a European Parliament plenary session? As the register is voluntary it is also unclear what the incentives are to participate and the degree to which business will fully disclose their many identities and access points across the EU public policy process.

So do we see a new business government arrangement in 2000s? Clearly the unobtru-sive nature of much lobbying activity has restricted our understanding of European business government activity and influence. Unlike the visible lobbying of rent-seeking industries in the US Senate and Congress and Political Action Committee contributions, most EU interest studies have focused on the trade associations and the visible logic of collective action (Eising 2007; Greenwood 2007). However, if we are to define codes of conduct and create databases of institutional lobbying activity it is important that we have a clear understanding of how and when interests make representation across the political institutions, along the policy process and for different policies. The political allocation figures (Fig. 12.2) above clearly illustrates that a number of mutually reinforcing political channels are utilized to influence the EU public policy process. However, the timing, take-up, and the style of activity have altered as EU procedural rules have changed and EU interests and functionaries learnt to trust one another.

In terms of a business–government relationship, the European Commission con-tinues to be the initial focus for agenda setting. Business has recognized that the European Commission is a significant policy entrepreneur with its right of initiative and continues to exert a huge influence on the formulation of the directive and during the consultation and co-decision process. What is sometimes less clear is its discretion to invite or exclude business interests groups from the table, and its ability to demand behavioral criteria from those that it does invite. Thus, the most signi-ficant development in lobbying in Brussels over the last twenty years has been the emergence of an elite pluralist arrangement where industry is perceived as an integral policy player but must fit certain political access and information criteria demanded by the EU institutions (Bouwen 2002; Coen 2007, 1998; Schmidt 2007). However, to compensate for the predominance of EU business representation the institutions have also been known to seek out and in some cases fund interest groups and countervailing ad hoc alliances (Mahoney 2004).

Significantly, the regulatory agency style of Brussels policy-making has produced the emergence of a trust-based relationship between insider firms and EU officials. Within this credibility game the Commission makes many of its attempts to build long-running relationships with interests, based on consistency of information exchanges, wide consultations, and conciliatory actions. Conversely, business must develop strategies that create reputations that will help them to gain access to the closed decision-making arenas. The result of this discretion politics is that business–government relations in Brussels are reliant upon both social capital and trust.

However, we must also be careful in our generalization of the EU institutions as there is much variety even between different Directorates (DGs) in the Commission. A study by Broscheid and Coen (2007) illustrated this by showing how Commission preferences for fora and/or direct action are a function of the informational demands of the Directorate, number of interests groups operating in the policy area, and the institutional capacity to process informational inputs, balanced against the legitimacy requirements of the policy domain. Thus in highly regulatory policy areas, where technical policy input defines the policy legitimacy and staffing numbers are low, they showed that the Commission create policy fora and committees to manage individual lobbying by business. However, in more redistributive policy domains they showed that the Commission sought to generate wider consultation and encouraged lobbying via associations, and collective groups with constituencies.

As already noted, individual direct lobbying of MEPs and European Parliament civil servants increased dramatically in the last ten years and consequently new political EU lobbying styles have emerged. First, as expected the greatest lobbying activity has congregated around the parliament committees secretariats where co-decision applies—such as single market and environmental legislation (Lehmann 2009). Accordingly, the greatest activity has tended to mirror the European Commission's legislative activity and has continued to focus on the technical aspects of the legislation. However, unlike the Commission the European Parliament is terribly understaffed in terms of policy expert support and much of the burden of drafting will fall on a few Rapporteurs, Shadow Rapporteurs, and assistants. As such there is a great risk of capture and a heavy reliance on the Commission officials.

Much like the Commission the nature of the policy will also dictate how the European Parliament requests information from business interests. In such a complex environment, business interests have often been forced to reformulate or re-emphasize economic competitiveness arguments (stated at the Commission) to focus on wider public goods such as regional employment consequences. This was perhaps most visible during the pharmaceutical patent debates and REACH proposals in

Chemical sector in the early 2000s (Earnshaw and Judge 2006). However, the more substantial difference between the European Commission's bureaucratic discretionary model and the European Parliament political environment is the growing use of the economic media and public opinion in lobbying the European Parliament pre-Committee hearing and plenary.

What this discussion illustrates is the importance of the policy and the type of institutional legitimacy required to deliver regulations in determining the business–government relationship. In the EU public policy context, there is huge variance in business political activity across regulatory and distributional issues and along the policy cycle. At the formulation stage, preference is for individual lobbying of the EU institutions and is supported by the potential sector consensus-building activity at the European federations. However, in line with concept of subsidiary much of the interpretation of EU directives is still the responsibility of the national regulatory authorities.

Hence we see in the recent liberalized sectors of telecommunication, energy, and financial securities a higher degree of political budget going into lobbying the national ministries and regulators (see Fig. 12.3; Coen and Thatcher 2008). National lobbying may also rise with the risk of major recession and a return to anti-competitive behavior and calls for state aid. Under these conditions we may see more EU legal lobbying occurring at the Competition directorate of the Commission and at the European court of Justice (see Bouwen and McCown 2007).

In looking for variance in allocation between national and EU lobbying channels, we must therefore look at the formal and informal delegation of policy-making powers to the EU (Pollack 2003; Franchino 2005). In policies where the outcome is market creating, standard harmonizing, trade, and competitiveness, we would expect post-Maastricht to see a high EU profile, while issues that touch on sovereignty such as fiscal and JHA issues are not surprisingly still dominated by domestic lobbying. We would also expect to see a distinction in lobbying strategy depending upon whether

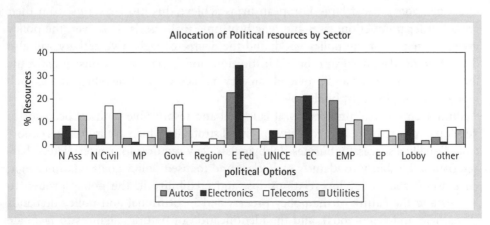

Fig. 12.3 Sector variance in lobbying activity in the EU

the market regulations were product or process regulation—as the incentives to collaborate or go it alone will vary dramatically on the nature of the common good available (Hix 2005).

THE ORGANIZATION OF EU BUSINESS–GOVERNMENT RELATIONS

How far can we develop a distinct micro-theory of the European large firm? As the above illustrated, the firm has evolved as a political actor in the EU and with this new political activity has come increased professionalization and organization of EU government affairs functions. In building a theory of the firm we must first understand what motivates large firms to go it alone in Brussels and the emergence of an information resource dependency between business and the EU institution. Secondly, we need to make sense of why as individual political action has increased—the incentives to participate in the lowest common denominator concessions of EU trade associations did not diminish but actually grew. In so doing it is hoped that we can explain the business rationale for new collective forms.

In attempting to understand the business–government relationship we must first accept that the EU institutions have a great deal of discretion in who they talk to. As a result policy-makers can often demand access goods to the policy process (Coen 1998; Bouwen 2004; Eising 2007). Hence, while the Commission at first glance looks open and accessible, a firm's effectiveness in influencing policy directly continues to be determined by its ability to establish a positive reputation in the European political process—: that is to say, the extent to which it can establish its reputation as a provider of reliable, sector-specific, and pan-European information (Broscheid and Coen 2003). Most large European firms achieve this insider status from their cross-border production, size, and length of time in Brussels. However, the policy cycle, the nature of the policy good, and the degree of legislative activity will also determine the demand from the EU institutions for direct input. Consequently, the level of access expected and provided can vary markedly for a single firm and as such lobbying strategies must be flexible.

With such political uncertainty, it is logical and responsible political behavior to develop a mix of direct and collective political strategies which are mutually reinforcing. Equally a successful business lobbying strategy requires four interrelated characteristics; the ability to identify early clear and focused policy goals (Gardner 1991; Greenwood 2007), develop relationships, and credibility in the policy process to understand the nature of the policy process and institutional and policy demands (Broscheid and Coen 2003), and the identification of natural alliances to facilitate access and redefine reputations. This requires political resources and expertise.

EU government affairs offices are often skeleton staffed with two to three permanent staff, and operate as an early warning function to headquarters. More significantly, many are empowered to directly mobilize experts from within the company and to commission expert advice from outside to company to respond to EU consultation calls. However, the most important functions of EU offices are to identify the potential EU policy consensus (and potential qualified majorities) and nurture relationships with EU officials in the EC Directorates, EP committees, and national permanent representations. In terms of a successful Brussels operation, seniority of EU directors helps in developing informal networks with other like-minded companies and EU interest groups, and may facilitate invitations to informal EU expert groups and high level fora—such as the C21 (Van Schendelen 2003; Gornitzka and Sverdrup 2008).

Perhaps equally important for political credibility, senior EU appointments are more likely to influence policy-making and strategic goals within their own company. In sum, for successful direct access it is important that firms have individuals who can operate within small policy communities as equals and have the political credibility to warrant invitations to select committees and industrial policy fora. Within this elite EU business/lobbying community we have seen a high degree of political learning and a convergence of lobbying strategy throughout the 1990s (Coen 1998, 2007; Woll 2008). What is clear is that creating credible working relationships with the EU institutions requires time, informational resources, and an element of "give and take" on behalf of firms and EU institutions. However, while trust and political legitimacy are developed through the provision of quick, reliable, and credible information over time, they can be lost in a much shorter period.

In assessing the logic of the EU business lobby it is important to note that multinational companies are not a single unitary actor, but are made up of a number of stakeholders and subsidiaries. As such, it is paramount that firms can identify their long-run political aims and provide consistent messages across the various EU and domestic institutions. To enable such focused and constant lobbying activity, firms need to establish clear lines of communication between the government affairs departments, technical line managers, public relations departments, board, and CEO. It is only by creating this distinct and centralized government affairs function that business can establish clear political accountability within the firm and credibility with EU officials; by monitoring the internal and external flow of information to managers and regulators (Willman et al. 2003). While focused information improves the credibility and the political weighting that business ascribes to the policy; consistency of message from all divisions of a company avoids the playing off of different groups by EU officials with differing competitiveness, environmental, and health and safety agendas. In fact, in the disaggregated EU public policy process it may actually be possible for large firms to have more information about the various directorate generals and European Committee positions than the EU functionaries.

With so much to manage in the EU policy process, we should see regulatory affairs as an informational post box and gatekeeper supplying information to the EU officials and receiving "policy credibility" from the quality of information from the company experts, and deriving "political credibility" from the CEO support. In a perfect world we would hope that EU institutions and business could reach a strategic awareness where industry would trust policy-makers enough to fully disclose information for a well-informed directive to be created.

In reality there is always a risk that the establishment of the gatekeeping function will result in asymmetric information flows that result in suboptimal policy-making. That is to say we might see a "policing focus" by the government affairs office (Willman et al. 2003). Such activity was observed in the early days of the single market program as many companies monitored the EU from national government affairs offices and in-house legal teams. Believing in the national veto at the Council of Ministers and embedded in their domestic political environment, few incentives existed for business to engage fully with the EU institutions (Coen 1997). However, this reactive and negative lobbying failed to establish relationships with EU officials and resulted in a number of political and legal clashes at the Commission and the ECJ (Mattli 1999; Bouwen and McCown 2007). The result, after a period of business compliance focus, was the discussed explosion in EU government affairs functions in Brussels, as firms recognized the cost of non-participation in standard-setting.

Recognizing the discretion of the EU officials in "who and when to consult," large firms initially established small monitoring operations staffed by ex-Commission officials (Gardner 1991; Hull 1993; Mazey and Richardson 1993). It was hoped that these informal networks would facilitate insider status, provide advance warning of proposed directives, and in the long run influence policy-making. However, industry quickly learned that such "quick fixes" had their limits—as the "revolving door" strategy while facilitating access to the EU institutions often alienated the HQ and domestic technical managers and potentially other directorate generals. Thus, by the mid-1990s there was a perception by industry that many EU affairs offices had gone native and that there was a need for the professionalization of the government affairs function. Over time and by managing the relationship with government and EU institutions directly, firms were gradually able to select appropriate senior managers within the firm to deal with specific informational requests. This has had the dual affect of reinforcing political credibility with the policy-makers for fast and effective information and developing a broader understanding of the policy-making process.

Accepting this level of sophistication, government affairs directors have noted that at different times along the policy process the level of management mobilized and the type of political good required from business alters. As such, in the early framing and agenda setting stages of a policy, CEO/commissioner contact is encouraged for the political momentum and political legitimacy engendered with the nation states and within the company. However, in the policy formulation and implementation stages it is the responsibility of the government affairs office to facilitate the appropriate middle managers to the policy committees.

Although large firms have established their credibility as policy actors in the EU, whether all firms who participate can attain the same favored access is open to debate. Rather, the parallel impact of increased EU business lobbying overload, coupled with a slowing down of the EU legislative activity in the 2000s, saw a fall in institutional demand for policy information and a shift towards "consensus politics through forums." This is a more focused and elite structure than the traditional corporatist arrangements of the 1970s or the open lobbying of the 1990s.

The upshot of forum politics and the multi-channel lobbying has been that EU institutions have become more concerned about the transparency in the EU policy process, while some of this call for change has been driven by democratic deficit debates and a desire for the European Commission and European Parliament to define their role vis-à-vis one another and their interest groups. The consequence is that direct lobbying by big business is coming under greater scrutiny, as it has been obvious to many that firms have been directly funding collective arrangements or fronting apparent ad hoc alliances to further their own individual access. It is hoped that the new transparency and regulation proposals will create greater disclosure and capture the individual lobbying footprints of business.

But what is the effect on traditional collective action logics? The above illustrated that large firms considered direct lobbying as the most effective means of influencing EU policy process, and that direct political action improved via establishing trust in the information provided and good political management of secondary collective channels. Significantly, the most common means of establishing an element of trust between EU officials and large firm was to attempt to foster European credentials. One strategy to create EU identity was to fund and participate in the EU trade federations. However, as firms became directly involved in the federations they sought to refine their functions and improve their policy-making impact.

As previously observed, business associations increased dramatically in number in the 1990s and currently accounted for almost two-thirds of all EU interests (Greenwood 2007). However, before we talk about a return to corporatism we must look beyond the growth statistics. Today we see a greater variation in the collective groupings available to business, ranging from the high-level business clubs like the European Round Table (Cowles 1995) and Transatlantic Business Dialogue (Coen and Grant 2001; Cowles 2001), high politics peak organizations such as Business for Europe, sector federations of national trade associations (Greenwood 2002a), and national chambers of commerce like AMCHAM (Cowles 1996). What is more, today much of the collective action growth is outside of the traditional sector and national cleavages and instead focuses on short-life issue alliances with small secretariats (see Mahoney 2004, 2007). As such the traditional analysis of business logic of collective action needs to be reassessed in the context of multi-level and multi-collective options.

While much focus in nation states has traditionally been on the logic of formation and overcoming free riding (Olson 1965; Moe 1980; Kimber 1993; Hart 2003; Streeck and Visser 2006), this has been less of an issue for EU collective action debates (Greenwood 2007). First and foremost, the EU institutions fostered and often funded the creation of many sector federations in the early days of the European Community, as a means of developing a functional "interest elite" that would work in parallel with the member states (Mazey and Richardson 1993). However, despite recognition of the value of structured corporatist system of consultation, the reality in Brussels was always a less formalized and pluralist policy-making system (Streeck and Schmitter 1991; Coen 1997). Secondly, the nature of membership of European federations, often combinations of national associations and large firms, has meant that entry costs would appear low to these established large political actors (Greenwood 2002b). Finally, once the initial decision to join has been made many large firms cease to continue the cost–benefit calculation of membership and may even fail to reach their rationality threshold (Kimber 1993).

So if the logic of formation and membership is less significant, the question becomes what is the logic of participation? As noted, there is a big difference between joining a federation and utilizing it to actively participate in the policy process (Jordan 1998; Lowery 2007). In the early days, many firms were frustrated with the role of trade associations in the EU policy process, feeling that they represented the lowest common denominator positions of their respective national associations (McLaughlin and Jordan 1993). As a result, in the 1990s sectors with high large-firm concentration ratios such as automobiles, chemicals, and pharmaceuticals encouraged the restructuring of European federations to foster direct firm membership, the rationale being that the new EU business associations would be more responsive to the informational demands of the EU institutions, that they would provide credible information with large end users and standard setters, and potentially be efficient organizations focusing on a limited range of consensus policy areas. The evidence is mixed for the success of firm-led association over traditional peak federations, with Eising arguing that the latter EU federations have more contact with the Commission than business-led groups (Eising 2004, 2007). However, this result may represent an under-counting of firm-led federations' impact and contact, as it fails to capture business direct representation, which should be seen as an accumulative and complementary effect with the EU federations.

The rise of such hybrid associations has challenged our traditional perception of EU collective action. First, what is beyond doubt is that these new collective arrangements provided firms with opportunities to develop their positive European credentials in the EU policy process. Accordingly, one EU rationale for active participation in collective channels is to develop a long-run reputation that can be discounted for direct lobbying access to the EU institutions. In Olsonian terms, membership and the continued high usage of European federations can in part be explained by the concept of the positive externality of reputation building for direct lobbying creating a private good incentive.

Secondly, given that most firms based in Brussels have limited political budgets, it is logical to assume that they prioritize political issues between core strategy that they lead and secondary issues in which they pool their expertise. Hence, in periods of high legislative activity, firms are more willing to share out the burden of the political representation to collective arrangements. Accepting greater resources at their disposal and the insider status of large federations, it is logical that EU federations are able to monitor a greater number of issue areas, with a greater level of expertise, and potentially gain more political coverage at lower cost for business.

Extending this concept of the logic of collective action, some argue that the rationale of firm-level participation at the EU federations is more a logic of the cost of non-membership than a calculus of the benefits (McLaughlin and Jordan 1993; Jordan 1998; Greenwood 2007). The costs may be linked to the reputation building and favored access for direct lobbying, the risk that the sector federation may become a countervailing voice to the outside firms' political preferences, and the loss of information and expertise. Overall, however, most firms surveyed saw positive benefits from active participation in the collective political channels, with 25 per cent of all their EU political resources going into national trade associations and EU federations, and recognition that these channels are mutually reinforcing direct access to the Commission and European Parliament.

Recognizing that federations are an important political channel to influence the policy process, what type of business collective action is most likely to thrive? First, as discussed in the second section, we must assess the nature of the political goods debated and the economic structure of the sector. As already alluded to, governance of a business federation is a function of uniformity of the membership: i.e. does it have to deal with the competing interests of network providers and service providers, does the association have large and small firms, manufacturers and retailers, etc. (Greenwood 2007: 69)? Thus, firms are more likely to participate directly in associations where clear goals can be identified and common ground found amongst a small group of key players—this would perhaps explain the success of the Association of European Automobile Constructors or the European Chemical Industrial Council. Equally important is the nature of the proposed legislation in as far as it is a collective or private good. As Fig. 12.3 illustrates, there is greater likelihood of collective action in policy areas that define products and markets, where incentives to collude are greater, than in sectors where the policy debates are about manufacturing processes or transposition of regulation into domestic markets.

The rise of long-run lobbying perspectives and sophisticated political business logics has challenged traditional forms of collective and direct individual action. As previously noted, in the interest-crowded EU public policy process, access improved for those that achieved credible political voice and political mass. The best means of achieving the latter was to establish some form of political alliance with rival firms, associations, and other public interests. In so doing, firms created "issue identities" for themselves. These alliances can be temporary ad hoc groups based around fast-changing single issues (Pijnenburg 1998) or more permanent groupings organized around formalized committees, fora, and even short-life trade associations (Greenwood 2007). This informality gives the European public policy its vitality and flexibility, allowing as it does for the development of informal relationships, the apportioning of favors, and the establishing of political trust.

CONCLUSION

Overall, the chapter is a story of the business lobby adapting to the changing EU institutional architecture and learning to lobby as an individual actor. The historical analysis leads to two significant observations: first, that the overall locus of business political activity has moved towards the EU institutions; and, second, that large firms see all the political channels as mutually reinforcing in an integrated lobbying strategy. In line with the complex multi-level pluralist system in which it operates business has learned to manage the political cycle and create different political identities as it moves along the formulation to delivery cycle and back and forth between EU and national political channels.

In terms of the large firm's logic as a political actor, a distinct European business–government model has evolved founded on information dependency and discretionary politics. Here the EU institutions have demanded increased specialized technical expertise to formulate policy and business has responded by developing individual direct representation strategies that build their goodwill and reputation in Brussels. Much of this business–government relationship has evolved incrementally with firms aware that misrepresentation and bad practice may result in exclusion from the policy process. Moreover, in professionalizing its political activity, the large firm has also altered the function and organization of many of the collective arrangements in Brussels and has learned to discount the cost of participation in one political channel for improved access in another.

So what of lobbying today? European business is faced with two new pressures. The first is a move towards a more formalized code of conduct and the introduction of European Parliament and European Commission accreditation. As business has learned to play "joined-up" lobbying along the EU policy process it is now time that the EU institutions move away from individual registration and competing definitions of what constitutes lobbying to audit, map, and monitor the business lobbying footprint across the life of a directive. The second threat is the current economic recession. As previously noted many government affairs departments have difficulty justifying and quantifying their lobbying, and their budget lines are often the first to be cut back in times of economic hardship. If this is the case it is possible that we will see a cutback on the new public relations activities at the European Parliament, a greater focus on the Commission with day-trip lobbying, and perhaps a greater reliance on trade associations for monitoring EU issues.

NOTE

1. This chapter is adapted from Coen (2009).

REFERENCES

BAUMGARTNER, F., and LEECH, B. 2001. "Interest niches and policy bandwagons: patterns of interest group involvement in national politics," *Journal of Politics* 63: 1191–213.
BERKHOUT, J., and LOWERY, D. 2008. "Counting organized interests in the European Union: a comparison of data sources," *Journal of European Public Policy* 15(4): 489–513.

BEYERS, J., and KERREMANS, B. 2007. "Critical resource dependencies and the Europeanization of domestic interest groups," *Journal of European Public Policy* 14(3): 460–81.

BOUWEN, P. 2002. "Corporate lobbying in the European Union: the logic of access," *Journal of European Public Policy* 9(3): 365–90.

—— 2004. "Exchanging access goods for access: a comparative study of business lobbying in the European Union institutions," *European Journal of Political Research* 43: 337–69.

—— 2009. "The European Commission," in D. Coen and J. Richardson, eds., *Lobbying the European Union: Institutions Actors and Policy*. Oxford: Oxford University Press.

—— and MCCOWN, M. 2007. "Lobbying versus litigation: political and legal strategies of interest representation in the European Union," *Journal of European Public Policy* 4(2): 422–43.

BROSCHEID, A., and COEN, D. 2003. "Insider and outsider lobbying of the European Commission: an informational model of forum politics," *European Union Politics* 4(2): 165–91.

—— —— 2007. "Lobbying activity and fora creation in the EU," *Journal of European Public Policy* 14(3): 346–65.

BUTT-PHILIP, A. 1990. *The Directory of Pressure Groups in the European Community*. London: Longmans.

COEN, D. 1997. "The evolution of the large firm as a political actor in the European Union," *Journal of European Public Policy* 4(1): 91–108.

—— 1998. "The European business interest and the nation state: large-firm lobbying in the European Union and member states," *Journal of Public Policy* 18(1): 75–100.

—— 1999. "The impact of US lobbying practice on the European business–government relationship," *California Management Review* 41(4): 27–44.

—— 2002. "Business interests and integration," in R. Bulme, D. Chambre, and V. Wright, eds., *Collective Action in the European Union*. Paris: Science-Po Press, 255–72.

—— 2007. "Empirical and theoretical studies in the EU lobbying," *Journal of European Public Policy* 14: 333–45.

—— 2009. "The European business lobby," in D. Coen and J. Richardson, eds., *Lobbying the European Union: Institutions, Actors and Policy*. Oxford: Oxford University Press.

—— and GRANT, W. 2001. "Corporate political strategy and global public policy: a case study of the transatlantic business dialogue," *European Business Journal* 13(1): 37–44.

—— and RICHARDSON, J. 2009. *Lobbying the European Union: Institutions, Actors and Policy*. Oxford: Oxford University Press.

—— and THATCHER, M. 2008. "Network governance and delegation: European networks of regulatory agencies," *Journal of Public Policy* 28(1): 49–71.

CONSTANTELOS, J. 2007. "Interest group strategies in multilevel Europe," *Journal of Public Affairs* 7: 39–53.

COWLES, M. 1995. "Setting the agenda for a new Europe: the ERT and EC1992," *Journal of Common Market Studies* 33(4): 501–26.

—— 1996. "The EU committee of Amcham: the powerful voice of American firms in Brussel," *Journal of European Public Policy* 3: 339–58.

—— 2001. "The transatlantic business dialogue and domestic business–government relations," in M. Cowles, J. Caporaso, and T. Risse, eds., *Transforming Europe: Europeanization and Domestic Change*. Ithaca, NY: Cornell University Press.

DE FIGUEIREDO, J. 2002. "Lobbying and information politics," *Business and Politics* 4(2): 125–30.

EARNSHAW, D., and JUDGE, D. 2006. "No simple dichotomies: lobbyists and the European Parliament," *Journal of Legislative Studies* 8(4): 1357–2334.

EISING, R. 2004. "Multilevel governance and business interests in the European Union," *Governance* 17(2): 211–46.

EISING, R. 2007. "The access of business interests to EU political institutions: towards elite pluralism?" *Journal of European Public Policy* 14(3): 345–75.

European Commission 1993a. "An open and structured dialogue between the Commission and special interest groups," Brussels, 93/C63/02.

—— 1993b. "Transparency in the Community," COM (1993) C1666/04 final.

—— 2001. "European governance: a white paper," COM (2001) 428 final.

—— 2006. "Green paper European Transparency Initiative," COM (2006) 194 final.

—— 2008. "European Transparency Initiative: a framework for relations with interest representatives," Register and code of conduct. COM 2008 323, May 27.

European Parliament. 2008. Resolution of May 8, 2008 on Development of the Framework for the Actitivies of Interest Representatives (lobbyists) in the European Institutions (2008/2115 (INI).

FRANCHINO, F. 2005. *The Powers of the Union: Delegation in the EU.* Cambridge: Cambridge University Press.

GARDNER, J. 1991. *Effective Lobbying in the European Community.* Deventer: Kluwer.

GRANT, W. 1993. "Pressure groups and the European Community: an overview," in S. Mazey and J. Richardson, eds., *Lobbying in the European Community.* Oxford: Oxford University Press.

GRAY, V., and LOWERY, D. 1997. "Reconceptualising PAC formation: it's not a collective action problem and it may be an arms race," *American Politics Quarterly* 25(3): 319–46.

—— and LOWERY, D. 2000. *The Population Ecology of Interest Representation: Lobbying Communities in the American States.* Ann Arbor: University of Michigan Press.

GORNITZKA, A., and SVERDRUP, U. 2008. "Who consults? The configuration of expert groups in the European union," *West European Politics* 31(4): 725–50.

GREENWOOD, J. 2002a. *Inside the EU Business Association.* Basingstoke: Palgrave.

—— 2002b. "EU interest Groups and their members: when is membership a 'collective action problem,'" in R. Balme, D. Chabanet, and V. Wright, eds., *L'Action collective en Europe.* Paris: Presses de Sciences Po.

—— 2007. *Interest Representation in the European Union.* Basingstoke: Palgrave.

GROSSMAN, E. 2004. "Bring politics back in: rethinking the role of economic interest groups in European integration," *Journal of European Public Policy* 11: 637–54.

—— and WOLL, C. 2007. "Associations matter: reconsidering the political strategies of firms in the European Union," at European Union Studies Association (EUSA), Biennial Conference, May 17–19, Montreal.

HAMADA, Y. 2007. "The impact of the traditional business–government relationship upon the Europeanization of Japanese firms," *Journal of European Public Policy* 14(3): 404–21.

HART, D. 2003. "Political representation among dominant firms: revisiting the Olsonian hypothesis," *Business and Politics* 5: 261–86.

HIX, S. 2005. *The Political System of the European Union.* London: Macmillan Press.

HULL, R. 1993. "Lobbying Brussels: a view from within," in S. Mazey and J. Richardson, eds., *Lobbying in the European Community.* Oxford: Oxford University Press.

JORDAN, G. 1998. "What drives associability at the European level? The limits of the utilitarian explanation," in M. Aspinwall and J. Greenwood, eds., *Collective Action in the European Union.* London: Routledge.

KIMBER, R. 1993. "Interest groups and the fallacy of the liberal fallacy," in J. Richardson, ed., *Pressure Groups.* Oxford: Oxford University Press.

KOHLER-KOCH, B., and EISING, R. 1999. *The Transformation of Governance in the European Union.* London: Routledge.

LAHUSEN, C. 2002. "Commercial consultancies in the European Union: the shape and structures of professional interest intermediation," *Journal of European Public Policy* 9(5): 695–715.

Landmarks Publications. 1993. *European Public Affairs Directory 1993.* Brussels:: Landmarks Publications.

—— 2003. *European Public Affairs Directory 2003.* Brussels: Landmarks Publications.

LEHMANN, W. 2009. "Lobbying the European Parliament," in D. Coen and J. Richardson, eds., *Lobbying the European Union: Institutions, Actors and Policy.* Oxford: Oxford University Press.

LONG, T., and LORINZI, L. 2009. *NGOs as Gatekeepers: A Green Vision, Lobbying the European Union. Institutions, Actors and Issues.* Oxford: Oxford University Press.

LOWERY, D. 2007. "Why do organised interests lobby? A multi-goal, multi-level theory of lobbying," *Polity* 39: 2954.

LOWI, T. 1964. "American business: public policy, case studies and political theory," *World Politics* 16: 677–715.

McLAUGHLIN, A., and JORDAN, G. 1993. "The rationality of lobbying in Europe: why are Euro-groups so numerous and so weak? Evidence from the car industry," in S. Mazey and J. Richardson, eds., *Lobbying in the European Community.* Oxford: Oxford University Press.

MAHONEY, C. 2004. "The power of institutions: state and interest groups activity in the European Union," *European Union Politics* 5(4): 441–66.

—— 2007. "Networking vs. allying: the decision of interest groups to join coalitions in the US and the EU," *Journal of European Public Policy* 14(3): 366–83.

MAJONE, G. 2005. *Dilemmas of European Integration: The Ambiguities and Pitfalls of Integration by Stealth.* Oxford: Oxford University Press.

MATTLI, W. 1999. *The Logic of Regional Integration.* Cambridge: Cambridge University Press.

MAZEY, S., and RICHARDSON, J. 1993. *Lobbying in the European Community.* Oxford: Oxford University Press.

—— —— 2005. "Interest groups and EU policy-making: organised logic and venue shopping," in J. Richardson, ed., *European Union: Power and Policy-Making.* New York: Routledge.

MOE, T. 1980. *The Organisation of Interests: Incentives and the Internal Dynamics of Political Interest Groups.* Chicago: University of Chicago Press.

OBRADOVIC, D. 2009. "Regulating lobbying in the European Union," in D. Coen and J. Richardson, eds., *Lobbying the European Union: Institutions, Actors, and Policy.* Oxford: Oxford University Press.

OLSON, M. 1965. *The Logic of Collective Action.* Cambridge, Mass.: Harvard University Press.

PIJNENBURG, B. 1998. "EU lobbying by ad-hoc coalitions: an exploratory case study," *Journal of European Public Policy* 5(2): 303–21.

POLLACK, M. 2003. *The Engines of European Integration: Delegation, Agency, and Agenda Setting in the EU.* Oxford: Oxford University Press.

RICHARDSON, J. 2006. "Policy-making in the EU: interests, ideas and garbage cans of primeval soup," in J. Richardson, ed., *European Union: Power and Policy-Making.* New York: Routledge, 3–30.

SANDHOLTZ, W., and ZYSMAN, J. 1989. "1992: recasting the European bargain," *World Politics* 95–128.

SCHARPF, F. W. 1999. "Legitimacy in the multi-actor European polity," in M. Egeberg and P. Laegreid, eds., *Organizing Political Institutions: Essays for Johan P. Olsen.* Oslo: Scandinavian University Press, 261–88.

SCHMIDT, V. 2007. *Democracy in Europe.* Oxford: Oxford University Press.

STREECK, W., and SCHMITTER, P. C. 1991. "From national corporatism to transnational pluralism," *Politics and Society* 19: 2133–65.

—— and VISSER, J. 2006. "Conclusions: organized business facing internationalization," in W. Streeck, J. Grote, V. Schneider, and J. Visser, eds., *Governing Interests. Business Associations Facing Internationalization.* London: Routledge, 242–72.

TRUMAN, D. B. 1951. *The Governmental Process: Political Interests and Public Opinion.* New York: Alfred A. Knopf.

VAN SCHENDELEN. R. 2003. *Machiavelli in Brussels: The Art of Lobbying the EU.* Amsterdam: Amsterdam University Press.

VOGEL, D. 1989. *Fluctuating Fortunes: The Political Power of Business in America.* New York: Basic Books.

WILLMAN, P, COEN, D., CURRIE, D., SINNER, M. 2003. "The evolution of regulatory relationships, regulatory institutions and firm behaviour in privatised industries," *Industrial and Corporate Change* 12(1): 69–89.

WILSON, G. 1990. "Corporations' political strategies," *British Journal of Political Science* 20: 281–8.

WOLL, C. 2006. "Lobbying in the European Union: from sui generis to a comparative perspective," *Journal of European Public Policy* 13: 456–69.

—— 2008. *Firm Interests: How Governments Shape Business Lobbying on Global Trade.* Ithaca, NY: Cornell University Press.

CHAPTER 13

BUSINESS POLITICS IN LATIN AMERICA

PATTERNS OF FRAGMENTATION AND CENTRALIZATION

BEN ROSS SCHNEIDER

> We don't have experience in the democratic game.... In the military regime, businessmen talked with at most four people: Figueiredo, Delfim, Galvêas, and the minister responsible for the sector. Decree laws resolved the rest. Today, the game is democratic ... Our main interlocutor, now, is Congress.
>
> (Antônio de Oliveira Santos, coordinator of the UBE (Dreifuss 1989: 44))

INTRODUCTION[1]

THE perception that business wields enormous power is widespread throughout Latin America. In a survey of politicians and leaders in civil society, 80 per cent

---

[*] For a list of abbreviations for this chapter, see Appendix 13.1 on p. 324.

mentioned that business exercised de facto power, and more respondents identified business than any other group or constitutional power (UNDP 2005: 155). However, the way business exercises power varies greatly across the region and sometimes within countries over time. For example, in Brazil, in a more pluralist, US-style pattern, relations are fluid and fragmented: business associations are mostly weak, especially encompassing associations, business people spend a lot on campaigns and lobbying, and they have easy access to government officials, in part because so many business people accept appointments to top government offices. In contrast, in Chile, in a more organized, structured, European-style (societal corporatist) pattern, relations between business and government are more formal, largely mediated through strong parties and business associations, and with little if any movement of business people into government positions.

More generally, business politics and participation in policy-making varies over time, across policy areas, and across countries along three interrelated dimensions. First, business participation can be collective and organized or dispersed and individual. Among industrialized countries, for example, business tends to be more organized in northern Europe and Japan, much less organized in the United States, with other English-speaking and southern Europe countries ranging in between (see Lehne 2006). Second, business input can be formal and open or informal and largely opaque. This dimension tends to co-vary with the organizational dimension but does not overlap completely. Participation through business associations is typically formal, structured, known to many, and often covered by the press. Personal networks, in contrast, involve very small numbers and are often largely invisible, even to other participants in policy-making.

Third, business input varies by the channels of influence that predominate in mediating business participation: deliberative or consultative councils, corporatist tripartite bargaining, lobbying, campaign and party finance, networks and appointments to government positions, and of course outright corruption. Business people will often avail themselves of a number of these channels simultaneously, but comparative analysis helps single out which are primary in particular countries. For example, Japan and other Asian countries have relied heavily on deliberative councils that bring together representatives of government and business to discuss a wide range of policy issues. Campaign contributions and legislative lobbying are more central to business politics in the United States and Japan than in most European countries, and obviously more important in democratic regimes than dictatorships. Lastly, the appointment of business people to top policy-making positions in government varies greatly cross-nationally, from thousands of appointments in the United States and many countries of Latin America to very few in most other industrialized countries.

How are these multifaceted and interconnected differences best characterized and conceptualized? The small comparative literature on business politics in Latin America provides limited help. One set of studies is too narrow empirically because it focuses exclusively on one or another dimension. For example, the volume organized by Francisco Durand and Eduardo Silva (1998) provides an excellent overview of business associations, but does not include much on elections, networks, or other forms of business–government relations (for other comparative studies, see Garrido 1988; Bartell and Payne 1995; Durand 1996; Schamis 1999). Another set of studies is too limited theoretically: Jeffrey Frieden's (1991) comparative study uses a deductive approach based on asset specificity and reduces business to sectoral actors with no consideration of more encompassing forms of business politics or the diverse preferences and activities of individual business people.

The alternative analytic framework offered here draws on the analogy of an investment portfolio where business distributes its political investments across a range of different activities depending on the opportunities and returns. Assessing these portfolios in different historical and national contexts allows us to identify two modal patterns, as well as permutations in between. In the more organized pattern (as in the pattern in Chile described earlier), business–government relations are largely mediated through formal channels like business associations, consultative councils, and political parties. In the more disorganized or fragmented pattern, these formal mechanisms are weaker and often displaced by more individualized, fluid, and informal relations mediated by personal networks, legislative lobbying, campaign contributions, and corruption.[2]

The major macro transformations in recent decades in Latin America—democratization and market reforms in the 1980s and 1990s, and the commodity boom of the 2000s—had important reverberations in relations between business and government. However, these reverberations have not completely made over preexisting patterns of business–government interaction, and important continuities persist in most countries; nor have the impacts of political and economic liberalization been the same across the region. The renewed power of legislatures and significance of elections has nearly everywhere drawn more attention and resources from business, especially in financing campaigns and later lobbying elected legislators. Yet, on other dimensions, democratization has had more uneven effects, displacing business associations, for example, in some countries (e.g., Mexico) and reinvigorating them elsewhere (e.g., Chile). Moreover, transitions to democracy marked dramatic shifts in some countries in the inclusion of business people in top government positions, though in opposition directions: inclusion in Mexico but exclusion in Chile and Argentina.

On the economic side, many observers expected that liberalization and the dismantling of state-led development and import substituting industrialization (ISI, roughly 1930s to 1980s) would deprive business of its usual government interlocutors and political access. Yet, while states have reduced some forms of intervention by eliminating programs and agencies, they have kept others and established new programs. So, while business and business associations may no longer be negotiating over protections and subsidies to import substituting industries, they are often in dialogue with government over trade agreements, subsidies for export sectors, and programs for technological development (see Pagés 2009). Overall, the analysis of business–government relations needs to be sensitive to the dramatic changes in the overall political economic context, but it should resist the temptation to ascribe too much, or unidirectional, force to these changes.

The rest of this chapter proceeds in several steps to analyze business politics in Latin America. The second section briefly reviews a general conceptual framework that distinguishes the sources of business preferences as well as a range of ways that business influences policy-makers. The third section takes these analytic building blocks and incorporates them into an examination of the dynamic, strategic interaction between business and government. This section develops the portfolio analysis of the range of political investments that business in Latin America typically employs, including lobbying, campaign finance, business associations, personal networks, and corruption.

SOURCES OF PREFERENCES, LEVERAGE, AND ACCESS

Scholars often mean different things when they say "business." Distinguishing among conceptual approaches to the analysis of business contrasts these meanings and illuminates the various ways that business can participate in policy-making: as capital, as sector, as firm, as association, and as individuals and participants in policy networks (Haggard, Maxfield, and Schneider 1997). These contrasting conceptions highlight the complexity of business interests and preferences as well as the variety of ways they can interact with, and influence, policy-makers (see also Martin 2006).

Through capital mobility, and especially episodes of capital flight, business can have an indirect, uncoordinated, effect as policy-makers try to anticipate policies that are likely to keep and attract capital (Mahon 1996; Maxfield 1997). While capital mobility imposes significant constraints on policy-makers, it is not a deliberate or organized form of business participation in policy-making. There have been fewer episodes of currency collapses and dramatic capital flight in the 2000s, compared with the late twentieth century, in part because the commodity boom allowed most countries to accumulate comfortable international reserves. However, short of financial melt down, more quotidian financial indicators such as interest rate spreads and bond ratings affect the movement and costs of capital for firms and governments, and depend in large part on investor perceptions of government intentions. In Brazil the election of Lula (Luis Inácio Lula da Silva) in 2002 provided a good example of investor fears and government responses. In the months leading up to the election, the spread in interest rates grew as Lula rose in the polls over fears of what policies a PT (Workers' Party) government might pursue (Vaaler, Schrage, and Block 2005). The post-election appointment of Henrique Meirelles, a former chief executive at BankBoston, to the Central Bank and other business people to top economic ministries, as well as fiscal and monetary moderation in the early months of the Lula government, had a reassuring effect on investors, and the spread steadily declined.

The contrasting corollary in other countries has been a visible correlation between a lack of external capital constraints and a range of policies antagonistic to international investors. Governments in Venezuela, Bolivia, and Ecuador all nationalized or threatened to nationalize foreign and domestic firms during the 2000s when the surge in oil prices meant these oil and gas exporters had little need for international finance. In Argentina, the Kirchner (Nestor) government (2002–8) was also antagonistic to some MNCs, less initially because of high commodity prices and international reserves but more because Argentina had just defaulted on international debts and did not have access to meaningful new credit. Thus, the actions and preferences of investors, both domestic and foreign (and the distinction is increasingly blurred by round tripping investment), significantly shape business–government interactions, even though these actions are not coordinated nor explicitly political.

The conceptual approach that focuses primarily on sectors is one of the most popular in the literature on international political economy and in many analyses of recent market-oriented reform in developing countries. This approach follows from the conventional Olsonian wisdom that businesses will be better able to overcome obstacles to collective action if they are small in number and homogeneous, as they usually are in capital-intensive sectors (Olson 1965).[3] Conceptualizing business as sector is often a useful 'first cut' because sectoral cleavages in Latin America are accentuated, and because many policies have uneven distributions of costs and benefits across sectors. Moreover, dramatic sectoral shifts in most economies over the past two decades, first out of manufacturing into services in the wake of market reforms and later into commodities and natural resources, have shifted the center of gravity of the private sector and the sectors out of which the largest firms have emerged (Schneider 2009a). These background shifts need to be factored in, but, taken alone, sectoral analysis can obscure other bases of business politics such as corporate structure, business associations, and business networks that regularly swamp sectoral considerations (Schneider 2004a: ch. 2, 2004b: 458–64).

In another conception, firms are the primary units of analysis, and business politics vary largely according to corporate structure. Two core features of corporate ownership, diversified business groups and MNCs, distinguish Latin America from other regions and have important consequences for business–government relations.[4] Diversified business groups have more encompassing interests which, combined with their huge size and small number, should in principle facilitate collective action, coordination, and regular direct contact with government. MNCs, because they can shift investment to other countries (exit), tend to be less committed interlocutors in longer term policy implementation and institution building. To the extent that MNCs influence policy more through anticipated reactions than deliberate political activity, MNCs resemble the effects of the first conception of business as capital. At a minimum ownership variables like multisectoral business groups and MNCs complicate simple deductions about business preferences on policy and straightforward predictions on their political behavior. Diversification and foreign ownership both open up exit options for firms in particular sectors. If, for example, policies threaten a stand-alone, single-sector firm, that firm is more likely to use voice and politics to change the policy. In contrast, MNCs and business groups are more likely to take the exit option because they can rely on investments in other countries or sectors.

In a network conception, the analysis turns to examining how individual business people can participate directly through appointment to government positions (or commissions and working groups) or close personal connections to top policy-makers in personal or policy networks (Teichman 2001). Personalized business-government networks can sometimes evolve out of long-standing social and kinship relations as well as common schooling and university training. More short-term network connections can also emerge out of career movement back and forth between the public and private sectors. As in the United States, most presidents in Latin America appoint thousands of people, including many from business, to top policy-making positions. There are some exceptions, notably Chile after 1990 and Mexico for most of the twentieth century, where presidents invited very few business people into government, but in most other countries business people circulate regularly in and out of government (as examined later). Such movement creates ready-made networks for sharing information and debating policy options. This network approach focuses more on the nature and extent of business access to government which is likely to be informal, individual, and opaque, and does not specify the kinds of preferences that get communicated beyond the likelihood that they are narrow and particular.

In a final conception, examined in the next section, the way business organizes and the longer institutionalization of business associations are primary factors in explaining patterns of business participation in policy-making. This consideration of various concepts of business also helps to highlight the very different sources of business preferences—based alternatively on firms, individuals, sectors, associations, or capital—and the wide range of mechanisms that can translate these preferences into pressures in politics, from capital flight to individual politicking.

PORTFOLIOS OF BUSINESS INVESTMENT IN POLITICS[5]

If business people have a range of potential preferences and a variety of political resources (funds, organization, or friends in high places), then how do they decide how to engage in politics? In principle, rational business people should balance their *portfolio* of political investments to take advantage of evolving opportunities by shifting political investments to activities that generate the greatest return. Where business concentrates its political investments is largely a function of the perceived opportunities for influence offered by the political system (see Tarrow 1998). Some aspects of the opportunity structure are relatively fixed by long-standing institutional features of the political system; other opportunities though can be created or closed off by individual policy-makers. So, while variations in overall patterns of business politics are relatively stable, they are not immutable and policy-makers can have decisive and relatively short-term impacts on those patterns. The rest of this section considers long-standing patterns and recent evolution in business investment in a range of activities including associations, consultative councils, legislative lobbying, campaign finance, networking, and corruption.

Associations

The major variations along this organizational dimension include whether associations are voluntary or state chartered (corporatist), whether they are encompassing or sectoral, whether they are based on production or employment relations, and whether they represent primarily large or small firms. In simplified terms, most of the thousands of business associations in Latin America are voluntary (save Brazil), sectoral, biased towards larger firms, and rarely geared toward bargaining collectively with labor. Where countries manifest greater variation is in the strength of broader encompassing associations (Table 13.1).[6] On this dimension countries like Mexico, Chile, and Colombia follow a more European or Japanese model of business organization compared to a more 'American' style of fragmentation in Brazil and Argentina. Among the remaining larger countries, Peru and Venezuela both had economy-wide encompassing associations in CONFIEP and Fedecamaras, respectively, though CONFIEP has faded in importance (Hernandez 2008). Almost all the smaller countries, with the significant exception of Uruguay, have economy-wide encompassing associations (see Durand and Silva 1998).

The mere existence of stable, well-staffed voluntary encompassing associations is one good indicator of the amounts prominent capitalists invest in collective action. The rough estimates of staff give a further proxy useful for comparing across countries the material investments members make in their associations. Other indicators of organizational strength would include the time business people invest in associations and the quality of internal representation. Although they cannot be summarized in a table, historical instances of organizational capacity to aggregate or reconcile member interests were more common in the histories of encompassing associations in Mexico, Chile, and Colombia than in Argentina and Brazil.[7]

Beyond economy-wide associations, wide variation also exists among encompassing associations for industry and for agriculture.[8] Agricultural associations were some of the first to form in the region though most had faded as organizations by the late twentieth century, save some in narrower sectors like coffee (Federacafe). Agricultural associations tended to be stronger in countries with less diversified agriculture and larger landholdings, as in Chile, Argentina, and Colombia (Smith 1969; Wright 1982). In industry, Chile and Colombia had the strongest voluntary associations in the region. The industry association in Argentina, UIA, enjoyed some periods of strength but after the 1940s always suffered from internal division and

Table 13.1 Voluntary encompassing associations

	Association	Scope	Staff
Strong encompassing associations			
Mexico	Coparmex (1929–)	economy-wide	30
	CMHN (1962–)	economy-wide	0
	CCE (1975–)	economy-wide	80
Chile	CPC (1935–)	economy-wide	8
	Sofofa (1883–)	industry	50
Colombia	Federacafe (1927–)	coffee	3,500
	ANDI (1944–)	industry	150
	Consejo Gremial (1991–)	economy-wide	3
Venezuela	Fedecamaras	economy-wide	20
Weak encompassing associations			
Argentina	ACIEL (1958–73)	economy-wide	0
	APEGE (1975–6)	economy-wide	0
	CGE (1952–)	economy-wide	10?
	UIA (1886–)	industry	50
	AEA (2002–)	economy-wide	8
Brazil	UBE (1987–8)	economy-wide	few to none
	IEDI (1989–)	industry	8
	Ação Empresarial (1990s–)	economy-wide	0
Peru	Confiep	economy-wide	

Note: Figures for staff are rough estimates for average total employment in the last quarter of the twentieth century. See Appendix 13.1 for abbreviations.

Sources: Updated and expanded from Schneider (2004a: 7); Hernandez (2008); Ortiz (2004).

competition from rival associations. Non-voluntary, corporatist associations in Mexico (through 1997) and Brazil gave industry federations the appearance of institutional strength, but behind the façade they were much weaker, in large part due to state controls on internal organization. These controls were especially debilitating in Brazil where the regional structure of representation gave marginal industry federations from states in the rural north-east control of the national industry confederation, CNI.

Business associations participate in policy-making in a number of ways. First, leaders of associations appear regularly in the press. Newspapers often assign reporters to cover business associations, and they contact associations almost daily for reactions to government announcements and breaking economic news. In addition, associations invest in their own press and dissemination departments, and call press conferences to announce policy positions. Some associations also have sophisticated research departments that collect data relevant to sectoral performance. Associations use the opportunity of announcing, say, monthly employment statistics to comment on policy issues of the day. Some leaders contend that this press presence may be the most important lever, albeit indirect, that business has to influence policy.[9] This exposure is quite different from countries like the United States where leaders of associations almost never appear in the mass media.

Leaders of associations also talk directly to policy-makers. Associations may invite officials to events or to make presentations, or associations may ask for appointments. For instance, an annual report to the members on the activities of the president of the economy-wide CCE in Mexico noted dozens of meetings with various cabinet ministers (CCE 1987). These meetings are often ad hoc and called to address conjunctural issues, but in some countries meetings are more routinized. Again in Mexico, the CMHN hosted monthly luncheons and the CCE monthly dinners mostly with ministers from the economic area. It is often unclear exactly what influence these meals have on policy, but they certainly expand access and dialogue.

In other cases governments institutionalize business input into policy-making or oversight councils. These fora, sometimes called consultative or deliberative councils, are typically granted functional authority over certain policy areas that can range from broad macro issues such as monetary policy and stabilization plans to labor issues like minimum wages and training, to narrow technical issues like animal husbandry. These councils have fixed membership that usually includes representatives from relevant ministries and business associations. A small number of councils also include representatives from labor or other organized social groups. In Venezuela, for example, various governments from the 1960s to the 1980s created 330 advisory commissions and 362 decentralized agencies, most with some representation by business associations (Monaldi et al. 2008: 383–4 citing Crisp 2000). Once invited to join councils, associations usually create or expand professional research departments to make sure their council representatives have the necessary background information (Silva 1996). Lastly, governments may grant complete policy authority, along with public resources, to associations. For example, the Colombian coffee confederation, Federacafe, had control over an export tax and other resources and was responsible for financing, promoting, and marketing Colombian coffee. Brazilian industry federations receive a 1 per cent payroll tax to promote worker training; the government collects the tax but turns it over to federations that decide alone how to spend it.

Fora and councils that bring business and government together merit more attention both because they have been so crucial to policy-making and development elsewhere, notably East Asia (Schwartz 1992; Campos and Root 1996), and because they continue to be an important and recurring locus for business–government interaction in Latin America. Deliberative or consultative councils proliferated into various policy areas over the decades of ISI, but over time many of these councils faded into disuse, and many were decommissioned in the wake of market reforms after 1990. However, some councils maintained their importance, and governments created new councils after the 1990s to manage new challenges of economic integration and globalization (Schneider 2009b). Most prominent among these were the councils set up to accompany trade negotiations, especially in Mexico (Thacker 2000);

Chile (Bull 2008); Colombia (Giacalone 1999); and later Brazil (Oliveira 2003). Other governments, especially in Chile, have created ongoing fora to deliberate on competitiveness, technology, and innovation (Muñoz 2000).

One of the more visible initiatives was the decision of the incoming Lula government in 2002 to create the Council for Economic and Social Development (CDES) (Doctor 2007; Vizeu and Bin 2008). The government structured CDES to have representation of labor and business (as well as government and civil society) but had very different approaches to the invitations to each side. Representatives from the labor side were union leaders, yet nearly two-thirds of the business members were not leaders of business associations.[10] The government preferred instead to invite individual businessmen, in a way that fits with the conception of business as network. Over the course of Lula's two terms, CDES had some influence in broad policy debates, but less than its proponents hoped, or critics feared.

Participation in deliberative councils is one of the sources of the wide variation across Latin America in the strength of business associations. As Olson (1965) would expect, most strong associations provide some selective benefit to members only, ranging from control over an export tax in the case of Federacafe, to a genealogical registry for cattle in Sociedad Rural Argentina, to monthly luncheons with ministers for CMHN. Furthermore, in most cases the most significant benefits are granted by the state. In cases where the state granted control over public funds to associations, firms had incentives to join the association and contribute to its institutional strength. Less tangible benefits, such as regular access to top policy-makers or to policy-making councils, also encouraged business people to join associations, as well as contribute to and participate in them.[11]

The consolidation of democracy across the region largely eliminated the pivotal role business associations sometimes played in regime change during the twentieth century. Previously business associations were prominent in clamoring for the end to democratic regimes in Chile and Argentina in the 1970s and supported authoritarian regimes in these countries as well as Mexico. On the side of democracy, Colombian associations sometimes rallied to support democratic governments in times of crisis in the 1960s, and Brazilian business, though more as individuals than association, helped convince the generals in the late 1970s to return to the barracks. By the 2000s, few associations were debating the merits of democracy. The exception was Fedecamaras in Venezuela, which joined in opposing Hugo Chávez in the early 2000s. This opposition reached its tragicomic climax when Pedro Carmona, the president of Fedecamaras, assumed the presidency in an unsuccessful, two-day coup against Chávez. But, in most of the rest of the region, the issue of whether or not business associations support democracy is no longer a major question.

Legislative lobbying

Democratization opened up more avenues for business participation in policy-making, particularly through political parties and congress. Systematic data are lacking, but available evidence and press coverage suggest that lobbying is increasingly routine. As business moves to invest more in lobbying the legislature, its influence tends to become more fragmented and particularistic, and therefore ineffectual on general issues, what Diniz and Boschi (2004) call an 'Americanization' of business politics. The sources of this fragmentation are several. For one, individual contributors are likely to seek legislators' assistance on issues relating specifically to their firms such as resolving particular administrative problems in the bureaucracy.

Moreover, business associations, by custom or legal restriction, do not contribute to political campaigns, and their influence with legislators is likely to be less than major contributors who tend to come from individual firms. An interesting exception, which tends to prove the general rule, is the sophisticated lobbying operation of the CNI, Brazil's national industry confederation. Its lobbying wing COAL (Coordenação de Assuntos Legislativos) grew from a small operation in Brasília in the late 1980s to a large and sophisticated lobby in the 1990s (interview with Carlos Alberto Cidade, director of COAL, May 27, 1995). By the mid-1990s COAL had twenty-one employees and accounted for close to half of CNI staff in Brasília (see Mancuso 2007). In contrast, legislative lobbying in the economy-wide CCE in Mexico was still incipient by 2003, in part because the legislature only began exercising a more active policy role after 1997 when the president's party lost its majority in Congress for the first time in many decades (interview with Luiz Miguel Pando, Director General, CCE, February 26, 2003).

Electoral politics, parties, and campaign contributions

In February 1993, at a private dinner with several dozen wealthy businessmen, President Carlos Salinas de Gortari asked them to donate $25 million each to the PRI to help finance the election of his successor (Oppenheimer 1998: 83–8). Press reports of the dinner generated heated debate and portended important changes in politics in Latin America (the possible privatization of the PRI, not least among them). For one, redemocratization in the region would inevitably lead to ever more expensive campaigns and require governments to decide how they would be financed. And, as the Salinas dinner made clear, big money was most likely to come from big business.

Over the last decade most of the large countries of Latin America reformed the legal framework for campaign finance (Griner and Zovatto 2004). Although complex and varied, several patterns emerge in campaign finance laws in the region (Payne et al. 2002). Most legal frameworks prohibit foreign contributions, maintain some public funding, limit maximum contributions, and provide some free media access. Smaller numbers of countries have a wide range of other restrictions including prohibitions on paid advertising, or contributions from government contractors and business associations, as well as different stipulations on eligibility for public funding. Taken together these laws represent a systematic effort to limit the private cost of elections and to reduce dependence on business contributions, both overall and by particular kinds of business. Nonetheless, a lot of money flows from business into elections, both legally and illegally. There are few studies of compliance, but sporadic evidence from Latin America, as well as experiences in other consolidated democracies, suggest that there are many ways to circumvent restrictions on business contributions.[12]

Several factors fragment and attenuate the influence of these contributions. Most contributions flow from individual business people to individual candidates which greatly narrows the interests represented and the ability of business to mobilize collective influence on issues of general interest to business. Several features though weaken this individualized influence. For one, turnover is very high in most legislatures (100 per cent in Mexico, by law) so that incumbents, once in office, have few incentives to heed their contributors. Moreover, very large contributors are likely, as in the United States, to give to both sides, as insurance to be sure the winner does not retaliate. In the 2002 elections in Colombia, for example, the grupo Santo Domingo, one of the four leading conglomerates, gave $300,000 to Uribe and $300,000 to his closest contender (Njaim 2004). Such electoral promiscuity is not likely to enhance contributors' policy influence, though it may keep channels of access open.

A study of campaign finance in Brazil listed more than a dozen scandals involving major alleged infractions of Brazil's electoral law in the twenty years since the return of freer and competitive elections in the 1980s (Fleischer 2002). The long list confirms several suspicions about campaign finance: (1) that laws are difficult to enforce and easy to circumvent; (2) irregularities and scandals involve all major parties, from left to right, and all levels, from municipal to presidential campaigns; and (3) in cases where the scandal reported alleged post-election favoritism for business contributors it was mostly in the form of individualized benefits, as in privatization policies, rather than collective influence on broad policy issues.

Business people could have more collective input through elections and legislatures if they had sustained, 'organic' connections to programmatic, pro-business political parties. However, such parties have historically been rare in Latin America (Gibson 1996). The best contemporary examples are found in Mexico and Chile. Northern business in Mexico was instrumental in creating the PAN, though business influence was diluted as the PAN evolved into one of the dominant mass parties of the 2000s (Mizrahi 2003). In Chile, business established close informal, financial, and programmatic ties with the two main parties on the right, UDI and RN (Fairfield 2007; Pribble 2008). However, these parties stand out as exceptions that highlight the rule rather than signal a coming trend.

Networks

In most countries informal personal relations connect at least some economic and government elites. These connections can result from family ties, attending the same schools (usually private) and universities, studying abroad, or overlapping in previous career stages. In Latin America, high socio-economic stratification and geographic concentration in capital cities facilitate the formation of elite networks. It is often difficult to tell what impact these networks have on policy-making, in part because the relations are informal and opaque, when not deliberately secretive. Analysts argue that intense networks can contribute to everything from shared world views to spot transactions and policies designed to favor only the firms of particular network participants (see Teichman 2001). At a minimum personal networks open up channels of access and communication. In terms of the portfolio analogy, to the extent that business people feel they have sufficient access through informal networks, they will have weaker incentives to invest in other formal channels like business associations or election campaigns.

The extent of networks is difficult to measure empirically. The most in-depth network analysis in Latin America covers Mexico during the years of PRI dominance (Smith 1979; Camp 1989; Centeno 1994).[13] This research documented the remarkable and long-standing absence of networks linking economic and political elites. On the other end of the spectrum, public and private elites in Colombia seem in most periods to be thoroughly networked and interconnected. Although not as extensively documented as in Mexico, many political elites in Colombia follow careers that weave in and out of government and private firms or business associations (Juárez 1995; Schneider 2004a: 148–50). Table 13.2 provides some further comparisons among recent governments in terms of the number of business people appointed to the cabinet. This table confirms both the expected expansion of business people in the Fox government in Mexico, as well as the continued patterns of business representation in governments in Colombia and exclusion in Concertación governments in Chile.

Some public–private network relations may result from decades of social interaction, others can be created overnight by political appointments of business people to government. In Mexico, the inauguration of Vicente Fox in 2000 transformed from one day to the next the relative absence of personal networks between business and government. Fox was himself an ex-businessman (and therefore had personal connections of his own to many business people) and also appointed other ministers from the private sector. Even in countries with fairly long-standing traditions of appointing business people as in Colombia, Brazil, and Argentina, practices can vary widely from one government to the next. In Brazil, for example, Presidents Fernando

Table 13.2 Business appointees in recent government cabinets

	President	Number of business appointees	Percentage of business appointees
Argentina	Kirchner	0	0
	Duhalde	1	8
	De la Rua	1	9
Chile	Lagos	0	0
Colombia	Uribe	7	54
Mexico	Fox	5	25
Peru	Toledo	7	27

Note: Compiled from government and periodical sources with data through 2005.

Collor and, as noted earlier, Lula appointed more prominent representatives of the private sector as ministers than did President Fernando Henrique Cardoso.[14]

From a broader comparative perspective, a common American pattern of appointing business people has emerged. It is not just a Latin American phenomenon because it is common in the United States as well as most of Latin America, and contrasts sharply with patterns in most of the rest of the world. For the most part these networks seem to bias policies generally in favor of business though not necessarily in particularistic ways. Some exceptions include Chile in the 1970s and Argentina under Menem. In these instances of "crony capitalism" (a term best reserved for these kinds of exclusive networks and particularistic policy benefits) political leaders appointed business people from a few of the largest conglomerates and thereby established very narrow and closed networks. Many of the early policies enacted by these governments in turn favored the few firms represented in these networks (Silva 1996; Etchemendy 2001; Teichman 2001; Schamis 2002).

Corruption

Beyond legal forms of participation in policy-making, business sometimes buys influence directly. For business participants, corruption, like legislative lobbying, is likely to be fragmented and individual (rather than collective) and designed to generate benefits for particular firms. According to indices compiled by Transparency International, levels of perceived corruption vary widely across Latin America. In the overall rankings, the countries in Table 13.3 cluster in three groups. A "cleaner" set that includes Chile, Costa Rica, and Uruguay is grouped around the least corrupt quartile. A middle group comprised of Brazil, Colombia, Mexico, and Peru hovers just above the median. And three countries perceived as more corrupt—Argentina, Venezuela, and Bolivia—cluster around the bottom quartile.

Overall it is difficult to relate these corruption rankings directly to different patterns of business politics. First, it is important to remember that these rankings are based on opinion surveys (and some rankings have been sensitive to scandals that appear in the media).[15] Second, they are aggregate measures that do not separate out specific forms of business corruption or gauge if business is the primary protagonist. However, it is still worth noting these rankings at least to signal the possibility that corruption is a more likely form of business influence in countries ranked toward the bottom than in those at the top of the list.

Portfolio distribution and opportunity structure

In the absence of a simpler way to capture a composite picture of cross-national variations, Table 13.4 offers a rough comparative assessment of how business distributes its political investments across major countries of the region. As noted at the beginning of this section, business people have incentives to rebalance their portfolios of political investments to take advantage of the opportunities offered by the political system. In countries where policy-makers pay less attention to associations, as in Brazil and Argentina, business tends not to invest much time or money in them.

Table 13.3 Perceived corruption in Latin America, 1996 and 2004

	1996			2004			Change in score 1996 to 2004
	Score	Rank	Percentile	Score	Rank	Percentile	
Low							
Chile	6.8	21	.38	7.4	20	.14	+ .6
Uruguay				6.2	28	.19	
Costa Rica				4.9	41	.28	
Medium							
Brazil	3.0	40	.74	3.9	59	.41	+ .9
Colombia	2.7	42	.77	3.8	60	.41	+ 1.1
Mexico	3.3	38	.70	3.6	64	.44	+ .3
Peru				3.5	67	.46	
High							
Argentina	3.4	35	.64	2.5	108	.74	− .9
Venezuela	2.5	48	.88	2.3	114	.78	− .2
Bolivia	3.4	36	.66	2.2	122	.84	− 1.2

Source: Transparency International index for 1996 and 2004. The surveys included 54 countries in 1996 and 145 in 2004.

Where government leaders have institutionalized business input through associations, then business people have strong incentives to invest in associations and build institutional capacity for long-term intermediation. This was evident historically in Chile, Colombia, and Mexico, and in the 1990s in trade negotiations, in particular in Mexico and Chile. These countries then tend to the more structured and organized end of the spectrum of business–government relations. Lacking a central role for associations, investments by business in Argentina, Brazil, and post-2000 Mexico tend to be more dispersed into more individual, fragmented, and often informal relations. Table 13.4 ranks business politics in descending order from more organized and structured to more fragmented and dispersed. Germany and the United States are also included for comparative benchmarks and representative examples of, respectively, more organized and more fragmented business politics.

The political evolution in Chile following democratization in 1990 offers a good illustration of the opportunity structure for business participation in politics. The Chilean political system in the 1990s continued to favor investment in associations, though the major sectoral associations gradually displaced the economy-wide CPC as the main policy discussions with the government shifted from macro issues to trade, competitiveness, and sectoral promotion (see Muñoz 2000). More importantly for a portfolio analysis, the Chilean political system does not offer many opportunities for alternative political investments (see Aninat et al. 2008). For example, the executive branch dominates in policy-making, but it is relatively insulated from direct lobbying and from personal networks since no business people have been appointed to Concertación cabinets. Moreover, the bureaucracy is more professionalized and

Table 13.4 Estimates of portfolio distribution

	Parties and elections	Lobbying Congress	Business associations	Networks	Corruption
Chile, 1990–	medium	low	high	Low	low
Mexico, 1990s	low	low	high	Low	medium
Colombia	medium	low	high	High	medium
Brazil 1990s	medium	medium	low	medium	medium
Argentina 1990s	medium	medium	low	medium	high
Mexico 2000–	medium	medium	medium	medium	medium
Germany	low	low	high	low	low
United States	high	high	low	high	low

Sources: Rough rankings based largely on preceding text. For the United States and Germany, see Lehne (2006). The estimates for the first two columns are the roughest. The rankings for the last three columns are derived from Tables 13.1, 13.2, and 13.3.

Weberian than the mean for Latin America, and perceived corruption is corresponding low (Chile is ranked the lowest in Latin America, just behind the United States (TI 2004: 4–5; see also Stein et al. 2005). Although they lack widespread individual access and influence that is common elsewhere in the region, Chilean business, as noted earlier, invests more in collective fashion in political parties. In sum, the Chilean political system is generally less porous and deflects or shunts business politicking into councils, associations, and parties, thereby making business politics in Chile more structured and organized. This is not to deny that business has great influence in Chile, but more to say that the influence is channeled in more organized fashion.

CONCLUSIONS

Although the range of political options and opportunities will vary, the portfolio framework could be extended to other regions, especially to identify common trends and significant contrasts. In broader inter-regional comparisons, several aspects of business–government relations in Latin America would likely stand out as distinctive. One particular aspect that sets the Americas, both North and South, apart from most of the rest of the world is the high number of business people appointed to top positions in the executive bureaucracy. Other differences stand out in comparisons with East Asia (though other south-east Asian countries resemble Latin America). For example, MNCs are a larger part of the private sector in Latin America than in East Asia which can complicate collective action, as noted earlier, and make policy-makers more sensitive to concerns over capital mobility. In addition, East Asian governments have relied more heavily on deliberative and consultative councils, providing associations with more input into policy implementation (if not always policy-making) (Campos and Root 1996). Despite these significant differences, business in most other developing and democratizing contexts has also, as in Latin America, shifted more political investments into parties and elections, though few business communities have developed close organic ties to established parties.

In comparison with more developed countries, another contrast stands out—the absence of similar levels of organization on the part of business and labor. For most developed countries, business and labor have similar levels of associational structure, coverage, and activity, often organized partly in response to one another (Schmitter and Streeck 1999), ranging from fragmentation of both business and labor in the more liberal economies such as the United States to concentration and centralization on both sides in northern Europe (with centralized business and fragmented labor, Japan is an important exception to this isomorphism). However, in Latin America the correlation is either negative or absent as labor is quite weak in some countries where business is best organized (Chile and Colombia) and strong where business is fragmented (Argentina), with some cases of greater isomorphism, as in Mexico (both sides concentrated) and Peru (both sides fragmented). A possible hypothesis for the lack of a clear relationship is the fact that labor relations are more closely mediated by the state in Latin America, and business and labor have historically rarely negotiated directly with one another without state accompaniment.

A core conceptual goal of this chapter was to elaborate a framework for classifying different patterns of business politics in the region by the intensity and prominence of business investment in a portfolio of political activities from associations to campaigns to bribery. Composite snapshots allow us to identify a continuum ranging from more organized, structured, and centripetal politics as in Chile to more fluid, dispersed, and centrifugal politics in Brazil, with other countries in the region in between. These variations raise important theoretical issues on the origins and durability of these patterns. The analysis in this chapter takes these variations largely as given; other work traces the origins of these variations back to accumulated state actions that either favored or discouraged organization and close collaboration in policy-making (Schneider 2004a). A core finding of that research was that the more state actors drew business associations into policy-making and the more government officials delegated responsibility for policy implementation to associations, the greater were business incentives to invest in the institutional capacity of these associations. Although policy-makers rarely had strengthening associations as a policy priority, the fact that these state actions affected business organization and participation in policy makes clear that these outcomes could in fact be objects of policy. At a minimum, strengthening incentives for collective action could be one of the important "externalities" that policy-makers consider when evaluating policy alternatives.

Variations in business politics also have important implications for policy-making. For one, more organized business interlocutors expand the range of instruments and mechanisms that policy-makers can use. The most noticeable cases are economy-wide policies such as stabilization, crisis management, and overall trade agreements where governments in countries with well-organized business sectors can engage in collective negotiations and implementation, as seen in Chile and Mexico in the 1990s, while governments dealing with more fragmented business communities (Brazil and Argentina) could not.[16] Business in less organized systems tends to concentrate political investments on narrower, particularistic benefits, which at the extreme tends to the divisive struggles of Olsonian distributional coalitions. Yet, business fragmentation can also give state actors greater autonomy and open up opportunities for policy-makers to extract more resources from business, as suggested by the higher rates of taxation in Brazil and Argentina compared to Chile (Fairfield 2007). Thus, while more concentrated, organized business politics expands policy options in some areas, it can narrow them in others.

APPENDIX 13.1 ABBREVIATIONS

ACIEL	Acción Coordinadora de las Instituciones Empresariales Libres, Argentina
AE	Ação Empresarial, Brazil
AEA	Asociación Empresaria Argentina
ANDI	Asociación Nacional de Industriales, Colombia
APEGE	Asamblea Permanente de Entidades Gremiales Empresarias, Argentina
CCE	Consejo Coordinador Empresarial, Mexico
CDES	Conselho de Desenvolvimento Econômico e Social, Brazil
CGE	Confederación General Económica, Argentina
CMHN	Consejo Mexicano de Hombres de Negocios
CNI	Confederação Nacional de Indústria, Brazil
CONFIEP	Confederación Nacional de Instituciones Empresariales Privadas, Peru
Coparmex	Confederación Patronal de la República Mexicana
CPC	Confederación de la Producción y del Comercio, Chile
Fedecamaras	Federación Venezolana de Cámaras y Asociaciones de Comercio y Producción
Federacafe	Federación Nacional de Cafeteros de Colombia
FIESP	Federação da Indústria do Estado de São Paulo
FTAA	Free Trade Area of the Americas
IEDI	Instituto de Estudos de Desenvolvimento Industrial, Brazil
PAN	Partido de Acción Nacional, Mexico
PRI	Partido Revolucionario Institucional, Mexico
PT	Partido dos Trabalhadores, Brazil
RN	Renovación Nacional, Chile
Sinduscon	Sindicato da Indústria da Construção Civil do Estado de São Paulo
Sofofa	Sociedad de Fomento Fabril, Chile

UBE	União Brasileira de Empresários
UDI	Unión Demócrata Independiente, Chile
UIA	Unión Industrial Argentina

Notes

1. I am grateful to Maria Florencia Guerzovich for research assistance and to David Coen, Kent Eaton, and workshop participants at the Interamerican Development Bank for useful comments on earlier versions. A more extensive version of this chapter is forthcoming in 2010.
2. These distinctions are similar to the conventional dichotomies of pluralism and corporatism (Schmitter 1974), but the portfolio approach goes beyond the single dimension of associations to consider a fuller range of political activities by business which may also vary from more fragmented and individualized to more centralized and collective.
3. Later approaches deepened the theoretical underpinnings with more elaborate conceptualizations of asset specificity: the more specific a firm's assets, the more likely it is to engage in collective action and politics (Shafer 1994).
4. For recent reviews on business groups, see Khanna and Yafeh (2007) generally and Schneider (2008) on Latin America. Firm size also differentiates business preferences in politics (Thacker 2000; Shadlen 2004). Another striking characteristic of firms of all sizes in Latin America is the persistence of family ownership and management. This variable has not been extensively researched or theorized, but there are good reasons to expect the political behavior of firms to differ according to whether or not they are run by family owners or professional managers.
5. Parts of a previous version of this section are summarized in Stein et al. (2005).
6. The table and other evidence on associations are drawn, unless otherwise noted, from Schneider (2004a).
7. Institutional or organizational strength refers to these internal characteristics—material resources and internal intermediation—not to the amount of power or influence of the association in the political system.
8. Commerce and finance are other major sectors with significant associational activity; however there is less variation across the region. Commerce associations tend to be weak, largely because they organize so many thousands of small retailers, except at the municipal level. Financial and banking associations in contrast tend everywhere to be strong and well organized, largely because they organize a small number of very large firms, except where they are divided between foreign and domestic firms, which was increasingly the case by the 2000s (Martinez-Diaz 2009).
9. Interview with Jorge Blanco Villegas, president of UIA, 1993–7, May 3, 2000. Analyses of Colombian associations emphasize their strong presence in the media (Urrutia 1983: 45, 82). Media exposure may be one of the factors that encourages some former association leaders to run for elected office.
10. Moreover, the government bypassed the national industry confederation whose president was not invited and included the heads of major state-level industry associations as well as sectoral associations in areas like banking, capital goods, and auto production.
11. Business also made significant collective investments in policy-oriented think tanks in some countries, including Colombia (ANIF for example), Argentina (FIEL and Fundación Mediterranea), Chile (IEP). Business-oriented think tanks were less prominent in Brazil

and Mexico, though some Mexican associations like Coparmex and CCE had large research and policy departments.

12. Another way that electoral politics opens up avenues for business influence is for business people to run for office themselves. In Brazil, for example, estimates of the percentage of deputies with business backgrounds range from a quarter to a half of deputies elected between 1985 and 2002 (see Schneider 2004a: ch. 4). In Mexico, former president Vicente Fox and many Panistas had business backgrounds. More permissive electoral systems and weak parties, as in Brazil, likely open more opportunities for business people to run for office.

13. The greater scholarly attention paid to networks in Mexico is partly the result of better data (the government published biographical information on all top policy-makers) and partly due to the importance of networks in intra-elite politics generally.

14. Marcílio Marques Moreira, Collor's minister of the economy in 1991–2, had a long career in banking. In his first term, Lula's main business appointees were Roberto Rodrigues (Agriculture), Luis Furlan (Development), and Henrique Meirelles (Central Bank).

15. See Sampford et al. (2006) for a full debate on the merits of perception-based corruption indices.

16. See Gerring and Thacker (2008) for a general defense of the benefits of centripetal over centrifugal political systems.

REFERENCES

ANINAT, C., LONDREGAN, J., NAVIA, P., and VIAL, J. 2008. "Political institutions, policymaking processes, and policy outcomes in Chile," in E. Stein and M. Tommasi, eds., *Policy Making in Latin America*. Washington, DC: Interamerican Development Bank.

BARTELL, E., and PAYNE, L., eds. 1995. *Business and Democracy in Latin America*. Pittsburgh: University of Pittsburgh Press.

BULL, B. 2008. "Policy networks and business participation in free trade negotiations in Chile," *Journal of Latin American Studies* 40(2): 195–224.

CAMP, R. 1989. *Entrepreneurs and Politics in Twentieth-Century Mexico*. New York: Oxford University Press.

CAMPOS, J., and ROOT, H. 1996. *The Key to the Asian Miracle: Making Shared Growth Credible*. Washington, DC: Brookings Institution.

CCE. 1987. "Informe de labores que el ing. Claudio X. González, Presidente del CCE, presenta al Consejo Directivo de Dicha Institución por el periódo 1985–87." México, DF: Consejo Coordinador Empresarial.

CENTENO, M. 1994. *Democracy within Reason: Technocratic Revolution in Mexico*. University Park: Pennsylvania State University Press.

CRISP, B. 2000. *Democratic Institutional Design: The Powers and Incentives of Venezuelan Politicians and Interest Groups*. Stanford, Calif.: Stanford University Press.

DINIZ, E., and BOSCHI, R. 2004. *Empresarios, interesses e mercado: Dilemas do desenvolvimento no Brasil*. Belo Horizonte: Editora UFMG.

DOCTOR, M. 2007. "Lula's Development Council: neo-corporatism and policy reform in Brazil," *Latin American Perspectives* 34(6): 131–48.

DREIFUSS, R. 1989. *O jogo da direita na nova república*. Petrópolis: Vozes.

DURAND, F. 1996. *Incertidumbre y soledad: reflexiones sobre los grandes empresarios de América Latina*. Lima: Friedrich Ebert.

—— and SILVA, E. 1998. *Organized Business, Economic Change, and Democracy in Latin America*. Miami: North-South Center Press.

ETCHEMENDY, S. 2001. "Constructing reform coalitions: the politics of compensations in Argentina's economic liberalization," *Latin American Politics and Society* 43b(3): 1–35.

FAIRFIELD, T. 2007. "The politics of taxing Latin American elites: the corporate income tax in Chile and interest income in Argentina," presented at Latin American Studies Association, Montreal.

FLEISCHER, D. 2002. "Financiamento de campanhas políticas: Brasil tenta regulamentação e melhor fiscalização," in G. Caetano et al., eds., *Dinero y política*. Montevideo: La Banda Oriental.

FRIEDEN, J. 1991. *Debt, Development, and Democracy*. Princeton: Princeton University Press.

GARRIDO, C., ed. 1988. *Empresarios y estado en América Latina*. México: CIDE.

GERRING, J., and THACKER, S. C. 2008. *A Centripetal Theory of Democratic Governance*. New York: Cambridge University Press.

GIACALONE, R. 1999. *Los empresarios frente al Grupo de Los Tres*. Caracas: Nueva Sociedad.

GIBSON, E. 1996. *Class and Conservative Parties: Argentina in Comparative Perspective*. Baltimore: Johns Hopkins University Press.

GRINER, S., and ZOVATTO, D., eds. 2004. *De las normas a las buenas prácticas: el desafío del financiamiento político en América Latina*. San José: Organización de los Estados Americanos/IDEA.

HAGGARD, S., MAXFIELD, S., and SCHNEIDER, B. R. 1997. "Alternative theories of business and business–state relations," in S. Maxfield and B. R. Schneider, eds., *Business and the State in Developing Countries*. Ithaca, NY: Cornell University Press.

HERNANDEZ, M. 2008. "The state, capital, and economic statecraft: the political economy of state–business relations in Peru and Chile," Ph.D. dissertation, University of Oxford.

JUÁREZ, C. 1995. "The political economy of economic policy reform in Colombia: technocratic bureaucracy and business–government relations, 1966–92," Ph. dissertation, University of California, Los Angeles.

KHANNA, T., and YAFEH, Y. 2007. "Business groups in emerging markets: paragons or parasites?" *Journal of Economic Literature* 45: 331–72.

LEHNE, R. 2006. *Government and Business: American Political Economy in Comparative Perspective*. Washington, DC: CQ Press.

MAHON, J. 1996. *Mobile Capital and Latin American Development*. University Park: Pennsylvania State University Press.

MANCUSO, W. 2007. *O lobby da indústria no Congresso Nacional: empresariado e política no Brasil contemporâneo*. São Paulo: FAPESP.

MARTIN, C. J. 2006. "Consider the source! Determinants of corporate preferences for public policy," in D. Coen and W. Grant, eds., *Business and Government*. Farmington Hills, Mich.: Barbara Budrich.

MARTINEZ-DIAZ, L. 2009. *Waiting for the Barbarians: The Politics of Banking-Sector Opening in the Emerging World*. Ithaca, NY: Cornell University Press.

MAXFIELD, S. 1997. *Gatekeepers of Growth: The International Political Economy of Central Banking in Developing Countries*. Princeton: Princeton University Press.

MIZRAHI, Y. 2003. *From Martyrdom to Power: The Partido Acción Nacional in Mexico*. Notre Dam, Ind.: University of Notre Dame Press.

MONALDI, F., GONZÁLEZ, R., OBUCHI, R., and PENFOLD, M. 2008. "Political institutions, policymaking in Venezuela: the rise and collapse of political cooperation," in E. Stein and

Mariano Tommasi, eds., *Policy Making in Latin America*. Washington, DC: Interamerican Development Bank.

Muñoz, O., ed. 2000. *El estado y el sector privado*. Santiago: Dolmen.

Njaim, H. 2004. "Financiamiento político en los países andinos: Bolivia, Colombia, Ecuador, Perú y Venezuela," in S. Griner and D. Zovatto, eds., *De las normas a las buenas prácticas*. San José: Organización de los Estados Americanos/IDEA.

Oliveira, A. 2003. "O papel da coalizão empresarial brasileira e as negociações da ALCA," dissertation, Departamento de Ciência Política, Universidade de São Paulo.

Olson, M. 1965. *The Logic of Collective Action*. Cambridge, Mass.: Harvard University Press.

Oppenheimer, A. 1998. *Bordering on Chaos: Mexico's Roller-Coaster Journey Toward Prosperity*. Boston: Little, Brown, & Co.

Ortíz, N. 2004. "Entrepreneurs: profits without power?" in J. McCoy and D. Myers, eds., *The Unraveling of Representative Democracy in Venezuela*. Baltimore: Johns Hopkins University Press.

Pagés, C. 2009. *Productivity in Latin America*. Washington, DC: IDB.

Payne, J. M., Zovatto, D., Carrillo, F., and Allamand, A. 2002. *Democracies in Development: Politics and Reform in Latin America*. Washington, DC: Inter-American Development Bank.

Pribble, J. 2008. "Protecting the poor: welfare politics in Latin America's free market era," Ph.D. dissertation, University of North Carolina at Chapel Hill.

Sampford, C., Shacklock, A., Connors, C., and Galtung, F., eds. 2006. *Measuring Corruption*. Aldershot: Ashgate.

Schamis, H. 1999. "Distributional coalitions and the politics of economic reform in Latin America," *World Politics* 51(2): 236–68.

—— 2002. *Re-Forming the State: The Politics of Privatization in Latin America and Europe*. Ann Arbor: University of Michigan Press.

Schmitter, P. 1974. "Still the century of corporatism?" *Review of Politics* 36(1): 85–121.

—— and Streeck, W. 1999. "The organization of business interests: studying the associative action of business in advanced industrial societies," MPIfG Discussion Paper 99/1 (originally distributed in 1981), Cologne.

Schneider, B. R. 2004a. *Business Politics and the State in 20th Century Latin America*. New York: Cambridge University Press.

—— 2004b. "Organizing interests and coalitions in the politics of market reform in Latin America," *World Politics* 56.

—— 2008. "Economic liberalization and corporate governance: the resilience of business groups in Latin America," *Comparative Politics* 40(4): 379–98.

—— 2009a. "Big business in Brazil: leveraging natural endowments and state support for international expansion," in L. Martinez-Diaz, ed., *Brazil as an Emerging Economic Superpower*. Washington, DC: Brookings Institution.

—— 2009b. "Business–government interaction in policy councils in Latin America: cheap talk, expensive exchanges, or collaborative learning?" Background paper prepared for the IDB. Washington, DC.

Schwartz, F. 1992. "Of fairy cloaks and familiar talks: the politics of consultation," in G. Allinson and Y. Sone, eds., *Political Dynamics in Contemporary Japan*. Ithaca, NY: Cornell University Press.

Shadlen, K. 2004. *Democratization without Representation: The Politics of Small Industry in Mexico*. College Park, Pa.: Penn State University Press.

Shafer, D. M. 1994. *Winners and Losers: How Sectors Shape the Developmental Prospects of States*. Ithaca, NY: Cornell University Press.

SILVA, E. 1996. *The State and Capital in Chile: Business Elites, Technocrats, and Market Economics*. Boulder, Colo.: Westview.

SMITH, P. 1969. *Politics and Beef in Argentina*. New York: Columbia University Press.

—— 1979. *Labyrinths of Power: Political Recruitment in Twentieth Century Mexico*. Princeton: Princeton University Press.

STEIN, E., et al. 2005. *The Politics of Policies (Economic and Social Progress in Latin America, 2006 Report)*. Washington, DC: Inter-American Development Bank.

TARROW, S. 1998. *Power in Movement: Social Movements and Contentious Politics*. New York: Cambridge.

TEICHMAN, J. 2001. *The Politics of Freeing Markets in Latin America: Chile, Argentina, and Mexico*. Chapel Hill: University of North Carolina.

THACKER, S. 2000. *Big Business, the State, and Free Trade: Constructing Coalitions in Mexico*. Cambridge: Cambridge University Press.

TI. 2004. *Transparency International Corruption Perceptions Index 2004*, http://www.transparency.org

UNDP. 2005. *Democracy in Latin America: Towards a Citizen's Democracy*. Buenos Aires: Aguilar, Altea, Taurus, Alfaguara (United Nations Development Programme).

URRUTIA, M. 1983. *Gremios, política económica y democracia*. Bogotá: Fondo Cultural Cafetero.

VAALER, P., SCHRAGE, B., and BLOCK, S. 2005. "Counting the investor vote: political business cycle effects on sovereign bond spreads in developing countries," *Journal of International Business Studies* 36: 62–88.

VIZEU, F., and BIN, D. 2008. "Democracia deliberativa: leitura crítica do caso CDES à luz da teoria do discurso," *Revista de administração pública* 42(1): 83–108.

WRIGHT, T. 1982. *Landowners and Reform in Chile: The Sociedad Nacional de Agricultura 1919–40*. Urbana, Ill.: University of Illinois Press.

CHAPTER 14

JAPANESE BUSINESS–GOVERNMENT RELATIONS

YUKIHIKO HAMADA

INTRODUCTION

BUSINESS interests have come to embody a significant force in the global politics. Large multinational firms have become independent political actors and affect the ways in which global agendas and legislations are shaped (Coen 1997, 1998; Greenwood 2003; Wilson 2003). As a consequence of this normalization, systematic comparisons of business interests become increasingly important. In this context, Japanese business–government model has attracted the interests of many scholars, who have produced a number of studies at national, international, and transnational levels (Zhao 1993; Katzenstein and Tsujinaka 1995; Belderbos 1997; Gilson 2000; Bobb 2001; Kewley 2002; Hamada 2007, 2008). One of the major lessons that has been drawn from the existing literature is the informal and private nature of the Japanese business–government relations, which make Japanese firms and business community unique and different from their European and American rivals. Traditionally, Japanese business–government model was often explained by the intertwined nature of government, bureaucracy, and business. Recent studies point out that the roles of business and mass participation have become more and more prominent in Japan. It appears that, since the early 1990s, Japan has entered a more pluralistic stage in its politics and policy-making process.

However, in a lobbying context, it is important to note that there is still no significant concept of direct lobbying in the Japanese policy-making process. Japanese business interests are often expressed through informal consultations and other informal means. Such business culture has affected the ways in which Japanese firms lobby both at home and abroad, and created a unique business–government model.

This chapter proceeds as follows: we shall first review major explanations of the Japanese business–government model. Where we depart from general treatment of participation of business interests, we especially focus on large Japanese multi-national firms' lobbying strategies within the policy-making process. Then, in order to highlight the nature of the Japanese business–government model, the pattern of Japanese business lobbying is explained in detail, with special attention to firms' preferences for collective lobbying through their business associations and their lobbying instruments. In addition, the chapter refers to the development of Japanese business interests in the US and Europe, and points out the enduring national business culture among Japanese firms in the age of globalization. In a wider sense, examination of these points will allow the opportunity to assess and clarify the enduring nature of the Japanese business–government model, existing debates, and the future research agenda for Japanese lobbying.

NATURE OF THE JAPANESE BUSINESS–GOVERNMENT MODEL

Speaking of the significance of the business culture that is underpinned by the historical and social legacies of the state, it is necessary to have an understanding of the traditional explanation of the Japanese policy-making process in order to fully capture the development of the Japanese business–government model.

Japan has few natural resources and depends on massive imports of raw materials. It must export to pay for its imports, and manufacturing and the sales of its services, such as banking and finance, are its principal means of doing so. For these reasons, the careful development of the producing sector had been a key concern of both government and industry throughout most of the twentieth century. Government and business leaders generally agree that the composition of Japan's output must continually shift if living standards are to rise. Government plays an active role in making these shifts, often anticipating economic developments rather than reacting to them. After the Second World War, the initial industries that policy-makers and the general public felt Japan should have were iron and steel, shipbuilding, the merchant marine, machine industries in general, heavy electrical equipment, and chemicals. Later they added the automobile industry, petrochemicals, and nuclear power and, in the 1980s, such industries as computers and semiconductors. Since the late 1970s, the government has strongly encouraged the development of knowledge-intensive industries. Government support for research and development grew rapidly in the 1980s, and large joint government-industry development projects in computers and robotics were started. At the same time, government promoted the managed decline of competitively troubled industries, including textiles, shipbuilding, and chemical fertilizers through such measures as tax breaks for corporations that retrained workers to work at other tasks.

Under such political conditions, the Japanese policy-making process is traditionally seen by the elitist perspective, which is based on the concept of tripartite power elites composed of the leaders of the ruling party (Liberal Democratic Party), the bureaucracy, and organized business. According to this perspective, these three major groups comprise a regular and effective alliance and control decision-making on major issues, although it emphasizes the bureaucracy rather than other political or economic leaders (Muramatsu, Mitsutoshi, and Tsujinaka 2001). Japanese political and business circles are inseparably connected to the bureaucracy, comprising a united power nucleus. Although Japan's economic development is primarily the product of private entrepreneurship, the government has directly contributed to the nation's prosperity. Its actions have helped initiate new industries, cushion the effects of economic depression, create a sound economic infrastructure, and protect the living standards of the citizenry. Thus, the relationship between government and business is as collaborators rather than as mutually suspicious adversaries. Indeed, so pervasive has government influence in the economy seemed that many foreign observers have popularized the term "Japan Inc." to describe its alliance of business and government interests. Whether Japan still fits this picture after several reforms in the 1980s and 1990s seems questionable, but there is little doubt that government agencies continue to influence the economy through a variety of policies.

Recent studies of Japanese politics point out that the roles of politicians, business, and mass participation have become more and more prominent. It appears that, since the early 1990s, Japan has entered a more pluralistic stage in its politics and policy-making process. For example, Blaker, Giarra, and Vogel (2002) argue that Japan is in many ways fragmented and pluralistic. It has without question a vertically organized society, however it is also structured horizontally and at each level there are numerous groups, fiercely assertive of their own interests, locked in competition with one another. In this sense, Japanese politics is sometimes described as "bureaucratic and mass inclusionary pluralism," "patterned pluralism," or "compartmentalized pluralism" in which the monopolistic role of the bureaucracy in the policy-making process has been kept intact. However the roles of other political actors have also become increasingly important, while the Western pluralist assumption that policy-making is carried out in free competition among various actors is still clearly hindered by the elite groups and hierarchically organized social structure (Zhao 1993; Tsujinaka 1997; Kono and Clegg 2001; and Muramatsu, Mitsutoshi, and Tsujinaka 2001). This political setting provides an institutional basis for firms and other interest groups to play their political function.

Under such political setting, where business and government are closely intertwined, the concept of harmony (*Wa*) is essential to maintain their relationship. That is, business-related policies are mostly drafted by the Ministry of Economy, Trade and Industry (METI), and METI traditionally stresses that business policy should serve the long-term interests of Japan to enhance its economic propensity and social stability through growing technological autonomy and the pursuit of a policy of international cooperation (Nester 1993; Vogel 1996; McCargo 2000). As a result, the Japanese business community also stresses that firms should serve the long-term interests of Japan as a whole. It emphasizes long-term profits through cooperating and networking with other countervailing groups. Japanese firms prefer to participate in one kind of meeting or another in the field in which they specialize or in related fields, in order to solidify and expand their social contacts. In addition, many Japanese business organizations show a strong tendency to develop close ties with other groups and firms whose immediate interests appear quite different from their own, demonstrating a Japanese characteristic of building as large a group of connections as possible, on the basis of what many Westerners might regard as minimum common interests (Kubota 1997). The concept of harmony traditionally expresses this norm and is deeply rooted in Japanese society. Under such political conditions, there is a clear lack of direct lobbying among firms' strategies within the Japanese policy-making process. Instead, it is crucial for firms to maintain an informal relationship with national policy-makers to secure their policy goals and quietly solve any problems. The Japanese business–government relationship is characterized by the extensive use of informal political activities by firms, which integrate their business interests into the policy-making process and make the boundary of public and private spheres blur. Informal settings are an important element of the Japanese business–government relationship in the way policy-makers can listen to and hear business interests which they might otherwise ignore.

Emphasis on harmony in the Japanese business–government relationship seems contradictory to the fundamental nature of business lobbying, in which business interests must exchange insider information for favored policy outcomes or put pressure on policy-makers to influence their decisions. Japanese firms seem to focus on maintaining stability in the policy-making process while they still need to conduct lobbying to feed their interests into politics. One important question is posed here. If emphasis on harmony is so important to Japanese firms, how can it be created and sustained within business lobbying practices? In order to answer the question, we begin by disaggregating Japanese firms' lobbying patterns, which enable them to incorporate lobbying and harmony.

LOBBYING PATTERN IN JAPAN

First, due to a long tradition of business activism and the existence of a hierarchically organized business community, Japanese firms show strong tendencies for collective action (Zhao 1993) through national business associations. These associations are well connected to each other and with politicians and bureaucrats. There are three different groups within the Japanese business community, each representing different hierarchical levels of economic groups. The top level is *zaikai* (the leaders of major economic organizations), the second is *gyokai* (the industrial groups), and the third is individual firms (Stockwin 1999; Yoshimatsu 2000). *Zaikai* are regarded as representative of big business interests including top economic organizations, such as the Japanese Federation of Economic Organizations (*Keidanren*), the Japanese Chamber of Commerce and Industry (*Nihon shoko kaigisho* or *Nissho*), the Japanese Committee for Economic Development (*Kauai doyukai*), and the Japanese Federation of Business Managers (*Nikkeiren*). *Keidanren* is regarded as the bastion of big business because its leaders are drawn from such circles and its corporate members occupy a disproportionate position of the whole. *Keidanren* has the most extensive range of interests and most intensive activities. It is concerned with numerous domestic issues, not only economic but also social and political as well as international problems. While *Keidanren* deals with the government, it does not have much to do with labor–management relations. This is left to the *Nikkeiren*. *Keizai Doyukai* is a more informal group, bringing together relatively progressive middle managers from somewhat less politically constrained companies. Unlike the three others, *Nissho* represents the interests of medium-sized or small business firms. It is not as fiercely independent or assertive as other *zaikai* organizations. It was created under national law, receives some state support, and cooperates more directly with the bureaucracy. Although each *zaikai* organization represents a different group within the Japanese business community, they all tend to maintain reasonably friendly relations with each other and cooperate closely on many matters including those that do not fall neatly into the jurisdiction of one *zaikai* organization or another. They are the heads of Japan's multinational corporations and exercise significant political power over Japanese politics. Although it is said to cost a few million dollars a year for a firm to send out one of its most senior officers as a *zaikai* leader, these positions are regarded as being highly prestigious and so they are actively sought after by Japan's top business leaders. Canon has chaired *Keidanren* since 2006, previously Toyota was the leader from 2002 to 2006. These *zaikai* leaders are often described as the Prime Ministers of the business community, and are invited to participate in many very important political events in Japan including, for example, state dinners for visiting heads of state.

Gyokai is equivalent to an industrial sector representing specific interests, which range from manufacturing to finance and from small to large sized industries. For example, gas (Japan Gas Council), electricity (JEITA: Japan Electronics and Information Technology Industries Association), automobile (JAMA: Japan Automobile Manufacturers Association), and steel (Japan Iron and Steel Federation), are considered among the most powerful *gyokai* in the business society. A *gyokai*'s function is to coordinate competitive interests among individual firms within their respective spheres. It is at this level that industries have close contact with responsible bureaucrats, as the *gyokai* represents the interests of a sector as a whole against governmental and foreign pressure. A *zaikai*, on the other hand, does not represent any particular industrial sector, however it mediates conflicts between *gyokai* and coordinates national economic goals with the government (Abe 1999).

Finally, since *zaikai* and *gyokai* are more politically powerful in Japan, individual firms tend to follow the decisions of their business associations. It is traditionally the case that an individual is seen as subordinate to the group to which he or she belongs. The effect of such traditional norm is that individual Japanese firms are reluctant to take initiatives and initiate lobbying on their own. Most lobbying is initiated collectively under the initiatives of business associations. This strong tendency for collective action inevitably leads to a clear lack of desire for direct lobbying among firms.

What is significant with these business groups at three different levels are their objectives and functions in the Japanese policy-making process. These groups have a different level of counterpart in the bureaucracy and among politicians. While *zaikai* interacts with high-level bureaucrats and the Liberal Democratic Party (LDP)/other parties' senior leaders, *gyokai* and individual firms communicate with bureaus and sections of the Ministries and certain politicians with interests in particular policy areas. It appears that top Japanese business leaders from these *zaikai* organizations continue to devote a large amount of their time to matters that are national in scope and far broader than any particular concerns directly related to the specific firms that continue to pay their salaries.

Second, informal networks are some of the most effective mechanisms by which to coordinate different interests and to achieve consensus among political elites. Given the centralized powerful bureaucracy and a long tradition that heavily values social harmony and cooperation, informal networks give firms broader options, provide more flexibility for bargaining and compromise, and reduce the risk of offending the domestic or international actors involved (Katzenstein and Tsujinaka 1995). Such networking is based on informal and personalized means, such as financial contribution, fine-dining, and offers of prestigious positions in the private sector to retired bureaucrats (*amakudari*). Some degree of informal networking between firms and policy-makers is prevalent in most countries. However, with regard to their usage, there is a clear difference in degree and scope of intensity between Japan and the EU. The use of personalized/informal networks for political influence and mobilization in Japan is a more visible and frequent activity than in many other industrialized countries.

Japanese businesses often exercise significant political power through financial backing of the political parties. This is especially so when we note that of Japan's three (previously four) principal *zaikai* organizations, only *Keidanren* plays a publicly acknowledged role in collecting funds from leading Japanese firms and major *gyokai* organizations. It used to distribute these funds mainly among Japan's conservative political parties, although it ceased its role in political fund-raising in 1994 after a series of political scandals involving big firms and politicians. Until 1993, donation quotas were assigned to each industrial organization, such as the Japan Iron and Steel Federation and the Federation of Electric Power Companies. Huge amounts were collected from affiliated companies, and then *Keidanren* distributed the donations through the National Political Association to political parties including the Liberal

Democratic Party and the now-disbanded Democratic Socialist Party. For example, the total annual amount of political funds handled by *Keidanren* in this process usually ranged from $120 to $140 million per year (Kubota 1997). Despite the fact that political donations to individual politicians or their personal fund-raising organizations were banned in 2000, for the 2002 national election campaigns, donations to political parties from firms and industrial organizations reached about $26 million. In 2004, a new method for political donations through *Keidanren* was introduced. It now provides guidelines as a reference for companies and industrial organizations when they make political donations. These guidelines comprise evaluations of the policies of political parties, indicating their practical strengths and track records. After referring to these guidelines, companies and organizations independently decide on the recipients and the amounts of their donations. Many *gyokai* organizations and individual firms continue to donate large sums of money to the political parties at both national and local levels. The rest of the financial contributions from the business world to the parties and politicians consist of membership fees and the purchase of tickets for fund-raising events. These tickets may well be sold unofficially through individuals using an informal person-to-person organizational structure. The business community tries to see its goals realized by having *Keidanren* unify and channel donations exclusively to those parties that accept its demands, not only in such areas as tax reform and industrial policies but also in diplomatic, defense, and security areas. In this sense, Japanese business interests can buy political influence.

Furthermore, Japanese business interests have a close network with bureaucrats as well, although manipulation takes a different form from the case of the business–politician network. While public employees are paid reasonably well and expect a decent retirement, and therefore have less acute needs for money than politicians, they are not immune to certain temptations. It is pointed out that they do enjoy fine wining and dining, especially when their own wages or pocket money exclude this, and it is nice to have an occasional round of golf at the expense of some big firms, especially if they bet on the game and win a lot of money when their host turns out to be a poor golfer. Then there are the real bribes (Woronoff 1986; Okumura 2000). Yet, more than anything, the bureaucracy is aided by the practice of *amakudari* (literally "descent from heaven"), which enable retired bureaucrats to move to the private sector and hold responsible and prestigious positions as second careers. This enables leaders of industries and big businesses to cultivate intimate relations and establish a close-knit social network with bureaucrats. For example, the Japan Shipbuilding Industry Association routinely imports high-ranking officials from the Ministry of Transport to fill its top positions. The Japan Association of Pharmaceutical Organizations makes it a rule to have former officials of the Ministry of Health and Wealth as its leaders. These ex-bureaucrats are valuable assets for an industry; through them the business world can maneuver officialdom into the decisions it prefers. The other side of the coin is that bureaucrats know that they are likely to end up occupying important positions in the corporate world, so they see no harm in developing and maintaining congenial relations with representatives of the business world. Out of

1,268 senior bureaucrats who retired from their Ministries in 2005, 553 (43.5 per cent) went to work for the industrial associations and other business organizations. From 1999 to 2004, about 3,700 retired bureaucrats took up senior positions in the business sectors. The exercise of such informal instruments to politicians and bureaucrats indicate that Japanese firms do not hesitate to buy access to the policy-makers and invest large sums of money to create favorable political environments for themselves.

Third, Japanese firms' style of consultative lobbying involves a wide range of behind-the-scenes consensus building (*nemawashi*). In contrast to the EU practice, the Japanese consultative process is characterized by mainly top–down one-way interaction, in which business actors are rather passive in terms of policy input contributions. This working style has deep roots in Japanese social norms and practices. This can be defined as a system of careful and thorough consultations, before a decision is arrived at by general consensus, to avoid open confrontation (Zhao 1993; Kono and Clegg 2001; Ohtsu and Imanari 2002). As discussed earlier, actions such as taking risks and initiatives, being assertive and inventive tend not to be rewarded within Japanese society, which values harmony (Zhao 1993). This tradition makes the Japanese uncomfortable with outspokenness in social gatherings, especially in a formal setting. The effect of these attitudes is evident at the negotiating table, where Japanese diplomats rarely make bold moves or propose new initiatives, and where a change in the personnel of Japanese delegation rarely alters the complexion or dynamic of the discussions. In other words, individual contact and connection may be casual in the beginning and may not necessarily result in obligation. Nevertheless, as personal connection deepens, mutual obligations based on mutual interests begin to mount, and individual consultation becomes necessary. Contacts and mutual trusts can be established for all negotiating parties, and disputes can be solved quietly through compromise. In practice, the results of these behind-the-scenes activities often take the form of a Ministry giving advice, suggestions, instructions, and warnings to business interests, although these are without statutory basis. As there are many retired bureaucrats in business due to the widespread practice of *amakudari*, they often help to deal with the policy guidance provided by the Ministries (Sugimoto 1997). This indirect style indeed reflects Japan's traditional cultural emphasis on the importance of maintaining harmony among the Japanese as well as with foreigners.

As a result, the Japanese business–government relationship is extremely consensual. Many Japanese firms are rather eager to accept the policy guidance provided by politicians and bureaucrats at the negotiation table to avoid open confrontation. The idea of extensive consensus building often slows the process of coordinating positions within the policy-making process. Thus, the informal way of maneuvering may sometimes provide mixed and uncertain messages externally, thereby creating confusion when communicating with foreigners. As Japan's economy matures further, the society will advance in the direction of greater political pluralism. Popular demand for more active political participation is expected to continue to grow. Japanese politics will move more toward a more inclusive direction. Policy debate in open forums will become more frequent, and special interest groups will be more proactive and skilful, thereby increasing their political influence. Nonetheless, in the immediate future and for some time to come, most of the basic characteristics of Japanese business lobbying are unlikely to change drastically.

JAPANESE BUSINESS LOBBYING ABROAD

Japanese business lobbying abroad is still a relatively new and much needed area of research in the discipline of public policy. Many existing studies of Japanese lobbying abroad take their cases from US and EU politics (Shinda 1989; Katzenstein and Tsujinaka 1995; Kewley 2002). There are a limited number of studies that focus on the roles of Japanese firms and their political capacities, such as in seeking strategic alliances and negotiating with other stakeholders (Hamada 2007). Most existing studies have tended to discuss the issue of how the government controls and administers the private sector in the context of FDI or trade policies (Belderbos 1997; Mason 1997; Gilson 2000).

UNITED STATES

Katzenstein and Tsujinaka (1995) considered the difference in the political strategies and tactics adopted by the American automobile and the Japanese electronics industries. They analyzed the difference in how American firms typically pursue their political objectives in Japan and how Japanese firms typically proceed in the USA, in terms of the difference in domestic structures of both countries. In short, the Japanese government spends a great deal of money and effort trying to create a favorable public climate in the US by investing in well-placed officials, many of them former members of the US government, who enjoy excellent access to key decision-makers. The attention to image building and creation of a favorable public climate in America are distinctive features of Japan's transnational relations with the United States, which are rooted in both the constraints under which foreign lobbies operate, as well as the political importance of a favorable public climate in Japan's domestic politics (Katzenstein and Tsujinaka 1995). Japan's lobbies in the American policy-making process reflect some characteristics of America's domestic structure. Due to the weakness of the American party system, Japanese lobbies, in times of political need, target individuals, Congressional districts and individual states rather than national political institutions. Since the 1950s, Japanese institutions and firms have spent an enormous amount of time, energy, and resources in mastering the American political process (Hansen and Mitchell 2000). The network of institutional and individual contacts they have built is both deep and broad. This lobbying strategy also corresponds in part to the Japanese domestic lobbying pattern in which firms must informally cultivate political channels with bureaucrats, politicians, and other stakeholders. It is claimed that there is little doubt that the Japan lobby in the United States is the largest and most effective foreign effort to influence legislation, policy-making, and public attitudes in this country (Uchida 2000). With its American face, the Japanese lobby has become almost integrated into the fundamental structure of advice giving, consultation, and governance in Washington (Shinda 1989; Katzen-stein and Tsujinaka 1995). Several cultural characteristics of domestic structures, such as the Japanese decision-making norm of reciprocal consent and the American notation of liberal pluralism, are only partly embodied in explicit regulations, but constitute nevertheless powerful cultural norms which define appropriateness with regard to the way decisions should be made in the political system. Japanese firms' approaches to the US policy-making process are partly an extension of their own domestic experiences, as well as being shaped by the political setting of the US. The Americanization of Japanese lobbying is also confirmed in several other studies. For example, Shinda (1989) investigated how the Japanese automobile industry lobbied the US government to ban the Domestic Content Bill in 1983. Similarly, Yoshimatsu (2000) looked at the internationalization of the Japanese automobile and electronics industries in the US markets.

These findings may imply that the theoretical foundation, which focuses on the transformation of domestic lobbying patterns and convergence with the hosting environment, seems also relevant and applicable for the study of Japanese business lobbies operating in other area of the world.

EUROPEAN UNION

In an EU context, there are some studies which look at the structure and actors of the European policy-making process in relation to Japanese business interests. For example, Kewley (2002) analyzed Japanese lobbying in the automobile industry since the 1970s and identified the gradual processes in which they have restructured their lobbying strategies. According to his observations, there was no significant Japanese lobbying at the European level until the 1980s: Japan did not view the Community as a whole, but preferred to conduct trade bilaterally with its constituent parts; the member states or their domestic industries. Most trade between Japan and the EC was conducted bilaterally at the member state level, whereby Japan agreed to accept Voluntary Restraint Agreements (VRAs) in its exports, or alternatively, export restraint was exercised by Japanese firms sectorally, known as Voluntary Export Restrictions (VERs). Thus, Japanese firms did not attempt to lobby the EC because their strategic trade objectives were being realized to a large extent through the acceptance of such agreements.

Yet since the 1980s, due to the severe economic conditions in the European market and Japan's aggressive export-oriented EC policies, the EC and some member states have become more hostile towards Japanese investment. Thus, it became increasingly important for Japanese firms to lobby to secure their policy objectives, and this was largely carried out indirectly through supportive member states, especially the UK, and in conjunction with the Japanese government and its Ministries, especially the Ministry of International Trade and Industry (MITI) (the Ministry of Economy, Trade, and Industry (METI) since 2001). On the issue of exports to the EC/EU, many decisions were at MITI's discretion: MITI handled negotiations to estimate European market growth, decided the scale of total Japanese exports, and allocated export quotas to individual firms. Under such conditions, participation of Japanese automobile firms in MITI's policy-making process was not usually exposed to the public, in that their more important contacts were often held at an informal level (Ando 2005).

Several studies have also been undertaken to examine troubled trade disputes between Japan and the EC during this period. For example, Belderbos (1997) dealt with various aspects of the internationalization of Japanese electronics firms and the role of trade policies in shaping Japanese firms' trade and investment behavior in the late 1980s and early 1990s. Similarly, Mason (1997) examined aggressive FDI patterns of the Japanese automobile and electronics industries in the European market and how they challenged and negotiated with EU institutions and firms to solve the trade-related disputes. Abe (1999) claimed that automobile disputes symbolized the troubled trade relations between Japan and the EC in the 1980s, and focused on Japan's automobile trade policy towards the EC to understand this transnational negotiation, with special attention to the power relationship between the automobile firms and MITI. More generally, Gilson (2000) clarified the processes that have mediated Japan–EU political relations since the 1950s by focusing on both the internal and external driving forces that have promoted change and development within this bilateral relationship over the past few decades.

These existing studies about Japanese firms in the EU provide some empirical understanding of their lobbying behaviors in certain sectors and policy areas. For instance, in the automobile sector, Japan and the EC signed an agreement in 1991 that stipulated that free trade in automobiles be completed by 1999 and set a transitional period to allow European manufacturers to adapt. Since the agreement, officials from the Japanese government and the Commission have held biannual meetings to control the flow of Japanese cars into Europe. Most case studies tend to set MITI as a key Japanese lobbying actor and argue that the accord of 1991 confirmed the role of MITI in trade control and, by avoiding commitment to restricting transplanted cars, the accord also allowed transnational development between Japanese firms and European actors. In addition, individual firms tended to rely on JAMA to express their opinions as a whole industrial sector rather than commenting independently on foreign trade issues.

Since the mid-1990s, the EU has institutionalized its bargaining position with business and strengthened the competences of its regulatory power. This has created a policy-making process with a number of access points at EU level. Besides, Japan's inability to disengage itself from the long-term economic downturn has eased European anxiety and hostility over the seriousness of the competitive challenge once posed by Japan. The recession also brought about a revision of the role of the Ministries. That is, the Japanese government has become more concerned with bringing foreign investment into Japan, and consequently the Ministries' abilities to influence firms' European market strategies have been diminished to some extent (Hughes 2001; Kudo 2001). In other words, MITI's role in the EU, that is providing a framework for communication and consensus building between government and business, has been significantly reduced and the mid-1990s was a significant turning point for Japanese firms in the EU, as most trade disputes between Japan and the EC/EU were resolved by the early 1990s. The EU regulatory issues, such as environmental policy and safety standards, have become more important concerns for Japanese firms in the EU since the mid-1990s. Besides, the automobile accord expired in 1999 and this included the elimination of national restrictions, such as the French 3 per cent registration limitation. Monitoring of automobile export levels was also completely abolished in 2000. Therefore, at face value at least, the EU market appears to have been liberalized.

Under such conditions, Japanese firms have become more proactive and tried to fully exploit policy channels. Many firms opened antennae offices in Brussels in the early 1990s to monitor EU affairs, although firms and business organizations in Brussels still have strong budgetary or personnel links with the Ministries. Furthermore, the recent elite pluralist environment of the EU policy-making process has encouraged Japanese firms to establish several forums and organizations, such as the EU–Japan Business Dialogue Round Table in 1995 and the Japan Business Council in Europe (JBCE) in 1998, although their policy successes have still been limited. With the creation of public affairs divisions in Brussels, staffed by those knowledgeable in the workings of the EU institutions, Japanese firms' lobbying campaigns may also be initiated directly with the Commission or the European Parliament. It is pointed out that Japanese firms with a high profile in the EU, such as Toyota, Sony, and Canon, are actively developing their own public affairs divisions and a localization policy is a primary factor in recruitment of personnel for these positions (Nakayama, Boulton, and Pecht 1999; Takahashi 2001). Belderbos (1997) argued that the Japanese manufacturing presence in Europe is still growing and firms are expected to continue investing at a slower pace. As Japanese subsidiaries become more established producers, they will increasingly be seen as insiders and judged less on their owner's nationality. Nevertheless, the prevailing view of Japanese firms as outsiders is changing, although it is doubtful if such firms will ever become fully naturalized. Similarly, Kewley (2002) concluded that, by the end of the 1990s, many Japanese firms still remained manifestly Japanese, but at the same time they were able to exploit policy channels in the EU more fully, although it was still uncertain whether these newly found advantages would be fully utilized.

More recently, Hamada (2007) explored the Europeanization of Japanese firms' lobbying strategies, and assessed how they have adapted to the constantly evolving

EU public policy-making system. With reference to the actor-based models of interest groups and Europeanization literature, his research provides an empirical investigation of interaction between traditional Japanese lobbying practices and the EU institutional environment in forming firms' preferences for particular lobbying strategies. Japanese firms have restructured their political behaviors to suit the EU policy-making process. However, the degree of such Europeanization of lobbying strategies has significantly varied across sectors and firms due to ranging influence from several institutional factors. The EU institutional environment does not affect the logic of Japanese lobbying to the same degree as European firms. Convergence of lobbying strategies may be apparent at the level of lobbying instruments, but below the surface, where the roots of leading Japanese firms remain lodged, there is a durable source of resistance. In other words, the underlying nationality of the firm remains the vitally important determinant in the nature of its lobbying strategy formulation, and is persistent in the face of Europeanization.

From existing observations, the development of Japanese business lobbying in the EU can be roughly divided into two stages: from the mid-1980s to 1993 (pre-Treaty of European Union) and from 1994 to the present day (post-TEU). The first period of Japanese lobbying is largely characterized by the EU–Japan trade disputes, strong initiatives of Japanese Ministries, and low associability and autonomy of firms, while the second period featured expanding EU regulatory competencies, and firms' growing awareness and efforts to blend into the European corporate landscape. This transformation of Japanese lobbying in the EU indicates that Japanese firms' strategies have become Europeanized to some extent and highlights their political capacities to learn and adjust to the hosting political environment.

Conclusion

This chapter identified the transformation of Japanese business–government model at home and abroad. As we discussed, Japanese business interests are traditionally and institutionally intertwined with the policy-makers, leading to a lack of direct lobbing among firms (Zhao 1993; Ohtsu and Imanari 2002). In short, Japanese lobbying is characterized by heavy reliance on national and sectoral organizations, financial and personalized instruments to access the policy-makers, and a passive and unconstructive negotiation manner in order to both maintain harmony and feed their views at the same time. In Japan, firms are not independent political actors within the policy-making process, and prefer lobbying through business associations. At the same time, it is important to note that many Japanese firms have been recognized as some of the largest in global industries such as electronics and automobiles. Outside Japan, they have to transform their traditional lobbying pattern to suit their hosting political environment to maximize their political interests (Shinoda 1989; Hansen and Mitchell 2000; Kewley 2002; Ando 2005; Hamada 2007). However, the degree of such transformation of lobbying strategies has significantly varied across sectors and firms due to ranging influence from several institutional factors. The underlying nationality of the firms still remains the vitally important determinant in the nature of the Japanese business–government model, and is much more persistent in the face of globalization.

The unique nature of the Japanese business–government model attracts a lot of academic interest. Every study builds on previous work, and this one is no exception. Also, every study is incomplete, in the sense of containing gaps and identifying questions that future studies can address. In concluding this chapter, we propose several topics for future research. There are a variety of straightforward ways in which empirical research on the Japanese business–government model could be extended. Future work could focus on some other sectors in which Japanese firms also actively operate and are at the vortex of interaction between internationalization and national characteristics, such as chemical and financial sectors. Different sectoral variables do matter and affect the business organization of firms. Thus, firms that are active in other sectors and touched in varying degrees by the globalization of competition should be considered to capture a comprehensive picture of the Japanese business–government model. In addition, given the difference between the Japanese policy-making process and those of other countries, it would be valid to investigate the ways in which American and European firms conduct lobbying in Japan and how they are converted into the Japanese business–government model. Many foreign multinational firms now have offices in Tokyo and have occupied a substantial market share in many industrial sectors and products. Whether and, if so, how these firms transform their traditional lobbying strategies to participate in the Japanese policy-making process would provide an interesting analysis for convergence of business–government models across different political systems.

Theorizing of the Japanese business–government model still needs to be advanced to keep track of the changing role of firms in the evolving global politics of the coming decade. Yet, such theorizing can only be of any real utility, for both scholars and practitioners, if it is predicated on solid and wide-ranging empirical research. It is in this spirit that this chapter has been written as we try to understand the causes and consequences of multinational corporate behavior.

REFERENCES

ABE, A. 1999. *Japan and the European Union*. London: Athlone Press.

ANDO, K. 2005. *Japanese Multinationals in Europe: A Comparison of the Automobile and Pharmaceutical Industries*, Cheltenham: Edward Elgar.

BELDERBOS, R. A. 1995. "The role of investment in Europe in the globalization strategy of Japanese electronics firms," in F. Sachwald, ed., *Japanese Firms in Europe*. Paris: Harwood Academic Publishers.

BELDERBOS, R. A. 1997. *Japanese Electronics Multinationals and Strategic Trade Policies.* Oxford: Clarendon Press.

BLAKER, M., GIARRA, P., and VOGEL, E. 2002. *Case Studies in Japanese Negotiating Behavior.* Washington, DC: United States Institute of Peace.

BOBB, J. 2001. *Business and Politics in Japan.* Manchester: Manchester University Press.

COEN, D. 1997. "The evolution of the large firm as a political actor in the European Union," *Journal of European Public Policy* 4(1): 91–108.

—— 1998. "The European business interest and the nation state: large-firm lobbying in the European Union and member states," *Journal of Public Policy* 18(1): 75–100.

GILSON, J. 2000. *Japan and the European Union: A Partnership for the Twenty-First Century?* Basingstoke: Macmillan.

GREENWOOD, J. 2003. *Interest Representation in the European Union,* 2nd edn. Basingstoke: Palgrave.

HAMADA, Y. 2007. "The impact of the traditional business–government relationship on the Europeanization of Japanese firms," *Journal of European Public Policy* 14(3): 404–21.

—— 2008. "Japanese business lobbying at home and abroad," in C. McGrath, ed., *Interest Groups and Lobbying in Latin America, Africa, the Middle East and Asia.* Lampeter Ceredigion: Edwin Mellen Press, 341–61.

HANSEN, W., and MITCHELL, N. 2000. "Disaggregating and explaining corporate political activity: domestic and foreign corporations in national politics," *American Political Science Review* 88: 911–29.

HUGHES, C. W. 2001. "Japan in Europe: Asian and European perspectives," in G. D. Hook and H. Hasegawa, eds., *The Political Economy of Japanese Globalization.* London: Routledge.

KATZENSTEIN, P. J., and TSUJINAKA, Y. 1995. " 'Bullying', 'buying', and 'binding': US–Japanese transnational relations and domestic structures," in T. Risse-Kappen, ed., *Bringing Transnational Actors Back In.* Cambridge: Cambridge University Press.

KEWLEY, S. 2002. "Japanese lobbying in the EU," in R. Pedler, ed., *European Union Lobbying.* London: Palgrave.

KONO, T., and CLEGG, S. 2001. *Trends in Japanese Management: Continuing Strengths, Current Problems and Changing Priorities.* Basingstoke: Palgrave Macmillan.

KUBOTA, A. 1997. "Big business and politics in Japan, 1993–95," in P. Jain and T. Inoguchi, eds., *Japanese Politics Today.* Melbourne: Macmillan.

KUDO, A. 2001. "Americanization or Europeanization? The globalization of the Japanese economy," in G. D. Hook and H. Hasegawa, eds., *The Political Economy of Japanese Globalization.* London: Routledge.

MCCARGO, D. 2000. *Contemporary Japan.* London: Macmillan.

MASON, M. 1997. *Europe and the Japanese Challenge.* Oxford: Oxford University Press.

MURAMATSU, M., MITSUTOSHI, I., and TSUJINAKA, Y. 2001. *Nihon no seiji* (Japanese Politics: Theoretical Perspectives and Reality), 2nd edn. Tokyo: Yuhikaku.

NAKAYAMA, W., BOULTON, W., and PECHT, M. 1999. *The Japanese Electronics Industry.* London: CRC press.

NESTER, W. R. 1993. *European Power and the Japanese Challenge.* Basingstoke: Macmillan.

OHTSU, M., and IMANARI, T. 2002. *Inside Japanese Business: A Narrative History 1960–2000,* Armonk: M. E. Sharpe.

OKUMURA, H. 2000. *Corporate Capitalism in Japan.* Basingstoke: Macmillan.

SHINDA, T. 1989. *America gikai wo lobby suru* (Lobbying in the American Congress). Tokyo: The Japan Times.

STOCKWIN, J. A. A. 1999. *Governing Japan,* 3rd edn. Oxford: Blackwell.

SUGIMOTO, Y. 1997. *An Introduction to Japanese Society.* Cambridge: Cambridge University Press.

TAKAHASHI, S. 2001. "The global meaning of Japan: the state's persistently precarious position in the world order," in G. D. Hook and H. Hasegawa, eds., *The Political Economy of Japanese Globalization.* London: Routledge.

TSUJINAKA, Y. 1997. "Nihon no seijitaisei no bekutoru tenkan: corporatism kara pluralism" (The changing nature of the Japanese political system: from corporatism to pluralism), *Leviathan* 20. Tokyo: Bokutakusha.

UCHIDA, M. 2000. *Seito, Atsuryokudantai, Gikai* (Parties, Pressure Groups, and Parliament). Tokyo: Waseda University Press.

VOGEL, D. 1996. "The study of business and politics," *California Management Review* 38(3): 146–65.

WILSON, G. 2003. *Business and Politics: A Comparative Introduction.* Basingstoke: Palgrave.

WORONOFF, J. 1986. *Politics the Japanese Way.* London: Macmillan.

YOSHIMATSU, H. 2000. *Internationalization, Corporate Preferences and Commercial Policy in Japan.* London: Macmillan Business.

ZHAO, Q. 1993. *Japanese Policymaking: The Politics beyond Politics.* London: Praeger.

CHAPTER 15

CHINA AND THE MULTINATIONAL EXPERIENCE

JONATHAN STORY

BUSINESS people ask of China: what do we need to know in order to do business in China? The answer provided here is that the transformation of China conditions every aspect of business, and that therefore the central consideration for top management of multinational corporations is to understand the linkage between the party-state's economic policies and record, the rapid evolution of the business system, and what this spells for the making and implementation of corporate strategy. The approach is to conceive of corporations as learning organizations, learning in this case how to operate in a China which is deeply engaged in learning what it means to modernize fast. In this chapter, I'll lead off by linking changes in the macro-context of China to changes in its business system; then briefly illustrate what this has meant, and continues to mean, for implementing corporate strategy and policies in China. In the final section, we discuss the futures of China as the key to making corporate policies there now.

CHINA'S TRANSFORMATION AND THE BUSINESS SYSTEM

Conceptualizing corporate strategy and policy in China requires us to bring together and examine the multiple linkages between China's changing context and corporate policies. We'll start by taking a broad brush to how China's transformation meshes with that of the world's; then discuss the process of transition towards a "socialist market economy"; introduce the concept of business system in its application to China; and then link these three dimensions of the global transformation, of China's transition, and the evolution of its business system to create to create the context in which corporate strategies and policies have to be implemented.

The interdependence of China's transformation and the world system

Let us start first with China's interdependence. Looking back over the past three decades since Deng Xiaoping emerged as the country's de facto leader, and launched the Open Door policy, we may say that China has been caught up in a double transformation: its own exit from the inherited Maoist economy, and the trans-formation of the global system, involving the collapse of the USSR, the retreat of alternative forms of government to "market democracy," the re-creation of the world market under the aegis of the Western powers, and the growth of the multinational industrial or service corporation (there is a huge literature on these topics: see Prahalad and Doz 1987; Huntingdon 1991; Stopford and Strange 1991; Hobsbawm 1994; Greider 1996; Whitehead 1996; Henderson 1998; Sally 1998; Kapstein and Mastanduno 1999; Lawton et al. 2000; Gilpin 2001;). China's own exit entails the transition from socialist command to a market economy under CCP direction, from autarky to interdependence, from a rural to an urban society, from membership of the international communist system to full participation in a global polity.

This double transformation, illustrated in Fig. 15.1, has produced over the years a fairly clear package of policies for China. In retrospect, China's leadership has adopted promptly to the change in the global state system. Collapse of the Soviet Union accelerated the exit from the command economy (Naughton 1996, 2007), encouraged the development of a multifaceted foreign policy (Lampton 2001; Medeiros and Fravel 2003; Shambaugh 2004; Goldstein 2005; Gill and Huang 2006), accentuated the leadership's determination to keep control of the process, and shaped China's determination to join all the key regional and global policy institu-tions. The CCP leadership resists demands, whatever their source, to "democratize" the regime, but leaves the option open for the future while widening the scope of liberties available to Chinese people. Defense of the principle of non-intervention in

Global system China →	The post–Cold War state system	The democracy wave	Re-creation of the world market	Growth of transnational corporations
Exit from the command economy	No alternative	Resist	Maximize benefits of participation in	Learn from
From autarky to interdependence	Develop multi-faceted foreign policy	Postpone	Open Door policy	Choice production & export location
Transition from rural to urban society	CCP control over process	Control widening of liberties	Maximize comparative advantage	Promote competitive market economy
Membership of global polity	Join all regional & global institutions	Firm advocate of non-intervention principle	Co-participate in setting policy	Make global corporations key allies

Fig. 15.1 A double transformation: China and the world

the internal affairs of states runs as a consistent leitmotif through both domestic and foreign policies. On the other hand, policy is designed to maximize the benefits of China's participation in global markets through deepening of the Open Door Policy, maximizing China's comparative advantage in abundant labor, and through active co-participation in global affairs. Over time, policy towards global corporations has evolved from seeking to accelerate the transfer of technology inwards to China, to promoting China as a choice location for foreign investment, while pushing ahead to develop a highly competitive domestic market. This sharply reduces the prospects of domination in the longer term of global corporations on China's markets, while also helping to make global corporations key allies for the regime in the global polity. China's adaptation is a magnificent achievement.

There were two key facts that the Chinese leadership observed over the decade following on the Soviet Union's collapse. Both were compatible with a Marxist vision of a world whose prime characteristic is conflict and competition. The first was the leaderships' recognition of US primacy—as Chinese analysts concluded at the time of the 1996 Taiwan Straits crisis—"the superpower is more super, and the many powers are less great" (Deng 2001). The second was the US-centered global capitalism, which Susan Strange has defined as "the power to shape and determine the structures of the global political economy within which other states, their political institutions, their economic enterprises, and (not least) their scientists and other professional people have to operate" (Strange 1988). This is the global structure which China's leadership is determined to have China join, and to exploit, in order to develop China as a leading world power. As President Jiang Zemin stated: "We must dance with the wolf" (Yu 1999).

The process of administrative and market transition

But the process of transition, beyond the early setting by Deng Xiaoping of a broad vision for China's emergence as a great power, was unplanned, and unanticipated. Ex post, we can say that the leadership had no design on how to escape from communism, comparable to Mao's design to destroy capitalism and to build socialism. Communist revolution was "a sweeping, fundamental change in political organisation, social structure, economic property control and the predominant myth of social order, thus indicating a major break in the continuity of development" (Neumann 1949). The agent for this transformation was the autonomous communist party-state: change in society and economy came as a consequence of its autonomy.

If fundamental, systemic change is the way into revolution, regime change is the way out (there is a huge literature on regime change: see Morlino 1980; Huntingdon 1968; Gurr 1968, 1970; Dunn 1972; Skocpol 1979; Linz 1978; Nordlinger 1981; Trimberger 1978; Tilly 1975, 1993; O'Donnell and Schmitter 1986; Whitehead 1996; Maravall 1997; Acemoglu and Robinson 2006). Regime change implies a substitution of the old for new norms, rules, and institutions. The problem is that the state is captured by the party and economy it has taken over. The center has to strive to re-acquire the autonomy it forwent, and to unravel the multiple bonds that tie it down. Separating politics, law, markets, business, and society—all fused under socialism—becomes a prime consideration for public officials. This has two consequences: first is the struggle over sequencing—what priority for policy, domestic or foreign, choice of personnel, or declaratory statements of intent? Second is the struggle over control of the agenda, and its content. The advantage lies with public officials, who enjoy a vast domain of policy resources to liberate in the future precisely because the state is so deeply engaged in the whole procedure of resource allocation. Public officials can chose when, how, and under what conditions to relinquish controls or to build up a new resource base.

In China's case, the only way out of Mao's legacy was one of trial and error, where successive leaderships learnt to tentatively explore the future (on a critique of the Big Bang approach applied in Central-Eastern Europe, and explicitly rejected by the Chinese leadership, see Murrell 1992; and for a concise account of the transition to market, see Qian 2000). Dengism suggested pragmatism, based on "seeking truth from facts" through Marxist-tinted spectacles. From the start, the idea of the Open Door policy was to open the Chinese people to learning from abroad, importing technologies and know-how, while creating a highly competitive "socialist market economy" (*Beijing Review* 1993) and promoting China as a prime location for production and export on to world markets. In this process, internationalization of relations across party-state, society, and government combined with policy initiatives "from below" and "from above" (on both bottom–up and top–down forces operating to generate policy change, see Zweig 2002). If we trace the origins of the transformation from below, we focus our attention on the discontented in society, how organized they are, what their appeal may be and the capacity of the state to crush, concede to, or convert them. When we focus on reform "from above," we assume that reform ushers forth from the brow of public officials and we take for granted that the state can implement its policy. In both cases, the political authority of the state, and its financial and administrative capability, is the key to success or failure.

Stylizing the process of the transformation of China's political-administrative system into five stages, we start with *the pre-transition phase* when performance of the inherited system is questioned with growing vehemence both inside and outside the regime (Brinton 1965; Rustow 1970). The proximate condition for breakdown of the old order is that the incumbent power is unable to resolve a growing list of problems, the dictator's death is pending, and opponents inside or outside of the regime gather strength. When Mao finally died in September 1976, China was a desperately poor country. Per capita income was 7 per cent of the US's; 60 per cent of the population survived on less than $1 a day, and international trade at 1 per cent GDP was the lowest out of 120 developing countries (see Maddison 1998).

There follows an *"hour of decision"* when a new team of reformers or revolutionaries come into office, and jettison some or all of the old ways. This "hour"—which may last for an indefinite period—is particularly delicate because uncertainty is rife about the sustainability of what all know to be an interim situation (Shain and Linz 1995). Struggles within the regime can escalate as incumbents anticipate an expected inrush of new participant groups to the arena of public policy, and try by all means to prevent such a development. In China, the "hour" lasted a number of years, as the costs of keeping China in a policy limbo awaiting Mao's death, and then awaiting the demise of the Gang of Four, rose sharply. The moment of decision struck in December 1978, when the Third Plenum of the 11th Chinese Communist Party Congress announced the shift in party focus from "class struggle" to "economic development." Hua Guofeng, Mao's chosen successor, insisted that "whatever instructions Chairman Mao has given, we all follow." Deng countered with the slogan "practice is the sole criterion of truth." The shift in ideology paved the way for Deng's market-oriented reforms.

The *third phase may be termed definitional*—new norms are elaborated and widely debated, and their limits explored. In China's transition, the norms that have changed have dealt with administration and the market, but not the political system. The key political detonator was the initial consolidation of Deng's position, and the ideological sleight of hand which defined Mao's leaps towards socialism as "premature" (Ma 2000; Qian 2000). In December 1978 at the Third Plenum of the 11th Central Committee, Deng Xiaoping announced the official launch of the Four Modernizations in the fields of agriculture, industry, science and technology, and national defense, the aim of which was to make China a great power in the twenty-first century. There were two dimensions to the regime's evolving economic policy: one was exit from the command economy towards some forms of state capitalist system; the other involved maintenance of the political status quo. Let us deal with these three stages of transformation, before discussing the fourth and fifth.

Exit from the command economy

As the leadership stepped up the pace of reform by opening up to imports of machinery and technology from the advanced industrial countries, official description of the Chinese economic system evolved in the light of internal policy struggles between the conservatives and reformers of the moment. As Susan Shirk (1992) has argued, the ideology of "balancism"—maintaining a semblance of internal party cohesion and unity—became the defining characteristic of how the CCP managed the process of reform. Since the Chinese leaders understood that losers in a reform process had the capability to block progress, the governing idea came to be to "leave no one worse off than before" (Shirk 1993). The implications of such a strategy are systemic preferences for small, incremental changes which allow for obstructions to be bypassed. Coherent and comprehensive reform proposals on paper may seem intellectually attractive, but are easy targets for obstruction, given the many veto points available for opponents and that are scattered across the length and breadth of the party-state.

This gradual evolution in policy orientation is traceable through the evolution of the party-state's vocabulary. In 1980, official documents described it as "a planned economy with commodity production and exchange" (Collection of Reform Drafts for China's Economic System 1988). By 1992, Deng stated during his famous southern tour two months after the Soviet Union's collapse that "Singapore enjoys good social order and is well-managed. We could tap on their expertise and learn how to manage better than them" (Ping 1993). This direction of policy was ratified at the 14th Party Congress in October 1992, where the leadership elaborated a program to transform the country into a "socialist market economy, under the rule of law." In the following decade, major changes in orientation were introduced at varied speeds, and in often very different ways, in foreign policy as in the country's economic, industrial, and financial structures. In foreign policy, the leadership elaborated a new foreign policy style to accommodate the realities of the post-Cold War world in a context of the continued salience of the US as the prime power in the global system, and as China's indispensable partner (the key statement is Qian 1997; see also Goldstein 2001). Through the East Asian financial crash of 1997–8, China developed rapidly as a major trading nation (Qian 2000; Yeh 2001; Flassbek et al. 2005); experienced remarkable improvements in resource allocation as markets become hyper-competitive (e.g. Yeh 2001; Heytens and Zebregs 2003; Naughton 2003; Poncet 2003; Young 2003; Zheng and Angang 2004); witnessed the emergence of private business as the prime engine of growth (International Finance Corporation 2000); became the choice target for inward direct investment for multinational corporations (UNCTAD 1999); and imported growing quantities of food, raw materials, and energy resources from around the world (Dong 2003; Trinh and Voss 2006). Not surprisingly, major economic battles within the regime were fought out over economic policy, one key decision by the leadership in March 1998 being to accelerate China entry to the WTO (Tucker 2000; Wang 2000; on the entry negotiations, see Fewsmith 1999; Zweig 2001). Entry in 2001 to the WTO entailed wholesale adoption of business norms elaborated over five decades in negotiations between the advanced industrial states. In 2003, the new leadership slightly modified the prevalent growthmanship by renewed emphasis on the social dimension of government policy. (The problem of poverty reduction has moved to the forefront of government attention, under the new leadership.)

In summer 2003, the leadership received a report analyzing thirteen major problems, including poverty, requiring urgent attention (South China Morning Post 2003; see also Angang et al. 2003). But the heart of the whole enterprise of transformation was for the party-state to keep the growth engine of China running—an achievement recorded by the doubling of national income in the decade 1998–2008.

Maintaining the political status quo

Going for growth was the regime's response to the shock of the Soviet Union collapse. The other was to stay in power, while transforming China into a market-driven system. The paradox of political continuity and economic transformation is the shrinkage of the party-state's monopoly of power in an ever more pluralist and dynamic social context. Despite central government censorship, China is awash in debates about public policy (Fewsmith 2001; Harwit and Clark 2001; Domenach 2002; Goldman 2005). A major challenge for the party-state has been, and continues to be, to control the ongoing transition from a rural economy (Wen 2006), on which possibly 900 million depend for a meager living, into a mainly urban society (China Investigation Report 2001; Yang 2005). Abundant surplus rural labor provided a key resource driving the country's long-term dynamic (Yao et al. 2005). The other side of the coin has been the development of an urban under-class, the urgent need for the development of social policies such as health, education, and social insurance, and above all the creation of jobs. Given the length of time required to put such policies into effect, and expectations of the public that the government has a responsibility to provide for citizen's needs (a detailed study on worker attitudes is provided by Nielsen et al. 2005), the leadership's prime social policy is economic growth. China is an Adam Smith country ruled by a Marxist-Leninist-Maoist party.

Deng was only too aware that there were limits as to how far a political process of de-Mao-ification could go (see Tu 1996, for a powerful statement on the need for a prolonged process of de-Mao-ification). The limits are drawn by the fact that reneging Mao risked shaking the regime's foundations (see Walden 2008, for a recent powerful statement to the effect that the time bomb under the regime is that Mao's record as a mass murderer will out). The problem was dexterously handled in a Central Committee document of 1982 entitled *On the Various Historical Issues since the Founding of the People's Republic of China*, in which Mao retained his status as a "great Marxist, proletarian revolutionary, militarist and general," but was criticized for starting the Cultural Revolution. With this definition available, the 1982 constitutional reform reaffirmed the "Four Cardinal Principles," guided by "Marxist-Leninist-Mao Zedong Thought": party-state hegemony; the leading role of the party; a unitary state; the concentration of powers; and democratic central-ism in the party. In the following years, the regime evolved away from Leninist mass organizations towards a "new authoritarianism" (Unger and Chan 1995), as sketched in the reform leader Zhao Ziyang's 1987 report to the 13th National Party Congress (NPC) (Rosen 1991). Not surprisingly, the Chinese communist leadership was aghast at the Polish comrades' initial willingness to accede in 1980–1 to the demands of Poland's non-official opposition, Solidarity, for union autonomy and political reform. Initially, they were attracted by Party Secretary Gorbachev's reforms in the USSR in the late 1980s, but so were the students who gathered to read a declaration in Tiananmen Square in May 1989, calling on the government to accelerate economic and political reforms (Nathan 2001)—the first known major push within China to reform the regime. The students wanted an end to corruption, more intra-party democracy, and a curb on the abuse of power by officials. Many leaders, notably Zhao Ziyang—former premier and leader of the communist party (CCP)—as well as party intellectuals sympathized with them, and understood that a market economy and political reform went together. As Wu Jiaxing, a young researcher at the Investigation and Research Division of the Communist Party's Central Office, had written, Deng's policies were "an express train toward democracy through the building of markets" (quoted in Rosen and Zou 1991). He was arrested in July on account of his association with regime reformers.

The student demonstrations on Tiananmen Square in May–June 1989, played out in the full glare of the global media which had turned up to cover Gorbachev's visit to Beijing, caused the party leadership to suffer its worse high-level split since the years of the Cultural Revolution. The key lessons learnt were encapsulated by two statements by Deng. First, "the CCP status as the ruling party must never be challenged. China cannot adopt a multi-party system" (quoted in Lam 1995). Second, "Two conditions are indispensable for our development: a stable environment at home and a peaceful environment abroad. We don't care what others say about us. The only thing we really care about is a good environment for developing ourselves" (quoted in Nathan 2001). In the terminology of regime change, China is still in a pre-transitional phase in terms of political evolution, defined as "mature post-totalitarian" (Linz and Stepan 1996). The implication is that China has experienced change short of redefining its key political norms, and that political development still lies ahead. Meanwhile, China has become a dictatorship with provisos: the leadership talks about democracy, "China's style" as a prospect, while celebrating the benefits of dictatorship as good for economic growth (*International Herald Tribune* 2005; *People's Daily* 2005). Civil society is growing fast, as indicated by the growth of non-governmental organizations, the fractious and decentralized lobbying arena (see Kennedy 2005), and the development of online petitioning (Reilly 2004). There is still far to go in creating a judiciary independent of the party-state (Keyuan 2000), which also presides over all levels of administration and all officially recognized associations. Politically, the regime is the same as it was, not having changed beyond recognition.

Implementing China's WTO commitments

The *fourth phase* overlaps in reality with the third in that norms become accepted, and the central task is more one of interpreting them into rules and implementing the rules. The *final phase* of consolidation opens when the now not so new political, market, and business system operates smoothly—so smoothly that a danger of institutional and ideational sclerosis sets in. Because this final phase of consolidation in China arguably rests somewhere in the future, we leave discussion of this to the last, after discussion of the business system, and the implications of China's transition for corporate management.

In the case of China, the fourth phase may be dated from the year of China's accession to the WTO, following over fourteen years of debates within the regime as well as in Tokyo, Washington, and Brussels about the desirability of China's joining the global trade club. In his speech to the National People's Congress on March 5, 2002, Prime Minister Zhu Rongji ran through a long list of problems faced by China, from corruption to unemployment and "deep-seated" difficulties in the economy. The country, said the Premier, was "facing new difficulties and severe challenges," and one of these was WTO entry (*People's Daily* 2002). Indeed, China's commitments to WTO partners was to reduce weighted average nominal tariffs from 11.1 per cent end 2001 to about 6.9 per cent by 2007, and to abolish most non-tariff barriers by 2006. This included a partial opening of telecommunications, banking, insurance, or films where US firms dominated internationally (Mattoo 2002). Beijing also committed to tighten up on patent infringements, with a 2005 deadline for compliance. China signed up to the Kyoto protocols, but as a developing country, and without an obligation to cut emissions until 2012. Both the US and the EU set up China trade monitoring bodies, and insisted on import surge protection for twelve years as well as the implementation of an anti-dumping regime to last fifteen years. In order to shore up foreign confidence in its commitments, Beijing agreed to apply trade policy uniformly across the country, and to enforce only those laws, regulations, and other measures that had been published beforehand and to make them available to the WTO. On worker and human rights, the US and EU member states entered explicit agreements with multinational corporations to respect the terms of the UN Global Compact.

At the time of entry, the consensus of economists was that entry on balance was beneficial to the world economy (Hertzel and Walmsley 2000; Tongzon 2001; Dorsey et al. 2003; Ianchovichina and Martin 2003; Wang 2003; Bhattasali, Li, and Martins 2004). But that is not how public opinion in the developed world saw it: as exports from China surged to account in 2007 for one-third of the US trade deficit, and for 85 per cent of the total extra-EU trade deficit, the country came to be seen as a threat to jobs and to global stability (Pew Global Attitudes Project 2007; Hall and Dyer 2008). Aggressive exchange rate management, and an undervalued currency, prompted a surge in China's growth rate from an 8 per cent average from 1998 to 2001, to a 10 per cent average in 2003–5, to over 11 per cent average in 2006–8. Successive government statements sourced "global imbalances," not in China's growing external surplus, but in the policies of President George W. Bush's Washington. The assessment that the country continued to be run as a "non-market economy" (Gilboy 2004) received contingent confirmation in China's salience as the prime target in terms of the number and severity of anti-dumping measures (Li 2005; Ushiyama 2007).

Multinationals based in the US, the EU, and Japan faced workforce concern at the prospective outsourcing of their jobs to a country seen as "sweat-shopping its way to success" (ICFTU 2006). Not least, China's entry to the WTO—the critics maintained—weakened international cooperation. Efforts to create a unified global trade regime repeatedly faltered because no agreement on farm trade could be reached between the US, India, China, and the EU.

A positive view on China's entry tells a not entirely different story. One of the main reasons for entry to WTO was to strengthen Beijing's powers over local governments, and to create a level playing field for all companies. The party-state's policies of modernization could only be implemented in the long run by creating a large internal market, overcoming local government-sponsored protectionism (Young 2000), and reducing the incentives for foreign companies to cherry-pick between provinces as preferred locations for investment (see Huang 2003 on cherry-picking provinces as locations for investment in the reform era). As Long Yongtu, China's chief negotiator at WTO, stated, we joined the WTO "to push forward economic reform . . . so that China can participate fully in economic globalization" (*Beijing Youth Daily* 2001). There was therefore every reason to consider that Beijing took its commitments in the WTO accession agreements seriously. Studies showed evidence that price behavior across the whole of China was becoming more interrelated (Naughton 2003), and cross-border mergers rose as the markets opened up to foreign corporate purchases of local companies (though measures in 2006 were introduced to protect Chinese "brand names"; see OECD 2006; Davies 2007). This translated into improved efficiencies in the Chinese economy, recorded by the rise in labor (much less in capital) productivity, wages, incomes, and imports. China's imports on goods alone by 2007 equaled in value nearly twice those of India, Russia, and Brazil together.

China's entry to the WTO symbolized not just a commitment of the leadership to reform of domestic institutions, but a return of China to the global economy after centuries of absence. The result has been to transform the Chinese and the world economy. China's exports have risen in volume while their relative prices have fallen, entailing adjustment costs for workers, capital, and management in China and around the world. The resulting changes in relative prices of world imports and exports have altered countries' terms of trade, while within countries some workers have gained and others have lost. Countries with an acquired advantage in skilled work, such as Germany, have benefited, while countries with low skilled labor—typically in southern Europe and Mexico—have suffered (Eichengreen and Tong 2006). More intense competition from China kept prices down (Kaplinsky 2006), and helped Western central banks' anti-inflationary policies (Rogoff 2006). In particular, China acted as an engine on growth for its Asian (Lall and Albaladejo 2003), Latin American (Lora 2005), and African suppliers: China's imports between 1997 and 2007 rose by 477 per cent, and 79 per cent of China's imports were sourced from other developing countries.

Despite these successes, China's vulnerability was its over-dependence on global markets. The reason for the huge surpluses accumulated since 2001 was not that foreign corporations found the Chinese market impenetrable, but that Chinese household and corporate savings rates aggregated year-on-year to 40–45 per cent of national income. Not surprisingly, the current account surplus mushroomed from 1.3 per cent GDP in 2001 to 11.5 per cent in 2007. In addition, inward direct investment flows amounted to 3.3 per cent GDP in 2001, rising to 4.4 per cent GDP by 2007. The Central Bank actively absorbed this huge inflow of funds, partly by accumulating foreign exchange reserves, partly by reinvesting abroad, and partly by accepting an expansion in the domestic monetary base. Foreign exchange reserves stood at a colossal $2 trillion by end-2008, and rising at an accelerating rate of over $500 billion dollars a year.

These assets give the Chinese state the means to recapitalize banks, continue preferential lending to enterprises within the party-state family, buy US Treasury bonds, bribe dictators, bail out Western banks, and purchase equity in mineral operations around the world. The counterpart to that was that foreign corporations in the China market seek a return on capital of 15 per cent per annum, whereas the returns for Chinese paper invested, say, in the US Treasury bond market are 4 per cent. As Charles Dumas of Lombard Research has demonstrated, China makes 1–2 per cent interest on its dollar reserves. It then loses regularly on the exchange rate as the dollar falls relative to the renmimbi, and suffers an inflation rate of 6 per cent per annum, for a total return in local currency of about minus 15 per cent. That is a loss, which Dumas calculates as amounting to about 7–8 per cent GNP a year (Dumas 2008). In other words, it was not China that was fleecing the world, but the great economic powers—and the US in particular—that were fleecing China.

The lesson for the party-state was clear enough. China's high savings rate, and not just a mercantilist exchange rate policy, was one of the prime sources of "global imbalances." Combined together, high saving and managed exchange rates made China maximally vulnerable to slowdown in its major markets of the US and the EU as the global financial meltdown of 2007–8 gathered strength. Rapid development of the internal market was the way to reduce the dangerous over-dependence on foreign export markets which characterized the years 2001–8. For the leadership, that meant pushing ahead on the broad WTO-based reform program to ensure more efficient financial, product, and labor markets, combined with continued massive investment in developing country-wide infrastructure to complement progress on product markets. It is time to introduce the concept of the business system.

China's business system

The term national business system has been coined by Richard Whitley to describe specific patterns of economic coordination and control in market economies (Whitley 1999). As Whitley (1998) puts it, "business systems . . . are distinctive ways of structuring economic activities with different kinds of actors following contrasting priorities and logics. They therefore vary in the sorts of activities and resources that are integrated, how they are coordinated and controlled, the nature of controlling groups and how they compete and cooperate."

Applied to China, we may say that China's business system has four key features (Guthrie 2006): first comes the *macro-context*, of institutional and policy at the central, provincial, local, city, and autonomy levels, particularly as they impact capital and labor markets. Transformation of the economy, as already discussed, entails a combination of top–down and bottom–up initiatives, prompting institutional changes at the highest level of government, and eventually applied nationwide. Such reforms include the development and implementation of legal instruments, new rules and regulations governing labor and capital markets, the effectiveness and cohesion of government policies at its five related levels, and how far the risks inherent to business are allocated between public and private agents. One of the key policy reforms over the three decades from 1978 to 2008 was in the realm of public finances. This dimension of the transition has involved a gradual separation of the budget from banking involving a move way from the mono-bank system of Mao's time, to a more complex financial system, over which the party-state continues to exert tutelage (the international organizations provided advice; see Jacobson and Oksenberg 1990; Lardy 1998; Xu 1998; Cargill and Parker 2001). Privileged financial circuits are embedded in the party-state family of financial institutions and companies. This is particularly evident in the development of the formal capital market (Heimann 2001; Green 2004; OECD 2005), the creation of Central Huijin to retain majority ownership in key financial institutions, and the regular recycling of ever expanding foreign exchange reserves to recapitalize banks. The bottom line is that the party-state aims to stay on top, and the financial system is a key tool to do so.

A crucial link in financial, corporate, and labor market reforms came in 1984 with the disbandment of Mao's communes, which had provided the backbone to Mao's experiment in social engineering. With their disbandment, through to the mid-1990s, township and village enterprises added over a hundred million jobs in rural China (Wong and Mu 1995), while private business activities provided over 90 per cent of the new jobs in the following decade. Surplus rural labor continued to be exploited as the key to China's longer term transformation and growth (Yao et al. 2005), but success there depended on the CCP managing the process of urbanization, through continued control over rural to urban labor movements, and acceptance of an accelerated inflow of people to cities. Inevitably, this was accompanied by the import of rural tensions to the cities, the transformation of city economic structures and social policies, and a feedback to incremental, but profound social changes for the longer term in rural China. The constant in policy has been the party-state's concern to control labor movements, the result of which is the paradox of labor scarcity in a China of plentiful labor supply, sharp rises in wages, and a declining sensitivity of economic growth to job creation. By the turn of the millennium, China's economy was creating eight million jobs a year, when twenty million was needed to absorb the urban workers laid off by industrial restructuring and the surplus rural labor.

The second feature of the business system is the way that *economic activities are coordinated among stakeholders*. In China, the party-state remains an indispensable coordinating mechanism for businesses, as government officials, local or central, run trade associations, allocate property rights, control access to land, licenses, financing, or a host of other policy instruments. It can be no surprise therefore that maintaining personal and regular contacts (*guanxi*) with officials is a central part of business people's activities. Not for nothing is the CCP known as the *Gongchan Dang*, "The Party of Public Assets." This translates into a corporate reform policy the objective and outcome of which is to keep capitalism within the communist party-state family (on the new business elite, see Pearson 1997; Dickson 2003). The high tide of corporate reforms was the decade from 1993 to 2003 (see Huchet 1999; Lu 1999; Sun 2005), and possibly beyond, involving efforts to create national champions to confront competition from the multinationals on Chinese and global markets (Nolan 2001; Huchet and Richet 2002); the creation of hybrid private–public "science and technology enterprises" (Lu 2000; Dahlmann and Aubert 2001); the fire-sale of local state enterprises; and above all the growth of private companies (see Cao, Qian, and Weingast 1999). Cultivating relations with officials is a central part of business leadership in China. But it is equally important to recall that the government has used markets as a decentralized coordinating mechanism to stimulate a growth (IFC 2000). Because the party-state is part of the marketplace where much truck, barter, and exchange is affected, there can be no surprise that corruption is rife, notably at local government level (Sun 2005).

In view of the leadership's objective to create a "socialist market economy," the major change in China's business norms results from entry to the WTO. Implementing WTO norms favors Beijing in its drive to create a huge and integrated internal market, and raises the stakes of for multinationals investing there. Here there is some difference between US and EU corporations, and overseas Asian corporations. Asian investors use China as an export platform onto global, particularly Western markets. US and EU corporations, by contrast, direct about two-thirds of output to the domestic market (see Tseng and Zebregs 2002; also Lemoine 2000). That is where Chinese corporations still keep a dominant position—controlling 85 per cent of domestic demand for industrial goods. Domestic corporations have less than 70 per cent market share in only two sectors—instruments and electrical and electronic machinery—and below 80 per cent in transport equipment and machinery. Up to the time of China's entry to the WTO, foreign corporations were doing particularly well in highly protected sectors. With entry to the WTO, and the gradual phasing out of tax and other advantages to multinationals, competition from mainland producers has become much more severe, as they have learnt to drive costs down, and productivity up. WTO entry provides the means to the leadership's aim which is to confirm China's rank as a pillar of the global economy.

The third feature of the business system is *changes at the level of the firm and factory*. Here we focus on ownership rights, and the implications for corporate governance of the constraints or discretion conferred on owners or managers by the financial, labor, or political systems in which they operate. Over time, the CCP has come round to recognize property rights, and has been eager to promote private business. But the monopoly party powers are visible in the financial and in the labor systems, where representation of workers runs through the All China Federation of Trade Unions (ACFTU) (Chan and Senser 1997; Chan 2001). Access to financial resources depends for private firms on family, friends, and internally generated revenues (Weidenbaum 1996; Pistrui et al. 2001; Redding 2002), whereas for firms operating within the extensive Communist Party corporate family, they run through privileged lending circuits (on the subject of informal banking, see Tsai 2002; Allen, Qian, and Qian 2005). In the 1980s, when powers in factories were returned to managers, and again during the extensive period of corporate restructuring in the 1990s, party officials representing the AFCTO had little reported say in factory life. More recently, this has changed as the leadership seeks to extend union membership into foreign-owned enterprises operating on the mainland.

Because firms are bundles of resources, under managerial direction, producing goods and services, sold in markets for a profit—as the late Edith Penrose (1995) used to argue—their personnel require time to expand the firm's collective learning process. The workforce's ability to learn is clearly related here to what is termed their "skillability"—the learning they have brought with them into the firm and factory, which are the locations where they develop collective competences specific to their particular operations. For foreign investors, the initial attraction for coming to China was the availability of cheap labor, especially in the economic zones. But wage costs have been rising fast in the industrialized zones of coastal China, on account of labor market rigidities, as mentioned, and in the longer run by 2030 as China's demography ages fast. The government's response has been to take action, particularly in higher education, to promote a more skilled labor force. Still, China is far from enjoying a comparative advantage as a source of skilled labor: only 0.6 people out of 1,000 are recorded as having science and technology backgrounds, compared to 0.3 in India. France has a figure of 5.4 per 1,000 (on China's technology policy, see Suttmeier and Yao 2004).

The business system's fourth feature is *the culture which permeates the business system*, such as mutual trust, patterns of authority, why people strive, and the identification of citizens with their country, city, or locality. This cultural dimension in the case of China may be presented in the following form (for a discussion of Max Weber's concept of rationality applied to China, see Redding 2002; also Redding and Witt 2007): Confucian ethics tend to legitimate paternalism in the household and patrimonialism in the state, and provide a moral justification for hierarchy, stressing reciprocal vertical obligations. Chinese civilization is predicated on individuals being socialized into a belief in the need for appropriate conduct in the interests of harmony, all within a dominant state structure with a mandate to preserve order. Given the limited trust between individuals, and between individuals and public officials, in China, the architecture of horizontal order is based on identity with family as the core social unit. The party-state's revival of Confucian ethics is a clear indication that it seeks to be a beneficiary of these age-old patrimonial values. China's modernization is to be based on traditional values, not on their destruction, as Mao intended and as convergence on Western ways would imply.

One of the reasons why the party-state under the post-2003 leadership has emphasized the social dimension of their policies is that the vertical order associated with Confucian values is predicated on reciprocity. The state or the owner is the source of authority, and the good worker is the obedient executor (Huo and Si 2001). Such values provide a measure of how much of a gamble it was for the leadership to abandon Mao's version of a-familial paternalism. Hence, the government's activism on labor markets, and its policy of growthmanship, including the high-risk strategy of entering the WTO in the midst of what must be ranked as one of the world's largest industrial shakeouts ever. Arguably, the challenge for the leadership, though, is not the pride Chinese feel in getting China to stand tall again in world affairs. It comes from the innumerable failings in public policies which affect citizens, such as the failure to take immediate action to alert the public about contaminated water; the innumerable occasions when local officials have abused their powers to confiscate land from peasants for construction, but without compensation; the vested interests perpetuating the second-class citizen status of the rural migrant workforce in cities. Indeed, one of the reasons that the leadership dances with danger is that its policies of growth have created two key effluents: one is the corrupt practices of public officials, and the other is pollution. No wonder that researchers in the Central Party School in Beijing have argued for the leadership to promote political reform (*Financial Times* 2008). The implication being made is that for trust to be restored in government, government has to be held accountable to the public. The same cultural assumptions of reciprocity are present in the workplace.

IMPLICATIONS FOR CORPORATE STRATEGY AND POLICY

Let us summarize the argument to date in three major points. First, we have observed ex post the country's deep interdependence with the rest of the world, as a result of Open Door policies pursued by the party-state since 1978 (Moore 2002; Zweig 2002). Second, China's political and economic transformation is conditioned by the leadership's realization that there was no precedent as to how to exit from the communism they had helped install in China over the previous three decades (Shirk 1993; Naughton 1995; Fewsmith 2001; Domenach 2002). Third is the evolution of its business system, a term coined by Richard Whitley (1999) to describe specific patterns of economic coordination and control in market economies. Business system are important for corporations because they secrete their own incentives for agents in markets and depend for their continuation on particular forms of policy processes (North 1991). The fourth dimension to be broached in this section is what this changing context implies for corporate strategies and policies of multinational corporations operating in China.

The four dimensions may be stylized, as in Fig. 15.2, where the political and market transformation of China is illustrated in the vertical line; the business system is

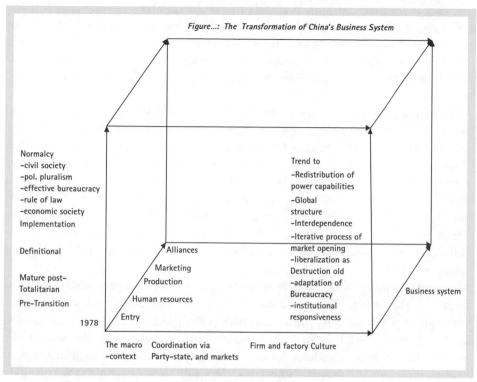

Figure...: The Transformation of China's Business System

Normalcy
–civil society
–pol. pluralism
–effective bureaucracy
–rule of law
–economic society
Implementation

Definitional

Mature post-
Totalitarian

Pre-Transition

1978

Alliances

Marketing

Production

Human resources

Entry

Trend to
–Redistribution of
power capabilities

–Global
structure
–Interdependence
–Iterative process of
market opening
–liberalization as
Destruction old
–adaptation of
Bureaucracy
–institutional
responsiveness

Business system

The macro   Coordination via   Firm and factory Culture
–context   Party-state, and markets

Fig. 15.2 The transformation of China's business system

represented in the horizontal line; and the implication for corporate strategies and/or for their implementation are illustrated in the diagonal line. The broad context of China's interdependence with the rest of the world is illustrated on the outer side of the box, and raises questions which senior management have to bear in mind such as possible longer term trends to the redistribution of capabilities around the world; the realities of interdependence of markets and politics; the iterative and partial processes of market opening around the world; the adaptation of state and corporate bureaucracies and institutional responsiveness—or lack of it—to changing world conditions.

The diagonal of Fig. 15.2 traces different features of corporate activities in China, such as market entry, human resources, production, marketing, etc. The figure represents the interrelatedness of corporate strategy and policy with political and economic developments in China, on the vertical, and the evolution of the business system, on the horizontal plane. The vertical axis traces the political transition, and locates our present position in terms of political development as mature post-totalitarian. The paradox of China is that in terms of economic policy, the country may be located as somewhere between the definitional phase—where there is still a vigorous debate about which norms should prevail as China goes forward: more efficiency in the markets? More national pride in the country's accomplishments and global standing? More accountability of public and corporate officials to the process of law, or to the public through elections?—and the implementational phase—where the Chinese leadership sees its purpose as vigorously promoting the rule of law, and actively creating a large internal market as a level playing field for all comers, along WTO norms.

The implication for corporate operations in China is straightforward: a central task of corporate strategy is to read the transition right, particularly as it affects the business system whose elements penetrate to the heart of corporate operations in China (Story 2010). On the outer vertical of Fig. 15.2 are listed some of the larger questions which our top managerial team should be asking themselves: what is happening worldwide in terms of the ongoing redistribution of capabilities? How is this affecting the global structure? How is China incorporated in the global, interdependent economy? Not least, how is the transition proceeding in China, and how does that process tie into developments in the world polity and economy?

We start with the top corporate team because a global corporation's strategy is shaped by the special features of the industry, and the top team's view of what constitutes right policy (the classic statement is Prahalad and Doz 1987; see Lawson and Story, this volume). In a nutshell, business leaders have to be able to scan the context, ask probing questions about it, elaborate a strategy, and implement it through policy. As the diagonal illustrates, the set of questions which the corporate top team have to elucidate is whether or not to go to China in the first place; if the answer is positive, where to locate; how to set about learning to deal with the party-state; how to manage human resources, production, marketing, and integrating China operations into worldwide operations. This is no easy task, as conditions across China vary greatly, and corporations have faced the different challenges as China has changed. To illustrate this, let us double back to the late 1970s, when China's opening coincided with a shift in global capitalism away from state activism towards open market policies (Nolan 2001; Yeh 2001; Flassbek et al. 2005). We will illustrate the evolution of the business system, as the transition proceeds up the vertical axis, through some examples of corporate experiences since 1980.

The changing business system and business policies over three decades

Foreign investors came to China for a host of reasons to exploit the opportunities opened up by government policy, as an expression of Greater Chinese patriotism, on account of the lure of cheap labor, and to take advantage of China's market potential, infrastructure development, and growing investment in human capital (see Fig. 15.3). In the 1980s, foreign direct investment trickled in, then surged after 1993. Entry to the WTO prompted a further influx. Most of this investment has bunched along the

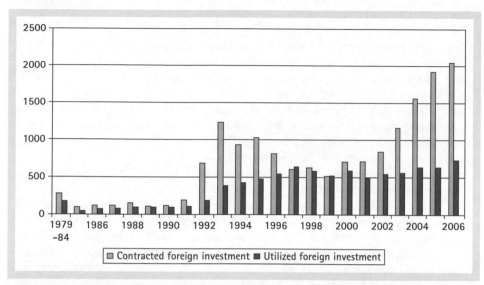

Fig. 15.3 Annual inflows of FDI to China: contracted and utilized amounts, 1979–2006 (US$ 100 million)

Source: China Statistics Yearbook (2006).

eastern coast, until Beijing launched into its huge infrastructure development in 1998 and across the length and breadth of China. Foreign enterprises played a key part in China's growth as a trading state, an emporium for Asian trade, and one of the region's two key currency countries.

As foreign corporations learnt about how, or how not to do business in China, successive governments in Beijing and in the provinces have learnt how to improve the climate for investors. Initially, joint venture (JV) was the party-state's preferred vehicle to attract foreign investors, and tap into Western technologies. The July 1979 law (see Box 15.1) stipulated that foreign capital must account for at least 25 per cent of the total capital of the JVs. Further adaptations came with experience, notably the 1986 law, allowing wholly owned foreign enterprises, and the 1988 law, which provided a more complete legal framework for foreign corporations, protection against expropriations, access to local markets, and a distribution of profits no longer dependable on partners' stakes. This cooperative form of JV became particularly popular among Hong Kong investors in the 1990s, accounting on average for about 20 per cent of inward investment. But the major change has been the popularity among Western corporations for wholly owned operations, which have come to represent about half of the total of actual commitments. This shift to wholly owned operations signals the replacement of overseas Chinese by Western corporations as the prime foreign investors on the mainland. Wholly owned foreign enterprises are the natural allies of Chinese private firms to strengthen property rights there.

Box 15.1 China's FDI regime has been progressively codified

1979 Law on Joint Ventures Using Chinese and Foreign Investment.

1982 Revised Constitution authorizes FDI in China.

1983 Regulations for Implementation of the 1979 Law provided more details on operations and preferential policies for JVs. Also law to protect trademarks.

1984 Law on patents. China starts signing agreements to avoid double taxation with trade partners. This leads to subscribing to international agreements on respect of intellectual property rights.

1985 Law on contracts with foreign enterprises.

1986 Law on Enterprises Operated Exclusively with Foreign Capital permitted the establishment of wholly foreign-owned enterprises in SEZs.
State Council notice on incentives to foster FDI using advanced technologies, and for exports. Later codified in the 1988 Cooperative JV law.

1990 Amendments to the 1983 and 1986 Laws, notably that the chairman of the board of a JV does not have to be appointed by Chinese investors. Protection provided from nationalization.

1993 Law on Unfair Competition, on holding company formula.

1994 Tax provisions to unify gradually the treatment of domestic enterprises and FFEs. Standard 33% corporate income tax and in designated cities; 18% in SEZs and technology development zones. Chinese organizations able to list as joint stock companies.

1995 Interim Provisions in Guiding FDI (revised 1997, and in 2002) classified FDI into four categories: projects are *encouraged* and *permitted* in designated industries that introduce new and advanced technologies, expand export capacity, raise product quality, and use local resources in central and western regions. *Restricted* and *prohibited* are projects in designated areas that make use of existing technologies, compete with domestic production or state monopolies, make extensive use of scarce resources, or are considered a danger to national safety and the environment (e.g. airports, nuclear power plants, oil and gas pipelines, subways and railways, water projects, aerospace, automobiles, defense, high-tech vaccines, mining, printing, shipping, satellite communications, tourism).

2000 Regulation permitting individuals to sign franchise contracts with foreign corporations.

2001 WTO commitments include non-discriminatory treatment of foreign and domestic enterprises, rules on IPR, elimination of requirements on FDI such as forex, technology transfer, local content, export performance. Sectoral commitments include national treatment for foreign firms, ending geographic and other restrictions in automobiles, telecommunications, life insurance, banking and distribution, and personnel, though the pay-off comes in terms of proximity to the market, listening to customers, and taking on the local competition.

This progressive transformation of the business context in China may be illustrated with reference to corporate experiences over the three decades. In the 1980s, multinationals knew little about China, and learning proved arduous for Nike, the US sportswear group. Michael Knight, the CEO and founder, saw the China of the early 1980s as an ideal platform from which to source manufacture and exports of shoes. The vision was of China as a low labor cost base, from which production could be geared up to produce one million units a month by mid-decade. As it turned out, Nike only reached 150, 000 units a month by end-1984, prompting Knight to sigh that China had to be one of the toughest places to do business in the world. Interpreted into the bottom line, what this meant is that the non-labor costs of operating there were nearly one-third higher than in Korea. In addition to labor costs at 10 per cent of Korea's came: the import of ex-pats to train, the problems of finding local suppliers, the difficulty of getting the staff to appreciate international quality standards, the discovery that the workforce in state economic enterprises had no incentive to improve, and unanticipated transport costs, to name just some. No wonder that Nike became interested in shifting its operations to a special economic zone, where free market conditions prevailed.

The emblematic story for that decade was Beijing Jeep. In May 1983, W. Paul Tippett, American Motor's chairman and CEO, asserted that the JV gave the company a "low-cost manufacturing base" to compete against the Japanese in South-East Asia. He was wrong. Beijing Jeep's foreign managers had annual production quotas set by state planners. Chinese factory managers were less concerned with efficiency than with welfare considerations. The real power, it turned out, lay with cadres in the municipalities, in government ministries, or in the party leadership. "The foreign companies that set up operations in China did not obtain the massive sales or the low-cost production of which they had dreamed" (Mann 1989). If ever there was to be a large, unified China market, wrote Jim Mann (1989) in his much acclaimed book *Beijing Jeep*, it was likely to be captured first of all by the Chinese themselves.

In the 1990s, Beijing launched its policy to create "national champions." The policy was informed by fear that China's corporations were dwarfed by global giants, then riding the wave of the 1990s merger boom (see Nolan 2002). By opening such a decentralized country to the multinationals, with their ability to pick and choose between local governments eager to attract their business, government policy seemed to be playing into the hands of the multinationals. China's national champions are minnows, the message ran, about to be devoured by the big beasts of the global corporate jungle.

Matters proved not quite so straightforward, as Whirlpool, the US home appliances giant, discovered when it entered the China market. Like many other rich country corporations which thundered into China in the early 1990s when growth was low at home, Whirlpool expected the China market to equal that of the US within a decade. By winter 1994–5, the US corporation had signed four joint ventures. Thereafter, about everything that could possibly have gone wrong went wrong. Whirlpool discovered too late that the four Chinese JVs had separate, non-complementary, and underdeveloped distribution networks. Bringing their production standards up to scratch cost heavily in terms of ex-pat salaries, and the absorption of scarce managerial resources. Above all, Whirlpool senior management gravely underestimated the local competition. In 1997, it pulled out of its refrigerator and air conditioner operations, citing overcapacity. The top ten producers' market share had reached 90 per cent of the market, with foreign brands accounting for 5 per cent only. Two years later, Whirlpool signed a deal whereby Kelon, along with Haier one of the prime domestic competitors, would sell Whirlpool washing machines under its own brand name. By 2001 Haier had fifteen design centers and forty-six manufacturing plants worldwide, plus 25 per cent of the US refrigerator market.

By the late 1990s, there were plenty of foreign investors with tales of woe. Chinese bureaucracy is a maze, the story ran. We had no idea how long it would take to negotiate a JV. Once we more or less owned the place, we discovered that our partner had a huge hidden agenda, which he revealed to us bit by bit. Trying to bring standards up to match our brand name has proven inordinately expensive. We thought we were buying into China, but we discovered that we could not sell outside the city walls. The plant has been regularly inactive for lack of power. The distribution system is a nightmare, and we are not allowed to set up our own. We failed to calculate demand correctly. As Wilfried Vanhonacker, then Dean of the China European Business School in Shanghai (CEIBs), has said: "Most companies that previously thought it would take three to five years to get out of the loss-making phase now think it will take nine to ten years to break even" (quoted in *Far East Asian Economic Review* 1997).

In the 2000s, as China becomes better known to foreign companies, so corporate policies have been shaped in the context of China's entry to the WTO. Chinese state enterprises, township enterprises, and private firms—foreign or local—have kept their specializations in textiles, shoes, or toys, and have won new positions in high-tech sectors such as electronics and household equipment. Fears about Chinese enterprises being devoured by the big beasts of the global corporate jungle have receded, as the government has used WTO norms to create a more level playing field between mainland Chinese firms and the multinationals. In 2001—the year China was brought into the WTO—only two "national champions" were included in the *Financial Times* 500, which ranks corporations by their market capitalization (*Financial Times* 2001). By 2008, that number had risen to twenty-five, placing China third behind the US and the UK. The combination of record growth rates and ever more competitive markets in China was clearly benefiting domestic players, too.

A common problem for multinationals in China in the 2000s is integration of the business units which have been negotiated across the length and breadth of the country at different moments in the past. Over time, the ways in which deals have been structured have grown more diverse, as the party-state has become less concerned about the legal form and more interested in what foreign investors bring to the party in terms of know-how and technology. In the 1990s, foreign investors followed the example set by Johnson & Johnson, the US pharmaceutical corporation, which decided to launch its oral care, baby, and female hygiene products under the wholly owned foreign enterprise formula (on the wholly owned formula, see Vanhonacker 1997). The formula allowed for greater control over operations, quicker expansion, less time spent on arduous negotiations with public officials and managers, and more protection over patents. Motorola, along with Nokia and

Ericsson a major force in China's huge mobile phone market, went even further, and created a hybrid wholly owned and JV operation: Motorola ran the integrated circuits and cell-phone operation itself, but entered JVs for marketing and sales. It thereby gave local partners a stake in the business, and managed to develop countrywide.

The party-state has learnt to hitch multinational corporate strategies to its own industrial purposes. There are many examples of this. One is BASF, the German petrochemical giant. Petrochemicals is par excellence government regulated. Once BASF had established a JV with Sinopec, it began lobbying for an integrated petrochemicals site. The JV took five years to negotiate, allowing BASF to begin construction in 2001 on eight downstream units and a central naphtha cracker. Production in Nanjing began in 2007, and is one of the biggest such undertakings in China. It has received $2.9 billion in investment, employs 1,400 people, and sells virtually all its output in China. Further investment planned in 2008 is aimed to boost output by 25 per cent over three years. This huge Nanjing production complex is set to rival Ludwigshaven as the focal point for BASF's global operations. BASF is on the way to creating a comprehensive basic-industry empire in China, with the government as partner.

Another example of shifts in party-state policies is provided by the ACFTU's taking on of Wal-Mart to organize union activities in twenty-two of the giant corporation's supercenters across China (Chan 2007). Until the leadership moved social policy up the list of national priorities, the ACFTU had a reputation as a branch of management. But workplace relationships came onto the radar screens of Western social auditors, as Nike and Reebok discovered when conditions among their sub-contractors in China, Indonesia, and Vietnam became headline news in the US. Nike at first argued that the sports-shoe icon was in the business of "marketing" shoes, not making them. The argument did not survive Nike founder and CEO Phil Knight being named a "Corporate Crook" in Michael Moore's book *Downsize This*, the interview Knight gave Moore for his film *The Big One*, and in his grilling by Congressional committees. In 1998 Knight pledged to impose more stringent standards for the factories that Nike hires to make its goods, including minimum age standards, factory monitoring, and greater external access to Nike's practices. The Nike case provided a powerful boost to the anti-sweatshop movement, backed by US and EU trade unions and non-governmental organizations. Sweatshop Watch in the United States, or Clean Clothes in Europe, used consumer pressure and education to get companies to adopt codes of conduct and improve working conditions. Former UN Secretary General Kofi Annan brought the subject up at the Davos summit in January 1999, and launched the Global Compact in 2000. The Pact appealed to businesses and other organizations to act ethically in the new global economy. Aware, as Joshua Cooper Ramo (2007) has suggested, that China's greatest strategic threat is its national image, the ACFTU took a leaf out of the global anti-Nike and anti-Wal-Mart movement, and targeted Wal-Mart as a high profile case. If the US wholesaler could be brought to accept unions, other foreign companies in China would have to follow suit.

WHAT DOES THE FUTURE HOLD?

Looking forward is what business and government alike have to do, in China, as elsewhere. So the question for corporate leadership—presently operating in a China where the political system is recognizably the same as before but WTO norms are being introduced in a highly competitive market environment—is: what does the future hold? A short answer is that China faces the challenge of putting global business norms into effect in the third, implementational phase. In the longer term, as the norms are converted into standard operating procedures, one possible future for China is to develop into an economic society, one of the five key characteristics of a democratic polity—the others being a vibrant civil society, a functioning legal system, a legitimate polity, and a viable state bureaucracy (the criteria for a consolidated market society, see Linz and Stepan 1996). Using the Linz–Stepan terminology, economic society—the context in which a mature business system operates—constitutes "a set of socio-politically crafted and socio-politically accepted norms, institutions, and regulations" that mediate between state and market. China is clearly not there yet. The shadow of an open future hangs over China's transition.

This can be gauged by China's positioning in the World Bank "ease of doing business in" rankings. As may be seen in Table 15.1, China ranks number 83 in the world in terms of the aggregate indicator measuring the ease of doing business in 178 countries, notably higher than Russia or India. But there is a long, long way to go to reach the status of the USA, which as the world's largest economy also has one of the top business climates in the world, just behind tiny Singapore and New Zealand. Moving up the world rankings is clearly in the realm of the possible for China, but the path ahead, in such a large and complex country, is long and arduous. Not least, anywhere along this path, breakdown and disaster is forever a present prospect. This is especially the case of China, where the regime is introducing economic society norms, but where the Communist Party is barely out of the pre-transition phase in terms of political change, along the state-administrative transformation path, illustrated in the matrix.

Hence we may legitimately ask the question: what happens if the Communist Party seeks to hold the fort at this point in China's transformation? And what happens if the Communist Party decides to change its governing norms—particularly, the leading role of the party in state and society. The degree of economic society achieved under a party dictatorship is clearly restricted, either in terms of civil society, of the rule of law, of political legitimacy, or of bureaucratic viability. It is by definition not consolidated, other than as an interim status of ill-defined duration. It is an economic society, bis, in a party-state monopoly, where all procedures become standard, and there is another game in town—more dictatorship or more democracy. The danger is as Douglas North argues, that there will tend to be increasing returns to groups which have nestled into the fabric of the original settlement and an incentive

Table 15.1 China in the "ease of doing business in" rankings

	Ease of doing business in	Starting business	Deal with licences	Employ workers	Register property	Get Credit	Protect investor	Pay taxes	Trade across frontiers	Enforce contract	Close business
Singapore	1	9	5	1	13	7	2	2	1	4	2
USA	3	4	24	1	10	7	5	76	15	8	18
Hong Kong	4	13	60	23	58	2	3	3	3	1	1
Taiwan	50	103	128	148	24	48	64	91	29	92	13
China	83	135	175	86	29	84	83	168	42	20	57
Russia	106	50	177	101	45	84	83	130	155	19	80
India	120	111	134	85	112	36	33	165	79	177	137

Source: IFC The Doing Business in Project, 2008 Rankings.

for them to preserve the existing constraints (North 1991). The danger is sclerosis, only to be undone by war, revolution, or free trade (Olson 1982).

Collapse is one of the four consistent narratives which have been replayed in various formats since the 1980s, or, at the latest, the early 1990s. But is has the advantage of being a narrative which the leadership continues to take very seriously. In the early 1990s, collapse was associated with the Soviet Union's disintegration, fears about the regime's legitimacy, the lack of any experience of how to marketize the economy, and on how to retain the party-state's urban constituency while controlling the countryside (Ming 1992; Fewsmith 1995; Goldstone 1995; *FBIS Daily Report* 1995; Baum 1996; Chang 2001; Hughes 2005). Since 2003, the leadership has taken seriously the many warnings coming from its own think tanks about the mounting tensions in the countryside, the rapid growth in inequalities, the pervasive corruption in all levels of government, or the political system's failures to deliver on environmental, health, or educational policies. (The problem of poverty reduction has moved to the forefront of government attention, under the new leadership. The SDRC submitted an outspoken report in summer 2003 to the leadership on thirteen major problems, including poverty, requiring urgent attention, see *South China Morning Post* 2003; see also Angang et al. 2003.)

China's acknowledged weaknesses flow into the second narrative of a country so caught up in the process of transformation that it cannot, and will not for decades be able to, assume the status of a great and responsible stakeholder in international affairs (Segal 1999; Domenach 2002; Shirk 2007). One version of this holds that the country is trapped halfway in the transition (Pei 2006), and is incapable of advancing much further on account of the multiple contradictions related to the Communist Party-state's shrinking monopoly on power in an ever more diverse and de facto pluralist society. Another version—alluded to above—would hold that China's structural trade surplus is not the result of purposive policy to pursue a beggar-thy-neighbor policy, so much as an expression of the widespread perception among Chinese people that they have to put aside savings for a rainy day. For the population to consume more, the Chinese have to get more optimistic about their collective future. Meanwhile, they prefer to be ruled by the devils they know, even though the system itself may be the source of the problem. It is as easy, this narrative holds, for foreigners to exaggerate China's potential as it is for the leadership's self-perception to be grander than the reality.

Then there is the third narrative of the rising China threat (Bernstein and Munro 1998; Timperlake and Triplett 1999; Geert 2000; Pillsbury 2000; Broomfield 2003; see also successive US Department of Defense reports on China's military power). The threat is not just inherent to the leadership's strategy to transform China into a modern, high-tech mastodon, dominating its region, in effect expecting neighbors to pay tribute to the millennial center of Asian life. It is seen as evidenced by the success to date of a leadership determined to harness all the vast resources of a huge country, ready to open the country to global influences and to encourage and foster the Chinese hunger for knowledge from the rest of the world. This, the argument runs with reason, is the true revolution that is transforming China and the world. It is visible in China's growth rates, the near inexhaustible supply of human labor, the high rate of savings, the hard work of millions of Chinese, the growth rates in both exports and imports, converting China into one of the world's prime production platforms and into becoming the central trade and business partner for the whole of Asia, East and South. And as the US Department of Defense regularly notes in its annual reports on China's military development, defense spending grows apace, as China moves—the expectation runs—to challenge the US in the longer run for primacy in world affairs.

But the fourth narrative looks and finds plenty of supporting evidence to suggest that China is set on an inevitable path to political development, where the giant country will become a democratic, pluralist, and market state, probably organized along federal lines in the manner of the United States, from which so much of the inspiration for a modern China has come (Overholt 1993; Gilley 2004; Guthrie 2006). The signs of China operating as a responsible member of the international society of states abound. So do the multiple indications of China's leadership to recast the state from being a chaotic, "planned" economy into being a regulatory state, under a developing rule of law. For all its failings, the party-state is both running as fast as it can to stay ahead of the game that it has set in movement, and is patient in that it uses time as its ally to transform the inherited harsh, authoritarian political culture of China into a culture which accepts an ever widening plurality of opinions and interests. Time is the leadership's ally in that the future is permanently being used as a place to locate present disagreements and unpleasant trade-offs, awaiting changed circumstances to revisit matters previously better left alone, and to see what can be done this time round. The method of governance is fundamentally empirical; but the vision for the long term is of China's full political development into becoming a modern state—an equal and responsible partner for the great powers of the world.

Which narrative will prevail is a question that all top management teams of multinational corporations investing in China should and do ask themselves. The only evidence about China's direction that we have lies in a history which we know is controversial, since it is the source of the multiple narratives about where China may be heading. What we can observe, bearing in mind the millennial history of China, and the recent past since 1978, is that the leadership fashions policy through mutual trade-offs between two broad and constantly changing coalitions of conservatives and reformers. It cannot stand pat even if it wanted to. In terms of the economic transition, we have also concluded that there has been a very successful transform-ation out of a command economy. But the present degree of economic society achieved under a party dictatorship is clearly restricted, either in terms of civil society, of the rule of law, of political legitimacy, or of bureaucratic viability. China's party state, we conclude, has to continue to move towards laying the institutional foundations of a constitutional order, if a market economy is to be consolidated.

There is in fact much more that we know about China's future than we give ourselves credit for. We know the tasks confronting China if it is to become a consolidated democracy, and how far the regime is from that. We know that the party's ideology is a barrier, but not insurmountable. We have evidence that widespread poverty, a mass peasantry, and a traditional political culture are not ideal materials to create a well-functioning constitutional democracy, even China-style. We know that the Chinese people are scared stiff of a return to the tragedies of the previous two centuries. We know that the party-state is only too well aware of the narrow way, and the many dangers, that lie ahead. We know that our four elements of the world's transformation—US pre-eminence, global markets, the Zeitgeist of "market-democracy," and the internationalization of production—bind China irreversibly into the global system. We know that the regime wants to join the lead group of powers in the world, and that the necessary but not sufficient condition for membership is creating a state under the rule of law. We know that the party's prime legitimation of its hold on power is that it is the sole guide available to chart China's road to prosperity. We know that the party-state is not keen on experimenting with Utopias, and that it prefers to feel its way into an uncertain future. We know that this has entailed, and will continue to entail, moving away from the command to the market economy, to deepening interdependence and away from autarky. We know that this creates major tensions in the rural–urban balance to be struck by the regime, and through the multiple opportunities that marketization creates for gross corruption.

We know therefore that while the political system changes little in appearance, a constant flow of legal and of economic policy measures are being implemented. Incrementally, we also know that these imply extensive changes in the political system. We need no reminding that political leaders are liable to moral failings, and that this is something that China truly shares with the rest of the world. We can only state as a probability the future timing or content of such measures, as each one is the outcome of political negotiations among the changing kaleidoscope of factions. Not least, we can only guess at the time such reforms will take to implement before China becomes a consolidated democracy. But we know that the regime's monopoly powers are shrinking, as the plural reality of China bursts into view, and that a frightened regime is therefore in danger of dithering between a policies of no rush, retribution, or of accelerated reform.

We also know rather more about China's emerging business system than we perhaps give ourselves credit for. Let us assume for the moment the convergence thesis, whereby China is converging in its business system on the developed countries of the world. Under these conditions, it is none too difficult to forecast the conditions which business people may expect going forward over the coming two decades. A convergent China, we may say, would look like a cross between the US and the EU: as a sovereign state, the central government and courts would exercise authority and jurisdiction over the provinces, while the provinces would cultivate their own gardens, much in the manner of European states, while proclaiming that their activities are in line with Beijing's mandate. But if we assume that China is crafting a Chinese-type of capitalism (Redding and Witt 2007), and in addition if we assume for the moment, that the leadership aims to create an efficient, market society, the corollary from the specific pathway taken by China as it moves to consolidate its economic order is that its emergent business system will take on particular features and structure economic activities in some ways rather than in others (Whitley 1998).

China's involvement in the global economy through trade, foreign direct investment, via the operations of global capital markets, or through the exchange of ideas and membership in international institutions does not mean that China will align on some idealized model. Rather, the multi-leveled impacts of China's involvement in the global economy will be mediated through local institutions and through a mutual learning process of adaptation to changing technologies, market structures, and public policies. We would expect not so much convergence as the emergence of a specific capitalism, "China-style." Getting to know this in detail is a prime task for top corporate leadership teams wishing to operate successfully in China.

REFERENCES

ACEMOGLU, D., and ROBINSON, J. A. 2006. *Economic Origins of Dictatorship and Democracy.* Cambridge: Cambridge University Press.

ALLEN, F., QIAN, J., and QIAN, M. 2005. "Law, finance and economic growth in China," *Journal of Financial Economics* 77: 57–116.

ANGANG, H., et al. 2003. "China economic growth and poverty reduction (1978–2002)," *IMF Seminars*, http://www.imf.org/external/np/apd/seminars/2003/newdelhi/angang.pdf

BAUM, R. 1996. "China after Deng: ten scenarios in search of reality," *China Quarterly*: 153–75.

Beijing Review. 1993. "Decision of the CCP Central Committee on some issues concerning the establishment of a socialist market economic structure." Adopted November 14, 1993. *Beijing Review*, November 22–8.

Beijing Youth Daily. 2001. *Beijing Youth Daily*, March 26.

BERNSTEIN, R., and MUNRO, R. H. 1998. *The Coming Conflict.* New York: Vintage Books.

BHATTASALI, D., LI, S., and MARTINS, W. J., eds., 2004. *China and the WTO Accession: Policy Reform, and Poverty Reduction Strategies.* Washington, DC: World Bank.

BRINTON, C. 1965. *The Anatomy of Revolution,* rev. edn. New York: Vintage Books.

BROOMFIELD, E. V. 2003. "Perceptions of danger: the China threat theory," *Journal of Contemporary China* 12(35): 265–84.

CAO, Y., QIAN, Y., and WEINGAST, B. 1999. "From federalism Chinese style to privatisation, Chinese style," *Economics of Transition* 7(1): 103–31.

CARGILL, T. F., and PARKER, E. 2001. "Financial liberalisation in China," *Journal of the Asia-Pacific Economy* 6(1): 1–21.

CHAN, A. 2001, *China's Workers under Assault: Exploitation and Abuse in a Globalizing Economy.* Armonk, NY: M. E. Sharpe.

—— 2007. "Organizing Wal-Mart in China: two steps forward, one step back for China's unions," *New Labor Forum* 16(2): 87–96.

—— and SENSER, R. E. 1997. "China's troubled workers," *Foreign Affairs* (March–April).

CHANG, G. C. 2001. *The Coming Collapse of China.* New York: Random House.

China Investigation Report. 2001. *China Investigation Report: A Study of Contradictions among the People under New Historical Conditions, 2000–2001. (Zhongguo Diaocha baogao, Xin xingshi xia renmin neibu maodun yanjiu 2000–2001.)* Beijing: Zhong-yang bianyiju chubanshe.

Collection of Reform Drafts for China's Economic System. 1988. *Collection of Reform Drafts for China's Economic System (1979–1987).* Beijing: CCP School Publishing House.

DAHLMANN, C. J., and AUBERT, J. E. 2001. *China and the Knowledge Economy: Seizing the 21st Century,* WBI Development Studies. Washington, DC: World Bank.

DAVIES, K. 2007. "China's investment watch," *OECD Observer* 260, March.

DENG, Y. 2001. "Hegemon on the offensive: Chinese perspectives on US global strategy," *Political Science Quarterly* 116(3): 344.

DICKSON, B. J. 2003. *Red Capitalists in China: The Party, Private Entrepreneurs, and Prospects for Political Change.* New York: Cambridge University Press.

DOMENACH, J.-L. 2002. *Où va la Chine?* Paris: Fayard.

—— 2005. *Où va la Chine.* Paris: Fayard.

DONG, L. Z. 2003. "An econometric study on China's economy, energy and environment to the year 2030," *Energy Policy* 31: 1137–50.

DORSEY, T., ROBINSON, D., YANG, Y., and ZEBREGS, H. 2003. "The impact of WTO accession," in W. Tseng and M. Rodlauer, eds., *China: Competing in the Global Economy.* Washington, DC: IMF.

DUMAS, C. 2008. *China and America: A Time for Reckoning.* London: Profile Books.

DUNN, J. 1972. *Modern Revolutions: An Introduction to the Analysis of a Political Phenomenon.* Cambridge: Cambridge University Press.

EICHENGREEN, B., and TONG, H. 2006. "How China is reorganizing the world economy," *Asian Economic Policy Review* 1: 73–97.

Far East Asian Economic Review. 1997. "Rethinking China," *Far East Asian Economic Review* December 18.

FBIS Daily Report. 1995. "Viewing China through a third eye," in translation in *FBIS Daily Report, China* Supplement, 19.

FEWSMITH, J. 1995. "Neoconservatism and the end of the Dengist era," *Asian Survey* 35(7): 635–51.

—— 1999. "China and the WTO: the politics behind the agreement," *NBR Analysis* 10(5): Essay 2.

—— 2001. *China Since Tiananmen: The Politics of Transition.* Cambridge: Cambridge University Press.

Financial Times. 2001. *Financial Times,* May 11.

—— 2008. "Think-tank urges checks on China rulers," *FT.com* February 19.

FLASSBEK, H., et al. 2005. "China's spectacular growth since the mid-90s: macroeconomic conditions and policy challenges," in *UNCTAD: China in a Globalizing World.* New York: UNCTAD, 1–44.

GEERTZ, B. 2000. *The China Threat: How the People's Republic Targets America.* Washington, DC: Regnery Publishers.

GILBOY, G. J. 2004. "The myth behind China's miracle," *Foreign Affairs* July–August: 33–48.

GILL, B., and HUANG, Y. 2006. Sources and limits of Chinese 'soft power,'" *Survival* 48(2): 17–36.

GILLEY, B. 2004. *China's Democratic Future: How It Will Happen and Where It Will Lead?* New York: Columbia University Press.

GILPIN, R. 2001. *Global Political Economy: Understanding the International Economic Order.* Princeton: Princeton University Press.

GOLDMAN, M. 2005. *From Comrade to Citizen: The Struggle for Political Rights in China.* Cambridge, Mass.: Harvard University Press.

GOLDSTEIN, A. 2001. "The diplomatic face of China's grand strategy: a rising power's emerging choice," *China Quarterly*: 835–64.

GOLDSTEIN, A. 2005. *Rising to the Challenge: China's Grand Strategy and International Security.* Stanford, Calif.: Stanford University Press.

GOLDSTONE, J. A. 1995. "The coming Chinese collapse," *Foreign Policy* (Summer): 35–44.

GREEN, S. 2004. The *Development of China's Stock Market, 1984–2002.* London: Routledge Curzon.

GREIDER, W. 1996. *One World: Ready or Not: The Manic Logic of Global Capitalism.* New York: Simon & Schuster.

GURR, T. 1968. "A causal model of civil strife: a comparative analysis using new indices," *American Political Science Review* 62: 1104–24.

—— 1970. *Why Men Rebel.* Princeton: Princeton University Press.

GUTHRIE, D. 2006. *China and Globalization: The Social, Economic and Political Transformation of Chinese Society.* New York: Routledge.

HALL, B., and DYER, G. 2008. "China seen as biggest threat to stability," *Financial Times* April 15.

HARWIT, E., and CLARK, D. 2001. "Shaping the internet in China: evolution of political control over network infrastructure and content," *Asian Survey* 41(3): 377–408.

HEIMANN, S. 2001. "Der Aktienmarkt der VR China (I), (II): Center for East Asian and Pacific Studies, Trier University, Germany," *China Analysis* 3.

HENDERSON, D. 1998. *The Changing Fortunes of Economic Liberalism: Yesterday, Today and Tomorrow.* London: Institute of Economic Affairs.

HERTZEL, T., and WALMSLEY, T. 2000. "China's accession to the WTO: timing is everything." GTAP Working Paper No. 13. West Lafayette, Ind.: Purdue University, Center for Global Trade Analysis.

HEYTENS, P., and ZEBREGS, H. 2003. "How fast can China grow?" in W. Tseng and M. Rodlauer, eds., *China: Competing in the Global Economy.* Washington, DC: IMF.

HOBSBAWM, E. 1994. *Age of Extremes: The Short Twentieth Century* London: Little Brown.

HUANG, Y. 2003. *Selling China: Foreign Direct Investment During the Reform Era.* New York: Cambridge University Press.

HUCHET, J.-F. 1999. "Concentration et émergence des groupes dans l'industrie chinoise," *Perspectives chinoises* 52 (March–April).

—— and RICHET, X. 2002. "Between bureaucracy and market: Chinese industrial groups in search of new forms of corporate governance. CEFC Working Paper No. 2, http://www.cefc.com.hk

HUGHES, C. R. 2005. "Interpreting nationalist texts: a post-structuralist approach," *Journal of Contemporary China* 14(43): 247–67.

HUNTINGDON, S. P. 1968. *Political Order in Changing Societies.* New Haven: Yale University Press.

—— 1991. *The Third Wave: Democratization in the late Twentieth Century.* Norman: University of Oklahoma Press.

HUO, P., and SI, S. 2001. "Employee responsibilities and rights in China," *Asia Pacific Business Review* 7(3): 35–56.

IANCHOVICHINA, E., and MARTIN, W. 2003. "Economic impacts of China's accession to the World Trade Organisation," World Bank Policy Research Working Paper, No. 3053. Washington, DC: World Bank.

ICFTU. 2006. *ICFTU Report for the WTO General Council Review of the Trade Policies of the People's Republic of China, Trade, Employment and Development in the People's Republic of China,* Geneva, April 4 and 6.

International Finance Corporation. 2000. *China's Emerging Private Enterprises: Prospects for the New Century.* International Finance Corporation.

International Herald Tribune. 2005. "White Paper on democracy," *International Herald Tribune* October 20.

JACOBSON, H. K., and OKSENBERG, M. 1990. *China's Participation in the IMF, the World Bank, and GATT: Toward a Global Economic Order.* Ann Arbor: University of Michigan Press.

KAPLINSKY, R. 2006. "Revisiting the revisited terms of trade: will China make a difference?" *World Development* 34(6): 981–95.

KAPSTEIN, E. B., and MASTANDUNO, M., eds. 1999. *Unipolar Politics: Realism and State Strategies after the Cold War.* New York: Columbia University Press.

KENNEDY, S. 2005. *The Business of Lobbying in China.* Boston: Harvard University Press.

KEVUAN, Z. 2000. "Towards the rule of law in China: experiences in the last two decades," *China Report* 36(4): 491–509.

LALL, S., and ALBALADEJO, M. 2003. "China's competitive performance: a threat to East Asian manufactured exports?" *World Development* 32(9): 1441–66.

LAM, W. W.-L. 1995. *China after Deng Xiaoping.* Singapore: Wiley.

LAMPTON, D. M., ed. 2001. *The Making of Chinese Foreign and Security Policy in the Era of Reform, 1978–2000.* Stanford, Calif.: Stanford University Press.

LARDY, N. R. 1998. *China's Unfinished Economic Revolution.* Washington, DC: Brookings Institution.

LAWTON, T. C., ROSENAU, J. N., and VERDUN, A. C., eds. 2000. *Strange Power: Shaping the Parameters of International Relations and International Political Economy.* Aldershot: Ashgate.

LEMOINE, F. 2000. "FDI and the opening up of China's economy," *CEPII* 11.

LI, Y. 2005. "Why is China the world's No 1 anti-dumping target?" in UNCTAD, ed., *China in a Globalizing World.* New York: UNCTAD, 75–104.

LINZ, J. 1978. *The Breakdown of Democratic Regimes: Crisis, Breakdown and Re Equilibration.* Baltimore: Johns Hopkins University Press.

—— and STEPAN, A. 1996. *Problems of Democratic Transition and Consolidation.* Baltimore: Johns Hopkins University Press.

LORA, E. 2005. "Should Latin America fear China?" I-ADB Research Department working paper series, No. 53.

LU, F. 1999. "State, market, and enterprise: the transformation of Chinese state industry," unpublished Ph.D. dissertation, Columbia University.

LU, Q. 2000. *China's Leap into the Information Age: Innovation and Organisation in the Computer Industry.* Oxford: Oxford University Press.

MA, S.-Y. 2000. "Understanding China's reform: looking beyond neoclassical explanations," *World Politics* 52: 586–603.

MADDISON, A. 1998. *Chinese Economic Performance in the Long Term.* Paris: OECD.

MANN, J. 1989. *Beijing Jeep.* New York: Simon & Schuster.

MARAVALL, J. M. 1997. *Regimes, Politics and Markets: Democratization and Economic Change in Southern and Eastern Europe.* Oxford: Oxford University Press.

MATTOO, A. 2002. *China's Accession to the WTO: The Services Dimension.* Washington, DC: World Bank.

MEDEIROS, E. S., and FRAVEL, M. T. 2003. "China's new diplomacy," *Foreign Affairs* November–December: 22–35.

MING, R. 1992. "Taizidang de disandiguo meimeng" ("The Third Reich fantasy of the princelings"), *Zhongguo zhiqun* 10: 39–41.

MOORE, T. 2002. *China in the World Market: Chinese Industry and International Sources of Reform in the Post Mao Era.* Cambridge: Cambridge University Press.

MORLINO, L. 1980. *Come cambiano i regimi politici: strumenti di analisi.* Milan: Franco Angeli.

MURRELL, P. 1992. "Conservative political philosophy and the strategy of economic transition," *Eastern European Politics and Societies* 6(1): 3–16.

NATHAN, A. J., ed. 2001. "The Tiananmen papers," *Foreign Affairs* 80(1): 2–49.

NAUGHTON, B. 1995. *Growing Out of the Plan: Chinese Economic Reform, 1978–1993*. New York: Cambridge University Press.

—— 1996. *Growing out of the Plan: Chinese Economic Reform, 1978–1993*. Cambridge: Cambridge University Press.

—— 2003. "How much can regional integration do to unify China's markets?" in N. Hope, D. Yang, and M. Lang, eds., *How Far Across the River? Chinese Policy reforms at the Millenium*. Stanford, Calif.: Stanford University Press, 204–32.

—— 2007. *The Chinese Economy: Transitions and Growth*. Cambridge, Mass.: The MIT Press.

NEUMANN, S. 1949. "The international civil war," *World Politics* 1: 333–4.

NIELSEN, I., NYLAND, C., SMITH, R., and ZHU, C. 2005. "Marketization and perceptions of social protection in China's cities," *World Development* 33(11): 1759–81.

NOLAN, P. 2001. *China and the Global Economy: National Champions, Industrial Policy and the Big Business Revolution*. Houndmills: Palgrave.

—— 2002. "China and the global business revolution," *Cambridge Journal of Economics* 26: 119–37.

NORDLINGER, E. 1981. *On the Autonomy of the Democratic State*. Cambridge, Mass.: Harvard University Press.

NORTH, D. C. 1991. *Institutions, Institutional Change and Economic Performance: Political Economy of Institutions and Decisions*. Cambridge: Cambridge University Press.

O'DONNELL, G., and SCHMITTER, P. 1986. *Transitions from Authoritarian Rule: Tentative Conclusions about Uncertain Democracies*. Baltimore: Johns Hopkins University Press.

OECD. 2000. *China in the Global Economy: Reforming China's Enterprises*. Paris: OECD.

—— 2005. *OECD Economic Survey: China, Chapter 3, Reforming the Financial System to Support the Market Economy*. Paris: OECD.

—— 2006. *Investment Policy Review of China: Open Policies towards Mergers and Acquisitions*. Paris: OECD.

OLSON, M. 1982. *The Rise and Decline of Nations: Economic Growth, Stagflation and Social Rigidities*. New Haven: Yale University Press.

OVERHOLT, W. E. 1993. *China: The Next Economic Superpower*. London: Weidenfeld and Nicholson.

PEARSON, M. 1997. *China's New Business Elite: The Political Consequences of Economic Reform*. Berkeley and Los Angeles: University of California Press.

PEI, M. 2006. *China's Trapped Transition: The Limits of Developmental Autocracy*. Cambridge, Mass.: Harvard University Press.

PENROSE, E. 1995. *The Theory of the Growth of the Firm*, rev. edn. Oxford: Oxford University Press.

People's Daily. 2002. "Full text of Premier Zhu's Government Work Report," *People's Daily* March 17.

—— 2005. "China issues white paper on political democracy," *People's Daily* October 19. A complete copy of the White Paper can be found on the *People's Daily* website, http://english.people.com.cn/whitepaper/democracy/democracy.html

Pew Global Attitudes Project 2007. www.pewglobal.org June 27: 43.

PILLSBURY, M. 2000. *China Debates the Future Security Environment*. Washington, DC: National Defense University Press.

PING, D. X. 1993. *Selected Works of Deng Xiao Ping*, 378, cited in W. Pien, H. W. Chow, and H. K. Peck, "Establishing a successful Sino-foreign equity joint venture: the Singaporean experience," *Journal of World Business* 34(3) (1999): 287–305.

PISTRUI, D., et al. 2001. "Entrepreneurship in China: characteristics, atrributes and family forces shaping the emerging private sector," *Family Business Review* 14(2): 141–52.

PONCET, S. 2003. "Measuring Chinese domestic and international integration," *China Economic Review* 14(1): 1–21.

PRAHALAD, C. K., and DOZ, Y.-L. 1987. *The Multi-National Mission: Balancing Local Demands and Global Vision.* New York: The Free Press.

QIAN, Q. 1997. "New security concept," *ARF* (July 27), www. shaps.hawaii.edu/security/china/qian-arf-9707.html

—— 2000. "The process of China's market transition (1978–98): the evolutionary, historical and comparative perspectives," *Journal of Institutional and Theoretical Economics* 156(1): 151–71.

RAMO, J. C. 2007. *Brand China.* London: The Foreign Policy Centre.

REDDING, G. 2002. "The capitalist business system of China and its rationale," *Asia Pacific Journal of Management* 19: 221–49.

—— and WITT, M. A. 2007. *The Future of Chinese Capitalism.* Oxford: Oxford University Press.

REILLY, J. 2004. "China's history activists and the war of resistance against Japan: history in the making," *Asian Survey* 44(2): 276–94.

ROGOFF, K. 2006. "Impact of globalization on monetary policy," paper prepared for symposium sponsored by Federal Reserve Bank of Kansas City, "The new economic geography: effects and policy implications," Jackson Hole, Wyo., August 24–6.

ROSEN, S., ed. 1991. "The Chinese debate on the new authoritarianism (l)," *Chinese Sociology and Anthropology* 23(2).

—— and ZOU, G. 1991. "The Chinese debate on the new authoritarianism (1)," *Chinese Sociology and Anthropology* 5.

RUSTOW, D. A. 1970. "Transitions to democracy: toward a dynamic model," *Comparative Politics* 2.

SALLY, R. 1998. *Classical Liberalism and International Economic Order.* London: Routledge.

SEGAL, G. 1999. "Does China matter?" *Foreign Affairs* 78(5): 24–36.

SHAIN, Y., and LINZ, J. 1995. *Between States: Interim Governments and Democratic Transitions.* New York: Cambridge University Press.

SHAMBAUGH, D. 2004. "China engages Asia: reshaping the regional order," *International Security* 29(3): 64–99.

SHIRK, S. 1992. "The Chinese political system and the political strategy of economic reform," in K. Lieberthal and D. Lampton, eds., *Bureaucracy, Politics and Decision-Making in Post-Mao China.* Berkeley and Los Angeles: University of California Press, 77.

—— 1993. *The Political Logic of Economic Reform in China.* Berkeley and Los Angeles: University of California Press.

—— 2007. *China: Fragile Superpower: How China's Internal Politics Could Derail Its Peaceful Rise.* New York: Oxford University Press.

SKOCPOL, T. 1979. *State and Revolutions in Comparative Perspective: A Comparative Analysis of France, Russia and China.* Cambridge: Cambridge University Press.

South China Morning Post. 2003. "A wake-up call for China's new leaders," *South China Morning Post* August 30.

STOPFORD, J., and STRANGE, S. 1991. *Rival States, Rival Firms: Competition for World Market Shares.* Cambridge: Cambridge University Press.

STORY, J. 2010. China Uncovered. What You Need to Know to Do Business in China. London: Pearson's.

STRANGE, S. 1988. *States and Markets.* London: Pinter.

SUN, P. 2005. "Industrial policy, corporate governance and the competitiveness of China's national champions: the case of Shanghai Baosteel group," *Journal of Chinese Economic and Business Studies* 3(2): 173–92.

SUN, Y. 2005. "Corruption, growth and reform: the Chinese enigma," *Current History* 104 (683): 257–63.

SUTTMEIER, R. P., and YAO, X. 2004. *NBR Special Report: China's Post-WTO Technology Policy: Standards, Software and the Changing Nature of Techno-Nationalism* No. 7, May.

TILLY, C. 1975. "Revolutions and collective violence," in F. Greenstein and N. Polsby, eds., *Handbook of Political Science*, iii: *Macropolitical Theory*. Reading, Mass.: Addison-Wesley, 483–555.

—— 1993. *European Revolutions, 1492–1992*. Oxford: Blackwell.

TIMPERLAKE, E., and TRIPLETT II, W. C. 1999. *Red Dragon Rising: Communist China's Military Threat to America*. Washington, DC: Regnery Publishers.

TONGZON, J. L. 2001. "China's membership in the World Trade Organization and the exports of the developing countries of E Asia: a computable general equilibrium approach," *Applied Economics* 33: 1943–59.

TRIMBERGER, E. K. 1978. *Revolution from Above: Military Bureaucrats and Development in Japan, Turkey, Egypt and Peru*. New Brunswick, NJ: Transaction Books.

TRINH, T., and VOSS, S. 2006. "China's commodity hunger: implications for Africa and Latin America, Deutsche Bank Research, June 13.

TSAI, K. 2002. *Back-Alley Banking*. Ithaca, NY: Cornell University Press.

TSENG, W., and ZEBREGS, H. 2002. "Foreign direct investment in China: some lessons for other countries," IMF Discussion Paper, PDP/02/3.

TU, W.-M. 1996. "Destructive will and ideological holocaust: Maoism as a source of social suffering in China," *Daedalus* 125(1): 149–79.

TUCKER, N. B. 2000. "The Taiwan factor in the vote on the PNTR for China and its WTO accession," *NBR* 11(2): 5–18.

UNCTAD 1999. "Les Delocalisations au cœur de l'expansion du commerce extérieur chinois," *Économie et statisitique*, 326–7. 1999–6/7. New York: UNCTAD, World Investment Reports (various).

UNGER, J., and CHAN, A. 1995. "China, corporatism, and the East Asian model," *Australian Journal of Chinese Affairs* 33: 29–53.

USHIYAMA, R. 2007. "Antidumping measures by Europe and the US against China are problematic," Japan Centre for Economic Reform Staff Report, February 8.

VANHONACKER, W. 1997. "Entering China: an unconventional approach," *Harvard Business Review* March–April.

WALDEN, G. 2008. *China: A Wolf at the Door?* London: Gibson Square.

WANG, Y. 2000. "China's domestic WTO debate," *China Business Review* 27(1): 54–62.

WANG, Z. 2003. "The impact of China's WTO accession on patterns of world trade," *Journal of Policy Modeling* 25: 1–42.

WEIDENBAUM, M. 1996. "The Chinese family business enterprise," *California Management Review* 38(4).

WEN, J. 2006. *Excerpts from Chinese Premier Wen Jiabao's Speech on Rural Issues*, posted January 20. Red Orbit: Breaking News.

WHITEHEAD, L. 1996. *The International Dimensions of Democratization, Europe and the Americas*. Oxford: Oxford University Press.

WHITLEY, R. 1998. "Internationalization and varieties of capitalism: the limited effects of cross-national co-ordination of economic activities on the nature of business systems," *Review of International Political Economy* 5(3): 449, 445–81.

WHITLEY, R. 1999. *Divergent Capitalisms: The Social Structuring and Change of Business Systems*. Oxford: Oxford University Press.

WONG, J., and MU, Y. 1995. "The making of the TVE miracle: an overview of case studies," in J. Wong, M. Rong, and Y. Mu, eds., *China's Rural Entrepreneurs: Ten Case Studies*. Singapore: Times Academic Press, 16–51.

XU, X. 1998. *China's Financial System under Transition*. London: Macmillan.

YANG, L. 2005. "Dark side of the Chinese moon: a review of Chen Guidi and Wu Chuntao, Zhongguo nongmin diaocha (Survey of Chinese Peasants). Beijing, People's Literature Publication Company," [publication suspended March 2004] *New Left Review* 32: 132–40.

YAO, S., FENG, G., LIU, A., and FU, G. 2005. "On China's rural and agricultural development after WTO accession," *Journal of Chinese Economic and Business Studies* 3(1): 59–78.

YEH, K. C. 2001. "China's economic growth: recent trends and prospects," in S. Chen and C. Wolf, eds., *China, the United States, and the Global Economy*. Santa Monica, Calif.: Rand Corporation.

YOUNG, A. 2000. "The razor's edge: distortions and incremental reform in China," *Quarterly Journal of Economics* 115(4).

—— 2003. "Gold into base metals: productivity growth in the People's Republic of China during the reform period," *Journal of Political Economy* 111(6).

YU, C.-S. 1999. "Jiang Zemin repeatedly expounds China's domestic and foreign policies in three internal speeches," *Ching Pao*, July 1, *FBIS*, July 9.

ZHENG, J., and ANGANG, H. 2004. "An empirical analysis of provincial productivity in China (1979–2001)," *Journal of Economic Literature Working Paper in Economics* 127.

ZWEIG, D. 2001. "China's stalled 'fifth wave': Zhu Ronghji's reform package of 1998–2000," *Asian Survey* 41(2): 231–47.

—— 2002. *Internationalizing China: Domestic Interests and Global Linkages*. Ithaca, NY: Cornell University.

PART IV

....

CHANGING MARKET GOVERNANCE

....

CHAPTER 16

THE RISE OF THE REGULATORY STATE[1]

MICHAEL MORAN

THE REGULATORY STATE AND BUSINESS POWER

REGULATION is at the heart of any relationship between business and the modern state in one obvious sense: in modern capitalist systems the way business engages with markets is conditioned by a state-backed regulatory framework. The most obvious form this takes is a set of rules governing market exchanges—the kind provided by, for instance, the system of commercial law. In this sense regulation of business life is ubiquitous in the modern market economy. But this chapter is about something more specific, and its character is conveyed by the phrase "regulatory state." The expression has become increasingly common in recent years, and is intended to mean something more than the traditional idea that the state provides a regulatory framework for the conduct of business life. It suggests the existence of a distinctive model of business–government relations: distinctive, for instance, from one where the state expects to replace the market economy with some more directive instruments, like public ownership. But it is here that the uncertainties begin, and they will recur in this chapter. There are two very different sources of our image of the regulatory state and what it implies for business: one is derived from a particular national experience; the other from the perceived experience of the wider economy of advanced capitalism in the last generation.

The single most important national system of democratic capitalism exists in the United States. American democratic capitalism has been distinctive not only in its scale and global influence. It has also pioneered a special kind of state–business relationship. That has created an American "regulatory state"—the most important formation on earth to deserve that title. As we shall see, this American regulatory state has a number of distinctive features: attitude to enterprise ownership; institutional forms; and historical trajectory.

We shall also see that the relationships developed between the regulatory state and business in America have often been very different from those suggested by the second source of the phrase: those that derive from attempts to summarize what has happened to the relationship between the state and business community in the wider world of advanced capitalism over recent decades. This latter image of the regulatory state contrasts it with more interventionist models of economic management—and therefore with more interventionist models of the relationship between the state and the business enterprise.

One of the quickest ways of appreciating what this latter image is trying to tell us about state–enterprise relations is to reflect for a moment on what lies behind the picture of a state as "regulator." It is a metaphor, and one borrowed from regulation in physical systems. In a physical system—like a steam engine or centrally regulated domestic heating—the regulator is a balancer keeping the system in some predetermined equilibrium. Applied to economic regulation this suggests that the state is a manager of the market system, but a manager that intervenes only to return it to some point of equilibrium. One of the most graphic images conveying this is provided by the highly influential work of Osborne and Gaebler (1992). They interpret long-term changes in the character of the modern state as involving a shift from "rowing" to "steering." In the former, the state either commanded large-scale resources, such as publicly owned industries, and used them to determine social and economic outcomes; or in the American instance which so concerned Osborne and Gaebler, it substituted direct ownership with regulation of a "command and control" variety, issuing specific regulatory commands backed by the force of law. By contrast, when it chooses to steer rather than row the state is transformed into a kind of social "pilot," guiding the systems of economy and society. This latter picture assigns the state a relatively subordinate role in its dealings with business, for it is responding to signals, in the manner of a pilot, from its environment—and in democratic capitalism a dominant part of that environment is made up of the business system.

But here the ambiguities and uncertainties multiply. The image of a "steering" state is not new, and some versions convey a very different meaning—indeed a sinister, anti-democratic meaning—from that involved in touching the tiller. The first great work of political theory, Plato's *Republic,* (circa 400 BC) offers an image of authoritarian political leadership in which an elite is pictured precisely in the language of the "pilot" of society. At the other end of the time span, one of the most brutally authoritarian governing systems of the twentieth century, that of Communist China, celebrated the leadership of the "Great Helmsman," Mao Tse-Tung—one of the most savage tyrants in a century of savage tyrants. Totalitarian steering of the kind practised by the Great Helmsman committed some of the greatest crimes recorded in human history (see Scott 1998.)

The very different meanings conveyed by the phrase "regulatory state" suggest that if we want to get an accurate sense of what it means in reality, and in particular what it means for the business enterprise, we should not start with theoretical accounts based on images of regulation; we should instead look at some real live states. That is the approach taken in this chapter. The most important example of a practicing regulatory state, as we have noted, is the United States. It dominates the chapter, for two obvious reasons: the very idea of modern business regulation is an American invention; and most of the important institutional innovations, and problems, in business regulation, are American in origin. We shall see that the history of the regulatory state took a fresh turn in Western Europe from the 1980s onwards, both at the level of the European Union and at the level of some individual member states. That fresh turn is indeed commonly pictured in the language of regulation as pilotage; examining this account is the purpose of the section that follows our examination of the United States. More recently, it has been argued that there has developed yet another variant of the modern regulatory state: one created by crisis and change in the Asian developmental state—in other words, in the state formation which for much of the generation before the 1990s produced the most successful variant of capitalism, at least measured by economic growth and export success. That is why the penultimate section of the chapter looks at this alleged transformation.

THE AMERICAN REGULATORY STATE: SNARLING AND SMILING AT BUSINESS

The relationship between the American regulatory state and the business enterprise is strikingly distinctive, viewed comparatively.

The simplest, but perhaps the most important, indicator of distinction is that this is a relationship with deep historical roots. The pre-industrial American economy was one where the state was closely involved directly in the conduct of economic life, for instance in the chartering of corporations. But the relationship with business took a special turn in the closing decades of the nineteenth century. That special turn was a reaction to a great economic revolution which spanned the generation following the end of the Civil War. This era saw the development for the first time of a significant plutocratic class in the United States, immortalized in the idea of the "robber barons" who emerged in the second half of the nineteenth century to dominate parts of the newly developing economy: for instance Carnegie in steel, Rockefeller in oil, Vanderbilt in rail (Josephson 1962.) The wealth of this class was fabulous by American historical standards, and the economic and political power that it was able to exercise was correspondingly great: "During the 1840s there were not twenty millionaires in the entire country; by 1910 there were probably more than twenty millionaires in the United States Senate" (Hofstadter 1972: 136).

The change was succeeded, in the last quarter of the nineteenth century, by an even more profound institutional development: the development of a new form of economic organization—new to American society, but also to the rest of the capitalist world. It consisted of giant corporations which captured and regulated markets in whole sectors, and which increasingly developed their own distinctive forms of internal organization (Lamoreaux 1985). They were a world away from that of the small farmer or storeowner who was the mythical center of the traditional American economy. These corporations were soon to pioneer new forms of internal divisional organization, which gave professional managers, rather than entrepreneurs, a central role (Chandler 1977: 6–12.) They were, in Chandler's arresting phrase, a "visible hand," which displaced much of the "invisible" hand of the market. The rise of these new giants was also associated with the emergence of new centers of financial power, publicly often demonized as the "Money Trust" allegedly organized on "Wall Street," the great financial district of New York City (Carosso 1973).

These great changes had political origins, and they had political consequences. The rise of the new giant corporations was not the result of some process of natural economic evolution; it reflected the exploitation of the political environment by creative entrepreneurs (Roy 1997: 10–20.) They turned the American state in a distinctive direction and may be said to have been the unintended progenitors of the American regulatory state—unintended because it was in response to the rise of the great new centers of American power that the clamor for regulation originated. The period was one of extraordinary social and economic change—and of corresponding stress, notably for the "old" economy and society of rural America, as it felt the impact of the new economic power and the new economic challenges. The most important political manifestation of this was Populism, a great movement of agrarian radicalism that reached its height in the 1890s. It arose out of the stresses and problems imposed on small business rural America by the momentous changes of the second half of the century, and was a reaction against the figures and institutions that seemed to be behind, and to benefit from, those changes: the new plutocracy represented in the public mind by the "Robber Barons"; the giant corporations that seemed to be able to control, rather than be controlled by, markets; the new centers of finance, and their perceived ability to control the terms on which small entrepreneurs could get credit. The ensuing crisis of legitimacy for big business was expressed in the view that, in place of small enterprises with a human face and spirit, there had been created corporations without a "soul" (Marchand 1998).

The single most important result of this hostility was the passage of the Sherman Act in 1890. This law was prompted by the furious debates over the alleged power of the trusts. It is agreed by scholars that the Act was aimed at the capacity of the new corporations to manipulate market competition, but critical interpretations have subsequently stressed the limited impact of the Act and its symbolic rather than substantive role. Critics of its effectiveness point to the extent to which the original proposals were shorn of sanctions during passage through Congress, and the extent to which later court interpretations created a jurisprudence which minimized the impact of the law on corporate combinations (Bowman 1996: 63–9). The Act nevertheless has claims to be the founding measure for a Federal regulatory state aimed at controlling corporate power. But it did not develop in isolation. It is a touchstone because it accompanied other events in the birth of the American regulatory state. The Progressive Movement was a kind of "twin" of Populism, but one focused more on creating efficient and honest administration, and one which had enduring roots in the professional classes being created in the newly urbanizing America (Foley 2007: 266–76.) To this period, thus, also belongs the creation of the Interstate Commerce Commission (1887–1995) from which we can date one of the characteristic forms of business regulation for the next century—rate and service regulation, which extended over time into industries created by new technologies, like airlines and telephones (Stone 1991). Likewise, the passage of the Food and Drugs Act 1906 inaugurated a key, and enduring, history of Federal regulation of both the food and pharmaceutical industries, leading to the establishment of a major regulatory agency, the Food and Drug Administration (Hilts 2003).

These are important episodes because they resonate through the political history of the regulation of business in America. Movements critical of the exercise of American business power have deep historical roots. There exists a strong and long established tradition of highly adversarial criticism of business institutions. This tradition exists in spite of, or perhaps even because of, the absence of the kind of root and branch opposition to capitalism represented by socialist movements in Europe, and in spite of the weakness of any American tradition of direct ownership of productive resources by the state.

The Great Crash of 1929, and the ensuing Great Depression, reignited this tradition of suspicion of big business, and especially of big business identified with the "money trusts" of Wall Street. This was an era of financial catastrophe, revelations of fraud, the collapse of production, and mass unemployment. Out of this came the "New Deal," shorthand for a series of social and economic reforms introduced under the Presidency of Roosevelt. The "New Deal" is a powerful symbol for a new relationship between government, business, and society, and a key development in the American regulatory state—but the meaning of that symbol, we shall see, continues to be contested.

The New Deal built on the foundations of populism and progressivism to create some of the key institutions of a *regulatory state,* and thus of a distinctively American way of ordering the relations between government and business. The heart of this new regulatory state was a series of Federal regulatory agencies. The most important of these were concentrated on financial markets and institutions: for instance, the Securities and Exchange Commission regulated stock markets; the Federal Deposit Insurance Corporation safeguarded small deposits in banks and, as a corollary, regulated the prudential conduct of those banks (Moran 1984, 1991).

The New Deal also established a highly distinctive *mode* of regulation that has ever since deeply shaped the relations between business, the state, and the wider political system. The most important feature of this mode is the dominance of the law and of legal argument. Formed by statute, in a culture where law was already central to the regulation of social relationships, the regulatory process soon became heavily shaped by the courts and by legal argument—a development confirmed by the adoption of the Administrative Procedures Act (1947), which greatly strengthened legalistic proceduralism.[2] Lawyers emerged as the key figures in negotiating the relationship between the new regulatory state and American business, both in the regulated enterprises and in the regulatory institutions. The law schools of the universities became important providers of skilled professionals for this new regulatory state (McCraw 1984: 243–4). We will in later pages see one consequence of this mode: the importation into the regulation of business of a distinctive feature of American legal culture—its reliance on adversarial argument between opposing parties as a means of determining outcomes.

The creation of new regulatory bodies and new, legally informed ways of thinking about business policy can be thought of as involving the imposition of constraints on business institutions—a common perception among critics of the New Deal in the business community. But this was not the whole story. Another feature of the regulatory state that the New Deal created reminds us that business institutions in America, whatever popular hostility they aroused, still entered the New Deal with formidable power resources. The most important resource was ideological: attachment to the market order still dominated the minds of most Americans (Galambos 1975). The aim of the New Deal was to stabilize, not replace, the business order (Foley 2007: 279). The institutional structure, and the actual practices of the new regulatory bodies, ensured that there was a great deal of cooperative regulation with business, market actors being encouraged to take responsibility for running their own regulatory affairs. A good example of the style of the new regulatory state is provided by the single most important agency established by the New Deal, the Securities and Exchange Commission. The Commission was designed to regulate the institution—stock exchanges—that had been at the heart of the scandalous collapses in 1929. But from the start the leadership of the Commission was drawn from the very markets where scandal had originated: its first chairman, Joseph Kennedy, founded the fortune of the Kennedy political dynasty by financial speculation in the 1920s. More important still, the Commission worked through a kind of "franchising" system: it delegated responsibility for regulation to the stock exchanges themselves, mostly restricting itself to authorizing and supervising these self-regulatory bodies (Seligman 1982: 103–23.)

In short, there is a contradictory history to the American regulatory state: a contradiction between a cooperative regulatory mode and a culture of adversarial suspicion. We can see the two at work in the great turn taken by regulation from the 1960s. This was the era when the interest of the regulatory state expanded to what is generally called the new "social" regulation: control of the environmental consequences of firm activity; control of health and safety in the workplace; control over (discriminatory) hiring and employment practices.

The new age of social regulation prompted an intensification of a key trait in the American system of business regulation: a further marked turn to the law, and indeed to a particularly adversarial form of law (Stewart 1988). Analysts like Vogel have established that, viewed comparatively, American regulation has long been more legalistic and punitive than regulation in most other large capitalist economies (D. Vogel 1978, 1986, 1989, 1996). But the advent of the new social regulation heightened these features. It strengthened a culture of what Kagan (2001, 2007) calls "adversarial legalism," the key features of which were a willingness to impose (often draconian) penalties on enterprises for breaches of regulations, and a readiness both on the part of the regulated and the regulators to resort to adversarial confrontation in courts to settle disputes. This readiness in turn reflects a wider culture of litigation, and the fact that, increasingly, institutions and groups not directly party to the regulatory process have shown a readiness to try to intervene by invoking law.

The contradictory inheritance continues to shape the politics of the relationship between business and the American regulatory state. The corporation is confronted by a two-headed beast: one with a smiling face, the other snarling at business. In recent decades—since the Reagan revolution of the 1980s—these contradictory aspects of the state have struggled for supremacy.

Business influence over regulation has been strengthened by a number of developments, notably by a paradigm shift within the intellectual world of the regulators themselves, and by a shift in the priorities of politicians. There has occurred a change in the balance of analytical skills represented in the agencies, and a change in perceptions of the character of the regulatory task. As we saw earlier, the great age of the institutionalization of the regulatory state was also the age of legal dominance over the regulatory process. But since the 1980s lawyers have been joined, and to some degree supplanted, by economists, and this has coincided with a shift in the way regulatory intervention is defended: justification is increasingly done in the language of microeconomic impact analysis (Eisner et al. 2006: 59–60.) A pioneer in this change was the great economist (and deregulator of airlines) Alfred Kahn, who liked to quip that for him airplanes were just "marginal costs with wings" (McCraw 1984: 224.)

This intellectual change has accompanied a growing lack of confidence in "command and control regulation": that system which relies on the enforcement of regulation by issuing down a legally backed hierarchy. The rise of economists and economics helped legitimate the deregulation movement, which produced liberalizing reforms in industries like telecommunications, airlines, and financial services. It also encouraged experiments with "soft" regulation: these include the attempt to use market style mechanisms (such as licensing systems allowing the purchase of "pollution permits" in environmental regulation). There developed a conviction that some areas of regulation were so technically complex that "command and control" was too blunt an instrument, thus prompting experiments in the delegation of regulatory authority to affected industries and enterprises, subject only to the achievement of broadly prescribed standards (Eisner, Worsham, and Ringquist 2006; Eisner 2007).

These paradigm shifts can call on that tradition in the American regulatory state which approved of close business involvement in self-policing. But they were reinforced by the wider ideological shifts of recent decades. Although these date mostly from the "Reagan revolution," some of their origins lie in the 1970s: the landmark deregulation of airlines, and of financial services, for instance, was well under way by the time that decade ended. But the Reagan presidency nevertheless marked a distinct change in the climate created by partisan politicians (Eisner, Worsham, and Ringquist 2006.) Every president since Reagan has at some period of office announced a temporary standstill on the making of regulations, usually expressed in the language of relieving the "burden" of regulation on business. And even the one president who publicly presented himself partly as an opponent of the Reaganite tradition—Clinton—also publicly endorsed Osborne and Gaebler's theory of a shift towards a "steering" government; indeed it is the appropriation of Osborne and Gaebler's language of "reinventing government" by the Clinton administration which made their work so well known and so influential. Every president since the start of the 1980s has talked the language of the "burden" of regulation on business, of deregulation, and of "soft" regulatory initiatives.

This is the aspect of the American regulatory state which has looked with a benign gaze on business in recent decades. But the other, snarling, face has also been in evidence. There is still life in the adversarial tradition, a tradition that is in part the product of the old populist suspicion of big business, and in part the product of the adversarial legal culture. Studies of American public opinion show a deep-rooted suspicion of big business, alongside an equally deep-rooted tendency to mythologize the virtues of small business (D. Vogel 1996; Dennis 2004). And for all the experiments with "soft" law, the revolution in regulation signaled by the advent of the new social regulation in the 1960s produced an irreversible juridification of the regulatory process, which has permanently exposed business to adversarial, punitive enforcement. Kagan and Axelrad's comparative study of regulatory enforcement paints a consistent picture of American distinctiveness: of a greater willingness to confront and to punish the corporation in the United States by comparison with experience in other leading capitalist democracies (Kagan and Axelrad 2000).

This exposure to the peculiarities of American legalism has taken a form which has been hugely damaging to the business enterprise. American liability law is distinctive in its expansive interpretation of liability for damages, and the result has been to expose enterprises to highly expensive lawsuits: the targets have been as diverse as asbestos and tobacco (Sicilia 2004). In a legal culture which is not only adversarial but also fiercely competitive, the potential rewards of successful cases have also stimulated the development of a highly aggressive branch of the legal services industry. Lawyers have invested some of their gains in one area (for instance asbestos) to fund cases in others (for instance tobacco). They have also used their wealth to fund, and try to influence, the competitive electoral system in order to defend the jurisprudential assumptions which support this thriving industry (Derthick 2005).

The continuing reality of adversarial implementation, combined with a vigorous, threatening industry staffed by liability lawyers, shows that, whatever the rhetoric of democratic politicians or academic theorists, the practical implementation of regulation is often anything but business friendly in the American regulatory state. One important reason the actual record of successive presidents does not match their deregulatory rhetoric is that there are powerful wider social forces driving continual regulatory intervention in the affairs of the enterprise. The most immediate manifestation is the way scandal functions as a driver of regulatory change. One of the most striking examples is provided by experience of financial regulation, notably of accounting and audit, in recent years. In the Sarbanes–Oxley Act of 2002 Congress transformed what had been a settled domain of self-regulation dominated by the industry into virtually a paradigm of traditional, adversarial command and control regulation. The moving force behind this was a series of financial scandals and collapses, of which the best known was the Enron Corporation. But "best known" is the appropriate phrase here. Business operates under the scrutiny of a highly competitive (and therefore aggressive) media system, which is constantly searching for scandals to discover and expose (Berry 1999: 120–30); and under a highly competitive political system in which legislators are constantly searching for scandalous regulatory failures to remedy. In other words, there are important features inscribed in the very character of the American regulatory state which are pushing it in the direction of deeper and wider controls over business, even as politicians and regulators talk the language of deregulation and light touch control.

The briefest characterization that we can offer of the American regulatory state is also the most obvious. It is *American:* that is, it can only be understood as a manifestation of very special American historical development, institutional innovation, and cultural patterning. Is the same true of our second great example?

The European Regulatory State: Crisis and State Building

The experience of business with the American regulatory state provides a kind of informal "benchmark" against which we can try to understand the European regulatory state—a formation that has its origins in the political economy of the 1970s. By that time, as we have seen, the American regulatory state had a number of well-established features. It had developed out of a long series of crises dating back over a century. It was marked by the linked traits inscribed in American political culture and American legal culture: that is, it was enmeshed in the institutions of democratic politics and it was commonly characterized in its enforcement practices by adversarial legalism. It thus presented two faces to business: a benign face which represented deregulation, liberalization, an emphasis on consultation with business, and light touch implementation; and a hostile face which represented the long history of suspicion of big business and a determination to settle economic disputes by adversarial challenge in the courts.

The most influential account of the rise of the regulatory state in Europe, that offered by Majone (1991, 1996, 1999), begins by invoking some of these American parallels, but we can see immediately that the American example is ambiguous: it leaves unsettled the question of whether a regulatory state is business friendly or business hostile. The most obvious sense in which Majone's model is American is that it is consciously Madisonian. It argues that the regulatory state is a necessary response to the complexities of economic government in democratic capitalism, and thus a necessary alternative to majoritarian models of democratic decision-making. As an alternative it offers insulation from majoritarian democracy—hence the Madisonian inspiration. Since the regulatory state is pictured as a functional response to high complexity in economic government, an obvious question is: why did it only develop in Europe after the 1970s? Complexity of this kind under democratic capitalism is, after all, hardly something new. Two novel conditions in the 1970s help explain the change. Both created a problem in relations between the European Union and the business system. The first sprang from the limits to state building in the new system of economic government being constructed in the European Economic Community (now the European Union.) On Majone's account the central governing institutions of this new system of economic government—notably its key executive agency, the European Commission—have been forced to depart from the command modes of control so common in the member states because of the character of the new "state": in particular, it lacks the fiscal resources and—partly as a result—the resources in skilled personnel directly to exercise control. It has thus been forced to appropriate the doctrine of subsidiarity, under which responsibility is delegated to lower levels and, in part as a result, the policies which are be implemented have to be worked out in consultation with the affected parties. As far as business is concerned, this means that it can expect to be closely involved in policy formulation, and to have a big say over policy implementation. The future in such a state seems to lie with business self-regulation. This expectation is reinforced by the second condition identified by Majone as a prompter of the rise of the regulatory state: the collapse of the Keynesian economic order following the end of the "long boom" in the advanced capitalist nations in the early 1970s. The exhaustion of Keynesianism also signaled the exhaustion of an age of direct, large-scale state intervention in economic life, and a turn to regulation in the "steering" sense identified at the beginning of this chapter.

These twin conditions—the turn to indirect modes of government via the doctrine of subsidiarity and the turn away from Keynesianism—combine to produce an (embryonic) European regulatory state: a mode of economic government which is "regulatory" in the twin sense that it relies on the promulgation of rules which are implemented elsewhere, and in the sense that it conceives the tasks of economic government as balancing and steering rather than direct control. Out of these twin forces come a European Regulatory State that practices economic government by establishing broad rules (like directives) in consultation with affected interests; these interests are then heavily involved in shaping the transposition of those rules into practical measures within individual national economies, individual sectors, and even individual enterprises.

It will be clear that this is a "business friendly" system of economic government, at least in intent. And it has another intended feature, which is designed to make it more business friendly still. We recall that the institutions and arenas of regulation in the US were heavily "politicized": that is, infused with the influences of democratic accountability and partisan political argument. Because they are faced with a power-ful Congress intent on oversight, agencies are constantly exposed to the influences of majoritarian democracy. The regulatory state movement in Europe, both at the level of the European Union and, as we shall see, at the level of important member states, has been driven by a very different force: the desire to "depoliticize"—which is to say, to take out of the partisan democratic arena issues formerly subject to democratic argument and to replace them with agencies that are insulated from the pressures of majoritarian democracy. The most important sign of this is the development docu-mented by Coen and by Thatcher: the spread of "non-majoritarian" regulatory agencies across the European Union, both in its most important member states and at the level of the Union itself (Thatcher 2002a, 2002b, 2005, 2007; Coen and Thatcher 2008). As far as the Union is concerned, the most important creation is the European Central Bank, an agency with an increasingly elaborate and wide mandate which controls a decision—determination of short term interest rates—formerly widely dispersed, and commonly controlled by democratically elected politicians (Macartney and Moran 2008; Moran and Macartney 2009). What is more it is an agency whose mandate has been shaped by pro-business ideologies, notably the object of controlling inflation and advancing "sound money" doctrines. This devel-opment exactly fits the pattern of what Majone calls "Madisonian democracy"—an emphasis on the technocratic settlement of policy problems through a process of adjustment between the affected parties.

Viewed in these terms, the European regulatory state looks a much more unam-biguously business friendly political formation than does its American counterpart. What is more a number of contingent features support this picture. In its search for partners in regulation the Commission has a well-documented history of seeking to involve business interests, notably the largest enterprises (Coen 1998, 2007). In addition the lobbying worlds which surround the making of regulatory policy at Union level are populated by a well-organized industry where some of the best-resourced actors are business institutions. Moreover, when we look at the European Regulatory State in American terms one key feature is missing: with the exception, discussed below, of the European Central Bank, it is hard to identify European regulatory agencies with anything like the clout, resources, or status that characterize the institutional giants of American Federal regulation. The complex systems of "double delegation" (Coen and Thatcher 2008) practiced in the European Union mean that even when agencies are created they are typically mired in complexities of multi-level governance. An instance is provided by the example of the European Chemicals Agency, created in 2007 to register and evaluate chemicals across the Union—a vital matter (European Chemicals Agency 2008).[3] Most of the detailed work is actually delegated to individual member states, while key parts of the industry—such as the production of pesticides—are regulated under an entirely different regime. In short, the institution which has given the American regulatory state "bite" in its dealing with business, the public regulatory agency, is a much more enfeebled animal in the European case. Moreover, Coen and Thatcher's study (2008) of the creation of EU wide networks of regulators—a second best solution to the problem of developing some Union wide regulatory capacity—suggests that these networks are of very limited use; they are certainly no substitute for the institutional giants of American regulation.

But this summary judgment that the European Regulatory State is business friendly is complicated by two developments, one at the level of the Union itself, and one in at least one important member state.

As far as the Union is concerned, whatever the rhetoric, it is not plain that the practice of EU-shaped regulation is indeed light touch. Much depends on the perspective of the affected interest. The diversity and complexity of business interests across the Union—divided by sector, by size, and by national regulatory traditions—means that the impact of regulatory intervention will be felt very differently by different groups. From the point of view of business regulatory systems that were historically weighted towards voluntary self-regulation, such as those of the UK or Ireland, many regulatory interventions—in areas as disparate as the regulation of product packaging and labeling, and the regulation of workplace safety—have been experienced as the creation of quite prescriptive systems of rules. More important still, the impact of the single most important regulatory agency created by the EU, the European Central Bank, has had complex and highly varying effects on business interests in different sectors. This is hardly a surprise because the Bank is trying to operate a single interest rate rule across a hugely diverse set of capitalist economies: consider the impact of a single interest rate regime on business communities as diverse in their market position, form of organization, and cultural understandings as those of the Germany, Spain, and the Republic of Ireland. Only by construing business "interests" at an almost metaphysical level of abstraction could the operations of the Union's interest rate regime be identified as unambiguously "business friendly." The developing institutional capacity and ambitions of the ECB are also changing its relations with business interests. The Bank has rapidly developed as an institution with its own highly distinctive organizational culture: it is a major promoter and shaper of banking systems, notably in the new accession states of the Union, and is also a rapidly developing center of expertise about both monetary policy and banking supervision and regulation (Moran and Macartney 2009). In short, it is in many instances superordinate, rather subordinate, in its dealings with key banking interests; indeed, in respect of the rebuilt private enterprise banking systems of the former communist autocracies it has been critical in the very construction of business interests (Johnson 2006).

This tendency for regulatory agencies to develop distinctive institutional cultures and powerful resources of expertise and information, independent of regulated interests, and often capable of imposing their will on those interests, is a well-documented feature of the American regulatory state. It is connected to another feature also well documented in regulatory systems: the importance of struggles for "turf" and influence in the systems of bureaucratic politics that are the natural by-product of the regulatory state. The process is well illustrated by the case of competition regulation in the EU, a critical part of the Union's area of competency in economic government. Wilks has called DG IV (the competent DG) the most powerful agency for the regulation of competition on earth (1999; and see also Wilks 2005; Wilks and McGowan 1996; Wilks and Bartle 2002). Under a succession of Commissioners it has also turned into one of the most abrasive, quite matching American regulators in its enforcement style. It has been involved in a series of high-profile confrontations with large firms, both European and American; it has, American fashion, used its powers to raid the offices of firms (in the search for evidence of collusion); and it has used its power to impose huge fines on large American and European multinationals, perhaps the most notable example being provided by its protracted battle with Microsoft.

The second big complication produced by the "business friendly" image of the European regulatory state is provided by the case of one member state, the United Kingdom. The UK is critical to understanding the regulatory state in part because Britain is a major national economy, and the most important financial center in the Union. But it also has a more analytical importance, because in the UK we have seen in recent decades the most ambitious attempt by any leading capitalist democracy to construct a new regulatory state. The relationship of business to this new regulatory order is puzzling and ambiguous. The puzzle may be stated as follows. On the one hand the British regulatory state exactly follows the kind of path we might have expected had we followed Majone's reasoning. After the end of the long boom in the 1970s the British economy, and the British system of economic government, entered a protracted crisis—in many ways the most serious crisis of any advanced capitalist economy. That was succeeded in the 1980s, under the prime ministership of Margaret Thatcher, by the implementation of some of the most radical reforms in the advanced capitalist world. The state attempted to withdraw from the direct control of large areas of economic life. The big symbols of that were the disavowal of Keynesian theories of active management of the macroeconomy, and the program of privatization of publicly owned enterprises—the most ambitious program of privatization in any large capitalist economy. The state also attempted to remove many restrictive practices in the economy. The most important examples were in labor markets and in financial markets—the latter symbolized by the "Big Bang" on the London Stock Exchange, which dismantled barriers to market entry and to price competition. The state also moved in the direction of relying heavily on reformed, or newly created, regulatory agencies to manage economic life. These agencies were constructed so as to ensure that areas of economic life that had hitherto been heavily politicized (that is, under the influence of democratic, partisan politics) were now to be run in a "depoliticized" fashion. The two most striking examples of this were: the gradual depoliticization of monetary policy, culminating in 1997 in the transfer of responsibility for setting short-term interest rates to an independent Monetary Policy Committee of the Bank of England; and the creation of a network of regulatory agencies to manage the newly privatized industries. This latter innovation—the creation of free-standing regulatory agencies—was soon extended to other parts of business regulation, either by the reform and integration of existing bodies (the experience of environmental policy) or by the creation of new free-standing institutions (the experience in broadcasting).

But if business believed that in the process it was getting a more compliant state, the experience of the two decades or so of the British regulatory state will have disabused it of that illusion. The turn to regulation in practice created new and formidable instruments of state control. There are four main reasons for this unpleasant outcome—unpleasant at least as far as business is concerned.

The first is that in key areas of economic life, of which the financial markets are the most important, the new agencies of regulation replaced systems of self-regulation that had been under the control of the actors in the marketplace. What is more, by replacing an informal, and often secretive, system by openly organized and explicitly empowered public bodies, the reforms forced into the public domain issues that could once be settled tacitly. The shift to statutory-based regulation also made the system look much more "American" in one other key respect: it made the courts and the law important in the implementation of regulation.

Second, whatever the ambitions of the creators, it has proved impossible to "depoliticize" the new systems of regulation. The history of the regulation of privatized industries is a particularly instructive example. The original theorists of regulation thought of it as a transitional arrangement, which would be succeeded by a "withering away of regulation" as market forces asserted themselves. In truth, regulation of privatization has become more complex, more detailed, and more entrenched. What is more, a whole set of public policy issues—to do with the appropriate levels of enterprise profit, and executive reward—have proved impossible to keep from the democratic public arena (for details, see Moran 2007: 95–123).

Third, this process of politicizing regulation has proved impossible to contain; it has spilled over into hitherto "depoliticized" domains in an often uncontrollable fashion. In whole areas of company law and company regulation recent decades have been an age of turmoil, of constant changes of rules, and of the intervention of democratic politicians into arenas like corporate governance. Of course business has fought back, and often fought back successfully; the fabulous enrichment of the corporate elite in recent decades shows that the most powerful have often been able to resist the complaints of democratic politics. But they have had to do precisely that: argue and resist, in fields that were once the domain of uncontested, silent acquiescence.

Fourth, and finally, the relationship between many of the new agencies and business has proved anything but easy, for at least some of the agencies have been far from business compliant. This is most evident in the field of the regulation of competition, maybe the single most important domain of regulation, especially for the large enterprise. The history of the regulation of competition for about fifty years after the Second World War was dominated by the Monopolies and Mergers Commission, which, as Wilks's (1999) history shows, was essentially a business friendly institution that expected to regulate in a cooperative fashion, especially in cooperation with the biggest firms. The successor institutions operate under very different mandates and with very different institutional cultures. They have been involved in a number of high-profile clashes with individual enterprises, often working in concert with Brussels regulators; these clashes show that the largest enterprises now have to operate in a very different way from the cooperative world of the old Monopolies and Mergers Commission.

The regulatory state in Europe does not quite match the extremes of smiling and snarling that we saw in the case of its American relative; nevertheless, as far as business is concerned it is a complex and moody animal to deal with. How far is the same true of the successor to the East Asian developmental state?

The Developmental State and the Regulatory State

We have thus far emphasized two features of the regulatory state: the degree to which it is rooted in distinct national and regional environments; and the extent to which it is the product of crisis and change. In the American case, this means crisis and change in the historically established character of regulatory institutions; in the European case it means the changes impelled by state building at the level of the Union and the crises of a Keynesian political economy. But the state formation which over the generation to the early 1990s proved most successful in delivering capitalist economic expansion—that practiced by the developmental states of East Asia—also entered a sustained period of crisis from the 1990s, albeit that the crisis took different forms, and was of different levels of severity, in individual systems. Debate of course exists whether a distinct "developmental state" of an East Asian—or even of a limited national—kind can indeed be identified (for debates on the single most important, Japanese, case: Johnson 1982; Samuels 1987; Babb 2001). What is more, there plainly are dangers in trying to assimilate distinct national and regional experiences into a single model of an East Asian developmental state. But two points do seem well established: that there existed in Japan, and in the smaller "Tiger" economies, a distinct kind of partnership between strong state agencies and business, especially big, organized business; and that from the 1990s this partnership entered a prolonged period of difficulty, typified by the great financial crisis of 1997, and the prolonged implosion of "post-bubble" Japan. Two forces seemed to be driving developmental states in a regulatory direction: in the case of the "Tigers" societal pressures unloosed by demands for greater democratization; and in the case of both Japan and the Tigers, pressures from global economic markets for more liberalization of markets and more transparency in the relationship between market actors and public agencies (Amyx 2004; Pirie 2005, 2007). The heart of these pressures for change could be traced to global financial institutions: because it was in the financial markets that the great 1997 crisis was located; because Japanese financial markets and institutions had become central to the global financial order; and because it was financial globalization that lay at the heart of the wider forces making for the transformed environment of developmental states.

On some accounts the conjunction of the crisis of the developmental state and the pressures of financial globalization have decisively pushed the former in the direction of the regulatory state. For Jayasuriya (2001, 2005) the heart of the matter lies in the evolution of one key regulatory institution, the central bank: throughout the 1990s central banks in developmental states (and in many other states) emerged as increasingly independent regulatory agencies with distinct mandates, normally attached to the goal of maintaining price stability. That emergence reflected the increasing hegemony of interests organized in the global financial markets, and was promoted by supranational agencies of global financial regulation. Alongside this a number of more contingent forces helped foster institutional innovations that made development states look more "regulatory." For instance, pressures from global economic actors and from global supervisory institutions challenged the characteristically discretionary and collusive modes of doing business that were part and parcel of the developmental state; and with an insistence on more transparent and formally specified rules went the creation of new agencies to formulate and police those rules.

That these are very important developments; that they arise from the crisis of the developmental state; that they represent a shift in the direction of a "regulatory state": all this looks incontestable. The more difficult questions are how great the changes have really been, and how far they represent a fundamental shift in the balance of power such as to marginalize the interests that controlled the developmental state. Here there are two grounds for skepticism about the extent of change. The first takes us back to an established theme: the ambiguous character of the regulatory state itself, simultaneously a "liberalizing" and a "controlling" project. The difficulty is encapsulated in the title of Steven Vogel's classic study of regulatory change in Japanese, and other, financial markets: "freer markets, more rules" (1996). In other words, the shift to a more openly regulatory mode in the financial markets of the former developmental systems does not necessarily entail a retreat in control of business by state agencies—in key respects it legitimates more comprehensive, more formal, and more detailed regimes of control.

The second ground for skepticism lies in the close examination of the experience of what entrenched interests have been able to do with the new institutional regimes. The problems are very well described in Walter's (2006) account of Japan. The key political constellations, and corrupt and collusive relationships, that lay at the heart of the Japanese development were those between a dominant political party (LDP), bureaucrats, and powerful corporate interests. Though these corrupt relationships give rise periodically to scandals, there is little sign that the forces that bind them together—exchanges of money, contracts, and policy favors—have significantly weakened. Babb (2001) shows how institutional change within the state sector is easily molded by the pre-existing bureaucratic elites. Of the "Tiger" economies, Singapore remains substantially resistant to one key disruptive influence—democratic politics. Only South Korea, which has experienced significant democratization and a significant political breakthrough by interests other than the corporate, might lay some claim to be undergoing significant transformation. The developmental state is thus undoubtedly in crisis. It may be dying, but its death agonies are prolonged, and are taking different forms. It is an open question whether it will be succeeded by anything that can recognizably be called a regulatory state.

Conclusion: The Regulatory State and Creative Destruction

I have argued in this chapter that the *idea* of the regulatory state is ambiguous, and likewise that the *practice* of the most important examples of regulatory states is ambiguous, especially in impact on business interests. The idea is ambiguous because the core image of governing which it offers—an idea of steering and control borrowed from physical systems—converts in political life into two very different images of the act of governing. The two are starkly contrasted in the images of "light touch" steering in the modern governance literature, and the more sinister images of authoritarian steering suggested by Plato's pilots or the murderous "Great Helmsman." More important still, I have argued that the modern image of a regulatory state has been appropriated and developed in very different national and historical circumstances, and its practice reflects those individual circumstances. Nevertheless, one common feature does emerge in the relationship between business interests and regulatory states: just as meaning and practice are ambiguous in general terms, so the impact on business interests in real live regulatory states is ambiguous. This ambiguity—or even better, contradictory character—is most starkly illustrated by the greatest of all regulatory states, the American, which from the perspective of business is a kind of two-headed beast, one with a benign face, the other snarling in a hostile fashion. But this tendency for the regulatory state to be simultaneously a friend and an enemy of business is, we have seen, also present in the case of the European Union and in the most important "regulatory (member) state" in the Union.

There are many reasons for the divided identity of these modern regulatory states, but the common feature of the cases examined here is that almost all work under conditions of democratic capitalism—albeit often a funny kind of democracy and a funny kind of capitalism. And beyond the particular national or regional settings, capitalist democracy imposes great forces on the regulatory state, which constantly unsettle its relations with business. Whatever the ambitions of political and economic elites to "depoliticize" regulatory decision-making, the influence of democratic competition constantly breaks in. That is the importance of the "democracy" in "capitalist democracy." But a key feature of these capitalist economies also constantly unsettles relations. All experience Schumpeter's ceaseless creative destruction. In other words, the processes of economic competition and innovation constantly destroy some business interests and create new ones. This creative destruction means that the identity of business interests is constantly being remade, and its relationship to the regulatory state constantly unsettled. There is no settled answer to the question: what does the regulatory state mean for business? There is no settled answer because both democracy and capitalism are dynamic, restless social creations, and the regulatory state is the product of both.

Creativity and destruction were never more apparent than in the great financial crisis of autumn 2008. The reader will immediately recognize destruction, as banks collapsed and the global financial system threatened to implode. Creativity might be thought less apparent. But in a few short weeks the regulatory state in Europe underwent dramatic change, and in its wake followed change in the US. Financial regulation in both the Eurozone and the UK had followed the principles of the regulatory state sketched by Majone: a Madisonian, technocratic ruling order which excluded democratic politicians in favor of non-majoritarian regulatory institutions. In the crisis of 2007–8 that regulatory state was weighed in the balance and found wanting. Confronted by crisis the bankers and the technocratic regulators froze, petrified like rabbits before a stoat. Now, the great agents of transformation are not the central bankers and financial regulators who until recently reigned supreme. The agents of transformation are democratic governments driven by fear of the electoral consequences of macroeconomic collapse. The crisis produced rapid learning and innovation—a common social function of any crisis. But it was politicians who learnt most rapidly, not central bankers still trapped in the mind world of the long boom. The epistemic convergence that occurred killed the old regulatory state—and is creating a new one. Across the capitalist world it turned banks into public utilities. Every big capitalist economy has taken significant public ownership stakes in the banking industry. The leader in innovation was the United Kingdom. That is not surprising, for the UK economy teetered most precariously on the extraordinary financial pyramid revealed by the crash of September–October 2008. But the UK was soon followed by other major EU economies, by frenzied coordination among the G7, and then—astonishingly—by the Bush administration in Washington. Even the crown jewels of the old regulatory state—central bank independence in setting short-term interest rates—may be lost to the politicians.

Old regulatory states are dying, and new, more democratically shaped, formations being born.

NOTES

1. I am grateful to the editors and to Iain Pirie for valuable comments on an earlier draft.
2. I owe this point to Graham Wilson.
3. I owe this example to Wyn Grant.

REFERENCES

AMYX, J. 2004. *Japan's Financial Crisis: Institutional Rigidity and Reluctant Change.* Princeton: Princeton University Press.

BABB, J. 2001. *Business and Politics in Japan.* Manchester: Manchester University Press.

BERRY, J. 1999. *The New Liberalism: The Rising Power of Citizen Groups.* Washington, DC: Brookings Institution Press.

BOWMAN, S. 1996. *The Modern Corporation and American Political Thought: Law, Power and Ideology.* Philadelphia: Pennsylvania University Press.

CAROSSO, V. 1973. "The Wall Street Money Trust from Pujo through Medina," *Business History Review* 47(4): 421–37.

CHANDLER, A. 1977. *The Visible Hand: The Managerial Revolution in American Business.* Cambridge, Mass.: Belknap Press of the Harvard University Press.

COEN, D. 1998. "The European business interest and the nation state: large firm lobbying in the European Union and member states," *Journal of Public Policy* 18(1): 75–100.

—— 2007. "Empirical and theoretical studies in EU lobbying," *Journal of European Public Policy* 14(3): 333–45.

—— and THATCHER, M. 2008. "Network governance and multilevel delegation: European networks of regulatory agencies," *Journal of Public Policy* 28(1): 49–71.

DENNIS, W. 2004. *The Public Reviews Small Business.* Washington, DC: National Federation of Independent Businesses Research Foundation.

DERTHICK, M. 2005. *Up in Smoke: From Legislation to Litigation in Tobacco Politics.* Washington, DC: CQ Press.

EISNER, M. 2007. *Governing the Environment: The Transformation of Environmental Regulation.* Boulder, Colo.: Lynne Rienner.

—— WORSHAM, J., and RINGQUIST, E. 2006. *Contemporary Regulatory Policy,* 2nd edn. Boulder, Colo.: Lynne Rienner.

European Chemicals Agency. 2008. "About ECHA," http://echa.europa.eu/home accessed May 25.

FOLEY, M. 2007. *American Credo: The Place of Ideas in US Politics.* Oxford: Oxford University Press.

GALAMBOS, L. 1975. *The Public Image of Big Business in America.* Baltimore: Johns Hopkins University Press.

HILTS, P. 2003. *Protecting America's Health: The FDA, Business, and One Hundred Years of Regulation.* New York: Alfred E. Knopf.

HOFSTADTER, R. 1972. *The Age of Reform: From Bryan to FDR*. New York: Knopf, 1st edn. 1955.

JAYASURIYA, K. 2001. "Globalization and the changing architecture of the state: the regulatory state and the politics of negative coordination," *Journal of European Public Policy* 8(1): 101–23.

—— 2005. "Beyond institutional fetishism: from the developmental to the regulatory state," *New Political Economy* 10(3): 381–7.

JOHNSON, C. 1982. *MITI and the Japanese Economic Miracle: The Growth of Industrial Policy 1925–75*. Stanford, Calif.: Stanford University Press.

JOHNSON, J. 2006. "Two-track diffusion and central bank embeddedness: the politics of euro adoption in Hungary and the Czech Republic," *Review of International Political Economy* 13 (3): 361–86.

JOSEPHSON, M. 1962. *The Robber Barons: The Great American Capitalists 1861–1901*. London: Eyre and Spottiswoode.

KAGAN, R. 2001. *Adversarial Legalism: The American Way of Law*. Cambridge, Mass.: Harvard University Press.

—— 2007. "Globalization and legal change: the 'Americanization' of European law?" *Regulation and Governance* 1(2): 99–120.

—— and AXELRAD, L., eds. 2000. *Regulatory Encounters: Multinational Corporations and American Adversarial Legalism*. Berkeley and Los Angeles: University of California Press.

LAMOREAUX, N. 1985. *The Great Merger Movement in American Business, 1885–1904*. New York: Cambridge University Press.

MACARTNEY, H., and MORAN, M. 2008. "Banking and financial market regulation and supervision," in K. Dyson, ed., *The Euro at Ten*. Oxford: Oxford University Press, 325–40.

McCRAW, T. 1984. *Prophets of Regulation*. Cambridge, Mass.: Harvard University Press.

MAJONE, G. 1991. "Cross-national sources of regulatory policymaking in Europe and the United State," *Journal of Public Policy* 11(1): 79–109.

—— 1996. *Regulating Europe*. London: Routledge.

—— 1999. "The regulatory state and its legitimacy problems," *West European Politics* 22(1): 1–24.

MARCHAND, R. 1998. *Creating the Corporate Soul: The Rise of Public Relations and Corporate Imagery in American Big Business*. Berkeley and Los Angeles: University of California Press.

MORAN, M. 1984. "Politics, banks and markets: an Anglo-American comparison," *Political Studies* 32(1): 173–89.

—— 1991. *The Politics of the Financial Services Revolution: The USA, UK and Japan*. Basingstoke: Palgrave Macmillan.

—— 2007. *The British Regulatory State: High Modernism and Hyper-innovation*, 2nd edn. Oxford: Oxford University Press.

—— and MACARTNEY, H. 2009. "Financial supervision: internationalization, Europeanization and power," in K. Dyson and M. Marcussen, eds., *Central Banking in the Age of the Euro*. Oxford: Oxford University Press.

OSBORNE, D., and GAEBLER, T. 1992. *Reinventing Government: How the Entreprenurial Spirit is Transforming the Public Sector*. Reading, Mass.: Addison Wesley

PIRIE, I. 2005. "Better by design: Korea's neoliberal economy," *Pacific Review* 18(3): 1–20.

—— 2007. *The Korean Developmental State: From Dirigisme to Neo-liberalism*. London: Routledge.

ROY, W. 1997. *Socializing Capital: The Rise of the Large Industrial Corporation in America*. Princeton: Princeton University Press.

SAMUELS, R. 1987. *The Business of the Japanese State: Energy Markets in Comparative and Historical Perspective*. Ithaca, NY: Cornell University Press.

Scott, J. 1998. *Seeing Like a State: How Certain Schemes to Improve the Human Condition Have Failed*. New Haven: Yale University Press.

Seligman, J. 1982. *The Transformation of Wall Street: A History of the Securities and Exchange Commission and Modern Corporate Finance*. Boston: Houghton Mifflin.

Sicilia, D. 2004. "The corporation under siege: social movements, regulation, public relations and tort law since the Second World War," in K. Lipartito and D. Sicilia, eds., *Constructing Corporate America: History, Politics, Culture*. Oxford: Oxford University Press, 188–220.

Stewart, R. 1988. "Regulation and the crisis of legitimization in the United States," in T. Daintith, ed., *Law as an Instrument of Economic Policy*. Berlin: de Gruyter, 97–133.

Stone, R. 1991. *The Interstate Commerce Commission and the Railroad Industry: A History of Regulatory Policy*. New York: Praeger.

Thatcher, M. 2002a. "Analysing regulatory reform in Europe," *Journal of European Public Policy* 8(5): 859–72.

—— 2002b. " Delegation to independent regulatory agencies," *West European Politics* 25(1): 125–45.

—— 2005. "The third force? Independent regulatory agencies and elected politicians in Europe," *Governance* 18(3): 347–74.

—— 2007. *Internationalization and Economic Institutions: Comparing European Experiences*. Oxford: Oxford University Press.

Vogel, D. 1978. *Lobbying the Corporation: Citizen Challenges to Business Authority*. New York: Basic Books.

—— 1986. *National Styles of Regulation: Environmental Policy in Great Britain and the United States*. Ithaca, NY: Cornell University Press.

—— 1989. *Fluctuating Fortunes: The Political Power of Business in America*. New York: Basic Books.

—— 1996. *Kindred Strangers*. Princeton: Princeton University Press.

Vogel, S. 1996. *Freer Markets, More Rules: Regulatory Reform in Advanced Industrial Countries*. Ithaca, NY: Cornell University Press.

Walter, A. 2006. "From developmental to regulatory state? Japan's new financial regulatory system," *Pacific Review* 19(4): 405–28.

Wilks, S. 1999. *In the Public Interest: Competition Policy and the Monopolies and Mergers Commission*. Manchester: Manchester University Press.

—— 2005. "Agency escape: decentralization or dominance of the European Commission in the modernization of competition policy," *Governance* 18(3): 431–52.

—— and Bartle, I. 2002. "The unanticipated consequences of creating independent competitive agencies," *West European Politics* 25(2): 148–72.

—— and McGowan, L. 1996. "Competition policy in the European Union: creating a federal agency," in G. Doern and S. Wilks, eds., *Comparative Competition Policy*. Oxford: Clarendon, 225–67.

CHAPTER 17

INTERNATIONAL REGULATORS AND NETWORK GOVERNANCE

PAMELA CAMERRA-ROWE
MICHELLE EGAN

INTRODUCTION

THE globalization of trade, the liberalization of financial markets, and technological change have created new regulatory issues in the international economy. These include the protection of intellectual property rights, the regulation of financial transactions, and the creation of industrial standards. These regulatory issues cannot always be sufficiently resolved by the action of a single nation state. In response, non-state actors, including private companies and international business associations, along with public officials, have created new forms of governance to create transnational regulations. These new forms of global governance have spawned a broad academic literature (Rosenau and Czempiel 1992; Reinecke 1998; Cutler et al. 1999; Prakash and Hart 1999; Donohue and Nye 2000; Held and McGrew 2003; Kahler and Lake 2004; Slaughter 2004; Coen and Thatcher 2005; Thatcher and Coen 2008) that raises important issues regarding accountability, transparency, equality, enforcement, and the role of the nation state.

This chapter will explore the rise of international regulation, the creation of transnational networks, and their implications for business and national governments. The chapter is divided into five parts. First, we examine the impact of globalization on business and the dilemmas it creates for business and governments. Second, we explore the wide range of formal and informal ways that business and government have sought to regulate the international economy. Third, we examine explanations for various types of global governance. Fourth, we analyze some of the issues raised by global governance including enforcement issues, democratic legitimacy, and accountability to the public. Finally, we conclude with some suggestions for future research.

GLOBALIZATION AND INTERNATIONAL REGULATION

The past four decades have seen enormous changes in the international economy. Financial markets have been liberalized, trade has increased, and communications networks have expanded. The changes are reflected in the increases in foreign direct investment and in the increasing flow of goods, services, and capital across borders. As a result of these changes, firms have created new global networks and rationalized production. While there have been earlier periods of globalization, this phase has been marked by its intensity and by the variety of transnational flows (Kahler and Lake 2003). Although not all firms or sectors have been affected by globalization, there are now well over 60,000 transnational corporations (TNCs) (Haufler 2001).

Traditionally, nation states have regulated the systems within which goods, services, and capital are produced and exchanged. They have been viewed as the only actor able to make binding decisions regarding public goods. They have established the rules regarding private property and exchange and provided a legal system to enforce contracts and to resolve disputes and regulate trade. Nation states also provided other public goods including health and safety standards, labor standards, and environmental regulations. These rules have been shaped by electoral and political factors within each nation state. But regulatory and other public goods issues now transcend national borders and there is no equivalent world government to regulate the international economy.

As with any market, the global economy needs rules in order to operate successfully (Cerny 2000). Without transnational rules, the risks of engaging in investment, production, and exchange can be very high. This is particularly true in the international economy, where the social distance between market participants is high (Kerwer 2005). Whereas, in the national market, lenders or firms might have known their customers and suppliers, this is often not the case in the international economy.

Moreover, new forms of products and services including twenty-four hour trading, and e-commerce have created new issues for regulators such as the protection of intellectual property rights. Finally, some public goods like environmental protection or protecting health and safety take on new dimensions with the increasing flow of goods across borders, as evidenced by the recent crises caused by various food products imported to the US from China.

Nation states can seek to construct global rules for the international system. However, they face some obstacles in creating these rules. First, in the international system, nation states have to find cooperative outcomes with other states. They may be unwilling or unable to do so because they have different priorities and different regulatory frameworks. Even if they are willing to create rules, there may be a considerable lag time in generating consensus around specific rules. Trying to find consensus among a number of states may not be the most efficient solution to regulating the international economy. Second, even if states agree on rules, it is difficult for nation states to supervise economic activities and enforce decisions in the international system because those rules fall outside the realm of their individual sovereign power (Reinecke 1998; Heritier 2002). States also do not have equal administrative or judicial capacity to enforce laws. Finally, both the international system and nation states themselves have become more fragmented, making it more difficult to provide unified response to global problems (Cerny 2000; Slaughter 2004).

Keohane (2001) suggests that political institutions have simply not kept pace with the changes in the international economy. Each country retains its own set of regulatory mechanisms and these vary widely. This has led to new forms of global governance, in which non-state actors seek to deal with interdependence problems. Private and semi-public regimes have become increasingly important in defining international rules and standards. These regimes vary considerably from transnational organizations such as the European Commission, World Trade Organization, and the International Monetary Fund to private authority regimes, which are transnational, cooperative networks of firms or business associations, which seek to provide public goods traditionally provided by the state (Cutler et al. 1999; Ronit and Schneider 2000; Mattli and Buthe 2005) The next section explores these various new forms of governance.

DIFFERENT FORMS OF GLOBAL GOVERNANCE

Governance, according to Rhodes (1997), involves voluntary networks of non-state actors, which, in addition to government, help to authoritatively allocate resources, exercise control, and coordinate social activities. They are generally characterized by horizontal interaction among equal autonomous actors, who are seeking public goods

(Schmitter 2000). Coen and Thatcher describe these networks as "non-majoritarian regulators." They are "unelected bodies that are organizationally separate from government and have powers over regulation of markets through endorsement or formal delegation by public bodies" (Coen and Thatcher 2005).

The networks can vary in terms of who initiates them, who takes part in the network, and the degree to which they are institutionalized (Cutler et al. 1999). Coen and Thatcher, for example, outline three types of non-majoritarian regulators. The first type is national independent regulatory agencies, which are national in scope and retain ties to the nation states. These would include networks of central bank officials such as the Basel Committee on Banking Regulation and Supervisory Practices. A second form of international regulatory network is the supranational regulatory agencies such as the European Commission or World Trade Organization. The third form is international regulation provided by private organizations or firms, also known as private authority government (Cutler et al. 1999; Coen and Thatcher 2005) These private non-majoritarian regulators are an "increasingly significant form of NMRs, which determine the rules under which private firms supply goods and compete with each other in the market" (Coen and Thatcher 2005: 331). These would include the International Accounting Standards Board (IASB) and private standards development organizations. While such private governance is often the result of delegated authority, in which states conditionally grant authority to non-state actors to act on their behalf to foster coordination, they are usually able to exert legitimate authority in regulatory agreements. We examine each of these in turn.

In the first case, networks of national government regulators have been set up to help regulate the international economy (Slaughter 2004; Coen and Thatcher 2005). These national government networks link regulatory counterparts from various nations to create global codes of best practices. They are generally networks of executive branch officials (Slaughter 2004). These have been particularly prevalent in the banking and financial sectors and include the Basel Committee and the International Organization of Securities Commissioners (IOSCO). The Basel Committee, for example, was set up by central bank governors in 1974 in order to set out the principles for supervising the international operations of banks. It was a reaction to the much more volatile macroeconomic environment of the 1970s. This forum was comprised of national bank supervisory officials. They sought to exchange information about regulatory structures and create international regulations for banks (Reinecke 1998). This was considered one of the central institutions in the new framework of global economic governance. For much of the 1970s and 1980s, the committee reacted to financial crises and tried to reinforce national systems of supervision by establishing home country responsibility (Picciotto and Haines 1999). Later, it issued minimum capital requirements for internationally active banks (Picciotto and Haines 1999).

The creation of the Basel Committee was followed by other transnational regulatory networks including the IOSCO, which was set up in 1984, and the International Association of Insurance Supervisors (IAIS), which was created in the 1990s. A Financial Stability Forum was created by the finance ministers and central bank

governors of advanced industrial countries in February 1999 and includes representatives of the Basel Committee, IOSCO, IAIS, and senior national regulatory officials
who are responsible for financial stability in important international financial centers
like London and New York (Slaughter 2004: 2).

The second form of international regulation is comprised of more formalized
supranational institutions. These include the World Trade Organization and the
European Commission. They are established by nation states in order to maintain
their regulatory capacity and solve transnational issues. In Europe, for example, the
nation states have delegated regulatory authority to the European Commission,
placing more emphasis on the use of authority, rules, and standard-setting, partially
displacing an earlier emphasis on public ownership, public subsidies, and directly
provided services with transnational regulatory coordination (Majone 1996). Not
only does the Commission draw up regulations that affect business, but the European
Court of Justice can resolve disputes regarding those decisions. National governments draw up the initial treaties and approve regulations through the Council of
Ministers. These organizations are discussed by David Coen in this volume.

Other international organizations have created voluntary rules or codes of conduct for businesses in the international system. For example, in the 1970s, the
Organisation for Economic Co-operation and Development (OECD) created a
voluntary Code for Multinational Enterprises, which included guidelines on disclosing information regarding their structure, activities, and policies and to issue financial
statements. The guidelines, which are applicable to companies operating in OECD
member countries, are not legally enforceable and do not displace local regulations.
However, in response, transnational firms did increase the amount of information
published along the lines specified in the guidelines. Similarly, the World Intellectual
Property Organization (WIPO) generated a proposal to resolve conflicts over internet
domain names. WIPO gave its recommendation to ICANN, a non-profit organization to administer and resolve domain name disputes.

Finally, there are transnational networks of firms or business associations that set
rules for the international system. Firms or business associations cooperate to create
rules to govern their own sector or specific issues within their sector (Spar 1999;
Ronit and Schneider 2000). For example, in order to regulate the internet, several
firms and associations have taken initiatives to enforce intellectual property rights
and secure exchange over the internet. One of the areas in which private authority
regimes are prevalent is the regulation of the internet. IBM, for example, launched an
infoMarket Rights Management project that used technologies to control the dissemination of its work after nation states failed to adequately regulate intellectual
property rights (Spar 1999). Other firms offer services to find and punish online
violations of intellectual property rights, and some business association seek to
license and monitor the use of internet property (Spar 1999: 40). Credit card
companies have sought to develop structures that will enable bank card transactions
to be conducted securely across the internet through the secure electronic transaction
protocol (Spar 1999: 46). All of these are examples of private authority regimes
designed to regulate internet use and protect both firms and consumers.

Another example of private interest government has emerged in the bond rating sector. Moody's and Standard and Poor's—the two largest debt rating agencies— have stepped in to provide information to securities issuers about the risks associated with their international investments (Sinclair 1999; Kerwer 2001). These agencies rate the creditworthiness of debtors and are responsible for keeping an eye out on who is violating norms of financial practice (Kerwer 2001: 285). They are able to exercise this power because of their ability to organize knowledge of capital markets. On the one hand, this provides them with power to influence international investment, but, on the other hand, as Kerwer points out, standards of creditworthiness are also enforced by public regulators so that the state is not completely absent from this process. Similarly, the International Federation of Stock Exchanges, which is a private organization, has created rules for securities market. These latter regulations often mirror those already produced by intergovernmental organizations such as the Basel Committee, the IOSCO, and the OECD.

Sectors with small numbers of large, internationally active firms and well-organized business associations also often engage in self-regulation in the international system. For example, Ronit and Schneider point to self-regulation in the dye and other colorant manufacturers industry. In this case, the Ecological and Toxicological Association of Dyes and organic Pigments Manufacturers (ETAD) developed international safety measure in the handling of colorants and in environmental safety. Their self-regulation at the global level is due in part to the smallness of the association and the global reach of all the members, which makes it easier to supervise and enforce these regulations (Ronit and Schneider 2000).

On the one hand, Knill and Lehmkuhl (2002) argue that self-regulation can be due to the weak capacity of states to create rules in the international system. However, on the other hand, Ronit and Schneider suggest that it can also be due to the imminent threat of regulation at the international level. This was true for example in the pharmaceutical industry in which the pharmaceutical companies created a code of pharmaceutical marketing practices and made them applicable internationally by the International Federation of Pharmaceutical Manufacturers Association in 1981 (Ronit and Schneider 2000). By contrast, a voluntary code of conduct generated by the WHO/UNICEF emerged after substantial pressure from transnational grass roots mobilization, as well as international organizations and business groups, in the wake of scandals and contamination of breast milk (Sikkink 1986). Such international regulation of transnational corporations still depends on states and non-state actors for implementation and monitoring.

Moreover, not only have firms and business associations organized globally, so too have non-governmental organizations. Environmental, health, and consumer safety groups have also lobbied international organizations for regulation of business and industry. As a result, firms and associations have sought to self-regulate. This can also be seen in the alcohol sector. Lobbying by consumer advocacy groups and the fear that the European Union could restrict alcohol advertising led the largest companies in the alcohol industry to create self-regulatory norms governing the advertisement of products to under-age drinkers (Camerra-Rowe 2005).

States may also delegate authority to private authority networks. They may do this in part for efficiency gains, since firms know more about the issues involved than the government officials. Standard-setting agencies, which are voluntary associations but are government funded, fall into this category. In the case of European standards, there are several non-state standards agencies, partially funded by the European Commission through contractual agreements. Governments may also willingly delegate regulatory responsibility to firms in order to use their technical expertise and resources or to use market forces as a mechanism to achieve some form of regulatory coordination. Failure to reach agreement would allow states to shift the blame (Cutler et al. 1999; Egan 2001; Beeson n.d.).

Transnational networks of firms may not make the rules themselves but influence governments to make transnational rules. Sell (2003), for example, discusses how the Intellectual Property Committee that represents twelve firms sought improved international protection for intellectual property rights and was able to create a proposal based on existing national laws, present it to the GATT Secretariat, and have it adopted. Similarly, the Transatlantic Business Dialogue has promoted regulatory cooperation in a range of issue areas, serving both as a transnational interest group and providing information and recommendations to governments on both sides of the Atlantic on regulatory issues such as mutual recognition and customs cooperation (Cowles 2001).

This discussion suggests that there are a wide array of private actor networks in the international system. Some of these are more institutionalized than others. Cutler et al. (1999) list six different types of private authority ranging from decentralized and informal practices to international private regimes. In the least formal case, firms over time create mutually recognized norms of behavior that guide the conduct of business in certain sectors. In the case of international private regimes, there is regular negotiation and interaction among firms or associations within a particular sector or issue area, the cooperation is more institutionalized, and the decisions are considered binding. But even here there will be differences in terms of the extent to which compliance is ensured. In some cases, they rely on other firms; in other cases, they depend on state enforcement. For example, companies seeking environmental credentials opt for ISO 14000 standards voluntarily and then seek independent certification and audits (Prakash 2000a). Others may seek state confirmation, as in the case of comfort letters from the European Commission that firms are not in violation with competition rules. Thus, private governance regimes may set standards, enforce rules, and provide services, varying widely across different regulatory regimes.

These different forms of international regulation and governance at a minimum suggest that the traditional line between public and private authority in the international system is blurred and that private firms and associations play an important role in establishing the rules which govern them in the international system. At the same time, it does not mean that states are not involved in the process. Firms often operate under the shadow of hierarchy (Scharpf 1999). For example, it is the threat of regulation by international organizations that leads to private authority government.

At other times, nation states still enforce regulatory standards. And at still other times, the regulations adopted by such networks reflect work already done by international organizations of states. In still other cases, states initiate the international network (Knill and Lehmkuhl 2002). Knill and Lehmkuhl provide a useful typology to differentiate different types of international governance based on the governing capacity of private and public actors. They suggest that there are four types of regulation—interventionist legislation is the one in which the capacity of the state is the greatest, followed by interfering regulation, regulated self-regulation, and private self-regulation. These different types suggest that we need to be careful in generalizing about the role of firms and associations in creating international rules.

What is clear however from the literature is that the types of regulation vary by sector and by issue. The ability of a sector to engage in private management depends on a number of factors including the market structure, the number of players involved and the issue area (Knill and Lehmkuhl 2002). Sectors with small numbers of firms, and particularly with a few large firms, often have an easier time organizing and monitoring members than sectors with large numbers of firms (Olson 1971). Private regimes do not have the legitimate authority to discipline other producers who violate norms, but if they are small enough they can better monitor whether firms are cooperating. While reputational effects and learning processes may foster compliance, litigation and adjudication may also safeguard compliance and enforcement with public policy objectives (Lehmkuhl 2008). Large transnational companies also are more likely to engage in self-regulation or be delegated authority by the state because of resource and informational advantages. Sectors with small, well-organized business associations also have advantages in engaging in self-regulation at the international level although Ronit and Schneider (2000) show that even larger associations, such as the International Chambers of Commerce, can create international regulations. Yet while collective action theory and political opportunity structures might also explain the varying levels of success of transnational business groups relative to labor, consumer, and environmental groups, diffuse groups may overcome such obstacles through selective incentives (Olson 1971).

Issues Raised by International Governance

International governance raises a number of issues that go to the heart of democratic governance. As we shift towards new mechanisms of governmentality, there are new dilemmas in terms of accountability, transparency, participation, equality, and legitimacy. The evolution of structural remedies to address a range of issues from market failures to public goods has meant a shift from command and control, interventionist measures to more flexible, decentralized, and fragmented norms and rules. For some, such "experimentalist governance" provides for more stakeholder participation; for others, such "government by proxy" serves to make horizontal coordination between public and private actors in service provision more complex, and undermines accountability as traditional hierarchical relationships are replaced with networks (see Kettl 1988; Sabel 2008).

Thus, one of the issues raised by the role of non-state actors in international regulation is accountability. In democratic nation states, people can hold elected officials accountable for their actions through elections. They can sanction actors if they are displeased with the rules that they make. However, transnational networks of public and private actors are not accountable to territorially defined citizens (Sørensen and Torfing 2001). Even in cases of the World Bank, IMF, WTO, or European Union, which one can argue are linked to national governments, they are not necessarily controlled by democratically elected politicians. And even if they were, Keohane (2001) argues, the organizations are more accountable to stronger states.

This raises a second issue, regarding the types of participants in the rule-making process. In national systems, a wide array of stakeholders can participate in the rule-making process either through the electoral system, or through their participation in institutionalized forms of interest group representation such as corporatism, or administrative hearings about rule-making, or lobbying. In the case of international governance, the problem is perhaps similar to that recognized by Lindblom and Dahl (1977) about the possibility of stakeholder bias in terms of institutional power and access. Consumers and others affected by the rules may not necessarily have a voice in the process, and any voice may be diffuse.

Third, rules determine winners and losers in the world economy. If industry is identifying the problem and devising solutions, they set the agenda and limit the options open to nation states. Sell, for example, shows that a small group of US-based multinational corporations who comprised the Intellectual Property Committee was able to convince GATT to adopt its politics on intellectual property rights. Sell argues that such rules can benefit the few at the possible expense of the many (Sell 2003: 191). Cutler et al. also show how merchants, their association, and corporations exercised historic influence on maritime transport law, which had distributional consequences (Cutler et al. 1999: 316). Beeson goes further, suggesting that it may be dangerous to rely on self-regulation by private actors to determine economic outcomes. Having shareholders formulate their own rules can lead to outcomes that may not be in the interest of consumers or the general public. Firms are private actors that are profit seeking (Cutler et al. 1999: 3–4). National governments, and particularly democratic governments, even if they give business a privileged position in rule-making, have to at least consider the electorate since they will be held accountable by the public (Lindblom and Dahl 1977).

A related issue raised by international governance is the problem of defining the public good in the international system. Regulations in the international system are a form of public good. Generally governments provide public goods based on what they deem to be the national public interest. However, the issue may be framed differently at the international level among participants. While a developed country might believe it is environmental protection, a developing country may suggest that it is economic growth.

A further problem is related to transparency and predictability. Governments typically follow both substantive and procedural rules. In contrast, these informal networks are flexible and open to many interpretations and uses. They also come in a wide array of forms. As Slaughter (2004) points out, these transnational networks tend to function with little or no "physical and legal infrastructure; most lack a foundational treaty and operate under only a few agreed upon objectives or bylaws. Nothing they do purports to be legally binding on the members and there typically are few or no mechanisms for formal enforcement or implementation. Rather, these functions are left to the members themselves" (48). This makes it difficult for individuals to understand exactly who is responsible for making the rules and how the rules were made. Voting patterns, political pressure, or economic monopoly may induce outcomes that diverge from socially accepted norms or legally required behavior. However, tort law and antitrust rules have the potential of ensuring that there is some supervision of private regulatory decision-making, and courts may also scrutinize standards and procedures that lead to the establishment of collective agreements.

Even if the process of international governance were accountable and transparent and inclusive, there is an additional problem of enforcement, monitoring, and compliance. Why would self-interested and competitive firms in the international system cooperate to create rules and agree to follow those rules? In the case of self-regulation, firms may find it in their self-interest to cooperate to create rules for the system to protect the reputation of their product or to avoid possible regulation by international organizations. Among small groups of firms, you may be able to monitor the participants, but in most cases you have to have some degree of obligation or trust among participants. Legal systems have also increasingly recognized private rule-making, but with procedural safeguards and government oversight in many instances. At the same time, there may be considerable flexibility in how states implement certain rules, with some states going beyond the stated minimum whereas other states may opt out of certain provisions (Falkner et al. 2005). Take for example the principle of mutual recognition of standards, which supposedly facilitates trade and eases problems created by different regulatory barriers by accepting consumer, health, and safety standards as equivalent. In practice, the principle has not been systematically applied given different perceptions of equivalence in national regulations. Applying the principle has high information, transaction, and compliance costs (Pelkmans 2002). In cases where international rules are made regarding the provision of public goods such as environmental protection or health and safety regulations, it may be even more difficult to enforce compliance since some firms may profit by not following the rules. As principal–agent theorists point out, shirking requires some form of deterrence. And even if there is enforcement by nation states, some nation states may lack the administrative and judicial capacity to enforce the rules.

Finally, some analysts have suggested that the rise of international regulation by private interest governance has led to a decline in the nation state and rule by transnational corporations in the international system. As the previous discussion makes clear, however, states are often involved in the process indirectly through their delegation of power, often with safeguards, and that they can withdraw their delegation of power to private actors. Moreover, as several authors have noted, the forms of international governance have also changed over time. In some cases, what begins as private rule-making leads to rule-making by international organizations; in other cases, private rule-making mirrors what has already been done in international organizations. As globalization fosters regulatory expansion through a host of new governance mechanisms, such regulatory diffusion allows specific states to expand their policy capacities at the international level (Levi Faur 2005: 7). The European Union has impacted global governance through transferring its regulatory approach in a range of issues areas from environmental standards to telecommunications (Egan 2001; Mattli and Büthe 2005; Drezner 2007) And closely related to the transfer of regulatory practices through global diffusion is the rise of new regulatory instruments that are often the direct result of changes in economic governance, new technology and production processes, and new investments and innovation at the national level. Mutual recognition is one example of a shift from direct intervention or harmonization to mutual cooperation among regulators based on the principle of regulatory equivalence. Instead of competition among rules, competition is based on markets and the performance of firms, as national rules are functionally equivalent. Such regulatory innovations can only work if there is mutual acceptance among regulators for fear of a race to the bottom as companies will seek out countries with low regulatory standards.

CONCLUSION:
FUTURE RESEARCH DIRECTIONS

Globalization has led to new forms of governance, providing considerable scope for firms and business associations to shape global rules in the international system. Given the regulatory and structural changes in the global economy, the implications for business and governments warrant further attention. There are different research agendas that this chapter brings together, with related interests concerning regulation, networks, and governance that fit within the broader frameworks of political economy and international relations. The emergence of work on transnational legal regimes, and their rule-making efforts in areas of regulatory cooperation, can fruitfully be combined with work on private governance to highlight the different modes of international governance. While the former is based on theories of international cooperation and bargaining, the latter is based on comparative public policy and business management. By utilizing both approaches, this chapter has drawn on a variety of perspectives including state–society relations, transaction-cost economics, theories of regulatory capture and delegation, and legal and democratic theory. As a consequence, this research has become truly interdisciplinary with scholars in economics, politics, and law focusing on the transformation of governance that is summarized in our conclusion around three themes: theories of regulation, theories of political institutions, and theories of collective action. A good deal of this research is based on strong empirical foundations with significant case study material. While there is attention given to different types of regulatory cooperation in different issue areas, with illustrative cases ranging from antitrust to financial markets, there is less debate on which rules and instruments, and which regulatory mechanisms work better in practice. It is useful not only to map out the range of governance regimes to regulate the international economy, but also to understand the conditions and instruments that foster better compliance and achievement of public policy objectives. Yet despite the expansion of markets, and the corresponding growth of global regulation, there are few quantitative studies that measure performance, accountability, or effectiveness of such international governance mechanisms.

Much of the research on governance regimes has drawn upon theories of regulation. The focus on transnational networks of regulation has primarily focused on the interests and outcomes derived from "regulatory" collective action (see Eberlein and Newman 2008). Since international regulatory negotiations, like domestic negotiations, can structure bargaining and affect outcomes, the dynamics of the bargaining game can reduce transaction costs, and provide information and credible commitments (Majone 1996). However, the bargaining outcome can also result in negative effects on general welfare, thereby generating outcomes that produce cartels, rents, and externalities (Hellman 1998). The emergence of such new forms of global governance provides new opportunity structures that creates new opportunities for collective action (Kitschelt 1986). Yet how institutions aggregate societal interests is a critical component of research on regulation. This partial replacement of public ownership, public subsidies, and directly provided services means that sovereign states have also become rule-takers as much as rule-makers (Jordana and Levi Faur 2004; Levi Faur 2005). Yet when markets alone cannot overcome coordination failures to achieve a positive outcome, states may play a role as catalysts in fostering rules and standards. Do states choose more flexible, market-based instruments of governance as opposed to rules-based regulation, applied in a uniform manner across sectors? What effect does the differential empowerment of states play in decisions within different regulatory regimes? Such questions are important, as states have often been assumed to be losing regulatory authority, and yet some have suggested that state power can be enhanced by globalization (Kahler and Lake 2003; Drezner 2007).

Whether these new institutional structures create adequate incentives to participate is closely linked to concerns that greater delegation to non-majoritarian institutions or private regimes might lead to reduced public scrutiny, transparency, and oversight. The issue of the legitimacy of new forms of regulatory governance has become, in recent years, a significant research area (Sabel 2008). While such new modes of governance, whether through the formalization of transgovernmental networks, the delegation of rule-making to international institutions, or the growth of private governance regimes, have only recently attracted attention as coordinating devices in managing markets, most attention has been given to issues of political control and democratic accountability rather than those of managerial control and efficiency. Certainly the expansion of non-state actors and their role in global governance indicate substantive shifts in rule-making, The emergence of civil society as legitimate and credible actors has predominantly focused on the institutionaliza-tion of business and firms, neglecting the growing role of environmental and social interest associations. But organizational resources can play a key role in shaping outcomes, and this can mean that participation seems limited to the participants in the sector and not necessarily consumers or others affected by the rules. Whether NGOs are perceived as legitimate social actors and can contribute through expert knowledge, issue framing, or social mobilization to international governance sug-gests that the growth of civil society may affect global governance.

Yet the efficiency of instruments and the efficacy of such international regulatory regimes is also important in allowing us to combine the insights from different literatures. The strong emphasis among constructivists on the role of norms, learning, and socialization in serving as important processes and preconditions for fostering compliance can also be applied to private governance regimes where reputation, trust, and credibility of participants are often key factors in fostering agreement on common norms and standards. Can reputation, peer pressure, and best practice be sufficient mechanisms to meet regulatory goals? Does benchmarking and best practice which characterize many corporate codes of conduct and transnational administrative net-works provide adequate safeguards? By contrast, interest-based approaches might focus on the cost–benefit of different types of institutionalized cooperation. Such rational calculations might address the willingness of states to reduce transaction costs and shift the regulatory burden by instruments other than law onto firms. States have used a variety of tools and regulatory strategies such as contracting out, manda-tory reporting requirements, and monitoring transgressions and disclosing informa-tion that shift the burden of compliance onto firms. Under what circumstances are private contributions better suited or more efficient to achieve public goods? While we know that more business-compatible approaches have emerged, through self-regulation at the firm, association, and sector level for example, we have paid less attention to the different ways that *firms serve as regulators* (Grabosky 1995).

Many of the assumptions about delegation of regulatory authority, new types of governance regimes, and transnational networks are based on the principal–agent models derived from American politics (Coen and Thatcher 2005; Gutnar 2005). Given the rationalist assumptions on which it is based, as a means to increase credible commitment, utilize policy expertise, and reduce information costs, there has been tremendous interest in the different institutional configurations as well as mechan-isms to exercise oversight and control. Yet most of this has involved institutionalized delegation to regulatory agencies, international organizations, or non-majoritarian institutions, with much less attention given to the "fiduciary principles" that exist within more private, informal, or self-regulatory fora. The issue of delegation to private governance regimes has often been viewed in negative terms. Yet the potential role of corporate organizations and economic associations can promote successful self-regulation (Lindberg and Campbell 1991). More attention needs to be given to the informal means of promoting compliance, the transferal of norms and diffusion of best practices (see Prakash 2000b). Nonetheless, most of the non-business literature continues to assume that self-regulation or private networks may produce less credible outcomes. Under what circumstances are private or non-state regimes more effective than state-based ones? What should be the reporting and monitoring requirements to ensure effective implementation and compliance? Has self-regulation, rather than law-based regulation, proven to be an adequate mechanism for regulating or disciplining market behavior?

Much of the literature on the frameworks of governance provided by the private sector focuses on their substitution for state authority, their legitimacy, and consequence for the provision of public goods. Greater attention to the expansion of rule-based relations and judicial management among private authority governance may highlight significant variation in terms of the role of market forces, and the relative effect of values, trust, and credibility as factors in fostering compliance with international norms and standards. Furthermore, as several authors argue, such delegation may shift adjustment costs and avoid dealing directly with externalities. However, the implicit assumption that private authority is more efficient warrants careful consideration. In the case of voluntary standards, which often become de facto market entry requirements in many areas of goods and services, the institutionalization of one particular rule or standard may in fact produce suboptimal regulatory outcomes. The famous case of QWERTY demonstrates the path dependent and irreversible effect of early standardization, and thus, international governance through private authority may not necessarily improve social welfare or generate efficiency gains (David 1985).

A second strand of research focuses on the role of political institutions in structuring outcomes. Scholars have focused on the operating rules and norms in different institutional arenas as well as the decision rules in shaping outcomes. There is considerable focus on the issue of compliance and implementation, as well as the impact of decision rules and veto points. Within each institutional setting, the decision rules and decision styles may affect regulatory outcomes. What seems to be of importance is whether these institutions create rules that are voluntary or mandatory, how verification of commitment or certification is carried out, and whether there is a consensus on a global or regional approach to the problem. Analyzing the distributional implications and effects of negotiations may link with the broader issues of whether state structure, varieties of capitalism, or economic openness for example affects institutional design and policy choices in different issue domains. Such pressures to foster international rules and standards may also be provided by contextual factors such as currency meltdowns, complexity of financial instruments, and environmental catastrophes, for example.

Institutional fragmentation is a key feature of the regulatory environment for business. Many firms have to take account of rules and standards that are developed in different arenas and fora. The impact of organizational fragmentation on both regulatory outcomes and the dilemmas this creates for business strategy deserve closer scrutiny. While international relations scholars have focused on how different institutional arrangements come into existence, and whether the institutional environment is the best available venue to foster regulatory cooperation, more work is needed on the impact of organizational fragmentation and differing governance regimes on business. Setting up new regional or transnational networks or governance regimes may make it possible to exclude certain interests, and the more competitive regulatory environment may provide strategic advantages for specific industries or sectors. While industry tends to share a general aversion to incompatibility or divergent rules, given the attendant costs of compliance, the rule-making environment may strategically disadvantage certain firms given their strategic assets and investments. It may also provide opportunities for forum shopping to promote specific regulatory outcomes. Given that differences in institutional norms and culture exist, the resulting institutional bias may also provide opportunities to shift their concepts, ideas, and preferences to specific institutional contexts (Riker 1980). The effect of institutional fragmentation in comparison to monopolistic organizational efforts to regulate the business environment might be worth considering in assessing the most efficient, credible, and legitimate outcomes. Bargaining power of participants may vary within these different institutional contexts, as the costs of veto may be more significant in a monopoly situation in contrast to a dense regulatory environment.

In focusing on the coordination of rules within different contexts, this might lead us to consider the impact of regulatory diffusion in the context of globalization. Several governance frameworks may lead to differing standards, as there are regional organizations, voluntary standards bodies, business associations, as well as networks of regulators that all engage in generating rules. And what are the effects on states and markets when rules collide? What are the effects of competition among rules in producing global public goods? On the one hand, competition between regulatory regimes has an additional advantage in that the coexistence of various rule-making authorities might introduce regulatory innovations that, once proven successful, can be copied by other authorities. On the other hand, regulatory competition may result in downward pressures and lead to a race to the bottom, although there are also examples that competition among rules can spur higher standards and learning processes (cf. Vogel 1995).

But in explaining the emergence of a range of transnational regulation, emerging from a variety of fora on the global level, from environmental management standards to antitrust cooperation, we have mapped out different institutional configurations, but more work needs to be done on whether the diffusion and internationalization of regulatory governance promotes public goods. To what extent are the decisions in line with collective interests or the interests of consumers? And how does one define collective good globally? What is the public interest in the international sphere?

As the relationship between public and private sectors evolves, the diversity of governance regimes and sectoral variations in regulating markets suggests that we should also take account of the temporal dimension in our analysis. These networks appear to change over time, with private and public actors playing different roles, and hence understanding how and why these changes occur, and the impact of a *temporal* logic on international governance has drawn less attention than the *spatial* reconfiguration and transformation of boundaries, markets, and regulation. In focusing on new international regulatory regimes, the relative costs, the time horizons, domestic constraints, and operating norms may all affect outcomes. While nation states are no longer always the most important actors in creating new international regulatory regimes, and there is a wider array of actors in regulating the international marketplace, the nature of global regulation requires collaboration among different actors. Such governance requires vertical and horizontal coordination across networks, institutions, and agencies, as the introduction of new products and methods of production, changes in market structures, and major transformations in the economic environment require new, innovative, and responsive coordinating mechanisms. The importance of these new forms of international governance and these transnational networks remains central to the study of business–government relations. The chapter raises some new avenues for research, and suggests that we need to focus on fully integrating different strands of research on business management and corporate social responsibility, regulatory agencies as coordinating mechanisms for international governance, private governance and voluntary standards as complements for international rule-making by states, and the diffusion and internationalization of regulatory rules and norms. Finally, many examples of the emergence of global governance in different issues and domains are often the result of the leverage and influence of particular advanced industrial states, and their respective firms. This raises important questions about the substantive influence of developing countries, the differentiation of states as rule-makers and rule-takers, and the importance of resources in the supply and demand of international economic regulations.

REFERENCES

BEESON, M. n.d. "Global governance," http://espace.library.uq.edu.au/eserv/UQ:10766/mb_enc.pdf

CAMERRA-ROWE, P. 2005. "Trouble brewing? EU and member state public health policy and the European beer industry," European Policy Paper No. 10, University of Pittsburgh, November.

CERNY, P. 2000. "Embedding global financial markets: securitization and the emerging web of governance," in K. Ronit and V. Schneider, eds., *Private Organizations in Global Politics*. New York: Routledge.

COEN, D., and THATCHER, M. 2005. "New governance of markets: regulation by non-majoritarian institutions," *Governance* 25(3): 329–47.

COWLES, M. G. 2001. "The transatlantic business dialogue: transforming the new transatlantic regulatory agenda," in M. Pollack and G. Schaffer, eds., *Transatlantic Governance in a Global Economy*. Boulder, Colo.: Rowman and Littlefield.

CUTLER, C., et al. 1999. *Private Authority and International Affairs.* SUNY Series in Global Politics. Albany, NY: State University of New York.

DAVID, P. 1985. "Clio and the economics of QWERTY," *American Economic Review* 75: 332–7.

DONOHUE, J., and NYE, J. 2000. *Market Based Governance.* Washington, DC: Brookings Institution.

DREZNER, D. 2007. *All Politics is Global: Explaining International Regulatory Regimes.* Princeton: Princeton University Press.

EBERLEIN, B., and NEWMAN, A. 2008. "Escaping the international governance dilemma? Incorporated transgovernmental networks in the European Union," *Governance* 21.

EGAN, M. 2001. *Constructing a European Market: Standards, Regulation and Governance.* Oxford: Oxford University Press.

FALKNER, G., et al., eds. 2005. *Complying with Europe: EU Soft Law and Harmonization in the Member States.* Cambridge: Cambridge University Press.

GRABOSKY, P. 1995. "Using non-governmental resources to foster regulatory compliance," *Governance* 8(4): 527–50.

GUTNAR, T. 2005. "Explaining the gaps between mandate and performance: agency theory and World Bank environmental reform," *Global Environmental Politics* 5(2): 10–37.

HAUFLER, V. 2001. *A Public Role for the Private Sector: Industry Self-Regulation in a Global Economy.* Washington: Carnegie Endowment for International Peace.

HELD, D., and McGREW, A., eds. 2003. *Governing Globalization: Power, Authority and Global Governance.* Oxford: Polity Press.

HELLMAN, J. 1998. "Winners take all: the politics of partial reform in postcommunist transitions," *World Politics* 50(2): 203–34.

HERITIER, A. 2002. *Common Goods: Reinventing European and International Governance.* Lanham, MD: Rowman & Littlefield.

JORDANA, J., and LEVI FAUR, D. 2004. *The Politics of Regulation: Institutions and Regulatory Reform in the Age of Governance.* Cheltenham: Edward Elgar and Manchester University Press.

KAHLER, M., and LAKE, D. 2003. *Governance in a Global Economy.* Princeton: Princeton University Press.

—— —— 2004. "Governance in a global economy: political authority in transition," *Political Science and Politics* 37(3): 409–14.

KEOHANE, R. 2001. "Governance in a partially globalized world," *American Political Science Review* 95(1): 1–13.

KERWER, D. 2001. "Holding global regulators accountable: the case of credit rating agencies," *Governance,* 18(3): 453–75.

KETTL, D. 1988. *Government by Proxy.* Washington, DC: Brookings.

KITSCHELT, H. 1986. "Political opportunity structures and political protest: anti-nuclear movements in four democracies," *British Journal of Political Science* 16(1): 57–86.

KNILL, C., and LEHMKUHL, D. 2002. "Private actors and the state: internationalization and changing patterns of governance," *Governance* 15(1): 41–63.

LEHMKUHL, D. 2008. "Control modes in the age of transnational governance," *Law and Policy* 30(3): 336–83.

LEVI FAUR, D. 2005. The global diffusion of regulatory capitalism," *Annals of the American Academy and Social Science* 598(1): 12–32.

LINDBERG, L., and CAMPBELL, J. 1991. "The state and the organization of economic activity," in J. L. Campbell et al., eds., *Governance of the American Economy.* New York: Cambridge University Press, 356–95.

LINDBLOM, C., and DAHL, R. 1977. *Politics and Markets*. New York: Basic Books.

MAJONE, G. 1996. *Regulating Europe*. New York: Routledge.

MATTLI, W., and BÜTHE, T. 2005. "Accountability in accounting? The politics of private rule-making in the public interest," *Governance* 18: 399.

OLSON, M. 1971. *The Logic of Collective Action: Public Good and the Theory of Groups*, rev edn. Cambridge, Mass.: Harvard University Press.

PELKMANS, J. 2002. "Mutual recognition in goods and services: an economic perspective," College of Europe Working Papers in Economics BEEP Briefing No. 2.

PICCIOTTO, S., and HAINES, J. 1999. "Regulating global financial markets," *Journal of Law and Society* 26(3): 351–68.

PRAKASH, A. 2000a. *Greening the Firm*. Cambridge: Cambridge University Press.

—— 2000b. "Responsible care: an assessment," *Business and Society* 39(2): 183–209.

—— and HART, J., eds. 1999. *Globalization and Governance*. London: Routledge.

REINECKE, W. 1998. *Global Public Policy: Governing without Government*. Washington, DC: Brookings Institution.

RHODES, R. 1997. *Understanding Governance: Policy Networks, Governance and Accountability*. Buckingham: Open University Press.

RIKER, W. 1980. "Implications from the disequilibrium of majority rule for the study of institutions," *American Political Science Review* 74: 432–46.

RONIT, K., and SCHNEIDER, V. 2000. *Private Organizations in Global Politics*. New York: Routledge.

ROSENAU, J. N. 1992. "Governance, order and change in world politics," in J. N. Rosenau and E.-O. Czempiel, eds., *Governance without Government: Order and Change in World Politics*. Cambridge: Cambridge University Press, 1–29.

—— and CZEMPIEL, O. 1992. *Governance without Government: Order and Change in World Politics*. Cambridge: Cambridge University Press.

SABEL, C. 2008. "Learning from difference: the new architecture of experimentalist governance in the EU," *European Law Journal* 14(3): 271–327.

SCHARPF, F. 1999. *Governing in Europe: Effective and Democratic?* Oxford: Oxford University Press.

SCHEPPEL, H. 2005. *The Constitution of Private Governance*. Oxford: Hart Publishing.

SCHMITTER, P. 2000. *How to Democratize the EU and Why Bother?* Lanham, MD: Rowman & Littlefield 2000.

SELL, S. 2003. *Private Power, Public Law: The Globalization of Intellectual Property Rights*. Cambridge: Cambridge University Press.

SIKKINK, K. 1986. "Codes of conduct for transnational corporations: the case of the WHO/UNICEF Code," *International Organization* 40: 815–40.

SINCLAIR, T. 1999. "Bond rating agencies and coordination in the global political economy," in Cutler et al., ed., *Private Authority and International Affairs*. Albany, NY: State University of New York, 153–68.

SLAUGHTER, A. M. 2004. *A New World Order*. Princeton: Princeton University Press.

SØRENSEN, E., and TORFING, J. 2005. "Network governance and post-liberal democracy," *Administration Theory and Praxis* 27(2): 197–237.

SPAR, D. 1999. "Lost in (cyber)space: the private rules of online commerce," in Cutler et al., *Private Authority and International Affairs*. Albany, NY: State University of New York, 31–52.

THATCHER, M., and COEN, D. 2008. "Reshaping European regulatory space: an evolutionary analysis," *West European Politics* 31(4): 806–36.

VOGEL, D. 1995. *Trading Up: Consumer and Environmental Regulation in a Global Economy*. Cambridge, Mass.: Harvard University Press.

CHAPTER 18

CREDIT RATING AGENCIES

TIMOTHY J. SINCLAIR

INTRODUCTION

HENRY Paulson, US Treasury Secretary in the last days of President George W. Bush's administration, made it clear when presenting the policy statement of the President's Working Group on Financial Markets in March 2008 that in the midst of the current market turbulence, officials, politicians and their advisers believe credit rating agencies "play a major role in financial markets," and that the work of the agencies must be improved in terms of the specific challenges faced in rating complex financial instruments like structured securities, and by avoiding the reality or appearance of conflicts of interest (Paulson 2008).

These comments, and the energetic reaction of European financial regulators to the perceived culpability of the agencies in the generation of the subprime crisis, point to the increasingly important job done by wholesale credit rating agencies in global markets. In fact, it was not too many years ago that rating agencies were little known outside the United States. Until the mid-1990s most European and Asian companies relied on their market reputations alone to secure financing. But this changed when the pressure of globalization led to the desire to tap the deep American financial markets and to a greater appetite for higher returns and thus risk. In these circumstances, the informality of the traditional old boys' networks is no longer defendable to shareholders or relevant to pension funds halfway around the world. The result is that an essentially American approach to market organization and judgment has become the global norm in the developed world, and increasingly, in emerging markets as well.

Ratings seem increasingly central to the regulatory system of modern capitalism and therefore to governments everywhere. Getting credit ratings "right" therefore seems vitally important to many observers. But in pursuing improvement in the rating system we need to appreciate the challenges and limits to rating. I argue, after due attention to the origins and work of the agencies, that our expectations of the agencies are founded on a limited rationalist or machine-like understanding of the workings of capital markets. A more appropriately social (and dynamic) view of markets makes the challenge of effective rating even more daunting. The increasingly volatile nature of markets has created a crisis in relations between the agencies and governments, which increasingly seek to monitor their performance and stimulate reform in their procedures.

Given the inherent challenges in rating it must seem paradoxical that rating is growing in importance as an approach to information problems in a variety of contexts outside the financial markets.[1] This form of regulation is increasingly important in health, education, and many other commercial activities. This being so, insights drawn from rating in the financial markets are likely to be relevant in many fields.

EMERGENCE

Rating agencies emerge after the Civil War in the United States. From this time until the First World War, American financial markets experienced an explosion of information provision. The transition between issuing compendiums of information and actually making judgments about the creditworthiness of debtors occurred after the 1907 financial crisis and before the Pujo hearings of 1912. By the mid-1920s, nearly 100 per cent of the US bond market was rated by Moody's.[2] The growth of the bond rating industry subsequently occurred in a number of distinct phases. Up to the 1930s, and the separation of the banking and the securities businesses in the United States with passage of the Glass–Steagall Act of 1933, bond rating was a fledgling activity. Rating entered a period of rapid growth and consolidation with this separation and institutionalization of the securities business after 1929, and rating became a standard requirement to sell any issue in the US after many state governments incorporated rating standards into their prudential rules for investment by pension funds. A series of defaults by major sovereign borrowers, including Germany, made the bond business largely a US one from the 1930s to the 1980s, dominated by American blue chip industrial firms and municipalities (Toffler 1990: 43–57). The third period of rating development began in the 1980s, as a market in junk or low-rated bonds developed. This market—a feature of the newly released energies of financial speculation—saw many new entrants participate in the capital markets.

Two major American agencies dominate the market in ratings. Both Moody's and S&P are headquartered in the lower Manhattan financial district of New York City. Moody's was sold in 1998 as a separate corporation by Dun and Bradstreet, the information concern, which had owned Moody's since 1962, while S&P remains a subsidiary of publishers McGraw-Hill, which bought S&P in 1966 (Abrahams 1996: 26; Moody's Corporation 2002). Both agencies have numerous branches in the US, in other developed countries, and in several emerging markets. S&P is famous for the S&P 500, the benchmark US stock index listing around $1 trillion in assets.

In the late 1960s and early 1970s, raters began to charge fees to bond issuers to pay for ratings. A number of scholars have suggested that charging fees to bond issuers constitutes a conflict of interest.[3] This may indeed be the case with the smaller, lower-profile firms eager for business. With Moody's and S&P, "grade inflation" does not seem to be a significant issue (although this has not stopped casual suggestions to the contrary). Both firms have fee incomes of several hundred million dollars a year, making it difficult for even the largest issuer to manipulate them through their revenues. Moreover, inflated ratings would diminish the reputation of the major agencies, and reputation is the very basis of their franchise.

DYNAMICS

Globalization has led to unprecedented financial volatility. One response to this development has been to separate central bank monetary policy from legislative and executive intervention. A second response has been to establish legislative constraints that impose discipline on fiscal matters. Less visible has been a shift in emphasis between what have come to be called "fire alarm" and "police patrol"-type regulation forms (McCubbins and Schwartz 1987: 427). The fire alarm metaphor suggests a problem-focused, episodic approach to governance. Like municipal fire departments, problems—like fires—only receive attention when they have been identified and called in by non-specialists. A framework is established—that fires will be reported by those who see them—which only requires occasional "enforcement." Inspections are infrequent (perhaps annually) and the emphasis is on self-regulation in self-interest. In the case of police patrols, a much more aggressive process of looking for law-breaking is characteristic. The idea here is that many problems never mature into crises because of surveillance and early intervention.

Paradoxically, while public institutions seem to be increasingly moving from the police patrol to the fire alarm approach under fiscal and competitive pressures, a tightening of governance is developing in the private realm, in which Thatcher and Stone Sweet (2002) identify a delegation of regulatory authority to non-majoritarian institutions (NMIs), in what Coen and Grant have called the "privatization of public policy" (2006). Bond or credit rating agencies are an example of this form of emerging private authority.

How should we understand these processes? Natural science seeks to establish universal laws, and considers specific events in terms of these laws. The objective in this case is always generalization. Many social scientists have also followed this path. The constructivist study of global finance has a different purpose. A constructivist approach to the politics of global finance examines the distinctiveness of particular events, institutions, and ways of thinking, and seeks to interpret and demonstrate their significance. The focus on understanding the particular—rather than positing universal laws about the politics of global finance "in general"—means that research design tends to be "realistic," and inductive (Ruggie 1998a: 34).

This approach draws on economic and organizational sociology as its inspiration. It does not adopt the assumption that there is a one-to-one match between imputed material interests and social action. The constructivist approach can complement the instrumental cause–effect focus of rationalism. The constructivist heuristic focuses on the processes through which the preferences and subsequent strategies of actors (such as corporations and states) are socially constructed, as features of intersubjective orders, which vary over time and space, and define the identity or nature of the actors in relation to others (Katzenstein, Keohane, and Krasner 1998: 681–2). The norms, identity, knowledge, and culture that comprise intersubjective structures—things held constant in Rationalism—are amongst the things that constitute or regulate actors in this theoretical orientation.[4] Both rationalism and constructivism are essential for understanding specific institutions.

By contrast with the Neorealist vision of an anarchy of self-regarding units, the notion of "embeddedness" identified by Granovetter (1992: 53), a key concept in economic sociology, sought to link institutions to the social relations in which they exist. In this understanding, economic life is not separate from society like a free-standing machine, but linked to historical and cultural circumstances, and therefore variable over time and space (Dobbin 1994). Change is linked to pervasive mental frameworks, which legitimate specific organizational forms (and negate others). Mental or intersubjective frameworks are just as consequential as other social structures. As W. I. Thomas noted in 1928, "If men [sic] define situations as real, they are real in their consequences."[5] Thomas was suggesting that people respond not just to objective things like mountains and automobile accidents, "but also, and often mainly," to their collective attribution of meaning to a social situation (Coser 1977: 521). As Coser suggests, if people think witches are real, "such beliefs have tangible consequences" (521).

The importance of mental frameworks is reflected within institutions. Meyer and Rowan argue organizations and how they are structured reflect not the efficient undertaking of their function but myths, or mental frameworks, that depict a public story about what the organization is supposed to be about (Meyer and Rowan 1977). Internal rules and organizational forms within institutions reflect "the prescriptions of myths" (349). These rules and organizational forms demonstrate that the organization is acting "in a proper and adequate manner" (349). By conforming to the myth, the organization protects itself from interrogation (1977: 349). For the organization, the key process is identifying the "societally legitimated rationalized elements," and then reconfiguring the organization around them (1977: 352). Organizations, Meyer and Rowan (1977) suggest, typically face dilemmas between the prescriptions of these elements and their own internal shared sense of what they are really supposed to be about, and also between diverse competing rationalized elements coming from different parts of society, such as government, interest groups, market associations, and so forth (355).

Professional judgment and analysis—and public expectations about its development and standards—is a key socially legitimated rationalized element of the mental framework of the rating agencies. One conception of how the rating mental framework can be understood in its wider social context is through what Peter Haas (1992) and his fellow contributors have called epistemic communities. Haas defines epistemic communities as "networks of knowledge-based experts" that address complex, seemingly technical problems (2). Haas observes that the "recognized expertise and competence" of these professionals give them an authoritative claim to be offering good advice (3). The control of expertise, he notes, is "an important dimension of power" (2). Haas suggests four features of epistemic communities: (1) a shared set of normative and principled beliefs; (2) shared causal beliefs; (3) shared notions of validity in the area of expertise; and (4) a "common policy enterprise," connected to enhancing human welfare (1992: 3). What epistemic communities do is neither guess nor produce data. Instead, epistemic communities interpret phenomena (4). Epistemic communities, Haas argues, are important in themselves. They are not epiphenomenal. They "convey new patterns of reasoning" to policy-makers, and "encourage them to pursue new paths of policymaking" with unpredictable outcomes (21). Although a subset of raters may share a conscious commitment to such beliefs, this conscious commitment to normative belief is a defining element of epistemic communities. An alternative concept, embedded knowledge networks, is elaborated below.

Embedded knowledge networks are analytical and judgmental systems that in principle remain at arm's length from market transactions. "Embedded" does not imply that embedded knowledge networks are locked in or institutionalized in finance, and thus simply resistant to change. "Embedded" does not suggest inertia, path dependency, or vested interests. Instead, it specifies that actors view embedded knowledge networks as endogenous rather than exogenous to financial globalization. Embedded knowledge networks are, therefore, generally considered legitimate rather than imposed entities by market participants. How embedded knowledge networks construct and reinforce this collective understanding of themselves is of great interest. Where institutions that are embedded knowledge networks in one society attempt to transplant themselves into others, they risk losing their embedded status, unless they recognize the necessity of getting the market actors in these other places to recognize their endogeneity. To return to the discussion of myth and mental frameworks, rating agencies must adapt themselves to public expectations of what they should be doing, as they expand from their American home base. But achieving endogeneity, and hence legitimacy, has been easier in some places than others for the major US bond rating agencies.

The role of knowledge in investment decision-making is at the heart of embedded knowledge network activity. Market actors are overwhelmed with data about prices, business activity, and political risk. A typical form of knowledge output is some sort of recommendation, ranking, or rating, which claims to condense these forms of knowledge. This knowledge output becomes a benchmark around which market players subsequently organize their affairs. Market actors can and do depart from benchmarks, but these still set the standard for the work of other actors, providing a measure of market success or failure. In this way, embedded knowledge network outputs play a crucial role in constructing markets in a context of less than perfect information and considerable uncertainty about the future. Rating agencies, acting as embedded knowledge networks, can be thought to adjust the "ground rules" inside international capital markets and thereby shape the internal organization and behaviour of institutions seeking funds. Their views on what is acceptable shape the actions of those seeking positive responses from them. This anticipation effect, or structural power, is reflected in the minds of capital market participants in terms of their understandings of the views and expectations of the agencies. In turn this acts as a base point from which business and policy initiatives are developed.

Bond traders and pension fund managers have seemingly contradictory views on rating agencies. They are at times critical of the work of the rating agencies. As Scott (1990) suggests in his research on the public roles played by the powerful and the powerless, in addition to a positive public discourse about the dominant, there is typically a "hidden transcript," a critique of power which exists as a sort of back-chat, spoken out of sight of the dominant (1990: xii). Back-chat only becomes public, suggests Scott, in times of crisis or unusual stress. But back-chat is just that. Financial market actors take the rating agencies seriously. Market participants usually treat the rating agencies and their views as matters of considerable interest. Rating agencies, especially Moody's and Standard & Poor's, have worked hard at creating their reputation for impartiality over the last century or so. In some situations where people surrender their own powers of judgment to an institution or to a group, the surrender may be quite fragile, as in the case of a fad or fashion (Bikchandani, Hirshleifer, and Welch 1992: 1016). The circumstances, including the longevity of the rating agencies, make their particular authoritative niche more resilient than that of most other non-state institutions. Their position within the capital markets provides them with considerable resources.

In addition to respect for the reputation of the agencies, there is also an awareness of the market influence of the rating agencies. Even if a trader or bond issuer does not respect a particular judgment of the rating agencies, they might anticipate the effect the judgment will have on others, and may act on that expectation, rather than their own views of the actual quality of the judgment itself. The intersubjective process described here is sometimes termed "Keynes's beauty contest," after J. M. Keynes's discussion of the similarities between financial market behavior and the tabloid newspaper beauty contests of the 1930s. In these competitions, the objective was not to guess who was the most attractive young woman, but to approximate best who was *generally thought to be* the prettiest by all competition entrants. With professional investment, Keynes argued, "We have reached the third degree where we devote our intelligences to anticipating what average opinion expects the average opinion to be" (Keynes 1936: 156).

Rating agency outputs comprise an important part of the infrastructure of capital markets. They are key benchmarks in the cognitive life of these markets: features of the marketplace, which form the basis for subsequent decision-making by participants. In this sense, rating agencies are important not so much for any particular rating they produce, but for the fact that they are a part of the internal organization of the market itself. So, we find that traders may refer to a company as an "AA company," or some other rating category, as if this were a fact, an agreed and uncontroversial way of describing and distinguishing companies, municipalities, or countries.[6]

A rationalist way to think about what rating agencies do is to see them as serving a "function" in the economic system. In this view, rating agencies solve a problem in markets that develops when banks no longer sit at the centre of the borrowing process.[7] Rating agencies serve as what Gourevitch calls "reputational intermediaries" like accountants, analysts, and lawyers, who are "essential to the functioning of the system," monitoring managers through a "constant flow of short-term snapshots" (Gourevitch 2002: 1, 11). Another way to think about the function of the agencies is to suggest rating agencies establish psychological "rules of thumb" which make market decisions less costly for participants (Heisler 1994: 78; Beckert 1996).

But purely functional explanations for the existence of rating agencies are potentially deceptive. Attempts to verify (or refute) the idea that rating agencies must exist because they serve a purpose have proven inconclusive. Rating agencies have to be considered important actors because people view them as important, and act on the basis of that understanding in markets, even if it proves impossible for analysts to actually isolate the specific benefits the agencies generate for these market actors. Investors often mimic other investors, "ignoring substantive private information" (Scharfstein and Stein 1990: 465). The fact that people may collectively view rating agencies as important—irrespective of what "function" the agencies are thought to serve in the scholarly literature—means that markets and debt issuers have strong incentives to act *as if* participants in the markets take the rating agencies seriously. In other words, the significance of rating is not to be estimated like a mountain or national population, as a "brute" fact which is true (or not) irrespective of shared beliefs about its existence, nor is the meaning of rating determined by the "subjective" facts of individual perception.[8] What is central to the status and consequentiality of rating agencies is what people believe about them, and act on collectively—even if those beliefs are clearly false. Indeed, the beliefs may be quite strange to the observer, but if people use them as a guide to action (or inaction) they are significant. Dismissing such collective beliefs, as structural Marxists once did, as "false consciousness" misses the fact that actors must take account of the existence of social facts in considering their own action. Reflection about the nature and direction of social facts is characteristic of financial markets on a day-to-day basis. Rating agencies are important in investment most immediately because there is a collective belief that says the agencies are important, which people act upon in markets, as if it were true. Whether rating agencies actually add new information to the process does not negate their significance, understood in these terms.

CRISES

Three main types of challenge to the power and authority of rating agencies can be identified. The first challenge—problems in rating organization—is the public discussion of problems that market actors (including government officials and financial reporters) see in how the agencies are organized, and in how they do their business. The two key elements are perceived conflicts of interest in how ratings are paid for, and the question of unsolicited ratings. The second sort of challenge— performance issues—is a more serious challenge than the organizational problems. The major issues here concern the lagging nature of rating, specific concerns about "split" ratings, and the lack of probabalistic quantitative analysis models in the rating process. The last sort of challenge to the power and authority of rating—rating crises—emerges from a series of high-profile failures to predict sudden bankruptcies or collapses of credit quality.

At the heart of all these challenges lies the key reality of the rating process: reputation cannot be bought off the shelf. Instead, the reputation of Moody's and S&P has been constructed over time through a combination of serving a need by offering to solve the information problem between buyers and sellers, and by providing that information in a reliable way, thus generating epistemic authority. Given that the reputational assets of the rating agencies are not natural, but reflect a process of construction, the question of the deconstruction or degrading of those assets is of vital importance. In what ways is this reputation susceptible to attack? Is rating reputation vulnerable to falling apart, or does it decline incrementally? The view offered here is that the rating agencies, as embedded knowledge networks, have a robustness which makes them resilient in the face of problems, issues, and crises in rating, but that for the rating agencies, a constant program of reinforcement by a variety of means makes good sense in an increasingly volatile world.

One of the commonplaces of the rating world, repeated in newspaper and magazine articles wherever the raters are a presence, is that work of the rating agencies is compromised by a conflict of interest inherent in charging the issuers of bonds for the rating work undertaken by the agencies. The problem inherent in issuer fees is that issuers are not actually the principals in rating. The principals—those for whom the rating work is done—are investors. So making issuers pay introduces the potential for issuers to influence the judgments of the agencies and undermine their commitment to giving a true account to investors.

The problem with making investors pay for ratings is that ratings are like the news, they are public goods. Once a rating is released by an agency there is no way for the creator to prevent investors, or intermediaries like banks who have not paid for the rating, from free riding on the rating. This makes it difficult for the agencies to get investors to pay for the full costs of rating. The dilemma for the agencies is the reconciliation of the public-good character of ratings with their need to earn revenue and make an appropriate return, while minimizing the potential for perceived conflicts of interest that degrade the reputation of the agencies.[9] The solution they arrived at was to charge issuers, because investors will free ride, but the agencies have to make sure issuers do not shape the rating process, which would destroy the reputational value of ratings (and thus the rating franchise).

The major agencies have been very successful in managing this dilemma. Smith and Walter suggest that internal operating procedures, and analysts' compensation policies that avoid linkage between salary and revenue streams, are designed to avoid conflict (2001: 43–4). If they were to give in to the conflict of interest inherent in their situation, where issuers pay for their own rating, they would probably find that their franchise as embedded knowledge networks would be seriously impaired. The best evidence for the viability of this position is the lack of any scandal related to conflict of interest, despite frequent comment in the financial and mainstream press about the issue. However, a more dynamic view of the rating industry suggests that conflicts of interest may become harder to manage in future if rating competition increases, driven by opportunities in emerging markets and by stock market sentiment about the agencies themselves (*Economist* 2001).

Things moved slowly as far as rating innovation was concerned in the era of rating conservatism that followed the Second World War. The biggest development was the introduction of issuer fees during the late 1960s by S&P (1968) and Moody's (1970) (*Bond Buyer* 1993: 5). Even then, however, as former S&P president Brenton W. Harries noted, congressmen did discuss the performance of the agencies and questioned rating officials about their work (5). Raters were never left alone to enjoy a sinecure. The hidden transcript may have been more hidden during these years, but it was still there, and raters knew about it then too. Today, near continuous expressions of concern about rating performance—about how good the rating agencies are at their business—have become normal. Newspapers, magazines, or online sites talk about the performance of the agencies and their failings.[10]

Three things are central to understanding the significance of this discourse of discontent. First, because there is a discourse at all, we have further confirmation of the importance of the agencies' role in financial globalization. The expression of the discourse of discontent happens because agencies cannot be ignored in these circumstances. The role of the agencies has a logic. They "fit" in the capital markets, even if they have made that place for themselves. Perceived failings in their work are too important to be ignored. Second, the rating discourse is very much framed within this logic of function. It is about improvement to the agencies, rather than their replacement. Third, the agencies have to deal with these expressions of the hidden transcript, but can fall back on the logic of their role to stiffen their resolve, especially versus issuers, who seem constantly to be engaged in an effort to become the principals of the agencies activities.

A common criticism suggests that the rating agencies are too slow, and apply the lessons of the past to the present, a bit like a general re-fighting the wars of his youth, even though technology and tactics have moved on substantially in the subsequent years. Market participants worry that the ratings they are looking at do not have much to do with the company whose balance sheet can move by billions in either direction in just a few hours. The traditional defense against this problem of timeliness was for the rating agencies to suggest they took a longer view, and wanted to offer ratings not just for today but that would have some ability to withstand the normal business cycle. They would cite their track record on defaults of rated debt.[11] Increasingly, "event risk," such as a merger or acquisition, came to be perceived as a vital ingredient in creditworthiness, and one to which the agencies should become more sensitive. More recently, the agencies have started to discuss the impact of market sentiment on issuers because of the Enron bankruptcy.

A less obvious, but interesting, performance issue arises when the agencies decide to treat specific financial instruments differently in their work, and where they split on rating an issuer.[12] In a world of increasingly sophisticated asset-backed securities and derivatives, having different views of the credit implications of these instruments calls into question one of the bedrock assumptions of the mental framework of rating orthodoxy: that there is a right way and a wrong way to understand specific economic and financial matters. Given that investment banks, regulators, and other parties may also differ on how to understand financial innovation, perhaps this has less negative impact on the agencies than the situation in which the agencies give different ratings on the same issuer or bond issue.[13] Given how sensationally they are sometimes reported in the financial press, it might seem that split ratings are very rare. In fact, split ratings are quite common. According to Cantor, Packer, and Cole, 50 per cent of all corporate bonds had different ratings from Moody's and S&P when issued. Despite this observation, split ratings challenge the idea that there is a knowable rating universe out there that the agencies are trying to reflect in their work. There are only a few diviners of this knowledge, and if the agencies cannot "get it right" with an accurate rating, what does this say about the quality of their staff or management? If some agencies are "less strict" than others, do the less stringent agencies reduce the reputational assets for the rest?

Most publicly, and most threateningly for the agencies, are the public rating crises. Enron and the subprime crisis are the most recent and damaging, and escalated government interest in the performance of the agencies. Enron and the other corporate financial scandals are a product of the basic incentives underpinning modern American (and global) capitalism. Just a few years ago the Texas-based energy trading corporation, which declared bankruptcy on December 2, 2001, was America's seventh-largest company (*Economist* 2002a: 9). At the start of 2001, Enron's market capitalization was $62.5 billion. By spring 2002, Enron stock was worth just pennies (Salter, Levesque, and Ciampa 2002). The "one big issue" raised by Enron's demise, according to the *Economist*, was the role played by auditors, who missed the exotic financial strategies pursued by the firm.[14] The question of who regulates accounting, conflict of interest problems when auditors are also consultants, and the rigor of America's GAAP standards, are all up for debate and action.[15] The big victim of the public panic about Enron is their auditor, Arthur Andersen.[16] What is interesting about the attack on Andersen is that it demonstrates that a high repute institution, whose only real asset is its reputation, can see that asset go up in a puff of smoke if circumstances are right. Enron was not the first time in recent years that Andersen had made significant errors. It survived these other problems. It is Enron that destroyed the company.[17]

Enron was a major crisis for the rating agencies too. They had got emerging markets "wrong" with the Asia crisis, and now here they had got it "wrong" in America itself by failing to warn investors of the Enron collapse. This was serious. No longer were the victims unknown citizens of foreign countries, but red-blooded American citizens, who had lost their pensions, jobs, futures. John Diaz, Managing Director at Moody's, defended the company's work in front of the Senate Committee hearing in March 2002. "Enron was an anomaly," he said; "its responses to our specific requests for information were misleading and incomplete." Moody's rating process, he observed, "was undermined by the missing information."[18] Ronald M. Barone, the S&P analyst on Enron for several years, used harsher language. He suggested Enron had made "what we later learned were direct and deliberate misrepresentations to us relating to matters of great substance."[19]

Former Securities and Exchange Commission Chairman Arthur Levitt—who had shown little enthusiasm for codification of the rules about rating agencies during the 1990s—called for "greater accountability" of the agencies, the requirement for the agencies to "reveal more about how they operate," an assessment of their "impact on the markets," and "new authority" for the SEC to "oversee" their work.[20] Much of the talk from the agencies focused on "speeding up" the rating process in response to market calls for change (Mahoney 2002; Moody 2002: H1; Wiggins 2002: 10; Wiggins and Spiegel 2002: 1; Zuckerman and Richard 2002: C1).

The SEC's role in creating and maintaining the environment in which the agencies operate was noted by White, who suggested the SEC's NRSRO designation was anti-competitive, and had "lured these rating agencies into complacency" (White 2002: 13). The Nationally Recognized Statistical Rating Organization designation—NRSRO—was introduced in 1975, as a way of reducing the regulatory capital requirements for bond issuers with bond ratings. At the Senate Committee hearings, Isaac C. Hunt, Jr., SEC Commissioner, defended the NRSRO designation as intended "largely to reflect the view of the marketplace as to credibility of the ratings [of an agency] rather than representing a 'seal of approval' of a federal regulatory agency."[21] He noted the 1997 proposal to codify NRSRO criteria had not yet been acted on by the Commission, that the Commission had not determined that the NRSRO designation was a "substantial barrier to entry" into the rating business, and observed that "Growth in the business of several credit rating agencies, not recognized as NRSROs suggests that there may be a growing appetite among market participants for advice about credit quality...and that this makes it possible for new entrants to develop a national following for their credit judgments." Nevertheless, the Commission determined to examine the competitive impact of the NRSRO designation. If greater supervision of NRSROs is needed, "additional oversight" could become a condition of NRSRO recognition of an agency.

A law professor called to give testimony at the Senate Committee hearings attacked the NRSRO designation vigorously. Macey argued that NRSROs, free of competitive forces as a result of their government designation, have incentives to "reduce costs as much as possible." They know that regulation creates a steady demand whatever they do.[22] Fees paid to the raters, he suggested, are better viewed as a form of tax, rather than a fee for service. Another lawyer, Schwarcz, suggested the anti-competitive effect of NRSRO designation, if any, was mitigated by the need of rating agencies to maintain their reputations with or without regulation. Further regulation would not be likely to materially improve on the effects of this reputational incentive.[23]

One of the distinctive things about the rating agency reaction to the Enron crisis is the effort to consult with interested parties about developing the rating process in order to avoid future Enrons. When Moody's announced their intentions, concerns were expressed about a "dramatic increase in the volatility of ratings" which could raise the price of debt, as investors started to perceive higher risk.[24] Moody's subsequently said that while it will incorporate stock and bond prices in its analysis, it will not "let market volatility displace fundamental credit analysis" (Dooley 2002: C16). Nor will it engage in "unannounced multinotch ratings changes."[25] According to Moody's, market analysts were concerned that changes to ratings should not disrupt the markets, although they did expect the agencies to pursue accounting issues and demand undisclosed data. Although Moody's still expect ratings to be valid through business cycles, they will in future be adjusted more frequently "in periods of heightened credit stress" (Dooley 2002).

What unites Enron with the subprime events of 2007/8 is the important role of extreme forms of financial innovation. In this case, securities were created out of underlying loans to residential mortgage borrowers with weak personal credit ratings. The holders of these structured securities had little understanding of the quality of the underlying assets. With the advantage of hindsight it is clear, as the Bank of England (2007: 5) notes, that this involved an underpricing of risk.

What distinguishes subprime and Enron, and makes subprime much more of a systemic threat, is the corrosive effect of market uncertainty on the valuation of securities. It was easy to dismiss Enron as a gang of bad guys engaging in illegal market manipulation in far off Texas, a "fly over" state. But the essence of the subprime crsis is not illegality, but the financial engineering at the heart of the global financial system.

The effect of uncertainty about the value of securities was to massively reduce activity in the capital markets, as investment banks looked nervously at each other. Given that the subprime market was worth only $0.7 trillion in mid-2007, out of total capital markets of $175 trillion, the impact of subprime is out of all proportion to its weight in the financial system (Bank of England 2007: 20). This strongly implies that an explanation for this systemic crisis cannot be deduced in rationalist terms. The subprime crisis is not a direct consequence of the subprime delinquencies of 2007. The crisis emerges not because subprime lending is so important. Plainly it is not so important. The paralysis that comes over global finance is a consequence of the social or intersubjective nature of markets, rather than the logical result of relatively minor problems with lending to the working poor. But this analysis of the subprime crisis cannot be assimilated by those socialized into an exclusively rationalist view of markets, in which events have logical causes. In this world, panics, crises, and collapses have to be explained as a result of specific failures rather than understood as a feature of the interactions of social life. It is necessary, in these circumstances, to find those institutions that did not do their jobs properly and make sure they do in future. This assumes, of course, that a proper job can be done and the problem solved.

It comes as no surprise then that the rating agencies have been subject to unprecedented criticism and investigation in the midst of the subprime meltdown. Congressional committees, the SEC, the European Parliament and Commission, the Committee of European Securities Regulators are conducting investigations, amongst others. A very senior rating official has indicated that the crisis over subprime ratings is the most threatening yet experienced by the agencies. This is a curious reaction, given that the rating agency business is now open to greater competition since NRSRO designation became subject to the Credit Rating Agency Reform Act of 2006. It suggests that the image of a movement from regulation to self-regulation, or from police patrol to fire alarm, has not created a world of autonomous non-state authorities as envisaged by International Political Economy scholars. What we see instead is a serious disciplining of the agencies by a regulatory state, intent on improving performance (Moran 2003: 1–11). The outcome of the subprime crisis is likely to be a reconstruction of the agencies along more "accountable" lines.

The problem with this development is that the agencies are not in a position to offer the capital markets a solution to the information problem about the underlying assets of these securities, as they are on their home turf of municipal, corporate, and sovereign rating. The agencies, like market participants, cannot know about the circumstances of each homeowner. The markets can apply the same financial tools to the structured offerings themselves. Because of this lack of information arbitrage in the case of structured bonds, all the agencies were doing was lending their reputation or brand to securities where they do not have a comparative advantage in information.

The other major criticism of the agencies that has emerged again with the subprime crisis is that they face conflicts of interest because they charge those they rate. This is, as noted, a perennial concern. It seems to be given added impetus by the fact that structured ratings generate about 40 per cent of rating agency revenues, on some reports. The reason the agencies charge the issuers of securities is that once information—the rating—is made public financial market participants are able to free ride and avoid paying for the costs of the rating system. This is precisely what drove the agencies to change their financial model at the end of the 1960s. They charge issuers because without doing this there could not be a rating system. What we see in rating, as in many other spheres of modern life, is a conflict of interest certainly, but no more so than exists in universities in which students pay tuition fees that support the salaries of the professors who grade their examinations. Rating agencies, like universities, manage this dilemma, in the case of the agencies through codes of conduct, and by de-linking analysis and remuneration.

CONCLUSIONS

Traditionally, the major bond rating agencies, Moody's Investors Service and Standard & Poor's, are anonymous, faceless institutions left alone to do their work by governments. Since the mid-1990s, however, this picture has changed, and the agencies and what they do have become of much greater interest to the regulatory state and to those of us concerned with the dynamics of global finance.

On the one hand, the demand for the work of the agencies has grown with the expansion of capital markets as the prevailing means of international financing. This has made the agencies more important than ever before, granting them significant power in some circumstances over those seeking bond financing. On the other, risks have grown for the agencies too. Financial innovation means the rule book is being reinvented continuously. Although change in global finance has increased the importance of the bond rating agencies, they are more vulnerable now to a sudden collapse in their franchise, as suffered dramatically by Arthur Andersen in late 2001.

The less important conclusion to be derived from the subprime crisis is that reforms are required to make global finance "work better." The more substantial conclusion is that global finance does not work as we think it works, that the most important dynamics are intersubjective, and that like a Hollywood movie, success cannot be guaranteed by mobilizing resources or technical skill. Given the reluctance of government regulators, market participants, and academics to confront the inherently social and relational character of global finance, we are likely to see more aggressive—and ineffective—efforts to reform these institutions as further crises emerge.

NOTES

1. On growth, see Sinclair (2005).
2. "Moody's History," available at www.moodys.com
3. Edward Comor strongly promoted this view during our many discussions in the early 1990s.
4. Ibid. (679–80). Also see Katzenstein (1996: 5–6).

5. Thomas and Thomas (1928), cited by Coser (1977: 521).
6. In a 1992 interview, President Leo O'Neill of Standard & Poor's explained how bond traders would, on the one hand, dispute particular ratings with S&P, and on the other, refer to companies unproblematically as AA, A, and so on. Ratings were the common sense of the markets.
7. See, for example, Wilson (1987: 321–59). Also see Wakeman (1997: 25–8).
8. Ruggie (1998b: 12–13). Ruggie draws on Searle (1995). See also Berger and Luckmann (1966).
9. For an excellent discussion of the conflicts of interest problem, see Smith and Walter (2001).
10. A few good examples from the last decade: Kilpatrick (1992: 1); *Economist* (1995: 53–4); House (1995: 245–9); Leftwich (1997: 2); Boley, von Dewall, and Hoekerd (2000: 22–3); and Wheatcroft (2001).
11. For example, Moody's Investors Service (2000).
12. For an example of the differences of view between the agencies on financial innovation, see French (1998: 12).
13. On split ratings, see Cantor, Packer and Cole (1997: 72–82).
14. Also see McNulty et al. (2002: 6).
15. On accounting reform after Enron, see Peel and London (2002); Smith and Schroeder (2002: C15); Lowenstein (2002: A22); Spiegel and Peel (2002); and *Economist* (2002b: 57–9); and Mayer (2002: 64–71).
16. Kulish and Wilke (2002: C1); Brown et al. (2002: C1).
17. On the astonishment among Andersen workers about their "death sentence," see O'Toole (2002: 12A).
18. Testimony of John Diaz, Managing Director, Moody's Investors Service, before the Committee on Government Affairs, United States Senate, March 20, 2002: 2–3.
19. Testimony of Ronald M. Barone, Managing Director, Standard & Poor's, before the Committee on Government Affairs, United States Senate, March 20, 2002: 2.
20. Levitt (2002: 29).
21. Testimony of Isaac C. Hunt, Jr., Commissioner, US Securities and Exchange Commission, before the Committee on Governmental Affairs, United States Senate, March 20, 2002: 2 and 4.
22. Testimony of Jonathan R. Macey, Cornell Law School, before the Committee on Governmental Affairs, United States Senate, March 20, 2002: 3.
23. Testimony of Steven L. Schwarcz, Duke University, before the Committee on Governmental Affairs, United States Senate, March 20, 2002: 2–3.
24. Louise Purtle, credit strategist at Deutsche Bank in New York, quoted in Zuckerman and Richard (2002).
25. Chris Mahoney, senior managing director, Moody's Investors Service, quoted in Dooley (2002).

REFERENCES

ABRAHAMS, P. 1996. "Dun & Bradstreet opts for divorce," *Financial Times*, November 1: 26.
Bank of England. 2007. *Financial Stability Report* 22: 5.
BECKERT, J. 1996. "What is sociological about economic sociology? Uncertainty and the embeddedness of economic action," *Theory and Society* 25: 803–40.
BERGER, P. L., and LUCKMANN, T. 1966. *The Social Construction of Reality: A Treatise in the Sociology of Knowledge*. New York: Anchor.

Bikchandani, S., Hirshleifer, D., and Welch, I. 1992. "A theory of fads, fashion, custom, and cultural change as informational cascades," *Journal of Political Economy* 100(5).

Boley, S., von Dewall, F., and Hoekerd, K. 2000. "Rating may be overrated," *The Banker* May.

Bond Buyer. 1993. "Profits, racism, quality of life, and other issues facing rating agencies," *Bond Buyer* February 26.

Brown, K., Bryan-Low, C., Mollenkamp, C., and Pacelle, M. 2002. "Andersen's Foreign Offices defect," *Wall Street Journal* March 22: C1.

Cantor, R., Packer, F., and Cole, K. 1997. "Split ratings and the pricing of credit risk," *Journal of Fixed Income* 7(3): 72–82.

Coen, D., and Grant, W. 1977. "Managing business and government relations," in D. Coen and W. Grant, eds., *Business and Government: Methods and Practice*. Opladen: Barbara Budrich Publishers.

Coser, L. A. 1977. *Masters of Sociological Thought: Ideas in Historical and Social Context*, 2nd edn. New York: Harcourt Brace Jovanovich.

Dobbin, F. R. 1994. "Cultural models of organization: the social construction of rational organizing principles," in D. Crane, ed., *The Sociology of Culture: Emerging Theoretical Perspectives*. Cambridge, Mass.: Blackwell.

Dooley, J. 2002. "Moody's planned overhaul of its ratings process includes effort to limit volatility, shorten reviews," *Wall Street Journal* February 13: C16.

Economist. 1995. "Rating the rating agencies," *Economist* July 15.

—— 2001. "In their drive for new revenues, credit-rating agencies are opening themselves up to conflicts of interest," *Economist* April 12, accessed from www.economist.co.uk

—— 2002a. "The real scandal," *Economist* January 19.

—— 2002b. "When the numbers don't add up," *Economist* February 9.

French, J. 1998. "Securitization wrinkle complicates ratings: Moody's, S&P differ on assets not transferred to trusts," *Wall Street Journal Europe* April 23: 12.

Gourevitch, P. 2002. "Collective action problems in monitoring managers: the Enron case as a systemic problem," *Economic Sociology: European Electronic Newsletter* 3(3), accessed June 12, 2002, at www.siswo.uva.nl/ES

Granovetter, M. 1992. "Economic action and social structure: the problem of embeddedness," in M. Granovetter and R. Swedberg, eds., *The Sociology of Economic Life*. Boulder, Colo.: Westview.

Haas, P. M. 1992. "Introduction: epistemic communities and international policy coordination," *International Organization* 46(1): 1–35.

Heisler, J. 1994. "Recent research in behavioral finance," *Financial Markets, Institutions and Instruments* 3(5).

House, R. 1995. "Ratings trouble," *Institutional Investor* October.

Katzenstein, P. J. 1996. "Introduction: alternative perspectives on national security," in P. J. Katzenstein, ed., *The Culture of National Security: Norms and Identity in World Politics*. New York: Columbia University Press, 51–6.

—— Keohane, R. O., and Krasner, S. D. 1998. "International organization and the study of world politics," *International Organization* 52(4): 681–2.

Keynes, J. M. 1936. *The General Theory of Employment Interest and Money*. London: Macmillan.

Kilpatrick, L. 1992. "Debt-rating's flaws," *Financial Times of Canada* March 30 – April 5: 1.

Kulish, N., and Wilke, J. R. 2002. "Indictment puts Andersen's fate on line," *Wall Street Journal* March 15: C1.

Leftwich, R. 1997. "Survey: mastering finance 3: evaluating the bond-rating agencies," *Financial Times* May 27.

LEVITT, A. 2002. "Who audits the auditors?" *New York Times* January 17: A29.

LOWENSTEIN, R. 2002. "Auditor independence: the SEC chairman doesn't get it," *Wall Street Journal* January 23: A22.

McCUBBINS, M. D., and SCHWARTZ, T. 1987. "Congressional oversight overlooked: police patrols versus fire alarms," in M. D. McCubbins and T. Sullivan, eds., *Congress: Structure and Policy.* Cambridge: Cambridge University Press.

McNULTY, S., MARTIN, P., MICHAELS, A., and PEEL, M. 2002. "Called to account," *Financial Times* January 12/13.

MAHONEY, C. 2002. *The Bond Rating Process in a Changing Environment.* New York: Moody's Investors Service.

MAYER, J. 2002. "The accountants' war," *New Yorker* April 22 and 29: 64–71.

MEYER, J. W., and ROWAN, B. 1977. "Institutionalized organizations: formal structure as myth and ceremony," *American Journal of Sociology* 83(2): 340–63.

MOODY, E. 2002. "Moody's looks at speeding ratings," *Ottawa Citizen* January 19: H.

Moody's Corporation. 2002. *2001 Annual Report.* New York: Moody's Corporation.

Moody's Investors Service. 2000. *Historical Default Rates on Corporate Bond Issuers, 1920–1999.* New York: Moody's Investors Service.

MORAN, M. 2003. *The British Regulatory State: High Modernism and Hyper-Innovation.* Oxford: Oxford University Press, 1–11.

O'TOOLE, D. 2002. "Where is justice for Andersen workers?" Letter to the editor, *USA Today* March 27: 12A.

PAULSON, H. 2008. Press release, March 13, available at www.treas.gov/press/releases/hp872.htm

PEEL, M., and LONDON, S. 2002. "Wall St. and regulators: watchdog to go as accountants return to principles," *Financial Times* January 18.

RUGGIE, J. G. 1998a. "Introduction: what makes the world hang together? Neo-utilitarianism and the social constructivist challenge," in *Constructing the World Polity: Essays on International Institutionalization.* New York: Routledge.

—— 1998b. *Constructing the World Polity: Essays on International Institutionalization.* New York: Routledge.

SALTER, M. S., LEVESQUE, L. C., and CIAMPA, M. 2002. "The rise and fall of Enron," paper prepared for the Faculty Symposium on Enron Corp., Harvard Business School, April.

SCHARFSTEIN, D. S., and STEIN, J. C. 1990. "Herd behavior and investment," *American Economic Review* 80(3).

SCOTT, J. 1990. *Domination and the Arts of Resistance: Hidden Transcripts.* New Haven: Yale University Press.

SEARLE, J. 1995. *The Construction of Social Reality.* New York: The Free Press.

SINCLAIR, T. J. 2005. *The New Masters of Capital: American Bond Rating Agencies and the Politics of Creditworthiness.* Ithaca, NY: Cornell University Press.

SMITH, R., and SCHROEDER, M. 2002. "Pitt's SEC plan for self-regulation of accountants may have pitfalls," *Wall Street Journal* January 18: C15.

SMITH, R. C., and WALTER, I. 2001. *Rating Agencies: Is There an Agency Issue?* New York: Stern School of Business, New York University.

SPIEGEL, P., and PEEL, M. 2002. "SEC set to mull range of rule reforms," *Financial Times* February 5.

THATCHER, M. and STONE SWEET, A. 2002. "Theory and practice of delegation to non-majoritarian institutions," *West European Politics* 25(1): 1–22.

THOMAS, W. I., with THOMAS, D. S. 1928. *The Child in America.* New York: Alfred A. Knopf.

TOFFLER, A. 1990. *Powershift: Knowledge, Wealth, and Violence at the Edge of the 21st Century.* New York: Bantam.

WAKEMAN, L. M. 1997. "The real function of bond rating agencies," in J. M. Stern and D. H. Chew, Jr., eds., *The Revolution in Corporate Finance*, 3rd edn. Oxford: Blackwell.

WHEATCROFT, P. 2001. "Don't give raters too much credit," *The Times* April 5, accessed from Lexis-Nexis, February 3, 2002.

WHITE, L. 2002. "Credit and credibility," *New York Times* February 24: 13.

WIGGINS, J. 2002. "S&P outlines ratings overhaul," *Financial Times* January 26/27: 10.

—— and SPIEGEL, P. 2002. "Enron's fall may spark credit rating rethink," *Financial Times* January 19/20: 1.

WILSON, R. S. 1987. *Corporate Senior Securities: Analysis and Evaluation of Bonds, Convertibles, and Preferreds*. Chicago: Probus Publishing Company.

ZUCKERMAN, G., and RICHARD, C. 2002. "Moody's and S&P, singed by Enron, may speed up credit downgrades," *Wall Street Journal* January 22: C1.

CHAPTER 19

INTERNATIONAL STANDARDS AND STANDARD-SETTING BODIES

TIM BÜTHE
WALTER MATTLI[1]

STANDARDS AND BUSINESS–GOVERNMENT RELATIONS

STANDARDS prescribe the behavior or characteristics of people or inanimate objects, often in technical terms. They play a central role in domestic and international product and financial markets. Standards for the sterility of medical instruments, for instance, prescribe safe methods for sterilizing instruments or spell out how long thereafter they may be considered sterile given specified packaging and storage conditions. Food standards may specify pesticide residue levels that are considered harmless for human consumption if found on the skin of an apple or prescribe methods for laboratory testing of beef or milk for artificial growth hormones (or natural components, such as fat content) so that food safety inspections and consumer labels provide reliable and comparable information—an increasingly contentious issue in international trade (e.g., Ansell and Vogel 2006; Büthe 2008c). Accounting standards specify how and when corporations may report profits or losses from business transactions and changes in asset values to make corporate financial reports comparable for investors within and across countries (e.g., Mattli and Büthe 2005a, 2005b). And standards for data privacy prescribe methods for safeguarding consumers' financial information and constrain the commercial use that airlines, retail stores, and other businesses may make of data that they have gathered about their customers' purchasing habits, for instance through transnational e-commerce (e.g., Henry Farrell 2003, 2006; Bignami 2005; Newman 2008). In short, standards are ubiquitous, shaping many facets of modern life.

Setting standards is consequently a form of writing or negotiating rules—rules that are usually intended to govern or shape the behavior of a far broader group of actors than those who directly participate in writing the rules (see also Kerwer 2005: esp. 620 ff.). As instruments of governance, standards are similar to norms, yet standards are explicit, which social norms need not be (Brunsson and Jacobsson 2000a: 12 f.). Standards also differ from government regulations in that the use of, or compliance with, a standard as such is not mandatory. Only if a standard is referenced or incorporated in a law or regulation does it become legally binding.[2]

Standards can be contested, and conflicts of interest are quite likely in standard setting since standardization almost always entails (at least for some) a change from previously differing practices. Nevertheless, standards often elicit compliance—convergence or harmonization of behavior or products in accordance with the stipulations of the standard—*even if compliance is not mandatory*. Why?

Focusing on businesses as the "target" whose practices or products many standards seek to change, we can identify five general reasons for compliance, with distinct implications for business–government relations.[3] First, businesses may adopt or implement a particular standard simply because it provides a superior solution to a technical problem (Brunsson and Jacobsson 2000b: esp. 127 ff.). In the early years of the electrical age, for instance, alternating current won out over direct current as the standard for electricity grids virtually everywhere because it had better physical properties, including that it could be easily transformed to higher or lower voltages, allowing greatly reduced losses in the transmission of electrical power over long distances (e.g., Hughes 1983). The cost savings of a superior technology in such cases can bring about convergence on a single standard by atomistic economic actors without any need for coordination (see also Büthe 2008b). When the preferences of private actors are aligned in this way (game theorists would consider it an example of a "harmony" game), governments matter only insofar at they must refrain from interfering with private choices—and keep others from doing so. In the case of direct versus alternating current, Thomas Edison and others whose patents gave them a great commercial stake in direct current technology sought to use their near monopoly position in the market and their influence with governments to block the adoption of the superior technology as the new standard. All of these attempts failed in the end, but only after protracted battles (see McNichol 2006).

Second, network externalities can create economic incentives for implementing a standard (Katz and Shapiro 1985). Network externalities arise whenever the usefulness of doing things in a particular way increases with the number of others who have made the same choice or when the value of a product increases with the extent to which complementary products are available. The larger the number of people who speak a language, for instance, the more valuable it is to know or learn that language (de Swaan 1988: 52 ff.). Similarly, having a cell-phone, fax machine, or network-able computer is only useful to the extent that it can send and receive a signal that allows me to connect with those with whom I want to communicate. These benefits of the size of the "network" are positive externalities to the extent that they are not reflected in the cost of producing nor the price of acquiring the good and therefore create an incentive to comply with the most commonly used standard. Some argue that such network externalities are quite rare (Liebowitz and Margolis 1994), but many find them to be pervasive (e.g., Tirole 1988; Shy 2001; Grewal 2008;). What are the implications for business–government relations? Network externalities can make compliance self-reinforcing, but governments can still help establish or reinforce the equilibrium by enshrining a standard (such as which side of the street to drive on) in laws or regulations. On the flipside, once network externalities reinforce the use of a particular standard, *not* switching to a different, technically or otherwise superior standard becomes individually rational even when it would be highly beneficial to switch if all (or many) did so (David 1985; Pierson 2000). Network externalities can thus create a need for politically costly government intervention to overcome "excess inertia," as illustrated by the (failed) attempts in the US to move from old imperial measures such as foot, mile, and gallon to the metric system (NIST 2002).

Third, information asymmetries in the market can create economic incentives for businesses to adopt standards. Standards reduce information asymmetries between buyers and sellers and thus can help overcome the "lemon problem" (Akerlof 1970), which depresses quality and size of markets. By producing to explicit and broadly recognized standards, a manufacturer may lose some ability to compete on quality or price, but standardization reduces customer uncertainty and the transaction costs that otherwise might arise from the need to test each item. And since this standardization is beneficial to the buyer, too, repeat or bulk buyers may demand compliance with certain standards as a condition for placing an order. In such private contractual relationships between buyer and seller, references to standards are used as a shorthand in communications to ensure consistent product quality or other characteristics of the goods or services or the conditions under which they are produced.[4] Governments need not have any direct role here, but they play an important supporting role in that private contractual promises of compliance with a standard are valuable (outside a tight reputational context, Milgrom, North, and Weingast 1990) only to the extent that they are enforceable in a rule of law system.

Fourth, social pressure or political-legal incentives from third parties may induce a company to comply with standards that are seen as embodying "best practice." A business that does not implement widely accepted standards for workplace safety may face higher insurance premiums and/or higher risks of being found negligent in the event of a workplace injury, even when the standards are not mandated by government regulation. More direct pressure from activist NGOs has led many businesses to commit at least rhetorically to various "fair trade" standards (Levi and Linton 2003; Cashore, Auld, and Newsom 2004; Kirton and Trebilock 2004; Jaffee 2007; Raynolds, Murray, and Wilkinson 2007). One key motivation for businesses to support such standards is to forestall (or minimize the scope of) government regulation. Moreover, companies may be assured a more prominent voice when standards are set (and updated) by non-governmental bodies than when they are fixed through government regulation (Haufler 2001). Government regulations may here induce adoption or use of a standard without mandating it, for instance by requiring that clothing that does *not* meet a standard for reduced flammability be labeled as "flammable" (WTO 2005: 33).

Finally, compliance with any particular standard may be outright required by laws or regulations, even when the standard itself might have been developed by a private body rather than a public (government) agency (e.g., Hamilton 1978; Salter 1988; Cheit 1990; Braithwaite and Drahos 2000). Business–government relations are naturally central to any analysis of what gets written into those laws and regulations—an issue discussed in greater detail in the literature on lobbying and the political power of business (e.g., Stigler 1971; Vogel 1989, 1996; Smith 2000) and in the chapters by Crouch, Hart, Schmitter, Vogel, and Wilson and Grant in this volume.

As the examples above illustrate, setting standards is an important means for shaping the behavior of firms and other economic actors. Governments may or may not be directly involved in this element of the governance of markets, though compliance with, or implementation of, a standard is often a function of public policy and business–government relations at other stages of what Abbott and Snidal (2009) have called the "regulatory process," consisting of agenda setting, negotiation of standards, implementation, monitoring, and enforcement. Those who are able to set standards that elicit compliance are therefore exercising power in the Dahlian sense of getting others to do something they would not otherwise do (Dahl 1957). This understanding of international standard-setting as an inherently political process (Mattli and Büthe 2003) calls for a systematic understanding of international standard-setting bodies and what enables some to win out over others when setting standards entails conflicts of interest.

In the remainder of this entry, we first differentiate two key problems that arise from economic interdependence and are commonly solved or ameliorated through standards. We then sketch how the international integration of product and financial markets has internationalized these problems and led to a shift from local and domestic to international standard setting. We then differentiate and discuss the operation of four types of bodies that set standards for the international economy.

COOPERATION, COORDINATION, AND STANDARDS

Demand for standards arises from interdependence—situations where the actions or choices of individuals, firms, or states mutually affect each other, though such reciprocal dependence need not be symmetrical (Keohane and Nye 1989: 9). It is analytically useful to distinguish two kinds of problems that arise from interdependence and may be addressed by setting standards: cooperation problems of the Prisoners' Dilemma (PD) type, where individually optimal behavior leads to collectively suboptimal outcomes, and coordination problems, where actors need to coordinate their choices to achieve the desired outcomes or benefits.

Cooperation problems of the PD type arise when individually optimal behavior leads to collectively suboptimal outcomes. The classic example of this problem is the "tragedy of the commons," pointedly presented in a now classic article by biologist Garrett Hardin (1968: 1244 f.): When a group of herders shares access to a pasture (the "commons"), each of them, when faced with the decision whether to let an additional animal graze the pasture, will trade off a benefit that accrues only to him against a cost that is shared among all of the herders. This balance of individually enjoyed benefits and shared costs makes it rational for each herder to keep increasing the number of animals from his own herd grazing on the common pasture *even beyond the point where overgrazing depletes or destroys the common resource (the pasture).* Under these circumstances, all would be better off in the long run if everyone were to exercise constraint. But every individual herder would be even better off by adding more animals to his herd *while everyone else exercised constraint.* Consequently, the cooperative outcome of everyone exercising constraint is not an "equilibrium" (is not sustainable) unless norms, contracts, or other measures counteract each individual's incentive to deviate from the cooperative behavior.

Figure 19.1 captures the essential logic of the so-called Prisoners' Dilemma in a stylized one-time interaction between two "players," each of whom chooses between two possible courses of action at the same time as the other player.[5] The collectively optimal outcome would be for each player to choose C (for cooperation), but without an ability by both to credibly commit to cooperation, each will be better off choosing D (for defection). Choosing D offers an even higher payoff (4) if the other player chooses C and avoids the worst one should the other player choose D. When both players adopt this "dominant strategy" (which is individually rational to do), the outcome will be the bottom right cell in Figure 19.1 (DD), which is worse for every actor than the outcome CC.

The problem is not just philosophical or historical. Many real world situations of interdependence have these characteristics, from overfishing or pollution of the world's oceans and the registration of unsafe ships by "flags of convenience" countries (e.g., Murphy 2004: 45 ff.; DeSombre 2006) to the breakdown of cartels such as

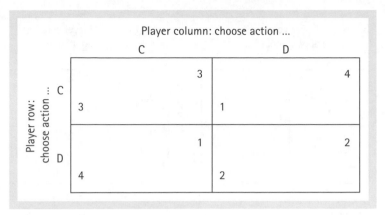

Fig. 19.1 Prisoners' Dilemma game

Note: Numbers indicate ordinal payoffs. Row = Column preferences: DC > CC > DD > CD. 1 equilibrium: DD.

OPEC (though cf. Griffin and Xiong 1997), money laundering by offshore financial centers (Simmons 2001: 605 ff.; Hülsse and Kerwer 2007), and the security dilemma in nuclear or conventional arms races (e.g., Jervis 1978).

Standards can ameliorate these problems by specifying precisely what constitutes cooperative behavior and how to measure it, thus facilitating detection of those who violate any agreement to cooperate. To overcome the incentives to engage in behavior of type "D," however, still requires monitoring and some form of enforcement—through anything from reputational mechanisms to coercion—which are often hampered by collective action problems (e.g., Olson 1971; Hardin 1982; Ostrom 1990).

Coordination problems are of a different nature (Snidal 1985a).[6] Here, actors need to coordinate their choices to achieve the desired benefits—which often does not happen automatically, even when there are no PD-type incentives. Commerce, for instance, requires a set of common or at least consistently convertible weights and measures (Bensel 2000; Spruyt 2001).[7] The choice of a technology with strong network externalities provides the purest example of a coordination problem: the transmission of television signals requires that sending and receiving equipment interpret information about picture resolution, brightness, color, and audio in the same or compatible ways (e.g., Abramson 1987, 2002; Austin and Milner 2001: 418 ff.); computers need a common language (or at least a finite set of languages that are sufficiently standardized to allow "translations") to communicate with each other to share files, display websites as intended by those who designed them, etc.

From a governance perspective, setting standards is often all that is required to solve coordination problems. Once a standard is widely established among a group whose members are interdependent, there is often little incentive for non-compliance. Producing television sets that will not be able to receive a signal or computers that cannot communicate with their peripherals makes little sense—though compliance is not

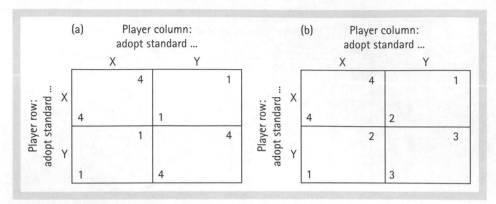

Fig. 19.2 (a) Simple coordination game;
(b) Coordination game without distributional conflict

Notes: (a) Row preferences = Column preferences: XX = YY > XY = YX; (b) Row preferences = Column preferences: XX > YY > XY > YX.

guaranteed if a business has a short time horizon and may therefore be less than truthful in what its advertisements claim about compatibility or even basic measurements, such as the screen size of a television.

Coordination problems can be "simple" when (a) actors are indifferent between the choices, and it only matters that, among those who are interdependent, everyone make the same choice—driving on the left or the right side of the road is one of the classic illustrations of this kind of coordination problem—or (b) all actors consider one choice clearly superior, but still may need a mechanism for assuring each other that there is agreement, since the overriding importance of coordinating on the same course of action might otherwise lead to a suboptimal equilibrium. Figures 19.2(a) and 19.2(b) capture the essential logic of the simple coordination problem.[8]

Coordination, however, often entails distributional conflicts, since the cost of adjusting to any particular new standard may differ across individuals, firms, or countries, for instance because of differing prior practices or because a standard may require (or foreclose) the use of a particular technology and thus raise or lower the value of related intellectual property rights. Coordination games with distributional conflict (as illustrated in Fig. 19.3) differ from simple coordination games in that there are several outcomes that are, as Krasner (1991) observed, "Pareto-improving"—that is, preferable to the status quo for some and at least equivalent to the status quo for all actors—but these outcomes differ in how much each actor benefits. When setting standards has such distributional implications, one should expect conflicts of interest over which standard will be chosen. And since the choice of a seemingly technical standard can lock in advantages for a long time to come (Moe 1990, 2005), the ensuing standards "battles" can be fierce.

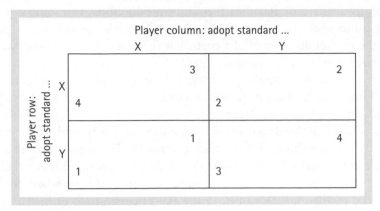

Fig. 19.3 Coordination game with distributional conflict

Note: Row preferences: X > Y; XX > YY > XY > YX; Column preferences: Y > X; YY > XX > YX > XY. 2 equilibria: XX, YY.

THE GLOBALIZATION OF STANDARD-SETTING AND THE RISE OF INTERNATIONAL STANDARD-SETTING BODIES

Both coordination and PD-type cooperation problems are common features of economic interactions. Economic globalization has therefore turned what were once local or at most national problems into international ones, increasing the economic and political salience of cross-national differences in standards and therefore the demand for *international* standard-setting.

Starting in the 1980s, divergent national standards became one of the most important non-tariff barriers to trade (NTBs, e.g., Ray 1987) and in the 1990s also prominent barriers to the international integration of financial markets. By 1998, cross-nationally divergent standards were estimated to result in $20–40 billion in lost sales of goods and services for the US alone (Mallett 1998–9). In some cases, differing standards were clearly introduced in order to protect domestic producers; in others, they simply reflected differences in taste or accidents of history. Regardless of intention, divergent standards became non-tariff barriers to trade when government regulations or local markets required compliance as a prerequisite for import or sale of a good, prohibiting imports or increasing the cost of production or entry for foreign producers.

Standards are not just non-tariff barriers to trade, however. They often fulfill multiple purposes, including non-trade-related and legitimate public policy purposes, such as workplace safety and consumer or environmental protection. The increasing prominence of standards as NTBs therefore rarely led to demands for their abolition. Instead, it led to increasing demands for the international harmonization of standards—and a spectacular shift of standardization activity from domestic to regional and international bodies (Mattli 2003: 200).

As recently as the early 1980s, each country produced its own standards without much regard to what others were doing. A few standards had come into global use through the market dominance of a particular firm's goods or licensed technology. But standards developed by genuinely international bodies were few and far between and mostly consisted of standards developed by a handful of intergovernmental organizations, such as the Codex Alimentarius Commission (a joint body of the UN Food and Agriculture Organization and the World Health Organization (WHO)), which had developed some food safety standards, and the International Telecommunications Union (ITU), which governed radio frequencies and standardized (some aspects of) related technologies. Today, for advanced industrialized and most developing countries, the overwhelming majority of new standards for product and financial markets are developed in the expert committees of international (or sometimes regional) standard-setting bodies.

In addition, globalization has led to a shift from intergovernmental to transnational (non-governmental) standardization, as it laid bare the procedural inadequacies and organizational limits of traditional intergovernmental standards bodies, most notably the excruciatingly slow pace of standard-setting and, increasingly, governments' lack of technical expertise and financial resources to deal with ever more complex and demanding standards issues. The result has been extensive (if sometimes only implicit) delegation of standard-setting authority to private international bodies. Some of these private international standard-setting bodies had long existed—the non-governmental International Electrotechnical Commission, IEC, was founded in 1906 to standardize electrical terminology, measurements, and technologies. But with few exceptions, such as the standards specifying the dimensions of shipping containers and credit cards, international standard-setters that develop through non-market institutionalized processes had little economic or political salience compared to domestic ones.[9] Today, these private bodies are for many industries the most important source of international standards.

A Typology of International Standard-Setting and Standard-Setting Bodies

To describe differences among international standard-setting bodies systematically and help explain differences in the outcomes of standardization in different settings, we develop a typology of international standard-setting bodies, which distinguishes the locus of regulation (the horizontal axis in Fig. 19.4), which is either public or private, from the institutional setting, which is either market-based or non-market-based (the vertical axis in Fig. 19.4).

Distinguishing these two dimensions yields four ideal types. It thereby clearly delineates as distinct phenomena—and draws analytical attention to—market-like

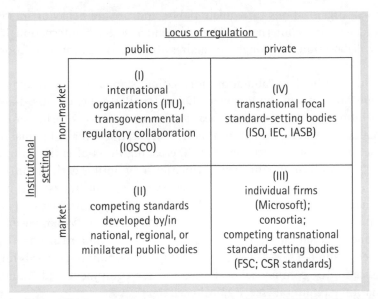

Fig. 19.4 Types of international standard-setting bodies (with examples)

international competition between public standard-setting bodies (bottom left, cell II) and non-governmental (private) standard-setting in an international focal institution, which does not entail market competition (top right, cell IV). These two types of standard-setting bodies play a prominent role in the international political economy. The global private standard-setting bodies IASB, IEC, and ISO, for instance, have set many of the key standards for global product and financial markets—and for most of these standards, one of these bodies is the essentially uncontested focal point (or what we call "focal institution") for standard-setting at the international level. Yet, until very recently, these standard-setting bodies have been largely overlooked in the literature, which has tended to focus on standard-setting in traditional intergovernmental organizations (cell I) or private market-based standard-setting (cell III).

We discuss each of the four ideal types, counter-clockwise from top left. For each type of standard-setting body, we describe the mode of standardization, analyze what constitutes power in each institutional setting given the standard-setting body's placement on the public–private dimension, and discuss to what extent each type of standard-setting can resolve coordination and PD-type problems that arise from international interdependence.

Public (governmental) non-market standard-setting bodies

Writing rules that organize and control economic or social behavior has traditionally been a key domestic policy function of governments. In addition, governments have long collaborated internationally ad hoc or through permanent international organizations to regulate public and private behavior in some issue areas characterized by international interdependence. Such international (governmental) collaboration has sought to address both cooperation and coordination problems.

Much international collaboration for setting standards has sought to solve cooperation problems of the Prisoners' Dilemma (PD) type, discussed above. The UN Convention on the Law of the Sea, for instance, deals with the problem that unsustainably overfishing the oceans is nonetheless rational for individual fishermen and in the case of some species even for the fishing fleets of entire countries. The treaty seeks to address this problem primarily by granting each country with an ocean shore an "exclusive economic zone" extending 200 miles (the new international standard), on the assumption that such property rights give every shoreline country an incentive to ensure sustainable fishing practices (Wijkman 1982). Similarly, the International Maritime Organization seeks to safeguard against shipowners imposing costs and risks on everybody else by setting common standards for training and certification of commercial seafarers, and for equipment and monitoring to reduce maritime pollution (see, e.g., Mitchell 1994).

In addition, governments have collaborated internationally to set standards in order to solve regulatory coordination problems. The ITU, for instance, was created to coordinate member states' allocation of radio spectrum—so that commercial or entertainment use of the airwaves in one country does not interfere with the use for emergency communications in a neighboring country—and to set standards for interconnectivity between national telephone networks, thus enabling international phone calls (Codding and Rutkowski 1982). As social scientists found when they begun to study these forms of international collaboration starting in the 1980s, even international organizations such as ITU, designed to address technical coordination problems, often entail distributional conflicts (Cowhey 1990; Wallenstein 1990; Krasner 1991). The coordination game with distributional conflict (Fig. 19.3 above) therefore often best captures the logic of international public standard-setting in non-market institutional settings.

Governmental (public) non-market international standard-setting can take place through (1) ad hoc agreements; (2) transgovernmental collaboration among specialized regulatory agencies; or (3) new or existing international (governmental) organizations (IOs).[10] Direct contacts and collaboration between public officials (incl. mid-level bureaucrats) charged with similar tasks in different countries—without going through the traditional channels and political hierarchies of international diplomacy (Keohane and Nye 1989: 34)—can be and often have become institutionalized as transgovernmental standard setting (e.g., Singer 2007). Each public official in such a transgovernmental network remains accountable to his or her domestic stakeholders through whatever political institutions each country has in place domestically (Slaughter 2004). Yet, their standards are not necessarily adopted unanimously nor, as standards, subject to domestic ratification. The transgovernmental network itself may therefore be considered the standard-setting body. Table 19.1 provides an overview of important standard-setting bodies of this kind.

Table 19.1 Transgovernmental international standard-setting bodies

Standard-setting body	Established	Type of standards	Participants in standard setting	Target audience of Standards
Basel Committee on Banking Supervision	1974	Capital adequacy standards	Central banks and banking supervisory authorities from 13 countries	Commercial banks
Consultative Committee for Space Data Systems	1982	Standards for data and information systems supporting space research	Space agencies from 11 countries with full voting rights ("member agencies"); 26 observer agencies from 19 countries; 100 + liaison organizations and industry observers	Space agencies and industry
IOSCO: Int'l Organization of Securities Commissions	1983	Standards for the operation and regulation of financial markets, incl. information exchange and non-financial disclosure requirement for private issuers	Financial market regulatory authorities ("ordinary members") from 109 countries + 11 associate members + 71 affiliate members. Most standards set in Technical Committee of members with largest, most advanced markets and in the Emerging Markets Committee	Capital markets, incl. operators and market participants

Notwithstanding the importance of some transgovernmental networks, formal international organizations are the more prominent kind of public international (non-market) standard-setting body. As the (by no means comprehensive) list of standard setting IOs in Table 19.2 illustrates, they vary considerably in their age, breadth of activities, and membership (see also Barnett and Finnemore 2004).

Who wins and who loses in conflicts of interest over the choice of global standards? Existing research suggests that outcomes of such conflicts of interest in intergovernmental settings are often well explained by the distribution of power in a traditional IR Realist sense of state power (Krasner 1991)—subject to five disclaimers: (i) incomplete information and information asymmetry may limit the usability of traditional (statist) power resources; (ii) the decision-making procedures of international organizations may reflect the international distribution of power at the time of the IO's inception rather than the contemporary distribution of power; (iii) if domestic stakeholders from a small or developing country face fewer collective action problems (e.g., due to more concentrated interests) they may be able to have substantial influence vis-a-vis their counterparts from ostensibly more powerful countries (ITC 2003); (iv) agency slack may allow an IO to set a standard that is

Table 19.2 Standard-setting international governmental organizations

Standard-setting Body	Established	Type of standards	Target audience	Member countries	Standards adoption process
ITU: International Telecommunications Union	1865	Information and telecommunication networking standards, esp. for int'l interoperability	Information and communication technology (ICT) industry	191	Intergovernmental multi-stage process
Universal Postal Union (UPU)	1874	Standards for international mail processing, including types/categories, postal fraud and crime prevention, and related technologies	Mail services providers (public and private) and their customers	172	Intergovernmental multi-stage process; final approval requires two-thirds majority vote
Bureau International des Poids et Mesures	1875	Metrological standards; int'l system of units (SI)	All industries	52	Intergovernmental multi-stage process
ILO: International Labor Organization	1919	Labor standards	Governments, employers, and workers of UN member states	182	Most matters decided by a simple majority of total no. of votes cast by individual delegates (each country: 2 gov, 1 employer, 1 worker representatives)
IMF: International Monetary Fund	1944	Standards for national financial systems and current account reporting	Government policy-makers, statistical offices	185	Weighted majority voting, mostly based on capital made available to the IMF
IMO: Int'l Maritime Organization	1948	Standards for international shipping (see text)	Owners, operators, and national regulators of ships and harbors	170 +	Varies
Codex Alimentarius Commission	1963	Food and food safety standards	Consumers, producers, domestic regulators, international food traders	187 (all WHO and FAO members)	Specialized committees with extensive private sector participation; final adoption by majority vote

closer to less powerful countries' preference (Hawkins et al. 2006); (v) the specialized standard-setting institutions' emphasis on technical expertise may constrain the exercise of traditional power resources (Schmidt and Werle 1993).

Setting standards in public international focal institutions has several advantages, most importantly that governments are able to establish a technical solution to interdependence-induced problems authoritatively. Second, insofar as the government agencies that develop standards are populated by a Weberian professional bureaucracy, public standard-setting bodies should seek a socially optimal technical solution that takes all stakeholders' interests into account. But government standardization also has clear disadvantages. First, public international standard setting in a single focal institutions tends to be very slow (Mattli 2003: 221 f.). Second, agencies may be captured by special interests and, like any other policy, government standards may be influenced through lobbying and might therefore privilege some actors (usually a small group of domestic producers with highly concentrated interests) over others. International standardization may thus become an overtly political process, undermining the benefits of standards that are based on public trust, though transparency in public standard-setting bodies may safeguard against some abuses. Third, government agencies increasingly lack the technical expertise to develop standards for highly specialized products and the practical experience to assess how feasible and efficient a particular technical solution may be. The recognition of this lack of expertise (or resources to acquire it) has led governments throughout the advanced industrialized countries to draw increasingly on the expertise of the private sector through delegating standardization implicitly or explicitly to non-governmental standards developing organizations (Egan 2001: 31 ff., 115 ff.; Mattli and Büthe 2003, 2005a; Büthe 2008c).

Public standard-setting bodies in market competition

Even when international standards are set by public bodies, these bodies need not be as comprehensively international as the set of countries where businesses may subsequently choose (or feel compelled) to comply with the standard. What we call market-based public international standard-setting entails competition between legislatures or regulatory agencies of individual states or competition between multiple regional or minilateral standard-setting bodies, each of which may internally be characterized by collaboration of the public non-market type. Such geographically limited regulatory solutions can come into competition with each other—sometimes after coexisting independently for many years—when exogenous or endogenous changes increase interdependence and thus create functional or political-economic incentives for a single standard for a broader set of countries or even for a single global standard.

Market-like international competition between public regulatory agencies or governmental standards is both a theoretical possibility and an empirical reality. From the 1960s to the 1980s, for instance, US public agencies such as the Environmental

Protection Agency and the Food and Drug Administration raised standards for consumer safety and environmental protection for products ranging from prescription medication and cosmetics to chlorofluorocarbons in spray cans and vehicle emissions—standards that then competed with less stringent standards in other countries (Vogel 2003: 558 ff.). Standards for determining the structure of a market, established by the European Union (EU) Commission to decide whether antitrust enforcement or the prohibition of mergers is warranted, similarly compete with (and have sometimes won out over) divergent standards in the US and other jurisdictions (Büthe 2007, 2008a); and the realm of international accounting standardization was characterized by competition between several inter- or transnational standard-setting bodies before the (non-governmental) IASB emerged as the focal institution in the late 1990s (e.g., Camfferman and Zeff 2007: 408 ff.).

The phenomenon of international competition among public standard-setting bodies is greatly understudied. Customary political economy assumptions suggest that states' market size is here an important power resource, at least when coordination problems are involved (see also Simmons 2001; Drezner 2005). To return to the above example of more stringent consumer and environmental standards developed in the 1960s–80s by US regulatory agencies: producers in other countries often ended up implementing these standards because they did not want to forgo the economies of scale from producing a single product for sale in the US (or even just California) and the rest of the world (see Vogel 1995; DeSombre 2000). Institutional Complementarity Theory (Mattli and Büthe 2003, mostly focused on private standard-setting and hence discussed below) offers an alternative view and suggests an institutional logic of power in standard setting. When PD-type cooperation problems are involved, standards will shape actual behavior at the international or global level only when there is monitoring and enforcement (what the World Bank has called "regulatory capacity"). When domestic (or regional) institutions differ, those with greater regulatory capacity will also have a greater chance of establishing their standards as global standards because, in cases of international competition among public standard-setting bodies, this capacity allows them to credibly threaten punishment of non-cooperative behavior. Indeed, Bach and Newman (2007: 829 ff.) find that the superior regulatory capacity of European public agencies (for controlling market access and for extraterritorial application of its laws and regulations) have repeatedly allowed EU standards to become effectively global standards (see also Newman 2008). EU competition policy and its standards for the permissibility of mergers among multinational firms, for example, effectively govern even mergers among US firms, because compliance with the EU merger regulation is a condition for EU market access, and few US firms want to forgo that access (Büthe and Swank 2006). Regulatory capacity thus is an important power resource for market-based public standard-setting, but note that the standard-setting *bodies* remain national, regional, or minilateral.

For those who participate in the domestic, regional, or minilateral standard setting, these standard-setting bodies have all the same benefits as international organizations of the public non-market type. And if standards are set among a smaller group of countries, whose societies (or at least governments) have more homogenous preferences, standardization can be faster and more efficient than in more comprehensive international public bodies. The flipside of international standard setting by a (sub)group of more homogenous countries, however, is that the resulting standard will inherently be further from the ideal point of those outside the group. This is one of the key concerns of developing countries about international standard setting by exclusive international organizations such as the OECD, even though nominally universal organizations, such as the UN and its suborganizations, can also be dominated by a small group of countries whose preferences are more homogenous than those of the general membership.

International standard-setting by public bodies is only part—and a declining part—of global regulation. Globalization, and specifically the international integration of product and financial markets, has led to (and in part has entailed) the rapidly increasing privatization of international standard-setting. This privatization has at the international or global level also taken either a market-based or a non-market-based path. We will briefly discuss the former, which has been analyzed at length in the literature in economics and other social sciences, then focus on non-market regulation, which has remained undertheorized.

Market-based private international standard-setting

Market-based private standard-setting entails rule-making by firms or other non-governmental bodies, competing individually or in small groups to establish their preferred technologies or practices as the de facto standard. A firm may seek, for instance, to make its copyrighted business model an essential component of service provision or make a technology the starting point for further product development if it has patented the technology, its engineers have great expertise in that technology, or it is more compatible with the firm's existing line of products than an alternative technology. A firm may achieve de facto standardization by using its existing market dominance, licensing intellectual property, pricing its technology temporarily below cost, or through the use of other business strategies (Gabel 1991; Besen and Farrell 1994).

This way of setting international standards has been very prominent in the Information and Communications Technology (ICT) sector. Microsoft, for instance, succeeded in establishing its Windows operating system as a de facto standard thanks to its market dominance and strong network effects (e.g., Grewal 2008: 198 ff.). Other classic examples include the standardization of the railroad gauge in the UK and the US in the 1800s (e.g. Taylor and Neu 1956; Kindleberger 1983: 384 f.), JVC's VHS format winning out over Sony's Betamax as the standard for videocassettes (Grindley 1995: esp. 75–89, 131 ff.), and most recently the Blu-ray standard for optical disc formatting winning out over the HD-DVD format.

Market-based private standard setting also characterizes Corporate Social Responsibility (CSR) and environmental sustainability standards, where standards developed by civil society-based NGOs compete for consumers' or purchasing managers' allegiance with alternative standards set (often defensively) by firms—a phenomenon for which Benjamin Cashore (2002) has coined the term "non-state market-driven governance." The Forest Stewardship Council, the earliest of the sustainable forestry standard-setting bodies, for example, can be traced back to proposals by high-end woodworking firms seeking to differentiate their products through certified ecological sustainability. It achieved its breakthrough as a global standard-setting body when political activism from environmentalist NGOs led major retailers like Home Depot in the US and B&Q in the UK to demand FSC certification from their suppliers all over the world (Bartley 2003: 443–5, 2007: 315 ff.). This marketplace success of the NGO-driven FSC (initially funded mostly by foundations and a few governments to placate environmentalist demands) allowed it to prevail over attempts to set such standards through an intergovernmental organization (Bartley 2007: 319 f.), but it also spurned the creation of alternative industry-driven standard-setters at the global and national level, with which it competes to this day (see also Cashore, Auld, and Newsom 2004; and Table 19.3).

Market-based private standard-setting has been the primary focus of economists (e.g. Katz and Shapiro 1985; Farrell and Saloner 1986; David and Steinmueller 1994; Matutes and Regibeau 1996), though it has in recent years also attracted analytical attention from other social scientists (e.g., Baron 2001; Gereffi, Garcia-Johnson, and Sasser 2001; Bartley 2003; Haufler 2003; Zysman and Newman 2006). There is consequently now an extensive literature on this mode of standard-setting (for comprehensive surveys, see Swann 2000; and Vogel 2008).

A particular specification becomes an international standard in market-based standard-setting as a function of the interaction between multiple entities, each of which seeks to promulgate a standard. The standard-setting *bodies* of the private market-based type vary from individual firms (e.g., Ronit and Schneider 2000) to civil society organizations, which greatly differ in their internal structures (e.g., Ahmed and Potter 2006; Meidinger 2006: 61 ff.) and may compete even when they have normatively principled rather than material objectives (Keck and Sikkink 1998; Lauterbach 2007). Particularly important standard-setting bodies for market-based private standardization have been consortia. Standards consortia are ad hoc strategic alliances of two or more firms, usually in the same industry, to develop a new standard. Established by private contract, they usually require unanimous approval from all current members before anyone can become a new member, since the individual participating firms share the often substantial costs of research and development in exchange for a stake in the intellectual property rights of the new technology. This allows a small and often exclusive group of firms to move fast in developing a common technological solution (particularly important where compatibility is desired)—which they then "deliver for *de facto* ratification to the market" (Mattli 2003: 223). Originally primarily a US phenomenon, today's consortia are often very multinational. Many of them lack the institutionalization or permanence of a standard-setting *body*, though there is great variation since each consortium is set up for a particular purpose (Büthe and Witte 2004: 32 f.).

Table 19.3 Private market-based standardization

Issue/standards	Type of standards	Target audience	Major competing standard-setters	Established; head office	Membership; governance	Notes
Forestry (standards for natural resource management and harvesting)	Process and performance standards	Forestry industry; consumers	Forest Stewardship Council (FSC)	1993, Mexico City; Bonn (Germany)	Complex muti-chamber stakeholder model with strong NGO participation (see Bartley; Cashore, et al.); offices in 46 countries; FSC-certified forests in 81 countries	Competing standards persist; see Rupert (2004)
			Programme for the Endorsement of Forest Certification (PEFC)	1999, Paris; Geneva	Started as confederation of European woodland owners' associations; umbrella organization for 26 approved and 8 not-yet-approved national forest certification schemes, which PEFC claims are used/recognized in 149 countries	
			Sustainable Forestry Initiative	1995, Washington; Arlington (USA)	Started by American Forest & Paper Association, since 2007 independent not-for-profit corporation; mostly US and Canada	
"High definition" (HD) optical disc format	Product standard	Producers of audio/video and computer equipment and media	Blu-ray Disc	2000; collaboration of Sony, Philips, and Panasonic	Industry consortium; jointly developed technology with variable patent rights; further format development via the open-membership Blu-ray Disc Association since 2002	After 2006–8 standards war, Blu-ray became the international standard
			HD-DVD	2000; Toshiba with NEC	Toshiba-led consortium; initially with support from Microsoft and many movie studios	

(cont.)

Table 19.3 (*Continued*)

Issue/standards	Type of standards	Target audience	Major competing standard-setters	Established; head office	Membership; governance	Notes
North–South distribution of gains from int'l trade; social and economic development; labor issues	Product and process standards; minimum prices	Importers and exporters; agricultural producers	Fairtrade Labeling Organizations International (FLO)	1997; Bonn (Germany)	Federation of 20 member labeling initiatives including European Max Havelaar and US/ Canadian TransFair labels, plus producer networks from 59 countries in Latin-America, Africa, Asia	Some FLO schemes used to compete; numerous other fair trade labels persist, mostly locally.
	Process standards	"Fair trade" organizations	International Federation for Alternative Trade	1989; Culemborg (the Netherlands)	Umbrella organization, representing and certifying 350 + organizations involved in the fair trade movement. Renamed World Fair Trade Org in 2008.	
			Fair Trade Federation	1994, Washington	Association of North American retailers and importers; certifies trading/business practices	

Private bodies often seek to establish their own solution to a technical problem as the de facto standard. Who prevails when their standards compete in the market? While market-based private standards setting is non-governmental, power still matters. But economic analyses suggest that power is here primarily a function of (a) the size of global or domestic markets controlled by those who support the standard and, most importantly, (b) the strategic decisions of the standard setting firm (or other body) regarding such issues as exclusive control over intellectual property versus licensing or the mix of political and commercial strategies. States can, of course, intervene in private market-based standard-setting, but if they do so after a de facto standard has already been established through market-based mechanisms, such interventions tend to be very costly and they may well fail, especially when the de facto standard solves a coordination problem. Power thus matters, but the kinds of resources required to influence global outcomes differ markedly from those in traditional international politics.

International standard-setting bodies of this type (or clusters of competing firms/bodies) are too numerous to attempt a comprehensive overview—for consortia alone, Gesmer and Updegrove (2009) currently claim to have identified 468 consortia, though many of those temporary collaborations do not last. Table 19.3 lists prominent examples of clusters of standard-setting bodies engaged in market-based private standardization.

Market-based private standard-setting bodies are attractive to firms. They allow firms to settle on a standard for their own products fast and without the need to compromise (though at the risk of losing out and having to pay adjustment costs later) and to fully capture the benefits from their investment in intellectual property (e.g., David and Steinmueller 1994: 238 ff.). In addition, this approach has the benefit for society of often preserving multiple alternative solutions in the early stages of the development of a new technology, which may be a period of great uncertainty about the optimal system (see Metcalfe and Miles 1994). But market-based private standard-setting also has clear disadvantages. First, competing firm-level standardization requires duplicate R&D efforts and expenditures. Second, a de facto standard may simply fail to emerge through the market process and a mass market product may therefore not materialize, as for example AM stereo radios (Berg 1989: 376 f.). Third, in markets for products with large network externalities (phones, computers, and many other communications and IT products), the choice of standard will be a function not so much of the technologies' objective technical qualities, but largely of consumers' desire to acquire the technology that will prevail in the end. This may lead to an early "tipping" of the market in favor of technologically inferior solutions (Mattli 2003: 203). Fourth, a firm that controls the technology (e.g., through IP rights) may deliberately introduce modifications in subsequent updates of the standard that put competitors' interconnecting components at a disadvantage (e.g., Ordover, Sykes, and Willig 1985). Finally, de facto standards—at least when they are proprietary—may not be suitable for adoption or referencing in government regulations lest such an endorsement be seen as undermining market competition, which limits the usefulness of de facto standards, notably for health and safety regulations.

Note that this form of standard-setting can be very effective for the kinds of issues where the main obstacle to collaboration is a coordination problem (with or without distributional conflict), because coordination usually constitutes a self-reinforcing equilibrium. By contrast, market-based regulation is quite likely deficient as a solution to PD-type problems. Although Coase (1960) showed that markets can be used to address PD-type problems, his theoretical conclusion only holds under ideal conditions that almost never pertain (e.g., Abbott and Snidal 2001: 348, 352 f.). Competing private standard-setting bodies rarely provide oversight nor mechanisms to prevent opportunistic behavior and ensure ongoing cooperation. If there are multiple standards and consumer information is limited, strict enforcement would raise the cost of (seeming) compliance and thus may risk driving potential adopters to seek participation in, and/or certification by, an alternative, less demanding standard setter (Spar and La Mure 2003; Sethi 2005; though cf. Prakash and Potoski 2006).

Non-market private international standard-setting

Market-based private rule-making processes have led to hundreds of standards spanning many industry sectors. Non-market private bodies, however, are responsible for the bulk of global private sector rules—literally thousands of standards. In contrast to market-based private global regulation, non-market private standard-setting entails deliberate rule-making by or through an international non-governmental organization that, for the issue in question, is *the* focal institution. These organizations often enjoy the privilege of tacit or explicit endorsement by governments, safeguarding their jurisdictional domains against competitive pressures. The transnational standard-setting bodies themselves, however, are—often adamantly—non-governmental.

Two prominent bodies of this type are the International Organization for Standardization (ISO) and the International Electrotechnical Commission (IEC): jointly they account for about 80 per cent of all international product standards.[11] ISO's standards include standards for freight container dimensions, paints and varnishes, screw threads, corrosion protection, thermal performance, and air quality measurement, as well as "ISO 9000"-series management standards. IEC standards include standards for radiation dosages for x-ray machines, dimensions and other characteristics of audio CDs, battery sizes, and standards for electromagnetic (non)interference. Credit and bank card dimensions are specified by a joint ISO–IEC standard. Little known until the mid-1980s, these two organizations have become prominent, in part due to the Agreement on Technical Barriers to Trade, negotiated during the Uruguay Round of the GATT. It obliges all WTO member states to use international standards as the technical basis of domestic laws and regulations whenever international standards exist. Another salient private global regulator is the International Accounting Standards Board (IASB), based in London. It sets global accounting standards, which public companies in more

than eighty countries now are required to use in their corporate financial reporting. The politics of private rule-making in these settings has been studied very little
until quite recently, even though for major parts of the international political
economy, non-market private standardization is the predominant mode of setting
international standards today.

Institutional Complementarity Theory (Mattli and Büthe 2003; Büthe and Mattli
2010) has been developed specifically to provide an analytical approach for understanding private international standard setting in focal institutions like ISO, IEC, and IASB. It
assumes that economic resources and technical expertise are prerequisites for effective
participation in non-market private standardization, at least as much as in public
international standardization. But unlike state-centric theories that treat domestic
political processes as a "black box," Institutional Complementarity Theory focuses
the analysis on how private sector interests have been organized at the national level
and how their domestic institutional arrangements, which may vary greatly, interact
with focal private organizations of standardization at the international level. Moreover, the theory does *not* assume that rule-making in private transnational organizations is simply a harmonious exercise of cooperation among technical experts, as
some have suggested based on sociological theories (Loya and Boli 1999). Rather,
international standards are usually more beneficial to some than to others, so that
distributional conflict is likely, which creates strong incentives to use quasi-scientific
arguments about technically optimal solutions in pursuit of other, usually commercial
objectives—important as technical norms and language may be in constraining *how*
this can be done (Büthe 2010). Institutional Complementarity Theory therefore portrays
and analyzes private non-market standard-setting as an often intensely *political* process
that involves bargaining, coalition building, and generally the strategic pursuit of often
high commercial stakes.

At the same time, Büthe and Mattli argue that private politics in transnational
standards-setting organizations follows an institutional logic that is distinct from
traditional international (governmental) politics. Cross-national differences in the
"complementarity between historically conditioned standardization systems at the
national level [and] the institutional structure of standardization at the international
level," rather than traditional power resources such as market size or military might,
put some countries at a substantial advantage vis-à-vis others in shaping international
standards (Mattli and Büthe 2003: 18). Institutional Complementarity Theory emphasizes the ease and speed with which information flows between the international
and domestic levels and especially the institutional capacity for aggregating preferences as crucial determinants of power in private non-market institutions, largely as a
function of the fit between domestic and international institutions. Mattli and Büthe
thus argue that differences in institutional complementarity explain much about the
cross-national distribution of switching costs when international standardization
involves harmonizing divergent domestic-level standards, resembling a coordination game with distributional conflict (2003: 11).[12] When the decision-making
procedures at the international level, for instance, call for (private yet) national
representation (as they do in ISO, IEC, and IASB), domestic institutions with a

Table 19.4 Private non-market (focal) international standard-setting bodies

Standard-setting body	Established	Type of standards	Target audience	Standard-setting process	Organizational structure
IEC: International Electrotechnical Commission	1906	Product and process standards	Firms (and public regulators) from all electrical and electronics industries	Common to ISO and IEC: multi-stage process with consensus procedures and supermajority voting among all national member bodies for final adoption	Common to ISO and IEC: decentralized structure of technical committees and working groups embedded in institutional hierarchy coordinated by central secretariat
ISO: International Organization for Standardization	1947	Product and process standards	All industries, except those covered by IEC		
IASB: International Accounting Standards Board	2001 (predecessor organization since 1973)	Accounting/ Financial Reporting standards (IAS/IFRS)	All industries, esp. publicly traded companies	Exposure drafts developed by Board members with input from staff and private sector recommendations. After a comment period, Board votes; adoption after exposure draft by supermajority of Board members	Members of Board are appointed and overseen by Trustees of IASC Foundation. Formal and informal liaisons with national private and public standard-setters. Funding is mostly by voluntary private-sector contributions
Int'l Auditing and Assurance Standards Board of the Int'l Federation of Accountants (IFAC)	2002 (predecessor organization since 1978)	International auditing standards	Auditors of private sector accounts in all industries	Similar to IASB; adoption requires two-thirds majority among quorum of at least 12 Board members	18 board members, appointed by the Board of IFAC: 10 from IFAC member bodies, 5 from private sector firms; 3 from government bodies

hierarchical structure and characterized by a high degree of coordination, which facilitate preference aggregation and hence the coherent projection of domestic preferences onto the international stage, should put stakeholders from such countries in a first mover position whereas fragmented domestic institutions put countries in a second mover position in the transnational development of technical standards. First movers set the standard in coordination games; second movers adjust and pay the switching costs.

Systematic empirical analysis, including the testing of the hypotheses derived from Institutional Complementarity Theory about non-market private internationals standardization, is still in its infancy. In large part, this is due to the enormous difficulty and cost of collecting comprehensive and systematic, unbiased data on transnational private sector standardization, since private international organizations have even fewer legal obligation than public ones to keep records that would allow public scrutiny, nor are they required to comply with "sunshine" clauses or principles.

Our recent research constitutes a first endeavor to establish systematic evidence about this central mode of standardization. Through business surveys conducted in the United States and several European countries across a broad range of industries, we have collected the first comprehensive set of data allowing for the scientific analysis of multiple aspects of international standardization in the central and expansive areas of global product standards and international financial reporting rules. The results of these empirical analyses (see esp. Büthe and Mattli 2010) are surprisingly robust and very consistent with Institutional Complementarity Theory. We find, for instance, that European firms are much more frequently involved in international *product* standardization than US firms and thus able to capture more of the gains from international collaboration, *because* hierarchical, high-coordination domestic private institutions, which have a long history in Europe, yield greater institutional complementarities when standardization becomes global than the fragmented domestic institutions for setting product standards in the US, which are market driven and characterized by a high degree of internal competition. In the case of global financial reporting standard-setting, there is a highly centralized institutional structure in the US, geared toward coordination and speaking with a single voice internationally, whereas institutional fragmentation characterizes European institutions at the national and regional level, due to historical legacies that also impede institutional adjustment. The empirical analyses show that the American private-sector interests are therefore more successful than European ones in influencing international accounting rules.

CONCLUSION

Those who set standards wield influence. Standard-setting is thus an inherently political activity. Yet, internationally as well as domestically, politics need not be governmental. In fact, an ever increasing share of this rule-making takes place in non-governmental and often private sector bodies, rather than public fora, decreasing the importance of business–government relations for the regulation of the global economy. Yet, the benefits of standardization are often unevenly distributed, which may lead to changes in both the structure of an industry and business–government relations. One of the earliest examples of product standardization illustrates the nuts and bolts of standardization and its distributional implications. The standardization of the thread width of screws (Whitworth 1841) allowed for enormous cost savings through economies of scale production, but it also increased competition and therefore allowed more efficient producers to drive out less efficient ones. To take a more contemporary example: *not* having standards for the shape or the placement of connectors on cell-phone batteries (which differ for virtually every model) may increase the price of production but also allows all producers to reap an even greater increase in profits from the sale of replacement batteries. The benefits from standardization, by contrast, would accrue mostly to consumers and (marginally) to the most efficient producers of batteries. When differences in standards fragment the market, market mechanisms without government regulation may not lead to the competition that is the essence of a market economy.

Notes

1. We thank Tammy Hwang for excellent research assistance. The research by Tim Büthe (corresponding author) was supported by a fellowship from the Robert-Wood-Johnson Foundation at the University of california, Berkeley.
2. This definitional distinction between standards and regulations was codified in the WTO Agreement on Technical Barriers to Trade (TBT). We adopt it because it is analytically and heuristically more useful than to speak of "voluntary standards" and "mandatory standards."
3. We do not discuss here standards set by a business for its own internal use.
4. Western brand-name sporting goods manufacturers have, for instance, long demanded that their developing country-based suppliers conform with labor standards that limit or prohibit child labor and "sweatshop" conditions, though their commitment to actual compliance has often been called into question (see, e.g., Bartley 2005; Locke, Qin, and Brause 2007; Mosley 2010).
5. For more discussion, including the name of the game, see Snidal (1985b) and Oye (1986).
6. As Fearon (1998) points out, however, negotiating a solution to coordination problems can raise PD-type cooperation problems, so the difference should not be overstated.
7. Coordination need not entail identical choices. An in-person meeting between a Chinese business executive and a Tanzanian government official to negotiate Chinese foreign direct investment in Tanzania might entail the former traveling south-west and/or the latter traveling north-east, but they must at a minimum converge in their expectations about each other's behavior for the meeting to occur.
8. Note that even in the version depicted in Fig. 19.2b, simple coordination is *not* a "harmony" game.
9. Standardizing the dimensions of freight containers in the late 1960s in fact played an important role in accelerating the international integration of product markets because it led to a spectacular reduction in long distance shipping costs by making it possible to stack

and move entire containers between ships, railroad cars, trucks, and storage, rather load and unload their content multiple times (Cudahy 2006; Levinson 2006; Hummels 2007: esp. 141).

10. Ad hoc agreements neither constitute nor establish standard-setting *bodies* and are therefore not discussed here.

11. Informal coordination and joint committees ensure cooperative rather than competitive relationship between ISO and IEC (authority contested by consortia for some technologies). See Table 19.4 for additional information.

12. Where international standards are intended to address a problem with PD characteristics, the analysis of standard-setting may need to be supplemented by an analysis of monitoring and enforcement (Abbott and Snidal 2009; Büthe 2008b).

REFERENCES

ABBOTT, K. W., and SNIDAL, D. 2001. "International 'standards' and international governance," *Journal of European Public Policy* 8(3): 345–70.

———— 2009. "The governance triangle: regulatory standards institutions and the shadow of the state," in W. Mattli and N. Woods, eds., *Politics of Global Regulation*. Princeton: Princeton University Press.

ABRAMSON, A. 1987. *History of Television, 1880–1941*. Jefferson, NC: McFarland & Co. Publishers.

—— 2002. *History of Television, 1942–2000*. Jefferson, NC: McFarland & Co. Publishers.

AHMED, S., and POTTER, D. M. 2006. *NGOs in International Politics*. Bloomfield, Conn.: Kumarian Press.

AKERLOF, G. A. 1970. "The market for lemons: quality uncertainty and the market mechanism," *Quarterly Journal of Economics* 84(3): 488–500.

ANSELL, C., and VOGEL, D., eds. 2006. *What's the Beef? The Contested Governance of European Food Safety*. Cambridge, Mass.: MIT Press.

AUSTIN, M., and MILNER, H. 2001. "Strategies of European standardization," *Journal of European Public Policy* Special Issue, 8(3): 411–31.

BACH, D., and NEWMAN, A. L. 2007. "The European regulatory state and global public policy: micro-institutions, macro-influence," *Journal of European Public Policy* 14(6): 827–46.

BARNETT, M. N., and FINNEMORE, M. 2004. *Rules for the World: International Organizations in Global Politics*. Ithaca, NY: Cornell University Press.

BARON, D. P. 2001. "Private politics, corporate social responsibility, and integrated strategy," *Journal of Economics & Management Strategy* 10(1): 7–45.

BARTLEY, T. 2003. "Certifying forests and factories: states, social movements, and the rise of private regulation in the apparel and forest products field," *Politics & Society* 31(3): 433–64.

—— 2005. "Corporate accountability and the privatization of labor standards: struggles over codes of conduct in the apparel industry," *Research in Political Sociology* 14: 211–44.

BARTLEY, T. 2007. "Institutional emergence in an era of globalization: the rise of transnational private regulation of labor and environmental conditions," *American Journal of Sociology* 113(2): 297–351.

BENSEL, R. F. 2000. *The Political Economy of American Industrialization, 1877–1900*. New York: Cambridge University Press.

BERG, S. V. 1989. "The production of compatibility: technical standards as collective goods," *Kyklos: Internationale Zeitschrift für Sozialwissenschaften* 42(3): 361–83.

BESEN, S., and FARRELL, J. 1994. "Choosing how to compete: strategies and tactics in standardization," *Journal of Economic Perspectives* 8(2): 117–31.

BIGNAMI, F. E. 2005. "Transgovernmental networks vs. democracy: the case of the European information privacy network," *Michigan Journal of International Law* 26 (3): 807–68.

BRAITHWAITE, J., and DRAHOS, P. 2000. *Global Business Regulation*. New York: Cambridge University Press.

BRUNSSON, N., and JACOBSSON, B. 2000a. "The contemporary expansion of standardization," in *A World of Standards*. New York: Oxford University Press, 1–17.

——— eds. 2000b. *A World of Standards*. New York: Oxford University Press.

BÜTHE, T. 2007. "The politics of competition and institutional change in the European Union: the first fifty years," in S. Meunier and K. McNamara, eds., *Making History: European Integration and Institutional Change at Fifty (State of the European Union, 8)*. Oxford: Oxford University Press, 175–93.

——— 2008a. "Institutional change in the European Union: two narratives of European Commission merger control authority, 1955–2004," manuscript, Duke University.

——— 2008b. "Power plays: why the plug for an international electrical outlet failed," paper presented at the Annual Meeting of the International Studies Association, San Francisco, March.

——— 2008c. "The globalization of health and safety standards: delegation of regulatory authority in the SPS-agreement of the 1994 Agreement Establishing the World Trade Organization," *Law and Contemporary Problems* 71(1): 219–55.

——— 2010. "The power of norms; the norms of power: who governs international electrical and electronic technology?," in D. D. Avant, M. Finnemore, and S. K. Sell, eds., *Who Governs the Globe?* New York: University Press.

——— and MATTLI, W. 2010. *Global Private Governance: The Politics of Rule-Making for Product and Financial Markets*. Princeton: Princeton University Press.

——— and SWANK, G. T. 2006. "The politics of antitrust and merger review in the European Union: institutional change and decisions from Messina to 2004," CES Working Paper 142. Cambridge, Mass.: Minda de Gunzburg Center for European Studies, Harvard University.

——— and WITTE, J. M. 2004. *Product Standards in Transatlantic Trade and Investment: Domestic and International Practices and Institutions*. Washington, DC: American Institute for Contemporary German Studies.

CAMFFERMAN, K., and ZEFF, S. A. 2007. *Financial Reporting and Global Capital Markets: A History of the International Accounting Standards Committee, 1973–2000*. Oxford: Oxford University Press.

CASHORE, B. 2002. "Legitimacy and the privatization of environmental governance: how non-state market-driven (NSMD) governance systems gain rule-making authority," *Governance* 15(4): 503–29.

——— AULD, G., and NEWSOMM D. 2004. *Governing through Markets: Forest Certification and the Emergence of Non-State Authority*. New Haven: Yale University Press.

CHEIT, R. E. 1990. *Setting Safety Standards: Regulation in the Public and Private Sectors*. Berkeley and Los Angeles: University of California Press.

COASE, R. H. 1960. "The problem of social cost," *Journal of Law and Economics* 1(1): 1–44.

CODDING, G. A., and RUTKOWSKI, A. M. 1982. *The International Telecommunications Union in a Changing World*. Dedham, Mass.: Artech House.

COWHEY, P. F. 1990. "The international telecommunications regime: the political roots of regimes for high technology," *International Organization* 44(2): 169–99.

CUDAHY, B. J. 2006. *Box Boats: How Container Ships Changed the World.* New York: Fordham University Press.

DAHL, R. A. 1957. "The concept of power," *Behavioral Science* 2(3): 201–15.

DAVID, P. A. 1985. "Clio and the economics of QWERTY," *American Economic Review* 75(2), paper and proceedings of the 97th Annual Meeting of the American Economics Association, 332–7.

——and STEINMUELLER, E. 1994. "Economics of compatibility standards and competition in telecommunication networks," *Information Economics and Policy* Special Issue, 6(3–4): 217–41.

DE SWAAN, A. 1988. *In Care of the State: Health Care, Education and Welfare in Europe and the USA in the Modern Era.* New York: Oxford University Press.

DESOMBRE, E. 2000. *Domestic Sources of International Environmental Policy: Industry, Environmentalists, and US Power.* Cambridge, Mass.: MIT Press.

——2006. *Flagging Standards: Globalization and Environmental, Safety, and Labor Regulation at Sea.* Cambridge, Mass.: MIT Press.

DREZNER, D. W. 2005. "Globalization, harmonization, and competition: the different pathways to policy convergence," *Journal of European Public Policy* Special Issue, 12(5): 841–59.

EGAN, M. 2001. *Constructing a European Market: Standards, Regulation, and Governance.* New York: Oxford University Press.

FARRELL, H. 2003. "Constructing the international foundations of e-commerce: the EU–US safe harbor arrangement," *International Organization* 57(2): 277–306.

——2006. "Regulating information flows: states, private actors, and e-commerce." *Annual Review of Political Science* 9: 353–74.

FARRELL, J., and SALONER, G. 1986. "Installed base and compatibility: innovation, product preannouncements, and predation," *American Economic Review* 76(5): 940–55.

FEARON, J. D. 1998. "Bargaining, enforcement, and international cooperation," *International Organization* 52(2): 269–305.

GABEL, H. L., ed. 1991. *Competitive Strategies for Product Standards: The Strategic Use of Compatibility Standards for Competitive Advantage.* London: McGraw-Hill.

GEREFFI, G., GARCIA-JOHNSON, R., and SASSER, E. 2001. "The NGO–industrial complex," *Foreign Policy* 125: 56–65.

GESMER and UPDEGROVE, LLP. 2009. "Standard setting organizations and standards list," http://www.consortiuminfo.org/links (last visited January 2, 2009).

GREWAL, D. S. 2008. *Network Power: The Social Dynamics of Globalization.* New Haven: Yale University Press.

GRIFFIN, J. M., and XIONG, W. 1997. "The incentive to cheat: an empirical analysis of OPEC," *Journal of Law and Economics* 40(2): 289–316.

GRINDLEY, P. 1995. *Standards, Strategy, and Policy: Cases and Stories.* Oxford: Oxford University Press.

HAMILTON, R. W. 1978. "The role of nongovernmental standards in the development of mandatory federal standards affecting safety or health," *Texas Law Review* 56(8): 1329–484.

HARDIN, G. 1968. "The tragedy of the commons," *Science* 162(3859): 1243–48.

HARDIN, R. 1982. *Collective Action.* Baltimore: Johns Hopkins University Press.

HAUFLER, V. 2001. *The Public Role of the Private Sector: Industry Self-Regulation in a Global Economy.* Washington, DC: Carnegie Endowment for International Peace.

——2003. "Globalization and industry self-regulations," in M. Kahler and D. A. Lake, eds., *Governance in a Global Economy: Political Authority in Transition.* Princeton: Princeton University Press, 226–52.

HAWKINS, D. G., et al., eds. 2006. *Delegation and Agency in International Organizations.* New York: Cambridge University Press.

HUGHES, T. P. 1983. *Networks of Power: Electrification in Western Society, 1880–1930.* Baltimore: Johns Hopkins University Press.

HÜLSSE, R., and KERWER, D. 2007. "Global standards in action: insights from anti-money laundering regulation," *Organization* 14(5): 625–42.

HUMMELS, D. 2007. "Transportation costs and international trade in the second era of globalization," *Journal of Economic Perspectives* 21(3): 131–54.

ITC (UNCTAD/WTO International Trade Centre) with the Commonwealth Secretariat (CS). 2003. *Influencing and Meeting International Standards: Challenges for Developing Countries.* Geneva: ITC/CS.

JAFFEE, D. 2007. *Brewing Justice: Fair Trade Coffee, Sustainability, and Survival.* Berkeley and Los Angeles: University of California Press.

JERVIS, ROBERT. 1978. "Cooperation under the security dilemma," *World Politics* 30(2): 167–214.

KATZ, M. L., and SHAPIRO, C. 1985. "Network externalities, competition, and compatibility," *American Economic Review* 75(3): 424–40.

KECK, M., and SIKKINK, K. 1998. *Activists beyond Borders: Advocacy Networks in International Politics.* Ithaca, NY: Cornell University Press.

KEOHANE, R. O., and NYE, J. S. 1989. *Power and Interdependence*, 2nd edn. New York: Harper Collins Publishers.

KERWER, D. 2005. "Rules that many use: standards and global regulation," *Governance* 18(4): 611–32.

KINDLEBERGER, C. P. 1983. "Standards as public, collective and private goods," *Kyklos* 36(3): 377–96.

KIRTON, J. J., and TREBILOCK, M., eds. 2004. *Hard Choices, Soft Law: Voluntary Standards in Global Trade, Environment and Social Governance.* Burlington, Vt.: Ashgate.

KRASNER, S. D. 1991. "Global communications and national power: life on the Pareto frontier," *World Politics* 43(3): 336–66.

LAUTERBACH, C. 2007. "The costs of cooperation: civilian casualty counts in Iraq," *International Studies Perspectives* 8(4): 429–45.

LEVI, M., and LINTON, A. 2003. "Fair trade: a cup at a time?," *Politics & Society* 31(3): 407–32.

LEVINSON, M. 2006. *The Box: How the Shipping Container Made the World Smaller and the World Economy Bigger.* Princeton: Princeton University Press.

LIEBOWITZ, S. J., and MARGOLIS, S. E. 1994. "Network externality: an uncommon tragedy," *Journal of Economic Perspectives* 8(2): 133–50.

LOCKE, R. M., QIN, F., and BRAUSE, A. 2007. "Does monitoring improve labor standards? Lessons from Nike," *Industrial and Labor Relations Review* 61(1): 3–31.

LOYA, T., and JOHN BOLI. 1999. "Standardization in the world polity: technical rationality over power," in J. Boli and G. Thomas, eds., *Constructing World Culture: International Non-governmental Organizations since 1875.* Stanford, Calif.: Stanford University Press, 169–97.

McNICHOL, T. 2006. *AC/DC: The Savage Tale of the First Standards War.* San Francisco: Jossey-Bass.

MALLETT, R. L. 1998–99. "Why standards matter," *Issues in Science and Technology* 15(2): 63–6.

MATTLI, W. 2003. "Public and private governance in setting international standards," in M. Kahler and D. A. Lake, eds., *Governance in a Global Economy: Political Authority in Transition.* Princeton: Princeton University Press, 197–229.

——and BÜTHE, T. 2003. "Setting international standards: technological rationality or primacy of power?" *World Politics* 56(1): 1–42.

———— 2005a. "Accountability in accounting? The politics of private rule-making in the public interest," *Governance* 18(3): 399–429.

———— 2005b. "Global private governance: lessons from a national model of setting standards in accounting," *Law and Contemporary Problems* 68(3/4): 225–62.

MATUTES, C., and REGIBEAU, P. 1996. "A selective review of the economics of standardization entry deterrence, technological progress and international competition," *European Journal of Political Economy* Special Issue, 12(2): 183–209.

MEIDINGER, E. 2006. "The administrative law of global public–private regulation: the case of forestry," *European Journal of International Law* 17(1): 47–87.

METCALFE, J. S., and MILES, I. 1994. "Standards, selection, and variety: an evolutionary approach," *Information Economics and Policy* Special Issue, 6(3–4): 243–68.

MILGROM, P. R., NORTH, D. C., and WEINGAST, B. R. 1990. "The role of institutions in the revival of trade: the law merchant, private judges, and the champagne fairs," *Economics and Politics* 2(1): 1–23.

MITCHELL, R. B. 1994. "Regime design matters: intentional oil pollution and treaty compliance," *International Organization* 48(3): 425–58.

MOE, T. M. 1990. "Political institutions: the neglected side of the story," *Journal of Law, Economics and Organization* Special Issue, 6(3): 213–53.

——— 2005. "Power and political institutions," *Perspectives on Politics* 3(2): 215–33.

MOSLEY, L. 2010. *Working Globally? Multinational Production and Labor Rights.* New York: Cambridge University Press.

MURPHY, D. D. 2004. *The Structure of Regulatory Competition: Corporations and Public Policies in a Global Economy.* New York: Oxford University Press.

NEWMAN, A. L. 2008. *Protectors of Privacy: Regulating Personal Data in the Global Economy.* Ithaca, NY: Cornell University Press.

NIST. 2002. "NIST metric information and conversions: a capsule history" http: //ts.nist.gov/ WeightsAndMeasures/Metric/lc1136a.cfm (last visited December 29, 2008).

OLSON, M. 1971. *The Logic of Collective Action: Public Goods and the Theory of Groups,* 2nd edn., with an added appendix. Cambridge, Mass.: Harvard University Press.

ORDOVER, J. A., SYKES, A. O., and WILLIG, R. D. 1985. "Non-price anticompetitive practices by dominant firms toward the producers of complementary products," in F. M. Fisher, ed., *Antitrust and Regulation: Essays in Memory of John J. McGowan.* Cambridge, Mass.: MIT Press, 115–30.

OSTROM, E. 1990. *Governing the Commons: The Evolution of Institutions for Collective Action.* New York: Cambridge University Press.

OYE, K. A. 1986. "Explaining cooperation under anarchy: hypotheses and strategies," in K. A. Oye, ed., *Cooperation under Anarchy.* Princeton: Princeton University Pres, 1–24.

PIERSON, P. 2000. "Increasing returns, path dependence, and the study of politics," *American Political Science Review* 94(2): 251–67.

PRAKASH, A., and POTOSKI, M. 2006. *The Voluntary Environmentalists: Green Clubs, ISO 14001, and Voluntary Environmental Regulations.* New York: Cambridge University Press.

RAY, E. J. 1987. "Changing patterns of protectionism: the fall of tariffs and the rise in non-tariff barriers," *Northwestern Journal of International Law and Business* 8(2): 285–327.

RAYNOLDS, L. T., MURRAY, D. L., and WILKINSON, J., eds. 2007. *Fair Trade: The Challenges of Transforming Globalzation:* Routledge.

RONIT, K., and SCHNEIDER, V. 2000. *Private Organizations in Global Politics.* London: Routledge.

RUPERT, O. 2004. *Forest Certification Matrix: Finding your Way through Forest Certification Schemes.* Brussels: Confederation of European Paper Industries.

SALTER, L. 1988. *Mandated Science: Science and Scientists in the Making of Standards.* Dordrecht: Kluwer Academic Publishers.

SCHMIDT, S. K., and WERLE, R. 1993. "Technical controversy in international standardisation," MPIfG Discussion Paper 93/5, March.

SETHI, S. P. 2005. "The effectiveness of industry-based codes in serving public interest: the case of the International Council on Mining and Metals," *Transnational Corporations* 14 (3): 55–100.

SHY, O. 2001. *The Economics of Network Industries.* Cambridge: Cambridge University Press.

SIMMONS, B. A. 2001. "The international politics of harmonization: the case of capital market regulation," *International Organization* 55(3): 589–620.

SINGER, D. A. 2007. *Regulating Capital: Setting Standards for the International Financial System.* Ithaca, NY: Cornell University Press.

SLAUGHTER, A.-M. 2004. *A New World Order.* Princeton: Princeton University Press.

SMITH, M. A. 2000. *American Business and Political Power: Public Opinion, Elections, and Democracy.* Chicago: University of Chicago Press.

SNIDAL, D. 1985a. "Coordination versus prisoners' dilemma: implications for international cooperation and regimes," *American Political Science Review* 79(4): 923–45.

——1985b. "The game THEORY of international politics," *World Politics* 38(1): 25–57.

SPAR, D., and LA MURE, L. T. 2003. "The power of activism: assessing the impact of NGOs on global business," *California Management Review* 45(3): 78–101.

SPRUYT, H. 2001. "The supply and demand of governance in standard setting: insights from the past," *Journal of European Public Policy* Special Issue, 8(3): 371–91.

STIGLER, G. J. 1971. "The theory of economic regulation," *Bell Journal of Economics and Management Science* 2(1): 3–21.

SWANN, G. M. P. 2000. *The Economics of Standardization: Final Report for Standards and Technical Regulations Directorate, Department of Trade and Industry.* Manchester: Manchester Business School Report.

TAYLOR, G. R., and NEU, I. D. 1956. *The American Railroad Network, 1861–1890.* Cambridge, Mass.: Harvard University Press.

TIROLE, J. 1988. *The Theory of Industrial Organization.* Cambridge, Mass.: MIT Press.

VOGEL, D. 1989. *Fluctuating Fortunes: Political Power of Business in America.* New York: Basic Books.

——1995. *Trading Up: Consumer and Environmental Regulation in a Global Economy.* Cambridge, Mass.: Harvard University Press.

——1996. *Kindred Strangers: The Uneasy Relationship Between Politics and Business in America.* Princeton: Princeton University Press.

——2003. "The hare and the tortoise revisited: the new politics of consumer and environmental regulation in Europe," *British Journal of Political Science* 33(4): 557–80.

——2008. "Private global business regulation," *Annual Review of Political Science* 11: 261–82.

WALLENSTEIN, G. D. 1990. *Setting Global Telecommunications Standards: The Stakes, the Players, and the Process.* Norwood: Artech House Publishers.

WHITWORTH, J. 1841. *On an Uniform System of Screw Threads: Communicated to the Institution of Civil Engineers, A.D. 1841.* London: J. Weale.

WIJKMAN, P. M. 1982. "Managing the global commons." *International Organization* 36(3): 511–36.

WTO (World Trade Organization). 2005. *World Trade Report 2005: Exploring the Links Between Trade, Standards, and the WTO.* Geneva: World Trade Organization.

ZYSMAN, J., and NEWMAN, A. L., eds. 2006. *How Revolutionary Was the Digital Revolution? National Responses, Market Transitions, and Global Technology.* Palo Alto, Calif.: Stanford University Press.

CHAPTER 20

TAMING GLOBALIZATION?

CIVIL REGULATION AND CORPORATE CAPITALISM

DAVID VOGEL

INTRODUCTION

THIS chapter explores the political dynamics of new forms of transnational non-state governance designed to make global firms more responsible and accountable. It begins by defining "civil regulation," describing its growth and placing its development, structure, and purposes in a broader historical and institutional context. It then explains the development of civil regulation as a response to the shortcomings of the global and national governance of global firms and markets. The third section describes how various policy entrepreneurs, led by non-governmental organizations (NGOs) and often supported by some national governments and international organizations, have, through a complex process of conflict and cooperation, persuaded large numbers of global firms to accept non-state regulatory standards.

The uneven impact of civil regulation, and the factors that underlie it, are then explored in case studies of relatively effective, moderately effective, and relatively ineffective private global regulations. These studies demonstrate that it has proven far easier to develop new regulatory instruments than to either persuade significant numbers of firms to adhere to them or to develop effective monitoring and enforcement mechanisms to assure compliance with them. This chapter concludes by specifying the changes in both corporate practices and public policies that would be necessary to strengthen the effectiveness of civil regulation and measurably contribute to ameliorating the current shortcomings of the governance of global firms and markets.

DEFINING CIVIL REGULATION

Civil regulations employ private, non-state, or market-based regulatory frameworks to govern multinational firms and global supply networks. A defining feature of civil regulation is that its legitimacy, governance, and implementation are not rooted in public authority. Typically operating beside or around the state rather than through it, civil regulations are based on "soft law" or private law rather than legally enforceable standards: violators typically face social or market penalties rather than legal sanctions (Abbott and Snidal 2000: 41–56; Kirton and Trebilock 2004: 3–33; Moth 2004). Civil regulation extends regulatory authority "sideways" beyond the state to global non-state actors (Haufler 2003: 226). Its recent growth reflects an expanded "public role for the private sector," as well as the growing importance of "private authority in global governance" (Haufler 2001; Hall and Biersteker 2002). Global corporate codes constitute part of an "emerging global public domain." Civil regulation does "not replace states, but...[rather] embed[s] systems of governance in broader global frameworks of social capacity and agency that did not previously exist" (Ruggie 2004: 519). It reflects the emergence of a more complex global "governance triangle," in which states are no longer the exclusive source of global regulatory authority (Abbott and Snidal 2009).

However, there are also important structural similarities between civil regulations and a subset of government regulations. Many governments employ voluntary agreements or market-based mechanisms as vehicles of business regulation. The market-based regulatory mechanisms typically employed by civil regulations, namely, producer certification, product labeling, third party auditing, and information disclosure, are also used by governments, especially in the area of environmental policy (Gunningham and Grabowsky 1998: 2003). However, the labeling, disclosure, auditing, and certification components of civil regulations are not subject to state scrutiny. Moreover, many "voluntary" agreements between firms and governments are voluntary in name only, as the state retains final legal authority (Brink 2001). This is not the case for civil regulations for which there is typically no state "backup." Rather, civil regulations rely primarily, if not exclusively, on voluntary compliance. As Grant and Keohane observe, "When standards are not legalized, we would expect accountability to operate chiefly through reputation and peer pressure, rather than in more formal ways" (Grant and Keohane 2005: 35).

THE DISTINCTIVENESS OF CIVIL REGULATION

Throughout the history of capitalism, business self-regulation has existed in parallel with government regulation; indeed, historically the former often preceded the latter. The medieval guilds exercised substantial regulatory authority, including controls over price, market entry, and quality. In contemporary economies, private regulations govern a wide variety of business activities, most notably in the areas of electronic commerce, maritime transportation, bond ratings, and financial services. Numerous technical standards have been developed by private organizations, and these play an important role in the global economy (Cutler, Haufler, and Porter 1999; Mattli 2003: 199–225).

But civil regulations are distinctive from traditional forms of industry self-regulation in three important respects. First, in contrast to many technical standards whose primary purpose is to lower the transactions costs of market transactions, civil regulations require firms to make expenditures that they would not otherwise make. They typically seek to protect interests not directly involved in the market chain by ameliorating some of the negative externalities of market transactions. Second, compared to traditional forms of business self-regulation, civil regulations are more likely to be politicized: they have typically emerged in response to political and social pressures on business, often spearheaded by national and transnational activists who have embarrassed global firms by publicizing the shortcomings of their social and environmental practices. Third, the governance of civil regulations is more likely to be transparent, contested, and to either formally or informally involve non-business constituencies—in contrast to traditional business self-regulation, which is typically exclusively governed and controlled by firms.

THE POLITICS OF CIVIL REGULATION

Civil regulation does not privatize business regulation in the sense of removing it from public scrutiny. Rather, it is associated with the development of new non-state, political mechanisms for governing global firms and markets. "Private governance helps empower global civil society by providing activist groups with political levers that exist outside state systems" (Falkner 2003: 79). The expansion of global civil regulation is closely linked to the emergence of a global "civil society," an increasingly sophisticated and extensive international network of NGOs based primarily in North America and Europe that monitor and seek to influence a wide range of global business practices (Keck and Sikkink 1998; Cohen and Rai 2000; Edwards and Gaventa 2001; Mayo 2005; Tarrow 2005).

"NGOs' role and influence have exploded in the last-half decade" (Mathews 1997: 53). NGOs have also become more global in scope: more than a thousand draw their membership from three or more countries. Many such organizations have become influential and legitimate global political actors. While much of their political activity has focused on public policies and institutions, over the last decade they have increasingly targeted business firms. The participants in the movement for global corporate accountability are wide ranging: they include unions, environmental organizations, human rights and labor activists, religious and consumer groups, student organizations, consumer groups, as well as social or ethical mutual funds and socially oriented institutional investors.

Global civil regulations are engaged in a non-state, market-based, variant of "trading up." By attempting to transmit more stringent regulatory standards from developed countries to firms, industries, and markets in developing ones, they are seeking to privatize the "California effect," a term coined to describe the dynamics of the transmission of more stringent standards among states via international trade (Vogel 1997). Their emergence and impact has been facilitated both by the growth of global brands which make firms more vulnerable to threats to their reputations in important consumer markets, and the expansion of international communications which enables activists to more easily acquire information about global business practices, and then to rapidly disseminate it.

The number and scope of global civil regulations began to expand significantly during the 1990s. Private regulations that define standards for "responsible" business practices now exist for virtually every global industry and internationally traded commodity, including forestry, fisheries, chemicals, computers and electronic equipment, apparel, rugs, coffee, cocoa, palm oil, diamonds, gold, toys, minerals and mining, energy, tourism, financial services, and athletic equipment, though most formally govern only a portion of these global products or sectors (Gereffi, Garcia-Johnson, and Sasser 2001: 56–65; Jenkins 2001; Koenig-Archibugi 2004: 234–59; Kolk and van Tulder 2005: 1–27). There are now more than 300 industry or product codes, nearly all of which address labor or environmental practices; many sectors and products are governed by multiple codes.

GOVERNANCE FAILURES AND THE GROWTH OF CIVIL REGULATION

Why has civil regulation grown? The growth of global civil regulation represents a political response to the recent expansion of economic globalization and the firms and industries that have fostered and benefited from it (Gereffi and Mayer 2006). During the last two decades, the dynamics of economic globalization have significantly transformed the international economic landscape in two respects. First, they have shifted the locus of manufacturing from developed to developing countries. Second, the production and supply networks of global firms increasingly transcend national boundaries: most international trade is now among firms or inter-firm networks.

The emergence of global civil regulation represents a political response to the structural imbalance between the size and power of global firms and markets, and the capacity and/or willingness of governments to adequately regulate them. According to this argument, economic globalization and the increased legitimacy and influence of neoliberal values and policies, has undermined both the willingness and capacity of governments to make global firms politically accountable. Civil regulation proposes to fill the regulatory gap between global markets and global firms on the one hand, and government regulation of multinational firms on the other. It is intended to "compensate for the decreasing capacities of national governments for providing public goods [as] ... internationalization yields an increasing gap between territorially bound regulatory competencies at the national level and emerging problems of international scope" (Knill and Lehmkuhl 2002: 42, 44).

The claim that the state is "in retreat" is contestable, as the scope and extent of state-based business regulation continues to expand in many countries, as well as at the international level. But the growth of civil regulation does reflect a widely shared perception that *the global economy is characterized by systemic regulatory failures or a structural "governance deficit"* (Newell 2002: 908). Arguably, the structure and scale of global production *has* challenged the existing capacities of governments to regulate the growing share of business activities that take place beyond their borders (Abbott and Snidal 2009). There are ways in which additional or more effective government controls over global firms and markets could address many, if not all, the criticisms of economic globalization, such as by trade agreements that link market access to improved national regulations, more extensive and better enforced international treaties, the extraterritorial application of national laws, and more effectively enforced regulations by developing country governments. *It is the inability or unwillingness of states to adopt or enforce them that has contributed to the development and growth of non-state-based governance institutions.* The growth of civil regulation essentially represents an effort to *extend* regulation to a wide range of global business practices for which the scope or effectiveness of national and international government authority currently is weak, limited, or nonexistent (Koenig-Archibugi 2004: 234–59).

THE POLITICAL DEMAND FOR CIVIL REGULATION

Where have civil regulations come from? Who has initiated them? The organizational or institutional sources of civil regulations vary widely (Gulbrandsen 2004: 75–99; Bartley 2003: 433–64, 2007: 297–351). They include NGOs such as the World

Wildlife Fund, Greenpeace, the Clean Clothes Campaign, Amnesty International, the Council on Economic Priorities, and Oxfam; trade associations for coffee, chemicals, mining, apparel, electronics, toys, and cocoa; trade unions such as the International Textile Workers Association; and international standards bodies such the International Standards Organization. Some civil regulations have been established with the support of national governments and interstate organizations, such as OECD, the World Bank, the International Finance Corporation, and the United Nations.

This in turn poses two additional questions: what has motivated NGOs and some governments to promote civil regulations, and why have many firms agreed to adopt or accept them? The motivation for Western NGOs is straightforward: they regard civil regulations as an important source of leverage over global business activity. The international impact, and thus the potential leverage, of many large Western firms are substantial. Changing the procurement policies and practices of firms such as Wal-Mart, Starbucks, and Home Depot would have major global social and environmental impacts, comparable to if not greater than that of many national regulations. At the same time, many NGOs have been repeatedly frustrated by their inability to strengthen international treaties. Thus, for global activists, lobbying corporations has come to represent a viable, though clearly second-best, alternative to pressuring for changes in public policies (Vogel 1978). While some NGOs continue to emphasize the "naming and shaming" of global firms, others have chosen to cooperate with firms and industry associations to develop voluntary standards and participate in their enforcement. Their willingness to enter into alliances with global firms has been critical to the emergence, legitimacy, and relative effectiveness of many civil regulations (Gereffi, Garcia-Johnson, and Sasser 2001: 56–65; Rondinelli and London 2003: 61–76; Pattberg 2005b: 589–610).

Some Western governments, especially in Europe, have played an important role in promoting civil regulations (Aaronson and Reeves 2002). Several European governments have indirectly promoted CSR by requiring companies that trade on their stock exchanges to issue annual reports on their social and environmental practices and encouraging, or in some cases, requiring, public pension funds to consider corporate social and environmental practices in making investment decisions. The procurement policies of some governments give preference to privately certified products. For its part, the EU has been a strong supporter of global CSR (Herrmann 2004: 205–32). Many aspects of civil regulation are consistent with the European approach to business regulation: the EU and many European governments make extensive use of voluntary agreements and soft regulation and frequently rely on private organizations to develop regulatory standards (Golub 1998; Joerges and Vos 1999; Egan 2001; Ansell and Vogel 2006).

In this context, an important advantage of civil regulations as a global regulatory vehicle is that their provisions are not currently governed by the WTO, whose rules primarily apply to regulations formally adopted by governments (Bernstein and Hannah 2008). For example, while state eco-labels are regarded by the WTO as (potential) technical barriers to trade, private product labels and certifications are not (OECD 2006). Likewise, firms can demand adherence to labor and environmental standards by their global suppliers as a condition for doing business with them; governments generally cannot make such requirements a condition for market access. This means that foreign producers who have been disadvantaged by private regulations or standards have no legal remedy: they must comply with them or risk losing export markets. The reliance of civil regulations on private, market-based standards and enforcement thus represents a major "loophole" in international trade law—one that civil regulation has attempted to exploit.

What about corporations? In some cases, industries have adopted or accepted private global regulations to avoid additional government regulation. For example, Responsible Care was adopted by several national chemical industry associations in part to forestall national laws establishing more stringent plant safety standards following the chemical plant explosion at Bhopal, India, in 1984. An international "Code of Pharmaceutical Marketing Practices" was developed by global drug firms as a response to the imminent threat of public regulation at the international level, including by the World Health Organization (Ronit and Schneider 1999: 252). The International Chamber of Commerce's Business Charter for Sustainable Development was initiated by global firms who feared that the 1992 Rio "Earth Summit" would lead to an expansion of global environmental regulations. But typically, firms have not agreed to accept civil regulations to avoid additional government regulation as there has been little prospect of additional regulations being enacted, let alone enforced, especially at the global level or by developing countries. The more than 3,500 firms who have signed on to the UN Global Compact did not do so in order to prevent the UN from adopting legally binding regulations for global corporations since there was no likelihood that it would do so.

Why, then, have an increasing number of global firms and industries accepted the legitimacy of voluntary regulations? Most civil regulations have their origin in citizen campaigns directed against particular companies, industries, and business practices (Klein 2002; O'Rourke 2005: 115–28; Bartley and Child 2007). Such campaigns have proliferated over the last decade, focusing on such issues as working conditions and wages, child labor, the income of agricultural workers, unsustainable forestry practices, business investments that support corrupt governments, and natural resource developments that adversely affect human rights and environmental quality. These public campaigns of "naming and shaming" have been directed at highly visible European- and American-based firms such as Nike, Home Depot, Shell, Ikea, C & A, Gap Inc., Tiffany & Co., Nestlé, Starbucks, Hennes & Mauritz, Rio Tinto, Freeport Mining, and Citibank, which then became public symbols of "corporate irresponsibility." Such widely publicized demonstrations of corporate irresponsibility have played a critical role in placing political pressures on global firms to act more "responsibly." Indeed, for many global firms CSR stands for "Crisis Scandal Response."

There is little evidence that more than a handful of consumers in Western countries actually care about how responsibly most of the products they consume are produced. Moreover, the public's attention span is both narrow in scope and limited in duration. Few of these public campaigns, even when accompanied by product boycotts, adverse media coverage, and pressures from socially concerned investors, have adversely affected either the sales or share prices of targeted firms (Vogel 2005: 46–74). Nevertheless, NGO-led public pressures and media exposes have had an impact: many firms have chosen to respond to them by either adopting industry self-regulations or participating in multi-stakeholder codes involving NGOs. Their motives are complex. Firms that market to consumers are particularly risk adverse as they are especially vulnerable to public criticisms that might adversely affect the value of their brands. "NGOs have become highly sophisticated in using market-campaigning techniques to gain leverage over recalcitrant firms" that sell directly to consumers (Gereffi, Garcia-Johnson, and Sasser 2001: 64). The most vulnerable firms, and the ones that have been most responsive to NGO pressures, are those with highly visible global consumer brands whose reputations are critical to their marketing strategies.

But even some global firms that do not market to consumers are concerned about their reputations: they value public approval and dislike negative media attention. For many global firms, CSR has become a component of their risk management policies and their marketing, public, employee, and investor relations. In some cases, the values and concerns of critics of economic globalization are personally shared by some executives, particularly those who manage corporations whose traditions and cultures have historically emphasized a strong commitment to corporate responsibility. Some firms have also developed or agreed to accept civil regulations in response to pressures from employees or in order to attract prospective employees (Battacharya, Sen, and Korschun 2008: 37–44).

This in turns raises a more interesting question. Why don't firms simply adopt their own codes of conduct? Why do they frequently encourage the formation of, or endorse, civil regulations that also govern their competitors? The two are not incompatible; many large global firms have also adopted their own regulations, and in some cases, these go beyond industry standards. But for "targeted" firms, industry-wide regulations make business sense. Adopting higher social or environmental standards can raise a firm's costs, while persuading their competitors to adopt similar standards creates a more level playing field. Moreover, the public often does not distinguish among the social or environmental practices of firms in the same industry. For example, in the fine jewelry industry, when some diamond retailers were accused of selling "blood diamonds" sold by warlords in conflict zones, the reputation of the entire industry was damaged.

In addition, "herd effects" play an important role in disseminating many management practices (Lieberman and Asaba 2006: 366–85). Accordingly, when an industry leader agrees to a voluntary code, other firms in its sector often decide that they should do so as well. This dynamic also operates across industries. The greater the number of global industries that agree to develop or accept voluntary codes, the more likely it is that other industries will follow their example. The growth of civil regulations among global firms and industries has thus created its own momentum: few global firms or industries headquartered in the United States or

Europe want to be regarded as less "responsible" or "enlightened" than their peers. As the *Financial Times* observed in describing the growth of industry-wide social standards, "Industries seek safety in numbers" (Maitland 2005: 1).

Finally, "corporate preferences are driven in part about norms about the appropriate approaches to [managing] a business" (Haufler 1999: 201). For many highly visible global firms, engaging in various forms of global CSR, including having a CSR office, issuing a CSR report, cooperating with NGOs, and agreeing to one or more voluntary industry codes has become an accepted and legitimate dimension of managing a global firm in a more politicized and transparent global economy (Dickerson 2002: 1431–59; Kollman 2006). The growth of civil regulation has not reduced the importance firms place on profit maximization; rather, many global firms have now concluded that it is now in their interest to profess their commitment to "good global corporate citizenship" by agreeing to a voluntary code of conduct.

The Effectiveness of Civil Regulations

Under what conditions have civil regulations been effective in addressing the regulatory and market failure they were established to address? A useful way of beginning to answer this critical question is to examine a few important case studies of civil regulations. This section looks at three categories of civil regulations: those that have been relatively effective, those whose impact has been mixed, and those that have been relatively ineffective in achieving their professed goals, and then seeks to explain these variations.

Relatively effective civil regulations: 'conflict diamonds' and labor practices in Cambodia

Two of the most important accomplishments of civil regulation have been to significantly reduce international trade in "conflict or blood diamonds" and to strengthen labor standards in the textile export sector in Cambodia. The issue of "conflict diamonds" first emerged during the late 1990s in connection with the civil war in Angola (Kantz 2007: 1–20). In 1998, at the request of the UN, Portugal, Russia, and the United States, the UN Security Council voted to prohibit the purchase of rough diamonds from UNITA, a rebel group, as their proceeds were being used to finance its civil war against the government of Angola. Similar trade restrictions were subsequently extended to diamonds from another conflict zone, Sierra Leone. In 2000, the US Congress passed the Clean Diamond Trade Act, which prohibited the import of "blood diamonds" from conflict zones. While both De Beers, which dominates the global diamond market (and which withdrew from Angola under pressure in 1999), and Tiffany & Co., a major diamond retailer, indicated their full support for these measures and declared that they did not deal in conflict diamonds, several NGOs expressed concern that their systems for monitoring the sources of diamond purchases was flawed.

Both De Beers and diamond retailers had an important reputational stake in assuring the public that they were not selling irresponsibly produced diamonds. In the case of De Beers, there was an additional motivation: their business strategy rests on controlling the supply of diamonds, which meant that the marketing of "conflict diamonds" threatened both their reputation *and* their quasi-monopolistic control of the global diamond market. In 2000, a joint resolution by an association of international diamond retailers declared a zero tolerance policy for trading in conflict diamonds and announced that any firm found to be doing so would be expelled from the World Diamond Council.

That same year, the Republic of South Africa launched the Kimberley Process (KP), named after the mining town at the heart of diamond production in the nineteenth century. KP brings together the world's major diamond producers and retailers, as well as diamond exporting and importing countries, seventy of whom have signed this agreement. KP has established a certification system which requires that all countries that trade or produce diamonds must issue certificates of origin that guarantee that the diamonds do not come from a conflict zone. While compliance by diamond exporting countries is not mandatory, each country that has endorsed the KP has agreed to on-site monitoring. The KP has expelled some countries for non-compliance, which effectively bans their diamond exports from states that have endorsed the KP—a trade restriction for which the WTO has granted a waiver.

Most diamonds are not individually certified; rather, bags of them are certified by and in the countries in which they are produced. The process is far from perfect, since some non-certified diamonds are smuggled into KP member countries, mixed with legitimate stones, and then re-exported. The existence of gaps in the enforcement of the KP means that illicit rough diamonds still find their way into global markets. Nonetheless, according to the KP, its members account for 99.8 per cent of all diamond production, though other estimates place the percentage of certified diamonds somewhat lower (Innocenti 2006: 2). But on balance, the KP has made substantial progress in addressing a major deficit in global economic governance. Equally important, its effectiveness appears to be steadily increasing as monitoring and enforcement are improving and the level of civil conflict in African diamond producing countries has declined. Accordingly, "KP stands as a positive example of active cooperation between governments, non-governmental organizations and the private sector" (Innocenti 2005a: 4, 2005b: 11).

Labor relations in Cambodia provide a second example of a relatively effective civil regulation. Improving working conditions in factories supplying products for Western retailers and manufactures has emerged as a major focus of civil regulation. Over the last decade, scores of private codes governing labor standards have been developed by global firms. Such codes primarily work through business-to-business markets: groups of Western firms establish standards for policies such as child labor, overtime, gender discrimination, wages, and freedom of association and then monitor the adherence of their suppliers through periodic inspections.

While several of these codes appear to have made progress in reducing some abuses, most notably unsafe working conditions and the employment of child labor, effective and credible enforcement remains a serious problem, especially with respect to wages and forced overtime (Vogel 2005: 75–109). This is due to both the large number of suppliers and subcontractors in major sectors and the fact that Western firms have conflicting incentives. They want to protect their reputations, but at the same time face competitive pressures to keep their costs as low as possible and to assure a rapid and continual flow of goods from their suppliers to retail outlets. While some firms have ended their contracts with suppliers who have violated their labor codes, their unwillingness to pay more for products produced by code compliant contractors also constrains the ability of the latter to improve their labor standards.

Between 1994 and 1998, apparel exports from Cambodia grew from virtually zero to more than half a billion dollars. The success of this industry attracted the attention of American textile unions for two related reasons: the unions were concerned about reports of abusive working conditions, and they wanted to bring these exports under the American textile quota system in order to protect domestic employment. While the United States had previously entered into a number of trade agreements that provided for penalties unless appropriate labor standards were enforced, it had never established positive incentives for countries that did so. It now decided to employ an economic carrot: the United States agreed to increase Cambodia's annual textile quota, provided that the Cambodian government was able to ensure substantial compliance with national labor laws and internationally agreed labor rights by *all* its apparel factories (Polaski 2003: 13–25).

As the Cambodian government lacked any enforcement capacity, monitoring compliance presented a formidable problem. While several private organizations were already monitoring the labor practices of suppliers to Western firms, their inspections lacked sufficient credibility to satisfy the American government. Accordingly, both the United States and Cambodia turned to the ILO, which for the first time agreed to establish a system for monitoring workplaces. (Previously, this intergovernmental organization had only reviewed the conduct of governments.) Financial support for the ILO was in turn provided by the American and Cambodian governments and Western apparel firms. For its part, the ILO agreed to make the results of all its inspections public.

At the outset, supplier participation in the ILO inspection program was voluntary. This presented a serious free rider problem, since non-participating firms faced lower costs, but enjoyed equal market access, as the American quota was awarded to the country as a whole. Subsequently, the Cambodian government agreed to limit exports to the United States to those firms that agreed to participate in the monitoring program. Because all producers involved in the inspection program stood to suffer if any major violations were reported, all now had a common stake in adhering to the labor provisions of the trade agreement. The agreement essentially aligned the influence of the American government with the interests of the Cambodian government, local producers, and Western retailers and manufacturers. The result was a measurable and cost-effective improvement in labor conditions in one of the world's poorest countries.

The US–Cambodia Textile Agreement formally expired with the end of the multi-fiber agreement. Yet the regulatory systems it established remain in place. Significantly, many Western firms, most notably Gap Inc., the largest purchaser of garments from factories in Cambodia, as well as Nike, continue to outsource from Cambodia, even though such products no longer receive preferential trade treatment. The fact that textile production in Cambodia has continued to increase demonstrates the importance of civil pressures for corporate accountability: those firms that continue to outsource from Cambodia presumably have a stake in maintaining responsible labor standards and a credible, transparent system for monitoring the compliance of their suppliers. The latter is particularly critical. If there is one aspect of the Cambodia monitoring program that can be singled out as indispensable to its success, it is the higher level of transparency that the ILO provided through its reports. The reports served a multiplicity of purposes in the hands of different actors and reinforced the common interests they shared (Polaski 2005: 16).

While some private labor regulations have become more transparent, few provide the detailed plant-by-plant disclosures of specific labor practices and conditions that characterize the work of the ILO in Cambodia. However, the Cambodian regulatory arrangement has yet to be effectively replicated in any other country, in part because no other country has been able to establish a credible system for monitoring supplier compliance. In addition, the multiplicity of both industry and firm labor codes has made it difficult for firms and NGOs to reach agreements on common standards.

Moderately effective civil regulations: fair trade and forest certification

In two other important cases of civil regulation, namely Fair Trade International (FTI) and the Forest Stewardship Council (FSC), the effectiveness of private global governance has been mixed. Both have attracted a significant number of business participants and have effective private compliance mechanisms. But when measured against the scope of global business activity in their respective sectors, their impact has been constrained by the limited number of producers who participate in them. Both FTI and FSC are market based: they employ private labeling and certification to align the interests of Western consumers with socially responsible global producers or exporters. Each represents a private response to a serious global governance deficit: the former seeks to ameliorate the impoverishment of farmers due to low global commodity prices, while the latter attempts to fill the regulatory gap created by the absence of an effective international forestry treaty.

In 1997, seventeen national Fair Trade certification programs in Europe, North America, and Japan established an international consortium, Fairtrade Labeling International. This organization certifies products produced in developing countries and then markets them to consumers in developed countries using the "Fair Trade" (FT) label. While this social label has been used to market several agricultural products, including bananas, cocoa, tea, flowers, oranges, nuts, sugar, chocolate, and most recently cotton, the most important ethical label is for coffee, an $80 billion industry and the world's second most widely traded commodity. The primary purpose of FT coffee is to increase the prices paid to farmers for this commodity, many of whose expenses barely cover the costs of production. FTI guarantees these farmers above world market prices for their products, a commitment that is financed by selling FT-labeled products at a premium price.

FTI exhibits both the strengths and weaknesses of consumer-based global governance. On one hand, there is a market for virtue: a growing number of consumers in the United States and Europe purchase FT coffee, often due to a sense of social commitment, and several coffee firms, such as Proctor & Gamble, as well as coffee retailers such as Starbucks, offer FT coffee, among other kinds, to their customers. Cafedirect, which only sells FT coffee, is the sixth largest British coffee brand, and nearly one-fifth of the British ground and roast coffee market is FT (Levi and Linton 2003: 419; Beattie 2006: W1). Thirty-five thousand firms sell FT coffee in the United States and sales have tripled since 1999, making it the fastest-growing segment of the specialty or premium coffee business (Alserver 2006: 5; Conroy 2007). In 2005, 60 million pounds of FT coffee were imported by the United States.

On the other hand, the economic impact of FT is limited by consumer demand for its products. Consumers typically purchase products on the basis of price, convenience, and quality, not on whether they were produced "responsibly"; most consumers are happy to benefit from the lower costs of production in developing countries. While FT coffee has an important advantage compared to other ethically labeled products, namely, that it is not more expensive than other premium coffees, though it is more expensive than commodity coffee, it still occupies a niche market. FT certified coffee represents only 2 per cent of American coffee sales, and up to 3.5 per cent in some European countries. Accordingly, while ethical labels have benefited some producers in developed countries, their overall redistributive impact remains limited.

Forestry regulation provides a second example of the strengths and shortcomings of market-based civil regulations. Frustrated by the failure of the 1992 Rio Summit to develop an effective international agreement governing forestry practices, a group of NGOs attempted to develop a private global forestry "treaty." Their efforts were supported by a number of foundations as well as the government of Austria, whose effort to develop a labeling standard for tropical forestry products was withdrawn following complaints from developing countries to the WTO. After several years of negotiations among foresters, scientists, and firms, the Forest Stewardship Council (FSC) was established in 1993, and began operations three years later. Arguably the most ambitious example of the "privatization of environmental governance," the FSC is an international private standard setting body (Cashore 2002: 514). Its goal is to create a global market for wood harvested in a socially and environmentally sound manner. The FSC has developed standards for forestry management and accredits and monitors organizations that in turn carry out assessments of wood production practices. It then issues certificates that guarantee a chain of custody for wood products from certified forests to their end users.

While originally conceived as a product labeling scheme, relatively few wood products sold to consumers are actually labeled, largely because relatively few consumers value certification. Nor, in contrast to FT products, are consumers willing to pay a market premium for certified wood. Rather, as in the case of labor codes that certify producers in developing countries, FSC operates primarily in the business-to-business market. It relies on sales of certified wood products to retailers and builders, rather than to individual consumers, few of whom have ever heard of FSC. For firms such as Home Depot, the world's largest retailer of wood products, their willingness to give preference to FSC certified products often represents a key component of their public commitment to CSR; many agreed to do so only after extensive grass roots pressures from activists, often accompanied by actual or threatened boycotts.

But many forestry firms regard FSC certification as too expensive and burdensome, especially because certified products do not command a price premium from either retailers or builders. In large measure as a response to FSC, more than forty industry-dominated alternative certification schemes have been developed, and their requirements are generally less stringent than those of FSC, though many have gradually been strengthened (Meidinger 2006: 47–97). In 2006, FSC's global market share of certified wood stood at 30 per cent, while that of the two major industry-based and governed certification schemes totaled 57 per cent (Pattberg 2006: 247). Worldwide, 4 per cent of all managed forests are FSC certified, accounting for 7 per cent of the global forest product market. This is an important accomplishment: the number of hectares of FSC certified wood grew from 500,000 in 1994 to more than 70 million in 2006, while between 1998 and 2006, the number of chain of custody certifications increased from 268 to 4,500 (Pattberg 2006: 248). However, virtually all FSC certified forests are located in temperate zones, and 84 per cent of them are located in Europe and North America, where forestry practices were already extensively regulated by governments.

FSC may well have improved the social and environmental management of temperate forests, especially in Europe and North America. But the most egregious forestry management practices are taking place in tropical forests, only 2.4 per cent of which are certified by the FSC or any other private certification scheme. The limited geographic scope of private forestry certification has seriously limited its ability to adequately address what is arguably the most critical forestry governance failure, namely, the accelerating rate of tropical deforestation (Dauvergne 1997, 2001). In fact, only 6–8 per cent of global timber production is traded and most of this trade occurs between environmentally sensitive developed countries, rather than from developing countries to developed ones, thus weakening the international leverage of Western firms and activists (Pattberg 2005a: 366–7).

Relatively ineffective civil regulations: curbing corruption

One of the most critical governance deficits in the global economy involves the misuse by developing countries of the royalty payments received from extractive industries. These payments are often squandered by corrupt government officials and, as a result, many of the people living in countries with the most abundant deposits of oil, natural gas, and minerals are among the world's most impoverished (Weinthal and Luong 2006: 35–43). In 2002, a global coalition of 200 NGOs launched a "Publish What You Pay" (PWYP) campaign to pressure global firms in extractive industries to reveal their royalty payments to host country governments (*Economist* 2005).

The results of this voluntary initiative have been disappointing (Davis 2005: 35–6). Only seven global oil companies, all based in Europe or the United States, have agreed to disclose their payments, and not all have actually done so, largely due to the opposition of host country governments. For example, when British Petroleum (BP) announced that it would disclose its royalty payments to the government of Angola, that government threatened to terminate BP's exploration rights and it took two years of negotiations before a compromise was reached. An equally striking limitation of PWYP is the failure of any state-based global energy firm to endorse it, even though such firms, as well quasi-private energy firms based in the former Soviet Union and Asia, account for a growing share of foreign investments in this sector, especially in Africa (Yeh 2006: 2). As a result, governments that benefit from the misuse of royalty payments from natural resources can continue to offer exploration or production concessions to global firms that have less demanding ethical standards.

The challenge faced by energy companies attempting to behave more responsibly in failed or highly corrupt states is illustrated by the experience of ExxonMobil in Chad. In 1998, an unprecedented agreement was reached among the government of Chad, one of the world's poorest countries, the World Bank, which helped finance ExxonMobil's $4.2 billion energy investment project, and several NGOs. Its terms provided that all royalty payments would be monitored and 80 per cent earmarked for education, health, and rural development (Useem 2002: 102–14). The agreement was hailed as groundbreaking and a model for responsible energy development.

But in December 2005, the government of Chad decided to take advantage of increased oil prices by breaking its terms (Polgreen 2005: A15; Cummins 2006: A4). It took a portion of the funds held in trust for development and allocated them to military spending, and also demanded increased royalty payments. The terms of the agreement were subsequently renegotiated, providing the government of Chad with more control over oil revenues. With oil revenues increasing, Chad repaid its loan from the World Bank and withdrew from the agreement. There has been no effort to establish similar programs in other countries, and for its part, ExxonMobil does not view the Chad program as a success. Nor is there any evidence that the agreement has improved the welfare of the citizens of Chad, which remains among the world's most corrupt countries and recently has faced increasing civil unrest. The Chad case illustrates an important limitation of global civil regulation, namely, the difficulty of promoting more responsible corporate practices when the objectives of civil regulations are opposed by host country governments.

There have also been other voluntary corporate initiatives to reduce corrupt payments. For example, concerned about numerous corruption allegations, forty-seven major global firms, representing $300 billion in global revenues, have signed a "zero tolerance" pact against paying bribes (Simpson 2005: A4–A8). But these firms represent only a small portion of MNCs, and their compliance with this pact is not independently monitored. For its part, the UN Global Compact has made eliminating corruption one of its ten key previsions, and along with the World Economic Forum, the International Chamber of Commerce, and an NGO, Transparency International, it has established a private regulatory standard: Business Principles for Countering Bribery. But these also lack any enforcement mechanisms or provisions for independent auditing.

Notwithstanding the endorsement of the Global Compact by more than 3,500 firms and the nearly fifty global firms who have signed a "zero tolerance" pledge, cases of corrupt payments by American and European firms continue to surface, though such payments are now more likely to be made public (Bonner and Perlez 2006: A6). There is no evidence that the extent of such payments has declined, and many continue to be made with the tacit approval of some Western governments (Williamson 2006: 5). The misuse of royalty payments by corrupt governments remains pervasive, as does the civil unrest such corruption often fosters. In short, the impact of these civil regulations on both business conduct and the citizens in developing countries whose welfare they were intended to enhance has been extremely modest, and, as a result, virtually all the regulatory and governance failures they were intended to ameliorate persist.

Analysis

In all three categories of cases, both the business case for compliance and the establishment of effective monitoring and enforcement mechanism parallel one another, and together explain much of the divergence in their effectiveness. Both were strongest in the case of the KP and the Cambodia agreement and weakest in the case of the various anti-corruption civil codes, with FTI and FSC falling in between. On balance, civil regulations have been most successful at influencing agenda setting; they have placed a wide array of global regulatory failures on the agenda of the international community. Many also have been relatively effective at the negotiation stage, persuading relatively large numbers of firms to subscribe to them. But for many civil regulations, implementation, and effective monitoring and enforcement represent a serious structural weakness.

CONCLUSION

The growth of global civil regulation and CSR has been both hailed as a highly promising solution to the shortcomings of state regulation and sharply criticized on the grounds that voluntary business regulations are inherently incapable of addressing market and regulatory failures—especially when these failures were created by global firms in the first place (Lipschutz and Rowe 2005; Savitz 2006). However, any realistic assessment of civil regulation should compare it not to an ideal world of effective global economic governance, but to actual policy alternatives. When compared to most government regulations in developed countries, civil regulation is clearly less effective. In fact, civil regulations exhibit many of the well-documented shortcomings of industry self-regulation at the national level, with which they share many important characteristics (OECD 1999; Lenox and Nash 2003: 343–56; Morgenstern and Pizer 2007). Both remain weaker than well-enforced command and control regulations in changing corporate behavior.

But the effectiveness of civil regulations *is* roughly comparable to that of many intergovernmental treaties and agreements, many of which are also based on soft law and the "naming and shaming" of non-compliant countries, and whose effectiveness in improving environmental protection, labor practices, and human rights is *also* mixed and uneven (Victor, Raustiala, and Skolnikoff 1998). In a number of important cases, most notably with regard to labor standards and forestry, civil regulations, for all their shortcomings, have been considerably *more* effective than intergovernmental treaties. At the same time, their scope is much more limited as they primarily affect the way some products exported to highly visible Western firms are produced.

But civil regulations are undoubtedly *more* effective than the labor, human rights, and environmental regulations of many developing countries. To be sure, the governance of civil regulations is uneven: many codes are not independently monitored and even those that provide for third party certification suffer many of the shortcomings that often characterize government regulation. But in many developing countries, they constitute the *only or the most* effective form of business regulation. The environmental, social, and human rights practices of firms in developing countries that either produce for global supply chains or are directly owned by Western MNCs are frequently better than those of domestic producers, and this is largely due to the impact of global civil regulations. If "accountability . . . implies that some actors have the right to hold other actors to a set of standards, to judge whether they have fulfilled their responsibilities in light of these standards, and to impose sanctions if they determine that these responsibilities have not been met," then civil regulations have clearly made some global firms *more* accountable (Grant and Keohane 2005: 29).

What would it take to make civil regulation a more effective form of global economic governance? Two factors are critical. First, the business case for compliance with civil regulations would need to become stronger (Vogel 2005, 16–45). Many developing country producers regard the civil regulations imposed by Western firms as a burden: meeting the requirements of Western codes raises their costs, but does not increase the prices they receive. (FT branded products are a notable though clearly limited exception.) This means that such firms have every incentive to do as little as possible to accommodate the demands of their Western contractors. Many have developed an adversarial relationship with private inspectors, and often seek to deceive them (Roberts and Engardio 2006: 50–8).

A similar logic holds for Western firms. They have accepted civil regulations for a variety of reasons, including public and peer pressures, changes in business norms, and in some cases a more sophisticated understanding of the basis for profitable business activities. But because the financial benefits of CSR remain for the most part either modest or elusive, few firms have integrated the standards of civil regulation into their core business practices. Many global CSR commitments and policies remain akin to corporate philanthropy or community or public relations, remaining on the periphery of the firm's business strategies (Porter and Kramer 2006: 78–92). They typically represent more a form of insurance against public opprobrium than a source of competitive advantage. As long as more "responsible" global firms do not enjoy consistently stronger financial performance than their less responsible competitors, and to date they do not, the incentives of firms to invest substantial resources into complying with civil regulations will remain limited, and the incentive of some firms to free ride on industry codes will remain a serious problem. Moreover, the growing economic prominence of MNCs based in non-Western countries, who face fewer domestic pressures from NGOs and who have been less willing to accept civil regulations, has exacerbated the competitive challenges faced by more responsible Western firms.

The second critical determinant of the future impact of civil regulation has to do with their relationship to governments. Some developing-country governments, such as Cambodia, recognize the value of civil regulation; others, such as Chad, do not. Unfortunately, the latter is more typical than the former: most developing countries tend to be indifferent to voluntary labor standards, and many are not supportive of codes that seek to reduce corruption. The KP is a notable exception, but that is primarily because it can be enforced by trade sanctions. In the case of FSC, the pattern is more mixed: some developing country governments closely cooperate with its rules, while others are indifferent to them (Espach 2006: 55–84). The laws of some countries, such as China, do not permit local firms to comply with labor codes that guarantee the right of workers to choose their own representatives, while some Central and Latin American countries have been unwilling or unable to protect independent labor organizations. In the long run, civil regulations must be more closely integrated into the domestic regulatory policies and the competitive strategies of developing country governments if they are to become more effective (MacGillivray, Sabapathy, and Zadek 2003; Zadek et al. 2005).

Equally importantly, developing country governments need to promote or at least permit the strengthening of civil society so that their citizens are able to define and defend their own social, political, and environmental interests vis-à-vis business firms, without having to rely on Western activists to do so in their name. This is particularly critical as the values and objectives of Western NGOs are not necessarily the same as those of many workers and citizens in developing countries. For example, in the important case of labor standards, Western NGO norms regarding overtime and child labor are often not shared by the workers in whose interests they purport to speak. This not only undermines the legitimacy and effectiveness of many Western imposed codes, but constitutes a democratic governance deficit in its own right.

The future effectiveness of, or demand for, effective civil regulations also depends on the policies of developed country governments. Some Western governments have assisted the development of civil regulations (WEO 1998; Nelson 2004; Ward 2004). But there is much more they could do to improve the behavior of global firms. For example, they could make greater efforts to promote compliance by developing country governments with the wide array of international treaties governing labor conditions and human rights that already exist as well as support legally binding standards for the conduct of global firms, both of which would "harden" public and private international soft law (Hertz 2004: 202–9; Zerk 2006; Ruggie 2007). They could also impose global corporate reporting requirements, develop procurement policies that give priority to more globally responsible firms, establish voluntary but legally enforceable labeling requirements and certification standards, and provide financial assistance to strengthen the regulatory capacity of developing country governments, as some countries have done. They could also support changes in trade rules that would integrate voluntary CSR initiatives into the WTO (Aaronson 2007: 629–59). Until the world's developed countries are willing to more closely integrate the norms of civil regulations into their domestic laws and international relations, the global regulatory failures private social regulation was intended to redress will persist.

Global business activity can only become more effectively governed if the inadequacies of both government regulation *and* civil regulation are recognized by both firms and governments. The effectiveness of global business regulation ultimately depends on the extent to which private and public authority, civil and government regulation, and soft and hard law, reinforce one another. Still, it would be misinformed to dismiss the political importance of civil regulation: its accomplishment may be uneven they but not inconsequential. In the final analysis, perhaps the most important contribution of global civil regulation has been to focus public attention on both the shortcomings of economic globalization and the lack of effective state-based regulatory instruments to ameliorate them.

References

AARONSON, S. A. 2007. "A match made in the corporate and public interest: marrying voluntary CSR initiatives and the WTO," *Journal of World Trade* 41: 629–59.

—— and REEVES, J. T. 2002. *Corporate Responsibility in the Global Village: The Role of Public Policy.* Washington, DC: National Policy Association.

ABBOTT, K., and SNIDAL, D. 2000. "Hard and soft law in international governance," *International Organization* 54: 421–56.

—— —— 2009. "The governance triangle: regulatory standards institutions and the shadow of the state," in W. Mattli and N. Woods, eds., *The Politics of Global Regulation.* Princeton: Princeton University Press.

ALSERVER, J. 2006. "Fair prices for farmers: simple idea, complex reality," *New York Times* March 16: Business Section.

ANSELL, C., and VOGEL, D., eds. 2006. *What's The Beef? The Contested Governance of European Food Safety.* Cambridge, Mass.: MIT Press.

BARTLEY, T. 2003. "Certifying forests and factories: states, social movements, and the rise of private regulation in the apparel and forest products fields," *Politics & Society* 31: 433–64.

—— 2007. "Institutional emergence in an era of globalization: the rise of transnational private regulation of labor and environmental conditions," *American Journal of Sociology* 113: 297–351.

—— and CHILD, C. 2007. "Shaming the corporation: reputation, globalization, and the dynamics of anti-corporate movements," Working Paper, Department of Sociology, Indiana University.

BATTACHARYA, C. B., SEN, S., and KORSCHUN, D. 2008. "Using corporate social responsibility to win the war for talent," *MIT Sloan Management Review* 49: 37–44.

BEATTIE, A. 2006. "Follow the thread," *Financial Times* July 22/23.

BERNSTEIN, S., and HANNAH, E. 2008. "Non-state global standard setting and the WTO: legitimacy and the need for regulatory space," *Journal of International Economic Law*: 1–34.

BONNER, R., and PERLEZ, J. 2006. "Controller charges mining company with filing false statements," *New York Times* January 26.

BRINK, P. ten, ed. 2001. *Voluntary Environmental Agreements: Process, Practice and Future Use.* Sheffield: Greenleaf Publishing.

CASHORE, B. 2002. "Legitimacy and the privatization of environmental governance: how non-state market-driven (NSMD) governance systems gain rule-making authority," *Governance* 15: 503–29.

COHEN, R., and RAI, S., ed. 2000. *Global Social Movements.* London: Athlone Press.

CONROY, M. 2007. *Branded! How the "Certification" Revolution Is Transforming Global Corporations.* British Columbia: New Society Publishers.

CUMMINS, C. 2006. "Exxon oil-fund model unravels in Chad," *Wall Street Journal* February 28.

CUTLER, A. C., HAUFLER, V., and PORTER, T., eds. 1999. *Private Authority and International Affairs.* Albany: State University of New York Press.

DAUVERGNE, P. 1997. *Shadows in the Forest: Japan and the Politics of Timber in Southeast Asia.* Cambridge, Mass.: MIT Press.

—— 2001. *Loggers and Degradation in the Asia-Pacific.* Cambridge: Cambridge University Press.

DAVIS, P. 2005. "Extracting transparency promises," *Ethical Corporation* May.

DICKERSON, C. M. 2002. "How do norms and empathy affect corporation law and corporate behavior? Human rights: the emerging norm of corporate social responsibility," *Tulane Law Review* 76: 1431–59.

Economist. 2005. "The paradox of plenty," *Economist* December 24.

EDWARDS, M., and GAVENTA, J., eds. 2001. *Global Citizen Action.* Boulder, Colo.: Lynne Rienner Publishers.

EGAN, M. 2001. *Constructing a European Market.* Oxford: Oxford University Press.

ESPACH, R. 2006. "When is sustainable forest sustainable? The Forest Stewardship Council in Argentina and Brazil," *Global Environmental Politics* 6: 55–84.

FALKNER, R. 2003. "Private environmental governance and international relations: exploring the links," *Global Environmental Politics* 3: 72–87.

GEREFFI, G., GARCIA-JOHNSON, R., and SASSER, E. 2001. "The NGO–industrial complex," *Foreign Policy* pp. 56–65.

——— and MAYER, F. 2006. "Globalization and the demand for governance," unpublished paper.

GOLUB, J., ed. 1998. *New Instruments for Environmental Policy in the EU.* London: Routledge.

GRANT, R., and KEOHANE, R. 2005. "Accountability and abuses of power in world politics," *American Political Science Review* 99: 29–43.

GULBRANDSEN, L. 2004. "Overlapping public and private governance: can forest certification fill gaps in the global forest regime?" *Global Environmental Politics* 4: 75–99.

GUNNINGHAM, N., and GRABOSKY, P. 1998. *Smart Regulation: Designing Environmental Policy.* Oxford: Clarendon Press.

——— ——— 2003. *Voluntary Approaches for Environmental Policy.* Paris: OECD.

HALL, R., and BIERSTEKER, T., eds. 2002. *The Emergence of Private Authority in Global Governance.* Cambridge: Cambridge University Press.

HAUFLER, V. 1999. "Self-regulation and business norms: political risk, political activism," in A. C. Cutler, V. Haufler, and T. Porter, eds., *Private Authority and International Affairs.* Albany: State University of New York Press.

——— 2001. *The Public Role for the Private Sector.* Washington, DC: Carnegie Endowment for International Peace.

——— 2003. "Globalization and industry self-regulation," in M. Kahler and D. Lake, eds., *Governance in a Global Economy: Political Authority in Transition.* Princeton: Princeton University Press.

HERRMANN, K. 2004. "Corporate social responsibility and sustainable development: the European Union initiative as a case study," *Indiana Journal of Global Legal Studies* 11: 205–32.

HERTZ, N. 2004. "Corporations on the front line," *Corporate Governance* 12: 202–9.

INNOCENTI, N. D. 2005a. "A positive example of co-operations on conflict stones," *Financial Times* June 28.

——— 2005b. "Accord on conflict diamond smuggling," *Financial Times* November 16.

——— 2006. "Time to review the monitoring system," *Financial Times* July 17.

JENKINS, R. 2001. "Corporate codes of conduct: self-regulation in a global economy." Geneva: UN Research Institute for Social Development.

JOERGES, C., and VOS, E., eds. 1999. *EU Committees: Social Regulation, Law and Politics.* Oxford: Hart Publishing.

KANTZ, C. 2007. "The power of socialization: engaging the diamond industry in the Kimberly Process," *Business and Politics* 9: 1–20.

KECK, M., and SIKKINK, K. 1998. *Activists beyond Borders.* Ithaca, NY: Cornell University Press.

KIRTON, J., and TREBILOCK, M. 2004. "Introduction: hard choices and soft law in sustainable global commerce," in J. Kirton and M. Trebilock, eds., *Hard Choices, Soft Law: Voluntary Standards in Global Trade, Environment and Social Governance.* Aldershot: Ashgate.

KLEIN, N. 2002. *No Logo: Taking Aim at the Brand Bullies.* New York: Picador.

KNILL, C., and LEHMKUHL, D. 2002. "Private actors and the state: internationalization and changing patterns of governance," *Governance* 15: 41–63.

KOENIG-ARCHIBUGI, M. 2004. "Transnational corporations and public accountability," *Government and Opposition* 39: 234–59.

KOLK, A., and TULDER, R. VAN. 2005. "Setting new global rules? TNCs and codes of conduct," *Transnational Corporations* 14: 1–27.

KOLLMAN, K. 2006. "The regulatory power of business norms: a call for a new research agenda," unpublished paper.

LENOX, M., and NASH, J. 2003. "Industry self-regulation and adverse selection: a comparison across four trade association programs," *Business Strategy and the Environment* 12: 343–56.

LEVI, M., and LINTON, A. 2003. " 'Fair trade': a cup at a time?" *Politics & Society* 31: 407–32.

LIEBERMAN, M., and ASABA, S. 2006. "Why do firms imitate each other?" *Academy of Management Review* 31: 366–85.

LIPSCHUTZ, R., and ROWE, J. 2005. *Globalization, Governmentality and Global Politics: Regulation for the Rest of Us.* London: Routledge.

MACGILLIVRAY, A., SABAPATHY, J., and ZADEK, S. 2003. *Aligning Corporate Responsibility and the Competitiveness of Nations.* AccountAbility, http://www.accountability21.net/publications.aspx?id=460

MAITLAND, A. 2005. "Industries seek safety in numbers," *FT Responsible Business, Special Report* November 18.

MATHEWS, J. 1997. "Power shift," *Foreign Affairs* January/February.

MATTLI, W. 2003. "Public and private governance in setting international standards," in M. Kahler and D. Lake, eds., *Governance in a Global Economy.* Princeton: Princeton University Press, 199–225.

MAYO, M. 2005. *Global Citizens: Social Movements and the Challenge of Globalization.* London: Zed Books.

MEIDINGER, E. 2006. "The administrative law of global private–public regulation: the case of forestry," *European Journal of International Law* 17: 47–97.

MORGENSTERN, R., and PIZER, W., eds. 2007. *Reality Check: The Nature and Performance of Voluntary Environmental Programs in the US, Europe, and Japan.* Washington, DC: Resources for the Future.

MOTH, U., ed. 2004. *Soft Law in Governance and Regulation.* Cheltenham: Edward Elger.

NELSON, J. 2004. "Leadership, accountability and partnership: critical trends and issues in corporate social responsibility." Report of the CSR Initiative Launch Event, Corporate Social Responsibility Initiative, Report No. 1. Cambridge, Mass.: John F. Kennedy School of Government, Harvard University.

NEWELL, P. 2000. "Environmental NGOs and globalisation: the governance of TNCs," in R. Cohen and S. Rai, eds., *Global Social Movements.* London: Athlone Press.

—— 2002. "Managing multinationals: the governance of investment for the environment," *Journal of International Development* 13: 907–19.

OECD. 1999. *Voluntary Approaches for Environmental Policy: An Assessment.* Paris: OECD.

—— 2006. *Informing Consumers of CSR in International Trade.* Paris: OECD.

O'ROURKE, D. 2005. "Market movements: nongovernmental organization strategies to influence global production and consumption," *Journal of Industrial Ecology* 9: 115–28.

PATTBERG, P. 2005a. "The Forest Stewardship Council; risk and potential of private forest governance," *Journal of Environment and Development* 14: 356–74.

—— 2005b. "The institutionalization of private governance: how business and nonprofit organizations agree on transnational rules," *Governance* 4: 589–610.

PATTBERG, P. 2006. "The influence of global business regulation: beyond good corporate conduct," *Business and Society Review* 111: 241–68.

POLASKI, S. 2003. "Protecting labor rights through trade agreements: an analytical guide," *UC David Journal of Law & Policy* 10: 13–25.

—— 2005. "Combining global and local forces: the case of labor rights in Cambodia," Global Economic Governance Programme Working Paper.

POLGREEN, L. 2005. "Chad backs out of pledge to use oil wealth to reduce poverty," *New York Times* December 3.

PORTER, M., and KRAMER, M. 2006. "Strategy and society: the link between competitive advantage and corporate social responsibility," *Harvard Business Review* December: 78–92.

ROBERTS, D., and ENGARDIO, P. 2006. "Secrets, lies and sweatshops," *Business Week* November 27.

RONDINELLI, D., and LONDON, T. 2003. "How corporations and environmental groups cooperate: assessing cross-sector alliances and collaborations," *Academy of Management Executive* 17: 61–76.

RONIT, K., and SCHNEIDER, V. 1999. "Global governance through private organizations," *Governance* 12: 243–66.

RUGGIE, J. 2004. "Reconstituting the global public domain: issues, actors and practices," *European Journal of International Relations* 10: 499–531.

—— 2007. "Business and human rights: the evolving international agenda," Working Paper of the Corporate Social Responsibility Initiative. Cambridge, Mass.: Harvard University.

SAVITZ, A. 2006. *The Triple Bottom Line: How Today's Best-Run Companies are Achieving Economic, Social and Environmental Success and How You Can Too.* San Francisco: Jossey-Bass.

SIMPSON, G. 2005. "Multinational firms unite to fight bribery," *Wall Street Journal* January 27.

TARROW, S. 2005. *The New Transnational Activism.* Cambridge: Cambridge University Press.

USEEM, J. 2002. "Exxon's african adventure," *Fortune* April 15.

VICTOR, D., RAUSTIALA, K., and SKOLNIKOFF, E., eds. 1998. *The Implementation and Effectiveness of International Environmental Commitments: Theory and Practice.* Cambridge, Mass.: MIT Press.

VOGEL, D. 1978. *Lobbying the Corporation: Citizen Challenges to Business Authority.* New York: Basic Books.

—— 1997. *Trading Up: Consumer and Environmental Regulation in Global Economy.* Cambridge, Mass.: Harvard University Press.

—— 2005. *The Market for Virtue: The Potential and Limits of Corporate Social Responsibility.* Washington, DC: Brookings Institution Press.

WARD, H. 2004. *Public Sector Roles in Strengthening Corporate Social Responsibility: Taking Stock.* Washington, DC: World Bank, International Finance Corporation.

WEINTHAL, E., and LUONG, P. J. 2006. "Combating the resource curse: an alternative solution to managing mineral wealth," *Perspectives on Politics* 4: 35–43.

WILLIAMSON, H. 2006. "West failing to curb bribery overseas," *Financial Times* September 26.

WEO. 1998. *Partnering to Strengthen Public Governance: The Leadership Challenge for CEOs and Boards.* Geneva: World Economic Forum.

YEH, A. 2006. "China ventures on rocky roads to trade with Africa," *Financial Times* June 20.

ZADEK, S., et al. 2005. *Responsible Competitiveness: Reshaping Markets Through Responsible Business Practices.* AccountAbility, http://www.accountability21.net/publications.aspx?id=358&terms=reshaping + global

ZERK, J. 2006. *Multinationals and Corporate Social Responsibility.* Cambridge: Cambridge University Press.

PART V

POLICY

CHAPTER 21

CORPORATE CONTROL AND MANAGERIAL POWER

PEPPER D. CULPEPPER

THERE is an interesting mismatch between theory and data in the political literature on corporate governance. On the one hand, important new scholarship has emerged in recent years about the political origins of corporate ownership patterns. These sophisticated arguments underline the predominant role of political coalitions and/or political parties in determining the outcomes of battles over patterns of ownership. This literature claims to show in detail that managers and large shareholders, who are a small minority in any political system, have to struggle with other political actors in order to get their way. And many of the opponents—unions, large pension funds, and parties of the left—should possess a superior ability to dominate the political agenda of democracies. Although these theories differ importantly among themselves, they agree on this point: the politics of corporate governance is something that looks like politics in any other part of a pluralist democracy, and should be understood as a contest among competing groups acting through parliament.

That, at least, is the theory. The interesting puzzle is that the data do not fit these theoretical expectations. Indeed, the facts about the politics of corporate ownership can be summarized far more succinctly: collectively, managers and blockholders rarely lose. Where liberalization of ownership is pushed by a party of the left and supported by an electoral system that creates durable majorities, as was the case in Italy 1996–2002, managers and blockholders nevertheless succeeded in maintaining highly concentrated private ownership. Where liberalization is pushed by a party of the neo-liberal right, as in the Netherlands between 1994 and 2006, managers succeeded in defeating government attempts to limit hostile takeover protections. Indeed, in the rare countries where we actually observe a breakdown of old owner-ship patterns—in France and Japan in the late 1990s—managers of companies are either leading the movement for change (in France) or indifferent to it (in Japan). These are not outlier cases, whose findings are part of the inevitably imperfect fit between theory and data in the social sciences. Instead, they raise a significant puzzle: if corporate governance is all about democratic politics, how is it that managers and blockholders almost always wind up on the winning side, regardless of who is in government?

Much of the answer lies in political salience. Unlike scholars of corporate govern-ance, most political actors do not care about the technical details of ownership and control of corporations, at least most of the time. Political parties may stake out ground on this issue for ideological reasons, as Cioffi and Höpner argue (2006). Yet any party program is an assembly of issues that some constituents care strongly about (such as abortion) or that many voters care at least somewhat about (such as taxes). In parties of the left, there is no group of voters which has this strong interest; labor unions certainly do not. And in parties of the right, which often encompass both managerial and shareholder interests (Callaghan 2009), shareholders represent more voters. There are only three groups that care strongly about the politics of ownership and control: managers (whose liberty as agents of shareholding principals is con-strained by these rules); blockholders (whose prerogatives to control corporations are affected by these rules); and minority shareholders (whose property rights are also affected by these rules). Yet two of these actors—managers and blockholders—have both small numbers and converging, concentrated interests. Members of the third group, minority shareholders, generally have diffuse interests and the problem of coordination inherent in large numbers. Given this interest calculus, it is not really all that surprising that managers and blockholders usually win.

The current chapter develops and expands this central point. The next section first reviews the existing literature on the politics of corporate governance. The scholarship discussed has provided an important corrective to work on the origins of ownership in the law and economics literature, which focused on the historical origins of legal systems as the primary determinant of contemporary patterns of share ownership and minority shareholder protection (La Porta et al. 1998; La Porta, López-de-Silanes, and Shleifer 1999). The new theories of politics in corporate governance bring in political agency and possibilities for change over time in individual countries, both of which were absent from the work on legal origins. And indeed, the new theories of corporate governance are not wrong about the politics they describe. They provide different and important lenses for explaining the politics of corporate governance during moments of high political salience. Their mistake lies in taking as a general condition what is really a special case: high political salience is rare and fleeting in the domain of corporate governance. To understand the real political dynamics of the field, we need to endogenize salience. When salience is low, which is the normal state of affairs, we see very different dynamics than during the extraordinary political moments when it is high. I illustrate these theoretical points through the example of the battles over hostile takeover regulation in the Netherlands between 1994 and 2006. The concluding section returns to the modern intellectual origins of work on the structural power of business (Lindblom 1978), considering how an emphasis on policy salience contributes to understanding the advantages enjoyed by business in lobbying in policy domains such as corporate governance.

Existing Theories of the Politics of Corporate Governance

Those scholars who write about the political aspects of corporate governance regulation typically stress two distinct ways of conceptualizing its political dynamics, though each runs through the parliamentary process. The first concentrates on the character of social coalitions that emerge to support legislation calling for change. This interest-based explanation has much to recommend it, and is indeed the default way of thinking for most political scientists: to explain outcomes, look at the interests behind them. The second sort of explanation is also interest based, but not premised on interest coalitions. Instead, this work stresses the importance of political parties—the usual makers of law in parliament—in determining the outcomes observed in corporate governance politics.[1]

Peter Gourevitch and James Shinn's (2005) recent book offers the most compelling statement of the coalitional view of corporate governance politics: "we explain corporate governance outcomes through public policy that is generated by the interaction of interest group preferences and political institutions" (10).[2] The outcome they are most interested in is the market for corporate control: can companies be bought against the will of existing management, and does that happen on a regular basis? While the question of markets for corporate control is sometimes conceptualized as being equivalent to the concentration or dispersion of share ownership, there are some systems in which managers or other shareholders can impede the emergence of hostile takeovers or other threats to their control. Thus, although the data gathered in their exercise are about ownership concentration, the real implicit variable for Gourevitch and Shinn, as for others in this literature, is the activity of the market for corporate control. Thus in the anomalous cases of the Netherlands and Japan, which appear in international comparison to have relatively diffuse shareholding, managers actually use other means to impede the development of an active market for corporate control. Gourevitch and Shinn have correctly identified the variable of greatest concern to scholars of the politics of corporate governance: whether one calls it corporate control or patient capital, as in the varieties of capitalism literature (Hall and Soskice 2001; Amable 2003), this characteristic of control is the outcome on which the national differentiation of systems of corporate governance fundamentally depends.

For Gourevitch and Shinn (2005; hereafter GS), the winning coalition determines the political outcome, i.e., whether markets for corporate control remain limited or become active. There are three potential coalition partners: shareholders, managers, and workers. None of the coalition partners has a unique interest. Workers may side with managers to form a corporatist coalition, when they favor employment protection; or they may instead side with shareholders against management, when the structure of their pension funds is such as to make them more interested in transparency than employment protection (this is the transparency coalition that gets much discussion in GS). Managers may align with workers (to protect themselves from shareholders) or with shareholders (to extract rents from workers). Similarly, shareholders may side with management or workers, depending on their preferences. Thus if the actors are clear but their preferences are indeterminate—which is a faithful rendering of political reality, if an unusual strategy for an interest-based theory—then any coalition is possible. And, in the GS telling, any coalition may win or lose.

However, GS rescue their theory from the realm of untestability by predicting an outcome of a conflict, conditional on a given winner. Thus, if owners and workers ally in a transparency coalition, and if the transparency coalition *wins*, then the outcome should be diffusion, or in different words, an active market for corporate control (2005: 23). Here we move from the frying pan of non-falsifiability to the fire of tautology, since it is not clear what measure of a transparency coalition's "winning" GS use that is independent of the outcome observed. The evidence on such measures is to be found in the dense analytic narratives contained in the later chapters of their book. In the case of France—one of the few cases of change widely accepted by scholars—GS note that many observers "see no political debate over corporate governance issues... That may be quite accurate as a description of the process, but politics plays an important role in allowing it to take place" (270). Well, OK, but what politics? What is it we can observe empirically and independently of the change being explained, to show that a transparency coalition wins in France? In the end, GS conclude their causal argument on France this way: "Overall, the decline of statist ideas on the left and right seem plausibly to explain the movement of French policy" (271). While that may be a correct statement, there is no connection here to the transparency coalition and no evidence of the actors involved in these interest coalitions as actually bringing about the change observed in France. This important example highlights a more general problem in the GS mode of explanation: it is unclear what evidence they could observe that would convince them of the predictions of their model. If the theory is supple enough to take the absence of clear coalitional mobilization in France as evidence that its predictions are borne out, then it is difficult to see how its predictions can usefully be falsified.

In sum, Gourevitch and Shinn elegantly characterize the different possible coalitions among interest groups in corporate governance politics. This is a valuable theoretical contribution. Yet their arguments about the causal determinants of change are difficult to operationalize empirically. Movement forward in this theoretical domain thus requires the deployment of workable empirical strategies. Two approaches seem likely to be most fruitful. The first is to define benchmarks of a "winning coalition"—benchmarks that are independent of the institutional outcomes to be explained by the theory. Of particular importance, given the contemporary state of debate, is how to measure the emergence of a winning transparency coalition, which should then move systems with inactive markets of corporate control toward having more active markets. The second empirical strategy is to subject the interest mechanisms that underlie the theory to scrutiny: is there evidence that actors behave in the political realm in ways consistent with the influence imputed to them? In the case of the transparency coalition, we would expect to see the interest groups that represent workers and shareholders—respectively, unions and minority shareholder associations—especially active in politics.

The partisanship literature is the primary political alternative to the coalitional approach. The pioneer in the partisan approach was Mark Roe (2003), whose book argues that social democracy is not compatible with dispersed ownership. In this view, social peace is the predicate of wealth creation, and countries that gave a prominent role to stakeholder views in politics in the post-war period created incentives for large blocks shareholding. This is because these systems made it difficult for managers to respond to concerns about shareholder value; blockholding was the alternative response to the agency problem facing shareholders. Roe's statistical work then used the significance of left parties in government as a measure of social democracy—which he equated with the stakeholder society—and demonstrated a correlation between the extent of blockholding and the degree of left party control.

Roe's work was pioneering in highlighting the connection between stakeholders and politics. Yet his use of social democracy as a conceptual umbrella for the stakeholder society is problematic. As John Cioffi and Martin Höpner (2006; hereafter CH) show in their work, the stakeholder society in places like Germany and Italy—and the large ownership blockholdings on which it was constructed—were politically assembled by friends of the right, not the left (cf. Höpner 2007). This is the background to Cioffi and Höpner's work on the contemporary period, in which they stress that parties of the left are, contra Roe, the fiercest opponents of patient capital and large blockholding. As an explanation of social change, moreover, they explicitly part company with Gourevitch and Shinn on the relevant actors for political change:

Center-left political actors have taken the lead in advancing corporate governance reform, rather than unions, shareholders, or other interest groups. Shareholders are too poorly organized (as in the United States) or too few in number (in Continental Europe) to constitute an effective coalition partner, while labor remains somewhat ambivalent and peripheral to the politics of financial system and corporate reform.   (Cioffi and Höpner 2006: 491)

Driven by economic changes that bring more of their voters to prefer increased transparency and attacks on patient capital, mainstream parties of the left passed legislation challenging the institutions of patient capital in multiple countries during the 1990s. Rather than being driven by interest groups, as GS claim, Cioffi and Höpner's view is that political parties are the striking arm of corporate reform in the advanced industrial countries.

Empirically, CH show very carefully how parties have pursued legislation in parliament. Their claim that these laws were the product of neither union power nor minority shareholders casts some doubt on the transparency coalition thesis of Gourevitch and Shinn. However, Cioffi and Höpner too easily accept legal change as evidence of institutional change. For example, in the Italian case they assert that "the decade of reform by the centre-left [begun in the 1990s] significantly altered Italian capitalism" (474). Beyond the Italian privatization reform (which affected only the ownership of formerly public companies), there was *no* effect of the left government's policies on the concentration of private shareholding concentration in Italy (Culpepper 2007). The work of CH suffers from the opposite problem to GS. GS stress empirical outcomes (correctly) but do little to show the empirical record of political change. CH, meanwhile, show the empirical record of legal change driven by political parties (correctly), but do not show the empirical changes they sometimes assert in the broader structure of the economy.

These shortcomings have a common root: the occupational inclination of political scientists to observe outcomes in capitalist democracies and then attribute them to democratic politics. It is impossible not to be sympathetic to such a view. If questions are important in their distributive implication, and if they are subject to political regulation, how can it be that their outcome is not a product of the interplay of democratic forces discussed by Gourevitch and Shinn and by Cioffi and Höpner?

THE PROBLEM OF SALIENCE IN POLITICS

One reason is that these scholars all emphasize the role of formal institutions—laws and regulations. Formal institutions are the bread and butter of political scientists and legal scholars, but they comprise only part of the institutional frameworks that structure advanced political economies (Hall and Soskice 2001). Where blockholders exercise control over large shares of companies, they generally dictate the rules of the game for the largest companies, which they control. Thus, in assessing why patient capital broke down in France but did not in Germany or Italy between 1995 and 2005, I have shown in previous work that legal change does not necessarily drive change in informal institutions (Culpepper 2005, 2007). Where blockholders and their managerial agents have concentrated economic power, governments have a limited ability to restructure patterns of private shareholding.[3] Those options they do possess—such as outright nationalization or imposing costs on concentrated ownership of firms—involve serious challenges to property rights. It is true that governments, which are the ultimate guarantors and regulators of property rights, could influence these informal institutions of private shareholding. Yet they do not and have not, notwithstanding the incentives discussed in GS and CH. Even taking account of the durability of informal economic institutions, it is not clear why governments rarely take such steps.

I argue that the answer to this puzzle lies in the role of political salience.[4] Political salience refers to how much the electorate in a democracy cares about a given political issue. Salience is a political construction, but it is one whose foundations generally lie in the structure of material interests. In the world of corporate control politics sketched by Gourevitch and Shinn, the three actors involved—managers, workers, and shareholders—all have an interest winning the political battle over the policy domain. This characterization is not true to the world we actually inhabit. In that world, there are many competing dimensions of politics that attract the attention of potential interest groups. Only those with very intense interests in the rules of corporate control are likely to be willing to pay attention to the complex area of corporate governance regulation. Workers with pension income invested in companies do not have this sort of interest. They are likely to be far more concerned about immediate issues of job protection and wages than the rules that govern companies in which their pension funds own shares. We should therefore expect that workers will be irrelevant voices in the politics of corporate control, both uninterested and unlikely to be heeded when they occasionally do express an interest. With the exception of institutional shareholders, minority shareholders have too small a stake to care. Large individual shareholders *do* care, and they have strong incentive to monitor managers and ensure that managers do not deviate too far from their policy preference. This intensity of preferences thus leads two groups—large shareholders and managers—to have a much more concentrated interest in the outcomes of policy reform than the other actors engaged in the corporate governance arena.

In the partisan world of Cioffi and Höpner, political parties of the left are particularly sensitive to the fact that regimes of patient capital favor managers and the blockholders who support them (where companies are large blockholders, managers are effectively also blockholders). Yet political parties have many policy priorities, and their highest priorities are generally those that win them the most votes, either with their core constituents or with crucial swing voters. In most cases, revisions to rules of shareholding and accounting do not have this sort of priority with parties. Party members may attempt to become policy entrepreneurs, investing in the acquisition of knowledge about the arcana of corporate governance in hopes of using that information draw wider attention to the issue area and to themselves. Yet given the low political salience of corporate governance issues more broadly, the entrepreneur's strategy is a long shot. We generally expect there to be a wide gap between party programs for reforming corporate governance and actual bills implementing that reform.

Recognizing the importance of policy salience helps to understand the poor fit between contemporary theories of politics and the actual politics of corporate ownership and control. First, recognizing the typically low public salience of corporate governance issues allows us to understand why models of coalitional and partisan politics frequently mischaracterize the political maneuvering we actually observe in this policy domain. Those models assume high salience, and at moments of high salience their projected lines of cleavage are indeed likely to emerge. Yet moments of high salience are rare, and thus these models cannot therefore be taken as general models of the politics of corporate governance.

SALIENCE AND THE POLITICS OF CORPORATE CONTROL: A DUTCH ILLUSTRATION

This chapter is not the appropriate forum for a full empirical examination of the role of business in the politics of corporate control.[5] To understand how low salience fundamentally empowers managers and thus affects the contours of corporate politics, this section draws on empirical work I have undertaken on the politics of reform in the Netherlands. The absence of blockholders in the Netherlands makes it a favorable empirical ground for theories that emphasize parliamentary politics and formal rules. Unlike in Italy or Germany, where powerful blockholders can ignore legislation intended to undermine their blockholdings, patient capital in the Netherlands has endured throughout the post-war period without strong concentration of ownership (De Jong and Röell 2005; Gourevitch and Shinn 2005). It seems reasonable to expect that managers in such a system, without the support of blockholding owners, would be heavily reliant on the support from the political system. Thus, the terrain is one that should be favorable for political theories.

Dutch companies, lacking large shareholders, have created a panoply of protections against hostile takeovers. These measures—notably preference shares, but also priority shares and share certification—all serve the function of weakening the effective capacity for control of ordinary shares acquired by a hostile suitor. In 1994, when the first purple coalition came to power in the Netherlands, Liberal Party (VVD) finance minister Gerrit Zalm made the strict limitation of takeover protections a consistent goal of his. The VVD was to control the finance ministry for the next twelve years, giving Zalm multiple potential opportunities to introduce and pass reforms of takeover legislation. He twice introduced such legislation to parliament—once from 1996 to 1998, and once from 2005 to 2006, during the implementation of the European Union's takeover directive. Both times he failed in the wake of a concerted lobbying effort by the organization of managers of Dutch listed companies, the VEUO. When he left office in 2006, he had been unable to introduce any legislation imposing time limits on the use of hostile takeover protections, and a majority of listed companies continued to use preference shares in 2006, a number virtually unchanged since 1993. Why, given his length of tenure and his importance in the government, did Zalm fail in achieving reform in the area of hostile takeover protections?

Gourevitch and Shinn attribute this outcome to the "triumph of the Netherlands' mangers-plus-workers insider coalition" (2005: 186). However, it is unclear the organizational representatives of workers—unions—cared much about the rules on hostile takeover protections. Most negotiations on the content of reform in the Netherlands took place either directly between the government and representatives of managerial organizations or within committees appointed by the government and dominated by managerial organizations. In neither of these fora did unions have any representation. Unions are represented in the Social and Economic Council (SER), the peak corporatist organization that advises the government on issues of general economic policy-making. Yet the SER was sidelined in the politics of hostile takeovers, and there is little evidence of direct union influence. The Labor Party, which Cioffi and Höpner would predict to *lead* the battle for reform, was very much ambivalent about change. Its role was important in defeating the first attempted reform in 1997–8, and it vacillated during the implementation of the EU directive in 2005–6, by which Zalm attempted to limit the duration of all takeover protection mechanisms. Neither Labor (the party) nor labor (the union organization) was a causal factor in defeating Zalm's attempted reforms. The coalition that triumphed was no manager–worker coalition, but simply a manager coalition—managers were the necessary and sufficient members of the coalition to secure its triumph.

Organized managers were able to repel Zalm's attempted reforms through concerted lobbying efforts and their ability to rely on expertise to persuade wavering politicians. In the first reform effort in the 1990s, representatives of the VEUO negotiated the measure with Zalm while simultaneously lobbying his parliamentary colleagues to kill the eventual bill through a procedural maneuver. In an interview with the author, he described the difference of the VEUO from the VNO-NCW, which is the peak lobbying employers' association: "they were not very loyal partners in making deals . . . Probably with the VNO-NCW we could have done business more easily, because they are used to compromise and sticking to compromise." The VEUO, which viewed the conservation of hostile takeover protections as its entire *raison d'être*, had no commitment to corporatist bargaining, only to defense of its members' prerogatives. The power of this lobbying, as summarized by a former VEUO leader, was based on information: "Look, Zalm is not mindless, he just doesn't have any practical business experience. So you offer him your expertise there. Because they are not mindless, you can clarify it for them." In the reform episode of 2005–6, the VEUO made similar use of its legal expertise, swinging the Labor Party to its side by convincing key lawmakers that there was no need for legislation to limit the duration of hostile takeover protections, since courts could always do this. In both instances, the lobbying offensives of the VEUO hung not on the threat of disinvestment—the old Lindblomian structural threat of business—but rather on reasoned (and self-interested) arguments buttressed by their access to substantial expertise.

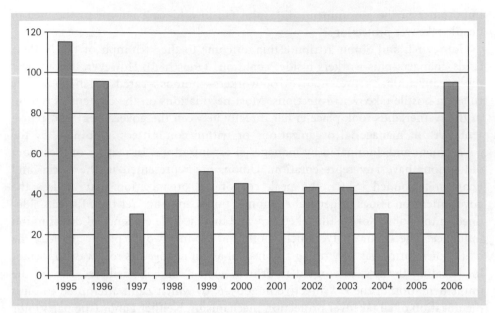

Fig. 21.1 Number of articles per year on takeover protection, 1995–2006

Notes: N = 679. A standard search protocol in Lexis-Nexis identified all articles on this topic in the four most widely read newspapers in the Netherlands—*De Telegraaf, Algemeen Dagblad, De Volkskrant*, and *NRC Handelsblad*, as well as the *Financieele Dagblad*, the business press equivalent of the *Financial Times* or the *Wall Street Journal*. The search terms used were "bescherming! [protection*] and (overname! [takeover*] or bod [bid])." Articles from *De Telegraaf* were only available through Lexis-Nexis from 1999. This search initially yielded 2,727 articles, many of which were on examination not relevant to the issue of takeover protection in the Netherlands. Articles were classified as relevant if they made some mention of the existing Dutch rules on hostile takeover protection. Roughly 25% of the articles (679 of the original 2,727) were relevant to the broader question of takeover rules in the Netherlands.

The ability to use information asymmetries to dominate the debate on reform depends on the generally low public attention paid to the issue of hostile takeover protections in the Netherlands. Fig. 21.1 shows the number of newspaper articles dealing with hostile takeover protection in the Dutch press between 1995 and 2006.

This figure shows the number of articles that appeared *per year* in all five papers on the subject of hostile takeovers. If only one article appeared per month on takeover protection in each of the five papers searched—an extremely low baseline—that would result in an annual figure of sixty articles. Fig. 21.1 illustrates that there were only three years during which the media paid attention to the issue of takeover protection: 1995, 1996, and 2006, which were the years of Zalm's most intense conflict with managers. Even during those three years, there was an average of 102 articles per year dealing with this topic, which means that on average Dutch newspaper readers saw fewer than two articles per month dealing with this subject. These are the sort of political conditions—those of extremely low salience—under which we would expect the lobbying capacity of business to be most successful.

CONCLUSION

Since 1990, managers in France, Germany, Italy, Japan, and the Netherlands have all faced challenges to their systems of ownership. During this time, managers have never lost a legislative battle that has then had effects on private ownership structure. In the first three countries, most of those battles have not taken place in parliament. In the Netherlands, they *did* take place in parliament, and organized managers won every time. In Japan, there was a breakdown of long-term shareholdings, which was tolerated by managers as a useful reallocation of capital. In terms of legal changes allowed, Japanese employer organizations have created the possibility for companies to adopt different board structure, but those organizations have opposed any attempts to make mandatory a move to American board structure (Gilson and Milhaupt 2005; Vogel 2006: 91–5). Once they engaged in political fights over hostile takeover protections, they succeeded in achieving their goals through the Corporate Value Working Group, an informal body convened by a government ministry, in which managerial interests were very well represented.

In all these cases, the politics of corporate control have been dominated by managers and managerial interests. This runs counter to the expectations that emerge from most of the existing literature on the politics of corporate control. Gourevitch and Shinn's coalitional analysis, while theoretically persuasive, does not capture the fact that the force behind the preservation of patient capital in the countries reviewed here is not a corporatist coalition between managers and workers, but managers alone. Rajan and Zingales (2003), who have importantly recognized the power resources of incumbents, nonetheless claim that the major source of financial development is the combination of trade and financial liberalization. The Dutch case, one of the world's most open economies in terms of both trade and investment, suggests that there are many other attributes of managerial power that must be considered. Cioffi and Höpner's analysis of the role of parties of the left in pushing for greater transparency in financial markets is a useful corrective to the mistaken conflation of the "stakeholder society" with "social democracy." Yet their political analysis suffers from an overly formalist structure, glossing over the fact that legal reforms in Germany and Italy were unable to promote a breakdown of existing models of patient capital (Culpepper 2005).

In this chapter I have suggested the failure of many of these theoretical approaches to explain the outcomes observed in national systems of ownership since 1990 lies in their neglect of policy salience. The fact that most people, most of the time, do not care about corporate governance is one of the most powerful factors which allows managerial organizations to dominate it. The complexity of the policy area, combined with the fact that companies constitute the productive tissue of the economy, makes their expertise in corporate governance issues a particularly potent lobbying weapon. Legislators will defer to this expertise in various ways, including in the process of bill-writing and in the decision about which issues to delegate to institutions of private interest governance. Absent a crisis or entrepreneurial effort which renders the rules of corporate control of high public salience, these advantages give managers and their political organizations a systematic advantage in promoting policies that are congruent with their interests and impeding the passage, implementation, and enforcement of policies they oppose.

Corporate politics is not always a low-salience affair. When events or political entrepreneurs give the area much higher salience, the existing literature acquires much surer explanatory footing. The characters of the coalitions described by Gourevitch and Shinn become important determinants of political victory, because the rules of corporate control become politicized. The swing of left parties in favor of transparency and away from supporting patient capital, which Cioffi and Höpner's work has demonstrated, becomes an important factor during these periods of high salience. When corporate politics acquires high salience because of a financial or accounting scandal, such as Enron in the United States or the crisis of 2008, this is especially damaging to managerial power, because it undermines a key source of managerial authority during times of low salience: expertise. Managers will try to influence the character of national discussion during such moments of high salience. Their ability to do so, I suggest, is likely to be contingent on the degree to which their expertise has been compromised. The more the politics of corporate governance is about the politics of financial malfeasance or systematic misperception of credit risks, the poorer the outlook for managerial victory.

The occasional increase in salience in the rules of corporate control is one reason managers do not always win. Even when they do win, managers in different countries may favor different particular arrangements: thus managers may be willing to accommodate a more active market for hostile takeovers because of the wide availability of golden parachutes. The lack of widespread availability of such insurance mechanisms for managers is one reason, among others, why German managers have not been quick to embrace the emergence of an active market for corporate control. So managerial advantages in the policy process are not likely to lead to regulatory convergence across countries over time.

The point of this chapter has been to underline that the literature on the politics of corporate governance has been too quick to conceptualize the policy arenas of capitalist democracies as democratic, but less quick to recognize some of the advantages of capital in the democratic arena. Charles Lindblom's enduring point about the structural advantage of capital—that business does not have to do anything, since politicians know that companies can disinvest if they do not like political decisions—is well remembered in theory. Yet Lindblom enumerated two other powers of business in capitalist democracies—special access to government and the capacity to bias citizens in favor of business preferences (1977: 189–213)—which are less frequently cited (for an exception, see Mitchell 1997). The importance of special access to government matters because of the informational expertise which business possesses and governments need in order to make good policy (cf. Bernhagen and Bräuninger 2005). Studies of the influence of American business on public policy have found that the capacity of framing to influence public opinion is one of the business community's most potent tools (Smith 2000; Guber and Boss 2007). Highlighting the variability of policy salience provides a way to better understand the conditions under which both lobbying and framing tools will be effective. The effectiveness of lobbying declines as salience rises, because rising salience directly increases the visibility of the process (the press starts to care more) and the incentive for policy-makers to develop alternative sources of information. Framing effects, conversely, should increase in relative importance for the business lobby as salience rises, because business is only able to win on high salience issues by bringing public opinion onto its side (Smith 2000).

While this chapter has illustrated some of these processes with empirical examples from recent developments in the Dutch politics of corporate control, these hypo- thetical relationships constitute a research program for the future rather than a set of firm empirical findings. As the chapter has shown, however, the current literature on the politics of corporate governance is faced with a set of empirical developments it has difficulty explaining. The way forward, I have argued, involves a return to the emphasis on the power resources of business and the effects of policy salience on these power resources. These claims also have implications for the literature on comparative political economy. The theoretical emphasis on the institutional differ- ences among types of capitalist democracies, as in the varieties of capitalism litera- ture, has resulted in the development of better conceptual tools for understanding the institutions of national political economies. That literature's emphasis of insti- tutional distinctions should not, however, overshadow commonalities in the way in which business influences economic policy across all different types of capitalist democracies (Swenson 2004). In the area of corporate control and corporate gov- ernance more broadly, there are good reasons to suspect that the political salience of the policy domain is an important variable for understanding the dynamics of political continuity and change.

NOTES

1. Yves Tiberghien's (2007) innovative work on political entrepreneurship in the area of corporate law fits neatly into neither of these conceptual categories. Its focus on the central role of politicians and bureaucrats in effecting institutional change brings it closer to the partisan approach, but its emphasis on the constraining role of inter- national investors on political action owes much to the coalitional mode of explanation. Like both, it tends to concentrate only on institutional changes in the formal legal sphere.
2. Other versions of the coalitional approach are Rajan and Zingales (2003) and Pagano and Volpin (2005).
3. Privatization can be used to affect the structure of shareholding, but the Italian attempt to do so failed in the late 1990s (Culpepper 2007).

4. The next few paragraphs summarize and draw on an argument developed fully in the manuscript of my forthcoming book. James Q. Wilson (1974, 1980) was a pioneer of the study of salience in American regulatory politics.
5. In addition to the previously cited work by Gourevitch and Shinn, Roe, and Cioffi and Höpner, see the following work for more complete empirical results on the political dynamics of changes and continuity in national systems of ownership: Culpepper (2005, 2007, forthcoming); O'Sullivan (2007); Deeg (2005); Tiberghien (2007); and Aoki, Jackson, and Miyajima (2007).

References

AMABLE, B. 2003. *The Diversity of Modern Capitalism*. Oxford: Oxford University Press.

AOKI, M., JACKSON, G., and MIYAJIMA, H., eds. 2007. *Corporate Governance in Japan: Institutional Change and Organizational Diversity*. New York: Oxford University Press.

BERNHAGEN, P., and BRÄUNINGER, T. 2005. "Structural power and public policy: a signaling model of business lobbying in democratic capitalism," *Political Studies* 53(1): 43–64.

CALLAGHAN, H. 2009. "Insiders, outsiders and the politics of corporate governance: how ownership structure shapes party positions in Britain, Germany and France," *Comparative Political Studies* 42(6).

CIOFFI, J. W., and HÖPNER, M. 2006. "The political paradox of finance capitalism: interests, preferences, and centre-left party politics in corporate governance reform," *Politics & Society* 34(4): 463–502.

CULPEPPER, P. D. 2005. "Institutional change in contemporary capitalism: coordinated financial systems since 1990," *World Politics* 57: 173–99.

—— 2007. "*Eppure, non si muove*: legal change, institutional stability and Italian corporate governance," *West European Politics* 30(4): 7843–802.

—— Forthcoming. *Quiet Politics: Business Power and Corporate Control*. Cambridge: Cambridge University Press.

DEEG, R. 2005. "Remaking Italian capitalism? The politics of corporate governance reform," *West European Politics* 28(3): 5213–48.

DE JONG, A., and RÖELL, A. 2005. "Financing and control in the Netherlands: a historical perspective," in R. K. Morck, ed., *A History of Corporate Governance around the World*. Chicago: University of Chicago Press, 467–506.

GILSON, R. J., and MILHAUPT, C. J. 2005. "Choice as regulatory reform: the case of Japanese corporate governance," *American Journal of Comparative Law* 51.

GOUREVITCH, P. A., and SHINN, J. 2005. *Political Power and Corporate Control: The New Global Politics of Corporate Governance*. Princeton: Princeton University Press.

GUBER, D. L., and BOSS, C. J. 2007. "Framing ANWR: citizens, consumers, and the privileged position of business," in M. E. Kraft and S. Kaminiecki, eds., *Business and Environmental Policy*. Boston: MIT Press, 35–60.

HALL, P. A., and SOSKICE, D., eds. 2001. *Varieties of Capitalism: The Institutional Foundations of Comparative Advantage*. New York: Oxford University Press.

HÖPNER, M. 2003. *Wer beherrscht die Unternehmen?* New York: Campus Verlag.

—— 2007. "Corporate governance reform and the German party paradox," *Comparative Politics* 39(4).

LA PORTA R., LÓPEZ-DE-SILANES, F., and SHLEIFER, A. 1999. "Corporate ownership around the world," *Journal of Finance* 54(2): 471–517.

—— —— —— and VISHNY, R. 1998. "Law and finance," *Journal of Political Economy*, 106(6): 1113–55.

LINDBLOM, C. E. 1977. *Politics and Markets: The World's Political-Economic Systems*. New York: Basic Books.

MITCHELL, N. J. 1997. *The Conspicuous Corporation: Business, Public Policy, and Representative Democracy*. Ann Arbor: University of Michigan Press.

O'SULLIVAN, M. 2007. "Acting out institutional change: understanding the recent transformation of the French financial system," *Socio-Economic Review* 5(3): 389–436.

PAGANO, M., and VOLPIN, P. 2005. "The political economy of corporate governance," *American Economic Review* September: 1005–30.

RAJAN, R. G., and ZINGALES, L. 2003. *Saving Capitalism from the Capitalists*. Princeton: Princeton University Press.

ROE, M. J. 2003. *Political Determinants of Corporate Governance: Political Context, Corporate Impact*. Oxford: Oxford University Press.

SMITH, M. A. 2000. *American Business and Political Power*. Chicago: University of Chicago Press.

SWENSON, P. A. 2004. "Varieties of capitalist interests: power, institutions and the regulatory welfare state in the United States and Sweden," *Studies in American Political Development* 18: 1–29.

TIBERGHIEN, Y. 2007. *Entrepreneurial States: Reforming Corporate Governance in France, Japan, and Korea*. Ithaca, NY: Cornell University Press.

VOGEL, S. K. 2006. *Japan Remodeled: How Government and Industry are Reforming Japanese Capitalism*. Ithaca, NY: Cornell University Press.

WILSON, J. Q. 1974. *Political Organizations*. New York: Basic Books.

—— ed. 1980. *The Politics of Regulation*. New York: Basic Books.

CHAPTER 22

CORPORATE SOCIAL RESPONSIBILITY AND GOVERNMENT

JEREMY MOON
NAHEE KANG
JEAN-PASCAL GOND

INTRODUCTION

OUR chapter title might appear oxymoronic as many definitions of corporate social responsibility (CSR) specify that it occurs beyond the requirements of government or the law (McGuire 1963; McWilliams and Siegel 2002). From this perspective CSR, often in the form of philanthropy, would be conceptualized as a form of *self-government* alongside a public system of government. Thus, government and CSR could coexist but reflect no obvious relationship. However, there is a view that CSR is not in a dichotomous relationship with government but, rather, it is embedded in systems of governance (Moon and Vogel 2008) reflecting social relations and hierarchies (Granovetter 1985) and state action (Polanyi 2001).

A recent typology distinguished "political" CSR theories which, in distinction to "instrumental, ethical and integrative theories', reflect "business's relationship with society and its responsibility in the political arena associated with this power" (Garriga and Melé 2004: 51). These theories include "corporate constitutionalism" (Davis 1967); "integrative social contract theory" (Donaldson and Dunfee 1994) and "corporate citizenship" (Davis 1973; Moon, Crane, and Matten 2005). Taking this political view of CSR and the firm further, Crane, Matten and Moon (2008) argue that corporations have very important, if not easily reconcilable, roles: in being like citizens, in governing human citizenship, and in constituting arenas for humans to play out their citizenship roles. These political views of CSR explain the focus on CSR and government.

However, CSR varies by context reflecting *governmental* factors (e.g., institutions, regulatory strategies) as well as *business* factors (e.g. leadership, firm, sector, company stakeholders) and *societal* factors (e.g. cultural and ethical norms, civil society institutions, social demands). Its specific manifestations and motivations therefore vary and an all-embracing definition is problematical. We see CSR as concerning the contribution of business to social (including environmental) welfare in the context of varied government–society–business relationships (the third section outlines debates about CSR).

Albareda, Lozano, and Ysa (2007) distinguish a range of explanations for recent governmental interest in CSR: globalization and the new economy (Zadek 2001); the welfare state crisis (Midttun 2005); the relational state and new governance (Moon 2002); new social demands (Kjaergaard and Westphalen 2001); national competitiveness and innovation (Hodge 2006); and sustainable development (European Commission 2006). Former UK Minister for CSR Margaret Hodge explained that "we [the government] want to see businesses take account of their economic, social and environmental impacts... [in order to]... ensure their longer term sustainability" (Hodge 2006: 100).

Our purpose is to distinguish different types of CSR–government relationship and to understand these in the context of broader state roles and government–business relations. We investigate these relationships comparatively, historically, and in terms of new institutionalism. We do so comparatively by investigating CSR and government in four types of political system on the assumption that CSR reflects features of respective national business systems, or varieties of capitalism, in which government roles are critical (Chapple and Moon 2005; Chapple et al. 2008; Matten and Moon 2008). Thus we consider CSR in the USA (the second section), in Europe (the third section), in transitional economies of East Asia, Eastern Europe, and South Africa (the fifth section), and globally (the sixth section). Our special focus on the USA is justified because, although business responsibilities have long existed throughout the world, in America the concept of CSR emerged as a basis for reflection on its relation to the wider purpose of the firm in the context of institutions of governance.

Our study is historical in that each section addresses the dynamic aspects of CSR in terms of the issues addressed and the modes adopted, as well as with reference to CSR–government relationships. There is, of course, a problem in retrospectively identifying CSR before the term was adopted in different national business systems (third and fourth sections). However, our approach is inclusive in order to bring to light the full range of business contributions to social welfare.

We locate CSR in the context of the new institutional theory. New institutionalism is a large literature (Hall and Taylor 1996; Campbell and Pedersen 2001; Schmidt 2002) and, given our interest in comparative and historical organizational analyses, we align with the historical and organizational institutionalism, rather than the rational choice variant. Therefore, we view CSR as an institution of rules, regulations, established practices, and values and norms embedded in the historical trajectory and organizational structure of the polity and political economy (Hall and Taylor 1996).

We distinguish six types of CSR–government relationship which reflect different balances of governmental and business responsibility (Table 22.1).

CSR as a form of *self-government* operates alongside government and conforms with a traditional, philanthropic view of CSR in which business makes discretionary contributions to society quite independent of government. These contributions often reflect more societal than governmental business relationships and thus the contributions of business are akin to those of citizens providing mutual support (Crane, Matten, and Moon 2008: ch. 2).

Governments can go further and *endorse* CSR through speeches and other means of attaching their imprimatur to business contributions to society (e.g., awards, kitemarks). In the 1990s Australian and Danish governments introduced peak business leaders' fora to enable government to engage business on topics of their responsibility. A stronger form of endorsement is in public procurement policies (McCrudden 2007) which encourage business responsibility through access to public

Table 22.1 Six government–CSR relationships

Relationship type	Features
1. CSR as self-government	Corporate discretion independent of but alongside government (e.g., philanthropic contributions to society, business strategies for CSR)
2. CSR as endorsed by government	Governments encourage CSR through rhetoric and selective policies (e.g., governmental imprimatur, public procurement)
3. CSR as facilitated by government	Governments provide incentives for CSR (e.g., subsidies, tax expenditures) or allocate organizational resources
4. CSR as a partnership with government	Governments and business organizations (and often civil society) combine their resources and objectives
5. CSR as mandated by government	Governments regulate for CSR (e.g., to report their social, environmental, and ethical impacts)
6. CSR as a form of government	Firms act as if they were governments where there are government deficits (e.g., in pre-welfare state; post-privatization; global governance; new/"wicked" issues)

Source: Adapted from Fox, Ward, and Howard (2002); and Crane, Matten, and Moon (2008).

sector markets which set requirements of product source and workforce compos-ition, for example.

Governments can *facilitate* CSR through subsidies to firms which adopt particular social policies (e.g., for employment or training of unemployed people) or to business associations which advocate, advance, and implement corporate social responsibility (Moon and Richardson 1985). A common form of facilitation is through tax incentives for corporate charitable giving.

The *partnership* relationship between government and CSR can reflect collaboration of governmental organizations with companies or with business associations. There is often a mix of resources such that governments bring fiscal and regulatory capacity whereas companies bring their networks, employees, and knowledge to bear in address-ing problems. This feature of new governance (Moon 2002) often entails partnerships with civil society organizations representing communities, religious or labor organiza-tions or the environment. They bring their close understanding of social expectations and of social problems as well as legitimation to the partnerships. Partnerships can be developed to address local issues (e.g., local economic partnerships); national issues (e.g., the UK's CSR Academy to improve SMEs' understanding of CSR); and even global issues (e.g. the US Apparel Industry Partnership, the UK Ethical Trade Initiative).

Although the idea of governmental *mandate* of CSR is counter-intuitive as it appears to obviate corporate discretion, there are a number of reasons to include this relationship. First, governments have used "soft law" to encourage CSR, often as a means of experimenting with new approaches to business responsibility. As noted by Ayres and Braithewaite (1992), the resource of regulation can be used in a variety of ways which fall short of coercion and punishment. For example, a number of governments have required companies to report their social, environmental, and ethical impacts without specifying what particular behavior they deem responsible. Second, a number of governments have underpinned various regulations with the rhetoric of CSR in order to legitimate these.

CSR as an *alternative* form of government is often negatively regarded as a usurpation of the proper responsibilities of government and as undermining the democratic accountability whether from the right (Friedman 1970) or the left (Monbiot 2001; Hertz 2002). However, companies often act in government-like ways which are not necessarily malign (Crane et al. 2008: ch. 3). First, corporations can provide social benefits (e.g., recreation opportunities, library and education facilities for workers, their families, and communities). This has happened in the nineteenth-century UK prior to the emergence of the welfare state (Moon 2004); following the reduction or withdrawal of government services (e.g., in Kenya, see Muthuri et al. 2008) or where there are serious governance deficits, often in developing countries as well as in transitional economies. Globalization is another sphere where governments, national or inter-national, have proved unwilling or unable to regulate cross-border activities. So, global companies have jointly or severally taken to governing environmental and social conditions in their supply chain by regulating other businesses (the sixth section). Companies can also act like governments in the way they address a host of new issues for which regulation may be premature or too blunt an instrument.

In reality government policies and CSR initiatives often reflect several of these relationships. Moreover, the relationships that we posit often overlie one another. Most obviously, CSR as self-regulation is fundamental to all the relationships. This holds even, paradoxically, where CSR is mandated by government. Partnerships often also reflect CSR as self-government, as endorsed by government and as facilitated by government (i.e., relationship types 1, 2, and 3—Table 22.1).

Having defined CSR, and identified various types of government–CSR relationships, we continue by introducing the American origins of CSR.

AMERICAN ORIGINS OF CSR

Although diverse forms of philanthropic activities have emerged in virtually all countries affected by the Second Industrial Revolution, the US provided the birthplace of the idea of CSR as we know it today (Bowen 1953; Heald 1970; Frederick 2006, 2008; Carroll 2008). Notwithstanding developments therein, in contrast to CSR in other countries, in the US it has mainly been "CSR as self government" (Relationship type 1—Table 22.1).

Four socio-cultural factors shaped the CSR doctrine and explain the maintenance of a strong interest in social responsibility in the US over the last century (Pasquero 2004: 259–62). First, CSR appeared to bridge the gap between private interests and the management of public good in an individualistic market: it avoided more socialized forms of regulation while limiting the moral failures and social damage of a pure laissez-faire system. (Bowen 1953: 14–21). Second, the idea of CSR was compatible with American traditions of democratic pluralism eulogized by de Tocqueville, where associations, pressure groups, and media lobby corporations in order to promote social causes. In this context, private initiatives drive the management of public good, and governmental regulation followed. Third, the notion of CSR drew on America's moralist and Puritan traditions. Social responsibility was presented as an application of Protestant ethics to economic life by some of its early promoters (Bowen 1953), thus illustrating Weber's (1930) thesis of the selective affinities of various branches of Protestantism and capitalism. Finally, CSR reflected the utilitarian and pragmatic ideals of America, a society that has always valued action and has seen corporations as a legitimate and important source of economic and social innovation.

The move of CSR from a businessmen's doctrine to an academic concept can be understood in the context of the emergence of the modern corporation as an organizational form (Chandler 1977), and the legitimation of American capitalism (Heald 1961, 1970; Carroll 2008). This transformation of social responsibility from philanthropy to CSR can be explained through a five-stage process (Table 22.2).

Table 22.2 The constitution of a social responsibility doctrine in the USA

Period	Stage of development	Key concepts	Corporate legitimacy	Main motivations
1880–1900	Embryonic. Emergence of philanthropy	Philanthropy rooted in paternalism	Not at stake—actions responding to individual motives	Mixed: religious (ethical roots), economic interest
1900–20	Corporate philanthropy as a pre-SR idea	Stewardship, public service mobilized by corporations	Criticism of corporations (muckrakers, etc.)	Public relations, favorable public opinion
1920–9	Constitution of the basic set of ideas on which the SR doctrine is built	Trusteeship, business as a partnership between capital, labor, management, community	Visibility of corporate activities. Managers' social prestige	Public relations, self-regulation, business case for ethics
1929–45	Collapse of corporate responsibility discourses	No new concept. State framing of Social Responsibility	Loss of credibility post-1929 crisis	Responding to govermental injunctions
1945–60	Resurgence of the SR doctrine, theorization of CSR	Resurgence of trusteeship, extension in business social responsibility	Restoration of corporate prestige, alternative to communism, legitimation of power	Superiority of self-regulation over public regulation, reinforcing public support for capitalism

Source: Adapted from Gond (2006: 20).

Philanthropic activities were driven by a mix of practical considerations and religious motives to "give back" to society (e.g., Andrew Carnegie's *Wealth 1889*). However, the diffusion of philanthropy and its transformation from a personal gesture to an organizational concern was critical to the birth of social responsibility as a modern ideology. As Heald (1970: 19) explains, "[w]hat the nineteenth century lacked, and what the twentieth was to supply, was a rationale—a concept of the relationship of business to the community—in which social responsibility was clearly seen as a charge not merely upon individual conscience and concern, but upon corporate resources as well."

During the Progressive years (1890–1920) the first antitrust laws to control business power and discipline markets were introduced. The corporate giants were attacked on multiple fronts: by reformists, fearful of threats to small merchants from big corporations (Cochoy 1999), by labor unions, by intellectuals, and ultimately by journalists (e.g., muckrakers who investigated corporate wrongdoing) (Pasquero 2005). Therefore, corporations began to acknowledge the importance of creating confidence in the "general public" in order to minimize the danger of governmental interference (Heald 1970: 27–34; Pasquero 2005: 88).

During the economic prosperity of the 1920s, the idea of social responsibility was consolidated through the concepts of trusteeship (i.e., obligations for managing others' property as if it was one's own and to care for society's needs through property management), and of business as a form of partnership (Bowen 1953: 33). Moreover, the emergence of a class of professional managers dissociated from corporate owners (Berle and Means 1932) gave rise to the first industrial codes of conduct as a means for managers to affirm their professional autonomy and to promote self-government and self-regulation (Heald 1970: 83–116).

From the onset of the Great Depression in 1929, corporations were criticized for their role in the financial catastrophe (Heald 1970). New Deal policies encouraged the adoption of new forms of self-regulation promoting a "legally framed" form of social responsibility (Pasquero 2005). This was a rare example of American CSR being mandated by government (relational type 5—Table 22.1).

The post-war resurgence of the idea of social responsibility was underpinned by the view that corporations had been critical to the victory in war and thus regained their social prestige. Social responsibility came to be theorized in academia, driven in large part by the Cold War context (Heald 1970: 271–308; Frederick 2006) in which some viewed CSR as an instrument to defend capitalism and oppose communism (Randall 1952). Others, however, saw CSR as a dangerous step toward socialism threatening the foundations of free capitalist societies (Friedman 1962, 1970). Nonetheless, in this period, the scale and range of social responsibility activities increased and expanded to new domains such as education.

This overview of the development of the social responsibility doctrine in the US reflects its strong socio-cultural and political embeddedness. It contextualizes the academic debates of the 1950s over the meaning of CSR to which we now turn.

DEFINING CORPORATE SOCIAL RESPONSIBILITY

Howard Bowen's (1953) *Social Responsibilities of the Businessman* marks the entry of the academic concept of CSR (Wood 1991; Carroll 1999, 2008; Frederick 2006; Crane et al. 2008a). Bowen delivers a systematic account of businessmen's self-perceptions of their social responsibilities, an analysis of the overlaps and mismatches of this doctrine with Protestant ethics, a historical study of the institutionalization of this doctrine in the US, and well-balanced and authoritative account of the potential and limitations of CSR as self regulation (Acquier and Gond 2007). Bowen conceptualizes social responsibility as a third way between pure laissez-faire and state regulation, and evaluates the potential of corporate action to enhance society's welfare. He provides a first definition of social responsibility as "the obligations for the business men to pursue those policies, to make those decisions, or to follow those lines of action which are desirable in terms of the objectives and values of our society" (6). Accordingly, most CSR definitions of the 1950s and 1960s stress those corporate activities that are oriented toward the broad social environment, beyond the technical, economic, and legal activities of business (Carroll 1999, 2008).

The subsequent academic debates were around the shortcomings of CSR such as the power over society that corporations may derive from this concept (Levitt 1958) or the agency problems that underlie and potentially undermine it (Friedman 1962, 1970). This latter debate partly replicates Dodd and Berle's controversy over the legal definition of corporate objectives. The corporation as a legal entity has been seen either as a shareholder creature dedicated to profit maximization or as serving a broader set of interests (for recent updates, see Freeman, Wicks, and Parmar 2004; Sundaram and Inkpen 2004). This debate, together with the emergence of business ethics as an academic field, underpinned the continuing controversy among and between the defenders and critics of CSR.

In the 1970s and 1980s, research moved from CSR's normative foundations to issues of CSR management. This shift was described by Frederick (1978) as a move from the "old" corporate social responsibility, or CSR-1, to the "new" concept of corporate social responsiveness, or CSR-2, and focused on the actual management of external pressures by corporate executives. Second, there was a move to the concept of Corporate Social Performance (CSP) (Carroll 1979; Wartick and Cochran 1985; Wood 1991) that integrated competing approaches to CSR such as Friedman's narrow economic view of CSR with ethicists' broad approach to CSR or CSR-1 and CSR-2. In line with Carroll's (1979) seminal integrative paper, several authors developed this line of research, refining the CSP framework to encompass developments in the strategy field and ethical theories (Wood 1991; Swanson 1995, 1999).

Most attempts to integrate CSR concepts and theories failed to provide a strong unifying paradigm (Gond and Matten 2007; Gond and Crane 2008). Some recent works persist with a positivist ideal (Schwartz and Carroll 2008) and CSP research moved from business and society relationships to the actual assessment of CSR impacts and policies. A third, empirical, research stream is mainly concerned with the analysis of the relationships between CSR and financial performance. It generated a corpus of more than 160 empirical studies that suggest a weak, but nevertheless positive, relationship between social and financial performance (Margolis and Walsh 2003; Orlitzky, Rynes, and Schmidt, 2003; Margolis, Elfenbein, and Walsh 2007; Orlitzky 2008).

Despite these important efforts at consolidating CSR research, the multiplication of concepts and theories for corporation–society relationships, the field remains fragmented (Waddock 2004; Gond 2006; Lockett, Moon, and Visser 2006). Figure 22.1 illustrates this through the unfolding of CSR concepts from corporate philanthropy to the more recent managerial (e.g., *Triple Bottom Line* coined by Elkington 1997; *Corporate Stakeholder Responsibility* proposed by Freeman, Wicks, and Parmar 2004) or more political (Scherer and Palazzo 2007, 2008; Crane et al. 2008b) conceptions of CSR.

As the new conceptualizations of CSR do not restrict the use of previous concepts this progression leaves a dozen or so current usages informing Garriga and Melé's (2004) observation that the CSR field "presents not only a landscape of theories, but also a proliferation of approaches, which are controversial, complex and unclear" (51).

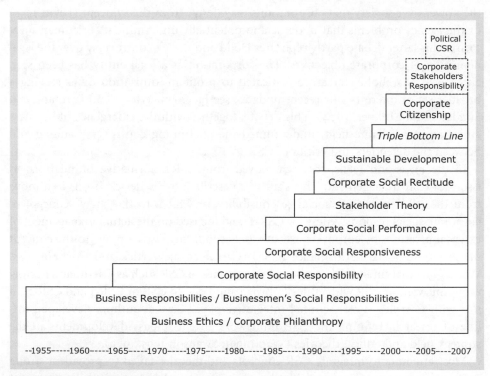

Fig. 22.1 Defining CSR, multiplying the concepts
Sources: Adapted from Mohan (2003).

Thus, Garriga and Melé (2004) more modestly mapped the field and classified the CSR theories and concepts into four categories: *Instrumental CSR theories, Political CSR theories, Integrative CSR theories,* and *Ethical CSR theories.*

Instrumental theories refer to research demonstrating CSR's contribution to corporate performance aligning CSR with the maximization of shareholder value (e.g., cause-related marketing—Varadarajan and Menon 1998; bottom of the pyramid—Prahalad and Hammond 2002). Political CSR focuses on theories stressing corporate power in CSR theorizing (e.g., corporate constitutionalism—Davis 1967; corporate citizenship—Logsdon and Wood 2002; Moon, Crane, and Matten 2005). Integrative CSR theories aim to integrate all business and society relationships into a single framework (e.g., Corporate Social Performance; Stakeholder Theory). Ethical theories encompass normative works defining the moral foundations of CSR (e.g., universal rights, sustainable development, normative stakeholder theories—Donaldson and Preston 1995).

This typology also brings difficulties. First, it reifies functionalism by defining perspectives on CSR according to Parsons's (1967) theory. Second, many categories overlap. Third, the typology is more retrospective than prospective. Gond and Matten (2007) aim to take CSR theory building forward by stressing the recurrent tensions in CSR research and adapting Burrell and Morgan's (1979) grid of analysis of social sciences paradigms to distinguish four alternative views on CSR. They see the *functionalist perspective* as focusing on regulative tools to integrate business and society. The *socio-political perspective* approach sees CSR as a power relationship, and focuses on CSR's role in the reconfiguring government, business, and society relationships (Moon and Vogel 2008). The *culturalist approach* is sensitive to the national, cultural, and institutional determinants of CSR and the translation of an American conception into multinational variants. Finally, they posit a *constructionist approach* that focuses on the social enactment of CSR as an organizational field.

Having discussed the US origins of CSR as self-regulation (relational type 1—Table 22.1), and its various evolutionary trajectories, we now address how CSR has moved to Western Europe and beyond, and highlight its relationship to government in this process of globalization.

European Traditions and Translations of CSR

Shared traditions and contrasting trajectories of CSR

Given that the "most similar" social, political, and economic systems to those in the US are in Western Europe, the question arises as to whether they have had a similar CSR history. Although there were instances of industrial paternalism and philanthropy, especially in the nineteenth century, there was little else to compare with the twentieth-century US developments. Does this mean that European businesses were necessarily less responsible than their American counterparts? In short, for most of the twentieth century, European business responsibilities were more "implicit" in wider, government-led, governance systems (Matten and Moon 2008). However, with changing roles of governments and modes of governance in the last quarter of the last century, and new institutional pressures and challenges faced by the MNCs, new forms of more "explicit" CSR have emerged, albeit with distinctive European features (Maignan and Ralston 2002; Matten and Moon 2008).[1]

There were some philanthropic traditions in Europe, particularly where industrialization preceded the welfare state such as the UK (Marinetto 1999; Moon 2004), the Netherlands (Cramer 2005), and France (Beaujolin and Capron 2005). This was sometimes associated with religious convictions of business leaders as well as reflecting some of the imperatives of industrialization, such as maintaining a loyal and functioning workforce (Rowlinson and Hassard 1993). Policies usually consisted of the provision of social and economic infrastructure for their workers and families, such as housing, education, and bathing and recreational facilities. However, the advent of the welfare state from the late nineteenth to early twentieth centuries tended to replace business provision. Where industrialization tended to parallel or follow the growth of the welfare state (e.g., Germany, Scandinavia), there was little evidence of the corporate philanthropy claimed explicitly by business in the US.[2] Rather, the responsibilities of business were driven or framed by the state in a style more reminiscent of the New Deal period in the US (second section above).

These contrasting trajectories of twentieth-century business responsibility can be understood with reference to the respective national business systems (Whitley 1999, 2002). European national business systems have tended to be characterized by more concentrated financial systems, more regulated education and labor systems, and cultural systems more skeptical about business and confident about government. This has informed differences in the nature of European firms which are more networked, directed, and sometimes publicly owned. European markets have been more organized and coordinated by varying balances of neo-corporatist and state forces, and their governance systems have reflected the influence of their stronger labor unions. As a result, the responsibilities of business have been implied in wider institutions of organizational responsibility be they state-led, norms endorsed and reinforced by business associations, or outcomes of neo-corporatist processes. These have covered many of the areas which in the US have been areas of corporate discretion such as environmental protection, health insurance, training, higher education, the arts, and community services (Matten and Moon 2008).

However, more recently European companies have taken more explicit responsibilities (i.e., the shift to relational type 1—Table 22.1) rather than rely on the legitimacy derived from their wider governance contexts. This we attribute to three related sorts of institutional change: first, shifts in the broad national governance systems, albeit at different rates and from different starting points (Moon 2002); second, organizational challenges associated with the imperatives of managing increasingly global corporations (DiMaggio and Powell 1983; Meyer et al. 1997; Meyer 1999, 2000); and, third the deliberate import and translation of CSR practices and objects from the US to Europe by the "CSR entrepreneurs" aiming either at reforming local institutions (e.g., Boxenbaum and Battilana 2005; Boxenbaum 2006) or at building new CSR markets (e.g., Boxenbaum and Gond 2006). Table 22.3 summarizes these developments in social responsibilities in Western Europe and enables comparison with Table 22.2.

As a result, the roles of governments have tended to decline in terms of size and change in terms of mode. First, the share of the economy accounted for by public sectors has tended to decline. Relatedly, the privatization of erstwhile public companies and utilities has led to increased expectations of business responsibility. Second, the prevailing trend towards deregulation has encouraged governments to rely less on their authority and more on markets, contracts for government, and partnerships with for- and non-profit organizations.

As European governments are no longer the only source of welfare, societies are increasingly turning to companies or, indeed, blaming them for their irresponsibility. The wider organizational fields of companies have changed in other ways such that labor unions are less able to secure nationwide employee protection and remuneration, and neo-corporatist policy-making systems have become less hierarchical and consensual, affording more business discretion and self-regulation (Molina and Rhodes 2002). Likewise, the greater "financialization" of European economies (Taino, Huolman, and Pulkkinen 2001) has encouraged companies to seek to differentiate themselves from their competitors and has given greater scope to the drivers of socially responsible investment. Third, consumers are including social estimations in their purchasing choices which has, in turn, led to the emergence of a set of new institutions under the broad umbrella of "fair trade" (Micheletti 2003).

Turning to organizational pressures for CSR (DiMaggio and Powell 1983; Meyer et al. 1997) three key factors can be noted. First, it is the subject of numerous "coercive isomorphisms" in the form of soft, social, and self-regulation. These include various intergovernmental initiatives (e.g., the OECD Guidelines for Multi-National Companies, the United Nations Global Compact) and collective business initiatives (e.g., the Global Reporting Initiative). Second, it is also the subject of "mimetic processes" whereby European businesses join business associations for CSR, sign up to new principles, codes, and standards (e.g., Business in the Community, UK). Third, new normative pressures for business responsibility and engagement have emerged with such issues as sustainable development (by environmental and development NGOs) and labor standards in supply chains (by human rights NGOs). These are not only highlighted by a sometimes critical media, but are then addressed by business and professional associations, business schools, business media, and non-government and government organizations with whom companies interact.

Finally, these trends have been reinforced by micro-processes of translations whereby entrepreneurial actors imported US-based CSR practices and products to European countries. Thus, CSR as an idea has travel from the US to other countries, and has usually been altered and transformed in this process to better fit social issues

Table 22.3 The changing social responsibility doctrine in Western Europe

Period	Stage of development	Key concept	Corporate legitimacy	Main motivations
1880–1900	Spread of industrialization; philanthropy	Self government: philanthropy/paternalism alongside regulatory state	Context of labor movements, industrial regulation	Mixed: religious, legitimacy, productivity
1900–45	Growth of welfare state; narrowing of business SR	Self-government: philanthropy/paternalism alongside various state forms	Contested by labor/socialist movements/governments; incorporated in fascist systems	Legitimacy (often linked with nationalism)
1945–80	Consolidation of welfare state; expansion of industrial state; growth of neo-corporatism; narrowing of business SR	Implicit role in enabling and mandating government / modest self-government in philanthropy	Incorporation in mixed economy / welfarism	Legitimized in social democracy / Christian democracy / liberalism / conservatism. Marginal values–led motivation
1980–2000	Liberalization/privatization/ globalization yields wider corporate discretion	Explicit CSR: community, market, workplace, environment	Global citizenship; focus on individual firm (as opposed to business)	Legitimacy, stakeholder approval, business strategy
2000–	Globalization and travel of CSR ideas and concepts	Translation of explicit CSR products and practices	Legitimating state reforms Developing CSR markets	Mixed motives (profit + SR) Business case approach

Source: Authors' own.

of the new context (Czarniawska and Joerges 1996; Latour 2005). Boxenbaum and Battilana (2005) highlighted the activity of innovators/translators in the process whereby the CSR practice of diversity management has been imported from the US to Denmark in the early 2000s. In a further study Boxenbaum (2006) analyzes the whole reconstruction process of "explicit" CSR during its move from US to Denmark. Finally, Boxenbaum and Gond (2006) have clarified the repertoire of micro-strategies of contextualization used by entrepreneurs to adapt Socially Responsible Investment practices built in US to France. This stream of research suggests that contemporary "explicit CSR" diffusion works not only through the diffusion of practices as such, but rather through micro-level processes of globalization "by the bottom," whereby explicit CSR is reconstructed to fit with and build on the traditional "implicit CSR" institutions.

Notwithstanding elements of convergence between West European and North American CSR, some differences persist. First, corporatist traditions continue to prevail and CSR in Europe is more closely organized with and through business associations, be they national or even European (e.g., CSR Europe). Second and most significantly in this context, West European CSR is much more closely aligned with government policies, both as objects of government policy and as partners with government (relational types 2 to 5—Table 22.1). This could be at the regional, national or EU levels. Albareda, Lozano, and Ysa (2007) conclude that all (fifteen) European governments' policies for CSR are "relational" in that they were designed to improve collaboration between governments and business and civil society stakeholders. These policies are generally intended "to improve awareness of the business sector, promote and facilitate voluntary initiatives, capacity building, stakeholder management, international standards, convergence and transparency, evaluation and accountability, tax and funding systems in addition to legislation." (Albareda, Lozano, and Ysa 2007: 395–6).

Having examined broad transatlantic CSR differences and some recent instances of convergence, we now examine intra-European contrasts.

Intra-European contrasts

The UK is regarded as leading in European (and global) CSR (Vogel 2005), and also as having the most advanced public policies for CSR (Aaronson 2003; *CSR Navigator* 2007). The UK combines well-established CSR as self-government with a wide range of government policies designed to encourage CSR often in the combined forms of endorsement, facilitation, partnerships and mandate (Moon 2004) (Table 22.4). Government policies also put great stress on the contribution of CSR to national competitiveness (Hodge 2006) and on the international responsibilities of UK companies, as illustrated by the Ethical Trade Initiative.

Perhaps reflecting their more embedded neo-corporatist industrial policies, Denmark, Finland, the Netherlands, and Sweden put greater stress upon co-responsibility for an inclusive society and dynamic labor market and thus CSR is more likely to reflect partnership relations with government. Sweden is also a leader in CSR,

Table 22.4 Changing government–business relations and CSR in Europe

	Direction of change (see Table 22.1)	Key drivers of CSR	Key issues of CSR
UK	From self-government to endorsement, facilitation, partnership, mandate	Firm, market, civil society, government	Global, domestic/ community, market, workplace, environment, legitimacy, sustainability
Denmark, Finland, the Netherlands, Sweden	From negligible relationships, self-government (the Netherlands) to partnership	Government, firm (the Netherlands)	Global, domestic/ competitiveness, legitimacy, labor markets, sustainability
Austria, Belgium, Germany, Luxembourg	From negligible relationships to mandate and partnership	Government, firm (the Netherlands)	Domestic (global)
France	From negligible relationships to mandate	Government	Domestic
Spain, Italy Portugal, Greece	From negligible relationships to endorsement	Firm, government, civil society (Spain)	Domestic

Sources: Adapted from Albareda, Lozano, and Ysa (2007); *CSR Navigator* (2007); Habisch et al. (2005).

although this is with a more narrowly confined policy focus including mandating (e.g., concerning transparency) and facilitation and partnership. In Denmark, a major CSR threshold was the state–business partnership to address labor market problems in the 1990s which remains a key focus of CSR (Morsing 2005). The Netherlands also illustrates the growth of CSR in the context of government but with less statist approaches to policy-making (Cramer 2005).

On the one hand Austria, Belgium, Germany, and Luxembourg have stronger government policies for CSR which tolerate less corporate discretion than in the UK, but on the other these tend to confine business obligations to the local "social market economy" whilst supporting measures for increased competitiveness (Albareda, Lozano, and Ysa 2007). Germany, like France (Beaujolin and Capron 2005), is a relatively late enthusiast for CSR and remains a relatively statist one. The government introduced numerous labor, social affairs, and governance laws, reflecting its own declining direct reach. However, some MNCs regard CSR as means of holding further and more intrusive regulation at bay (Habisch and Wegner 2005). Government-led CSR partnerships have recently emerged in the fields of education, work–life balance, and development (*CSR Navigator* 2007: 21).

In the Mediterranean countries, CSR is more likely to reflect policies to establish a new consensus about respective responsibilities rather than drawing upon longer traditions of business responsibility in partnerships. This reflects CSR as a partnership with government (relational type 4—Table 22.1), or what Albareda, Lozano, and Ysa (2007) refer to as an "agora" model. These mainly reflect firm and government drivers, though in Spain Catholic social societal ethics are also significant (Fernandez and Melé 2005).

Overall, whilst differences exist, greater convergence might be expected given the interest of the European Union in CSR. Since the Lisbon Summit (2000) the EU has looked to business, and specifically CSR, to fill the gap between the objective of economic competitiveness and the goal of increased social and economic standards. This broad goal has informed various uses of CSR including the global positioning of the EU as an "ethical power"; a European Model for combining economic success with social responsibility; assisting integration through enlargement; and creating more and better jobs as a means of improving confidence and trust in business. The EU Commission has sought to assist CSR understanding through the publication of Green Papers and facilitation of discussion (e.g., the Multi-Stakeholder Forum on CSR 2004). There has been a shift since the initial EU focus on environmental issues and mandatory modes to a greater emphasis on the social through CSR as self-government endorsed and facilitated by the Commission (e.g., 2006).

We now turn to consider the wider adaptations of CSR.

WORLD ADAPTATIONS OF CSR

We explore CSR's adaptation in the rest of the world, focusing on East Asia, Eastern Europe, and South Africa. "Adaptation" signals a greater rupture than "translation" discussed in Western Europe. Our chosen regions are all dynamic, undergoing dramatic changes associated with globalization and neo-liberalism. Thus we pass over non-Western cases where CSR is becoming more prominent in business–society–government relations by virtue of translation (e.g., India, Malaysia, and several Central and South American countries) and where CSR reflects only imported practices of MNCs (typically where markets do not function, civil society is marginalized or suppressed, governments are non-democratic, and there is no rule of law).

We discuss changes in the national governance systems, governmental roles, government–business relations, and, more specifically, government and CSR, with reference to East Asia (Japan, Korea), former socialist economies (China and Poland), and South Africa. The choice of national case studies is not meant to be representative but indicative of the role of CSR in fast changing government–business–society relations. Whilst significant variations exist *within* each of our sets of examples, we illumine regional differences between the three as well as their commonalities as non-Western societies and economies. Compared to Western European CSR, the role of the government figures more heavily than markets and civil society.

East Asia: Japan and Korea

In Japan and Korea, the role of the government has traditionally been developmental (or interventionist) supported by a Weberian type of bureaucracy. Governments have fostered the growth of local capital through protectionist trade and industrial policies (Johnson 1982; Amsden 1989; Wade 1992; Evans 1995; Woo-Cumings 1997). Thus, despite being privately owned, large corporations in Japan and Korea were perceived to be pseudo-public institutions (Mafune 1988; Kim 1997). It was not uncommon for owner-managers of large firms in these countries to proclaim their responsibility for long-term national growth, rather than simply for short-term individual profit. Such government–business relationships informed government–CSR relationships.

Like in Western Europe, CSR was largely "implicit" as opposed to "explicit." The dominant relationship was "CSR as mandated by government" (Table 22.1) and this focused on promoting social responsibility of business for national growth. This was most evident in employment relations, given the importance of workers as human capital and of maintaining industrial peace in economic development. The most notable state measures were support of long-term employment, and the promotion of firm-level social welfare schemes (e.g., academic grants to the children of employees, provision of secondary education on company premises, provision of dormitories, medical facilities), as well as social protection measures (e.g., legal sanctioning of priority of wage claims over creditors in case of bankruptcy; You and Chang 1993). Thus, CSR was geared towards welfare and social protection for the workers and their families, which, in turn tied workers' interests to those of companies. Notwithstanding certain "pathologies" associated with the lack of attention to quality of employment and work–life balance (e.g., long working hours, flexible working; Fukukawa and Moon 2004; Welford 2004) and weak representation rights within the firm, large corporations in Japan and Korea acted as the functional equivalents of the welfare state.

Since the late 1980s and early 1990s, with globalization, neo-liberal ideology and liberalization policies of deregulation and privatization, the traditional role of Japanese and Korean government has undergone a conversion or redeployment. Granted that Japan and Korea are still associated with comparatively strong states (Vogel 1996; Weiss 2002), it is easy to overlook the impact of globalization (Ohmae 1990, 1995) on the change in emphasis from government as a developer (governing and even bypassing the market) to a greater regulatory role to facilitate the market and address its failures (Woo-Cumings 1999; Tiberghien 2002; Kang 2008).

These changing roles have informed a more marked division of labor between the government and business with implications for CSR. Corporations are viewed increasingly in terms of property/ownership, with responsibility first and foremost for profit maximization for shareholders, whilst the government is responsible for supporting, which includes "moralizing," the new market arrangements. The latter entails not only the creation and expansion of the welfare state, but also, as a complementary new governance measure, promoting CSR through facilitation and endorsement (Table 22.1). For instance, in Korea where the pace of change is faster, large corporations have begun to question and challenge the traditional employment practices, and advocate more labor market flexibility premised on more individualistic and marketized views of employment relations (e.g., short-term contracts, performance-based pay). Meanwhile, the government has introduced unemployment benefits and promoted dialogue between the employers and unions by formulating tripartite commissions (Kong 2006), and endorsing the codes of conduct stipulated by international organizations such as the ILO and OECD as the "best practice." Thus, the traditional relationship of "CSR as mandate" (relational type 5—Table 22.1) now overlaps with "CSR as self-regulation" (relational type 1—Table 22.1) and "CSR as endorsement" (relational type 2) (Table 22.5).

More recently, reflecting the worldwide diffusion and growth of CSR practices as a new and complementary mode of governance (seventh section), the key CSR issues of interest to the government, have diversified not only regarding employment relations (e.g., diversity of workplaces, work–life balance), but also broader issues. These include corporate governance to enhance transparency and accountability, following the 1997 Asian financial crisis, and sustainable development, in response to the growing international and regional concerns for climate change and the status of East Asian tigers as large carbon emitters, and as a means of addressing the growing scarcity of resources (e.g., energy, water). Government CSR agendas are strongly influenced by the emergence of non-state actors and their growing power (e.g., investors, NGOs, international organizations) which have influenced the shaping of corporate governance reforms (Tiberghien 2002).

Table 22.5 Changing government–business relations and CSR in transitional economies

	Change in CSR–government relationship (Table 22.1)	Key drivers of CSR	Key interests of CSR
Japan and Korea	From mandate to self-government, endorsement, facilitation	State, foreign investors, NGOs, international organizations	Diversity in workplace, corporate governance, sustainable development
China and Poland	From mandate to self-government, continued mandate	State, foreign investors, the EU (Poland)	Corporate governance, sustainable development
South Africa	From negligible relationships to self-government, partnerships	State, foreign investors, MNCs, the development community (international organizations, NGOs)	Social development (health, education, poverty reduction, etc.), sustainable development

Former socialist: China and Poland

In former socialist economies such as China and Poland, governmental roles have undergone a dramatic conversion since the late 1990s, becoming less "statist" and more "developmental." Previously, the state was *the* actor (i.e. through state-owned firms) but privatization has required governments to work with the fast growing private sector. Reflecting the tight public–private relationship (or obscure distinction between public and private), the view of the firm is as a pseudo-public institution, and many of the employment practices that existed prior to transition are still mandated by the government (e.g., employee protection, occupational health and safety).

Notwithstanding their common backdrop of socialism, recent liberalization, and new governmental roles, there has nonetheless been some divergence of government–CSR relations. The Chinese government adopts a more developmental role than does that of Poland, and it prioritizes economic and sustainable development, with a twin focus on corporate governance (transparency and accountability) and the environment. However, the implementation gap between state mandate and enforcement is considerable such that the most advanced everyday CSR practices in China are enacted largely by foreign investors and MNCs. The civil society remains closely bound to the state and is conspicuously absent as a driver of CSR. Thus, the model of CSR as partnerships is yet to emerge.

The Polish government is also undergoing conversion, towards a weak "regulatory" mode compared to the Chinese "developmental" mode. This is because Poland, like Eastern Europe in general, has undergone rapid governmental as well as economic change, as well as Poland's "big bang" approach to economic liberalization (Chang and Rowthorn 1995). Thus, although the government–business relations have been more marketized there are doubts about the capacity of the post-socialist Polish state in this new political economy. As a result, CSR was left to the voluntary initiative of the private sector, and mainly existed as self-governance (relational type 1—Table 22.1). More recently, however, due to the influence of EU, stronger regulatory mechanisms are being developed. CSR has entered the policy arena in a more concrete manner (e.g., the interministerial working group on CSR; *CSR Navigator* 2007), which suggests that government–CSR relations will take on stronger dimensions of endorsement and facilitation (relational types 2 and 3—Table 22.1). However, despite the EU influence, the kind of partnership that is common in Western Europe is unlikely to emerge in Poland soon, for the civil society remains comparatively weak.

South Africa

Although difficult to generalize, the traditional role of African government has been predatory (i.e. extracting profits from the private sector, see Evans 1995). Thus, CSR was absent from governmental agendas and virtually non-existent. There is no shortage of examples of corporate complicity in political corruption, environmental destruction, labor exploitation, and social disruption (Visser, Middleton, and

McIntosh 2005: 19). Rare CSR initiatives came from the MNCs, who generally reacted to pressure from international organizations and NGOs and where was CSR as a form of government (relational type 5—Table 22.1; Muthuri et al. 2008).

However, post-Apartheid South African governments have experimented with enabling rather than developmental or regulatory models of CSR relationships. This shift is perhaps explicable given its institutional endowments: namely, the absence of the strong state traditions of East Asia and Eastern Europe, and the presence of a civil society. The view of the firm is that of a social institution, given the diverse set of pressing social development issues. The government recognizes that the private sector is well placed to contribute to address development agendas through CSR. However, CSR related issues advanced by the government are focused primarily upon its policy framework on Black Economic Empowerment (BEE), which seeks to redress inherited socio-economic inequalities (*CSR Navigator* 2007). The government does not explicitly mandate CSR outside the BEE framework, although there is an encompassing legal framework with regard to CSR-related areas (e.g., environment, social standards). However, the government also brings a partnering relationship through the multi-stakeholder processes that the BEE and some issue-specific initiatives chart reflecting the legacy of international and civic organizational involvement in African development.

As in Western Europe, whilst variations exist, the wider adaptations of CSR also reflect a common interest in promoting CSR through new combinations of self government, endorsement, facilitation, and partnership.

We now turn to the global level.

GLOBAL INSTITUTIONS OF CSR

Globalization and CSR

Globalization has not only challenged national government capacities, it has also informed CSR developments. This includes the management of cross-national MNC supply chain responsibilities regarding labor standards, human rights, environmental impacts, business ethics, and corporate governance.

The question arises as to why global CSR institutions have emerged. After all, the anti-globalization movement draws strength from the view of corporate responsibility for the *negative* aspects of globalization. Under globalization companies can access capital, labor, and raw materials relatively free from the regulation of its price and use. Thus for MNCs globalization is a strategy emphasizing self-interest, market reliance, competition, and economic liberalization. Although this has arguably made for greater rates of economic growth, wider distributions of resources, and increased consumer, employee, and investor choice, these dynamics are also associated with increased corporate social *ir*responsibility (Tulder and Zwart 2006).

Moreover, given the significance of the national contexts for CSR we have observed, it might be expected to be undermined by globalization.

Our answer to this question lies in a confluence of business, NGO, and governmental motivations. Individual companies and business associations have recognized certain imperatives for improved governance of international business. These in part derive from the risks for the MNCs epitomized by the reputational damage of sweat shops, health and safety failures, and human rights abuses. These risks have extended to threats to shareholder confidence and value; increases in liability; imperatives for reputation management; and complex systems of labor management. These threats increase with the globalization of information critical of MNCs associated with new technologies available to media organizations and civil society movements (Castells 1996, 1997, 1998).

NGOs, frustrated by continuing global governance deficits, have looked to business, individually and collectively, to address a host of international issues (e.g., environment, human rights, labor rights, corruption—Newell 2000, 2002; Bartley 2003). Although many NGOs remain critical of corporations, others engage with MNCs through the medium of CSR in order to raise standards of business and the fabric of society, be it in fighting corruption (e.g., Transparency International), in more sustainable use of natural resources (e.g., World Wildlife Fund for Nature), or in respect of human rights (e.g., Amnesty International).

National and international governmental organizations now see CSR as an opportunity to encourage business responsibility across borders and to participate in improving global governance (Knill and Lehmkuhl 2002). In addition to the national government initiatives for global business responsibility noted above (e.g., the UK's Ethical Trade Initiative; the USA's Apparel Industry Partnership), international governmental organizations, including the United Nations, the World Bank, the OECD, the G8, Climate Change Summits, have done likewise. The power of international governmental organizations to mandate CSR is modest, and they often depend on national governments to monitor, censure, and even prosecute, companies (e.g., OECD Guidelines for Multinational Enterprises). Significantly, the UN Human Rights Commissioner, John Ruggie, recently concluded that it is not possible to set binding human rights norms for companies and that this responsibility belongs to governments. Ruggie nevertheless sees a role for social regulation and self-regulation of companies and employs the language of CSR when he recommends that they improve their due diligence and add grievance procedures to such business-led initiatives as the Voluntary Principles on Security and Human Rights. Notwithstanding these limitations, the symbolic power of international governmental organizations reinforces the significance of legitimacy as a motive for business global responsibility.

Global institutions for CSR

As a result of the conjuncture of these motivations, there has emerged a variety of new institutions for global CSR and institutions for global governance which involve CSR (Table 22.6).

Table 22.6 Institutions for global CSR

	CSR institutions (examples)
CSR institutions within companies	The Nestlé Business Principles Unilever's sustainable agriculture guidelines

CSR institutions among companies	International business associations
	   (e.g., the World Business Council for Sustainable Development,
	   International Business Leaders' Forum)
	Sector-based associations (e.g., the Electronics Industry Citizenship
	   Coalition, the Equator Principles (finance))
	   Issue-based associations (e.g., Business Coalition on HIV Aids)
	   Region-based associations (e.g., CSR Europe, European Alliance on
	   CSR)

Multi-stakeholder CSR institutions	Global Reporting Initiative, Kimberly Process, the
	   OECD Guidelines for Multinational Enterprises, the UN Global
	   Compact

We should note some overlap, mutual reference, and convergence among these different institutional forms. Thus the OECD Guidelines make explicit reference to the ILO, the UN Global Compact, the Equator Principles, the UN Principles for Responsible Investment, the Global Reporting Initiative, and the prospective ISO 26000 CSR standard.

CSR institutions within companies

There is a trend of more MNCs taking responsibility for their supply chains through self-government. Thus the Nestlé Business Principles claim to have the same environmental, safety, and health standards around the world as in Switzerland. These are devised to assist managers; to enable supply chains to be audited or evaluated; to assist in the regulation of suppliers; and to enable companies to report their performance.

Some company systems are designed in partnership with civil society and governmental organizations. Thus Unilever's tea sustainability policy is in partnership with the UK's Department of International Development and the Kenya Tea Development Agency. CSR as self-government can extend to CSR as government where governmental or civil society institutions are weak. This applies in the nature of many cross-border activities which are difficult for national governments to regulate.

CSR institutions among companies

Business organizations also collaborate to create institutions which embody basic CSR principles and assist individual companies meeting these. *The World Business Council for Sustainable Development* is made up of over 200 CEOs from thirty-five countries and over twenty sectors, and is networked with over fifty national and regional business associations. It participates in policy debates, develops the business case for sustainable development, and focuses on projects in developing and emerging markets. Other institutions are more regionally, issue-, and sectorally focused (Table 22.6).

These institutions are mainly about self-government through collective means. As they have become more institutionalized they have increasingly figured as interlocutors with international civil society and governmental organizations in wider institution building.

Multi-stakeholder CSR institutions

There are numerous multi-stakeholder institutions which develop standards for responsible business. The *Global Reporting Initiative* (GRI) consists of individuals and representatives of accounting, business, civil society, and governmental organizations. It encourages reporting, particularly on sustainable development and transparency, and over 1,500 corporations claim to report against GRI frameworks.

Some multi-stakeholder institutions have emerged directly from business initiatives. The *Marine Stewardship Council* was formed by Unilever and the World Wildlife Council to address the depletion of world fish stocks. It became an independent institution in 1999 with members from business, charity, and governmental organizations. Its label guarantees that the respective fish have been caught from well-managed fisheries and do not contribute to environmental problems.

International governmental organizations combine their powers to endorse, facilitate, and partner business and other organizations to build CSR institutions. The *UN Global Compact* (UNGC) provides a business framework of ten principles in the areas of human rights, labor rights, the environment, and anti-corruption. It numbers over 4,000 companies along with business associations, local and global NGOs, local and global trade unions, foundations, public sector organizations, and academic institutions. Whilst criticized for its lack of teeth (Knight and Smith 2008), recently 400 signatories were de-listed for a failed or inadequate reporting. The UNGC is also developing partnerships in the areas of advocacy; social investment, and philanthropy; and core business, particularly around employment and entrepreneurship.

Ruggie (2004: 499) describes the emergence of these developments as a fundamental shift from the idea of the "public" in international sphere being exclusively associated with sovereign states to one in which the very system of states "is becoming embedded in a broader and deepening transnational arena concerned with the production of global public goods." This is consistent with wider developments in global governance (Rosenau 2005).

The system is uneven in terms of the actors (governmental interest varies enormously, NGO capacity is very unequally distributed, many companies don't participate). It is also uneven in terms of issues covered. Moreover, the enforcement of agreed standards relies almost entirely on self-government. Even where governments have assumed some formal monitoring responsibility, they are reluctant to sanction business (e.g., OECD and corruption) (Levy and Kaplan 2008; Scherer and Palazzo

2008). Conversely, their multi-stakeholder nature requires agreement over standards and their mobilization and enforcement to be deliberative and consensus based. The emphasis on "soft" law means that their effectiveness depends on the extent to which the inherent norms are understood and spread among businesses. Transnational businesses are more likely to be signed up, at least, to standards of responsible business than those which are confined to a single country (Chapple and Moon 2005).

CSR and New Governance

CSR is not only a feature of contemporary business and management but also of systems of government and governance albeit in very different and dynamic national and international contexts. This confirms Moon's UK conclusion that CSR had "moved from the margins of governance to occupy a more mainstream position, entailing partnerships with government and non-profit organizations" (2002: 406). The association of CSR and government should not be regarded as oxymoronic.

We have highlighted the range of CSR–government relationships (Table 22.1). CSR as self-government sits alongside a functioning system of liberal market governance, but it also underpins other CSR–government relationships. Governments are increasingly making CSR policies, from encouraging, through facilitation and partnering, to mandate through "soft regulation." CSR as government is also evident, mainly associated with underdeveloped governance systems and issues, or "between" the developed and the developing worlds.

Although the USA was the cradle of CSR, in Western Europe there has been the clearest development from CSR as self-government, to that which is also strongly encouraged, facilitated, and partnered by government. In the rest of the world, there has been a relatively recent growth of CSR as self-government as well as CSR as government, and where governments have encouraged CSR there has been a greater emphasis on mandate-type policies. But national configurations of CSR are increasingly connected to the emerging global systems of governance. Thus, national companies, business associations, NGOs, and governments are connected through international institutions through commitments to global standards, adopting of global practices, and participation in these new governance entities.

There is a paradox here. On the one hand, CSR is part and parcel of a more liberalized environment emphasizing autonomy and "bottom–up" and problem-oriented, multi-sector governance instruments. On the other hand, many governments are exploiting CSR for their own purposes. We characterize these developments as a maturation of CSR in which, from the perspective of corporations, there is a shift from the relative isolation of CSR as self-government to a contribution to governance which is more engaged and socially regulated and "light touch" governmentally regulated.

Looking to future research, there is a need for greater evaluation of CSR's contribution to governance and of the role of government policies therein. How and why does CSR improve governance? Do government policies stimulate improvements in business social performance? Second, there is a need for comparative research into the compatibility, convergence, difference, or divergence of government policies for CSR. This is important for companies whose business straddles national boundaries and for policy-makers to understand their effectiveness. Third, these questions could be investigated in tandem with inquiry about the nature of CSR development from simple self-regulation. For instance, Streeck and Thelen (2005) identify five mechanisms and modes of institutional change, namely layering (when new institutional material is placed on top of existing ones), drift (when existing institutions are not actively maintained/deliberately neglected, and gradually disappear), conversion (when old institutions are redirected, redeployed, or reinterpreted with respect to new goals, functions, and purposes), displacement (when existing institutions are replaced by, and actors defect to, new ones), and exhaustion (when institutions deplete and breakdown). Bearing in mind that change never occurs as neatly as the modes seem to suggest this is one way of embedding CSR in the broader political economy literature.

Notes

1. We suggest that all national systems of CSR have some balance of implicit and explicit features (Matten and Moon 2008).
2. Though in Germany, particularly, there were adaptations to traditions of social responsibilities being collectively met through guilds, particularly for industrial apprenticeships.

References

Aaronson, S. 2003. "CSR in the global village: the British role model and the American laggard," *Business and Society Review* 108: 309–38.

Acquier, A., and Gond, J.-P. 2007. "Aux sources de la responsabilité sociale de l'entreprise: (re)lecture et analyse d'un ouvrage séminal: Social Responsibilities of the Businessmen d'Howard Bowen 1953," *Finance contrôle stratégie* 10(2): 5–35.

Albareda, L., Lozano, J. M., and Ysa, T. 2007. "Public policies on corporate social responsibility: the role of governments in Europe," *Journal of Business Ethics* 74: 391–407.

Amsden, A. H. 1989. *Asia's Next Giant: South Korea and Late Industrialization*. New York: Oxford University Press.

Ayres, I., and Braithewaite, J. 1992. *Transcending the Deregulation Debate*. New York: Oxford University Press.

Bakan, J. 2004. *The Corporation: The Pathological Pursuit of Profit and Power*. London: Constable.

BARTLEY, T. 2003. "Certifying forests and factories: states, social movements, and the rise of private regulation in the apparel and forest product field," *Politics and Society* 31(3).

BEAUJOLIN, F., and CAPRON, M. 2005. "Balancing between constructive harassment and virtuous intensions," in A. Habish, J. Jonker, M. Wegner, and R. Schmidpeter, eds., *Corporate Social Responsibility across Europe*. Berlin: Springer 95–108.

BERLE, A. A., and MEANS, G. 1932. *The Modern Corporation and the Private Property*. New York: McMillan.

BOWEN, H. R. 1953. *The Social Responsibilities of the Businessman*. New York: Harper and Row.

BOXENBAUM, E. 2006. "Corporate social responsibility as institutional hybrids," *Journal of Business Strategies* 23(1): 45–64.

—— and BATTILANA, J. 2005. "Importation as innovation: transposing managerial practices across fields," *Strategic Organization* 3(4): 355–83.

—— and GOND, J. P. 2006. "Importing socially responsible investment in France and Quebec," DRUID Working Paper, available at www.druid.dk

BURRELL, G., and MORGAN, G. 1979. *Sociological Paradigms and Organizational Analysis: Elements of the Sociology of Corporate Life*. Newcastle: Athenaeum Press.

CAMPBELL, J., and PEDERSEN, O. 2001. *The Rise of Neoliberalism and Institutional Analysis*. Princeton: Princeton University Press.

CAPDEVILA, G. 2007. "Politics: 'Global Compact Lacks Teeth'—NGOs," *IPS* (Inter Press Service) http://ipsnews.net/news.asp?idnews=38453 accessed August 25, 2009.

CARNEGIE, A. 1889. "Wealth," *North American Review* 148(391): 653–65.

CARROLL, A. B. 1979. "A three dimensional conceptual model of corporate social performance," *Academy of Management Review* 4: 497–505.

—— 1999. "Corporate social responsibility: evolution of a definitional construct," *Business and Society* 38: 268–95.

—— 2008. "A history of CSR: concept and practices," in A. Crane, D. Matten, A. McWilliams, J. Moon, and D. Siegel, eds., *The Oxford Handbook of CSR*. Oxford: Oxford University Press, 19–45.

CASTELLS, M. 1996. *The Information Age: Economy, Society and Culture*, i: *The Rise of the Network Society*. Oxford: Blackwells.

—— 1997. *The Information Age: Economy, Society and Culture*, ii: *The Power of Identity*. Oxford: Blackwells.

—— 1998. *The Information Age: Economy, Society and Culture*, iii: *End of Millennium*. Oxford: Blackwells.

CHANDLER, A. 1977. *The Visible Hand: The Managerial Revolution in American Business*. Cambridge, Mass.: Harvard University Press.

CHANG, H.-J., and ROWTHORN, B., eds. 1995. *The Role of the State in Economic Change*. Oxford: Clarendon Press.

CHAPPLE, W., and MOON, J. 2005. "Corporate social responsibility in Asia: a seven country study of CSR website reporting," *Business and Society* 44: 415–41.

—— GOND, J.-P., ORLTIZKY, M., and LOUCHE, C. 2008. "The influence of institutional varieties of capitalism on corporate stakeholder responsibility," paper presented at the Academy of Management Conference, Anaheim.

COCHOY, F. 1999 *Une histoire du marketing: discipliner l'économie de marché*. Paris: La Découverte.

CRAMER, J. 2005. "Redefining positions in society," in A. Habish, J. Jonker, M. Wegner, and R. Schmidpeter, eds., *Corporate Social Responsibility across Europe*. Berlin: Springer, 87–96.

CRANE, A., MATTEN, D., and MOON, J. 2008. *Corporations and Citizenship*. Cambridge: Cambridge University Press.

———— McWILLIAMS, A., MOON, J., and SIEGEL, D., eds. 2008a. *The Oxford Handbook of Corporate Social Responsibility*. Oxford: Oxford University Press.

———————— 2008b. "Introduction," in A. Crane, D. Matten, A. McWilliams, J. Moon, and D. Siegel, eds., *The Oxford Handbook of CSR*. Oxford: Oxford University Press, 3–15.

CSR Navigator (Public Policies in Africa, the Americas, Asia, and Europe). 2007. The Deutsche Gesellschaft für Technische Zusammen-arbeit (GTZ) and the Bertelsmann Stiftung.

CZARNIAWSKA, B., and JOERGES, B. 1996. "Travels of ideas," in B. Czarniawska and G. Sevón, eds., *Translating Organizational Change*. Berlin: Walter de Gruyter, 13–48.

DAVIS, K. 1967. "Understanding the social responsibility puzzle: what does the businessman owe to society?" *Business Horizons* 10: 45–50.

——— 1973. "The case for and against business assumption of social responsibilities," *Academy of Management Journal* 16: 312–23.

DiMAGGIO, P., and POWELL, P. 1983. "The iron cage revisited: institutional isomorphism and collective rationality in organizational fields," *American Sociological Review* 48: 147–60.

DONALDSON, T., and DUNFEE, T. 1994. "Towards a unified conception of business ethics: integrative social contracts theory," *Academy of Management Review* 19: 252–84.

——— and PRESTON, L. E. 1995. "The stakeholder theory of the corporation: concepts, evidence and implications," *Academy of Management Review* 20(1): 65–91.

ELKINGTON, J. 1997. *Cannibals with Forks: The Triple Bottom Line of the 21st Century Business*. Oxford: Capstone Publishing.

EU Commission. 2006. Communication from the EU Commission "Implementing the partnership for growth and jobs: making europe a pole of excellence on corporate social responsibility," available at www.foretica.es/imgs/foretica/rse_eu.pdf

EVANS, P. 1995 *The Embedded Autonomy: States and Industrial Transformation*. Princeton: Princeton University Press.

FERNANDEZ, J., and MELÉ, D. 2005. "Spain: from a paternalistic past to sustainable companies," in A. Habisch, J. Jonker, M. Wegner, and R. Schmidpeter, eds., *Corporate Social Responsibility across Europe*. New York: Stringer, 289–302.

FOX, T., WARD, H., and HOWARD, B. 2002 *Public Sector Roles in Strengthening Corporate Social Responsibility*. Washington, DC: The World Bank Group.

FREDERICK, W. C. 1978. "From CSR 1 to CSR 2 : the maturing of business & society thought," Graduate School of Business Working Paper. University of Pittsburgh.

——— 2006. *Corporation, Be Good! The Story of Corporate Social Responsibility*. Indianapolis: Dog Ear Publishing.

——— 2008. "Corporate social responsibility: deep roots, flourishing growth, promising future," in A. Crane, D. Matten, A. McWilliams, J. Moon, and D. Siegel, eds., *The Oxford Handbook of CSR*. Oxford: Oxford University Press, 522–31.

FREEMAN, R. E., WICKS, A. C., and PARMAR, B. 2004. "Stakeholder theory and 'The Corporate Objective Revisited,' " *Organization Science* 15(3): 364–9.

FRIEDMAN, M. 1962. *Capitalism and Freedom*. Chicago: University of Chicago Press.

——— 1970. "The social responsibility of business is to increase its profits," *New York Times Magazine* September 13: 32–3, 122–6.

FUKUKAWA, K., and MOON, J. 2004. "A Japanese model of corporate social responsibility?" *Journal of Corporate Citizenship* 16: 45–59.

GALLAGHER, M. E. 2005. *Contagious Capitalism: Globalization and the Politics of Labor in China*. Princeton: Princeton University Press.

GARRIGA, E., and MELÉ, D. 2004. "Corporate social responsibility: mapping the conceptual territory," *Journal of Business Ethics* 53: 51–71.

GOND, J.-P. 2006. "Contribution à l'étude de la performance sociétale de l'entreprise: fondements théoriques, construction sociale, impact financier," Ph.D. thesis, Department of Management Studies, Université Toulouse I—Sciences Sociales.

—— and CRANE, A. 2008. "Corporate social performance disoriented: saving the lost paradigm?" *Business and Society* doi: 10.1177/0007650308315510.

—— and MATTEN, D. 2007. "Rethinking the corporation–society interface: beyond the functionalist trap," ICCSR Research Paper Series 47, University of Nottingham.

GRANOVETTER, M. 1985. "Economic action and social structure: the problem of embeddedness," *American Journal of Sociology* 91: 481–510.

HABISCH, A., and WEGNER, M. 2005. "Germany: overcoming the heritage of corporatism," in A. Habisch, J. Jonker, M. Wegner, and R. Schmidpeter, eds., *Corporate Social Responsibility Across Europe*. Berlin: Springer.

HALL, P., and TAYLOR, L. 1996. "Political science and the three variants of new institutionalisms," *Political Studies* 44: 936–57.

HEALD, M. 1961. "Business thought in the twenties: social responsibility," *American Quarterly* 13(2): 126–39.

—— 1970. *The Social Responsibility of Business: Company and Community, 1900–1970*. Cleveland: Case Western Reserve University Press.

HERTZ, N. 2002. *The Silent Takeover*. London: Arrow.

HODGE, M. 2006. "The British CSR strategy: how a government supports the good work," in J. Hennigfeld, M. Pohl, and N. Tolhurst, eds., *The ICCA Handbook on Corporate Social Responsibility*. London: John Wiley and Sons.

JOHNSON, C. 1982. *MITI and the Japanese Miracle: The Growth of Industrial Policy*. Stanford, Calif.: Stanford University Press.

KANG, N. 2008. "Institutional change in the state-led model of capitalism: corporate governance in France and South Korea," Ph.D. thesis, Faculty of Social and Political Sciences, University of Cambridge.

KIM, E. M. 1997. *Big Business, Strong State: Collusion and Conflict in South Korean Development, 1960–1980*. New York: SUNY Press.

KING, L. 2000. *The Basic Features of Postcommunist Capitalism in Eastern Europe: Firms in Hungary, the Czech Republic, and Slovakia*. New York: Praeger Publishers.

KJAERGAARD, C., and WESTPHALEN, S.-Å. 2001. *From Collective Bargaining to Social Partnerships: New Roles of Social Partners in Europe*. Copenhagen: The Copenhagen Centre.

KNIGHT, G., and SMITH, J. 2008. "The global compact and its critics," in J. Leatherman, ed., *Discipline and Punishment in Global Politics*. Basingstoke: Palgrave Macmillian.

KNILL, C., and LEHMKUHL, D. 2002. "Private actors and the state: internationalization and changing patterns of governance," *Governance* 15(1): 41–63.

KONG, T. Y. 2006. "Globalization and labor market reforms: patterns of response in northeast Asia," *British Journal of Political Science* 36: 359–83.

LATOUR, B. 2005. *Reassembling the Social: An Introduction to Actor-Network Theory*. Oxford: Oxford University Press.

LEVITT, T. 1958. "The dangers of social responsibility," *Harvard Business Review* 36: 41–50.

LEVY, D., and KAPLAN, R. 2008. "Corporate social responsibility and theories of global governance: strategic contestation in global issue arenas," in A. Crane, D. Matten,

A. McWilliams, J. Moon, and D. Siegel, eds., *The Oxford Handbook of CSR*. Oxford: Oxford University Press, 432–51.

LOCKETT, A., MOON, J., and VISSER, W. 2006. "Corporate social responsibility in management research: focus, nature, salience and sources of influence," *Journal of Management Studies* 43: 115–36.

LOGSDON, J., and WOOD, D. 2002. "Business citizenship: from domestic to global level of analysis," *Business Ethics Quarterly* 12(2): 155–87.

McCRUDDEN, C. 2007. *Buying Social Justice: Equality, Government Procurement and Legal Change*. Oxford: Oxford University Press.

McGUIRE, J. 1963. *Business and Society*. New York: McGraw-Hill.

McWILLIAMS, A., and SIEGEL, D. 2002. "Corporate social responsibility: a theory of the firm perspective," *Academy of Management Review* 26: 177–227.

MAFUNE, Y. 1988. "Corporate social performance and policy in Japan," *Research in Corporate Social Performance and Policy* 10: 291–303.

MAIGNAN, I., and RALSTON, D. A. 2002. "Corporate social responsibility in Europe and the US: insights from businesses' self-presentations," *Journal of International Business Studies* 33 (3): 497–514.

MARGOLIS, J. D., ELFENBEIN, E., and WALSH, J. P. 2007. "Does it pay to be good? A meta-analysis and redirection of research on the relationship between corporate social and financial performance," paper presented at the Academy of Management, Philadelphia, US.

——— and WALSH, J. P. 2003. "Misery loves companies: whither social initiatives by business?" *Administrative Science Quarterly* 48: 268–305.

MARINETTO, M. 1999. "The historical development of business philanthropy: social responsibility in the new corporate economy," *Business History* 41: 1—20.

MATTEN, D., and MOON, J. 2008. " 'Implicit' and 'explicit' CSR: a conceptual framework for a comparative understanding of corporate social responsibility," *Academy of Management Review* 33(2): 404–24.

MEYER, J. W. 1999. "The changing cultural content of the nation-state: a world society perspective," in G. Steinmetz, ed., *State and Culture: New Approaches to the State after the Cultural Turn*. Ithaca, NY: Cornell University Press, 123–43.

——— 2000. "Globalization: sources and effects on national states and societies," *International Sociology* 15: 233–48.

——— BOLI, J., THOMAS, G., and RAMIREZ, F. O. 1997. "World society and the nation state," *American Journal of Sociology* 103: 144–81.

MICHELETTI, M. 2003. *Political Virtue and Shopping: Individuals, Consumerism, and Collective Action*. New York: Palgrave Macmillan.

MIDTTUN, A. 2005. "Realigning business, government, and civil society: emerging embedded relational governance beyond the (neo)liberal and welfare state models," *Corporate Governance: The International Journal of Business in Society* 5(3): 159–74.

MOHAN, A. 2003. "Strategies for the management of complex practices in complex organizations: a study of the transnational management of corporate responsibility," Ph.D. thesis, University of Warwick.

MOLINA, O. and RHODES, M. 2002. "Corporatism: the past, present and future of a concept," *Annual Review of Political Science* 5: 305–31.

MONBIOT, G. 2001. *Captive State: The Corporate Takeover of Britain*. London: Pan Books.

MOON, J. 2002. "Business social responsibility and new governance," *Government and Opposition* 37(3): 385–408.

——— 2004. "Government as a driver of CSR," ICCSR Research Paper Series 20, University of Nottingham.

—— CRANE, A., and MATTEN, D. 2005. "Can corporations be citizens? Corporate citizenship as a metaphor for business participation in society," *Business Ethics Quarterly* 15(3): 427–51.

—— and RICHARDSON, J. J. 1985. *Unemployment in the UK: Politics and Policies*. Aldershot: Gower.

—— and VOGEL, D. 2008. "Corporate social responsibility, government, and civil society," in A. Crane, D. Matten, A. McWilliams, J. Moon, and D. Siegel, eds., *The Oxford Handbook of CSR*. Oxford: Oxford University Press, 303–23.

MORSING, M. 2005. "Denmark: inclusive labor market strategies," in A. Habisch, J. Jonker, M. Wegner, and R. Schmidpeter, eds., *Corporate Social Responsibility across Europe*. New York: Stringer, 23–36.

MUTHURI, J., MOON, J., and CHAPPLE, W. 2008. "Implementing 'community participation' in corporate community involvement: lessons from Magadi Soda Company in Kenya," *Journal of Business Ethics* 85: 431–44.

NEWELL, P. 2000 "Environmental NGOs and globalization: the governance of TNCs," in R. Cohen and S. Rai, eds., *Global Social Movements*. London: Athlone Press.

—— 2002. "Managing multinationals: the governance of investment for the environment," *Journal of International Development* 13: 907–19.

OHMAE, K. 1995. *The End of the Nation State*. New York: Free Press.

ORLTIZKY, M. 2008. "Corporate social performance and financial performance: a research synthesis," in A. Crane, D. Matten, A. McWilliams, J. Moon, and D. Siegel, eds., *The Oxford Handbook of CSR*. Oxford: Oxford University Press, 113–34.

—— RYNES, F. L., and SCHMIDT, S. L. 2003. "Corporate social and financial performance: a meta-analysis," *Organization Studies* 24: 103–441.

PARSONS, T. 1967. *Sociological Theory and Modern Society*. New York: The Free Press.

PASQUERO, J. 2004. "Responsabilité sociale des entreprises: les approches nords-américaines," in J. Igalens, ed., *Tous responsable*. Paris: Editions d'Organization, 257–72.

—— 2005. "La responsabilité sociale de l'entreprise comme objet des sciences de gestion: un regard historique," in M.-F. Bouthillier-Turcotte and A. Salmon, eds., *Responsabilité sociale et environnementale de l'entreprise*. Sillery: Presses de l'Université du Québec, 80–112.

PETERS, B. G. 1996. "Shouldn't row, can't steer: what's a government to do?" *Public Policy and Administration* 12(1): 51–2.

POLYANI, K. 2001. *The Great Transformation: The Political and Economic Origins of Our Time*. Boston: Beacon Press, 1st edn. 1944.

PRAHALAD, C. K., and HAMMOND, A. 2002. "Serving the world's poor, profitability," *Harvard Business Review* 80(9): 48–58.

RANDALL, C. B. 1952. *A Creed for Free Enterprise*. Boston: Little, Brown and Company.

ROSENAU, J. 2005. "Globalisation and governance: sustainability between fragmentation and integration," in U. Petschow, J. Rosenau, and E. Ulrich von Weizsäcker, eds., *Governance and Sustainability: New Challenges for States, Companies, and Civil Society*. Sheffield: Greenleaf Publishing.

ROWLINSON, M., and HASSARD, J. 1993. "The invention of corporate culture: a history of histories of Cadbury," *Human Relations* 6: 299–326.

RUGGIE, J. 2004. "Reconstituting the global public domain: issues, actors and practices," *European Journal of International Relations* 10(4): 499–531.

SCHERER, A., and PALAZZO, G. 2007. "Towards a political conception of corporate responsibility: business and society seen from an Habermasian perspective," *Academy of Management Review* 32(4): 1096–120.

SCHERER, A., and PALAZZO, G. 2008. "Globalization and corporate social responsibility," in A. Crane, D. Matten, A. McWilliams, J. Moon, and D. Siegel, eds., *The Oxford Handbook of CSR*. Oxford: Oxford University Press, 413–31.

SCHMIDT, V. 2002. *The Futures of European Capitalism*. Oxford: Oxford University Press.

SCHWARTZ, M. S., and CARROLL, A. B. 2008. "Integrating and unifying competing and complementary frameworks," *Business and Society* 47(2): 148–86.

SHIN, J.-S., and CHANG, H.-J. 2003. *Restructuring Korea Inc*. London: RoutledgeCurzon.

STREECK, W., and THELEN, W. 2005 *Beyond Continuity: Institutional Change in Advanced Political Economies*. Oxford: Oxford University Press.

SUNDARAM, A. K., and INKPEN, A. C. 2004. "The corporate objective revisited," *Organization Science* 15(3): 350–63.

SWANSON, D. L. 1995. "Addressing a theoretical problem by reorienting the corporate social performance model," *Academy of Management Review* 20: 43–64.

—— 1999. "Toward an integrative theory of business and society: a research strategy for corporate social performance," *Academy of Management Review* 24: 506–21.

TAINO, R., HUOLMAN, M., and PULKKINEN, M. 2001. "The internationalization of capital markets: how international institutional investors are restructuring Finnish companies," in G. Morgan, P. Kristensen, and R. Whitley, eds., *The Multinational Firm*. Oxford: Oxford University Press, 153–71.

TIBERGHIEN, Y. 2002. "Political mediation of global economic forces: the politics of corporate restructuring in Japan, France, and South Korea," Ph.D. thesis, Department of Political Science, Stanford University, Calif.

TULDER, R. VAN, and ZWART, A. VAN DER. 2006. *International Business–Society Management: Linking Corporate Responsibility and Globalization*. London: Routledge.

VARADARAJAN, P. R., and MENON, A. 1998. "Cause-related marketing: a coalignment of marketing strategy and corporate philanthropy," *Journal of Marketing* 53(2): 58–74.

VISSER, W., MIDDLETON, C., and MCLNTOSH, M. 2005. "Corporate ctizenship in Africa: introduction," *Journal of Corporate Citizenship* 18: 8–20.

VOGEL, S. 1996. *Freer Markets, More Rules: Regulatory Reform in Advanced Industrial Countries*. Ithaca, NY: Cornell University Press.

VOGEL, D. 2005. *The Market for Virtue: The Potential and Limits of Corporate Social Responsibility*. Washington, DC: Brookings.

WADDOCK, S. A. 2004. "Parallel universes: companies, academics, and the progress of corporate citizenship," *Business and Society Review* 109(1): 5–42.

WADE, R. 1992. *Governing the Market: Economic Theory and the Role of Government in East Asian Industrialization*. Princeton: Princeton University Press.

WARTICK, S. L., and COCHRAN, P. L. 1985. "The evolution of the corporate social performance model," *Academy of Management Review* 10(4): 758–69.

WEBER, M. 1930. *The Protestant Ethic and the Spirit of Capitalism*. London: Routledge.

WEISS, L., ed. 2002. *States in the Global Economy: Bringing Domestic Institutions Back In*. Cambridge: Cambridge University Press.

WELFORD, R. 2004. "Corporate social responsibility in Europe, North America, and Asia," *Journal of Corporate Citizenship* 17: 33–52.

WHITLEY, R. 1992. *Business Systems in East Asia: Firm, Markets and Societies*. London: Sage.

—— 1999. *Divergent Capitalisms: The Social Structuring of Change of Business Systems*. Oxford: Oxford University Press.

WOO-CUMINGS, M. 1997. "Slouching toward the market: the politics of financial liberalization in South Korea," in M. Loriaux, M. Woo-Cumings, and K. Calder, eds., *Liberalizing Finance in Interventionist States*. Ithaca, NY: Cornell University Press.

—— 1999. *The Developmental State.* Ithaca, NY: Cornell University Press.

WOOD, D. J. 1991. "Corporate social performance revisited," *Academy of Management Review* 16: 691–718.

YOU, J.-I., and CHANG, H.-J. 1993. "The myth of free labor market in Korea," *Contributions to Political Economy* 12: 29–46.

ZADEK, S. 2001. *The Civil Corporation: The New Economy of Corporate Citizenship.* London: Earthscan Publications Ltd.

CHAPTER 23

THE STATE, BUSINESS, AND TRAINING

JASON HEYES

HELEN RAINBIRD

INTRODUCTION

SKILLS and knowledge are seen as engines of economic growth and social development and a policy arena in which the state and the organized interest groups have a legitimate interest (ILO 2003). Historically, governments and business interest organizations have had an interest in vocational education and training (VET), but the way in which social institutions have developed has varied according to the historical process of industrialization and state formation (Sheldrake and Vickerstaff 1987; Green 1990). Brown argues that "[w]ithin capitalist economies we find variations in historical and economic conditions; cultural, political and social mores; constellations of political interest groups and social classes; and in labour markets, which shape skill formation policies" (2001: 30). Research on comparative training systems and their relationship to labor markets, work organization, and economic performance (for example, Maurice, Sellier, and Silvestre 1986; Ashton and Green 1996; Whitley 1999; Brown 2001; Rubery and Grimshaw 2003) has a clear link both to the wider debate on varieties of capitalism, the role of social institutions in economic performance, and the impact of globalization on nation states (Crouch and Streeck 1997; Hall and Soskice 2001).

At the level of the nation state, VET is an example of a policy arena in which there is both "market" and "state" failure and represents an arena in which public policy may be devolved to private interest government (Schmitter and Streeck 1985). The rationale for involving employer and employee interests groups lies in the fact that "straight-forward (state) intervention may be based on highly imperfect information and comprehension of problems, and may meet resistance from employers and unions to the extent that policy objectives may not be met" (Grant 1985: 130). In his analysis of the limits to neo-liberalism in skill formation, Streeck (1989) argues that the free contract for labor in capitalist economies makes it difficult for employers to secure a return on their investment in training, because it is embodied in individual workers who may leave the company for a rival employer. Because of this uncertainty, employers acting rationally have a tendency to invest less than they ought to in their own best interests because of the "free rider problem." It is in this context that state intervention may involve forms of compulsion, such as the operation of training levies, and institution building, to overcome the problem of free-riding. It is also the case that smaller companies are less likely to have the capacity to train, in the form of in-house trainers and expertise, than large companies with a well-resourced training function. Sectors in which small companies predominate or have difficulty in organizing training because of technology and work organization (for example, the site-based nature of the construction industry) also benefit from collective approaches to organizing skill formation. Size and sector are therefore likely to influence the benefits that are perceived from business interest representation in training institutions.

The resolution of the problem of state and market failure in the provision of workforce skills varies in different national VET systems. The extent to which business interests (and those of trade unions) are incorporated varies, according to whether VET is delivered through the education system (and therefore seen as competence of the state) or through different forms of dual model (e.g., apprenticeship, labor market, and training programs) in which young employees or trainees undergo a period of learning in the workplace and therefore come within the competence of the employer. In this chapter, we consider the typologies which have been applied to characterize national vocational training systems, which tend to focus on the respective roles of the state, interest organizations, and the degree of coordination between different levels of social institutions. Moreover, these national institutional systems are not static but have been evolving in response to internal and external pressures (Bosch and Charest 2010).

This discussion must be located in the context of globalization and its real and perceived effects on national economies. The increasingly international nature of markets for capital, production goods, and services, on the one hand, and of production chains, facilitated by communication and information technology, and the capacity of multinational companies to locate production activities internationally, on the other, has given rise to a perception amongst policy-makers and national governments that knowledge, education, and skills are a source of competitive advantage underpinning economic performance (see, e.g., Commission of the

HM Treasury et al. 2004; European Communities 2005). The nature of these changes and their implications for work modernization, employers' competitive strategies, and workforce skills and qualifications are contested.[1] Nevertheless, this is the context in which education, training and workers' access to training throughout their working lives have come to be seen as maintaining the competitiveness of national economies and companies. This perception is reflected in educational policy; the traditional policy arena of VET; and in the opening up of the continuing vocational training of the workforce as an arena for policy intervention and for the extension of the scope of collective bargaining.

Economic and political internationalization has a dual impact on national interest groups. The first of these is that globalization and liberalization, combined with the emergence of regional political blocs, raise important questions about the evolution of nation states and nationally based systems of business interest organizations (Schneider and Gröte 2006: 5). Of the regional political blocs, the European Union is the most developed and shows most evidence of development towards a multi-level system of governance (Marginson and Sisson 2004; Schneider and Gröte 2006). The European Commission's Involvement in matters relating to training is well-established: the 1957 Treaty of Rome identified the need for cooperation between member states of the European Economic Community on vocational training and its contribution to the harmonization of working conditions and standards of living. Training policy has implications for lobbying activity as well as associational activity, both in relation to policy-making and to new arenas for collective bargaining at EU level. The second area of impact on national interest organizations is the pressure which derives from the interests of multinational firms (Schneider and Gröte 2006: 8). Companies' mobility across borders devalues the benefits of membership of nationally based associations (Traxler 2006: 93). They learn to engage in policy-making at different levels through international market governance mechanisms (e.g., European Union institutions) and are developing a growing awareness of the need for "trans-national self-regulation" (Coen and Grant 2006: 14). One consequence is that MNCs may be represented in associations and also represent their own interests directly to government (Schneider and Gröte 2006: 9).

In addition to these two impacts of internationalization on interest groups, we identify a third which has significance for training and skill development. Large companies, in particular, have "structured sets of social relationships through which orders are transmitted, making companies into social institutions and not just clusters of exchanges" (Crouch and Streeck 1997: 2). Where this also involves a process of managing a workforce across borders, analyses of training and skills development must consider interactions with different national business systems and systems of skill formation.

The approach adopted in this chapter is to focus on the involvement of business interests in social institutions rather than the lobbying activity of business interest associations. In other words, drawing on Wilson's (2001) identification of the dual motives for interest group studies, we are not examining interest groups as a form of political participation and their lobbying activities in relation to training as an arena of policy-making, even though this would make an interesting study and we are not aware of any current research in this area. Rather we are adopting what he identifies as the sociological perspective on interest groups (2001: 11), which involves examining how relationships are structured and organized between the state and business in relation to training policy.

This chapter is divided into five sections. In the first section we discuss why training and skill formation are considered to be central to economic competitiveness and company performance and the ways in which business interests may be involved in social institutions and policy-making in this arena. In the second section we explore the political economy of training and skill formation, identifying the strengths and limitations of different approaches and typologies. The third section extends the analysis of business and social institutions by examining the emerging supranational level for economic and employment policy. Here, the principal focus is on the European Union as a regional bloc in which training policy has played a significant role as an arena of social dialogue between organized interest groups at European level. In the fourth section we examine the training and human resource management practices of multinational companies, exploring the extent to which they intersect with national institutional arenas in which business interest groups operate. The conclusion assesses continuity and change in the relationships between the state and business interests in the field of vocational training.

Why is Training Important?

It has long been recognized that skills and knowledge have the potential to make an important contribution to economic performance and the competitiveness of organizations. Studies have pointed to the influence that training may have on labor productivity (e.g., Mason, Van Ark, and Wagner 1994) and trading performance (Webster 1993) and skills and knowledge have come to be seen as crucial determinants of economic growth. Neoclassical economic theories that emphasized the exogenous influence of technology (e.g., Solow 1956) have recently been challenged by "post-neoclassical" theories that emphasize instead human capital as an endogenous determinant of growth (Romer 1990; Gemmell 1996). Interest in the relationship between training and competitiveness extends beyond the field of economics to the areas of management, employment relations, and HRM. Researchers have regarded training as a vital accompaniment to systems of production based on principles of quality and flexibility (e.g., Streeck 1992; MacDuffie and Kochan 1995). Skills and knowledge have also been seen as potential core organizational resources that can be exploited so as to secure competitive advantages. The "resource-based" perspective on strategic HRM suggests that organizations that are able to develop their employees in ways that cannot easily be copied by their competitors (Barney 1995) may secure an ongoing competitive advantage over their rivals.

The potential benefits of training are not restricted to organizations. Since the 1960s neoclassical economists (Becker 1964; Mincer 1974) have sought to demonstrate that the lifetime earnings potential of individual workers is fundamentally determined by investments in education and training that result in the accumulation of skills and knowledge, or "human capital." The assumptions, concepts, and theoretical content of human capital theory have been subject to a considerable amount of criticism (see, e.g., Bowles and Gintis 1976), yet few would challenge the view that those who are able to benefit from education and training will tend to enjoy more opportunities in the labor market and, on average, higher earnings, than those who have relatively little education and training. In recent years training has also come to be seen as a means by which workers might insure themselves against the risk of job loss, which is often assumed to have increased as a result of shifts in the international division of labor, increased capital mobility, greater uncertainty, and more frequent and widespread restructuring of industry (Beck 2000; Rifkin 2000). Commentators have suggested that jobs have become more insecure, that workers can expect to change job more frequently than in the past and that they therefore need to equip themselves with a portfolio of skills so as to maximize their "employability." Evidence (Auer and Cazes 2000) that average job tenure has remained stable over time suggests that the claims made in respect of increased job insecurity have been exaggerated. Nevertheless, the view that individuals should bear greater responsibility for ensuring their ongoing "employability" has become a common theme of policy rhetoric at national and (as discussed below) European levels. The European Commission also regards training as contributing to the goal of social inclusion, an issue that has taken on a new significance as a consequence of recent increases in intra-European migration, particularly in the wake of the accession of the "A8" and "A2" economies. In this context, issues relating to the equivalence and transparency of qualifications, and the extent to which they are recognized by employers, are also likely to become increasingly important.

GOVERNANCE AND TRAINING

The belief that training is a vital determinant of economic performance has encouraged a considerable amount of comparative international research that has, among other things, sought to describe and account for differences in the extent of VET provision, the relationship between skills supply and employers' production strategies, and the implications of different sites of learning (e.g., the workplace, schools, and colleges). While some studies (e.g., Caillods 1994) have examined national VET systems in relative isolation, others have sought to understand how government policies, regulatory institutions, and investment patterns in respect of VET relate to, and are conditioned by, other social and economic phenomena. A number of these studies (Ashton and Green 1996; Crouch, Finegold, and Sako 1999; Brown 2001) have attempted to explain why some countries have developed into "low-skill" economies while others have become "high-skill" economies, and in so doing have sought to explain how training systems have come to acquire their current characteristics. It has been suggested that the interplay of state, employer, and trade union actions has had an important influence in this regard by shaping the institutional context of skill formation (Ashton and Green 1996; Ashton, Sung, and Turbin 2000). The key social agencies also commonly feature in attempts to distinguish between different "models" of training. A number of comparative studies (see, e.g., Caillods 1994; Heidemann et al. 1994; ILO 1998; Ashton, Sung, and Turbin 2000; Winterton 2000) have focused on the respective responsibilities of national governments, employers, and trade unions in respect of VET. These studies have examined, for example, the extent to which employers and trade unions participate in national, regional, or sectoral institutions charged with tasks relating to the regulation of training, such as distributing training investment funds and setting training and accreditation standards. These studies have drawn attention to the extent to which decisions relating to training are discussed, negotiated, or co-determined by employers and worker representatives, as opposed to being taken by employers unilaterally. On the basis of such considerations, the UK and US "training systems" have been identified as examples of a "voluntarist" or "market-led" model of VET, in which decisions relating to training are generally left to employers, with trade unions having little or no formal involvement (ILO 1998; Ashton, Sung, and Turbin 2000). By contrast, training systems in countries such as Austria, Germany, and the Netherlands, where employers and unions both have a formal role in the regulation of training, have been defined as "corporatist" or "co-operative" (ILO 1998: 69; Eaton 2000). A third model, defined by Ashton, Sung, and Turbin (2000) as the "developmental state model" and by the ILO as a "demand-led, state-driven" system, is exemplified by South Korea and Singapore, whose national governments have provided institutional and financial support for education and training and coordinated their provision so as to promote economic development. The ILO has also identified a "supply-led, state-driven" system, which is characterized by the state taking on primary responsibility for providing training, with little or no pressure applied on employers. The ILO associates this model with a number of transition and developing economies However, according to Ashton, Sung, and Turbin (2000) the financial crises and subsequent IMF-imposed economic restructuring and liberalization experienced by countries such as Chile and Mexico, have resulted in responsibility for skill formation increasingly coming to rest with foreign capital, with the supply and demand for skills largely being coordinated by market forces. They suggest that these developments represent the emergence of a "neo-market model" of education and training.

Other studies have sought to locate training systems within a broader analysis of differences in the way capitalism is organized within different national social formations. The "business systems" approach to this issue (Whitley 1999) attempts to link wider social institutions with work organization at enterprise level and the extent to which interest groups have a vested interest in entrenching particular sets of social relations. Whitley argues that differences in the forms of economic organization observed across nation states can be explained in terms of the influence of interdependent political, financial, labor, and cultural institutions. Well-developed public training systems that involve inter-employer and employer-union collaboration are said to be associated with less "manager-worker separation" than in countries where public training systems are weak or absent, as well as business growth strategies that place emphasis on skills and innovation, and collaborative hierarchies that involve market regulation and risk sharing. In a similar vein, the "varieties of capitalism" analysis associated with Hall and Soskice (2001) focuses on attempts by firms to "develop relationships to resolve coordination problems" in respect of industrial relations, vocational training, corporate governance, inter-firm relations, and the day-to-day management of the employment relationship. According to Hall and Soskice, "co-ordinated market economies" (CMEs), such as Germany, have developed institutions that promote investment in industry and company-specific skills, discourage the poaching of skilled labor, encourage inter-firm collaboration, and facilitate the production of goods and services that require a highly skilled workforce. Liberal market economies (LMEs), such as the US and UK, by contrast, combine weak labor market regulation with a lack of institutional support for apprenticeships and the development of specialized skills. As a consequence, it is claimed that LMEs are likely to be oriented towards the production of goods and services that require general or low-level skills while CMEs are likely to produce goods and services that require higher-level company or industry-specific skills.

The studies referred to above are largely concerned with the governance of training, although the term tends not to be used explicitly. The concept of governance has been operationalized in a variety of ways (Rhodes 1996), although the most common areas of enquiry are the functions and capabilities of the state and its relationship to civil society; the practice of policy-making, including a focus on actors, interests, and processes; policy implementation, including the delivery of services and the relationship between providers and users; and normative assumptions about how societies, organizations and institutions should be governed (Daly 2003: 119). A major focus of enquiry has been the extent to which responsibilities for the delivery of government policies are being redistributed from the state to non-governmental actors (e.g., businesses, NGOs) and the associated implications for the distribution of power and exercise of authority. The governance literature extends the well-established interest of economists in evaluating the relative implications of organizing economic activity through markets, hierarchies, and networks, applying these distinctions to a broader set of concerns relating to public policy and administration. While there has been little explicit engagement with the governance debate in the VET literature (and vice versa), the distinction between markets, hierarchies, and networks closely approximates the distinction between "voluntarist"/"market-led," "developmental state"/"state driven," and "corporatist"/"cooperative" models of VET and both literatures share a concern with issues relating to interest coordination, the degree to which social agencies (including those representing business interests) are involved in policy development, and the organization of service provision. However, the analytical range of the governance literature is greater in that it focuses attention on "linkages among the community, civil society, local and regional governance, the state and the supranational level" (Daly 2003: 123). Comparative international analyses of VET, by contrast, tend to focus on national training systems, while neglecting variations within countries and the articulation between sectoral, regional, national, and supranational levels.

A core concern of the governance literature is the extent to which the authority and capacity of national governments is being eroded. This issue should be of particular concern to those with an interest in VET as the forces that are invoked by those who seek to account for alleged changes in the capacities and orientations of national governments are also said to be magnifying the importance of skill formation. According to Cerny (1995: 620) greater economic openness and capital mobility are encouraging a transition from welfare states towards "competition states," in which the focus of public policy becomes the promotion of activities "that will make firms and sectors located within the territory of the state competitive in international markets." The implication of the thesis advanced by Cerny is that the national governments of the developed economies will embrace neo-liberalism, seeking to weaken employment and labor market protections while attempting to boost the supply of skills as part of a broader strategy designed to meet the needs of businesses. An alternative analysis is provided by Jessop (2002), who argues that the "Keynesian national welfare states" of Western economies are (to varying degrees) giving way to "Schumpeterian workfare post-national regimes" (SWPRs), which are said to involve the creation of conditions that benefit business through measures designed to develop skills, knowledge and innovative capacity, cuts in social expenditure, and attempts to increase the "flexibility" of labor markets.

What are the implications for VET? If Cerny is correct, it would seem that the strong institutions that have underpinned the "high skill accumulation strategies" (Ashton and Green 1996) of economies such as Germany are likely to be threatened and the scope for cooperation between employer and trade union organizations will become more limited. By contrast, Jessop regards neo-liberalism as but one variety of SWPR and argues that SWPRs may develop in ways that are compatible with neo-corporatist and state-led approaches to organizing economic activity. His arguments in this regard bear some similarities to those of Hall and Soskice, who argue that globalization is only likely to encourage liberalization in LMEs "since firms that coordinate their endeavours primarily through the market can improve their competencies by sharpening its edges" (Hall and Soskice 2001: 57). In CMEs, by contrast, "governments should be less sympathetic to deregulation because it threatens the nation's comparative institutional advantages" (Hall and Soskice 2001: 58). Moreover, Hall and Soskice argue that, since both employers and workers derive advantages from strong institutions they are likely to take a common position in defence of regulation, preferring institutional reform to deregulation and liberalization. While Hall and Soskice do not discuss in detail the implications of their claims for VET, they would appear to imply that the VET systems of CMEs such as Germany will remain relatively stable, while those of LMEs may become even more market driven.

Contrary to the predictions of Hall and Soskice, there is evidence that political support for deregulation and threats to corporatist institutions are emerging in CMEs and that policy-makers have become more receptive to neo-liberal policies developed in LMEs, particularly as far as workfare-oriented labor market policies are concerned (Heyes 2004). However, the adoption of neo-liberal policies should not be regarded as an inevitable response to developments at the level of the international economy. Globalization is a contradictory and contested phenomenon (Clarke 2004: 29) and national politics, the balance of social forces, and the interaction of the strategies pursued by key social actors continue to be important in determining the extent and pace of globalization, the policies adopted by governments, and the extent to which they favor the interests of labor or capital.[2] In accounting for change and continuity in national VET policies and practices it is therefore essential to recognize the continuing importance of national politics.

THE SUPRANATIONAL LEVEL, MULTI-LEVEL GOVERNANCE AND THE EU

As noted, the governance debate has directed attention toward institutions, processes, and relationships that operate at, and potentially link, the sub-national, national, and surpra-national level. Commentators have increasingly come to refer to "multi-level governance," a term that, according to Peters and Pierre (2001: 7–8), refers to "negoti-ated, non-hierarchical exchanges between institutions at the transnational, national, regional and local levels" and to the "relationships between governance process at these different levels." Interest in multi-level governance has been stimulated by an alleged weakening of the steering capabilities of national governments, the emergence of new forms of sub-national governance and the challenges posed by supranational institu-tions (Peters and Pierre 2001), and the European Union in particular. Ongoing Euro-pean integration has led to the creation of new vertical relationships that involve the EC and the EU member states, and new horizontal relationships that involve coordinated actions by actors in different member states (for a detailed analysis and discussion, see Marginson and Sisson 2004). Somewhat surprisingly, the implications of European integration for the governance of training has received little attention to date, despite the importance attached to training in European social policy debates. Education and training have come to be seen as critical to ensuring the future competitiveness of EU member states and, by extension, the EU as a trading bloc. In the wake of the 2000 Lisbon Summit, during which "the European Council acknowledged that the European Union was confronted with a quantum shift resulting from globalisation and the knowledge-driven economy" (European Commission 2002: 3), the EU adopted the "Lisbon Agenda," the objective of which is to make Europe "the most competitive and dynamic knowledge-based economy in the world, capable of sustainable economic growth with more and better jobs and greater social cohesion" (2002: 3). Three strategic objectives were set for European education and training systems, encompassing basic skills, vocational and higher education, and lifelong learning: first, improving their quality and effectiveness; second, facilitating the access of all; and third, opening up education and training systems to the wider world (European Commission 2002: 4). These ambitions were further elaborated at the 2002 Barcelona European Council, which established that the European approach to education and training should become a "world reference" by 2010. The resulting "Education and Training 2010" agenda involves making education and training in Europe a "world-wide reference" for quality; facilitating the movement of citizens within the EU; validating qualifications, knowledge, and skill validated for the purpose of further learning; providing Europeans with better access to lifelong learning; and helping Europe to cooperate with other regions so that it becomes the "most-favoured destination" of students, scholars, and researchers (European Commission 2002: 50).

These objectives have been pursued through a variety of channels. The European Employment Strategy's (EES) employment guidelines, which have been developed with the aim of ensuring that the employment and social policies of EU member states are oriented towards meeting the objectives of the Lisbon agenda, include a number of measures relating to VET. The guidelines for 2005–8 mention objectives such as improving the matching of labor market needs, improving investments in human capital, ensuring inclusive labor markets, making work pay for job seekers, and improving productivity and quality at work. The governments of EU member states provide the EC with annual National Reform Programme reports (previously National Action plans) that provide information about future intended actions and progress over the previous twelve months.[3] The progress of the EU as a whole is reviewed by the EC in an annual Joint Employment Report, the most recent of which emphasized that Europe remains "behind schedule" (Council of the European Union 2008: 6) in terms of its progress towards meeting objectives relating to lifelong learning.

The European Commission regards social dialogue at European and national levels as an important channel through which progress towards the Lisbon objectives can be made. Since the mid-1980s the peak-level European employer and trade union organizations, the ETUC, CEEP, and BusinessEurope (formerly UNICE), have expressed support for a partnership approach to training and have engaged in inter-professional social dialogue on training-related matters (Heyes 2007). At the 2002 Barcelona European Council the peak-level organizations presented an agreed "Framework of Actions for the Lifelong Development of Competencies and Qualifications" (ETUC et al. 2002), which was intended to contribute to the implementation of the Lisbon strategy by providing a boost to actions relating to education and training. The joint statement asserted the need for "an intensification of dialogue and partnership" and identified four priorities: the "identification and anticipation of competencies and qualifications needs"; "recognition and validation of competencies and qualifications"; "information, support and guidance"; and "mobilising resources for the lifelong development of competencies." For the period 2002–5, the member organizations of ETUC, UNICE, and CEEP were directed to promote the framework at national level, draw up annual reports on national actions with respect to the four priorities, and evaluate the impact on companies and workers. The framework agreement thus represented a new development in the role of the social partners at European level, providing them with an enhanced role in implementation and evaluation.

Alongside the inter-professional social dialogue, training has been discussed by a number of the thirty-five (to date) sectoral social dialogue committees (SSDCs). Training and lifelong learning have been the most frequent topics of discussion for the SDDCs and by 2006 all but eight SDDCs had either undertaken initiatives or had plans to do so in the future (European Commission 2006a). The work of the SSDCs in relation to VET has tended to focus on the sharing of information and the issuing of joint statements that emphasize the importance of training to employers and encourage affiliated organizations and their members to engage in training. A number of SSDCs, for example those covering the electricity, footwear, and chemicals sectors, have initiated studies of current and possible future skills requirements in their sectors. Some, including those covering the electricity, hotels and restaurants, road transport, and postal sectors, have issued recommendations to guide practice within member states. A small number of SSDCs, including those for the construction, private security, and personal services and sea fishing sectors, have also developed training materials and other informational resources for use within member states (EC 2006a).

While the peak-level employer and union organizations are clearly devoting a considerable amount of attention to issues relating to VET, their ability to alter practices across Europe is limited in several respects (see Heyes 2007). While the social partners have since 1991 been able to substitute binding agreements for proposed legislation by the Commission, the Maastricht Protocol on Social Policy states that this does not apply to vocational education and training. The ability of the peak-level organizations to influence concrete practices is therefore entirely dependent on the willingness and capacity of their affiliates to act on their recommendations. It should be borne in mind that the peak-level employer and union organizations do not have the authority to force or, in some cases, even advise their national affiliates to act in accordance with sectoral or inter-professional recommendations and guidelines issued at the European level (Keller and Bansbach 2001). Moreover, social dialogue in respect of some sectors is entirely absent, reflecting either a lack of a representative employer organization or unwillingness on the part of employers to enter into negotiations (Keller 2003). The limitations of the power and authority of the peak-level organizations is apparent in the agricultural sector, which to date has been the only sector in which a full-blown European agreement on VET has been reached. In only five member states (Denmark, Sweden, Finland, the UK, and Austria) have there been "negotiations on the possibility of transposing the agreement to the national context" (European Commission 2006b: 99) and the practice of undertaking skills assessments, one of the agreements main recommendations, has yet to become common in Member States other than France (2006b).

The impact of the inter-professional Framework of Actions for the Lifelong Development of Competencies and Qualifications is also questionable. Progress at national level has been documented in three annual follow-up reports (ETUC et al. 2003, 2004, and 2005) and an evaluation report (ETUC et al. 2006). The last of these reviewed activities undertaken since the implementation of the Framework and highlighted those that the national-level social partners considered to be most significant. However, the origins of a number of the areas of social partner involvement and government schemes contained in the report pre-dated the implementation of the Framework of Actions and the report did not specify which activities had been undertaken as a direct consequence of the implementation of the Framework. Furthermore, little information was provided about the outcomes of the activities undertaken and the extent to which they had been successful in meeting their objectives. Therefore, while it is likely that the Framework of Actions has had a stimulating effect, its precise consequences remain unclear.

The limits of the European Commission's authority in the area of VET must also be acknowledged. Article 150 of the European Community treaty stipulates that member states of the EU retain sole responsibility for the content and organization of vocational training provision within their national borders and explicitly rules out an imposed "harmonisation of the rules and regulations of the Member States." In any case the EC has come to reject "top–down" regulation of employment and social policy in favor of the so-called "Open Method of Coordination" (OMC), which is intended to encourage the diffusion of "good practices" through information sharing, benchmarking, and mutual learning. The operation of the principles of the OMC are evident in the various recent programs and initiatives under which VET has been addressed, including the EES, the Copenhagen process, and the Framework of Actions. However, in the absence of sanctions and "hard laws," the impact of recommendations and guidelines issued at the European level depends on the extent of voluntary cooperation by national-level actors. It is therefore probable that national politics and the strategies of national-level social agencies will remain the dominant influences on VET policies and practices within EU member-states and that VET policies, practices, institutions, and outcomes will continue to differ substantially across the EU (Heyes 2007).

Looking beyond the European Union, the International Labor Organization (ILO) represents a further potential supra-national influence on training at national level. The ILO views vocational training as fundamental to the promotion of "decent work" to the extent that it is vital to the maintenance and enhancement of worker "employability," social inclusion, and equality in the labor market (ILO 2001). The organization has developed a number of instruments relating to vocational training, including the Paid Educational Leave Convention of 1974 (No. 140) and the Human Resources Development Convention of 1975 (No. 142, revised in 2004). The ILO also views the issue of training as fertile ground for social dialogue and has called upon national governments to develop long-term training strategies "which are formulated in consultation with the social partners and are integrated with economic and employment policies" (ILO 2000: para. 19). The extent to which the exhortations of the ILO have significantly influenced national practices is difficult to evaluate in the absence of systematic evidence. The effectiveness of ILO conventions is ultimately dependent on the willingness of the national governments of member countries to ratify them and implement policies that are in keeping with their recommendations. However, in developing and transitional economies in particular, the ILO has a direct influence on national practices through its technical cooperation projects. These projects, which are guided by the recommendations contained in the Human Resources Development Convention, aim to help national governments address specific training needs by developing new capacities, training policies, strategies, institutions, and delivery mechanisms.

Multinational Companies, National Business Systems and Training

As Schneider and Gröte (2006: 5) observe, the impact of internationalization on business interest organizations concerns whether an association's increasingly internationally oriented members retain an interest in national interest organizations. This is because their internal resources, size, and geographical spread mean that they are less dependent on national and international associations than nationally based companies. The implications of internationalization for the management of labor and for skill formation vary. Many companies engage in international activity, but the process of internationalization does not necessarily involve the direct management of labor in another country (Hendry 1994). Where companies export through an agent or distributor, or sell a brand name through licensing arrangements, these arrangements take the form of a contract for services with another company. In contrast, where a company engages in foreign direct investment, investing in a green field site, through acquisition or joint ventures, the company is confronted by the challenges of managing labor regulated by a different set of national institutions.

The main challenges to national institutions and systems of business representation from internationalization and globalization come from multinational companies. Nevertheless, there are different definitions of multinational companies. Edwards and Rees (2006: 46–7) contrast the approach adopted by economists, with one which gives more weight to power relations. Whereas the former focuses on the coordination of production without using market exchange and involves the firm managing across national boundaries through foreign direct investment, the latter allows the control exercised by multinationals over the production chain to be taken into consideration, outside the formal legal boundaries of the firm, as discussed by Klein (2001) in her analysis of branded goods. Multinationals are more likely to exercise an influence over the labor management practices of directly owned operations than over those of sub-contractors, although the nature of power relations in supply chains means that they have the potential to do this as well.[4]

There are two main bodies of literature analyzing the HRM strategies and, as a subset of these, training strategies in multinational companies. The first of these focuses on the strategic aspects of managing human resources across borders and, in particular, the problems of managing and rewarding expatriates (for example, Evans, Hodkinson, and Unwin 2002; Harris, Brewster, and Sparrow 2003; Scullion and Linehan 2006). More significant for our analysis is the second approach which focuses on the transfer of HRM and training practices across borders. In discussing the influence of social institutions on the training and employment practices of multinational companies, two main sets of influences have been identified. The first focuses on the company's home country, or "country of origin effects" which we have discussed in some detail in the section on training and political economy, above. With multinational companies, the following questions arise. When companies invest in other institutional environments, do they transfer practices from their country of origin?

The second set of influences focuses on the country in which the company invests. These "host country effects" concern practices relating to recruitment, training, wages, work organization, and industrial relations are affected by a range of environmental influences that derive from local social institutions. As far as training and skill formation are concerned, these institutions affect the availability of suitably trained and educated labor and institutional and legal influences on company practices, such as requirements to recruit local labor, to train (Rubery and Grimshaw 2003: 218) and to consult and involve employee representatives on training. There are variations in the extent to which employment relations and training are regulated by law in different countries, which raise a series of questions about the company's relationship to the host country. Are multinational companies able to pay premium rates of pay and poach educated and trained workers from other domestic employers? What is their bargaining power vis-à-vis the nation state and can they avoid compliance with national regulations?

Edwards (2004) has identified two further sets of influences within a "four influences" framework. "Dominance effects" (Smith and Meiskins 1995) refer to the way in which the HRM practices of dominant economies are emulated by other companies. Examples of this can be seen in the widespread adoption of the management practices of US companies in the post-war period and, more recently, the dissemination of Japanese management practices. Finally, Edwards (2004) argues that the development of internal management structures within MNCs based on regional structures may replace "host country effects." Although regionalization is evident in many MNC organizational structures, it is particularly in evidence in the development of the "Eurocompany" (Marginson 2004).

A final factor relating to multinational companies concerns the role of the supply of well-qualified labor and institutional infrastructures in their locational decisions. In newly industrializing economies in Asia, such as Singapore, South Korea, and Taiwan, the state has played a prominent role in promoting and sustaining investment in skills to support industrialization, learning from the experience of the advanced economies and multinational companies. The developmental state provides a distinctive model for promoting skill formation, which has allowed these economies to speed up the process of industrialization, develop specialized niches in the world market and anticipate future skills needs, whilst attracting multinational investment in their economies (Ashton and Green 1996: 156–8). The relationship between the developmental state and multinational companies raises fundamental questions about the respective roles of the state and companies in innovation and skill formation, and for the relationship between private and public interests.

The discussion in this section considers the extent to which the internationalization of companies' activities leads to convergence in training and HRM practices or whether institutional structures, located in the nation state, continue to structure local practices. The research on the strategies of multinational companies suggests that practice is contingent on a range of factors relating to the characteristics of the home and host countries of the companies, as well as their strategies and sources of competitive advantage. Social institutions governing vocational education and training systems and other aspects of the employment relationship impact on the organization of work. As Whitley (2000) notes, national business systems are "linked to the nature of firms, interest groups, and dominance governance principles of 'rules of the game' in different societies, which in turn stem from different patterns of industrialisation" (88). Nevertheless, the transformation of a prevalent system will be limited by the extent to which work system characteristics are integrated with institutional arrangements (114).

Conclusion

Vocational education and training systems are rooted in national social institutions. In this chapter we have considered the implications of internationalization, liberalization, and the activities of multinational companies for changes in the relationship between the state, business, and these nationally based training systems. Early debates on the role of knowledge and skills in competitive strategies in the developed economies suggested that the threat from emerging economies such as China and India was from low wage costs, but the experience of other newly industrializing countries in Asia suggests that where the state takes a more strategic and developmental role in training and industrial policy, a new model of skill formation may be emerging.

In the face of globalization, in both its real and perceived effects, national governments have modernized their education and training systems. On the basis of a ten-country comparative study of training systems, Bosch and Charest (2010) identify that apprenticeship systems have mainly survived in countries with strong dual systems, such as Germany and Denmark. Elsewhere, the state is taking an increasing role in the provision of vocational training through the education system. This comes at a time in which there is a neo-liberal agenda promoting the marketization of higher education systems; the growing role of the workfare state and conditionality of welfare benefits (Peck 2001); and a shift in policy discourse towards individual responsibility for lifelong learning and employability (Rainbird 2002).

The emergence of regional blocs has the potential to create a new arena for state/business relations, the most developed being the European Union. We have therefore spent some time discussing the emergence of a system of multi-level governance of training in the EU. In the light of increasing internationalized nature of MNE activities, we have explored their relationship to nationally based labor forces and the education and training systems which shape the supply of labor. Although the changed conditions of competitiveness in the twenty-first century have prompted the International Labor Organization to issue new recommendations on training, the extent to which they influence nation states and nationally based associations remains to be seen. As far as self-regulation is concerned, there is a potential role for training in relation to the emergence of companies' concerns with corporate social responsibility. However, self-regulation has not been particularly effective in enforcing minimum labor standards, so it is difficult to see how it could have an impact on training. Finally, the international migration and "poaching" of qualified labor is an arena in which market failure emerges on an international level. At present, regulation is emerging on a piecemeal basis, often through the actions of professional organizations (Bach 2007), trade unions, and bilateral agreements between nation states. Employers and their associations have had little input in this arena.[5]

At the beginning of this chapter, we drew attention to Wilson's (2001) distinction between interest group studies as a form of political participation and a sociological approach to the understanding of the role of business interests in social institutions. Our analysis suggests that the policy arena of vocational education and training raises many questions which could be addressed from both these perspectives. Moreover, the developments analyzed in this chapter have implications for the way comparative international research in respect of training is conducted. Despite the attention given to industrial relations actors and institutions, the comparative literature on training has largely failed to keep pace with developments in comparative industrial relations research, which, as Strauss (1998) notes, has developed beyond "parallel descriptions" of institutions and practices within different countries in order to connect with developments at supra-national and sub-national levels (see Locke 1992). By contrast, research in the area of vocational training continues to focus on nation states and the policies of national actors, which are generally treated as undifferentiated across economic sectors[6] (Heyes 2002). Furthermore, a fixation with "national models" of training has encouraged a related tendency towards overlooking pressures for change. Viewing training as a potentially contested focus of multi-level governance may encourage a richer analysis—one that is sensitive to the articulation of the different levels at which the interests of business, employers, and policy-makers are expressed and given force, and the range of political, social, and economic pressures that may serve to reshape these interests over time.

NOTES

1. For critical analyses of these concepts see, e.g., Rees (2000); Keep and Rainbird (2000); Thompson, Warhurst, and Callaghan (2001): on the debate on the new forms of work organization, the "learning organization" and knowledge work, respectively.
2. For a detailed critical assessment of the arguments put forth by Cerny and Jessop, see Hay (2004). For a skeptical analysis of the impact of globalization on European welfare states, see Navarro, Schmitt, and Astudillo (2004). For a discussion of the continuing influence of national politics on industrial relations practices, policies, and institutions, see Hamann and Kelly (2003).
3. The reports are available at http://ec.europa.eu/employment_social/employment_strategy/national_en.htm
4. The ability of multinational companies to exercise influence over labor relations in suppliers is evident where they wish to demonstrate their corporate social responsibility credentials through enforcing adherence to international labor standards.
5. Personal communication, Colleen McNeil-Walsh, doctoral student, Birmingham Business School, University of Birmingham, working on the international migration of South African nurses to the UK social care sector.
6. For an exception, see Debrah and Ofori (2001).

REFERENCES

ASHTON, D., and GREEN, F. 1996. *Education, Training and the Global Economy.* Cheltenham: Edward Elgar.
—— SUNG, J., and TURBIN, J. 2000. "Towards a framework for the comparative analysis of national systems of skill formation," *International Journal of Training and Development* 4(1): 8–25.
AUER, P., and CAZES, S. 2000. "The resilience of the long-term employment relationship: evidence from industrialized countries," *International Labour Review* 139(4): 379–408.
BACH, S. 2007. "Going global? The regulation of nurse migration in the UK," *British Journal of Industrial Relations* 45(2): 383–403.
BARNEY, J. 1995. "Looking inside for competitive advantage," *Academy of Management Executive* 9(4): 49–61.
BECK, U. 2000. *The Brave New World of Work.* Cambridge: Polity Press.
BECKER, G. S. 1964. *Human Capital: A Theoretical and Empirical Analysis, with Special Reference to Education.* Chicago: University of Chicago Press.
BOSCH, G., and CHAREST, J. 2010. *Vocational Training: International Inernational Perspectives.* London: Routledge.
BOWLES, S., and GINTIS, H. 1976. *Schooling in Capitalist America: Educational Reform and the Contradictions of Economic Life.* New York: Basic Books.
BROWN, P. 2001. "Skill formation in the twenty-first century," in P. Brown, A. Green, and H. Lauder, *High Skills, Globalisation, Competitiveness and Skill Formation.* Oxford: Oxford University Press.
CAILLODS, F. 1994. "Converging trends amidst diversity in vocational training systems," *International Labour Review* 133(2): 241–57.
CERNY, P. G. 1995. "Globalization and the changing logic of collective action," *International Organization* 49(4): 595–625.

CLARKE, J. 2004. "Dissolving the public realm? The logics and limits of neo-liberalism," *Journal of Social Policy* 33(1): 27–48.

COEN, D., and GRANT, W. 2006. "Managing business and government relations," in D. Coen and W. Grant, eds., *Business and Government: Methods and Practice*. Opladen: Barbara Budrich Publishers.

Commission of the European Communities. 2005. *Communication from the Commission to the Council and the European Parliament: Common Actions for Growth and Employment. The Community Lisbon Programme*. COM(2005) 330 final.

Council of the European Union 2008. *Joint Employment Report 2007/2008*, available at http://bancadati.italialavoro.it/BDD_WEB/bdd/publishcontents/bin/C_21_DocEuropea_786_documenti_itemName_0_documento.pdf accessed August, 18 2009.

CROUCH, C., and STREECK, W. 1997. *Political Economy of Modern Capitalism*. London: Sage Publications.

——FINEGOLD, D., and SAKO, M. 1999. *Are Skills the Answer? The Political Economy of Skill Creation in Advanced Industrialised Countries*. Oxford: Oxford University Press.

DALY, M. 2003. "Governance and social policy," *Journal of Social Policy* 32(1): 113–28.

DEBRAH, Y. A., and OFORI, G. 2001. "The state, skill formation and productivity enhancement in the construction industry: the case of Singapore," *International Journal of Human Resource Management* 12(2): 184–202.

EATON, J. 2000. *Comparative Industrial Relations: An Introduction*. Cambridge: Polity Press.

EDWARDS, T. 2004. "The transfer of employment practices across borders in mutli-national companies," in A.-W. Harzing and J. Van Ruysseveldt, eds., *International Human Resource Management*, 2nd edn. London: Sage.

——and REES, C. 2006. *International Human Resource Management: Globalization, National Systems and Multinational Companies*. Harlow: Pearson Education Ltd.

ETUC, UNICE, and CEEP. 2002. *Framework of Actions for the Lifelong Development of Competencies and Qualifications*, available at http://www.etuc.org/a/580

ETUC, UNICE/UEAPME, and CEEP. 2003. *Framework of Actions for the Lifelong Development of Competencies and Qualifications: First Follow-up Report*, available at: http://etuc.sydesy.com/a/1123

——————2004. *Framework of Actions for the Lifelong Development of Competencies and Qualifications: Second Follow-up Report*, available at: http://www.etuc.org/a/650

——————2005. *Framework of Actions for the Lifelong Development of Competencies and Qualifications: Third Follow-up Report*, available at: http://www.etuc.org/a/901

——————2006. *Framework of Actions for the Lifelong Development of Competencies and Qualifications: Evaluation Report 2006*, available at: http://www.etuc.org/a/2319

European Commission. 2002. "Detailed work programme on the follow-up of the objectives of education and training systems in Europe," *Official Journal of the European Communities*, 2002/C 142/01.

——2004. *Recent Developments in the European Inter-professional Social Dialogue 2002–03*. Luxembourg: Office for Official Publications of the European Communities.

——2006a. *Recent Developments in the European Sectoral Social Dialogue*. Luxembourg: Office for Official Publications of the European Communities.

——2006b. *Industrial Relations in Europe 2006*. Brussels: European Commission.

EVANS, K., HODKINSON, P., and UNWIN, L., eds. 2002. *Working to Learn: Transforming Learning in the Workplace*. London: Kogan Page.

FERNER, A., 1998. "Country of origin effects and HRM in multinational companies," *Human Resource Management Journal* 7(1): 19–37.

GEMMELL, N. 1996. "Evaluating the impacts of human capital stocks and accumulation on economic growth: some new evidence," *Oxford Bulletin of Economics and Statistics* 58(1): 9–28.

GRANT, W. 1985. *The Political Economy of Corporatism*. Basingstoke: Macmillan.

GREEN, A. 1990. *Education and State Formation: The Rise of Education Systems in England France and the USA*. Basingstoke: Macmillan.

HALL, P. A., and SOSKICE, D. 2001. "An introduction to varieties of capitalism," in P. Hall and D. Soskice, eds., *Varieties of Capitalism: The Institutional Foundations of Comparative Advantage*. Oxford: Oxford University Press.

HAMANN, K., and KELLY, J. 2003. "The domestic sources of differences in labour market policies," *British Journal of Industrial Relations* 41(4): 639–64.

HARRIS, H., BREWSTER, C., and SPARROW, P. 2003. *International Human Resource Management*. London: CIPD.

HARZING, A.-W. 2004. "Strategy and structure of multinational companies," in A.-W. Harzing and J. Van Ruysseveldt, eds., 2004. *International Human Resource Management*, 2nd edn. London: Sage.

HAWORTH, N., and HUGHES, S. 2003. "International political economy and industrial relations," *British Journal of Industrial Relations* 41(4): 665–82.

HAY, C. 2004. "Re-stating politics, re-politicising the state: neo-liberalism, economic imperatives and the rise of the competition state," *Political Quarterly* 75(1): 38–50.

HEIDEMANN, W., KRUSE, W., PAUL-KOHLHOFF, A., and ZEUENER, C. 1994. *Social Dialogue and Further Education and Training in Europe: New Challenges for Trade Unions*. Berlin: Ed Sigma.

HENDRY, C. 1994. *Human Resource Strategies for International Growth*. London: Routledge.

HEYES, J. 2002. "Training, social dialogue and collective bargaining: issues for comparative research," Conference on Training, Employability & Employment, Monash University Centre, July, 11–12, 2002.

—— 2004. *The Changing Role of Labour Ministries: Influencing Labour, Employment and Social Policy*. In-focus Program on Social Dialogue Paper No. 6. Geneva: International Labor Office.

—— 2007. "Training, social dialogue and collective bargaining in Western Europe," *Economic and Industrial Democracy* 28(2): 239–58.

HM Treasury, Department for Work and Pensions, Department for Education and Skills. 2004. *Supporting Young People to Achieve: Towards a New Deal for Skills*. London: HM Treasury, Department for Work and Pensions, Department for Education and Skills.

International Labor Organization. 1998. *World Employment Report 1998–99: Employability in the Global Economy—How Training Matters*. Geneva: International Labor Office.

—— 2003. *Learning and Training for Work in the Knowledge Society*. Report IV. Geneva: International Labor Office.

JESSOP, B. 2002. *The Future of the Capitalist State*. Cambridge: Polity Press.

JORDAN, A. 2001. "The European Union: an evolving system of multi-level governance . . . or government?" *Policy & Politics* 29(2): 193–208.

KEEP, E., and RAINBIRD, H. 2000. "Towards the learning organization?" in S. Bach and K. Sisson, eds., *Personnel Management: A Comprehensive Guide to Theory and Practice*. Oxford: Blackwell.

KELLER, B. 2003. "Social dialogues: the state of the art a decade after Maastricht," *Industrial Relations Journal* 34(5): 411–29.

—— and BANSBACH, M. 2001. "Social dialogues: tranquil past, troubled present and uncertain future," *Industrial Relations Journal* 32(5): 419–34.

KLEIN, N. 2001. *No Logo*. London: Flamingo.

LOCKE, R. M. 1992. "The demise of the national union in Italy: lessons for comparative industrial relations theory," *Industrial and Labor Relations Review* 45(2): 229–49.

MACDUFFIE, J. P., and KOCHAN, T. A. 1995. "Do US firms invest less in human resources? Training in the world auto industry," *Industrial Relations* 34(2): 147–68.

MARCHINGTON, M., GRIMSHAW, D., RUBERY, J., and WILLMOTT, H., eds. 2003. *Fragmenting Work, Blurring Organizational Boundaries and Disordering Hierarchies*. Oxford: Oxford University Press.

MARGINSON, P. 2004. "The Eurocompany and European Works Councils," in A.-W. Harzing and J. Van Ruysseveldt, eds., *International Human Resource Management*, 2nd edn. London: Sage.

—— and SISSON, K. 2004. *European Integration and Industrial Relations: Multi-Level Governance in the Making*. Basingstoke: Palgrave MacMillan.

MASON, G., VAN ARK, B., and WAGNER, K. 1994. "Productivity, product quality and workforce skills: food processing in four European countries," *National Institute Economic Review* 1: 62–83.

MAURICE, M., SELLIER, F., and SILVESTRE, J.-J. 1986. *The Social Foundations of Industrial Power*. Cambridge, Mass.: MIT Press.

MINCER, J. A., 1974. *Schooling, Experience and Earnings*. New York: Columbia University Press.

NAVARRO, V., SCHMITT, J., and ASTUDILLO, J. 2004. "Is globalisation undermining the welfare state?," *Cambridge Journal of Economics* 28: 133–52.

PECK, J. 2001. *Workfare States*. New York: Gildford Press.

PETERS, G., and PIERRE, J. 2001. "Developments in intergovernmental relations: towards multi-level governance," *Policy & Politics* 29(2): 131–5.

RAINBIRD, H. 2002. "No rights, just responsibilities: individual demand for continuing training," in K. Evans, P. Hodkinson, and L. Unwin, eds., *Working to Learn: Transforming Learning in the Workplace*. London: Kogan Page.

REES, C. 2000. "Training and new forms of work organisation," in H. Rainbird, ed., *Training in the Workplace: Critical Perspectives on Training at Work*. Basingstoke: Macmillan.

RHODES, R. A. W. 1996. "The new governance: governing without government," *Political Studies* 44: 652–67.

RIFKIN, J. 2000. *The End of Work*. Harmondsworth: Penguin Books.

ROMER, P. 1990. "Endogenous technological change," *Journal of Political Economy* 98: 71–102.

RUBERY, J., and GRIMSHAW, D. 2003. *The Organisation of Employment: An International Perspective*. Basingstoke: Palgrave.

SCHMITTER, P., and STREECK, W., eds. 1985. *Private Interest Government: Beyond Market and State*. London: Sage.

SCHNEIDER, V., and GRÖTE, J. R. 2006. "Introduction: business associations, associative order and internationalisation," in W. Streeck, J. R. Gröte, V. Schneider, and J. Visser, eds., *Governing Interests: Business Associations Facing Internationalisation*. London: Routledge.

SCULLION, H., and LINEHAN, M., eds. 2006. *International Human Resource Management*. Basingstoke: Palgrave Macmillan.

SHELDRAKE, J., and VICKERSTAFF, S. 1987. *The History of Industrial Training in Britain*. Aldershot: Avebury.

SMITH, C., and MEISKINS, P. 1995. "System, society and dominance effects in cross-national organisational analysis," *Work, Employment and Society* 9(2): 241–67.

SOLOW, R. M. 1956. "A contribution to the theory of economic growth," *Quarterly Journal of Economics* 70(1): 65–94.

STEDWARD, G., 2003. "Education as industrial policy: New Labour's marriage of the social and the economic," *Policy & Politics* 31(2): 139–52.

STRAUSS, G. 1998. "Comparative international industrial relations," in K. Whitfield and G. Strauss, eds., *Researching the World of Work: Strategies and Methods in Researching Industrial Relations.* Ithaca, NY: Cornell University Press.

STREECK, W. 1989 "Skills and the limits to neo-liberalism: the enterprise of the future as a place of learning," *Work, Employment and Society* 3(1): 89–104.

——1992. "Productive constraints: on the institutional conditions of diversified quality production," in W. Streeck, *Social Institutions and Economic Performance: Institutional Studies of Industrial Relations in Advanced Capitalist Economies.* London: Sage.

THOMPSON, P., WARHURST, C., and CALLAGHAN, G. 2001. "Ignorant theory and knowledge-able workers: interrogating the connections between knowledge, skills and services," *Journal of Management Studies* 38(7) :923–42.

TRAXLER, F. 2006. "Economic internationalisation and the organisational dilemma of employer associations: a comparison of 20 OECD countries," in W. Streeck, J. R. Gröte, V. Schneider, and J. Visser, eds., *Governing Interests: Business Associations Facing Internationalisation.* London: Routledge.

WEBSTER, A. 1993. "The skill and higher educational content of UK net exports," *Oxford Bulletin of Economics & Statistics* 55(2): 141–59.

WHITLEY, R. 1999. *Divergent Capitalisms: The Social Structuring and Change of Business Systems.* Oxford: Oxford University Press.

WILSON, G. K. 2001. "The dual motives of interest group studies," paper presented to the ECPR research conference, University of Kent, Canterbury, September.

WINTERTON, J. 2000. "Social dialogue over vocational training in market-led systems," *International Journal of Training and Development* 4(1): 26–41.

CHAPTER 24

SOCIAL POLICY AND BUSINESS

CATHIE JO MARTIN

INTRODUCTION

BUSINESS and social policy are terms seldom linked positively in the lexicon of daily life. We often assume, intuitively, that firms wish to avoid taxes, big government, and the welfare state: business managers need to think about the bottom line, first and foremost, and spending on the social needs of workers and other citizens is not at the top of their to-do list. But in fact, employers' engagement in the social world has been extensive, seemingly inconsistent with this conventional wisdom, and important to public policy. Many companies provide health or training benefits for their own workers, and some support government programs for the social needs of the broader citizenry.

This chapter seeks to ascertain the full measure of the relationship between business and the welfare state and to understand when employers reluctantly accept, tolerate, or even actively pursue the provision of social benefits. We first review the relevant literature to pinpoint business motivations for supporting the creation of social benefits, either within the firm or by the state. We then explore the institutional conditions that encourage employers to cast a sympathetic eye on the welfare state. We suggest that employers have varied reasons for accepting and even seeking the provision of social benefits, ranging from mitigating labor unrest to securing productivity enhancements. Higher levels of employer organization, somewhat unexpectedly, make firms and national business communities *more likely* to support social programs. The structure and strategies of government and, in particular, the structure of party competition have been profoundly important both to the organization of employers and to their subsequent involvement with the social arena. These insights into the relationship between employers and the social realm have important consequences for our thinking about the expansion of the welfare state, for the sources of corporate preferences, and for the development of business as a social class.

THE BENEFITS OF SOCIAL PROTECTIONS FOR EMPLOYERS

Why might employers actually desire social policies? As a starting point, it is important to reinforce that firms want profits, first and foremost; indeed, the claim of this chapter is *not* that companies are motivated by altruism to support social issues (although many corporations do participate in various charitable activities). Companies look unfavorably on policies—social and otherwise—that increase their costs of production, interfere with their profitability, or interfere with managerial control. All things being equal, we would expect firms to oppose increased tax burdens or policies to raise the wage floor of collective bargaining (Block 1977; Lindblom 1977; Jacobs 1988; and for critical appraisals, Przeworski and Wallerstein 1988; Swank 1992).

Yet all things are not equal and employers might support social policies when they believe that the benefits outweigh the costs. Thus this chapter investigates the situations in which companies view social supports as contributing to their bottom lines. Several broad motivations might bring companies to develop social benefits for their own workers or to support government programs to provide a social good.

First, firms that might otherwise oppose social spending might be pressured into it by other actors. Just as partners in any long-term relationship learn to make the requisite accommodations, companies might determine that social benefits to keep employees happy would be a positive boon for workplace stability and productivity. Firms with highly organized workers might be forced into such accommodations; alternatively, companies might create these programs in order to keep unions at bay (Jacoby 1977; Ferguson 1984; Bowman 1985; Gordon 1991). Governments also might choose to create social policies when confronted with highly organized labor movements that seek to alter the balance of power between capital and labor with high levels of social redistribution. Thus scholars have noted that countries with a high degree of union organization and working-class participation in government through left parties tend to have larger welfare states (Korpi 1980; Stephens 1980; Hicks and Swank 1992). At the same time, one often finds broad cross-class coalitions between segments of business and segments of labor in countries. In these countries, business is persuaded to join the political coalitions in support of social benefits because they recognize the likelihood of certain types of legislative outcomes, alter their expectations accordingly, and seek to make an impact on the outcomes (Hacker and Pierson 2002).

Firms may also support social policies because they are more susceptible to governmental pressures; for example, those employers who sell to the public sector have been shown to be significantly more likely to offer political support for governmental policies (Dobbin 1992; Grier Munger, and Roberts 1994; Martin 1995). For example, a British manager rationalized his company's participation in active labor market programs for the long-term unemployed: "The firm's business is heavily tied to the Ministry of Defense and to the government. So we felt obliged to support a new, and very key program for the Blair government" (Martin 1995).

Second, employers might discover social regulations to be in their strategic interests: if they can better afford the burdens of social mandates than their competitors, they might see the imposition of these mandates as a mechanism by which they could gain a competitive advantage. Or they might simply be better able to afford the burdens of social spending and, therefore, be more willing to accept these burdens. Wilensky (2002), for example, found national affluence to be a significant determinant of a country's level of social spending (Wilensky 2002). Larger firms with a greater amount of organizational slack have been shown to be more to take advantage of these selective advantages (Jacobs 1988; Gordon 1991). Alternatively, in countries with smaller firms, managers might prefer governments to provide social benefits in order to take responsibility for the social risks associated with work (Baldwin 1990).

Finally, social benefits may make a positive contribution to the production process, in that they may have relevance for economic productivity and profitability. The most prominent contribution of social protections to economic production is in the area of education and skills development. A US Census Bureau study sought to isolate the contribution of workforce training to employees' productivity, and found that a 10 per cent increase in educational attainment improves productivity by 8.6 per cent, while an equal increase in capital stock value only produces a 3.4 per cent rise in productivity (Applebome 1995: 22).

The link between skills and economic productivity has grown in recent decades with technological changes in manufacturing, the decline of Fordist production strategies, and the incredible expansion of the service economy. In manufacturing sectors, consumer tastes now demand variety (and shorter production runs) and computer technologies call for a worker with a jack-of-all-trades skills set rather than an assembly-line automaton; therefore, many manufacturing workers must now possess the mental agility to adapt to their everchanging tasks. Investment in new skills has also become more critical with economic transition, because significant retraining is necessary to bring individuals up to date in the new economy. Just as the passage from agriculture to manufacturing production drove post-Second World War expansion of education and training, "de-industrialization," or the decline in manufacturing employment, has pressured policy-makers to expand training, job placement, and related services to assist those in transition from traditional industrial jobs (Iversen and Cusack 2000). Increases in unemployment rates more generally automatically swell (passive) unemployment compensation and pressure policy-makers to provide increased access to training and labor market services (Hicks 1999; Huber and Stephens 2001; Swank 2002).

With the transition to services, a growing percentage of jobs are also requiring post-secondary education: Service sector jobs represent about 69 per cent of total employment among the EU 15, and high-skilled service sector jobs are growing the most rapidly (OECD 2005). While 29 per cent of American jobs required post-secondary education (associate degree or post-secondary vocational award and higher) in 2000, 31 per cent will require these degrees by 2010 and positions requiring only work-related training are growing more slowly (12 per cent) than those requir-ing bachelors' degrees (22 per cent) (Hecker 2001). A survey by the Business Council of New York State (1998) found 45 per cent of companies reporting a moderate or severe gap between newly hired workers' skills and employers' needs. Sixty-four per cent of a National Association of Manufacturers' sample favored the creation of "a national, business-run remedial education program" (Towers Perrin 1991: 30).

This perceived link between skills training and productivity drove the education and training initiatives that were a centerpiece of Tony Blair's first term, and the administration lobbied employers vigorously to participate in the effort. Vocational training has historically received limited support in Britain, and Blair hoped to develop non-academic programs that would better train workers for real jobs. Employers were asked to help with the development of a template of requisite skills in each industrial sector, and Blair set out to create networks of firms organized into "Sector Skills Councils" that would be licensed to establish skills standards for workers in their industry (Secretary of State for Education and Skills 2005: 6–20).

Other types of social programs also contribute to worker productivity, by indir-ectly fostering the development of worker skills and/or productivity. Unemployment insurance gives future labor force participants the economic security to defer work in order to invest in skills formation with training (Estevez-Abe, Iversen, and Soskice 2001; Mares 2001). Pensions help to ease older, less productive workers out of the labor force (Quadagno 1988; Myles 1989; Mares 2001).

Quality child care and flexible family leave policies have been adopted to expand support for working women, to curb absenteeism, and to improve retention rates. Concerns about potential labor shortages have caused managers to think about investing in future workforce. Mothers with children and good child care could fill the labor gaps. Thus, 55 per cent of a Fortune 1000 sample favored work/family policies to offset potential future labor shortages (Galinsky and Friedman 1993). Work/family policies claim to increase productivity on the assumption that happy parents make happy workers. New mothers in firms with flexible leave policies and health care expressed greater satisfaction, had lower levels of absenteeism, took less time off during pregnancy, and were more likely to return to their jobs (Hawthorne 1993). AETNA's Denise Cichon explained the connection between quality day care and absenteeism: "The better the quality of care, the less likely it is to have a breakdown in care" (interview with author). Work/family policies claim to reduce turnover, which is enormously expensive for a company, as hiring new workers may cost as much as 93 per cent of a yearly salary. AETNA calculated saving $2 million in 1991 by not having to hire and train replacement workers, because 91 per cent of its workers return after taking a family leave (Verespej 1993).

In the United States, the only advanced industrial country lacking national health insurance, employment-based health insurance has been the norm; yet American business is deeply ambivalent about this burden. On the one hand, health benefits are argued to make for more productive workers and the expansion of firm-based plans was initially justified on these grounds (Hacker 2002). Worker productivity has driven the recent interest in preventive health care, and less comprehensive medical plans that are cheaper in the short term have been shown to be less cost effective in the long run (Porter and Teisberg 2006). Yet the health burden has been steadily growing and employers have increasingly asked for a larger government role in the regulation if not provision of health insurance. During the Clinton health reform cycle, American manufacturers expressed concern about the enormous costs of their health benefits, compared to the burden of firms in countries with national health insurance. Health care was found to add $700 to the price of an American-made car, but only $200 to an auto made in Japan, and health costs for each hourly Canadian steelworker were calculated to be $3,200 a year, compared with $7,600 a year for comparable US workers (Williams 1991). A 1991 Harris poll found two-thirds of its corporate sample at least somewhat accepting of an employer mandates to provide health insurance, although much of this corporate support disappeared during the Clinton health financing legislative battle ("Leaders Look at Health Care" 1991; Martin 2000).

Institutions and Employers' Interests in Social Protections

Despite the varied benefits of social policies for economic production and productivity, these social benefits tend to be under-supplied due to a collective action problem. Firms that provide benefits cannot always be assured that their workers will remain loyal to the company. Such firms—that develop the skills of their workers or provide work–family benefits for young parents—run the risk that their workers will leave the firm when the benefits are no longer needed. Trained workers have an incentive to take jobs at other companies where training is not provided and that can, consequently, pay higher wages.

Employers' ability to provide social benefits is becoming less tenable, at precisely the moment when certain social needs are more pressing than ever. While changes in the organization of work and the transition to the post-industrial economy are demanding higher levels of human capital investment, global competitive pressures are limiting private firms' ability to fund their workers' social needs. Competition in global markets with countries with lower wage structures makes it more difficult for firms in high-wage countries to sustain increases in their total rates of compensation. Pressures of global competition have placed the system of employer-based health insurance in the United States under considerable stress in recent years, because many firms feel that they simply cannot afford to provide health benefits. By 2004 nearly one-fifth of working Americans lacked health insurance (up from 16.3 per cent in 1996) and over half of these 45.5 million uninsured Americans had jobs (Employee Benefit Research Institute 2005).

The degree to which employers embrace the provision of social benefits (both to their own workers and to citizens in general) is influenced by several types of institutional structures: the structure of the welfare state; the institutions for coordinating employers; and the institutional structures of the state. Thus, the difficulties individual firms face in providing social benefits to their workers can be resolved by institutional, collective arrangements, and the following pages delve into how institutions work to strengthen employers' commitment to social policies.

First, social programs may well meet needs of capitalist economies, but the congruence of some employers and the welfare state is partially influenced by the form and the mechanisms by which social benefits are provided. Esping-Andersen (1990) identifies three fundamental types of welfare regimes—a social democratic, Christian Democratic, and liberal one. Social democratic systems rely heavily on universal social assistance and direct benefits programs that designate the entire eligible population as beneficiaries; this means that most of the programs that raise the incomes of poor people are programs that also raise the incomes of the middle class. While public spending levels are quite high in these countries, the quality of public services and benefits are also high and the absence of means-tested programs means that social provision is not stigmatized as an intervention for marginal citizens. Historically there has been an enormous amount of support for these universal benefits in Scandinavian countries, both by employers and by the public more generally. The Danish Conservative Party, representing urban employers, began supporting comprehensive and compulsory social provision after its Workers' Commission was impressed by Bismarck's social experiments. The extensive public system of social provision was aided by the strong organization of Danish business, and ironically the Social Democrats opposed many of these early social reforms (Møller 1992).

Christian Democratic systems (in Germany, Austria, France, etc.) rely heavily on social insurance for benefits such as unemployment insurance, health, and pensions. Although the programs are nearly universal in covering individuals at risk, the transfers are made on the basis of social contributions, which reinforces status differentials—higher paid individuals get better benefits. In addition, the programs are often tied to work and/or unions, therefore, the male breadwinner typically does better than his wife who works inside the home. Social spending levels are quite high in these countries, but they are much less redistributive and spending is often geared toward enhancing the productivity of the core economy and keeping workers stable rather than equal. This emphasis on productivity has brought employers to offer strong support for social programs, as they may use these programs for their own needs (Thelen 2004), but the emphasis on work has created a dualism between labor market participants and those marginal to the core economy (Martin and Thelen 2007).

Finally, liberal welfare regimes (found in the United States and Great Britain) provide benefits through social insurance programs for middle-class workers and means-tested state assistance for poor people. This dual provision system stigmatizes those receiving support from government, because these public benefits are not viewed as "earned" through social contributions like social insurance benefits for workers (Esping-Andersen 1990). A huge component of the liberal system is privately provided, largely through work: employment-based programs for health, pensions, and even child care evolved through collective bargaining negotiations and were supported by employers in the core economy as a substitute for wage increases. In liberal countries, employers have, therefore, been quite supportive of social benefits for their own workers but are much less enthusiastic about programs for the socially excluded (Stevens 1986; Martin 2000; Hacker 2002).

Related to the question of who benefits from social programs is the issue of how these programs are implemented and funded; consequently, Goodin and Rein (2001) suggest that greater attention be paid to the "pillars" of the welfare state—market, state, and community/family. While some natural affinities link regimes to pillars (liberal welfare regimes often depend on the market, corporatist welfare regimes often rely on the community/family, and social democratic welfare regimes often rely on the state), welfare states can combine in odd ways. Employers tend to believe more in social programs that are administered by non-state entities, which are considered more effective (Vogel 1978). But Danish employers backed government provision of social benefits at a very early stage, in part because the small firms wanted government to assume social risks (Baldwin 1992) and this permitted easier legislation of future government programs.

In some other continental European countries, highly organized labor and business associations—extending across most of the economy—developed collective social benefits for broad categories of workers. In such situations, employees pay into health and pension funds that are administered by the social partners and training is coordinated by industrial sector associations (Esping-Andersen 1990). Bismarck, advisor to Kaiser Wilhelm II, invented a "welfare monarchy" system of government-administered social insurance that would prevent more radical solutions to the ills of the day and tie the industrial worker firmly to the state. Bismarck's compulsory social insurance drew considerable backing from German employers, yet somewhat surprisingly, German employers diverged from Bismarck's original plan in successfully demanding that *firms* rather than government administer old age pensions and industrial accident insurance. In an impressive policy shift Bismarck caved in to business demands and created corporative associations to administer workmen's compensation and other benefits, even while trade unionists and leftists denounced Bismarck's plan as blatant political machination (Bowen 1947: 154–6; Rimlinger 1971: 108–13, 117–22).

In countries such as the United States, a greater share of social provision was left up to individual firms (Quadagno 1988). Beginning in the 1920s, some companies sought to create social benefits for their workers in order to keep labor happy (and to prevent the spread of unionization), to keep workers healthy, and to move older employees out of the workforce to make way for younger, more productive labor. Some American firms sought to develop social provision to curb labor unrest; to this end, the National Civic Federation offered technical advice to firms about the development of child care, housing, health, and training programs (Weinstein 1968: 17–19). Many large manufacturers developed old age pensions, so that by 1935 these plans purported to cover as much as 80 per cent of the workforce, although in reality a much smaller proportion met the service requirements (Myles 1989: 29, 12–13; Gordon 1991: 171). Over 400 firms offered on-site health care to their workers by 1926 (Brandes 1976: 99). The popularity of this welfare capitalism combined with the relative absence of national social legislation added up to a shadow welfare state in the American political economy (Stevens 1986). Yet this private provision of social benefits has led to a lower level of benefits, even when factoring in the large private welfare state (Esping-Andersen 1990; Hacker 2002).

Employers' views of the welfare state will also be influenced by how social welfare systems interact with institutions for economic coordination. As scholars working on the "varieties of capitalism" have noted, core institutions enhance employers' support for social policies by fostering a relationship between social protections and certain types of competitive strategies (Kitschelt et al. 1999; Estevez-Abe et al. 2001; Hall and Soskice 2001; and Swenson 2002). National economies can be sorted into two broad varieties of capitalism with different employer competitive strategies, and divergent views of the fit between social protections and economic production. Employers in coordinated market economies (CME) realize that in addition to deriving economic advantage from physical and factor components, they can enhance their competitive positions with institutional arrangements that encourage information exchange and consensus. Consequently, CME firms choose to compete in high-skills market niches and desire government interventions that contribute to the expansion of skills, such as high levels of social protection and policies fostering cooperative labor relations. Alternatively, in liberal market economies (LME) labor–management relations are contentious, neither workers nor employers have incentives to invest in skills, and competitive strategies entailing a high-skilled, productive workforce are discouraged (Visser and Hemmerjck 1997; Hall and Soskice 2001; Huber and Stephens 2001).

Estevez-Abe et al. (2001) argue that social protections can be used by society to encourage the development of skills; indeed, this skills dimension is at the heart of welfare states. Some countries have created high levels of protections against employment (i.e., regulations to prevent layoffs) and unemployment (i.e., benefits after termination of work). These protections make workers more willing to invest in a type of skills development that one might not find in an area where there is less security; indeed, young workers will be willing to delay entering the workforce to pursue lengthy vocational training programs and to develop skills that are highly specific to their industries or even to their firms. These investments in specific skills are risky, making workers vulnerable to layoffs and market fluctuations; but high levels of social protection enable workers to take the gamble. In countries such as liberal market economies without high levels of social or employment protections, workers will choose instead to invest only in general skills that enable rapid retooling. Over time, employers in countries with high levels of social protections have moved into market niches with high value-added products that are created by highly skilled workers. These employers have come to rely on the social protections that enable new entrants into the labor force to acquire the skills necessary to these sectors of production.

A second set of institutions that influences business attitudes toward social benefits concerns the coordinating capacities of employers for political ends: business associations have a second powerful impact on firms' preferences for social policies by influencing how people think about their interests (Friedland and Robertson 1990: 32). Firms have multiple objectives, many intermediate goals coexist with the primary ambition of profit maximization, and a range of policies might be in a company's objective interests (Thompson 1982: 233; Fligstein 1990). Decision-making almost always occurs under conditions of bounded rationality in which full information is not available (Powell and DiMaggio 1991). Firms must make strategic decisions in developing policy preferences and even companies with the same economic characteristics may develop very different political profiles (Yoffie 1984: 45; Hillman and Hitt 1999).

Employers' associations shape firms' preferences under these ambiguous circumstances because groups influence our cognitive processes: they channel new ideas that change their member's perceptions of interests and they foster broader political identities (Snow et al. 1986: 464–81). Groups also have affective benefits, in offering friendship and other types of solidarity goods. When firms are organized collectively, individual managers from diverse sectors come to identify with one another and to set a priority on shared concerns and interests. The institutional context also contributes to the mobilization of interests, in structuring the groups in which people air their grievances and decide to take action. Thus business associations not only represent their members' interests, but also shape their preferences (Turner 1982; Grimm and Holcomb 1987: 105–18; Martin 2000).

Empirical evidence supports this claim that membership in groups expands employers support for social policies. In a study of sixty randomly selected companies' positions on the Clinton health plan, I found that membership in any group was a significant determinant of American firms' support for employer mandates (Martin 1995, 2000). Respondents indicated that they were often confused about health reform before their groups addressed the issue and most were followers rather than leaders in this area. Members were invited to participate by contacts in the area and joined for a variety of reasons, but once in the group they were exposed to a host of new information and their outlooks often changed accordingly. Managers considered groups especially helpful in exposing them to new information about and analysis of the larger health system; for example, two human resource professionals in a large Midwestern company, who were transferred to the benefits division "to inject activism" into company policy, immediately joined groups "to get up to speed on the health issue" (Martin 2000). The solidarity effects of small group participation also seemed to bring opposing interests closer together in the quest for health solutions. Thus, a member of the Iowa Leadership Consortium recalls how the group learned to work together, before it subsequently endorsed a state-wide play or pay plan:

This has been an incredible process. To go through the process of people walking through the door who are obviously going to have conflict. Doctors talking to businessmen. Twenty to forty people sitting down together and staying focused on a complex issue for a long time. One thing that made it work is that they decided to take the sacred cows and leave them at home.   (Martin 2000)

Not all groups are equally likely to foster employers' support for social policy; instead, certain characteristics of groups—specifically the scope, exclusivity, and degree of centralization—tend to increase employers' willingness to support social provision. In thinking about the characteristics that draw employers to favor social provision, it is helpful to think of two poles in employer organization: "pluralist" groups and "corporatist" associations. With pluralist groups, firms tend to belong to multiple groups and the groups overlap in function. Thus the groups are rather narrow in scope, are not exclusive representatives of their members, and are not hierarchically organized into a centralized peak association. General Motors may well belong to the Automobile Manufacturers' Association, the National Association of Manufacturers, and the Chamber of Commerce, and while the auto association has a more limited focus than the other two, all the groups more or less do the same thing. Thus, pluralist groups tend to compete with one another for members, are highly risk averse, and have a limited capacity to foster cooperation.

Corporatist groups, found in many continental European countries, are organized into a hierarchy, with a peak association at the head. These groups are functionally specific and hierarchically ordered; consequently, there is virtually no overlap in membership at each level of the hierarchy. At the top of the pyramid is a peak employers' association that brings everyone together and cooperates closely with labor and with government.

Countries with corporatist associations generally have higher levels of support for government intervention in general and social policy in particular. Corporatist associations are more centralized, more encompassing, less voluntary, and less competitive than their pluralist counterparts and should be better able to promote collective action for shared goals (Schmitter 1981; Wilson 1990). Political deliberation should be of higher quality in social corporatist groups, because the associations focus participants' attention on broader, shared concerns; in contrast, pluralist interest groups tend to concentrate on the particularistic self-interests of their members. This is not to say that business interests are a priori less diverse in countries with a high level of corporate organization; indeed, significant material cleavages divide employers in all advanced, industrialized countries that are related to the firm's size, labor intensity of the production process, exposure to foreign trade, skill level of the workers, etc. (Ferguson 1984; Gourevitch 1986). But the aggregation at a higher level allows participants to find common ground more easily. For example, encompassing associations have been found to be more likely to accept wage or income restraints in order to achieve the broad, collective goal of price stability. As we show, this broader definition of political aims may extend to the social realm, with associations desiring policies for skills upgrading, human capital development, and solidarity (Streeck 1992; Visser and Hermerijck 1997; Martin 2000).

These cognitive benefits of association are reinforced by the norms of cooperation, trust, and "social partnership" that develop in these groups (Katzenstein 1985; Crouch 1993; Rothstein 2000). Indeed, corporatist institutions have an economic logic (their encompassing organization of functional economic interests internalizes "externalities") and a political logic (sustained interaction enhances accommodation among social partners) that facilitate a search for the public good (Putnam, Leonardo, and Nanetti 1993; Visser and Hemerijck 1997). Norms of reciprocity, trust, and public-regarding behavior tend to be reinforced at multiple levels of social corporatist systems: centralized collective bargaining over wages and conditions of work, explicitly tripartite policy-making forums (commissions, boards, committees), and decentralized relations of business–labor exchange such as works councils. Thus corporatist interactions and highly organized business associations foster relatively supportive views of social policy among member firms.

Participation in these corporatist groups helps to overcome the limits to collective action by binding firms to negotiated decisions and bringing members to trust that they will not be punished for committing to longer term goals (Streeck 1992; Putnam, Leonardo, and Nanetti 1993; Visser and Hermerijck 1997; Rothstein 2000). Members receive assurance that they will not be punished for committing to these broader goals because corporatist peak associations adjudicate among conflicting demands and bind firms to negotiated decisions. When peak associations include most firms in a country, members do not have the luxury of leaving and joining another group should the association not satisfy narrow policy demands. Thus encompassing groups are more likely to cultivate norms of trust and cooperation and to generate support for broad collective concerns than associations with a more narrow membership (Katzenstein 1985; Streeck 1992: 265–84; Visser and Hemmerijck 1997; Rothstein 2000: 235–60).

The benefits of corporatism extend beyond the characteristics of the groups to the manner in which business and labor are brought into the policy-making process. In pluralist systems, social partners provide input primarily through the legislative process; however, in corporatist settings they may also serve on advisory commissions of administrative governmental agencies, and develop rules and regulations through the collective bargaining process (Mosley, Keller, and Speckesser 1998: 2). Iterative corporatist patterns of interaction create a positive sum game for business and labor in tripartite or collective bargaining settings: because the groups foster a long-term perspective and guarantee compliance, each side is more willing to take positions that will benefit the broader economy (Wilensky 1976; Streeck and Schmitter 1985; Crouch 1993; Hicks and Kenworthy 1998; Mosley, Keller, and Speckesser 1998).

Consequently, countries with encompassing employers and labor organizations are more likely to produce collectively beneficial outcomes than those without such groups (Wilensky 1976; Streeck and Schmitter 1985; Kendix and Olson 1990; Crouch 1993; Hicks and Kenworthy 1998). Although much of the conventional writing on the welfare state held that weak or divided business led to greater social provision because strong employers defeat social initiatives (Castles 1978; Korpi 1980), the logic of corporatism suggests that well-organized managers are more likely to favor broader, more universal welfare states (Streeck 1992; Martin 2000).

My study of 107 randomly selected Danish and British firms provides empirical evidence of the importance of corporatist associations in shaping employers' views of active labor market policy (Martin 2005). Danish firms belonging to corporatist employer associations were significantly more likely to participate and to identify their association as their most important source of information about labor market and HR issues. Although associations in both countries supported active social policies, belonging to a pluralist association in Britain did not play the same role. When asked to state their most important source of information about HR issues and labor market policy, 31 per cent of the Danes identified an employers' association, as opposed to 14 per cent of the Brits. In comparison, 30 per cent of the British firms identified trade press and internet sources as opposed to 4 per cent of the Danish companies. The Danish associations educated their members in informal discussion groups for their members as well as in formal corporatist settings. One manager recalled planning a "talk show" to teach firms about the programs, in which a TV star interviewed former welfare recipients who had successfully made the transition to the world of work (December 20, 2000). Conversely, British firms were significantly more likely to participate when policy experts in their relatively larger human resources departments educated them about the benefits of participation.

High levels of business organization has also been shown to be a significant determinant of cross-national differences of welfare state spending. Thus, Duane Swank and I found the centralization and coordination of employers as well as the integration of employer organizations in corporatist policy-making fora to be strongly associated with levels of spending on social and active labor market policies (Martin and Swank 2004).

The fact that American firms are so poorly organized to secure their collective political concerns has made them more hostile to social programs than their counterparts in continental Europe. The business voice in America is quite fragmented, as trade associations in each industry are not formally united under the auspices of an economy-wide peak association but operate as independent agents. This weakness in political organization means that American managers have a more difficult time finding common ground than their counterparts elsewhere (Wilson 1990). Corporate cohesion eludes even the big umbrella associations, due to replication and redundancy, as too many groups claim peak status and none has jurisdictional monopoly. Fearful of alienating members, associations resort to a least common denominator politics: expressing broad, inoffensive principles and but seldom taking the lead on more politically contentious ventures. Thus, despite a powerful reputation, large employers in America are so politically fragmented that they have difficulty achieving collective political positions (Martin 2000).

In the area of health reform private policy expertise grew considerably in the years leading up to the proposed Clinton Health Security Act and managers did much to put the issue on the public agenda. Yet the absence of a unifying policy-level business group prevented managers from contributing much support for comprehensive reform at the point of legislation. Although the National Association of Manufacturers and the Chamber of Commerce both initially offered support, minority factions forced the two groups to switch directions, despite Clinton's assurances that corporate concerns about the plan could be addressed (Martin 1997; see also Wilson 1996 on physicians' interests; and Skocpol 1997).

BUSINESS AND THE STATE

Perhaps at this point the reader is convinced that employers under some conditions support social policies; perhaps the reader also believes that the organization of employers is broadly determinative of corporate preferences. Yet employers do not organize in a vacuum; rather, they often need a catalyst to help them band together in search of a collective social good. A final part of our story, therefore, concerns the catalyst.

It is our contention that the agency of government bureaucrats and the structure of competition in the political realm are of vital importance to the organization of business and the representation of employers' social preferences. Agency matters in that politicians and bureaucrats may mobilize employers to serve their goals: because bureaucratic goals vary over time, major periods of corporate organization may occur when state actors have particularly activist agendas and the greatest need for business assistance (Martin 1991, 1994; Schneider 2004). In this vein Garon (1987) finds that bureaucratic repression of labor organization varied in accordance with the Japanese government's national goals, and the fortunes of the labor movement shifted accordingly. The 1920s in the United States were a period in which both government and business were engaged in "a search for order" and social programs were part of that broad effort (Hawley 1966; Wiebe 1967).

State structure also matters enormously to the way in which employers engage with the welfare state, and the rules of partisan competition have been shown to be

particularly important. As Iversen (2005) has recently shown, the strategic calculations of both politicians and employers with regard to social policies are deeply
influenced by the structure of party competition. In multi-party systems governed by
proportional representation, political parties develop closer ties to interest groups
(whether these be employers, farmers, Catholics, or workers) than two-party systems
constructed around winner-takes-all rules of competition. Therefore, while parties in
a two-party system tend to hug the political center in an effort to capture the
allegiance of the median voter and alter their political positions to satisfy the partisan
flavor of the month, parties in a multi-party system are more likely to make credible
commitments to their long-term voters that they will stand by their policy promises.
Voters in the latter system have greater confidence that if a party promises to take
care of their social needs in their old age, the party will remain committed in the
future. This stability of electoral politics has made citizens of countries with PR
systems more willing to support the development of the welfare state, because they
believe that they will, themselves, eventually be the beneficiaries of the social system.
This critical linkage between electoral systems and social protections has contributed
to the evolution of national production regimes: countries developing proportional
representation systems in the early twentieth century have invested more heavily in
skills—a prerequisite for coordinated market economies—than those with single
member district plurality systems (Iversen 2005).

The structure of party competition also contributed mightily to the organization
of national employers' associations at the dawn of the twentieth century (Martin
2006; Martin and Swank 2008). In brief, multi-party systems (subsequently with
proportional representation) were more likely to produce social corporatist associations while non-proportional two-party systems were more likely to produce
pluralist associations. The structure of party representation mattered to the origins
and evolutions of business organization, in shaping the incentives of both employers
and party activists. Multi-party systems tend to cover corporate interests more
completely than do two-party systems: a single business party (as well as a single
labor party) is more likely to emerge in such a system and the entire business
community is more likely to be united within a single party organization. The
dedicated business parties in multi-party systems can make credible commitments
that they will set a high priority on their members' interests. Because most managers
belong to the party and the party is more targeted to the interests of employers (i.e.
coverage of interests is high), the party has an easier time figuring out its priorities.
These dedicated business parties help to aggregate and to unify broad corporate
interests; therefore, they may assist in developing the collective voice of business. In
addition, dedicated business parties have incentives to form alliances with parties
representing workers, farmers, and other interests in order to join the ruling coalitions; and one might expect these parties to transfer this spirit of cooperation to
employers' associations. Highly organized employers' associations may emerge to
coordinate labor and industrial relations systems and to help with state development
strategies. At the same time, although employer organizations in multi-party systems
enhance cooperative arrangements with labor and implement party goals, these

organizations tend to leave the realm of electoral politics to the parties. Therefore, their activities may be viewed as more legitimate.

In two-party systems, employers generally have no singular partisan home. The large umbrella parties tend to cut across class lines and employers (as well as other groups) are often dispersed across parties. When employers are dispersed across parties, a common corporate voice may be more difficult to establish: party leaders have fewer incentives to try to unify employers around policy issues and they must attend to a wide variety of constituents. Party leaders experience greater difficulty in making credible commitments to their various constituent groups because they have incentives to formulate positions that appeal to the medium voter (Downs 1957). Therefore, systems of two-party competition tend to create "representation gaps": interest groups are imperfectly represented by the parties, some constituencies may find that no party meets their interests, and this is why voter turnout tends to be lower in two-party systems. Since protections against social risks often involve paying in now for future benefits—pensions are the classic example—future governments might logically renege on past commitments in order to appeal to voters (Iversen 2005). Party leaders may also have incentives to seek the formation of employer associations in two-party systems, but the characteristics and functions of these groups should differ from those of multi-party systems. Political entrepreneurs in the party most closely aligned with business may seek the development of broad employers' associations to compensate for the party's inability to represent fully employers (Martin and Swank 2008).

Duane Swank and I found quantitative and qualitative evidence of this relationship in the origins of employers' associations at the end of the nineteenth century. Our historical quantitative analysis reveals party system characteristics to have a strongly significant impact on employer association, independent of other factors such as high levels of union mobilization. The absence of proportionality and two-party systems, coupled with federalism and attendant political economic fragmentation, are systematically associated with low levels of employers' organization and low levels of social corporatism in the early (and later) decades of the twentieth century. These factors had a significant and independent impact on employers' organization (Martin and Swank 2008).

Historical qualitative case studies confirm that party competition was important to the development and subsequent trajectories of national employers' associations. In both Denmark and the US, for example, business organization was partially a top–down process, in that party leaders encouraged employers to form associations; yet the dynamics of multi-party competition (later associated with proportional representation) reinforced employer coordination in Denmark, while two-party competition hindered business cooperation in the United States. NAM's initial structure and policy positions reveal a deep interest in economic coordination and social cooperation. The leadership promoted "industrial betterment ideas" and a cooperative stance toward organized labor (Search 1901: 23–4; Martin 2006). Yet NAM's corporatist ambitions were dashed on the shoals of the two-party system; in particular, NAM's organizational growth was constrained by the failure of Congress to legislate the association's agenda of economic development. Because employers lacked a dedicated business party to represent their interests in a coalitional government, NAM's concerns were viewed as Republican rather than as business issues (Search 1901:13). After nearly a decade, the organization finally abandoned its initial corporatist vision, and adopted anti-labor and laissez-faire liberal rhetoric (Martin 2006). In Denmark, alternatively, a moderate faction of the Danish Right Party (Højre) desired a politics of coordination in order to further the interests of the moderate faction of the party and to enhance Højre's negotiating position with other parties in parliament. It sought to strengthen its message of cross-class cooperation with a message of labor–management coordination (Bindslev 1937–8; Dybdahl 1969: 14–15). Niels Andersen (a Højre member of parliament and construction employer) helped to create the Danish Employers' Federation of 1896 in order to demonstrate that Højre offered a meaningful middle way to lead the country to technological industrial development and labor peace between employers and workers (*Arbejdsgiver Foreningen Gennem 50 Aar 1946*).

Conclusion

These insights into the relationship between employers and the social realm have important consequences for our thinking about the expansion of the welfare state. Scholarship has fully explored the contribution of working class power to social policy outcomes (Korpi 1980; Stephens 1980) and economic historians have studied the development of welfare state capitalism in the United States (Wiebe 1967; Weinstein 1968). Yet, for many years, the impact of employers' strategic needs and organization on the development of welfare states was sorely neglected. Important work in this area in the past decade now signals that this is an exciting new research topic in political science and is likely to remain so in the post-industrial era, when investment in human capital has become more critical than ever (for example, see Castles 1978; Streeck 1992; Martin 1995, 2000; Hall and Soskice 2001; Swenson 2002; Hacker 2002; Mares 2003; Thelen 2004; Iversen 2005; Pontusson 2005).

In addition, the relationship between employers, labor, and the state in the arena of social provision contributes to our understanding of the construction of business as a social class. Corporate preferences are presented in this chapter as somewhat fluid, socially constructed, and receptive to political influences (see also Katzenstein 1985 and Gourevitch 1986), and one might credibly argue that managers are particularly susceptible to varying interpretations of their interests in the social realm. Attitudes to the welfare state have been mediated by the associations and political parties representing employers in political life. Corporatist mechanisms of coordination allowed some twentieth-century employers to develop a distinctive set of competitive strategies and to work toward national economic goals (Hall and

Soskice 2001). Party politics had a major impact on the creation of these distinctive types of organization and on the range of competitive strategies available to employers, because non-proportional, two-party and proportional multi-party systems had different capacities for realizing employers' interests in economic development goals. Thus the development of business as a social class has been a journey through uncharted territory, deeply influenced by the institutional landscape.

What might we conclude about the future of employers' support for and participation in the social political realm? Certainly, the future of collective capitalism may be on the decline in the twenty-first Century. The very concept of the "national economy" is becoming increasingly suspect: multinational corporations (with total sales approaching the GDP of small states) now seek such diverse and distant locales to create components of their final products that the "Made in America" appellation, for example, loses all meaning (Berger 2006). In like mode, nations may experience greater difficulty retaining their privileged position in organizing politics, as supra-national political structures—both public and private—come to replace traditional state structures (Slaughter 2004). Under such conditions, states may have greater difficulty building coalitions of employers to endorse their social agenda; yet the institutions governing corporate life may continue to involve employers in the pursuit of their social interests.

REFERENCES

APPLEBOME, P. 1995. "Study ties educational gains to more productivity growth," *New York Times* May 14: 22.

BALDWIN, P. 1992. *The Politics of Social Solidarity.* Cambridge: Cambridge University Press.

BERGER, S. 2006. *How We Compete.* New York: Doubleday.

BINDSLEV, A. 1937–8. *Konservatismens Historie i Danmark.* Odense: Kulturhistorisk forlag.

BLOCK, F. 1977. "The ruling class does not rule," *Socialist Revolution* 3.

BOWEN, R. 1947. *German Theories of the Corporate State.* New York: McGraw Hill.

BOWMAN, J. 1985. "The politics of the market: economic competition and the organization of capitalists," *Political Power and Social Theory* 5: 35–88.

BRANDES, S. 1976. *American Welfare Capitalism.* Chicago: University of Chicago Press.

Business Council of New York State. 1998. *1998 Business Council Survey of Employer Perspectives on Workforce Preparedness,* http://www.bcnys.org/whatsnew/1998/relsurv.htm

CASTLES, F. 1978. *The Social Democratic Image of Society.* London: Routledge & Kegan Paul.

CED. 1987. *Children in Need.* New York: Committee for Economic Development.

CROUCH, C. 1993. *Industrial Relations and European State Traditions.* New York: Oxford University Press.

DIMAGGIO, P., and POWELL, W. 1991. "Introduction," in Powell and DiMaggio, ed., *The New Institutionalism in Organizational Analysis.* Chicago: University of Chicago Press.

DOBBIN, F. 1992. "The origins of private social insurance," *American Journal of Sociology* 997: 1416–50.

DOWNS, A. 1957. *An Economic Theory of Democracy.* New York: Harper.

DYBDAHL, V. 1969. *Partier og Erhverv.* Aarhus: Universitets Forlaget i Aarhus.

Employee Benefit Research Institute. 2005. "Estimates from the March Current Population Survey," 2005 Supplement.

ESPING-ANDERSEN, G. 1990. *Three Worlds of Welfare Capitalism*. London: Polity Press.

ESTEVEZ-ABE, M., IVERSEN, T., and SOSKICE, D. 2001. "Social protection and the formation of skills," in P. Hall and D. Soskice, eds., *Varieties of Capitalism*. Cambridge: Cambridge University Press.

FERGUSON, T. 1984. "From normalcy to new deal: industrial structure, party competition, and American public policy in the Great Depression," *International Organization* 38(1): 41–94.

FLIGSTEIN, N. 1990. *The Transformation of Corporate Control*. Cambridge, Mass.: Harvard University Press.

FRIEDLAND, R., and ROBERTSON, A. F., eds. 1990. *Beyond the Market Place: Rethinking Economy and Society*. New York: Aldine de Gruyter.

GALINSKY, E., and FRIEDMAN, D. 1993. *Education before School*. New York: Scholastic Inc.

GARON, S. 1987. *The State and Labor in Modern Japan*. Berkeley: University of California Press.

GOODIN, R., and REIN, M. 2001. "Regimes on pillars," *Public Administration* 79(4): 769–801.

GORDON, C. 1991. "New deal, old deck: business and the origins of social security," *Politics and Society* 19(2).

GOUREVITCH, P. 1986. *Politics in Hard Times*. Ithaca, NY: Cornell University Press.

GRIER, K., MUNGER, M., and ROBERTS, B. 1994. "The determinants of industry political activity, 1978–1986." *American Political Science Review* 88 December.

GRIMM, C., and HOLCOMB, J. 1987. "Choices among encompassing organizations," in A. Marcus, A. Kaufman, and D. Beam, eds., *Business Strategy and Public Policy*. New York: Quorum Books.

HACKER, J. 2002. *Boundary Wars*. New York: Cambridge University Press.

—— and PIERSON, P. 2002. "Business power and social policy: employers and the formation of the American welfare state," *Politics & Society* 30(2): 277–326.

HALL, P., and SOSKICE, D., eds. 2001. *Varieties of Capitalism: The Institutional Foundations of Comparative Advantage*. Cambridge: Cambridge University Press.

HAWLEY, E. 1966. *The New Deal and the Problem of Monopoly*. Princeton: Princeton University Press.

HAWTHORNE, F. 1993. "Why family leave shouldn't scare employers," *Institutional Investor* March: 31.

HECKER, D. 2001. "Occupational employment projections to 2010," *Monthly Labor Review* November: 57–84.

HICKS, A. 1999. *Social Democracy and Welfare Capitalism*. Ithaca, NY: Cornell University Press.

—— and KENWORTHY, L. 1998. "Cooperation and political economic performance in affluent democratic capitalism," *American Journal of Sociology* May, 6: 1631–72.

—— and SWANK, D. 1984. "On the political economy of welfare expansion," *Comparative Political Studies* 17: 81–119.

HILLMAN, A., and HITT, M. 1999. "Corporate political strategy formulation," *Academy of Management Review* October 4, 24: 825–43.

HUBER, E., and STEPHENS, J. 2001. *Development and Crisis of the Welfare State: Parties and Policies in Global Markets*. Chicago: University of Chicago Press.

IVERSEN, T. 2005. *Capitalism, Democracy, and Welfare*. Cambridge: Cambridge University Press.

—— and CUSACK, T. 2000. "The causes of welfare state expansion," *World Politics* 52(3): 313–49.

JACOBS, D. 1988. "Corporate economic power and the state," *American Journal of Sociology* January 4, 93: 852–81.

JACOBY, S. 1977. *Modern Manors*. Princeton: Princeton University Press.

KATZENSTEIN, P. 1985. *Small States in World Markets*. Ithaca, NY: Cornell University Press.

KENDIX, M., and OLSON, M. 1990. "Changing unemployment rates in Europe and the USA," in R. Brunetta and C. Dell'Aringa, eds., *Labor Relations and Economic Performance*. New York: NYU Press, 68–91.

KITSCHELT, H., LANGE, P., MARKS, G., and STEPHENS, J., eds. 1999. *Continuity and Change in Contemporary Capitalism*. New York: Cambridge University Press.

KORPI, W. 1980. "Social policy and distributional conflict in the capitalist democracies," *West European Politics* 3: 296–315.

"Leaders Look at Health Care." 1991. *Business and Health* 9(2): 8–9.

LINDBLOM, C. 1977. *Politics and Markets*. New York: Basic Books.

MARES, I. 2001. "Firms and the welfare state," in P. Hall and D. Soskice, eds., *Varieties of Capitalism*. Cambridge: Cambridge University Press, 184–212.

MARTIN, C. J. 1991. *Shifting the Burden: The Struggle over Growth and Corporate Taxation*. Chicago: The University of Chicago Press.

——1994. "Business and the new economic activism: the growth of corporate lobbies in the sixties," *Polity* (Fall).

——1995. "Nature or nurture? Sources of firm preference for national health reform," *American Political Science Review* December, 89: 898–913.

——1997. "Mandating social change: the business struggle over national health reform," *Governance* 10(4): 397–428.

——2000. *Stuck in Neutral: Business and the Politics of Human Capital Investment Policy*. Princeton: Princeton University Press.

——2004. "Reinventing welfare regimes," *World Politics* 57(1): 39–69.

——2005. "Corporatism from the firm perspective," *British Journal of Political Science* 35(1): 127–48.

——2006. "Sectional parties, divided business," *Studies in American Political Development* 20 (2).

——and SWANK, D. 2004. "Does the organization of capital matter?" *American Political Science Review* 98(4): 593–611.

————2008. "The political origins of coordinated capitalism," *American Political Science Review* May.

——and THELEN, K. 2007. "The state and coordinated capitalism: contributions of the public sector to social solidarity in post-industrial societies," *World Politics* October.

MØLLER, I. H. 1992. *Den danske velfaerdsstats tilblivelse*. Frederiksberg: Samfundslitterature.

MOSLEY, H., KELLER, T., and SPECKESSER, S. 1998. *The Role of the Social Partners in the Design and Implementation of Active Measures* 27. Geneva: International Labor Office.

MYLES, J. 1989. *Old Age and the Welfare State*. Lawrence, Kan.: University Press of Kansas.

OECD Observer. 2005. "Civilian Employment," *OECD in Figures*, Supplement: 16–17.

PONTUSSON, J. 2005. *Inequality and Prosperity: Social Europe vs. Liberal America*. Ithaca, NY: Cornell University Press.

PORTER, M., and TEISBERG, E. O. 2006. *Redefining Health Care*. Boston: Harvard Business School Press.

PUTNAM, R., LEONARDI, R., and NANETTI, R. Y. 1993. *Making Democracy Work*. Princeton: Princeton University Press.

QUADAGNO, J. 1988. *The Transformation of Old Age Security*. Chicago: University of Chicago Press.

RIMLINGER, G. V. 1971. *Welfare Policy and Industrialization in Europe, America, and Russia*. New York: John Wiley & Sons.

ROTHSTEIN, B. 2000. "Trust, social dilemmas and collective memories," *Journal of Theoretical Politics* 12(4): 477–503.

SCHMITTER, P. 1981. "Interest intermediation and regime governability in contemporary Western Europe and North America," in S. Berger, ed., *Organizing Interests in Western Europe.* Cambridge: Cambridge University Press.

SCHNEIDER, B. R. 2004. *Business Politics and the State in Twentieth-Century Latin America.* Cambridge: Cambridge University Press.

SEARCH, T. 1901. "President's Report," *Proceedings of the Sixth Annual Convention of the National Association of Manufacturers.* New York: NAM Bureau of Publicity.

Secretary of State for Education and Skills. 2005. *14–19 Education and Skills* February.

SKOCPOL, T. 1997. *Boomerang: Health Care Reform and the Turn against Government.* New York: W. W. Norton.

SLAUGHTER, A.-M. 2004. *A New World Order.* Princeton: Princeton University Press.

SNOW, D., ROCHFORD, E. B. Jr., WORDEN, S., and BENFORD, R. 1986. "Frame alignment processes, micromobilization, and movement participation," *American Sociological Review* 51: 464–81.

STEPHENS, J. 1980. *The Transition from Capitalism to Socialism.* Atlantic Highlands, NJ: Humanities Press.

STEVENS, B. 1986. *Complementing the Welfare State.* Geneva: International Labor Organization.

STREECK, W. 1992. *Social Institutions and Economic Performance.* Beverly Hills, Calif.: Sage.

——and SCHMITTER, P. 1985. *Private Interest Government.* Beverly Hills, Calif.: Sage.

SWANK, D. 2002. *Global Capital, Political Institutions, and Policy Change in Developed Welfare States.* New York: Cambridge University Press.

SWENSON, P. 2002. *Capitalists against Markets.* New York: Oxford University Press.

THELEN, K. 2004. *How Institutions Evolve.* New York: Cambridge University Press.

TOWERS PERRIN. 1991. "Today's dilemma: tomorrow's competitive edg," produced for the National Association of Manufacturers, obtained from Towers Perrin, November.

TURNER, J. 1982. "Towards a cognitive redefinition of the social group," in H. Tajfel, ed., *Social Identity and Intergroup Relations.* New York: Cambridge University Press.

VERESPEJ, M. "Clinton's first legislative child: will family leave trigger more government mandates?" *Industry Week* 242(5): 57.

VISSER, J., and HEMERIJCK, A. 1997. *"A Dutch Miracle": Job Growth, Welfare Reform, and Corporatism in the Netherlands.* Amsterdam: Amsterdam University Press.

VOGEL, D. 1978. "Why businessmen distrust their state," *British Journal of Political Science* 8: 45–78.

THOMPSON, G. 1982. "The firm as a 'dispersed' social agency," *Economy and Society* August 3, 11: 233.

WEINSTEIN, J. 1968. *The Corporate Ideal in the Liberal State: 1900–1918.* Boston: Beacon Press.

WIEBE, R. 1967. *The Search for Order.* New York: Hill & Wang.

WILENSKY, H. 1976. *The "New Corporatism," Centralization, and the Welfare State.* Beverly Hills, Calif.: Sage.

——2002. *Rich Democracies.* Berkeley: University of California Press.

WILLIAMS, W. 1991. "United States Senate Committee on Finance hearing on health care costs, April 16, 1991," *Healthwise* 2: 2.

WILSON, G. 1990. *Business and Politics,* 2nd edn. Chatham, NJ: Chatham House.

——1996. "Interest groups in the health care debate," in H. Aaron, ed., *The Clinton Plan and the Future of Health Care Reform.* Washington, DC: Brookings Institution.

YOFFIE, D. 1984. "Corporate strategies for political action," in A. Marcus, et al., eds., *Business Strategy and Public Policy.* New York: Quorum Books, 43–60.

PUBLIC–PRIVATE PARTNERSHIPS IN BUSINESS AND GOVERNMENT

CARSTEN GREVE

PUBLIC–private partnerships (PPPs)—understood here primarily as institutionalized long-term infrastructure contracts between public sector and private sector actors— have gained increasing interest in the OECD world and the developed world (Osborne 2001; Hodge and Greve 2005). Some have hailed it as "worldwide revolution in infrastructure provision and project finance" (Grimsey and Lewis 2004), others have called it "pink privatization" (Levi-Faur 2004), whilst the European Commission has welcomed PPPs as "innovative solutions towards the procurement of public services" (McCreevy 2005).

The purpose of this chapter will be to examine the various definitions and categories of the concept of PPPs, the nature of the recent debate in the disciplines of economics, political science, and sociology, the business side of the partnerships in terms of the companies involved worldwide, and the regulatory perspective from a government point of view of how to steer, govern, and regulate partnerships. The chapter will close with some remarks on future research agendas.

The first section will deal with the definition challenges. Some scholars conceive of PPPs in a very broad manner that tries to encompass nearly all sustained activities between business actors and formal political actors from traditional political institutions. Some also point to various historical collaborations that in hindsight can be termed partnerships. There may be some good reasons for doing this, such as keeping the mind open to new types of cooperative arrangements, but there are also downsides in terms of lack of clarification about the type of partnerships examined. The other extreme is the more narrow PPP conception of private finance arrangements in mainly physical infrastructure settings that have been popular in the United Kingdom in particular, but that are gaining interest elsewhere also. Other people claim that the "new" item on the partnership agenda is the attention paid to risk management and innovation. The section will try to specify the different meanings and discussions related to various definitions and conceptions of PPPs.

The second section will try to trace the recent debates in academia and in practice about where PPPs are headed. A brief overview of the main contributions, arguments, and evidence from the disciplines of economics, political science, and sociology will be offered. Some of the debate has revolved around the question of whether PPPs are a continuation of already known contractual forms of governance, and whether new forms of organizations bring new results in terms of performance with them. Economists tend to be slightly optimistic about the prospects of PPPs for physical infrastructure projects while political scientist have raised concerns over the democratic aspects of partnerships (but have also pointed to the opportunities for collaboration), and sociologists have wondered about how the partnerships are enacted in real life organizations and how the informal rules that structure relationships are influenced by the new partnerships.

The third section will examine in more detail how different firms around the world have seized on partnerships as a vehicle to start doing (big) business with government. Investors looking for safe investments and firms looking for new and stable customers for their products and solutions have turned their attention to government actors to let governments endorse projects that involve private sector activity. The way business tries to push for PPPs on the policy agenda, and the way businesses are structured—in networks and consortia—to bid for partnership deals are some of the main topics of the third section.

The fourth section turns the attention to the government side and asks how governments pursue the policy of PPPs and also how they try to find ways of regulating PPPs once they are established, including how that regulatory challenge is influenced by the debate on the nature of "the regulatory state" in recent years.

The fifth section concludes the chapter by making remarks on future research agendas, and trying to identify the areas in which researchers need to be more active, for example on examining the business perspective.

Defining Public–Private Partnerships

Defining PPPs has traditionally caused a lot of problems, but there seems to have been a consensus among the basic ideas in recent years. If we start with the "big" debates first, the relationship between what is public and what is private has been troubling and challenging researchers for years. In some of the broadest definitions, a PPP is simply any type of relationship where actors from the public sector and the private sector interact. Historically minded scholars and observers have been quick to point out numerous examples from history where public and private sector activities have been blurred and merged (Wettenhall 2003, 2005).

In more recent times, the term "PPP" has had a number of different meanings. The term was first used for urban renewal projects and regional development projects with industry. The term has also been used to describe how civil society actors and voluntary "third sector" organizations interact with the public sector in numerous ways. Finally, there has been a heap of research on public policy networks which are sometimes described as PPPs. In this chapter, we will concentrate on a fourth meaning of the term that has occupied the political economy literature most, and which is also the specific term many governments, firms, and international organizations use: here PPPs are understood as long-term infrastructure contracts which combine the efforts of public sector actors and private sector actors.

Recently, the number of definitions that has addressed around this type of PPPs has increased (Klijn and Teisman 2005; Skelcher 2005; World Bank 2007). The European Union's version of the definition is:

PPPs are forms of cooperation between public authorities and businesses, with the aim of carrying out infrastructure projects or providing services for the public. These arrangements which typically involve complex legal and financial arrangements have been developed in several areas of the public sector and widely used within the EU, in particular in the areas of transport, public health, public safety, waste management and water distribution. (European Commission 2005)

The European Union calls these partnerships "institutionalized partnerships" (European Commission 2005). A definition from the research community concerns the same factors: "A form of structured cooperation between public and private partners in the planning/construction and/or exploitation of infrastructural facilities in which they share or reallocate risks, costs, benefits, resources, and responsibilities" (Koppenjan 2005: 37).

There are some borderlines to be drawn to the concepts of "privatization" and "contracting out/outsourcing." Most observers seem to acknowledge that PPPs follow on from the concepts just mentioned, and that PPPs are a part of a larger "privatization family" which includes asset sales, contracting out, vouchers, and private sector development (Hodge 2005). Some observers see contracting out as being very close to PPPs, and PPPs are merely a more sophisticated extension of contracting out arrangements (Skelcher 2005). Others are aware of the "language games" that are being played, and Stephen Linder (1999) suggested that "a grammar of multiple meanings" could be attached to PPPs.

The question whether PPPs are an extension of the privatization debate, or privatization in new disguises depends how you define PPPs. A definition of PPPs that focuses on infrastructure projects would emphasize that PPPs are new. A definition of PPPs that has a broader view of public–private collaboration, like Chris Skelcher's (2005) definition, for example, would see PPPs as including contracting out/outsourcing practices. So it depends how far you cast the net of definition.

If we focus on long-term infrastructure contracts, there are arguments as to why it is new: the preferential use of private finance, high deal complexity, the focus on risk, and altered governance and accountability assumptions. The private finance has been most evident in the UK experience with the Private Finance Initative (PFI). The UK started to use PFI in 1992 (although there also tales of earlier deals) as a way to overcome the problem of financing new public infrastructure and services without having to raise taxes (Terry 1996). Over 700 PFI projects have been signed since 1992, and a number of them have been completed already (HM Treasury 2006). The basic idea is that the government can arrange for a new infrastructure project to be completed, but the government does not have to pay for the project up front. Instead it uses finance that the private sector has made available. The contract normally lasts from twenty to thirty years. The government pays the money back over time. It works like a "mega credit card." The supposed benefit seen from a government's point of view is that the financing does not appear on the balance sheet. The Eurostat statement in the European Union in 2004 confirmed that private finance projects are "off the balance sheet." In times when European governments have to comply with the Maastricht criteria, PPPs seem an attractive option. The finance and the "off balance sheet argument" have been seen as main motivation for governments to enter into PPP deals (World Bank 2007). As we shall see below, there are critics to this position, and the strong economy of some countries in the 2000s has also had an impact on the attraction for some governments at least. High complexity is a second characteristic of PPPs. In a straightforward contracting out arrangement, a government signs a deal with a private provider in order to get a certain product or service delivered. The specification is done prior to the deal, so in principle, the provider just has to comply with the instructions given in the contract to deliver the product or service in question. In a PPP arrangement, this is different. Government and business will in principle be in a dialogue in the design phase, the decision phase (they both have to agree to the deal), the building phase, the financing phase, and the operations and maintenance phase. This is "in principle" because, at least in the European Union, there has to be a formal tendering round where the government is getting in bids like a "normal" contracting out arrangements. This is because the principle of competition and transparency is a key element in EU law, and PPPs do not change that. Therefore, the decision is not a one-on-one arrangement, but a formal arrangement according to EU procurement rules. Because of the intense involvement of both partners in many aspects of the collaboration, the deals tend to be highly complex. There are often many partners on each side (several government departments may cooperate on the project from the government), and many partners on the private side (a main contractor will often work with many sub-contractors plus the finance actors and the designer/architecture actors). And the partners do often want to safeguard their collaborative actions so they take precautions in contractual matters to prepare for a situation where the contractual arrangement breaks down. This means that contracts get relative complex because despite the good intentions and rosy words, the partnership remains a business arrangement and a transaction, often involving billions of euros or dollars, which both partners cannot afford not to safeguard in some way. The focus on risk is a third factor that is new. Identifying risks were never a strong side of governments in the past. Governments often took on risks without knowing it, and it was often assumed that the government would step in and save a project if it got into financial difficulties. The new thing is that governments are beginning to identify risks in the PPP projects, and the private sector has been quick to put a value on the identified risks. The private sector is used to identifying and putting a value on risks. After all, this is what insurance companies do almost by definition. A list of risks would include, for example, design and construction risks, maintenance risks, planning risks, regulation and legal change risks (see Department of Treasury, Victoria, 2001).

In the official parlance of the PPP literature, the public sector and the private should share the risks. Governments aspire to place risks "where it is most appropriate" as the UK National Audit Office (2000) has called it. In reality, this often means that the private sector agrees to take on a large part of the risks against a sizeable compensation. In principle, the new focus on risks should provide better projects because of a presumed more detailed and informed analysis of risk factors. Skeptics have pointed to the private sector's advantage because it knows the "risk game" better than the government. Projects can end up being more costly because of the new identified risks. The altered governance and accountability assumptions are the fourth factor that signals the "new" in PPPs. Discussions on accountability are galore, but there seems to be agreement that "the privatized state" calls for a more complex accountability system than the hierarchical accountability arrangements that include ministerial responsibility that have been the case in the "old government days" (Stone 1995). A few PPPs in a country will not rock the boat, of course. But there is a sense that the accountability relationships are changing when an institutionalized PPP is in charge of a large infrastructure project, and the actual providers and operators first answer to the institutionalized PPP unit before they answer to the government. As Donald F. Kettl (1993) already pointed out many years ago, the presence of a contract put a new link in the chain between government and providers. The conflicting role of the Ministry of Finance in many countries has also been noted: Ministries of Finances are supposed to be stewards of the sound economies, yet they are often also advocates for PPP projects which, almost by definition, carry huge risks with them. In the UK, the 700+ deals make it a potentially very complex matter to find out who is in charge if a project goes wrong.

GOVERNMENT DEBATES ON PUBLIC–PRIVATE PARTNERSHIPS: FROM FINANCE TO INNOVATION?

Why have governments become interested in PPPs? Is it because the privatization trend has died out or at least slowed down, is it because the contracting deals were too inflexible, or is it because governments and businesses have succumbed to "third way" type of arguments and decided that it is better to collaborate than to compete? The literature has so far concentrated on three types of arguments for PPPs: economy, planning, and innovation (Flinders 2005). First, governments face economic pressure and have to run very tight budgets. Many countries in the European Union are struggling to meet the Maastricht criteria. The tight budget situation is known in countries all over the world. The first argument for PPPs has been that private finance can come to governments' rescue so that new projects can be build without making the government raise taxes from citizens. As we have seen, the economic argument and the availability of private finance used to be the main argument for PPPs. In the new member states of the European Union, the private finance argument is likely to be the continuing argument for a foreseeable future (World Bank 2007). But as many countries are experiencing stronger economies, the need for private finance may become less obvious. The debate has therefore shifted in recent years to the other arguments: planning and innovation. Second, planning has been highlighted as an argument for PPPs. The idea is that the "whole-of-life" cost analysis of a project will provide better outcomes. Because private sector actors "stay on" in the project and are responsible for operations and maintenance, they will be less likely to build a poorly designed or constructed infrastructure facility, and they will continue to be responsible for the facility for the duration of the contract period. This should be understood as opposed to a "normal" situation where a government puts out a contract, specifies the designs, lets the private sector consortium build the facility, and then assumes overall responsibility for the project as soon as the facility has been constructed. The government will not—in the stylized version—set money aside for maintenance, but do repairs and maintenance only when it is absolutely needed in order to save money. A private partner will, on the contrary, be directly responsible in a PPP arrangement, and therefore the assets will be better looked after. This is the main argument from the "whole-of-life" project perspective. There has been little debate to date as to why governments could not simply adopt an equal planning horizon, or conduct a financial model that would ensure continuing attention to its facilities. It seems strange in a way that long-term planning is here associated with the private sector, and the short-term outlook is associated with the public sector. A third argument in favor of PPPs has been that projects become more innovative when the combined minds of both public sector actors and private sector actors are united in an infrastructure project. The usual "synergy" arguments apply here. The public sector may be good at some things, but not other things, and the private sector can then step in and help so the project is more complete in the end. In the context of the contracting out discussion, the businesses have often complained that the formal contracting out did not allow for private sector innovation to be applied. When a government has issued a tender (or Request for Proposal in the American jargon), the government has been forced to make the contract very detailed, and companies have had to comply with the requirements in the contract. The contractual situation has been changed within the European Union with the introduction of the "competitive dialogue" where partners are allowed to enter a dialogue under certain conditions. Again the transparency principle and the competition principle that the European Union is built on warn against any closed deals between public sector actors and private sector actors. In the private sector's view, the innovative solutions that a private company may have picked up from its experience in other sectors, or from an innovation unit within the company itself, have not been allowed to come forward in the restricted contracting out arrangements if the government purchaser has not specified it in the contract. There is discussion of the innovative capacity in the literature, and there are again few reasons why innovation should only be a matter of PPPs and why governments cannot be innovative themselves. Indeed, governments have experimented with innovation in products and services for years (Borins 2000) and have now started on "innovative governance" perspectives (Hartley and Moore 2008). Summing up this part, there seems to be four main arguments for PPPs, but none of them seems convincing enough to make the case for PPPs on their own. It can be argued that the arguments have shifted over time (Flinders 2005), so that finance was the first period with PPPs, planning and whole-of-life perspectives are the preferred argument at the present time, while innovation is likely to be the key argument of the future.

Sceptics have discussed whether many of these arguments are applicable to the majority of PPP projects. They claim that there is little evidence that the deals will actually be less expensive in the end, and that PPP projects are often compared with old practices in the public sector. They also claim that private sector parties sometimes "abandon the ship" and are getting bought up by other companies, or do only what is in the contract and not a lot more, which can be very inflexible. They finally claim that PPPs are not necessarily innovative and that the private sector only brings along tried and tested concepts to the table that they have picked up in other projects, so the actual innovations in the specific projects are less visible.

PPPs have been prolific in the anglophone countries mostly. The trend took off in the UK in the 1990s, and the UK remains the country where most PPP projects are in place. In North America, the picture is more complex, as there have been experiences with PPP-type arrangements for a number of years, but they have not necessarily been labeled as PPPs. Some provinces in Canada have sophisticated PPP programs in place. Australia is also a remarkable country for PPPs. The PPP evolution began in the 1990s, mostly in the states of New South Wales and Victoria. In Victoria, Hodge (2005) listed nearly 50 PPP projects. Prolific examples in Australia are the link road in Sydney, the City Link project in Melbourne, but there are also hospitals and prisons as PPPs in Australia. In Europe, PPP projects have occurred most frequently in the Netherlands where relatively many infrastructure projects have been designed as PPPs (Van Ham and Koppenjan 2001; Klijn and Teisman 2005; Koppenjan 2005). In the rest of Europe, the picture is more constrained. In Austria, the city of Vienna has experimented with PPPs and there has been a failed PPP project with radio communication equipment for rescue services and the police (Hammerschmid 2007). In Germany, PPPs have been slow to take off, mainly due to the usually good workings of the public sector, but Germany also needs huge investments in infrastructure in the coming years (700 billion euros until 2012 according the European Commission (McCreevy 2005). Germany has welcomed foreign PPP companies, for example in a town where a British company has taken over the local government administration. In Spain the PPP examples focuses on the health sector, mainly a couple of hospitals. In Italy, there are signs of a few PPP projects. In the Nordic countries, PPP projects are relatively rare. Sweden can report very limited experience, Norway has experiments with a few roads, and Denmark has only two official projects (a primary school and a new national archive) although a handful of projects are in the pipeline. PPPs seem attractive to the new EU member states, and have already taken off in countries like the Czech Republic, Poland, and Hungary. Both Poland and Hungary have built motorways in the PPP formula (World Bank 2007). In the developing countries, PPPs, or private sector development, have attracted attention, and there is a new forum organized by the World Bank. The IMF is also advocating PPPs, but adopts a realistic view. The OECD (2005) has welcomed PPPs, but has also warned against too optimistic a view of what can be achieved. The European Union published a Green Paper on Public–Private Partnerships in 2005, and is continuing to follow the development. The overall impression is that PPPs are here to stay, but that the countries' enthusiasm varies. Deloitte has developed a "maturity model" of PPPs, and claims that the anglophone countries of the UK, Australia, and Ireland are the countries with the most sophisticated PPP models and most activities. From a comparative political economy perspective, researchers must be vary about such models, given the "varieties of capitalism" literature that focuses on divergence of market economy models. It would seem that PPPs are mostly associated with "liberal market economies" and less associated with "coordinated market economies." One argument could be that liberal market economies have a greater need to talk about "partnerships" because the focus has been on competition, while coordinated market economies are almost defined by being partnership economies so there is less need to embrace a "new" concept of PPPs.

Do PPPs work or not? Predictably, there exists some controversy in the literature. One key problem is that many of the deals are thirty-year contracts, so in essence we cannot safely know the answer to "do they work or not?" until 2020 when the first deals begin to have run their course. This has not stopped the debate, and it is raging. Overall, the assessment of the development so far has been mainly positive in the sense that PPPs have been delivered on time and have been delivered to the budget. This is the conclusion Cambridge economist Michael Pollitt (2005) reached in his reading of the National Audit Office's material of ten UK cases. And this is also the view shared by a host of government organizations, consultancy companies, and finance institutions (PriceWaterhouseCoopers 2004; KPMG 2005; Deloitte 2006; Partnerships UK 2007). There are also skeptics. British researcher Jean Shaoul (2005) has been the most vocal in criticism. Recently, the UK HM Treasury's calculations have been questioned. Reports from Australia suggest a cautionary tale too.

The Business of Public–Private Partnerships

Businesses are intensely involved in PPPs, and a new "PPP industry" appears to have grown up. In selected countries, PPPs are "big business." Surprisingly, this point has not been discussed to a large degree in the literature on PPPs to date. The literature seems have to have concentrated on issues on the financial arrangements, the complexity of the many actors involved, and the question of whether PPPs can deliver the promised outcomes. Yet, it is a fact that certain parts of the private sector have committed themselves substantially to PPP issues. The main private sector participants include project sponsors, i.e., initial providers of equity, construction contractors, hard facility ("FM") contractors, soft facility management contractors, lenders (banks, financial institutions), financial advisors, legal advisors, technical advisors, and insurance advisors (Partnerships UK 2007: 21). In the UK case, the top five lenders in the period 2004–7 were Bank of Scotland, SMBC, RBS, Dexia,and NB Capital (2007: 25). The top five construction contractors were Carillion, Balfour Beatty, Skanska, AMEC, and Boris. The top ten contractors covered projects with a total capital value of £8.1 billion, or 63 per cent of the market for construction in PPP projects (Partnerships UK 2007: 26). The top five hard facility management contractors were Skanska, Balfour Beatty, Mitie, AMEC, Interserve. The top five financial advisors were PriceWaterhouseCoopers, Deloitte, Grant Thomson, KPMG, and Ernest and Young (2007: 28). PriceWaterhouseCoopers had a portfolio of £7,55 million for the period 2004–7, followed by Deloitte with £2,140 million.

There are no known estimates for the world market, but it seems clear that there are market shares to be gained in potential PPP countries in the new European member states, in developing countries (see World Bank 2007). Further expansion in North America and Australia can also be anticipated as well as Asia. These businesses are therefore likely to grow even more in the future.

The question is how the private sector will affect the evolution of PPPs in different countries. It seems probable that countries that want to renew their infrastructure will receive offers and suggestions for PPP projects from the already established market players in the UK and elsewhere. Therefore, governments will have to come up with good arguments as to why governments should build infrastructure projects themselves instead of entering into a PPP. British scholar Patrick Dunleavy (1997) formulated the question some years ago when he asked: "Can governments be best in the world?" Dunleavy pointed to the fact that governments were striving to be "world class" in public service production, yet governments only have their own "market" to practice on, whereas international companies specialize in particular markets and are able to offer standardized products and specially made products because of economics of scale. Take the construction contractor Skanska as an example. Skanska is originally a Swedish company, but now has offices around the world. Its subsidiary company Skanska UK is, as we have seen, the biggest hard facility management contractor in the UK PPP market with a total capital value of £1.4 billion. On its website, Skanska UK presents itself as "the leading PFI/PPP service provider in the UK," and furthermore states:

From the successful completion of the country's first PFI scheme in the late 1980's, Skanska's portfolio is now in the excess of 3 billion GBP, covering health care, custodial, education, transport, and defence sectors. We build in-house teams responsible for the development of design, construction, operation and hard facilities services. With investment financing and operational management through our sister company Skanska Infrastructure Development, we further enhance "the Skanska solution."   (Skanska 2008)

In theoretical terms, Skanska, PriceWaterhouseCoopers, National Bank of Scotland, are the market leaders in the PPP market. They form the "conceptions of control" in Fligstein's (1996, 2001) terms. They "structure the perception of how the market works." Although it is not a stable group as such, the dominant market players seem to agree on issues like: private finance is helping infrastructure projects, risks should be shared among partners, and PPP contracts should be safeguarded. The identity of the PPP market has been shaped by the early adopters in the UK and other leading countries. In Australia, Marquarie Bank has played an important role as well. Fligstein's three other factors affecting a market—property rights, governance structures, and rules of exchange—are all evolving and have not yet been settled in most countries (except again maybe for the UK). Property rights are disputed in most countries. The Danish tax authorities first made a ruling on the tax status of PPP projects in 2007, almost nine years after the PPP concept had first been introduced in a government document (Danish Ministry of Finance 1999). That would echo the situation in many countries. The European Union has refrained from making any particular rules for PPPs, except to state in 2004 that PPPs can be treated as "off balance sheet" units. Governance structures for PPPs are not clear in most countries outside the UK. Is it the Ministry of Finance that is in charge, or it is other ministries? How do audit offices treat PPP projects in the national accounting systems? Not clear at all. Again, the European Union is still undecided about the governance structures for PPPs, and one priority is that PPP rules most not interfere with competition rules that the European Union holds in high regard (European Commission 2004). The point about lack of adequate governance structures is also pointed out by the World Bank (2007). Rules of exchange are defined by "who can transact with whom and the conditions under which the transactions are carried out" (Fligstein 1996: 658). This has caused great difficulties in some countries. Who are actually the partners that can enter a PPP contract? How many government departments can be aboard the agreement? What is the legal nature of the institutionalized PPP (the PPP company), and what are the subsidiary partners' relation to the main contractual partner? These issues are less than crystal clear and therefore the PPP market can best be described as a developing market, or a market under construction. The PPP market has not yet reached the state of a stable market, characterized by Fligstein (1996: 659) as: "In markets, the goal of action is ensure the survival of the firm. No actor can determine which behaviours will maximise profits (either a priori or ex post), and action is there directed towards the creation of stable worlds."

The PPP market is so far dominated by international firms: the financial advisors are the well-known top five big consultancy firms in the world. They were also active in the privatization era in the 1980s and the 1990s. These firms have brought their insights from earlier public–private policies into the new world of PPPs. The legal advisors are big legal firms, like Grant Thornton, which are also international players. The construction contractors are world market players as well; Skanska and others have been mentioned. There is some way to go before it is a "globalized market" in Fligstein's (2001) terms where a few companies dominate the world market, but in some areas, like financial advice, it is close to being a globalized market. Recent interest from the World Bank and the IMF in promoting PPP as a solution to developing countries also points to a global perspective for PPPs in the longer run. Advice from the leading states in the UK and Australia is also highly sought after. The National Audit Office in the UK has a stream of visitors. HM Treasury in the UK has entered the Partnership UK company with the private sector in promoting and advising on PPPs, and is in itself a PPP! The advice of the Australian government has been sought by provincial governments in Canada and elsewhere. The exact amount of this commercially based government advice is not known, but it should be added to the picture of the "market for PPPs."

Public–Private Partnerships
and the Regulatory Challenges

A key to the future development of PPPs seem to lie in the regulatory framework that will surround the PPPs. This is what Fligstein refers to as property rights, governance structures, and rules of exchange. The "regulatory state" has grown in size and import- ance in many other areas of public policy in recent decades (Levi-Faur and Jordana 2004). The market for PPPs has not been institutionalized fully yet. The market for PPPs is still in its early stages in many parts of the world, while it seems more developed especially in North America, Australia, and the UK. Areas where the PPP regulatory framework is only partially developed are the European Union (minus UK), Asia, and developing countries. The regulatory framework can develop in several ways. One way is to make the contract the centerpiece for regulation and accountability. This has been the practice so far. The individual contracts will be the way to regulate PPP activity, and consequently an improved regulatory framework means improved PPP contracts.

Another way to go is to institutionalize regulatory agencies around the PPP deals, and to empower them with specific mandates to scrutinize PPP behavior. The agencies in the UK already lead the way in this respect. HM Treasury has a special unit for PPPs, but is both the endorser and the controller, which leaves it with a potential conflicting role. Much expertise has been gathered in the UK National Audit Office which has maintained a value-for-money policy towards PPPs.

A third way is to engage the international organizations and to make international rules for PPPs. The European Union has been trying to wrestle with the regulatory framework, but has, as we have seen, not yet found an adequate framework. The World Bank (2007) is calling for more activity and engagement from the international organizations. The UN has its own policy towards PPPs. The OECD has so far been hesitant towards making recommendations, but there are some developments and activities going on inside the OECD (summer conference on PPPs in 2006, high-level meeting in 2008).

A fourth way is for the market players to regulate themselves. This is going on to a certain extent already as there are professional fora where the industry debates common problems. There is a way to go still towards exposing the deals that have not gone well. Reading material from organizations like Partnerships UK, or the reports of the global consultancy firms, there are some admissions of cases that have not evolved as predicted, but the main part of the material on PPPs is presented in a positive light. The industry has made a huge effort to portray what Baumgartner and Jones (1993) call a "positive policy image." The stories connected with PPPs as well as the technical workings of the PPPs are presented as new and exciting, while the failures of specific projects are not so vivid (but see Shaoul 2005 for an alternative view). The European Commission could be one organization where there could be a call for more involvement of the industry, given the Commission's interest in finding alternative ways of regulating, but the European Commission Green Paper mostly focuses on the possibility of new centralized EU rules, or the relationship with the already existing rules for competition and public procurement. There are as yet few elaborate "industry codes" on how to conduct business affairs in PPPs.

The whole idea of regulation can potentially conflict with the synergy idea that still surrounds much PPP discussions, but as Klijn and Teisman (2005) have shown, mutual conflicts continue to exist in PPPs, and public actors and private actors do not easily share the same objectives.

Conclusions

PPPs have been on the policy agenda for many governments and businesses around the world in recent decades. The history of collaboration between public and private partners goes back a long way in history, but the recent focus on what the European Commission calls "institutionalized PPPs," long-term infrastructure contracts, has some new characteristics, mainly the extended use of private finance, high contractual deal complexity, risk sharing, and altered accountability mechanisms. Since the 1990s PPPs have blossomed around the world, especially in the UK, North America, and Australia, while developments in the European Union (including the new member states), Asia, and the developing countries have been more constrained.

The main reasons for choosing PPPs are need for private finance (often to keep activities off balance sheet), planning and whole-of-life costing, and innovation in project-making. The reasons seem to shift in periods, for "private finance" was the initial argument, planning and whole-of-life considerations are now the main argument, and innovation and bringing new solutions to the table are likely to be the argument of the future. Skeptics claim that these reasons do not always create better project results. The evidence so far suggests that PPPs are delivered on time and to the budget, but there are many qualifications to be made to that statement, and it is still early days given the twenty- and thirty-year contracts that often characterize PPPs. PPPs are still mainly an anglophone phenomenon, and the greater need for "partnerships" in liberal market economies may seem plausible, while coordinated market economies already have institutionalized connections between the public sector and the private sector, and therefore do not see the point in enthusing over the partnership concept. Having said that, there are signs that the new member states of the European Union, and the developing countries, are finding PPPs a likely part of a solution for their need for investment in infrastructure in the future. International organizations have been slow to endorse PPPs, but the World Bank, OECD, the UN, and the European Union are all working on PPP policies. It seems clear that what PPPs miss so far in many countries is what Fligstein refers to as governance structures (as well as property rights and rules of exchange). Most governments, with the exception of the UK and Australia, have not established adequate institutional frameworks (governance structures) to guide PPP activity yet. The European Commission has tried to propose rules for the European Union, but so far only some recommendations from a EU Green Paper exist, and the European Union has to balance PPP policy with the more general competition policy and public procurement rules that guide action between the public sector and the private sector. A new "PPP industry" seems to be emerging, and many of the main players, for example the big consultancy firms that were also active in the privatization era, dominate the market for PPPs up to now. There appears to be a conception of control between the main players about private finance, risk, and the contractual complexity, and the policy image of the PPPs is still mainly positive. The regulatory challenge is huge, and so far the contract is the center of attention, but following the UK, countries are looking to building institutions that could regulate PPPs, and international organizations are also debating how to construct inter-national frameworks for PPP regulation. There are few signs yet of self-regulation within the PPP industry.

The PPP debate has engaged government actors, especially in the "advanced PPP countries," but the main drive could be seen to come from the business side. Businesses are thriving in the emergent PPP market, and businesses seem overall to have been better able to organize themselves in networks and business organizations to push the PPP agenda ahead. There are signs, however, from the main international organizations that an international regulatory framework might be under way, so that both governments and businesses can be assured that PPPs will be regulated internationally.

References

BAUMGARTNER, F., and JONES, B. 1993. *Agendas and Instability in American Government.* Chicago: University of Chicago Press.

BORINS, S. 2000. "Loose canons and rule breakers, or enterprising leaders? Some evidence about innovative public managers," *Public Administration Review* 60: 498–507.

Danish Ministry of Finance. 1999. *Budgetredegørelse* [Budget report]. Copenhagen: Schultz.

DELOITTE. 2006. *Closing the Infrastructure Gap.* Deloitte Study Report.

Department of Treasury, Victoria. 2001. *Partnership Victoria.*

DUNLEAVY, P. 1997. "The globalization of public service production: can governments be 'best in the world'?" in A. Massey, ed., *Globalization and Marketization of Public Services.* London: MacMillan.

European Commission. 2004. Green Paper on Public–Private Partnerships and Community Law on Public Contracts and Concessions, COM/2004/327/Final.

—— 2005. Communication from the Commission to the European Parliament, the Council, the European Economic and Social Committee and the Committee of the Regions on Public–Private Partnerships and Community Law on Public Procurement and Concessions, COM/2005/0569/Final.

FLIGSTEIN, N. 1996. "Markets as politics: a political-cultural approach to market institutions," *American Sociological Review* 61(4), 656–73.

—— 2001. *The Architecture of Markets.* Princeton: Princeton University Press.

FLINDERS, M. 2005. "The politics of public–private partnerships," *British Journal of Political and International Relations* 7: 215–39.

GRIMSEY, D., and LEWIS, M. 2004. *The World Wide Revolution in Infrastructure Provision and Project Finance.* Cheltenham: Edward Elgar.

HAMMERSCHMID, G. 2007. "Legitimizing the failure of a public–private partnership project: media accounts in the twilight zone of public and private sector logic," paper for the EGOS colloquium Vienna, July 5–7, 2007.

HARTLEY, J. and MOORE, M. H. 2008. "Innovations in governance," *Public Management Review* 12(1).

HM Treasury. 2003. *PFI: Meeting the Investment Challenge.* London: HMSO.

—— 2006. *PFI: Strengthening Long Term Partnerships.* London: HMSO.

HODGE, G. 2005. "Public–private partnerships: the Australasian experience," in G. Hodge and C. Greve, eds., *The Challenge of Public–Private Partnerships.* Cheltenham: Edward Elgar, 305–31.

—— and GREVE, C. 2005. *The Challenge of Public–Private Partnerships: Learning from International Experience.* Cheltenham: Edward Elgar.

———— 2007. "Public–private partnerships: an international performance review," *Public Administration Review* 67(3), 545–58.

KETTL, D. F. 1993. *Sharing Power: Public Governance and Private Markets.* Washington, DC: Brookings.

KLIJN, E.-H., and TEISMAN, G. 2005. "Public–private partnerships as the management of co-production," in G. Hodge and C. Greve, eds., *The Challenge of Public–Private Partnerships: Learning from International Experience.* Cheltenham: Edward Elgar, 95–116.

KOPPENJAN, J. 2005. "The formation of public–private partnerships: lessons from nine transport infrastructure projects in the Netherlands," *Public Administration* 8(1): 135–57.

KPMG. 2005. *OPP markedet i Danmark* [The PPP Market in Denmark]. Copenhagen: KPMG.

LEVI FAUR, D., and JORDANA, J., eds. 2004. *The Politics of Regulation.* Cheltenham: Edward Elgar.

LINDER, S. 1999. "Coming to terms with the public–private partnership: a grammar of multiple meanings," *American Behavioral Scientist* 43(1): 35–51.

McCREEVY, C. 2005. Speech by Charlie McCreevy, European Commissioner for Internal Market and Services, November 17, 2005.

National Audit Office (UK). 2000. *Examining the Value for Money of Deals under the Private Finance Initiative.* London: HMSO.

OECD. 2005. *Modernising Government.* Paris: OECD.

—— 2008. *Public–Private Partnerships: In Pursuit of Risk Sharing and Value for Money.* Paris: OECD.

OSBORNE, S., ed. 2001. *Public–Private Partnerships.* London: Routledge.

Partnerships UK. 2007. *PFI: The State of the Market.* London: Partnerships UK.

POLLITT, M. 2005. "Learning from the UK private finance experience," in G. Hodge and C. Greve, eds., *The Challenge of Public–Private Partnerships: Learning from International Experience.* Cheltenham: Edward Elgar, 207–30.

PriceWaterhouseCoopers. 2005. *Delivering the PPP Promise: A Review of PPP Issues and Activity.* London: PriceWaterhouseCoopers.

SHAOUL, J. 2005. "The private finance initiative or the public funding of private profit," in G. Hodge and C. Greve, eds., *The Challenge of Public–Private Partnerships: Learning from International Experience.* Cheltenham: Edward Elgar, 190–206.

SKANSKA. 2008. "Skanska is a leading PFI/PPP provider in the UK," Skanska UK, available at www.skanska.com accessed February 25, 2008.

SKELCHER, CHRIS. 2005. "Public–private partnerships and hybridity," in E. Ferlie, C. Pollitt, and L. Lynn, eds., *The Oxford Handbook of Public Management.* Oxford: Oxford University Press, 347–70.

STONE, B. 1995. "Administrative accountability in the westminster democracies: towards a new conceptual framework," *Governance* 8(1), 505–25.

TERRY, F. 1996. "The private finance initiative: overdue reform or policy breakthrough?" *Public Money and Management* January–March: 9–16.

VAN HAM, H. and KOPPENJAN, J. 2001. "Building public–private partnerships: assessing and managing risk in port development," *Public Administration* 4(1): 593–616.

WETTENHALL, R. 2003. "The rhetoric and reality of public–private partnerships," *Public Organization Review: A Global Journal* 3: 77–107.

—— 2005. "The public–private interface: surveying history," in G. Hodge and C. Greve, eds., *The Challenge of Public–Private Partnerships: Learning from International Experience.* Cheltenham: Edward Elgar.

World Bank. 2007. *Public–Private Partnerships in the New EU Member States.* Washington, DC: World Bank.

CHAPTER 26

ENTREPRENEURSHIP AND SMALL BUSINESS POLICY

EVALUATING ITS ROLE AND PURPOSE

FRANCIS J. GREENE
DAVID J. STOREY

INTRODUCTION

Van Praag and Versloot (2007) argue there is evidence of four economic benefits of entrepreneurship. First, entrepreneurs and small businesses make a positive contribution to job generation. Second, they are integral to innovatory processes that bring new ideas and new products or services to the market. Third, they promote productivity and economic growth. Finally, entrepreneurs and small business owner-managers are an important outlet for people seeking higher "utility"—either in terms of achieving greater income or job satisfaction.

Such evidence is reassuring to public policy-makers since public policy in this area has become increasingly fashionable. Such policies began in the United States in the 1950s, took off in Europe in the 1980s, and are now found in all developed countries.

The aim of this chapter is to review the extent to which public policy can enhance entrepreneurship and so garner the economic benefits identified by van Praag and Versloot. To achieve this aim the chapter has four sections. We begin by addressing the conceptual confusion caused by the different definitions of "entrepreneurship and small business (public) policy." Following Hart (2003), we take "public policy" to be the intended use of powers by government to impact on societal outcomes. We then follow Lundstrom and Stevenson (2007) and suggest that entrepreneurship policies focus upon individuals who are not yet business owners; here the policy objective is to shift them into becoming business owners. In contrast, small business or "small and medium sized enterprise" (SME) policies focus upon existing businesses.

Second, we pose the question of whether, and under what circumstances, potential entrepreneurs and small business owners are appropriate beneficiaries of funding from taxpayers. The traditional response to such a question is to re-emphasize the case made by van Praag and Versloot, and by the OECD (2005), that such individuals and enterprises create and sustain dynamic, flexible, and innovative economies throughout the world. We review that evidence.

However, even if entrepreneurs and small business owners provide these benefits, the central question remains: Why should the taxpayer have to pay to make this happen? Our third task is then to clarify the theoretical justification underlying entrepreneurship and small business public policy. Although the term is rarely, if ever, used by politicians, the basis for public policy in this and many other areas is "market failure," of which there are two relevant forms here (Storey 2003). The first are constraints, normally information imperfections, and second is externalities. Amongst the information imperfections relevant for entrepreneurship policy is that some individuals—particularly amongst "disadvantaged" groups (e.g., the young; women)—may be unaware of how to go about starting a business. Public funding may then be justified on the grounds that providing such information enables businesses to be established. In the context of established (small) businesses, information or advice provided from public funds may lead businesses to expand faster/become more competitive, leading to enhanced societal outcomes. The second theoretical justification relates to the presence of externalities. These are the unpriced costs or benefits of a particular activity. Traditionally, externalities have been seen negatively: a business pollutes the environment but this cost is not captured in its pricing, forcing the government either to tax or regulate the polluter. However externalities can also be positive and provide unpriced benefits to society. These are often referred to as "spillovers." The classic spillover in an entrepreneurial context is knowledge, which is argued to be a key ingredient for economic growth (Acs and Armington 2006). The spillover argument, at its most basic, is that business owners and potential business owners accumulate knowledge at no cost to themselves by observing the success and failure of others. They then use that knowledge to adjust their own behavior, which may mean they either start a business or change the strategy of that business. However that "unpriced" information would not be available to them without other firms starting, failing, or growing and that it is, therefore, potentially an appropriate use of public money to stimulate the creation of new firms on the grounds that this provides unpriced benefits to actual and potential business owners.

Our final area of interest is in charting how public policy-makers have historically approached entrepreneurship and small business policy. We contrast two nations: the United States and the United Kingdom. We chose the US for three reasons. First, it has the longest established set of enterprise policies in the world. Second, other nations, either in the developed or developing world, have long looked to the US as an exemplar of "enterprise." Third, Dennis (2004) argues that the US provides low levels of financial assistance to entrepreneurs and small business and has few barriers to actually starting a business.

By contrast, Dennis argues that most European countries have comparatively high barriers to starting a business and spend considerable sums of public money on encouraging entrepreneurship and small businesses. The UK is of interest because, although it has few barriers to starting a business, its level of actual support is comparable to other European countries. Indeed, the UK has perhaps been at the forefront of European efforts to improve entrepreneurial propensity and capacity (see Dannreuther 1999 for a review of EU enterprise policy). It also differs from the US in that its dedicated enterprise policy regime only really began in the early 1980s. Also, whilst the US has had a fairly stable set of enterprise policies, the UK has constantly rearranged its policy "deckchairs."

Against these differences, we compare the enterprise policies of these countries. What we find is that the US appears to spend less on enterprise support. It is difficult, however, to be certain about this because—unlike the UK—the US does not publish data on the overall costs of enterprise support. The US also appears to spend more on "hard" (financial) than "soft" (e.g. training, mentoring) support. Both countries, however, appear to have generally weak enterprise evaluation cultures, although the UK arguably has a greater number of appropriate evaluations.

We conclude the chapter by asserting that entrepreneurship and small business policy is unlikely to diminish in scale in the foreseeable future. Our interpretation of the evidence from observing policy impact in the two countries with the longest experience in this area is the need to be much clearer about the role, purpose, and value of specific policies. Given the current evidence available we are unconvinced that taxpayers have had, or currently obtain, value for money in this area of public policy.

DEFINITIONS OF ENTREPRENEURSHIP AND SMALL BUSINESS POLICY

Entrepreneurship policy

As far back as 1959 Edith Penrose described entrepreneurship as "a slippery concept" and some years later Coleman (1973)—clearly a man with a sense of humor—said "the joys of defining 'entrepreneurial' could fill a whole volume" (111–12). Amongst the contents of such a volume could be the personal characteristics or traits of that individual—such as the need to be in control or the need to achieve. The European Commission's (2003) Green Paper on Entrepreneurship appears to have some sympathy with this view:

Entrepreneurship is first and foremost a mindset. It covers an individual's motivation and capacity, independently or within an organisation, to identify an opportunity and to pursue it in order to produce new value or economic success. (5)

Unfortunately for the Commission, there is very little evidence to link particular "mindsets" with entrepreneurial activities. Gartner (1989) is widely viewed as having had the last word on the matter:

A startling number of traits and characteristics have been attributed to the entrepreneur. A psychological profile of the entrepreneur assembled from these studies would portray someone larger than life, full of contradictions and conversely so full of traits that (s)he would have to be a sort of generic "Everyman." (57)

Other research has explored the cognitive biases and decision-making processes involved in entrepreneurship. Here attention has focused upon the optimism or risk orientation of entrepreneurs. This also has produced very mixed results (Delmar 2000). Finally, other research has sought to equate entrepreneurship with certain types of behaviors such as being innovative, but again the patterns that emerge are not consistent. Current practice amongst researchers seems to be to equate entrepreneurship with a particularly set of behaviors grouped around the setting up of a new business. Daily et al. (2002) defined (independent) entrepreneurship as:

The process whereby an individual or group of individuals, acting independently of any association with an existing organisation, create a new organisation. (389)

The concentration then has been on *how, why,* and *where* individuals interested in setting up a business (nascent entrepreneurs) come to set up their own business (entrepreneurship). There is also an interest in developing both an awareness and appreciation of the entrepreneurial option. The advantage of this approach to entrepreneurship is that it covers three different but integral elements of entrepreneurship: society (e.g., population, economy, education), the business (e.g., types of new business), and the individual (e.g., cognitive biases).

This is the approach favored by Lundstrom and Stevenson (2007). They argue that entrepreneurship is focused around three distinct phases: awareness, nascent, and start-up activities. Hence, they define entrepreneurship policy as:

policy aimed at the pre-start, the start-up and early post-start-up phases of the entrepreneurial process, designed and delivered to address the areas of motivation, opportunity and skills, with the primary objective of encouraging more people in the population to consider entrepreneurship as an option, move into the nascent stage of taking actions to start a business and proceed into the entry and early stages of the business. (105)

Public policy is then viewed as a catalyst to enable individuals to realize their entrepreneurial propensities and capacities. Entrepreneurship policy has a role in primary, secondary, and tertiary education; the promotion of entrepreneurship in the media and in society; the reduction of administrative, legislative, and regulatory barriers; and actual support for people to set up in business.

Limiting entrepreneurship policy to the start up and early stages of business development has two disadvantages. First, although someone sets up a new business it does not mean they continue to be innovative or dynamic. Indeed, most people who set up a new business do not seek to grow their business. Neither are they likely to be particularly innovative. Much of what new businesses offer is humdrum, either because it focuses on personal (e.g., clothes, food, entertainment) or living needs (e.g., house repair).

The second is that, whilst it is clear that entrepreneurship as reflected in fast growth businesses such as Google clearly has major economic significance, the case is much less clear for the average start up. The reality of policy is that it is the latter that are more likely to be stimulated by policy than are Google's. This distinction is recognized by the National Commission on Entrepreneurship which defines "entrepreneurs as leaders of small companies that are based on innovation and are designed to grow quickly—often at an annual rate of 15–20 percent" (quoted in NGA 2004: 6). Hoffmann (2007) also argues for a similar definition—"entrepreneurship ... is actually about creating a dynamic economy, which ensures that people can start new ventures and subsequently develop these new ventures to become high-growth firms" (140). Hart (2003) has also stated: "the domain of entrepreneurship policy is large. It encompasses activities at several levels of government, from local to national (and perhaps beyond)" (4). Equally, because the term "entrepreneurship" is so malleable, it is often applies to differing organizational forms such as intrapreneurship or social entrepreneurship.

Small business policy

If there are definitional issues about entrepreneurship, there are also similarly irksome difficulties in defining a small business. Qualitatively, small businesses seem to have particular attributes. First, they are usually seen as independent and autonomous. Second, they are often seen as price takers rather than price makers. Finally, the same individual(s) generally combine ownership with control (Bolton 1971).

Public policy, however, finds it difficult to operationalize policies about the "feel" of businesses. Instead, small businesses policy is delivered to enterprises below a specified size threshold. Hence, in the US, small businesses are defined as those with fewer than 500 employees whilst in the European Union it is SMEs with fewer than 250 employees.[1] Because these limits include nearly all businesses, public policy-makers have sought to further disaggregate small businesses into further size bands. In the EU, for example, enterprises are disaggregated into micro businesses (0–9 employees), small businesses (10–49 employees), medium-sized businesses (50–249 employees), and large businesses (250 + employees).

Lundstrom and Stevenson (2007) argue that small business or SME policy is quite different from entrepreneurship policy. They suggest SME policies are focused around the post-start-up phase of the *existing* business and its survival/growth. They say:

The primary aim of small business policy is to level the playing field for small firms through measures to overcome their disadvantages in the marketplace resulting from their "smallness" and "resource poverty," and to improve their competitiveness. (105)

This implies SME public policy has two functions. The first is to ensure smaller firms are not disadvantaged by the (anti)competitive behavior of (large) businesses. The second is, by managing the activities and behaviors of SMEs (e.g., export orientation, innovation propensity), to maximize the benefits to society of such firms achieving their full potential. There are two main advantages for policy-makers with such an approach. First, the clear and identifiable focus upon the business as the unit of analysis means it is relatively easy to track and follow such entities. In this sense the "target population" is easy to identify. Second, the owner-manager has a clear understanding of the expected impact on his or her business in terms of costs (tax, employment regulations) and benefits (e.g., availability of grants, loans).

There are, of course, disadvantages with such an approach. First, a harmonized international understanding of small businesses is impossible when there is no common definition of firm size (OECD 2005). Second, concentrating on the business can ignore the individual. After all, businesses are just forms of coping with the market (Coase 1937); it is people who *do* business. Unfortunately, each business is not owned by a single person; instead some businesses are owned by several people and some people own several businesses. Third, within the group defined as small businesses there is considerable heterogeneity, so that the policies likely to impact upon a small software house are likely to differ sharply from those of concern to a hairdresser employing the same number of staff. Finally, although clear limits can be placed upon who is "in" and who is "out," does this make for good policy? One basic rationale—as we shall see—for small business policy is that such businesses are "resource constrained." Some might argue, though, that small firms have behavioral advantages over larger firms (e.g., greater flexibility) so the case for providing taxpayers' support is less clear.

Despite these conceptual difficulties, there are three distinct areas of public policy towards enterprises. The first is "macro policy." Here the focus is upon creating a macroeconomic environment comprising low and stable interest rates, low inflation, and high aggregate demand. It may also include providing tax incentives, an appropriate legal framework (e.g., intellectual property rights), competitive markets (e.g., business regulations), and attracting and retaining particular individuals (immigration and emigration issues). Public policy, therefore, has a role in ensuring that the "rules of the game" are understood by individuals and that the nature of incentives are robust and clearly signal appropriate entrepreneurial opportunities (Baumol 1990).

Increasingly, however, as Lundstrom and Stevenson (2007) suggest, public policy-makers across the world have seen the need to identify and target particular policies either aimed specifically at entrepreneurship or small businesses. We now turn to examine the rationale underpinning this policy area.

REASONS FOR SUPPORTING SMALL BUSINESSES AND ENTREPRENEURS

The main reasons for supporting small businesses and entrepreneurs are shown in Table 26.1. Historically, the most important of these has been their contribution to job generation. Birch (1979) was the first to demonstrate that smaller businesses were responsible for a high proportion of the net new jobs in the US economy.[2] At the time, the Birch findings were criticized on the grounds of data quality (Storey and Johnson 1987) and analytical approach (Davis, Hatiwanger, and Schuh 1996). Over time there has been an improvement in data quality and, using the Birch approach, his key findings have been reproduced for Sweden (Folster 2000), the US (Acs and Mueller 2008), Portugal (Oliveira and Fortunato 2006), Germany (Wagner 1997), and the Netherlands (van Stel and Suddle 2008).[3]

A second reason for the public policy interest in small business and entrepreneurship is their contribution to economic development through enhancing productivity by raising entry and exit. Productivity gains are argued to come about in two ways. The first is a direct gain because a new business is more efficient or offers higher quality (e.g., better customer experience) and therefore displaces existing less efficient businesses. The indirect effect of (potential) entry is to exert a threat to incumbent businesses, disciplining them to provide more innovative or cheaper offerings to customers. Newer businesses have been found to have major productivity benefits (e.g., Disney, Haskel, and Heden 2003). There is also evidence that, in the long run, new businesses provide additional employment growth in both single country (e.g., Germany; Fritsch and Mueller 2007) and international studies (e.g., Carree and Thurik 2008).

As well as enhancing productivity, fast growing small businesses make a direct contribution to economic growth (Storey 1994; Cognetics 2000). Frequently, but by

Table 26.1 Summary of the advantages of entrepreneurship and small businesses

Contribute towards employment growth	Plenty of empirical evidence to suggest that smaller business is responsible for net job generation in developed economies
Contribute to economic development	Productivity gains from competition (dynamic selection and disciplining effects of new entrants); importance of fast growth businesses; contribution to innovation; development of new industries
Contribute to sustainability	Increase consumer choice; productive outlet for independent individuals; seedbed for social entrepreneurship
Large political constituency	Nearly all businesses are small; represent a large proportion of employment and payroll turnover; large numbers of owner-managers and self-employed individuals

no means always, these fast growth firms are in the new industries. Jovanovic (2001) reported that four of the largest US companies in terms of market capitalization in 1999 were less than twenty years old. Equally, for smaller economies, there is evidence to suggest that one company can make a dramatic economic contribution: Nokia was responsible for a great deal of the economic growth experienced by Finland in the 1990s.

Another important reason why smaller businesses are able to contribute to economic growth is their innovative capacity. Although expenditure on formal Research and Development continues to be primarily undertaken by larger businesses, there is now persuasive evidence that smaller businesses play an important role in developing the innovatory capacity of an economy (OECD 2005). There are two key reasons for this. The first is that the nature of competitive advantage has changed. Prior to the 1980s competitive advantage was seen primarily in terms of lowering of costs. In that context, large firms, able to reap scale economies, would always out-perform small firms. However, if competitive advantage reflects informational advantages in the form of knowledge capital, the pendulum then swings back in favor of flexible and responsive smaller firms (Audretsch and Thurik 2004). Alternatively expressed, smaller businesses have behavioral characteristics—creativity, originality, independence, autonomy, and openness—that are potentially more attuned to modern economic conditions. In contrast, large businesses are seen as bureaucratic, rule bound, hierarchical, and conformist (Audretsch and Beckman 2007). Being closer to the market and having greater flexibility allows smaller businesses to be potentially more dynamic relative to larger more stable businesses.

Whilst the picture painted is plausible the empirical evidence on the innovatory contribution of small businesses is not consistent. In their summary of the economic literature, van Praag and Versloot (2008) show small firms are no more likely to invest in innovation than larger businesses but that the quality of any innovations may be higher (e.g., higher levels of patent activity). Equally, although entrepreneurs have higher levels of commercialization activity, it is unclear whether this leads to subsequent widespread economic benefits. Finally, entrepreneurs are also more likely to adopt low innovation strategies.

Sustainability benefits

A third reason for interest in small businesses and entrepreneurs is that they may provide for economic sustainability rather than additional economic growth. There are a variety of dimensions to these advantages. First, smaller businesses provide choice and variety to consumers and, therefore, serve as a bulwark against exploitation from larger businesses. They are often also key assets in communities because of the personalized way that they tend to run their business. Equally, not everyone sees themselves as suited to employment or feels that they have ready access to mainstream employment. Indeed, the empirical evidence indicates that the self-employed are more satisfied with their work than waged workers (Blanchflower and Oswald 1998). This also extends to workers. Forth, Bewley, and Bryson (2006) find that employees in smaller businesses were more likely to be "happier" and more trusting of managers than those working in larger enterprises.

Setting up and running a business may also be a productive outlet for an individual or groups in society who are disadvantaged in some way either because of limited labor market experience (e.g., young people) or because of real or perceived discrimination (e.g., women; minorities). Finally, many businesses seek to act as agents of social change by integrating social and environmental concerns into their business operations (Tracey and Phillips 2007). Hence, they may reflect the local indigenous culture of an area (e.g., farmer's markets) but also the importance of other cultures (Fair Trade goods such as tea and coffee).

It would be misleading, however, to believe that entrepreneurship and small businesses are unalloyed agents of social good. Entrepreneurship has its "dark" side. Again, there are various dimensions to this. First, the bulk of the evidence points to entrepreneurs and smaller businesses' owner-managers having, all else equal, lower incomes than those in the waged sector (Hamilton 2000). Hence, they may be "happier" but they are also likely to be poorer; persist with an "entrepreneurial" opportunity when they would be better off working for someone else (Gimeno et al. 1997); or face greater uncertainty about their incomes (Parker 2004).[4]

Workers in smaller businesses are also likely to receive lower wages than comparable employees in larger businesses (McNabb and Whitfield 2000). International evidence from the US (Brown and Medoff 1989), Germany (Wagner 1997), and the UK (Belfield 1999) also indicates that small business employees are likely to enjoy fewer fringe benefits (e.g., health insurance, a company pension scheme, a profit sharing scheme, a travel scheme, or merit/bonus-related pay). Meanwhile, Hasle and Limborg's (2006) review of safety issues in smaller businesses also concludes that small business workplaces have higher accident rates and poorer safety records. Finally, the evidence is that smaller businesses are less likely to provide *formal* training for their employees than larger businesses—although they may provide more informal training.

A core political constituency

A final set of factors explaining the scale and focus of entrepreneurship and small business public policy reflects the direct democratic influence of entrepreneurs and small business owners. In every economy in the world at least 95 per cent of its businesses are small businesses. The percentage, however, is often higher. In the United States, the SBA (2007a) estimates that of the 26.8 million businesses in the United States, only 17,000 (0.3 per cent) businesses were large businesses in 2004 (<500 employees). The SBA also estimates that small businesses employ about half of all private sector employees and were responsible for more than 45 per cent of the US's private payroll. Similar claims can be made about other economies. In Japan, for instance, small businesses made up 99.7 per cent of businesses, contributed 71 per cent of employment, and more than half of all manufacturing shipments in 2004 (<300 employees) (JSBRI 2006). In essence, as the OECD (2008a) documents, small businesses make up nearly all businesses and typically represent at least 50 per cent of total employment in any given economy.

There are also large numbers of self-employed in very many countries. In Mexico, the OECD (2007a) estimates that in 2005, self-employment stood at 35.6 per cent of the total civilian population. In Greece it was even higher at 36.4 per cent whilst in Italy it was 27 per cent. From a political perspective, the sheer number of people employed in small businesses and the large numbers of owner-managers or self-employed individuals means that they represent a very sizeable constituency to any politician.

So, Why have Entrepreneurship and Small Business Policies?

Even if small businesses and entrepreneurship provide jobs, build economic growth, and offer sustainability benefits this, of itself, is not sufficient to justify the use of taxpayers funds. In this section, we discuss the types of justifications usually associated with policy interventions in this area. These are largely grouped around notions of market failure. We complement this section by examining some of the reasons why intervention may not be judicious.

Market failure is the economically accepted basis for public policy interventions. Storey (1982) argued that market failure occurs in the absence of perfect competition, fully informed consumers, where there are externalities, and where demand fails to reflect willingness to pay. Even when these situations occur it does not imply that intervention should take place: public policy-makers have to show that their favored intervention leads to improved social outcomes, net of the costs of intervention. Table 26.2 identifies instances of market failure and then provides examples of entrepreneurship and small business policies that seek to address these failures. It focuses on two main types of market failure. The first is constraints faced by a small business or by an individual considering establishing a new business. These reflect information imperfections. For example, young people might be ignorant of the entrepreneurial option because they are not taught about entrepreneurship at school. Financiers may be wary of providing funds for a new business because its owner has no prior business experience; the transactions costs of collecting information on the owner are high relative to the sum requested; there may be differences in opinion over the risk–return relationships; and if the financier believes that the entrepreneur is "hiding" their true intentions. The key point is that these

Table 26.2 Justifications for public policy interventions

	Entrepreneurship policy	Small business policy
Resource constraints		
Information is imperfect and asymmetric	Individuals are ignorant of the benefits of starting a business	Small business owner–managers are ignorant of the benefits of obtaining expert advice from outside specialists
Finance	Disadvantaged groups (e.g., young people with no prior labor market experience) are denied start up finance because of expected higher default rates	Equity gaps exist because of economies of scale in the provision of finance (e.g., high transaction costs for finance dissuade financiers from offering small "packages" of equity)
Physical premises	Absence of suitable start up premises	Planning laws prevent the changes of use needed to reflect changing market requirements
Business development services	Support needed to guide some individuals through the complexities of business registration	Difficulties in overcoming exporting in international markets
Training	Some individuals lack the necessary skills to set up and manage a business	Small business owner–managers are unwilling/unable to afford off-site training for their employees even if better-trained workers would enhance business performance
Risk and uncertainty	Individual is unable to accurately assess the risk of starting a business and so may be discouraged from starting	Small businesses under-invest in R&D or capital because of uncertainty of the returns from R&D or prospects for the economy
Failure to appropriate returns from innovation	A potential business owner cannot adequately protect/patent its ideas and so does not develop them	Small business owner–managers believe that their idea/project is easily reverse engineered and therefore not profitable for them to develop
Externalities		
Network externalities	A start up gains intangible benefits from being located close to existing or new businesses	The "small business" capabilities are shaped by the network that it works within: the greater the nature of trust within the network, stronger the "small business" capabilities
Knowledge externalities	New business is able to take advantage of (redundant) knowledge spillovers (e.g., Xerox inventions (e.g., graphical user interface, mouse, Ethernet) taken advantage by new businesses like Apple and Microsoft)	Knowledge spillovers (e.g., incumbent business failing) signal to existing businesses likely returns from particular projects
Demonstration or learning externalities	Individual setting of up a business in a deprived area acts as a role model to others in the area	Championing of a particular technology demonstrates value of technology to other businesses

information imperfections may prevent the business starting or prevent the expansion of an existing business leading directly to a loss of welfare not only for the business owner but for society more widely. On these grounds it may be reasonable for politicians, acting on behalf of society, to use some public funds to lower information barriers, enable businesses to start and expand, and thus benefit society.

Table 26.2 also identifies other resource constraints which might lead the entrepreneur to either not invest (set up their business) or to sub-optimally invest. Examples include the lack of availability of suitable premises (which leads to policy-makers providing dedicated science parks or other incubator units) and "soft" support (e.g., mentoring) to develop the business.

Such sub-optimal investments often arise in a market failure framework because it is very difficult for the entrepreneur to fully realize the benefits of their investment. For instance, an owner-manager may be reluctant to incur the cost of training workers if they leave before any benefits accrue because they have become more attractive to another employer willing to pay higher wages.

The "knowledge" economy brings with it particular policy challenges. Most goods like a house or a car come with certain property rights which allow us to exclude others. But "knowledge" has intangible properties that make it difficult for any one individual to easily claim property rights. Table 26.2 points to three types of positive externalities that arise because no one can fully capture the full benefits of knowledge and learning. These are network, knowledge, and learning externalities. Policy-makers may judge that these spillovers effects are important to support. For example, in a deprived area of an economy, the existence of a successful entrepreneur from that community has the wider (unpriced) benefit in that she or he acts as a positive role model to others in the community. Equally, there are distinctive intangible benefits from businesses working together formally or informally (e.g., the Emilia Romagna region of Italy, Piore and Sabel 1984; or Silicon Valley, Saxenian 1994).

Intervention issues

The above has emphasized that there is an a priori case for government intervention when there is clear evidence of market failure. Whether that intervention actually takes place depends on the answer to a second question: is the intervention likely to lead to improvement for both society as a whole or only for certain groups?

Unsurprisingly the specific public policy "recipe" for addressing market inefficiencies varies markedly. In the UK and the US, for example, public policy-makers often do not share in the risks of the business. Bennett (1996) argues that this promotes risk aversion amongst public policy-makers and perhaps explains why policy-makers have a better record of picking "losers" rather than "winners." Equally, if competitive advantage is increasingly dependent on the access to intangible sources of information—what Storper and Venables (2002) have called the entrepreneurial and innovatory "buzz" of urban environments—then it is difficult to see how governments can easily find or successfully "animate" social networks so that new combinations of products and processes "emerge."

Even if there is a theoretical justification for public intervention, and it can be appropriately shown that the public policy-maker has a role, there is often the need to guard against unintended consequences. Blanchflower and Wainwright (2005) argued that one consequence of affirmative action programs in the US was that some wives were used as fronts for their husband's business because they could benefit from positive gender discrimination. Equally, very many programs have significant unintended consequences. This may be in terms of employment (e.g., employment legislation limits taking on extra workers); deadweight (businesses getting subsidies to undertake actions that they would have undertaken without the subsidy); or displacement effects (subsidized businesses displacing non-subsidized businesses purely because of the subsidy and not because of any other competitive advantage).

For all these reasons policy-makers also face real challenges in designing and implementing publicly funded programs targeted at entrepreneurs and small businesses. Mole and Bramley (2006) provide a succinct overview of the menu of choices open to the policy-maker once a decision to intervene has been made. The five choice areas are:

1. Who delivers ... public, private, or quasi?
2. What "type"... generic, standards, tailored, regulated, face-to-face, e-based?
3. How is it rationed ... time, sector, price, market segmentation?
4. How is it integrated ... into other economic and social programs?
5. How is it funded ... by charges, by donations, directly from public funds?

This choice framework can be illustrated with reference to enterprise education. Point (1) raises the question of who delivers such education—schools or universities—and who should get support—for example science or arts students. Point (2) asks what is the most effective way of communicating these skills and who should do it—former entrepreneurs or qualified teachers? Point (3) is the crucial rationing question: it asks if this type of education is so valuable, whether students are prepared to pay for it, or what else needs to be eliminated from the curriculum in order to accommodate its inclusion. Point (4) asks about the links between enterprise education and other public programs. This is on the grounds that generating enthusiasm for enterprise in schools and colleges will be of only limited value if the cost of starting a business is high, or the macroeconomic conditions are unfavorable, or if the tax regime is oppressive. Finally, point (5) asks about how such programs are funded.

The above choice framework is therefore the third step in the chain. The first is to identify the market failure; the second is the political decision to intervene and the third is the range of choices associated with the intervention. Parker (2004) summarizes thus:

Governments invariably face conflicting aspirations and objectives. They want to target resources to achieve focus but are unable to pick winners; they want to make assistance selective to control budgetary costs but wish also to both remain inclusive and avoid spreading resources too thinly; and they want policies to make a big impact for political reasons whilst minimizing costs and program deadweight losses. These trade-offs are deep-rooted and probably inescapable.   (2004: 269)

ENTREPRENEURSHIP AND SMALL BUSINESS POLICY DEVELOPMENTS: A COMPARISON OF THE UK AND THE US

In this section, we compare and contrast UK and US enterprise policies. We examine five areas. First, we briefly detail the evolution of UK and US enterprise policies. We then assess the costs of such support, where the emphasis of such support lies, and whether these programs appear appropriately evaluated. Finally, we look at key "entrepreneurial outcomes" in the two countries.

The evolution of US and UK enterprise policy

It is tempting to regard the US as not having a dedicated range of public enterprise policies. This rests on the US being intrinsically pro-enterprise (Acs and Stough 2008). This would be a misconception. The US has had formal policies in this area far longer than any other developed country. This began with the creation of the Small Business Administration (SBA) in 1953. As the lead or "host" agency responsible for small business and entrepreneurship matters the SBA's aim is and was to "aid, counsel, assist and protect, insofar as is possible, the interests of small business concerns" (SBA 2007b). By 1954, the SBA was making direct business loans, guaranteeing bank loans to businesses, helping to get government procurement contracts for small businesses, and helping business owners with management and technical assistance and business training.

These policy concerns remain. The SBA's portfolio covers finance (e.g., 7(a) Loan Program); access to federal contracts (e.g., Prime Contracting Assistance Program); counseling, training, and the education of nascent and actual entrepreneurs (e.g., Small Business Development Centers); and advocacy programs (e.g., Regulatory Enforcement Assistance).

By contrast, Greene, Mole, and Storey (2008) have argued that the UK only really began to develop enterprise policies in the early 1980s. Prior to that, the focus was on larger firms. The reason for the switch to enterprise policies remains contested. Two views stand out. One is that the UK government believed that there was a need to mimic the US pro-enterprise focus. The second was that around one in eight adults was unemployed in the early 1980s and self-employment seemed a positive mechanism for getting people back to work (Birch 1979).

Since the early 1980s, the pace of enterprise initiatives has accelerated (Greene 2002) but the focus of such policies has tended to vacillate between using enterprise policies to improve productivity, reduce unemployment, or as an alternative mechanism by which people can realize their own aspirations. The net result of this is that, unlike the US, particular initiatives have appeared to come and go—only to return when conditions again are suitable.

Cost and emphasis

Although UK enterprise policies have taken longer to mature, it is now more transparent on the actual cost to the taxpayer of enterprise support. The most recent estimate is that, for 2003/4, the cost of enterprise support was £10.3 billion (PACEC 2005). This is made up of four main components: central government programs run by diverse departments such as Trade and Industry, Culture, Media, and Sport and government bodies such as the Learning and Skills Council (£3.9 billion); regional government programs (£0.4 billion); tax incentives (£3.6 billion); and agricultural subsidies (£2.4 billion). For the same year, the UK population was around 60 million. This equates enterprise support to being about US$276 per head (if a pound sterling is worth 1.5 US dollars).

By comparison, the figure for the US is unknown. No information on a comparable basis is collected by the US government. Part of this is because of the difficulty of collecting such information across government departments and issues in finding comparable tax incentive and agricultural subsidies data. Our own estimates suggests that, in for 2005, tax incentives were $8 billion (Guenther 2005). The OECD (2008b) also estimates that US agricultural subsidies were $41 billion. Finally, there is central and regional government expenditure on enterprise support. We are unable to identify the contribution of the various US department of state to enterprise support. For the SBA— the "lead" US enterprise department—we estimate, using Kalman and Elliott (2006), that the SBA's total outlay (expenditure) in 2005 was $2.5 billion. In total, our best estimate is that the US spent $51.5 billion on enterprise support. There were around 296 million people in the US in 2005. This means that per capita the cost of enterprise support was $174 per person. This is far less than the UK expenditure on enterprise support.

It is also clear that the emphasis between the two countries differs. In the US, the bulk of enterprise support is largely in terms of improving access to finance. For example, the US's biggest program by size is the 7a program. In 2005, these loan guarantees amounted to $20 billion. By contrast, the UK loan guarantee program is much smaller. The UK would also seem to spend comparatively more on "soft" support (e.g., training and mentoring).

Evaluation

The evidence above seems to indicate that the US spends less on its enterprise support than a European country such as the UK. The question remains, however: is the money well spent? To answer this requires appropriate evaluations of programs and policies. Ideally, this should be done by randomized trials where people either get the treatment (the policy) or nothing. This allows for the net effect of the policy to be identified. If cost, complexity, or ethical issues intervene (e.g., concerns about people being denied a policy), there exist a range of quasi-experimental techniques that statistically control for differences between the treatment and control groups (OECD 2008c).

Unfortunately, the level of evaluation in developed economies remains modest. The more typical approach is to evaluate based upon the judgments of recipients of support. This is generally true of both the UK and the US. However, there does seem to be a greater interest in undertaking sophisticated policy evaluations in the UK than in the US. Illustrative of this is that, since 1981, the UK's loan guarantee scheme has been evaluated five times. There have also been evaluations, *inter alia*, of other programs (e.g., Wren and Storey 2002; Fraser 2003).

By contrast, Gu, Karoly, and Zissimopoulos (2008) suggest that the publicly available evaluations of various US enterprise support schemes remains underdeveloped. They can only find one study—Benus (1994) —that "appropriately" evaluates a particular enterprise Program. Other evaluations such as Lerner's (1999) evaluation of the Small Business Innovation Research (SBIR) program controls for differences between the treatment and a control group but, significantly, does not control for unobservable (e.g., motivation) differences between these two groups. The various evaluations of the Small Business Development Centers (SBDC) (e.g., Chrisman, Nelson, Hoy, and Robinson 1985 to Chrisman, McMullan, and Hall 2005) also fail to take full account of possible sources of bias because they compare rather than match SBDC clients with "typical" businesses.

Outcomes

Evaluation problems obviously make it difficult to effectively assess the outcomes of enterprise policies. The absence of a holistic statement on policy, patchy data, and shifting policy objectives combine to make comparative outcome assessments difficult.

Nevertheless, recognizing all these limitations, Table 26.3 identifies nine policy outcomes. They are selected on the grounds that, in aggregate, they reflect current policy objectives in the two countries, and the data used can be considered to be broadly comparable.

Using some measures, most notably the "ease of doing business" indicator, both countries perform well; it is relatively easy and inexpensive to start and operate an enterprise in both countries. The US, however, seems to perform more strongly, particularly in terms of higher nascent rates (GEM rates), women co-owner rates, and fast growth firm ("gazelles") concentrations. On the other hand, the UK would seem to be more entrepreneurial in terms of its start up rate, business ownership rate, and in terms of the share of business R&D undertaken by businesses with 250 or

Table 26.3 UK and US enterprise outcomes

	UK	US
Position in World Bank *Ease of Doing Business* 2007[a]	Sixth out of 178	Third out of 178
New firm formation rat[b]	8.7%	13.2%
"Death" rate	8.6%	10.8%
"Churn" rate (start ups + deaths)	17.3%	24%
Women co-owner rates[c]	34.1%–41.2%	48%
GEM Total Entrepreneur Activity rates[d]	5.5%	9.6%
Gazelle concentration[e]	Very low	A handful of gazelles have become household names within two decades of start up
Share of business R&D (<250 employees)[f]	18.6%	14.3%
Business ownership rates[g]	01.112	0.101

[a] World Bank (2008).

[b] Birth and death rates (as a percentage of total number of enterprises) 2003 or latest available year (OECD 2007b: table C7).

[c] Source: Carter and Shaw (2006: 6–7).

[d] GEM (2008: table 1).

[e] Jovanovic (2001) reports that immediately prior to the Stock Market crash of 1999, four US businesses—Cisco System, Dell, MCI, and Microsoft—had been established for less than 20 years but had grown to a size whereby their valuation was equivalent to 13% of US GDP. No non-US enterprise achieved that level of growth since start up. Since 1999 Google has joined that list.

[f] Share of business R&D by size and class of firms, 2005 (OECD 2007b: table A6).

[g] EIM Compendia database (van Stel 2005).

fewer employees. Finally, Table 26.3 shows the UK has a higher churn rate than the US primarily because of its higher business death rate.

Overall we conclude that, although there look to be differences between the countries in terms of enterprise outcomes, it is not clear that one country is clearly more "enterprising" than the other.

To summarize: in both the UK and the US considerable sums of taxpayers' money is spent on support for small businesses and entrepreneurs, particularly through the provision of tax incentives, and also with much funding directed towards agriculture. On our estimates, the US appears to spend less on enterprise policies but we strongly suspect there is considerable "under-reporting." Clearly, there is a need for the US authorities to specifically identify enterprise costs across departments. What is also clear is that the US spends more on improving access to finance. This is odd because there is little evidence of the effectiveness of this spending (Parker 2004). Finally, our outcome measures imply that although there are differences between the two countries, these are hardly sufficient to clearly distinguish one country as being more "entrepreneurial" than the other.

CONCLUSIONS

This chapter asks whether the prevailing interest in small business and entrepreneurship public policy is warranted. We began by introducing some of the difficulties and tensions in defining entrepreneurship and small business policy. We concluded that current definitions included the local to the supranational firm and from the "mom and pop" store to the leading edge innovative fast growth businesses. It is unlikely in our view that any single definition is ever going to be satisfactory. Probably the least unsatisfactory, at least from a public policy viewpoint, is the approach of Lundstrom and Stevenson (2007). They suggest a temporal definition, largely placing entrepreneurship policy around pre-start-up activities and SME policy around post-start-up activities. Even here, though, such a definition is likely to remain a blunt instrument, if only because successful economies (and policies) may only result when entrepreneurship increasingly spills over into existing businesses.

In contrast, the high economic and social value placed by policy-makers on small business and entrepreneurship is much clearer. Three main contributions are normally highlighted—job creation, economic growth, and economic sustainability. Equally, it would be naive, given the sheer weight of people either seeking to run their own business or, more importantly, actually running their own business, to ignore the importance of this core electorate to public policy-makers.

The chapter then explored the market failure based rationale for public support towards small businesses and entrepreneurs and how it also links with political imperatives. In comparing and contrasting the UK with the US, we show that US policies matured quicker and have been far more stable in their policy objectives over time.

A second key US/UK difference is that the former seems to focus more heavily on providing "surrogate" finance. A third difference is that the UK, unlike the US, has documented taxpayers' funding of small business and entrepreneurship. Our own estimates—based on official UK government estimates and available US information—tend to suggest that the US spends less on direct assistance than European countries such as the UK. However, in the absence of appropriate evaluations, it is difficult to establish if this money is well spent. Neither country has a formal mechanism for taking a "bird's eye view" of expenditure in this area. Overall, our conclusions are in line with a former member of US Council of Economic Advisors and former Director of the Congressional Budget Office. Holtz-Eakin (2000) said:

There seems to be widespread support for special help to small businesses which is manifested in preferential tax treatment of these enterprises. However, consideration of the standard efficiency and equity criteria for such subsidy provides little support for such policies. (290)

Notes

1. This is not the only way the EU defines size of businesses (see http://ec.europa.eu/enterprise/enterprise_policy/sme_definition/index_en.htm). Besides employment, they also define an SME as an enterprise as having an annual turnover not exceeding 50 million euros or not exceeding a balance sheet valuation of 43 million euros.
2. He showed that two-thirds of the increase in employment in the US, 1969–76, was in firms with less than twenty workers.
3. Nevertheless, the key Davis et al. criticism remains valid: that the "results" depend heavily upon whether a base year or final year weighting system is used.
4. Parker (2004: 14–18) however emphasizes that studies reaching this conclusion have primarily used official data, yet one of the key "benefits" of self-employment is the greater opportunity for income under-reporting, compared with employees. He quotes non-response rates to official surveys being virtually twice as high amongst the self-employed as amongst the employed.

References

Acs, Z. J, and Armington, C. 2006. *Entrepreneurship, Geography, and American Economic Growth.* Cambridge: Cambridge University Press.

—— and Mueller, P. 2008. "Employment effects of business dynamics: mice, gazelles and elephants," *Small Business Economics* 30(1): 85–100.

—— and Stough, R. 2008. "Introduction," in Z. J. Acs and R. Stough, eds., *Public Policy in an Entrepreneurial Economy: Creating the Conditions for Business Growth.* New York: Springer, 1–22.

Audretsch, D. B., and Beckman, I. A. M. 2007. "From small business to entrepreneurship policy," in D. B. Audretsch, I. Grilo, and R. A. Thurik, eds., *Handbook of Research on Entrepreneurship Policy.* Cheltenham: Edward Elgar, 36–53.

—— and Thurik, R. 2004. "A model of the entrepreneurial economy," Discussion Papers on Entrepreneurship, Growth and Public Policy, Max Planck Institute, 1204.

Baumol, W. J. 1990. "Entrepreneurship: productive, unproductive, and destructive," *Journal of Political Economy* 98: 893–921.

Belfield, C. R. 1999. "The behaviour of graduates in the SME labour market: evidence and perceptions," *Small Business Economics* 12(3): 249–59.

Bennett, R. J. 1996. "Memorandum submitted by Robert Bennett," in *Business Links, Trade and Industry Committee, Fifth Report HC302–II.* London: HMSO.

Benus, J. M. 1994. "Self-employment programmes: a new reemployment tool," *Entrepreneurship Theory and Practice,* 19(2): 73–86.

Birch, D. 1979. *The Job Generation Process.* Cambridge, Mass.: MIT Program on Neighborhood and Regional Change.

Blanchflower, D. G., and Oswald, A. J. 1998. "What makes an entrepreneur?" *Journal of Labor Economics* 16: 26–60.

—— and Wainwright, J. 2005. "An analysis of the impact of affirmative action programs on self-employment in the construction industry," NBER Working Papers 11793. National Bureau of Economic Research.

Bolton, J. 1971. *Report of the Committee of Inquiry on Small Firms,* Cmnd. 4811. London: HMSO.

BROWN, C., and MEDOFF, J. 1989. "The employer size–wage effect," *Journal of Political Economy* 97(5): 1027–59.

CARREE, M. A., and THURIK, A. R. 2008. "The lag structure of the impact of business ownership on economic performance in OECD countries," *Small Business Economics* 30 (1): 101–10.

CARTER, S., and SHAW, E. 2006. *Women's Business Ownership: Recent Research and Policy Developments.* London: BERR.

CHRISMAN, J. J., McMULLAN, E., and HALL, J. 2005. "The influence of guided preparation on the long-term performance of new ventures," *Journal of Business Venturing* 20(6): 769–91.

—— NELSON, R. R., HOY, F., and ROBINSON, Jr., R. B. 1985. "The impact of SBDC consulting activities," *Journal of Small Business Management* 23 (3): 1–11.

COASE, R. H. 1937. "The nature of the firm," *Economica* 4: 386–405.

COGNETICS. 2000. *Business Almanac.* Cambridge, Mass.: Cognetics.

COLEMAN, D. C. 1973. "Gentleman and players," *Economic History Review* 26: 92–116.

DAILY, C. M., McDOUGALL, P. P., COVIN, J. G., and DALTON, D. R. 2002. "Governance and strategic leadership in entrepreneurial firms," *Journal of Management* 28(3): 387–412.

DANNREUTHER, C. 1999. "Discrete dialogues and the legitimisation of EU SME policy," *Journal of European Public Policy* 6(3): 436–55.

DAVIS, J. J., HATIWANGER, J., and SCHUH, S. 1996. "Small business and job creation: dissecting the myth and reassessing the facts," *Small Business Economics* 8(4): 297–315.

DELMAR, F. 2000. "The psychology of the entrepreneur," in S. Carter and D. Jones-Evans, eds., *Enterprise and Small Business.* Harlow: Pearson Education, 132–54.

DENNIS, W. J. 2004. "Creating and sustaining a viable small business sector," paper presented at School of Continuing Education, University of Oklahoma, October 27.

DISNEY, R., HASKEL, J., and HEDEN, Y. 2003. "Restructuring and productivity growth in UK manufacturing," *Economic Journal* 113: 666–94.

European Commission. 2003. *Green Paper: Entrepreneurship in Europe.* Brussels: European Commission.

FOLSTER, S. 2000. "Do entrepreneurs create jobs?" *Small Business Economics* 14(2): 137–48.

FORTH, J., BEWLEY, H., and BRYSON, A. 2006. *Small and Medium-Sized Enterprises: Findings from the 2004 Workplace Employment Relations Survey.* London: DTI.

FRASER, S. 2003. "The impact of investors in people on small business growth," *Environment and Planning C* 21: 793–812.

FRITSCH, M., and MUELLER, P. 2007. "The effect of new business formation on regional development over time: the case of Germany," *Small Business Economics.*

GARTNER, W. B. 1989. " 'Who is an entrepreneur?' is the wrong question," *American Journal of Small Business* 12(1): 11–32.

GIMENO, J., FOLTA, T. B., COOPER, A. C., and WOO, C. Y. 1997. "Survival of the fittest? Entrepreneurial human capital and the persistence of underperforming firms," *Administrative Science Quarterly* 42: 750–83.

Global Entrepreneurship Monitor (GEM). 2008. *2007 Executive Report.* Babson/London: GEM.

GREENE, F. J. 2002. "An investigation into enterprise support for young people: 1975–2000," *International Small Business Journal* 20(3): 315–36.

GREENE, F. J. MOLE, K. F., and STOREY D. J. 2008. *Enterprise and Economic Development.* London: Palgrave.

GU, Q., KAROLY, L. A., and ZISSIMOPOULOS, J. 2008. *Small Bussiness Assistance Programs in the United States: An Analysis of What They Are, How Well They Perform, and How We Can Learn More About Them*, WR-603-EMKF. Santa Monica, Calif.: Rand Corporation.

GUENTHER, G. 2005. *Small Business Tax Benefits: Overview and Economic Rationales.* CRS Report for Congress. Washington, DC: Congressional Research Service.

HAMILTON, B. H. 2000. "Does entrepreneurship pay? An empirical analysis of the returns to self-employment," *Journal of Political Economy* 108(3): 604–31.

HART, D. M. 2003. "Entrepreneurship policy: what is it and where it came from," in *The Emergence of Entrepreneurship Policy: Governance, Start-Ups, and Growth in the US Knowledge Economy.* Cambridge: Cambridge University Press, 3–19.

HASLE, P., and LIMBORG, H. J. 2006. "A review of the literature on preventive occupational health and safety activities in small enterprises," *Industrial Health* 44(1): 6–12.

HOFFMANN, A. N. 2007. "A rough guide to entrepreneurship policy," in D. B. Audretsch, I. Grilo, and R. A. Thurik, eds., *Handbook of Research on Entrepreneurship Policy.* Cheltenham: Edward Elgar, 140–71.

HOLTZ-EAKIN, D. 2000. "Public policy toward entrepreneurship," *Small Business Economics* 15 (4): 283–91.

Japan Small Business Research Institute (JSBRI). 2006. *White Paper on Small and Medium Enterprises in Japan 2006: Small and Medium Enterprises at a Turning Point: Strengthening Ties with Overseas Economies and Population Decline in Japan.* Tokyo: JSBRI.

JOVANOVIC, B. 2001. "New technology and the small firm," *Small Business Economics* 16(1): 53–5.

KALMAN, Z., and ELLIOTT, D. J. 2006. *Small Business Administration: A Primer.* Washington, DC: COFFI.

LERNER, J. 1999. "The government as venture capitalist: the long run impact of the SBIR programme," *Journal of Business* 72(3): 285–318.

LUNDSTROM, A., and STEVENSON, L. A. 2007. "Dressing the emperor: the fabric of entrepreneurship policy," in D. B. Audretsch, I. Grilo, and R. A. Thurik, eds., *Handbook of Research on Entrepreneurship Policy.* Cheltenham: Edward Elgar, 94–129.

MCNABB, R., and WHITFIELD, K. 2000. "'Worth so appallingly little': a workplace-level analysis of low pay," *British Journal of Industrial Relations* 38(4): 585–609.

MOLE, K. F., and BRAMLEY, G. 2006. "Making policy choices in non-financial business support: an international comparison," *Environment and Planning C: Government and Policy* 24(6): 885–908.

National Governors Association (NGA). 2004. *A Governor's Guide to Strengthening State Entrepreneurship Policy.* Washington, DC: NGA.

OECD. 2005. *Small and Medium Enterprise & Entrepreneurship Outlook.* Paris: OECD.

—— 2007a. "Self-employment rates: total', http://fiordiliji.sourceoecd.org/pdf//fact2007pdf// 06–01–04.pdf

—— 2007b. *OECD Science, Technology and Industry Scoreboard 2007: Innovation and Performance in the Global Economy.* Paris: OECD.

—— 2008a. *Measuring Enterpeneurship: A Digest of Indicators.* Paris: OECD.

—— 2008b. *Producer and Consumer Support Estimates: OECD Database 1986–2007,* http://www.oecd.org/document/59/0,3343,en_2649_33727_39551355_1_1_1_1,00.html accessed September 3.

—— 2008c. *Framework for the Evaluation of SME & Entrepreneurship Policies and Programmes.* Paris: OECD.

OLIVEIRA, B., and FORTUNATO, A. 2006. "Firm growth and liquidity constraints: a dynamic analysis," *Small Business Economics* 27(2–3): 139–56.

PACEC. 2005. *Small Business Service Mapping of Government Services for Small Business Final Report.* Cambridge: PACEC.

PARKER, S. C. 2004. *The Economics of Self Employment and Entrepreneurship.* Cambridge: Cambridge University Press.

PENROSE, E. T. 1959. *The Theory of the Growth of the Firm.* New York: Wiley.

PIORE, M., and SABEL, C. 1984. *The Second Industrial Divide.* New York: Basic Books.

SBA. 2007a. *How Important are Small Businesses to the US economy?* http://app1.sba.gov/faqs/ faqindex.cfm?areaID=24

—— 2007b. *SBA: 50 Years as America's Small Business Resource,* http://www.sba.gov/50/ history.html

SAXENIAN, A. 1994. *Regional Advantage: Culture and Competition in Silicon Valley and Route 128.* Cambridge, Mass.: Harvard University Press.

STOREY, D. J. 1982. *Entrepreneurship and the New Firm.* London: Croom Helm.

—— 1994. *Understanding the Small Business Sector.* London: Routledge.

—— 2003. "Entrepreneurship, small and medium sized enterprises and public policies," in Z. J. Acs, and D. B. Audretsch, eds., *Handbook of Entrepreneurship Research.* Dordrecht: Kluwer, 473–511.

—— and JOHNSON, S. 1987. *Job Generation and Labour Market Change.* London: Macmillan.

STORPER, M., and VENABLES, A. J. 2002. "Buzz: the economic force of the city," paper presented at the Druid Summer Conference on "Industrial dynamics of the new and old economy—who is embracing whom?" Copenhagen/Elsinore.

TRACEY, P., and PHILLIPS, N. 2007. "The distinctive challenge of educating social entrepreneurs: a postscript and rejoinder to the special issue on entrepreneurship education," *Academy of Management Learning and Education* (AMLE) 6(2): 264–71.

VAN PRAAG, C. M., and VERSLOOT, P. H. 2007. "What is the value of entrepreneurship? A review of recent research," *Small Business Economics* 29: 351–82.

VAN STEL, A. J. 2005. "COMPENDIA: harmonizing business ownership data across countries and over time," *International Entrepreneurship and Management Journal* 1(1): 105–23.

—— and SUDDLE, K. 2008. "The impact of new firm formation on regional development in the Netherlands," *Small Business Economics* 30: 31–47.

WAGNER, J. 1997. "Firm size and job quality: a survey of the evidence from Germany," *Small Business Economics* 9(5): 411–25.

World Bank. 2008. *Ease of Doing Business Indicators,* http://www.doingbusiness.org/ economyrankings/ accessed March 18.

WREN, C., and STOREY, D. J. 2002. "Evaluating the effect of 'soft' business support upon small firms performance," *Oxford Economic Papers* 54: 334–65.

CHAPTER 27

....

CONSUMER POLICY

BUSINESS AND THE POLITICS OF CONSUMPTION

....

GUNNAR TRUMBULL

INTRODUCTION

....

SOME of the most significant regulatory constraints businesses face today are intended to shape and protect the consumer markets into which they sell their products. By almost any method of accounting, these product market regulations are more numerous and more diverse than nearly any other form of industry regulation—including labor and environmental regulations. Such product market regulations range from product liability standards, through truth in advertising and labeling, product testing and safety, standardization of products and contracts, up to forced removal of products from the market accompanied by intrusive investigative powers for oversight agencies. For nearly every advanced industrialized country, this barrage of consumer product regulation emerged in the late 1960s and 1970s. How individual countries approached these new regulatory issues, however, differed across countries. While some countries emphasized the importance of transparency and information to enable consumers to protect themselves, others placed heavy burdens on producers to ensure that products that arrived in the consumer marketplace were safe. How can we explain this sort of regulatory variation? And where do such consumer protection policies come from?

Policy researchers have offered two classes of theories of consumer regulation. One emphasizes the role of business in proposing and shaping consumer protection policies. Their interests in doing so may be varied. Businesses may use regulation to block out incumbents, to promote economies of scale in production, to create an advantage in export markets, or to reassure wary customers of the quality of their products. A second set of theories emphasizes the discretion and initiative of regulators. Responding to real consumer concerns, entrepreneurial administrators design new policies to protect the interests of diffuse groups in society that would not otherwise have a voice in the policy process. Each of these accounts implies a specific political logic to consumer policy formation. In the business-interest theories, product markets are shaped in ways that mirror the priorities and interests of the production system. In the policy entrepreneurship theories, policy-makers enjoy wide discretion in designing national regulatory approaches, subject to some degree of electoral scrutiny. What both approaches share is a view of consumer protection as derivative of the existing—business or administrative—regulatory regimes.

Through a comparative study of the emergence of consumer protection policies in France and Germany during the 1970s, I show that neither of these classes of theories explains the patterns of regulation that emerge. On the one hand, business interests were nearly identical across the two countries, yet regulatory outcomes were starkly different. On the other hand, national regulators that advocated consumer protections faced strong societal pressures as they selected the regulatory trajectory their country would follow. In France, in particular, consumer policy was characterized by significant experimentation, failure, and reassessment. While both producers and regulators did play an important role in the regulatory process, consumer groups were also highly influential. Their influence derived from two sources. First, consumers were surprisingly well-organized for such a diffuse and overlapping set of societal interests. Second, the new policies had to be perceived as a legitimate reflection of the broader consumer interest, and consumer group engagement in the policy process secured policy legitimacy. This meant that consumer groups played a central role in helping to define what the relevant consumer interests were and therefore how they should be protected. The participation of consumers, with their own distinctive economic and organizational priorities, helped to create a set of regulatory responses that were not merely reflections of existing production or regulatory regimes.

In many ways, the policy process by which the new consumer protections were designed resembles classic interest group politics. Policy-makers, subject to conflicting external pressures, worked to design policies that reconciled the policy preferences of organized business and consumer groups. What is distinctive about the process of consumer policy formation is that the core struggle was over an idea: the very conception of who the consumer was and what role he or she played in the modern economy. Was the consumer an economic actor with the same status as other economic actors—workers, suppliers, manufacturers? Was the consumer a social actor deserving of special protections from the vicissitudes of markets? Were they simply another interest group in society, on a par with religious, welfare, and occupational groups that also organized to defend their specific interests? This struggle over the consumer ideal mattered because it would, in turn, dictate what kinds of regulatory solutions would be seen as legitimate and appropriate. If the consumer was mainly an economic actor, then the goal of national policy should be to ensure that markets were working efficiently, that risk and information were shared evenly, and that competition was maintained. If, on the other hand, the consumer ideal was one of a social actor, then appropriate regulatory responses should work to insulate the consumer from market risks. At the root of the French and German consumer policies that emerged in the 1970s and early 1980s was an interest group fight over the very idea of who the consumer was.

THE POLITICS OF CONSUMER PROTECTION

Consumer policy confounds standard approaches to explaining regulatory policy. First, it does not fit standard interest group explanations. Consumers are perhaps the most diffuse interest group in society, and yet they are highly protected in all of the advanced industrialized economies. Organized industry interests have opposed nearly every step in regulating consumer markets, yet it is the more diffuse set of consumer interests that have tended to prevail. Second, more obscure and complex areas of regulation are thought to be subject to greater industry influence, verging to outright capture. Few areas of regulation are more arcane than product market regulation, yet cases of outright industry capture are surprisingly rare. Third, consumer politics does not fit standard models of regulatory competition. Consumer products flow readily across borders, and yet national regulations seem to defy the race-to-the-bottom dynamic that has characterized other areas of interjurisdictional regulation. In his work on consumer regulation, *Trading Up*, David Vogel (1995) finds just the opposite: states may compete for higher rather than lower regulatory standards for consumer products. A core question remains concerning the sources of variation in national approaches to regulating consumer product markets. Where do consumer politics come from?

Two broad sets of arguments have dominated policy analysis. The most common approach to consumer protections is to attribute them to the interests and political pressure of producers. One reason that this sort of productionist view of consumer protection has been so persistent is that it draws its intellectual roots from both the left and right. Leftists and economic liberals agreed on the constitutive role of business in shaping the consumer sphere. For leftist social theorists of the immediate post-war period, patterns of modern consumption were understood to reflect the priorities of producers, conveyed through modern marketing, advertising, and consumer-oriented culture (Horkheimer and Adorno 1944; also Galbraith 1958). The efficiencies of mass production seemed to require a new social organization empha- sizing mass consumption (Habermas 1991: 189). This neo-Marxist critique was mirrored on the right by regulation theorists trained at the University of Chicago. During the 1960s and 1970s, they would argue that the difficulties of organizing diffuse interests gave industry a disproportionate influence in public policy (Olson 1965; Stigler 1975; Peltzman 1976). While the left and right disagreed about what business influence implied for public policy and democracy, they agreed that con- centrated business interests set the rules in the consumer marketplace.

A more recent variation of the productionist argument has emphasized the trade interests of producers. As global trade has increased, possibilities for institutional arbitrage under free trade appear to have led regulators to be especially attentive to the interests of trade-exposed business. It is argued (Vogel 1995; Murphy 2004) that this sort of regulatory competition can, under the right circumstances, lead business to favor stricter standards of consumer and environmental regulation. Yet, while they are undoubtedly correct about the potential advantages of higher standards of regulation, historically, industry has commonly opposed regulation that they later came to see as advantageous (Coleman 2001). One of the most interesting cases of this phenomenon was the 1962 Kefauver–Harris amendments to the US Food and Drug Act, which imposed far higher standards on US pharmaceutical firms than did similar regulation in Europe or Japan. Drug companies spent much of the 1960s and 1970s fighting these new restrictions. By 1995, when New Gingrich proposed to roll back strict US drug standards, the drug industry opposed him, arguing that the stricter rules had made US drugs more competitive.

The second approach to explain consumer protection has tended to focus on the discretion enjoyed by policy-makers, seen as policy entrepreneurs, and the intellec- tual and institutional constraints on the kinds of solutions they propose. Some have attributed a high degree of discretion to policy-makers, understood as entrepreneur- ial problem solvers (Wilson 1980; Majone 1996). Others have seen consumer regula- tions emerging out of existing national legal and regulatory traditions (Joerges, Falke, and Micklitz 1988; Micklitz 1990). A third, sociologically oriented set of researchers has traced distinctive national regulatory responses to deep institutional or cultural traditions (Douglas and Wildavsky 1982; Beck 1992; Sassetilli 1995).

What has commonly been overlooked is the role of consumers themselves in setting consumer protection policies. Indeed, one of the surprises of recent research into consumer policy has been the relatively high degree of mobilization that has characterized this highly diffuse set of interests. Researchers of collective action have long taken consumers as the archetypal illustration of the challenge of organization diffuse interests. As if fulfilling the prophecy, no researcher in the new social movements literature has ever written a paper on consumer mobilization. Vibrant national consumer movements emerged at the same time as the environmental, feminist, and peace movements of the 1970s (MacLachlan 2002; Cohen 2003; Hilton 2003; Theien 2004), but the explicitly material interests of consumers fit poorly with the socially activist, post-materialist emphasis of the social movement literature (Inglehart 1977; McCarthy and Zald 1977; Tarrow 1998). Research into trade liberalization also found little evidence of consumer mobilization in favor of greater trade freedom (Destler and Odell 1987).

Yet, by the 1970s, consumer groups in most of the industrialized nations were organizing political protests, coordinating producer and retail boycotts, undertaking independent product tests, taking manufacturers to court, and organizing massive grassroots informational and protest actions. Many of the product market regulations that have become the focus of recent trade contention have their roots in this period. Recent attention to European food regulation has begun to uncover the role of organized consumers in advocating specific protections, often in opposition to organized business interests. Alistair Young (2003) has found a central role for consumer NGOs in Europe's response to genetically modified foods. Bernauer and Caduff (2004) also trace the roots of Europe's ban on hormone-treated beef to consumer boycotts in France, Germany, and Italy in the early 1980s. They propose "endogenizing public perceptions" by focusing on the role of consumer NGOs in setting consumer protection policy.

Building on their work, I argue that organized consumer groups are influential in policy formation in part because consumer policies are new at the time, and policy-makers need for them to be seen as legitimate by the broader public. For any new consumer policy to succeed, the public has to believe the new regulations are appropriate, proportionate, and fair. While these standards are relevant to other areas of regulation, they are especially important to policy formation in consumer markets, for two reasons. First, most consumer policies implemented since the 1950s have been highly innovative, either because the products to which they applied were new, or because the move to an affluent consumer society lowered public forbearance of product-related losses. Second, consumer policies commonly extend government regulatory intervention into areas of formerly purely contractual agreement. More than almost any other kind of economic exchange, consumers have real choices about how and with whom they contract for products and services. This contractual freedom creates a high bar for legitimate government intervention. In order for this kind of state intervention to be seen as legitimate, both by producers and by the consuming public, the process by which it emerged also has to reflect legitimate interest inputs.

The result was a policy process in which producers and regulators played an important role, as has traditionally been noted, but in which organized consumers were also critically important. Any issue in consumer policy always potentially has three actors in play: regulators, consumers, and producers. Each of these actors brings some degree of legitimacy to the process. Producers bring detailed knowledge about the impact that regulation will have on consumers, on competition, and on the broader economy. Regulators bring political legitimacy, insofar as they are acting with a common understanding of legislative initiatives adopted through democratic processes. Consumers, insofar as they mobilize for certain kinds of reform, bring the legitimacy of mass mobilization, of street democracy. Indeed, the very challenge of organizing the diffuse consumer interest means that successful cases are seen to reflect legitimate underlying concerns. No single class of actors has sufficient standing to ensure that regulatory or self-regulatory outcomes are perceived as legitimate. Effective, legitimate regulation required collaboration between at least two of the three actors involved. In the rest of the chapter, I show how this process evolved in France and Germany.

Defining the Consumer Interest

As consumers were first becoming the focus of national regulatory protections in the 1970s, three distinct strategies were considered for protecting them. The first model interpreted the consumer as an economic actor with a status analogous to other actors in the economy, including workers and suppliers. In this model, consumer protection should be a private contractual matter so long as the conditions for market failure have been eliminated. From this analysis came two primary policy prescriptions. First, the state should step in to eliminate information asymmetries that could lead to market failure. Government responses would therefore focus on consumer education and the provision of accurate product information, including strict regulation of truth in advertising, product labels, and consumer contracts. A rigorous program of comparative product testing was also a central element of this approach. The second prescription was to ensure that consumers, as economic actors, enjoyed real choice. This meant creating conditions for real product competition, and ensuring the availability of quality goods. This approach, borrowed from the British initiative launched in the 1960s by the Maloney commission, was adopted by Germany as its dominant strategy of consumer regulation. Referred to as the "information strategy," it led to a set of policies that emphasized accurate information as a solution to consumer grievance. Given adequate information and choice, the consumer, understood as an economic actor, should have the necessary tools to defend his or her own interests.

The second model, familiar from the US consumer experience, interpreted the modern consumer as having an entirely new set of societal interests. In this view, consumer interests constituted a new set of political rights to be incorporated into the existing legal and institutional framework of the country. Consumer rights were, in essence, new rights of citizenship. The challenge to consumers was therefore to mobilize politically, to push for new legal protections, and to ensure that existing protections would be adequately enforced. For consumer groups, this approach called for political mobilization, grassroots activism, and often direct confrontation with industry in order to draw attention to problems requiring regulatory response. Product-related risks would be allocated—through a strict standard of liability, aggressive safety testing, and product recall actions—entirely to producers. Moreover, consumers should be granted rights as a legal class so that they might effectively enforce their new rights through the courts. This indemnity approach eventually came to be adopted in France.

A third model, adopted in the Scandinavian countries, construed the consumer as a newly emerging societal interest group, analogous to other interest groups such as welfare recipients, war veterans, or industrial laborers. In this model, consumers who were adequately organized would be able to defend their own interests through ongoing negotiations with other economic actors in society. This "Swedish model," based on that country's early post-war experience with consumer protection, stressed the challenges of consumer collective action as the primary source of their plight. The solution, therefore, was to assist consumers in their effort to represent their own interests. Consumer representatives should be granted access to important decision-making forums. The government might then grant binding legal status to the outcome of consumer–producer negotiations. In administrative matters, a "consumer ombudsman" would be appointed to spearhead new consumer initiatives, and to launch discussions with other economic interest groups. Ideally, the "Swedish model" would rely on consumer and producer representatives to negotiate mutually agreeable solutions that would require minimal government regulatory intervention.

Each of these views entailed both an analysis of the problem that consumers faced, as well as a set of policy prescriptions for overcoming the problem (Hall 1993; Muller 1995). What was surprising about this process, however, was that each of the major actors—consumer groups, producers, and state policy-makers—appears to have been fully aware of the alternative models. Through a series of research visits, policy studies, and public debates, each of the models drew advocates and detractors in a way that made the models themselves the focus of political contestation (Stone 1989; Boltanski and Thévenot 1991). Indeed, each model came to be associated with the particular country—Britain, Sweden, or the United States—in which it had already been successfully deployed.

The cases of France and Germany illustrate the differences entailed by adopting different models (Joerges, Falke, and Micklitz 1988: ch. 2; Fily and Guillermin 1992: 47). France has adopted an approach to consumer protection that systematically embraces a strategy of indemnity. It created administrative bodies to monitor for dangerous products and granted them strong powers to investigate and to ban products from the market. The French legal system has imposed a strict standard of liability on producers for product-related loss. Consumer groups have been granted a group status to file lawsuits on behalf of the general consumer interest. Regulations governing product safety have also embraced a strict standard, requiring that producers take account in the design process any likely misuse of a product by end consumers. By contrast, efforts to promote accurate product information have been weak: French efforts to promote informative labels have mainly failed; advertising enjoys broad latitude for creativity and exaggeration; the terms of sales contracts have not been subject to specific regulation; and consumer groups have focused more heavily on mobilization and legal advising than on providing consumers with accurate technical information about products.

In Germany, an information strategy has been adopted for protecting consumers. Advertising is highly regulated for misleading content. Product quality labels are widely employed and, in some product categories, required. Comparative product tests are supported by both the state and producers. The terms of consumer contracts have been standardized. A network of hundreds of consumer advice centers distribute technical information about products—typically free of charge. By contrast, regulations to indemnify against product-related loss have tended to place a high burden on the consumer. Germany's product liability standard allows producers to exonerate themselves if they have followed accepted industry standards. Group consumer actions are allowed only in cases related to accurate information provision (especially advertising and consumer contract regulation) but not for product liability. Products must meet a safety standard of reasonable use, not likely misuse. State agencies can only recommend, but not compel, that products be withdrawn from the market.

These systematic differences in approach to consumer protection are not merely academic; there are signs that they have had real impact on product markets. Germany's information strategy has provided consumers with subsidized access to accurate product information. As they share the burdens of product-related loss with producers, they have incentives to use information as a means to manage this risk. Consumers injured by defective products tend to receive extremely low compensation, even in the rare case of a successful liability suit. One example of the impact of these incentives is the popularity of Germany's product testing magazine, *Test*. One million Germans subscribe—compared to 260,000 for its French analogs. Accordingly, 80 per cent of German companies report relying on *Test* results when designing or testing new products (Stiftung Warentest data; *Die Welt*, December 2, 1994). This combination of carrot (information access) and stick (risk sharing) has led German consumers to favor better quality, more highly engineered products. It has also led them to shun entirely new types of products for which useful information is typically not yet available.

French consumers face a very different set of market constraints. In principle, they are indemnified against risk for all product classes, so even the most radically innovative products and services entail no risk premium.[1] Conversely, consumers have little access to or incentive to acquire technical product information, and so make purchasing decisions with less knowledge about hidden product qualities such as design and engineering refinement. This combination of indemnity (legal protection) and ignorance (low access to accurate information) has led French consumers to discount engineering and design quality. As one set of legal researchers observe: "if price is more easily observed than quality, competition may be skewed toward less expensive, lower quality products" (Beales, Craswell, and Salop 1981: 510). The French approach has also led consumers to favor products with qualities that are clearly visible, including radically innovative products.

The different outcomes in France and Germany cannot be traced purely to producer interest, because producers in the two countries expressed the same interests. Industry publications and public statements show that producers in both countries shared the same preferences over these policy models. Producers most strongly favored the information model, as it implied a minimal impact on business and came with the potential for creating more discerning and loyal customers. Producers' second choice was the "Swedish" or negotiation model. While this approach implied a greater impact on business practice, it had the advantage of offering a non-regulatory approach to consumer protection. A French businessman noted of this approach: "A good experiment is better than bad regulation" (*Les Echos*, July 13, 1982: 6). The least favored option for producers in both countries was the "US model" treating consumer interests as political rights. This approach was particularly worrisome because it threatened potentially unlimited regulatory intervention in the core functions of production: design, quality, pricing, and distribution.

Given these common producer rankings, why did France and Germany end up embracing different policy models? Specifically, how did Germany end up with the information model, the top preference for producers, while France ended up with the indemnity model, the lowest preference for producers? To understand how each country came to the policy outcome it did, we need to take into account not just producer interests but also the activities and preferences of organized consumers.

Consumer interest organization mattered for three reasons. First, while producers in the two countries had identical preferences with respect to consumer policy, consumer groups ranked their policy preferences differently (see below). Second, the way in which consumer and producer groups were organized also proved decisive in their ability to make their preferred solution work successfully. French producers, for example, clearly preferred to negotiate directly with consumers over a system of direct government regulation. Yet, after a period of experimentation, it became clear that they lacked the associational capacity to make such a negotiation strategy succeed. Third, the political influence of consumer and producer groups was critical, and their influence was again a direct result of their strategies of organization. This factor was most important in the case of consumer interests. The growing grassroots mobilization of the French consumer group over the course of the 1970s gave them increasing influence with national regulators. Conversely, the political weakness of Germany's technically oriented consumer associations meant that their preferences were rarely reflected in national policy. To understand how national policies evolved, we need to look at both producer *and* consumer interest. But what were the consumers' interests, and from where did they come?

Consumer Organization and Policy Preference

Beginning in the early 1970s, consumer groups in both France and Germany organized to defend the interests of consumers. Their actions included political mobilization, boycotts, price surveys, informational campaigns, the staffing of local consumer

centers, product testing, arbitration, legal action, and participation in new government bodies and in drafting new legislation. Government funding to consumer
groups grew tenfold over the course of the 1970s. These consumer groups were
granted access to government ministries and consultative bodies. They organized
to protest dangerous products, to boycott expensive products, to lobby for transparent pricing and content labels, to advocate new legislation, to perform comparative
product tests, to address consumer grievances, and to educate and inform the
consuming public. One of the popular contemporary books on the consumer
movement in France evokes how significant the new movements seemed at the
time: "The Third Estate revolted in 1789, the Russian proletariat in 1917. Are we at
the dawn of an equally radical struggle? It's not impossible" (Neirynck and Hilgers
1973: 236).

Consumer organization was not entirely new to Europe. During the nineteenth
century, consumer leagues and cooperative societies emerged that linked farmers and
small producers directly to consumers (Furlough 1991; Thompson 2001). What
distinguished the new movements of the 1970s, however, was their narrow focus on
issues of affluent consumption (Hilton 2003). As they became wealthier, consumers
were increasingly perceived to have their own distinct interests, apart from those of
labor or of the women's movement. Those interests were potentially diverse: price,
suppression of fraud, quality, safety, availability, information, political voice, access
to justice, legal status as a class, and many others. The challenge of post-war
consumer mobilization was to craft from this broad new issue space a specific agenda
capable of galvanizing the diffuse consumer interest. The issues that national consumer movements chose to emphasize therefore depended on their organizational
strategy. French and German consumer mobilization strategies were markedly
different.

In France, consumer groups mobilized an active grassroots constituency that
undertook often-militant campaigns against industry and in favor of government
reform. In a 1976 poll, 2 per cent of French citizens reported belonging to such
organizations. Roughly twenty national consumer associations and an estimated 860
affiliated local unions gave the French consumer groups the organizational capacity
to take on ambitious group actions, including price surveys, boycotts, and political
protests. Vocal public criticism of specific products and producers helped them
to attract attention and new members. While these groups received some state
funding, much of their financial support came from membership dues and journal
subscriptions.

Like France, Germany experienced the emergence of a large number of national
and state-level consumer organizations during the 1960s and 1970s. State-level
consumer associations sponsored a network of hundreds of consumer information
centers charged with advising consumers in their purchases. If France's consumer
movement portrayed itself as antagonistic to business, Germany's movement was
more accommodating. Most of Germany's consumer associations had few individual
members, and many actively blocked private individuals from joining. Their concern
was that individual members would radicalize or distort the consumerist agenda,

diverting them from their goal of protecting the weakest members of the consuming public. Instead, the associations developed strong technical skills that gave them a respected voice in policy-making and industry standard setting. Financial support came primarily from the national and state governments, rather than membership fees.

These organizational strategies emerged from a combination of institutional and ideational factors. Institutionally, their different mobilization strategies depended on the ability of consumer groups to create coalitions with other economic actors. Two proved to be critical: labor unions and retailers. In France over the course of the 1970s, labor unions moved to form their own affiliated consumers' association. France's umbrella labor-oriented consumer group ORGECO gradually divided into new consumer groups with direct affiliation with specific labor unions: FO, CGT, and CFDT. Each formed their own national associations and local consumer unions, and provided both financial resources and membership lists to the new consumer groups. Though these new labor-oriented groups were not the only ones to mobilize grass-roots members, they did contribute substantially to the dynamism of France's consumer movement. In Germany, by contrast, labor unions showed little interest in the consumer movement. The labor movement felt that it was already performing the most important role in consumer protection—namely, ensuring rising wages and increased purchasing power for workers. Repeated attempts by the AgV to draw labor unions into consumer issues mainly failed.

The second potential coalition was with the growing retail sector. In France, consumers groups began to work collaboratively with the new large-scale retailers. Both sides had an interest in collaboration. Consumer groups had found repeatedly through price surveys that large-surface-area stores offered lower prices than traditional small retailers. The large-scale retailers, for their part, often drew on consumer groups to support their applications to open new retail sites. Not only did consumers have two representatives on each of the Departmental Commissions of Commercial Town-Planning (CDUC) that decided new retail permits, they also often mobilized their membership in rallies to support new store openings. It is telling that when the first French *Salon des consommateurs* was organized in Paris in 1974, it took place in a new retail facility built by the cooperative music chain FNAC. In Germany, a retail-consumer coalition never emerged. Part of the problem was Germany's highly restrictive retail opening hours, set by the Store Closing Law. Germany's consumer groups fought bitterly against this legislation, on the grounds that women needed more time to shop. This fight antagonized Germany's retail associations, which uniformly supported the closing time restrictions. It also antagonized Germany's powerful white collar union representing retail, insurance, and banking. Whereas French consumer groups were able to draw support from a set of powerful economic actors, their German counterparts found themselves relatively isolated.

Divergent approaches to mobilization also grew out of different cultures of protest. Consumer movements in both countries emerged in the wake of the 1968 student protests and were shaped by their legacy. In Germany, 1968 activism had emphasized post-materialist values and a critique of consumer society that had its roots in the neo-Marxist heritage of the Frankfurt School. For students and workers who had mobilized around issues of world peace and the environment, the explicitly materialist concerns of Germany's consumer associations held little allure. In France, the emphasis of the 1968 protests was on social justice and a critique of capitalism and the power of big business. This slightly different set of preoccupations left a culture of protest that fitted more comfortably with material concerns of the consumer movement. Such differences were reinforced by the intellectual leadership of the consumer movements in the two countries. In Germany, early leaders of the consumer movement like Gerhard Weisser and Otto Blume (both founders of the AgV) were trained in philosophy and sociology. With their roots in the social systems theories of Talcott Parsons and Nicholas Luhman, they interpreted the consumer movement as an integral component of the broader social and economic structure of modern society. In France, by contrast, the consumer movement was dominated by social activists. Leaders like Henri Estingoy, of the Institut National de la Consom- mation, and François Lamy of the Federal Consumers' Union (UFC), were by nature suspicious of business and favored confrontation as a means of forging a new consumer identity.

The different organizational strategies adopted by the consumer movements in France and Germany caused them to prefer slightly different approaches to consumer protection. In both countries, the negotiation model was seen as the preferred approach, although for somewhat different reasons. In France, activist consumer groups with broad grassroots support saw themselves as legitimate representatives of all consumers. They imagined a world in which they, rather than the state, would negotiate directly with producers to set contractual and quality standards for consumer products. During a short period from 1978 to 1983, France experimented with this sort of negotiated protection. In Germany, where the consumer groups were less confrontational and more technically oriented, they saw themselves representing consumer interests in nearly every economic function of society: in policy formation and enforcement, in technical standards setting, in macroeconomic decision-making, even on company boards of directors. In these roles they would serve as a conduit, aggregating consumer interests and representing them in the realms of policy and production.

Beyond the negotiation approach, preferences diverged. For French consumer groups, their strong second preference was a strategy of political protection. They were in a strong position to influence government policy because of their grassroots mobilization. Consumer activists with roots in the labor movement understood that weaker economic interests could leverage their organization by mobilizing, not directly against business, but through the state in order to affect business. Moreover, consumer groups worried that the information model risked depoliticizing the consumer movement. If consumer protection became a technical matter of testing, labeling, and informing, there was little reason for organizing consumers as a coherent political constituency. The very purpose of their movement would disappear.

For German consumer groups, their strong second preference was for the information model. This approach played to their strengths in technical matters. Although they would have little policy input, they would still play an expansive role in consumer protection through advisory centers, product testing, and consumer education programs. Most importantly, it allowed them to avoid a politicized confrontation with German industry. German consumer groups explicitly aimed to keep consumer issues from becoming political. They worried that the consumer interest would become distorted through a political contest; they also seem to have recognized that their political weight was insufficient to achieve a meaningful political response. As AgV editors wrote in 1974 (*Verbraucherpolitsche Korrespondenz* (*VK*), July 23, 1974: 8): "No one desires a state managed consumer; any bureaucratization of consumer protection should be rejected."

CONSUMER INTEREST VERSUS PRODUCER INTEREST

The ways in which French and German consumer markets have been regulated—France's emphasis on indemnity and Germany's emphasis on information—emerged from the conflicting preferences of consumers and producers over what broad strategy of consumer protection to pursue (see Table 27.1).

In Germany, both producers and consumers were wary of the political approach. A struggle, therefore, occurred between the information approach which producers preferred and the negotiation approach which consumer groups preferred. As both consumer and producers had ruled out an explicitly political fight over the indemnity approach, the German policy debate focused on whether or not solutions would incorporate consumers as an equal negotiating partner with industry. Some early government initiatives suggested that this might be the case. In 1973, for example, consumers were invited to join high-level "concerted action" negotiations to set

Table 27.1 Consumer and producer preferences for consumer protection strategies

	Ranking (producers, consumers)		
	Information	Negotiation	Indemnity
Germany	1.2[a]	2.1	3.3
France	1.3	2.1	**3.2**

[a] 1 is the highest ranked preference, 3 is the lowest ranked preference. Policy outcomes are marked in bold.

levels of wages, prices and money supply (*Die Welt*, October 25, 1978). In 1974, the Economics ministry forced Germany's standards association to accept consumer representatives on its technical committees (Joerges et al. 1989: 186). In an experiment that ultimately failed, the government of the state of North-Rhein Westfalia brought consumer and producer groups together to negotiate a broad range of issues relating to consumer protection (*VK*, July 23, 1974: 8). Industry actively opposed this sort of negotiated approach, even when its goal was a better informed consumer. During the 1960s, for example, Germany's consumer groups had persistently negotiated with producer associations to develop standard labels for a variety of consumer goods. The goal was to negotiate a voluntary set of standards that would bear the endorsement of consumer associations (*VK*, February 25, 1964: 8; *VK*, July 25, 1965: 8; *VK* December 15–25, 1967: 2–4). They did show some limited success: in labels for shoes and wool products, for pantyhose and for sausage.

By the early 1970s, however, consumer groups were already seeing significant defeats in the battle for a negotiated approach to consumer protection. In 1974, Germany's product labeling association RAL invited consumers to participate on an equal basis with producers in setting labeling standards (RAL-Testate) for products. But industry balked at the plan, and the economics ministry quickly withdrew financial support from the organization (Bopp-Schmehl, Heibült, and Kypke 1984: 86). Consumer groups were also commonly invited to participate in the negotiation of new consumer legislation. It became clear, however, that their voice did not carry as much weight as their industry counterparts. When legislation to regulate consumer contracts was negotiated in 1974, for example, consumer groups participated actively. Yet, they were far outnumbered by industry associations, and few of their ideas were incorporated into the final legislation (Schatz 1984: 68). Other initiatives failed outright. In 1973, the AgV lobbied unsuccessfully for consumer representation on Germany's monopoly commission (*VK*, September 4, 1973: 3–4). An ambitious plan to incorporate consumers in industry co-determination also failed (*VK*, February 6, 1973). By the late 1970s, these failures put an end to consumer-group hopes for a negotiated approach to consumer protection, although they would continue to play a vital though supporting role providing consumers with accurate product information.

In France, consumer and producer groups had more strongly divergent preferences. As in Germany, French producers favored the information strategy most and the political strategy least. French consumer groups, like their German counterparts, favored the negotiation strategy most. Unlike Germany's consumer groups, however, they least favored the information strategy. The result was a complex set of policy experiments, in which French consumer policy skipped from an information approach, through an experiment with negotiations, to a protection approach. Indeed, one of the puzzles of French consumer policy is that they arrived at a policy solution that offered the worst combined preference ranking. How did this happen?

Early efforts at consumer protection in France focused on providing consumers with accurate information about products. Product labeling (1972), advertising (1973), and consumer education (1977) were core areas of policy emphasis. When

Christiane Scrivener was appointed the country's first Secretary of Consumption in 1976, her agenda (Scrivener 1976) emphasized the benefits of informed consumers for the entire economy: "consumers who are better informed [are] an inducement to greater product quality and consequently greater exports." France's main consumer groups, who in 1975 came together to issue a manifesto of consumer rights, began with the right to information and training ("Pour une loi-cadre de la consommation," propositions presented by the national consumer organizations, April 1975). Consumer groups were also wary that an information strategy alone could provide consumers with adequate protections. In 1970, for example, France's peak industry association CNPF undertook a joint project with the National Consumption Institute to devise informative product labels within the newly created French Association for Informative Labels. Although hundreds of label templates were created, consumers were disappointed that the voluntary standards were rarely used in practice. Henry Estingoy (1971), head of the INC at the time, wrote of the results: "we don't sense delirious enthusiasm among the industrial sectors."

While French administrators experimented with consumer information strategies, the French consumer movement was blossoming. A typical example was the Federal Consumers' Union (UFC), which formed its first local union in 1973. By 1980, it had 170 local unions with 40,000 grassroots members (Daujam 1980). A survey conducted in 1984 found that France's eleven national consumer associations had by then created a total of 682 local consumers' unions (*Bulletin Interieur de Documentation de la Repression des Fraudes—BID*, August 1985: 64). As they mobilized, these groups increasingly sought a seat at the negotiating table with producers. Interestingly, French producers seem to have viewed these groups as harbingers of a new economic order. A business survey conducted in 1977 found that 59 per cent of companies expected the development of a dialogue with consumer groups—indeed one-quarter of respondents reported already having met with consumer groups. More than a third of all companies felt that such a dialogue with consumers should extend to issues of product design and quality (*LSA*, May 6, 1977: 45–6). Two years later, the Chamber of Commerce in Limoges (*Ecodis*, February 11, 1980) wrote: "for the moment . . . these [consumer] groups represent a minority. But we don't know how they will evolve. We must consider ways to . . . dialogue with them in order to guide the movement by favoring the development of those [groups] that seem serious and truly representative." The mobilization of France's consumer groups, and industry's apparently willingness to sit down at the table with them, set the state for France's experiment with negotiated consumer protections.

France's experiment with consumer–producer negotiations lasted for five years, beginning with the appointment of René Monory as Economics Minister 1978. Monory, a trained economist who described himself as France's "consumption minister," advocated consumer-industry "concertation" as the solution to consumer grievance (*Ecodis*, February 11, 1980). The CNPF responded by convening a series of monthly negotiations with consumer groups beginning in the fall of 1979 to discuss topics as diverse as consumer contracts and quality standards. Separate sectoral negotiations generated new standards in retailing, advertising, and construction. Amid this flurry of activity, consumer groups grew frustrated with spotty implementation of the new voluntary standards. In 1980, the eleven major national consumer associations boycotted further negotiations until an enforcement mechanism was put in place. A national debate ensued concerning whether agreements negotiated by associations could be made mandatory. Amid overwhelming opposition from industry and from the ministry of justice, the Mitterrand administration instead created a novel new administrative mechanism: the quality contract. Quality contracts, negotiated between individual companies and accredited consumer groups, were legally binding. By some measures, they were a success. Hundreds of quality contracts were signed over the ensuing years, especially in the furniture and travel sectors.

Yet, the quality contracts covered only a small segment of the total consumer market. The failure of this and similar initiatives made it clear that the dream of a negotiated approach to consumer protection was not going to produce satisfactory protections for consumers. In 1983, the Mitterrand administration changed course. It began implementing administrative protections for consumers, including a new Consumer Safety Commission (1983) with broad oversight and policing powers, and the new General Direction for Competition, Consumption, and the Repression of Fraud (1985). This shift in strategy set the trajectory for France's current state-centered approach to consumer protection, in which the government is assumed to take full responsibility for insulating consumers against product-related risk.

CONCLUSION

One implication of this interest-based account is that both productionist and regulatory accounts of consumer protection play a less determinative role than most observers have suggested. Producers have sometimes achieved their preferred goals, as in Germany. But the French case offers a cautionary tale about the limits of industry influence. One of the surprises of consumer protection policy is that, even for this most diffuse set of interests, concentrated producer groups are not necessarily able to achieve their preferred policy outcomes. Business is not without impact on policy. But when they were effective at influencing policy outcomes, it was less through unilateral influence than through a give-and-take interaction with regulators and organized consumers. It remains a theoretical puzzle, and raises important questions about the limits of the influence of concentrated interests, that consumers were able to exert even the amount of influence they did over the newly forming consumer protection policies.

National regulators also appear to have played a less independent role in setting policy than is commonly asserted in instances of new policy formation (Heclo 1974; Pierson 1994). While French and German regulators did genuinely puzzle over alternative approaches to managing consumer markets, their choices were intended in large part to balance the conflicting interests of producer and consumer groups. New experiments emerged in part by weighing the proposals put forth by industry and by organized consumer groups. If one set of experiments appeared to be failing—as happened repeatedly in France—they initiated a new set of experiments based on a less favored policy approach. Regulators were at least as much facilitators in an essentially interest-based policy process as they were designers and initiators of new policies. Nor were national cultural or regulatory traditions determinative. Because regulatory traditions tend to be multiple and overlapping, advocates of very different approaches to consumer protection were able to find institutional precedents for their preferred solutions. In Germany, for example, producer groups wishing to portray the consumer as an economic actor pointed to the country's intellectual tradition of ordo-liberalism. By contrast, advocates of a "Swedish" interest-group approach pointed to Germany's tradition of neo-corporatism and worker co-determination. Cultural and regulatory traditions thus became tools in the struggle over the consumer identity, with advocates of different approaches drawing on different symbolic resources.

This account challenges the role that ideas and interests are normally thought to play in the formation of new areas of policy. During times of radical policy innovation, interests are assumed to recede and the force of ideas is thought to increase (Heclo 1974; Hall 1993). The case of consumer protection suggests a different mechanism. Rather than serving as paradigms that constrained the way policymakers and economic actors thought about the consumer interests, ideas about modern consumption played a more instrumental role. And, far from being suspended during the formative policy period, economic actors contested aggressively, fighting for one set of policy ideas over another. Indeed, because the stakes were understood to be high at the moment when the consumer interest was being defined, business and consumer groups were especially active. It was only after the initial struggle over the basic conception of the consumer interest was settled that ideas proved to be determinative. Each subsequent consumer policy, from mad cow disease to phthalates in children's toys to the regulation of genetically modified organisms, has followed the basic logic of consumer protection laid down in the decade lasting from the early 1970s to the early 1980s.

Given that national consumption regimes did not emerge as a direct reflection of producer priorities, the institutional features of consumer markets may prove to be an important independent element of national systems of capitalism. In particular, post-war regulation of product markets in France and Germany appears to have created a systematic bias in consumer choice along dimensions that are relevant to national systems of production and distribution. In the case of Germany, the focus of consumer protection policies on information appears to reinforce an orientation toward high-quality, highly engineered products. German consumers demand quality and shun innovation—precisely the product qualities that Germany's labor and capital markets appear suited to produce. French consumers, who are in principle insulated from product-related risk and know relatively little about their technical details, readily accept both innovative and inexpensive products, and tend not to prioritize hidden qualities like incremental improvements and careful engineering. To the extent that demand conditions matter for producer strategies, and that national systems of product market regulation are subject to path dependencies that perpetuate their distinctiveness, such national demand-side conditions may work to sustain distinctive national approaches to industrial capitalism.

NOTE

1. Because the indemnification model requires active state monitoring of consumer markets, product failures that have occurred in France have tended to have significant political repercussions.

REFERENCES

ADAMS, M. 1984. "Ökonomische Analyse des Gesetzes zur Regelung des Rechts der Allgemeinen Geschäftsbedingungen AGB-Gesetz," in M. Neumann, ed., *Anspruche, Eigentums- und Verfügungsrechte: Arbeitstagung des Vereins für Socialpolitik, Gesellschaft für Wirtschafts- und Sozialwissenschaften in Basel 1983*. Berlin: Duncker & Humblot.

BEALES, H., CRASWELL, R., and SALOP, S. C. 1981. "The efficient regulation of consumer information," *Journal of Law and Economics* 24(3): 491–539.

BECK, U. 1992. *Risk Society: Towards a New Modernity*. London: Sage Publications.

BERNAUER, T., and CADUFF, L. 2004. "Interest group politics and industrial competition as drivers of environmental and consumer regulation," *Journal of Public Policy* 24(1): 99–126.

BOLTANSKI, L., and THÉVENOTI, L. 1991. *De la justification: les économies de la grandeur*. Paris: Gallimard.

BOPP-SCHMEHL, A., HEIBÜLT, U., and KYPKE, U. 1984. *Technische Normung und Verbraucherinteressen im gesellschaftlichen Wandel*. Frankfurt am Main: Haag & Herchen Verlag.

BOYER, R. 1997. "The variety and unequal performance of really existing markets: farewell to Doctor Pangloss?" in J. Rogers Hollingsworth and R. Boyer, eds., *Contemporary Capitalism: The Embeddedness of Institutions*. Cambridge: Cambridge University Press.

CAMPBELL, C. 1989. *The Romantic Ethic and the Spirit of Modern Consumerism*. Malden, Mass.: Blackwell.

COHEN, L. 2003. *A Consumer's Republic: The Politics of Mass Consumption in Postwar America*. New York: Knopf.

COLEMAN, T. 2001. "Quality and competition: the political economy of the wine sector," paper presented at the annual meeting of the Society for the Advancement of Socio-Economics.

DARLING, J., and PUETZ, J. 2002. "Analysis of changes in consumer attitudes towards products of England, France, Germany and the USA, 1975–2000," *European Business Review* 14(3): 170–83.

DAUJAM, F. 1980. "Information et pouvoir des consommateurs: le rôle de l'union fédérale des consommateurs," doctoral thesis presented to the faculty of economic and social sciences, University of Toulouse.

DE MOOIJ, M., and HOFSTEDE, G. 2002. Convergence and diversity in consumer behavior: implications for international retailing. *Journal of Retailing* 78: 61–9.

DESTLER, I. M., and ODELL, J. S. 1987. *Anti-Protection: Changing Forces in United States Trade Politics.* Washington, DC: Institute for International Economics.

DOUGLAS, M., and WILDAVSKY, A. 1982. *Risk and Culture: An Essay on the Selection of Technical and Environmental Dangers.* Berkeley: University of California Press.

ESTEVEZ-ABE, M., IVERSEN, T., and SOSKICE, D. 2001. "Social protection and skill formation," in P. Hall and D. Soskice, eds., *Varieties of Capitalism.* New York: Oxford University Press.

ESTINGOY, H. 1971. "Promouvoir la fonction consommation," *Vos Clients,* 9.

FILY, A., and GUILLERMIN, P. 1992. "Les Politiques de la consommation dans les États membres de la CEE," *Revue de la concurrence et de la consommation* 70.

FRIDERICHS, H. 1974. "Aufgaben der Verbraucherpolitik," *Bulletin des Presse- und Informationsamtes der Bundesregierung* 146: 1465.

FURLOUGH, E. 1991. *Consumer Cooperation in France: The Politics of Consumption, 1834–1930.* Ithaca, NY: Cornell University Press.

GALBRAITH, J. K. 1958. *The Affluent Society.* London: H. Hamilton.

GHOLZ, E. 1996. "Getting subsidies right," paper presented at the Annual Conference of the American Political Science Association, Boston.

HABERMAS, J. 1991. *The Structural Transformation of the Public Sphere: An Inquiry into a Category of Bourgeois Society,* trans. Thomas Burger. Cambridge: MIT Press.

HALL, P. 1993. "Policy paradigms, social learning, and the state: the case of economic policy-making in Britain," *Comparative Politics* 25: 275–96.

HARDIN, R. 1982. *Collective Action.* Baltimore: Johns Hopkins University Press.

HECLO, H. 1974. *Modern Social Politics in Britain and Sweden: From Relief to Income Maintenance.* New Haven: Yale University Press.

HILTON, M. 2003. *Consumerism in Twentieth-Century Britain: The Search for a Historical Movement.* Cambridge: Cambridge University Press.

HOFSTEDE, G. 1980. *Culture's Consequences.* Thousand Oaks, Calif.: Sage.

HORKHEIMER, M., and ADORNO, T. 1994. *The Dialectic of Enlightenment.* Stanford, Calif.: Stanford University Press.

HUME, D. 1748. *Essays, Moral and Political.*

INGLEHART, R. 1977. *The Silent Revolution: Changing Values and Political Styles among Western Publics.* Princeton: Princeton University Press.

JOERGES, C., FALKE, J., MICKLITZ, H., and BRÜGGEMEIER, G. 1989. *Die Sicherheit von Konsumgütern und die Entwicklung der Europäischen Gemeinschaft.* Baden-Baden: Nomos.

KOGUT, B. 1991. Country Capabilities and the Permeability of Borders. *Strategic Management Journal,* 12: 33–47.

KURZER, P. 2001. *Markets and Moral Regulation: Cultural Change in the European Union.* Cambridge: Cambridge University Press.

LASCHET, W. 1987. "Verbraucher sind auch Kunden," in H. Piepenbroch and C. Schröder, eds., *Verbraucherpolitik Kontrovers.* Cologne: Deutscher Instituts-Verlag.

LOCKE, R. 1991. "Building trust," paper presented at the Annual Conference of the American Political Science Association.

LUNDVALL, B. 1988. "Innovation as an interactive process: from user–producer interaction to the national system of innovation," in G. Dosi, ed., *Technical Change and Economic Theory.* London: Pinter.

McCARTHY, M., and ZALD, M. 1977. "Resource mobilization and social movements: a partial theory," *American Journal of Sociology* 82(6).

MacLachlan, P. 2002. *Consumer Politics in Postwar Japan*. New York: Columbia University Press.

Majone, G. 1996. *Regulating Europe*. London: Routledge.

Micklitz, H. 1990. *Post Market Control of Consumer Goods*. Baden-Baden: Nomos Verlagsgesellschaft.

Muller, P. 1995. "Les Politiques publiques comme construction d'un rapport au monde," in A. Faure, G. Pollet, and P. Warin, eds., *La Construction du sens dans les politiques publiques: débats autour de la notion de réferentiel*. Paris: Éditions L'Harmattan.

Murphy, D. 2004. *The Structure of Regulatory Competition: Corporations and Public Policies in a Global Economy*. Oxford: Oxford University Press.

Nadel, M. 1971. *The Politics of Consumer Protection*. Indianapolis: Bobbs-Merrill.

Neirynck, J., and Hilgers, W. 1973. *Le Consommateur piégé: le dossier noir de la consommation*. Paris: Éditions Ouvrières.

Nelson, P. 1970. "Information and consumer behavior," *Journal of Political Economy* 78: 311–29.

Olson, M. 1965. *The Logic of Collective Action: Public Goods and the Theory of Groups*. Cambridge, Mass.: Harvard University Press.

Peltzman, S. 1976. "Toward a more general theory of regulation," *Journal of Law and Economics* 19: 211–40.

Pierson, P. 1994. *Dismantling the Welfare State*. New York: Cambridge University Press.

Porter, M. 1990. *The Competitive Advantage of Nations*. New York: The Free Press.

Robertson, P., and Yu, T. 2001. "Firm strategy, innovation, and consumer demand: a market process approach," *Managerial and Decision Economics* 22: 183–99.

Sartori, G. 1991. "Changes in the pattern of demand, consumer learning and firm strategies: an examination of postwar economic growth in the United States and France," in *Technology and Productivity: The Challenge for Economic Policy*. Paris: OECD.

Sassetilli, R. 1995. *Power Balance in the Consumption Sphere: Reconsidering Consumer Protection Organisations*. European University Institute Working Paper, Florence.

Schatz, H. 1984. *Verbraucherinteressen im politischen Entscheidungsprozess*. Frankfurt: Campus Verlag.

Scrivener, C. 1976. "Le Droit des consommateurs à l'information," *Allocutions ministérielles: Secrétariat d'État à la consommation*. Paris: Economics and Finance Ministry.

Soskice, D. 1996. *German Technology Policy, Innovation, and National Institutional Frameworks*. Discussion Paper FS I 96–319, Wissenschaftzentrum Berlin, Berlin.

Stigler, G. 1975. *The Citizen and the State: Essays on Regulation*. Chicago: The University of Chicago Press.

Stone, D. 1989. "Causal stories and the formation of policy agendas," *Political Science Quarterly* 104(2): 281–300.

Strassner, S. 1992. *Verbraucherinformationsrecht*. Saarbrücken: ÖR Verlag.

Swidler, A. 1986. "Culture in action: symbols and strategies," *American Sociological Review* 51(2): 273–86.

Sykes, A. O. 1995. *Product Standards for Internationally Integrated Goods Markets*. Washington, DC: Brookings Press.

Tarrow, S. 1998. *Power in Movement: Social Movements and Contentious Politics*. Cambridge: Cambridge University Press.

Theien, I. 2004. *Affluence and Activism*. Oslo: Akademica.

Thompson, N. 2001. "Social opulence, private asceticism: ideas of consumption in early socialist thought," in M. Daunton and M. Hilton, eds., *The Politics of Consumption: Material Culture and Citizenship in Europe and America*. Oxford: Berg.

VOGEL, D. 1995. *Trading up: Consumer and Environmental Regulation in a Global Economy.* Cambridge, Mass.: Harvard University Press.

—— 1999. "When interests are not preferences: the cautionary tale of Japanese consumers," *Comparative Politics* 31(2): 187–207.

VON HIPPEL, E. 1976. "The dominant role of users in the scientific instrument innovation process," *Research Policy* 5: 212–39.

WILSON, J. Q. 1980. "The politics of regulation," in J. Q. Wilson, ed., *The Politics of Regulation.* New York: Basic Books.

YOUNG, A. 2003. "Political transfer and 'trading up'? Transatlantic trade in genetically modified food and US politics," *World Politics* 55: 157–84.

ZYSMAN, J. 1983. *Governments, Markets and Growth.* Ithaca, NY: Cornell University Press.

CHAPTER 28

MEDIA ECONOMICS AND THE POLITICAL ECONOMY OF INFORMATION

JILL J. McCLUSKEY

JOHAN F. M. SWINNEN

INTRODUCTION

The ... press appears to me to have passions and instincts of its own. ... In America as in France it constitutes a singular power, so strangely composed of mingled good and evil that liberty could not live without it, and public order can hardly be maintained against it.

(Alexis de Tocqueville 1835)

ALTHOUGH households are flooded with information through hundreds of television channels, internet access, multiple newspapers, and radio, the public is said to be poorly informed on many issues important to business and government when public opinion differs from experts' views. For example, despite the guarantees from experts that genetically engineered food is safe, many consumers are opposed to it. Similarly, the benefits of free trade and the importance of international specialization according to comparative advantage have been demonstrated centuries ago by Adam Smith and David Ricardo and since then, many studies and publications have supported these arguments. Yet, non-governmental organizations oppose trade liberalization, and mass demonstrations are held against the World Trade Organization and the perceived consequences of globalization. In both cases the public is said to be poorly informed and public opinion biased.

Imperfect information is of course not a new issue in economics. However, most of the extensive literature on imperfect information (e.g., important contributions by, for example, Akerlof 1970; and Stiglitz 1993) focuses on the effects of imperfect information and says little about the supply of information. Often there is an implicit assumption in this literature that information provision is neutral. This assumption is not realistic. In reality most information is not provided by institutions whose objective is to foster the public good, but by organizations that have an internal incentive to select certain information items and certain forms of information over others in their distribution activities. Information is provided either by private sources with their own objectives, including profits, or by public sources that may formally be charged with providing objective information, but may have incentives to bias the information.

Supply of information through commercial media has increased rapidly over the past decades. Commercial mass media has become the key information broker in our society, and it is where most people obtain their information. Mass media has become an important factor in influencing public opinion.[1] Yet the media is criticized as being sensationalistic and biased in its reporting, giving demonstrators prime time coverage and ignoring careful analyses.

This impact of the media is well understood by leaders in politics and business. Increasingly, the most important ally of governments is no longer the police or the military; it is the media. Hence, a prime target of political organization is control over the media, as witnessed, for example, by recent maneuvering of the Putin administration in Russia. The first target of a military coup or a popular uprising is no longer the police station, but the television station. Similarly, businesses are well aware of the potential impact of the media for their activities and sales. Extensive media coverage affects consumer perceptions on products and risk, and consequently demand for business services and products.

Given these important effects it is surprising how little attention economists have paid, until relatively recently,[2] to how the industrial organization of the media industry and the structure of the information market affects the quantity and quality of information supply; and what the implications are. Recently however an important, and rapidly growing, literature has emerged on this issue, analyzing the impact of media structures and ownership on information distribution and economic welfare. This chapter reviews the emerging literature on the economics of the media and its implications for business and government.

STRUCTURAL CHANGE IN MEDIA MARKETS

On the supply side of the information market, private commercial sources of information are increasingly important globally. While in the United States, news coverage has always been largely in the hands of commercial companies, the emergence of private companies as the dominant source of information is a relatively new phenomenon in Europe (Anderson and Coate 2005). Until relatively recently, European television and radio broadcasting were largely in the hands of state broadcasting companies, and companies publishing daily newspapers and popular journals were often closely aligned with political parties.[3]

The origins of these differences go back several centuries and relate directly to different paths of political development. Starr (2004) explains how centralizing absolutist regimes in seventeenth-century Europe used communications to consolidate their power. They sought control of the press not only by censoring it but also by limiting it exclusively to printing guilds, which were concentrated in the national capital. The use of monopolistic state controlled organizations was applied to the early newspapers, to postal systems, to the telegraph, and later, in the twentieth century, to national broadcast monopolies. Interests in state and nation building were driving forces in development of the media, often leading to state monopolies or other direct state involvement. In contrast, private enterprises played a much greater role in the United States from the beginning. The Revolutionary period in America created an alliance between patriots and printers that elevated freedom of the press to high symbolic importance. US postal policies were designed to subsidize newspapers of all kinds instead of taxing opposition newspapers as in Europe. The suspicion of centralized power in the United States carried over to the press and kept it highly decentralized. While there have certainly been periods with attempts to control the press, the press in America enjoyed a much larger degree of political autonomy throughout much of the eighteenth, nineteenth, and twentieth centuries than in Europe.

However, in the past two decades the media ownership structure has changed dramatically in Europe. Commercial television and radio stations are now dominant in the market. The written press has gradually devolved itself of the patronage of the political parties and is driven more by commercial than political objectives. Also in other regions of the world, such as in emerging and developing economies, there is significant growth in private and commercial media, albeit major differences continue to exist in media structure among countries (O'Neil 1998;

Carrington and Nelson 2002). For example, state ownership of the media is still much more important in low income countries than in high income countries (see Table 28.1).

In countries where commercial media has been traditionally important, such as in the United States, there are also important changes in the media market structure (Alterman 2008). The ownership of the main media has changed, as reflected in takeovers of the main media by industrial and financial concerns and the role played by global investors. There are important relations between various media sources. Some of the major players offer the gamut of media product categories: television stations, newspapers, magazines, movie production, and internet (Peers 2007).

New players have emerged in the media market. There are a growing number of alternatives to the traditional channels, including 24-hour media with the emergence of CNN, pay-per-view, satellite, cable, and internet blogs. Viewers under 35 are less attracted to major networks and newspapers (Pew Research Center for People and the Press 2002). This is important since advertisers generally target younger audiences. Related to these changes, the traditional media are becoming less dominant. For example, the major US networks have been losing market share since their peak in the 1950s. In the 1980s, the establishment of CNN eroded the market share of the major networks. CNN offered something different in terms of instantaneous reporting. A younger generation ("Gen Net," the children of the Baby Boomers) are more likely to get their news from the internet or alternative sources than the network news shows their parents watch (Pew Research Center for People and the Press 2000).

Traditional media, such as newspapers, are losing their markets and becoming less profitable. Newspaper classified advertising, an important revenue source, has lost ground to internet sites such as e-Bay (for selling used items), Craigslist (for services), and job websites, such as Monster.com. Newspapers have created websites that receive online advertising revenues, but it is not enough to offset the losses from falling circulation and print advertising (Alterman 2008). As with the network television news shows, the average newspaper readers is nearing retirement age.

There is also a blurring of lines between professional media sources and amateur media. As Tapscott and Williams (2006) discuss, media customers become media "prosumers" by co-creating goods and services rather than simply consuming the end product. Consumers, who formerly only received information from the media, now use blogs, wikis, and chat rooms to add their voices to the debate. Not only are these new sources increasingly important—for example, certain internet blogs get more hits than elite media websites, such as the *Wall Street Journal* website—it also fundamentally changes the nature of the market.

Moreover, there is a blurring of the lines between news and entertainment, and this blurring goes in two directions. Serious news programs cover more celebrity news, while entertainment shows include more serious topics. In fact, in the United States, Jon Stewart's *Daily Show*, a humorous review of the main news that is televised daily on Comedy Central network, is now a major source of news information for the younger generation.

Table 28.1 Indicators of press freedom and share of state ownership of the media

	Income level[a] GNI/cap	Press freedom score[b]	Press freedom category[b]	Ownership share of the state in press[c]	Ownership share of the state in television[c]
High-income countries					
United States	44 710	16	Free	0.00	0.34
Sweden	43 530	11	Free	0.00	0.51
United Kingdom	40 560	19	Free	0.00	0.60
Japan	38 630	21	Free	0.00	0.39
Belgium	38 460	11	Free	0.00	0.41
Germany	36 810	16	Free	0.00	0.61
Canada	36 650	17	Free	0.00	0.00
France	36 560	21	Free	0.00	0.43
Italy	31 990	25	Free	0.00	0.61
Israel	20 170	29	Free	0.00	0.36
Slovenia	18 660	21	Free	0.00	0.54
Average	*35 157*	*19*		*0.00*	*0.44*
Middle-income countries					
Hungary	10 870	21	Free	0.00	0.20
Mexico	7 830	48	Partly free	0.00	0.27
Chile	6 810	30	Free	0.00	0.30
Russian Federation	5 770	75	Not free	0.15	0.96
Turkey	5 400	49	Partly free	0.00	0.00
Bulgaria	3 990	34	Partly free	0.00	0.75
Algeria	3 030	62	Not free	0.57	1.00
Peru	2 980	42	Partly free	0.00	0.00
Ukraine	1 940	53	Partly free	0.15	0.14
Philippines	1 390	46	Partly free	0.44	0.18
Average	*5 001*	*46*		*0.13*	*0.38*
Low-income countries					
Cameroon	990	67	Not free	1.00	1.00
Côte d'Ivoire	880	68	Not free	0.64	1.00
India	820	35	Partly free	0.00	0.88
Senegal	760	46	Partly free	0.51	1.00
Zambia	630	64	Not free	0.74	1.00
Uzbekistan	610	91	Not free	1.00	1.00
Kenya	580	59	Partly free	0.00	0.45
Lao PDR	500	81	Not free	1.00	1.00
Togo	350	74	Not free	1.00	1.00
Niger	270	58	Partly free	1.00	1.00
Ethiopia	170	77	Not free	1.00	1.00
Uganda	130	54	Partly free	0.58	0.61
Burundi	100	77	Not free	1.00	1.00
Average	*447*	*65*		*0.71*	*0.90*

[a] World Bank (2004, www.worldbank.org).
[b] Sussmann and Karlekar (2002).
[c] Djankov et al. (2003).

INDUSTRIAL ORGANIZATION OF THE
MEDIA AND WELFARE

The obvious question is how this increased market provision of news affects welfare. An important issue is the interaction between private and public media organizations and implications for social welfare (Berry and Waldfogel 1999a, 1999b; Motta and Polo 1997; Goettler and Shachar 2001; Brown and Alexander 2005). Berry and Waldfogel (1999a) discuss that the public good nature of radio can result in the classic problem of under provision (e.g., the value exceeds the costs of some radio broadcasts, but they are not provided). They find that public supported radio sometime alleviates the problem of under provision, but it depends on the size and preferences of the market. In some larger markets, the public radio station crowds out commercial programming.

Traditionally, broadcast media programs have been considered public goods, e.g., non-rival and non-excludable, with various implications for social efficiency and public regulation. Technology has changed this: digital broadcasts can be encrypted, so they are now excludable. At the same time, the marginal cost of an additional user is still zero. If the airwaves are a public resource and the content providers have market power, there is the potential for losses in welfare due to the associated reduction in supply (or increase in nuisance advertising). Anderson and Coate (2005) show that since the monopoly broadcaster does not face competition, the equilibrium level of advertising is higher. However, industry concentration has been decreasing over time in markets where the private sector provides information. One can consider the example of broadcasting of sports events. Hoehn and Lancefield (2003) compare the role of sports in the European and American broadcasting value chains. They write that US television markets are generally considered to be highly competitive in comparison with their European counterparts. They state that the major difference in Europe lies in the status of public service broadcasters who are generally financed with a compulsory license fee (except Spain) and advertising (except the UK). Major broadcast rights in Europe tend to migrate to pay television platforms (Hoehn and Lancefield 2003). Government officials worry about whether pay television should be allowed to capture rights to events that historically have been broadcast on free-to-air stations (Noll 2007). The United States has almost complete penetration of cable and satellite, which has resulted in greater choices of sports broadcasts and reduced prices to consumers.

Recent analyses of the industrial organization of the media have focused on the fact that the media is a classic example of a "two-sided market" with readers and advertisers (Anderson and Gabszewicz 2005). A two-sided market is one where the participants on each side care directly about the number of participants on the other, i.e., there are network externalities. Network externalities occur when usage in one end-user market makes a product more attractive to another market. In media markets, network externalities occur from the number of readers/viewers that can make the media product more attractive to advertisers. This externality will be reflected in the price to end-users. For example, the price of a newspaper will likely be below the marginal cost of production and delivery in order to increase circulation and advertising revenues. In the extreme is the case of free newspapers that bring in revenue entirely based on advertising.

In analyzing a two-sided market model of commercial broadcasting and how well commercial broadcasting fulfills its role of providing programming to viewers and permitting advertisers to contact potential customers, one must consider both the social benefits and costs of advertising (Crampes, Haritchabalet, and Jullien 2009). The benefits are that firms can inform consumers about their products, and the costs are the nuisance costs to viewers. The implications for welfare depend on the benefit cost ratio (Anderson and Coate 2005). Gabszewicz, Laussel, and Sonnac (2004) analyze competition between two private television stations that derive their profits from advertising. They assume that consumers have an aversion to advertising, so the advertising ratios play the role of prices in the standard horizontal differentiation models. They find that as advertising aversion increases, the channel profiles are closer to each other.

Bias

Media bias can take various forms, and there is no generally accepted definition. Anand, Di Tella, and Galetovic (2007: 637) write that "[t]he phenomenon of bias in the media appears to be quite different than, say, a statistician's notion of bias— because bias lies in the eyes of the beholder (consumer)." Others define bias as the "absence of balance resulting in one side of a story receiving unwarranted attention" (Baron 2006: 4) or in other words, "sins of omission—cases where a journalist chose facts or stories that only one side of the . . . spectrum is likely to mention" (Groseclose and Milyo 2005: 1205). In terms of political bias, Sutter (2001) defines media bias in terms of the media outlet's position on the political spectrum relative to the views of the median voter. Gentzkow and Shapiro (2007: 3) develop a "slant" index, which measures "differences in news content that . . . would tend to increase a reader's support for one side of the political spectrum."

Many empirical studies analyze political bias in the media. A survey by the American Society of Newspaper Editors (ASNE) in 1999 revealed that 78 per cent of the public believed there was bias in news reporting. Groseclose and Milyo (2005) measure media bias by computing an index for various media outlets based on a comparison of the number of times the media outlet cites various think tanks and other policy groups with the citation counts of members of US Congress. They find that there is diversity among US media outlets with substantial liberal bias in news reporting.[4] In contrast, d'Alessio and Allen (2000) do not find significant bias.

Hamilton (2004) examines bias based on data from Pew Center surveys and finds that both self-identified liberals and self-identified conservatives see media biases towards the opposing side. It seems that bias is perceived relative to one's ideology. Personal assessments of bias may be affected by one's personal ideology (Vallone, Ross, and Lepper 1985; Gentzkow and Shapiro 2004).

Studies have identified several possible theoretical explanations for the existence of bias. Bias can be induced by supply and/or demand factors. It can be due to ideology or partisan politics, where owners, editors, or journalists present stories that support particular world views. It can also result from falsehoods or from information hidden or distorted by sources or journalists eager for a scoop or under pressure to attract attention, or due to consumer preferences.

The most obvious source of bias is preferences from the owners, editors, or journalists who may affect the news coverage (Bovitz, Druckman, and Lupia 2002). This bias is most evident in mass media owned by the state, such as in totalitarian countries (such as China and North Korea) and many developing countries where the state continues to control mass media. In those countries the media is used by the government to disseminate the political communication of the ruling parties and to control information which may threaten their legitimacy or their hold on power. One source of evidence is a measure of freedom of the press. Freedom House (Sussmann and Karlekar 2002) assigns an index of freedom of the press and rates each country with one of the three designations: "free," "partly free," and "not free." By these rankings, all the developed countries of Western Europe and North America have a "free press," while the press situation in the less developed countries is more mixed and certainly less free on average. In particular, in countries such as China and Colombia, the press is considered not free (Table 28.1).

However, also in less rigorously controlled media regimes, such bias can be important. In many European countries, until recently, much of the non-state-owned printed media and television stations were owned or closely related to political parties; and the different media expressed the preferences of their parties. Similarly, public television organizations were often influenced by the parties in government. An interesting illustration is Italy, where the main leader of the right-wing political parties, Silvio Berlusconi, owns much of the commercial TV stations and control of the public TV stations—and their political news coverage—switches when left or right wing parties take over government. Governments can also put strong pressure on them not to publish stories. Gentzkow and Shapiro (2008b) discuss several examples, including the political and legal pressure used by the US government on CBS not to broadcast the Abu Graib photographs during the Iraq War or on the *New York Times* not to publish the Pentagon Papers during the Vietnam War.

Owners of commercial media may wish to impose their personal preferences on their media reporting. In doing so they may face a trade-off between political objectives (i.e., using the media to express the owners' ideological bias) and commercial objectives (McCluskey and Swinnen 2004; Mulainathan and Shleifer 2005). Commercial objectives may be affected, first, by potential consumers' distaste for bias, or the negative utility they get from consuming media products which differ from their personal political preferences. Second, as discussed earlier, commercial media's profitability depends not only on consumers, but to a large extent also on its advertising revenues. Bagdikian (1992) writes, "As mass advertising grew, the liberal and radical ideas—in editorials, in selection of news, and in investigative initiatives—became a problem. If a paper wished to attract maximum advertising, its explicit politics might create a disadvantage" (129–30; reprinted in Gabszewicz, Laussel, and Sonnac 2001). Gabszewicz, Laussel, and Sonnac (2001) show that the media's incentives to appeal to a larger audience and hence be more attractive to advertisers may induce editors to moderate the political messages they display to their readers.

The importance of attracting large numbers of readers or viewers may in itself also lead to bias. One mechanism is explained by Strömberg (2004a) who argues that media coverage is biased towards large groups as the media is more likely to cover issues that are of interest to them. This bias can result from the need to attract as much readers as possible or from economies of scale in the media. Kuzyk and McCluskey (2006) provide empirical support for Strömberg's theoretical model with content analysis of media coverage of the US–Canadian lumber trade dispute. The coverage of the trade dispute was largely negative, which coincides with the interests of the vast majority of readers.

Other empirical studies find that there is a bias towards "negative coverage" in mass media in a variety of policy and public interest areas, such as trade policy and globalization (Swinnen and Francken 2006) and food safety (Swinnen, McCluskey, and Francken 2005). Marks, Kalaitzandonakes, and Konduru (2006) find that reporting on globalization was positive early on but switched to more negative in recent years. McCluskey and Swinnen (2007) explain that negative news coverage is likely to dominate positive news stories because of demand side effects. Their argument is based on the premise that consumers use the information from positive media stories to take advantage of opportunities from positive shocks and use the information from negative stories to avoid negative shocks. If utility is concave, the marginal loss in utility from not consuming the first bad news story is greater than the marginal gain in utility from consuming the first positive news story. As a result, consumers will choose to consume more negative stories than positive stories.

Spatial models of firm location provide a consumer-driven rationale for bias based on product differentiation. Mullainathan and Shleifer (2005) argue that readers or viewers have a preference for news that is consistent with their initial beliefs, and that media organizations have therefore an incentive to bias their reporting towards confirming their readers' or viewers' initial beliefs. When readers are heterogeneous in their beliefs, accuracy increases due to cross-checking of facts across newspapers. This is a "wisdom of crowds" argument (Surowiecki 2004) that aggregation of signals reduces noise. Anand, Di Tella, and Galetovic (2007) assume that facts are not always verifiable, and that consumers have heterogeneous ideologies. They find that when facts are verifiable, there is no bias. However, when a news item comprises information that is mostly non-verifiable, then consumers may care both about opinion and editorials, and the media firm's report will contain both these aspects. The diversity of opinion and editorials results in a differentiated products market. A dynamic version of this type of argument can be made when media organizations attempt to obtain a reputation for accuracy induces bias in reporting. Gentzkow and Shapiro (2006) consider the Bayesian consumer who is uncertain about the quality of an information source. The consumer infers the source is of higher quality when its report conforms to the consumer's prior expectations. Consequently, media first slant their reports toward the prior beliefs of their customers in order to build a reputation for quality.

Others have focused on other aspects of the supply side of the media market to explain bias. Baron (2006) explains that bias may be related to the availability of potential journalists who are willing to work for lower wages in positions in which they can advance their careers or demonstrate influence by exercising the discretion granted by new organizations. Dyck and Zingales (2002) and Baron (2005) focus on the relationship between journalists and their sources of information as the reason for media bias. Sources may release partial information that supports their preferences, or journalists may use partial information to reward sources for providing information. Baron (2005) models how the competition between information sources affects the news report. Private information may be held by two sources with opposing views. The sources have incentives to reveal only information that supports their own views, and it is costly for the media to obtain additional information from independent sources. Dyck and Zingales (2002) argue that to induce a source to reveal information, the journal provides a positive spin to stories to reward the source for providing the information.

An interesting empirical study on these issues is by Gentzkow and Shapiro (2007). They use data from a large set of US media and come to the conclusion that "newspapers' actual slant is neither to the right nor to the left of the profit maximizing level on average." While their results are consistent with Groseclose and Milyo's (2005) findings that the average newspaper's language is similar to that of a left-of-center member of Congress, they estimate that the profit maximizing average slant is also left-of-center on average. They conclude that the slant (or bias) in newspapers is strongly related to the political distribution of their potential readers, much more so than to the political preferences of their owners or the journalists.

Competition may play an important role in media organizations' trade-off between ideology and profits. Some researchers, such as Baron (2006), show that bias can persist in the face of competition. Gentzkow and Shapiro (2006, 2008a) argue that competition reduces supply side induced bias because it increases the likelihood that erroneous reports will be exposed ex post, but argue that the impact of competition on demand side induced bias is less clear. Mullainathan and Shleifer (2005) in their two-firm location model show that price competition results in greater product differentiation—e.g., more "slanting" of news. When advertising revenues are included in the product differentiation models of media, minimum differentiation can result (Gal-Or and Dukes 2003; Gabszewicz, Laussel, and Sonnac 2004; Barros et al. 2004).

IMPACT

A key question is, of course, to what extent these characteristics of the media, including bias, are affecting business, society, and government. There are a variety of insights coming out of studies on these issues.

Mass media affects *advertising and business communication strategies*. There is a two-way interaction between the business community and the media. We explained above that the media's profitability depends to a large extent on its advertising revenues and that the media's incentives to be more attractive to advertisers may induce the political bias of the media.

In addition, businesses also actively interface with the media for advertising, for public relations purposes, and as part of their corporate social responsibility (CSR) commitments (Anderson and Gabszewicz 2005; Baron 2007; Siegel and Vitaliano 2007). For example, firms search for media environments in which their products are advertised to reflect favorably on their corporate identities, including ethical and environmental practices. Through media placement, firms use their advertising budgets to encourage programming and publications to maintain high standards with which that associate their corporate identities. Many major companies such as McDonalds, Motorola, Nike, Wal-mart, and British Petroleum (BP) are trying to improve their corporate reputations with CSR communication strategies and publish annual reports on social responsibility, which are often reported on by the media. Media coverage of CSR is more valuable than corporate annual reports because consumers may perceive the annual reports authored by senior corporate management as biased, while media coverage may be perceived as more independent.[5] Eccles and Vollbracht (2006) discuss that the image of reality created by the media has become a key factor influencing firms' stakeholders. As a result, firm engage in strategic communication management. Firms closely monitor the media's agenda and provide journalists with stories addressing the relevant issues from their point of view.

These business strategies, and also public policy, are important as studies show that the mass media has an important impact *on consumer and voter attitudes*. Some recent studies have analyzed the impact of media on voter attitudes and come to interesting, and sometimes conflicting, conclusions. Strömberg (2004b) finds that entry of the radio increased voter turnout between 1920 and 1940. However, Gentzkow (2006) finds that the entry of television in the US since the 1950s had a strong negative effect on voter turnout in elections and on citizens' knowledge of politics. The effect was strongest for local elections. The author explains this result by arguing that television substituted for newspapers and radio which had more political and/or local information, compared to the mainly national news coverage of television, and that entertainment offered by television substituted for "hard news." George and Waldfogel (2006) come to similar conclusions that as major media (such as the *New York Times* in their study) with mostly national news crowd out local newspapers, information on and interest in local politics declines. These findings contrast to some extent with DellaVigna and Kaplan's (2007) findings that the spread of Fox News on cable TV over the past decade in the US had a positive effect on voter turnout, in particular among republicans.

DellaVigna and Kaplan (2007) not only argue that the spread of Fox News increased voter turnout but also that the increasing reach of their partisan message did affect voting behavior. This is consistent with Gentzkow and Shapiro's (2004) findings that exposure to media with different (political) biases does affect viewers' (or readers') beliefs. These findings conflict with arguments that viewers/readers anticipate the bias of the media source and use this to discount the information they receive. The conclusion from these and related behavioral studies is that, even when viewers know that the media sources are biased, they insufficiently discount the information to fully take into account the bias. Exposure to media can thus systematically alter beliefs and voting behavior.

There are also a series of interesting studies on media effects on consumers focusing on technology and food safety issues. Based on a political economy model of the media, McCluskey and Swinnen (2004) discuss the implications of information distribution through the media on consumer acceptance of biotechnology. On the empirical side, Marks, Kalaitzandonakes, and Zakharova (2003) find that the vast majority of consumers receive information about food and biotechnology primarily through the popular press and television. Studies show that media coverage influences demand for products. For example, Johnson (1988) and Negin (1996) show how (biased) media coverage of product contamination by pesticides resulted in unnecessary consumer panic and major losses for business in the United States. Similarly, studies show that media coverage of the BSE outbreak in Europe and its effects on food safety significantly reduced meat demand, and that younger people, and households with young children, were the most susceptible to such negative media coverage (Verbeke, Ward, and Viaene 2000) and that business advertising had only a minor impact on meat demand compared to negative media coverage (Verbeke and Ward 2001).

More generally, a series of recent studies examine the direct impact of media on *social behavior and public attitudes*, including on educational achievements of children, on gender attitudes, and on violence, using innovative empirical approaches and new data. Some of these studies challenge common wisdom. For example, Dahl and Dellavigna (2007) find that the growth of violence in the media reduces rather than increases violence in society. While laboratory experiments generally find that media violence increases aggression, Dahl and DellaVigna claim that these results cannot be extended to actual violence because of substitution effects between consumption of media and participation in violence which is strong due to self-selection. As a consequence, they estimate that in the short run violent movies deter almost 1,000 assaults on an average weekend in the United States. Gentzkow and Shapiro (2008a) challenge the widespread belief that television is detrimental to cognitive development and academic achievement. Applying an innovative methodology to long-run US data, they find that television does not cause harm but instead raises cognitive and educational development of children. This positive effect is strongest for children from households where English is not the primary language, for children whose mothers have less than a high school education, and for non-white children, indicating that the cognitive effects of television exposure depend on the educational value of the alternative activities that television crowds out. Jensen and Oster (2007) find that the spread of modern media is affecting attitudes in developing countries, using evidence from the growth of cable television and its effect on gender attitudes in India. They find the introduction of cable TV is associated with significant increases in women's autonomy, decreases in the acceptability of physical abuse, and decreases in preferences for male children; as well as increases in female school enrollment and decreases in fertility via increased birth spacing.

It is already clear from these findings that mass media has a significant impact on society and plays an important role in public policy. It does so in a variety of ways. However, there is substantial debate on the effectiveness of various impacts of mass media on government policy. One mechanism is *the agenda setting effect* of the media. In foreign policy, this agenda setting effect has sometimes been referred to as the "CNN factor" (Hawkins 2002). It refers to the process by which the media influences policy by invoking responses in their audiences through concentrated and emotionally based coverage, which in turn applies pressure to governments to react. Similarly, the absence of media coverage reduces priority in agenda setting (Jakobson 2000). In this logic, public officials react to media news because they see it as a reflection of public opinion (Kim 2005). However others have questioned the importance of these effects (Natsios 1996) and argue that the media is more likely to follow politics than lead it (Strobel 1996). A more nuanced argument is forwarded by Robinson (2001) who explains that the media can be a powerful source in leading policy-makers but primarily when there is great uncertainty or limited information.

Other studies have focused more explicitly on the media's impact on the *effectiveness of lobbying*. It is well known that benefits of import protection and other trade distortions are typically highly concentrated, while the costs are widely spread. Several political economists, starting with the influential work of Downs (1957), have argued that this is a key reason for sub-optimal policy-making in general, including trade interventions. Recent studies analyze whether this political economy process is reinforced or weakened by mass media. Some argue that mass media will reinforce the power of special interest lobbies over unorganized interests and that coverage of policy issues will mirror interests of dominant political and commercial powers, not the readers' interests (Bennett 1990). Others (e.g., Strömberg 2004a) argue that mass media weakens the power of special interest lobbies relative to unorganized interests. With news production exhibiting increasing returns to scale and demand depending upon the relevance of the contents to the various groups of readers, there are cost and revenue advantages to covering issues that are important to a wide audience rather than those that appeal to narrow interests. There is some support for the latter argument in empirical work (e.g., by Kuzyk and McCluskey 2006). A prediction from this line of reasoning is that policy-makers will be more responsive to the electorate in countries where a free press has a strong presence.

Another element is the media's impact on *political accountability*. Besley and Burgess (2001, 2002) show that in developing countries an electorate which is better informed by mass media strengthens incentives for a government to be responsive. Mass media play a substantial role in increasing political accountability; a finding which is consistent with Drèze and Sen's (1990) earlier work on comparing government reactions to crises in China and India. Djankov et al. (2003) analyze global data and find that government ownership of the media is generally associated with fewer political and economic rights. Stapenhurst (2000) and Ahrend (2002) find evidence that a lack of press freedom increases corruption. However the fact that a free press and good governance are positively correlated in a cross-section analysis does not necessarily reflect causality (Besley and Pratt 2002). A recent study by Snyder and Strömberg (2008) attempts to correct for this potential bi-causality and, using data on US media coverage and activities of members of Congress, concludes a positive causal effect of press coverage on citizen knowledge, politicians' actions, and public policy.

Several recent studies have taken these general arguments further and have analyzed explicitly the impact of media on development through its *impact on reducing corruption in public policy*. Influential studies by Reinikka and Svensson (2004, 2005) find that increased information flows to beneficiaries of public programs through mass media strongly reduced corruption in the implementation of public policy in several African countries. Francken, Minten, and Swinnen (2009) find similar results in Madagascar.

A study by Olken (2007) on the impact of the media on policy governance focuses on the impact of the media on social and political activities—in line with the earlier discussed studies showing changes in voter behavior—and how this affects governance in public policies. Using data from Indonesia, he finds that increased access to mass media reduces social capital but that this reduction in social capital had little influence on governance of public programs.

Media also influences development policy in high-income countries, in particular through its impact *on humanitarian and foreign aid*. Several studies have analyzed the impact of rich country media coverage of poverty, humanitarian crises, and natural disasters on aid flows. Van Belle, Rioux, and Potter (2004) and Kim (2005) find that a higher level of media attention to developing countries problems leads to more aid in several developed countries. Others find that foreign policy and domestic political considerations are more important than media in aid allocations. Eisensee and Strömberg (2007) argue that disaster relief decisions are driven by news coverage of disasters and that the other newsworthy material crowds out this news coverage. They criticize some of the earlier work for not addressing endogeneity problems in determining causality. Accounting for endogeneity issues, they find that media attention to humanitarian crises and natural disasters affects aid allocations. Further, media coverage is strongly influenced by other newsworthy events.

CONCLUSIONS

Until recently economists had paid relatively little attention to how the industrial organization of the media industry and the structure of demand and supply of information in modern societies affect welfare. The information market has changed dramatically in recent years, and the literature on the economics of the media is rapidly growing. In this chapter, we reviewed key insights from this expanding literature.

The structure of the media differs significantly across countries and over time. Across countries, on average, the press is less constrained by the state in countries with higher incomes. Over time, commercial media have grown in importance and new forms of media have emerged. Traditional media, such as newspapers, came under pressure at the beginning of the twentieth century with the arrival of first radio and later television. In turn, radio and television came to face new competition from internet-based information sources.

The welfare effects of the structure of the media market, including the importance of competition, are complex. It is important to take into account various factors, such as the mix of public and private media companies in a single market; whether information is excludable—which depends on technology; the importance of advertising, or, more generally, the two-sided nature of the market where the participants of each side of the market are affected by the participants on the other side. In addition to this, even when media organizations are not directly competing in the product market, they may be competing in the information market: two media organizations may target fully separate sets of potential buyers for their product (e.g., newspapers). However, as information spreads rapidly across market boundaries once it is released, they may be competing through the information market.

It is obvious that in totalitarian states governments control the media and can enforce bias in their reporting. However, even in more democratic regimes, governments may attempt to influence the media in their reporting. This can be accomplished through a variety of mechanisms: partial ownership of the media, threats of legal action, reduced access to government sources, or even bribery.

There is widespread belief even in societies with a "free press" that most, if not all, media organizations are still "biased" in one way or another. Theoretical papers have identified several sources of bias. On the supply side, they point at influence of governments, owners, and journalists. On the demand side, preferences of media consumers are important as they may prefer media products which reflect their prior beliefs or interests. Empirical studies come to mixed conclusions on the existence of bias in the media and point out that the measure of bias crucially depends on the point of comparison. The "truth" or an "unbiased presentation" is easy to identify in theory but hard in reality. Recent studies suggest that, in environments with a largely free and commercial press, bias in the media seems to reflect mostly bias in consumer preferences (ideology) rather than bias in owner or journalist preferences.

Mass media has major effects on society. In addition to political tactics and military actions, it affects voter attitudes, agenda setting in politics, and the implementation of public policies. It affects decisions on budget and aid allocations. It affects business communication strategies and advertising plans. It affects social behavior and has an influence on consumer attitudes.

However, an important conclusion which is coming out of the recent studies is that in most cases these influencing effects are bi-directional and complex. Citizens who receive information from the media anticipate that this information from media sources is likely to be biased. Moreover, their own biases in their personal preferences and beliefs affect the media's reporting strategies to convince these consumers to buy their media products. Similar complex interactions occur between media and politicians and between media and business. Only some of the most recent studies try to account for the endogeneity of many relations and are using more sophisticated data and statistical methods to disentangle several of the potential causal effects. A further complication, which has so far received limited formal attention, is the difference between short-term and long-term effects. Hence, while this emerging literature is yielding a rapidly growing rich set of research findings, there is much work left to do in order to provide a more solid base of conclusions and insights.

NOTES

1. Mass media is not only important from the perspective of information provision, but also from the perspective of time allocation and consumption. The average TV watching time per day is between 3.5 and 4 hours in the US, the EU, and Japan—which means that most leisure time is spent watching TV (Anderson and Gabszewicz 2005).
2. Important exceptions are, for example, contributions by Coase (1974) and Spence and Owen (1977).
3. Hamilton (2004) argues that prior to the twentieth century also in the United States an important share of the newspapers had explicit affiliations with political parties.
4. Interestingly, Groseclose and Milyo (2005) find that the *New York Times* is biased (in the liberal direction). Almost a century earlier, the *New York Times* coverage of the Russian Revolution was argued to be "riddled with bias and inaccuracies" by a 1920 study by Lippman and Merz—as reported in Starr (2004).
5. Although, as discussed previously, the independent media can still be perceived as politically biased.

REFERENCES

AHREND, R. 2002. "Press freedom, human capital and corruption," DELTA Working Paper No. 2002–11. Paris: OECD, Economics Department.
AKERLOF, G. 1970. "The market for 'lemons': quality uncertainty and the market mechanism," *Quarterly Journal of Economics* 84: 488–500.

ALTERMAN, E. 2008. "Out of print: the death and life of the American newspaper," *New Yorker* pp. 48–59.

ANAND, B., DI TELLA, R., and GALETOVIC, A. 2007. "Information or opinion? Media bias as product differentiation," *Journal of Economics and Management Strategy* 163: 635–682.

ANDERSON, S. P., and COATE, S. 2005. "Market provision of broadcasting: a welfare analysis." *Review of Economic Studies* 724: 947–72.

—— and GABSZEWICZ, J. J. 2005. "The media and advertising: a tale of two-sided markets," CEPR Discussion Papers 5223.

BAGDIKIAN, B. H. 1992. *The Media Monopoly*, 4th edn. Boston: Beacon Press.

BARON, D. P. 2005. "Competing for the public through the news media," *Journal of Economics and Management Strategy* 142: 339–76.

—— 2006. "Persistent media Bias," *Journal of Public Economics* 90: 1–36.

—— 2007. "Corporate social responsibility and social entrepreneurship" *Journal of Economics and Management Strategy* 163: 683–717.

BARROS, P. P., KIND, H. J., NILSSEN, T., and SØRGARD, L. 2004. "Media competition on the internet," *Topics in Economic Analysis & Policy* 41, article 32.

BENNETT, W. L. 1990, "Toward a theory of press–state relations in the United States," *Journal of Communication* 40: 103–25.

BERRY, S., and WALDFOGEL, J. 1999a. "Public radio in the US: does it correct market failure or cannibalize commercial stations," *Journal of Public Economics* 712: 189–211.

—— —— 1999b. "Free entry and social inefficiency in radio broadcasting," *RAND Journal of Economics* 30: 397–420.

BESLEY, T., and BURGESS, R. 2001. "Political agency, government responsiveness and the role of the media," *European Economic Review* 45: 629–40.

—— —— 2002. "The political economy of government responsiveness: theory and evidence from India," *Quarterly Journal of Economics* 117(4): 1415–51.

—— and PRATT, A. 2002. "Handcuffs for the grabbing hand? Media capture and government accountability," CEPR Working Paper No. 3132, 39.

BOVITZ, J., DRUCKMAN, N., and LUPIA, A. 2002. "When can a news organization lead public opinion? Ideology versus market forces in decisions to make news," *Public Choice* 113: 127–55.

BROWN, K., and ALEXANDER, P. J. 2005. "Market structure, viewer welfare, and advertising rates in local broadcast television markets," *Economics Letters* 863: 331–7.

CARRINGTON, T., and NELSON, M. 2002. "Media in transition: the hegemony of economics," in *The Right to Tell.* Washington, DC: World Bank.

COASE, R. H. 1974. "The market for goods and the market for ideas," *American Economic Review* 64: 384–91.

CORNEO, G. 2006. "Media capture in a democracy: the role of wealth concentration," *Journal of Public Economics* 90(1–2): 37–58.

CRAMPES, C., HARITCHABALET, C., and JULLIEN, B. 2009. "Advertising, competition and entry in media industries," *Journal of Industrial Economics* 57: 7–31.

CURTIS, K., McCLUSKEY, J., and SWINNEN, J. 2008. "Risk perceptions of biotechnology in developing nations and the political economy of the media," *International Journal of Global Environmental Issues* 8: 77–89.

DAHL, G., and DELLAVIGNA, S. 2007. "Does movie violence increase violent crime?" Mimeo, UC Berkeley

D'ALESSIO, D., and ALLEN, M. 2000. "Media bias in presidential elections: a meta-analysis," *Journal of Communication* 50: 133–56.

DELLAVIGNA, S., and KAPLAN, E. 2007. "The Fox News effect: media bias and voting," *Quarterly Journal of Economics* 122(3): 1187–234.

DJANKOV, S., McLIESH, C., NENOVA, T., and SHLEIFER, A. 2003. "Who owns the media?," *Journal of Law and Economics* 46: 341–81.

DOWNS, A. 1957. *An Economic Theory of Democracy.* New York: Harper and Row.

DRÈZE, J., and SEN, A. 1990. *The Political Economy of Hunger.* Oxford: Clarendon Press.

DYCK, A., and ZINGALES, L. 2002. "The corporate governance role of the media," in R. Islam, ed., *The Right to Tell: The Role of Mass Media in Economic Development.* Washington, DC: World Bank.

ECCLES, R. G., and VOLLBRACHT, M. 2006. "Media reputation of the insurance industry: an urgent call for strategic communication management," *The Geneva Papers* 31: 395–408.

EISENSEE, T., and STRÖMBERG, D. 2007. "News droughts, news floods, and US disaster relief," *Quarterly Journal of Economics,* 122(2): 693–728.

FRANCKEN, N., MINTEN, B., and SWINNEN, J. 2009. "Media, monitoring, and capture of public funds: evidence from Madagascar," *World Development* 37(1): 242–55.

GABSZEWICZ, J. J., LAUSSEL, D., and SONNAC, N. 2001. "Press advertising and the ascent of the pensée unique?," *European Economic Review* 45: 645–51.

————2004. "Programming and advertising competition in the broadcasting industry," *Journal of Economics and Management Strategy* 134: 657–69.

GAL-OR, E., and DUKES, A. 2003. "Minimum differentiation in commercial media markets," *Journal of Economics & Management Strategy* 123: 291–325.

GENTZKOW, M. 2006. "Television and voter turnout," *Quarterly Journal of Economics* 121(3): 931–72.

——and SHAPIRO, J. 2004. "Media, education, and anti-Americanism in the Muslim world," *Journal of Economic Perspectives* 183: 117–33.

GENTZKOW, M., and SHAPIRO J. 2006. "Media Bias and Reputation," *Journal of Political Economy* 11420: 280–316.

————2007. "What drives media slant? Evidence from US daily newspapers," NBER Working Paper, No. 12707.

————2008a. "Preschool television viewing and adolescent test scores. Historical evidence from the Coleman study," *Quarterly Journal of Economics* 123(1): 279–323.

————2008b. "Competition and truth in the market for news," *Journal of Economic Perspectives,* 22(2): 133–54.

GEORGE, L., and WALDFOGEL, J. 2006. "The *New York Times* and the market for local newspapers," *American Economic Review* 96(1): 435–77.

GOETTLER, R., and SHACHAR, R. 2001. "Spatial competition in the network television industry," *RAND Journal of Economics* 32: 624–56.

GROSECLOSE, T., and MILYO, J. 2005. "A measure of media bias," *Quarterly Journal of Economics* 120(4): 1191–237.

HAMILTON, J. T. 2004. *All the News That's Fit to Sell: How the Market Transforms Information into News.* Princeton; Princeton University Press.

HAWKINS, V. 2002. "The other side of the CNN factor: the media and conflict," *Journalism Studies* 32: 225–40.

HOEHN, T., and LANCEFIELD, D. 2003. "Broadcasting and sport," *Oxford Review of Economic Policy* 194: 552–68.

JAKOBSEN, P. V. 2000. "Focus on the CNN effect misses the point: the real media impact on conflict management is invisible and indirect," *Journal of Peace Research* 372: 131–43.

JENSEN, R., and OSTER, E. 2007. "The power of TV: cable television and gender attitudes in India," NBER Working Paper 13305.

JOHNSON, F. R., 1988. "Economic costs of misinforming about risk: the EDB scare and the media," *Risk Analysis* 82: 261–20.

KALAITZANDONAKES, N., MARKS, L. A., and VICKNER, S. S. 2004. "Media coverage of biotech foods, and influence on consumer choice," *American Journal of Agricultural Economics* 865: 1238–46.

KIM, J. S. 2005. "Media coverage and foreign assistance: the effects of US media coverage on the distribution of US official development assistance ODA to recipient countries," Mimeo, Georgetown Public Policy Institute.

KUZYK, P., and MCCLUSKEY, J. J. 2006. "The political economy of the media: coverage of the US–Canadian lumber trade dispute," *World Economy* 295: 637–54.

LIPPMAN, W., and MERZ, C. 1920. "A test of the news," *New Republic* August 4.

MCCLUSKEY, J. J., and SWINNEN, J. F. M. 2004. "Political economy of the media and consumer perceptions of biotechnology," *American Journal of Agricultural Economics* 86: 1230–7.

—— —— 2007. "Rational ignorance and negative news in the information market," LICOS Centre for Institutions and Economic Performance Discussion Paper 191/2007.

MARKS, L. A., KALAITZANDONAKES, N., and KONDURU, S. 2006. "Globalization in the mass media," *World Economy* 295: 615–36.

—— —— and ZAKHAROVA, L. 2003. "Media coverage of agrobiotechnology: did the butterfly have an effect?" *Journal of Agribusiness* 211: 1–20.

—— KALAITZANDONAKES, N., WILKINS, L., and ZAKHAROVA, L. 2007. "Mass media framing of biotechnology news," *Public Understanding of Science* 162: 183–203.

MOTTA, M., and POLO, M. 1997. "Concentration and public policies in the broadcasting industry: the future of television," *Economic Policy* 25: 294–334.

MULLAINATHAN, S., and SHLEIFER, A. 2005. "The market for news," *American Economic Review* 95: 1031–53.

NATSIOS, A. S. 1996 "Illusions of influence: the CNN effect in complex emergencies," in R. I. Rotberg, and T. G. Weiss, eds., *From Massacres to Genocide: The Media, Public Policy and Humanitarian Crises.* Washington, DC: The Brookings Institution, 149–68.

NEGIN, E. 1996. "The Alar 'scare' was for real: and so is that 'veggie hate-crime' movement," *Columbia Journalism Review* 353: 13–15.

NOLL, R. 2007. "Broadcasting and team sports," *Scottish Journal of Political Economy* 543: 400–21.

OLKEN, B. 2007. "Do television and radio destroy social capital? Evidence from Indonesian villages," Mimeo, Harvard University.

O'NEIL, P. H. 1998. *Communicating Democracy: The Media and Political Transitions.* Boulder, Colo.: Lynne Rienner Publishers.

PEERS, M. 2007. "Murdoch's next focus: business-news battle," *Wall Street Journal* August 2: A2.

Pew Research Center for the People and the Press. 2000. "Internet sapping broadcast news audience," http://people-press.org/reports/pdf/36.pdf

—— 2002. "Public's news habits little changed by September 11: Americans lack background to follow international news," http://people-press.org/reports/display.php3?ReportID=156 accessed April 21, 2008.

REINIKKA, R., and SVENSSON, J. 2004. "The power of information: evidence from a newspaper campaign to reduce capture." World Bank Policy Research Working Paper 3239. Washington, DC: World Bank.

—— —— 2005. "Fighting corruption to improve schooling: evidence from a newspaper campaign in Uganda," *Journal of the European Economic Association* 3(2–3): 259–67.

ROBINSON, P. 2001. "Theorizing the influence of media on world politics," *European Journal of Communication* 16(4): 523–44.

SIEGEL, D. S., and VITALIANO, D. F. 2007. "An empirical analysis of the strategic use of corporate social responsibility," *Journal of Economics and Management Strategy* 163: 773–92.

SNYDER, J. M., and STRÖMBERG, D. 2008. "Press coverage and political accountability," Mimeo, MIT.

SPENCE, M., and OWEN, B. 1977. "Television programming, monopolistic competition, and welfare," *Quarterly Journal of Economics* 91: 103–26.

STAPENHURST, R. 2000. "The media's role in curbing corruption," WBI Working Paper 37158. Washington, DC: World Bank.

STARR, P. 2004. *The Creation of the Media: Political Origins of Modern Communications.* New York: Basic Books.

STIGLITZ, J. E. 1993. *Information and Economic Analysis.* Oxford: Oxford University Press.

STROBEL, W. P. 1996. "The media and US policies toward intervention: a closer look at the 'CNN Effect,' " in C. A. Crocker, F. O. Hampson, and P. R. Aall, eds., *Managing Global Chaos.* Washington, DC: USIP Press.

STRÖMBERG, D. 2001. "Mass media and public policy," *European Economic Review* 45: 652–63.

—— 2004a. "Mass media competition, political competition, and public policy," *Review of Economic Studies* 71: 265–84.

—— 2004b. "Radio's impact on public spending," *Quarterly Journal of Economics* 119: 189–221.

SUROWIECKI, J. 2004. *The Wisdom of Crowds.* New York: Doubleday.

SUSSMANN, L. R., and KARLEKAR, K. D., eds. 2002. *The Annual Survey of Press Freedom.* New York: Freedom House.

SUTTER, D. 2001. "Can the media be so liberal? The economics of media bias," *Cato Journal* 20: 431–51.

SWINNEN, J., and FRANCKEN, N. 2006. "Trade summits, riots, and media attention: the political economy of information on trade and globalization," *World Economy* 295: 637–54.

—— McCLUSKEY, J., and FRANCKEN, N. 2005. "Food safety, the media and the information market," *Agricultural Economics* 32: 175–88.

TAPSCOTT, D., and WILLIAMS, A. D. 2006. *Wikinomics: How Mass Collaboration Changes Everything.* New York: Penguin Publishing.

Television Bureau of Advertising. 2003. *TV Basics 2003: A Report on the Growth and Scope of Television,* http://www.tvb.org/rcentral/mediattrendstracks/tvbasics, accessed October 19.

TOCQUEVILLE, A. DE. [1835] 1969. *Democracy in America,* ed. J. P. Mayer, trans. G. Lawrence. Garden City, NY: Doubleday. Original work published in 1835.

VALLONE, R., ROSS, L., and LEPPER, M. 1985. "The hostile media phenomenon: biased perceptions and perceptions of media bias in coverage of the Beirut massacre," *Journal of Personality and Social Psychology* 49: 577–85.

VAN BELLE, D. A., RIOUX, J., and POTTER, D. M. 2004. *Media, Bureaucracies, and Foreign Aid: A Comparative Analysis of the United States, the United Kingdom, Canada, France and Japan.* New York: Palgrave Macmillan.

VELDKAMP, L. L. 2006. "Media frenzies in markets for financial information," *American Economic Review* 963: 577–601.

VERBEKE, W., and WARD, R. W. 2001. "A fresh meat almost ideal demand system incorporating negative TV press and advertising impact," *Agricultural Economics* 25: 359–74.

—————— and VIAENE, J. 2000. "Probit analysis of fresh meat consumption in Belgium: exploring BSE and television communication impact," *Agribusiness* 16: 215–34.

World Bank 2004. "World development indicators: the information age," available at http://www.worldbank.org

CHAPTER 29

ENVIRONMENTAL AND FOOD SAFETY POLICY

WYN GRANT

In a broad sense business has seen a change in the challenges that it faces in its relationship with government. At one time, the political agenda was dominated by issues arising from the politics of production: labor relations, incomes policies, claims for co-determination, etc. These issues have not disappeared, but they have been partially displaced by a new set of issues that may be conceptualized in terms of a politics of collective consumption. These include negative externalities from production that may take the form of public goods, as well as the consumption choices that are available on a more individual basis. Environmental and food safety policy fall centrally within these new form of politics. They may demand responses at different levels of government (global or regional) or new forms of regulation in which state action is supplemented by self-regulation by firms. What unites both environmental and food safety policy is a concern by firms for the integrity and reputation of their brands which are seen as a valuable asset to be protected and enhanced. "Choice editing, whereby businesses make environmentally and socially sound sourcing decisions on behalf of their customers is... a particularly important trend. Choice editing can strengthen brands by reinforcing consumer trust" (Food Ethics Council 2007: 4).

Four broad themes will be addressed in this chapter. First, there is a set of challenges to business from non-governmental organizations (NGOs) concerned with environment and food related issues. Against a background of a general decline in the strength of trade unions, these public interest groups have become the main countervailing political force to business. Second, there is the emergence of an entirely new set of regulatory actors, most notably the EU. Multi-level governance has become a key feature of the regulatory process. Third, there is the reaction against command and control regulation and its perceived limitations and a search for new policy instruments, although one must be careful of exaggerating the extent to which government has been replaced by governance (Jordan, Wurzel, and Zito 2005). A fourth underlying theme is the economic and political significance of globalization in the food chain, particularly in terms of debates about trade liberalization. It should be noted that in the context of food, where images are consumed as well as the substance itself, "Globalisation is as much about the mobility of information as it is of people and material" (Lowe, Phillipson, and Lee 2008: 228).

FOOD SAFETY REGULATION

Changing attitudes towards food safety have to be understood within the context of broader social changes:

Growing awareness of the environmental and social costs associated with the provenance and processes of food production is itself associated with broader changes in modern societies towards what social scientists term reflexive consumption, whereby people think of themselves as active, discerning consumers whose choices contribute to their sense of identity.

(Lowe, Phillipson, and Lee 2008: 228)

As old forms of identity associated with class or workplace become less salient, consumption and its associated cultural meanings become more significant, reinforcing the importance of self-expression through consumption that is possible in an affluent society where globalization extends both the knowledge of cuisines and their availability.

Food safety regulation has its own distinctive characteristics. In particular, "few other areas of public policy so directly, personally and continually affect the well-being of every citizen" (Ansell and Vogel 2006: 4). "Food scares" over BSE and salmonella outbreaks have given consumers an increased sense of vulnerability and have reduced their trust in the regulatory system. This has translated, in Northern Europe at least, to a substantial resistance to the introduction of genetically modified (GM) crops and foods, fanned by effective interventions by non-governmental organizations. "The [NGOs] that comprise the anti-GMO movement have taken center stage in the European contestation over genetic engineering and the politics of food. Their influence has been pervasive" (Ansell, Maxwell, and Sicurelli 2006: 97). Whereas in other areas of activity, such as ameliorating climate change, NGOs may be prepared to negotiate and arrive at shared solutions with business, the association of food with risk means that they are less willing to do so in this area. This is not just about perceptions of personal risk but about conceptions of food as a "liminal substance" that links humans and nature (Atkinson 1991).

Opposition coordinated by NGOs has substantially restricted the commercial planting of GM crops in Northern Europe, although they are widely grown in North America, Latin America, and China. This is a rare example of successful political resistance to the spread of globalization, although it reflects the extent to which the food chain has become one of the primary sites of resistance to globalization (Coleman, Grant, and Josling 2004). Opponents of GM crops claim that they are both a health and environmental hazard. However, NGOs are also very active in environmental issues which like food safety are a highly contested terrain which can be occupied by those opposed to the process of globalization and the multinational companies with which it is associated. This is consistent with a politics of collective consumption where attention is switched from personal gains or losses to negative externalities that affect a society as a whole. In the US, against the background of a favorable climate for business during the Bush administration, the contest between business and environmental groups produced "an extended period of policy gridlock in which neither environmental groups nor business groups have succeeded in attaining their goals" (Kamieniecki and Kraft 2007: 330).

REGIONAL AND DOMESTIC REGULATION

Effective regulation that commands widespread trust can then become an important mechanism to restore consumer confidence. In the context of the GM debate, it was argued that regulatory agencies in the USA, in particular the Food and Drug Administration (FDA), commanded wider confidence than European arrangements, hence facilitating the introduction of GM crops. Other factors were certainly important and in any case it has been argued that "despite an impressive record of achievement" federal food safety policy is in urgent need of modernization to meet new challenges (Hoffman 2005: 3). Nevertheless, the FDA model was one of the inspirations behind the creation of a European Food Safety Authority (EFSA), although its responsibilities are confined to risk assessment rather than risk management.

"For many years the EU approach in relation to food legislation was mainly based on the objective of ensuring free movement of foodstuffs through the common market...the process of developing food legislation was...slow, fragmented and characterized by the different national traditions of the Member States" (Ugland and Veggeland 2006: 612). Following, the BSE crisis, food safety policy was given an institutional home in DG SANCO (Health and Consumer Protection). An EU Food Law was also developed (General Food Law Regulation, EC 178/2002). MacMaoláin (2007: 277) argues that "consumer protection and human health preservation are not the primary concerns of EU food law. Free movement remains in the top spot." Even so, food regulation has become deeply embedded in the European integration process, rather than simply being an offshoot of the Common Agricultural Policy (CAP). Domestic food law is developed within the context of EU law. Nevertheless, this activity takes place within a system of multi-level governance and enforcement is largely the responsibility of member states and often locally controlled officials. Inevitably, "this results in wide variations across countries in how EC/EU food safety legislation has been implemented and enforced" (Skogstad 2001: 490).

Federal legislation governing food in the USA dates from 1886. The best resourced agency is the United States Department of Agriculture's Food Safety and Inspection Service (FSIS). Because the Secretary of Agriculture has a responsibility to ensure the examination of every meat and poultry carcass to be sold as food in interstate commerce, this requires a continuous inspection service in plants, although the effectiveness of those inspections has been called into question. The FDA is responsible for poisoning and toxic materials and deals with outbreaks of life threatening diseases such as salmonella. The Environmental Protection Agency (EPA) deals with pesticide residues. What one thus finds is a pattern of agency fragmentation not uncommon in the USA:

[The] United States in no sense operates an "integrated food safety system." Rather, Congress has allocated tasks and resources among several agencies with discrete, although sometimes interrelated authorities and responsibilities. These boundaries and connections are largely the result of legislative decisions made decades ago, when food production was almost exclusively domestic and the distinctions among producer sectors were much easier to discern. (Merrill 2005: 39)

Environmental policy

Like food safety policy, environmental policy had a slow and haphazard development in the EU, in part because it initially had no specific basis in the treaties, a defect remedied by the Single European Act. It also took some time for the Environment Directorate-General (originally DG XI) to be become established and influential within the internal politics of the Commission. Business interests were able to lobby against DG XI proposals by using other directorate-generals, such as that concerned with the internal market and industrial affairs, to argue their position within the Commission. The increasing strength of Green parties within some member states such as Germany and the admission of member states with a "green" orientation such as Austria and Sweden strengthened the case for effective environmental policies. The European Parliament, which gained greater influence within the decision-making process over time, was also generally well disposed to environmental initiatives. However, the defeat of proposals for a carbon tax in the mid-1990s showed the continuing influence of business interests. As with food safety policy, implementation and enforcement of environmental policy at member state level was a continuing problem, although the new member states from Central and East Europe were given extensive derogations from the application of Community environmental policy. Nevertheless, the EU liked to see itself as setting the international pace on policies to combat climate change, an area of policy where its stance contrasted with that of the US.

The EPA in the US was established in 1970. Its influence in the policy-making process has fluctuated under different administrations, but a certain momentum is maintained by the range of regulatory instruments at its disposal regardless of the political climate. However, the George W. Bush administration appointed to the EPA "a long list of individuals who had previously worked for or lobbied on behalf of the oil, natural gas, coal mining, timber, chemical, manufacturing, pesticide, electric power and cattle industries or served at libertarian think tanks and advocacy centers" (Peterson 2004: 247). These "appointees share Bush's pro business approach to 'free market environmentalism'" (Peterson 2004: 247–8). Agencies such as EPA implement environmental policy through detailed regulations which have the effect of law. It would appear that business groups "have been very successful in influencing environmental policies within executive-branch agencies, especially during the... Bush administration" (Furlong 2007: 178).

INTERNATIONAL REGULATION

"Command and control" regulation still has its place in environmental and food safety policy, but it is increasingly recognized that it is by itself insufficient and in some cases counter-productive. Transaction costs associated with such forms of regulation can be high, particularly in terms of enforcement and outcomes may be suboptimal. In particular, it imposes "uniform reduction targets and technologies which ignore the variable pollution abatement costs facing individual firms. In practice, marginal costs of pollution vary widely among industries" (Golub 1998: 3). Better results may be obtained by policy instruments that make use of the price mechanism such as taxes or emission trading schemes. However, Zito (2000: 101) makes the point that "Industrial groups have tended to support voluntary agreements and even command and control instruments over an environmental tax because industry can negotiate and consult with government during the policy implementation." Even more effective in certain cases may be voluntary agreements with firms or sectors or allowing firms to develop their own systems of self-regulation. Thus, even in areas that are strictly regulated and where the potential risks are high, supplementary systems of private regulation may develop. In the highly regulated area of synthetic pesticides, retailers have placed additional prohibitions or restrictions on the use of pesticides, making use of contractual mechanisms as an enforcement device.

Where there is public regulation, it often takes place at a global or regional level. The decisions of the World Trade Organization (WTO) can influence environmental regulation if it is seen as a barrier to trade. After complaints by developing companies, the Sanitary and Phytosanitary Standards (SPS) Committee of the WTO began discussing private standards imposed by retailers and there was also a joint information session on the subject in 2007 between the United Nations Conference on Trade and Development (UNCTAD) and the WTO. There are some serious tensions between environmental policy and trade policy which at their most fundamental level "call into question many commonly held 'liberal' assumptions about the relationship between free trade generally and the common well-being" (Whiteside 2006: 87). For environmentalists, free trade is inextricably linked with economic growth and hence a source of the planet's problems, not least because the growth of trade requires the growth of freight transport. Some advocates of freer trade are uneasy about trade policy institutions becoming involved in environmental questions. The solution might seem to lie in impartially applied rules, but the difficulty with the precautionary principle is that it enshrines uncertainty as a norm which is just what a rule-based regime seeks to reduce. Insofar as "the precautionary principle validates scientific *uncertainty* as a reason to restrain trade, it shakes the foundation of international agreements" (Whiteside 2006: 86).

There are also potentially tensions between the WTO and its Disputes Settlement Body (DSB) and food safety standards. Cases considered by the DSB such as that on beef hormones (the presence of which was used by the EU as a justification for restricting meat imports from the USA in the absence of adequate scientific evidence) show that governments do not have to justify their choice of a given level of protection to the DSB. "It also held that the burden of proof was on the complainant to show that there was no justification for the measures. This appears to mean that complainants have to show both that a measure was not based on international standards and that the risk assessment on which it was based was inadequate" (Young and Holmes 2006: 293).

International bodies specifically concerned with food safety date back to the Office International des Epizooties (OIE) established by international treaty in 1924 to deal with infectious animal diseases. It harmonizes import and export regulations for animals and animal products as well as dealing with fish. Together with the International Plant Protection Convention (IPPC) that has dealt with plant products since 1952 "These treaties provide much of the scientific consensus that underlies domestic food safety systems" (Phillips 2001: 38). The Codex Alimentarius Commission, responsible for processed food, represents another attempt to harmonize standards in a way that facilitates international trade and the protection of consumers. It was created in 1963 by the Food Agricultural Organization (FAO) and the World Health Organization (WHO) to develop food standards and to promote the coordination of international governmental and non-governmental food standards work. One of the strongest drivers for the adoption of Codex principles is the growth of global food trade. "Codex plays an important part in agri-food trade because its standards, guidelines and recommendations are in the Sanitary and Phytosanitary and Technical Barriers to Trade Agreements of the WTO" (Phillips 2001: 39). It has become a global reference point for the international food trade and has a considerable impact on the decisions made by food processors and producers. In particular, its standards provide maximum residue limits (MRLs) for residues of pesticides or veterinary drugs in foods; general standards for food additives and contaminants; and codes of practice governing the production, transport, and storage of individual foods or groups of foods.

The Codex introduced the Hazard Analysis and Critical Control Point (HACCP) food safety management system which is now widely used. In the EU, some of the HACCP principles have become mandatory through directive EC/93/43 and other measures. Similarly, in the United States, the FSIS required meat and poultry plants to implement HACCP systems from 1998 (Dyckman 2005: 98). In the Global South, WHO and FAO have been involved in capacity-building initiatives in relation to HACCP. For example, an FAO program to adopt HACCP standards across the coffee production and processing chain was completed in 2004 in countries such as the Ivory Coast, Kenya, and Uganda (Garcia and Carruth 2006: 422).

Nevertheless, even within Europe "implementation of HACCP remains highly incomplete...It appears that implementation of HACCP varies strongly across countries, food industry sectors, and types of firms" (Bernauer and Caduff 2006: 87). International standards might appear to be the solution to a situation in which internationalization heightens consumer perceptions of risk and uncertainty, yet national regulation becomes less effective. "The most obvious solution, international food standards, is likely to be highly contested in the light of the diversity of cultures...each with different ideas and interests with respect to food" (van Waarden 2006: 37). The outcome is often a complex system of multi-level governance in which responsibilities are not necessarily shared out in a rational way, either between different levels or between public and private forms of regulation.

In the area of environmental policy the United Nations (UN) has played a key role in shaping the agenda. The precautionary principle was endorsed in the Rio Declaration on Sustainable Development and has subsequently become an important policy rule, particularly in the European Union (EU). Its interpretation is controversial, but "This principle means that the absence of scientific proof for a risk of environmental harm is not a sufficient reason for failing to take preventative action" (McEldowney and McEldowney 2001: 10). Thus, according to the European Commission, "Recourse to the precautionary principle presupposes that potentially dangerous effects deriving from a phenomenon, product or process have been identified, and that scientific evaluation does not allow the risk to be determined with sufficient certainty" (European Commission 2000: 4). Although precautionary reasoning may in practice be recognized in US law, "The United States appears reflexively anti-precautionary" and the administration of George W. Bush waged "a concerted campaign against the precautionary principle itself" (Whiteside 2006: 63). There are limits to the extent to which the UN can shape the environmental agenda.

The UN also encountered resistance from the US on the subject of global warming. Nevertheless, it has also been a major driver of the debate on climate change through the Intergovernmental Panel on Climate Change (IPCC), which assesses the available scientific evidence and hence frames the debate. The IPCC is a scientific intergovernmental body set up by the World Meteorological Organization (WMO) and by the United Nations Environment Program (UNEP). Action on climate change can affect some of the most powerful and economically important sectors in the global economy (Newell and Paterson 1998). Sectors such as coal, oil, motor vehicles, and energy-intensive industries may combine both to question how much climate change is occurring and to restrict and limit any policy actions that might impinge on their interests.

BUSINESS RESPONSES TO NEW CHALLENGES

Both the increasing importance of international bodies in these policy areas and the growth in global trade in food calls forth new kinds of responses by business. The initiative is often taken by multinational corporations which are the most directly affected bodies and have the resources to act. Such activities often form part of a broader corporate responsibility agenda. By taking its own initiatives, business can avoid more onerous or intrusive forms of imposed regulation. Private systems of regulation may also be more attuned to the specific commercial needs of business, particularly in terms of protecting product reputation and the integrity of a brand.

The World Business Council for Sustainable Development (WBCSD) was founded on the eve of the 1992 Rio Earth Summit to encourage business to become involved in sustainability issues which are framed in terms of the three pillars of environmental, social, and economic. Giving a rough equivalence to these different dimensions means, of course that, for example, environmental needs have to be balanced against considerations of economic viability. In 1995 the Council merged with the World Industry Council for the Environment, a branch of the International Chamber of Commerce. It is a CEO-led, global association of some leading 200 companies with an exclusive membership which can be obtained only by invitation of the executive committee. The international distribution of member companies is shown in Table 29.1 with European companies predominating. The core teams in its "focus areas" such as Energy and Climate include such well-known companies as BP, General Electric, General Motors, KPMG, Sony, Toyota, Unilever, and Vodafone. Its role is partly one of advocacy, to participate in policy development to ensure that the right framework conditions exist for business and that it can still operate, innovate, and grow. It also seeks to demonstrate the business contribution to sustainable development. Internally, it provides a forum within which business leaders can work with their peers to find business opportunities and solutions.

Not surprisingly, the WBCSD has attracted criticism as an example of "greenwash," receiving a Greenwash award from CorpWatch in 1997. CorpWatch suggests

Table 29.1 WBSCD member countries by country/region, 2007

Country/region	Number of companies
Europe	78
United States	39
Japan	28
Australasia	8
Other Asia	7
Canada	5
Korea	5
China	3
Russia	3
South Africa	2
Middle East	1

Source: Calculated from WBCSD data.

that WBCSD pronouncements are characterized by a "carefully crafted tone of heartening ambiguity":

The overall tone of recent WBCSD pronouncements is one of reassurance; to governments and NGOs, reassurance that business understands and is voluntarily taking action; and to their members reassurance that things are changing but not that fast; that some actions is needed, but not that much.

(http://www.corpwatch.org/article,php?id=471 accessed December 12, 2007)

A development like the WBCSD is perfectly consistent with the theory of "ecological modernization." This predicted that "a cleavage begins to open up not between business and environmentalists, but between progressively, environmentally aware business on the one hand and short-term profit takers on the other" (Weale 1992: 31). As Weale notes (1992: 75), "There is no one canonical statement of the ideology of ecology modernisation as *The General Theory* is a source for Keynesianism." Its significance for business–government relations in the area of environmental policy is that embedding it in the decision-making process is seen as a win–win situation. At a fundamental level, "the argument emerged, notably in the Brundtland report, that environmental protection to a high level was a precondition of long-term economic development" (Weale 1992: 31). More specifically, it doesn't make economic sense for business to use scarce resources inefficiently. Using energy inefficiently is simply wasteful, while pollution may represent resources that could have been recycled or used for alternative products. Pollution control creates opportunities for new enterprises.

That the goals of business and government should appear to be complementary in this way is welcome news for both. However, ecological critics would argue that there is still a fundamental tension between economic growth and the carrying capacity of the planet, particularly manifested by climate change. Under the umbrella of ecological modernization, business can undertake ameliorative projects while continuing with conduct that is inimical to sustainability.

Private regulation

In the area of food safety, a number of important regulatory initiatives have been undertaken by groupings of firms. In an effort to limit their liability and protect their reputations, firms in the food chain have sought to "pursue any potential vulnerabilities in a food chain right back to its origins...The result is a spreading, extra-territorial 'private' regulation of food chains by downstream firms, accompanied by a proliferation of private standard setting" (Lowe, Phillipson, and Lee 2008: 227). As economic power has flowed down the food chain to retailers, the initiators have often been supermarkets. This reflects "a pendulum movement during the 1990s in which the deregulation in food markets and the disappearance of representative (production-based) corporate organisations were largely replaced by large-scale retailer's organisations" (Thankappan and Marsden 2005: 7). The retailers become an important source of state legitimacy and a key mechanism "on behalf of the state in delivering consumer rights and choices. Reciprocally, the regulatory state has become critically dependent upon the continued economic dependence of the retailers in their role as the providers of quality food goods" (Marsden, Flynn, and Harrison 2000: 28) Thus:

It seems that public food safety regulation is becoming less detailed and less prescriptive. At the same time, important forms of private regulation are more detailed, with a high degree of intervention curtailing freedom of regulated firms. For food manufacturers and producers, private retail-driven food safety standards may be similar to public food laws, confronting the organization with external requirements and specifications.   (Havinga 2006: 529)

One of the most important private systems of regulation is what was originally EurepGap but was reconstituted in 2007 as GlobalGap, which seeks to facilitate global trade in fresh fruit and vegetable products through a benchmarking system. Many of its members are global players in the retail industry and source food products from around the world. It was set up in 1997 as an initiative of retailers belonging to the Euro-Retailer Produce Working Group (EUREP). In the wake of food safety scares such as BSE, EurepGAP was driven by the desire to reassure consumers. It was considered that there was a need "for a commonly recognised and applied reference standard of Good Agricultural Practice which has at its centre a consumer focus" (http://www.eurepgap.org/Languages/English/about.html accessed June 7, 2006).

Technically speaking GlobalGAP is a set of documents suitable to be accredited to internationally recognized certification criteria such as ISO Guide 65. GlobalGAP's scope is limited to practices on the farm and once the product leaves the farm other Codes of Conduct relevant to food packing and processing become operative. GlobalGAP members include retailers, farmers, and growers and associate members from the input and service side of agriculture. Governance is by sector specific steering committees which have 50 per cent retailer and 50 per cent producer representation with an independent chairperson. The work of the committees is supported by FoodPLUS, a not-for-profit limited company based in Germany. Despite the efforts to make it a global organization, American participation remained limited. There were just three full members in the United States in 2008, the only retailer being the relatively small upscale East Coast chain, Wegmans Food Market. Although it remained preponderantly European, the small American membership contrasted with twelve members in Latin America, seven in Africa, four in Asia, and even three in New Zealand. These figures perhaps reflect survey evidence that suggests that "European consumers are more concerned about food safety and process attributes of food than American consumers" (Thankapan and Marsden 2005: 31).

Another retailer driven initiative is the Global Food Safety Initiative (GFSI) launched in 2000 under the auspices of the Food Business Forum (CIES) in the wake of the 1999 Dioxin Crisis. (Dioxins are a group of chemicals that increase the risk of cancer. Animal feed was contaminated by them in Belgium leading to the withdrawal of eggs and chickens from the market.) It is a global network of food safety experts and their trade associations. It was driven by the need of retailers to make of an assessment of their suppliers of private label products and fresh products and meats. "There are many of these standards and suppliers...many customers may be audited many times a year, at a high cost and little added benefit" (http://www.foodsafety.sgs.com/global_food_safety_initiative_gfsi_foodsafety accessed August 10, 2009). GFSI does not undertake any accreditation or certification activities but encourages the use of third party audits based on its own benchmarking standards. It issues regularly revised Guidance Documents containing agreed criteria against which any food safety standard can be benchmarked. It aims for consistency and objectivity in the benchmarking process. It sees itself as a knowledge sharing forum for participants in the food chain and a mechanism for the delivery of improved standards of food safety. Although this is not stated, its existence would imply that public international coordination arrangements do not meet all the needs of commercial actors.

The British Retail Consortium (BRC) Global Standard was initially driven by the need to meet the legislative requirements of the EU General Product Safety Directive and the UK Food Safety Act. Its main function is to evaluate manufacturers of retailers own brand products. It quickly evolved into a Global Standard and most Scandinavian retailers will only consider business with suppliers who have gained certification. By 2007 there were four regularly revised standards for food, identity preserved non-genetically modified food ingredients, packaging, and consumer products. There has been some criticism of the fact that these standards exceed the requirements of legislation, although this is not untypical of such private systems of regulation. "It has been argued...in recent discussions in the WTO SPS Committee, that private-sector standards may be more stringent than government regulations" (http://www.unctad.org/Templates/Page.asp?intItemID=4285&lang=1 accessed August 24, 2007).

The development of these private systems of governance is not without its costs. They may not overcome asymmetry of information problems for the consumer:

The danger of proliferating schemes by individual supermarkets, on top of the existing national assurance programs and umbrella initiatives such as EUREP...is that the consumer will be left more confused than ever. Research...shows that consumers are completely baffled by the range of schemes, logos and claims that surround the food industry. (Thankappan and Marsden 2005: 45)

Moreover, it has been argued that "the oligopsony power of European retailers have been strengthened by producer-led food safety and quality assurance schemes" (Food Ethics Council 2005: 5). Thankappan and Marsden (2005: 56) warn that "sustainability as a set of quality standards may provide leverage for large enterprises to control markets and raise barriers to competition." Because well-capitalized farmers are better able to implement standards and codes of practice evolved by private systems of governance, the economic competitiveness of more marginal farmers may be undermined with implications for farm structure. They may also pose challenges for producers in the Global South: "Several of these standards for food...combine food safety with environmental, health and workers' health and safety requirements, which makes compliance a very tall order for developing-country producers and exporters" (http://www.unctad.org/Templates/Page.asp?inItemID=4285&lang=1 accessed August 24, 2007).

NATIONAL REGULATORY STYLES: THE CASE OF BIOPESTICIDES

Vogel (1986) presented an analysis of contrasting national styles of regulation in environmental policy in Britain and the United States. His analysis has been somewhat overtaken by subsequent developments as the more discretionary style he identified in Britain has been modified by the increasing extent to which British regulation is shaped by the more standards driven approach of the EU. Nevertheless, the concept of different national approaches remains worth exploring as it can set the context within which government–business interactions in food and environmental policy take place.

Pesticide policy offers a good arena for exploration of these issues as it straddles both food policy and environmental policy. From a food policy perspective, pesticide residues on fresh foods are a major concern as, even if they are deemed to be safe, they may deter consumers from eating fruit and vegetables, which is thought to be desirable in terms of preventive health. From an environmental perspective, there is a particular concern about water pollution by pesticides, both in terms of the contamination of the water supply and possible effects on aquatic life. Ever since the publication of *Silent Spring*, the impact of extensive synthetic pesticide use on biodiversity, particular bird populations, has also been a subject of concern.

Biopesticides offer an environmentally friendly alternative to synthetic pesticides. They are mass-produced, biologically based agents used for the control of plant pests. Examples would be predatory insects, nematodes, or naturally occurring substances such as plant extracts or insect pheromones. Microbial control agents such as bacteria, protozoa, or fungi are safe to humans and vertebrate wildlife. Unwanted direct effects on non-target organisms are likely to be rare. They produce little or no toxic residue and can be applied to crops using the same equipment used to apply chemical pesticides. They are a means of promoting sustainable pest management.

However, just because something is natural does not mean that it is safe and these products still need to be regulated. One of the problems for biological control agents is that the regulatory system has been constructed to deal with synthetic pesticides which remain dominant in the market. Microbial biopesticides represent less than 1 per cent of the global market for agrochemical crop protection (Hajek 2004: 331). Hence it is no surprise that regulators have little experience of dealing with biological control agents and tend to ask questions that are only relevant to synthetic pesticides. Nevertheless, there are some interesting and significant national variations in outcomes from the regulatory process. Data on microbial biopesticide agents from Agriculture and Agri-Food Canada (Kabaluk and Gazdik 2005) and from the EPA indicates that more than 200 products are being sold in the USA, compared with only sixty in the EU and five in the UK. Why has the US regulatory system been more successful at facilitating the registration of biopesticides and getting them on to the market?

The companies that develop and produce biopesticides are typically small or at most medium-sized companies. They might be start-up companies on a science park, spinning off from an idea developed in a university. They cannot afford the well-staffed regulatory affairs departments maintained by agrochemical companies. Often regulatory work is undertaken by the owner/manager or perhaps by a recent doctoral graduate. They have little familiarity with the regulatory system and how it operates. They cannot turn to industry associations for help as they have limited resources and no full-time staff (the International Biocontrol Manufacturers Association, IBMA, in Europe; The Biopesticide Industry Alliance, BPIA, in the USA). They can hire consultants to help them, but they can be expensive. Hence, they are substantially dependent on an encouraging and supportive response from the state regulatory agency.

Research based on visits to the Biopesticides and Pollution Prevention Division (BPPD) of the Office of Pesticides Programs of the EPA and the UK's Pesticides Safety Directorate (PSD) suggest that there are substantial differences in bureaucratic resources, organizational culture, rules, market structure, and supporting policy measures which, taken together, help to explain differences in policy outcomes. (There is a complex and changing division of responsibility for regulation in the EU, but in general terms the EU approves active substances and member states regulate products). The BPPD was established in 1995 and has twenty staff in its Microbial Pesticide Branch and twenty-three in its Biochemical Pesticide Branch. The formation of the BBPD was the result of pressure from the biopesticides industry: "Biopesticides industry as a whole pushed. Fifteen years ago no one paid us any attention. Fell on a few ears. [It was] staff who were really interested, senior leadership at a political level within the [EPA]" (Interview, BPPD, Crystal City, Va., November 18, 2005).

In contrast PSD does not have a biopesticides division but a small team with other responsibilities. There is a Biopesticides Champion but it is a part-time post. Following pressure from the Better Regulation team in the Cabinet Office concerned about the low rate of registration of biopesticides in the UK, the PSD adopted a Pilot Project to facilitate their registration in 2005, later succeeded by a Biopesticides Scheme. This offers reduced registration fees compared with synthetic chemicals and pre-registration meetings. However, it should be noted that 70 per cent of biopesticide firms in the US can be classified as small businesses under Small Business Administration and hence are exempt from review fees paid to the EPA (Schneider 2006).

PSD staff members see themselves as "scientific regulators." Hence, they are keen to extend their scientific knowledge and have embraced the regulation of biopesticides in that spirit (Greaves 2009). The stance of BPPD staff was more proactive. It was evident from the interviews conducted with a number of staff members that there was a strong identification with the division, perhaps reinforced by their location away from the rest of EPA in a federal building mostly occupied by the Department of Homeland Security. One respondent commented in interview:

We do things differently from the rest of the office, we have a one stop shop, don't farm out anything on economic or ecological efficacy or health effects. Have our own chemists, economists, toxicologists, cut down on amount of bureaucracy, helps us to implement things. Have all personnel in one division, all on the same floor, much easier if person is sitting in cubicle across floor.

Although as a government agency they are prevented from promoting a product or technology, it is noticeable that they went to look for samples of recent approved products during interviews. This reflected a commitment to the mission of the division. As one respondent put it:

We are pro-biopesticides. We believe strongly that there's a role to create a division just dedicated to them. One person about to retire worked with very small companies, perhaps given them too much tender loving care. Help to make sure everything is right.

Language of this kind was not used at PSD. PSD has an "Information Section." It does not have an Ombudsman who answered questions such as "How to find a consultant, how long will registration take, how much will it cost, how do I get a registration number? The fact that they speak to a human being and get a good referral, someone that is live, speaking their language [the Ombudsman spoke French and Spanish] and usually giving them accurate information."

There is an important rule difference between the US and the UK in that the EPA does not require that biopesticides be tested for efficacy before they are approved. This is a legislative requirement in the UK and it is all viewed as necessary to write the label that accompanies the product. An alternative view is that the market can decide whether a product is efficacious or not. Firms do have to undertake some efficacy testing of a new product for marketing purposes in the US (and the BPPD can call in data), but it need not be as protracted or as expensive as the testing required for product registration.

The US offers a substantial internal market for biopesticide products which permits economies of scale. The EU does not have an internal market in biopesticide products because there are twenty-seven national regulatory authorities and mutual recognition generally fails to work. An attempt to overcome this problem by dividing Europe into three "eco zones" where a product registered in one member state would be approved in all the others in the zone ran into resistance from some member states and the European Parliament. The variety of climatic conditions in the USA also creates opportunities for a range of biological products.

There is also more external policy support in the USA. The Interregional Research Project (IR-4) program was started by the Directors of the State Agricultural Experiment Stations (SAES) in 1963 and has been administered since then by USDA. IR-4 works closely with EPA: "IR-4 is our best mechanism, so helpful." In 1995 the program was updated to include a focus on biopesticides and since then $2.85 million has been provided for biopesticides research. They have an employee whose only role is to help get biological pesticides registered. Funding can be provided to help small companies get the data they need for registration. IR-4 also supported the growth of the industry trade association, BPIA. For its part, BPPD has provided $100,000 for a Biopesticide Demonstration Program to persuade growers of their advantages. The sums involved are not large, but they may be sufficient to ensure that a product gets developed, registered, and marketed. The UK, in contrast, operates a relatively rigid market failure doctrine on such matters so that new actives which have been developed with public money cannot afford to meet product registration costs.

What emerges from this comparison is that the US adopted a more pragmatic and supportive approach to biopesticides policy than the UK. The UK did start to catch up with initiatives taken some seven years after the US, but even then the resources available were more limited and the commitment appeared to be less strong. The same area of environmental policy can thus still be regulated very differently from one country to another even though the Organisation for Economic Co-operation and Development (OECD) is attempting to harmonize biopesticide regulations. At present, however, a biopesticides manufacturer can face very different regulatory arrangements in different countries, illustrating the limits to the extent that globalization overcomes differences in political regimes.

Climate Change

The attitude of leading companies towards climate change has shifted markedly over time. This reflects both an increasing acceptance of the scientific consensus on climate change and recognition that companies were suffering reputational damage as a result of denying the phenomenon of global warming. "As the scientific consensus grew stronger, some CEOs began to believe that carbon limits were inevitable and that being early movers would earn them a prominent role in designing the rules." Moreover, in the US, "Some preferred federal rules to the emerging hodgepodge of state-level requirements" (Layzer 2007: 109).

A number of leading fossil fuels companies in the United States had combined in the Global Climate Coalition (GCC) or "Carbon Club" run out of the office of the National Association of Manufacturers in Washington, DC. It engaged in an extensive television advertising campaign in the USA in the run-up to the Kyoto Conference in 1997 that contributed to the American decision not to endorse a global agreement on carbon emissions. "Early business responses to climate change were hindered by the prevalence of pessimistic economic models—which business associations touted—and by limited understanding and evidence of the potential of new technologies and policies to lower the cost of mitigation" (Dunn 2002: 28).

However, one by one, companies started to desert the coalition. Dupont was among the first to leave, followed by BP in 1997. In 1998, Royal Dutch Shell left, stating that it viewed itself as an energy rather than an oil company. It was followed by Ford in 1999, whose chairman said that he expected to preside over the demise of the internal combustion engine. In the early months of 2000, Daimler Chrysler, Texaco, and General Motors all left. One factor that weighed in the minds of companies was the loss of credibility and financial damage that the tobacco industry suffered as a result of denying the link between smoking and health. The GCC announced that it would confine its membership to trade associations then "deactivated" itself in 2002 claiming that its views were embedded in those of the Bush administration. Some of the exiting companies, such as BP, Shell, and Dupont joined the Business Environment Leadership Council founded by the Pew Center on Global Climate Change which by 2007 had forty-five leading corporations in membership representing $2.8 trillion in market capitalization (http://www.pewclimate.org/companies_leading_the_way_belc accessed December 17, 2007). This body accepts that enough is known about the science and environmental impacts of climate change to take action to address its consequences. "The most important point of corporative relevance regarding the economics of climate change is that, however, the costs and benefits add up, they will be spread unevenly across different sectors of the economy, and even potentially within sectors" (Dunn 2002: 30). It is easier to identify losers than potential winners, including the energy-intensive manufacturing industries, such as steel, glass, aluminium, paper, and ceramics as well as the power companies. However, in many ways the energy production companies are in a more advantageous position than the intensive users:

[Overall] we can talk about the power sector being differentiated from the industrial sector in three main ways: i) it is more capable, at least in principle, of reducing carbon emissions fairly substantially in the short term (through fuel switching from coal to gas); ii) it does not suffer from the same exposure to international competition; and . . . iii) it is generally more able to pass on the costs of the Scheme to its customers.

(Environmental Audit Committee 2007: 31)

As far as companies that have an incentive to take action on climate change are concerned, "Insurance and reinsurance companies are confronted with enormous liabilities from rising weather-related claims" (Dunn 2002: 31). The Association of British Insurers in the UK has launched a Climate Change initiative that is attracting global support. The insurance industry is strongly placed to influence the conduct of its policy holders and sees climate change as a market opportunity rather than a threat. The renewable energy sector should also benefit from the search for carbon neutral means of power generation. However, its firms are "relative newcomers to the policy process" (Dunn 2002: 30), are generally smaller companies, and lack the government relations divisions of big corporations or well-developed trade associations. Nuclear power can claim to be carbon neutral and has seen the climate change debate as a window of opportunity to revive the industry, but nuclear energy is a terrain highly contested by NGOs because of problems of waste disposal and fears about accidents. The sectoral differentiation of greenhouse gas emissions would benefit from a policy approach that is differentiated by industry. The negotiations on an international post-2012 framework for climate change will include a provision for "global sectoral agreements" pioneered by the WBCSD. This will require the leading companies in energy intensive sectors such as paper, cement, steel, and aluminium to meet and agree on industry-wide pacts to cutting their greenhouse gas emissions. Many industries favor such agreements, viewing them as preferable to alternatives such as a global patchwork of emission regulations. Any competitive disadvantage is removed by committing the biggest companies in a given sector to cut their emissions by similar amounts to their peers. This form of private interest governance is feasible because it is not unusual in many sectors to have ten to fifteen companies responsible for more than 50 per cent of economic activity in that sector.

Emissions trading schemes (ETS), such as that run by the EU, are seen as a market-friendly way of allowing markets and firms to adjust to the need to reduce greenhouse gas emissions. However, the commodity of emission credits exists by virtue of political decision-making and there is a potential for a massive resource transfer from industry to government. Moreover, the markets for energy production are not fully competitive. There is often an oligopolistic structure of firms and coal and has sit on top of the market and effectively set the electricity price.

The civil aviation industry has been the focus of particular controversy in the context of global climate change debates. It has strongly resisted the proposed extension of the EU's ETS to civil aviation. The industry claims that the attention it has received is disproportionate to its level of emissions, but its critics point to the absence of any tax on aircraft fuel (kerosene) and the emissions impact of journeys made by travellers going to and from airports. Low-cost airline Ryanair responded with a "capitalist aggressive" response, launching outspoken attacks on green groups. However, Ryanair admitted that the onslaught from environmental campaigners against low-cost flying is affecting sales. Howard Millar, Ryanair deputy chief executive, said in December 2007 he was "concerned" about the negative publicity gathering around the airline sector and admitted demand for flights was being impacted "at the edges" (http://www.guardian.co.uk/business/2007/may/31/theairlineindustry.environment accessed December 17, 2007). The more general point here is that those who deny that there is a climate change problem are losing the argument and that the issue is being "framed" by scientists and NGOs rather than business.

The first major emissions trading system, the EU emissions trading scheme launched in 2005, is generally acknowledged to have been a failure in its first phase. There has been a lack of scarcity in the market, prices have been highly volatile, and have fallen below €1 a tonne. "It appears to us that Phase 1 will have very little impact on carbon emissions across the EU" (Environmental Audit Committee 2007: 3). Indeed, carbon emissions are increasing in rapidly developing and increasingly energy-intensive economies like Spain, but they will be able to buy credits relatively cheaply. Many economists consider that a carbon tax would be a more efficient solution, but that solution is generally unpopular with business.

CONCLUSION

The challenges that face business have shifted from those that are predominantly economic in character and concerned with the production process itself to a new politics of collective consumption centered on public goods and external bads. This is uncertain and challenging territory for business as it is populated by NGOs that may be less amenable to negotiations at the margin of the kind that was possible with trade unions who were formerly the main countervailing groups to business. Of course, that is not to deny that "The centrality of business in negotiating, structuring and implementing regimes of international economic governance is all too obvious to negotiation participants" (Newell and Levy 2002: 84). Nevertheless, those business coalitions that tried to deny the phenomenon of climate change have been supplanted by groupings that admit the existence of the problem and seek to engage in a constructive dialogue about solutions. MacMaoláin (2007: 1) argues that "Manufacturers and producers are agile and adept at putting pressure on local and European politicians to maintain outdated and unsustainable systems of production preventing improvements in food quality." Nevertheless, the successful resistance to the commercial introduction of GM crops in Northern Europe shows that multinational business can suffer significant setbacks, although it may still win this particular argument in the long run.

A failure of food safety control can do serious damage to the reputation of a business. The increased reliance on regional or even global food chains can enhance the vulnerability of businesses. A series of food scares, particularly in Europe, has made consumers more sensitive to food quality and food safety issues. One response has not been greater state regulation, but rather the opening up of a space for retailers to go beyond state regulation, either through their own in-house policies or through collective activities such as GlobalGap setting standards for the certification of agricultural products around the globe. What one sees in this area are new forms of governance initiative by firms or new forms of collective activity rather than the use of traditional trade associations, although these still have their role. In general, however, the challenges faced by business demand innovative forms of response that often bypass the state.

What is also evident is that key government–business relationships are often conducted at the regional or global rather than the national level. The globalization of the food chain requires such a response, while problems such as climate change require effective action at a global level, not least to avoid competitive distortions. However, differences in national regulatory arrangements in the environmental and food safety areas persist and can pose significant challenges for business. This calls forth complex systems of multi-level governance which require sophisticated handling and continuous development by both government and business.

NOTE

This chapter draws on research conducted as part of the Rural Economy and Land Use Programme (RELU), funded by the UK Research Councils.

REFERENCES

ANSELL, C., MAXWELL, R., and SICURELLI, D. 2006. "Protesting Food: NGOS and Political Mobilization in Europe," in C. Ansell and D. Vogel, eds., *Where's the Beef? The Contested Governance of European Food Safety.* Cambridge, Mass.: MIT Press, 97–122.

—— and VOGEL, D. 2006. "The contested governance of European food safety regulation," in C. Ansell and D. Vogel, eds., *Where's the Beef? The Contested Governance of European Food Safety.* Cambridge, Mass.: MIT Press, 3–32.

ATKINSON, A. 1991. *Principles of Political Ecology.* London: Belhaven.

BERNAUER, T., and CADUFF, L. 2006. "Food safety and the structure of the European food industry," in C. Ansell and D. Vogel, eds., *Where's the Beef? The Contested Governance of European Food Safety.* Cambridge, Mass.: MIT Press, 81–95.

COLEMAN, W., GRANT, W., and JOSLING, T. 2004. *Agriculture in the New Global Economy.* Cheltenham: Edward Elgar.

DUNN, S. 2002. "Down to business on climate change: an overview of corporate strategies," *Greener Management International* 39: 27–41.

DYCKMAN, L. J. 2005. "The current state of play: federal and state expenditures on food safety," in S. A. Hoffman and M. R. Taylor, eds., *Toward Safer Food: Perspectives on Risk and Priority Setting.* Washington, DC: Resources for the Future, 82–104.

Environmental Audit Committee. 2007. House of Commons Environmental Audit Committee Second Report of Session 2006–7, *The EU Emissions Trading Scheme: Lessons for the Future.* London: The Stationery Office.

European Commission. 2000. "Communication from the Commission on the precautionary principle," Commission of the European Communities, Brussels.

Food Ethics Council. 2005. *Power in the Food System: Understanding Trends and Improving Accountability.* Brighton: Food Ethics Council.

—— 2007. "'Food miles' or 'food minutes': is sustainability all in the timing?" Brighton: Food Ethics Council.

FURLONG, S. R. 2007. "Business and the environment: influencing agency policy-making," in M. E. Kraft and S. Kamieniecki, eds., *Business and Environmental Policy.* Cambridge, Mass.: MIT Press, 155–84.

GARCIA, G., and CARRUTH, R. A. 2006. "Multilateral governance of food safety in global food industries ad food systems: the role of FAO, WHO and Codex Alimentarius in regulatory harmonization," in R. A. Carruth, ed., *Global Governance of Food and Agriculture Industries.* Cheltenham: Edward Elgar, 392–430.

GOLUB, J. 1998. "New instruments for environmental policy in the EU: introduction and overview," in J. Golub, ed., *New Instruments for Environmental Policy in the EU.* London: Routledge, 1–29.

GREAVES, J. 2009. "Biopesticides, regulatory innovation and the regulatory state," *Public Policy and Administration* 24(3): 245–64.

HAJEK, A. 2004. *Natural Enemies: An Introduction to Biological Control.* Cambridge: Cambridge University Press.

HAVINGA, T. 2006. "Private regulation of food safety by supermarkets," *Law and Policy* 28(4): 515–33.

HOFFMAN, S. A. 2005. "Getting to risk-based food safety regulatory management: lessons from federal environmental policy," in S. A. Hoffman and M. R. Taylor, eds., *Toward Safer Food: Perspectives on Risk and Priority Setting* Washington, DC: Resources for the Future, 3–22.

JORDAN, A., WURZEL, R., and ZITO, A. 2005. "The rise of 'new' policy instruments in comparative perspective: has governance eclipsed government?" *Political Studies* 53(3): 477–96.

KABALUK, T., and GAZDIK, K. 2005. *Directory of Microbial Pesticides for Agricultural Crops in OECD Countries.* Aggassiz: Agriculture and Agri-Food Canada.

KAMIENIECKI, S., and KRAFT, M. E. 2007. "Conclusions: the influence of business on environmental politics and policy," in M. E. Kraft and S. Kamieniecki, eds., *Business and Environmental Policy.* Cambridge, Mass.: MIT Press, 329–47.

LAYZER, J. A. 2007. "Deep freeze: how business has shaped the global warming debate in Congress," in M. E. Kraft and S. Kamieniecki, eds., *Business and Environmental Policy.* Cambridge, Mass.: MIT Press, 93–126.

LOWE, P., PHILLIPSON, J., and LEE, R. P. 2008. "Socio-technical innovation for sustainable food chains: roles for social science," *Food Science and Technology* 19: 226–33.

MCELDOWNEY, J., and MCELDOWNEY, S. 1996. *Environment and the Law.* Harlow: Addison Wesley Longman.

MACMAOLÁIN, C. 2007. *EU Food Law: Protecting Health and Consumers in a Common Market.* Oxford: Hart Publishing.

MARSDEN, T., FLYNN, A., and HARRISON, M. 2000. *Consuming Interests: The Social Provision of Foods.* London: UCL Press.

MERRILL, R. A. 2005. "The centennial of US food safety law: a legal and administrative history," in S. A. Hoffman and M. R. Taylor, eds., *Toward Safer Food: Perspectives on Risk and Priority Setting.* Washington, DC: Resources for the Future, 23–43.

NEWELL, P., and LEVY, D. 2002. "Business strategy and international environmental governance: toward a neo-Gramscian synthesis," *Global Environmental Politics* 3(4): 84–101.

—— and PATERSON, M. 1998. "A climate for business: global warming, the state and capital," *Review of International Political Economy* 5(4): 679–703.

PETERSON, M. A. 2004. "Bush and interest groups: a government of chums," in C. Campbell and B. A. Rockman, eds., *The George W. Bush Presidency: Appraisals and Prospects*. Washington, DC: Congressional Quarterly Press, 226–64.

PHILLIPS, P. W. B. 2001. "Food safety, trade policy and international institutions," in P. W. B. Phillips and R. Wolfe, eds., *Governing Food: Science, Safety and Trade*. Montreal and Kingston: McGill-Queen's University Press, 27–48.

SCHNEIDER, W. R. 2006. "Microbial and biochemical pesticide regulation," paper presented at the REBECA (Regulation of Environmental Biological Control Agents) Workshop on Current Risk Assessment and Regulation Practice, Salzau, Germany, http://www.rebeca-net.de/

SKOGSTAD, G. 2001. "The WTO and food safety regulatory policy in the EU," *Journal of Common Market Studies* 39(3): 485–505.

THANKAPPAN, S., and MARSDEN, T. 2005. "The contested regulation of the fresh fruit and vegetable sector in Europe," The Centre for Business Relationships, Accountability, Sustainability and Society (BRASS), Working Paper Series No. 27, University of Cardiff.

UGLAND, T., and VEGGELAND, F. 2006. "Experiments in food safety policy integration in the European Union," *Journal of Common Market Studies* 44(3): 607–24.

VAN WAARDEN, F. 2006. "Taste, traditions, transactions and trust: the public and private regulation of food," in C. Ansell and D. Vogel, eds., *Where's the Beef? The Contested Governance of European Food Safety*. Cambridge, Mass.: MIT Press, 35–59.

VOGEL, D. 1986. *National Styles of Regulation: Environmental Policy in Great Britain and the United States*. Ithaca, NY: Cornell University Press.

WEALE, A. 1992. *The New Politics of Pollution*. Manchester: Manchester University Press.

WHITESIDE, K. H. 2006. *Precautionary Politics*. Cambridge, Mass.: MIT Press.

YOUNG, A. R. and HOLMES, P. 2006. "Compatibility or clash? EU food safety and the WTO," in C. Ansell and D. Vogel, eds., *Where"s the Beef? The Contested Governance of European Food Safety*. Cambridge, Mass.: MIT Press, 281–305.

ZITO, A. R. 2000. *Creating Environmental Policy in the European Union*. Basingstoke: Macmillan.

CHAPTER 30

NETWORK UTILITIES

TECHNOLOGICAL DEVELOPMENT, MARKET STRUCTURE, AND FORMS OF OWNERSHIP

MARTIN CHICK

THE largest section of the industrial economy of most persistent concern to governments is that of the network-containing industries (electricity, water, telecommunications, gas, trams and light railways, railways, post and telecommunications). Government interest in these industries dates from at least the middle of the nineteenth century. These industries have been at the heart of political debate concerning forms of ownership (nationalization, privatization) and economists and politicians have frequently been at odds over the appropriate pricing and investment rules, and industrial structure for such industries. Often characterized by lumpy, sunk distribution and transmission investments giving rise to natural monopoly characteristics and enjoying large potential economies of scale, investment in these industries has consistently outpaced that in manufacturing industry. As Foreman-Peck and Millward observed of the United Kingdom, in 1900 railways' fixed assets alone were larger than those in the whole of manufacturing industry, and "from as early as 1850 the capital stock in the network industries exceeded that in manufacturing and this was still the case in 1960" (Foreman-Peck and Millward 1994: 2). More generally, by the 1960s, public enterprise accounted for about 10 per cent of GDP in most countries, about 20 per cent of annual capital formation, and less than 10 per cent of employment. Its scope did not change much over the next thirty years (Millward 2005: 173).

While historians have tended to focus on the policy changes and shifts in ideology concerning the ownership of these industries, for economic historians a fundamental "driver" of such debates has been the technological development and economic characteristics of these industries. It was their economic and technological underpinnings which initially occasioned local government involvement with the utility network industries, and the technological and economic characteristics of these industries often pushed them to larger, ultimately nationwide industrial structures, well before politicians began to implement policies of nationalization. Equally, it was the economic consequences of the technological developments within these industries which provided the opportunity for reintroducing competition into regulated and nationalized monopoly markets, well before political talk of privatization and liberalization became fashionable. Yet while economic historians argue that technological developments were a necessary prerequisite for shifts in political ideology concerning such industries, they were not sufficient in themselves. Indeed some economic historians such as Peter Temin accord a much greater role to ideology over technological development in itself in promoting, in this case, the break-up of AT&T in the United States. Whatever the case-by-case arguments, it does seem likely that without the economic and public finance difficulties which afflicted many national governments from the 1970s, many politicians would have been less interested in pursuing programs of privatization and deregulation which sought to exploit some of the potential for increased competition made possible by previous technological developments. This was as true of manufacturing industry as of the network utilities.

Much of this interplay between technological development, economic change, and shifts in political ideology is evident in the network utility industries and perhaps, above all, in the fuel and power industries. These industries included non-network industries like coal and oil, which often attracted protection and public ownership (partial, in the case of oil) because of political concern with unemployment (coal) and national security (oil, coal). Considerations of national security also prompted government involvement in the airline industry, as well as in a network utility like telecommunications. These issues will be considered in this chapter, but its prime concern is that of the economic historian, namely with the influence exerted by the economic and technological developments in network utilities on the timing and form of government involvement with these industries since the mid-nineteenth century. While because of their quantitative and persistent importance this chapter concentrates on the network utilities rather than on manufacturing industry, many of the fashionable shifts in political opinion concerning the trade-off between economies of scale and competition that typify the nationalization program and the regulatory debates, are also germane to broader industrial and competition policy.

Many of the early commercial initiatives in what became network utilities were taken by private individuals and enterprises rather than by local or national governments. Perhaps because of the protection offered by limited liability legislation, the ability to raise finance on capital markets, and to locate in suitable urban markets, private enterprise seemed willing to take the risk of moving from an *ex ante* interest in the industry to an *ex post* irrevocable commitment to it by literally sinking capital into cable and pipe networks. In the early stages of such competitive investment, there is some evidence of over-investment in capacity, but once laid the combination of the high sunk costs of the distribution system and the low marginal costs of production were likely in an integrated system to make it possible to deter new entrants. It was often at this point, with the early entrepreneurial risks taken, and with the political interest in utility output growing, that local authorities would become involved in the industry. Not only were there beneficial spillovers from the provision of piped water, but the existence of economies of scale in production and distribution allied to the ratio of sunk : marginal costs did make these industries likely candidates for price regulation. However, it did not necessarily make them natural monopolies, that status being a function of the relation between the given state of the technology, the size of demand, the number of firms, and the movement of costs over each range of output.

When local authorities did enter these industries, they either did so immediately in their own right or, more commonly, by granting franchises to undertakings on the condition that at the end of a prescribed period the local authority would have the right to purchase the private company. The 1870 Tramways Act inaugurated the system of providing limited period franchises which was initially usually for twenty-one years but was subsequently extended to forty-two years in 1888 (Byatt 1979: 8). In Western Europe, such municipalization was strongest in areas of greatest urbanization, namely in Britain and Germany, but less so in the more rural France, Belgium, Spain, and Italy (Millward 2007a: 19–20). In France municipalization was virtually unknown, much greater use being made of the concession system, and the French regulatory regime was tougher than that in Britain. In Paris, by 1889, the six *concessionaire* electricity companies in Paris were on eighteen-year leases, but the French regulatory regime often offered much shorter leases (Millward 2005: 77, 82). In the United States, municipalization in electricity supply reached its peak in 1921 when there were 2,581 municipal systems. However many of these systems were small, accounting for 41 per cent of all electric systems, but generating only 4.7 per cent of the total power output. During the consolidation movement of the 1920s, many small town systems were to be sold to private companies. For the most part, this consolidation of companies and enlargement of the system occurred at the level of the state. So long as transactions remained within state boundaries, so in the Federal system were the industry's dealings with government likely to remain at state level. Thus, the essentially state-based development of the electricity supply industry in the United States contrasted with that of the gas industry, where the move of the industry from a coal to natural gas base shifted the industry into exploiting the economies of scale available on interstate pipelines and subjecting them thereby to Federal regulatory overview/jurisdiction.

In Britain, discoveries of commercially viable natural gas were made later than in the United States. As a consequence, and illustrative of the relationship between the economic and technological characteristics of an industry and its industrial structure, it was not until the second half of the twentieth century that the industry moved towards regional and national grids. Until then, the limited production economies of scale of coking coal-based gas and its high transport cost limited the range of its natural monopoly system. In contrast, in electricity generation, there was a much earlier technological and economic case for moving to supplying a larger area, but by the early twentieth century the ability to do so was constrained by the municipal form of ownership and the structure of important urban sections of the industry. Although the optimal area for electricity supply had grown as a result of technological improvements and increased scale economies in electricity generation, the local authorities made little effort to cooperate with each other and were particularly reluctant to cooperate with private companies in adjacent areas. The response of the national government was to initiate the construction of the larger, interconnecting natural monopoly, national grid, so as to increase the size of the market available to electricity producers. Accompanying this use of a natural monopoly to reduce the market power of local and municipal monopolies, the Central Electricity Board, which was established in 1926 by the Conservative Baldwin government to oversee the construction of the national grid, was given powers to close compulsorily the most inefficient power stations. Yet, the Baldwin government sought to play up the fact that industrial restructuring had been effected without any substantial interference with the form of ownership within the industry.

Thus, technological developments and available economies of scale shaped the industrial structure of the electricity supply industry at the national level in the centralized British political system and at the state level in the Federal United States. While in Britain, national and local governments had devised a mix of instruments for the regulation of utilities, in the United States the basis of regulation emerged from intermittent judicial decisions (Hunter 1917; Phillips 1984: 80; Viscusi, Harrington, and Vernon 2005: 363). In both Britain and the United States one response to the macroeconomic difficulties of the 1930s was to widen the scope of regulation as part of a developing industrial policy. Just as the economic difficulties of the 1930s were to see the British government take a greater interest in measures to initiate structural change in non-network-containing industries like coal mining, so too in the United States in the mid-1930s was there an extension of the scope of regulation. Indeed, the combination of the Supreme Court's 1934 ruling in *Nebbia v New York*, that an industry need not have a monopolistic structure to be regulated, and the politically protecting response to the economic depression of the early 1930s, widened the scope of regulation to cover at Federal level surface freight transport including trucks, water barges, oil pipelines, broadcasting, and telecommunications; at state level, oil production; and at interstate level, electricity and natural gas commerce. When immediately after the Second World War the French and British governments nationalized the major utilities like electricity and gas as well as extractive industries like coal mining, ownership was transferred from municipal and private hands to those of the central state. In contrast in the United States utilities remained as investor-owned utilities (IOUs) mainly regulated at state level. In 1944, the Supreme Court ruling in the *Hope Natural Gas* case left to the state commissions the determination of the rate base and the rate of return (Joskow and Schmalensee 1986). Yet, although the forms of ownership and point of regulatory impact differed on either side of the Atlantic, there was a similarity between forms of industrial structure driven by an economic and technological impetus. Thus, in the immediate post-war period, as the French and British governments moved to nationalize their gas, coal, and electricity industries as vertically integrated national monopolies, so too in the United States was vertical integration the dominant structure of state-based IOUs.

In addition to economic and technological considerations encouraging increased state interest and involvement in leading industries, there were also wider political concerns, notably with national security, which occasioned early state involvement. The influence of national security factors depended in part on the stage of political and economic development of the state or nation, and, most obviously, its foreign relations and policy. Thus while the railways in Britain were run by private companies throughout the nineteenth century, in a continental Europe pitted with wars of national unification, the railway system was nationalized in Prussia in 1879, in Germany in 1919, in Sweden in 1939, and in France in 1937. Similar considerations of national security encouraged state ownership of the postal and telecommunications services. Security considerations were also adduced for the establishment of national airlines and national government shareholdings in oil companies like British Petroleum and Azienda Generale Italia Petroli (AGIP). Among the reasons for the nationalization of industries in France in the 1940s was that of promoting national security through economic modernization (Millward 2005: 96).

The decision to nationalize industries in monopoly form, whether in the United States, France, or Britain, raised interesting questions concerning the appropriate basis for pricing output. That some form of price regulation would occur was inevitable given the monopoly structure of these industries and the claims of marginal cost pricing as the basis for nationalized industry pricing were pushed by welfare and industrial economists (Chick 2007: ch. 4). Not only would marginal cost pricing accurately signal to marginal consumers the resource cost of their marginal consumption, but the use of long-run marginal cost pricing at peak hours would reduce the capacity requirements of industries with non-stockable output such as electricity and telecommunications. While charging at long-run marginal cost (LRMC) would also expose more distant consumers to the costs of connection, these one-off costs could have been borne by the state or indeed by the industry itself, classically in a two-part tariff. However, other features of marginal cost pricing were unattractive to politicians, clashing as they did with other protective and redistributive motives for nationalization. In Britain, there was concern that using marginal, rather than average, cost pricing would put a stop to any cross-subsidizing intentions within the multi-pit cost structure of the coal-mining industry as well as exposing high-cost pits to competition not only from more efficient pits but also from the relative prices of other substitute fuels (oil). Within utilities, there were also likely to be differences in the cost of supplying urban and rural consumers because of differences in available economies of scale. Pricing at marginal cost in increasing returns industries was also likely to leave price below average (and therefore) total cost. Suggestions from economists like James Meade that profits in diminishing returns industries (where demand resulted in marginal cost pricing being above average costs) be used to offset losses in increasing returns industries did not hold much appeal for the nationalizing Labour government in Britain. The main concern of politicians like Herbert Morrison was explicitly to use the nationalized industries as an instrument of redistribution, in which the cross-subsidies implicit in average cost pricing were specifically favored.

Similar cross-subsidizing elements were also present in regulation in the United States. While in contrast to the "break-even" requirement in Britain the basis of regulation in the United States specified a rate of return based on capital assets, this also contained an important, averaging, cross-subsidizing component. Again this reflected political and regulatory concern as to the physical and financial availability of output. Such cross-subsidizing was easier within monopolies, and this may go some way to explain why mid-twentieth-century nationalization and regulation was often accompanied by the restructuring of the affected industries as monopolies. It was only in France, and then only in the electricity supply industry so as to take the edge off peak-hour demand and to encourage the modernization of industry, that progress was made in the adoption of marginal cost pricing (Chick 2002). Thus, with the exception of EDF, many utilities whether nationalized or regulated had their output priced in relation to average rather than marginal cost during the later 1940s, the 1950s, and the 1960s as these industries were used in part as instruments of redistribution.

Just as this chapter has argued that much of the organizational and market structure of industries like telecommunications, gas, electricity, and railways arose out of their technological and economic characteristics to which politicians then responded with a number of forms of social control, so too will it be argued that for all of the political noise surrounding the deregulation and privatization of industries from the 1970s and 1980s respectively, it was important developments in the technological and economic bases of these industries which underpinned many of these changes and aspirations for change. Similarly, just as local, state, national, and federal government responses to the development of these industries had been shaped by the capabilities of each form and level of government itself, so too were changes from the late 1960s affected by a changed perception of the capabilities of government. One source of political anxiety regarding the capabilities of governments concerned the ability of the public finances to sustain government expenditure and borrowing during the 1970s. However, this was not a new concern. In Britain, the 1961 White Paper had required nationalized industries to move away from covering costs to earning a stated rate of return on their assets (Cmnd. 1337 1961). If this rate of return on existing assets mimicked to some extent US-style regulation by offering guidelines as to the permitted returns on existing assets, the 1967 White Paper moved from the *ex post* to the *ex ante* in specifying the test discount rates which were to be attained before fixed capital investment projects could be undertaken (Cmnd. 3437 1967). In France, similar moves were made in the Nora Committee of 1966 and the subsequent Contract of 1970 negotiated between EDF and the government to allow, and require, nationalized industries to ease their pressure on the public finances by earning higher regulated returns on capital. Had British governments not introduced price controls on nationalized industry output as part of their anti-inflationary measures in the 1970s, thereby pointing perhaps to the need in the British system for a more independent industrial regulator, there was not per se any obvious reason why nationalized industries like electricity, gas, and telecommunications could not have continued as publicly owned monopolies making efficient financial contributions to the public purse. Where, as in Britain, nationalized industries like coal mining and railways encountered financial difficulties, this was mainly because of the emergence of strong competitive substitutes, in these cases oil and motor vehicles (and from airlines in the USA) respectively. Certainly, issues of public finance do not shed much light on why deregulation occurred in the United States during the 1970s, although they may provide much of the context just as general dissatisfaction may have done in the 1930s. The public finance problems help to explain why politicians became interested in change, just as dissatisfaction in the 1930s and experience of war provided a context in which politicians could seek change. Yet, just as in the mid-twentieth century many of the technological and economic factors making for larger, more concentrated industrial and market structures were already in place, so too in the 1970s technological developments underpinned the changes and deconcentration which did occur. This was certainly true of airlines, telecommunications, and electricity, all of which were variously deregulated, privatized, and liberalized in the US and the UK from the 1970s.

That airlines, especially in Europe, should have enjoyed some protection from international competition and a regulated fare structure was mainly the result of government concerns with the security of airplanes themselves and also of the airspace above each nation. Arising out of early government concerns with the security of the skies above their populations, governments had moved both to assert property rights over the "national" sky and, given the security and military significance of airlines, had also moved to promote the development of a national airline, be it KLM, Sabena, Air France, Alitalia, British Airways, or British European Airways. The partial segmenting of the market between national carriers each of which dominated its domestic market restricted competition and reduced the ability to exploit the economies of scale available on technologically improved and larger aircraft. This was less the case in the quantitatively and geographically larger and more homogeneous US market, and there big airlines like TWA, United Airlines, and American Airlines did develop and posed an increasing competitive threat to European national airlines. One European response was to establish a price cartel in 1945, the International Air Traffic Association (IATA), which effectively protected its national airlines from American competition, as well as from each other, by setting prices sufficiently high to protect high-cost airlines such as Air France with its

Caravelle and BOAC and BEA with their expensive Comet, Britannia, Trident, and VC10 aircraft. In economic terms, there was no substantial natural monopoly component in the airline industry, and the ability to limit international competition in this industry and to deny the cheaper fares and larger consumer surplus to citizens came under increasing strain from the late 1960s as higher per capita incomes financed an increase in international holiday travel. As technological developments resulted first in the replacement of the twin-engined monoplane of the 1930s by the DC-4s and Lockheed Constellation of the 1950s with their better pressurization, bigger payloads, and ability to travel longer distances, and then in the development of wide-bodied jets in the 1960s, the losses in terms of economic efficiency (and price) of the preservation of national carriers, price regulation, and the restriction of competition became increasingly evident. Eventually in 1965 the British government approved forty-six new licenses for independent airlines and abolished the monopoly of BOAC and BEA on scheduled services. By 1969, there were 5.7 million sun-starved Britons on foreign holidays and half were on package tours. However, the IATA-regulated scheduled services remained intact, although under increasing pressure (Millward 2005: 10, 180, 238, 240).

As in airlines, so too in telecommunications, where technological developments gave rise to a proliferation of available terminal value added network services (VANS), alongside the long-standing core activity of voice communication, while the development of mobile phones circumvented the sunk natural monopoly land-line network. With the bursting out of more and diverse forms of communication, a state-owned telecommunications monopoly appeared an increasingly inadequate and unnecessary means of safeguarding national security. Quite why the industry should be a state-owned monopoly with its terminal equipment supplied and even owned by the PTO which also set technical standards for all equipment became increasingly difficult to justify, especially when a large, competitive equipment and service—providing industry without any natural monopoly component was evidently so practicable.

In electricity, the relationship between technological development and industrial restructuring was more complex than in either airlines or telecommunications. The major technological developments in the industry from the end of the 1960s concerned not the technological progress of the industry, but the very lack of it. Rather than experiencing any major leap forward, thermal generation experienced what Richard Hirsh has termed "technological stasis," while nuclear power disappointed those who had seen it as a source of electricity "too cheap to meter." Technological and construction problems bedeviled the nuclear power industry such that from 1972 to 1975 the cost per kilowatt of new nuclear capacity rose 80 per cent while the cost of new coal-fired power plants doubled (Anderson 1981: 70). In the United States, in conventional thermal generating stations the economies of scale and technological advances which had caused electricity unit output costs and prices to fall during most of its lifetime began to dry up. Thermal efficiency gains in traditional steam turbine generator technology reached a new plateau, and economies of scale in building power plants ceased accruing. Thermodynamic theory limited steam systems to a maximum efficiency of about 48 per cent, while in practice, metallurgical problems appeared in boilers and turbines when efficiency reached 40 per cent. With their costs rising, companies were forced to approach state utility commissions for rate reviews (Joskow 1974). This contrasted sharply with the small number of applications for rate review during the Golden Age. Whereas in 1963 only three cases were being reviewed nationwide, in 1969 the number had increased to nineteen, and by 1975 it had shot up to 114. Rates to the average residential consumer more than doubled from 2.1 cents per kWh (in unadjusted terms) in 1969 to 4.4 cents in 1979. In the same period, rates for industrial customers increased from 0.9 cents to 2.6 cents per kWh (Anderson 1981). Moreover, as the issue arose as to who should bear the rising capital cost of nuclear power, the traditional regulatory assumptions came under increasing strain. Regulators began to squirm as they struggled to square their traditional obligation to provide utilities with a "fair" return with their reluctance to visit sharp price rises upon utility customers. It was precisely the regulatory inability to bridge the gap between what appeared to be fair to the company under original cost principles and what appeared to be fair to consumers in these circumstances that produced institutional breakdown, and opened up the possibility of a true "passing of the public utility concept" (Averch and Johnson 1962; Stigler and Friedland 1962; Stigler 1971; Kahn 1988: xxvi–xxviii, echoing Gray 1940). In the wake of the Three Mile Island accident, the imposition of increased safety requirements imposed unwanted higher costs on the nuclear industry, not least as load factor fell as plant stayed out of service for longer, but this was not the main cause of the industry's difficulties. More generally in the fuel and power sector, further dissatisfaction with regulation arose from the electricity peak-time "brownouts" (reduced voltage) on the East Coast in the summers of 1967–71, as well as from the natural gas supply failures which arose from a long-standing over-extension of regulation across the industry (Hirsh 1999: 59).

It was against this background of technological development (or the lack of it in the case of electricity) that the wider public finance and macroeconomic problems began to breed dissatisfaction with the existing way of doing things. In the United States and Britain, disgruntled politicians began to give a more receptive hearing to academic criticisms of regulation. Stigler and Posner's criticism of the capture of regulators by the regulated had its counterpart in Britain in concerns that sponsoring governments had become industry's, rather the consumer's, voice in government. Economists like Averch and Johnson criticized the gold-plating effects of capital-based regulation, while the problems of the nuclear industry pointed up the political limits to placing risk upon consumers in the regulatory system. The agency problems that existed between regulators and the regulated, and between ministers and public corporations, were well recognized by the 1970s, and in part were seen as arising from asymmetries of information which arose in turn from the often monopoly structure of the agent in the principal–agent relationship between government/regulators and industries. That the presence of a natural monopoly component within an industry necessarily required all of that industry being given monopoly status was also questioned more publicly, these criticisms reiterating those made by the likes of Horace Gray in the United States in the 1940s. Echoes of the 1940s were also heard increasingly loudly in the public reopening of the debate on the respective merits of marginal and average cost pricing. Pre-eminent among the evangelists of the marginalist cause in the 1970s was Alfred Kahn, the Cornell Professor of Political Economy, whose books on the economics of regulation appeared in 1970 and 1971 (Kahn 1988). Kahn's emphasis on the merits of marginal cost pricing chimed well with similar concerns with the size and distribution of the consumers' surplus, the precise location of the natural monopoly boundaries in increasingly multi-product utilities such as telecommunications, and as such the ability to distinguish between sustainable and contestable markets being evinced by other economists such as Baumol, Willig, and Sharkey (Baumol 1977; Baumol, Panzar, and Willig 1982; Sharkey 1982; Crew and Kleindorfer 1986: 26; Kahn 1988: 11–12).

In the United States, the translation of the economists' criticisms of the basis of the structure and practices of industrial regulation and of political dissatisfaction with their performance was eased by the willingness of some of the academic critics to become involved in the process of deregulation itself. Most importantly, Alfred Kahn took the opportunity to implement his ideas on pricing and competition, first as chairman of the New York State Public Service Commission (NYSPSC) from July 1974 and then, from 1977 as President Carter's appointment as the chairman of the Civil Aeronautics Board. Famously characterizing airplanes as marginal costs with wings, Kahn oversaw the deregulation of the airline industry in the United States following the Congressional passing of the 1978 Airline Deregulation Act. The often brutal success of that deregulation confirmed to many politicians the available increases in the consumers' surplus which might be flushed out by a program of deregulation. Often strange coalitions emerged among those for whom the interests of consumers became of heightened political and economic interest during the 1970s. Political support for deregulation cut across party lines with Ford, Carter, and Edward Kennedy among its high-profile backers. Kennedy was chair of the Subcommittee on Administrative Practice and Procedure of the Judiciary Committee, in which capacity he met Stephen Breyer, special counsel to the Subcommittee and an ardent advocate of regulatory reform. Breyer was a professor of administrative and antitrust law at Harvard and had worked in the Justice Department's Antitrust Division in the late 1960s at the time when it was beginning to get involved in regulatory proceedings. It was Breyer who, on joining the Subcommittee staff in the spring of 1974, urged Kennedy to consider airline regulation as a subject for investigative hearings. In such conditions, and given its earlier supply failures, it was difficult for the gas industry to avoid the regulatory eye. It certainly did not help the industry that Stephen Breyer had co-authored work with the economist Paul MacAvoy arguing for the deregulation of natural gas (Breyer and MacAvoy 1974; Derthick and Quick 1985: 35–40). In the same year, 1984, that AT&T was dismantled, so too was access to gas pipelines liberalized and natural gas well-head prices significantly decontrolled. A year later airline rates were completely deregulated with the abolition of the Civil Aeronautics Board on January 1, 1985. In the electricity supply industry, while the first, almost unintentional steps were taken in the 1978 Public Utility Regulatory Policies Act (PURPA) towards liberalizing the electricity markets, it was not until the 1992 Energy Policy Act and the subsequent orders issued by the Federal Energy Regulatory Commission (FERC) that efforts were made at a Federal legislative and regulatory level to promote the liberalization of electricity markets in the United States.

While privatization in the UK patently was concerned with the transfer of ownership, there was a complex relationship, born of experience, between privatization and efforts to promote the liberalization of former nationalized industry markets. In the fuel and power markets, efforts were made in the 1982 Oil and Gas (Enterprise) Act and the 1983 Energy Act to encourage competition. Both pieces of legislation reflected the outlook of the new Energy Secretary, Nigel Lawson, whose arrival in the Department of Energy in September 1981 marked a sharp break with its past practices. However, efforts to encourage competition in the industry were hampered by the incumbents' market power and by their continued influence over access to the grid. While British Gas's statutory monopoly on the pipeline system had been removed in the Oil and Gas (Enterprise) Act of 1982, it had been left free to deter and exclude entrants by setting uneconomic access charges. Similarly, in the 1983 Energy Act, the Central Electricity Generating Board (CEGB) had been left able to restructure tariffs so as to deter entry into potentially competitive markets (Newbery 1999: 178, 193). The outcome of these thwarted efforts to promote competition and to change ownership were instructive and influential in shaping the privatization of the electricity supply industry. They were taken to demonstrate the difficulty of promoting competition in markets dominated by an incumbent publicly owned monopoly. Separating out the grid component was a necessary but not sufficient condition for the promotion of competition to supply across the grid. The incumbent's power to influence access to the grid also had to be weakened.

If the attempted liberalization of energy markets in the absence of the effective restructuring of the industry was unsuccessful, no markedly greater success was achieved by efforts to promote competition through privatization. Whatever the short-term benefits of privatization (and these had to be set against the future income forgone from the privatization of profitable industries) there was a genuine interest in restructuring the industries through privatization into competitive forms. As it happened, information asymmetries and electoral time constraints made their influence felt, and the transfer of ownership took priority over the introduction of competition (Kay and Thompson 1986; Moore 1986; Chick 1994). British Telecom was privatized in 1984 as a vertically integrated monopoly owning the entire existing network to which Mercury as its sole licensed competitor was granted a time-limited access. Notoriously, British Gas was privatized in 1986 as a licensed monopoly. Any aspirant entrants were left to negotiate access terms with British Gas and unsurprisingly none of the ten attempts to secure access between 1982 and 1990 proved to be successful (Newbery 1999: 176, 193). Entry only occurred in 1990 after the Office of Fair Trading had forced British Gas to contract for no more than 90 per cent of new gas supply in 1989.

The consequence of the failed attempts to secure liberalization without privatization, and to obtain significant industrial and market restructuring as part of the process of privatization, was to push policy-makers in the 1989 Electricity Act to secure the desired industrial restructuring before the privatization of the electricity supply industry. The bare bones of such a restructuring required the competitive sections of the industry (e.g., generation, marketing, and retail supply) to be separated from the regulated sections (distribution, transmission, system operation) and access to the grid to be allowed on a fair basis for all (Joskow 2005: 38). Arrangements also needed to be made for an Independent System Operator (ISO) to manage the operation of the entire network. An early proposal for restructuring the CEGB was that generation should be split between five fossil fuel companies which together would jointly own a nuclear company. However, the government had misgivings over the practicability of being able to split the CEGB in this manner, and especially of being able to do so before the summer of 1991, the likely date of the next general election. The government was also resistant to a substantial break-up of the CEGB since it wished to privatize the nuclear power stations and to complete four Pressurized Water Reactors (PWRs). As such, it decided to group the twelve nuclear stations with a large fossil generation company, National Power.

In analyzing the processes and outcomes of industrial and market restructuring of the electricity supply industry in Britain and the United States, a number of comparative points and issues are worth emphasizing. The first concerns the civil nuclear power industry and the issue of risk. One set of risks concerned the future unknown costs of decommissioning and fuel reprocessing as well as the apportioning of risks in the construction of Sizewell B and three further PWRs. To finance the construction of the nuclear stations, very long contracts would need to be negotiated between National Power and the regional electricity companies (RECs) and both the cost and allocation of risk was uncertain (Henney 1994: 54, 59, 63, 141). Being unwilling to dupe shareholders about the full costs of nuclear power in the same way as successive governments had misled parliament, the government was forced to withdraw the nuclear power component from the privatization issue. However, it did not then alter the structure of the industry which no longer had to support the nuclear program. In the Electricity Act of 1989, National Power accounted for 60 per cent and PowerGen for 40 per cent of conventional generation capacity in the newly privatized industry. Sixty per cent of National Power and PowerGen was subsequently sold to the public in March 1991, with the balance sold in March 1995. At privatization, all twelve nuclear stations were placed in Nuclear Electric. Subsequently in 1996 the five newer advanced gas-cooled reactors were privatized as British Energy. The seven old Magnox reactors were moved to the publicly owned British Nuclear Fuels plc, the fuel reprocessing company. The British government had used public ownership to absorb the nuclear reactors which the market would not accept. This use of public funds and ownership to overcome what was a stranded asset problem provided a neat point of comparison with the attempts in the United States to introduce competition into the electricity supply industry (Gilbert and Kahn 1996: 185–6; Gilbert, Kahn, and Newbery 1996: 18; Newbery 1999: 153, 202–3, 260; Hunt 2002: 39, 264).

In the United States, while the 1978 PURPA legislation had been passed, its prime motive had not been market liberalization. Rather, fashionably embracing the marginal concept, the PURPA required utilities to purchase power from certain types of approved independent power producers called Qualifying Facilities (QFs) at the utility's avoided cost. The subsequent QF output was not subject to price regulation. Avoided cost was taken as being the cost which the utility "avoided" by not having to build its own plants, although that avoided cost could be set sufficiently high by state regulators so as to make these contracts highly lucrative for their owners (Hunt 2002: 257). QFs qualified on the grounds of their environmental friendliness, with co-generators and renewable energy facilities being the most favored forms of production. What gave PURPA its bite was the technological development of combined-cycle gas turbine (CCGT) which, deemed to be environmentally friendly, was given the QF imprimatur. Similarly, a co-generator used a small version of a utility's turbine generator, and, while lacking economies of scale, it benefited from the mass production of several of its key components. Its capital cost was between $800 and $1,200 per kw in 1986, which compared favorably with fossil fuel turbine generators, and was generally lower than the cost of nuclear units which ranged from anywhere between $932 and $5,192 per kw at the beginning of 1984. At such a cost, with prices unregulated, and utilities required to buy from QFs, the maths proved attractive. By 1992, 60 per cent of new capacity in the United States was being built by Independent Power Producers (IPPs) using mainly co-generation and renewable energy facilities. Nowhere were IPPs more active than in California, where by 1990, of about 56,000 MW of Californian capacity, 9,412 MW came from QFs. In 1991, non-utility companies in the Golden State provided one-third of the state's electricity, and 21 per cent of all of the electricity produced by IPPs in the United States (Joskow and Jones 1983; Hirsh 1999: 6, 93, 102–3; Joskow 2005). Yet while this marked a significant break with the traditional, regulated, vertically-integrated industry supplying a captive market and subject to cost-of-service regulation, it was not, nor was it ever intended to be, the spearhead for a fundamental restructuring of the industry and its markets. The impact of the IPPs remained at the level of the state, and then varied between states, and they sold on long-term contracts to the utilities (Crew and Kleindorfer 1986: 205).

Just as the development of CCGT reduced the cost of new entry into state-based electricity markets in the United States, and enabled avoided cost-based returns to be earned on capital assets, in so doing it highlighted the difficulties for the nuclear industry in earning an adequate return on its much larger actual and proportionate investment. While able to price itself into markets on the basis of its low marginal costs, it was then dependent on the price set in the market in the hope of recovering its sunk costs from a sufficiently large producers' surplus. Under historical regulatory arrangements, a reasonable return on such sunk investment was effectively guaranteed. Now, with nuclear capital and operating costs higher than expected, and CCGT causing prices to fall in electricity markets, deregulation effectively reneged on what many in the nuclear industry regarded as implicit contracts between them and the regulatory authorities.

Both regulatory hesitancy about passing on nuclear construction and operating costs to consumers and the encouragement given by PURPA to CCGT new entrants had undone the anticipated returns from nuclear investments leaving them with stranded assets and stranded costs. In addition, the contracts signed with QFs based on what the states and their utility commissions judged to be the utility's avoided costs could also be viewed as stranded contracts that locked the utilities into taking higher cost power than they would have done left to their own devices. Nowhere was this more so than in California, where in the post-1978 PURPA period, most of the early dealings with the QF new entrants centered on long-term contracts along the lines of what the European Commission was later to dub the single-buyer model. Under this arrangement, the existing integrated area monopoly bought from competing generators under life-of-plant contracts, the length of contract offering a safeguard against the potential monopsony power of the utility to manipulate its purchase price from the independent generator. Prices were decided and then regulated through a form of auction so as to determine the lowest cost offering. These contract prices were then passed on to the final customers as part of bundled tariffs and in general this limited form of competition kept risk with the customer. The risk borne by the QF was that while free of rate-of-return regulation and therefore offering the incentive of retaining profits arising from cost-reducing innovation, the outcome of new technology was uncertain and its costs less recoverable than in the case of regulated firms. While PURPA legislation applied to all states, nowhere were its possibilities relished more than in California. Yet the risks borne by customers of the early post-PURPA contracts signed with QFs became evident as many of these contracts were themselves revealed as stranded costs, as prices dropped well below the exaggerated estimates of future avoided costs originally made by state regulators (Gilbert and Kahn 1996: 201, 204; Newbery 1999: 260; Hunt 2002: 42, 257). The irony was that those states in which the potentially stranded costs and contracts contributed strongly to their electricity prices being higher than in other states were the very same states which were interested in exploiting the reforming opportunities offered by the Energy Policy Act of 1992, which were in turn to throw up yet more problems of stranded costs and assets. In 1995, while the average price of electricity in the United States was 6.9 cents/kWh, it was 9.9 cents/kWh in California, 10.3 cents/ kWh in Massachusetts, and 10.5 cents/kWh in Connecticut. Residential prices in those three states were 11.6 cents, 11.4 cents and 12 cents, exceeded only by New York at 14 cents/kWh, compared to the US average of 8.4 cents/kWh (Newbery 1999: 260; Hunt 2002: 257). California's efforts to secure cheaper electricity were, through a series of misjudgments and arguably nefarious behavior, to leave the state experiencing blackouts in 2000 and 2001.

The difficulties arising from stranded contracts affecting nuclear power arose because of the need in the United States for the IOUs at the very least to recover their capital cost. In Britain, these costs were simply absorbed by the state and the better parts of the nuclear industry subsequently privatized. In France, until fairly recently, any temptations to embrace such "Anglo-Saxon" notions as privatization and liberalization had been resisted. In fending off the efforts from the European Commission to liberalize, or at least open up, the French electricity market, the weighty presence of a nuclear-dominated form of generation allowed the low marginal costs of both nuclear and hydro to be used to deter new entrants. For the French, the main pressure for liberalization, but not privatization, has come from the European Commission. In December 1996 the Electricity Directive was drawn up by the European Commission requiring each member state gradually to open its market to competition, to a minimum of 33 per cent by 2003, and restructuring electricity generation by a single company to 50 per cent (Clifton, Comin, and Díaz-Fuentes 2007: 5). The main French responses to the European directives came in legislative acts passed in February 2000, January 2003, and August 2004, but often the European Commission's approach suited the French aims. While the European Commission's Second Directive in 2003 moved towards the creation of a single European electricity market by toughening the independent regulation of access to national and cross-border transmission systems and links, the European Commission was often unable to move directly against the dominant incumbent in the national economy. The European Commission did not push privatization as a route to restructuring and liberalization, and while developing conditions of access to the transmission system, it did little to move against dominant incumbents in Spain, Germany, Belgium, Portugal, as well as France. The relationship between the European Commission and the national electricity industries was not unlike that between the FERC and the state-based IOUs in the United States. The European Commission could encourage and cajole certain behavior, but it could not enforce it (Glachant and Finon 2005: 181; Newbery 1999: 4). While in the 2003 Electricity Directive the European Commission was to move against the single buyer and require the regulated third party access (TPA) model for access to distribution networks, the persistent presence of a dominant incumbent could act as a steady deterrent to new entrants. In France non-EDF suppliers served about 15 per cent of the eligible market in 2004, and the 2003 Directive required that all non-household customers could freely choose their electricity supply by 1 July 2004. Full market opening to include all household customers was to follow by 1 July 2007 (Jamasb and Pollitt 2005: 23–4).

It is only recently that the French government has moved to a French-style privatization of EDF, its previous reluctance to do so reflecting an approving view of the performance of EDF, such that neither its public ownership nor its national monopoly structure were seen as a source of weakness in the economy. In this view, it is supported by productivity data. While the annual growth rate of Total Factor Productivity (TFP) in the electricity supply industry in Britain was, at 2.54 per cent p.a., superior to that in the United States (1.85 per cent p.a.) between 1960 and 1979, the British performance slipped to 1.78 per cent p.a. for 1979–89, and 1.22 per cent p.a. in 1989–97. In contrast, in the United States, the industry's TFP improved to 2.6 per cent in 1979–89 before falling slightly to 2.55 per cent. On this basis, the total factor productivity performance of the electricity industry in Britain was better as a nation-alized than as a privatized industry, and during the period of deregulation, privatiza-tion, and liberalization its productivity performance fell significantly below that of the industry in the United States. However, in both countries the TFP performance lagged considerably that of the French nationalized electricity monopoly. In France, the electricity supply industry experienced an annual growth rate of TFP of 3.08 per cent in 1960–79, this increasing to 4.17 per cent in 1979–89 before falling back to 3.09 per cent p.a. in 1989–97. For the entire period 1960–97, the annual growth rate of TFP was 2.05 in Britain, 2.2 per cent in the United States, and 3.38 per cent in France (O'Mahony and Vecchi 2001; Weyman-Jones 2003; Millward 2005: 276).

The economic characteristics of network industries, with their initial high sunk costs and subsequent marginal costs often being below average costs at most levels of demand, led potential investors to seek credible assurances that adequate returns would be earned on any investment undertaken. Regulation and public ownership were but differing responses to these problems of uncertainty and commitment. That the social benefits of such investment could exceed private benefits, and that the output of such industries was regarded as essential to everyday life, made it likely that some form of government involvement would ensue. Where major projects with the same mix of sunk and marginal costs, such as the Channel Tunnel between France and England, were largely privately financed, the experience was not encouraging. The Channel Tunnel cost £5 billion to construct, twice as much to finance, and shareholders never recovered their investment. That the social benefits, in the presence of ferry and airplane substitutes, were minimal vindicated the UK Treasury's unwillingness to become involved (Gourvish 2006).

That public ownership faded as an approach to influencing the behavior of these industries reflected as much public finance and agency difficulties as any intrinsic problem in public ownership as such. Public finance problems arose in part out of relative productivity problems which were fundamental to the labor-intensive personal services component of the public sector. In the 1970s and 1980s these problems were exacerbated by the increase in the number of those drawing unemployment benefit. Agency problems arose from a fundamental paradox bedeviling nationalization. Governments took network industries into public ownership on the assumption that ownership would enhance their control over industries for whose performance they were politically responsible. In fact, public ownership by enhancing responsibility only seemed to weaken control as it strengthened the industry's position in its relationship with government (Chick 1998: chs. 4, 5). That industries were usually nationalized in monopoly form, with that monopoly extending either side of the natural monopoly network component of the industry, simply exaggerated the asymmetries of information bedeviling the government (principal) – agent (industry) relationship in the industry. Yet similar agency problems afflicted relations between regulators and the regulated in the United States, and recent evidence from Europe, where even supposedly liberalized network industries are increasingly characterized by vertical integration, suggests that the balancing of a wish to secure consumers' interests through competition with a concern to provide producers with sufficient incentive to invest in the industry's productive and distributive capacity is still very much work in progress. The conjunction of high sunk costs, low marginal costs over much of the range of output, and the political sensitivity of network utility output is likely to provide the durable basis for government involvement with these network industries, irrespective of changes in fashionable political approaches to forms of ownership and regulation, for many years to come.

REFERENCES

ANDERSON, D. 1981. *Regulatory Politics and Electric Utilities*. Boston, Mass.: Auburn House.

AVERCH, H., and JOHNSON, L. L. 1962. "Behaviour of the firm under regulatory constraint," *American Economic Review* 52: 1052–69.

BAUMOL, W. 1977. "On the proper tests for a natural monopoly in a multiproduct industry," *American Economic Review* 67(5): 809–22.

——PANZAR, J., and WILLIG, R. 1982. *Contestable Markets and the Theory of Industry Structure*. New York: Harcourt, Brace, Jovanovich.

BREYER, S., and MacAVOY, P. 1974. *Energy Regulation by the Federal Power Commission*. Washington, DC: Brookings Institution.

BYATT, I. 1979. *The British Electrical Industry 1875–1914*. Oxford: Clarendon Press.

CHICK, M. 1994. "Nationalisation, privatisation and regulation," in M. Rose and M. Kirby, eds., *Business Enterprise in Modern Britain*. London: Routledge, 315–38.

——1998. *Industrial Policy in Britain*. Cambridge: Cambridge University Press.

——2002. "Le Tarif Vert retrouvé: the marginal cost concept and the pricing of electricity in Britain and France, 1945–1970," *Energy Journal* 23(1): 97–116.

——2007. *Electricity and Energy Policy in Britain, France and the United States since 1945*. Cheltenham: Edward Elgar.

CLIFTON, J., COMIN, F., and DÍAZ-FUENTES, D. 2007. "Transforming network services in Europe and the Americas: from ugly ducklings to swans?" in J. Clifton, F. Comin, and D. Díaz-Fuentes, *Transforming Public Enterprise in Europe and North America: Networks, Integration and Transnationalisation*. Houndmills: Palgrave, Macmillan.

Cmnd. 1337. 1961. *The Financial and Economic Obligations of the Nationalised Industries*, London: HMSO.

Cmnd. 3437. 1967. *Nationalised Industries: A Review of Economic and Financial Objectives*, London: HMSO.

CREW, M., and KLEINDORFER, P. 1986. *The Economics of Public Utility Regulation*. Cambridge, Mass.: MIT Press.

DERTHICK, M., and QUIRK, P. 1985. *The Politics of Deregulation*. Washington, DC: Brookings Institution.

FOREMAN-PECK, J., and MILLWARD, R. 1994. *Public and Private Ownership of British Industry, 1820–1990*. Oxford: Clarendon Press.

GILBERT, R., and KAHN, E., eds. 1996. *International Comparisons of Electricity Regulation*. Cambridge: Cambridge University Press.

——————and NEWBERY, D. 1996. "Introduction," in R. Gilbert and E. Kahn, eds., *International Comparisons of Electricity Regulation*. Cambridge: Cambridge University Press, 1–24.

GLACHANT, J.-M., and FINON, D. 2005. "A competitive fringe in the shadow of a state-owned incumbent: the case of France," *Energy Journal*, Special Edition pp. 181–204.

GOURVISH, T. 2006. *The Official History of Britain and the Channel Tunnel*. London: Routledge.

GRAY, H. 1940. "The passing of the public utility concept," *Journal of Land and Public Utility Economics* 16(1): 8–20.

HENNEY, A. 1994. *A Study of the Privatisation of the Electricity Supply Industry in England and Wales*. London: EEE.

HIRSH, R. 1989. *Technology and Transformation in the American Electric Utility Industry*. Cambridge: Cambridge University Press.

——1999. *Power Loss: The Origins of Deregulation and Restructuring in the American Electric Utility System*. Cambridge, Mass.: MIT Press.

HUNT, S. 2002. *Making Competition Work in Electricity.* New York: John Wiley.

HUNTER, M. 1917. "Early regulation of public service corporations," *American Economic Review* September 7: 569–81.

JAMASB, T., and POLLITT, M. 2005. "Electricity market reform in the European Union: review of progress towards liberalisation and integration," *Energy Journal,* Special Edition pp. 11–41.

JOSKOW, P. 1974. "Inflation and environmental concern: structural change in the process of public utility price regulation," *Journal of Law and Economics* 17(2): 291–327.

—— 2005. "The difficult transition to competitive electricity markets in the United States," in J. Griffin and S. Puller, eds., *Electricity Deregulation: Choices and Challenges.* Chicago: University of Chicago Press, 31–97.

—— BOHI, D., and GALLOP, F. 1989. "Regulatory failure, regulatory reform, and structural change in the electrical power industry," *Brookings Papers on Economic Activity: Microeconomics,* pp. 125–208.

—— and JONES, D. 1983. "The simple economics of industrial cogeneration," *Energy Journal* 4(1): 1–22.

—— and SCHMALENSEE, R. 1986. "Incentive regulation for electric utilities," *Yale Journal on Regulation* 4(1): 1–49.

KAHN, A. 1988. *The Economics of Regulation: Principles and Institutions.* Cambridge, Mass.: MIT Press. First published in two volumes: *The Economics of Regulation: Principles and Institutions,* i: *Economic Principles,* 1970; ii: *Institutional Issues,* 1971. New York: John Wiley & Sons.

KAY, J., and THOMPSON, D. 1986. "Privatisation: a policy in search of a rationale," *Economic Journal* 96(381): 18–32.

LYNCH, F. 1984. "Resolving the paradox of the Monnet Plan: national and international planning in French reconstruction," *Economic History Review,* 2nd ser. 37(2): 229–43.

McCRAW, T. 1984. *Prophets of Regulation.* Cambridge, Mass.: Belknap Press of Harvard University Press.

MILLWARD, R. 2005. *Private and Public Enterprise in Europe: Energy, Telecommunications and Transport, 1830–1990.* Cambridge: Cambridge University Press.

—— 2007a. "Cross-border investment and service flows in networks within Western Europe, c.1830–1980," in J. Clifton, F. Comin, and D. Díaz-Fuentes, *Transforming Public Enterprise in Europe and North America: Networks, Integration and Transnationalisation.* Houndmills: Palgrave, Macmillan.

MILLWARD, R. 2007b. "Explaining institutional change in the networks: Britain in comparative perspective, 1945–90," in J. Clifton, F. Comin, and D. Díaz-Fuentes, eds., *Transforming Public Enterprise in Europe and North America: Networks, Integration and Transnationalisation.* Houndmills: Palgrave, Macmillan.

MOORE, J. 1986. "Why privatise?" in J. Kay, C. Mayer, and D. Thompson, eds., *Privatisation and Regulation: The UK Experience.* Oxford: Clarendon Press, 78–93.

NEWBERY, D. 1999. *Privatization, Restructuring and Regulation of Network Utilities.* Cambridge, Mass.: MIT Press.

O'MAHONY, M., and VECCHI, M. 2001. "The electricity supply industry: a study of an industry in transition," *National Institute Economic Review* 177(3): 85–99.

PHILLIPS, C., Jr. 1984. *The Regulation of Public Utilities.* Arlington, Va.: Public Utilities Reports.

SHARKEY, W. 1982. *The Theory of Natural Monopoly.* Cambridge: Cambridge University Press.

STIGLER, G. 1971. "The theory of economic regulation," *Bell Journal of Economics and Management Science* 2(1): 3–21.

Stigler, G. and Friedland, C. 1962. "What can regulators regulate? The case of electricity," *Journal of Law and Economics* 5: 1–16.

Viscusi, W. K., Harrington, J., and Vernon, J. 2005. *Economics of Regulation and Antitrust.* Cambridge, Mass.: MIT Press.

Weyman-Jones, T. 2003. "Yardstick competition and efficiency benchmarking in electricity distribution," in L. Hunt, ed., *Energy in a Competitive Market.* Cheltenham: Edward Elgar, 35–60.

CHAPTER 31

....

ENDOGENOUS TRADE PROTECTION

A SURVEY

....

CHRISTOPHER S. P. MAGEE

STEPHEN P. MAGEE

....

INTRODUCTION

....

THIS chapter surveys the literature on the political economy of trade policy. We organize the discussion around five propositions:

1. Lobby groups representing the interests of business have incentives to affect both election outcomes and gain influence over politicians in office.
2. Governments are thus influenced to care about more than just maximizing social welfare.
3. Lobby groups organize along industry lines to affect trade policies in the short run but along factor lines to influence long-run trade policies.
4. Global markets are becoming more powerful than nation states.
5. Openness (and good economic policies generally) are more important than democracy for economic success.

The first two propositions listed above are widely accepted. The first is just a statement about the ways in which interest groups can influence government policies. The second proposition is the central point made in the political economy literature, and it explains the existence of policies that transfer income within a country while clearly reducing national welfare. Governments choose trade (and other) policies that are not welfare maximizing because policy-makers are affected by political as well as economic considerations. One of the ways in which political considerations enter into the decision-making process is when businesses and other interest groups become organized to put pressure on the government. Proposition three discusses how interest groups will be organized in their lobbying over trade policy. Our discussion of these propositions provides a survey of the recent literature on the political economy of trade policy. For an earlier survey of the political economy of trade policy see Rodrik (1995), and for a recent survey of EU lobbying see Coen (2007).

The last two propositions are more recent and more controversial. Both of these effects are weakening protectionist forces globally. In proposition four, we discuss the evidence that globalization has weakened the autonomy of nation states. Because the list of recent economic success stories includes several authoritarian governments and because interest groups can gain influence over policies in both democracies and autocracies, we argue in proposition five that democracy is not a necessary condition for economic success. Good economic policies, such as openness, are a necessary condition, however, and as such, appear to have a larger impact on whether a country develops a strong economy than does its political system. Nations with global economic strategies and high literacy we call "globalist states." They have become models for economic success in the twenty-first century.

Lobby Groups Representing the Interests of Business Have Incentives to Affect Both Election Outcomes and Gain Influence over Politicians in Office

As Magee and Magee (2004) discuss, James Madison warned against the problem of interest groups in Federalist Paper No. 10. The basic idea is that political power can create wealth and economic wealth can create political power. It is this mutual attraction between power and money that motivates wasteful redistributive activity and results in inefficient policies such as trade protection. Individuals and groups devote resources to predatory redistribution as long as the expected gains exceed the costs.

Interest groups representing firms can affect government policies either by getting sympathetic candidates into office or by gaining influence over politicians in power. There are well-developed models of endogenous trade policies based on each of these channels. The Magee, Brock, and Young (1989; hereafter MBY) model assumes that businesses and other interest groups contribute money to affect election outcomes. There are two parties: a protectionist party and a proexport party. Import-competing industries give money to the protectionist party in order to advance its chance of winning the election. A larger tariff offered in the protectionist party's platform provides a stronger incentive for the protection-desiring interest groups to contribute money, and their donations increase. The party is a Stackelberg leader of the interest groups, and it chooses a tariff that maximizes its chance of winning election. In doing so, it has to weigh the gain in votes from having more money to spend as it raises the tariff in its platform against the votes that are lost as the tariff's distortions reduce economic welfare. Magee (1997) provides a more extended summary of the MBY results.

Several results emerge from this work. One is the compensation effect. When there is an economic downturn, the rate of return to economic activity falls. Capital and labor rationally transfer time and effort out of economic activity and into political lobbying. Politicians increase inefficient policies such as protection that partially offset the downturn effect, thereby partially compensating or offsetting the initially negative drop in the rate of return. The negative of this is that a global economic downturn could lead to global lobbying for import protection. An example is the disastrous US Smoot–Hawley tariff of 1930, which ignited a world trade war that deepened and extended the Great Depression. Compensation effects have been observed by Williamson (2003) in the rise and fall of world tariffs from 1789 to 1938; by Brainard and Verdier (1997) in the political economy of declining industries; by Rama (1994) in trade policy in Uruguay 1925–83; and by Bilal (1998) in increased demand for trade protection with regionalism.

Another result from MBY is that endogenous politics leads to increasing returns to capital worldwide and polarization of country capital–labor ratios. Since both capital and labor attempt to influence democracies, capital has more influence in the political systems of advanced countries while labor has more influence in poor countries. Politics thus increases the rates of return to capital (both physical and human) in advanced countries through more favorable policies (leading to even more capital accumulation) and decreases the rates of return to capital in poor countries (in some cases trapping them in poverty). With globalization, capital is thus attracted to countries where wealth is already abundant, making them richer. This explains that tariff rates decrease the higher the income of advanced countries because of a special-interest lobbying effect: the power of the pro-export factor, capital, rises relative to labor, the protectionist factor, the higher the level of economic development.[1] Chiu (1998) finds the MBY effect of increasing returns to factor endowments in a Grossman and Helpman (1994) model.

The most extensively studied model in which interest groups gain influence over politicians already in office is the Protection for Sale model of Grossman and Helpman (1994; GH hereafter). Most recent studies of government–business relationships in trade policy are conducted within the framework of this model. There are several reasons for its popularity. One is that the model is tractable, so it can be modified and extended easily in order to analyze many government policies. A second reason is that it is seen as providing microfoundations for earlier models of endogenous trade policy, such as the tariff function approach of Findlay and Wellisz (1982). That model assumes that tariffs are a function of political contributions, with greater contributions leading to higher levels of protection. The tariff function is posited in a black-box manner, however, while the tariff that emerges in the GH model, as in MBY, comes from the interaction of utility-maximizing agents. Finally, the GH model has found some empirical support in recent years from a number of studies that attempt to estimate it. Eicher and Osang (2002), for example, present a unified theoretical framework in which they can test the GH model against the tariff function approach. While both models perform well empirically, J-tests suggest that the GH model provides a much better fit for the data. Empirical work that builds on the GH model is discussed below.

The Grossman and Helpman (1994) model adopts a very simple basic structure in order to remain tractable. All consumers are assumed to have identical preferences that are quasilinear and separable by industry:

$$u = c_0 + \sum_{i=1}^{n} u_i(c_i), \tag{1}$$

where c_i is consumption of good i (sector 0 is the numeraire) and u_i is the subutility function for sector i. Since the utilities are separable by industry, demand for each good depends only on the good's price. The numeraire good is produced using only labor, with constant returns to scale, and one unit of labor produces one unit of the good. Since the price of the numeraire is set to one, the wage paid to labor also equals one.

The political interactions rely on the menu-auction work of Bernheim and Whinston (1986). Some industries are assumed to be successful in overcoming the free-rider problem so that they are able to form lobbies, while others are not. Lobby formation is taken as exogenous in the model. The lobbies offer the government policy-maker a contribution schedule in which greater contributions are offered in exchange for more favorable trade policies. The government policy-maker is assumed to have a utility function that values both contributions and social welfare:

$$G = \sum_{i \in L} C_i(\mathbf{p}) + aW(\mathbf{p}), \tag{2}$$

where $C_i(\mathbf{p})$ is the industry i contribution, L is the set of industries that have formed a lobby, and W is social welfare. The parameter a is the weight that the policy-maker places on aggregate social welfare relative to contributions. When the lobbies offer truthful contribution schedules, the equilibrium tariff for industry i is

$$\frac{t_i}{1 + t_i} = \frac{I_i - \alpha_L}{a + \alpha_L} \cdot \frac{z_i}{e_i}, \tag{3}$$

where t_i is the ad valorem tariff rate, I_i is an indicator variable that equals one if industry i is organized and zero otherwise, α_L is the fraction of the country's population that is represented by an organized industry lobby, z_i is the inverse import–penetration ratio (domestic output over imports), and e_i is the absolute value of the price elasticity of import demand. This is a "modified Ramsey rule" for tariffs. Tariffs are more costly for society when the import demand elasticity is larger. Since policy-makers dislike imposing welfare costs on voters, there are smaller equilibrium tariffs on products with high import demand elasticities.

There are a number of ways that the model has been extended since its publication. First, the model assumes that tariffs are set unilaterally in a small country. Grossman and Helpman (1995) consider the case in which tariffs are negotiated internationally and countries have a terms of trade incentive for protection. Most of the conclusions of the small country unilateral tariff case carry over to the results of international negotiations. Industries receive higher tariffs when they are large, politically organized, have inelastic import demand, and have a government that values campaign contributions highly. An industry also receives high protection in this model when the exporting industry in the foreign country is smaller, not organized politically, and has elastic export supply.

A second simplification in the GH model is that lobby formation is taken to be exogenous. The first paper to endogenize lobby formation within this framework was Mitra (1999). Mitra assumes that there are fixed costs to lobby formation. The owners of sector-specific capital in each industry decide whether or not to organize politically by considering the expected gains from organization against the costs. There are several interesting new results. The tariff that an already organized industry receives may actually decline as the government begins to care more deeply about campaign contributions. When government affinity for contributions rises, the gain to political organization increases, and thus sector-specific capital owners in more industries are encouraged to form lobbies. The greater lobbying competition may result in a lower equilibrium tariff even though the government now cares less about social welfare.

Magee (2002a) introduces endogenous lobby formation in a slightly different way. In the first stage, lobbies bargain with the government policy-maker over a contribution schedule, which reveals the tariff the industry will receive in exchange for each amount of contributions given. The paper shows that this interaction between lobby and policy-maker results in a tariff function that has some of the characteristics typically assumed in the literature: tariffs increase with contributions but at a decreasing rate, and the tariff is zero if contributions are zero. It thus provides microfoundations for the Findlay and Wellisz (1982) tariff function approach. The individual firms in the industry (taking the tariff function as given) decide whether to cooperate with the other firms in the industry lobbying effort or to defect from the effort, in which case they are punished by noncooperative behavior from the other firms in the future. In that way, lobby formation becomes a profit-maximizing choice made by individual firms.

Hoffman (2005) points out a time consistency problem in the GH framework. Once the government has set trade barriers, firms have no incentive to contribute. If the contributions come first, the government has no incentive to implement trade barriers that lower social welfare. Thus, there is a prisoner's dilemma in lobbying, and in the static equilibrium there are no contributions and no tariffs. Using a political support function from Hillman (1982), Hoffman shows that an equilibrium with contributions and positive tariffs can be sustained in an infinitely repeated game if the players are sufficiently patient. If there is a chance of a politician being removed from office, it makes cooperation between the firm and politician more difficult. Thus, stable dictatorships have more redistribution and higher trade barriers than do democracies or fragile dictatorships. The conclusion differs from Staiger and Tabellini (1987) who argued that the government could not commit not to surprise workers with protection since surprise protection is less costly than anticipated protection. The workers realize the government has a time consistency problem and they anticipate protection, which leads to higher protection. Thus, discretion in their model leads to higher tariffs.

Do interest groups try to gain influence over government policy-makers directly, as in GH, or do they try to affect election outcomes, as in MBY? Bronars and Lott (1997) find that, despite a large decline in contributions received during their last election cycle, retiring legislators do not change their voting patterns. They interpret this evidence to mean that PAC contributions do not change politicians' behavior. They also note that major political action committees claim that they almost never give to both candidates in the same election.

Stratmann (1998) argues that the timing of contributions suggests interest groups try to influence both elections and congressional votes. He finds that farm PACs increased contributions around the times of farm subsidy votes in Congress as well as near the primary and general elections. Welch (1980) also found evidence that interest groups donated more money to likely winners than they did to candidates in close races. Groups would contribute primarily to the latter if they wanted only to influence elections. Snyder (1992) also notes that PACs tend to donate heavily to senior incumbents who face little electoral opposition.

Magee (2002b) finds that PAC contributions have a significant influence on policy positions for only one out of five issues examined. That result suggests that on most issues, interest groups focus on election outcomes. There may be a split between ideological groups and economic or investor PACs, such as firms. Magee (2007) shows that defense industry firms contributed heavily to safe incumbents, suggesting they wished to gain influence, while the more ideological peace PACs gave money primarily to challengers in close races, indicating a focus on elections. Thus, while interest groups have an incentive both to sway elections and to gain influence, the jury is out on how much emphasis groups place on each strategy.

Governments Care about more than just Maximizing Social Welfare

This proposition is probably considered a stylized fact given the proliferation of government policies (such as the US sugar quota) that reduce national income while transferring wealth to well-organized interest groups. One way that researchers have attempted to show that labor and business groups influence trade policy decisions is by linking PAC contributions to legislators' votes in Congress. Baldwin and Magee (2000), for example, show that business PAC money swayed representatives to vote in favor of both the NAFTA and GATT Uruguay Round implementation bills while labor money influenced them to vote against the two bills. Other papers, such as Stratmann (1991 and 2002), have also found a significant link between congressional votes and PAC contributions. The conclusion that campaign contributions allow interest groups to influence representatives' votes is not universal, however. Levitt (1995) and Bender and Lott (1996) both review the literature and find that the effect of PAC contributions on congressional voting is minimal.

One way of attaining a measure of how much the government cares about social welfare in its trade policy decisions is by estimating the Grossman and Helpman (1994) model empirically. The parameter a in equation (2) provides an indication of the weight placed by government policy-makers on welfare relative to contributions. The first papers to test the GH model empirically were Goldberg and Maggi (1999) and Gawande and Bandyopadhyay (2000). They and others testing the model write the equilibrium tariff from equation (3) in a form that is empirically estimable:

$$\frac{t_i}{1 + t_i} = \gamma \frac{z_i}{e_i} + \delta I_i \frac{z_i}{e_i} + \varepsilon_i, \tag{4}$$

where $\gamma = \frac{-\alpha_L}{a+\alpha_L}$, $\delta = \frac{1}{a+\alpha_L}$, and ε_i is an error term added to the equation to account for factors outside the model that affect tariff rates. Once the parameters γ and δ are estimated, they can be used to calculate the underlying parameters in the model a and α_L. The Grossman and Helpman model predicts that $\gamma < 0$, $\delta > 0$, and $\gamma + \delta > 0$.

Both papers conclude that the empirical evidence is consistent with the predictions of the theory. In particular, protection decreases with the variable $\frac{z_i}{e_i}$ in unorganized industries ($\gamma < 0$) and increases with the variable $\frac{z_i}{e_i}$ in organized industries ($\delta > 0$). In both papers, the prediction that $\gamma + \delta > 0$ finds only weak support. The sum of the two coefficients is positive, but it is not statistically significantly different from zero. Both papers also explore adding alternative variables into the regressions that the existing literature suggests should affect protection levels, such as concentration levels in the industry and changes in import penetration. In Goldberg and Maggi (1999), these extra variables did not significantly improve the fit of the basic empirical model based on a strict interpretation of the GH theory. In Gawande and Bandyopadhyay (2000), the expanded model was found to be a better fit for the data by one test (the Akaike information criterion) but the sparse GH specification was preferred by a different measure (the Schwarz information criterion). One surprising result in both papers, discussed further below, is that the government is estimated to value social welfare much more highly than it values contributions.

There are a number of complications the papers had to address in estimating equation (4). The first is what protection measure to use. The GH model describes levels of protection chosen unilaterally, but US tariffs are determined through multilateral negotiations in the GATT/WTO. Thus, Goldberg and Maggi (1999), Gawande and Bandyopadhyay (2000), and most subsequent studies have used nontariff barrier coverage ratios as the measure of protection. This is clearly an imperfect measure of protection, but it appears to be the best that is available for the United States. Facchini, van Biesebroeck, and Willmann (2006) argue that there is an important distinction between testing the model based on tariffs and using nontariff barriers: tariffs allow the government to capture the tariff revenue while quota rents from nontariff barriers often go to foreign exporters. They argue that using nontariff barriers to test a model based on tariffs is likely to lead to biased coefficient estimates. Maggi and Rodriguez-Clare (2000) also show that allowing the government to use nontariff barriers (quotas and VERs) to redistribute income and introducing a cost of public funds dramatically changes the predictions of models such as GH. Thus, testing GH using data on nontariff barriers can be problematic.

Several papers have tested the GH model using tariff data. Mitra, Thomakos, and Ulubasoglu (2002) use data on several different protection measures (including tariffs) in Turkey, and they also find general support for the predictions of the GH model. Like Goldberg and Maggi (1999) and Gawande and Bandyopadhyay (2000), they find that the government places a much greater weight on social welfare than on campaign contributions. Interestingly, the government cared more about social welfare during periods of democracy in Turkey than during periods of dictatorship.

Another paper that tests the GH model using tariff data is McCalman (2004). He estimates the model using tariff data for Australia from the late 1960s and early 1990s. Australia was considered by the GATT to be a country midway between developing and developed so it had greater flexibility in setting its tariffs unilaterally than did the United States and other GATT members. The GH model is also meant to apply to a small country, which more clearly fits the case of Australia than of the United States.[2] McCalman finds results that are similar to Goldberg and Maggi (1999). The weight placed by the government on social welfare is estimated to be over 40 times larger than the weight on contributions, and 88–96 per cent of the population is estimated to be represented by a lobby.

A second difficult issue is how to determine which industries are organized. The issue of which industries are counted as organized can have a large impact on the results, as several of the papers discussed below reveal. The data consist of three-digit SIC industries, and every one of these industries had positive campaign contributions. Goldberg and Maggi (1999) argue that many contributions are given to influence domestic policies, however, and the contributors may not make an effort to influence trade policy. They consider an industry as organized if it has more than $100 million in contributions in the 1981–2 election cycle. Any threshold level chosen will be somewhat arbitrary, but they argue that there is a natural break in the data at that point. Gawande and Bandyopadhyay (2000) regress PAC contributions per firm as a share of industry value added on bilateral import penetration interacted with industry dummies. Positive coefficients on the industry dummy variables indicated that the industry was organized with respect to trade policy. This method assumes that organized industries respond to higher import-penetration with greater lobbying efforts. This assumption relates to the compensation effect from Magee, Brock, and Young (1989) in which firms compensate for greater competition from foreign suppliers by getting the government to provide higher tariff protection. They provide evidence of a compensation effect by showing that declines in the price of US imports relative to its exports are correlated with increases in protection levels between the 1920s and 1980s.

Two other difficulties in estimating the model arise. One is that the key explanatory variables are endogenous. The import penetration ratio is affected by the level of protection, and so it can not be treated as an exogenous regressor. Both Goldberg and Maggi (1999) and Gawande and Bandyopadhyay (2000) set up systems of equations in which the inverse import penetration ratio and the industry organization variable are both endogenous. A final difficulty is that the elasticities are estimates and thus are measured with error, and measurement errors in explanatory variables lead to biased coefficient estimates. Goldberg and Maggi (1999) solve this problem by bringing the elasticities over to the left-hand side of equation (4) before estimating it. Gawande and Bandyopadhyay use an errors-in-variables correction they develop based on Fuller (1987).

While the results are broadly supportive of the GH theory's predictions, the estimates provide several surprises. First, the coefficient estimates imply that the underlying parameter a (the weight placed by the government policy-maker on social welfare relative to contributions) in the model is extremely large. Goldberg and Maggi's estimates mean the government values a dollar of social welfare fifty to seventy times greater than it values a dollar of campaign contributions. The basic model estimated in Gawande and Bandyopadhyay (2000) implies that $a = 3175$, so that the policy-maker values welfare thousands of times more than contributions. In practice, then, these estimates suggest that the government is for all practical purposes welfare maximizing. As Gawande and Bandyopadhyay point out, this extremely high estimate conflicts with other studies showing that efficiency losses from protection are many times greater than what is spent by lobbies to obtain it. It also seems to contradict much of the literature on political economy written over the past forty years, where the government is often found to be responsive to lobbying and to enact policies such as trade barriers that reduce social welfare. As Gawande and Pravin Krishna (2003: 213) explain, "The primary explanation offered in this literature is that suboptimal policies are chosen because policies are not set by those who seek to maximize economic efficiency."

The government is estimated to place such a high weight on social welfare because of a need to reconcile the obvious gains to firms from lobbying for tariff protection with the low levels of protection actually given by governments in developed countries. The producer and consumer distortions caused by tariffs are very small at low levels of protection and these are the only costs of trade barriers in the GH model. Thus, if the government puts any significant weight on contributions in its utility function, it should be willing to give out considerable protection.

The conclusion that the government must really care mostly about welfare is related to the question asked by Gordon Tullock (1972) and later investigated by Ansolabehere, de Figueiredo, and Snyder (2003): "Why is there so little money in US politics?" They show that the value of gaining a share of influence over government policies is so great that firms should give much more money to politicians than they do. Given the gains to firms of lobbying in the GH model, we should see much more generous contributions and much higher levels of protection than are actually observed in practice. To explain the low tariffs within the context of the GH model requires that the government be fairly close to a welfare maximizer (or that the share of the population represented by a lobby be very high, which many studies also find).

The low level of protection may be a result of free riding rather than government benevolence. The GH model treats lobby formation as exogenous: some industries are able to overcome the free-rider problem and lobby in such a way as to maximize the gains to all the specific factor owners in the industry. Other industries are assumed to be unorganized and unable to lobby at all. In Gawande and Bandyopadhyay (2000), more than two-thirds of industries are classified as politically organized. If even organized industries are not perfectly able to overcome the free-rider problem that Mancur Olson (1965) identified as critical to lobby formation, then contributions will be less generous and tariff protection smaller than if firms cooperate fully in the lobbying effort. Thus, estimates of the value placed by the government on social welfare would not need to be so high in order to explain the low observed levels of protection. Gawande and Magee (2009) extend the Grossman and Helpman model to include the possibility of free riding by firms in organized industries. Lee and Magee (2002) estimate the extent of free riding in lobbying for US trade policy, and they find that free riding is extensive. Their direct estimates showed free riding ranging from 57 to 86 per cent. Simulations based on their model show that the tariff would have increased from the actual level of 3.4 per cent to nearly 59 per cent if free riding on trade policy had been eliminated.

The conclusion that the government largely maximizes welfare is counter to the intuition of most scholars of the political economy of trade policy. There is also some empirical evidence, even within the GH framework, that contradicts it. Kee, Olarreaga, and Silva (2007) look at foreign lobbying in the United States. Foreign lobbying is likely to focus on preferential access rather than reductions in MFN tariffs, which would then benefit all exporters to the US rather than just those lobbying. They estimate a GH model for foreign lobbies (from countries in the Western hemisphere) and find that the US government grants five times as much weight to foreign lobby contributions as it does to forgone tariff revenue in its objective function. They find that foreign lobby contributions significantly affect US tariff preferences across industries and across countries and conclude (93) that "market access is up for sale and foreign lobbies are buying it."

The Kee, Olarreaga, and Silva result that the US government cares more about contributions than about welfare differs markedly from a different study that looks at how foreign lobbying affects US tariffs and nontariff barriers. Gawande, Krishna, and Robbins (2006) estimate a GH model augmented to include foreign lobbies. They find that having an organized domestic political lobby raises protection while a foreign political presence reduces trade barriers. The government appears to place approximately equal weight on a dollar of contributions received from domestic lobbyists and a dollar from foreign lobby groups. Neither domestic nor foreign contributions receive anywhere near the weight placed on social welfare in the government's utility function, however. When they add plausible extra variables to the simple model (concentration ratio, per cent unionized, capital–labor ratio, wage, and scale), the augmented model is preferred to the parsimonious model based on both the Akaike information criterion and Schwarz information criterion.

Several papers have tried to explain the surprising benevolence of governments in setting their trade policies. Gawande and Krishna (2005) describe how policy-makers, even ones who are responsive to lobbying and campaign contributions, might end up choosing policies close to free trade because pro-tariff lobbying by import-competing industries is countered by pro-trade lobbying from the users of imported intermediate goods. The paper finds that tariffs are higher in industries with lobbying from pro-tariff groups and tariffs are lower when there is lobbying by organized groups using imported goods to produce output (downstream users of imported goods, such as car producers lobbying over steel tariffs). The estimated weight on social welfare for policy-makers falls when downstream users are included in the estimation, but it remains unrealistically high, at between 125 and 500 times larger than the weight placed on contributions.

Gawande and Hoekman (2006) show that policy uncertainty can help explain the puzzle that governments appear to be welfare maximizing in the estimation. They apply the GH model to the protection and subsidies given to agricultural industries, and they find that organized sectors receive greater protection (if import competing) and larger subsidies (if exporting). Just as in the papers that estimate the GH model using protection given to manufacturing industries, the weight policy-makers are estimated to place on social welfare dwarfs that on contributions (42 to 100 times larger weight on welfare). Introducing policy uncertainty, however, greatly reduces the weight placed on social welfare (relative to contributions) for policy-makers that is implied by the estimates. Because there is uncertainty about whether lobbying will be effective in influencing government policies, firms are less generous in the theoretical model when offering their contribution schedules to the policy-maker. Thus, greater uncertainty leads to lower equilibrium protection for any given weight on social welfare in the government utility function. The low observed levels of protection in the data can be explained as a result of the uncertainties in the lobbying process rather than as a result of a welfare-maximizing government.

Mitra, Thomakos, and Ulubasoglu (2006) investigate the surprisingly large weight estimated to be placed on social welfare in the government utility function by examining which industries are classified as politically organized. They argue that it is unrealistic to assume that an industry organized for one purpose (lobbying over domestic policy) is not organized for lobbying over trade policy. Since every industry has positive PAC contributions, they suggest that all industries should be treated as if they are organized. If all industries are organized, then the two explanatory variables in equation (4) collapse down to one (because $I_i = 1$ for all industries) and there is only one coefficient estimated. With only one coefficient estimated, it is not possible to use it to calculate separately the two underlying parameters from the GH model (a and α_L). Instead, they present what the implied value of a is for different assumed values of α_L. They show that treating every sector as organized politically does reduce the estimated weight placed on social welfare by the government. When $\alpha_L = 0.9$ (close to the estimate in Goldberg and Maggi 1999), for example, the estimate of a lies between 0.75 and 5. At higher levels of α_L, the government becomes close to a pure contributions maximizer. Using Turkish data, they find that even if only 10 per cent of the population is represented by a trade lobby, then welfare and contributions receive equal weight in the government's utility function. If 55–66 per cent of the population is represented, then the government is close to maximizing only contributions. Thus, they are able to obtain more realistic estimates of the parameters if they assume that all industries are organized.

Imai, Katayama, and Krishna (2007a) also view the way that industries are divided into organized and unorganized as driving many of the results in tests of the GH model. They argue that misclassification of industries into politically organized or unorganized in tests of the GH model means the estimates of it in Goldberg and Maggi (1999) and Gawande and Bandyopadhyay (2000) are inconsistent. In the GH model, only industries that are organized politically receive tariff protection, so this paper argues that industries with higher protection are more likely to be organized. For those industries, there should be a positive relationship between the inverse import penetration ratio and protection. Using the data from Gawande and Bandyopadhyay (2000), they perform quantile regression and show that there is no evidence of a positive relationship between the inverse import penetration ratio and protection for high-protection industries. In fact, the coefficient estimates are almost always negative, which is not consistent with the GH model predictions.

A second surprising result is that the fraction of the population estimated to be represented by an import-competing lobby, α_L, is very high. Goldberg and Maggi (1999) estimate that α_L is between 84 and 88 per cent, while Gawande and Bandyopadhyay (2000) find that it is very close to 100 per cent. But only 23 per cent of the population owned stocks and mutual funds in some form in 1990, according to Gross (2004). It thus seems unlikely that nearly all Americans were represented by industry lobbies in the early 1980s, which would have required them to own the sector-specific capital in import-competing industries. There is also a contradiction pointed out by Mitra, Thomakos, and Ulubasoglu (2006: 189): "it does not seem realistic to have such a high proportion of the population to have an incentive to organize in the presence of a government that does not seem to care much about contributions."

It is possible that the estimates suggesting that the government values mainly social welfare and that a large fraction of the population is politically organized come from a bias caused by using nontariff barriers to estimate a model of tariff formation, as Facchini, van Biesebroeck, and Willmann (2006) point out. They extend the GH model to allow only partial government capture of rents from protection, and they estimate this model. It suggests that the government appropriates only about 72–5 per cent of potential rents from trade policy. The paper also shows that this augmented model estimates a much smaller percentage of the population that is represented by a trade-related lobby (34 per cent) than did Goldberg and Maggi (over 80 per cent). The paper still finds an extremely high weight placed by policy-makers on social welfare relative to contributions. Eicher and Osang (2002) find similar results (a smaller share, 26 per cent, of the population represented by a lobby and a very large weight placed by the government on social welfare) when they estimate the GH model using a minimum distance estimator.

Several recent papers have argued that the empirical evidence is not as supportive of the GH model as early studies suggested. Ederington and Minier (2007), for example, point out that the GH model assumes that countries can use only trade policies to redistribute income, and thus it rules out domestic taxes and subsidies. Empirically, however, domestic taxes and subsidies remain policy options. When domestic policies are incorporated into the GH model, the model predicts free trade (only domestic subsidies/taxes are used because they are more efficient transfer mechanisms) unless raising revenues through taxes is sufficiently costly. They also point out that the GH model predicts negative protection for unorganized industries, but industries classified as unorganized actually receive positive protection. Most empirical papers add a constant into the estimating equation, and justify it by assuming there are other reasons for protection. They find that protection decreases in $\frac{z_i}{e_i}$ for unorganized industries and suggest that this is consistent with GH. A decreasing tariff means that deviations from free trade are decreasing in $\frac{z_i}{e_i}$, however, while the GH model actually predicts that deviations from free trade are increasing in $\frac{z_i}{e_i}$ (the import subsidy is predicted to get larger). The authors point out that this empirical pattern does not make economic sense because it suggests that tariffs are increasing with the deadweight costs of protection. They show that if other political motivations for protection are added into the government's utility function, then the model no longer predicts that protection is decreasing in $\frac{z_i}{e_i}$ for unorganized industries.

Imai, Katayama, and Krishna (2007b) point out that many of the predictions from the GH model that are tested empirically could arise in other models as well. They set up a model in which organized industries receive quota protection if imports rise above a certain level, and some (randomly determined) industries are organized while others are not. Then they generate a simulated data set based on their model and run the Goldberg and Maggi (1999) and Gawande and Bandyopadhyay (2000) estimates of the GH model. The estimates seem to provide support for the GH model even though the data are generated from a simpler alternative model. They find similar estimates to Goldberg and Maggi and Gawande and Bandyopadhyay in that the estimated weight on social welfare is too high and the fraction of the population represented by a lobby is estimated to be large as well. Thus, they show that the results supporting GH in empirical tests are consistent with a simpler model in which the government protects organized industries if imports rise above some cutoff level.

Given the strict assumptions that are necessary to create a tractable model, it is actually somewhat surprising that the GH model has received the empirical support found in the literature. As Goldberg and Maggi (1999: 1151) explain, "tests of the strict versions of trade models traditionally yield disastrous results for the theories under investigation." One part of the GH model that dramatically simplifies real-world conditions is the labor market, where identical workers all receive the same wage and do not have any incentive to lobby for protection. Matschke and Sherlund (2006) add unions into the GH model. The unions bargain over wages and employment with capital owners and both capital owners and unions can lobby the government for trade protection. They test the model using the same data and find that the GH restrictions can be rejected empirically in favor of the labor-augmented model. The labor-augmented model also finds lower estimates of the percentage of population represented by a lobby (65–75 per cent) and the weight on social welfare in the government utility function (309– 25 times larger than the weight on contributions) than does the pure GH model. While the augmented model estimates a smaller weight on social welfare in the government utility function, it is still large enough that the government remains close to welfare maximizing.

Bradford (2003) also develops a model that is similar to GH but with labor involvement in lobbying. In his model, the government maximizes votes, which increase from workers whose industry receives protection and increase with campaign contributions but decrease as tariffs reduce consumer surplus. The model predicts that protection will be higher in sectors with more workers but not necessarily in sectors with more output (greater output could raise or lower protection). Estimates of the model suggest that politicians find contributions to be about 15 per cent more valuable in terms of votes they can buy than is consumer surplus. The estimates also suggest that there are frictions in lobbying, so that the costs to lobby groups are greater than the money received by politicians. Transaction costs for producer lobbies are estimated to be 14.4 per cent. While protection is estimated to increase with employment in each industry, there is no statistically significant evidence that protection increases with industry output, contrary to the predictions of GH.

In conclusion, the early empirical work testing the GH model suggests that the government in the United States is close to welfare maximizing. This result is not one we expect to withstand further scrutiny, however, given the difficulties in estimating the model we describe above and the empirical evidence showing that political money influences trade policy decisions.

Lobby Groups Organize along Industry Lines to Affect Trade Policies in the Short Run but along Factor Lines to Influence Long-Run Trade Policies

The vast majority of lobby groups representing businesses are organized at the firm level (AT&T Inc. Federal PAC) or at the industry level (American Bankers Association). As Olson (1965) points out, there are very few lobby groups that have organized successfully to represent business interests as a whole. The National Association of Manufacturers, for example, is much weaker as a lobby group than is General Electric, whose PAC spent over $2 million in the 2006 election cycle. While groups representing individual firms in some cases lobby for policies that will favor only their own firm, in other cases they will join together in pursuit of a common policy goal. This joint effort is particularly relevant for trade policy, where protection is a public good for all firms in an industry.

Theoretically, there are two ways in which lobby groups might coalesce over trade policy. The Stolper–Samuelson theorem states that trade benefits the abundant factor in a country and harms the scarce factor. If capital is abundant and labor scarce in the United States, then trade benefits all capital owners and harms all workers (regardless of industry). The key assumption driving this result is that factors of production are perfectly mobile across industries within the country. An alternative prediction comes from the specific-factors model, in which some factors are assumed to be immobile across industry lines. Within that framework, factors that are specific to import-competing industries are harmed by international trade while factors specific to exporting industries gain from trade. Thus, lobby groups will coalesce along factor lines over trade policy if factors are perfectly mobile, and they will coalesce along industry lines if they are immobile.

The first paper to test the predictions of the two models was Magee (1980). He used testimony before the House Ways and Means Committee by lobby groups in order to identify their position on the Trade Act of 1974. In nineteen out of twenty-one cases, the business and labor groups within an industry took the same position on the trade bill, which is consistent with the prediction of the specific factors model. This provided strong evidence that the perfect mobility assumption of Stolper–Samuelson was flawed.

Beaulieu and Magee (2004) re-examine this question using data on PAC contributions around the time of the NAFTA vote. If exporting industries support the trade deal while import-competing industries do not, the former should give money to representatives voting for NAFTA and the latter to representatives voting against it. If all businesses support deals liberalizing trade while labor unions do not, there should be a large split between firm and labor PACs in terms of which representatives receive contributions. The results differ from Magee (1980) in that (after controlling for representative characteristics such as party), exporting industry PACs gave only a slightly higher fraction of their contributions to pro-NAFTA representatives than did PACs from import-competing industries. Corporate PACs, on the other hand, gave significantly more money to representatives supporting NAFTA than did labor groups. Thus, lobbying over NAFTA appeared to coalesce along factor lines while lobbying over the 1974 Trade Act did so along industry lines.

One explanation for the different results is that NAFTA was intended to be a permanent agreement, and thus long-term considerations about its effects would shape interest groups' calculations on whether or not to support it. Since interest groups could expect the 1974 Trade Act to be modified within a decade, support for it depended on shorter term considerations and over a short time period mobility across industry lines is more limited. Magee, Davidson, and Matusz (2005) provide some evidence for this interpretation. They show that in sectors with high levels of turnover (more factor mobility), business groups gave much more of their PAC money to pro-NAFTA representatives than did labor groups. In sectors with low turnover, this same split between business and labor contributions was considerably smaller. Low turnover industries showed a much larger split, on the other hand, between import-competing and exporting industries.

The ability of lobby groups to gain through redistributive policies depends on the discretion that governments have over their policy choices. The next section argues that national governments are facing more and more constraints on their policy choices.

GLOBAL MARKETS ARE BECOMING MORE POWERFUL THAN NATION STATES

To make our case that nation states are losing their traditional powers, we first examine where states came from. Carneiro (1970) has a rich political economy theory of "circumscribed population growth" in which Peru emerged as the first South American nation around 3000 BC. He posits that necessary conditions for the emergence of states were population growth leading to competition for resources with neighboring cultures; a state leader who would lead wars against contiguous neighbors; and geographical barriers to prevent the escape of the chiefdom's own population from taxation. Wars are critical to nation building. While wars existed long before states, he says that no early state was without war. Carneiro argues that nation states may have started in Peru because its populations were located in mountain valleys and could not escape taxation because of desert on the east and the Pacific ocean on the west and rival populations in neighboring valleys north and south. States formed later in populations without geographical barriers such as Brazil, where the population could escape taxation by moving farther into the rain forest.

In the nineteenth century it became apparent that national military success would grow out of economic power and that came from the national infrastructure of universal education, law, and public goods. The national borders that protected these valuable national infrastructures from free riding by foreigners were also used as economic protection for local firms against cheap imports.

This history gives insight into globalization today. In *The Structure of Scientific Revolutions*, Thomas Kuhn (1962) says that paradigm shifts are largely invisible to contemporaries. Is it possible that we have missed the driving force behind globalization? Since nations were formed 5,000 years ago out of military necessity—conquer or be conquered—the disappearance of nations through globalization today can be explained by the decline in military threats from neighboring countries. There has been no world war and with the *Pax Americana* of the last sixty years, there were essentially only two real military rivals—the American and Soviet spheres of influence because of the Cold War. Excepting small regional conflicts, within the US orb of American hegemony, there were nonexistent military threats to nations. The only external threats were foreign goods and World Cup qualifications. So, economically inefficient trade protection has become archaic and is being washed away by a sea of global capital mobility.[3] Carneiro's military conditions for national boundaries have disappeared. Kuhn's invisibility effect is that countries are becoming less important and we did not know why, having forgotten the original military motivations for nation states

Figure 31.1 confirms the decline in armed conflict after 1991.[4]

The implication is that if major future military threats to the world re-emerge, we can expect a strengthening of national boundaries and a rapid retreat from globalization. Absent that, national politics will continue to be weakened by globalization and economic protection will continue to disappear. These arguments are consistent with the vast political science literature on the relationship between peace (or cooperative relationships) and countries' bilateral trade. Pollins (1989) is one of many studies showing that political and military cooperation between nations increases their trade flows. A reversal of the trend toward lower conflict would mean a return to trade barriers and a reduction in trade flows.

Thomas Friedman (1999) argues that globalization has already placed countries that wish to participate in world markets in what he calls a "golden straitjacket." The need to appeal to global investors limits their economic policies to only those approved by the world market. Thus, they are in a policy straitjacket, but it is a

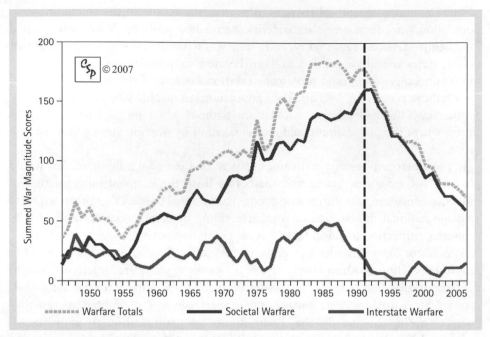

Fig. 31.1 Global trends in armed conflict, 1946–2006

"golden" one because these beneficial policies lead to increased wealth. Rodrik (2000) expands on this idea by arguing that there is an "impossible trinity" in which only two of the following three can be chosen: nation states, mass politics, and an integrated global economy. If nations exist and they are integrated into the world economy, the golden straitjacket means they have given up the ability to choose their own policies (i.e., mass politics). The only way to have both global integration and mass politics in which citizens choose economic policies is to have the policies determined through global federalism. In that case, nation states have ceased to exist in a meaningful sense.

The economics of why nations lose power comes from Coase (1960), who developed a powerful proposition showing the weakness of government policies even in a closed domestic economy. He argued that in the presence of well-defined property rights antipollution laws are irrelevant—economics and not laws will determine the level of pollution in a country. Polluters will just get sued by the public and pay tort damages in court equal to the harm done to society, but these damages are less than the cost of the polluters cleaning up the pollution (otherwise, they would not have polluted).

The same process explains why government policies regulating business are getting weaker with globalization. When the economic benefits of avoiding government rules exceed the costs, firms change countries. And because the national success stories of the last century were global (Krugman 2004: 368), globalist economic policies are being copied because they work. The power of benefit–cost economics makes global markets dominate national economic policies. The twentieth-century Realist theory of international relations asserted that politics dominates economics. That pattern is being reversed in the current period of globalization.

Evidence of this is the finding in Magee, Brock, and Young (1989) that economic factors dominate political factors in explaining tariff rates across ten advanced countries and nineteen countries. The MBY tests showed that 53 per cent of the variability in tariff rates was explained by industry (economic) factors and only 20 per cent of the variability in tariff rates was explained by country (political) factors. The current globalization parallels the United States in the 1890s when the rise of national corporations created a national market and eclipsed the power of the US states, leading to the ascent of the US government as the locus of political power.

Evidence of global corporations eclipsing nation states is that the largest 350 global corporations account for 28 per cent of world output.[5] American multinationals have become the new British East India Companies, extending US culture, technology, and economic ideas globally. Globalization has added Schumpeter's waves of creative destruction to politics so that governments are losing their power over global finance, communications, and their own economies. Strange (1992) agrees that globalization is leading to the marginalization if not the irrelevance of governments. She notes that increasing capital mobility, the technological revolution, and the decreasing costs of transportation and communication are all reducing the power of nation states.

One sign of the decline in importance of national governments is that national boundaries have ceased to define the area for which there is free trade in goods and services. The past several decades have seen an explosion of regional trade agreements in which free trading areas have been expanded beyond national boundaries. By July of 2007, some 380 regional agreements had been notified to the WTO.[6] In effect, optimal country size appears to be increasing.

Openness (or Good Economic Policy More Generally) is More Important than Democracy for Economic Success

Krugman (2004) argues that globalization (nations producing for the world market rather than embracing self-sufficiency) drove virtually every national economic success story in the past century. At the same time, authoritarian rule describes the governments of several recent globalist success stories such as China, Singapore, Hong Kong, and Chile. Table 31.1 shows GDP per capita growth rates from 1980 to 2006 for the Asian Tigers, China, and Chile. It also shows the average Polity score for each country from 1980 to 2005. This score can range from −10 (a dictatorial regime) to 10 (democracy).[7] China and Singapore are ranked as autocracies (negative polity

Table 31.1 Per capita GDP growth rates and democracy for selected countries, 1980–2006

Country	Real GDPPC growth rate, 1980 to 2006 (%)	Average polity score, 1980 to 2005	Notes
Chile	3.00	3.46	Strongly autocratic prior to 1989
China	8.63	−7.00	Consistently autocratic
Indonesia	3.12	−3.27	Strongly autocratic prior to 1998
Korea	5.78	3.35	Autocratic prior to 1987
Malaysia	3.50	3.58	Weakly democratic, 1980 to 2005
Singapore	4.38	−2.00	Consistently autocratic
Taiwan	5.35	2.50	Autocratic prior to 1991
Thailand	4.49	5.77	Weakly democratic before 1992
World	1.13	1.13	

scores) every year, and four more of the countries were autocracies during the 1980s. Yet all of these countries have experienced very rapid growth in income per capita, with China, the least democratic, leading the pack.

We do not want to argue that democracy hinders economic development. In fact, countries with higher polity scores in 1980 had significantly faster GDP per capita growth between 1980 and 2006. Nonetheless, the ability of countries such as China and Singapore to achieve remarkable economic growth over long periods of time means that democracy is not a *necessary* condition for economic success.

The most economically successful nations in the late twentieth century are those, like the globalist countries in Table 31.1, that have embraced globalization. Rosecrance (1996) describes some of them (the archetypal examples are Hong Kong and Singapore) as virtual states. These countries, along with Taiwan and South Korea, comprised the first wave of Asian Tigers. Starting as relatively poor countries with low wages, they embraced exports to highly developed countries. While the Tigers started with manufacturing exports, they realized that these sectors would ultimately be lost to even lower-wage countries. So they poured heavy funding into primary, secondary, and university education to upgrade their labor force to advanced country levels. They also strengthened property rights to attract foreign capital to both modernize their countries and to employ skilled labor. Their enlightened strategy was to invest in people rather than manufacturing capacity. The second wave of Asian Tigers consisted of Thailand, Malaysia, and Indonesia.[8]

Such states got their name from American virtual corporations. A virtual corporation consists almost entirely of skilled marketing and management. They outsource their production to low-wage countries. Nike is an example of a virtual corporation, because it does not make shoes—it markets them. Nike buys its shoes from low-wage countries. The virtual states are similar in that they outsource their manufacturing and their core competence is skilled labor. South Korea produces a lot of its manufacturing offshore. Instead of protecting domestic labor by limiting immigration, virtual states encourage entry by foreign labor. While these policies appear

Draconian, they are generally embraced at home because of the government's dedication to creating an advanced economy through education. Most virtual states, such as Hong Kong and Singapore, are smaller nations, which are always more dependent on world markets.

The virtual states described above are national versions of virtual corporations. Strategic alliances are also becoming an increasingly important feature of American virtual corporations. The global parallel is that nation states are also engaging in strategic alliances by forming regional trading blocs. Excessively competitive or failing industries demonstrate similar behavior. Firms have to merge in highly competitive industries. Globalization generates similar competitive pressures for nations to merge into trading blocs that eliminate inter-country barriers to trade. Thus, optimal country size is rising. Even more ambitious nations are increasing country size by creating complete economic unions (e.g., the EU) while anti-global states are decreasing theirs and becoming more protectionist (the splintering of the former Soviet republics).[9]

The most enlightened globalist governments have avoided capture by protectionist groups (either business or labor) so that their policies do not harm market efficiency. Rather, the governments provide an efficient legal system since well-defined property rights are critical for well-functioning capital markets. The development of a strong legal system and emphasis on education by the globalist governments is important because most of the world's wealth consists of intangible capital: 78 per cent of the world's wealth is intangible capital; 18 per cent is physical capital; and 4 per cent is land capital. About 57 per cent of intangible capital is due to a country's rule of law and 36 per cent is due to education (human capital). Human capital is the present value of education, the intensive factor driving the information revolution. The countries, whether democratic or not, that have strong legal systems and develop the human capital of their residents, like the globalist countries in Table 31.1, are succeeding economically.

CONCLUSION

We began this chapter by examining two ways that business and labor groups can shape government policies. They can try to affect which candidates win election, as in the Magee, Brock, and Young (1989) model, or they can try to gain influence over politicians who are in office, as in the Grossman and Helpman (1994) model. There is some empirical evidence favoring each type of strategy for special interest groups representing firms. Magee (2007) shows that defense industry political action committees gave overwhelmingly to safe incumbents during the 1996 House of Representatives elections, suggesting that they were trying to gain influence over politicians already in office. Stratmann (1998) finds that farm PACs increased their contributions around the time of both farm subsidy votes in the House and around the time of primary and general elections. The increase at the time of the general election was considerably larger than during the weeks surrounding the farm subsidy votes, however, which might indicate a greater focus on affecting election outcomes for farm PACs.

Next we considered a proposition that seems self-evident to most researchers in political economy: governments are not purely welfare maximizers. Despite the near consensus on this proposition, the early empirical estimates of the Grossman and Helpman (1994) model have seemed to contradict it. The GH model abstracts from policy uncertainty and the free rider problem, however, and there are a number of difficulties in estimating the model, such as identifying which industries are organized politically and dealing with endogenous variables. Thus, it seems likely that these early empirical results will not lead to a paradigm shift overturning the proposition.

The third proposition examines how groups organize their lobbying efforts, whether they coalesce along industry lines or along factor lines. In the short run, factors are relatively immobile, and thus firms' trade policy stance depends on whether they are in an import-competing or exporting industry. Thus, some firms favor trade liberalization and others stronger protection. In the long run, however, capital is mobile across industries. For capital-abundant countries, then, all capital owners should favor liberalization based on the Stolper–Samuelson theorem.

Proposition four argues that globalization is weakening nation states. It is now much more difficult to tax and regulate businesses that can easily move across the border to a lower tax or less regulated country. As a result, countries are limited in the policies they can choose. If they wish to participate in world markets and attract foreign investment, they must don a "golden straitjacket" that constrains policies to be those approved by global investors. Businesses whose desired policies are consistent with those favored by the global market find their lobbying goals easier to achieve. Although some remain successful, protectionists are fighting an uphill battle to hold onto their trade barriers.

Our last proposition examines the necessary conditions for economic success. We argue that certain economic policies are critical for rapid economic development: an embrace of globalization, an emphasis on education, and the development of a legal system that protects property rights. There are cases of both democracies and autocracies that have followed these globalist policies and achieved rapid economic growth. Thus, we argue that it is good economic policy, rather than the type of government a country has, that drives economic success.

RESEARCH AGENDA

The political economy literature on trade policy in the past fifteen years has moved toward presenting and testing formal economic models, with many of the empirical papers estimating the Grossman and Helpman (1994) model. Two advantages of this type of research over empirical work that is more loosely based on theory are that the estimation can uncover structural parameters and the empirical and theoretical work are closely linked. The disadvantage is that assumptions necessary to make a theoretical model tractable may be unrealistic and limiting when it comes to empirical estimation. In the Protection for Sale model, for example, tariffs are set unilaterally by policy-makers in a small country and the tariff choice is influenced by interest group campaign contributions. These assumptions mean that the model is less relevant for cases where tariffs are determined by multilateral negotiations and for countries in which there is state funding of elections. Grossman and Helpman (1995) allow tariffs to be set multilaterally, but estimates of this model are rare because of the extensive data requirements.

Empirically, one need is for continued improvements in data on the restrictiveness of trade barriers across countries and industries and on elasticity measures. A good recent improvement in the data available comes from Kee, Nicita, and Olarreaga (2008, 2009), who provide estimates of elasticities and of the restrictiveness of trade barriers. Second, it would be useful to have a range of theoretical models that can be tested against each other in order to determine which model provides the best fit for the data. Eicher and Osang (2002) provide one example of a paper testing theoretical models against each other directly, and their approach could be followed in testing more recent models.

There are a number of ways in which the existing models can be extended theoretically. While there have been a few models with endogenous lobby group formation and imperfect cooperation between firms in their lobbying efforts, greater attention paid to the issue of which industries are successful in overcoming the free-rider problem seems warranted. Such models might reveal industry characteristics that could be included in empirical estimates of the determinants of tariff protection across sectors. Developing tractable models in which interests groups give money both in order to affect election outcomes, the focus of Magee, Brock, and Young (1989), and in order to gain influence over politicians in office, the focus of Grossman and Helpman (1994), might also be useful. Incorporating elections directly into the model could allow a more well-developed policy-maker utility function than that in the GH model, which merely assumes that the policy-maker values both contributions and social welfare. Given that the dominant political economy model of tariff formation is now fifteen years old, it seems time for the next generation of theoretical models to emerge and be tested against the older work.

Notes

1. This is in addition to the standard explanation that the more advanced the country, the less dependent it is on tariffs for sources of revenue.
2. Magee and Magee (2008), however, argue that the United States is a small country in world trade and has too small of a market share to influence world prices through its trade policies.

3. The average daily turnover is $3.2 trillion in foreign exchange markets (Bank for International Settlements 2007), which is nearly one-quarter of the over $13 trillion annual gross domestic product of the US (*CIA World Factbook*).
4. The trends in armed conflict data come from http://systemicpeace.org/
5. Frieden and Lake (1995: 135). There were 16,000 multinational corporations in the world in the early 1990s.
6. http://www.wto.org/english/tratop_e/region_e/region_e.htm
7. The GDP per capita growth rates are calculated using data from www.imf.org The polity scores are from the Polity IV data set downloaded from http://systemicpeace.org/
8. Globalist European countries with high literacy are also virtual states. Switzerland has as much as 98 per cent of Nestlé's productive capacity located abroad. Holland now produces most of its goods outside of its borders and England started becoming more globalist in the 1980s.
9. The formation of trading blocs is endogenous. Magee and Lee (2001) show that the continental countries most devastated by the Second World War (Germany, Italy, and France) had the fastest capital growth after the war and formed the more pro-export EEC while countries with slower capital growth in the same period ended up in the less pro-export EFTA.

REFERENCES

ANSOLABEHERE, S., FIGUEIREDO, J. DE, and SNYDER, J. 2003. "Why is there so little money in US politics?" *Journal of Economic Perspectives* 17(1): 105–30.

BALDWIN, R., and MAGEE, C. 2000. "is trade policy for sale? Congressional voting on recent trade bills," *Public Choice* 105: 79–101.

Bank for International Settlements. 2007. *Evolving Banking Systems in Latin America and the Caribbean: Challenges and Implications for Monetary Policy and Financial Stability.* Basel: Bank for International Settlements.

BEAULIEU, E., and MAGEE, C. 2004. "Four simple tests of campaign contributions and trade policy preferences," *Economics and Politics* 16(2): 163–87.

BENDER, B., and LOTT, J. 1996. "Legislator voting and shirking: a critical review of the literature," *Public Choice* 87(1–2): 67–100.

BERNHEIM, D., and WHINSTON, M. 1986. "Menu auctions, resource allocation, and economic influence," *Quarterly Journal of Economics* 101(1): 1–31.

BILAL, S. 1998. "Why regionalism may increase the demand for trade protection," *Journal of Economic Integration* 13(1): 30–61.

BRADFORD, S. 2003. "Protection and jobs: explaining the structure of trade barriers across industries," *Journal of International Economics* 61: 19–39.

BRAINARD, S. L., and VERDIER, T. 1997. "The political economy of declining industries: senescent industry collapse revisited," *Journal of International Economics* 42(1–2): 221–37.

BRONARS, S., and LOTT, J. 1997. "Do campaign donations alter how a politician votes? Or, do donors support candidates who value the same things that they do?" *Journal of Law and Economics* 40(2): 317–50.

CARNEIRO, R. L. 1970. "A theory of the origin of the state," *Science* 169: 733–8.

CHIU, Y. S. 1998. "Politics, structure of protection and welfare," *Review of International Economics* 6(3): 472–87.

COASE, R. H. 1960. "The problem of social cost," *Journal of Law and Economics* 3: 1–44.

COEN, D. 2007. "Empirical and theoretical studies in EU lobbying," *Journal of European Public Policy* 14(3): 333–45.

EDERINGTON, J., and MINIER, J. 2008. "Reconsidering the empirical evidence on the Grossman-Helpman model of endogenous protection," *Canadian Journal of Economics* 41(2): 501–16.

EICHER, T., and OSANG, T. 2002. "Protection for sale: an empirical investigation. comment," *American Economic Review* 92(5): 1702–10.

FACCHINI, G., BIESEBROECK, J. VAN, and WILLMANN, G. 2006. "Protection for sale with imperfect rent capturing," *Canadian Journal of Economics* 39(3): 845–73.

FINDLAY, R., and WELLISZ, S. 1982. "Endogenous tariffs, the political economy of trade restrictions, and welfare," in J. N. Bhagwati, ed., *Import Competition and Response.* Chicago: University of Chicago, 223–34.

FRIEDEN, J., and LAKE, D. 1995. *International Political Economy*, 3rd edn. New York: St Martin's.

FRIEDMAN, T. 1999. *The Lexus and the Olive Tree.* New York: Farrar, Straus, Giroux.

FULLER, W. 1987. *Measurement Error Models.* New York: Wiley.

GAWANDE, K., and BANDYOPADHYAY, U. 2000. "Is protection for sale? A test of the Grossman-Helpman theory of endogenous protection," *Review of Economics and Statistics* 82: 139–52.

—— and HOEKMAN, B. 2006. "Lobbying and agricultural trade policy in the United States," *International Organization* 60(3): 527–61.

—— and KRISHNA, P. 2003. "The political economy of trade policy: empirical approaches," in J. Harrigan and E. K. Choi, eds., *Handbook of International Trade.* Malden, Mass.: Blackwell, 213–50.

—— —— 2005. "Lobbying competition over US trade policy," NBER Working Paper 11371.

—— —— and ROBBINS, M. J. 2006. "Foreign lobbying and US trade policy," *Review of Economics and Statistics* 88(3): 563–71.

—— and MAGEE, C. 2009. "Free riding on protection for sale," submitted to *Journal of International Economics.*

GOLDBERG, P., and MAGGI, G. 1999. "Protection for sale: an empirical investigation," *American Economic Review* 89: 1135–55.

GROSS, D. 2004. "Buy stock, vote Bush: does investing really make you more Republican?" http://www.slate.com/id/2105743/ accessed October 31, 2007.

GROSSMAN, G., and HELPMAN, E. 1994. "Protection for sale," *American Economic Review* 84: 833–50.

—— —— 1995. "Trade wars and trade talks," *Journal of Political Economy* 103(4): 675–708.

HILLMAN, A. 1982. "Declining industries and political-support protectionist motives," *American Economic Review* 72(5): 1180–7.

HOFFMAN, M. 2005. "Discretion, lobbying, and political influence in models of trade policy," *Journal of Policy Reform* 8(3): 175–88.

IMAI, S., KATAYAMA, H., and KRISHNA, K. 2007a. "A quantile-based test of protection for sale model," Mimeo.

—— —— —— 2007b. "Protection for sale or surge protection?" Working Paper from http://www.econ.psu.edu/~kkrishna/research.html accessed October 19, 2007.

KEE, H. L., NICITA, A., and OLARREAGA, M. 2008. "Import demand elasticities and trade distortions," *Review of Economics and Statistics* 90(4): 666–82.

—— —— —— 2009. "Estimating trade restrictiveness indices," *Economic Journal* 119: 172–99.

—— OLARREAGA, M., and SILVA, P. 2007. "Market access for sale," *Journal of Development Economics* 82: 79–94.

KRUGMAN, P. 2004. *The Great Unraveling: Losing our Way in the New Century.* New York: Norton.

KUHN, T., 1962. *The Structure of Scientific Revolutions*. Chicago: University of Chicago Press.

LEE, H.-L., and MAGEE, S. 2002. "Three simple measures of endogenous free riding in protectionist lobbies," Mimeo, University of Texas at Austin.

LEVITT, S. 1995. "Policy watch: congressional campaign finance reform," *Journal of Economic Perspectives* 9(1): 183–93.

McCALMAN, P. 2004. "Protection for sale and trade liberalization: an empirical investigation," *Review of International Economics* 12: 81–94.

MAGEE, C. 2002a. "Endogenous trade policy and lobby formation: an application to the free-rider problem," *Journal of International Economics* 57(2): 449–71.

—— 2002b. "Do political action committees give money to candidates for electoral or influence motives?" *Public Choice* 112: 373–99.

—— 2007. "Influence, elections, and the value of a vote in the US House of Representatives," *Economics and Politics* 19: 289–315.

—— DAVIDSON, C., and MATUSZ, S. 2005. "Trade, turnover, and tithing," *Journal of International Economics* 66(1): 157–76.

—— and MAGEE, S. P. 2004. "The Madison paradox and the low cost of special-interest legislation," in D. Nelson, ed., *The Political Economy of Policy Reform*. New York: Elsevier, 131–54.

—— —— 2008. "The United States is a small country in world trade," *Review of International Economics* 16(5): 990–1004.

MAGEE, S. P. 1977. "Information and the multinational corporation: an appropriability theory of direct foreign investment," in J. Bhagwati, ed., *The New International Economic Order: The North-South Debate*. Cambridge, Mass.: MIT Press, 317–40.

—— 1980. "Three simple tests of the Stolper–Samuelson theorem", in P. Oppenheimer, ed., *Issues in International Economics*. London: Oriel Press, 138–53.

—— 1997. "Endogenous protection: the empirical evidence," in D. C. Mueller, ed., *Perspectives On Public Choice: A Handbook*. New York: Cambridge University Press, 526–61.

—— and LEE, H.-L. 2001. "Endogenous tariff creation and tariff diversion in a customs union," *European Economic Review* 45: 495–518.

—— BROCK, W., and YOUNG, L. 1989. *Black Hole Tariffs and Endogenous Policy Theory*. New York: Cambridge University Press.

MAGGI, G., and RODRIGUEZ-CLARE, A. 2000. "Import penetration and the politics of trade protection," *Journal of International Economics* 51: 287–305.

MATSCHKE, X., and SHERLUND, S. 2006. "Do labor issues matter in the determination of US trade policy? An empirical reevaluation," *American Economic Review* 96(1): 405–21.

MITRA, D. 1999. "Endogenous lobby formation and endogenous protection: a long run model of trade policy determination," *American Economic Review* 89: 1116–34.

—— THOMAKOS, D., and ULUBASOGLU, M. 2002. "Protection for sale in a developing country: democracy vs. dictatorship," *Review of Economics and Statistics* 84(3): 497–508.

—— —— —— 2006. "Can we obtain realistic parameter estimates for the 'protection for sale' model?" *Canadian Journal of Economics* 39(1): 187–210.

OLSON, M. 1965. *The Logic of Collective Action*. Cambridge, Mass.: Harvard University Press.

POLLINS, B. M. 1989. "Does trade still follow the flag?" *American Political Science Review* 83(2): 465–80.

RAMA, M. 1994. "Endogenous trade policy: a time-series approach," *Economics and Politics* 6(3): 215–32.

RODRIK, D. 1995. "The political economy of trade policy," in P. B. Kenen et al., eds., *Handbook of International Economics*. New York: Elsevier, 1457–94.

—— 2000. "How far will economic integration go?" *Journal of Economic Perspectives* 14(1): 177–86.

ROSECRANCE, R. 1996. "The rise of the virtual state," *Foreign Affairs* 75(4): 45–61.

SNYDER, J. 1992. "Long-term investing in politicians; or, give early, give often," *Journal of Law and Economics* April, 35: 15–43.

STAIGER, R., and TABELLINI, G. 1987. "Discretionary trade policy and excessive protection," *American Economic Review* 77: 823–37.

STRANGE, S. 1992. "States, firms and diplomacy," *International Affairs* January, 68: 1–15.

STRATMANN, T. 1991. "What do campaign contributions buy? deciphering causal effects of money and votes," *Southern Economic Journal* 57(3): 606–20.

—— 1998. "The market for congressional votes: is timing of contributions everything?" *Journal of Law and Economics* 41(1): 85–113.

—— 2002. "Can special interests buy congressional votes? Evidence from financial services legislation," *Journal of Law and Economics* 45(2): 345–73.

TULLOCK, G. 1972. "The purchase of politicians," *Western Economic Journal* 10: 354–5.

WELCH, W. P. 1980. "The allocation of political monies: economic interest groups," *Public Choice* 35: 97–120.

WILLIAMSON, J. G. 2003. "Was it Stolper-Samuelson, infant industry or something else? World tariffs 1789–1938," NBER Working Paper 9656 (April).

CHAPTER 32

COMPETITION POLICY

STEPHEN WILKS

UNDERSTANDING COMPETITION POLICY

COMPETITION policy is a complex policy field which requires knowledge of competition law and economics as well as familiarity with the framework of policy and the agencies of enforcement. There are large literatures dealing with the law and the economics but surprisingly little work which provides an overall assessment of policy. Unfortunately, discussion of competition policy is therefore segregated into rather insular sub-specialisms. This chapter presents an outline of the main elements of policy but also seeks to cover new ground by presenting a distinctively "political economy" analysis of competition policy. It argues that competition policy is simultaneously a growing area of legal regulation, a core component of economic policy, and a mode of balancing public and private power in contemporary liberal democracy. There is, as yet, no single study that brings these dimensions together in a book-length analysis, although students might like to refer to Doern and Wilks 1996; Amato 1997; Cini and McGowan 2009; and Wilks 1999. It is significant that all these studies were written before the full ascendancy of neo-liberal, free market capitalism, what Glyn (2006) has termed *Capitalism Unleashed* although the 2008 financial crisis may lead to capitalism being constrained with implications for the ideological underpinning of competition policy.

In a familiar regulatory paradox we have also seen "antitrust unleashed." The paradox is that the expansion of the free market has been accompanied by more regulation. This should come as no surprise to students of Polanyi (1944) and the paradox has been brilliantly captured by Gamble (1994) and Vogel (1996). This curious partnership between expanded markets and more intensive regulation has been restated by Levi-Faur (2005) in his thesis of "regulatory capitalism" but, while Gamble stressed the power of the state, Levi-Faur and Braithwaite stress the regulatory role of large corporations joined with the state in regulatory networks (Braithwaite 2008: ch. 1). Here we have a further paradox for competition policy. A great expansion in policy powers and enforcement is accompanied by a great increase in the global power of large corporations. Competition policy has developed, and been enforced, in ways that benefit and support large global corporations. We come back to that insight in the conclusion.

Competition policy is an atypical policy sector which aims at creating and reinforcing systems rather than specific goals, and it is about means rather than ends. The systems in question are first, a comprehensive system of legal regulation of the commercial activities of companies, and second, the system of freedom to compete in a market economy. The two systems are, of course, substantially integrated and in sum could be regarded as an "economic constitution" which is itself an ideological construct. The ideological basis of a liberal, capitalist, free market economy is also the foundation of competition policy which therefore only makes sense in a state committed to the free market. States whose economies are based on an alternative system of public ownership and state planning, or on common ownership and cooperative working, would have no need for competition policy. In that sense, and unlike universal policy areas such as health or education, competition policy is acutely ideological and evaluation of policy cannot logically be detached from evaluation of the costs and benefits of a free market system.

Accordingly the second section gives a brief account of the development of modern competition policy, exploring its relationship with the ascendancy of liberal market economies and proposing the concept of an "economic constitution." The next three sections seek to capture the essence of policy by looking at the regulation of companies, of governments, and at the curious absence of international institutions. The following two sections turn to much more practical aspects of policy by looking at the agencies in the major national jurisdictions and then turning to the "reinvention" of competition policy as a supply side policy aspiring to mobilize competition to increase national competitiveness. The conclusion summarizes the arguments and identifies theoretical approaches which constitute some of the most promising areas for research.

EVOLUTION OF POLICY TOWARDS AN "ECONOMIC CONSTITUTION"

We first consider the gradual evolution of legal frameworks before emphasizing the recent "turn to economics" and then conceptualizing competition policy as part of the "economic constitution" that promises to lock in the post-1980s emancipation of market forces. Competition law, especially in its earliest incarnation of "antitrust," has a venerable tradition going back to the Sherman Antitrust Act of 1890. The global economic history of antitrust is captured admirably in Freyer (1992, 2006). By the early twenty-first century competition law had become an elaborate legislative framework constraining commercial behavior operated through networks of agencies, courts, procedures, codes, and professional practices. As an apparatus of enforcement, competition law is essentially unconcerned with ideological or distributional issues. It is preoccupied with due process and with interpretation and enforcement of the statutes although some of the best authoritative texts, such as Whish 2008, do locate the technical law within a framework of governmental intentions. There is a powerful legal community in the UK, Europe, and the USA which has a defining influence over the evolution of competition law and embraces the enforcement agencies, the courts, the big law firms, and academics. The participants in this legal community are often adversaries, but are united in a shared support for the legal discourse of competition law. The influence of this legal industry lends itself to analysis through the theoretical lens of "epistemic communities," a concept which suggests that policy-making is driven by international communities of experts who share an epistemology (Haas 1992), in this case a common legal discourse. The epistemic communities approach has been used productively to analyze change and convergence in competition law (Drahos and Van Waarden 2002; Wilks 2004). But however the legal system is analyzed, the reality is of a substantial and growing apparatus of legal regulation which provides a framework of rules and expectations which influences competitive behavior and competitive strategies for all companies operating in the US and Europe. As noted later, competition law exemplifies a process of "juridification," of creeping legalization in which formerly free and innocent commercial activities become subject to judgments of illegality.

In contrast, the economic system is far less well established. Oddly, economics played a small part in the design and operation of competition policy until relatively recently. In the UK economic tests were not incorporated fully into British law until the Competition Act of 1998. Competition policy was conceived in terms of legal freedoms to participate in the market and to trade fairly. Policy was enforced with laxity and hesitation and was not driven by economic goals of efficiency, productivity, and growth (Wilks 1999). In the post-Thatcherite world of free markets and neo-liberal principles competition economics has come into its own but has only gradually been fully incorporated into the definition and enforcement of policy.

Since the early 1990s, however, economic tests have become more important and economic analysis has become more sophisticated and more effectively incorporated into the operation of the law. The major innovations in economic analysis have originated in the US, articulated through US academic research and absorbed by the enforcement agencies and, of especial importance, by judges (Kovacic 2003). The doctrine which has become most influential has been described as a "post-Chicago synthesis" which "predominantly sticks with the single goal of (allocative) efficiency and reinforces the focus on quantifiable, short term welfare effects" (Budzinski 2008: 301). One influential text therefore defines competition policy as "the set of policies and laws which ensure that competition in the marketplace is not restricted in such a way as to reduce economic welfare" (Motta 2004: 30). The test is based on the effect of a particular business practice on the welfare of those who consume the product in question. In practice this tends to emphasize short-term price effects, which allows scope to accept efficiency enhancing behavior, but each case is assessed in its merits. There are therefore very few absolute or per se tests of illegality. Areas such as RPI (resale price maintenance) and cartel behavior (market sharing and price fixing) are almost always illegal but otherwise legality depends on economic analysis; behaviors such as loyalty discounts, bundling products together for sale, or supply chain mergers may be legal or illegal depending on the circumstances. In this uncertain world economic expertise and advice starts to become as important as legal advice.

Accordingly, competition agencies have increased their employment of econo-mists, companies and their advisers mobilize economic analysis, and there has been a startling growth in economic consultancies (Neven 2006). These changes reflect a much deeper transition in the role of competition policy. We are not experiencing a simple incremental progression but rather a major paradigmatic transition which has redefined competition policy as a foundational economic policy at the heart of rivalry between nations over industrial competitiveness. The transition originated in the abandonment of "industrial policy" and the shift from selective intervention in the 1970s and early 1980s to a non-interventionist free market policy in the 1990s and 2000s. As economic ideology was transformed so the basis of competition policy moved away from a concern with industrial organization and the SCP (structure/conduct/performance) paradigm (Hay and Morris 1991) and towards a more micro-economic and game-theoretic concern with economic welfare. This transformation involved, in effect, a shift from the maintenance of a prima-facie competitive industrial structure (for instance maintaining four or more competitors in a specific market) to a more applied concern with economic efficiency. Following the Thatch-erite emphasis on the efficiency of markets in the abstract, the new competition economics promised a way to "correct" markets in practice, in order to ensure that efficiency was delivered. Thus competition policy has become a key supply side policy and has taken over the mantle of 1970s-style industrial policy (Beath 2002). In Europe competition policy has been linked to the Lisbon competitiveness agenda and the Competition Commissioner, Neelie Kroes, has declared that "competition policy is the new industrial policy" (Kroes 2006).

An understanding of competition policy therefore requires appreciation of the system of legal regulation, and a perspective on how that system has been affected by the introduction of economic tests and by political demands to use the system to pursue goals of economic policy. However, these legal and economic perspectives tell only half the story. Competition policy must also be understood as an expression of political goals and, more fundamentally, as a quasi-constitutional element in the operation of liberal democracy. Competition policy, as argued elsewhere (Wilks 1999: 347–9), should be seen as an expression of industrial politics, as a constituent of a post-Thatcherite political settlement defining the relative power of the public and private sectors and as a way of regulating and legitimating private power.

The debate about the balance between public and private power in the economy is long-standing and complex (Shonfield 1965; Lindblom 1977; Moran 2006). Competition policy can be employed to control private power through market-enforcing measures to curb monopoly, cartels, and the exploitative behavior that they allow. It can also be used to control state power by preventing state monopolization (through nationalization), state-induced cartels, and state intervention and subsidies. This quality of competition policy locates it as a potential foundation of liberal democracy itself. The relationship between democracy and the market is symbiotic. Market systems are conventionally regarded as supportive and even constitutive of liberal democracy (Friedman 1962; Lindblom 1977; Bernhagen 2007) but concentrations of market power, the growth of market inequalities, and the marketization of many aspects of public life mean that private economic power can become a threat to democracy (Dryzak 1996). As the private sector expands, and under contemporary neo-liberalism the public sector becomes more dependent and more deferential (Marquand 2004), so the need to police the public/private boundary becomes acute. This political dimension of competition policy is rarely emphasized in the literature but one stimulating treatment comes from the former Italian Prime Minister Giuliano Amato who writes that antitrust law was seen:

as an answer (if not "the" answer) to a crucial problem for democracy: the emergence from the company or firm, as an expression of the fundamental freedoms of individuals, of the opposite phenomenon of private power; a power devoid of legitimation and dangerously capable of infringing not just the economic freedom of other private individuals, but also the balance of public decisions exposed to its domineering strength.   (Amato 1997: 2)

This constitutional quality of competition policy effectively leads it to define the commercial and the constitutional obligations of corporate citizens in return for their freedom to operate as private actors within national markets. In this setting competition policy can therefore be seen not just as a series of cases that attack individual examples of exploitative behavior, but as a coherent economic constitution. The concept of a "constitution" is itself complex. Political scientists associate the concept with a territorial agreement about the rules of governance which operates at the level of the state and provides the basis for the rule of law. But constitutions operate at many levels, from the UN to a company's articles of association, and can cover economic and human rights issues as well as law and politics.

The defining characteristics of constitutions are that they embody an agreement (or acceptance) among all interested parties about the principles and procedures which should govern an area of life, and those principles and procedures are enforced by some equivalent of a judicial system. Constitutions therefore bind participants in a state or organization and channel their behavior. They represent the consolidation of a set of principles which could be described as "hegemonic," but of course constitutions can be changed. They change either through gradual evolution as part of a judicial process of interpretation and precedent; or they change through major amendments which tend to be crisis driven and for which exceptional procedures come into play.

Presenting competition policy as having a constitutional quality may seem portentous but it reflects the important ordoliberal foundations of the social market economy (Gerber 1998) and the almost clichéd view that antitrust is an indissoluble part of the US "constitution," for Shonfield (1965 329) "a form of national religion." But the concept takes on a special meaning in the European setting where competition policy is built into the founding Treaties. It has become accepted that the Treaties should be regarded as the constitution of Europe and of course the process of adopting a formal constitutional version of the Treaties has dominated European Union politics since 2005. The incorporation of articles requiring free competition and control of state aid reflect the origins of the European project as essentially an economic venture and competition policy has enjoyed the integrationist support of the European Court. Indeed, the constitutional standing of the competition rules was underlined by the remarkable French amendments to the Reform Treaty in June 2007 where the Treaty objectives in Article 3 were amended to delete the requirement for "a system ensuring that competition in the internal market is not distorted." This downplayed the allegedly neo-liberal competition principle but did not, of course, remove the substantive articles. The Treaty debate has reawakened interest in the "economic constitution" of Europe (Laurent and Le Cacheux 2007), in the role of the competition provisions as one element of that economic constitution (OECD 2005), and in the question of what sort of market the constitution requires (Jabko 2006). We return to the implications of this constitutional approach in the conclusion but first turn to a more detailed examination of competition policy in operation.

REGULATING COMPANIES

The prime focus of competition policy is private sector companies and the legality or otherwise of their trading behavior and competitive strategies. In effect, of course, companies are "regulated" by their markets so that in a world of perfect competition companies have virtually no discretion and must simply respond to market signals. In practice perfect markets are a theoretical abstraction, all markets are imperfect, and most are characterized by oligopoly which allows bigger companies to exert market power. In this everyday setting the job of competition policy is to ensure that market forces are not overridden or neutralized. The basic principle of business conduct is "freedom to contract" with the expectation that all contracts are prima facie legal and it is not always easy to define when a contract will breach competition rules. This is especially difficult because competition laws are written in very general terms and are capable of being interpreted as constraining a wide range of commercial activity. Thus section 1 of the grand-daddy of all competition legislation, the 1890

Sherman Antitrust Act, declares that "Every contract, combination in the form of trust or otherwise, or conspiracy, in restraint of trade or commerce" is illegal, while Article 81(1) of the European Treaty prohibits "all agreements between undertakings ... which have as their objective or effect the prevention, restriction or distortion of competition." Since the majority of contracts "restrict trade" it is difficult to see what would not be caught by an expansive enforcement of these provisions.

The absurdities that would be generated by a strict interpretation and enforcement of such laws have given rise to a "rule of reason" approach in all jurisdictions. In other words, regimes have applied competition law in a "reasonable" fashion which has varied substantially between jurisdictions depending on political priorities, the creation and determination of enforcement agencies, the rigor of the courts, and the prevailing economic doctrine. The competition rules have at times virtually been ignored and have been treated as a merely symbolic reassurance for competitors and for the public. Indeed, Galbraith felt that the prevailing oligopolistic structure of industry in the US made antitrust ineffective; to attack oligopoly would be "to suppose that the very fabric of American capitalism is illegal" (Galbraith 1952: 58). But the pendulum has swung away from Galbraith's fascination with planning and in today's neo-liberal markets, competition policy has become a key consideration in the competitive strategies of all large corporations, especially those in highly regulated or concentrated industries.

The enforcement of law is conventionally analyzed through the three routes of: agreements between companies; mergers between companies; and abuse of a dominant position by a single company. In Europe these areas are covered by Article 81, by the Merger Regulation, and by Article 82, and the following discussion rests mainly on the European regime (see also Wilks 2005b, 2009). Control of agreements between companies is the bread and butter of competition policy. Agreements will be subject to an "effects-based" appraisal designed to determine the effect of the particular agreement on the relevant market. Virtually all authorities are nowadays more tolerant of "vertical" agreements (between different stages in the supply chain) than of "horizontal" agreements (between companies at the same stage in the supply chain). Since 2003 cases are no longer notified to the authorities but when they come, via investigations or complaints, each case is assessed on its merits and it is not always possible to predict the results although there are some well-established expectations which are enshrined in legal precedents, guidelines, or formal exemptions. Thus, export bans are typically illegal, franchise agreements are usually legal, while refusal to supply can be legal or illegal depending on the circumstances.

The agreements that are regarded as the most malevolent and damaging are cartels. A cartel is a more or less formal agreement between the major firms in an industry to organize the market. It may involve geographical or product sharing, fixing of prices, allocation of sales volumes, or restriction of production or innovation. Historically cartels have had a mixed reception. Up to, during, and immediately after the Second World War they were an accepted and normal way of organizing many industrial sectors, competition was regarded as "wasteful," and cartels were regarded as a rational device to create efficiency and stability. Cartels were organized by trade associations or even governments and were formal agreements, in some cases enforceable at law, with the result that Europe has a legacy of "cartel tolerance" (Harding and Joshua 2003: 270). The redefinition of cartels as malevolent took place during the 1950s as European competition law was being created. This generated heated debate, especially in Germany (Gerber 1998; Freyer 2006: 262–71). Whilst the Americans talk of "antitrust" the Germans talk of cartels and the enforcement agency is called "The Cartel Office" (Bundeskartellamt, BKA). Since the late 1980s discovery, suppression, and punishment of cartels has come to the forefront in competition enforcement. They are now regarded as indefensible, exploitative, and economically inefficient. The first substantial fines against cartels were imposed in Europe in 1986, and from the mid-1990s DG Comp gave top priority to anti-cartel investigations. The rhetoric is blood-curdling—cartels have been described as "cancers on the open market economy" (Monti 2000)—but they can be very lucrative and they still exist in secret in many industrial sectors. The European Commission has exposed deliberate and systematic law breaking, sometimes undertaken by highly respected companies, and has imposed swingeing fines on cartels in industries such as vitamins, lift equipment, switchgear, and plasterboard.

Merger control provides a second area of company regulation. It came relatively late to the UK where the first merger legislation was enacted in 1965 and came even later to Europe where the Merger Regulation was not finally enacted until 1989. This is a highly visible regulatory area marked by paradox and inconsistency. The paradox emerges from the way in which enforcement of policy against agreements and nineteenth-century trusts (which were effectively super cartels) provoked subsequent merger waves. Commercial practices which were illegal between separate enterprises became cheerfully acceptable when brought within a single enterprise and it was logical for large enterprises to eliminate their competitors through mergers and (sometimes hostile) acquisitions. The inconsistency arises from the operation of policy which in all jurisdictions allows the vast majority of mergers and blocks very few. In the ten years 1998–2007 the EU blocked only twelve mergers (Wilks 2009). This is despite the fact that there is no consensus that mergers lead to greater efficiency and persuasive evidence that they do not (Motta 2004: ch. 5). Moreover, merger control only applies to transactions. It may therefore block or dissuade the creation of a firm with a large market share whilst ignoring the fact that in some other industries firms have built up larger market shares on the back of organic growth.

Merger control is the glamorous face of competition policy. It becomes headline news and is the subject of high politics and high strategy by household name companies and their chief executives. Mergers comprise the theatre of industrial politics where charismatic and egotistical actors engage in battle. For instance, the 2006 UK BSkyB/ITV partial merger pitted James Murdoch (Sky) against Richard Branson (Virgin) in attempts to control Michael Grade (ITV) and such encounters become the stuff of legend (Burrough and Helyar 1990). On a less melodramatic level merger control provides a key parameter of the "market for corporate control" through which the stock market appoints and replaces chief executives and management teams. In assessing prospects for mergers and acquisitions companies and their advisers will take full account of the "regulatory risk" of a merger being referred to the competition authorities. A blocked merger is a major setback but even a permissive competition investigation in itself highly undesirable with huge transaction costs and delays which could jeopardize the deal. In addition the control regime varies significantly between jurisdictions ranging from the benign British environment, where mergers are encouraged and control is efficient and relatively predictable, to the far more problematic settings of Germany and Japan where hostile mergers are anathema and merger control is uncertain and politicized.

The third route of company regulation is provided by control over exploitative behavior by large companies, termed under Article 82 "abuse of a dominant position." Size and a large market share in itself is not illegal under competition law; indeed, size should reflect superior performance and a large market share will be a reward for success, which is the argument advanced by firms such as Tesco, Wal-Mart, and Microsoft. But high levels of concentration in a market do constitute warning signals and a large market share suggests some degree of dominance and market power which could be abused. Here competition policy is at its weakest. The law on how to identify, attack, and remedy abuse of market power is weak in most regimes and enforcement is patchy. Large companies have substantial economic power, they may enjoy efficiency benefits through economies of scale and scope, competitors and suppliers are typically reluctant to make complaints, and they also enjoy political power. The economic and political influence of large companies comes together in a quasi-mercantilist form through the prestige of "national champions" which embody the competitive aspirations of nation states. Governments, and competition agencies, have been hesitant to take on major market dominant companies.

The ultimate response to market dominance is the break-up of large companies. The legendary deployment of those powers was seen in the "trust-busting" of the 1890s with the dissolution of the Standard Oil Trust. Dissolution remained on the US antitrust agenda until the 1980s with the partial break-up of the Bell telephone system in the AT&T case and the ultimately abandoned case against IBM (Fisher, McGowan, and Greenwood 1983). Since IBM, break-up of such dominant companies as Boeing or Microsoft has not been contemplated and in Europe there has never been company dissolution through competition policy. Under European law, companies with a market share of 50 per cent are assumed to be dominant and with 40 per cent plus may be dominant. Such companies are periodically prosecuted for various types of exploitative behavior such as refusal to supply or predatory pricing (the Tetra-Pak predatory pricing cases of the early 1990s are a good example; Whish 2008: 733). In European law dominant companies are expected to meet a higher standard of responsible behavior in the "special responsibility" doctrine (Whish 2008: 183–6) which is not found in US law. Increasingly also, large companies, individually or collectively, have been subject to investigation through sector market inquiries which are a particular feature of the UK regime but which are now also being developed by the European authorities. Market inquiries allow the competition agencies to make a thorough, unrushed assessment of potentially problematic markets. The Competition

Commission has thus undertaken high-profile inquiries into groceries and airports with the subtext of examining the roles played by Tesco and by BAA and its Spanish owner, Ferrovial.

Through these three routes of regulation of agreements, mergers, and dominant positions a modern competition regime is able to regulate private companies by maintaining market disciplines and sustaining competition. But this is not the perfect competition of economic textbooks. It typically tolerates oligopolistic markets so that competition is often constrained and adequate rather than vigorous. Competition economists (especially in Germany) used to employ the concept of "workable competition" (Budzinski 2008: 298) as the realistic goal of policy and this remains a fair characterization of the compromises and pragmatic judgments made by the enforcement agencies when they use their discretion to attack mainly the most blatant and damaging practices by companies.

REGULATING GOVERNMENTS

Competition policy has a counter-intuitive role in regulating governments as well as companies. Many free market critics of big government believe that government itself is a major source of market imperfections and would regard this dimension of competition policy as crucial (Prosser 2005). Regulation of government operates at two levels. At an abstract or constitutional level competition policy defines the boundaries of public power. At the more applied level it limits the range of industrial policy options.

The constitutional level defines a private sector, a market realm which is governed by economic law and within which the writ of the state does not operate. This dimension is almost invisible in Anglo-Saxon countries where limited government and the free market is virtually taken for granted. In countries with a state tradition, however, and particularly in Germany, this dimension is quite fundamental and was elaborately explored and defined through the post-war ordoliberal theorizing of the Frieberg School (Gerber 1998). Ordoliberalism (constitutional liberalism) requires an institutional framework that would protect competition (Budzinski 2008: 305) and it therefore prescribed cartel laws with universal and quasi-constitutional status which would bind governments just as stringently as they would bind companies. The German cartel laws therefore grew out of the rootstock of the social market economy which strictly limits state intervention in, and control of, the private sector and which was legitimated by the post-war German economic miracle. This tradition might nowadays be regarded as an historical curiosity but that would be to underplay its continuing role in Germany and in the wider EU economic constitution as the German influences over competition policy were reproduced at the European level in the design of law and the culture of DG Comp.

At the applied level competition policy had, until the financial crisis of 2008, simply eliminated the traditional tools of industrial policy as can be seen in the three main areas of state-owned utilities, state regulation, and industrial subsidy. Competition policy does not prohibit state ownership but it does insist that state companies should compete fairly in the market and that the state should not create monopolies through legislation. This has created conflict and confrontation in the area of public utilities which were traditionally operated or regulated by the state in the form of a monopoly, often justified by efficiency arguments derived from the need for a single supplier in network markets characterized by "natural monopoly." In gas, electricity, water, post, rail, and, most successfully, in telecommunications these state-sponsored monopolies have been eliminated or modified on the basis of challenge by the competition authorities. This is very much work in progress but sectoral regulatory regimes designed to increase competition have been developed across Europe in all these industries (Jordana and Levi-Faur 2004; Thatcher 2007). In a second applied area, that of state regulation, competition policy has been inspired by the proposition that many market constraints have been created by government regulation. Competition authorities have therefore attacked state-created or state-sanctioned restrictive practices in areas like the professions, public procurement, environmental standards, and land use planning.

In the case of state subsidy, the third applied area, European governments are heavily constrained by the EU "state aid" rules. This is a regime unique to Europe and, although administered by DG Comp, it could be argued that it falls outside a strict interpretation of competition policy. On the other hand the criteria for assessing state aid are firmly expressed in terms of effects on competition so it seems right to include them as part of a broadly defined competition policy. The EU state aid regime is therefore a supranational competition policy which prevents governments from granting preferential treatment to companies when that aid distorts competition. This applies most clearly in cases of outright industrial subsidy as in subsidies to declining industries (such as coal or shipbuilding) or for industrial rescues (the motor industry or Northern Rock). The rules also apply to less obvious cases such as tax breaks, employment aid, preferential purchasing, or state guarantees. In fact the largest and highly controversial case concerned the removal of state guarantees to the depositors in German public banks (Landesbanken and Sparkassen). These traditional guarantees involved a huge hidden subsidy, in the shape of a lower cost of borrowing, which was challenged by the Commission and will gradually be eliminated in a process that will take twenty years from 1996 (Wilks 2005b: 124). Of course, not all state aid is prohibited. Some aid for innovation or regional development may be pro-competitive and again, each case has to be assessed on its merits.

Although the state aid regime derives from Treaty provisions (Article 87, TEC) the enforcement powers are far less effective than for Articles 81 and 82 and the level of cooperation from member sates can be minimal. Control is often by negotiation as much as by formal legal processes and the Commission has to wage a permanent campaign. The Lisbon process (for a more competitive European industry) has added weight to state aid control and the Commission maintains a "name and shame" system in the shape of a "state aid scoreboard" (CEC 2008) which indicates a downward trend in aid across the member states but certainly not complete elimination.

The way in which competition policy has become so effective in disciplining governments since the late 1980s has produced a transformation in microeconomic policies across Europe. It is little short of extraordinary that the whole industrial policy and planning debate that obsessed European political economists from 1945 to 1985 has become otiose, rendered redundant by the remorseless expansion of competition policy. All those debates about indicative planning, selective intervention, sectoral policy, and industrial promotion along the lines of MITI were embodied in studies ranging from Shonfield (1965) to Wilks and Wright (1987). In those years competition policy was a trivial distraction. In the early days of the twenty-first century the pendulum has swung to the opposite extreme. Industrial policy is anathema and competition policy is the dominant paradigm. One major question, explored further below, is whether the incorporation of competition policy into an economic constitution will freeze the pendulum at the neo-liberal end of its arc.

GLOBALIZATION AND THE RETARDED INTERNATIONAL REGIME

Globalization has had a paradoxical effect on the industrial economics of competition policy, simultaneously accentuating problems through increased international concentration and resolving them through enlarged markets. In political and regulatory terms, however, globalization has presented severe challenges which curiously have not resulted in the creation of effective international regulatory institutions.

The level and dynamics of globalization are a contested area but statistics on FDI (foreign direct investment) and cross-border mergers testify to a continuing increase in corporate internationalization (Glyn 2006: 100). As far as competition policy is concerned, globalization within markets is important but so also is globalization of markets. The reach of markets has been extended by the global trend towards privatization which has brought many formerly state-controlled activities into competitive markets, and by the collapse of communism which has opened up new markets from the Ukraine to Shanghai. As countries have moved more firmly into the ambit of market economies so they have enacted competition laws and created competition agencies. A functioning competition regime is a condition for joining the EU and is also an entry ticket for the OECD. A detailed survey indicates that in

1973 only twenty-seven countries had competition laws but the figure had grown to 101 by 2004 (Kronthaler and Stephan 2007: 140). Among these is the highly symbolic example of China whose competition laws came into effect in August 2008.

Competition policies are confronted with a range of cross-border issues. Restrictive practices and abuse of dominance take on an international dimension as the characteristic industrial structure of advanced capitalist economies moves from domestic oligopoly to international oligopoly in regional or international markets. Mergers become global in scale and can affect dozens of countries, whilst cartels, which always had an international dimension, appear to be intensifying. Utton (2006: 31) notes that "international cartels have once again become an important feature of the world economy." Some of these cartels are state sponsored, with OPEC being the prime example, others are private cartels which become visible through successful prosecutions and appear especially prevalent in extractive industries, chemicals, and biotechnology. Thanks to more effective enforcement these cartels are more visible in the US and Europe but they are undoubtedly widespread and global.

Dealing with this range of international issues through over 100 national competition jurisdictions appears highly problematic. It is therefore remarkable that there is no global competition regime comparable to the WTO (World Trade Organization). The GATT/WTO machinery has been in place for over fifty years and has been successful in reducing tariffs and opening markets. The ideological focus and practical effects of the international organizations that pursue the free market "Washington consensus" have been extensively criticized (Stiglitz 2002: 16, 216), but they might be thought also to favor international enforcement of competition principles. For some participants, however, open markets actually eliminate the need for an international competition regime. Completely free trade, so the argument goes, will enhance competitive pressures, open markets, and eliminate oligopolistic abuses. Hence no need for a competition policy. This argument has some purchase but could also be construed as a license for corporate irresponsibility and it is widely accepted that competition policy remains necessary (Utton 2006: 4), which renews the question of why international treaties and institutions have not been created in the competition area.

Proposals for international regulation of competition go back to the International Trade Organization included in the 1944 Havana Charter. The US Senate refused to ratify the Charter and instead the GATT was created without powers to regulate international competition (Utton 2006: 107). US opposition to an international treaty has been sustained and includes its rejection of a WTO competition competence in 2003 (Doern 1996: 307; Freyer 2006: 299). It is worth dwelling on the three motivations for US opposition which throw light on future developments. The first is historical and rests on the fact that for over forty years from 1944 US-style antitrust was "the only game in town." Very few countries had competition laws and the developed market economies that did had weak and marginalized enforcement. The US had actually exported its antitrust principles to Germany (Djelic 1998: 169–71) and to Japan (Hadley 1970) but by the time these regimes had become effective they had evolved to become rather different from the US with its private litigation and judicialized system (Freyer 2006).

A second factor has, until very recently, been the ability of the US to exercise unilateral extraterritoriality in the enforcement of its antitrust laws. Where actions taken abroad affect the American economy the US antitrust agencies may proceed against the companies concerned challenging, for instance, a merger or agreement made in a foreign country. So long as the companies wish to trade in the US there will be pressure to comply and, in addition, national competition agencies have tended to support the US authorities and have not sought to apply their own laws extraterritorially. But this US dominance is changing with two dramatic recent cases rebounding on the US. In 1997 the huge Boeing/McDonnell Douglas merger was approved by the FTC but was initially opposed by the European Commission and was only allowed with a conditional agreement after outspoken protests from the US government and threats of a trade war (Damro 2001). In 2001 the unthinkable actually happened when the GE/Honeywell merger, again approved in the US, was blocked in Europe and was eventually abandoned. This was similarly a huge merger, the largest in the world to date, and again it caused great consternation and a rupture in EU–US relations. In fact the EU decision, based on the conglomerate effects of the merger, was widely criticized as protectionist and economically illiterate so that "far from strengthening the standing of EU policy, this high profile case has exposed its weaknesses" (Morgan and McGuire 2004: 51). The EU has now moved closer to US merger criteria but the case illustrates both the potential for interstate conflict and the growing vulnerability of the US to extraterritorial application of the reinforced competition laws in other jurisdictions.

In the light of these developments we might have expected more intense efforts to create an international treaty and a more accommodating posture from the US. This introduces a third reason for US opposition which is that the independent competition agencies are very reluctant to open the Pandora's Box of political regime redesign. Instead they prefer to negotiate a series of bilateral cooperation agreements such as the EU–US Bilateral Cooperation Agreement signed in 1991 by US and EU officials. This Agreement became controversial when it was overturned by the ECJ in 1994 on the grounds that the European Commission was not competent to sign international treaties. The competition agencies succeeded in having the Agreement ratified in 1995, thus creating a formal cooperative framework which protected their discretion and avoided the unpredictable process of negotiating a treaty between their respective governments. For Damro this episode can be explained in principal–agent terms as the two agents (the competition authorities) seeking to avoid a redefinition of their discretionary authority by their principals (the national governments) (Damro 2006: 173, 189). This explanation is certainly consistent with the pattern of agency independence and network autonomy seen in the network of European competition agencies (Wilks 2004, 2007). The overall outcome is a series of agreements between national competition authorities which creates a messy and politically weaker regime of international governance.

The current position of international competition policy can still therefore be characterized as the loose "regime" (as opposed to institution) that Doern analyzed in 1996, pointing out that regimes tend to be dominated by existing vested interests with less minority protection than typically afforded by institutions (Doern 1996: 317). This loose regime does involve substantial inter-country cooperation structured by a series of bilateral agreements which involve exchange of information, harmonization, and increasingly "positive comity." This is a technical term which provides for a voluntaristic system in which authorities in country A can proceed to enforce policy in the interests of country B. Dialogues about the form, success, and future of international cooperation take place in a number of settings including the WTO and the Competition Law and Policy working groups of the OECD which has also set up a useful forum for cooperation and dialogue known as the ICN (International Competition Network). There have been a series of proposals for more formal international institutions including Scherer's 1994 proposal for an International Competition Policy Office within the WTO (Scherer 1994; Utton 2006: 119) and a string of proposals from Eleanor Fox (2001). As yet there is no sign of an international agreement and although Utton (2006 132) concludes his study with the observation that "the pressures for a more internationally acceptable mechanism for resolving competition problems are likely to become irresistible" the reality is still of over a hundred parallel national jurisdictions poorly coordinated and dominated by the big, developed free market economies. The major exception to this picture of balkanization is the EU with the central role of DG Comp and the smooth coordination of enforcement across the Union through the ECN (European Competition Network) (Wilks 2005a, 2007). The EU offers an alternative approach to competition regulation and enforcement which has become more admired and emulated than the US (Freyer 2006: 300).

THE AGENCIES AND THE INSTITUTION

The most useful approach to evaluating competition policy is to gain an understanding of the design and operation of the competition agencies which interpret and enforce policy. The global norm, reflecting the quasi-constitutional status of antitrust, is that enforcement is entrusted to independent agencies (Wilks with Bartle 2002). The classic benchmark is provided by the US FTC (Federal Trade Commission) which was created in 1915 as an independent regulatory commission with all the traditional characteristics of the US "fourth branch of government" (see Calkins 2006). The US divides enforcement between the FTC and the Antitrust Division of the DoJ, both of which are regarded as prestigious and effective. The enforcement agencies are ranked annually on the basis of a reputational survey undertaken by the *Global Competition Review*. The elite agencies are listed in Table 32.1 which shows the

Table 32.1 The elite competition agencies

	GCR banking
Europe, DG Competition	5.0
UK, Competition Commission	5.0
US Federal Trade Commission	5.0
US Department of Justice	4.5
Australian Competition and Consumer Commission	4.0
France, Competition Council	4.0
Germany, Federal Cartel Office	4.0
UK, Office of Fair Trading	4.0

Note: Ranking on a 5 point scale where 5 is "elite" and 4/4.5 is "very good."

Source: Global Competition Review (2007: 3).

six leading jurisdictions and, despite the fact that the reputational method contains many biases, it illustrates how far the UK and European agencies have progressed.

These agencies enjoy adequate legal powers but they also need organizational resources including effective leadership, a reasonable budget, and talented staff. Ambitious leadership is important. Antitrust leaders such as Robert Pitofsky, Clinton's very effective chairman of the FTC 1995–2001, are hardly household names but agencies have had highly visible representatives such as Alan Fels, chairman of the ACCC from 1991 to 2003 (Brenchley 2003), or Lord (Gordon) Borrie who was the face of the OFT during his sixteen years as Director General of Fair Trading (1976–92, Wilks 1998: 285). DG Comp is rather a different case. Here the Commissioner is a significant national politician and the competition portfolio has attracted some very effective, high-profile, and crusading leaders from Leon Brittan to Mario Monti and, since 2004, Neelie Kroes. It is important how such leaders define their role and motivate their staff. There is a continuum stretching from high-profile activism, exemplified by Alan Fels, through to a passive, residual regulatory stance which is seen in a number of agencies and was almost part of the system in the JFTC (Japan Fair Trade Commission) up to the early 1990s (Wilks 1994).

A less tangible but fundamental aspect of agencies is their determination and self-definition as an "enforcement agency," rather than a passive regulator. This combination could also be termed an "organizational culture" and can be analyzed in terms of incentives, norms, and repertoires of expected behavior. This cultural dimension is hard to capture and is conventionally ignored in profound legal analyzes and arcane economic recommendations but in its importance is magnified by the independence of the agencies. The regulatory systems are designed so that government ministers and sponsor departments are kept at arm's length, allowing agencies extensive autonomy and exceptional room to deploy their discretion in a manner analogous to central bank independence. That discretion is further removed from control by politicians and the electoral process by the oversight of the courts, often specialized economic courts such at the European CFI (Court of First Instance) and the UK CAT

(Competition Appeal Tribunal). When exercising discretion, making choices, and assessing risk, the leadership, the staff, and the resources come together in a culturally determined pattern which leads an agency to be bold and proactive, or risk averse and passive. The enforcement culture of the agencies may be difficult to measure but it becomes quickly apparent to those who deal with the agencies and is partially captured by the reputational rankings of the GCR. Thus DG Comp has a vigorous enforcement culture, as does the FTC and the Netherlands Competition Authority.

This discussion of "the agencies" and of "agency" should be located within a broader structural framework which interprets the agencies and competition policy itself as part of a wider political economy. Here the core questions are about why competition agencies have been given such a striking degree of independence and the implications of that independence for their effectiveness and deployment of power. Agency independence can be seen as a conscious technique of statecraft (Flinders and Buller 2006) and can be explained through principal–agent (P–A) theory. P–A theory offers a perceptive and refreshingly political interpretation of why governments grant independence to regulators (Thatcher and Stone Swee 2002; Gilardi 2007). The three key elements are expertise, blame avoidance, and "credible commitment," in other words convincing the regulatees that the regulatory rules will be applied stringently and objectively. This approach offers a plausible interpretation of why independence is granted to competition regulators (Wilks with Bartle 2002) but it is far less effective in explaining how the principals (elected governments) either alter or retract grants of autonomy. This chapter therefore argues that the P–A approach, whilst revealing, is less effective than an approach which analyzes competition policy as "an institution" which in turn is strengthened and protected by a quasi-constitutional status. The creation of independent competition regulators has taken on a self-perpetuating quality: they are able to consolidate and extend their independence to the point where it would be very difficult for elected governments to re-establish direct control. This applies in the UK and in Europe such that "the European Commission "has "escaped" its agency constraints to take on a constitutional status as a "trustee" of a particular economic system" (Wilks 2005a: 433). Principal–agent rationales are not completely suppressed, governments retain influence over "their" competition agencies (not least through budgets and senior appointments), and governments, especially in the UK, retain the ultimate authority to abolish independent agencies and to redesign the system. The argument, however, is that the threshold for intervention by principals has been raised to an extremely high level. To repoliticize competition policy would require a crisis and the sort of exceptional action that is normally associated with constitutional amendments.

This thesis of extreme independence for the competition agencies invites parallels with the independence enjoyed by central banks. As in the case of the banks, the implications of independence are first, that the agencies will pursue the goals defined in their legislative foundations; but secondly, that they will do so on the basis of the exercise of judgment, discretion, and political priorities. It therefore becomes important to analyze who is appointed to lead and manage competition agencies, and what sort of ideological programs they might be expected to favor. At the European level the recent Commissioners, Mario Monti and now Neelie Kroes, have appeared far more sympathetic to an "Americanization" agenda and have come to lead a DG that has taken on a very neo-liberal coloration (Wigger and Nölke 2007; Wigger 2007: 117). This presents a specific example of what Streeck and Thelen (2005: 4) see as a general transformation of capitalist economies towards "liberalization" which

puts us on the alert that in studying liberalization as a direction of institutional change, we should expect also to observe changes in institutions intended to reembed the very same market relations that liberalization set free from traditional social constraints.

In other words, having freed the market from state ownership, planning, intervention, subsidy, and social disapproval, the neo-liberal project seeks to consolidate the gains of liberalization. This is precisely the role being played by a strengthened and constitutionalized competition policy.

Whilst we can theorize the ascendancy of competition policy as part of an historic redesign of economic institutions the privileging of competition in the neo-liberal reforms provides the rationale for institutional transformation. Competition is the dynamic force within market economies which creates incentives, drives behavior, and, by delivering efficiency, maximizes welfare. It has become a principle of policy in many fields and has been diagnosed as a major driver of productivity and competitiveness. This has involved a "reinvention" of competition policy, moving it from concerns with fair markets and symbolic reassurance to become a front-line economic policy designed to deliver economic growth. This reinvention of competition policy is discussed with a particular focus on the UK which provides an especially clear model.

THE REINVENTION OF COMPETITION POLICY IN THE UK

The ascendancy of market ideas from the Reagan and Thatcher governments onwards should have produced policies to encourage competition almost as a matter of course. In the event the benefits of promoting competition were not fully appreciated and incorporated into the UK economic policy agenda until the work of Michael Porter and his Harvard School theories began to impact on the British Treasury. Porter's (1990) study of *The Competitive Advantage of Nations* argued that it is companies, not nations, which compete and that their competitive success is closely related to the competitive environment in their home economies, including the intensity of competition. The Treasury and the DTI examined the implications for the UK economy (Porter and Ketels 2003). They drew the rather obvious conclusion that intensified competition within the UK economy was desirable and that, accordingly, Britain's sedate, minimalist, and under-resourced competition policy should be strengthened.

Moving from analysis to legislation required political initiatives of which the Conservative government of John Major seemed incapable. The curious delay in legislating for a strengthened UK policy is explored in Wilks (1999: 308–25). The logjam was broken by Gordon Brown and the 1998 Competition Act which comprehensively reformed British law on restrictive practices and abuse of dominance and aligned it with European legislation. The reform of British law, and especially the 1998 Act, are conventionally characterized as "Europeanization" (Cini 2006) but in fact the Labour government was marching to the tune of the "Battle Hymn of the Republic" rather than the "Ode to Joy." Whilst the 1998 Act was taken virtually off the shelf and represented a bi-partisan consensus between the Conservatives and Labour on moving towards a European model, the 2002 Enterprise Act was transatlantic in its inspiration and US in its orientation.

After its election in 1997 New Labour, under the direct leadership of Gordon Brown, developed a distinctive and sophisticated microeconomic policy. Their supply side approach was centered on the importance of improving productivity in the UK economy and was inspired by international comparisons of labor productivity and the "productivity gap" with Germany, with France, but, above all, with the USA. The Treasury and the DTI developed a forcefully argued, comprehensive, and consistent productivity strategy which revolved around five "drivers" of productivity: competition, innovation, investment, skills, and enterprise. The anchorage of competition policy in the productivity agenda is consistent with the long-term alignment of the UK and American models of capitalism in the Anglo-Saxon model. The 2002 Enterprise Act therefore completed the process of reinvention of UK policy by creating the tripartite system of independent competition bodies (the OFT, the CC, and the CAT), basing merger control on the US-style and purely economic principle of SLC (substantial lessening of competition) and creating a US-style criminal cartel offence. Labour ministers exhibited something of the zealotry of the newly converted. They not only wanted a good competition regime, in the spirit of targets and benchmarking they wanted "the most effective competition regime in the OECD" (DTI 2001: 15).

The reinvention of UK competition policy, as essentially an industrial policy designed to encourage productivity, creates acute ambiguities in the enforcement of policy for the tripartite system of independent agencies. There are various dimensions to this ambiguity but here we can restrict ourselves to two systemic problems: the first can be termed the "fallacy of composition," the second is the divergence of goals of the principal and the agent. The fallacy of composition arises from the disjuncture between microeconomic policy and policy goals that are essentially macroeconomic. While competition enforcement can perhaps be linked to efficiency and even productivity in individual firms or market sectors it is theoretically demanding to try to link it to whole-economy labor productivity, to an international productivity gap, or ultimately to economic growth. This makes it hard to establish success or failure and poses problems for policy design. The Treasury has established to its own satisfaction, based on what has now become a formidable body of research (Mayhew and Neely 2006), that high levels of competition are conducive to higher levels of international competitiveness. But it is in fact difficult to establish links between competition policy, levels of competition, and productivity. The OFT's review of the evidence remarks that "there is a voluminous literature linking competition to productivity. Far less has been done directly linking competition *policy* to productivity" (OFT 2007: 39, emphasis in original). Productivity criteria are not therefore built into individual case decisions and there is a disconnect between the overall goals of policy and its practical enforcement on the ground. The consumer welfare standard increasingly being applied may deliver long-term productivity growth, but this is an article of faith, and there are cogent reasons why it might not.

The second systemic problem is a disjuncture between the policy goals of the government and of the OFT which can be expressed in P–A terms. The government wanted and expected to see the active implementation of a policy that would improve productivity and contribute to growth. The OFT appears unable to deliver those goals but, more worryingly, appears to be working to a different set of goals. The main evidence for this conclusion is threefold. First, the OFT has proved to be hesitant in its use of its now very substantial powers. Second, it has been distracted by its second function of consumer protection and has allowed consumer priorities to bias and in some cases to hijack its competition functions. Third, even within its competition enforcement, the resort to the post-Chicago goals of emphasizing consumer welfare has detracted from efforts to encourage long-term productivity growth within industries. The result is that the government may lose patience with the competition authorities that it has created. The P–A literature has a lot to say about the problem of "shirking" which occurs when agents fail to achieve the goals of their principals or redefine those goals. In the case of the OFT the quasi-constitutional status of competition policy analyzed above means that there is very little that the government can do about any shirking that it identifies. It could reduce budgets and attach less priority to the policy area but it would require a crisis for government to legislate to redesign the system. Whilst the 2008 credit crunch and recessionary risk could provide such a crisis it is probably more plausible to look for change following the next UK general election in 2010.

Conclusions: Competition Policy
in 2010—and 2020

This chapter has charted the growth in global salience of competition policy over the past two decades. In the early 1980s competition policy, where it existed, was a weak or marginal area of business regulation in virtually every jurisdiction. The most influential model of capitalism at that time was Japan whose industrial policy was celebrated, growth rates were the envy of the world, and competition policy was ineffectual so that "over the whole of its existence there has been a huge gap between the powers available to (the JFTC) and the actual enforcement of those powers" Sanekata and Wilks 1996: 102). The two most effective competition regimes were in the US and Germany, the European powers were underutilized, and the Commission was still engaged in the long campaign just to secure a regulation to control mergers.

The position twenty years later is radically different. The most influential model of capitalism has become the neo-liberal, financially globalized, free market, Anglo-Saxon model. The US was (until the 2007–8 credit crunch) the engine of the world economy and the UK had gone from the sick man of Europe to achieve its own economic miracle with sixty-two consecutive quarters of growth up to 2008 with a rejuvenated, strong, and well-resourced competition regime. In Europe competition officials noted that the EU has developed in fifty years the sort of sophisticated and effective regime that took over a hundred years in the US. Perhaps the greatest evidence of the impact of competition policy is the way in which it channeled the corporate strategy of every major business corporation.

As noted in the introduction, competition policy is a complex field with a particular technical interest to specialist lawyers and economists and a great practical interest to anyone concerned with business strategy. This chapter has taken a broader approach and has introduced a series of issues which are aspects of traditional political economy such as the balance of public and private power and the design of economic policy. At its very broadest competition policy can be seen as a foundation of mega-corporate global capitalism. Both Freyer (2006) and Braithwaite see antitrust as enabling the growth of large corporations and as underpinning the post-neo-liberal development of global regulatory capitalism (Braithwaite 2008: 19, 197). At a lower level of abstraction this chapter has stressed three areas which will be constitutive of the shape and success of policy over the longer term. They are competition policy as an independent institution; competition policy as a global regime; and competition policy as an economic constitution.

The theme of competition policy as an institution has been developed at several points above (see also Wilks 1999: 2). It suggests a universal yet tacit assumption permeating market societies that competition is a necessary and benign aspect of economic life that needs to be protected. This justifies the related aspect which again has been stressed repeatedly above, namely that competition policy is entrusted to independent agencies and courts operating with legal and normative safeguards to insulate competition enforcement from intervention by "politics," whether politicians or politically powerful companies. In this sense competition could be likened to the emphasis in all market economies on monetary stability which is similarly regarded as a universal norm and entrusted to independent central banks. This institutional quality means that the competition policy world is both insulated and capable of deciding its own future. The networks, communities, ideas, and incentives that operate within that world require detailed analysis, but it can be suggested that the competition policy community may be overly self-satisfied and complacent.

The second theme, competition policy as a global regime, was addressed in the fourth section. Competition policy operating in a series of national jurisdictions is clearly inadequate for controlling globalized markets. The conflicts and weaknesses which will become steadily more apparent will generate strong pressures for convergence but also strong national reactions from countries and multinational corporations. Two aspects of this area of uncertainty are worth emphasizing. The first is that Europe provides a remarkable example of a functioning cross-border regime. For all European countries, including the UK, competition policy is designed and guided at the European level, especially for large companies, with the national authorities important chiefly for the way in which they enforce European policy and negotiate within the European network. The second is the key role played by the United States in sanctioning or opposing negotiations over a possible international treaty, and in disseminating its own model of antitrust doctrine and enforcement to its allies and trading partners. The transatlantic influence of competition economics is particularly important.

The third theme, of competition policy as an economic constitution, raises the question of "what sort of market" is being embedded in regulatory institutions. Competition policy has been presented as a "meta-policy" which is about rules and systems rather than about concrete policy objectives. As such it can be seen from a "constitutional" perspective as a way of structuring the operation of markets and the relationship between the individual and the market and the state and the market. Viewing competition policy as part of an economic constitution for the developed market economies leads into a series of theoretical avenues which invite further research. We can briefly review four avenues.

First, a constitutional role for competition policy means that the agencies enforcing it must necessarily have an exceptional degree of independence. But it could be argued that the constitutional principle allows an even greater level of independence for the competition authorities because their activities are (at least in Europe) defended by the constitutional court. This avenue leads towards theories of agency independence and regulatory networks (Braithwaite 2008; Coen and Thatcher 2008; Gilardi 2008). Second, competition policy can be expected to develop its own dynamic and to evolve as a relatively self-contained system of regulation that is influenced by governments but which is driven by legal and economic discourses. The principle of competition becomes a constitutional objective to be defined by economic expertise and protected by the courts and an apparatus of legal procedure and precedent. This suggests a juridification of the economy in which law may become self-referential and inaccessible and may lose sight of the original goals which competition was intended to achieve. This takes research into questions of professional influence, disciplinary development, and legal sociology (Teubner 1987).

The third avenue is to consider the economic model that constitutional commitments to undistorted markets and unrestricted competition imply. This is an important and rapidly developing area of research stimulated by the turn to economics and the Americanization reviewed above. The traditional Frieberg School ordoliberal prescriptions argued in favor of an economic constitution that was mainly about establishing a legal framework that limited state intervention and market dominance to achieve "workable competition." It did not prescribe a particular economic model. More recent economic theories espouse an ideal of consumer welfare and cohere around a "post-Chicago synthesis." There has been concern expressed about the potential dominance of one, unduly neo-liberal model (Budzinski 2008) and about an excessive move to liberalization being embodied in competition enforcement (Wigger and Nölke 2007). Here the research avenue invites analysis of the competing economic models embodied in national varieties of capitalism (or varieties of regulatory capitalism) with the concern that an economic model appropriate for competition policy in the Anglo-Saxon developed economies is far less suitable for incorporation into policy in coordinated market economies (or in the developing world) (Hancke, Rhodes, and Thatcher 2007).

A fourth intriguing research avenue is presented by an international political economy critique of the "new constitutionalism." This is a neo-Gramscian line of argument which argues that the governments and institutions that have succeeded in creating a global neo-liberal hegemony (what Gill 2000 calls "disciplinary neo-liberalism") are eager to embed them in global constitutional arrangements. They seek to "lock in" the key neo-liberal drivers such as free trade, equal treatment, privatization, free capital movement and the sanctity of private property by incorporating them into constitutional arrangements. The power of capital is being incorporated in legal and political frameworks which are depoliticised and defended by the rule of law and international organizations (Gill 2005; Cerny 2008). A clear example is the debate over the constitution of the WTO (Trachtman 2006). This is a fertile research theme which is extremely ambitious since it locates competition policy within an analysis of global capitalist relations. It considers foundational questions within a Polanyiesque tradition (Polanyi 1944) and addresses the questions raised above about the balance between public and private power. The new constitutionalism argument is expressly concerned to emphasize the consolidation of private power. Which allows us to end with the classic question of political science which is to ask in whose interests competition policy operates: does it benefit consumers and economic growth, or does it benefit large corporations and the legal profession? In practice, of course, competition policy could serve many ends and the aim of this chapter has been to provide a manifesto for further research which will bring politics back in.

REFERENCES

AMATO, G. 1997. *Antitrust and the Bounds of Power: The Dilemma of Liberal Democracy in the History of the Market*. Oxford: Hart.

BEATH, J. 2002. "UK industrial policy: old tunes on new instruments?," *Oxford Review of Economic Policy* 18(2): 221–39.

BERNHAGEN, P. 2007. *The Political Power of Business*. London: Routledge.

BRAITHWAITE, J. 2008. *Regulatory Capitalism*. Cheltenham: Elgar.

BRENCHLEY, F. 2003. *Allan Fels: A Portrait of Power*. Milton: Wiley.

BROADBERRY, S., and O'MAHONEY, M. 2004. "Britain's productivity gap with the United States and Europe: a historical perspective," *National Institute Economic Review* 189: 72–85.

BUDZINSKI, O. 2008. "Monoculture versus diversity in competition economics," *Cambridge Journal of Economics* 32: 295–324.

BURROUGH, B., and HELYAR, J. 1990. *Barbarians at the Gate*. London: Random House.

CALKINS, S. 2006. "Ninety years and two days in forty-five minutes," Federal Trade Commission 90th Anniversary Symposium, *Antitrust Law Journal* 72: 1183–203.

CEC. 2008. *Report from the Commission: State Aid Scoreboard*, COM(2008) 304, available at http://eu.europa.com/comm/competition/state_aid

CERNY, P. 2008. "Embedding neoliberalism: the evolution of a hegemonic paradigm," *Journal of International Trade and Diplomacy* 2: 1–46.

CINI, M. 2006. "Competition policy," in I. Bache and A. Jordan, eds., *The Europeanization of British Politics*. Basingstoke: Palgrave Macmillan.

—— and McGOWAN, L. 2009. *Competition Policy in the European Union*, 2nd edn. Houndsmills: Macmillan.

COEN, D., and THATCHER, M. 2008. "Network governance and multi-level delegation: european networks of regulatory agencies," *Journal of Public Policy* 28: 49–71.

DAMRO, C. 2001. "Building an international identity: the EU and extraterritorial competition policy," *Journal of European Public Policy* 8: 208–26.

—— 2006. "Transatlantic competition policy: domestic and international sources of EU–US cooperation," *European Journal of International Relations* 12: 171–196.

DJELIC, M.-L. 1998. *Exporting the American Model: The Postwar Transformation of European Business*. Oxford: Oxford University Press.

DOERN, B. 1996. "The internationalization of competition policy," in B. Doern and S. Wilks, eds., *Comparative Competition Policy*. Oxford: Clarendon Press.

—— and WILKS, S., eds. 1996. *Comparative Competition Policy: National Institutions in a Global Market*. Oxford: Clarendon Press.

DRAHOS, M., and VAN WAARDEN, F. 2002. "Courts and (epistemic) communities in the convergence of competition policies," *Journal of European Public Policy* 9: 913–34.

DRYZEK, J. 1996. *Democracy in Capitalist Times*. Oxford: Oxford University Press.

DTI. 2001. *Productivity and Enterprise: A World Class Competition Regime*. London: HMSO, Cm 5233.

EISNER, M. 1991. *Antitrust and the Triumph of Economics*. Chapel Hill: University of North Carolina Press.

EYRE, S., and LODGE, M. 2000. "National tunes and a European melody? Competition law reform in the UK and Germany," *Journal of European Public Policy* 7: 63–97.

FISHER, F., McGOWAN, J., and GREENWOOD, J. 1983. *Folded, Spindled and Mutilated: Economic Analysis and US v IBM*. Cambridge, Mass.: MIT.

FLINDERS, M., and BULLER, J. 2006. "Depoliticization: principles, tactics and tools," *British Politics* 1(1): 1–26.

FREYER, T. 1992. *Regulating Big Business: Antitrust in Great Britain and America 1880–1990*. Cambridge: Cambridge University Press.

—— 2006. *Antitrust and Global Capitalism*. Cambridge: Cambridge University Press.

FRIEDMAN, M. 1962. *Capitalism and Freedom*. Chicago: University of Chicago Press.

FOX, E. 2001. "Antitrust law on a global scale: races up, down, and sideways," in D. Esty and D. Geradin, eds., *Regulatory Competition and Economic Integration*. Oxford: Oxford University Press.

GALBRAITH, J. K. 1952. *American Capitalism: The Concept of Countervailing Power.* Boston: Houghton Mifflin.

GAMBLE, A. 1994. *The Free Economy and the Strong State: The Politics of Thatcherism,* 2nd edn. London: Macmillan.

GERBER, D. 1998. *Law and Competition in Twentieth Century Europe.* Oxford: Clarendon Press.

GILARDI, F. 2008. *Delegation in the Regulatory State: Independent Regulatory Agencies in Western Europe.* Cheltenham: Edward Elgar.

GILL, S. 2005. "New constitutionalism, democratization and global political economy," in R. Williams, ed., *The Global Governance Reader.* London: Routledge.

Global Competition Review. 2007. "Rating enforcement," *Global Competition Review* 8: 5.

GLYN, A. 2006. *Capitalism Unleashed.* Oxford: Oxford University Press.

HAAS, P. 1992. "Introduction: epistemic communities and international policy coordination," *International Organization,* 1: 3.

HADLEY, E. 1970. *Antitrust in Japan.* Princeton: Princeton University Press.

HALL, P., and SOSKICE, D. 2001. "An introduction to varieties of capitalism," in P. Hall and D. Soskice, eds., *Varieties of Capitalism: The Institutional Foundations of Comparative Advantage.* Oxford: Oxford University Press.

HANCKE, B., RHODES, M., and THATCHER, M., eds. 2007. *Beyond Varieties of Capitalism.* Oxford: Oxford University Press.

HARDING, C., and JOSHUA, J. 2003. *Regulating Cartels in Europe: A Study of Legal Control of Corporate Delinquency.* Oxford: Oxford University Press.

HAY, D., and MORRIS, D. 1991. *Industrial Economics and Organization,* 2nd edn. Oxford: Oxford University Press.

JABKO, N. 2006. *Playing the Market: A Political Strategy for Uniting Europe 1985–2005.* Ithaca, NY: Cornell University Press.

JORDANA, J., and LEVI-FAUR, D., eds. 2004. "The politics of regulation in the age of governance," in J. Jordana and D. Levi-Faur, eds., *The Politics of Regulation.* Cheltenham: Edward Elgar, 1–28.

KOVACIC, W. 2003. "The modern evolution of U.S. competition policy enforcement norms," *Antitrust Law Journal* 71: 377–478.

KROES, N. 2006. "Industrial policy and competition law & policy" speech at Fordham University Law School, September, Europa press release.

KRONTHALER, F., and STEPHAN, J. 2007. "Factors accounting for the enactment of a competition law: an empirical analysis," *Antitrust Bulletin* 52: 137–63.

LAURENT, E., and LE CACHEUX, J. 2007. *What (Economic) Constitution Does the EU Need?* OFCE Document de Travail, at www.ofce.sciences-po.fr

LEVI-FAUR, D. 2005. "The global diffusion of regulatory capitalism," *Annals of the American Academy of Political and Social Science* 598: 12–32.

LINDBLOM, C. 1977. *Politics and Markets: The World's Political-Economic Systems.* New York: Basic Books.

McGOWAN, L. 2005. "Europeanization unleashed and rebounding: assessing the modernization of EU cartel policy," *Journal of European Public Policy* 12: 986–1004.

MARQUAND, D. 2004. *The Decline of the Public.* Cambridge: Polity.

MAYHEW, K., and NEELY, A. 2006. "Improving productivity: opening the black box," *Oxford Review of Economic Policy* 22: 445–56.

MONTI, M. 2000. Opening speech at the Third Nordic Competition Policy Conference, Stockholm, September.

MORAN, M. 2006. "The company of strangers: defending the power of business in Britain, 1975–2005," *New Political Economy* 11(6).

MORGAN, E., and McGUIRE, S. 2004. "Transatlantic divergence: GE-Honeywell and the EU's merger policy," *Journal of European Public Policy* 11: 39–56.

MOTTA, M. 2004. *Competition Policy: Theory and Practice.* Cambridge: Cambridge University Press.

NEVEN, D. 2006. "Competition economics and antitrust in Europe," *Economic Policy* pp. 741–91.

OECD. 2005. *Competition Law and Policy in the European Union.* Paris: OECD.

OFT. 2007. *Productivity and Competition: An OFT Perspective on the Productivity Debate.* London: OFT.

POLANYI, K. 1944. *The Great Transformation.* Boston: Beacon.

PORTER, M. 1990. *The Competitive Advantage of Nations.* London: Macmillan.

—— and KETELS, C. 2003. *UK Competitiveness: Moving to the Next Stage.* DTI Economics Paper No. 3. London: DTI and ESRC.

PROSSER, T. 2005. *The Limits of Competition Law: Markets and Public Services.* Oxford: Oxford University Press.

SANEKATA, K., and WILKS, S. 1996. "The Fair Trade Commission and the enforcement of competition policy in Japan," in B. Doern and S. Wilks, eds., *Comparative Competition Policy.* Oxford: Clarendon Press.

SCHERER, F. M. 1994. *Competition Policies for an Integrated World Economy.* Washington, DC: Brookings.

SCHMIDT, V. 2002. *The Futures of European Capitalism.* Oxford: Oxford University Press.

SHONFIELD, A. 1965. *Modern Capitalism: The Changing Balance of Public and Private Power.* Oxford: Oxford University Press.

STIGLITZ, J. 2002. *Globalization and its Discontents.* London: Penguin.

STREECK, W., and THELEN, K. 2005. "Introduction: institutional change in advanced political economies," in W. Streeck and K. Thelen, eds., *Beyond Continuity: Institutional Change in Advanced Political Economies.* Oxford: Oxford University Press.

TEUBNER, G. 1987. "Juridification: concepts, aspects, limits, solutions," in G. Teubner, ed., *Juridification of Social Spheres: A Comparative Analysis in the Areas of Labor, Corporate Antitrust and Social Welfare Law.* Berlin: de Gruyter.

THATCHER, M. 2007. *Internationalization and Economic Institutions.* Oxford: Oxford University Press.

—— and STONE SWEET, A. 2002. "The theory and practice of delegation to non-majoritarian institutions," *West European Politics* 25: 1–22.

TRACHTMAN, J. 2006. "The constitutions of the WTO," *European Journal of International Law* 17: 624–46.

UTTON, M. 2006. *International Competition Policy: Maintaining Open Markets in the Global Economy.* Cheltenham: Edward Elgar.

VICKERS, J. 2003. "Competition economics and policy," *European Competition Law Review* 24: 95–102.

VOGEL, S. 1996. *Freer Markets More Rules: Regulatory Reform in Advanced Industrial Countries.* Ithaca, NY: Cornell University Press.

WHISH, R. 2008. *Competition Law,* 6th edn. Oxford: Oxford University Press.

WIGGER, A. 2007. "Towards a market-based approach: the privatization and microeconomization of EU antitrust law enforcement," in H. Overbeek et al., eds., *The Transnational Politics of Corporate Governance Regulation.* London: Routledge.

—— and NÖLKE, A. 2007. "Enhanced roles of private actors in EU business regulation and the erosion of Rhenish capitalism: the case of antitrust enforcement," *Journal of Common Market Studies* 45: 486–513.

WILKS, S. 1994. *The Revival of Japanese Competition Policy and its Importance for EU–Japan Relations*. London, RIIA.

—— 1996. "The prolonged reform of United Kingdom competition policy," in B. Doern and S. Wilks, eds., *Comparative Competition Policy: National Institutions in a Global Market*. Oxford: Clarendon Press.

—— 1999. *In the Public Interest: Competition Policy and the Monopolies and Mergers Commission*. Manchester: Manchester University Press.

—— 2004. "Understanding competition policy networks in Europe: a political science perspective," in C.-D. Elhermann and I. Atanasiu, eds., *European Competition Law Annual 2002: Constructing the EU Network of Competition Authorities*. Oxford: Hart.

—— 2005a. "Agency escape: decentralization or dominance of the European Commission in the modernization of competition policy?" *Governance* 18(3): 431–52.

—— 2005b. "Competition policy: challenge and reform," in H. Wallace, W. Wallace, and M. Pollack, eds., *Policy-Making in the European Union*, 5th edn. Oxford: Oxford University Press.

—— 2007. "Agencies, networks, discourses and the trajectory of European competition enforcement," *European Competition Journal* 3(2): 437–64.

—— 2009. "Competition policy: towards an economic constitution?," in H. Wallace, W. Wallace, and M. Pollack, eds., *Policy-Making in the European Union*, 6th edn. Oxford: Oxford University Press.

—— with BARTLE, I. 2002. "The unanticipated consequences of creating independent competition agencies," *West European Politics* 25: 148–72.

—— and WRIGHT, M., eds. 1987. *Comparative Government–Industry Relations: Europe, the United States and Japan*. Oxford: Clarendon Press.

General Index